JAN RYPKA

HISTORY OF IRANIAN LITERATURE

Written in collaboration with

OTAKAR KLÍMA, VĚRA KUBÍČKOVÁ, FELIX TAUER,
JIŘÍ BEČKA, JIŘÍ CEJPEK,
JAN MAREK, I. HRBEK AND J. T. P. DE BRUIJN

Edited by

KARL JAHN
(University of Leyden)

D. REIDEL PUBLISHING COMPANY
DORDRECHT - HOLLAND

DĚJINY PERSKÉ A TADŽICKÉ LITERATURY
First published by Nakladatelství Československé akademie věd, Praha 1956
Translated from the German by P. van Popta-Hope, and enlarged and revised by the authors

Printed in The Netherlands by D. Reidel, Dordrecht

Frontispiece:

The Prophet, seated on Burāq, passing over the Kaʿbah at Mecca on his miraculous night-journey. From Or. 6810, a copy of the Khamseh of Niẓāmī dated 900/1494–5, which bears autograph notes of the Mughal Emperors Jahāngīr and Shāh Jahān. (*By courtesy of the Trustees of the British Museum.*)

FOREWORD

Some justification seems to be necessary for the addition of yet another *History of Iranian Literature* to the number of those already in existence. Such a work must obviously contain as many novel features as possible, so that a short explanation of what my collaborators and I had in mind when planning the book is perhaps not superfluous. In the first place our object was to present a short summary of the material in all its aspects, and secondly to review the subject from the chronological, geographical and substantial standpoints – all within the compass of a single volume. Such a scheme precludes a formal and complete enumeration of names and phenomena, and renders all the greater the obligation to accord most prominence to matters deemed to be of greatest importance, supplementing these with such figures and forms as will enable an impression to be gained of the period in question – all this is far as possible in the light of the most recent discoveries. A glance at the table of contents will suffice to give an idea of the multifarious approach that has been our aim. We begin at the very first traces of evidence bearing on our subject and continue the narrative up to the present day. Geographically the book embraces Iran and its neighbouring countries, while it should be remarked that Iranian literature in its fullest sense also includes Indo-Persian and Judeo-Persian works. The absence of a section on modern Afghan literature must be compensated by the works of H. J. de Dianous and A. Gerasimova and G. Girs (cf. Bibliography, B VIII). New substrata of our subject are laid bare in the extensive contribution on Tajik literature and in that on folklore, though in respect of the former it must be admitted that Soviet works on the subject have not been taken into account. New, in relation to the German version of our book, is the separate section on scholarly literature.

Another feature that may be regarded as an innovation consists in the references to Iranian (mainly modern studies), Russian and Soviet sources. It cannot be denied that this has been done before in the West, but such references are mostly rare and inadequate. The result of this omission in other works has been that important factual material and a multitude of valuable opinions have been lost to the reader unacquainted with these spheres of learning. Of course one must not censure unjustly, for it must be borne in mind that in the meantime the measure of Iranian studies in the country itself and in the Soviet-Union has increased out of all proportion compared with the achievements of former times. This advance is indeed highly gratifying.

The present version of the *History of Iranian Literature* differs from its predecessors in various and in some cases special ways. As can be seen from the Bibliography (B 1) it resembles most closely the second Czech edition (1961) which, however, in its turn varies considerably in compass and detail from the original edition (1955) and the German version (1959). It is clear that a work of this kind requires constant revision and emendation in order to bring it up to date, not to mention the rectification of the errors that are bound to creep into an opus covering such a wide field, however conscientiously the authors endeavour to avoid them. It lies in the nature of things that a History of this kind can never be regarded as being definitively concluded. Moreover a considerable period of time was required before the manuscript was ready for the press. This lapse of time, together with the distance separating those engaged on the work, could not but have some disadvantages. Some of the authors, prompted by experience, even completely altered the arrangement of their contributions. In view of the years that have passed since the publication of the original edition, it is not surprising that many a reversal of opinion has taken place, and it has unfortunately been impossible to incorporate all of these in the present volume. In certain cases, however, they are mentioned in the notes. Many of these revised views may be accounted for by the appearance of numerous new publications and reports of recent investigations, the results of which we have also regrettably been obliged to omit.

An extensive use has therefore been made of this material in the Bibliography. The latter, though only providing a selection of titles, occupies an unusually large amount of space and has been acclaimed with enthusiasm by the critics of the former editions. The object of this Bibliography was obviously not only to present a collection of works, but as it were to expand the range of the book itself, for it enables the reader to pursue his interests further in any given direction. In order to facilitate orientation, an alphabetical list is given of the special subjects included in the Bibliography, arranged according to the individual poets and prose-writers, only very occasionally according to the works themselves in cases where they are better known than their authors. Learned prose, as such instantly recognizable, has already been assembled in the relevant section of the Bibliography, always under the name of the author in question. Amphilological figures such as ʿOmar Khayyām, Avicenna and others, are dealt with, as is fitting, both in the section on polite literature and in that on scholarly prose. Textual or note references to a passage in the Bibliography are made by means of a special capital letter for each section.

The zeal demonstrated by Iranian scholars for research and composition, which has found valuable support in the activity of the native publishing houses, added to the large amount of specialized study being carried on outside Iran, has obliged the authors of the *History of Iranian Literature* to exercise the utmost restraint in their choice of works to be enumerated. The stream of new publications has waxed and is still waxing to such an extent that it seems to be boundless. Quality, up-to-dateness and importance have had to be the decisive factors for selection. In order to keep pace with this tumultuous advance, and at the same time to confine the size of the Bibliography to reasonable limits, some sort of compromise had to be sought: some of the titles appearing in previous editions have to our great regret been dropped so as to make way for new ones. Older titles of special significance have of course been retained. It should be mentioned that in recent years Iranian bibliography has flourished exceedingly thanks to the efforts of men such as Iraj Afshar, to whom one cannot be adequately grateful. Further particulars are to be found in our Bibliography (B 1). An excellent supplementary source to our own selection for the non-Persian works is J. D. Pearson's *Index Islamicus*, published in the years 1906–1955, 1956–1960 (see Bibliography, B 1). In consequence of an alteration in the date of publication of Volumes 7–9 (1343–1344 A.H. = 1964–1966 A.D.) of *Rāhnāma-i kitāb*, it has alas been impossible to make use of this excellent bibliographical periodical to the extent we should have liked. On the other hand we have been able to enlarge the section dealing with the classical period by the addition of a selection of good Georgian works, albeit only such as were provided with a summary in Russian.

The term 'New Persian' (or 'Neo-Persian') is usually denoted by 'Persian'; similarly, for the sake of brevity, by 'verse' is to be understood 'distich' or 'couplet'. As regards the indication of dates according to the solar Hijra system, it has been deemed sufficient to omit the 'A.D.' equivalent since a simple calculation, $x+621$ (e.g. 1343 solar + 621 = 1964 A.D.) will remove any doubt. On the other hand it was considered imperative to quote lunar dates next to those of the Christian era throughout. If here or there an error has crept in despite the extremely careful revision that has been carried out, we may perhaps be excused in view of the very large number of dates given and of the general uncertainty as to their accuracy.

This foreword cannot be brought to a close before mention has been made of all those persons who have given us their advice and assistance. Their number is however so great that it is alas impossible to give them their due by alluding to them all by name. We must therefore appeal to our friends in East and West to be content with this general but no less heartfelt assurance of our most sincere gratitude.

Nevertheless it would not be right to omit mentioning certain persons who have expended an immense amount of time and trouble in the preparation of this English edition. First and foremost we should like to offer our warmest thanks to Professor Dr Karl Jahn of Leyden University for the disinterested enthusiasm he has brought to bear on the work. After making the acquaintance of the first (Czech) edition of the *History of Iranian Literature*, he at once conceived the plan of having the book translated into English. Through unavoidable circumstances several years elapsed between the completion of the translated text and the actual going to press. And again it is thanks to the untiring efforts of Professor Jahn that the production of the book has now been entrusted to the well-known firm, D. Reidel Publishing Company of Dordrecht, Holland. Nor should his supervision of the translation be underestimated, for his expert knowledge of the subject has many a time stood the translator in good stead in the solution of knotty problems.

After some initial hesitation, Mrs. P. van Popta took on the extremely arduous and difficult translation of the major part of the book and the revision of the remaining sections. Our hearty thanks are due to her for the successful accomplishment of this task, and also for the countless hours of labour involved in the reading of the proofs – not to mention the patience she exhibited in respect of the many alterations and additions made to the text during the course of the translation, which frequently necessitated a recasting of whole portions of the manuscript.

For the adaptation of the Bibliography and the genealogical tables to the requirements of the Anglo-Saxon world, as well as for assistance at other stages of the work, we are deeply indebted to Mr. J. T. P. de Bruijn. Our thanks are also due to Mr. J. P. H. Bosman who compiled the Index, and to Mr. A. H. Nauta who gave invaluable assistance with the revision of the proofs. We should therefore like to take this opportunity of expressing our great appreciation of the punctilious manner in which these exacting portions of the work have been carried out.

During the period when the completed English manuscript was no longer in our hands, a number of new facts and opinions came to light which it seemed a pity not to include. These have been printed separately at the end of the book and are referred to in the text by means of marginal asterisks.

Finally we must not omit to mention the willing and reliable co-operation we have received from the publishers during the production of the book, especially from Mr. H. J. Lek, head of the editorial department.

It now only remains for us to offer our best wishes to the *History of Iranian Literature* on its new flight to far-off lands, in the hope that it will contribute to the spreading of a knowledge of and love towards one of the most glorious literatures of the world.

June, 1967 JAN RYPKA

Any effort on my part to help towards the realization of this English edition of Professor Rypka's *History of Iranian Literature* is amply repaid by the knowledge that it has been expended with the aim of increasing the circle of readers of what will surely become a standard work by one of the most shining lights among modern orientalist scholars, whose erudition will never cease to be an inspiring example to his former pupils – not least to the undersigned.

KARL JAHN

TABLE OF CONTENTS

LIST OF ABBREVIATIONS

Abh. — Abhandlungen

Abt. — Abteilung

ADTD — *Ankara Üniversitesi, Dil ve Tarih-Coğrafya Fakültesi Dergisi*

Ak. der W. und der L. — Akademie der Wissenschaften und der Literatur

AN SSSR; AzSSR; Gruz SSR; TadzhSSR; Uzb SSR — Akademiya Nauk SSSR (=USSR); Azerbaydzhanskoy SSR; Gruzinskoy (= Georgian) SSR; Tadzhikskoy SSR; Uzbekskoy SSR

Annali (Napoli) — *Annali dell' Instituto universitario orientale di Napoli*

Antol. — *Antologia tadzhikskoy poezii* (see Bibl., D IIa)

AR — *The Asiatic Review*

Arb. — A. J. Arberry, *Persian Books, Catalogue of the Library of the India Office* (see Bibl. B I)

Arm. — *Armaghān*

ArOr. — *Archiv Orientální*

ASAW — *Abhandlungen der Sächsischen Akademie der Wissenschaften zu Leipzig*

b. — *ibn* ['son']

B. — Berlin

BAS — *Baroi adabiëti sotsialisti* (see Bibl., D IIIb)

BEO Damas — *Bulletin d'études orientales.* Institut français de Damas

BI — *Bibliotheca Indica*

bibl. — bibliography

BOE — *Bibliothèque orientale Elzéverienne*

BSL — *Bulletin de la Société de linguistiquede Paris*

BSO(A)S — *Bulletin of the School of Oriental (and African) Studies*, London

CAJ — *Central Asiatic Journal*

CAR — *Central Asian Review*

coll. publ. — collective publication

cont., contin. — continuation(s)

CPL — A. J. Arberry, *Classical Persian Literature* (see Bibl., B v)

DAN — *Dokladī Akademii Nauk SSSR*

DRAN — *Dokladī Rossiyskoy Akademii Nauk*

ed. — edition, edited, editor

EI — *Encyclopaedia of Islam* (see Bibl., B I)

Ermit. — see below, *s.v.* 'Gos. Erm.'

Ethé — H. Ethé, *Neupersische Literatur* (see Bibl., B v)

Fihrist — Ibn an-Nadīm, *Kitāb al-Fihrist*, ed. by G. Flügel (Leipzig 1871–2)

FĪZ — *Farhang-i Īrān-zamīn*

FO — *Folia Orientalia*

GAL — C. Brockelmann, *Geschichte der arabischen Literatur* (see Bibl., B I)

GIPh — *Grundriss der iranischen Philologie* (see Bibl., B, p. 757)

GM(N)S — E. J. W. Gibb Memorial (New) Series

Gos.Erm. — Gosudarstvennïy Ermitazh, Leningrad

GSAI — *Giornale della Società asiatica italiana*

Ḥikmat — 'A.-A. Ḥikmat's translation of *LHP*, III (see Bibl., B v, *s.v.* 'E. G. Browne')

Hist.-filol.Medd. — *Det Kgl. Danske Videnskabernes Selskab. Historisk-filologiske Meddelelser*
Horn — Paul Horn, *Geschichte der persischen Literatur* (see Bibl., B v)
hrsg. — herausgegeben
İA — *İslam Ansiklopedisi*
IAN OGN; —*OON*; —*OLY* — *Izvestiya Akademii Nauk SSSR, otdeleniye gumanitarnïkh nauk*; — *otdeleniye obshchestvennïkh nauk*; — *otdeleniye literaturï i yazïka*
IC — *Islamic Culture*
IEFD — *İstanbul Üniversitesi, Edebiyat Fakültesi, Türk Dili ve Edebiyati Dergisi*
IHRC Procs. — *Proceedings of the Indian Historical Records Commission*
IIFL — Georg Morgenstierne, *Indo-Iranian Frontier Languages* (Oslo 1929–1956) (Instituttet for sammenlignende kulturforskning)
ILG — Jan Rypka *et al.*, *Iranische Literaturgeschichte* (see Bibl., B v)
IPTL — Ye. E. Bertel's, *Izbrannïye trudï*: *Istoriya persidsko-tadzhikskoy literaturï* (see Bibl., B v)
Isl. — *Der Islam*
Ist.Uzb. — *Istoriya Uzbekskoy SSR* (see Bibl., D ia)
IVV — Institut vostokovedeniya Akademii Nauk SSSR
Izv. — *Izvestiya*
Izv.Tadzh. — *Izvestiya otdeleniya obshchestvennïkh nauk Akademii Nauk Tadzhikskoy SSR*, Dushanbe
JA — *Journal asiatique*
JAH — *Journal of Asian History*
JAOS — *Journal of the American Oriental Society*
JASP — *Journal of the Asiatic Society of Pakistan*
JPHS — *Journal of the Pakistan Historical Society*
JRAS — *Journal of the Royal Asiatic Society*, London
J(R)ASB — *Journal of the (Royal) Asiatic Society of Bengal*
JRCentr.AS — *Journal of the Royal Central Asian Society*
Karatay — F. E. Karatay, *İstanbul Üniversitesi ... kataloğu* (see Bibl., B i)
Kit. — *Kitābhā-i māh* (see Bibl., B i)
Kl. — Klasse
Krïmskiy — A. Krïmskiy, *Istoriya Persii* (see Bibl., B v)
Krïms'kïy (Ukr.) — A. Krïms'kïy, *Istoriya Persiyi* (see Bibl., B v)
KS — *Kratkiye soobshcheniya Instituta vostokovedeniya Akademii Nauk SSSR*, resp. *Instituta narodov Azii*
KSIE — *Kratkiye soobshcheniya Instituta etnografii*
L. — Leningrad
LGU — Leningradskiy gosudarstvennïy universitet
LHP — E. G. Browne, *A Literary History of Persia* (see Bibl., B v)
Lit.Ir. — *Literatura Irana X–XV vv.* (see Bibl., B via)
lith. — lithograph
Lpz. — Leipzig
M. — Moscow
MDASh — *Majalla-i Dānishkada-i adabiyyāt-i Shīrāz*
MDAT — *Majalla-i Dānishkada-i adabiyyāt-i Tihrān*
MEA — *Middle Eastern Affairs*
MEJ — *Middle Eastern Journal*
Mél. — *Mélanges*
Memoirs ASB — *Memoirs of the Asiatic Society of Bengal*
MSOS — *Mitteilungen des Seminars für orientalische Sprachen, Westasiatische Studien*, Berlin
MS(S). — manuscript(s)
MTA — Magyar Tudományos Akadémia (Hungarian Academy of Sciences)
M. va M. — *Maorif va Madaniyat* (see Bibl., D iiia)
MW — *The Muslim World*
NAA — *Narodï Azii i Afriki*
Namuna — *Namunahoi adabiëti tojik* (see Bibl., D iia)
n.d. — not dated
NDAT — *Nashriyya-i Dānishkada-i adabiyyāt-i Tabrīz*
NKNI — *Nukhustīn kongre-i navīsandagān-i Īrān* (Tehran 1325)
NO — *Nový Orient*
NY — *List of Works in the New York Public Library* (see Bibl., B i)
OCM — *Oriental College Magazine*

OITL — I. S. Braginskiy, *Ocherki iz istorii tadzhikskoy literaturï* (see Bibl., D IIa)
OLZ — *Orientalische Literaturzeitung*
OM — *Oriente moderno*
per. — perevod, perevël ('translation', 'translated')
Przegl.Or. — *Przegląd Orientalistyczny*
PV — *Problemï vostokovedeniya*
RANL — *Rendiconti della Academia nazionale dei Lincei, Scienze morali*
red. — redaction, redactor
REI — *Revue des études islamiques*
repr. — reprinted
RES — *Revue des études sémitiques*
rev. — revised
RK — *Rāhnamā-i kitāb*
RMM — *Revue du monde musulman*
ROr. — *Rocznik Orientalistyczny*
RRAL — *Rendiconti della Reale academia de Lincei*
RSO — *Rivista degli studi orientali*
Sabk — Muḥ. Taqī Bahār, *Sabk-shināsī* (see Bibl., B IV)
Ṣafā — Dh.Ṣafā, *Ta'rīkh-i adabiyyāt dar Īrān* (see Bibl., B V)
Sb. — *Sbornik*
SBAW — *Sitzungsberichte der Akademie der Wissenschaften*
Shiblī — Shiblī Nuʿmānī, *Shiʿru'l-ʿAjam* (see Bibl., B V)
ShS — *Sharqi surkh* (see Bibl., D IIIb)
s.l. — *sine loco*
ŞM — *Şarkiyat Mecmuası*
Sobr. vost. rukop. — *Sobraniye vostochnïkh rukopisey Akademii Nauk Uzbekskoy SSR*, Tashkent
Spraw. Pols. Ak. Umiej — *Sprawozdania Polskiej Akademii Umijetnosci*
SSh — *Sadoi Sharq* (see Bibl., D IIIb)
St. — Stalinobod (Stalinabad)
Storey — C. A. Storey, *Persian Literature* (see Bibl., B V)
SV — *Sovetskoye vostokovedeniye*
T. — Tashkent
Thr. — Tehran
TIE — *Trudï Instituta etnografii*
TIYa — *Trudï Instituta yazïkoznaniya*
TM — *Türkiyat Mecmuası*
TMIV — *Trudï Moskovskogo Instituta vostokovedeniya*
TOV — *Trudï Otdela Vostoka*, Gos. Erm., Leningrad
trad. — traduction, traduit
TS — *Tojikistoni soveti* (see Bibl., D IIIb)
TTK — *Türk Tarih Kurumu*
UAS — *Uralic and Altaic Series (Indiana University Publications)*
übers. — übersetzt
Univ. — university publications, in particular: *Intishārāt-i Dānishgāh-i Tihrān*
UZIV — *Uchënïye zapiski Instituta vostokovedeniya Akademii Nauk SSSR*, Moscow
v., vv. — vek, veki ('century', 'centuries')
VoIst. — *Voprosï istorii*
WZKM — *Wiener Zeitschrift für die Kunde des Morgenlandes*
ZDMG — *Zeitschrift der Deutschen Morgenländischen Gesellschaft*
ZfA — *Zeitschrift für Assyriologie*
ZIV — *Zapiski Instituta vostokovedeniya Akademii Nauk SSSR*
ZKV — *Zapiski kollegii vostokovedov pri Asiatskoy Muzeye Akademii Nauk, Leningrad*
ZVORAO — *Zapiski vostochnogo otdeleniya Russkogo arkheologicheskogo obshchestva*

≅ — indicates that the work referred to has been lithographed or printed several times in India, in Iran or in other Oriental countries.

(For a supplementary list of abbreviations, used only in the section on Persian Learned Literature, see p. 423, note 2)

GUIDE TO PRONUNCIATION

The spelling of Persian names, titles etc. in this work is based on a system of strict transliteration from the Arabic script. Geographic, ethnic and dynastic names, however, are usually given in a form which is current in English.

In pronouncing the transliterated Persian words the following rules should be observed:

1. *ā, ī* and *ū* are long vowels approximately like the English vowels in *barred, beat* and *booed*; the ancient *majhūl* vowels *ē* and *ō* (like English *ai* and *oa* in *raid* and *road*) have been disregarded as far as New Persian is concerned, with the exception of the section on Indo-Persian literature (pp. 711–734) | *au* and *ay* are diphthongs.
2. *zh* = French *j* in *jour*.
3. *ṭ* = *t* | *th* and *ṣ* = *s* | *ẓ*, *ḍ* and *dh* = *z*.
4. *gh* and *q* (Arabic *ghayn* and *qāf*) constitute a single phoneme in modern Persian: a voiced or unvoiced uvular plosive sounding like German *g* in *Tage* | *ḥ* = *h*, pronounced in all positions | *kh* = Scottish *ch* in *loch*.
5. ʾ and ʿ (Arabic *hamza* and *ʿayn*) represent a *hiatus* between two vowels or the lengthening of a preceding short vowel before a consonant; otherwise they are to be disregarded in pronunciation.

In the section on Ancient and Middle Iranian literature (pp. 1–67) some additional rules have been applied:
1. *ə* = a short intermediate vowel approximately like English *u* in *but* | *ą* = a nasalised vowel like French *en* | *ṛ* (in Old Iranian and Old Indic) = a retroflected *r* used as a vowel.
2. *ṣ* (in Khotanese and Old Indic) = *sh*.
3. *th* = English *th* in *thing*.
4. *ṅ* = *ng*.

In the section on Tajik literature (pp. 483–605) a different system of transliteration has been adopted, based on the current orthography of the Tajik language. The following rules are only valid in that section:
1. *o* (Persian *ā*) and *e* are always long vowels | long *ī* is exclusively used at the end of a word; the short *i* in that position marks the *izofa* (*iḍāfat*) | *ū* = a labialised long vowel lower than *u* and higher than *o* | *ë* = *yo* (Persian *yā*) | *ĭ* (in diphthongs) = *y*.

2. ʿ = cyrillic ъ written both for etymological *hamza* and *ʿayn* | ʾ = cyrillic ь, the so-called *alomati judoī*, a punctuation point placed before ё, я (*ya*) and ю (*yu*): *e.g. bisʾёr*.
3. *gh* and *q* are still separate phonemes in Tajik.
This system has also been applied to names and titles belonging to the older periods of Tajik literature when the Arabic script was still in use: *e.g. Badoeʿ-ul-vaqoeʿ* instead of *Badāyiʿuʾl-vaqāyiʿ*.

In Turkish words:
1. *ı* (in the Latin alphabet of Turkey), *ï* (in the Turkic languages of the Soviet Union) = an unrounded intermediate vowel like Russian ы (here also transcribed as *ï*).
2. *c* = *j* | *ç* = *ch* | *ş* = *sh*.
3. *ğ* = *y* (with front vowels) or a very weakly pronounced guttural (with back vowels).

ERRATA

P. 133, line 7: Ibn-i Murfarrigh *must be* Ibn-i Mufarrigh
P. 133, line 32: OF MIDDLE AND PERSIAN VERSE *must be* OF MIDDLE AND NEW PERSIAN VERSE
P. 259, line 11: *Tārīkh-i must be Ta'rīkh-i*
P. 274, note 6: Ivanow *must be* Ivanov
P. 306, line 15: *BAZ-GĀSHT must be BĀZ-GASHT*
P. 307, line 32: *baz-gāsht must be bāz-gasht*
P. 558, line 35: Abdurauf *must be* Abdurrauf
P. 658, line 17: *mathnavī must be Mathnavī*
P. 722, line 4: *mathnavī must be Mathnavī*
P. 733, note 2: Abdulvahab *must be* Abdul Wahab
P. 739, line 13: Ibn Abu'l-Khayr *must be* Ibn Abi'l-Khayr
P. 740, note 1, line 3: *read* 'Qissai Yusuf u Zulaykha'

OTAKAR KLÍMA

AVESTA. ANCIENT PERSIAN INSCRIPTIONS

MIDDLE PERSIAN LITERATURE

I. ANCIENT EASTERN-IRANIAN CULTURE

A. THE BEGINNINGS OF IRANIAN CULTURE

It is only possible to estimate the time of the birth of Iranian culture by analogy with the literatures and cultures of other Indo-European peoples; for there is a complete absence of written documents dating from the time when the Aryans settled in Iran and built up their first centres of culture and civilisation. Even the Indians were unacquainted with the art of writing for a long time after their advent in India and, like them, the Iranian Aryans entrusted the fruits of their minds only to the memory and handed them down by word of mouth from generation to generation. Works of popular origin such as songs, proverbs, riddles, myths and sagas were not written down and underwent many changes in the course of oral transmission. Social development was determined by the transition from nomadic sheep-farming to cattle-breeding and agriculture and eventually crystallised into a three-class system which was maintained for many centuries to come. These classes were the priesthood, whose sole task it was to occupy itself with matters of religion; the nobility, viz. princes, tribal leaders and warriors; and finally the peasantry, who found a subsistence in stock-farming and the cultivation of the soil. Later on a class of artisans and merchants developed, referred to in the Avesta as *hūtai.* Slavery had existed in Iran since time immemorial, the slaves being members of subjugated races and, above all, prisoners of war. The Avesta mentions land servants and distinguishes two classes of these: the first lived permanently in their master's house (the *Vaēsas*), the others worked on the farms as labourers, earned a daily wage and were known as *Pairyaētars* ('itinerants'). The Avestan *Vidēvdāt* states that the fee for the ritual cleansing of a servant was lower than that for the farmer and his wife, but higher than that for the farmer's children. Religion was a matter of the highest importance, for its servants and dignitaries ordered *ex professo* not only the relations between man and God but also between man and his neighbour.

Religion did not possess the restricted scope it does today, but embraced also the authoritative foundation of law, justice, public morals, culture, and economic order. The religious dignitaries established and maintained the socio-religious orders, the *ṛtam*. Their ritual performances were accompanied by songs and hymns, invocations and prayers. At their sacrificial ceremonies they united adherents of the Aryan congregations, thus fostering a community spirit. Of all the manifestations of their imagination and emotion nothing has been preserved in the original form, with the sole exception of a few rhythms and numerous sagas – the latter adapted to the requirements of subsequent generations.

B. THE FIRST STATES

The first mature states in the Aryan Iranian region may have sprung up in the east of the country, as would appear from the Avesta, where at one moment mention is made of the countries on the river Haētumant (Hilmand) and around the lake of Kąsaoya (Hamun in Sistan) and at the next of those on the other side of the Oxus (Amu-Darya) and of the lake of Vourukasha (maybe Lake Aral). There is no doubt that the tradition according to which the Aryan tribes migrated from their former homeland *Airyanəm vaējah* to other parts of Iran is very old. Many scholars believe this country of origin to have been situated to the north-east of Iran. Samarkand, Merv, Balkh (the ancient Baktra of the Greeks) and Sistan are perhaps the first centres of Aryan culture in Iran. This was the scene of ancient mythical Iranian history, which was to be moulded in its greatest form in the work of Firdausī.

The settlements lying further to the west suffered a long time under Semitic pressure. It is probable that the fabulous monster of the Avesta, the Dragon King *Azhai Dahāka*, was the symbol of oppression emanating from Akkad and penetrating to the east beyond the Median frontier. Moreover, between Babylon and Fars there existed for many hundreds of years an important state populated by a non-Indo-European people, Elam, which for a long time withstood the attacks of its neighbours. The eastern Aryan kingdoms certainly suffered in their turn under the invasions of the Central Asian nomads, for whom the Aryans had always employed the name *Tūra*. Among these are the Indo-European and non-Aryan tribes living on the other side of the Yaxartes (Syr-Darya) and belonging to a group of peoples to whom, owing to a regrettable error, the name of Scythians had been given already in ancient times. The natural aversion and spontaneous animosity which existed between the settled and the nomadic portions of the population is the most characteristic trait in the mutual relations of the Iranians and the Tūra. *The antithesis between the two regions has become the foundation and the main feature of Iranian national tradition, viz. a dualistic conception of the world and of history*. This contrast is already evident in the Avesta, in fragments and echoes of the sagas, and reached its climax as regards artistic treatment in the epic work of Firdausī. As a people the Iranians are virtuous, intelligent and order-loving, with a veneration for work, light and all that is good, while the Tūra are a people of evil, cunning, violence, destruction, addicted to the powers of darkness, war, robbery, and obscurity. And this social, economic and historical disparity contributed in large measure to the formation of dualism in the spiritual life of the Iranians. The second component was the religion of Zarathushtra, one of the most important religious reforms in the history of the world.

C. ZARATHUSHTRA

The history of Zarathushtra and the inception of his religion are uncertain. It is probable that the Prophet and creator of the Iranian dualistic doctrine appeared somewhere in an East-Iranian kingdom before the commencement of Persian history as we know it. Experts date his life in the 6th century B.C., though no adequate proof has as yet been brought to light. The grounds for this dating can be found in the traditional Parsee church chronology, which reckoned the time between Zarathushtra and Alexander the Great as three hundred years. But this chronology is not reliable, and up till now we possess no other key to the correct timing of events than the Parsee. It is not even known whence the Prophet came. Some traditions put his birthplace in north-western Iran. From his youth on he was acquainted with the harsh absurdities of the old ritual which led to the excessive slaughtering of cattle for the innumerable sacrifices and orgiastic revelries held in honour of the ancient idols. At such orgies especial honour was paid to the genius of the intoxicating drink *haoma*. The old cult reduced the peasant class to a state of poverty and resulted in a harmful strengthening of the power of fortune-tellers and magicians, *Karpans*, whose influence had also to be taken into account by the *Kavais*, the tribal rulers. Zarathushtra is said to have gone into 'voluntary exile' in his twentieth year in order to be able to work as a preacher of new conceptions. But it was not until ten years later that he was granted a revelation of the highest, sole and true God *Ahura Mazdā*, whereby also his own mission became evident. After considerable further toil his dogmas were accepted by the ruler Vishtāspa (somewhere in eastern Iran) who became his follower and patron and an apostle of the new religion. In his seventy-seventh year Zarathushtra was put to death by the Turanians on their invasion of Iran; according to a more recent tradition he was slain before the fire-altar at Balkh. The story of his life was very soon adorned with numerous legends and miraculous episodes. In the Younger Avesta Zarathushtra appears as an example of perfect humanity. The *Fravardīn-Yasht* portrays him for us in the following inspired words:

Zarathushtra was the first who thought what is good, who spoke what is good, who did what is good, who was the first priest, the first warrior, the first cattle-breeder, the first revealer, the first who got the revelation, who first deserved and first took possession of the cattle and of the wages and of the word, the obedience to the word, and dominion, and all the good things made by Mazdā, that originated from the genuine religion. He was the first who turned away his face from the Daēvas and human race, who first in this world pronounced the praise of Asha and refused to worship the Daēvas, and confessed himself a worshipper of Mazdā, an adherent of Mazdā, one who hates the Daēvas, and obeys the law of Ahura, who first in this world preached against the Daēvas, who first in this world declared the Daēvas unworthy of sacrifice and prayer. He was the first who gave all the good things of life with success, the first prophet in the world. From him we first heard the right word, containing the whole revelation. He was the master and teacher of living creatures, the praiser of the genuine religion, the greatest, the best, the fairest, the first seeker of the religion that is best of all. (Yt. XIII, 87–91; after Wolff)

In essence Zarathushtra's teaching is dualistic. The true God of Virtue, Light, Life, *Ahura Mazdā*, is opposed to the arch-demon of Evil, Darkness and Death, *Angra Mainyav*. Its first manifestation is described at the beginning of the 30th Yasna as follows:

In the beginning there were two spirits, twins, who were according to the dream revelation called the Good and the Evil in thought and word and deed. Between them those rightly chose whose behaviour was good and not bad. And when these two spirits met, for the first time they established Life and Death and stated that finally the unbeliever should suffer from the worst existence while the orthodox would be rewarded for his good thought. (Ys. 30, 3–4; after Bartholomae)

They have divided the whole universe between them and, aided by spiritual beings and by men, they continue the struggle against each other until the end of the world. God is in reality only *Ahura Mazdā*, the Wise Lord; the Demon is not a God. The ethical postulate of the victory of Good required a belief in the ultimate victory of the forces of Good. Ahura and his heavenly host protect Truth, Good, Justice, useful work and all qualities on which the order of Good is founded. The ancient Aryan idols became *Daēvas* (Demons), but in later times several of them were rehabilitated and accorded a place among the followers of Ahura, in particular the spirit of the intoxicating drink *haoma* and the ancient divine fighter of monsters and redeemer of mankind, the Indo-Iranian Hercules, *Indra*, for the people were not easily able to relinquish their ancient gods. It is the moral duty of Man to aid Ahura in his struggle against the Evil One and inexorably to combat everything which the arch-demon has created and everything he employs as a means to victory; to avoid falsehood, to kill harmful creatures, to vanquish the enemies of faith, to fulfil his duties properly and especially to work. Agriculture was regarded as the most meritorious form of labour. The *Vidēvdāt*, the Law against Evil Spirits, says:

> *To him who tills the earth, Spitama Zarathushtra, neither with his left arm nor with his right one, says the earth: "Thou shalt stand leaning at the door of the stranger and among those who beg for food; those will pass round you who will be bringing the food to those who have profusion of good things."* (III, 28–29; after Wolff)

Work is the most powerful instrument in the struggle against evil, next to the magical power of the words of prayer. The *Vidēvdāt* says, moreover:

> *When the corn is set to be threshed, the Daēvas start sweating for anguish, when the mill is prepared, the Daēvas cease to be content, when the flour is worked up into dough, the Daēvas groan, when the dough is prepared for baking, the Daēvas emit winds from anxiety.* (III, 32; after Wolff)

Among the important duties of human beings were of course also participation in religious services, belief in the priests, and obedience to superiors. Of the elements, Fire was worshipped as a symbol of purity, light, and warmth; of the animals the cow, the dog and the cock were revered. Mazdaism inspired the Iranians with a strong religio-national consciousness, built up a strictly organised system of social collectives, the privileges and duties of which were narrowly defined, while their spirit contained something of militarism. The Iranians regarded themselves as God's people, the chosen of Ahura, whereas other nations belonged to the Evil Spirit. It was for this reason that, when it ultimately became victorious, the religion supported a marked tendency to arrogance, intolerance and proselytism. In this form, however, Mazdaism only appeared in the Sasanian period. Family life was highly esteemed. Asceticism was repudiated because, according to Iranian views, it weakens men in the struggle against the forces of Evil.

D. AVESTA

I. THE 'GĀTHĀS'

The oldest Iranian language in which we possess a relatively large number of documents is that of the Avesta, i.e. the collection of sacred books of the Mazdaistic religion. According to Parsee tradition, however, only a small proportion of these has been preserved. Another regrettable circumstance is that the sacred text was committed to writing only at a very late date, probably under the Sasanians in about the 4th century A.D., and that, moreover, a spelling was employed which tended considerably to obscure the true form of the language. As regards the wealth of forms and the nature of the syntactical constructions, it may be said that the Avestan language entirely attains the level of the ancient Indian Vedic language, viz. in the texts which in all probability can be attributed to the first period of the Mazdaistic creed. These texts, which are written in verse form, are known as *Gāthās* ('sung strophes') and are said to have been composed by Zarathushtra himself. There is no plausible reason for doubting this. They appear to be metrical formulations of the basic principles of the Prophet's preaching, containing the quintessence of his dogma. Occasionally we encounter in the *Gāthās* a more personal note, an emotion, joy or disillusion. We catch a glimpse of the difficulties surrounding the Prophet's life; he fights against the powerful Karpans, he sees his work almost frustrated, he is overcome by despair:

> *To what land to flee, whither to flee shall I go? They separate me from the clans and the confederates, nor does the peasantry seek to please me, nor those who are the evil rulers of the country. How to thee, Ahura Mazdā, am I to render satisfaction?*
>
> (According to R. P. Dewhurst)

But finally his teaching triumphs. In the last chapter of the *Gāthās* we witness his success in the marriage of his youngest daughter Pouruchistā with Jāmāspa, the wise counsellor of Vishtāspa. The *Gāthās* contain altogether 248 strophes in 17 chapters of the Yasna. Yet, it is not certain whether these chapters consist of the strophes in the original arrangement or whether they are the result of subsequent editing.

2. 'YASNA', 'VISPRAT'

The *Gāthās* are to be found in the first part of the Avesta, in a collection of liturgical prayers which accompanied the main religious service. They are called *Yasna*, 'liturgy'. The language of this book, as also of the other portions of the Avesta, is a dialect closely related to that of the *Gāthās*, nevertheless frequently revealing a poverty of forms that is no doubt the result of the evolution of the language. This language is known as Younger Avestan. In the most recent parts there are even errors to be found of such a kind as to provide evidence of the language having been quite dead at the time they were written. The most arresting part of the *Yasna*, apart from the *Gāthās*, is the *Homyasht*, in which is described the revelation of the idol Haoma to Zarathushtra. It also bears witness to the fact that after the death of the Prophet the religion began, at any rate in certain respects, to revert to the old conceptions, which were deeply rooted among the people and held in great esteem.

At the time of the first pressing of haoma, Haoma approached to Zarathushtra, as he was concerned with the sacred fire, while he sang the Gāthās. Zarathushtra asked him: "Who art thou, man, who art of all the visible world the most beautiful in thine own body of those whom I have seen, the glorious immortal?" Thereupon answered Haoma, the holy one who drives death afar: "I am, Zarathushtra, Haoma, the holy and driving death afar. Take me to the sacrifice, Spitama, press me for the drinking. Sing toward me praises as the other helpers of God will praise me." Thereupon spoke Zarathushtra: "Haoma be praised!" (Y. IX, 1–3; after Wolff)

The greatest part of the *Yasna*, however, consists only of litany-like invocations. Even more monotonous are the contents of another collection of prayers and invocations, the *Visprat* ('All Arbitrators or Patrons'). Of the prayers the best-known and most frequently recited is the strophe *Ashəm vohu:*

Asha is the highest Good; it shall be granted us according to our desires, Asha for the best Asha. (Y. XXVII, 14; after Wolff)

The meaning of some of the words in the Avesta is still not exactly known. According to Bartholomae, for instance, three meanings of the word *Asha* occur in this prayer: justice, the right to Paradise, righteousness.

3. THE 'YASHTS'

Compared with the *Yasna* and the *Visprat*, the collection of the *Yashts*, 'Songs of Praise', is of considerably greater interest. The *Yashts* are religious hymns glorifying certain of the gods of the Avestan pantheon. The most important are those in praise of the gods who protect the Avestan people in their struggle against enemies and bring aid and redemption to its leaders. Into these hymns the religious singers wove fragments from the popular heroic epics, thereby preserving many an epical tradition from the pre-Zarathushtran period. The fifth *Yasht* celebrates in song the spirit of a mythical river which is represented by a fair maiden *Arədvī Sūrā anāhitā* ('the strong immaculate Arədvī'), the personification of the fertilising power of the waters. This goddess imparts strength to the heroes of Good in their combats. The description of this deity is interesting and is characteristic of the imaginative power of the singer:

Worship, O Spitama Zarathushtra, this powerful pure Arədvī, spreading afar, bringing health, fighting against the Daēvas, devoted to Ahura's doctrine, who deserves to be worshipped by the creatures of the earth, to be praised by the creatures of the earth, augmenting zeal, augmenting herds of cattle, augmenting farms, augmenting wealth, augmenting fields; she can always be seen – this powerful pure Arədvī – in beautiful maiden's form, very strong, well-developed, girded high, tall in form, of glorious lineage, nobly born, wearing a precious well-adorned golden mantle. As needed, she holds a bunch of barəsman twigs in her hand. Being proud of her gold four-cornered ear-rings, the noble powerful pure Arədvī wears her necklace round her fair neck. Tightly has she girded her waist in order that her breasts may be well-shaped and pleasing. The powerful pure Arədvī fastened a golden diadem set with one hundred jewels on her head. The diadem is in eight parts, formed like a chariot's frame with beautiful fillets, good in size and well-fashioned. The fillet stands out in it. The powerful pure Arədvī wears a garment made of three hundred female beavers that drop four young ones each, as the female beaver is most beautiful when its fur is thickest. The beaver is an aquatic animal. If rightly dressed at the proper time the hides radiate their golden and silver lustre on to the beholders.

(*Yasht* v, 125 *et seq.*; after Wolff)

The extraordinarily prosaic tone of the last words gives us reason to suppose that some intrepid person has inserted an instructive gloss in prose into the poetic hymn. This occurs not infrequently in the Younger Avesta.

In the eighth *Yasht* the angel *Tishtrya*, the deified star Sirius, comes to the fore. It is he who brings moisture to the earth, after having vanquished the demon of drought, *Apaosha:*

We worship Tishtrya for whom waters, pools and rivers long, in fountains and in running streams, snow-waters and rain-waters: When will the bright and glorious Tishtrya rise for us? When will the springs thick as a horse run here? When will they flow to the beautiful places and houses and pastures, to flood with their powerful growth?

(*Yasht* VIII, 41 *et seq.*)

The hero of the tenth *Yasht* is *Mithra*, the God of Light, who proclaims the rising of the sun, the Protector of Order, of Fidelity, of the Oath. Later on Mithra was worshipped in a mystery religion which spread throughout the whole of the Roman Empire and was cultivated especially in the lodges of soldiers and merchants. This *Yasht* contains a great many descriptions of battle-scenes.

The thirteenth *Yasht* is in praise of the guardian angels of the faithful Iranian clans and tribes, the *Fravashais*, represented as women. This is the army of Ahura that descends once a year from Heaven to its native haunts and is there worshipped by the faithful. These are probably the souls of dead ancestors who were worshipped as gods.

The fourteenth *Yasht* is in celebration of *Vərəthraghna*, the genius of victory, corresponding to *Indra* of the Indians. He revealed himself to Zarathushtra in ten different forms: as the wind, a bull, a horse, a camel, a boar, a fair fifteen-year-old youth, a bird of prey *vārəgan*, a ram, a he-goat, and a warrior. The following is the poet's description of the bird of prey:

catching his prey from below, tearing it from above, who among the birds is the swiftest, the quickest of them that fly forward. He alone among living creatures overtakes an arrow in flight, however well it has been shot forth; who, ruffling up his feathers, flies up at the first break of dawn, seeking his evening meal at nightfall, his morning meal at daybreak. In his flight he brushes the clefts of the mountains, he lightly touches mountain peaks and the river valleys and the summits of trees; he listens to the voices of the birds. (*Yasht* XIV, 19 *et seq.*; after Wolff)

The poet is fond of watching Nature and observing the lives of beasts, birds and quadrupeds. He longs to have a power of sight as sharp as

the golden-collared vulture that can perceive a piece of flesh as large as a fist even across eight countries. (*Yasht* XIV, 33; after Wolff)

The feather of this bird acts as a charm:

Zarathushtra asked Ahura Mazdā: "O, Ahura Mazdā, most beneficent Spirit, Maker of the visible world, the most dignified in the order. If a curse is cast upon me, a spell told upon me by the enemies who hate me, what is the remedy for it?" Ahura Mazdā answered: "Take a feather of that bird vārəngan with spread wings, O Spitama Zarathushtra! With that feather thou shalt rub thy own body, with that feather thou shalt curse back thy enemies." (*Yasht* XIV, 34–35; after Wolff)

In the seventeenth *Yasht Ashai vaṅuhī* is extolled as the Giver of Happiness and of Prosperity arising from pious devotion. She it is also who is the patroness of Marriage.

The most important *Yasht* in the heroic epic is the nineteenth, containing songs of praise in addition to the mythical story of the *Khvarənah* ('glory'). Heroes and saints were surrounded by the Khvarənah, which endowed them with the divine blessing and legitimacy. The Khvarənah abandoned kings who had sinned, and their good fortune deserted them. Heroes of non-Iranian descent never succeeded in the permanent possession of the Khvarənah. The last to wear the nimbus in the Avesta are Zarathushtra and his royal patron Vishtāspa. One day the halo will be granted to the last of God's helpers at the Last Judgement, Saoshyant and his companions

in order to restore mankind, which will then never grow old and never die, never decay and never rot, will ever live and ever increase and act according to its will.
(*Yasht* XIX, 89; after Wolff)

All the forces of Good will unite in the struggle against the powers of Evil and will vanquish them. This is the old story of the end of the world and of the struggle to be made by the gods to achieve final victory over Evil. But this sombre hymn ends nevertheless on an optimistic note: there is a more perfect creation to come and the victory of Good is assured. In this *Yasht* we find the names of the principal heroes, from the first king of the Iranian saga Haoshyaṅha (Hūshang) up to Vishtāspa, the first Mazdaist on the Iranian throne. Of all these valiant heroes the most famous is Kərəsāspa (Garshāsp in New Persian poetry) who freed Iran from numerous demons and even fought with the dragon, as is related in the *Hōmyasht* of the *Yasna*:

> *He was a young man famous for his strength, had curly hair and swung his club; he smote the horny dragon, the horse-swallowing and men-swallowing, full of poison, yellow of colour, over whom yellow poison flowed as high as a spear. On his back Kərəsāspa cooked his meal in an iron cauldron at the time of noon. And the monster felt warm and began to sweat. Then he rushed from under the iron cauldron and upset the boiling water. Affrighted rushed headlong the valiant Kərəsāspa.*
>
> (*Yasht* IX, 10 *et seq.*; after Wolff)

After his brother, the legislator Urvākhshaya, had been assassinated, Kərəsāspa killed his murderer according to the ancient law of blood-revenge and tied his body to a carriage to be dragged to his home, as is related in the fifteenth *Yasht* (28). This description reminds one of the similar scene in the *Iliad*, where Achilles avenged himself in the same way on the dead Hector for the death of Patroclos. It may be that this is an ancient Indo-European custom.

The remaining *Yashts* are of more recent date and, as regards their contents, on the whole less important. In the *Yasna* there are two very old *Yashts*, one in praise of *Haoma* and the other of *Sraosha*, the angel who guards in their sleep those who labour and fulfil the will of God.

4. 'VIDĒVDĀT'

The *Vidēvdāt*, 'the Law against Evil Spirits', draws the attention not only of linguists and students of religion, but also of theologians, folklorists, and jurists. In a very long section, which begins with extremely ancient sagas concerning the creation of the Iranian countries and the reign of the mythical king *Yima Khshaēta* (Jamshēd), we find an exposition of the precepts of religious law, namely the laws laid down by the priests to regulate the relations between the two worlds, the material and the supernatural, as well as between man and man. These rules were based on diverse beliefs, customs and superstitions of the ancient religion of Iran. Attention is drawn to purity and of the care to be bestowed on fire and other elements specially subject to pollution by contact with the dead body; a description is given of the purification ceremony of those who are obliged to handle corpses; verses of the Gāthās are quoted which are effective against Evil Spirits; instructions are given as to the care of different breeds of dogs and other domestic animals; various transgressions against the social order, violation of contracts etc. are discussed.

In the nineteenth chapter a legend of Zarathushtra is related of how he was tempted by the evil spirit Angra Mainyav to abandon the true faith and follow him. In return Zarathushtra was promised fame and wealth. But the Prophet repelled him and his demons by the words of prayer. The *Vidēvdāt* contains many cultural and historical details and gives a deep insight into the life of the Mazdaistic religious community, its morality, its creed and its often very curious superstitions. Particularly interesting is the account given of the demons, swarms of them being present in Nature around the Iranian, the main feature in whose character must be an unflinching caution in his struggle against the forces of Evil. From this follows the emphasis on everything that tends to make man wary and on the alert: on obedience to virtuous beings, on the usefulness of domestic animals, notably the dog which defends (man) against brigands, and the cock which chases away darkness and arouses men to prayer and work, and on the good elements, particularly Fire, which banishes demons.

The saga in the second chapter of the *Vidēvdāt* is an unexcelled sample of an ancient saga in which we find a reflection of the fear of the 'Untergang des Zeitalters' (The Fall of the Era), also typical of the nordic hymns in the Edda, together with the hope of salvation and transition to the paradisiacal age to come:

Zarathushtra asked Ahura Mazdā: "O Ahura Mazdā, most beneficent Spirit, Maker of the visible world, the most dignified in the order! Who was the first mortal before myself, Zarathushtra, with whom thou, Ahura Mazdā, didst converse, whom thou didst teach the law of Ahura, the law of Zarathushtra?" Ahura Mazdā answered: "The fair Yima, the great shepherd, O holy Zarathushtra. He was the first mortal before thee, Zarathushtra, with whom I, Ahura Mazdā, conversed, whom I taught the law of Ahura, the law of Zarathushtra. O Zarathushtra, I, Ahura Mazdā, told him: 'Well, fair Yima, son of Vīvahvant, be thou the preacher and the bearer of my law.' And the fair Yima, O Zarathushtra, replied to me, saying: 'I was not born, I was not taught to be the preacher and the bearer of thy law.' Then I, Ahura Mazdā, said thus to him, O Zarathushtra: 'Since thou wantest not to be the preacher and the bearer of my law, make my worlds thrive, make my worlds increase, undertake to nourish, to rule, and to watch over my world.' And the fair Yima replied to me, O Zarathushtra, saying: 'Yes, I will make thy worlds increase, I will nourish and rule and watch over thy world. There shall be, while I am king, neither cold wind nor hot wind, neither disease nor death.' Then I, Ahura Mazdā, brought two implements to him: a golden arrow and a whip adorned with gold. Behold, here Yima bears the royal sway. Thus under the sway of Yima, three hundred winters passed away, and the earth was filled with small animals and big animals, with men and dogs and birds and with red blazing fires, and there was no more room for small animals and big animals and men. Then I warned the fair Yima, saying: 'O fair Yima, son of Vīvahvant, the earth has become full of small animals and big animals, of men and dogs and birds and of red blazing fires, and there is no more room for small animals, big animals and men.' Then Yima stepped forward, towards the luminous space, southwards, to meet the sun, and he rent the earth with the golden arrow and lashed it with the whip, speaking thus: 'O Spənta Ārmaiti, kindly open asunder and stretch thyself afar, to bear small animals and big animals and men.' And Yima made the earth grow larger by one-third than it was before, and there came small animals and big animals and men, at his will and wish, as many as he wished. Thus, under the sway of Yima, six hundred winters passed away, and the earth was filled with small animals and big animals, with men and dogs and birds and with red blazing fires ..." (*Vidēvdāt* II, 1–12; after Wolff)

And the saga goes on to tell how Yima with his divine weapons tore the earth asunder and passed his hand over it, thus enlarging it by two-thirds. But the number of creatures likewise increased and the earth again became too small for them. At Ahura's command Yima made the earth still larger, this time by three-thirds. The ancient character and origin of this story is proved by the three-fold repetition of the action and by the fairy-tale-like tone, as well as by its simplicity – so characteristic of the myth. Plot and *dramatis personae* appear only in outline; space and time are accorded the same function as in a fairy-tale. It may be that we are dealing here with a reflection of ancient Iranian history, a memory of the time when the Aryans were seeking new dwelling-places.

The second part of Chapter II describes how Yima was granted a revelation on the occasion of a gathering of gods and heroes in his native land Airyanəm vaējah:

the evil mankind of this world will suffer from winters and masses of snow will fall and only one-third of the animal world will be saved. Before this winter the earth used to have pastures with much grass; now when the snow melts, waters will flood the earth which will appear inaccessible for the world in those places where now a ram's foot-prints can be seen. (Vd. II; 22–24; after Wolff)

Ahura commands Yima to build a subterranean asylum for the descendants of small and large beasts and men and dogs and birds and of red flaming fire, also of plants and victuals, where the creatures would survive this catastrophe as in a paradise. Yima appears here as the redeemer of creation, who will save all creatures in his subterranean fortress Var. It is interesting that the Soviet archaeologist S. P. Tolstov discovered the remains of a settlement in Central Asia to which the description of Vara in the Avesta can well be applied.

Cleanliness and physical health were of immeasurable value to the ancient Iranians. The *Vidēvdāt* establishes the fees to be paid for purification and medical treatment (IX, 37 *et seq.*). The scale of charges demonstrates the different grades in the social ladder and the economic importance of the population of the various districts of Iran.

The priest paid with his blessing, the power of which was believed to be as great as the most effective remedy, the king paid with a camel, the provincial governor with a stallion, the village mayor with a bull, the farmer with a cow in calf. The charge made for a housewife was a heifer, for a servant a milch cow, for a child a lamb. The transactions were clinched by word of honour, by a handshake or by mortgage. Violation of law and justice was punished by flogging, although later it was possible for the culprit to get himself free by paying a ransom. The *Vidēvdāt* contains detailed instructions regarding purification, notably in connection with uncleanliness arising from funeral obsequies. The nineteenth *frakart*, 'chapter', gives the legend of the temptation of the Prophet by the Evil Spirit:

> *From the north, from the north rushed forth Angra Mainyav, the Daēva of the Daēvas, who brings all sorts of death. And thus spoke the crafty evil-doer Angra Mainyav, bringing all sorts of death: "Druj, rush down upon him, destroy the holy Zarathushtra!" The Druj came rushing along. Zarathushtra chanted aloud the Ahuna Vairya ... he offered up prayers to the good waters of the good Dāitya and professed the doctrine of the worshippers of Mazda. The Druj dismayed, rushed away. ... And the Druj ... said to Angra Mainyav: "O Angra Mainyav! I see no way to kill him, Spitama Zarathushtra, so great is the glory of the holy Zarathushtra." Zarathushtra saw from within his soul: "The evil-doing Daēvas ... take counsel together for my death." Up started Zarathushtra, forward went Zarathushtra, ... swinging stones in his hand, stones as big as a house, ... "At what on this wide, round earth, whose ends lie afar, at what dost thou swing those stones?" Thus Zarathushtra answered Angra Mainyav: "O evil-doer, Angra Mainyav, I will smite the creation of the Daēva. I will smite the Nasu, a creature of the Daēva. I will smite the Pairika Khnąthaiti, till the fiend-smiter Saoshyant comes up to life out of the lake Kąsava, from the east, from the east." Again to him said Angra Mainyav: "Do not destroy my creatures, O holy Zarathushtra! Thou art the son of Pourushāspa. ... Renounce the good doctrine of the worshippers of Mazdā, and thou shalt gain such a boon as the king Vadhagan gained." Thus in answer to him said Spitama Zarathushtra: "No, never will I renounce the good doctrine of the worshippers of Mazda, in order that the body, the life, the power and the senses should not separate."* (Vidēvdāt XIX, 1–7; after Wolff)

The twenty-second *frakart* narrates how Angra Mainyav afflicted Ahura Mazdā with 99,999 diseases. Ahura begs the spirit Aryaman and the Holy Word to heal him.

5. MINOR TEXTS

The *Vidēvdāt* also contains additions of later date. Besides these texts there is to be found in the Avesta a collection of prayers, and similar formulae, the so-called *Khvar-*

tak Apastāk (Khorda Avesta, 'Small Avesta'). There are also a considerable number of fragments scattered in Middle Persian books; as well as this there are also several texts all of a religious nature, written in the Avestan language but nevertheless not incorporated in the Avesta, such as the *Nīrangistān*, *Argəmadaēchā*, *Hādōkht-nask*, etc.

6. TRADITIONS REGARDING THE ORIGIN OF THE AVESTA

As to the origin and history of the Avesta, only a few short accounts have been preserved in the Iranian Parsee tradition. The teaching of the Prophet is said to have been written down by his son-in-law, pupil and follower Jamāspa. Two official copies were lost immediately after the invasion of Alexander the Great. These had been copied from the archetype, which was written with gold ink on ox-hide parchment and was kept in the royal treasure-chambers. It is said that subsequently the Parthian king Valgash and the founder of the Sasanian dynasty, Artakhshēr I Pāpakān (224–241) had the scattered fragments of the text collected; tradition mentions the wise Magian Tansar, an expert on the Avesta, in connection with the first Sasanian edition. But it was only under Shāhpuhr II (309–379) that the collection, arranged by the theologian Āturpāt, son of Mahrəspand (c. 340) was given ecclesiastical recognition. It is not yet certain to what extent these traditions may be regarded as authenticated historical truth. The account given by Āturpāt, son of Mahrəspand, may nevertheless have some truth in it, for in the 4th century the Zoroastrian church had to fight against considerable competition from Manichaeism and from Christianity. These churches possessed extensive canons of their already well-ordered scriptures. Perhaps these traditions serve to explain why the Avesta was for so long not committed to writing. The life of Āturpāt was later embellished by a religious legend: in order to prove the authenticity of his collection of Avestan texts, Āturpāt subjected himself to a divine judgement during which molten metal was allowed to trickle over his bare chest, and he withstood this ordeal. According to a saga, this was the same means of proving the divine mission as that to which Zarathushtra had once submitted himself in Heaven before the throne of God. The establishment of Manichaean missions and the fact that shortly after its inception Manichaeism was able to boast of a rich theological literature, gave rise to the systematization of the Mazdaistic canon during the Sasanian period. Mānī himself is said to have written seven books (all in Aramaic, with the exception of one in Persian). He appears to have accused the Persian priesthood of having brought disorder into the Holy Scriptures. Several theological schools (Zurvanites and Gayōmardites) and sectarian movements also induced official theologians to work on the Avestan canon. According to tradition the canon contained in the Sasanian period twenty-one *nasks* ('sections') of which only a small part has been preserved. The oldest Avestan manuscripts in existence today date only from the 13th and 14th centuries, most of the others being of far more recent origin.

7. BEGINNINGS OF IRANIAN PHILOLOGY. SIGNIFICANCE OF THE AVESTA

As early as the 17th century a number of Avestan manuscripts found their way to Europe. The French scholar Abraham Hyacinthe Anquetil Duperron was the first to attempt a translation of the Avestan texts (1771) after a sojourn in the Indian Parsee colonies (1758–1761), where he had become acquainted with the Zoroastrian religion from native priests. Sceptical scholars of the 18th century, however, declared his translation to be a forgery, maintaining that it was another specimen of the predilection for the moral teachings of oriental sages current in this period of Enlightenment. After a long and learned dispute the authenticity of Anquetil's Avesta was established in 1826, after the Dane R.K. Rask had brought other manuscripts of the original from India and explained the nature of the newly-discovered literature. He thus laid the foundation for the study of Iranian philology, the further development of which has largely been due to his compatriot Niels L. Westergaard, who was the first to publish the Avesta, the Frenchman E. Burnouf, who attempted to explain the *Yasna* with the aid of the Sanskrit translation, and of the German scholars Martin Haug and Friedrich Spiegel. Research on the Avesta then continued hand in hand with the study of Middle Persian, which had been initiated in 1793 by the French orientalist A. Silvestre de Sacy, who deciphered inscriptions and legends on coins, and with Indo-European comparative philology. It was the modern grammatical school of German linguists that first brought complete elucidation of the Avestan text and set both the grammar and the vocabulary on a firm and steady foundation for posterity. It is fitting here to commemorate the greatest investigator of our subject, Christian Bartholomae (1855–1925), who, on account of his critical faculty and all-round knowledge of the problem, may be described as the founder of modern Iranian studies.

From the standpoint of theology, cultural history and linguistics, the Avesta forms a highly interesting and, for the study of philology and history of Iran, an unusually important text. It contains ideas and conceptions from different epochs in the development of Mazdaism, and its languages reflect various periods in the history of Iranian. It may be only due to an unpropitious stroke of fate that the preserved portions of the Avesta cannot compete with the scriptures of Judaism and Christianity on the grounds of their ethical content and profundity of thought. For not even single parts of the extant portions can be considered to be on a level with single parts of the Bible, such as the Pentateuch, the Prophets, the Psalms or the Gospels. The chief significance of the Avesta lies in the fact that for the first time in history it gave form to dualism, the harsh antithesis of two entities which reveal themselves in the universe and which, owing to the relationship between them, determine the nature and way of the world and its origins and history. But it was just this character that made it impossible for dualism to assume a leading position in the subsequent religious development of humanity, for this was reserved for monotheistic religions.

II. THE CULTURE OF THE ANCIENT MEDES AND PERSIANS

A. THE MEDES AND PERSIANS

The real history of Iran commences with the mention of the wars between the Akkadian Semites and the Aryan inhabitants of western Iran in the 9th century B.C. and with the founding of the Median kingdom – the capital of which was Hagmatāna (Greek Ecbatana, known today as Hamadān; the name denoted originally 'place of meeting' – at the close of the 8th and the beginning of the 7th century B.C. It is mainly due to the work of two scholars, the German Ferdinand Justi (1837–1907) and the Czech Justin Václav Prášek (1853–1924), that the history of the earliest Aryan powers in Iran, the Medes, and their even more renowned successors the Persians, is now not only clear to us in outline but with a wealth of detail as well. After the catastrophic invasions by the savage brethren of the Medes, the Scythians, the Medes, in conjunction with the Babylonians, succeeded in destroying the kingdom of their Assyrian oppressors and in establishing the first Iranian empire. With the exception of a few proper names of rulers, generals and cities and about three appellatives (*tigris*, 'arrow', *spaka*, 'dog', *tetaros*, *tatyras*, 'pheasant', *cf.* the New Persian *tadarv*, Czech *tetřev*, 'woodcock'), the language of the Medes is unfortunately unknown to us since no Median records have been preserved. In the 6th century the Persian kingdom, which originated in a part of the present-day Fars and had annexed part of Elam, began to grow in importance. In Akkadian texts it was called *Anzān*. The standard of culture in both kingdoms, until the year 550 B.C. under the hegemony of Media, was at first not very high. But there too the social organisation was on the whole the same as that to the east of the Iranian mountain country. As well as the corps of religious functionaries (Magians) there was the ruling military aristocracy, among which there were seven families who greatly influenced the politics of the new dynasty in Persia. Economically the most important class in the community was the peasantry who cultivated the land, and the nomad herdsmen who bred the cattle. The heads of the state in western Iran were the kings (*Khshāyathiya*) who sought to come to an understanding with the powerful nobles but on every possible occasion furthered their own ends. A culture gradually developed thanks to the infiltration of Semitic, Elamitic and Urartian elements. In both kingdoms there was a large population of slaves, whose position within the framework of the original patriarchal system was fairly tolerable. But only Greek texts make any mention of these slaves; there are no Iranian records in existence concerning this class.

B. THE ACHAEMENIDS. CHARACTER OF THEIR GOVERNMENT AND LANGUAGES OF THEIR REALM

About the middle of the 6th century B.C., Kūrush, better known as Cyrus (the Greek version of his name), a ruler descended from the Persian family of Hakhāmanish (Achaemenes), conquered the last of the Pādshāhs of Media, his overlord Astyages, and founded an empire in Western Asia, the great Persian realm. His military actions put an end to the independence of Babylon, Lydia, and other states; his son Cambyses conquered Egypt and penetrated as far as Ethiopia. This new state was, however, threatened by collapse as a result of the stormy rebellions roused by the usurper Gaumāta during Cambyses' stay in Egypt. But the unity of the empire was restored and maintained by Prince Dārayavahush (Darius), a member of a collateral line of the ruling dynasty and a capable and courageous organiser. The restoration of the kingdom forms the subject of his most famous record, the *inscription at Bahistan* (Bīsutūn). Persian inscriptional literature was flourishing at the time and this work was the finest and most important product of Iranian epigraphy. The Persians adopted the Akkadian pattern for their cuneiform inscriptions, but their alphabet differs from the latter in that it is syllabic and phonetic. No books dating from the Achaemenid period are in existence today. The language of the Old Persian dynasty has only survived in inscriptions. Compared with Old Indian and the language of the Zoroastrian *Gāthās* it is characterised by a poverty of forms; but it must be remembered that the contents of the inscriptions consist largely in stereotyped ceremonious expressions and that the number of inscriptions is small. The spirit of the inscriptions is significant. The king's 'declaration of power' is a monumental manifesto of oriental despotism. The king reigns by the grace of Ahura Mazdā; he is the supreme and only rightful king on earth; opposition to him or denial of his right is a 'lie' (*drauga*). According to old Iranian morals, the 'lie' is the greatest sin of all. With the help of God Darius fights his enemies and severely punishes usurpers. To him the noble generals are slaves (*bandakā*) and their primary duty is loyalty. As Ahura Mazdā stands to his retinue in heaven, such also is the relationship on earth between 'the King of Kings, the great King, King of the countries from Ethiopia to India' and his courtiers, vassals, and subjects. In the Achaemenid kingdom the form of government was wholly determined in accordance with the relationship between the king and his subjects, i.e. in proportion to their strength. It became weaker as the people became aware of the king's weakness, and increased in strength when the king was a firm and powerful despot.

In addition to the Old Persian language of the court, other languages too were used in the Achaemenid kingdom for official purposes. Thus Akkadian and Elamite were also used in the royal inscriptions of which there are versions in these two languages as well as in Old Persian. Egyptian, Greek, Aramaic and the language of the Scythian subjects, whom the Persians called Sakas, and other dialects were also officially recognised. In its dealings with the Jews the royal chancellery employed Aramaic, as is testified by several biblical references. The Jews certainly spoke Aramaic as early as the 5th century and particularly in those countries bordering on Palestine. A fragment of a translation of the Bahistan inscription into Aramaic has been found among some Jewish documents in Elephantine in southern Egypt. We may certainly assume that Aramaic clerks were to be found at the royal chancellery at the time of the Achaemenids. The Aramaic language was already spreading throughout western Asia during the Achaemenid period and became the common language of the chancellery ('Official Aramaic', *cf.* W. B. Henning, 'Mitteliranisch', in *Handbuch der Orientalistik*, I, 4, I, p. 21 *et seq.*). Just as they tolerated the languages of the subjugated peoples, the Persians also showed consideration in regard to their religions. We have no accounts of religious persecutions in the Achaemenid period and the excesses of Cambyses in Egypt can more probably be attributed to his despotic character. Later on the Achaemenid kingdom gradually declined owing to the lack of capable rulers, to numerous intrigues at the royal court and to the mingling of heterogeneous elements, as well as to the vast expansion of the kingdom, the comparative freedom of the leaders and of the satrapies, and, not in the last place, to the economic disharmony of some of its districts.

C. THE INSCRIPTIONS OF THE ACHAEMENIDS

The most ancient text known up to now in the series of Achaemenid inscriptions is that of King Ariyāramna, the great-grandfather of Darius I (about the year 600 B.C.). His successor Arshāma also caused some inscriptions to be composed, but of those only a single one has been preserved. But the two inscriptions are probably not genuine. From the period of Cyrus the Great we possess only a few short inscriptions from Murghāb, and some investigators even doubt their authenticity. The most valuable and longest inscriptions date back to the reign of Darius I. They consist partly of accounts of his accession to the throne and assumption of power, partly of descriptions of his building projects – edifices, statues, cornices, pillars, reliefs, halls, vaults and rocks, all testified to in his own autobiography. Besides the huge *inscription in the rock at Bahistan*, of particular interest to us is the *foundation charter of the Susa palace*, which gives a description of its erection. It contains a complete list of the building materials used, while mention is made of craftsmen from various countries. The cultural importance of the contents of this charter make it a particularly interesting and fascinating monument.

Several inscriptions have also been left by Khshayārshā (Xerxes). Of special historical interest is the *Charter of Persepolis*, which informs us that of all his sons Darius chose Xerxes (according to Herodotus he was not the eldest) as his successor, and further the so-called *Daiva inscription*, which justifies the conclusion that at any rate at the time of Xerxes a religion strongly influenced by Mazdaism existed at the Achaemenid court. After that time linguistic errors appear in the inscriptions which, according to Herzfeld, shows that the language had developed and that that of the monuments had gradually become unfamiliar to the composers of the later inscriptions. The most recent inscriptions date back to Artakhshathrā II (Artaxerxes Mnemon) and Artakhshathrā III (up to 338 B.C.) and are written in an already extinct Old Persian. The language evolved rapidly from a synthetic mode of expression to an analytic. The old cases and verbal forms disappeared and their functions were taken over by syntactical constructions. Iranian had in fact become a different kind of language. The engravers of the last inscriptions of King Artaxerxes III already thought and spoke in Middle Persian. Their knowledge of the phraseology of Old Persian was no longer based on a living colloquial language but was founded on knowledge acquired from the standard expressions found in the earlier cuneiform inscriptions. A typical example is an inscription on a silver dish belonging to King Artaxerxes I, dating from a hundred years earlier, which, though it enables us to guess at the meaning, is impossible to translate since it is entirely ungrammatical. This definitely proves that in the year 400 B.C. the Old Persian of the Achaemenid inscriptions was already a dead language. The old case-endings were replaced by prepositional constructions; verbal forms (optative, perfect, imperfect, pluperfect, aorist, future, etc.) disappeared with amazing rapidity. While as regards structure the language of the *Gāthās*, Young Avestan and Old Persian remind one of Sanskrit, Middle Persian already has a method of expression very similar to New Persian. Here investigation reveals a maze of problems most difficult of solution. It is not always possible to say where the inherent tendencies that affect the evolution of a language lead to and what can be attributed to other, also non-Indo-European languages and where both factors meet and supplement each other. One can only say that the causes were manifold and varied. It is probable that the natural development, the economic and cultural exchanges between separate satrapies and the mingling of the races and dialects in Iran gradually built up a new system of linguistic expression and thus formed a *lingua franca* which by its simplicity appealed to the Iranians as well as to speakers of other languages. Another important question is that of the pre-Aryan substratum and its influence, but unfortunately we are still only at the initial stages of investigation into this matter.

The style of the Achaemenid inscriptions is arid and stereotyped. The king begins by mentioning himself with all his titles, next his ancestors, and goes on by giving a concise announcement of the purpose for which the inscription has been composed. The conclusion contains a prayer to the deity for protection. For example, in *the inscription of Artaxerxes II at Hamadān*, we read:

> *Saith Artaxerxes, the Great King, King of Kings, King of Countries, King in this earth, son of Darius the King, of Darius (who was) son of Artaxerxes the King, of Artaxerxes (who was) son of Xerxes the King, of Xerxes (who was) son of Darius the King, of Darius (who was) son of Hystaspes, an Achaemenian: I built this palace by the favour of Ahura Mazdā, Anāhitā and Mithra. May Ahura Mazdā, Anāhitā and and Mithra protect me from all evil, and that which I have built may they not shatter nor harm.* (Kent, *Old Persian*², p. 154 *et seq.*)

This is probably the meaning of the inscription, which abounds in errors. In other inscriptions the king commences with his confession of faith (e.g. Xerxes in the *Alvand inscription*):

> *A great god is Ahura Mazdā, who created this earth, who created yonder sky, who created man, who created happiness for man, who made Xerxes king, one king of many, one lord of many.* (Kent, *Old Persian*², p. 152)

Valuable historical information is given in a dry and rather pompous style but with a distinct attempt at accuracy and detail in the *Bahistān inscription* of King Darius I. Let us hear the tale of Cambyses and Gaumāta in a literal translation:

> *Saith Darius the King: This is what was done by me after that I became king. A son of Cyrus, Cambyses by name, of our family – he was king here. Of that Cambyses there was a brother, Smerdis by name, having the same mother and the same father as Cambyses. Afterwards, Cambyses slew that Smerdis. When Cambyses slew Smerdis, it did not become known to the people that Smerdis had been slain. Afterwards, Cambyses went to Egypt. When Cambyses had gone off to Egypt, after that the people became evil. After that the Lie waxed great in the country, both in Persia and in Media and in the other provinces. Saith Darius the King: Afterwards, there was one man, a Magian, Gaumāta by name; he rose up from Paishiyāuvādā. A mountain by name Arakadri – from there 14 days of the month Viyakhna were past when he rose up. He lied to the people: I am Smerdis, the son of Cyrus, brother of Cambyses. After that, all the people became rebellious from Cambyses, went over to him, both Persia and Media and the*

other provinces. He seized the kingdom; of the month Garmapada nine days were past, then he seized the kingdom. After that, Cambyses died by his own hand.

(Kent, *Old Persian*², p. 119 *et seq.*)

To the same Darius who had defeated the Magian the whole kingdom brings building materials for the erection of a splendid residence in Susa. All the districts contribute the best that they possess: earth, gravel, clay tiles, cedar-wood, teak-wood (?), lapis-lazuli, cinnabar, grey-stone, stone pillars, precious stones, gold, silver, lead and ivory. And craftsmen of every nation work on the building to put on record the power and the fame of the kingdom whose capital is being unearthed from the ruins today with so much trouble. The king is not blind to the achievements of his artists and craftsmen, on the contrary, he proclaims and glorifies in his charter the artistic powers of his subjects and thence of their native lands. This is the sole evidence so far of the righteous attitude of the Persian rulers towards other peoples. In other inscriptions too we find expressions for stones, wood-carving, halls, and pillars.

D. TRACES OF THE LOST LITERATURE

No other records of Old Persian have been preserved. It is known with certainty that the ancient Persians possessed national songs, namely heroic sagas, myths and similar works. It may be that some elements of them appear in an altered form in works of the poets who later elaborated the Old Iranian Kings' Saga, and also in those of several Greek writers (Xenophon, Herodotus, Ctesias, etc.). The most valuable of all is the story of *Zariadres*, written by Chares of Mytilene and handed down to us by Athenaios. That court chronicles existed in ancient Persia is proved by the Book of Esther in the Old Testament; King Ahasuerus (Xerxes?) had the history book *Sēfer Hazzikhrōnōt* read aloud to him when he was unable to sleep. The Bible interprets the name with the added gloss *dibrē hayyāmīm*, 'Chronicle'. The first term is a striking reminder of the Greek names of this kind in the Sasanian period, *basilika apomnemoneumata*, 'Royal Memoirs', in the works of Agathias. Perhaps the old title of the royal annals was still preserved at the time of the Sasanians.

E. OLD PERSIAN LEARNING IN EUROPE

The Persian cuneiform inscriptions were seen in the 17th century for the first time by Pietro della Valle, who brought back news of his discovery to Europe. Attempts to decipher the inscriptions proved to be in vain. Carsten Niebuhr (second half 18th century) was the first to produce carefully written copies; from these the German F. Grotefend deciphered a few words and established the value of some of the characters. Then the English investigator H. C. Rawlinson succeeded in finally deciphering the inscriptions. Next to the Champollion deciphering of the Egyptian hieroglyphics, the work of Grotefend and his successors is the greatest triumph of European oriental scholarship in the 19th century. This success also led to the possibility of reading Babylonic and Elamite texts and thereby to the foundation of Assyriology. Thanks to the excavations carried out by numerous scientific expeditions to Iran – in the first place those of J. de Morgan and E. Herzfeld – more than twenty further inscriptions have been discovered in the present century.

III. THE MIDDLE PERSIAN ERA

A. THE ARSACIDS

I. ALEXANDER THE GREAT, THE SELEUCIDS, THE PARTHIANS

In consequence of the victory of Alexander the Great (330–323 B.C.) vast changes were wrought in Iran. Many centuries later Persian tradition still refers to the fall of the Achaemenid kingdom as the greatest catastrophe that ever befell Iran. Alexander abolished the privileged position of the Iranian elements and endeavoured to form a new nobility by amalgamating the ranks of his officers with the Iranian feudal aristocracy who had finally joined forces with him. But after his sudden death (323 B.C.) Iran fell to his capable and energetic general Seleukos and became part of a new Asiatic empire having Syria as its centre. The Greek element penetrated unhindered into the most easterly provinces of this new kingdom; Greek towns arose in the regions between the Tigris and the Indus, Hellenic colonisation spread as far as the Yaxartes. Greek became the language of the ruling classes, the army, the townsmen, the merchants, as well as being employed in treaties, inscriptions and legends on coins. Parsee writers assure us that the Zoroastrian religion was on the decline, that disbelief was rampant and the number of sects on the increase. Iran was ostensibly broken up into 240 lesser princedoms. Arab writers call these lesser kings *mulūku'ṭ-ṭavā'if*, 'kings of the tribes'. Nothing remains of the language of the Achaemenid dynasty. But a dangerous rival to Greek arose in the form of the Semitic language Aramaic, which in earlier times had been the colloquial tongue in use throughout western Asia. The gifted, vigorous, intelligent and enterprising Semitic element achieved great influence owing to the new conditions, particularly in the economic world because in relation to trade, manual labour and agriculture, it possessed the wealthiest districts, namely Syria and Babylonia. And yet the successors of Seleukos were unable to maintain the kingdom in its original dimensions. About the year 250 B.C. two kingdoms arose in eastern Iran, that of the Greek military aristocrats with Baktria as its centre, and the kingdom of the native population in Parthia that was founded by the Arsacid tribe. At first the situation of the new Parthian state, lying as it did between the Seleucids and the Baktrian Greeks, was difficult, but eventually international relations took a turn in its favour. The dissolution of the Baktrian kingdom and its final disappearance, due to the migration of the peoples of Central Asia, liberated Parthia towards the east; in the west the Romans contributed to its relief by paralyzing the Seleucid kingdom by their victories and finally conquering it (64 B.C.). Parthia defended itself against the attacks of the Central Asian peoples and was a serious antagonist of the Roman Empire right up to its end in 224–227 A.D.

2. THE LITERATURE OF THE PARTHIAN ERA

We have but little information about the literature of Iran in the time of the Arsacids. There was no lack of heroic poetry, but unfortunately nothing authentic has been preserved. Nevertheless, it had an influence on Armenian epic poetry, a fragment of which is preserved in a part of the hymn to Vahagn, an ancient Armenian heathen idol (=Iran. *Vṛthraghna*). Middle Persian, especially in the Arsacid period, affected Armenian, for we find about 1500 loan words from the Iranian of the time. Just as nothing has been preserved of the belles-lettres, there is also a complete absence of records of didactic prose. During the early period of the Parthian kingdom, the leading class, a group of noble families, possibly of Scythian origin, was entirely occupied with the formation and organisation of the state. The influence of Greek culture was very strong. The kings specially favoured Greek literature. In his biography of Crassus, Plutarch relates an episode from life at the Arsacid court in which a curious contrast is evident between the spirit of barbarism on the one hand and a noticeable appreciation of Greek culture on the other, though the latter was only conveyed through a tragedy of violent passions and by a depraved group of Greek actors. It so happened that at the time of Crassus' defeat King Orodes was staying at the Armenian court, and the Greek actors were just then giving a performance of Euripides' *Bacchae*. When the arrival of messengers was announced, bringing with them the head of Crassus as a trophy from the battlefield of Carrhae, the actor Jason held up the head of the Roman to the public and amid the cheers of the whole assembly recited the verses of the Maenads, who were intoxicated with fury and lust by tearing to pieces the body of the slanderer Pentheus. According to Plutarch, Orodes' host, the Armenian Arsacid Artavazd, himself wrote Greek tragedies. But this period of downfall, invasions and wars was by no means favorable for the creation of literary works. The kings and the nobility spent their time in hunting, games and contests, affairs of law and administration; the majority of their officials were secretaries of Aramaic origin and were entirely responsible for the formation and normalisation of the documentary style. Hardly anything is known about the priesthood. During the second half of the Arsacid period certain attempts are said to have been made to edit the fragments of the sacred Mazdaistic writings, but nothing has been preserved of the Mazdaistic religious literature of the Arsacid period. Of official royal inscriptions only a few Greek ones remain. That there was a national religious renaissance after about the year 50 A.D. may perhaps be proved by the gradual corruption of the Greek legends on the coinage and the traditional report about King Valgash (Vologeses), who is said to have ordered scattered fragments of the Avesta to be collected. Unfortunately these reports are very lacunary, no chronology is given and, still worse, the successors of the Arsacids, the Sasanians, suppressed intentionally and tendentiously everything about the Parthians that might have put them in a favourable light and even tried to make them contemptible. It is quite possible that much of what is nowadays ascribed to the Sasanians had already been introduced by the Parthian Arsacids.

3. THE EARLIEST RECORDS OF MIDDLE IRANIAN LITERATURE

These appear as early as the 5th century B.C. They consist of words derived from the Persian and transferred into Aramaic found in the *Jewish manuscripts on papyrus in Elephantine* and Iranian proper names, as well as some appellatives occurring in the texts of Aramaic inscriptions, papyri and later books of the Bible and in the works of Greek authors, albeit often in a modified form. As a result of the predominance of the Aramaic element in Iran after the death of Alexander the Great, an alphabet was eventually formed, based on the western Semitic consonantal script, for the composition of Middle Iranian records. The differences between the Semitic and the Middle Iranian, formerly *Chaldaeopahlavi*, nowadays known as *Pahlavik* script, are comparatively small. The earliest documents ever written in this 'Parthian' script are fragments of deeds found on erstwhile Parthian soil and now being published by Soviet investigators. They appear to date from the 2nd century B.C. After these there follows another document also written in the Arsacid alphabet, namely a purchase deed drawn up in the year 87 B.C. or thereabouts, and discovered in 1909 in Avrōmān in the Kurdish Zagros mountains. The original copy of this deed, which is written on parchment, is in Greek; on the reverse side there is a more recent but unfortunately illegible translation into Middle Iranian. Of another document from Avrōmān only the Greek text has survived, and of a third – dating from the year 300 or 400 of the Seleucid era, viz. 12 B.C. or 90 A.D. – only the Middle Iranian text. According to Rostovtzeff it may have been written in the year 53 A.D. (Henning, 'Mitteliranisch', p. 29). It is composed in a very arid style and states that Pataspak, the son of Tīrīn, has sold half of his vineyard to a certain Avīl, the son of Bashnīn, for 65 *dirhams*. Five witnesses are mentioned, whose names are probably all Iranian. The style of the document immediately betrays a peculiar characteristic of Middle Iranian texts, namely an intermingling of Semitic words and moreover not only in legal and economic matters (MZBN, 'seller', ZBN, 'buyer', ShHD, 'witness') but also for concrete objects and general expressions (KRM', 'vineyard', BRY, 'son'). But this peculiar characteristic of Middle Iranian orthography, namely the mixing of Iranic and Semitic expressions, occurs not only in the documents of Avrōmān but also on the coinage. Instead of the Iranic *shāh*, 'king', they write the Aramaic MLK' (*malkā*); instead of *zan*, 'woman', NYShH (*nishsheh*); instead of *pit* (*ar*), 'father', we find 'BW (*abū*) or even '*Bitar* with the Iranic suffix *-tar*. Semitic words are used for the most common topics of everyday life and even for pronouns and prepositions. We thus find this peculiar manner of writing in all the Iranic-written works up to the time of the Arab dominion and again in Middle Persian texts that came into being during the New Persian period. Exceptions to this are formed by the surviving fragments of the Manichaean writings discovered in Central Asia. Since the inception of Iranian studies in Europe a painful uncertainty has prevailed as to the proper nature of the writing and the language written in this 'mixture'. Earlier investigators maintained that this Middle Iranian was in reality a mixed language not only as regards the writing but also phonetically; that is, that the Semitic words were also pronounced in a Semitic manner. But this view was repudiated by the research work of Th. Nöldeke, C. Salemann and Chr. Bartholomae, and the more recent experts E. Herzfeld and H. S. Nyberg. These scholars have proved convincingly that the mixture had penetrated into the writing only and that phonetically the language is purely Iranic, the written form having been built up entirely artificially by the use of Semitic elements employed exclusively as ideographs. For instance they wrote LḤM' (*laḥmā*), but pronounced it *naghn*, *nān*, 'bread'. But as the Semitic words are not ideograms in the sense of Sumeric or Chinese symbolic characters, but are written with a consonantal alphabet, H. Junker correctly coined them *heterograms*. The Iranic, phonetically written words were called *eteograms*. For example KLB' (*kalbā*) is the heterogram for the Iranic eteogram *sag*, 'dog'. Finally both ways of writing were used simultaneously in the texts. Here we are confronted with the difficult problem of how this very strange manner of writing came into being. The most natural answer, to my mind, is that the scribes (*dipīrān*), all-powerful in matters of culture, were of Aramaic origin, equally versed in Aramaic and Persian; and because the other classes of the population were absolutely dependent on them when it came to the compilation of manuscripts, they strove to fortify the monopoly of their position by inventing a system of writing and orthography which could not be adopted for general purposes without great difficulty. It is true that in course of time Iranian elements did penetrate into the bureaucratic and notarial sphere and indeed finally dominated it completely; but the manner of writing had to be preserved at any cost or else the royal archives as well as all the records, writings and deeds etc. would all have become illegible and useless. Thus for the Persians too it was subsequently no longer possible to reform the manner of writing.

4. MIDDLE IRANIAN DIALECTS

The collective term *Pahlavi* is generally used for the Middle Iranian dialects. This name is derived from the word *Pahlav*, 'Parthian'. It would therefore only refer to the dialect that we rightly ascribe to the Parthians, i.e. the language of the Pahlavik versions of the Sasanian inscriptions and to the so-called North-western dialect found in the Manichaean fragments from Turfan. As a rule the name Pahlavi is used for the language of the Mazdaistic books and for all Middle Persian works written with the mingling of heterograms and eteograms. Ibn al-Muqaffaʿ, already calls Pahlavi the language of the north-west, knowing as he did what the word originally meant, for Media proper had finally become the core of the Arsacid kingdom as against Fars in the south-west, the cradle of the Sasanians. As a matter of fact we can distinguish the following Middle Iranian languages: (1) Middle Persian, the language of the Sasanians and their subjects in Fars; (2) Parthian, the so-called north-western or northern dialect, these two languages form the western group; (3) three eastern languages, Soghdian, Khvarezmian and Khotanese Saka. There are numerous fragments of literary works preserved in these languages. The Old Ossetic can be studied only in proper names. The problems of the Iranian dialects spoken in the ancient reigns of the Kushans, the Hephthalites and in Tokharistan are not yet solved. Investigators speak of the remnants of Kushano-Hephthalite, Middle Baktrian and Eteo-Tokharian records. Present-day native experts are getting accustomed to use the name Pahlavi for the preliminary stage of some of the modern West-Persian dialects. To use the word *fahlaviyyāt* for poetry in dialect is out of date.

5. INSCRIPTIONS FROM ARSACID TIMES

Several inscriptions dating from the Arsacid period have been preserved in Iran. The contents of the inscriptions on the Sarpul relief are not yet known. The last Parthian king, Artabanus V, ordered a tombstone with an inscription to be built in Susa for his governor (215 A.D.). Inscriptions likewise dating from the end of the Parthian period have been discovered near Birjand in eastern Persia. Two important epigraphic monuments have been found in the temple of Zeus Megistos in Dura. The greatest triumph of the investigators, however, was the discovery of ostraca near the site of the ancient Parthian residence Nisa, not far from Ashkhabad in Turkmenistan. They were discovered thanks to Soviet expeditions and have for the most part been taken in hand by Soviet experts, too (D'yakonov, Lifshits, and Vinnikov). As for their contents, they are chiefly documents dealing with the supply of wine and date from the period between 100 and 29 B.C. It is probable that these texts found at Nisa are written in Parthian mingled with heterograms. The Parthian kings used Greek in their inscriptions as well. The most important Greek inscription was made by King Gotarzes (about 46–50 A.D.), who celebrated his victory over his rival Mithradates. This inscription can be found on a mountain at Bahistān and is accompanied by a rough relief showing a horseman with a spear, the rider being festooned by a winged goddess of Victory. As regards Parthian inscriptions discovered during the last decade, see Henning, 'Mitteliranisch', p. 41 *et seq.*

6. COINS OF THE PRE-SASANIAN PERIOD

The Parthian coins bear Greek legends; only since the reign of King Valgash I (51–79 A.D.) do the names of Parthian kings appear in Pahlavi script on the coins beside the Greek inscriptions, to which fact Justi draws attention. That Aramaic predominated on the coinage is proved by the discovery of coins dating from the second half of the 4th century B.C., the inscriptions on which have been deciphered by M. A. Levy. The legend of a coin struck in Cilicia contains the name *Mazdī*, indicating perhaps the satrap and general of the last Achaemenids and of Alexander the Great, *Mazaios*. According to the inscription he was lord of the region on the near side of the Euphrates and Cilicia. With the exception of his name the legend is purely Aramaic. On all the Parthian coins the name of the ruler is given only in Semitic (*malkā*, 'king', *malkīn malkā*, 'king of kings', *malkā rabbā*, 'great king'). From the same Aramaic script that had been the origin of *Pahlavik*, there also arose in south-western Iran a script for Middle Persian known by the name of *Pārsīk*. In its earliest form it is to be found even earlier than *Pahlavik*. In the first half of the 3rd century B.C. were struck the earliest coins of the *Frataraka*, the princes of Fārs (who may also have held high religious offices). The earliest issues are the coins of Bagadāta, the first Frataraka of Istakhr, near the old Persepolis. In the course of their development these two alphabets diverged more and more from one another and their different forms are finally found in the Sasanian inscriptions. Only the proper names in the legends on the Parthian coins are Iranic, all the rest is Semitic. The Middle Iranian phonetic form of the Zoroastrian deities appears on the coins of the kings of Kushān (on the frontier between India, Iran and Central Asia). The title of these rulers, *raonano rao*, formerly read as *shāhiāno shāh*, is nowadays interpreted as coming from the Khotanese Saka language as *ṣṣaunānu ṣṣau*, 'prince of princes'. The legends on these coins were inscribed in an only slightly modified Greek alphabet.

B. THE SASANIANS

The Arsacids were succeeded in Iran by a new dynasty, this time from Fars, namely the Sasanians. Their reign began between 224 and 227 A.D. and lasted until the year

652. The written records of the Sasanian epoch at our disposal today are all monumental in character. So far no original manuscripts of books on the Mazdaistic religion or other documents have been found, with the exception of a few scant remnants.

I. INSCRIPTIONS

The most important are the inscriptions of kings and dignitaries (3rd and 4th centuries A.D.), at first trilingual (Greek, south-west Persian or Sasanian, north-west Iranic or Arsacid), later bilingual (in the two Iranic dialects), and finally only in the Sasanian language. The earliest inscriptions date from the founder of the dynasty, Artakhshēr I Pāpakān. In Naqsh-i Rustam, not far from Persepolis, there is a rock-carving representing the king and the god Ahura Mazdā (Ōhrmazd) seated high on horseback. Under the horse's hooves lie the last two members of the disenthroned ruling house of the Arsacids, Ardavān and Valgash.

Underneath the carvings one can read the following inscriptions: "This is the image of the worshipper of Mazdā, the divine Artakhshēr, the King of Kings of the Iranians, of divine descent, son of the divine King Pāpak", and "This is the image of the god Ōhrmazd." The son of Artakhshēr, Shāpūr I, known in history as the conqueror of the Romans and the patron of Mānī, had inscriptions carved in the rock at Naqsh-i Rajab near Persepolis and near the village of Ḥājjīābād. Shortly before the Second World War inscriptions were also discovered dating from the time of this ruler which throw a new light on the revival of the Zoroastrian religion and the relationship between Persia and Rome. In the Ḥājjīābād inscription the king boasts of his skill in the ancient Persian national sport, archery. The longest royal inscription is to be found in Pāykūlī, though only fragments of it have survived. Herzfeld has made a successful attempt to reconstruct this bilingual document, which originates from the reign of King Narseh (*c.* 294). Another inscription derives its name from Rostovtzeff's suggestion of *Res gestae divi Saporis*, because its contents and importance remind us of Augustus' inscription at Ancyra. In three languages it sings the glories of the victorious wars waged by King Shāpūr I against the Romans (the emperors Gordian III, Philip, and Valerian). It mentions the foundation of the fire temples and enumerates imperial and court dignitaries during the reigns of the first three Sasanians. At the beginning we find a list of the provinces of Shāpūr's empire. Higher dignitaries also had inscriptions made. In Naqsh-i Rustam, Naqsh-i Rajab and on the walls of the temple Kaʿba-i Zardusht at Persepolis were found inscriptions of Kartīr, a Mazdayasnian priest of high rank. On his last monument especially he described his career and related that he had persecuted Jews, Christians, Nasoraeans, Maktīks, Brahmans, Buddhists and Manichaeans. We are entitled to judge that it was owing to his activities that the Zoroastrian doctrine became the state religion of the Sasanian Empire. It was undoubtedly he who ordered Mānī to be imprisoned, thus causing his death. A long but not yet thoroughly investigated inscription at Sar Mashhad is rightly attributed to him. Of less importance are the inscriptions of the kings Shāpūr II and Shāpūr III in Ṭāq-i Būstān, of the Sasanian Shāpūr Sakānshāh in Persepolis and of two officials, Kāvar and Slūk, to be found in the same place. Unfortunately the inscriptions are illegible here and there as they have suffered damage in the course of time. The language is clumsy and the style dry. They are few in number and in most cases we have no further information as to the circumstances under which they were made. This predilection for inscriptions prevailed also among persons of humbler station. Travellers often left their signatures at the places they visited, as did also the Zoroastrian visitors to the Kanheri caves in Salsetta near Bombay. "In the name of God! In the year 378 after Yazdkart, in the month of Āpān, on the day of Mihr, fellow-believers arrived at this spot...", followed by their names. According to the dating still customary among the Parsees today, they arrived there on November 24, 1009. But another inscription shows that even earlier, on October 10th, a group of Parsees visited the same Buddhist temple. And others came in the year 1021. The reason for their visit to this cave is not known.

Valuable remains of Middle Persian documents have been excavated in the course of the last decades at *Dura* on the Euphrates. This town was an important seat of Western Asian Hellenism and in post-Alexandrian times it was called 'Europos'. These remains consist of fragments of parchment documents containing correspondence dating from early Sasanian times. They include important references to the building projects in that town which was situated on the frontier between the Roman Empire and the Sasanian state, and was more exposed than any other to the consequences of the destructive wars between the two great powers. We also gather from these fragments details concerning the decoration of the buildings, particularly the paintings. It may be that Persian painters were also responsible for the frescoes in the synagogues there. At any rate they immortalised themselves in Middle Persian inscriptions on the walls of the synagogue. Among the ruins of Dura, ostraca have also been found bearing texts written partly in Pahlavik and partly in Pārsīk (i.e. Sasanian Pahlavi). One of these refers to the delivery of wine to the officers of the Persian occupying forces, and another to a letter of credit of the Iranian Shāpūr to the Roman Pacuvius; the witnesses of both parties are also given.

2. OTHER RECORDS. SEALS, GEMS, COINS, DOCUMENTS

Of the other remains mention must certainly be made of the stone *talisman* discovered in Baghdad, the inscription on which contains a confused incantation. But our attention is more especially drawn to the *seals*. The fondness at that time on the part of those in power for precious stones led to the manufacture of carvings and engraved figures which were used as seals. There are beautiful examples of *gems, cameos* and *intaglios*, most of them bearing inscriptions, the materials employed being ruby, amethyst, lapislazuli, cornelian and sardonyx. The seals show portraits of their owners, often very expressively and artistically carried out. Some of them belonged to rulers or dignitaries, but most of them to Magians. The inscriptions encircling the pictures (though not all gems were provided with legends) contain the name of the owner, his official title and often a probably superstitious formula supposed to bring him health, success and happiness, or to solicit confidence in him. Thus such an inscription often ends with the words *farrakhv bād*, 'may he be happy!' The text on the seal of Queen Dēnak, mother of the shāhs Ōhrmazd III and Pērōz (about the year 457) ends: *Pat tanish apastān*, 'have confidence in her person!' Henning separates the last words in a different way, namely, *tan shāpəstān*. His opinion is that the seal belonged to the queen's head-eunuch, who was allowed to use a seal with her image ('Mittel-iranisch', p. 45, note 3). And elsewhere we read *afzūn shnōm*, 'may his joy increase!', or *yōm shappīr*, viz. *rōzh vēh*, 'good day, happiness!' From the Sasanian period quite a number of coins bearing Middle Persian legends and likenesses of the rulers have survived. The pictures on the coins exhibit an interesting monumental realism which occasionally calls forth a feeling of absurdity. For the deciphering of seal and numismatic inscriptions we are indebted to the investigators A. D. Mordtmann, P. Horn, G. Steindorff, and B. Dorn, who have published reproductions of the coins preserved in the collection of General J. de Bartholomaei at St. Petersburg. The governors of the provinces also caused coins to be struck.

The legends contain only the name and title of the ruler; now and then the word *mazdēsn* calls attention to the fact that the sovereign was a worshipper of Mazdā. A particularly interesting personality was Pērōz, the brother of Shāpūr I, governor of Khurasan, who adopted the title of *vazurg Kushānshāh*, 'Great Kushān-Shāh'. His coins carry the text: 'Mazdā-worshipper, divine Pērōz, great Kushān-Shāh', or the more modest 'Pērōz the King'. He was a patron of Mānī but was at the same time a friend to Buddhism, which at that time had spread considerably in eastern Iran. Otherwise nothing has been preserved of the official eastern Iranic literature. Official documents are rarely available, and then only in translations, e.g. royal edicts. We have, for example, the manifesto of Yazdkart II to the Armenians, ordering them to renounce the Christian faith and to adopt Mazdaism, in two varying versions, one being by the historiographer of the revolt of Vardan Mamikoni against the Persians, Elisha Vardapet, and the other by the chronicler Ḷazar Pharpeçi.

C. MIDDLE PERSIAN BOOK-LITERATURE

I. PAHLAVI LITERATURE

There is a great wealth of Middle Persian book-literature, usually known as Pahlavi literature. The language is also called book-Pahlavi. Its subject matter is largely religious, only a few works being of a secular character. Book-Pahlavi is richly interlarded with Semitic heterograms. Occasionally the heterograms are replaced by an Iranic phonetic version, but some forms are written only heterographically, while others again are found only in the phonetic form. The style is terse, even dry, especially in the religious texts, while now and then it is even vague and incomprehensible. The authors of most of the books are unknown; often, it is true, the texts contain the name of the author in the title, but it is by no means certain that the person mentioned was in fact the author of the book; and indeed it has often been proved later that the name given was erroneous. The names of the copyists are sometimes, but not always, preserved in the colophons of the copies. The beginnings of this literature go back to the Sasanian period; the publication of the Avesta necessitated at the time explanations and appendices in Middle Persian. But the earliest texts too have come down to us only in later copies, versions and redactions from the Arab period (after the year 650). Many monuments of religious literature contain translations of Avestan texts but a far greater part consists of *treatises on morals or dogma, commentaries, polemics, apologies, responses*, etc. In the Arab period Iranian Zoroastrian writers turned to new alphabets and attempted to use them for writing down Middle Persian texts phonetically. The writings in the Avestan alphabet are called *Pāzand*, those in the Arabic consonantal writing are called *Pārsī*. It is easy to understand that the influence of post-Sasanian Persian often played a part here. These works were written down at a time when Middle Persian was no longer being spoken, the language was continuing to develop and the post-Sasanian forms were affecting the pronunciation of the old ones through their phonetic character. In addition to Pārsī and Pāzand versions we find Middle Persian books also in translation and elaborations in *New Persian*, in *Sanskrit* and *Gujarātī*, though the two latter appear only in India. Of the New Persian works the most famous is the *Zartusht-nāma*, a legendary biography of the Prophet consisting of 570 couplets and written by the Zoroastrian priest Zartusht Bahrām Pazhdū in 1278. In Sanskrit, in addition to many other works, there is the extremely important *Translation of the Avestan Yasna*, the greater part of which was written by the Parsee Nēryōsang and completed later (about the 13th century). The translator based his work – very freely here and there – on the Middle Persian version and not on the Avestan original. His Sanskrit too reveals that it was not the work of a first-rate scholar. The Parsee settlers in India translated Middle Persian books into Gujarātī and indeed not only parts of the Avesta but other works as well, both religious and secular. In India, Gujarātī became their colloquial language, thus replacing their native Iranic tongue. Imitations and paraphrases of Middle Persian works were also composed in Gujarātī. In the 17th century the poet Rustam Peshōtan Hōrmazdyār composed books dealing with *Zartusht* and *Syāvakhsh*. In the 19th century there appeared a Gujarātī paraphrase of the *Bundahishn*. All these more recent works are only important in so far as they show the development of the traditions and the modifications in the conception of the themes up to the time of their composition.

2. MIDDLE PERSIAN TRANSLATIONS OF THE AVESTA (ZAND)

Translations have survived of the *Yasna*, the *Visprat* and the *Vidēvdāt*, as well as of a few shorter texts. They are arranged in the manuscripts of the Avesta in such a way that an Avestan paragraph (*lemma*) is followed by its translation, the latter being nearly always literal and for that very reason often inaccurate and ambiguous. For this reason too many translators explain various passages by means of glosses, which, however, very often do not elucidate the sense at all. Sometimes the translation is too free. Many words were not rightly understood. The translators were handicapped by their inadequate knowledge of the declensions and syntax of Avestan, with the result that they tried in vain to guess the meaning of the sentence. Nevertheless these translations formed the most important clue to the comprehension of the Avesta in the first stages of Iranistic studies in Europe. For the translation of the Avesta into Pahlavi the word *Zand* is used, and investigators in the 18th and 19th centuries erroneously referred to the sacred text as *Zendavesta* and to the language as *Zend*. It is reasonable to assume that the translations of the Avestan books increased in number after the 6th century because of the necessity of combating sectarian and heretical tendencies in the Sasanian kingdom. According to some reports the Mazdakite movement in particular firmly maintained that it was called to convey to the people the true and original meaning of the Avesta, which had become obscured and altered by the priesthood; this is also evident from references in the glosses to the translations. It is said that in the time of the *Dēnkart* there were translations of nineteen Avestan *nasks*. These however later got lost.

D. RELIGIOUS PAHLAVI LITERATURE

1. RELIGIOUS TEXTS

More fascinating than the *Zand* are the religious texts, containing as they do the often interesting views of the Mazdaists concerning the world, life, work, culture, instruction on the faith and its mysteries, and also a wealth of material for the study of popular customs, superstitions, practices, etc. Such folklore yields valuable information, for instance the sections dealing with the calendar. One chapter of the *Andarz of Āturpāt, son of Mahraspand*, offers advice to fellow-believers as to what they should undertake or leave undone on each day of the month in order that everything may prosper to the satisfaction of mankind and the deity. We learn something about customs, amusements, relatives, duties, the relations to one's neighbour, etc. Reminiscent of Dante's *Divina Commedia* is the *Artāk Virāz* (formerly erroneously read as *Vīrāf-nāmak*), 'The Book of Artāk Virāz', with its theme of wanderings through the supernatural worlds of heaven, purgatory, and hell. The author, as is so often the case, was an unknown theologian who described in a fascinating, though at times monotonous manner, the dream-vision of the saint Artāk ('just', 'orthodox') Virāz, in order to show the faithful the consequences of their good and evil works in heaven, purgatory and hell. The priest Virāz is said to have been elected by a synod of Magians on account of his moral and religious integrity to act as messenger from mortals to the kingdoms above and below this world and to bring from thence the true doctrine of life and faith to the Mazdaistic church. That was a time of decadence, disbelief and uncertainty. Seated on the throne of the 'Seer', surrounded by Magi and the army, Virāz fell into a supernatural slumber after drinking a goblet of intoxicating *mang*. While he was asleep his soul wandered into the other world and was there a witness of the retributions and punishments for the dead. After seven days his soul returned. When he awoke Virāz sent for his scribe in order to dictate an account of his strange experiences. The Pahlavi text fixes the time of this legendary event broadly to the period of religious decline. The Pāzand version places it in the age of Vishtāsp shortly after the death of Zoroaster; the New Persian translation still later, namely during the reign of Artakhshēr Pāpakān. The writer pays most attention to the punishments of hell. A whole chapter is devoted to each of the sins, the introductions being written according to a stereotyped formula. The guides of the seer are *Srōsh*, an angel and messenger of the gods, who protects the community of believers at night, and *Ātur*, the angel of the sacred fire. They explain to him what this or that one of the condemned had done during his lifetime and why he was being punished in that way. The punishments themselves were carried out by demons, who tortured the condemned in horrible fashion. The scenes reflect the cruelty for which the Persians were notorious in their treatment of wrong-doers and criminals, to whom they applied the most outrageous methods of torture. For something similar has been described in the documents written in Syriac on the Persian Christian martyrs. The Mazdaists are generally known for their remarkable sense of justice. This is demonstrated by several episodes; for instance, the case of a man who held adulterous relations with the wife of a fellow-believer. Punishment was inflicted over the whole of his body excepting one foot, for with this foot he had crushed harmful animals on his way to the woman. Another sinner was also not punished on one foot because he had tossed a bundle of straw with it to a hard-working ox. Some of the sins are not considered as such according to present-day principles, as for example the wearing of wigs and talking while eating. As an instance we may quote the description of Huvarsht, one of the celestial spheres:

When I put forth the third footstep on Huvarsht, there where good deeds are received with hospitality, there I arrived. There is the radiance which they call the highest of the highest; and I saw the pious on thrones and carpets made of gold; and they were people whose brightness was like unto the brightness of the sun. And I asked Srōsh the pious and Ātur the angel, thus: "What place is this? And who are those souls?" Srōsh the pious and Ātur the angel said thus: "This is the sun track; and those are the souls who, in the world, exercised good sovereignty and rulership and chieftainship."

(M. Haug)

Terrible is hell, according to the Persian description:

I also saw the greedy jaws of hell, like the most frightful pit, descending in a very narrow and fearful place; in darkness so gloomy, that it is necessary to hold by the hand; and in such stench that everyone whose nose inhales that air will struggle and stagger and fall; and on account of such close confinement, no one's existence is possible.

(M. Haug)

At the end of his wanderings Virāz sees Satan himself in hell:

Then I saw the evil spirit, the deadly, the world-destroyer, whose religion is evil, who ever ridiculed and mocked the wicked in hell, and said thus: "Why did you ever eat the bread of Ahurmazd, and do my work? and thought not of your own creator, but practised my will?" So ever he shouted to the wicked very mockingly. (M. Haug)

With the exception of the motif, the work cannot be compared to Dante's *Divina Commedia*, either as regards its poetic form or the majestic manner in which the Italian genius unfolded the picture and the criticism of the whole life of the Middle Ages for his contemporaries and for all generations to come.

2. THE 'ANDARZ' BOOKS. MORALISING, APOCALYPTIC, AND ESCHATOLOGICAL LITERATURE

There is a fairly large amount of moralising literature containing ethical teachings and admonitions, advice and indications for a correct conduct of life, always accompanied by dogmatic articles. Such writings were called *Andarz*, 'teachings', or *Pand-nāmak*, 'book of counsels'. Āturpāt-i Mahraspandān, a famous theologian to whom we have already referred, is said to be the author of the booklet *Andarz-i Āturpāt-i Mahraspandān* which contains teachings intended for his son Zartusht. To this Zartusht was attributed the script *Pandnāmak-i Zartusht* (or *Chītak Andarz-i pōryōtkēshān*, 'Book of Counsels by Zartusht', or 'Selections of teachings of the first teachers of faith'). It offers moral instruction together with dogmatic religious teachings and amounts thus to a kind of brief catechism. Another work ascribed to Āturpāt is *Vāchak ēchand-i Āturpāt-i Mahraspandān*, 'A few words of A., the son of M.'. It is not certain, however, whether it was written by the compiler and redactor of the Avesta or by a grandson bearing the same name. They are mentioned by the eminent Mazdaist theologian of Khusrau's time, Bakhtāfrīt, himself the composer of a book of proverbs in collaboration with another theologian, Āturfarnbag; with him and others Bakhtāfrīt wrote a commentary on the Avesta and took part in the decisive dispute with the heretic *Mazdak*. Another *Andarz* was connected with a character in the Old Iranian saga, *Ōshnar*, the wise counsellor of Kay Kā'ūs, a king in remote antiquity. King Khusrau I Anōsharvān also bequeathed advice and admonitions to his people in the book *Andarz-i Khusrau-i Kavātān*, 'Teachings of Kh., son of Kavāt'.

The names of the orthodox theologians of the time of Khusrau occur in the *Vahuman-Yasht*, which proves that apocalyptic and eschatological literature has left its mark. This Yasht describes the revelation of the God Ōhrmazd to Zoroaster concerning the future of the Iranian kingdom and its faith. The several periods of Mazdaistic history are here compared to the branches of a tree composed of various metals of differing values. The golden branch represents the first period of the religion, that of Vishtāsp, the silver one that of his grandson Artakhshēr Kay-shāh, the steel branch the epoch of Khusrau I, the one with the iron alloy that of the rule of the demons descended from the race of Aēshma. In another vision the tree of history has seven branches. This proves that in Iran belief was held in the world epochs through which mankind had to pass, each of these epochs being worse than the foregoing one. We find this view, though in poetic guise, in Ovid too. In the *Vahuman-Yasht* there is also a concise account of the Mazdakite movement. Another work of an apocalyptic nature is the *Ayātkār-i Zhāmāspīk*; most of it is preserved only in the Pārsī and Pāzand versions but the beginnings go back as far as the 6th century. The framework of the story is a dialogue between King Vishtāsp, the first Zoroastrian on the throne of Iran, and his wise vizier Zhāmāsp who, according to tradition, was the son-in-law of the Prophet. The king sets certain questions to the sage concerning the future; the soothsayer foretells the future fate of the Faith and the disasters that will befall the country of Iran. The writer includes within this framework several details borrowed from sagas and history, geography, and ethnography. He speaks of real and of fictitious peoples, and also of Indians, Chinese, Turks, Arabs, the inhabitants of Barbaristān, i.e. peoples of East Africa and Abyssinia, but also of people with eyes and ears in their breasts, of dwarfs, bow-legged and dog-headed people, thus reminding us of the mediaeval fantasies of Mandeville. He further tells of dwellers in mythical places (such as Kangdiz, a castle that the Iranian prince Syāvakhsh had built in Turkestan when he lived as an exile with King Afrāsyāb; Var, a subterranean fortress belonging to the 'handsome shepherd' Yima, and Ērān-vēzh, the primeval home of the Avestan peoples). The work also provides a list of the Sasanian kings (incomplete like all the others and here and there inaccurate in its chronological data), and closes with a description of the signs that will appear in the world on the occasion of the coming of future prophets, the sons of Zoroaster and the judges of mankind. The work bears evidence of having only reached its final form in the Arab period. For the rest eschatological and apocalyptic texts are also to be found scattered about in other books. Remarkable descriptions are given in the 24th chapter, for instance, of the work of Zātsparam, *Chītakihā*, which contains a representation of events at the Last Judgment. We find a similar account in the 30th chapter of the *Bundahishn*. According to the most recent researches it appears that Jewish and Christian eschatology are either of Persian origin or that in the last stages of development they were strongly influenced by the Persian.

3. COLLECTIONS OF TRADITIONS AND POLEMIC TREATISES

Many important works, the writers of which are known, have been preserved from the Arab period. The most comprehensive of these writings is the *Dēnkart*, 'Documents of Religion', a collection of numerous facts on doctrines, moral precepts, historical and literary traditions belonging to the field of Mazdaistic religion. It originally consisted of nine books but in the course of time the first two have been lost. There are two noteworthy accounts of the history of the Avesta (to be found in the last chapter of Book III and in Book IV). According to the first account King Vishtāsp commanded the Avesta to be put down in writing, the original copy to be kept in the royal treasury and two copies in the archives of the so-called fortress of documents. Alexander the Great gave orders after his victory for one manuscript to be burnt but the other to be translated (?) into Greek. Of the other copies only fragments have survived. On his accession to the throne Artakhshēr I ordered these to be collected and completed, the task being entrusted to the priest Tansar. According to another account King Vishtāsp had the documents on religion collected and Dārā (Darius III) ordered two standard manuscripts of each to be made. Later on the fragments of the sacred scripts were collected and completed, first by the Arsacid Valgash, then by Tansar and finally by Āturpāt, son of Mahraspand. There is also mention of a new revision of the Avesta and the Zand as ordered by King Khusrau I Anōsharvān. In Book V we find a biography of Zoroaster, treated again, and this time far more fully, in Book VII. It may perhaps be a translation, and the contents the residue of the *Nask Spand*, which had dealt with the life of the Prophet. This biography contains large numbers of legends recounting his birth, childhood, youth, the visit to Heaven and the triumph at the court of Vishtāsp. Books VIII and IX give a list of the contents of the *Nasks* of the Sasanian Avesta.

The style of the *Dēnkart* is often obscure and in general reminiscent of the Jewish *Talmud.* The compilation of the *Dēnkart*, according to Book III, was undertaken by the theologian Āturfarnbag at the time of Caliph al-Ma'mūn (813–833) and completed during the last quarter of the 9th century by Āturpāt, the son of Hēmēt. Āturfarnbag is also the hero of the small book *Mātagdān-i gizāstak Abālish*, 'The Story of Abālish the Accursed', which relates the course of a debate before the Caliph al-Ma'mūn in the year 825. In this debate the wise Magian succeeded in answering the seven questions put to him by a heretic. Abālish, whose name, according to Schaeder, is of Arabic origin (from Abū Laythin and, to be exact, from the exclamation *yā Abā Laythin*), was a sceptical thinker on religion, who held as many doubts about the meaning and efficacy of the dogmas of the Zoroastrian religion as about the effect of the practices based on them. He asks Āturfarnbag how it is that although fire and water were created by Ōhrmazd they possessed a destructive force; he also asks whether there exists a greater sin than to defile fire and water by contact with a corpse and whether the punishments inflicted on human beings were ordained by Ōhrmazd or by Ahriman (in the former case the suffering involved by the punishment would not proceed from the Evil One, and in the latter case the one inflicting the punishment would not be acting according to the will of Ōhrmazd). Abālish evidently attacks the fundamental principles of faith by pointing out with great perspicacity the inconsistencies between dogma and practice. How can ablutions with cow's urine be of any avail when followed by another washing with water, although cow's urine is said to possess the most effective cleansing powers? Abālish does not conceal his doubt as to the effectiveness of the adoration of sacred fires and that of the sacred rope-girdle (*Kustīk*). He is astonished that the corpse of a pure believer can defile whereas that of an impure unbeliever does not. Of course Āturfarnbag answers these impertinent questions satisfactorily; in any case at the end of the debate caliph and listeners pronounce him the winner. Abālish is representative of the movement prevailing in Iran at the time of the Abbasid caliphs. Its followers were known as *Zindīqs*. Among them were free-thinkers who tried to undermine the dogmas of Islam and other religions, secret dualists and also Manichaeans and supporters of other beliefs, all of them hostile towards the doctrine of the state. To these also belonged the famous writer Ibn al-Muqaffaʿ.

Among these Zindīqs there reigned a spirit of freedom that contributed to the flourishing of philosophy and supported the Persian element in its national and cultural endeavours. For this reason the Zindīqs were persecuted in the eighth decade of the 8th century by the Arab government and some were put to death.

A favourite form of treating religious subjects is that of the question and answer. The book *Dātəstān-i dēnīk*, 'Religious Decisions', by the head of the Zoroastrian priesthood in Fars and Kirman, Manushchihr, was compiled in this form. It contains answers to ninety-two questions drawn from the field of religious themes, including good works and sins, traditions and duties of the priests, ceremonies and privileges of the priesthood, the relation between good and evil beings, the responsibility of believers, the fate of the human soul, etc. The Magians were greatly troubled at that time not only by the problems raised by the Islamic government but also on account of adversaries among their own ranks. We have already witnessed this in the debate with Abālish, against whom the Magians appealed to the Moslem powers for protection. But innovators also appeared from time to time among the orthodox believers who, however, met with a stubborn resistance on the part of the clerical leaders with their strict regard for observances. One of these reformers was Zātsparam, the brother of Manushchihr and head of a religious community in Sirkan in Kirman. He introduced new ordinances for purification which, however, did not please his subordinates. The believers took their complaints to Manushchihr who, in *three letters*, settled the dispute in favour of the discontented orthodox members. In the first letter he replied to the discontents, in the second he came to an understanding with his brother, and in the third pronounced an open verdict rejecting the innovations. The letters were composed in the year 881.

Zātsparam himself was one of the religious writers. In his work *Chītakihā*, 'Selected Treatises', he deals with religious themes in three short articles, the first of which contains a legendary biography of Zoroaster. Another writer of that period was the Magian Martānfarrakhv, author of the *Shkand gumānīk vichār*, 'Explanation that Dispels Doubts'. Of greater importance in this connection are the polemics directed against Moslems, Jews, Christians and Manichaeans (this last part is unfortunately incomplete, as the last portion of the work has been lost). The question-and-answer form is also to be found in a fascinating little encyclopaedia on religious matters, *Dānāk u mēnōkē khrat*, 'The Sage and Celestial Wisdom', in which the sage puts sixty-two questions on religion to the spirit of celestial wisdom and receives in return answers and explanations. The *Bundahishn*, 'The Original Creation', is a valuable compilation of religious stories, studies on local surroundings, mythical and legendary traditions. We learn about the creation of this world, of the advent of Ahriman on earth, the Last Judgment, the resurrection of the body, the country of Iran with its rivers, mountains, lakes, rulers and heroes, the religious significance of the elements and creation in general and finally also about traditional chronology. There are two recensions of the *Bundahishn* extant: one of these has been handed down in manuscripts of Indian origin, the other, earlier and more detailed, originated in Iran. For this reason it is known as the *Iranian* or *Great Bundahishn*. Of great importance for the study of Persian epical material is the treatment of ancient heroic sagas, which often elucidate things only occasionally mentioned in the Avesta. According to a note at the beginning of the book the real title is *Zandākāsīh*, 'The Doctrine that explains Religious Subjects'. The name *Bundahishn* was given to the text because it describes the original state of Creation before the Evil One entered the world. Persian tradition holds that during the first three thousand years Creation existed in a purely spiritual state. Then the evil spirit Ahriman found his way into the world, but he was bewildered on seeing light. The good God Ōhrmazd first offered him peace but when Ahriman refused they agreed to carry on a conflict for nine thousand years, for Ōhrmazd knew that at the end of that time the power of the Evil One would have been destroyed. By the power of prayer he then banished the demon back into darkness where he remained for a further three thousand years. During this space of time Ōhrmazd created the material world, namely sky, water, earth, vegetation, beasts and Man in succession. Neither did the Evil One remain idle, for he created wicked beings for his future army in the struggle against the powers of Good. Then, urged by the she-devil *Jēh*, he summoned his strength and penetrated through the heavens down to the earth. There he threw Creation into a state of chaos, brought destruction, death and disease, misery and calamity into the world, thus adding the bad qualities of Creation to the good ones. This was the beginning of the mingling (*gumēzhishn*) of the two, which will last until the end of the world. The *Bundahishn* further depicts the struggle between the good spirits and the demons, with the defeat of the latter, the story of the first man and woman, *Mihrē* and *Mihriyānē*, who committed the original sin by obeying the lusts of the flesh instead of first offering thanks to Ōhrmazd for their creation. From the descendants of these two stemmed the monarchs of ancient Iran, who introduced civilisation and built up a powerful kingdom. In the sagas these kings are called *Pēshdādians*, 'the first rulers'. They were greatly troubled by those nations that had been stirred up by Ahriman against the Iranians, in particular the Turanians, whose king *Frāsyāp* (Afrāsyāb) even defeated the Iranian shāhs. Finally, however, thanks to the second Iranian dynasty, the *Kayanids*, the danger from the side of the Turanians was brought to a stand. At last, three thousand years before the end of the world, the prophet Zoroaster came and brought the true faith to the Iranians. The *Bundahishn* contains lengthy genealogical trees of all these mythical kings and of the family of Zoroaster. Most fascinating are its descriptions of the last days of the world, of the universal catastrophe that will bring about the downfall of the wicked. The world will be purged by the firebrand arising from the stream of molten metal that will flow over the whole earth. In similar manner the end of the world is also described in the Bible and still more recent traditions, such as the heathen- (*Edda*) and Christian-Germanic (*Muspilli*). Ahriman is rendered harmless, hell is purged and all creatures are set free. Then only will the world remain perfect and good for ever. The *Bundahishn* gives information on natural phenomena and their significance, the human body, sacred fires, harmful animals, the calendar, and chronology. It also contains a long list of demons – briefly, it is a compendium of practically all that is worth knowing in the world past and present, seen of course from a deliberately dogmatic religious standpoint. The sole motive of the author is to show believers the relation of creation to Ōhrmazd and to the true religion. In the form in which we know it today it originated during the Arab supremacy in Iran. The *Great Bundahishn* makes mention of the end of the Sasanian kingdom and of the Arab plunderers. The latest recension dates apparently from the 12th century.

Sins, good deeds, ceremonies, customs and the meaning of the sacred texts are discussed in the *Shāyist nē shāyist*, 'What one may and may not do'. The *Mātagdān i Yavisht-i Friyān*, 'The Story of the Friyānid Yavisht', is a collection of riddles within the framework of a religious legend. The subject is a contest in riddles between the young but wise Zoroastrian saint and the wicked enchanter *Akht*. Aided by good, supernatural beings, the god-fearing Yavisht solves the riddles put to him by Akht and so saves his town from destruction, but Akht is unable to guess the riddles given him by Yavisht, even with the help of the arch-demon, who with cynical mockery leaves him in the lurch. In the end Akht is killed by the winner. The subject is also briefly mentioned in the fifth *Yasht* of the Avesta. *Yōishta*, as he is called there, a Fryanid, sacrifices to the river-goddess *Arədvī sūrā* a thousand horses, a thousand bulls and a thousand rams on an island in the river Raṅhā, in order with her aid to defeat the crafty and beguiling *Akhtya*, who for malicious reasons had asked him ninety-nine difficult questions. The Middle Persian legend is thus nothing other than a completion of the passage in the Avesta.

The *Antiphon* played an important role during the latter part of the period when the Indian Parsees were dependent on their Iranian brethren in the faith for information on religious and disciplinary questions. Iranian Magians sent to the Indian communities either discussions on such problems in the form of collections of short treatises or in the form of letters (*maktūb*). Both forms were given the name *Rivāyat*. These *Rivāyats* sometimes include very valuable comments on the position of religion, on the social and cultural conditions of the faithful, as well as dogmatic, moral and literary details. The *Rivāyats* were supplemented in India by the local priests. From Iran the Magians sent manuscripts of the Avesta and Middle Persian books to India, but the earliest copies of Indian origin date only from the first quarter of the 14th century. In the 15th century the Iranian Magians already wrote in post-Sasanian Persian. The first post-Sasanian Persian *Rivāyat* dates from the year 1478. But as recently as 1768 an Indian Parsee from Surat journeyed to the town of Yazd in Persia for answers to seventy-eight questions which he had brought with him.

E. SECULAR LITERATURE

Secular literature written in the book-language is on the whole scarce and consists entirely of prose. But this does not exclude the possibility of some of these records having originally been cast in poetical form. E. Benveniste endeavoured to reconstruct the epic *Ayātkār-i Zarērān*, 'The Book of the Heroic Deeds of the Son of Zarēr', as a poem. This little book is one of the earliest Middle Persian literary productions of its kind. It was perhaps written at the time when Persia, after the catastrophic defeat of King Pērōz in the year 484, was being seriously threatened by the Hephthalites or

White Huns. It gives an account of the religious war between King Vishtāsp and the heathen ruler Arjāsp of Turan at the time of Zoroaster. The heathen wanted Vishtāsp to renounce the new faith, but the king refused. He ultimately emerged victorious from the war, which at one point appeared to be going favourably for the infidels; he took Arjāsp prisoner, punished him and sent him as a crippled man back to his country in disgrace. The knights in the retinue of Vishtāsp were intended by the author to represent model types of the Iranian feudal nobility and to have risked their lives for Ērānshahr, just as the heroes of old had done at the time of Zoroaster. This story had very likely an older prototype which was revised in accordance with the time when danger from the Huns was imminent. It may be that at the same period the Parthian version of the work *Vīs u Rāmīn* was revised. This work has survived only in the post-Sasanian Persian poetical form.

I. HISTORICAL BELLES-LETTRES

The most successful work of secular literature is undoubtedly the historical story *Kārnāmak-i Artakhshēr-i Pāpakān*, 'Book of the Deeds of Ardashīr, son of Pāpak'. It was written round about the year 600 and glorifies the heroic founder of the dynasty. Its historical content is in any case intermingled with many national sagas; even the fabulous motif of the fight with the dragon that was killed by the valiant prince in the same way as the Babylonian dragon by the prophet Daniel, was not omitted. *Artakhshēr* was the son of a shepherd named *Sāsān* and descended from Dārā, the last Iranian Shah, son of Dārā. He was in the service of Prince *Pāpak*, a vassal of the Parthians in Fars. Pāpak's attention was once called to this young shepherd in a dream and after ascertaining his descent he gave him his daughter in marriage and adopted their son. In his youth Artakhshēr was educated in all the chivalric skills and morals. Later he was held in arrest at the court of the jealous *Ardavān*, the last of the Arsacids. He was treated in an unworthy and humiliating fashion by the king and his family. Once while hunting wild asses a quarrel arose between Artakhshēr and the arrogant son of Ardavān, who laid false claim to an animal killed by a masterly shot from the former. The father settled the matter in favour of his son and punished Artakhshēr by letting him work in the stables and excluding him from further pleasure in the hunt. But a clever slave girl, named *Artadukht* in another work, fell in love with the boy and divulged to him the prophecy of the royal astrologer, namely that he who in those days should leave the royal court would become the ruler of the Iranian Empire. The girl then took a number of valuables from the royal treasury and fled with Artakhshēr to Fars. Ardavān pursued them in vain; Artakhshēr collected an army, defeated the neighbouring lords, slew Ardavān in a decisive battle and founded a new empire, the Sasanian. In this form the plot of the story is already very old. Essential elements of the beginning of Artakhshēr's career are given in a Greek legend about Saint *Gregory Lusavorich*, the apostle from Armenia, written by Agathangelos. At any rate further details subsequently found their way into the story of Artakhshēr. For instance aṭ-Ṭabarī informs us that Artakhshēr was the son of Pāpak, whose parents were Sāsān, a priest in the fire temple at Istakhr, and his wife *Rāmbahisht*. The Byzantine historiographer Agathias tells us that Pāpak was a shoe-maker who, while studying the future in the stars, recognised in the common soldier Sāsān, who happened to come to his house, the father of the future king of Iran. He thereupon gave up his wife to him so that Artakhshēr was born. This version may perhaps originate from the Christian Persians. In the second part of the narrative are described the birth and youth of *Shāpūr*, the son of Artakhshēr, and of his grandson *Ōhrmazd*, who ruled in succession. The language of the narrative is simple and the style animated.

At the time of the Sasanians historical belles-lettres were very popular. Tales of famous historical events connected with the dynasty and its vicissitudes, and also anticipating as it were its tragic end, are told with the addition of romantic and fantastic episodes as in the *Mazdak-nāmak* (see below) and the *Vahrām Chōpēn-nāmak*. The latter work recounts the story of the notorious usurper of the 6th century, who first led the Persian troops from victory to victory but, after having been insulted by Ōhrmazd IV ,rebelled and for a time occupied the Persian throne. Finally he was defeated by Khusrau Parvēz with the help of the Byzantines, when he fled to the Turks and was assassinated there. Neither of these two works has been preserved in its original form; they were, however, translated into Arabic. We have come to know them from the Arabic chronicles and also from Firdausī's epic.

2. INSTRUCTIVE WORKS ON POLITICAL AFFAIRS

A favourite species of literature was called into being by the need for guidance in the principles of state government and state politics. These provided information about the state, its traditions, history, politics and organisation, often in a variegated medley. Of many of such works we unfortunately nowadays only possess the titles in Arabic catalogues and encyclopaedias. Ibn al-Muqaffaʿ, already mentioned above, translated the *Āyēn-nāmak*, 'Book of Regulations', into Arabic; he also interpreted another book, *Tāj-nāmak*, 'Book of the Crown', which consists of treatises on royal documents, ordinances, and edicts. In the choice of such books the translator perhaps combined patriotism and national pride with the requirements of his Arab masters, who were convinced that it was necessary and useful for their supremacy in Persia to be acquainted with the practices of the ancient national regime and to select from these those customs that they themselves could apply. The *Gāh-nāmak*, 'Notitia dignitatum', was a syllabus of state dignitaries representing about six hundred ranks. An interesting little political and religio-ethical work, which moreover contains valuable historical and cultural details, is the *Letter of the Priest Tansar to the King of Tabaristan,*

Gushnasp. According to an old tradition Tansar was a teacher of law who lived at the time of Artakhshēr I and strove for the revival of the Zoroastrian faith. The treatise ascribed to him has only survived in a Persian translation from the Arabic version of Ibn al-Muqaffaʿ. The framework consists of the counsels given by the sage to the ruler, as Gushnasp had to decide whether he would become subordinate to the new lord of Iran. Christensen points out most convincingly that the letter was only written after the year 556, that is during the reign of Khusrau I, for some of the regulations mentioned by the author did not yet exist at the time of Artakhshēr. The expansion of the kingdom, as alluded to in the letter, refers rather to the growth of his dominion after the fall of the kingdom of the Hephthalites. Since Yaman is not mentioned among the districts of Persia, the letter must have been written before the year 570. The epistle describes many features of religio-political usage, the proceedings against the apostates, the ordinances concerning the succession to the throne, the relationship between the King of Kings and his most important vassals, etc. Under the name of Artakhshēr there is another script that bore the form of a will. It is not clear under what heading we must rank the lost book *Pēshīnakān-nāmak*, 'Book of Ancestors', or 'Book about Ancestors', and whether the matter it contained was politically edifying or whether it was a chronicle interwoven with examples and anecdotes (Arab. Pers. *ḥikāyat*). The *Siyāsat-nāma*, by the Seljuq vizier Niẓāmu'l-mulk (11th century, see p. 221), contains a passage from the *Pēshīnakān* relating how the Persian kings pronounced judgment seated on a high platform so that they could survey the crowd of petitioners. This they did because it often happened that if the proceedings of the trial took place in a hall of the palace separated from the other rooms by walls and curtains, the petitioners were often held back by extortionate sycophants in an antechamber and were not permitted to appear before the Shāh. A story taken from court circles is *Khusrav-i Kavātān u rētakē*, 'Khusrau, son of Kavāt, and a page': a boy schooled in the sciences, in religion, music, games, horsemanship and literature challenges his master, the King of Kings, to put him to the test. He passes this test with flying colours. After a thrilling adventure in which he captures two lions, he is made governor of a district. It is evident that Middle Persian belles-lettres have a predilection for examples of perfect knights, loyal to the death towards their lords and masters (like *Zarēr* and his son *Bastvar*), and at the same time brought up in chivalric morals and courtly arts and excelling in clearness of judgment and energy like Artakhshēr, and reliable like the page of Khusrau.

Of less importance among secular prose are two small works, *Shahrəstānihā-i Ērān*, 'Iranian Towns', and *Avdihā u sahīkihā-i Sakastān*, 'Curiosities and Wonders of Sīstān'. The first contains a list of towns in Iran (altogether one hundred and ten) and their founders. We learn that most of these towns were founded by Sasanian kings. The last of them, Baghdad, was built by the second caliph of the Abbasid dynasty, Abū Jaʿfar Manṣūr. In the 'Wonders of Sīstān' we are fascinated by the references to the period of the Iranian sagas and the beginnings of the Zoroastrian faith. They tell of the river Hilmand, whose praises were already sung in the Avesta, of lake *Frazdān* and of lake Hāmūn, here called *Kayānsīh,* in which lies the semen of Zoroaster, guarded by Fravashis. We read further of the mountain *Ōshdāshtar,* in short of the beauties of the native land of the future successors to Zoroaster in the office of prophet, of whom it is said in the orthodox traditions that one is born every 1000 years. The last of these future saviours, *Saoshyant,* will also be the judge at the Last Judgment.

3. LEGAL WRITINGS. PAPYRI

Various social institutions, privileges and duties are dealt with in the book of social law, as West once called it. Of this book only fragments are now in existence, but it certainly goes back to the Sasanian period. The fragments were published in Bombay in 1901 and were recognised as belonging to the Sasanian book of law, *Mātagdān-i hazār dātəstān*, 'Book of the Thousand Judgments'. In Europe it was taken in hand by Chr. Bartholomae, who did much to elucidate its contents. The existence of juridical writings at the time of the Sasanians is also proved by the Syriac version of such a legal codex as that of the Metropolitan Ishōʿbukht for the use of Christians. It contains interesting items of information regarding social and economic conditions, the mutual legal relations of husband and wife, and regulations concerning slaves, etc. The verdicts pronounced by legal authorities in relation to family rights are instructive and valuable. Though the family was polygamous, in reality monogamy was already quite common. The poor man had no means with which to buy a wife. The wife and the slaves (*anshahrīk*) were both legal entities. If there were several wives, then one of them was the privileged mistress of the house. In ancient Persia it was not only permissible but was considered as religiously desirable for a father to marry his daughter, a son his mother, and a brother his sister. A husband (particularly later on) could give his wife partnership in his fortune but he could also dismiss her or hand her over to another man. Further we learn about agricultural produce and the management of real estate and slaves. The landowner granted portions of his estate in usufruct to his slave, who cultivated it for himself and for his master, but he remained bound to the soil and could be sold or given away with the estate. Other verdicts refer to capital, the income of wives, instalments and securities, provision for children, the relations between shareholders and companies, inheritance, oaths, etc. In social life use was made of polite forms of address with which letters to persons of rank were to begin and end. A list of such forms has come down to us under the title *Apar advēnak-i nāmak nipēsishnīh*, 'On How to Write Letters'. We also possess a model of an ordinary marriage contract (in a copy dating from the year 1278). It begins with a date, prescribes the reciprocal treatment of the parties and decrees the payment of 3000 drachmas as the price of the bride. The remains of most of the papyri discovered in Fayyum in Egypt largely concern private life, but the contents are often obscure. To judge by the better preserved fragments, we have to do here with the correspondence between those taking part in the government of occupation which Persia forced on the Egyptians in the years 617–629.

In one fragment for instance we are given the lists of wine and other articles of consumption for several days of the month; in another there may be an announcement that a dignitary had left for a distant place and was therefore unable to receive visitors; yet another refers to orders and delivery of wine etc.

The fragments are for the greater part untranslatable, containing as most of them do only a few lines or even words, with frequent gaps in between.

4. THE 'FRAHANGS'

Mention must be made of the *lexicons* which explain by means of phonetic Iranic readings the Semitic heterograms and the Iranic archaisms (*pseudo-heterograms*) held to be Semitic heterograms. They are called *frahangs* ('schools'). They were probably intended both as guides for the students in the schools for scribes and as handbooks for writers and readers of documents in general. Thus in the *Frahang-i oīm* Avestan words are explained by the Middle Persian equivalents. A *fragment of a frahang* has also been discovered in *Turfan. Frahang-i pahlavīk* edited by H. Junker is the most comprehensive of these lexicons, as well as being the most perfectly preserved. It is compiled in a practical manner according to word-families. The chapters deal severally with entries connected with subjects such as the elements of nature, the earth and its subdivisions, the waters, fruits, foods, vegetables, animals, birds, beasts of prey, parts of the human body, family relationships, offices or ranks, occupations, arms, calligraphy, metals, law, verbs and other parts of speech, time, months, and numbers. The Berlin Assyriologist Erich Ebeling also took this text in hand and endeavoured to establish the etymology of the Semitic heterograms and, more in particular, to determine their origin.

It has long been known that the heterograms belong to an eastern Aramaic dialect, a sister-language to Syriac, the language of the Babylonian-Talmudic Gemara and to Mandaean, but a definite solution to this problem has not yet been found. In the heterographic vocabulary Ebeling found words that were undoubtedly Akkadian and had apparently survived in that dialect up to Parthian times, for we find them here and there in other eastern Aramaic texts. But it is not really certain whether all the words claimed by Ebeling to be Akkadian do in fact stem from that language.

Of special interest to philologists are those words in the *Frahang* that, owing to the unusual way in which they are written, could no longer be read in Iranic and were therefore held to be heterograms. Among these is strangely enough the name of the god *Ōhrmazd* (in the Avesta *Ahurō Mazdå*) which was written in such a way that later scribes read it as *Anhōmā* and took it to be a heterogram. This was indeed indicated by the script, for the letters could represent more sounds than one, so that the version *'whrmzd* might easily and without further thought be read as *'nhwm'*.

5. POETRY IN THE MIDDLE PERSIAN PERIOD. LYRICAL POETRY AND MUSIC

The research carried out during the last few decades has proved that Middle Persian literature also included poetry. Post-Sasanian Persian writers doubted the existence of poetry and in so far as they made use of examples of poetry in the Middle Persian language, they attached no great value to them because they found just those qualities lacking which became fully developed only in Persian literature, such as complicated rhythms and impeccable rhymes, as well as an abundance of imagery and figures of speech. New Persian prosody is quantitative, a principle that was adopted from the Arabs. The prosodic principle of the Iranian Middle Ages was that of counted syllables combined perhaps with attention to accent. It is true that Persian poetry is beyond comparison with the relics of Middle Persian poems. The beauty of the imagery and its harmony, the wealth of rhythms and the melodiousness of its rhyme are not to be found in the Middle Persian epoch, which is why Persian poets of later times speak contemptuously of the poetic imagery used before the Arab conquest. It is evident from the relics that have survived that though rhyme did exist, it did not occur often. In its stead there was here and there merely some assonance. The verses contain 5 to 11 syllables; there are also poems in which the verses show a constantly differing number of syllables, especially in the rhythmically composed Manichaean fragments. In the first chapter of the *Iranian or Great Bundahishn* Nyberg discovered a *fragment of the hymn to Zurvān,* a deity worshipped as the forefather of the universe in Sasanian times by a school of speculative theologians. Benveniste analysed the Manichaean fragments of Turfan and found poetical imagery in them here and there. He also made an attempt to reconstruct metrically the *tale of Zarēr* and that of the battle between the goat and the tree (*Drakht-i asūrīk*). The great master of Semitic epigraphy, M. Lidzbarski, proved convincingly that Mānī wrote Aramaic poems which were later translated into Middle Persian. He demonstrated this by reference to a hymn in which the dualistic prophet proudly acknowledged Babylon as his native country. Here follow literal translations of the two poems:

Hymn to Zurvān

Time is more powerful than both the creations
Time is the measuring-rod for the validity of religious work
Time is more blessed with treasures than those especially favoured by Fate,
Time has more knowledge than the well-instructed.

Our span of life vanishes away
When the time for it is ordained,
Even the magnificent will come to naught
The soul cannot escape from it,
Not when it ascends
Nor when it descends
Nor even when it goes down below the world. (after Nyberg)

Hymn of Mānī

A grateful scholar am I
For I come from the land of Babel,
From the land of Babel I hail,
And at the gate of truth I have stood.
A proclaiming pupil am I,
For from the land of Babel I have departed
I have gone from the land of Babel
So that I may utter a cry in the world created on the Earth.
(after Müller-Andreas)

The hymn to Zurvān contains four strophes, the first two consisting of two verses, the other two of four. In the first two strophes the verses have eleven syllables, in the third each has nine, while the last has verses of eight syllables. The verses of each separate strophe are in rhyme. Nyberg is of the opinion that there is an obvious connection between this poem and New Persian poetry in the *hazaj* rhythm and the quatrain strophes of Bābā Ṭāhir. Andreas maintains that in the poem by Mānī the verse has eight syllables.

New Persian writers traced the origin of artistic poetry back to the Sasanian king, Bahrām V Gōr ('the onager', a kind of wild ass, because hunting this animal was a favourite pastime of the king, 420–438). According to Arab and Persian scholars it was in fact he who composed the first Persian verses:

man-am ān shīr-i shala
man-am ān babr-i yala,
man-am ān Bahrām-i Gōr,
man-am ān Bū-Jabala

I am that bloodthirsty lion,
I am that ferocious tiger,
I am that Bahrām Gōr,
I am he whom men call Abū-Jabala.

There are several variants of the text of this poem.

The famous New Persian anthologist, ʿAufī, states that he saw and read the complete collection of the works of this king in Bukhara. There is a tradition that Bahrām recited the first verses in a discourse of love with his wife *Dilārām*. He spent his youth at the court of the Arab king in al-Ḥīra and there became acquainted with Arabic poetry. At his court there later lived the beautiful harpist of Greek descent, *Āzāda*, his favourite. A later New Persian scholar, Daulatshāh (d. 1494), repeats some of these statements and adds other information concerning the pre-Arab beginnings of poetry in Persia. One of his sources establishes the existence of poetry at the time of King Khusrau II (591–628). On the wall of the palace that this Shāh had had built for his beloved and lady musician, Shīrīn, in Qaṣr-i Shīrīn, a Persian couplet could still be read at the time of the Amīr ʿAḍudu'd-daula, of the Buyid family, about the year 950. Daulatshāh also tells us that the Amīr of Khurasan, ʿAbdu'llāh of the Tahirids (828–844), received an old book depicting the love of *Vāmiq and ʿAdhrā*, composed by ancient sages and dedicated by them to King Khusrau I. But the Amīr ordered it to be destroyed, saying that the Koran and the Tradition were sufficient for good Moslems, and that this book, written as it was by Magians, was accursed and harmful. Perhaps these accounts were invented later, at a time when it was a matter of importance to put Persian poetry on a level with its then more favourably placed Arabic rival, especially as regards its age. However that may be, it is certain that the poetry of the Middle Persian epoch flourished under Sasanian rule. It is indeed probable that it already prospered under the Arsacids. It seems also to have carried influence in the neighbouring state of Armenia. The Armenian historiographer Mosēs of Khorene quotes a portion of the *Hymn to Vahagn*, the ancient Iranian *Vərəthraghna*, Indian Vṛtrahan or Indra, who was worshipped in the Tarōnian Ashtishat on the Euphrates. In the imagery employed we find products of poetical imagination similar to those in the sacred texts of the ancient Indians:

Heaven and earth were in the throes of labour
The scarlet sea was in agony
The sea gave birth to a small red reed,
Out of the stalk of the reed arose smoke
Out of the stalk of the reed broke out a flame
Out of the flame there arose a child
The child had fiery hair and a beard of fire
And his eyes were two suns. (after Justi)

Benveniste assumes that this hymn, like others similar to it – for example Vahagn's fight with the dragon – was influenced in its composition by Arsacid hymns. V. Minorsky, by a thorough analysis of the plot of *Vīs u Rāmīn*, came to the plausible conclusion that the model for the New Persian work can be traced back as far as the Arsacid period. But in the very preface to this New Persian version the writer expresses his dissatisfaction about the primitiveness of the pre-New Persian poetry. It is interesting to note that the authors of Middle Persian texts were often described in New Persian books as sages, wise men and such like. There is a valuable piece among the Turfan fragments of Manichaean origin that bears a lyrical character, a miniature in a mood of nature, behind which we can perhaps detect religious mystery:

Radiant sun and gleaming full moon
They shine and glitter from the trunk of that tree.
Splendid birds strut about there joyfully;
There the dove and the many-coloured peacock give themselves airs.

A missing word in the fourth line has been felicitously filled in by H. Junker. From numerous later references it is known that the Persians possessed many lyrical poems dating from as early as Sasanian times. These were sung in their country. Music and song were very popular in Persia. The singing was accompanied by stringed instruments. King Artakhshēr Pāpakān (according to the *Kārnāmak*) used to sing charming songs whilst playing his own accompaniment on the *vīn*, a kind of guitar. Mānī set great store by singing and was assiduous in introducing temple music into his religious services. Persian singers excelled in their art and in the Islamic period they influenced the development of music and song among the Arabs. Ibn Misjaḥ of Mecca, who studied the Persian songs sung by Persian craftsmen hired to repair the Kaʿba sanctuary, introduced Persian music into the Arab world. Persian women singers taught Arab musicians to play the lute, while at feasts their melodies moved Arab poets to tears, though they were unfamiliar with the Persian language. During the reign of Hārūn ar-Rashīd (786–809) the famous lute-player Sunayd of Fars acted as judge at musical competitions.

In New Persian literature there are poetical texts of this kind that appear to be in outmoded language, so that at a first glance it is obvious that they are ancient linguistic monuments whose origin can be traced back to Sasanian times. Their age is revealed especially by their content and their purpose. One of these texts is the hymn contained in the chronicle *Taʾrīkh-i Sīstān* (composed between 1277 and 1281), which was sung by Zoroastrian priests in a fire temple and was composed metrically in the ancient language. The metre goes back to the pre-Arab period. In the book *Naurūz-nāma*, erroneously attributed to ʿOmar Khayyām, there is a poem consisting of a New Year's wish that was recited by the chief priest before the royal throne. The language of this poem proves beyond doubt that it belonged to the Sasanian period. Ch. Rempis has interpreted these interesting relics of ancient poetry and demonstrated their Middle Persian origin by reference to their language and prosody.

The popularity of Persian epic poems in other countries besides Persia is illustrated by an interesting episode taken from the life of Muḥammad. A merchant from Mekka, a certain Naḍr ibn al-Ḥārith, while on one of his journeys bought at al-Ḥīra a copy of the history of the war between Rustam and Isfandiyār, and on returning to Mecca he read this epic saga to his compatriots, who showed more appreciation for it than for the sermons of the prophets. Muḥammad, without considering his name worthy of mention, swore in the thirty-first Sura of the Koran that this merchant would be punished by God for his infamy. The spread of Persian material in other countries is further proved by the existence of a fragment of the *Saga of Rustam* in a Sogdian version. This runs as follows:

> *Rakhsh agreed. At once Rustam turned back. When the demons saw this at once they swiftly smote the horsemen and the foot-soldiers together. To one another they cried: "The chieftain's courage is now broken, with us he will be unable to fight longer. Let him not flee away, yet kill him not, but take him alive that we may torture him most cruelly!" The demons greatly incited one another; together they called out. They started in pursuit of Rustam. Then Rustam turned.* (Bailey)

The metrical aspect of Middle Persian poems is mentioned in only one single source, and this again a foreign one. In the annotations to the work of the Greek prosodist Hephaistion it is stated that the *Ionicus a maiore*, viz. a Greek verse measure consisting of two long and two short syllables (— — ∪∪), is also known as the *persicus* because there were Persian stories composed in it. What Middle Persian verse looked like in this rhythm, we do not know.

6. FOREIGN INFLUENCES IN MIDDLE PERSIAN LITERATURE

A comprehensive discussion of the influence of Persian literature on other literatures would lead far beyond our present scope. Conversely traces of the influence of foreign literatures in Persia go as far back as pre-Sasanian times. Apart from the fact that the motif of the *Artāk Virāz-nāmak* appears many centuries earlier in oriental literatures, we read in the *Dēnkart* a report stating that King Shāpūr I caused translations of Greek and Indian works to be made, which translations were to be incorporated into a collection of religious texts. The Sasanians gathered information about the past partly from sagas, partly from Greek historical works. If it is true that works such as those mentioned in the *Book of Esther*, for instance, were destroyed at the time of Alexander the Great and the turbulent period following his death, then the only explanation that can be given for the contents of the letter written at the behest of Shāpūr II to the Roman emperor is that the Persians must have gained all their knowledge of their own ancient history from Hellenic sources. The Shāh namely commanded Constantine to concede to him all those districts that had once been in the possession of Persian kings and in the course of time had become Roman provinces:

adusque Strymona flumen et Macedonicos fines tenuisse maiores meos, antiquitates quoque vestrae testantur. But the Shāh could not have derived this knowledge from Old Persian cuneiform scripts or other ancient documents, although he does use the word *quoque*. Many cultural treasures have passed through Persia. By way of example we may mention that during the Sasanian epoch, most of all perhaps during the last centuries of its existence, entertaining Indian reading matter was translated into Middle Persian. The most famous specimen is undoubtedly the Arabian collection of fairy-tales *Alf layla va-layla*, 'Thousand and One Nights', concerning which al-Mas'ūdī informs us that:

> *The case with them (viz. some legendary stories) is similar to that of the books that have come to us from the Persian, Indian (Var. Pahlavi) and the Greek and have been translated for us, and that originated in the way that we have described, such as for example the book 'Hazār Afsāna', which in Arabic means 'thousand tales', for 'tale' is in Persian 'afsāna'. The people call this book 'Thousand Nights (Var. Thousand Nights and One Night)'. This is the story of the king and the vizier and his daughter and her servant-girl; these two are called Shīrāzād and Dīnāzād (Var. and her nurse; and his two daughters).* (after E. Littmann)

The original doubt as to the authenticity and veracity of this information was dispelled by thorough investigation, which proved definitely that the book was really written in Persia after an Indian model, was translated into Arabic in the 9th century, but was later expanded by numerous interpolations until it reached its present length. This is an excellent example of how Persia was instrumental in passing on works of cultural value.

7. PERSIAN INFLUENCES ON OTHER LITERATURES

An open question remains in my opinion the influence of oriental literature (especially that of Persia) on that of mediaeval western Europe, in particular chivalric epic poetry and court epics. In Europe these problems have been studied by Fr. von Suhtscheck and Franz Rolf Schröder, and in the east by the Parsee investigator, Sir J. C. Coyajee. Their view is that the motifs of Persian heroic poetry are to be found in chivalric epic cycles and particularly in the Arthurian legends. The first two of these scholars have made a closer study of the connection with the characters in *Parzival*, Wolfram von Eschenbach's famous epic poem. Suhtscheck discovers here Persian material, while Schröder suspects that use is being made of works that originated in Neo-Manichaean circles in southern France, to which Wolfram himself moreover refers. The problem can be solved if it is possible to prove that the work of the otherwise unknown Provençal poet Kyôt, mentioned by Wolfram as his model, really did exist and that

Kyôt was a Manichaean or that he at least composed his poems under Manichaean influence or in the spirit of Manichaeism. It would not be impossible for the Manichaeans of southern France to be capable of elaborating material of Persian origin.

Coyajee sees the Persian sagas reflected in those of the Arthurian cycle. As matters stand at present it is evident that the assertions of these scholars are in many cases not yet capable of proof.

8. LITERATURE OF THE LAST CENTURY OF THE SASANIAN ERA

Not until the last century of the Sasanian era do the names of authors appear in Middle Persian literature. Owing to the suppression of the social movement and the consolidation of the ruling power under Khusrau I Anōsharvān ('immortal soul') Persia became a powerful absolute monarchy, a national and imperialistic kingdom. Khusrau found his main support in the well-organized and loyal class of officials, who belonged to the nobility, and in the knightage, from which his mother Nēvāndukht is said to have been descended. According to some traditions he ordered a collection to be made of *sources and sagas dealing with the ancient kings of Iran*, thus laying the foundation for the royal saga, the most eminent version of which is to be found in the work of Firdausī. An important achievement during his reign was the establishment of a Persian colony in Yemen in southern Arabia, whence several epical narratives by later historiographers have been handed down to us, albeit in an Arabic version. These reveal to us the mentality, customs and character of the adventurous knights *Vahriz*, *Zīn*, *Marzvān*, and *Khurrakhusrau*, founders of the colony and conquerors of the Abyssinians, whom they had driven out of Yemen. It was thanks to Anōsharvān that for centuries Persia was regarded by all the kings and viziers of the east as a pattern of a well-organized kingdom. Khusrau's vizier Vazurgmihr, son of Bukhtak, who according to Persian tradition was the perfect type of a wise minister, was the author of a book of instructive proverbs, *Ganj-i shāhagān*, 'Royal Treasury', and hero of the story *Chatrang-nāmak*, 'Book on Chess'. This interesting little work relates how the Indian king *Dēvasārm* sent chessmen together with other valuable gifts to Khusrau and challenged him either to explain the rules and the essence of the game of chess or else to pay him a handsome tribute. Vazurgmihr discovered the principle of the game in three days' time and moreover invented a new game, *Nēv-Artakhshēr* (*Nard*, a kind of backgammon). He then set out for India taking this new game with him, and in the name of the Shāh made a similar challenge to Dēvasārm. The Indian king, of course, had no such clever vizier, neither were his courtiers of any assistance, so that he had to admit himself defeated and to pay tribute to Persia. This small book demonstrates the importance of the relationship between India and Persia at that time. The name *chatrang* testifies to the Indian origin of the game of chess (in Sanskrit *chaturangam*, 'army of four classes, namely infantry, cavalry, chariots, and elephants'). After the death of the Shāh, Vazurgmihr fell a victim to his successor Ōhrmazd IV. It was also Khusrau who offered sanctuary in his kingdom to the last Greek heathen philosophers who had left their native land. In the town of Gundīshāpūr he founded a school of medicine at which the majority of the physicians were Syrians. An enterprise with far-reaching results was the translation of the Indian *Pañchatantram*, a collection of stories and fables compiled at Khusrau's desire by his physician, Burzōē of Nīshāpūr. This translation, *Kalīlak u Dimnak*, in its Syriac version became a source for numerous instructive and entertaining collections of narratives in mediaeval Europe. Under Ōhrmazd IV the Arab *Fihrist* makes mention of the teacher Sagzanbarī. Persian poetry and music reached their highest point of development during the reign of Khusrau II Parvēz (591–628), Ōhrmazd's son. We are informed about this by Arabic writings and New Persian treatises; this kind of information is, however, mostly an echo of traditions written down in Middle Persian books towards the end of the Sasanian era and during the first centuries of the Arab dominion. Court entertainments and pleasures were accompanied by the singing of poems called *srōt i khusravānīk*, 'royal songs'. And indeed there was enough that called for celebration! The Shāh lived in a splendid residence in Ctesiphon on the river Tigris and his court was rich in treasures and wonders of superiority. Poets celebrated his fair wife Shīrēn, his black horse Shabdēz, his banner *Dirafsh i kāvayān* set with gems, his white elephant, his parks and throne, his 'cow's treasure' (one hundred containers of gold, silver and jewels which had been ploughed up by a common peasant; the treasure is said to have belonged to Alexander the Great), his *ganj-i vāt āvurt* (this treasure was sent by the Greeks on vessels from besieged Alexandria to Constantinople, but the wind drove it towards the Persian coast), and many other curiosities. The celebration required several poets. In Khusrau's period there were three poets who remained in the memory of later epochs: they were Nigīsā, Bārbad, and Sarkash. Some traditions consider Nigīsā as the first composer of royal songs, other traditions designate Bārbad, who was the court minstrel (*muṭrib* or *changī*) of Khusrau II. He came either from Marv or Jahram near Shiraz. His activities at the royal court are veiled in romantic legends. His rival and head of the bards, Sarkash, knew Bārbad's art and, being afraid of losing his rank, he tried hard to prevent the young and gifted poet from approaching the king. But Bārbad used a trick. He gained the confidence of the guard of the park and, hidden in green clothing among the leaves of the trees, he watched the king who was opening the feast in his park. When the king lifted his bowl of wine for the first time, Bārbad sang the song *Yazdān āfarīd*, 'God created', then the song *Partav-i Farkhār*, 'The Splendour of the Town of Farkhār', and during the third draught he sang *Sabz andar sabz*, 'The Green Man in the Verdure'. The king, enthralled by these beautiful songs and verses, ordered the singer to be sought. Having finished his song, Bārbad came out of the thicket and bowed to the Shāh. Then he became the head of the royal singers and the court poet. He is said to have composed seven royal chants, thirty *laḥns* and three hundred and sixty songs that used to be sung during the feasts every day. According to Moslem authors these songs held their popularity even in several following centuries. It is interesting to note that the number of these works conforms to that of the days in a week, in a month and in a year. The names of some of the songs have been preserved and indicate to a certain extent the nature of their inspiration. *Yazdān āfarīd* is perhaps a religious chant. Firdausī calls the song *Paygār-i gurd*, 'Hero's Fight'. But Bārbad also gathered inspiration from tales and myths, e.g. *Kēn-i Ēraj*, 'Revenge for Ēraj', *Kēn-i Syāvakhsh*, 'Revenge for Syāvakhsh'. In other songs he celebrated the wonders of the royal court, e.g. *Bāgh-i Shahriyār*, 'Shahriyār's garden', *Aurangīk*, 'Throne Song', *Haft ganj*, 'Seven treasures', etc. But he also chose themes relating to the seasons of the year and holidays, e.g. *Naurōz-i vazurg*, 'Great New Year's Day'. He was sometimes inspired by natural phenomena and moods, as *Sarvistān*, 'Cypress Garden', *Ārāyishn-i khvarshēd*, 'Beauty of the Sun' or *Māh apar kōhān*, 'Moon over the Mountains'. Bārbad is said to have been poisoned by his enemy Sarkash.

Arabic sources have preserved information on other kinds of Persian literature, the value of which is completely lost for us nowadays. I cannot say whether all the works enumerated by the Arabs belong to the last century of the Sasanian period or whether some of them were composed as late as the intermediate era, between the occupation of the empire and the beginning of the 10th century. Al-Masʿūdī mentions the book *Sakīsarān* (?) with a description of the fight between Isfandiyār and Rustam, the book *Hazār afsāna*, 'Thousand Tales' and the book of *Farza and Sīmās*. The latter is mentioned also by the chronicler Ḥamza al-Iṣfahānī, who includes it in the range of seventy writings said to have been translated into Persian under the latter Arsacids. There he enumerates also *Sindibād-nāma*, 'The Book of Sindibād', known from the Arabian Nights. An-Nadīm's *Fihrist* lists stories and romances, e.g. the fairy-tale of *Dārāb and the Golden Statue*, the *History of Seven Viziers* (which was an original version of or parallel to the History of Ten Viziers, known from the popular Persian book *Bakhtyār-nāma*), *On the Orphan Rōzveh*, *On the Bear and the Fox*, *On Nimrod, the King of Babel*, books of stories and amusement, etc. Many instructive books were written as well as books on political principles and methods of ruling, full of ideas of the foremost Sasanian kings; sometimes these ideas were only ascribed to the kings. In this category we can find *Ardashīr's Testament*, *Wise Maxims of Vazurgmihr*, *Kisrā's Testament*, that existed in several versions, *Zādānfarrukh's Instructions for his Son*, etc. The Persians also wrote theoretical works on archery (one such is by Bahrām Chōbēn rather than by Bahrām Gōr), on the game of polo that was very popular among the nobles and courtiers, but also books about warfare, the siege of towns and fortresses, filing troops, horsemanship, the use of war engines, beasts of burden during campaigns, the use of fire, oil and engines in war, etc. According to Arab information there was even no lack of obscene works, e.g. the book of *Banyān-dukht* or of *Bahrām-dukht*. Many well-known literary works had come from India; they were translated into Persian and then into Arabic, for instance *Kalīla u Dimna*, two books of *Sindibād*, especially the famous legend of *Bilauhar and Būdāsaf (Yūdāsaf)* that reached Europe and is still known under the title of *Barlaam and Josaphat*. We cannot say anything about the book that was found in the possession of the famous commander Afshīn, Bābak's conqueror. Afshīn was interrogated soon after his victory, being under suspicion of having intrigued against the state and against religion. He died miserably in prison in 841. His house contained not only some statues of gods but also a work called *Zarāva*, which contained heretical doctrines. We do not know when the book was written or by whom.

Firdausī, who refers to some of the above-mentioned authors, mentions in addition to Vazurgmihr and Burzōē the court singers of Khusrau II, son of Ōhrmazd, Sarkash and Bārbud, the latter of whom came from Nishapur and composed more than thirty original melodies for the king. During the reign of the last of the Sasanians, Yazdkart III (633–652), a country nobleman of the name of Dānishvar compiled, in conjunction with the Magian Farrukhān and the courtier Rāmīn, a comprehensive work on the history of Iran since the earliest times up to the death of Khusrau II (628). This book, entitled *Khvatāy-nāmak*, 'Book of Kings', was translated into Arabic in the 8th century by Ibn al-Muqaffaʿ and in the 10th century into New Persian by several Zoroastrians. Later historians and poets drew from it as being the most important source of information concerning ancient Persian sagas and historical events. The Russian scholar, Baron V. R. Rosen, proved that although this Middle Persian chronicle was in the first place translated by Ibn al-Muqaffaʿ, many other versions appeared later on, some of which made use of his old translation; others again inserted episodes drawn from Middle Persian books and yet others compared the different versions and endeavoured to reconstruct the *Khvatāy-nāmak* in its genuine and original form, for these authors were quite well aware that the first translators had omitted many things. Evidence of the existence of the chronicles and annals (known by the Arabs as *kutub as-siyar va't-tavārīkh*) is frequently given by Islamic authors, who had seen them with their own eyes in the homes of Iranian magnates and men of culture. Al-Masʿūdī relates that in the year 915 he had seen in Istakhr a large illustrated book that included in its contents the history of the Sasanian kings, their governments and their edifices. There was a portrait of each king, so that following generations could see the kind of crown he wore, what his festive robes were like and even how his beard had been curled. This book is said to be a copy of the one found in the year 731 in the Persian royal treasury in which the illustrations were carried out in gold, silver and copper on fine parchment or paper. Ancient Persian chronicles are also said to have been preserved in Shīz in Media Atropatene, the illustrations – according to the geographer al-Istakhrī – corresponding to the pictures of the Persian kings carved in the rock in the neighbourhood of Shapur. The existence of official chronicles is also alluded to by the Byzantine chronicler Agathias (*c.* 570) who, thanks to the intermediation of the then famous dragoman Sergios and with the permission of the Persian authorities, succeeded in deriving from them important facts and especially dates.

9. LITERATURE OF THE SECTARIANS AND DISSENTERS. ZURVANISM. CHRISTIANITY

No sectarian or heretical literature has survived from the period before the Arab conquest. Later writers maintain that the father of the national communist movement, *Mazdak* (c. 500), composed a book entitled *Dēsnād* in which he expounded his doctrines, but this has disappeared. For after the Mazdakites had been exterminated (524–525) their books were burnt. The Middle Persian document known by the Arabs as *Kitābu Mazdaka* (in the original *Mazdak-nāmak*) is a tendentious belletristic work that relates the history and end of the movement, written to meet the demands of the ruling classes. Its contents have come down to us in the later New Persian books *Siyāsat-nāma* and *Fārs-nāma*. Mazdak is represented as a Magian who misleads people by assumedly correct explanations of the Avesta and also by other deceptive means in order to gain the confidence of King Kavāt and the upper classes. He professes to be able to converse with the Spirit of the sacred fire and to receive instructions recited by the Spirit in a human voice. In reality he conceals close to the fire-altar one of his followers who, from his subterranean hiding-place, communicates in his own voice instructions apparently proceeding from the deity. He succeeds in deluding the king, but the young successor to the throne, Khusrau Anōsharvān, conspiring with the Magians, exposes the trickery and turns his father against the all-powerful reformer. The conspiracy is successful, Mazdak and the heads of the movement fall into the trap and are put to death. This story was translated by Ibn al-Muqaffaʿ into Arabic and retold in verse form by Abān al-Lāḥiqī.

Nor is it possible for us to gather any information about the various theological movements from original writings. There are only scattered references in the book-literature to prove that some works passed through the hands of Zurvanite theologians (e.g. the *Iranian* or *Great Bundahishn*). More important is the chapter from the Zurvanite Dogmas to be found in King Yazdkart's manifesto to the Armenians. This reveals the tendency to transform Mazdaistic dualism into monotheism. For the rest we are dependent for our knowledge of the sectarian doctrines entirely on what we are told by ash-Shahrastānī, al-Bīrūnī, and other Arab writers.

The spread of Christianity in Iran was very slow, possibly already from the time of the apostles (the Apocrypha relate that several apostles were at work in the Persian empire), reaching the Semitic districts of the kingdom and Susiana earlier. In the other regions there were only very few Christians. There is a legend about the acts of the Apostle Thomas at the court of King Gondophares in eastern Iran, and history records a few persecutions in the Sasanian period, the greatest of these being about the year 340 under Shāpūr II. After the end of the 5th century, tolerance was shown towards the Nestorians, a Christian sect that had been persecuted by the orthodox emperors in Byzantium. Its mission was not limited to Iran but extended as far as Central Asia and in the first half of the 7th century even reached China. The missionaries were

Syrians (the Nestorian inscription in the Chinese Si-ngan-fu dating from the year 781 was written both in Chinese and in Syriac) and they brought with them the Syrian script from which the alphabets of several Central Asian and Eastern Asian peoples originated. Later on Persians also took part in the missions. Their names appear on Nestorian tombstones in Siberia. As well as in Syriac the Christians composed their religious literature in various Iranic languages, among them being Middle Persian and Sogdian. Among Christian writings in Middle Persian the most important is the *Psalter*, but unfortunately only a fragment of it has survived. It was discovered at Bulayiq near Turfan and entrusted to F. C. Andreas for examination. After his death it was published as part of the Andreas literary legacy by his Danish pupil Kai Barr (1933). Its archaic Pahlavi script shows that it is a copy of a translation carried out some time during the second half of the 6th century and written down in the customary Middle Persian manner, making use of heterograms. This translation was made neither from the original Hebrew text nor from the Greek Septuaginta, but from the Syriac, the ecclesiastical language of the eastern Christians. The *Psalter* is thus an unusually important document, particularly on account of its ancient forms and orthography and because, being a contemporary work, it demonstrates the language and spelling of the Sasanian period. Its script is also of the greatest importance, being less complicated than that of the book-literature, while numbers of words are here more legible and more accurately formed.

10. MIDDLE IRANIAN MANUSCRIPTS

The records of Middle Iranian Mazdaistic literature are dispersed among numerous libraries and collections. The most important collections of Avestan and Middle Persian manuscripts are to be found in the University Library at Copenhagen and the libraries at Bombay, the State Library at Munich, and the Bibliothèque Nationale at Paris. A small number of older and more important texts belong to other institutions and to individual Parsee scholars. Ancient manuscripts, especially those that were written in Iran, are conspicuous for their beautiful calligraphy. The writers always begin with the formula *pat nām-i Yazdān*, "In the Name of God", just as did the Islamic copyists, and ended their books with the phrase *frazhaft pat drōt u shātīh u rāmishn*, "concluded in peace, happiness and joy". Many of the manuscripts have at the end a *colophon*, added by the scribe, stating where, by whom and from what model the copy has been made. This information is very important for fixing the date of a manuscript. The Manichaean fragments from Turfan are for the main part preserved in Berlin, to a smaller extent in the capital cities of the states that took part in the Turfan expeditions. Many of the book-texts and fragments from Turfan have not yet been published. Older editions are gradually being replaced by newer ones, which profit by the knowledge gained from recent discoveries in Turfan and Iran. The Indian

Parsee editions were originally practically worthless; but since the Parsee scholar K. R. Cama has become acquainted with the technique and methods practised in Germany, the quality of scientific investigation among the Parsees has noticeably improved, though it has not yet reached European level. Translations from the Middle Persian are far from numerous. The old translations of the English scholar E. W. West no longer fulfil modern requirements. Nowadays publishers include the original texts with the translations, so that investigators in other fields can also consult the Iranian sources.

F. DISCOVERIES IN CENTRAL ASIA

In the last decade of the 19th century, travellers in Chinese Turkestan found some documents belonging to ancient literatures. Their discoveries were an incentive to the most important European institutes to undertake expeditions to the Central Asian countries, especially Chinese Turkestan, with the result that great numbers of cultural monuments were brought to light. A study of these records revealed them to be the remains of literatures containing a wealth of information on the peoples that inhabited Central Asia before the Mongol Empire came into existence. These peoples possessed their own states, civilisations and cultures. They exercised mutual influence in matters pertaining to trade and politics as well as religion and were in their turn affected by the neighbouring cultural powers of India, Persia, and China. The world religions such as Buddhism, Manichaeism and Christianity existed side by side and vied with one another in the production of literature. The Uighurian texts belong to the Turkish element, and to the Iranian belong the relics of Middle Persian, Sogdian and Sakian manuscripts. Of the then newly-discovered Indo-European languages the one that drew the most attention was the so-called Tokharian. Fragments of texts in Indian languages (Sanskrit and Prakrit) have also been found.

1. MANICHAEAN DOCUMENTS

In addition to the Buddhistic Mahāyāna and Nestorian Christianity, the Manichaean religion especially was widespread in Central Asia. Its adherents made use not only of Middle Persian dialects, but also of Sogdian, Uighurian, and Chinese. Thanks to F. W. K. Müller and his contemporaries Carl Salemann and F. C. Andreas, who were the first to decipher the Middle Persian Manichaean fragments discovered in the Turfan oasis, a portion of these fragments has now been published and elucidated. To W. B. Henning great credit is due for having published and elucidated several of the Manichaean fragments. The work of these investigators has provided new authentic sources for the study of Manichaeism and new texts for Iranistic and Indo-European studies. These have brought about a revolution in linguistics, the history of literature and in theology.

The *Manichaean Middle Persian fragments* are written partly in the south-western and partly in the north-western (Parthian) dialect. From time to time one also comes across a Sogdian phrase. From a literary point of view the content is somewhat heterogeneous. These fragments contain liturgical hymns, prayers, sections on cosmogony, episodes from the life of Mānī and legends dealing with the acts of the first Manichaean missionaries, polemics with dissenters, accounts of the death of Jesus reminiscent of the Passion as described by the Evangelists, fragments of a work on eschatology and descriptions of the cosmic drama, as well as on the mythical foundation of doctrinal theology. Many of the fragments would appear to prove that they were in fact originally composed in the form of poetry and in the Aramaic language. Mānī, the great Babylonian-Iranian theosopher and representative of Asian-Hellenistic gnosticism, was born in 216 A.D. His family, of Iranian descent, lived either in Mardinū, in the region of the ancient Kūthā, or in Avrūmyā in southern Babylonia. Mānī was brought up among the baptists of his homeland. Later he became acquainted with other religious and philosophical opinions and created a doctrine of universal salvation that was intended to unite all the foremost religions of the contemporary world. He presented his teachings to King Shāpūr I, as they were extraordinarily well suited to the purpose of becoming the state religion of the Iranian empire. The king undoubtedly thought this plan over, but finally he chose the traditional Zoroastrian dualism. Mānī travelled a great deal and spread his doctrine especially in the countries of Central Asia. After his return to Iran he became the victim of the Magians' intrigues and died in prison on 6 March 276. He wrote mainly in Aramaic and laid special stress on his Babylonian origin, but he also wrote in Middle Persian, for according to Arabic accounts his dogmatic-eschatological book *Shāhpuhrakān* was composed in Persian. According to Schaeder (*Urform und Fortbildungen des manich. Systems*, p. 147 *et seq.*) and Henning, ('Mitteliranisch', p. 73) Mānī not only introduced a variant on the Palmyranian script for his Persian works but he also put into practice an improved spelling and did away with heterograms. Yet these reforms were not accepted by the Persians (and not only for religious reasons!) and their use was confined to Mānī's followers. The Manichaeans also possessed a rich *collection of letters*, many of which have been ascribed to Mānī. But from fragments of some of these letters one can conclude that this attribution was wrong and that the letters were more likely written later by the authors and adherents of the Dēnāvarian heterodoxy (this Manichaean sect did not recognise the Archegos with his residence in Babylon as the head of the whole church). These forgers concealed their activities by making use of the name of the founder of their religion.

The Manichaeans also practised the art of *belles-lettres*, especially fables and parables. Among the Turfan documents there are fragments of tales in which indications for moral behaviour and the duties of practical life are given in belletristic form. In fragment No. 45 we find the familiar motif of a mother who weeps excessively over her dead child:

> *Up to now I have not known that I was killing my spiritual son (the soul of my dead son) when mourning for his death. Therefore I shall mourn no longer in order that his soul may live.* (after W. Bang)

We find this motif occurring in several literatures. The commandment is connected with the moral law of Zoroaster, according to which immoderate weeping for the dead is a sin. The Sogdian Manichaean fragments contain the *story of a pearl-borer* who played on his lute all day long for his employer and in the evening received his wages without having bored a single pearl. A version of this same story is often met with in India and also in the Arabic *Kalīla u Dimna*. The Uighur version gives a Manichaean conception of the Buddhist *legend of Bodhisattva* which, after finding its way across Iran, Syria and other Arab countries, took shape in Europe in the legend of *Barlaam and Josaphat*. The authentic literature gives only a few, though valuable, details on the history of Manichaeism. Comparatively common are accounts of the lives of famous missionaries as, for instance, Mar Amū, the apostle of Central Asia, though these stories are of a legendary nature. The *historical fragments* in the Parthian language are also legendary. One of them relates the wonders that took place at the death of Mānī; these show considerable resemblance to those which according to biblical tradition occurred at the death of Jesus.

As early as the Sasanian period Persia won fame through the pictorial decorations to its manuscripts, which also served as models to the neighbouring oriental countries. The most famous work of all, outstanding on account of the magnificent execution of its illustrations, was the *Artang* (or *Arzhang*, sometimes also known by other names), composed by Mānī in a cave somewhere in Turkestan. It contained virtually an encyclopaedia of the sage's cosmological doctrines, while the pictures represented single portions of his fantastic globe and scenes taken from the cosmic drama, from the first meeting of Light and Darkness up to the tragedy of primitive Man, the birth of aeons and the battles with the giants. This work was admired by Abu'l-Ma'ālī in the treasure-chamber of the shāhs of Ghazna as late as the year 1092, but subsequently it was lost. In later centuries his followers adorned edifices and rocks in Turkestan and southern Siberia with portraits of Mānī and his disciples.

2. SOGDIAN LITERATURE

It has already been stated that the Manichaeans and Christians in Central Asia also made use of the Sogdian language and in this connection it is right that mention should likewise be made of those Central Asiatic sister-languages of Middle Persian that played a more modest part in the history of Iranian culture. *Sogdian* was spoken not only in Sogd (Samarkand) where Iranian was the native language, but was also used by merchants in the adjoining districts, so that it formed an important vehicle of expression in the heart of Asia. Although it was actually the language of the regions of Bukhara, Samarkand, Tashkent, Alma-Ata, important documents have been found east of Pamir, in Chinese Turkestan, Kashgar and Yarkand, as well as to the south of Lake Lob-nor and in the Uighurian Karabalgasun. In this last place an inscription of the local Khāqān shows a Sogdian version as well as an Old Turkic and a Chinese one. The most ancient documents are represented by the so-called Ancient Letters, found near the Chinese wall at Tun-huang; they date from the beginning of the 4th century A.D. To the Christians can be attributed fragments of a translation of the New Testament and the partly preserved legend on the discovery of the Holy Cross by the Empress Helen, the fragment of Saint George's Acts, etc. Manichaeism appears in fragments of theological works, mainly of later origin, in which the dogmatic theories are often distorted. Most of the works in Sogdian were written by Buddhists. They consist of translations from Indian languages (*Vesāntarajātakam*, *Sūtra of the monk Dīrghanakha*, *Sūtra of Causes and Effects*).

3. REMAINS OF KHVAREZMIAN LITERATURE

Like the Sogdian language, the sole descendant of which is the Yagnobi language found in the valley of the Yagnob, a tributary of the Zarafshan, Khvarezmic, of which the present-day Khiva in Uzbekistan was the centre, also became interlaced with the Turkic language and nationality. There is very little left in Khvarezmian. Except for a list of days, months, feast-days, some names of stars and signs of the zodiac (in works by al-Bīrūnī) there are only a few legends on coins still in existence, scanty scraps that have been excavated by Soviet archaeologists; and words and sentences from late Moslem times in legal books (in works by at-Tarjumānī in the first half of the 12th century and al-Ghazmīnī in the 13th). Khvarezmian glosses have also been discovered in a manuscript of Zamakhsharī's lexicon at Constantinople. If the credit for deciphering and investigating the Sogdian texts is due to the Frenchmen R. Gauthiot and E. Benveniste and the Germans F. W. K. Müller and H. Reichelt, it is also certainly due to the Soviet investigators and expositors of archaeology and linguistics, S. P. Tolstov, A. A. Freyman and S. L. Volin for having discovered and fathomed the Khvarezmian civilisation. Other workers in this new field of linguistic research were A. Z. V. Togan and W. B. Henning. Tolstov subjected the district of ancient Khvarezm to an extensive archaeological study (1937–1947) and from the finds excavated there reconstructed a picture of the culture of a one-time important nation and state, which only the Mongol invasion brought to a tragic end. Whereas the most ancient Sogdian records so far known are dated in the 4th century A.D., Tolstov is of the opinion that the oldest remains of the Khvarezmian scripts go back to the 3rd century A.D.

4. SAKIAN LITERATURE

The third of the newly-discovered languages belonging to the Iranic family is the Khotanese Saka, formerly also known as 'Nordarisch'. This is one of the Scytho-Iranic dialects at its Middle Iranian stage of development. The first traces of it are found in a few expressions in Central Asia dating from the first three centuries of the Christian era. Relics of manuscripts discovered in the Chinese Turkestan region of the ancient Khotanese kingdom date from a later period (7th to 10th century). The large majority of fragments and finds indicate that these relate to translations of Sanskrit works and to a small extent also of Tibetan. The contents consist of *religious legends* and *Buddhist texts*, *epics* (e.g. a version of the saga of *Rāma*), articles on medicine, etc. The following description of Spring may be taken as a sample of this poetry and its style:

> *Spring has come; in the earth it is warm. The many-coloured flowers have blossomed on all the trees. The creeper has burgeoned; they sway about exceedingly in the wind. The wind from the trees smells sweetly. The lotus-pools have blossomed, the springs, the ponds and the hills. The birds sing many a most lovely song. The waters have flowed on the green bank at the fountain. The days are clouded, the living beings are hot exceedingly.* (Bailey)

In Maralbashi (east of Kashgar) some written records have been discovered, the language of which is apparently a Sakian dialect. There were certainly several of these. Of those spoken in India hardly anything has been preserved. We are indebted mainly to E. Leumann, Sten Konov and H. W. Bailey for their investigations relating to the Sakian documents.

Up till now Central Asia has produced no remains of *Sarmatian*, a younger form of the Scythian dialect (traces of which have been handed down to us in a few words to be found in Herodotus), and perhaps the one most closely related to Khvarezmian. Present-day *Ossetic* is the only Iranic language to be found north of the Caucasus. Of *Middle Ossetic* we possess only a few words in a tomb inscription, written in Greek letters and excavated in the basin of the river Zelentshuk in the Kuban area. It dates from about the 11th or 12th century. The forms found in these words justify our taking them to be the preliminary stage of the present-day *Digor* (Western Ossetic) dialect. The study of Ossetic has been successfully commenced by H. Hübschmann and Vsevolod Miller; Soviet scholars, in particular V. I. Abayev, are making good progress.

IV. THE PERIOD OF TRANSITION TO NEW PERSIAN LITERATURE

(The Advance of Islam and the Beginnings of New Persian)

After the dissolution of the Sasanian Empire, Islam began gradually to spread in Iran, and in its wake there followed the language of its sacred texts, namely Arabic. Arabic expressions found their way into Persian. Gradually too the religion of Muḥammad gained the upper hand so that in due course adherents of the old Zoroastrian faith were in the minority. A number of the latter emigrated to India. In northern Iran the native princedoms remained in existence right up to the 15th century and were ruled by descendants of the old nobility of the Sasanian period. Middle Persian was used in this area at least up to the 11th century, especially in inscriptions on monuments (*Mīl-i Rādkān*). The Pahlavi inscriptions were found at the towers of Lajim and Resget. The Pahlavi inscription of the Persian Christians at Quilon in southern India dates from the 9th century, those on the crosses are more recent. The Persians entered the service of the Arabs and not seldom occupied important posts in the government and at court (Barmakids). Under the Ummayads (661–750) the financial organisation was in particular the work of Persian officials. The Persian element became more actively prominent in the Abbasid period (after 750), namely in rebellions that were frequently based on communist movements. The majority of cultured Islamic Persians were clandestinely true to the old faith or to Manichaeism, and from time to time persecution from the side of the fanatical caliphs was directed against them. But it was these very men who had taken upon themselves the task of translating the most mature and important of the Middle Persian literary creations into Arabic, thus making them accessible to the Islamic world. The greatest of these men was Rōzveh, son of Dādōē, better known by his Muslim name ʿAbdu'llāh Ibn al-Muqaffaʿ (died about 757), who translated the *Pañchatantra* of Burzōē and the chronicle *Khvatāy-nāmak* by Dānishvar into Arabic. The Arabic version of the *Khvatāy-nāmak* later became the main source of information on the past history of Persia for Arab and Persian scholars. The Zoroastrian experts on the old literature sometimes found favour in the eyes of the Turkish and Persian sultans, who gave them the work of translating the collections of ancient traditions and more especially of 'adapting' them in such a way as to procure legitimacy for themselves! Many an amīr, shāh and sulṭān of Turkish origin learnt then to his surprise and satisfaction that he was a direct descendant of Jamshēd, Manushchihr, Isfandiyār or some other figure of ancient mythology, or, at the very worst, at least of the Sasanians. About the year 950 such Zoroastrian script-experts translated into New Persian the chronicle that Firdausī used as source for his *Shāh-nāma.*

As early as the second half of the Sasanian period, Middle Persian underwent a gradual change phonetically as well as in accidence and syntax. Slowly the preliminary stages of the New Iranian languages and dialects were developing. Details of this development are not as yet sufficiently clear, but it can safely be said that the oldest form of the New Persian language of the cultured, the so-called *Darī*, already existed in the 7th century. By the end of the 10th century New Persian is sufficiently developed to produce such splendid fruits as the poems of Rūdakī, Daqīqī and above all that grand heroic poem, Firdausī's *Shāh-nāma*, the most valuable and monumental of all, enhancing as it does the glory of the fables of all previous generations. But even in the 10th century there were still persons in Istakhr who were able to read Middle Persian inscriptions on monuments dating from the Sasanian period. This is attested by an inscription of 'Aḍudu'd-daula, a ruler of the Buyid tribe, which he ordered to be made in the Arabic language and in Kufic script in the old Persepolis in the year 955. In this, the oldest Muslim inscription in Persia, the amīr ends his account of the victory over Isfahan and Khurasan with the following phrase: "And he commanded that a man be brought before him who could read all these inscriptions on these monuments." We do not know what he expected of this, but it is certain that the expert in question was one of the very last of those capable of reading and explaining the dry and wordy phrases of the ancient shāhs. This was perhaps the reason why 'Aḍudu'd-daula mentioned him, for this unknown reader of inscriptions was no doubt a *rara avis* in his kingdom. And although in his time there was no lack of persons who were familiar with Middle Persian books, yet the Middle Persian language was in itself already a thing of the past; the future belonged to its heir, New Persian.

March 1967

JAN RYPKA

HISTORY OF PERSIAN LITERATURE
UP TO THE BEGINNING OF THE 20TH CENTURY

For my wife Maria, without whose cooperation
this work would never have been accomplished

I. INTRODUCTION

A. THE PERSIAN LANGUAGE (DARĪ)

The Persian written language, the records of which go back to the 1st / 7th century, was based on South-West Middle Persian, which constituted the chief source of the language of the court, official correspondence and of the upper ranks in the Sasanian period. On the one hand it adopted elements from other Iranian dialects, but on the other it followed its own natural development. We find this South-Western language preserved in that form of Sasanian inscriptions which are written in *Pārsīk*, as well as in the dialect employed in the Manichaean fragments found in Turfan. The idiom of the latter, on account of its similarity to the Sasanian language, is known as the South-West Middle Persian of the Turfan documents.

Since the Achaemenid period Fars had been the centre of western Persian culture, of state and cultural traditions and, certainly since the Sasanians, also of religion. It was also in the Sasanian period (up to 650 A.D.) that all phonetic changes took place, and this resulted in the transformation of Middle Persian into the oldest form of the Persian written language; the process may be said to have been complete in the 7th century. Among old Iranian tongues Middle Persian is distinctive in that in the morphology it replaces synthetic constructions by analytic. For this reason there exists a far slighter difference between Middle Persian and post-Sasanian Persian than between Middle and Old Persian. Ever since the Sasanian epoch the vocabulary of Persian had been affected by other Iranian dialects, mainly those of N.-W. Persia (Median), which from the second century B.C. had been strongly influenced by the dominant Parthians. While the local dialects of Fars had kept free from the influence of dialects of the erstwhile Parthian regions, the forms of written Persian absorbed north-western elements; there thus arose in Iran an antithesis between the local south-western dialects of Fars and the Persian written language, which was exposed to powerful influences from the north-west.

Notes on pp. 120–125

After the fall of the Sasanian Empire the prospects of a better future for the Persian nation were transferred to the regions where the power of the Arabs was advancing but slowly and with difficulty, in the north-east part of Iran. As early as the 8th century the longing of the Iranian people for their former independence manifested itself here in major and minor revolts, and it was here that in the year 822 the first Islamic Iranian state, that of the Tahirids, came into existence and with it – at any rate not later – the real Persian literature. The situation of the Iranian languages round about the year 750 is explained to us by Ibn al-Muqaffa‘[1]: according to his account quoted in the *Fihrist*, *Pahlavī* was spoken in Media and Azerbayjan, *Fārsī* in Fars, *Darī* in the east of the country. This last was the original language of intercourse among the ruling classes of the late Sasanian period and the court language of the residence in al-Madā'in. Doubtless it was also the language of the entire state administration. As a result of the decline and ultimate disappearance of the Parthian language in Khurasan, of the final safe establishment of Khurasan after the downfall of the Hephthalite empire at the time of Khusrau I Anūshirvān in the 6th century, of the immigration of the Manichaeans – who had been persecuted by the Sasanians – and of the Zoroastrians under the Arabs, this Darī gained solid ground in eastern Persia, where the eastern trading centre Balkh rose to be the centre. Thus Darī is the first form of the Persian written language in the lapse of time between the 7th and 10th centuries.

It is a language distinct from that of the Medes of the Jibal region to the north-west and from that of Fars in the south-east and which maintains itself by obstinate resistance to the infiltration of Arabic elements. The Persian written language becomes enriched step by step with various dialectical elements and in its first phase gradually frees itself from all remnants of language reminiscent of Middle Persian. If now and then an old form or ancient construction finds its way into such works as the *Shāhnāma* or *Vīs u Rāmīn* this must be considered as merely dependence on persianised Middle Persian texts and on popular tradition. It is important to realise where the first creators of Persian literature and persons with whose names the first records of Persian are associated sprung from: they came from Merv, Herat, Balkh, Gurgan, Ṭūs, Bādghīs, Sogdiana (Sughd) and worked in Sistan, Khurasan, and Transoxania. Conversely, Persian influences the Middle Persian language of the Parsees in the phonetic transcription of Zoroastrian works (*pāzand*). In the 4th/10th century a Persian literature appears also in the western Persia of the Buyids, the written language becomes stabilised and develops into a general means of expression in the whole of Iran. It cannot be claimed that the Persian written language is the sole continuation of one or other Middle Persian dialect, for the forms of written language are ultimately due to selection. Yet this much may be said, namely that the fundamentals of Persian are of south-western origin, connected with the dialects of the dynasties (the Achaemenids and later the Sasanians) ruling from the very beginning of Persian history. In due course an abundance of north, western, and in lesser degree eastern elements were added.

Present-day Iranians are now again giving the name of 'Darī' to their written language. Probably this expression is originally meant to denote the language of intercourse of the temporal rulers at the end of the Sasanian epoch. As such it developed into the first literary form of Persian up to the beginning of the first blossoming of Persian literature at the court of the Samanids in north-eastern Iran.

I. THE ARABISING OF PERSIAN[2]

The language in which Islamic Persia first begins to write has remained essentially the same and at the same stage of morphological development from the earliest beginnings up to the present day. Only now and then do we notice a progressive use of contractions, simplifications, or a relinquishing of older forms. Greater changes occur in the vocabulary. The existing stock of Persian words did not meet the demands of the new way of life, and for this reason certain Persian expressions fell into disuse as being snperfluous on political and religious grounds. On the other hand the language had not become sufficiently flexible, especially when one bears in mind the astonishing creative capacity of Arabic, which had at its disposal ready-made expressions that were often more pregnant than the Persian equivalents. Thus we observe a slow but constant penetration of Arabic words into Persian, which latter as a result becomes a mixed language, in particular as regards the manner of speech of the higher classes and the whole of its literature, which again represents a medium of expression for these classes only, in contrast to popular idioms that were less influenced by Arabic.

This permeation, which with increasing pomposity turns into a pronouncedly morbid growth at the end of the Mongol period (actually nothing other than an international Arabic transposed into the unimpaired system of the Persian language) continues unchanged under the Timurids and even survives the Safavids. Again, it is necessary to lay emphasis on the fact that this distorted idiom could only be understood by a small and limited number of educated people.

Meanwhile the language also adopted a series of Mongol and Turkic[3] words. When in the course of its political unification the Safavid renaissance paid heed to the requirements of the people, it was done exclusively on religio-political grounds and resulted in a generally comprehensible Shīʿite propaganda literature. The intense confusion with which we are presented in the 18th century is the cause of the revolution which in the 19th century manifests itself in a systematic renunciation both of the overbearing influence of Arabic and also of other extravagances. Yet, neither then nor ever before did the development of the languages of prose and poetry run a similar course.

But one may not look upon the general characteristics of any given period as symbolical without making certain reservations. Even when artificiality and Arabic influence were at their height there appear masters who find satisfaction in relative simplicity, and vice versa. The Persian revolution and European currents put an end to old

Notes on pp. 120–125

mannerisms once and for all and confine coquetry with Arabic foreign words within rational, indispensable proportions.[4]

The extreme simplicity of the morphology and syntax of the Persian language and the permeation of the latter with Arabic words were from the start decisive in making of this language the international idiom of eastern Islam.

2. THE RELATION OF DIALECTS TO PERSIAN LITERATURE

Up to the time of the separation of the western Iranians (Persians) from those of the east (Tajiks) there existed a common written language which was, it is true, subject to a certain historical development and to regional peculiarities. But this uniformity is not without its exceptions. The result of the long-continued independence of Tabaristan was that local writers employed the dialect of their district (e.g. the original *Marzbān-nāma* [see p. 223] and the *Nīkī-nāma*, 'The Book of Beauty', written in verse form by the same author; the poet Amīr Pāzvārī and others later on); E. G. Browne[5] cites a number of writers in the Ṭabarī dialect, grouped around Qābūs and quite unknown to the *tadhkiras*; up to the first half of the 11th century these were attempts to raise the local dialects of western Iran and of the adjacent Azerbayjan to the level of a written language.[6] From the 3rd / 9th century M. F. Köprülü mentions a certain Muḥammad b. Saʿīd Bayhaqī, who composed poetry in the dialect of Bayhaq, the present Sabzavār.[7] Anṣārī (see p. 234)[8] wrote prose and Bināʾī (Bannāʾī, see p. 284) a *qaṣīda* in the vernacular of Herat and three other pieces in the vernacular of Samarkand.[9] We possess a few verses in the dialect of Shiraz by Saʿdī and Ḥāfiẓ[10]; by Nāṣiru'd-dīn Khatīb an Arabic-Persian-Shirazian *qaṣīda-i mulammaʿ* (composed before 782/1380–81).[11] Occasional use was made of dialects by erudite poets of later periods, frequently for comic or satirical purposes, e.g. ʿUbayd-i Zākānī, Busḥāq, Qārī, Ṣabūḥī Birjandī, and others. A few avowedly dialectic poets must be included in the circle of authors of popular literature (e.g. Bābā Ṭāhir, Sharaf-Shāh Gīlānī, Amīr Pāzvārī, and others, not omitting Shāh ʿĀshiq, a confectioner from Shiraz, mentioned by dr. Ghanī)[12], sometimes in that of folklore. Verses written in dialect are known as *fahlaviyyāt.*[13] Finally passing reference must be made here to the ancient idiom of the Persian Jews with biblical and religious literature in the Hebrew letters.

3. THE SCRIPT

One of the consequences of the advance of the Arabs and the penetration of Islam into Iran was the gradual introduction of Arabic script. Compared to the complicated script of the Middle Persian period (*Pahlavī*), the Arabic possessed the advantage of exceeding simplicity, so that its acceptance amounted to progress. Persian left out the

Arabic emphatic consonants as it had no need of them, but otherwise adopted the system as it stood. Several essentially Persian consonants (*p*, *ch*, *g*) absent in Arabic, were reproduced at first by those most nearly approximating to them in sound (*b*, *j*, *k*); a more exact differentiation is of later date (the most recent is the case of *k-g*). The Arabic system of writing has no short vowels, but this formed no impediment to the change-over as the same applies to the Pahlavi system. The length, however, is indicated, and it is just this abundance of long vowels that marks the structure of Persian. On the whole, therefore, Arabic script proved to be a suitable medium. It can nevertheless not be denied that as a result of the above-mentioned shortcomings the old pronunciation was sometimes forgotten and in various places was superseded by an incorrect one. We may reckon as a serious defect the inadequate graphical system of Persian syntactical 'connexus', known as *iḍāfat*, 'status constructus' (genitive and adjectival connection). The Arabic words retain their original orthography, but this latter does not affect the actual pronunciation of sounds unknown in Persian; for this reason the Iranians also pronounce Arabic words in the Persian manner. This gradually built-up system remained uninfluenced by the changes in political and religious conditions in Iran, and this state of affairs still continues, apart from a few small details not worth mentioning.

Arabic script has the advantage of an almost stenographic terseness, and is moreover extremely ornamental, both of which factors are lacking in Latin script. Artists soon became aware of its aesthetic importance and raised fine penmanship to one of the highest ranks in the field of Iranian art. The calligraphy, the miniature, binding and paper together provide splendid opportunities for the bibliophile. Here too the Persians demonstrate their mastery. But the ornamental factor in the script was not overlooked by the artists in words, the poets, who therefore sometimes associated the ideas expressed in the poem with the letter-forms. When such a poem is transcribed into Latin script or Azbuka it loses in efficacy, seeing that the letter-form is inseparably connected with the thought to be expressed. An even greater drawback is formed by the 'advantage' of the stenographic compactness which offers only too great a scope for obscurity of meaning. Besides this there are the difficulties of learning the Persian script and of adapting it to the demands of the industrialisation of book-printing technique (written and printed letters being in principle one and the same), and not in the last place the impossibility of indicating shades of difference in sound and of establishing their values at all. Both these factors are essential for the standardisation of language and also for all deviations from the standard, in particular for the conception of slang (e.g. in present-day literature) and for purposes of dialectology.

These are the main reasons why the Turkish peoples and the Tajiks sought to rid themselves of this impediment by replacing it on the one hand by Latin script (in the case of the Ottoman Turks) and on the other by Azbuka (the Turkish peoples of the Soviet-Union and the Tajiks). In Iran also there was no lack of voices clamouring for reform; Mīrzā Malkum-Khān (1833–1905) may be mentioned as being the first of

Notes on pp. 120–125

these. There is no doubt that at the present day the number of these voices is increasing, but, as compared with the radicalism of the Tajiks, such efforts meet with but little response from the side of the Iranians. Conservatism, regard for a more than one thousand-year-old tradition and a highly important classical literature, esteem for the advantages already discussed and many more things – all these are more potent motives than that of reform, even if this implied no more than a number of modifications, the more so when the adoption of the Latin alphabet as the universal one was concerned. The foreigner may in no case remain oblivious to the point of view of the Iranians.[14]

It may also be remarked that Judeo-Persian literature has from time immemorial used the Hebrew script.

B. NATIONAL INDIVIDUALITY

National individuality is an extremely important factor; it determines ways of living and thinking, distinguishes these from those of other nations, and endows each nation with its own peculiar traits. Obviously this will be reflected in the literature. In this place it is only possible to bring forward some of the more conspicuous features among all those that stand in an immediate relationship to national individuality.

I. THE CONCEPTION OF UNITY AND ITS REVERSE – REGIONALISM

The history of Iran unfolds itself in an unceasing interplay of centripetal and centrifugal forces. But however and whenever Iran (and here I have in mind Iran in the more restricted sense, viz. Persia proper) fell a prey to dismemberment, it nevertheless each time succeeded in retrieving its unification. In addition to economic considerations, geographical factors will certainly have played a part, and it may be that a specimen of that statesmanship of which al-Jāḥiẓ (d. 255/869) spoke in very high terms to the Sasanian Iranians is at the base of it. This unity was not destroyed even later under almost entirely foreign dynasties because, although war was being waged by usurpers, the state was nevertheless ruled by Iranians whose deeply rooted feeling of political homogeneity and national community spirit is beyond all doubt. The territory of the north-eastern Iranians, the Tajiks, which from early times had been in greater or lesser degree independent, when it was not for the time being actually predominant, however gradually acquired a different character.

The centripetal tendency is evident in the unity of Persian literature from the points of view of language and content and also in a sense of civic unity. Even the Caucasian Niẓāmī, although living on the far-flung periphery, does not manifest a different spirit and apostrophises Iran as the Heart of the World.[15] Though the diversity of peoples and tribes that inhabited Iran was undoubtedly a stimulant to divergent trends, yet Iranian culture smoothed out all these differences and had such an attraction and overpowering influence, even on non-Iranians, that the latter were frequently inspired by the same sentiments as the Iranians proper. On the other hand an extensive territory like Iran cannot be expected to show such a degree of uniformity that the inhabitants of widely scattered districts should be alike in their mental and physical abilities. Regional idiosyncrasies in the literature cannot therefore be ignored. Despite a general uniformity, certain regions do, in their literature, distinguish themselves from the others (see p. 111 *et seq.*). Even Iranian historians of literature differentiate between various styles (viz. the eastern, western, and Indian), although the relevant theory does not appear to have been worked out sufficiently clearly.

2. RELIGIOUS ELATION AND ITS NATURE

From time immemorial up to the present day history goes to show that the Iranians are a spiritually gifted people. If this were not so it would be difficult to account for the appearance in that country of so many fanatics, reformers, and heretics. A. J. Arberry[16] attributes it to the centuries of great suffering and disillusion which have brought about "in the Persian character an admirable serenity and detachment from material things". But let us beware! We must not allow ourselves to be led astray by the popular religious movements and ferments which so frequently occur in the history of Iran: it is a common custom to use religious watchwords as a cloak to conceal protest against oppression and social disharmony in general.[17] Karl Marx was already aware of this when he maintained that the whole history of the Orient passes before us under the flag of religious history.[18] Thus one may regard religious fanatics not merely as seekers of the transcendental but also as men striving at the same time after a more righteous order of things in this world (e.g. the Ismāʿīlīs; the founders of the Safavid dynasty at the end of the 13th century counted among their numbers also members of the Akhī brotherhood who permitted regicide and exhibited certain communistic traits; Bābism etc.). This explains the ease with which the heretics were able to obtain followers. Be that as it may, however, in Iran a powerful religious feeling can easily turn into fanaticism – in the case of the lower classes as a result of ignorance, in that of the priesthood from inner impulse or from the desire to remain in power. In such cases the populace is incited by the priesthood, the priesthood in its turn by the ruling class. The lively interest of the Iranian in religious speculation is infallibly reflected in his poetry, which is deeply permeated with mysticism. Even today this is the way in which the Iranian prefers to seek his entertainment and it is also one of the reasons why he has from olden times been fond of poetry: in it he discovers himself. Nevertheless not every poet need be a Ṣūfī!

3. THE SHĪʿA

The Iranian adapted himself easily to Islam but he moulded this faith according to his own nature. He no longer professed Sunna, although it was on this religious conviction that the great Iranian Muḥammad al-Ghazālī (d. 505/1111) had laid an ineffaceable mark. On the other hand Persian scholars had from olden times supported the theology of the Shīʿa, especially since the rise of the Safavids, when the doctrine of the 'Twelve Imams' was declared the sole state religion within the Safavid Empire.

This old-established inclination towards Shīʿa exposes two important component traits of the national character: nationalism and monarchistic legitimacy. In the former is expressed a conscious turning away from the Arabs, in the latter the ancient Iranian doctrine of the *farr*, the 'halo surrounding kings and heroes and endowing them with legitimacy'. Without this it is impossible to rule legally over Iran. In this doctrine we also find expression of the conviction that at no time can humanity dispense with a leader. This may perhaps give rise to the impression that the Shīʿa, although not of Iranian origin, is nevertheless ultimately an expression of Iranian mentality. The question is however not so simple and straightforward. Above all Transoxania and Afghanistan should be borne in mind, for here the Sunna is firmly established. Although in Transoxania there was also a run towards the Shīʿa, this concerned the sect of the 'Seven Imams' (Ismāʿīliyya) which was founded on other political and social hypotheses than the Shīʿa of Persia. Moreover, in Persia too a not inconsiderable portion of the population professed the faith of Sunna. On the whole it can be said that the Shīʿa in one form or the other must have possessed a certain attraction for Iran, varying according to the political and social circumstances at any given juncture, and that its influence and form acted reciprocally. The Shīʿa, which, as the non-official form of Islam of the unprivileged classes of the population, had previously espoused the cause of the oppressed with numerous popular heterodoxies, succeeded later (as the state religion) in uniting the nation, yet ultimately it lost its élan.[19]

4. THE TOLERANCE OF PERSIAN POETRY[20]

It does inestimable credit to Persian poetry that, apart from some altogether inferior and on the whole insignificant specimens, it did not become the wrestling-ground of ecclesiastical fanaticism, although the Iranian priesthood, which in this respect already possessed a considerable Sasanian tradition, frequently kindled and fed the religious sentiments of the people up to passionate heat. The poets rise above a narrow-minded view, they adhere rather to the spirit than to the letter, they guide towards moderation, tolerance, liberalism, now and then to complete freedom of thought and to revolt against the belief in revelation. In this connection mention should be made on the one hand of the healthy influence of the Iranians on the rise of the Muʿtazila, and on the other hand of the fall in power of the latter from the time of the reactionary Caliph al-Mutavakkil (232–247/847–861), surrounded by his Turkish guards. Neither are racial or national pride inherent to the poetry; only occasionally do we come across a thrust at the Jews or the Christians, and this can usually be attributed to economic interests. There was certainly antagonism on the part of the Iranians towards the Arabs (*shuʿūbiyya*, p. 130) on political grounds, be it understood, and towards the Turks (Tatars) and Mongols on account of their cruelty and perfidy and the well-founded fear they aroused in the Persians.

5. ADAPTABILITY AND LATE EUROPEANISATION

The adaptability common to all Iranians can be associated with the exceptional giftedness of the race. The Iranian is quick of comprehension and can learn with extreme ease. This has its advantages but also its dangers. History and experience go to show that when thrust into Turkish surroundings he frequently becomes absorbed by the Turkish power of assimilation without, however, the sphere of Iranian culture being thereby injured: rather the contrary. Once he finds himself in a new situation, he aims at swift accommodation. Such is the attitude of the present-day Iranian when put face to face with European civilisation, and such was his attitude when, as a consequence of the Arab invasion, the nation was subjected to new political, social, and economic conditions. Although passionately fond of his language, he nevertheless allowed it to become arabised because this was the easier way – and one for which certain analogies from former times are to be found in Iran – of solving the problem that was forcing itself upon his attention. Over and above this the Arabic language had the unusual advantage of a truly astonishing plasticity. But mental versatility leads to a certain superficiality. I am not aware if Persian literature has produced any coherent exposé of the nature of Cicero's 'Cato Maior *de senectute*'; but there are nonetheless a large number of poems in which the poet laments old age and misery. They are however inspired only by sentiment and are entirely lacking in method.[21]

The Iranian's mental flexibility and the ease with which he can adapt himself play their part in his present-day rapid europeanisation. But the change appears to be taking place on the surface, as if the spirit itself follows but arduously and unwillingly. It is also true that European civilisation is much farther removed from the non-materialistic Iranian mentality than are Islam and its culture. The recent, and to all appearances very late, conversion can be explained by the various obstacles, mostly exceedingly difficult, with which the Iranian had to struggle in re-fashioning life to suit modern times. The centuries-old conservatism of Persian literature forms no contradiction to this. It merely bears evidence of the fact that the feudal tradition continued practically unchanged for the same length of time, for no revolution in literature would have been possible until the latter had detached itself from the old basis.

Notes on pp. 120–125

6. ARTISTIC PERCEPTIBILITY, NATURE, AND INBORN DISPOSITION FOR POETRY

From time immemorial the artistic perceptibility of the Iranian has found expression in sublime monuments of fine art, but to no less an extent in its literary works; it is as if the age-old struggle against the surrounding desert had compelled him to create beauty around him. The desert evokes horror, nature as animated by plant and animal life inspires admiration, and both horror and admiration find constant expression in the works of the poets. But their comprehension of nature follows a different path from ours. The manner of expressing the relation to nature is undoubtedly beautiful, it abounds in splendour, but it is visually decorative, conventional, static, in the lyrics even stereotyped [22] – general characteristics of Persian poetry as well as of the fine arts. The visual decorative impulse can in reality indicate a certain romantic feeling for nature [23], in as far as nature is here placed in inner relation to the human emotions, whether it be in order to express them actively or to meditate on them passively. Despite all the conservatism and conventions there is here nevertheless no lack of vitality. H. Ritter [24], here treading new paths, establishes three characteristics within whose bounds Niẓāmī portrays nature: humanised animation of nature, transposition of spatial juxtaposition into a causal relationship, and the choice of images in accordance with human moods. Such is the case with Niẓāmī, and it is certainly also true of other great epic writers and finds an analogy in lyric poetry. A perfect parallel to the Persian poet's attitude to nature presents itself above all in the Persian miniature.

The enthusiasm with which the Iranian, irrespective of the social class to which he belongs, approaches poetry, is generally known. Thanks to this elemental emotion in the whole of the nation, the love of poetry, be it active or passive, is evident and alive in Iran today as scarcely anywhere else in Europe. Sometimes it is impossible to resist the impression of a mania for writing verse. The question may be raised whether in the present-day persistence we are not faced with a kind of remnant of the Middle Ages. One is justified in entertaining well-founded doubts about this, even though the novel and the short story are gaining ground as a means of giving expression to modern times at the expense of poetry. But the love of poetry, the pleasure in the euphony of the Persian language, enhanced by an enchanting rhythm, the art of the idiom and grandeur of substance – all this is innate in the Iranian [25] – that is the reason to my mind why the inviolability of a Persian poem will always be higher than in the West. Whether this hypothesis is correct will be proved by the subsequent development of the newly awakening culture in Iran. But we can certainly give as our retrospective opinion that it is hardly imaginable that a nation which under Islam created such valuable poetic literature, could ever exist at all without poetry – the less so as it was a nation with a centuries-old high cultural standard, as has been proved by the written documents which have been handed down to us. The cause of this is not only artistic perceptibility but also in like measure the tenderness and flexibility of the Iranian spirit, which extends almost to oversensitivity. It is quite inconceivable that such characteristic traits could have been produced only by the subversion accompanying the Arab invasion or by a possible admixture of foreign blood in the early history of Islam. On the other hand it cannot be denied that "Persian poetry is a product of Persian-Arabic culture: Iranian characteristics are no doubt outstanding in it but Islam has given them a new shape and colour."[26]

7. THE SPIRIT OF ISLAM

The manner in which the spirit of Islam finds expression in the literature exposed to its influence is fully discussed by G. E. von Grunebaum.[27] The religious sentiment of the contents, the influence of the *Koran* and the *Ḥadīth* do not, in his opinion, *a priori* constitute conclusive evidence of a relation between the literary production of the Faithful and Islam as a religious and socio-political system. As to the outer form, the tendency towards language bound by a certain rhythm (poetry) and ornamental prose cannot be denied, but this is a phenomenon which on the one hand was already apparent in Arabic in pre-Islamic times and on the other was enriched by modifications from the side of Moslem Iran, subsequently, it is true, becoming general. The inward form shows a certain incoherence of composition. We find sudden contrasting transitions which Von Grunebaum wishes to explain not as a genetically Arabic but rather as a specifically Islamic phenomenon on account of the relationship between the literary and the philosophic-theological conception of Islam. That the literary principles of the Islamic peoples do not include a wider expansion of poetical creativity is due to religious scruples aiming at an avoidance of conflict with the dogma of the *creatio ex nihilo*. Persian literature, on the other hand, as represented by its epic poetry, never adopted this point of view and thus the whole world of Iranian myth and legend – and in fact all the fiction belonging to the Persian tradition – are to be found in the Islamic phase of Persian literary development. Characteristic of Islam is the erudition displayed in the poetry and in fact in belles-lettres as a whole.

8. THE RELATIONSHIP BETWEEN POETRY AND PROSE. PROBLEMS OF LITERARY HISTORY

Persian literature is distinguished by its fundamentally poetical character, manifested of course chiefly in its poetry. Narrative prose is relatively less in quantity, but here too verses have been lavishly inserted. Muḥammad Bahār[28] points out that the number of verses occurring in prose works shows a steady increase from the earliest preserved documents onwards. In various fields of knowledge instructive literature is without doubt exceptionally important, mature and extensive, but it is poetry and not

Notes on pp. 120–125

prose that characterises Persian literature. From the fact that the fine arts are a no less valuable aspect of Islamic Iran than is the poetry, it can be theoretically assumed that the same indissoluble partnership existed in pre-Islamic Iran. This would be one of the most convincing *a priori* proofs of the continuity of the poetry, even if we had no direct examples at hand. Research on prose is far in arrear of that on poetry, although in the latter field too the wide range of problems many times surpasses the actual results achieved. For a history of literature may not be limited to mere biographies and anecdotes in the manner of the ancient *tadhkiras* ('anthologies'), but must consist of an evaluation and linking up of the separate manifestations, and that not merely in the case of the most eminent but also – and perhaps in even greater measure – of the mass of minor figures. Of course it cannot be denied that all this is a dream of the far future. That on the other hand an exhaustive knowledge of the lives of the poets is of inestimable value for an understanding of their works requires no long and wide discussion. But in regard to the poetry of the Islamic peoples there is also a special circumstance that renders biographical and political details – even the smallest – indispensable, as is evident from the most recent studies on Ḥāfiẓ. A knowledge of such facts is the only possible means of making good the deficient chronology of the *dīvān* poetry and of thereby attaining a deeper understanding of the poet and his development, for instance by gaining wider and more plausible information from his own mouth. So far this stage has by no means been reached.

9. THE INFLUENCE OF ṢŪFISM

The development of thought was formed and for a part deformed by the permeation of Ṣūfism into the poetry, that same Ṣūfism which, it is true, originally sprang from a popular movement aimed against orthodoxy and oppression but which then subjugated Persian poetry, divested it of a sense of reality and gave it, alas, a somewhat monotonous constitution. It must be borne in mind that the Persian lyric begins in a sphere of vigorous reality, yet soon becomes involved in a mysticism which is frequently also quite incompatible with Islam, and, whilst professing mystic love, becomes to such an extent obsessed by eroticism that it is not always possible to draw a reliable dividing line between real and supermundane love. For here we come up against one of the greatest difficulties of Persian lyric poetry – its ambiguity. There are but few poets who remain untouched by Ṣūfism in one form or another. But yet it is alas all too often uncertain whether these images do or do not conceal other thoughts. But that again is a trait characteristic of Iran, which has an analogy in the Shīʿite *taqiyya*, 'prudence', 'fear', 'dissimulation'. On the other hand it must not be forgotten that behind the Ṣūfī veil conceptions are frequently hidden which contemporary society would scarcely have endured or tolerated in their naked form. Supported by the neuter structure of the Persian language, Ṣūfism distorts heterosexuality to homosexuality, and considers earthly love as metaphorical, transcendental love on the contrary as real, just as elsewhere, thanks to the conception of pantheism, it indulges in paradoxes. It reaches its zenith round about the 12th–13th century, but, on account of its constant repetitions, or because it gets lost in its own astonishing subtleties, the further it progresses the more monotonous become the lyrical thoughts which occur in its themes, constricted as they likewise are by convention. The romantic epic, on the contrary, yields but gradually to Ṣūfism and professes heterosexuality without reserve. The didactic epic appears in the light of ethics rather than in philosophic speculation.

In addition to the many unique values and beauties which Ṣūfism possessed, it was also the breeding-ground of a number of pernicious features, such as the belief in the inconstancy of the world, the inevitability both of fate and of the course of events in general. There were some poets who put up resistance in the form of passivity, quietism, and asceticism which turned its back upon the world, a retreat into the world of self, letting outward events take their course. Against this pessimistic conception of the world others, proceeding from the self-same presumption, set the principle of hedonism (*carpe diem*) unless it was that this concealed an attack on the existing religious and social order. In one or other of these aspects the Iranian, known from olden times for his particular fondness of imparting advice, found consolation and support for his moral and practical behaviour: lyric and didactic poetry provided him with such counsel in abundance. It sounds almost paradoxical that this trait should also form one of the reasons for the unusual vigour of the poetry, in which it is reflected and shown to be common to the whole nation, though this does not necessarily imply that the advice was always followed up.

A. J. Arberry sums it up in the following manner[29]: It was inevitable that the many catastrophes which afflicted Iran in chain-like succession should have affected the inner life of the Iranian. Uncertainty and instability in all things are constantly to be observed, therefore the soul thirsts after consolation and peace. These can be imparted by the preacher and by the poet, each in his own fashion. The Ṣūfī (Arberry has in mind Maulavī and others like him) says that the soul separated from its Beloved must suffer and tarry in order to attain the return to Him. But there is also another solution: to take pleasure in worldly treasures; even when one cannot possess all these oneself, one must nevertheless love life and overcome grief!

10. LACK OF HUMOUR. THE 'SATIRE'

To a person of cheerful disposition the questionableness and uncertainty of life which arose from the atrocious oriental despotism – states of mind which moreover were nourished by Islam, especially the gloomy Shī'a – were oppressive. What was a human life? Thrones collapsed, persons came into prominence and then disappeared as they had come, but no far-reaching improvement followed. There was only an occasional

Notes on pp. 120–125

escape from the worst forms of horror and outrage. Anger, despair and a complete feeling of impotence engendered pessimism. Mysticism followed the same track. But seldom, compared with this mood, do we hear in the literature the sound of humour, which in private life the Iranian nevertheless possesses in abundance! A favourite form of humour is that of the anecdote, usually brimming over with witticisms.[30] That nevertheless under certain circumstances a laugh can penetrate even to the most serious-minded is proved by Niẓāmī in his story of the Seventh Princess in the *Haft Paykar* and here and there by Saʿdī in the *Gulistān*. From time to time a real humorist appears. Satirists, if the authors of slanderous writings can be so designated, appear in enormous number from the earliest times up to the most recent: for the *hajv*, the so-called 'satire', is very closely associated with the aristocratic system. Yet it must be admitted that our hitherto incomplete knowledge of literary documents and an excessive emphasis on the Ṣūfi impulse are obstructive to a correct comprehension of humour, irony, and similar mediums of expression.

11. THE INFLUENCE OF DESPOTISM AND FEUDALISM

The sociability, courtesy and serviceableness of the Iranian turn not infrequently into an obsequious servility, adulation, and corruptibility. An all too clear echo of this is to be found in the *qaṣīda* and in panegyrics in general. But we may not judge too hastily: it was inevitable that a thousand years of feudalism, autocracy and tyranny should leave certain traces on the Iranian character. Against this background we also see the relations between the lovers – either real or allegorical – often carried to the point of self-degradation of the lover[31]; Safavid despotism even stamped the relation as one of dog and master. Renunciation of the world, preached unceasingly by the poets, is surely nothing other than a direct echo of the feeling of servitude. From the despotic relationship originate the ceaseless complaints of injustice on the part of those in power and of heaven, there is no true conception of liberty.[32]

An excrescence of feudalism is the exuberant growth of envy. That it actually was rife among the court poets is proved by the perpetual bitter complaints of all the panegyric writers of importance, whose life was poisoned by this immature but for that reason all the more malicious gang. A similar dissonance in the same orchestra is the literary brigandry that was perpetrated to such an extent that it has been accorded a scholastic evaluation in works on poetry.[33]

12. EXTRAVAGANCE

Excessive emotions and exaltation scarcely ever penetrate to the European mind through the mask of traditional courtesy. But the literature and manifestations of a religious kind undoubtedly betray a tendency in that direction. The hyperbolism of the poetical language is sufficient proof of this. But it is not the only one. In the flight to unattainable heights the poet as it were loses the feeling for logical sequence of thought. Further on (see p. 102) we shall encounter this peculiarity again in another light. In the oriental mind imagination is always given priority over logic. One of the functions of metaphor consists in creating an intensified world of hyperbolism, always aesthetically perceptible to the reader, whether the tendency be towards the grotesque or towards idealisation. Meanwhile the dramatic factor in Persian lyric poetry is absent.[34]

13. EROS AND ITS EXPRESSION: ALLEGORY AND SYMBOLISM. ABSTRACT CHARACTER OF THE LYRIC. HOMOSEXUALITY

The intensity and depth of the erotic feelings of the Iranian are demonstrated in the romantic epic. But the latter is not their only setting, for in point of fact all lyric poetry is permeated with eroticism as it were to the last thread, and to such an extent that every theme – even when showing no connection with mysticism – is or can be projected into the sphere of eroticism. Wine plays a similar rôle. In Persian poetry the direct manner of expression gives place entirely to the veiled, whatever the subject may be. The motive for composing a *ghazal* and similar forms of poetry is not usually known and, apart from very rare exceptional cases, cannot be deduced from the content. Thus it is always difficult and in most cases impossible – unless we are dealing with known and avowed mystics – to determine when the conception of love or of wine indicates the actual thing and when on the contrary the poet has in mind a metaphor, an allegory, whether in a factual or transcendental sense. This too we must regard as the expression of a certain insincerity, of a tendency to present unpleasant things in a polished form, to conceal disagreeable truths and even to indicate them by their direct opposites, a disposition for affectation and the traditional courtesy. But it is frequently merely a question of fear. Allusions to contemporary events and situations must of course be well disguised; for the allegory (like derision) is a weapon forced by slavery and oppression into the hands of the socially weaker for use against their oppressors. On the other hand it must not be forgotten that the allegory, enhancing as it does the poetic semi-obscurity, thereby magnifies the effect of a thought. Iranian poets make use of this medium up to the present day, nowadays it is true in a manner more lucid to us, because we stand in a closer relationship to them.

It is relevant here to mention the symbolical manner of expression, viz. certain constant metaphors, which require no explanation and as such assume the meaning of the subject under comparison, although the literal meaning of the word continues to be used unaltered in common speech. Thus, for instance, the lips are symbolised by the ruby or by sugar, dark locks by the hyacinth, hand-writing stands for down, the cypress for an upright figure, etc. Ṣūfī poetry gladly adopted this custom and created a whole nomenclature of symbols, which were metamorphosed into the transcendental. Thus, for example, wine means ecstasy, the dark lock everything that conceals the reality of God, the eyebrows indicate the attributes of God, in as far as they veil the true Being of God; an idol represents the manifestation of God's beauty, etc. "The use of this metaphorical language does not in itself constitute a poetical achievement, which only comes into being by the manner of application of these metaphors, their combination, contraposition and so on."[35]

The increasing power of Ṣūfism and the all-devouring metaphorical or allegorical eroticism leave an abstract impress on lyric poetry. This finds response in the essentially imaginative nature of the Iranian mentality. An accompanying phenomenon is that of generalisation, both in lyric and in epic poetry. Persian poetry depicts neither the object of love in its individual beauty nor a landscape nor a natural object in their characteristic features. However fine may be the details painted in, yet the subject is nothing other than a hyperbolic abstraction of beauty and in no sense a concrete picture. The Persian miniature is also merely another manifestation of the same idea, making use of a different technique. The portrait and the landscape in non-abstract, non-idealised form constitute its weak side. It is indeed not easy to say to what extent lyric poetry consists of a masterly variation on conventional themes and where actual experience begins – in as far as in any given case such was intended at all – nor what is merely a play of phantasy and what is reality. In general it can be said that in the course of time the presentation of reality gradually lessens, and not until the 11th/17th and following centuries does it timidly begin to gain ground again (see p. 295). Vagueness is carried to such an extent into the lyric poetry that it is usually a sheer impossibility to guess the sex of the Beloved. The language itself contributes to this uncertainty in that it possesses no grammatical distinction between the genders: *yār*, *dūst*, etc. can just as well indicate the male as the female loved one. There is no doubt that love towards fair youths (slaves from distant or foreign tribes)[36] in poetry is a legacy which goes back to the Arab poets (often of Persian origin) from court and town, and it had its origin in a degenerate life of pleasure and in the prudery of Islam in relation to the female sex. At any rate it is a phenomenon which was wide-spread in Iran from the earliest times. With the establishment of Persian influence under the first Abbasids, it encroached into the neighbouring caliphate, where it began to supersede the natural healthy heterosexual eroticism of the ancient Arabic *qaṣīdas*. Nevertheless, this should not be exaggerated.[37] For the rest this is one of the most intricate problems and one which has hardly ever been accorded serious attention. Moreover, it is a question which is impossible to answer uniformly for the whole duration of Persian literature, both on social as well as on literary-theoretical grounds. Translators into European languages have generally taken refuge in a feminine interpretation, and maybe not always wrongly. The romantic epic was openly heterosexual from the start and remained so for a long time, as is the case in occasional parts of the heroic epic and the epic of chivalry.

C. CONSERVATISM AND CONVENTION IN PERSIAN LITERATURE

I. THE CONNECTION WITH FEUDALISM

Islamic Iran was and remained up to the most recent times a feudal structure, whose institutions have undergone no essential changes. The old Iranian aristocrats and landowners had to withdraw from their former position of social monopoly under the pressure of numerous invasions and of internal disruption. They were replaced by foreign invaders and native upstarts. Thus, generally speaking, we find simply another picture of the old feudalism, even if the fiefs assumed other forms and names. In view of such circumstances it is not surprising that classical poetry and literature as a whole have not undergone any great change even in the course of many centuries. Except during the wave of Arabic influence now swelling, then ebbing away again, the language remains essentially the same. In the same way there is scarcely a noticeable change in subject-matter.[38] The whole field is governed by convention. The authors are scholars, their public consists of the ruling class and the intelligentsia dependent on it – especially in the first centuries of Persian literature. But gradually the scene changes: the increasing power of the towns cannot fail to cause a reaction, both with regard to the production of literature and to a reshuffling within the circle of readers. This is a phenomenon of unusual importance because, in the struggle of the urban population against the ruling classes of the aristocracy[39], we must see an essential motive for the development of Persian literature. Only the uneducated – certainly the largest portion of the population – appear to have had no share in the process and are in fact completely excluded from it. Life flows on steadily in the old channels and those who direct it have certainly no occasion to abolish its feudal institutions. Dynastical changes bring scarcely any improvement in this direction, riots among the subjects have no decisive or lasting effect. According as the economic basis and consequently the organisation of society takes form, a reaction in literature becomes evident, both as regards the subject-matter and the manner of expression. For the same reason innovations produce not the slightest result, as is proved by the attempts of the language-reformer and enemy of the aristocracy, Ṭarzī Afshār from Azerbayjan at the beginning of the 11th/18th century.[40] Lack of originality on the part of the writers becomes compensated by increased artificiality and arabising of the language. As a result of this the distance between this literature of the aristocracy and the broad masses of the people widens more than ever into an unbridgeable gulf. The masses are obliged to satisfy their needs with their own simple folk-literature, which is generally overlooked or even entirely disregarded by the more highly educated classes and those they had trained up to their own level. Yet even in these circles it did not fail to arouse a certain response, the more so as the exponents of popular literature belonged to different social classes,

Notes on pp. 120–125

notably in the earliest periods (see p. 128). A remarkable opinion is held by I. S. Braginskiy[41], who holds that it was not at the court of the Samanids with its *razm u bazm*, 'battles and banquets', but rather in the simple oral literature of the masses that the written poetry of the feudal period was born.

2. OFFICIAL ISLAM AS A RESTRAINING FACTOR

It is impossible to close one's eyes to the fact that the centuries-old imprisonment within old traditions in Persia had resulted in an increasing backwardness. The economic causes of this have been exhaustively discussed by I. Reisner.[42] But did not official Islam also contribute to this stagnation? There is no doubt that it did, and that in no small measure, as is proved by the history of all Islamic nations. It put a restraint on life in that its social axioms were in practice converted into their exact reverses. On the other hand, the fact may not pass unnoticed that it was the Shīʿa that possessed in its *mujtahids*, 'priests competent to practice divine service', an instrument thanks to whom it was unnecessary for it to bind itself so strongly to the past as the Sunna. This is certainly a progressive, though unfortunately purely theoretical aspect of the Shīʿa. Islam, which in the first centuries had shown merit in the spreading of culture in the Orient, neglected the natural sciences, did not concern itself with public morals and took no heed of the position of the common people[43], which thus remained stagnant at the level attained in the Middle Ages.

3. CONSERVATISM OF THE ORIENTAL CONCEPTION OF THE RELATION BETWEEN WORD AND THOUGHT

Having analysed the causes of conservatism in classical literature, it would not be right to pass it by unnoticed or to underestimate its influence. With some knowledge of ancient indigenous opinions, we even incline to the view that the classical Oriental does not repudiate this conservatism, which to him does not at all imply stiffness, inflexibility and uniformity, but an essential feature that he consciously retains. For we must admit that the Oriental understands creative originality as something quite other than the Westerner. Whereas the latter regards it as a kind of absoluteness of the new, the former is satisfied with a different mode of expression or a further deepening of existing material, a refinement of presentation and expression, etc. In short the Oriental puts more emphasis on the 'how' than on the 'what'.[44] Not multiplicity but subtlety! Ibn Khaldūn[45] makes the pertinent remark that the art of writing, either in verse or prose, is based not on ideas but only on words. The content of the *ghazal* is limited to what the old masters treated with such consummate grace. The aim of the later poets consists in conveying the same content but in still more flowing words and more elegant turns of phrase. Since the time of the Timurids it appears to have been possible to write *ghazals* according to prescription. But it was then already a period of manifest literary decline. A twilight was setting in that not even the glory of the metaphor – which remained of course constant – was able to dispel. Herein lies the immense difference between the spirit of the West and that of the classical East: the culture of word and form as against the fetish of content. Regarded in such a light, this conservatism now appears to us as something quite different, for it will no longer be understood as mere ossification or dull monotony. Conversely the ancient oriental poet might regard his western colleague from his own standpoint: compared with his own niceties of speech, that frequently lead to over-refinement, western poetry must needs appear to him unspeakably coarse. The constant re-use of themes, customary in the Orient, must not grow into a mere soulless copying, to which in the hands of a master it has in fact never descended. Here too there exists, on the part of the poet, an honest wrestling with his work within the given limits. In this fundamental difference of approach between East and West, whether one gives priority to content or to form, lies the difficulty – almost the impossibility – for the Westerner of altogether understanding Persian (and Turkish) poetry. This also accounts for a certain lack of competence on the part of western critics in relation to the Persian and Turkish classics.

4. THE DIFFICULTIES OF THE WESTERNER IN COMPREHENDING PERSIAN AND OTHER ORIENTAL AUTHORS

In respect of minuteness of observation and perceptibility a European scholar will never be able to equal a cultured Iranian man of letters.[46] Thus many things must seem to him to coïncide and to be of a more uniform nature than they appear to the oriental observer. He will not easily grasp the points of difference between individual poets, especially lyric poets, when examining their artistic characteristics, quite apart from the finer shades of meaning. It is in any case certain that we should be making a great mistake were we to judge this poetic individuality by the standards of modern literature. For the Westerner it is difficult, maybe well-nigh impossible, to enter into the spirit of ecstasy which is, as it were, the daily bread of this poetry. It will therefore not do to overlook or ignore native opinion, either traditional or modern, e.g. as found in the various *tadhkiras*, in Jāmī's *Bahāristān* or in the work of present-day critics. By this we do not refer to the flattery of contemporaries or the superficial assessments so often perpetrated by indigenous aesthetes and literary historians of today, as for instance "that is, or is not, Ḥāfiẓ' style", etc. What we want are facts and proofs, not merely feelings or impressions – these to be used to the last instance, when no other concrete method of identification is possible. Thus dr. Shafaq[47] claims that authorities on Persian literature recognise Ḥāfiẓ' verse immediately and grasp its melody. And yet there is so much that has been forged and distorted, particularly in the case of Ḥāfiẓ!

Notes on pp. 120–125

The only safe criteria here, as everywhere else, are of course the oldest manuscripts.[48]

The disparity between works of widely differing periods of time is infallible. For meanwhile the underlying social conditions will have altered. Does not the dissimilarity between poets of the Samanid and Safavid periods strike the eye at once? But now and then we must also be content with smaller lapses of time. For instance, how different from each other are the lyrics of Rūdakī, of Farrukhī and again those of Saʿdī when simplicity is gradually abandoned in favour of a more complicated style. Even if, as often happened, development was limited only to the use of words or to a refining of conventional images, we must expect to find the results of growth and of differentiation in literary aims through the centuries.

There were several contributory factors to this, besides unceasing social and economic happenings: increasing education and a tradition embracing more and more predecessors, the schools of poets which grew up around the great masters, the dissension and attaining of independence of differing currents of thought (Ṣūfistic or philosophical), regional differences, and so on.

5. MEN OF GENIUS AND EPIGONES: THE EUROPEAN SCHOOL

From time to time geniuses are born who, as interpreters of the present and prophets of the future, occupy a commanding position in one or the other kind of poetry, not only in their own epoch and in that of their immediate successors, but also for centuries to come. Their works represent both an eloquent expression of their own time and an achievement of higher creative individuality. Thus there still appear imitations of the *Shāh-nāma*; the appreciation accorded to Saʿdī's *ghazal* poetry steadily increases as time goes on; Ḥāfiẓ does not cease to be the model for lyric poets; the imitators of Niẓāmī are myriad; in Ṣūfism Maulavī retains his commanding position, etc. The conservative Vaḥīd Dastgirdī[49] (d. 1361/1942) proclaims point blank that one of the preliminary conditions to becoming an accomplished Persian poet must be to tread in the footsteps of the old masters, and he positively repudiates foreign models, viz. the Indians of the 17th century and Europeans from the beginning of the 20th century onwards. He does not even consider folk-poetry to be a suitable basis for the renaissance of literary verse, but on the contrary regards the study of Arabic, theory of literature and mysticism as indispensable elements of the poet's education. There has never been a lack of great talent in Iran, though the same cannot be said of the care given to preliminary training, and this has led to the progressive deterioration of Persian literature down to the present-day decline. Such is the significant view of a poet, uninfluenced by Europe, who, if not consciously quoting the opinions of the eminent Niẓāmī ʿArūḍī in the middle of the 6th/12th century (see p. 221) at least instinctively enters into his spirit and at any rate best exposes the fundamental pre-requisites of a Persian *adīb* (writer in the classical style). The greatest masters are formed by personal genius against this background and their traditions cannot be relinquished without straying on to untrodden paths. Seen from this standpoint it can be understood that the creative sphere of action of epigones is of course restricted, in fact anything that exceeds the bounds is barely tolerated, when permitted at all. These fetters can only be shattered by a genius who, however, in his turn immediately establishes new standards that are unsurmountable for others.

The European school in Iran refuses to be bound in this way by classical tradition. In its attempts to draw close to European movements it inevitably comes more or less within the scope of European criticism.

D. POETRY AND ITS FORMS

Preponderance of Poetry

Until recently Persian poetry was superior to prose in quantity and quality, and it is poetry that gives to Persian literature its specific character. Verse permeates belles-lettres and very often also didactic and learned prose. As in the case of poetry, so too in the case of literary prose a distinction must be made between the inward and the outward form. The inward form is common to poetry and literary prose.

I. THE OUTWARD FORM

a. *Fundamental Concepts*

Poetry, i.e. 'metrical' literature, is determined by the following outward signs: (a) the measurement of syllables according to length, that is quantitative prosody, and (b) rhyme. The nature of the rhyme in addition to specified metres (viz. purely outward criteria) and of course the content make possible a division into lyrical and epic poetry. The unit of the poem is always the distich (*bayt*), which falls into two semi-distichs (*miṣrāʿ*) that agree with the rules of prosody as regards the number of syllables and are connected by one thought, in certain cases by one thought and its underlying argument. This connection can also, however, be the result of merely formal, rhetorical measures, such as parallelism (*muvāzana*), the harmony of common images (*murāʿātu'n-naẓīr* or *tanāsub*, see pp. 100, 107), and so on. More rarely a number of thoughts grouped together grammatically covers two or more *bayts*. Seeing that each distich is to a certain extent independent, the logical connection of the poem is not so clear and obvious as in European poetry, particularly in the *ghazal*, the unity of which is apparently or in fact only based on rhyme and metre.

It is true that in the poetry of recent times we witness a slackening of all established rules of prosody and poetics, in fact now and then they are thrown overboard altogether. In some cases such poetry has become entirely free verse, restricted by no bounds whatsoever.

b. *Metrics*

In pre-Islamic Persian versification, the syllables (or the accents) were counted, as is always the case in folk-poetry, though only very exceptionally in classical poetry (e.g. *Dīvān-i Ḥaydar* in the satires on Khvājū).[50] It must, however, be noted that to the modern-trained Iranian scholar the principle of syllable-counting does not appear to be an adequate explanation of popular and Middle Persian prosody. It is true that Adīb Ṭūsī[51] sees in syllable-counting the fundamental principle of popular poetry, but at the same time points out in it the more or less free quantity, the accentuation, verse-feet and caesura. Similarly P. N. Khānlarī[52] advances free quantity and clearly defined accentuation as two connected principles of popular poetry and traces them, as does Adīb Ṭūsī, back to Middle Persian poetry. The *dīvāns* of Amīr Pāzvārī in the Ṭabarī dialect (see p. 74) and Mullā Parīshān in the Kurd language are written syllabically.[53] Examples of an accentuating Tajik ten-syllable verse are cited by A. N. Boldïrev[54]; a recent Ṣūfi *qaṣīda* of fourteen syllables in the Shushtarī dialect has been noted by B. V. Miller.[55] The problem is so far not altogether clear. But however it may be, the ancient metrical procedure was abandoned under the influence of Arabic poetry and quantitative measuring (*ʿarūḍ*) was adopted in its stead. In its essentials it corresponds fairly well with that of the Greeks and Romans. Persian prosody is distinguished from the classical by the metrical structure, the unconditional metrical equality of all semi-distichs in one and the same separate poem (*monokōla*), by an almost entire absence of caesura, by hiatus without elision (at the most with contraction in certain cases like *k*(*i*) + vowel, third person singular of the perfect, etc.), by the rhyme and over-long syllables. The function of the expiratory accent is reduced to a purely individual factor.[56]

The metres, of which there are a great many, are with the exception of the *rubāʿī* (see p. 96) all taken from Arabic prosody, though selected and with slight modifications; at least this was the general opinion until recently, agreeing as it did with the views of the earliest Persian metricians[57] who, it is true, showed strong arabising tendencies. A few metres of Arabic poetry, notably the most frequently encountered and most characteristic (*ṭavīl*, *basīṭ*, *kāmil*, *vāfir*, *madīd*), appear hardly ever in Persian poetry. It can rather be said that the metres that do occur are employed seldom or never in Arabic. The reason for this lies undoubtedly in the difference of syllabic structure of the Persian and Arabic languages. Any kind of versification other than these fixed traditional verse metres is entirely unknown in Persian classical literature.[58]

The poet is not expected to invent new metres, he is limited to the use of the immutable ones already in existence. The reduction to a minimum of the anceps positions typical of the Arabic metrical pattern is also connected with the disparity between the Persian and the Arabic syllable. As opposed to this, Persian versification introduces extended long syllables: the closed long syllable before the following consonant is measured within the verse as a long syllable plus a short one (as in fact they always were in the ancient language, something like the French mute *e*). An exception is formed by the closed long syllables with final *-n*, either from the strong nasal tone with which this vowel appears to have been pronounced already in early times[59], or else a kind of reaction to the Arabic *tanvīn*. Poetic licence is practically excluded[60], metrical errors lead to the rejection of the verse as of something quite impossible. An orientalist who pays no attention to the rules of prosody foregoes a valuable means of interpretation and indeed often falls into errors. This is particularly true of older Oriental scholars, who sometimes ignored the unconditional rigourousness of the Persian (and Turkish) metrical canons. A peculiarity of Persian is the *baḥr-i ṭavīl* (*ionicus a minore*, ∪∪ – – *ad infinitum*), that was used not simply for purposes of jesting, as Ye. E. Bertel's suggests[61] – basing his assumption on one case in Ṭarzī Afshār – but rather for reproducing 'general moods'.[62]

c. *Rhyme in Relation to Form*

Rhyme too is subject to strict and complicated rules, from which modern poetry has certainly to some extent broken loose[63], just as it has from the ossified system of classical metre and prosody. These rules are likewise taken from the Arabic and adapted to Persian. Whereas the former has command of an enormous wealth of rhymes, the study of any given Persian *dīvān* or – more clearly – epic will demonstrate that Persian rhyme is ultimately reduced to a number of constantly recurring clichés which exhaust the whole rhyming capacity of the language. The result was that in this field there were soon very few discoveries left to be made by the poets. But the rhyming capacity of Persian is considerably increased by the addition of Arabic loan words. The rhyme is often followed by the refrain (*radīf*), thus giving a certain lengthening of the rhyme line and introducing variety into the stale stock of rhymes, all of which forms sometimes an extra burden for the poet, sometimes, on the other hand, perhaps an alleviation. In the case of longer metres rhyme is also permitted within the semi-distich; but, apart from the opening verse, this rhyme is separate from the continuous ones. The arrangement of the rhyme is either continuous at the end of each distich or in pairs (*mathnavī*). In the latter case the rhyme connects not distichs but semi-distichs, and in such a way that each distich contains its own pair of rhymes. The first method is characteristic of the whole of lyric poetry, the second of the epic.

(I) FORMS OF LYRIC POETRY

(a) At least fifteen distichs (according to others only seven or ten), with a rhyme pattern *aa*, *ba*, *ca*, etc., form the *qaṣīda* ('purposive' poem), viz. with a panegyric, elegiac, satirical[64], didactic, or religious content. They usually have a purely lyrical introduction, commonly called *nasīb* but, when tinged with eroticism, *tashbīb* or *taghazzul*. From this introduction the poet proceeds, after a suitable transitional portion (*gurīz-gāh*), to the praise of the person to be eulogized. The panegyric can also often be explained by the desire of the poet to present an ideal model to the person addressed. The most famous masters of the Persian eulogistic *qaṣīda* are Rūdakī, ʿUnṣurī, Farrukhī, Muʿizzī, Anvarī, Khāqānī, ʿUrfī, Qāʾānī. Orientalists were formerly inclined to regard this form as only hollow praise, at the best mere biographical and historical material and therefore as a source which, despite its extravagant idealisation, is certainly of very great value and unsurpassable as regards the accuracy of the names and titles of the eulogised persons.[65] This is a prejudiced view which is still but unwillingly relinquished. The *qaṣīda*, a form of purely Arabic origin, had already on its native soil undergone considerable development, conditioned by changes in the social structure: from the poetry of the Bedouins to that of the towns and feudal times. Not until it was in its later stages did it reach the Iranians, when only scanty and entirely anachronistic vestiges were left of the original Bedouin features.[66] Nevertheless the panegyric was nothing new to the Persians. It had its roots in a centuries-old tradition and had already been mentioned by Xenophon.[67] There is no doubt that a panegyric could be sold more easily to the Persians than to the Arabs.[68] The court-poet served not one master but all those who in succession came into power either by intrigue or by force, being sometimes in the employ of several masters at the same time, while the latter were not as a rule on particularly amicable terms with one another. Nevertheless it would be idle to underestimate the achievements of these poets, for apart from the brilliant use of words of the panegyric writers, there are exordia of real poetic charm, exceptionally fine comparisons with masterly theoretical embellishments, philosophical and Ṣūfistic meditations, ethical counsels and serious warnings, pictures of nature, many and varied descriptions, etc. The Iranian is passionately fond of imparting advice, a trait already evident in Pahlavi literature. But the panegyric also had its social significance: it formed a means of subsistence for the poet and a reinforcement of the art of pure poetry and provided a basis for the development of the latter. It is a magic circle: the poets – with the exception of itinerant singers, the Sheikhs of the Orders, and others like them who set no store on being able to stand at the side of a master – did not write for the ordinary people, for there was no market to be found there for their poetry. This became the more evident in proportion as the tones of feudal poetry became more elevated, thus affording still less satisfaction to the masses both as regards language and spirit. Poets could therefore exist only thanks to the favour and the gifts of the court and its environment. Soviet scholars present a very dispassionate judgement on this maecenic system of patronage, even to the point of denying its value altogether (cf. pp. 108, 142).[69] Certain prominent persons, we know, certainly saw through the falseness of the panegyrics and adopted a negative (e.g. Kay-Kā'ūs, author of the *Qābūs-nāma*) and even hostile (the vizier Niẓāmu'l-mulk) attitude towards the court-poets. There are of course *qaṣīdas* which are altogether devoid of encomium (Nāṣir-i Khusrau is usually cited as an example; see however p. 189). Finally it may be mentioned that the *qaṣīda* commands a greater range of lyrical themes than the somewhat restricted *ghazal*. Now and then we come across *qaṣīdas* containing an enumeration of technical expressions (*iṣṭilāḥāt*) having bearing on some special field, for instance philosophy, poetics, music and other similar subjects connected with the theme in question, and rendered into verse in scholarly fashion.[70] It should also be noticed that of all lyrical forms the *qaṣīda* was the one least influenced by Ṣūfism.

(b) The same rhyme pattern, but with five to fifteen distichs (Kamāl Khujandī, Jāmī, 'Ubayd-i Zākānī, Shāh Ni 'matu'llāh, Shāh Qāsimu' l-anvār and Kātibī regularly show seven distichs, in striking resemblance to the sonnet) forms the *ghazal*, the truest and most pleasing expression of lyricism, particularly of the erotic and mystical but also of the meditative and even of the panegyric (Ḥāfiẓ).[71] Whereas the *qaṣīda* represents the poetry of the court, the *ghazal* springs from the cultural life of the town. "With the earlier masters, such as Sa'dī, Amīr Khusrau and Ḥasan of Dihlī, its almost invariable theme was love. Khvājū sang of other matters as well, such as the transitoriness of the world, while Salmān excelled in rhetorical artifices and novel comparisons and similes. Ḥāfiẓ combined the merits of all, adding to them a charm all his own"; thus E. G. Browne renders Shiblī Nu'mānī's description of the development of the *ghazal*.[72] Yet this view cannot be considered as in any sense accurate. It has so far not been made clear whether the *ghazal* originated from the *qaṣīda* by relinquishing the sung *taghazzul* (*nasīb*)[73], or by direct adoption of the Arabic *ghazal*, without its being at first regarded in Persian literature as a complete and independent poetic form[74], or whether it sprang from some pre-Islamic Persian form of song.[75] There are also other possibilities. The greatest masters of the *ghazal* are Sa'dī, Ḥāfiẓ, Ṣā'ib. The traditional opinion of orientalists (with the exception of Friedrich Veit, 1908[76] and several other more recent investigators) regarding the lack of unity of content of the verses appears latterly to be wavering and in need of revision, at any rate in relation to Ḥāfiẓ, in whom the *ghazal* reaches its peak (see p. 269[77]). Modern Oriental criticism even draws attention to the fragmentary nature of the thought in the 'Indian' (Safavid) *ghazal*.[78]

(c) If the opening verse *aa* in the pattern of the *ghazal* or *qaṣīda* is absent, thus leaving only *ba*, *ca*, *da*, etc., we get the *qiṭ'a* or 'fragment', which is usually of a philosophical, ethical or meditative character. Poets excelling in this type of verse are Anvarī and Ibn-i Yamīn. The *qiṭ'a* was popular for use in improvisations, a touchstone for new poets, but also a harbour of refuge for their more experienced colleagues, who were so frequently required to dispel the peevishness and boredom of their masters.[79]

As a consequence the introduction of unaccustomed arbitrary themes was permitted. In the *qiṭʿa* the poet often tells of his own personal experiences.

(d) The quatrain (*rubāʿī*) has an epigrammatic character with the rhyme plan *aaba*, though less frequently the not so expressive *aaaa* is encountered. It is an ancient pre-Islamic indigenous form[80], still alive in the rhythmic variation *dū-baytī*, 'double distich', of popular chanted poetry. As a genuine expression of the Persian ingenuity the *rubāʿī* is to be found in the earliest Persian poets such as Shahīd, Rūdakī, Abū-Shakūr of Balkh, etc., and in thousands of others up to the present day. In the 11th and 12th centuries A.D. it begins to occupy an important place in Khurasan and Transoxania. It is significant that ʿOmar Khayyām (d. 1122), world-famous as a writer of *rubāʿīs*, came from eastern Iran! "As regards subject-matter quatrain literature includes all genres of poetry with the exception of the epic."[81]

(e) There are also separate verses (*fard*) *aa* or *ab*, containing momentary flashes of greater or less brilliance on the part of the poet which he was unable to utilise in any other way.

In the above-cited series of forms the poet arranged his lyrical creations, in alphabetical order of rhyme for each kind, in his *dīvān*[82] (almost always in a single *dīvān*, by exception in several, e.g. Amīr Khusrau, Jāmī). This same procedure was also followed later by those who collected the scattered poems together after the death of the poet. (Only very seldom does one find the initial letter of the poetic form in question being used as a basis for the arrangement instead of the rhyming letters.) Thus the chronological sequence of a poet's oeuvre, apart from the *qaṣīdas*, which can be dated thanks to intrinsic or other elements, has become impossible to establish and insight into the poet's artistic development lost. The alphabetical principle was developed to such an extent by Muḥammad Qazvīnī in his edition of Ḥāfiẓ that it is possible to find any given verse at once (independently of him J. Rypka, first in the treatise on Labībī). R. Lescot[83] pointed out that this method of arrangement – at any rate in the case of Ḥāfiẓ – permits the presentation of poems similar as regards metre or rhyme, or bearing a close thematic and consequently, as is evident, temporal relation to each other. The subject-matter of a *dīvān* underwent modification according to the importance attached to one poetic form or another during the period in which it was conceived.

(f) Finally a few remarks on some less common strophic forms (*tarjīʿ-band* 'return-tie' and *tarkīb-band* 'composite-tie'). Certain strophes such as *takhmīs*, 'five-line verse', or *tasdīs*, 'six-line verse', were commonly employed as variations on a given *ghazal*. Modern poets also willingly make use of strophic forms, in particularly the *musammaṭ* (*aaaa x*, *bbba x*, *aaaaa x*, *bbbba x*, etc.) the masters of this form being Manūchihrī (first half of the 5th/11th century) and Qā'ānī (first half of the 13th/19th century). Chr. Rempis[84] declares the strophe to be a pre-Islamic form.

(g) Very occasionally one comes across the *mustazād*, 'supplemented'[85], characterised by the refrain (in the familiar sense) after each semi-distich and resembling the tone of a folk-song. It spread considerably in the revolutionary poetry of the 20th century.

It is relevant at this point to make mention of a very popular custom, that of writing imitations of poems by other poets, more rarely of one's own, *istiqbāl*, now and then *javāb*, 'reply', in Turkish known as *naẓīra*. Verse measure, rhyme and number of verses must correspond with those of the original. The poet strives to imitate or surpass the latter (in the case of a difficult rhyme even by extension of the number of verses), occasionally by the use of parody.

(2) SUBSTANCE OF LYRICAL FORMS

By way of summing up and completion a few words are required regarding the subject-matter. With the panegyric (*madīḥa*) and the satire (or rather libellous writings in verse: *hajviyya*) are associated the nenia (*marthiya*) and elegy, with few exceptions entirely in the feudal spirit, or at least in its sphere. A note of sincerity can be felt in the prison-poems (*ḥabsiyya*), particularly those of Mas'ūd-i Sa'd and Falakī (pp. 196, 209). Poems of advice are very popular, though their effect is little more than a pleasant sensation aroused by fine words. Love, tippling and meditation gradually assume tones of mysticism, or at least of semi-mysticism or allegory, whether it be to veil the actual facts or to comply with poetic convention. Ṣūfī poets too undoubtedly employ anacreontic methods of expression, of course in a symbolic sense. Mood, poetic individuality and conception of the world result in hedonistic intoxication, revolt, unbelief or a turning away from the world. Complaints about their fellow-men, their surroundings, their rulers and the base behaviour of the latter, the mental dullness and the jealousy of their contemporaries in literary and other circles, fill the poets only too often with anger and despair; but the poets also know how to defend themselves by attack and criticism. Praise of self is the order of the day ('Urfī is renowned in this respect). Here and there we find parodies and travesties (Busḥāq, Qārī, etc.) Coherent descriptions of nature belong especially to the *qaṣīda*, shorter ones are to be found everywhere, though always within the framework of statics and convention (see p. 87). To treat of everyday things would not have been consistent with the aristocratic self-respect of the poet and the eminence of the poetic art (as opposed to the Indian style, see p. 295) and for that reason we seek in vain for bucolic and such-like themes. Somewhat different are short descriptions (*vaṣf*, *tauṣīf*) of objects of seigniorial pleasure, sometimes standing alone, sometimes in other contexts. Letters in verse-form find their way even into diplomatic correspondence. Not even puzzles (*lughz*), logogriphs (*mu'ammā*) and chronograms (*ta'rīkh*), viz. verses or single words, the numeral letters of which indicate the year of the event, are scorned – the great Jāmī writes four essays on logogriphs! But they occur on a larger scale in periods of decadence. The first chronogram appears in Abū-Shakūr's *Āfarīn-nāma* (see p. 144). Of great value are the betting and quarelling songs, *tenzons* (*munāẓara*), which Asadī introduced into the *qaṣīda* – as opposed to the Arabic *tenzons* of al-Jāḥiẓ[86] which were composed in prose

– being again a form which, judging by its origin, goes back to pre-Islamic Iran.[87] The *munāẓara* had no influence on the Provençal *tenzon* or the Old French *Débats et Disputes*. The similar conditions under which they came into existence or the similarity in character of mediaeval literatures led in Iran and Provence to the same result.[88] The wealth of epigrammatic quatrains of the most diverse kinds provides the best reflection of Persian wit and keenness of intellect.

From the foregoing it is quite clear that nearly everything – content and form – was embraced by convention.

(3) THE FORM OF THE EPIC AND DIDACTIC POEM

Here we are solely concerned with the *mathnavī*, 'a series of distichs rhyming in pairs' (*aa*, *bb*, *cc*, etc.). It contains the whole of heroic, historic and romantic epic poetry, together with the didactic poetry of more considerable compass. This essentially Persian form, the only possible one for more extensive subjects if the same verse measure is to be used, was adopted by the Arabs, but gained no footing with them.[89] They were not particularly fond of the epic. Not every metre, however, is suitable for this purpose. For this reason epic and didactic poetry embrace a far more limited range of verse-measures, which correspond with those used in lyric poetry, but on principle only the shorter ones (10–11 syllables). The heroic verse rhythm is the *mutaqārib* (see p. 154, but also pp. 144, 175, 177, 251), which is certainly an Arabic adaptation of an old verse-measure from the Persian popular poems *à la Russe* '*bïlina*'. There is a great deal of didactic poetry, which however is markedly one-sided in character in that it is mainly concerned with Ṣūfistic religio-philosophical and ethical themes, often following in the wake of heresy, unbelief and insurrection.[90] As far as I know, there is nothing that reminds one of such works as the Georgics, yet there are erudite *mathnavīs* on prosody, astrology, calligraphy, etc.[91]

The popular passion plays were also written in verse (according to A. Krïms'kïy[92] authenticated only since the beginning of the 19th century). Apart from these there is an entire absence of dramatic poetry in classical literature, whereas in the case of modern writers the inspiration has come from Europe. In the works of 'Ayyūqī, 'Irāqī and Maktabī paired rhyme is interspersed with *ghazals* (see pp. 177, 213, 255).

d. *Strictness of Form. Efficiency of the System*

Despite the lack of originality and the unrelaxing strictness of all rules relating to form and metre, it can be shown that the work of the poet was in no sense rendered more difficult by the prosody. The Persians were able to manipulate these principles so that the latter were in complete conformity with the structure and spirit of the Persian language. There are grounds for assuming that in some cases the poets have transposed suitably modified popular and even *Pahlavī* poems into the Persian prosody, thereby proving themselves true both to national and feudal standards (see p. 154). The fact that the so recently formed quantitative metrics were suited to the structure of the Persian language can best be gathered by a consideration of the large range of literary production, both individual and collective. The only reproach to be levelled at the Persian metrics is the neglect – to a certain extent inevitable – of the expiratory accent of the Persian language. The fact that all rules, whether metric or otherwise, soon became stringent, finds a parallel in the rigid social conditions and is based on the conservatism discussed above. Yet as soon as changes began to take place in the economic and social structure in Persia attempts were made to unfetter poetic technique and introduce new forms (19th–20th century).

e. *Takhalluṣ*

Finally it should be mentioned that, with the exception of the shortest forms of poetry (though very seldom, as far as I can ascertain, in the old *qaṣīdas*[93]), the poet signed himself by an adoptive name (*takhalluṣ*, '*nom de plume*'), formed either after the name of his patron or after his own character traits, occasionally too according to circumstances. In the *ghazal* this custom came into more general use only later (6th/12th century), though sporadically, it is true, at the end of a lyrical song as early as Daqīqī.[94] This would presumably prove that originally the *ghazal* was not an independent poetic form.[95] V. A. Eberman[96], however, allows for the possibility of the *takhalluṣ* having already been one of the characteristic features of pre-Islamic Persian poetry. It was of course no precaution against literary forgery. In point of fact there are so many plagiarised and falsely attributed verses and poems that historians of literature are faced with the greatest difficulties of identification, for instance in the case of some of the *mathnavīs* of ʿAṭṭār. The *dīvān* that bears the name of Shāṭir ʿAbbās Ṣabūḥī is from beginning to end a plagiarism from poets of the Safavid epoch and others.[97]

2. THE INWARD FORM OF THE POETRY

By the inward form of poetry is meant the precise expression of a *pointe*, in each verse in respect both of the thought to be expressed and of the rhetoric. But the definition is not yet complete, for, if this were so, there would be no fundamental difference between Persian (or Turkish) poetry on the one hand and occidental poetry on the other. The West likewise "points" its thoughts to the utmost and has at its disposal a range of tropes and figures that is in no way poorer. The real difference lies rather in the spontaneity of the West and its contrary in the Orient. While the Idea in each verse must have its *pointe* (*nukta*) – and a very emphatic one at that – there must also be a mutual relationship between the separate concepts in one and the same verse, whether it be in connection with the contents of the verse or without regard to the latter. This law of the two-fold *nukta* may nowhere be disregarded because it is this in the first place that, in the eyes of the Iranian, marks the verse as real poetry. The *pointe* of the thought subordinates emotion to intellect. The importance of the expression of emotion thus occupies a place far behind that accorded to it by the West. The second *nukta*, that of expression, demands the use of one of the exceedingly numerous figures or tropes created by oriental theory, as an integral completion of each of the verses.[98] Tropes which consist merely of a transference of the literal meaning into imagery do not as a rule suffice to bring a Persian or Turkish verse to perfection. While the occidental poet is able to transport his reader by a simple metaphor or a single simile, in the case of the oriental poet both belong rather to the thought as such.[99] But in addition the thought demands a formal completion in the manner of a rhetorical embellishment (*melismus*), in many cases a combination of several. It is also important that the metaphors and similes should be entirely apposite, which however does not mean that the *tertium comparationis* should always be too obvious.

a. *Characteristic Embellishments. Excess of Rhetoric*

Persian prosodists have worked out to the point of subtle nicety the theory of tropes and figures, which will often be found to correspond with ours. Frequently, however, others can be distinguished which are strange to us. The cause is to be found partly in an exaggerated mania for complexity and partly in the immutable fact that the Persian poet expresses himself in a different manner from the Westerner. It is here only possible to touch lightly on the trope *ḥusn-i taʿlīl* 'aetiology', i.e. the invented imaginary poetical 'explanation' of some phenomenon, as an example, but in particular the most frequently occurring figure, *tanāsub* or *murāʿāt-i naẓīr*, 'harmony of the similar', viz. an intentional accumulation of homogeneous images or concepts in one distich frequently combined with the more or less complicated trope *īhām*, 'amphibology'.[100] In contradistinction to the figures known only to oriental theorists, it would be possible to quote converse cases, especially imitative sounds, which seem to have eluded oriental rhetoric, although examples of onomatopeia, alliteration and assonance can be furnished without difficulty from poetic texts. Several embellishments on the other hand enjoy great popularity, e.g. parallelism (*muvāzana*), but above all hyperbole (*mubālagha*) and a hyperbolic method of expression in general (*ighrāq*), which certainly reflect the most specific mental gifts of the Oriental (see p. 84) and can already be cited from the Avesta. *Aḥsanu'sh-shiʿri akdhabuhu va khayru' l-kalāmi mā būligha fīhi* "the most beautiful poem, the most untruthful and the most admirable language – that in which there is exaggeration." "From countless examples could be shown what the exorbitance of these image leads one to suppose: that this poetry is unaware of the correct relationship between the poetical ego and the world, mankind and itself, which is what constitutes the true character of great poetry."[101] Yet this is an extreme and too rectilinear conclusion, in which it is difficult to agree with H. H. Schaeder. Puns arise from numerous homonyms, thanks above all to the special structure of the Arabic language, with the vocabulary of which Persian is surfeited. The writing too also lends itself particularly well to playful tricks.

Thus each verse is in itself a completely worked out and independent miniature.[102] Some poets have indulged in formalism to the point of intolerable mannerism (Fattāḥī), others to a lesser degree; in the hands of masters of the word, of ingenuity and of good taste, the art of poetry, enhanced by a complete co-ordination of rhetorical media, attains a brilliance generally unknown to the West, at the same time, however, having the great disadvantage of being impossible to translate into another language, with the exception of Turkish. It is just by the art concealed behind his apparent simplicity that Saʿdī demonstrates his calculated deliberation. It is surprising to find even Firdausī making such copious use of rhetoric and not less so Maulavī, although he dictated most of his verses.

Though it must be acknowledged that the Persians took over this rhetorical equipment from the Arabs, a restriction must nevertheless be made, for at the same time it is necessary to realise to the full the part played by the Persians in the Arabic poetry of the 2nd/8th and 3rd/9th centuries. V. A. Eberman[103] has already shown that the hyperbole overlapped from Persian into Arabic poetry.

b. *Prerequisites for the Poet*

The art of rhetoric, combined with pointed thought, unconditionally exacts the careful consideration and weighing up of each word in a verse. All this ingenuity must obviously balance up the lack of originality of thought and in general the conventionality and triteness of the images, embellishments, and themes. Within this enchanted circle the Persian poet must find a means of expressing himself.

To write a real *shiʿr*, 'poem', the poet of classical times was obliged to submit unquestioningly to all the prescribed rules. It is not at all a question of writing only according to one's emotions. To be a Persian poet was at the same time to be a scholar, in fact even more. The biographies of the poets state in each case that he was versed in "all branches of learning", viz. theology, philosophy, jurisprudence, natural sciences – including astronomy and mathematics – medicine, in addition of course to the literary disciplines, viz. grammar, poetics, and rhetoric. Over and above this he was obliged to have read through several tens of thousands of Arabic and Persian verses and to know several thousand by heart, in order as it were to get into the closest possible touch with the approved patterns. Thus the art of poetry categorically necessitates an extensive training, it is a scholarly occupation, one branch of knowledge among the rest. Only in this way, according to Niẓāmī ʿArūḍī, could the poet endow

Notes on pp. 120–125

his verses with that which constitutes poetry: the art "of drawing appropriate conclusions from images of phantasy, so that as a result a small thing appears large and a large thing small, or that good resembles evil and evil good. By playing on the imagination the poet arouses feelings of displeasure or pleasure and produces accordingly a depressing or enlivening effect which invests him with influence on important affairs." [104]

In their views regarding the scholarly character of the poet and the art of poetry, the Persians are the pupils of the Arabs, both laying emphasis upon it in like manner as do "the Alexandrians, the humanists of the Renaissance and their heirs, the classicists of the sixteenth and seventeenth centuries".[105]

c. *Peculiarities in the Train of Thought*

This compression of so much mental labour and ingenuity can be more easily appreciated by means of the eye than of the ear, through the mind than through the emotions, on longer acquaintance than on a first reading. Thus, a Persian poem should be read in a different manner from that customary to the European, less as a whole, more as filigree work, for it is full of finely-wrought details, with no strictly logical sequence of verses in any given poem as is common in the West. It is as if the poets exhausted themselves to such an extent by giving form to such refinement that the fitting together of a whole escapes them. Variations in the order and number of verses in one and the same poem, according to the manuscript, are no special exception. The circumstance that now and then certain pieces were written down or copied from memory was bound to lead to mistakes often being made, however admirable the achievement may have been in itself. As the same lack of logic such as we are accustomed to can also be observed in Arabic poetry, it is quite plain that the Iranians, in addition to other things, have also taken this 'molecular structure'[106] from the same source. It is probable that, despite all the mental labour involved in details, the Persian poet is led far more by the imagination than by logic, both as regards description and abstract speculation. Whatever may be the nature or extent of this imagination it may well be that it is nevertheless subject to certain laws (see pp. 95 and 269), which T. Kowalski perceives in the association of ideas. The same scholar extends this assertion of absence of system to the whole literary and scientific production of the Islamic peoples and explains it by a tradition having its foundation on the one hand in Arabic poetry and on the other in the Koran. Even in modern prose W. Lentz states[107]: "Instead of developing one idea from the other, the author likes first of all to strew them about in apparently haphazard fashion, subsequently taking up first one, then the other, without in the meantime losing sight of the remainder."

Opposed to this we find the appearance of tautology, viz. the lack of progress in the line of thought, irrespective of whether it occurs within a distich or in the immediate continuation of the same, being a sure indication of an inferior versifier or of subsequent interpolation, above all in epic poetry.

d. *Craftsmanlike Modelling of the Form*

Be it as it may, let us not condemn all this formalism, conservatism, and traditionalism. That the consequences were, and were bound to be, such as they were lies in the laws governing historical phenomena. It is only important to realise that what we are here confronted with is not without precedent. Greek poetry can furnish us with evidence. "The power of form is demonstrated in Greek poetry perhaps more strongly than anywhere else. With an unequalled educative influence as long as new life was striving to find its form, and for a long time beneficent in that it endowed minor poets with style and grace, it ultimately had a mummifying effect and prematurely suffocated new talent. Greek poetry has the merits of a competent and consciously practised craft: it had to be learnt, and the rules, once recognized, had to be put into practice."[108]

e. *The Attitude of the Older Orientalists*

To the older generation of orientalists the formal side of Persian (and Turkish) poetry either remained hidden or was not known to them in its full extent. They sought and overestimated the mental content without taking notice of shades of form. The reason for this is perhaps that the old oriental commentators regarded the latter as self-evident and at most drew attention to it in isolated verses (e.g. Sūdī on Ḥāfiẓ). It is certainly no small matter for the Westerner to transfer himself into a world so far removed by differences in artistic conception, quite apart from the by no means slight difficulties with which he is faced on account of language, culture and in some cases too the lapse of time. Hence it follows that the European critic may on no account ignore the judgement of his native colleague, for otherwise his opinion cannot but be inexpert and arbitrary. Not until the europeanising movements manifest themselves in Persian poetry is he provided with a basis for his view. The philologist on the other hand finds an important aid to text-criticism in rhetoric, which nevertheless cannot be applied to all poets in the same degree.

f. *Applicability of the Old Forms to Modern Life*

Do the old forms offer to the modern poet a pliable tool for the expression of thought so diametrically opposed to the former, largely feudal way of life?[109] Here too a struggle between convention and progress will be inevitable, a struggle which in my

Notes on pp. 120–125

opinion is nevertheless destined *a priori* to result in a change or in a relinquishing of the old forms. If these forms appeared immutable, even inseparable from Persian poetry, this was only so as long as the economic foundation of intellectual life remained unaltered. As the feudal-aristocratic form of life declines, it is inevitable that the forms of poetry associated with it and originating from it should also yield, since they are not adequate to the demands of anew and different order of society. This is an unequivocal and reliable prognosis, whether the course of the coming literary development be gradual or precipitate.[110]

g. *Exclusive Nature of the Poetry*

If we take into consideration the artificial technique of the poetry as sketched above, we are bound to acknowledge the fact that this in itself is an infallible sign of a literature which appeals purely to educated circles and to the upper classes, but in no way to the masses of the people, who therefore find themselves obliged to satisfy the natural hunger for stimulating thoughts, magic watchwords and in general for a universally intelligible literature, in the song, either anonymously or through their own popular poets. The literary poet could only in very exceptional cases treat his public to such popular strains – in the political satire[111] and now and again in Ṣūfism. Thus it is an art far removed from the common people, it is a court or feudal art, destined for the highest classes and their adherents, which with the development of the towns spreads to the urban population.

*

h. *The Nature of Poetical Experience*

Finally let us consider one of the fundamental questions: the reality of experience in the Persian lyric of the classical period, viz. until the rise of the European school. It is not possible to agree altogether with the conjecture that the contents reflect only phantasy or imagination and not reality, but neither can one refute it entirely. The premises just expounded cover a wider span. Formalism, virtuosity, and convention tend, it is true, to a purely verbal play on images. But this would not at all be doing justice to Persian poetry, for within these limits too there are innumerable cases "where the experience, though unreal, is nevertheless encased in the innermost recesses of the soul"[112], thus representing no mere artistic verbalism or 'poeticism'. On the other hand one cannot doubt the existence of experiences inspired by pure reality, not merely products of the poetic imagination. If, in the course of the development of the lyric, the reality of experience perhaps appears to weaken and even to dwindle away altogether while yielding to artificiality or to mere artisanship, the fact must nevertheless not be overlooked that the experience is very frequently and completely disguised in allegory or metaphor. Though thus concealed, it does nonetheless exist. Moments of reality from daily life appear however now and then in the Safavid period (see p. 295) and still more pronouncedly under the transformed conditions of the 19th century. There is no straightforward answer to the question as to the nature of poetical experience. In all probability the suppositions necessary to substantiate a more trustworthy judgement have not yet been given. There can be no question of a uniform solution, not even in the case of one and the same poet, where one can observe a constant play between the two poles of reality and imagination.[113]

j. *The Specific Nature of Persian Poetry*

In his study on the imagery of Niẓāmī, H. Ritter[114] more than once raises the problem of the specific nature of Persian poetry – that which distinguishes it essentially from any other. The general picture sketched above is still only a partial and non-exhaustive answer to the given question, for our point of departure was formed rather by the peculiarities of Persian literature in relation to the literatures of Europe. Occasional mention has been or will be made of the lack of originality apparent in this or that example. But only by tracing the originality or its absence in Persian poetry can we get to the root of the question regarding the intrinsic character of this poetry. The main point is the relation between Arabic and Persian literature. This is an extremely complicated and difficult problem because from olden times the two literatures have been interwoven with one another. Some features that appear to be characteristic of the one later turn out to have been adopted from the other. There is a good deal of truth in the tendency shown by some scholars of Arabic to attribute primacy to the Arabs, but it is not the whole truth: the findings of research on Ancient and Middle Persian literature, which is constantly progressing, as well as knowledge of the prominent part played by Iranians during the beginnings of Arabic literature, enable us to perceive that the current flowing from the Iranians to the Arabs was no less important. The further one penetrates into the subject the more clearly does one realise that many a feature has been distorted by the arabising tradition (e.g. in Persian metrics). E. G. Browne and Ye. E. Bertel's[115] have pointed to the unity of the two literatures, especially in the first centuries of the Hejira and for a considerable time afterwards, and the subject receives an even greater emphasis in the words of H. Ritter, according to whom it is impossible to study New Persian literature apart from the Arabic and equally so to write its history solely on the basis of Persian records. And Arabic literature should certainly also be approached in like manner. "The language frontiers must not be allowed to form boundaries for the historian of oriental literature."[116] But such research cannot pursue a course of aprioristic conjecture, it can only proceed from the basis of a searching comparison of the concrete phenomena just as H. Ritter himself has shown in the case of metaphor in Niẓāmī's poetry. To him we owe richly detailed observations which expose new channels in the problems of non-scholastic rhetoric and poetics, and which give a deeper insight into the psychology of the Persian poet. Of great value is the work of U. M. Daudpota [117], though not everything that he ascribes to Arab influence can be incontestably accepted as such, and he does not always attain the same niceties as are to be found in H. Ritter's treatise, with which unfortunately he was unacquainted. The influence of Hellenism on the forming of the Iranian and Arab spirit has been pointed out by E. G. Browne, H. H. Schaeder, G. E. von Grunebaum [118], and others.

Yet we must not consider all similar phenomena as due to one influence, for in Arabic and Persian literature and also elsewhere there are many common signs which are not the consequence of a direct impact from one side or the other, but spring from similar general conditions. As such, for instance, can be regarded the general mediaeval view of the world and its material elements as something immutable, static; and further the common feudal basis with its accompanying conservatism which affects literary themes almost to the point of petrifaction, irrespective of whether one regards selection of subjects or treatment.

In contrast to the Iranian, the Arab is not attracted to the epic.[119] Not until the Iranian poet took it in hand did the *disjecta membra* of the little story of *Laylī and Majnūn* become a really integrated work of art. This is also proved no less convincingly by the infinite number of epic poems of a narrative character in Persian literature. Nor did Ṣūfism find in Arab countries the same fertile soil as it did in Iran, where a great deal of the poetry became saturated with it, even though sometimes only superficially or apparently. In general this luxuriant growth of Ṣūfism (quite apart from its social importance) springs from the inclination of the Iranian towards the phantastic, which not infrequently led to licentiousness, as can be gathered, for instance, from the romances and tales of folk-literature. Whilst the truest medium of expression of the Arab spirit is the *qaṣīda* in the widest sense of the word (thus not only the panegyric), the lyrical way of thought of Iran finds its appropriate form in the *ghazal*.

In his summary of the characteristics of Persian literature H. Ritter[120] draws attention to the fact "that the poetic comparison, that fills such an important rôle in Arabic poetry, appears here – in the case of Niẓāmī or of Persian poetry as a whole – to be almost entirely suppressed in favour of the direct figurative mode of expression, the metaphor, *istiʿāra*, or of the metaphorical simile." Certainly it is true that in Persian poetry the metaphor fulfils the most manifold functions and constitutes its most delightful ornament.

There is a striking contrast between the specific features of Persian and European poetry. In his study on this subject H. Ritter [121] selects Goethe and demonstrates that in his case "the effect of Nature on Man is as it were directly transmitted to the hearer. The poet transports us in the most vivid manner to the same situation in which he found himself, and now the same natural phenomena affect us as directly as they affected him, his metaphors suggest as it were to us only the special manner in which

Nature has affected him and must affect us. If, for instance, the Persian analyses the Night into its separate physical phenomena, the important thing for him is not so much to suggest a certain immediate emotional effect to the reader as responsive subject, by seeking to transfer him to a certain situation. He achieves his object in a more roundabout way. The physical phenomena are robbed of their immediate effect by this modified interpretation. It is only in metaphorical transformation that they again acquire this effect. Thus he is at liberty to invent afresh phenomena which have no equivalent in reality at all."

A second fundamental difference is that the German poet feels not the least necessity to motivate the juxtaposition of phenomena by an imaginary bond, thus as it were legitimising their mention in the poem: "The Persian obtains his effect of mood by the animating interpretation of natural objects in a sense corresponding to the desired* mood."

"In place of a juxtaposition (like Niẓāmī) of comparisons pregnant with emotion, which in their totality evoke the desired state of mind", Goethe places in juxtaposition words laden with emotion, words "of which a Niẓāmī would first have to justify each single one by a complete image and by placing it in a clearly comprehensible logical sequence."[122] Whilst the European poet chooses his words according to form, for instance for reasons of sound, the Persian poet is led by rhetorical considerations. The figure *murā'āt-i naẓīr* (=*tanāsub*), 'harmony of images associatively connected with a fundamental expression'[123], represents together with the metaphor the most important tool of the Persian poet; in it he includes other figures and tropes such as paranomasia, antithesis, etc.

Whereas the European poet experiences and portrays Nature dynamically, his Persian counterpart senses and describes it purely visually, with at the same time a tendency towards the decorative. The spatial, temporal, and physiological connection gives way before an imaginary new interpretation and this new association of things has a stronger, more inevitable, more 'matter-of-fact'-effect than the natural one. This apperception of the phantasy can be witnessed in Arabic poetry in the Abbasid epoch – though used to a comparatively slight extent – and is clearly a manifestation of Persian or Greek blood.[124]

H. Ritter takes only Niẓāmī and Goethe as basis of his deductions, yet one can nevertheless rightly assume that the inferences obtained are of general value. In other respects the knowledge of the subject quoted in the title is rather too rudimentary to warrant its being accorded more attention than has already been done in this narrow framework. It can only be added that the Iranians, however much they may have adopted from others, handled the material in their own manner and carried it to the point of perfection. Thus, all this borrowing in no sense diminishes the artistic value of their poetry.

k. *Poets' Centres and the Division of Poetry into Periods*

V. Zhukovskiy[125] and others have already observed that in the eastern world the art of poetry was concentrated and flourished above all at the courts of the rulers or under the patronage of highly-placed persons. In point of fact the poet was drawn there by the chance of attaining fame, by the political atmosphere and especially by the pecuniary reward. But this was not all. One must bear in mind that not only the courts but also the towns were in increasing measure becoming focal points of literature. The fact that the feudal lord and the towns were ceaselessly engaged in political and economic struggles against each other was of necessity reflected in the literature of the day. And this forms one of the most important motives for the stir that became evident within classical Persian literature. Thus the opinion that the writing of poetry was concentrated exclusively at the courts is reduced to its proper proportions. Moreover, we also know from the poets themselves that the part of Maecenas, as played by the princes, should not be over-idealised.[126] But despite all, the fact remains that the responsibility for the material welfare of a large number of the poets devolved upon the court, which in its turn needed and employed them for purposes of propaganda. It was there that men of literature met together. By regarding the duration of any given dynasty (e.g. the Safavids) as a cultural unit, we obtain a valuable method of division into literary periods. For it cannot be denied that, particularly as a result of the advent of great new dynasties (e.g. Samanids, Safavids, and Qajars[127]), new cultural and literary ideals were formed. The revolution was not so much brought about by the founders of one dynasty or another, who are rather to be regarded as the bearers of a change in public opinions and convictions. They would otherwise never have risen to such heights or have been able to maintain themselves there (Tīmūr, the Qajars). For they needed the constant support of certain masses even though these were at times armed foreign upstarts; but they too erected boundaries between that which already existed and that which was about to come into being (e.g. the Mongols). All thus must be seen, it is true, against the background of the above-mentioned conservatism.

E. PROSE

Although neither as regards quantity nor as regards quality does Persian prose reach the heights attained by the poetry until about the end of the 19th century, it must by no means be ignored, especially as it contains many a distinguished work and commands admiration moreover by virtue of its sheer bulk. If it is true to say of Persian poetry that the problems it evokes have not in a true sense been adequately investigated, then how incomparably more so is this the case with the prose. We are not concerned here with a detailed discussion of scientific prose, but now and then it is no easy task to draw a dividing line between the latter and literary prose. This is not only because verses frequently creep into the most erudite works, but because even scientific writings are often borne by the poetic spirit and style, which of course is more artificial than suitable (e.g. the history of Vaṣṣāf). The intermingling of prose and verse is peculiar to some works of the greatest artistic value (Saʿdī's *Gulistān*, 'Rose Garden', Jāmī's *Bahāristān*, 'Spring Garden'), and also others. The poetical strain is predominant especially in tracts with a Ṣūfistic tendency, just as Ṣūfism, in virtue of its essential nature, shows a general inclination towards poetry and finds in versified works its most frequent and most monumental vehicle of expression. Moreover, many a prose work of the sectarians (e.g. Bahā'u'llāh's *Kalimāt-i maknūna* 'Hidden Words') belongs rather to the realm of literature than to that of theology.

The whole of belletristic and related prose of the classical period can be divided purely according to form into the following general sections (partly after H. Ethé):

A. Fiction:

1. Tales of heroism and chivalry;

2. Separate fairy stories and tales;

3. Collections of narratives, anecdotes and fables, united in a common framework: (a) by means of a superimposed story (e.g. *Ṭūṭī-nāma* 'The Book of Parrots'), (b) by means of a constantly recurring theme, sometimes non-tendential (*al-faraj baʿda'sh-shidda*, 'Joy after Suffering'), sometimes of an instructive nature (Saʿdī's *Gulistān* 'Rose Garden');

4. Allegorical tales;

B. Meditations:

1. Essays, including those of Ṣūfī origin (especially on the subject of love);

2. Biographies of Ṣūfīs;

3. Ethical works, including politics;

4. Diplomatic, official and private epistolography, viz. collections of letters and letter-writing manuals;

C. Works closely connected with A and B:

1. Biographies and anthologies (*tadhkira*);

2. Theory of literature (especially poetics and style);

D. Scholarly works in poetical style, consisting largely of historiography;

E. Memoires. – It may be mentioned that in classical prose also there is no lack of translated literature.

There is an enormous quantity of prose-literature, belletristic or serious as well as erudite. Unfortunately most of it is at present only known to exist from catalogues and similar inventories, occasionally inadequately scheduled. It has been summarised by the admirable H. Ethé[128], and more recently and thoroughly by H. Ritter (who discusses mainly writings on "profane and mystic love" and the works of the four bearers of the genetic name Suhravardī).[129] In the present outline we can concern ourselves only with the most important works.

For purposes of general characterisation the following remarks can be made: seen as a whole, the course of development can be traced from simplicity of expression, style and substance to the utmost extremes of 'arabising', to an intolerable form of 'poetry-making', pomposity and over-complicated periods, in which *saj*ʿ, 'rhyme' (actually sentences or parts of sentences rhymed by harmonious cadences) appears rather as something quite inevitable than as a decorative accessory, because without it the sentence would be less comprehensible than it already is. Not until the 19th century did the tide turn to some extent. Poetry follows a similar course although there are certain differences: prose at its zenith is disproportionately permeated, even satiated, with Arabic and baroque elements, while at its lowest point it approaches more nearly the popular genre. The background of classical prose is of course again to be found in the feudal structure of society, to serve which almost the whole of the literary output is produced. In the prose, too, flashes of humour and sarcasm are encountered but seldom (e.g. ʿUbayd-i Zākānī).

The prose of the European school is adequately characterised by its name. If we regard it in the light of old-established tradition, it is easy to discern that – more than is the case with poetry – it has alienated itself from everything in classical literature that had preceded it. This proves above all how lastingly the changed political and economic circumstances had penetrated into the life of Iran, and perhaps also how firmly rooted in the Iranian is the feeling for classical poetry, with the result that the latter so hesitatingly assumes new forms. It is true that in the approximation to everyday speech, that is to a commonly comprehensible written language, modern prose and poetry are on the whole in agreement; but, from the point of view of substance and form, it was in prose that the more pioneering and forceful advance was made towards new ideals with new media. Nowadays the European conception of the novel and the story has already been accepted by the Iranian as a matter of course. Translations from European languages are becoming more and more common, the daily newspaper has become as familiar to everyone as his daily bread. The contemporary spirit also determines the direction to be followed by scientific publications. To this struggle for a literary reform we can also finally accredit the initial stages of a dramatic literature. The feudal social structure yields gradually to Western conceptions. With the industrialisation of the country the first stir of socialism begins to manifest itself.

I. THE RANGE OF PERSIAN LITERATURE

The subject of Persian literary history is the literary production in this language, beginning with its earliest manifestations and continuing up to the present day. This period corresponds fairly approximately with the duration of Islam in Iran. The present chapters deal only with poetry in the narrow sense of the word and with literary prose. But it is not permissible even for such a restricted survey to limit itself to writings associated only with the ruling noble and urban classes, for in this way the predominating majority of the nation would be excluded, viz. the masses of the people, who, driven by the same innate necessity as the 'upper' classes, wish to give free rein to their longing for expression of emotions and experiences by means of euphonious and impressive words. Most of the resulting utterances have not been committed to paper but are folk-poems handed down by word of mouth, though not in all cases anonymously. They are equivalent in value, relatively speaking, to the literature of the 'upper' classes and on this account, in order to complete the literary picture of a nation, they must not be passed by unnoticed.

But it would be erroneous to classify Persian literature according to period and social class only, for equal emphasis can be laid on the anthropo-geographical division. In the first place, certainly there is the written Persian literature of the Iranians themselves. But especially in the first centuries of Islam the Iranian converts played a very real part in the development of Arabic literature and later on also made considerable contributions to it. This category should therefore be included in our review, for it is also, in effect, Persian literature, though written in the Arabic language. The synoptical nature of the present work permits only of a very concise treatment of this portion. But while limiting ourselves to the written works of Persian literature, we must not lose sight of the fact that historic Iran – widely expanded as it was – embraced various Iranian tribes, dialects and even languages. To the literary historian these idioms are less important because, with few exceptions, they were not able to hold their own and yielded to the sovereignty of a uniform written language (see p. 74). Yet there were also tribes living in Iran of ethnically non-Iranian origin, whose members, although they possessed a foreign, non-Iranian native tongue, were creatively engaged in Iranian literature, and of these we must mention in the first place the Azerbayjan Turks. The significance of this will become clearer if we bear in mind that the boundaries of the Moslem kingdom of Iran fluctuated very considerably in the course of time: according to where power prevailed, Central Asia and Khvārazm gained the upper hand, only to lose it later on. Under the Safavids Iraq was lost, shortly afterwards Afghanistan and finally the Caucasian provinces. As far as the ethnically Iranian frontier districts were concerned, they yielded to the pressure of progressive Turkish infiltration. All these provinces, to whatever nationality they belonged – and sometimes they were no longer subject to the state sovereignty of Iran at all – added to no mean extent to the wealth of Persian literature.

However, the sphere of action of Iranian culture and especially the community feeling of the dervish orders extended far beyond the extreme boundaries of the kingdom, by which is meant Ottoman Turkey and North-West India. These enormous territories were not only closely related to Persian literature, but they also took an active part in its creation – the Ottoman Turks to a slighter degree but the Indians in such abundance that we can actually speak of an Indo-Persian literature.

The consequence of all this is that Persian literature, similar to the Arabic and Ottoman Turkish literatures in the East or the Latin and Greek in the West, is a complex whole originating in the common endeavour of a number of nations, stretching from the Mediterranean to far beyond the borders of India. Its anthropo-geographical constellation lends to the literature an astonishingly rich power of expression, great variety, and wide dissemination. To this may be added the share contributed by Iranians to Arabic literature. The resulting 'Persian' literature thus forms a part of the collective achievement of the important races and peoples that came into contact with each other through Islam, an achievement which has in the past so notably enriched human civilisation. Despite its international character Persian literature forms a unity guaranteed by the Persian language and by the predominance of the Iranian spirit. Nevertheless it would not do to ignore regional peculiarities and characteristic distinctions. Ye. E. Bertel's[130], whose method is here followed, distinguishes four main districts: (1) Transcaucasia, (2) Central Asia, (3) Iran and (4) India.

This regional division approximates in principle to the Persian view of certain styles in poetry (*sabk*), and forms at the same time a roughly sketched periodisation.

In more extensively worked out histories of literature attention is also devoted to the literary 'schools'. But such a method presupposes the possession of accurate factual material, and I am not certain whether, as regards oriental literatures – including Persian – we possess adequate preliminary studies, which we certainly cannot dispense with in view of the intricate problems involved in this subject.

2. STYLES OF POETRY AS INTERPRETED BY M. BAHĀR AND S. NAFĪSĪ[131]

In Persian literary criticism reference is frequently made to a Khurasanian (Turkestanian) and an Iraqian style. From the earliest times up to the present day opinions have differed as to their respective merits. The Iraqian poets themselves occasionally concede the greater worth to the eastern movement, at other times they become vexed by it or ironic. It must be clear that during the first phases of Persian quantitative verse* Iraq was exposed to a strong influence from Arabic literature, considerably stronger than was Khurasan. This resulted on the one hand from the proximity of Baghdad, on the other from the unceasing flow of Arab men of letters to the courts of the Buyids. Yet the Buyid 'Aḍudu'd-daula (d. 372/983), himself an Arabic verse-writer, had at most interest only for the ancient Sasanian syllable-counting poetry in the Ṭabarī dialect. Nonetheless, thanks to the patronage of the highly cultured vizier Ṣāḥib-Ismā'īl b. 'Abbād (d. 385/995), also a writer, Persian poets too appear at the courts of the Buyids, such as Manṣūr Manṭiqī, Bundār (both from Ray), later Qaṭrān, Bakhtyārī and Ghaḍā'irī, in the 11th century the famous Manūchihrī in Southern Caspia. Yet at the earliest dawn of Persian poetry there had been, in the district of Fars and in Iraq up to the borders of Gurgan and Khvārazm, just where Arabic influence was predominant, no symptoms of an imminent literary awakening.

It was a different matter however in distant Khurasan, to which just on account of its remoteness priority must be accredited as regards time, for here there were already signs of activity at the beginning of the 2nd/8th century. Closely associated with this district are the names of Abū Ḥafṣ Sughdī, Abu'l-ʿAbbās Marvazī, Ḥanẓala Bādghīsī, Muḥammad ibn Vaṣīf Sijzī, and others. The focal points of the arabising movement in Bukhara and Nishapur were not able to check the Persian movement, which was gaining ever greater favour with the emirs and other eminent men, the more so because it was in accordance with their centrifugal tendencies which gained success in the same measure that Baghdad exhibited signs of weakening. Thus for a hundred-and-fifty years after the Arab invasion we find in Transoxania, Nishapur and Tukharistan a swarm of men of letters who no longer write exclusively in Arabic, but also in Persian or only in Persian. Iraq and the neighbouring territories remain on the contrary still backward, until, at the time of the Ghaznavids and Seljuqs, here too a change sets in. We encounter a succession of first-rate poets such as Ghaḍā'irī, Manūchihrī, Qaṭrān, Masʿūd of Ray, Fakhru'd-dīn Gurgānī, Jamālu'd-dīn Iṣfahānī, Khāqānī, ʿImādī Shahryārī, Kamālu'd-dīn Ismāʿīl, Mujīr, and others. But the eastern part of the country is continually ahead of the western districts and even at the time of Sanjar the great poets of Iraq and Azerbayjan are still now and then seized with yearning for Khurasan. From the time of the Seljuqs onwards development proceeds slowly, keeping a similar pace in Khurasan and in Iraq. In prose-writing the Arabic *sajʿ* becomes even more popular, and in increasing measure poetical embellishments are made use of and the language becomes more 'poetical'. At each step verse quotations are introduced, synonyms accumulate, the hitherto existing proportion of Arabic words is increased by superfluous and incomprehensible items, titles and headings are enlarged, long periods employed with evident satisfaction, etc. Poetry writing also becomes more complicated by the use of learned Arabic terms, difficult tropes, extravagances, subtleties and, in short, everything that tends to transform simplicity and clarity into their opposites. Along these untrodden paths new ways are sought, which however lead downwards rather than upwards. Muḥammad Bahār [132] avers that all this is a sign of the time and not of the place, for poets writing at the same time in Khurasan, such as Imāmī of Herat, Kamāl of Khujand, Shams of Ṭabas, Sayf of Isfarang, Nizārī, and others, do not differ in any way from their contemporaries in Iraq, in Fars and Azerbayjan, just as formerly Ghaḍā'irī of Ray, Qaṭrān of Tabriz and Manṣūr Manṭiqī of Dāmghān were not different from ʿUnṣurī and Farrukhī, even though there are many who consider Manūchihrī of Dāmghān superior to the Khurasanians or Ghaḍā'irī to ʿUnṣurī. This movement continues up to the time when the Mongols reduced Khurasan to a heap of ruins. Scholars and men of letters, in so far as they escaped being murdered, fled in all directions, to Isfahan, Shiraz, Baghdad and to other regions where material prosperity and intellectual culture had been spared from the Mongol storm. As a result of the overthrow of Baghdad the Arab influence declined and all local rulers, whether Turks or Persians, were patrons of the Persian language and literature. The poetry emanating from the ruined cities of Khurasan found a home in the west and a vehicle of expression in the 'Iraqian style'.[133] But it must be realised that the difference as compared with the style of Khurasan is determined neither by the country nor by the prevailing taste but by the period only. It is a literary technique which Iraq – left relatively unmolested by the Mongols – adopted from the devastated Khurasan and by which it regenerated and carried on Persian verse and prose, since the depopulated Khurasan was for a long time incapable of doing so. The Mongol invasion, it is clear, opens up a new period in literature.

A third style – the 'Indian' as it is called nowadays[134] – was added to the first two from the time of the Amīr Khusrau Dihlavī. This was evoked both by time and by place, without however being thereby restricted within narrow limits. Rather can it be said that under the Safavids, thus much later, it spread like an avalanche to Khurasan and Turkestan as well as to Iraq, until in the second half of the 18th century it was irretrievably banned from Persia.

The styles of Khurasan and Iraq have both been used side by side up to our own day, independent of time and place, according only to personal preference and mood and consequently promiscuously. As examples we may cite such eminent poets of the Qajar renaissance as Ṣabā and Shaybānī from Kashan, Mijmar and Surūsh from Isfahan, Qā'ānī from Shiraz, who were to such an extent addicts of the Khurasanian style that their work shows no trace whatsoever of the Iraqian, although they all hailed from the western half of Persia.

This was originally the opinion held by Muḥammad Bahār, but he appears to have modified it later because his *Sabk-shināsī*, II, 359, places the beginning of the Iraqian orientation in poetry and artificial prose style (*sabk-i fannī*) already in the Seljuq period, in connection with the greater influence of Arabic literature. This would certainly imply a radical change from the former view, a complete swing-around in fact, because then the Iraqian movement would have been conditioned not only by the period but also by the country and by its taste, since we are dealing with the time of the Ghuzz raid in Khurasan (548/1153).

Quite different, however, in nature is the terminology of the modern scholar, professor Sa'īd Nafīsī. The period from the known beginnings of Persian literature in the *darī* language up to the end of the 5th/11th century he designates as realism, which is gradually succeeded by naturalism. Simultaneously to this we also find the *taṣavvuf* (Ṣūfism) appearing. Since its doctrines may not be revealed to all and sundry, it is distinguished, as may readily be understood, by a multitude of symbols. Thus symbolism proceeds hand in hand with Ṣūfism and naturalism. In the case of Ḥāfiẓ, one of the greatest of Persian symbolists, intensified symbolism grows into impressionism (8th/14th century), which really flourished mainly from the 10th/16th up to the end of the 11th/17th century. With the Isfahan poets of the 12th/18th century the tide turns again to the former naturalism, whereas the 13th/19th century was more inclined towards realism. Romanticism, in the opinion of S. Nafīsī, has not the same significance in Persian as in European literature; in essence it is in the former only a naturalism of exaggerated emotions and fantasies. The mysticism and didacticism found in parables and short stories are also, in his opinion, based on a similar romanticism.

If we compare S. Nafīsī's view with Bahār's classification as mentioned above, we find the following parallels: realism is nothing other than the Turkestanian or Khurasanian style up to Niẓāmī, Khāqānī, Kamālu'd-dīn Ismāʿīl and their contemporaries in the 6th/12th century. From then on begins the Iraqian style, viz. naturalism. ʿUrfī (second half of the 10th/16th century) inaugurates the Indian, impressionistic manner. Symbolism and romanticism do not take up any particular stand, but permeate each other, the former mostly in conjunction with the *taṣavvuf*.[135]

3. THE DEVELOPMENT OF LITERATURE IN POLITICAL-HISTORICAL SEQUENCE

The Asiatic School

A. *The Pre-Mongolian period*

a. *the Arab occupation*: continuation of Iranian culture;

1. two different streams: the indigenous (continuation of the Middle Persian and folk-literature, first signs of Persian syllabic poetry in Khurasan and Transoxania), and the movement prepared to co-operate with Islam (Iran's literary tradition in Arabic garb);

2. the Shuʿūbiyya as a turning away on the part of the Iranian aristocracy from the Caliphate, which was in the throes of disintegration, and the former's re-association with the Persian language for the purpose of upholding power (the language as a means to political and social agreements, the rise of native regional principalities); lyrical poetry and didactic epic; establishment of quantitative prosody;

3. codification of the national epic tradition and climax of the latter in the feudal heroic epic (symptom of the decline of Sasanian chivalry).

(1st to 4th/7th to 10th century)

b. *the Turkish Ghaznavid dynasty* (transference of the centre from Bukhara to Ghazna) *and the Great Seljuqs*: panegyric poetry; further suppression of the old Iranian aristocracy by the Turks; growth of urban power: maturing of the romantic epic; resistance to feudalism: Ṣūfism, *ghazal*. (5th/11th century).

c. *Sanjar and the collapse of Iran, the Atābegs and Khvārazm-Shāhs*: panegyrism at the royal and princely courts at its peak, simultaneously with the romantic epic, the latter as a vehicle of expression of the urban population; the first great mystics, similarly a product of the towns; the Iraqian style in poetry. (6th/12th century).[136]

Notes on pp. 120–125

B. *The period from the Mongol invasion up to the 'return' in the second half of the 12th/18th century*

a. *the Īl-Khāns and disintegration*: general material and cultural decadence of the northern half of Iran; decline of the panegyric; later climax of historiography; climax of Ṣūfī poetry (Maulavī) and of the *ghazal* (Saʿdī) at the periphery.

(7th/13th century up to third quarter of the 8th/14th century).

b. *Tīmūr, his successors and the disintegration*: centre in Samarkand and Herat; the Turkish feudal lords; despite all its artificiality, interest in literature spreads; transition of the romantic epic and the romantic short story to mysticism.

(last quarter of the 8th/14th century up to the end of the 9th/15th century)

c. *the Safavids: rigid despotism.* Shīʿite fanaticism, wars, buildings; aversion to secular literature in Iran and new centre at the Moghul court: Indian style; alienation of Central Asia and India.[137] (10th/16th to beginning of the 12th/18th century)

d. *the Afghan invasion, Nādir-Shāh and Karīm-Khān Zand*: parallel to the economic situation at first steady decline, then from the middle of the 12th/18th century onwards a change in the form of a 'return' to the old schools of poetry.

(beginning to end of 12th/18th century)

C. *19th century. The Qajar dynasty*: the re-unification of Persia guarantees a certain peace, but increases backwardness and all-round decadence; in connection with this, rivalry between Russian and British imperialism, infiltration of economic influence of both powers (the bourgeoisie, with increased economic power, seizes feudal property): Persia falls into a semi-colonial position.

a. up to the appearance of Nāṣiru'd-dīn (1264/1848): beginning of financial economy and a striving towards europeanisation (army, press); continuation of the 'return'; resurrection of the panegyric; high level of the *ghazal*, general tendency towards a more straightforward manner of expression in poetry; reform of official prose by Qā'im-maqām.

b. up to the assault on Nāṣiru'd-dīn (1313/1896): increasing political and economic pressure on the part of England and Russia; period of transition, attempts at reform, among them *Dāru'l-funūn* 'Polytechnic College' in the field of culture, introduction of European sciences. Native and emigrant press; new notes in poetry, pessimism, discontent; simplification of prose style, significant rôle of translations from European belles-lettres, the first belletristic proseworks of the new movement.

D. *20th century*. Constitutional struggle under the last Qajars. Partition of the country between England and Russia into spheres of political influence (1907); First World War; post-war imperialistic exertion on the part of England; deposition of the Qajars, Riḍā-Khān founds the hereditary Pahlavi dynasty; assertion of sovereignty, influx of European civilisation, industrialisation; more and more rigid military dictatorship of Riḍā-Shāh, his resignation and Iran's entry into Second World War on the side of the Allies; revival of political and cultural activity under Shāh Muḥammad Riḍā; the significance of the Tūda party. – Repercussion in culture and literature:

a. up to the appearance of Riḍā-Khān (1299/1921): very rapid growth of journalism during the constitutional struggle; poets and writers as political factors; newspapers as the chief literary tool in this period; popular forms of poetry, interest of poets in topical affairs, and the turning away from Ṣūfism; first historical novels following European models.

b. the dictatorship of Riḍā-Shāh (up to 1319/1941): feverish building up of industry, transport and the Trans-Iranian railway; school and language reforms; censorship; declining standard of the daily press; increase of prose production (novels and short stories); dissension between the 'traditionals' and the 'progressives' in poetry.

c. Resignation of Riḍā-Shāh (1319/1941), end of dictatorship; growth of liberal and communistic press, further development of literary prose, in particular of the short story; increase in subjects taken from everyday life both in prose and poetry; popular idiom; repercussions in literature of the two ideologies in world politics.

4. MUḤAMMAD BAHĀR'S[138] CLASSIFICATION OF PROSE INTO PERIODS ACCORDING TO STYLE

1. *The Samanid period* is characterised by simplicity, conciseness, freedom from mannerisms and metaphors, Persian expressions preponderant; e.g. the History of Balʿamī (Persian adaptation of Ṭabarī's work); *Ḥudūduʾl-ʿālam* 'The Frontiers of the World'. (300–450/10th to middle of 11th century)

2. *The Ghaznavid and first Seljuq periods* are distinguished by lengthy sentences under the influence of Arabic prose and by an increase in the proportion of Arabic words; e.g. Bayhaqī's History, *Kalīla u Dimna.*
(450–550/middle of 11th to middle of 12th century)

3. *The second Seljuq and the Khvārazm periods*, marked by parallelism, rhyme,* mannerism, rhetorical embellishments, e.g. Ḥamīdī's *Maqāms*, 'Sittings, facetiae', *Marzbān-nāma.* (550–600/middle of 12th to beginning of 13th century)

4. *The period of the Iraqian style and of rhetorical prose* expands the range of rhetorical mannerisms and fastidious Arabic expressions, erudite terms, which makes it more difficult of comprehension; e.g. Nasavī's *Nafthatuʾl-maṣdūr*, 'The Expectoration of the Consumptive', *At-tavassul ilaʾt-tarassul*, 'The Way to Correspondence', by Bahāʾuʾd-dīn Baghdādī, the prose portions in ʿAufī's *Lubābʾul-albāb*, 'The Quintessence of Hearts', the same writer's *Javāmiʿuʾl-ḥikāyāt*, 'The Necklaces of Anecdotes', ʿUtbī's (Yamīnī's) History in the translation of Jurfādaqānī, Juvaynī's *Taʾrīkh-i Jahān-gushāy*, 'History of the World Conqueror', and the History of Vaṣṣāf, viz. of 'The Panegyrist' ʿAbduʾllāh, etc.
(600–1200/beginning of the 13th to end of the 18th century)

5. *The period of the 'return' in literature* imitates the style of the *Gulistān*, of Khvārazm

Notes on pp. 120–125

prose and the History of Bayhaqī, e.g. the official correspondence of Qā'im-maqām and Nashāṭ, Sipihr's *Nāsikhu't-tavārīkh*, 'The Abolisher of earlier Historical Works'; Riḍā-qulī Hidāyat's works and *Nāma-i dānishvarān*, 'Book of the Learned Men'.[139]

(1200–1300/end of 18th up to end of 19th century)

6. *The period of the straightforward style of writing*, such as the essays of Malkum, the translation of J. Morier's 'The Adventures of Haji Baba of Ispahan', *Kitāb-i Aḥmad*, 'Ahmad's Book' and others by Ṭālibūf, 'The Three Musketeers' in the translation of Muḥammad Ṭāhir-Mīrzā, articles in the better newspapers.

(1300/end of 19th century up to the present day)

I agree with professor S. Nafīsī that in each period the simple, straightforward style of writing had its adherents.

5. ZARRE'S DIVISION INTO PERIODS[140]

Abu-l'-Kasim Zarre bases his classification solely on economic criteria. His pattern is as follows:

I. *The period of Asiatic economic policy of common property, after the break-up of the clan community*: Ancient Persian literature.

II. *The feudal period* (approx. 2nd to 19th century)

1. the rise and establishment of feudalism: 2nd to 8th century
2. its full development: 9th to 15th century
3. its stagnation and decline: 15th to 19th century.

III. *The period of infiltration of capitalistic conditions into Iran and the rise of national liberation movements*: approximately from the second half of the 19th century up to the present day.

The oldest period I shall leave out of the discussion. Taking the economic background as his starting-point, Zarre connects the Sasanian period to the Islamic and reveals a close association between the literatures of the two epochs as regards the epic poetry (in addition to primitive mythological elements and Sakian heroic sagas), but he ignores – at least in the scheme of his classification – their differences of language and the revolution brought about by the Arabs, notably factors which may not be separated from the acknowledged principle. When later on he expresses the opinion that the usual classifications refer only to such superficial elements as script and political forms, it appears as if he is unwilling to realise that, even if this were the case, which in fact it is not, these are only symptomatic designations of the real cause. On the other hand he maintains rightly and admissibly that the deeper one penetrates into pre-Islamic Persian literature, the more compelling becomes the hypothesis that the literature of Islamic Iran must be regarded in its historical development as the direct successor of the pre-Islamic, certainly a conception the significance of which lies not in its novelty but in the emphasis laid on it and in the support it receives from the economic background. In any case Zarre's qualification requires a more exhaustive treatment and further details in the classification.

*

6. SOURCES FOR THE HISTORY OF PERSIAN LITERATURE

1. Actual records, in manuscript or print:
   a. belles-lettres,
   b. scientific writings.
2. Indigenous dictionaries with quotations from the poets.
3. Records:
   a. of Arabic literature,
   b. of the literature of all the Turkish peoples, in so far as they contain mention of Persian literature,
   c. Turkish or Arabic commentaries on Persian works.
4. a. *Tadhkiras*, viz. anthologies of the works of native poets and scholars in addition to biographical data, actually a kind of rudimentary history of literature compiled from the feudal and religious viewpoint of the ruling classes; all too frequently they lead to an empty torrent of words at the expense of actual biographical data, to unreliability and incompleteness. Characteristic traits are at best too much generalised, as a rule they convey nothing and it is hardly possible to glean from them anything of fundamental value. The authors of the *tadhkiras* failed to penetrate to the essential being of the poets because they regarded such as of secondary importance or, for whatever reason it may be, because they shunned further communicativeness. The weakness of their specimens is astonishing. H. Ethé[141] enumerated fifty *tadhkiras* compiled according to the most varied principles: since then (1904) we have become acquainted with others (see p. 316). Despite all their defects they are nevertheless extremely important and in many cases the only sources;
   b. anthologies without biographical data (*safīna* 'boat', *majma*ʿ 'collection', *jung* 'miscellany', *bayāḍ* 'album', *intikhāb* or *muntakhab* 'selection', etc.).
5. Works on literary history and criticism by
   a. indigenous or
   b. oriental scholars and men of letters of modern times,
   c. orientalists.
6. Catalogues of manuscripts and prints.
7. Suitable material appertaining to the auxiliary branches of history.
8. Works of fine art.
9. Accounts of travel by Europeans.

NOTES

1. *Fihrist*, ed. Flügel, 13, 1–10.
2. Cf. Sabk, 1, 250 *et seq.*
3. Cf. Köprülü (B IV); Ṣafā 2, 329. Now subjected to an exhaustive treatment by G. Doerfer (B IV). Bausani, *Storia* (B V), 481, sees in the introduction of Mongolian words in prose and verse (e.g. in Vaṣṣāf, Pūr-i Bahā) unsuccessful attempts at realism. But when Maulavī wrote verses in Turkish, or Qāsimu'l-anvār in Gīlānic or Azerbayjanian, they were addressing themselves to the masses (Bertel's, IPTL, 524). *
4. An ancient, almost pure Persian is purposely employed in the heroic epic (Firdausī, Asadī, and others). Among later poetry and prose writers the names may be mentioned of Davānī (p. 314), Yaghmā (p. 334), Vaqār (cf. NDAT, 7, 1334, 327); other examples of this extremely 'pure' Persian (*pārsī-i sāda*) could easily be found.
5. 'Some Notes' (B VIa).
6. Bertel's, *Nizami*, 39 *et seq.*
7. *İA*, 1, 640a. Cf. also W. Ivanow (B VIa).
8. Ivanow, *Tabaqat* (B VIb).
9. A. Mirzoyev, *Binoī*, 416.
10. Ḥāfiẓ, ed. Brockh., No. 572; ed. Rosenzweig, 3, pp. 227–8; ed. Qazvīnī-Ghanī, No. 438. Adīb Ṭūsī, *Du ghazal* (B VIb). Sa'dī, *Gulistān*, ed. R. M. Aliyev, 22. M. J. Maḥjūb, *Vīs u Rāmīn*, 20_2.
11. Ghanā, Baḥth, 1, 313.
12. *Ibid.*, 1, 123.
13. Adīb Ṭūsī, *Fahlaviyyāt*.
14. Cf. 'Dar bāra-i taghyīr-i khaṭṭ-i fārsī', *Sukhan*, 11, 1339, 3–7; see also RK 3, 1339, 128, No. 91: Jalāl Āl-i Aḥmad, *Chand nukta dar bāra-i khaṭṭ va zabān-i fārsī*, 1339.
15. *Haft Paykar*, ed. Ritter-Rypka, 6, 24 *et seq.*
16. *Pers. Lit.*, 222.
17. Bartol'd, 'K istorii krest'. dvizheniy' (B II), 61–2: "The economic struggle between the various elements of the urban population and in particular between the town and the village." For the character of the anti-Abbasid revolts, cf. Minorsky, 'Iran', 184 (B II).
18. Tardov, *Ferdousi*, 142.
19. Minorsky, 'Iran', 196, 199_4, 200. A good survey is given by N. D. Miklukho-Maklay, *Shī'izm* (B III). For a detailed account of the Shī'a parties cf. Ṣafā, 'Firaq-i shī'a' (B III). One has of course to take an unprejudiced view of the Shī'a in relation to individual pre-Safavid poets.
20. Cf. Abdullah, *The Value* (B IV), 4 *et seq.*
21. Regarding the Ottomans cf. Ettore Rossi, 'Parafrasi turca del "De Senectute" ... (1559)', *RANL*, 1937, Ser. VI, vol. XII, fasc. 7–10.
22. Cf. Shiblī, 4: 165, 169, 171.
23. Ritter, *Die Bilderspr.*, 7, 44.
24. *Ibid.*, 57_1.
25. Mīr Afḍalī, *Rūzgār-i nau*, 5/3, 53, holds the same opinion.
26. Abdullah, *op. cit.*, 2.
27. *The Spirit* (B VIa), 101 *et seq.*
28. Sabk, 2, pp. 69, 119, 248, 270, 299 *et seq.* etc., in almost every analysis of each period and of separate works.
29. *Pers. Lit.*, 224–229.
30. Cf. Kuka (B VIa) and Yār-Shāṭir, *Shi'r* (*ibid.*), 234 *et seq.*
31. The cruel Beloved was often called *Turk*, cf. Ritter, *Das Meer*, 365; Yār-Shāṭir, *op. cit.*, 153, 157

etc. On the Turkish male Beloveds see Ṣafā 2, 71 *et seq.*; Shiblī, 4, 145; 5, 58. 'Love' in the course of the centuries, Ritter, *op. cit.*, 369. The lover as *sag*, 'dog': I. Braginskiy, *Ocherki*, 247; Bausani, *Storia* (B v), 457; cf. below, pp. 295. *et seq.*

32. This does not contradict Maimanat Mīr Ṣādiqī's article 'Āzāda va āzādagān', *Sukhan*, 11, 1339, 793–802. *

33. von Grunebaum, 'The Concept' (B iv), German in *Kritik und Dichtkunst*, Wiesbaden 1955, 100 *et seq.*, Vaḥīd's essays Arm. 7, 201; 8, 244, 275; 15, 633; 21, 201; Shiblī, 4^2, 106 *et seq.*

34. Ritter, *Die Bilderspr.*, 36 *et seq.* Cf. below, p. 270, and H. Massé, *Le roman de Wîs et Râmîn*, 14.

35. *Ibid.*, 29.

36. Cf. above, note 31.

37. In Bausani's sympathetic inquiry, *Storia* (B v), 408 *et seq.*, it is a question of inoffensive customs. Important evidence: Shams-i Qays, *Al-Muʿjam* (B iv), 306, according to which eros in the *ghazal* refers only to the woman. An undoubtedly concrete case of a beautiful woman: Bertel's, IPTL, 453.

38. Shiblī, 4, 142–4, 149, 156, points out how great was the influence on the Persian stock of expressions of the former policy of war, the fondness for the chase, etc. This character is also reflected in the similes and metaphors, but in the further course of development after the second half of the 6th/12th century – and particularly after the Mongol-Tatar invasions (4, 156–7) – it underwent a change.

39. Cf. O. L. Vil'chevskiy, 'Noviy istochnik' (B ii) based on a MS dated 584/1188 on the anti-feudal spirit of the urban population.

40. Bertel's, *Tarzi Afshar*, 122.

41. Antol.[1], 8.

42. I. Reisner, 'K voprosu' (B ii).

43. W. E. Hocking: von Grunebaum, *Med. Islam* (B ii), 343.

44. Very appositely stated by Al. Bausani, *Storia* (B iv), 51: not a direct expression of emotion but disguised.

45. LHP 2, 86.

46. Cf. Annemarie Schimmel, 'Alman gözüyle divan edebiyatı', *ADTD*, xi/2–3, 1953, 355 *et seq.*

47. *Taʾrīkh-i adabiyyāt* (B v), 335.

48. Less categorical: V. F. Minorsky, 'Tekstï persidskikh klassikov', *KS*, 65, 1964, 105–111.

49. Arm. 18, 81 *et seq.*; 8, 77; 19, 291.

50. Ḥaydar against Khvājū: Krïmskiy, 3, 104; idem, *Khafïz*, 16; Ghanī, *Baḥth*, 1, 375.

51. *Tarānahā* (B via), 1, 98 *et seq.*, rsp. 2, 168.

52. *Taḥqīq* (B iv), 38 *et seq.*

53. Bahār, *Shiʿr* (B via), 71, where the former *dīvān* is described as a valuable work of poetry.

54. 'K fol'kloru Tajikistana. Epicheskaya traditsiya u Tajikov', *Trudï Tadzh. Bazï*, AN SSSR, St.-L., 3, 1936; 'Ustnïy epos Tajikistana', *Al'manakh "Druzhba narodov"*, 1, M. 1939, 299 *et seq.*

55. Miller, *O dialekte.*

56. J. Rypka, 'La métrique' (B iv).

57. A diametrically opposite view is held by von Grunebaum, *Kritik* (B iv), 18, who regards the exact reverse as plausible, viz. Persian influence on the technical refinement of the early Arabic-Mesopotamian poetry. "At least two, possibly three of the metres by which the poetry of the Land between the two Rivers is distinguished, the *ramal*, the *mutaqārib* and maybe also the *khafīf*, might be considered as adaptations of Persian (*pahlavī*) metres to satisfy the demands of the Arabic language."

58. An exception is Shihāb (d. 1215/1800), see p. 309.

59. Nöldeke, 'Über den vokal. Nachhall' (B iv), 494 *et seq.*

60. Shiblī, 4, 92 *et seq.* draws attention to several irregularities in the ancient poets and the consequent unavoidable doubling of the consonant.

61. Bertel's, *Tarzi Afshar*, 123.
62. Yu. N. Marr in the essay 'Vïrazheniye fonetiki stikha...' (B IV), 139. I am not aware whether the 'Predvaritel'noye soobshcheniye o Terzi Afshare' (mentioned in the same work, p. 140), that is based on Tamaddun's article (*Īrānshahr*, 3, 721–8) and in which Marr cites further proofs for *baḥr-i ṭavīl*, has in fact been published. From my own notes I quote the following examples: Nāṣir-i Khusrau, *Baḥr-i ṭavīl*, 'a prose romance' (?), Lith. Khair-ābād 1292/1875 (Arb.); *Dīvān-i Ṣāmit*, Lith. Tehran 1348/1930, 2–11; Farrukhī, Arm. 6, 493–5.
63. Viṣāl (d. 1262/1845–6) was already reproached with similar slackness, see *NDAT*, 7, 1334, 221, line 3.
64. The satire (*hajv*, *hajviyya*, see p. 84) or rather the libellous poem, is directed against the enemies of the patron or of the poet, frequently against the patron himself as soon as he becomes niggardly with regard to remuneration or tardy in paying it.
65. Chaykin, *Asadī*, 149.
66. Cf. Shiblī, 5, 2–18, where an attempt is made to show the development of the *qaṣīda*. Its progress in the period from Kamāl Ismā'īl up to Salmān Sāvajī: *ibid.*, 2, 5. Recently A. J. Arberry, *CPL*, 8–12, where Arabic examples of several varieties of the Persian *qaṣīda* are quoted. But the Persians also had influence on the development of the Arabic *qaṣīda*, cf. von Grunebaum, *Kritik* (B IV), 2: pleasant scenes taken from the *qaṣīdas* of al-A'shā, a contemporary of the Prophet and one of the great masters of the Arabic *qaṣīda*, reveal Sasanian inspiration.
67. Kyrupaideia, ed. A. Hug, Lpz. 1900, ed. min. ster.: 1/2, 1; 1/4, 25; 11/2, 13; Strabon, ed. H. Meineke, Lpz. 1866, ed. min. ster.: XV 733, 18 (to which Mrs. Dr. R. Dostálová kindly drew my attention).
68. Shiblī, 5, 89; Krïmskiy, 3, 98. Poets such as Ẓahīr Fāryābī are not ashamed to cadge unabashed: Shiblī, 2, 181.
69. For far more moderate and certainly fair views see M. I. Zand, *Shest' vekov* (B V), 44 *et seq.*
70. Cf. Bibl. *s.v.* Findariskī (philosophy); Vaṣṣāf (poetics); Qivāmī Ganjavī, LHP 2, 47–76 (poetics); 'Abdu'llāh Jauharī (alchemy); F. Meier, *Mahsatī*, 61; Sanā'ī's *qaṣīda* with a list of birds: Bert., IPTL, 86, 439.
71. But also already earlier, e.g. Ḥasan Ghaznavī, cf. I. S. Braginskiy, 'O vozniknovenii' (B VIa), 97; Niẓāmī: cf. J. Rypka, *Chand ghazal*, No. 12, 14, 19.
72. LHP, 3, 293 = Shiblī, 2, 188; on the development of the Persian *ghazal* in detail: Shiblī, 5, 27 *et seq.*; 4, 96 *et seq.*
73. Bertel's, *Pers. poez. v Bukh.* (B VI a), 32.
74. Ateş, *İA*, *s.v.* 'Gazel'.
75. Arberry, *Ḥāfiẓ*[1], 22: mentioned only as a traditional possibility. Regarding poetry and song or music: *ibid.*–Well summarised by F. Meier, *Mahsatī*, 85 *et seq.* – I. S. Braginskiy, *K vozniknovenii gazeli* (B IV) 94 *et seq.*, persists in the opinion that the *ghazal* was an independent art form as early as the 10th century, as against the view of A. M. Mirzoyev, *Rūdakī*, 71 *et seq.* (Russian 66 *et seq.*) who assumes a gradual development from lyrical poems, but does not regard the *ghazal* as having originated in the *nasīb* of the *qaṣīda*. I consider the latter theory as correct, for lyrical verse must already have existed, parallel with music, before the panegyric *qaṣīda*. But is this controversy not merely one of terminology? Mirzoyev traces the course of the *ghazal* and shows how, beginning with Rūdakī, it gradually took shape and was transformed through the centuries, mainly under the influence of the stormy development of the towns at the time of the Seljuqs, to which Ye. E. Bertel's has already drawn attention. In the 10th century it had not yet taken on the form known to us today, yet the lyrical verses it contained became more and more clearly characterised by certain specific peculiarities: the independence of the individual verses and the *takhalluṣ*. Whereas in the earliest lyrical poems (*ghazals*) the verses are connected with each other, later on they become independent. In the 10th century, he upholds, there was no independence of the verses as regards content, not even in the 13th century was this always so. Still he discerns a rational and logical connection in Sa'di

(13th century). This was to be otherwise in the case of Ḥāfiẓ (14th century) where the relation was so weak that one could omit verses or alter their sequence without damaging the poem as a whole. But in spite of this Mirzoyev does not admit that in Ḥāfiẓ, apart from a purely formal unity, there is no connection at all between the verses – he considers the subject-matter as a whole to form a unity. In his opinion this circumstance gives Ḥāfiẓ the opportunity for a greater variety of thought than was the case with his predecessors.–The second peculiarity is the *takhalluṣ*: at first we do not find it occurring at all, but gradually its use becomes a rule though it is not yet regularly inserted in the last verse, this latter custom being first introduced by Ḥāfiẓ.

76. 'Des Grafen von Platen...', 4, 149.

77. Lescot, *Chronol.*, 61 (= 5 off-print); Arberry, *op. cit.*, 29; idem, *Orient Pearls*, 704 *et seq.*; Wickens, *The Persian Conception*, 239.

78. Shiblī considers this phenomenon a disadvantage (5, 57). He imagines the circumstances to be such that the poet is unwilling to let any of the ideas arising in his mind escape him; as opposed to the diffuseness of European poets, the Iranian compresses each thought into a single verse (2, 245). Of a uniform nature is the *ghazal* of Niẓāmī (Bertel's, *Nizami*², 1956, 237), and of Sa'dī ("to the point of exhaustion of the theme set up at the beginning", Arm. 19, 421).

79. Ṣafā, 2, 348. On the value of the improvisation see Shiblī, 4, 121 *et seq.*

80. Bausani, *Storia* (B v), and previous to him T. Kowalski and M. F. Köprülüzade, consider the possibility of the quatrain's having been of Turkish origin. Bausani's 'La quartina', *ibid.* 527 *et seq.*, is a thorough and original analysis of this form of poetry. Bertel's, IPTL 549 *s.v.* '*rubā'ī*', contributes a large number of valuable considerations to the history of the development of the *rubā'ī*. F. Meier, in a recent and penetrating study, *Mahsatī* 1–27, takes nevertheless a critical attitude towards the above opinion regarding the origin of the quatrain and is inclined rather to accept evidence of Arabic influence (p. 12).

81. F. Meier, *Mahsatī*, 22.

82. The word *dīvān* as implying a collection of poetry, is of comparatively modern usage. The earlier use of the word indicated a collection of written works, whether of poetry or prose (W. Ivanow, *Problems*, 70). It is interesting to note that in the mediaeval literature of the Kurds, which was closely related to Ṣūfism, it became the custom for pupils to use the *takhalluṣ* of their masters and to incorporate their verses in the latters' *dīvāns* (O. L. Vil'chevskiy, 'Noviy istochnik', 103).

83. *Chronol.* 61 (= 5 off-print).

84. 'Die ält. Dichtungen' (B VI a), 239.

85. 'The increment poem', LHP 2, 43; 'Zusetzling', Rückert-Pertsch (B IV), 80.

86. al-Jāḥiẓ: Daudpota, *The Influence* (B VI a), 60.

87. Eberman, 'Persï' (B VI a), 126, 153; and A. J. Arberry, *Pers. Lit.*, 202; cf. also Zarre, *Ocherk* (B V), 56.

88. Chaykin, *Asadi*, 133 *et seq.*

89. On Arabic poems in the *mathnavī* form, called by the Arabs *muzdavij* (short verses, usually in the *rajaz aa bb* etc.), see von Grunebaum, *Islam* (B II), 180 and idem, *Kritik* (B IV) 24: a form that was adopted by the Arabs from the later period of Sasanian poetry round about the year 700.

90. Shiblī is of the opinion that the essential characteristics of Persian didactic poetry are not sufficiently appreciated by Europeans in that the latter ignore the difficult and restricted conditions on which didactic poetry is founded (5, 141 *et seq.*) and forget how carefully the poet had to tread in order to be able to find a suitable expression in face of the violence and wickedness of the upper classes (*ibid.*, 143 *et seq.*).

91. Cf. *Calligraphers and Painters* by Cāḍī Aḥmad, son of Mīr Munshī (ca. A.H. 1015/A.D. 1606), transl. by V. Minorsky, Washington 1959, 17 *et seq.* Versified treatises on diverse branches of learning are further dealt with in professor Tauer's section of the present work.

92. *Teatr*, 30 *et seq.* (Bibl. F) according to Ett. Rossi–Al. Bombaci, *Elenco di drammi religiosi persiani*,

Città del Vaticano 1961, p. XV, since the end of the 18th century.

93. Yet already in Rūdakī, *JRAS*, 1926, 222 v. 75, and I. S. Braginskiy, 'O vozniknovenii gazeli' (B VIa), 98.

94. Nöldeke, *Das iran. Nationalepos*, 147. When it occurs in Rūdakī it is certainly a forgery, cf. Mirzoyev, *Rudaki* (Russ. 1958), 10 *et seq*.

95. Daudpota, *The Influence* (B VI a), 64.

96. 'Persī' (B VIa), 126, 153. Bertel's, IPTL, 519, gives evidence of the *takhalluṣ* in the Ṣūfī lyric as early as the 5th/11th century. Seeing that the Ṣūfī poets, if they were town-dwellers, had close relations with craftsmen, Bertel's has in mind an analogy with the custom prevalent among these latter of signing their works by name. Al. Bausani, *Storia* (B V), 408, inclines to the supposition brought forward by A. Ateş according to which the origin of the *takhalluṣ* should be sought in emotional self-exhortation of the poet in Ṣūfī lyric poetry.

97. Bibl. *s.v.* 'Ṣafā'ī'.

98. Theoretically this is already considered necessary by Ibn al-Mu'tazz (d. 908); cf. Arberry, *CPL*, 11, and J. Rypka, *Forma* (B VI a).

99. Far-fetched, imaginary comparisons, based purely on phantasy, are characteristic of Azraqī (born c. 465/1072, p. 195). He was unjustly censured for this by his contemporaries and was in this respect a predecessor of 'Am'aq and especially of Bīdil and other poets of the 'Indian' movement (cf. Al. Bausani, *Note su Mirzā Bedil* (E VII), 192, Note 2.

100. I cannot agree with Shiblī when he asserts that Salmān Sāvajī was the first to contribute to the greater spread of this figure (2, 236 *et seq.*), for we already find it occurring frequently in works of the earliest Persian poets.

101. Goethe, 115.

102. From the very beginning of their creative period the poets perform with such accomplishment that "time passes and the quality of the poet's verse remains constant" (Hādī Ḥasan, *Researches* [B VIa], 56 *ad vocem* Falakī).

103. 'Persī' (B VI a), 137.

104. Horn, *Gesch. der pers. Lit.* (B V), 50 *et seq*.

105. von Grunebaum, 'The Aesth. Foundation' (B IV), 326.

106. Kowalski, *Na szlakach islamu* (B VIa), 109 *et seq*. Cf. above p. 81 *et seq*.

107. *Beobachtungen* (C), 167.

108. E. Bethe, *Einl. in die Altertumswissenschaft*, ed. A. Gercke & Ed. Norden, Lpzg.-B., 1, 1912, 296.

109. A. Kasravī sees in the classics an obstacle to the development of a modern literature, and therefore recommends that the former should be forgotten: Bibl. *s.v.* 'Kasravī', '*Ḥāfiẓ*'.

110. A contrary view is supported by Sayyid Abu'l-Qāsim Injū-i Shīrāzī in his anthology *Safīna-i ghazal*, Tehran 1336, where he holds that traditional forms cannot be a hindrance to the further development of Persian poetry because the value of any artistic work is dependent on the profundity of its contents (PV 1959/2, 246).

111. Bertel's, *Pers. poez. v Bukh.* (B VI a), 25.

112. Rypka, *Bāqī als Ghazeldichter*, Pr. 1926, 76.

113. On reality (*vāqi'iyyat*) in the *ghazal* see Shiblī, 5, 60. The same author alleges (5, 50) that faint signs of the phenomenon can already be found in Khusrau and Sa'dī; the realistic movement, he avers, was started under Ṭahmāsp I by Sharaf-jahān and found more support than did that of Fighānī.

114. *Die Bilderspr.*, 1, and elsewhere.

115. LHP, 1, 274 *et seq.*, 341 and elsewhere; Bertel's, *Pers. poez. v Bukh.* (B VI a), 55_1.

116. *Die Bilderspr.*, 21; 2.

117. *The Influence* (B VI a).

118. LHP, 1, Index *s.v.* 'Greece'; Schaeder, 'Die isl. Lehre' (B VI a), 192–201; idem, 'Der Orient und das griech. Erbe', *Die Antike*, 4, 1928, 226–65; von Grunebaum, 'Islam and Hellenism', *Scientia*,

44, 1950 (= von Grunebaum, *Islam*, 1955, 159–67); idem, 'The Aesth. Foundation' (B IV), 323 *et seq.*
119. Daudpota, *l.c.*, 65.
120. *Die Bilderspr.*, 4.
121. *Ibid.*, 55.
122. *Ibid.*, 56.
123. 'Das Prinzip der beziehungsreichen Bildwahl', *ibid.*, 25, 44, 50, 57.
124. *Ibid.*, 6 *et seq.*, 14.
125. *Enveri*, p. x *et seq.*; Shiblī, 4, 112 *et seq.*, 117 *et seq.*
126. This is also made clear by the 'prison poems' (*ḥabsiyya*) of the most famous poets. Regarding the position of the poets at the court in the 4th–6th/10th–12th century, see Falsafī (B VIa), 159–180.*
127. Cf. *idhā taghayyara's-sulṭānu, taghayyara'z-zamānu*, 'a change of sultan brings a change of the times'. The *Marzubān-nāma*, ed. Muḥ. Qazvīnī 19, p. 21; cf. also Ye. E. Bertel's, 'Lit. na pers. yazïke' (D IIa), 203 (= in German transl. 185, "4"). I. S. Braginskiy divides it into centuries in 'K probleme periodizatsii istorii persidskoy i tadzhikskoy literatur', *Trudï XXV mezhdun. kongressa vostokovedov*, II. M. 1963, 349–56.
128. *GIPh.*, 317 *et seq.*
129. *Philol.* VII and IX (B VIa, b).
130. Bertel's, 'Lit. na pers. yaz. v Sr. Az.' (D IIa) 200 *et seq.* Cf. Shiblī, 4, 112 *et seq.*, 117 *et seq.*
131. Bahār, *Bāz-gasht* (B VIa); Nafīsī, Foreword to *Shāh-kārhā* (C).
132. Bahār, *ibid.*, 444, 446, 448.
133. Ṣafā, 2, 344, regards the poetic style of the second half of the 6th/12th century as being the forerunner.
134. Thus at least in India, cf. Bahār, *ibid.*, 446.
135. I very much regret not having been able at least to 'touch up' the above classification according to the essay of A. N. Boldïrev and I. S. Braginskiy, 'Soobrazheniya o periodizatsii klassicheskoy persidsko-tadzhikskoy literaturï', *NAA*, 1965/2, 100–110. This essay would seem to conclude the erstwhile attempt at periodisation by these Soviet scholars. I therefore earnestly recommend it to the attention of the reader.
136. In the introduction to his translation of *Būstān* (p. XXI *et seq.*) K. Chaykin regards the second half of the C-period, with Niẓāmī and 'Aṭṭār at the summit, as a period of decline and points to the acute social-economic crisis in Iran during the same epoch – a crisis which led to the Mongol occupation. The social conditions before and after the Mongol invasion gave rise to a new style, the exponents of which associated themselves (in the case in point the author of *Būstān*) with the old tradition, already forgotten by their immediate predecessors.
137. This estrangement, that began under the Safavids and in course of time led finally to the literature of Tajikistan becoming independent, is considered by M. I. Zand, in his thorough-going review of our book (*SV*, 1957/6, 150–55), to constitute a more decisive turning-point in the division into periods than the Mongol invasion. He would therefore prefer to place the beginning of the B-period at this bifurcation.
138. *Sabk*, 2, p. "j".
139. On this work *ibid.*, 3, 371.
140. *Ocherk* (B V), 26.
141. *GIPh.*, 213 *et seq.*; TL, 1, 781–923.

II. THE BEGINNINGS OF PERSIAN LITERATURE

A. THE ARAB OCCUPATION

The origin of Persian literature is shrouded in a dense mist that for a long time appeared to be impenetrable. That a remarkable insight into the subject has been obtained in recent years is the result of research, based on more or less fortuitous fragments or incidental references in ancient Arabic writers; further thanks to newly discovered records connected with the very earliest periods; and finally the improved methods used in examining the material we have inherited.

Persian literature begins at the time of the downfall of the Sasanian empire, brought about by the Arab invasion, under the omen of Islam in its initial stages, though in point of fact there is evidence of its existence somewhat earlier. But it is wrong to attribute its coming into being exclusively to Islam, the influence of which was felt increasingly later on. The Persian kingdom of the Sasanians, although outwardly a great power, succumbed all too rapidly under the Arab assault. It had become vulnerable partly as a result of the continual and exhausting struggle against Byzantium and the Hephthalites, partly owing to the disturbed situation at home. Internal disintegration was caused by peasant uprisings, the outcome of long-continued subjugation and constant warfare; and while all this was going on below, palace revolutions were taking place at the top. Moreover the knights, who formed the foundation of the Sasanian state, were already yielding to the power of the monarch. The Arab invasion bore the character of a rapacious conquest, a result of the fusion of the Arabs, united in Islam, under the leadership of the merchant aristocracy. It was not in vain that penniless intruders sought out countries which abounded in wealth of all kinds. Pillaging continued under the Umayyads and the oppression of the nation increased. The equality of rights proclaimed by Islam soon showed itself to be but mere propaganda; the masses of the people were further exploited by taxation, for the feudal system of the Sasanian period was simply carried on by the new rulers under a different flag: Sasanian despotism acquired under the Caliphs the appearance of a feudal-theocratic state. The principle of canonic democracy became subordinated to this form but at the same time it caused the downfall of the old aristocracy. The Sasanian knighthood suited neither the Arabs nor Islam, and was therefore doomed to be gradually absorbed into the lower classes. In addition it was becoming more and more threatened by the pressure of the steadily expanding towns.[1] When thanks to the eastern Iranian revolt under the leadership of Abū-Muslim power came into the hands of the Abbasids, the Iranian influence on matters concerning the Caliphate became far-reaching and the economic situation of Iran improved, but the condition of the agrarian serfs showed no change and peasant risings were constantly breaking out.[2]

The Arab victory brought with it the destruction of the Sasanian empire, but this same fate did not befall Persian culture. But there is no doubt that it constituted the greatest revolution in the whole history of Iran; many institutions were ruined, many took a new turn. Yet let us not lay the blame for all disaster on the aggressors and occupying forces alone, for to be quite fair we must charge a considerable portion of the cultural losses and the further consequences of the radical change to the Iranian proselytes themselves. We may even go to the point of regarding the Arab conquest as not entirely a misfortune. A. Zarre[3] observes that the Caliphate, by uniting the various Iranian districts under a common flag – thus binding them together economically – indirectly contributed to the spread of Persian to territories where hitherto other Iranian languages had been in use.

With the exception of religion the Arabs had nothing to offer. The Persians on the other hand had much to give, for after the catastrophe brought about by Alexander and the further progress of Hellenism they underwent under the Sasanians a national unification and rebirth, built up on the strongly accentuated principle of Mazdaïsm, which was continually stirred into flame by the fanatical priesthood, exactly as occurred *mutatis mutandis* more than one thousand years later under the Safavids. The Arabs had no need to spread the new faith by means of the sword; the intolerance of the Zoroastrian priesthood, manifold common factors in the elementary religious ideas of Parsism and Islam, the hatred on the part of the oppressed and the confused state of the country as a whole – wearied moreover by dynastic strife – were all grist to their mill. There was also a great disparity between rich and poor, between powerful and weak; there was of course social strife (Mānī, Mazdak), which gained in force as a result of the increasing austerity of feudalism and its burden which fell ultimately on the shoulders of the most needy. The everlasting wars of the Sasanians led inevitably to heavy taxation of the people. The urban population, part of the ambitious aristocracy and of the intelligentsia were, in addition to avowed malcontents, the first to accept the doctrine of Muḥammad. It was not Allah they were seeking, but advantage: the desire for material gain or the natural wish to remain in power drove them into the arms of the conquerors, who at first welcomed everyone willing to place himself on their side and gave him a reward because they had need of supporters. So many flocked to his side that Caliph ʿUmar I is said to have been alarmed. Nevertheless they were followers in name only, for not until the following generation did the population really become Moslem. Although this meant a great step 'forward' in the spreading of the new religion and all that it implied, neither financial pressure nor the effort towards active collaboration was for a long time able to fill the still considerable breaches, the less so when the proselytes began to realise that the new doctrine of faith promised more than it gave. The loudly proclaimed equality of its converts with the Arabic rulers soon proved to be a flagrant lie; proselytes advanced only in the ranks of the *mavālī*, 'clients', and this social disappointment certainly proved a setback to hopes and desires. The small land-owners (*dihqāns*) and a portion of the people, particularly in outlying and hardly accessible districts, remained true for a long time to the faith of their fathers, some – the materially secure – from a sense of national pride, others in virtue of an obstinate persistence, strengthened in its steadfastness by the priesthood, which was nevertheless gradually losing its supremacy though not its influence. As B. Spuler[4] convincingly shows, there was need of "a real inner impulse to eliminate Zoroastrianism definitively. It had its origin just as much in mysticism as in the religious ethics of the Shīʿa in their attitude of opposition to the State at that time."

In spite of all the 'peaceful penetration' on the part of Islam, we must not imagine that the situation in the occupied country was idyllic. In point of fact excesses were perpetrated frequently by both sides. It is certainly not by chance that the history of the years 682 and 697[5] records the exodus of a large number of adherents of Zoroastrianism to the islands of Hormuz and Diu, and thence later on to Sanjan. Nonetheless in due course Islam succeeded in taking root so deeply that at last only very vague memories of the past remained. But it was soon evident that a highly developed culture is far too powerful a factor to be concealed or eventually to disappear entirely – an analogy to "Graecia capta ferum victorem cepit et artes intulit agresti Latio". Although the political subjugation of Iran was actually completed in a very short time, Persian cultural supremacy did not yield; at the most it can be said to have changed its form. For a long time the old social structure continued to exist, the Sasanian bureaucratic order remained and with it the Persian bureaucrats; for half a century after the invasion tax registers were kept in the Persian language because the Arabs, in their primitive state of social development, were not capable of providing the necessary management.

I. THE ANCIENT CULTURE AND ITS CONTINUATION

The geographical position was decisive for the preservation of the national culture. Of course the western regions, situated as they were nearer to or in the immediate vicinity of the Arab centres, were the first to suffer defeat. The provinces on the Caspian Sea kept up their independence for a long time, but their position did not allow of their becoming a centre in the evolution of the national cultural life of Iran. The most important, though differing, rôles were played by the distant and vast Khurasan, together with Central Asia, and the inaccessible Fars. The north-eastern regions, which had held out obstinately against the Umayyads, became the main fulcrum of the Abbasids, by whose accession to the throne the Iranian element acquired a decisive influence in the empire of the Caliphs and its cultural life. The preservation of the old civilisation is referred to in a notice about the 'Persian' library in Merv at the beginning of the 3rd/9th century, for an acquaintance with its treasures was considered also by Arab scholars to be indispensable. Outwardly less pugnacious, but in the preservation of the ancient culture uncommonly conservative, was the mountainous district of Fars, where, together with the old tradition, the fire-altars and fortresses of the patriotic nobles were kept up for a long time. There it was possible for many elements of Persia's past to find refuge. As late as the 4th/10th century Ḥiṣnu'l-Jiṣṣ was still standing in the district of Arrajān, in which it is alleged that manuscripts containing the history and portraits of Persian kings and high dignitaries, all fire-worshippers, of the Mūbads and others, the same as those depicted in relief in the rock-carvings near Shapur, were placed and carefully guarded by the garrison of the fortress. This is the interpretation given by K. Inostrantsev and A. Christensen of the relevant passage in the works of Iṣṭakhrī, whereas W. Barthold[6] on the other hand doubts whether Iṣṭakhrī was thinking of a library or archives in the citadel. In his opinion there is no proof of the Arabs having so sought to destroy the ancient culture that its elements had to be hidden away from them in fortresses, and Iṣṭakhrī may rather have had in mind lecture notes based on oral instruction. But according to Barthold such a school was also of importance for the preservation of the true national tradition. Finally the three scholars are in agreement as regards the extreme importance of these records for the history of the preservation of the epic and historical tradition. Cultivated by the priesthood of Fars and guarded by the conservative landed nobility, it thus in literary form survived the fall of the Sasanian kingdom by several centuries. It was to such places that amateurs of Persian antiquity turned for information. There are also other accounts, such as that of Mas'ūdī[7] (303/915–6), who was shown by an eminent person in Iṣṭakhr (Fars) a book containing a notice to the effect that it had been composed in 113/731 from works discovered in the collections of the Persian kings and translated from Middle Persian into Arabic for the Caliph Hishām (724–43). This magnificent volume is said to have contained much information on Persian science, history, architecture and public institutions, and was illustrated with portraits of the Sasanian rulers. In this way at least fragments of Middle Persian literature were saved, but on the other hand a far greater portion passed over into Arabic literature, in which there even came into being a special kind of literature, known as *adab*[8], namely instruction on correct and successful behaviour in any given situation. In Persian garb this portion even found its way back again to Iran ('books of advice', the best-known being

Notes on pp. 137–138

'Aṭṭār's or Sa'dī's *Pand-nāma*), and a considerable quantity of ethical-didactic literature ranging from the prosaic *Qābūs-nāma* to the highly artistic *Gulistān* etc.[9] Meanwhile *adab* was not the only domain of the Iranian mind in Arabic literature. It is true that A. J. Arberry[10] emphasises the impossibility of isolating specific Persian (Iranian) elements in Arabic culture and literature because Arabic culture was a confluence of many streams, and already in Sasanian literature we are not even able to separate the Greek and the Aramaic contribution with certainty. Nevertheless there is not the slightest doubt concerning the powerful contribution made by the Persians to the Arabic conception of history. In similar manner the Persians paid their share to geography, administration, ceremonial, biography, exegesis, dogmatics, jurisprudence, and in large measure to mysticism, all of which should be seen not as outstanding individual achievements only but above all as the fruit of ancient Iranian culture. It is to be regretted that the Iranian traditional literature in Islam and in the Arabic translation has only been preserved in incidental fragments or in mere titles – the information thus gained being generally of all the greater importance. And not even this much would have come down to us had it not been for the appearance of the Shu'ūbiyya (the party of adherents to the doctrine of the superiority of the non-Arabs to the Arabs), a movement in which the hitherto subjugated Persian nation was able to raise its head, this time entirely under the cloak of Islam, and proudly point to Iran's illustrious past – as it certainly had every right to do. Thus the Iranians gradually became reconciled to the new religion, though not to the loss of their independence and specific national character.

The view that the old literature had died out before the new came into existence, as if the invasion had torn away the threads of Persian literature leaving a gap of at least a hundred and fifty years, if not even more, is a serious error. The ancient literary traditions did not disappear, but lived on; for in certain poetic turns of expression, occurring in Xenophon[11], there is an obvious affinity to be found between Achaemenid antiquity and Persian custom, via the Sasanians, right up to modern times! Middle Persian literature progresses undisturbed in the hands of the Zoroastrian priesthood and devotees, imbued of course with a religious tint; and meanwhile Persian literature has begun to manifest itself. We possess in fact examples of Persian from the 1st/7th century; on the other hand there can be no doubt of the continued existence of folk-literature if we bear in mind that the nation, viz. the masses of the people, preserved its most essential characteristics and went on living in its own way, because the population as a whole had not for a single instant relinquished its mother-tongue. Both these phenomena, namely the continued existence both of literary poetry of the ancient indigenous kind and of folk-poetry, must not be forgotten, for they proved the idea of a 'rebirth' of Persian literature to be a fallacy and merely a fictitious invention of later epochs. It is probable that the converts very soon began using Arabic script; this is a sign of servility but also of an activistic movement. Arabic script, compared with the extremely complicated

Pahlavi, provided a more perfect graphical system and consequently became a better tool of progress. The third movement, represented jointly by the old and new bureaucracy and by the nobility willing to collaborate, followed the new rulers (for a knowledge of the Arabic language was not a matter for the common people) and maintained its rights on the one hand by direct participation in the field of Arabic literature, on the other by introducing Arabic elements into Persian – in neither case, however, immediately after the collapse of the Sasanian empire. The Persian share in the Arabic literary movement had its advantages. In view of the esteem in which poetry was held by the Arabs, the Iranians, by their performance both as poets and as reciters [12], found just in Arabic the best way to free themselves from the humiliating position of *mavālī*, 'clients', for as such they were regarded at the time of the Umayyads even if they embraced the Islamic faith. But in addition to personal advantages there were also those of general value, for in the Arabic language Iranian patriotism found an excellent means of propaganda. It is really astonishing to witness the speed and degree of perfection with which the Iranians mastered the language – by no means an easy one for them – when we consider that a number of outstanding names in Arabic literature of the first ('golden') Abbasid century are Persian. Thus Arabic literature finds its way on to the international stage and loses its originally purely national character. When the adherents of the Shuʿūbiyya write in Arabic, they introduce Iranian subjects and interests into Arabic literature no longer unconsciously but with a purpose. A still greater emphasis was laid on everything Iranian when part of the nobility and the well-to-do classes, who at first had bowed before the new rulers, began to draw away from them when they sensed the advancing downfall of Baghdad – again from the same motives as those that had at first attracted them, namely the preservation of influence and retention of possessions in their own country. *

The polymorphism of Persian literature in this period, as has been shown, increases the task of the literary historian to no slight extent, because, apart from the output of folk-literature, he must trace not only the origin and development of Persian literature as such, but must also include in his examination works belonging to Arabic literature in as far as they are of Iranian authorship, especially because they represent an essential part of Iranian literary production, at least when looking back from a present-day standpoint. Over and above this the scholar must retrace the echo of the Sasanian tradition as revealed in Arabic literature of the same period. As regards the theoretical accuracy of this conception there can be no difference of opinion, but in the realisation of such a far-reaching task there will be many obstacles to be overcome, in the case in point the synoptical character of the present opus. The last two points will therefore be discussed only as far as their main features are concerned. A separate portion of the book, however, will be devoted to folk-literature.

Notes on pp. 137–138

2. THE EXISTENCE OF A MIDDLE PERSIAN POETRY

It was formerly the custom to doubt the very existence of Middle Persian poetry. Nowadays, however, we can furnish examples of it. It is not sufficient to regard Middle Persian literature as an organism incorporating Greek knowledge and elements of Indian culture. Even if at a first glance it may appear from the preserved fragments to consist exclusively of didactic prose, this cannot be the case, seeing that the literature of no nation is complete without poetry. Records have been handed down to us of the poetic oeuvre of Bahrām Gōr (420–38): ʿAufī states that there is an Arabic *dīvān* from his hand, al-Masʿūdī that he wrote numerous Arabic and Persian verses (according to tradition there are some rather dubitable Arabic verses and one single Persian verse which, in the form in which it has been handed down, is unmistakably forged). There are also references to a distich on the wall of the castle Qaṣr-i Shīrīn, dating from the time of Khusrau Parvēz (590–628), to the original form of the romance *Vāmiq u ʿAdhrā*, allegedly dedicated to the Shah Anōsharvān (531–79), and to *Vīs u Rāmīn*, another romance. These references are in themselves sufficient proof of the actual existence of Middle Persian poetry and render an enumeration of further evidence unnecessary. However distorted these pieces of information may be, they may nevertheless not be ignored, and even less rejected, at least if one considers them as an echo of an old tradition, which thus in its own manner intimated that there was in fact poetry in existence at that period. U. M. Daudpota[13] records an account by Abū-Hilāl al-ʿAskarī (d. 395/1004–5) of such a large quantity of poetry of the 'ancient Persians' that it could not even be collected in books. Simultaneously with the decline of the language, Persian poetry is said to have gradually disappeared, leaving behind nothing other than Arabic 'on their tongues'. In a number of Arabic sources and elsewhere special attention is drawn to Nigīsā, Sarkash and Bārbad, evidently names of prominent musicians, singers and also of poets[14] at the court of Khusrau Parvēz (590–628). On official feast-days *surūd-khvāns*, 'singers', sing songs or panegyrics (*surūd-i khusravānī*) in verse-form at the court of the Shāh. The Arabs learn singing and music from Persian men and women, although they do not understand the words. We even possess pieces of genuine Middle Persian poetry. For a number of years a series of eminent scholars has been engaged in the elucidation of the problem of Middle Persian prosody. We already know the main features of such prosody: syllabic principle (verses containing five, six, eight, eleven syllables as main types), quantity non-existent; according to the latest view of W. B. Henning the verses are accentuated and rhymed, though not unconditionally.[15] E. Benveniste[16] considers the metrics of the Avesta, of Middle Persian and of Persian folk-poetry to be closely related, in so far as the last-named is not influenced by scholarly prosody. H. S. Nyberg[17] already earlier pointed to a certain formal connection between Middle Persian and Persian poetry, while Chr. Rempis[18] has now rightly established that the Persian *mathnavī* and Persian strophic poetry originate in Middle Persian. E. Benveniste, and subsequently

Ye. E. Bertel's[19], come to the conclusion that Moslem Iran merely adapted its autochthonous syllabic metrics to quantitative Arabic prosody. Attempts to scan Middle Persian poetry (as a concrete example we may take the New Year's homage paid to the Sasanian ruler by the chief *Mōbad*, contained in the *Naurūz-nāma*, see p. 191) or the earliest Persian verses (e.g. the hymn – in essence certainly pre-Islamic – of the Zoroastrian priests in the fire temple at Karkūy in honour of Hūsh-i Garshāsp, or Ibn-i Murfarrigh's satiric verses, both preserved in the *Sīstān-nāma*) according to the standard of the ancient Arabic *rajaz*[20] are tantamount to the introduction of an entirely foreign and anachronistic element, viz. quantity, into these and similar works. Fakhru'd-dīn Gurgānī (see p. 178) contests on principle the possibility of the existence of Middle Persian poetry as a 'profession' (as he says) because there was ostensibly neither metre nor rhyme. Assuming that we do not yield to doubt as to whether he was acquainted with the *Pahlavī* language at all (and at the most his knowledge cannot have been more than superficial), we shall nonetheless give not the slightest credit to his assertion because, educated as he was in the already fully-developed Arabic-Persian system of metrics, he did not consider verses not conforming to the same prosody as poetry at all. In the same sense ʿAufī and Shams-i Qays, author of a distinguished work on poetics in the first half of the 7th/13th century, consider the songs of Bārbad as being without metre or rhyme – rather too late a testimony to merit serious attention. The fact that so lamentably little Middle Persian poetry has survived, even if we include discoveries which will certainly take place in the future, is due to several causes: the violent convulsions of the state and of religion, continual blows of fate (for – as Vaḥīd Dastgirdī[21] puts it – Iran is the land of political catastrophes), disregard and antagonism on the part of the Moslems towards the ancient poetry, later a revolution in taste, unfamiliarity with the institution of rhapsodists and the lapse of time. Even less would have been preserved had it not been for the Zoroastrian priesthood, by whom books on religion were held to be of such great consequence. Middle Persian profane scripts suffered considerably, a fact very much to be regretted, because there is no doubt that these works in particular would have afforded a more extensive and deeper insight into the content of Sasanian poetry.

3. THE FIRST SPECIMENS OF PERSIAN VERSE. CONTINUITY OF MIDDLE AND PERSIAN VERSE

Let us begin by establishing the fact that, as far as can be ascertained, the first beginnings of Persian literature are to be found in the eastern part of Iran, thus at a distance from Baghdad, the seat of Arabic culture. Some records have come down to us of the first beginnings of Persian poetry, a few verses and names of poets have also been preserved; but despite the great importance of the alas extremely sparse new material thus furnished, they are only adequate for forming a rough impression if need be.[22] As the development of a language is effected by minor changes and gradual transitions, it would be naïve to presuppose an exact date for the division between two periods. This would not be possible even if we had an abundance of specimens at our disposal. At the most we could speak of the first, slightly more distinct signs of the new literature, which does not mean that the older period had come to an end, for the transition is very gradual. We find, moreover, that during the earliest period progress took place in the old native spirit and that the arabising trend only set in later, for no other course of development was logically possible; this applies both to examples of folk- and of literary poetry, anonymous or identified. For the methodical treatment of almost the whole of this material we are indebted to Chr. Rempis[23], who, in exceptionally scholarly manner, has at the same time reconstructed the badly corrupted oldest fragments. These are a couple of anonymous poems dating from the period previous to 21/642, both based on syllable-counting and rhyme, one being a late Middle Persian *mathnavī*, the other early Persian strophes. We thus witness examples of two phases of language evolution taking place without doubt almost simultaneously and in conformity with each other in respect of prosody. Whilst the knell of the old is being sounded, the new sets forth on its course, thus clearly affording a proof of continuity. The picture that subsequently clearly emerges proves that round about the middle of the 3rd/9th century the syllabic principle of Persian poetry begins to yield to the Arabic principle of quantity[24] – not a faultless one at first when compared with the strict rules that were imposed later on – but we see that in the course of the next half-century these imperfections are removed. All this provides a true reflection of the progress of the arabising influences. In a few cases it is impossible to accept the traditional dating without reservation, criticism, and correction. As an example we may take Abū-Ḥafṣ Ḥakīm of Sughd, in whose case Chr. Rempis[25] rightly pronounces judgement in favour of the 1st/7th century in respect of the twelve-syllabic verse which was already unimaginable in the 3rd/9th century. In this assertion he finds support in part of the tradition. The earliest document that can be dated with certainty may be considered to be three (four?) satirical hemistichs by Yazīd b. Mufarrigh al-Ḥimyarī.[26] As the poet died in the year 68/688, it is possible that they date back to the time of the Caliphate of Muʿāviya I (41–60/661–80). Biting sarcasm is also to be found in four verses cited by Ṭabarī, which the inhabitants of Balkh sang on the occasion of the defeat of Asad b. ʿAbdu'llāh in 119/737.[27] Both the former and the latter are monorhyming and contain seven and eight syllables respectively. These may be divided by a caesura but they cannot be compared with the Arabic measure *rajaz*. In all respects the picture conforms with the plan sketched above and is all the more valuable since we are here obviously concerned with poetry that is partly literary, partly popular, both of which varieties thus continue to make use of traditional Middle Persian technique. This truly national popular feature possesses however a still further importance, which should perhaps be brought forward with even more emphasis, namely the content, for it is just this that must have greatly influenced the arabising movement in Persian literature and Arabic literature itself. But in other specimens (800–900) both the metrics and the rhyming rules already begin to suffer defeat by the arabising tendency. The next case is a little less obvious: the identity and the period of the poet are established, though in respect of language and probably also of subject-matter they are at variance with the preserved example. And yet I am of the opinion that ʿAufī's account need not be rejected when he records that in 193/809 ʿAbbās of Merv (d. 200/815–16) greeted the 'Caliph' al-Ma'mūn, a half-Iranian and Iranophile, with a Persian *qaṣīda*, for at that juncture its excessively arabised form must indeed have aroused justified suspicions as to the authenticity of the document. As al-Ma'mūn did not ascend the throne until 198/813, ʿAbbās must still have addressed him as prince. It is immaterial whether this is an error in calculation of time or in the narrative. A greater difficulty is presented by the outward and inward form, which may have been felt by ʿAufī himself, for he remarks that up to the Tahirid and Saffarid period no more *shiʿr-i pārsī*, 'Persian poems', were written. Above all the actual existence of the poet ʿAbbās Marvazī must be emphasised; this is proved by the geographer Ibn Khurdādhbih who preserved two Persian six-syllabic distichs, rhyming in pairs, under the name of Abu'l-Yanbaghī al-ʿAbbās b. Ṭarkhān, the latter being probably none other than the above-mentioned ʿAbbās Marvazī. We owe this ingenious piece of identification to W. Barthold[28], who was the first to draw attention to this passage at all. Let us not reject the good with the bad but take the view that ʿAufī's account is probably authentic, though with the restriction that the *qaṣīda* was fundamentally remodelled and adapted to suit current taste later on when Persian poetry had changed its countenance.

B. THE POETS OF THE TAHIRID AND SAFFARID PERIODS

An important piece of information is contained in a passage from Ṭabarī, but unfortunately it is not followed up by a quotation from the text; Ṭabarī states that from elderly people in Maragha he has heard 'Persian' (*bi'l-fārsiyya*) verses which we may assume to have been syllabic, by Muḥammad b. al-Baʿīth (d. 235/849–50); although in his own time b. al-Baʿīth was esteemed as a poet, he may already have fallen into oblivion in the Samanid period. At the same time it is hereby proved that at this early epoch verse-writers were by no means rare, so that one more or less made no difference. There is also a record of the poet Abu'l-Ashʿath of Qum, likewise in the time of the Tahirids (205–59/820–72). The latter were an admirable dynasty of Khurasanian-Persian descent whose members, simply out of consideration for the purely Persian masses living on their territory and notwithstanding their apparently strong pro-Arab leanings, could not and did not take up such an indifferent or hostile at-

Notes on pp. 137–138

titude towards the Persian language as is frequently supposed. In the advice given to his son, the enlightened aristocrat Ṭāhir demands the most accommodating attitude towards the simple working people. It is true, however, that here the presence of utilitarian motives cannot be denied. About his son ʿAbdu'llāh we learn that during the time he was working in Baghdad, Egypt, etc., he was fond of being surrounded by Arab poets and that he rewarded them generously. As ruler too he adopted the attitude of patron of science and culture for all. He too shows his good-will towards the people, particularly the agrarian element, in spite of all the opposition which, as aristocrat and believer, he set up against the radical social reforms, which were concealed under the cloak of heresy.[29] Ḥanẓala of Bādghīs (d. not earlier than 248/862–3) we find represented by quantitative verse. Then follow the Shīʿite Saffarids (253–90/867–903) who had risen directly from the popular ranks of Sistan. Their rule bore a military character; generous towards their regiments, consciously strict towards themselves, they introduced order into the land. From their period we already possess clearer fragments of a quantitative nature from the works of the poets Muḥammad b. Vaṣīf as-Sijzī (287/900), Bassām Kūrd Khārijī and Muḥammad b. Mukhallad as-Sijzī: in these fragments Arabic verse-metres can easily be recognised, though they are not without defects and possess a freedom which would have been inadmissible in the classics. All this agrees with the theoretical conception of the increasing influence of Arabic models on the activistic movement, which, engaged as it was in attaining a higher degree of perfection, increased its range up to the point where it supplanted the old indigenous technique altogether. In reviewing the preserved texts one must certainly never lose sight of the possibility of corruption and the still greater probability of later 'emendations' or violations, especially when the poetry found its way through the *tadhkiras* or works on poetics (e.g. Fīrūz al-Mashriqī and Abū-Salīk Gurgānī, both belonging to the Saffarid period); this can easily be demonstrated by a poem attributed to Bahrām Gōr (see p. 132), which was originally syllabically measured and subsequently adjusted to quantitative verse.

C. CONTINUOUS FLOW OF LITERATURE. PERSIAN WRITERS IN ARABIC LITERATURE (750–850)

Neither before nor after the beginning of the new era – for as such must the Arab invasion here be regarded – is there an abundant flow of records, at any rate not to the extent that one might wish. Yet there can be no possible doubt as to the continuity of literature during the two phases. Persian poetry follows on directly after Middle Persian, there is no gap between them. Even if we possessed no information on the existence of Middle Persian poetry, we should still be obliged to take it for granted since the most elementary consideration excludes the possibility of the poetical talent manifested by the Iranians after the adoption of Islam having descended like a thunderbolt for the first time under Islam or having been called into existence by the benevolence of Islam. We can at the most admit with H. R. Roemer[30] "that it was Arab domination that gave the Persian mind a new impetus"; yet even this supposition is not needed, for the disproportion between the two periods is merely an optical illusion, arising in the one case from the scarcity and in the other from the later abundance of our sources. The picture is completed by the accounts and conclusions from early Arabic literature, to which the Iranians certainly contributed in the most varied fields, not in the last place in poetry. Its 'Golden Age' reached its final form at the zenith of Abbasid culture (ca. 750–850), to which the Iranians had made an essential contribution, for personalities such as the prose-writer 'Abdu'llāh b. al-Muqaffa' (put to death ca. 142/759–60), the jurist and first of the four orthodox Imāms Abū-Ḥanīfa (d. ca. 150/767), the grammarian Sībavayhī (d. between 166–194/782–809), the sceptic, poet and satirist al-Bashshār b. Burd (put to death 167/783), the poet Abū-Nuvās (d. 198/810)[31] and others can be counted amongst its most shining examples. *

NOTES

1. Barthold, *Shu'ūb.* (B II), 252 *et seq.*, "as an inevitable result of the development of urban life".
2. Ivanov, *Ocherk* (B II), 37 *et seq.*; see also LHP, I, 308–36.
3. *Ocherk* (B V), 44.
4. 'Iran und Islam' (B II), 231.
5. W. Jackson, *GIPh*, II, 698 f.; D. Menant, *Les Parsis*, P. 1898, IX, 12. Conversely A. Pagliaro, *EI*, 3, 1109a.
6. Inostrantsev, *Pers. lit. trad.* (F) 8 f.; Christensen, *L'Iran*² (B II), 68; Barthold, *Shu'ūb.*, 263.
7. Mas'ūdī, *Tanbīh*, BGA 8, 106, l. 5 *et seq.*
8. von Grunebaum, *Islam* (B II), 47; 56; idem, *Med. Isl.*, 250 *et seq.*
9. Arberry, *Pers. Lit.*, 202.
10. *Ibid.*, 205 *et seq.*
11. Xenophon: *ibid.*, 203.
12. Eberman, 'Persī' (B VIa), 114; Daudpota, *The Influence* (B VIa), 38 (cf. nevertheless 6!); Zhukovskiy, *Enveri*, XIII *et seq.*; LHP, 2, 373; Bertel's, *Nizami*, 1956, 125₃. *
13. *The Influence* (B VIa), 2.
14. Not of course quantitative! Cf. Shiblī, 4, 83.
15. Cf. Arberry, *CPL*, 9.
16. 'Le mémorial de Zarêr', *JA*, 1932, 292.
17. 'Ein Hymnus auf Zervān', *ZDMG*, 82, 1928, 225.
18. 'Die ält. Dichtungen' (B VIa), 239.
19. Benveniste, *Le mémorial* 293; Bertel's, *Pers. poez. v Bukh.* (B VIa), 39 *et seq.*
20. *Ta'rīkh-i Sīstān*, ed. Bahār, 37 (6) (tanātanantan-tan); von Grunebaum, 'Eine Bemerkung' (B VIa), 226; Sabk, 2, 240, last line *et seq.*

21. Arm., 5, 342 *et seq.*, and elsewhere.
22. Cf. A. N. Boldïrev, 'Iz istorii' (B IV).
23. Rempis, 'Die ält. Dichtungen', 233. M. Bahār, *Shi'r* (B IV), rich in content, but tendentious and not always clear.
24. M. Bahār, *Shi'r*, 57 *et seq.* quotes four seven-syllabic, unrhymed hemistichs of a poet named Abū-Ṭāhir aṭ-Ṭayyib b. Muḥ. al-Khurāsānī 'Khusravānī' (round about the middle of the 4th/10th century).
25. *Op. cit.*, 220 *et seq.*
26. For further information on him see al-Jurjānī (al-Curcānī), *Die Geheimnisse der Wortkunst*, transl. H. Ritter (B IV), 4 *et seq.* Latest contribution to an interpretation of Yazīd b. Mufarrigh and Muḥ. b. Vaṣīf (see above, p. 136): F. Meier, *Mahsatī*, 9–11.
27. Daudpota, *The Influence*, 5 ("of *rajaz* character").
28. Barthold, *To the Question*, 837, though both here and in the Arab. text incorrectly "Abu't-Taqiyy". Correct are S. Nafīsī, *Rūdakī*, 3, appendix 11 (M. I. Zand); M.-N. Osmanov, *Iz istorii* (B V), 110; cf. further 'A. Iqbāl, 'Du shā'ir-i 'aṣr-i qadīm', *Yaghmā*, 11, 1337, 457–9.
29. Krïms'kïy (Ukr.), I, 29 *et seq.*; ad 'Abdu'llāh b. Ṭāhir, *ibid.*, 36 *et seq.* (41!). Cf. Daudpota, *The Influence*, 172, against LHP I, 346 *et seq.*
30. Roemer, 'Probleme', 97 (= 3 off-print).
31. On Abū-Nuvās' *Fārsiyyāt* see M. Mīnuvī in the bibliography; on the comical aim of his persianising cf. Boldïrev, *op. cit.*, 80. *

III. THE SAMANIDS

(Middle of 3rd/9th century to end of 4th/10th)

With the rise of the Samanids, originally a noble family from Balkh, a dynasty came into power that was not only Iranian but moreover one with pronounced feelings for Iranian legitimacy. Although during the reigns of the two preceding regional dynasties it became evident that the disintegration of the Caliphate had already set in, Baghdad lost its supremacy to a still greater extent at the time of the Samanids. This dynasty formed a focal point for all the creative forces – both political and cultural – of the eastern Iranians, who were striving for independence in a far-lying yet extremely vigorous part of the realm of the Caliph whose power there was merely theoretical. A powerful factor was certainly to be found in the culture of Eastern Iran, which had been left behind by Buddhism in Central Asia and represented a civilisation of a higher order than that in the chivalric state of the Sasanians.[1] The Samanid dominion, which under Ismāʿīl (279–295/892–907) united a large part of Iran, represents the zenith of a Central Asian feudal kingdom, the last reflected splendour of the glory of the Sasanians.[2] A general characterisation is given by A. Yakubovskiy[3]: in the state and local administrative machinery we find a repetition of the Abbasid Caliphate, the same applying to court life and to the constellation of the armed forces. The army consisted of slaves of different nationalities, predominantly Turks, and of proletarian volunteers (*ghāzī*). The old aristocratic families of Iran kept their hold on the large estates almost until the end of the dynasty. It is true that irrigation works enabled large areas of land to be cultivated, but the expenditure thereby involved and the burden on agriculture in general led to an increase in the number of small holdings and to a rural proletariat. These were the foundation stones of the Samanid state, and on them depended the prosperity of the nobles and the wealth of the state treasury. The urban population, which took on a definitive feudal form towards the end of the 4th/10th century, was better off. Crafts, bazaar and caravan trade enjoyed special protection from the Samanids, albeit to the vexation of the nobility. The dynasty attempted to pacify these malcontents by incorporating them into the civil service but was not able to eradicate their fundamental dissatisfaction with the central governmental system. The opposition became more and more marked and the Samanids tried to quell it by seeking support from the aristocracy in the struggle against the mutinous masses, while against the nobility they employed slaves (*ghulām*) from which a new, Turkish aristocracy arose. Although these abuses and revolts ultimately led to the fall of the Empire[4] – the resistance of the Turkish guards and the priesthood was upon the whole insignificant, except in cases when the ruler appeared to them to be insufficiently Sunnitic – yet one cannot deny that the Samanid rule was one of the most successful and was even regarded as ideal by subsequent generations. Thanks to the economic basis and the ambitious policy of the regents and their viziers, cultural life was able to develop in abundance while the intelligentsia was no longer to be found exclusively in the upper classes. Bukhara and Samarkand became centres whose influence was felt far and wide in the Iranian and Turkish world. As regards industry, behind which Chinese influences were at various times at work, particular importance may be attached to the manufacture of excellent paper – a necessary adjunct to a vigorous cultural development. From the biography of Avicenna we learn not only about the magnificent Samanid library, but also of the superabundance of manuscripts, in fact we may conclude by mentioning their relatively low price.

A. LITERATURE IN THE SAMANID PERIOD

It is thus not to be wondered at that under such favourable material conditions a great impetus was given to literary life. The increasing estrangement from Baghdad found an echo in a hitherto unknown number of Persian poets and authors. To express this more succinctly: under the patronage of this dynasty learning and literature, cultivated by both Arabs and Persians, flourished in Transoxania and Khurasan. The Iranians wrote prose in Arabic and verse in both Arabic and Persian. Not until the second half of the Samanid century did the Persian language penetrate into learned prose. Compared with the Buyids in Western Iran, a fundamental difference strikes one here. For although the Buyids only came into power towards the middle of the 4th/10th century, viz. much later than the Samanids, their authority extended right up to the centre of the Caliph's empire; in fact they, the Persian Shīʿites, wielded such influence over the Prince of the Faithful that he became a mere puppet in their hands. On the other hand the yoke of the neighbouring Baghdad with its pro-Arab influence lay so heavily on their shoulders that for a long time Western Iran remained hardly perceptible in the field of Persian literature. But once more we must note the fact that early Persian literature cannot be properly judged or understood without reference to the Arabic, which ran parallel to it. As regards authors of Iranian descent who wrote in Arabic, we are confronted with the unusual phenomenon of a literature written in two languages. And that is not all, for we must constantly bear in mind how essential was the influence of the Iranians on the Arab writers themselves.[5]

I. POINTS OF CONTACT BETWEEN PERSIAN AND CONTEMPORANEOUS ARABIC POETRY. CHARACTER OF THE LATTER. FUNDAMENTAL TRAITS OF THE EARLIEST PERIOD IN PERSIAN POETRY

At this point it will be useful to take a closer look at the character of the Persian poetry of the activistic movement, which under the Samanids took on a definable form, by following the treatise of Ye. E. Bertel's' entitled *Persidskaya poeziya v Bukhare.* Its beginnings and first blossoming fall within the early and middle Abbasid period (750–1000 A.D.).[6] The Iranians receive, but they also have something to give, and through their nationals writing in Arabic they exert a considerable influence particularly on Abbasid literature. Among the elements they receive there can frequently be found much of what they themselves have given or are still giving. The early Persian period falls at the time when the economic position of the Arabs has so altered that the most specific vehicle of expression of the intrinsically national, ancient Arabic literature, namely the Bedouin *qaṣīda,* loses its immediate impact on the settled population of the towns. Meanwhile, however, from the old patterns a fixed canon has come into existence which, already of course ossified and unpliable, is now also applied to the new forms of Islamic society, particularly to urban life. But with the rise of the towns the Persian element intervenes. A compromise takes place, partly by an artificial rendering of the naturalistic nomadic themes and partly by the introduction of new subjects that appeal to the urban upper classes, aristocrats, and rulers. The poet is no longer the herald of his tribe, as was the case with the pre-Islamic Bedouins, but becomes now the spokesman of the privileged classes. The poetry does not for the time being suffer any loss of reality, because it includes in its images all the things in their own surroundings in which those circles could take an interest. On the soil of north-eastern Iran a vigorous literary life soon springs into existence. The grandees of Iran approach the Arab lords first of all by means of the latter's language and take an active part in this movement. But with the weakening of the political power of the Arab rulers they show a tendency towards the *Shuʿūbiyya* and once again towards Iranian nationalism, not so much from purely patriotic motives as because they quite rightly foresee that Baghdad eventually will not be able to forestall the independence of such outlying provinces as Khurasan, Transoxania, and Khvārazm, whose rulers, once independent, will be incapable of evading the influence of the native Iranian population, the latter preferring to confer the right to its former power henceforth on its own aristocracy than on foreign upstarts. The old Iranian nobility, debased as it had been by the Arabs, must therefore endeavour to attain its end in an anti-Arab agreement with the people. Whereas before this turn of the tide the grandees had themselves occupied most of the literary posts, in the course of time the educated classes succeeded in making themselves heard – people well versed in Arabic and later also in Persian poetry, professional poets, *kātibs* ('writers', 'secretaries') from the towns, all of course under the patronage of their masters. The poet has to extol the latter in extravagant panegyrics and to entertain them by depicting scenes from their lives, which revolve around *razm u bazm* ('fighting and feasting'), and to defend them by pouring scorn upon their enemies. In short, he has to dance to the tune of the aristocrats whose bread he eats – bread which could be bitter enough at times, as is evident from many a sigh expressed in verse –, for he lives in constant fear of competition, of falling into disgrace and of old age. Into the immorality of the court and through the door of his fear of the uncertain morrow and of old age, creep the poet's circumspection and – as a consequence and not seldom in union with it – an unworldly, mystical note. Nonetheless, oriental feudal courts continued to be the centres where poetry sprang up and flourished, for a sound economic background has always been an essential condition for the production of literature. It was the task of the court poets to greet their feudal masters with songs of praise on the occasion of public audiences and on Moslem as well as national feast-days, to offer congratulations on important family events, to bewail the dead, to scoff at and scorn the enemy, to accompany their masters on campaigns of war and to the hunt, to enliven drinking parties with song and play, etc. Both sides had equally strong interests – the princes in the propaganda, notably the establishment and extension of their power, the poets in acquiring fame and pecuniary reward, above all the latter. An eloquent example of this state of affairs is given by the following: as soon as the Caliphate began to split up into smaller principalities, the poets and scholars were on the one hand seduced from one court to another, and on the other hand they themselves sought their own advancement. The *ghazal*, which was to become the main vehicle of expression of Persian lyricism a few centuries later, was in these early times not yet in existence. According to Ye. E. Bertel's it owes its origin in the first place to the amatory introduction to *qaṣīdas* when sung in small intimate circles (see p. 95), as opposed to the complete *qaṣīdas* recited before an audience. The singing is an integral element introduced to heighten the effect of such a love-*nasīb*, which in this manner breaks away from the *qaṣīda*, then by degrees rids itself of the singing altogether and becomes the independent *ghazal*. Unfortunately it became all too easily pervaded with homosexuality, but one must constantly bear in mind the influence under which this phenomenon had infiltrated into Arabic poetry at the beginning of the Abbasid era (see p. 86). – Contrary to the supporters of the theory that Persian poetry originated at the courts, I. S. Braginskiy (see p. 122) holds the opinion that the *ghazal* existed in an independent form as early as the 4th/10th century and is derived from folklore. It is at any rate certain that the song, whether of the folk or artistic variety, must have existed from time immemorial. – The Arabic *qaṣīda* undoubtedly demanded a quantitative metre (*ʿarūḍ*); in other respects its adoption and imitation presented no difficulties, as the song could serve as a basis for the *nasīb*. Moreover the panegyric was not foreign to the pre-Islamic period, being a logical sequence of the attitude of despotism towards culture.

The imitation of Arabic poetry, a knowledge of which became imperative for the Persian poet when the ancient native tradition (with the exception of folk-poetry) had ceased to hold, was extended both to content and to form. Quantitative prosody, rules of rhyme and word embellishments were translated, at first imperfectly but later on with increasing bravura. A certain essential unity can be discerned both in the ideology and the themes. Among the Abbasid poets who had a particularly decisive influence on the Persians, the first place must be accorded to al-Mutanabbī (303–54/915–65).

In the epic and quatrain, on the other hand, the Persian poet goes his own way from the very beginning, for here he was led by a firmly established, centuries-old popular indigenous tradition. This originality becomes evident already in the style and language of the epic and in the rhythm of the quatrain. Though the *mathnavī* did begin to put in an appearance with the Arabs (they adopted it but designated it by the term *muz-davij*), the quatrain was and remained somewhat alien to them.[7]

As characteristic features of this earliest period of Persian poetry Ye. E. Bertel's mentions the following: influence of folk poetry, whose simplicity and realism form such a pleasant contrast to the later tyranny of diametrically opposite trends; entire absence of religious subjects in the lyrical poetry; bilingualism of Persian poets[8] (e.g. Abu'l-Ḥasan Shahīd from Balkh, one of the earliest of the Samanid period, Abū-Bakr Muḥammad ʿAlī al-Khusravī from Sarakhs, Abū-ʿAbdi'llāh Muḥammad b. ʿAbdi'llāh Junaydī); translations from Persian into Arabic, and vice versa. Though we are in possession of detailed information concerning the Arabic cultural policy of the Samanids, when it comes to the real Persian literature of that period we have to rely on somewhat scanty scraps which, although relatively more numerous than those of the foregoing periods, are nevertheless not so plentiful as to provide more than a rough outline and that only of the principal features – not to mention fragments from minor poets. The sole exception is the heroic epic.

2. SOME NAMES

Where lyrical poetry is concerned, one reads more names and mere fragments than actual specimens, for the compilers of anthologies (the first dates from the beginning of the 7th/13th century) cater for contemporary taste and the lexicographers in turn for their specific requirements. Only in cases where the extant remnants of any one poet's works have been collected and edited individually is it possible to form an opinion of the whole and to draw more reliable conclusions as to their literary value than those obtained by generalising on the grounds of a haphazardly chosen fragment.[9] Of the multitude of names that have been handed down to us whose bearers

Notes on pp. 166–171

lived in Samanid times, we may add to those already mentioned in the first place the bilingual Abū-Shakūr of Balkh (b. 303/915–6), an excellent poet who, though often regarded as a predecessor of the much younger Rūdakī, was in fact his contemporary. Only 192 scraps of verse have remained of his whole output, among them three *mathnavīs*. One of these, named *Āfarīn-nāma* (written in 333/944–5), is probably of a didactic nature and is composed in the *mutaqārib*[10] metre; the other two are in *hazaj* and *khafīf* measures and were certainly known to Niẓāmī. The likewise bilingual Amīr Abu'l-Ḥasan b. Ilyās Āghāchī from Bukhara came from a high military circle; Ḥakīm Khabbāz of Nishapur sprang from the artisan class and probably started his career as a baker but later on changed over to the science of medicine. More sagas than facts are known about Rābi'a (Zaynu'l-'Arab) bint Ka'b-i Quzdārī Balkhī, a renowned poetess who lived at the end of the period of Samanid supremacy or the beginning of the Ghaznavid era.[11] She is even said to have lived at the same time as Rūdakī. She writes in Arabic (in conformity with her extraction) and in Persian. Her love affair with the slave Baktāsh inspired Riḍā-Qulī-Khān Hidāyat to compose the romantic epic *Gulistān-i Iram* or *Baktāsh-nāma* (see p. 340).

Other poets and prose writers will be mentioned later as occasion arises, for to my mind there is no useful end to be served in giving merely a long list of names.

3. RŪDAKĪ, (DAQĪQĪ), KISĀ'Ī

The first really great poet and one who outshone his whole environment was Abū-'Abdi'llāh Ja'far Rūdakī, also a singer and musician.[12] The myth according to which he is said to have written 1,300,000 distichs and moreover to have been blind from birth can be exploded by correct interpretation of the evidence. In respect of the first assertion the number is thus reduced to 100,000[13](!) or a little more, while logical calculation, together with Daqīqī's testimony and that of the *Shāh-nāma*, go to show that he became blind later on.[14] He himself speaks of his erudition. His great popularity with Amīr Naṣr II (301–31/914–43), whose Ismā'īlitic views he shared[15], earned him the wealth that became proverbial among later court poets. But the winds turned against Ismā'īlism and the fall of the vizier Abu'l-Faḍl Bal'amī (326/937–8) also caused the fall of Rūdakī who had certainly long been an object of envy on the part of court hirelings. As an old man he laments the feebleness of age and complains of his distressed condition, in which it is true he died in 329/940–1.[16] Of his *dīvān* only a few authenticated poems and verses are left and everything else circulated under his name can be attributed to Qaṭrān, who lived about a hundred years later. We must therefore rather take the subsequent appreciation accorded to him as decisive in ranking him as a master of the sparkling *qaṣīda*-panegyrics and to an equal degree of the *taghazzul* ('ghazal')-eroticism, meditation and wisdom – from hedonism to pessimism. His verse is adorned by a simplicity which the completely antithetical taste of the periods of mannerism that followed were incapable of comprehending, although ʿUnṣurī, who lived about a hundred years later, acknowledged that in the *ghazal* Rūdakī has no rival. Certainly we are told that the magical power of his verse, his singing and his lute-playing were able to persuade the king, after a stay of several years, to leave Herat and return to Bukhara; but this directness of style was already too far removed from later generations of poets to exert its erstwhile overmastering force. When the most pompous verbalist, Vaṣṣāf[17], composed an imitation of this poem four-hundred years later, he obviously did so only on account of the above moving anecdote, which must surely have appeared incredible in view of such modest verses.[18] Since Rūdakī had nothing to offer to satisfy the increasing demands of a literary taste intent on artificiality, the *dīvān* was lost. Moreover we may not overlook the fact that its effect rested in the main on the combination of verse, music, and song. Nevertheless it was Rūdakī who laid the foundation for the Khurasanian panegyrics in the line ʿUnṣurī – Muʿizzī – Anvarī.[19] The same straightforward style is to be found in his epic poems. In the first place there is *Kalīla u Dimna*[20], the well-known collection of Indian 'Bidpāi' fables, which ʿAbdu'llāh b. al-Muqaffaʿ translated from the Middle Persian into exemplary Arabic prose. This translation became the basis for subsequent adaptations. To Asadī's dictionary we owe the fact that of the lost work at least a number of verses have been preserved. These, though they do not permit a closer inspection of the contents of the poem, yet confirm anew the characteristic simplicity established by his lyrical poetry. This also typified Rūdakī's *Sindbād-nāma*[21], a story of the king's son and the seven viziers, which had followed a course similar to that of 'Bidpāi' from Indian into Middle Persian, thence to Arabic and Persian prose. No more than a few verses of this epic have survived, while of the other six there is but one single title in existence: *ʿArā'isu'n-nafā'is*, 'The Brides of the Jewels' (i.e. the jewels resembling the charming brides).[22] To Rūdakī is attributed the dictionary *Tāju'l-maṣādir*, 'The Crown of Infinitives', that may have been known to Asadī (p. 164) but has since then disappeared.[23]

Another outstanding poet who appeared at the Samanid court, certainly considerably younger than Rūdakī, is Daqīqī. But since his greatest importance lies in the field of the epic he will be discussed later on in that context (see p. 153 *et seq.*).

The life of Abu'l-Ḥasan (Abū-Isḥāq?) Kisā'ī of Merv (b. 341/953) followed a curious course, for up to his fiftieth year he was a frivolous waster. He paid flattery first and foremost to the Samanids but also to the Abbasids and Sultan Maḥmūd, all of whom were Sunnites; later on he became a strict ascetic and a passionate Shīʿite, and was the first to extol the Twelve Imāms, for that reason repeatedly incurring the displeasure of the Ismāʿīlite Nāṣir-i Khusrau (b. 394/1003–4, see p. 186 *et seq.*). He dedicated himself to mystical contemplation up to a great age. Although the actual motive for his inward conversion cannot be established, no doubt at all may be entertained as to its sincerity.

4. PROVINCIAL POETS AT THE COURTS OF THE ĀL-I MUḤTĀJ IN CHAGHĀNIYĀN, ZIYARIDS AND BUYIDS

It would be an easy matter to expand the list of lyric writers who grouped themselves around the earlier and later Samanids. More names however would convey but little, and the evaluation accorded them in handbooks on the subject – with the exception of Ye. E. Bertel's' standard treatise mentioned above[24] – is usually based on inadequate data. There is but one sure way of correcting this state of affairs, namely by monographical treatment of each separate poet. Nowadays, thanks to the Tehran editions of Asadī's dictionary and to the *tadhkiras*, one has more reliable material to go by, despite all its one-sidedness owing to lexicographical, aesthetic, and social considerations. Let us now turn to the poets themselves.

As well as at Bukhara we find poets appearing at the courts of the rulers of Chaghāniyān in Juzjān, the Ziyarids in Tabaristan, the Buyids in Western Iran. The Āl-i Muḥtāj of Chaghāniyān patronized Abu'l-Ḥasan ʿAlī b. Muḥ. Munjīk from Tirmidh (second half of the 4th/10th century), whose insults and impudence offered a favourable opportunity to the lexicographers to show to advantage the peculiarities of language which were so welcome to them; such a picture can of course lay no claim to completeness or fidelity. Fragments found in the *tadhkiras* and elsewhere, as well as the express testimony of the anthologists, show him as having been in fact an outstanding panegyrist, though a verse of Sūzanī's[25] leads one to the conclusion that Munjīk had a special proclivity towards the satire.

The fact cannot be ignored that western dynasties, such as the ʿAlīids, Ziyarids and Buyids, notwithstanding their vigorous political traditions, made on the whole the smallest contribution to the development of literature.[26] The Ziyarid Shamsu'l-maʿālī Qābūs b. Vushmgīr (366–403/976–1012), an impetuous man but a brilliant writer of Arabic, was surrounded by a number of poets whose names are known to us and who wrote in the Ṭabarī dialect; several of them wrote besides in the common literary language, e.g. Abu'l-Qāsim Ziyād b. Muḥammad al-Qamarī al-Jurjānī and Abū-Bakr Muḥammad b. ʿAlī al-Khusravī from Sarakhs (d. before 393/1002). It was also under the Ziyarids that the poet Manūchihrī (d. 432/1040–41) started his career.

The courts of the Buyids (333–447/945–1055) appear to present a surprising picture. They were a purely Iranian dynasty from Daylam and rose to such great power that they obtained sovereign rule over Iraq as well as the western half of Persia and even held the Caliphs of Baghdad in check: pioneers of the Persian Shīʿa, five hundred years before the Safavids! Western Iran, however, was too much exposed to the influence of Baghdad to allow the Buyid residences of Ray, Isfahan and Shiraz to become focal points of Persian literature. At least three of the Buyid Shāhanshāhs were themselves writers of Arabic verse, such as ʿAḍudu'd-daula (d. 372/983), the most famous of all and the last patron of al-Mutanabbī (see p. 143). His bearing on Persian poetry was of a peculiar nature: he was fond of syllabic verses in the Ṭabarī dialect. Nonetheless the literary movements from Khurasan obtained the upper hand and found fertile soil especially in the adjacent territory of Ray: the 'Ṣāḥib' Ismāʿīl b. ʿAbbād from Ṭālaqān (326–85/938–95), vizier to the Buyids Mu'ayyidu'd-daula and Fakhru'd-daula, was as enlightened and cultured as he was generous. He possessed a library so extensive that apparently about four hundred camels would have been required for its removal when the Samanid Nūḥ II (365–87/976–98) was trying to induce him to enter his service. The *Kitābu'l-aghānī*, 'The Book of Songs', a thesaurus of Arabic poetry by Abu'l-Faraj Iṣfahānī (d. 356/967), accompanied him on all his journeys. But the fact that during his viziership (977–995) there were several poets writing either in Persian or in both languages, points to his having borne a favourable attitude towards works in Arabic as well as in Persian. When the poet Badīʿu'z-zamān from Hamadan, a youthful prodigy at improvising Arabic verse (d. 398/1008) and later famous for his *Maqāmas*, appeared at the age of twelve before the 'Ṣāḥib', he was given three Persian verses from the *dīvān* of Abū-Muḥammad Manṣūr b. ʿAlī Manṭiqī from Ray to translate. The boy immediately recited his translation. But what interests us particularly here is that it was certainly not by mere chance that verses by Manṭiqī, whom A. Mirzoyev regards as an eloquent example of the high standard to which lyrical poetry had risen in the 10th century[27], were selected for the test. Manṭiqī's genius for rhetoric was intended to render the task more difficult rather than more easy. And he, the bilingual panegyrist of the vizier, was in fact renowned as a rhetorical virtuoso, thanks to the proximity of the Arab metropolis.

Among the bilingual poets we may mention Khusravī of Sarakhs (see p. 143), who, however, associated himself more closely with the Tabaristan Ziyarid Amīr Shamsu'l-maʿālī Qābūs b. Vushmgīr. In the service of the 'Ṣāḥib' we also find the brilliant panegyrist Kamālu'd-dīn Bundār of Ray (d. 401/1010; according to E. G. Browne[28] his poetry was written between 997 and 1029), who in addition to composing Persian and Arabic verse also wrote in the Gīlakī dialect. As late as the 12th century the poet Ẓahīr Fāryābī boastfully compared himself to him. At the courts of the Buyids Avicenna put his political ingenuity to the test. Among the later poets Kiyā Ghaḍā'irī (i.e. the maker of majolica) from Ray (d. 425–6/1034–5) stands out; in reality he was a spy in the service of Sulṭān Maḥmūd of Ghazna at the court of the latter's Buyid rivals.[29]

5. GENERAL CHARACTERISTICS OF THE FIRST PERIOD

What now can be said to characterise the earliest period of the Persian literature with an arabising tendency, viz. the time from the Arab conquest and the first native dynasties up to the appearance of Sultan Maḥmūd of Ghazna? Let me finish and complete the foregoing sketch by quoting Ye. E. Bertel's'[30] masterly summary, here recapitulated shortly and concisely: (1) Persian poetry has many points of contact with contemporary Arabic verse and constitutes a literature in two languages; the dependence of Persian poetry on Arabic is thus the natural outcome, but on the other hand the Persian spirit penetrates deeply into the latter; (2) Persian as an effective literary language demonstrates the powerlessness of the Baghdad Caliphate and the loss of attraction of the latter for the Iranian aristocracy; (3) feudal ideology permeates the whole of poetry, from the organisation of literary life up to the themes themselves; (4) the *ghazal* still exists only as a component part of the *qaṣīda*[31]; (5) the *qaṣīda*, either panegyric or 'satirical', is the main poetic form; (6) the eulogy grows into an idealisation which in its turn becomes a set of stereotyped phrases; (7) the didactic epic undergoes considerable development, in contrast for the time being to the heroic, though in both cases the Iranian spirit is evident, as opposed to the *qaṣīda* with its arabising tendency; (8) the *rubāʿī*, a specific kind of Persian folk-poetry, has not as yet found its way into the literature of the aristocracy; (9) all subjects revolve around the theme of *razm u bazm*, 'fighting and feasting'; (10) as there was a general absence of danger of war, subjects dealing with peace and with the pomp and circumstance of the court predominate; (11) the static feeling does not permit any deeper development of the theme; thence follows the self-sufficiency of each couplet; (12) religious subjects are of subordinate importance because the prosperous aristocrat has no need to look forward to a state of bliss in the world to come when he can taste to the full of earthly joys in this world, even though this may be contrary to the laws of Islam (the pleasures of wine!); (13) as regards descriptions, no convention has as yet been formed, although there are already signs pointing towards such; the range of subjects suitable for expression in verse is certainly more limited than in Arabic poetry, but is not as yet canonised; (14) the function of poetry is reduced to two antithetic elements: on the one hand aesthetic entertainment, by which the poet enters into the mental sphere of his masters, and on the other a means of livelihood and dependence. Signs of meditation, discontent and criticism later take form in antifeudal Ṣūfism; (15) as opposed to this feudal classicism, the Ghaznavid period is characterised by a feudal romanticism.

In the above summary Ye. E. Bertel's ignores the folk-element, to which I. S. Braginskiy on the contrary accords his main attention.[32]

B. THE EARLIEST MONUMENTS

There are in existence a few records, not really belonging to the field of literature, still less ranking as examples of belles-lettres, which nevertheless deserve mention in virtue of their being the oldest first-hand documents[33] committed to writing in the Persian language. They are the following: inscriptions of Tang-i Azao in Hebrew script dating from the year 752–3 A.D.[34]; the private letter of a Jewish merchant, written in Hebrew script and found in Dandan-Uylïq near Khotan, dating maybe also from as early as the 8th century; signatory inscriptions of Jewish witnesses concerning a church in Malabar, dating from the early 9th century; a Jewish-Persian legal document from the year 1020 from Hormshir in Khuzistan. There are also a contract dealing with the sale of a piece of ground dating from 501/1107, discovered in the country of Khotan (?); entries on the title page of a Kūfī copy of the Koran concerning the birth of three children, between 561–67/1165–71; records, six in number, from Bāmiyān, one of which dates from 607/1211. (Copies of old letters and records, from as early as the Ghaznavid and Seljuq periods, have survived in various collections of documents and historical works.) To these later dates belong also the Kūfī inscriptions of Khurram-ābād (in Luristan) from 513/1119 and Georgian coins from 1210.

Of a literary, though not belletristic, nature are also the following: a commentary on Ezechiel in Hebrew script, a translation of the Psalms in Syrian script, discovered in Bulayïq (Turfan), and fragments in Manichaean script; these are very ancient Persian monuments but none of them are dated.

I. THE EARLIEST POETRY AND PROSE, INCLUDING THE WORKS OF AVICENNA AND AL-BĪRŪNĪ

It is possible on the other hand to affix dates to the following: verses from Ibn Khurdādhbih (d. 230/844)[35]; twenty-seven defective verses in a Manichaean manuscript dating from the first half of the 4th/10th century; fragments from Bilauhar and Būdāsaf are derived either from Rūdakī or from members of his circle[36]; *Risāla-i aḥkām-i fiqh-i ḥanafī*, 'On the Ḥanafī doctrine of Law', by Abu'l-Qāsim Iṣḥāq b. Muḥ. Samarqandī (d. 342/953), composed about 320/932, the manuscript dating from 795/1392–3[37]; the old preface to Abū-Manṣūr's *Shāh-nāma* in prose (which was actually Firdausī's source), from 346/957–8; Abū-ʿAlī Muḥammad Balʿamī's translation, properly speaking a partly abridged and partly enlarged revision of the chronicle of Ṭabarī, from 352/963[38]; an abridged translation of Ṭabarī's commentary on the Koran, executed by a group of Transoxanian scholars under the Samanid Manṣūr b. Nūḥ (350–65/961–76), the oldest manuscript of which was discovered in Ardabil and dates from 606/1209[39]; two *risālas*: *Istikhrāj dar shinākhtan-i ʿumr*, 'The Knowledge of Life in Extract', and *Shash faṣl*, 'Six Chapters', on the astrolabe, by Abū-Jaʿfar Muḥ. b. Ayyūb Ḥāsib Ṭabarī, the latter written about 354/965, the manuscript dating from 372/982–3[40]; *Kashfu'l-Maḥjūb*, 'The Unveiling of the Concealed' (Ismāʿīlitic) by Abū-Yaʿqūb Sijistānī, still alive about 360/970; Abū-Naṣr Ḥasan b. ʿAlī Qumī's *Kitāb-i madkhal dar ʿilm-i nujūm*, 'Introduction to Astronomy', dates from 365/975, the manuscript from 1231; *Ḥudūdu'l-ʿālam*, 'The Boundaries of the World', by an anonymous author (Ibn Farīghūn?)[41] from 372/982–3; *ʿAjā'ibu'l-buldān*, 'The

Wonders of the Lands', by Abu'l-Mu'ayyad Balkhī, written for the Samanid Abu'l-Qāsim Nūḥ b. Manṣūr (365–87/976–97), of which unfortunately only a rump has survived, and that moreover corrupted by a later hand. From the same author there was a work entitled *Kitāb-i Garshāsp*, the probable source of Asadī's *Garshāsp-nāma* (despite several differences) (see p. 165), to be found in very condensed form in the *Sīstān-nāma*, which according to M. Bahār is part of a lost *Shāh-nāma* in prose, but in the opinion of M.-N. Osmanov[42] a separate work by Abu'l-Mu'ayyad. G. Lazard (BVIb) has recently discovered three manuscripts which, to judge both by the style and by the writing, are of very ancient origin: (1) *Dānish-nāma*, 'The Book of Knowledge' (medicine in verse-form!) by Maysarī, written in 367–70/978–81 (MS Paris, dated 852/1448); (2) *Kitāb-i Hidāyatu'l-muta'allimīn*, 'The Book of Guidance for Learners' (medicine), by Abū-Bakr Rabī' b. Akhavaynī Bukhārā'ī, written about 370/981 (MS Oxford, dated 478/1085); (3) a commentary on Kalābādī (Ṣūfistic, MS Peshavar, dated 473/1081).

There is uncertainty as to the date of the pharmacopoeia *Kitābu'l-abniya 'an* ḥaqā'iqi'l-adviya*, 'The Book on the Rudiments of the Real Nature of Medicines', by Muvaffaq Abū-Manṣūr b. 'Alī Haravī (surviving in a MS dated 447/1056 from the pen of the poet Asadī of Ṭūs, a magnificent ancient Persian document in book form); some scholars, among those of recent date also Muḥammad Bahār[43], place it in the period of the Samanid Manṣūr b. Nūḥ (350–65/961–76), others – in particular Muḥammad Qazvīnī – at an undeterminable date with 447/1056 as *terminus ad quem*.

This survey would not be complete without at least mention being made of Avicenna and al-Bīrūnī, although in the course of their fertile and extremely influential scholarly activity they wrote on the whole only exceptionally in the Persian language (assuming also that the relevant surviving scripts are authentic). Nevertheless we are concerned here with valuable specimens of Persian prose, in respect of time close to those cited above. Abū-'Alī ibn Sīnā (Avicenna; b. 370/980 near Bukhara; d. 428/980 in Hamadan), was a physician, natural scientist and philosopher, who also wrote verse in Arabic and Persian. The polyhistor Abu'r-Rayḥān Muḥ. al-Bīrūnī (b. 362/972–3 in Khvārazm, d. 443/1051 in Ghazna) is unique among the Islamic scholars on account of his uncompromising love of truth, his precision, and critical spirit.[44] Thus he explains historical phenomena by economic causes and considers certain aspects of religion to be incompatible with science.[45] It is striking that both these outstanding figures of Moslem erudition attached importance to rendering knowledge accessible to those of their compatriots who were unacquainted with the Arabic tongue. It is no less surprising that at this early period they were capable of writing a clear, robust scholarly Persian prose – Avicenna in his concise philosophical encyclopaedia *Dānish-nāma-i 'Alā'ī*[46], 'The Book of Knowledge', dedicated to the Kakuyid 'Alā'u'd-daula of Isfahan, and two further essays (according to M. Bahār[47] the style is in keeping with the period, the authorship probable), and Bīrūnī in *At-tafhīm li-avā'ili ṣinā'ati't-tanjīm*, 'Information on the Beginnings of the Art of Astrology'.

Speaking generally, with the decline of the political power of Baghdad the knowledge of the Arabic language on the part of the feudal lords and their satellites also diminishes and they now make use of the vernacular of the people, who had never known Arabic. Thus the first Persian prose came into being.[48]

All the works enumerated are distinguished by their lucid straightforward 'Samanid' style and are in general void of rhetorical embellishments, whereby the percentage of Arabic loan-words is small.

But this is not yet all: we also possess records, unfortunately somewhat lacking in precision and lucidity, of other books, no longer extant. Bīrūnī states that the sectarian Bih-āfarīdh wrote a book in the Persian language for his followers (about 132/749–50). Between 170–7/786–94 Manke translated Shānāq's book on medicine from Sanskrit into Persian, evidently still in Pahlavi script, because Abū-Ḥātim of Balkh was entrusted with the translation into 'Persian', viz. Islamic Persian and thus Arabic script.[49]

C. THE EPIC TRADITION OF IRAN[50]

The first authenticated official Sasanian text of the traditional epic of Iran (*Khodāy-nāma*, 'The Book of the Kings') appeared approximately in its present form under Khusrau Anūshirvān I (531–79), the last one soon after the accession to the throne of Yazdagird III (632–51), thus shortly before the dynasty came to an end. This redaction contained the history of Iran from the very earliest beginnings and is a mixture of truth and legend. The revival of the old tradition, namely when already in the first half of the 8th century Persian historical works were translated into Arabic, signifies one of the earliest stages in the awakening of national sentiment on the part of the Iranians. Mas'ūdī records the translation of a history of the Sasanians for the Caliph Hishām (already mentioned, see p. 129). Some of the translators confined themselves to popular sagas connected with the Sasanians, including the heroic deeds of the Sistanian Rustam (the latter began to appear in the epic poem at the time when the Arsacids were succeeded by the Sasanians). The first of the *Khodāy-nāmas* translated into Arabic is the work of Ibnu'l-Muqaffa', an Iranian, renowned far and wide as one of the best Arabic stylists (put to death ca. 142/759–60). The Middle Persian original has not survived and unfortunately the same fate befell the translation just mentioned, as well as eight other translations or editions (*Siyaru'l-mulūk*, viz. *Khodāy-nāma*, in New Persian *Shāh-nāma*). Of these Mūsā b. 'Isā al-Kisravī's edition was especially renowned, for it even rivalled that of Ibnu'l-Muqaffa'.[51] Only some scattered fragments in Arabic chronicles have been passed down to us. The Persian prose version of the epic, that probably constitutes only one part of the whole, namely the extract on

Garshāsp by Abu'l-Mu'ayyad from Balkh, has been already referred to (see p. 150). This author was preceded by Mas'ūdī from Merv (before 355/965–6) with a poem of similar content which, however, was not immediately designated as *Shāh-nāma*. From this *mathnavī* three verses have been preserved in the epical *hazaj*. From Firdausī himself we learn that he owed the material for his conception of Rustam's death to a certain Āzād-Sarv, a poet who in his turn lived with an Iranian patriot named Aḥmad b. Sahl in Merv; on another occasion (*à propos* the story of the Ashkanians) he quotes as authority a *dihqān* from Chāch in Transoxania. These then were the forerunners of the most important prose version of the *Shāh-nāma*, the source actually used by Firdausī – namely the product of a group of four Eastern Iranian Zoroastrians who had collaborated on the initiative of Abū-Manṣūr Muḥammad b. 'Abdu'r-Razzāq, the feudal ruler of Ṭūs, doubtless also in the spirit of the latter's social opinions. This committee made use of the *Khodāy-nāma* in Pahlavi as well as of other ancient documents and completed its task in 346/957. There is some uncertainty as to the *Shāh-nāma* – testified to only by Bīrūnī – of the poet Abū-'Alī Muḥammad b. Aḥmad from Balkh, whom W. Barthold[52] wishes to identify with Muḥammad b. Aḥmad Daqīqī (see below). Other scholars hold differing opinions, none of which, however, are regarded by M.-N. Osmanov as sound.[53]

Notwithstanding all the names that have been quoted, we are unable to disclose the indirect and direct sources otherwise than fragmentarily. A very great deal of material has been lost, either through the unpropitiousness of the times or because the great master put all others into the shade. But we must at any rate not ignore the factors of oral tradition and folklore, from which it is certain that Firdausī borrowed appropriate matter to a very large extent.

The bare facts we have brought forward will suffice to leave no one in doubt as to the feudal and aristocratic mould into which the whole of the written tradition was cast.[54] W. Barthold[55], whom I follow here and there, has already shown that "in Moslem Persia, as also in the pre-Moslem period beginning with the Achaemenid epoch, epical poetry, the literary treatment of epical themes and their transference to historical personages was concentrated in Eastern Iran". But in whatever part of Iran the 'sagas' may have originated, some of them at any rate can be proved to form part of the common heritage of the entire Iranian nation from the earliest times onward. Finally it can be shown that in Iran epical poetry continued to be written longer than anywhere else and only gradually ceased to exist in the 11th to 12th centuries, contemporaneously with the fall of the chivalric nobility and the accompanying rise of the towns.

Yet the epical tradition was not limited to Eastern Iran. Shāh-mardān's *Nuzhat-nāma-i 'Alā'ī*, "Alā'ī's Book of Pleasure', shows that it also existed in Western Iran, and that it was a tradition peculiar to this region and different from that of the East. It took shape in two prose summaries: the first, a voluminous work dating from 977 to about 1010, was collected by Rustam Lāriyānī, to all appearances a historiographer at the court of the Buyids; the second was written by Pīrūzān, 'the teacher', at the command of his Kakuyid Amīr between 1040 and 1050. About seventy years later Shāhmardān reproduced Pīrūzān's version in abridged form in his *Nuzhat-nāma* (1120); he was already acquainted with the eastern tradition from the works of Abu'l-Mu'ayyad Balkhī and Firdausī and is conspicuous on account of a special tendency to explain the myths in a rationalistic manner. With the break-up of the Buyids and their literature in the Persian language, the western tradition fell into decay and thus did not attain to an artistic treatment in verse-form as did the eastern tradition in Khurasan in the *Shāh-nāma*.[56]

With V. Minorsky[57] one must draw attention to pre-Islamic culture which, next to non-Islamic inspiration, formed a beneficent counterweight to Ṣūfī quietism. The influence of the Iranian epic went hand in hand with the belief in the Imāms. This upheld the national consciousness already in the *shuʿūbiyya* and was to the advantage of those rulers who prided themselves on their Persian origin. The most renowned subjects of Moslem-Iranian heroic and romantic poetry can be traced back to indigenous tradition or to purely secular material (Firdausī, Niẓāmī, etc.).

D. DAQĪQĪ

An outstanding figure at the close of the Samanid period is Abū-Manṣūr Muḥammad b. Aḥmad Daqīqī of Ṭūs (though Balkh, Bukhara and Samarqand are also sometimes mentioned as his birthplace). He was born at any rate before the middle of the 4th/10th century and died between 366/976 and 370/981. He wrote poems to the glory of the Samanids and their governor in Khurasan, one of the Chaghāniyān princes. The theory according to which he had become converted to Zoroastrianism must be rejected; for, based as it is on a certain lyrical fragment, it proves no more than the romantic interest of a liberally-minded Moslem conforming to the cultural trends of Samanid policy that consciously followed in the wake of the Sasanian tradition.[58] The importance of Daqīqī from the standpoint of literary history lies not in his lyrical poetry, although the latter surpassed the average and enjoyed the high esteem of his contemporaries, but in his endeavours – still clearly discernible today – on behalf of the Iranian national epic by which he prepared the way for Firdausī's *Shāh-nāma*. His work contains a little under one thousand verses dealing with the introduction of the new religion by Zoroaster under Gushtāsp and with the conflict arising between him and Arjāsp on account of it; but thanks to Bīrūnī we know with certainty that he actually wrote more than this number, even though the figures given in other records (9000 and even 20000 couplets) must appear exaggerated.[59] All that has been preserved has been incorporated by Firdausī in his work. That the author of the *Shāh-nāma* judges Daqīqī's work severely is not without reason: the fragment is duller and more monotonous as regards style, and falls short of the elegance and richness of imagination to be found in Firdausī[60]; the eloquent panegyrist and lyricist proves to be a poor narrator. It may be asked for what reason Firdausī used inferior verses, not his own, and of secondary importance at that? He could have done the same thing with other extracts from the same poet! Did Firdausī wish to disparage the value of the more ticklish passages at a later period, when with the fall of Samanids religious liberty came to an end, and, by maintaining silence, himself remain free from all suspicion? The same kind of evasion seems to be provided by the dream with which Firdausī introduces the insertion: Daqīqī is said to have appeared to him in a dream and to have besought Firdausī to include the verses in his *Shāh-nāma*; but the latter hastens to add that he himself had better verses! Why and when Daqīqī began to work on the epic, why and when it came to a standstill, is not known; but there is good reason to suppose that his sudden death was not the first signal for Firdausī to take over his work on the *Shāh-nāma*.[61] The usual assumption, that both poets had drawn their material from the same text, viz. the prose version of Abū-Manṣūr's committee, is contested by M. Bahār[62], who regards the lost prose *Shāh-nāma* of Abu'l-Mu'ayyad (see p. 150) as Daqīqī's source. Admittedly Daqīqī alone cannot have invented the verse metre and style characteristic of the epic, but he must nevertheless have contributed his share to both elements for Firdausī to have been provided with a complete ready-made pattern. Daqīqī or his predecessors were able to use popular heroic songs, particularly the dirges on Siyāvūsh[63], as a basis, for these used to be sung in Bukhara by folk singers with musical accompaniment; they arranged the style to suit literary purposes and adapted the songs to the most appropriate Arabic verse-measure (*mutaqārib* or *hazaj*). They thus satisfied the requirements of aristocratic aesthetic theory and yet continued to preserve pure Iranian tradition in their works (Ye. E. Bertel's[64], but only as regards Daqīqī). According to E. Benveniste[65] the *mutaqārib* is a sequel to the Middle Persian *hendekasyllabus* and is not derived from Arabic prosody. The same may be the case with other Persian metres.

When still quite a young man the poet was assassinated by his Turkish slave. Later sources sought to reveal an erotic relationship, but the real motive may have been of a different kind, in particular his unmalleable character, which the *Shāh-nāma* underlines all too clearly.

E. FIRDAUSĪ

Daqīqī's fragment has its origin in the feudal spirit in its purest form; the vassals serve their masters, display their chivalrous courage and remain faithful to the grave, with complete disregard of their own death and destruction. Disputes are settled more frequently by duel than by battle, for personal encounter exhibits the virtues of chivalry more clearly. All these features are of course also to be found in Firdausī; he lays stress on Iranian legitimacy, of which the distinctive mark is the hereditary *farr*. The Sasanians inherited it from former dynasties, the Samanids from the Sasanians, and had therefore a legal claim to the possession of Iran.[66] In his love-scenes however Firdausī partly changes over into a romantic style. The somewhat younger ʿUnṣurī lapses into it altogether[67] and Gurgānī's heroes even violate the principle of loyalty in the midst of amorous intrigues.

Like a giant, not only of earlier times but of the whole of Persian literature, arises Abu'l-Qāsim Manṣūr (? Ḥasan, Aḥmad ?) Firdausī of Ṭūs (more accurately perhaps of the village Vāzh, near Ṭābarān, part of the city of Ṭūṣ). His name has been known long since in Europe and also far beyond the boundaries of Iranian culture from numerous works of orientalist scholars and from translations. The millenial celebrations in 1934 proclaimed the fame of the writer of the *Shāh-nāma* literally throughout the world. Biographical details concerning the classical poets of the East are certainly not conspicuously plentiful. Firdausī is in many respects an exception: apparently there are sufficient data but they are of a much more recent period (the earliest date from a century after the death of the poet) and are full of uncertain elements and even sagas; after a critical rejection of all the historical contradictions, impossibilities and sentimentality there is but little remaining. All that one has to build on are the allusions scattered about by the poet himself in the *Shāh-nāma*, although this material is not always unequivocal and, in consequence of the very poor reconstructions of the text that have been made up till now[68], is in no sense sufficiently reliable. Data taken from the epical poem *Yūsuf u Zalīkhā*, proved since to have been forged, are quite useless for biographical purposes. On the ground of more or less definitive combinations, Firdausī's birth has now been placed between 320–4/932–6, officially (according to Th. Nöldeke[69]) in the year 934, although the years 326/937–8, 329/940–1 or 331/942–3 are also occasionally given. By birth and conviction a small landowner (*dihqān*) in his native province, with no means at his disposal (he is glad to be exempt from paying taxes) he no doubt devoted himself to literature and poetry from his early youth onwards, and possibly also to epic-writing; but he began his main work only after reaching manhood. He derived his material from Abū-Manṣūr's redaction of the traditional epic of Iran (see p. 152) but M.-N. Osmanov[70] shows that he also made use of numerous other sources, undoubtedly supplemented to a great extent by oral tradition.[71] Neither he nor Daqīqī was familiar with Middle Persian. Firdausī probably started work in 365/975–6, that is before the death of his predecessor. Supported both morally and materially by people of high rank and by friends, he worked for several decades at his masterpiece, mostly in his native town.

Firdausī is said to have gone to Baghdad in order to present the first version of the *Shāh-nāma*, dated 384/994–5, to the Buyid Prince Bahā'u'd-daula, as the representative of a strong Iranian power. This can in fact be proved by reference to the work itself, though admittedly it is impossible to determine which portions were concerned. But the prince's response was apparently not such as Firdausī had hoped for. If the evidence for this journey is only to be found in the connection with *Yūsuf u Zalīkhā*, supposedly Firdausī's second epic poem, then it is a hypothesis that stands or falls with the authenticity of the latter work. Firdausī's stay in Khān-Lanjān (near Isfahan), where he is said to have offered a second version of the *Shāh-nāma*, dating from 389/998–9, to Ḥākim Aḥmad b. Muḥammad b. Abī-Bakr, the feudal ruler there, can be rejected altogether for the simple reason that it concerns a stay that has been constructed out of a misconstrued alien postscript in a *Shāh-nāma* manuscript.[72]

In the meantime the Samanid supremacy, in the spirit of which the *Shāh-nāma* had been written, was nearing its close. It collapsed completely on the defeat of the Samanids by the Iligh-Khān in Transoxania and by Maḥmūd of Ghazna in Khurasan. The work must have been influenced by the radical change in political circumstances, for in Sultan Maḥmūd the poet evidently thought to find the ardently longed-for man of the 'unification and re-birth of Iran'. As soon as Maḥmūd came into power Firdausī, then fifty-eight years old, despatched at intervals portions of his poem to Ghazna, and accompanied it each time by panegyric verse. This custom was started somewhere about the middle of the work. Strangely enough the Samanids are only mentioned once in the *Shāh-nāma*.[73] Were such parts deleted after the political reversal, or was the old regime already dying out to such an extent that the poet felt he could no longer count on the support of the dynasty? It is remarkable that Firdausī sings the praises of Maḥmūd and complains of his own distress in one and the same breath! Yet he never utters a single word of thanks, possibly because he had nothing to be grateful for. It is generally assumed that Firdausī finally completed his monumental work in the year 400/1009–10.[74] Apparently he took this redaction personally to Ghazna but again without success. Did in fact the violent quarrel between the poet and the Sultan break out, a quarrel which according to the legend led the former to write a bitter satire, with disastrous consequences for himself? It is said that he was obliged to flee from the wrathful Sultan's vicinity and wander restlessly from place to place in the regions of Iran until, after long years of vagabondage and penury, he finally obtained pardon and returned to Ṭūs, only to die there. The story goes on to relate that the dead poet was just being borne to his grave when a caravan entered the city gate, laden with rich gifts from Maḥmūd. This is obviously a case of distorted reality combined with sentimental fiction. The famous satire seems to be mainly a mere assembly of verses (*c.* 100) taken from various parts of the *Shāh-nāma*.[75] Furthermore we hear that all but six of its verses were destroyed. Where, then, do the present hundred verses come from? Although it is quite certain that the poet met with bitter disappointments at the court of Maḥmūd, it is not clear that they were accompanied by an open conflict. What was the cause of this disfavour? Sultan Maḥmūd, an enemy of the Shīʿa and of Ismāʿīlism in particular, may have been prejudiced if the court camarilla suspected the poet of leanings in that direction. But the change in Maḥmūd's politics as a whole must also be taken into account. By fighting against the Iligh-Khān the Sultan exhibited a quasi-accommodation to Iranian patriotism. Conversely, the Iranian patriots' idea of a struggle between Iran and Turan suited the policy of Ghazna. But from the year 401/1010–11 onwards a change set in: another vizier was appointed, the court chancellery conducted its correspondence in Arabic instead of Persian and sought closer relations with Baghdad; Firdausī, who because of his distressed circumstances enjoyed the support of Maḥmūd's people until his work was finished, now became the victim of the new political trend, for the *Shāh-nāma* ceased to be an object of further interest to the court. That he sought refuge with other rulers was not so much on account of political persecution as because he was an old man, hard pressed by necessity. Thus the story that he was obliged to flee, first to Herat and then to Tabaristan until he was beyond the sphere of influence of Maḥmūd and reached the Buyid Bahā'u'd-daula or the latter's son, does not seem to be quite in accordance with the facts. At the most it can be concluded that he wandered from court to court, although not even such an Odyssey is necessarily true. But it is certainly not in concordance with the historically certifiable data contained in the prefatory songs to some of the *Yūsuf u Zalīkhā* manuscripts that he composed this epic only towards the end of his life at the request of the Buyids. Sources depicting the conflict and its consequences are prejudiced and hostile towards Maḥmūd. The end of the poet's life is veiled in obscurity. The manifold complaints about his neglected old age lead one to assume that he actually was exposed to want, if not to real distress. A further development in the policy of Ghazna does not take place until 415/1025, and this likewise is reflected in a change of vizier. A more favorable wind might then have blown for the poet, but he had died in the meantime, perhaps in a foreign land (411/1020–1 or 416/1025–6). This was the origin of the familiar sentimental legend of the caravan and the gifts.

There are many gaps, obscurities and riddles in the life of Firdausī. Much has been elucidated but there still remains far more to be done. Renewed investigations, new sources, progressive and ever more reliable interpretations, and above all a critical edition of the *Shāh-nāma*, could yield further results. The most important disclosure of recent times is the certainty that Firdausī had never been in Khān-Lanjān and that the romantic epic *Yūsuf u Zalīkhā*, based on the 12th Sura, about Joseph, son of Jacob, and his experiences, is erroneously ascribed to him (Shīrānī, Qarīb, Mīnuvī, Khayyām-pūr, Nafīsī)[76]; thus for instance in the quite unreliable preface to the *Shāh-nāma* of Bāysunghur[77], dating from 829/1425–6. Other authorities from the same period – some of them of greater importance – such as Ḥāfiẓ-i Ābrū, Jāmī and Daulatshāh, remain silent, and not a single manuscript of the epic is available in which Firdausī is quoted in the script. The untenability of opinions from other quarters can be proved by a series of intrinsic and extrinsic reasons that are irrefutable. The style alone (e.g. the coordination of synonyms) makes it impossible to attribute the poem even to a contemporary of Firdausī. It is not an anonymous work (dated about 476/1083, Mīnuvī; 484/1092–3, Shīrānī), but was composed by Amānī, an otherwise unknown poet from Khurasan, after 476/1083 (S. Nafīsī)[78] and was dedicated to Abu'-l-Favāris Shamsu'd-daula Ṭughān-Shāh, the son of the famous Seljuqid Alp-Arslan Muḥammad. We will only add that according to the encyclopaedia *Haft Iqlīm* (1002/1594) no one before ʿAmʿaq of Bukhara (d. 543/1148–9, see p. 200) had worked out this theme in the form of an epic poem.[79] For the rest this alleged work of Firdausī's has no particular value nor does it in any way come up to the level of genius of the great epic writer. H. Ritter, who like A. T. Tagirjanov[80] will not altogether relinquish the idea that Firdausī was the author, is of the opinion that the poem was undoubtedly written before 385/995–6, but he repudiates as unfounded the traditional view that it was written only after Firdausī had incurred the anger of Sultan Maḥmūd, that is to say after the completion of the *Shāh-nāma*.

In the great majority of manuscripts the *Shāh-nāma* comprises from 48,000 to 52,000 distichs, only sporadically 55,000 or more. If this fact is in itself sufficient to provide philology with an important task[81], then the immense problems surrounding the *Shāh-nāma* and its creator surely make a critical edition one of the most urgent requirements of Iranian studies. And in view of the vast extent of the research involved, collective work will inevitably be called for. It is therefore extremely gratifying that Soviet scholars are now about to obey this call.[82] The invaluable glossary of Fritz Wolff will form a notable aid to the text-criticism. Needless to say, the earliest manuscripts will have to be consulted and the feudal recensions of Ḥamdu'llāh Qazvīnī (753/1334–5) and the 'Bāysunghurian' *collegium* (829/1425–6) relinquished, especially as the latter in particular was obliged to comply with the demands and suit the taste of its by no means unintelligent master. There can be no doubt that in these two recensions, stupidly enough, no distinction was made between all the redactions prepared by the poet himself.

The story of the *Shāh-nāma*, divided according to the different rulers into fifty parts of very varying lengths, constitutes an epopee of mankind based on the history of Iran from the time of the first mythical king to the downfall of the Sasanians. From an often astounding mass of detail it becomes increasingly apparent how accurately the poet adheres to his sources without giving free rein to imagination or subjectivism. While the first mythological or legendary kings of that period belong to the primitive Indo-Iranian social order, the Kayanids must be classified as belonging to a later, purely Iranian period beginning with the founding of a monarchical regime among the Aryan immigrants in Eastern Iran (9th century B.C.) and closing with the appearance of Zoroaster. Up to Manūchihr the names of the kings can also be found in the Avesta; from then on, following the introduction of a legend[83] concerning the princes of Sistan and Zabulistan, a reversal takes place in these cycles: the heroes Zāl, Rustam and Isfandyār become the real subject of a detailed presentation, while the legendary Kayanids, though originally Eastern Iranian tribal chieftains, are all accorded secondary roles; opposite to them stands Afrāsyāb at the head of Turan. With the kings Dārāb and Dārā the epic passes on to Alexander. While this strange and originally hostile figure also acquired a more friendly aspect in the long run, from Pseudo-Callisthenes onwards, the *Khodāy-nāma*, that took the part of the Sasanians, merely mentions the Arsacids (Ashkānīs) in passing. Firdausī is not familiar with the Greek-Baktrian period and compresses the Arsacids, as an epoch of anarchy, into some twenty double-rhymed verses. The history of the Sasanians follows in twenty-eight parts which, though not entirely dispensing with the historical element, are closely interwoven with popular sagas. The opinion that this portion degenerates into a rhymed chronicle is not therefore quite in accordance with the truth. Speeches and letters of kings and eminent persons, intermingled with wisdom and counsels – a favourite variation already in old Persian literature and adopted in the earliest Islamic times by Arabic literature – alternate with events to compensate the scarcity of facts and are doubtless partly derived from the model itself. There is profound truth in the view of ancient Iran that sees in the *Shāh-nāma* the history of its own past; all that is required is to strip it of every naïve interpretation that does not get to the real root of the historical truth. This is indeed a valuable historical document which, thanks to faithful adherence to past tradition and in spite of its display of fantasy and allegory, "lays bare facts that are of importance not only to history but also to prehistory for the investigation of primitive formations"; better than all Arabic and other sources, the *Shāh-nāma* elucidates social conditions and life under the Sasanians and also explains several historical details.[84] But this extremely valuable book must of course be read with understanding. Only modern methods of research based on economic and social data reveal how very right the ancients were in regarding the *Shāh-nāma* as a historical work.

It is obvious that, bearing in mind this chronological sequence as the unifying basic conception of the whole, the connection between the separate parts, unlike a work of fiction, could not be particularly close. Indeed, it is properly speaking "one long chain of chronologically arranged episodes". Externally they are held together by fixed formulas indicating commencement, transition and close, standard *epitheta ornantia*, hyperboles, archaic expressions – the whole a legacy from the literary tradition of an earlier developed epical style of narration.[85] But there are still other factors that bring unity into this immense mass of verse. These are the three fundamental conceptions of ancient Iranian morality: the contrast between Good and Evil, and the final victory of the former, also expressed in the religious dualism Ormuzd-Ahriman and thus resolving *a priori* the ever-old struggle between Iran and Turan (originally no doubt the struggle between the resident farmer and the nomadic herdsman), a thread that winds through a considerable part of the epic; the idea associated with it of the absolute necessity of a legitimate line of succession, since only by means of an heir can the ruler obtain *farr*, the 'aureole of divine descent' (in addition justness is indispensable, for the good ruler is an essential element of the national faith[86]); finally the purely

Notes on pp. 166–171

feudal conception of the unconditional honour, loyalty and duty towards his lord incumbent upon the vassal, which nevertheless does not prevent the hero from uttering occasional angry outbursts against his sovereign nor from defying him. The duty of retaliation, of revenge, is the chief motive for all the warlike events with which the *Shāh-nāma* is interwoven. It must however be added that in the same way that revenge ordains the mythical happenings, justice predominates under the Sasanians.

That wars and battles fill the greater part of the book is inherent in the nature of the heroic epic. In the very diversity of these descriptions Firdausī reveals his masterly skill.[87] The mythical heroes possess superhuman strength (the chief figure Rustam is a giant), the others are supernormal. Armed conflicts are often reduced to duels. In contrast to this there are the festivities, chiefly banquets and carousals, where moderation was not always observed, as indeed is befitting to heroes; in times of peace, courage and skill find vent in the hunt. Dramatic effect is prominent in the tragedy of Rustam and Suhrāb, the motif being the quarrel between father and son. Indeed the conflicts, with the accompanying dialogue and monologue, are distinguished by dramatic moments.[88] Comparatively little space is devoted to love but these passages form a climax both emotionally and otherwise, because woman is not inferior to man either as regards sagacity or heroism. Inviolable chastity is typical. Love-scenes and lyrical interludes provide a romantic element in Firdausī's heroic epic. Of course the perceptibility of the artist in relation to the material is not always of the same quality, for it could not easily be otherwise; it would be beyond human power to handle such vast material in a consistently poetical manner. But this by no means alters the fact that no other nation possesses an equally magnificent epic of the kind, embracing as does the *Shāh-nāma* the entire historical tradition, from the obscure age of myths down to the middle of the 7th century.

The views and descriptions are anachronisms[89] and, where geography and ethnography are concerned, fantastic ones at that; they can be traced back to the cultural ideas of those times. For instance Turan, the arch-enemy of Iran, is identified with the Turkish world[90], against which moreover the Sasanians were already fighting about the year 628. G. V. Ptitsïn[91], it is true, maintains that Firdausī's geography is correct in both the 'historical' and the legendary part, at any rate in respect of Eastern Iran and Central Asia. Love towards Iran, its antiquity and its history, towards its feudal system, its unbridled, valiant knighthood, yet, at the same time, a seemingly antithetical love towards an Iran with a strong central royal power capable of protecting the small *dihqāns* against the insatiability of the grandees – this latter may be regarded as a direct consequence of Firdausī's double position, first as a member of a proud aristocracy and secondly as a quite insignificant *dihqān* or small estate-owner, a member of that class whose landed property was already doomed – such ideas, so easy to understand when uttered by a small *dihqān* himself, form the foundation of the whole work. The *dihqān* has due respect for the work of the peasant but is little concerned in the craftsmen; yet the conservative landowner cannot ignore the latter's tendency to unrest and progress.[92] In the heroes of the *Shāh-nāma* too the true Iranians are reflected, albeit in a highly idealised light. They show a care-free gaiety, are boastful, loquacious and courageous. There are numerous realistic features characterising not only the persons but also here and there some of the stories. Naturally reality cannot be the central pivot of an epic of this kind. When Firdausī selected his material he was guided by factual and aesthetic considerations as well as psychological in order not only to give the actual facts but also to motivate them.[93] Firdausī is not exactly fond of the Arabs, but this is not at the expense of his religiosity[94], Shīʿite-tinted as it was. Firdausī does not explain away the fundamental duality of his sources but keeps any features liable to offend the Moslem reader in the background. Of course the feeling of pride based on the old Iranian religion was inseparable from that aroused by Iran's past. Firdausī as a Moslem had to avoid the conflict between the two religious ideologies. From the fact that he was not accused of holding secret Magian doctrines, one is inclined to assume that to cherish simultaneously both political and religious-patriotic feelings of pride was quite usual in those times. In this connection G. E. von Grunebaum[95] moreover points out that the poet draws no general conclusions from the events he describes nor does he interpret the facts in the light of any given synthesis. Firdausī's view of the past is lacking in unity because he is a reverer of the Iranian past and at the same time a Moslem. He conceals the antithesis of these two views by a slight touch of melancholy, evoked in him by the instability of things which always, in his opinion, show a tendency towards the less favorable, more wicked. His concrete manner of representation without a theoretical re-interpretation, the absence of a unifying synthetic background prove however in the end to be a great blessing, since they permit every epoch to rediscover itself in the past and thus to keep the past alive. Because the poet makes no attempt at synthetic unification, his work has become the common property of all Iranians and has contributed in no small measure to the strengthening and consolidation of the national consciousness. For the rest this was the ultimate aim of the poet himself.

The antiquity of the language corresponds with that of the events, as is shown by comparing it with contemporary lyrical poetry including that ascribed to Firdausī. His epical poetry, like that of Daqīqī, is linked on to folk and artistic tradition. This is also expressed by the *mutaqārib* verse-metre (see p. 154) which on the whole is admirably suited to the spirit of the Persian language though its immutable Bacchius-sequence (∪ — —) offers insufficient scope for an unlimited choice of words (including proper names). Poetic élan, conciseness (the latter not without exceptions), simplicity, absence of bombast are the basic qualities of the style of the *Shāh-nāma*; the hyperboles on the other hand are a typically oriental accessory.

The *Shāh-nāma* is of extreme importance. Its patriotic value has been referred to above and cannot be sufficiently emphasised. In depicting the illustrious past the poet appeals for a rebuilding of erstwhile greatness. It is a call to action, virility, and diligence, in which he perceives a remedy for the growing quietism of mysticism.

Among the heroes of the *Shāh-nāma* there is not a single one lacking confidence in his own strength.[96] He is quite aware of the omnipotence of Fate, yet his commands are not to evade difficulties but to fight against them until evil is overcome. This call to action lent strength to the nation whenever it had to raise itself up again after disintegration and subjugation. *Tavānā buvad har-ki dānā buvad*, "powerful is he who rules in virtue of his knowledge": this is the motto of the publications of the Iranian Ministry of Education. The proclamation of the right of reason and emphatic stress on the significance of knowledge represent a progressive component of Firdausī's work.[97]

A brief reference to its literary recognition may be made here. Firdausī's work was always held in the highest esteem and was often imitated. Towards the end of the 5th/11th century and at the beginning of the following a reaction to the heroic epic and to Firdausī seems to have been noticeable – at least this is how M. Mīnuvī[98] explains the 'Ṭoghānshāh' romance, *Yūsuf u Zalīkhā*, with its condemnation of the pre-Islamic heroes; he is supported in this opinion by the nagging of the panegyrist Muʿizzī. Still earlier ʿUnṣurī and Farrukhī had carried on a polemic discussion with Firdausī, maintaining it was senseless to extol the deeds of warriors long since dead while there were so many living fighters in the army of Sultan Maḥmūd; they even accused Firdausī of having idealised the Zoroastrians[99] – but these are insignificant deviations from the general conviction and in most cases even imposed eye-service.

Fragments of separate lyrics have also been preserved under Firdausī's name, but the question of their authenticity inevitably arises.[100]

F. EPIC POEMS CONNECTED WITH THE 'SHĀH-NĀMA'

The heroic epical (Asadī's 'Garshāsp-nāma'), the semi-historical, religious and historical. Extracts from the 'Shāh-nāma'. Translations, adaptations, etc.

Analogous to the group of cyclic poems that surround the works of Homer are the various epics that encircle the *Shāh-nāma* even up to the present day. According to their contents they can be divided into secondary epics (romances of chivalry and adventure) and historical epics, the form of both types being dependent on the verse-metre and especially on the style of the *Shāh-nāma*, whereby the historical epics not infrequently degenerate into grotesque anachronisms (thus for instance Ṣabā's epic composed at the beginning of the 19th century). Dhabīḥu'llāh Ṣafā[101] devoted his attention to chivalric, historical and religious epics alike. Maryan Molé has rightly observed that one may no longer be content with the traditional opinions, which in a manner as contemptuous as it is superficial, dispose of the whole subject of the followers of Firdausī who form a large and thus not fortuitous link in the chain of literary productions. A series of secondary epics (I will not enumerate all of them) appears in the 5th/11th to 6th/12th centuries. Among the earliest are the *Garshāsp-nāma* (author: Asadī), *Burzū-nāma* (author: ʿAmīd ʿAṭā'ī), *Bahmān-nāma* (author: Īrānshāh b. Abi'l-Khayr or Jamālī Mihrījirdī), and *Kūsh-nāma* (by the same author), all of which date from towards the end of the 5th/11th century; the *Farāmurz-nāma* appears to have originated at about the same time. To that period, between the first crusades and the Mongol invasion, belongs the religiously biased *Jahāngīr-nāma* (according to Ṣafā, by Qāsim Mādiḥ of Herat)[102], to the early Timurid era the *Sām-nāma* which though in some versions a brazen plagiarism of Khvājū's *Humāy va Humāyūn* (see p. 260) is, in Ṣafā's opinion, very likely a work by Khvājū himself and for the rest more a court romance than an epic[103], although written in *mutaqārib*. Various redactions are nevertheless characteristic not only of the *Sām-nāma* but of a large number of the epics in this category. The most comprehensive of them is the *Burzū-nāma*, dating from the 5th–6th/11th–12th century and containing 65,000 distichs. General features: the secondary epics, some of them anonymous, aimed at completing the work of Firdausī who claimed to have by no means exhausted the whole of the national tradition and in fact encouraged others to do so.[104] There is, however, a fundamental difference, for the writers of post-Firdausī epics, though indeed developing mythical Iranian subjects, are no longer inspired by the greatness of Iran's past. They are mainly concerned in providing entertaining descriptions of the motley and incredible adventures that befall the hero of the moment; he is always the greatest of all, no one can be compared to him (for instance, Asadī's Garshāsp surpasses even Rustam). The indisputable and facile victories are only detrimental to the poetic side of the work. With the exception of the *Kūsh-nāma* all the cyclic epics extol the heroes of Sistan, which is not surprising if we bear in mind that the Sistan saga constitutes the actual heroic legend of the *Shāh-nāma*. By means of a complicated continuation and expansion of the legendary versions, their heroes are all presented to us as relatives of Rustam, which, in virtue of their being heroes, is as it were compulsory for them. Beginning with the *Garshāsp-nāma* the heroes of these epics set out in stereotype fashion on a journey to foreign lands, mostly to India, where a vast field of adventure awaits them and where the atmosphere is pregnant with wonders and magic, where hermits (Brahmans) discuss the problems of the world and of life. The framework is similar to that of the Alexander romance of *Pseudo-Callisthenes*. Though the influence of the latter is already noticeable in Firdausī (and no doubt also still earlier), in particular as regards the person of Alexander, it manifests itself patently to a greater extent in the secondary epics and – as stated by H. Massé[105] – most conspicuously in the *Garshāsp-nāma*. In the *Faramūrz-nāma* it is especially evident. A further motif of all the secondary epics is the conflict between the father and son who are unknown to one another.

It is certainly typical of the intense seriousness of Firdausī's nature that this conflict has a tragic end in the *Shāh-nāma* only. In Firdausī's narrative no allusions are made to Islam. It is true that in a few external details there is evidence of Zoroastrianism but this is based on a monotheism acceptable to both the Islamic and the Zoroastrian doctrine of faith. The same attitude is revealed in the *Garshāsp-nāma* and *Bahmān-nāma*, the earliest epics, whilst in the more recent ones religious aspirations begin to increase in strength. The heroes are transformed into champions of faith, until in *Jahāngīr-nāma*, with its extreme arabising tendency, Islam is depicted in downright fanatical colours. The last offshoot of this movement is the *Khāvarān-nāma*[106] in which – the victory of the Safavid Shīʿa being already imminent – the epic tradition becomes Shīʿitic and the Imām ʿAlī takes the place of the chief hero. The *Garshāsp-nāma* and the *Kūsh-nāma* possess certain distinguishing marks: the first has strong didactic tendencies (on this account Asadī is called *Ḥakīm*, 'the Sage'), and the second brings forward not the struggle, as one of the fundamental elements, but the conception of the legitimate line of succession that forms the driving force of the action. Chivalric epics were important as expressing the spirit of the time, for the old Iranian knighthood was already approaching its irrevocable disappearance. Very promising perspectives are offered to mythological research and a further investigation of Iranian sagas. The older view that all these epics were merely void fantasies can no longer be accepted in such measure; one only needs to refer to the *Garshāsp-nāma*, between which and the others there is in this respect no fundamental difference. Finally it should be mentioned that some of the secondary epics belong to the field of folk literature.

Next in order of time to the author of the *Shāh-nāma*, at least so far as we know at present and as long as it is not proved that the *Shahryār-nāma* may be attributed to the poet Farrukhī (see p. 176)[107], is Abū-Manṣūr ʿAlī b. Aḥmad Asadī (born in Ṭūs about the beginning of the second decade of the 11th century), whose life and true significance have been critically reviewed by K. Chaykin.[108] The assumption that there were two Asadīs, father and son, has already been rejected by Badīʿu'z-zamān Bushrūya'ī,[109] for the author of the heroic epic *Garshāsp-nāma* (9000 verses) and of the oldest extant Persian lexicon (*Kitāb-i lughat-i Furs*) cannot be separated from the poet of several *tenzon-qaṣīdas*, the earliest records of this kind in Persian verse – a thesis generally accepted today. The epic *Garshāsp-nāma* was composed by Asadī in 456–8/1064–6 and was dedicated to Abū-Dulaf, a prince in Transcaucasian Nakhjavān. How long he stayed there, far from his native Ṭūs, has not been ascertained. Some time after 1072 he appeared in Ānī, passing through on the way from an unknown place of residence. He died round about the end of the eighth decade of the 11th century; according to Riḍā-qulī-Khān, as early as 465/1072–3.[110]

Asadī draws our attention for more than one reason. By quoting in his lexicon a large number of illustrations from the poets up to date, he provides literary historians with an opportunity, up till then unique and considerably more exhaustive and deeper than that offered by the oldest *tadhkiras*, of penetrating to the beginnings of Persian literature. Thanks to his calligraphic skill a very ancient Persian literary document has been preserved for us (see p. 150). He rehabilitated an old autochthonous form by introducing the tenzon into Persian verse. No less an achievement is finally the *Garshāsp-nāma* which, although it already inaugurates the secondary epic, nevertheless continues along the lines of the heroic epic and forms the last offshoot of the method adopted by Daqīqī, Firdausī, and their predecessors. He has therefore much in common with Firdausī – and this literary similarity between Asadī and the creator of the great *Shāh-nāma* is what the alleged relationship is based on – but he also reveals characteristics of his own. Asadī's *Garshāsp-nāma* draws from the oral tradition of Sistan and also from the *Kitāb-i Garshāsp* of Abu'l-Mu'ayyad Balkhī (see p. 150).[111] It can be shown that Asadī kept to his model just as faithfully as did Firdausī without letting his imagination run riot. He says himself in his introduction that he wanted to supplement the great poet of Ṭūs in those parts that the latter had purposely omitted and to preserve a portion of the Iranian saga that would otherwise probably have been lost. His language, although on the whole following in the track of the *Shāh-nāma*, in no way equals the magnificent simplicity of the model, because on the one hand he purposely uses words which for Firdausī were already out of date, and on the other hand indulges in scholasticism. Erudition and religious principles – Asadī is even called *Asadu'l-ḥukamā'*, 'Lion of the Wise', on that account – suppress warmth of feeling. The aims of these two differ completely: whereas Firdausī paints pictures which in their powerfulness remain matchless in the literature of the world, Asadī merely fills up a gap that in fact is only imaginary. When Firdausī omitted the *Garshāsp-nāma* it was obviously only because he, very rightly, did not want to duplicate the figure of Rustam. As Marquart and Herzfeld have already stated, Rustam is identical with Garshāsp (certainly a later stage in the development of the legend of Garshāsp; and, more exactly, M. Molé[112] who regards it as a later adaptation of the orthodox Zoroastrian version).

Under the influence of the *Shāh-nāma* semi-historical and historical epics were also produced. Among these we reckon several Alexander books and epics dealing with members of the Prophet's family, Shī'ite in tendency, written now and then within the compass of popular literature. Careful consideration deserves to be given to the opinion of H. Massé[113], namely that the philosophical discussions of the Brahmans (here 'hermits') lead to the creation of the Ṣūfi-didactic epic in the 6th/12th century (see however p. 236), for not less than one third of the *Garshāsp-nāma* is taken up by didacticism. In practically all the truly historical epics poetical value is lacking. Every one of the rulers of Iran, but also those of 'Turan', longed to be immortalised in a *Shāh-nāma*, *Shāhanshāh-nāma*, *Pādshāh-nāma* or something of the sort[114], and this longing has not altered in the course of time. The poets, always on the look-out for material advantage, were lavish in their praises, which often reached fabulous heights. Therefore, even from the historical point of view, all these numerous epics cannot be assessed very highly, to say nothing of those works that were substantially (or literally) copies of Firdausī. There are however exceptions, such as the *Ẓafar-nāma* of Ḥamdu'llāh Mustaufī of Qazvin, a historically valuable continuation of the *Shāh-nāma* right up to the date when it was written (735/1335), consisting of 75,000 distichs and representing the work of fifteen years. Naubakht's narrative extends from the time of the Arab occupation up to the present day. He iranises the language of his epic to the extent of excluding all Arabic expressions, thereby imbuing it with a strong national spirit.

But with all this the significance and influence of the *Shāh-nāma* are in no way exhausted. There remain to be mentioned the poetry and prose extracts, numerous translations (of importance for text-criticism of Firdausī is Bundārī's translation into Arabic dating from the beginning of the 7th/13th century[115]), recastings and their reverberations among the masses at home and in neighbouring countries. The popular Russian love-story, *Yeruslan Lazarevich* (i.e. Rustam the son of Zāl-i zar) is derived from these.

G. PERSIAN AUTHORS IN ARABIC LITERATURE (850–1000)

During the period between about 850 and 1000 A.D. a large number of Iranians again played a part in Arabic literature. Here follow at least the most important of them: the two leading traditionalists, Muḥammad al-Bukhārī (d. 256/870) and Muslim of Nishapur (d. 269/883), together with further authorities in this field – the polyhistors ʿAbdu'llāh b. Qutayba of Merv (d. 276/889–90) and Abū-Ḥanīfa Dīnavarī (d. 282/895), the historian Aḥmad al-Balādhurī (d. 279/892), the historian and theologian Abū-Jaʿfar Ṭabarī (d. 310/923), the physician and encyclopaedist Abū-Bakr Muḥammad b. Zakariyyā ar-Rāzī ('Rhazes', d. 313/925), the Shīʿite theologian Muḥammad b. Bābūya (d. 381/991), the lexicographer Ismāʿīl al-Jauharī (d. 392/1002), the author of the affected *Maqāmas*, Badīʿu'z-zamān Hamadānī[116] (d. 398/1008) and others. Besides these a detailed history of literature records an immense number of Iranians who wrote poems in Arabic or in the two languages. Yet R. Blachère rightly observes that as the Iranian renaissance flourished, its deeper influence on Arabic literature gradually waned.[117]

NOTES

1. Barthold, 'Shuʿūb.' (B II), 262.
2. *Ibid.*, 252.
3. Yakubovskiy (B II), *Makhmud*, 53–72.
4. B. G. Gafurov, 'O prichinakh' (B II), 55: "The Samanid Empire, tool of the supremacy of the

powerful feudal aristocracy, was not able to withstand the pressure from without and fell into disintegration because it found no support among the people, whose interests and expectations were violently and irreconcilably opposed to those of the feudal nobility."

5. Shiblī, 4, 108.

6. Shiblī, 4, 97.

7. *Muzdavij*: cf. above, p. 123_{89}; *rubāʿī* in the foregoing sense: Ye. E. Bertel's, IPTL, 88, 107 *et seq.* and above, p. 123_{81}.

8. Likewise von Grunebaum, *Kritik* (B IV), 27, though with the additional remark that in the 11th century the issue was already decided and Persia no longer contributed directly to Arabic literature. For information on the translations in the 10th century: M. I. Zand, *Iskusstvo perevoda* (B VIa).

9. It appears that even today Iranian scholars are contemplating tackling this problem (see Bibl. under Ṭāhirī Shihāb, Dabīr Siyāqī); earlier however Rypka/Borecký (*q.v.*). *

10. Cf. p. 98. Also Bertel's, IPTL, 150 *et seq.*

11. Thus Ye. E. Bertel's, in agreement with ʿAufī, cf. F. Meier, *Mahsatī*, 41. The latter has recently devoted a large study to this poetess (*ibid.*, 27–42). Further references: M. Ishaque; Rādūyānī, *Tarcumân*, 144–8; Dh. Ṣafā, *Ta'rīkh*, 1, 452–4.

12. Born 850–60 (M. I. Zand, *Sokhibqiron*, 15) at Rūdak near Samarkand. Muḥ. Muʿīn, 'Rūdagī yā Rūdakī?', *Yaghmā*, 12, 1338, 53 *et seq.*

13. ʿAbb. Iqbāl: Bertel's, 'Lit. na pers. yaz. v Sr. Az.' (D IIa) 206_1. In his essay 'Baʿze mas'alahoi tarjimai holi Rūdakī', *SSh*, 1966/1, 126–30, A. Tagırjanov contributes the following to the problems arising around Rūdakī: (1) following an invitation the poet (b. 850–60) is said to have gone to the Samanid court at Samarkand in his youth where he served first Naṣr I (acc. Tagirjanov 842–82) and subsequently several other rulers; Naṣr II (914–42) thus cannot enter the picture; (2) the assumption that Naṣr II with his train, including Balʿamī and Rūdakī, were converted to Qarmatism is thus an error – they had no association with this sect; (3) Rūdakī is said to have been born blind, and not to have become blind or, having been blinded, expelled from the court; (4) as to a rational assessment of the number of verses, the author arrives at a total of 13 × 10,000 (as opposed to the traditional '1,300,000'), viz. 130,000, a figure that at any rate more nearly approximates to the bounds of possibility.

14. Thus also Nafīsī, *Rūdakī*, 554. The same scholar persisted in this opinion again recently in his essay 'Chand nukta-i tāza' (*q.v.*) and even laid emphasis on a blindness caused by violence. He claims his theory to be substantiated by an archeological find in Rūdakī's grave, when this was discovered and opened up (cf. below, note 16). Blindness from birth is on the other hand corroborated by Badīʿu'z-zamān Furūzānfar in the essay 'Shiʿr va shāʿirī-i Rūdakī' (*q.v.*), that appeared in one and the same celebration number of the *MDAT*. *

15. Probably only outwardly in order to gain the favour of Naṣr II and his circle: A. Ye. Bertel's, *Rudaki*, 78. Cf. A. N. Boldïrev, 'Bïl-li Rudaki ismailitom?', *ArOr.*, 30, 1962, 541–2: no more than as a follower of the average Shīʿa. *

16. In conformity with Samʿānī's *Kitābu'l-ansāb*. For a report on the grave discovered at Panchrūd near Rūdak cf. R. Amonov, *Qabri Rūdakī*.

17. Cf. Sabk, 3, 103 *et seq.*

18. Thus Daulatshāh (9th/15th century), who was only able to account for the effect – to him incredible – produced by the poem by its having been set to music. Niẓāmī ʿArūḍī (6th/12th century), a man of fine feeling, speaks very highly of the poem, cf. Yār Shāṭir, *Shiʿr-i fārsī*, 103 *et seq.* For a detailed account see M. Muʿīn, *Yak qaṣīda-i Rūdakī* (*q.v.*). As early as the 12th century Rūdakī's simplicity did not satisfy the 'innovators': Bertel's: IPTL, 485.

19. Bertel's, *op. cit.*, 212. A. Mirzoyev, *Rūdakī*, 73 *et seq.* (Russian 69 *et seq.*) calls special attention to Rūdakī's enormous influence on the further development of Persian poetry and this can certainly not be contested. But to prove it he quotes the *istiqbāls* of Sanā'ī and Ḥāfiẓ, in both cases replies to Rūdakī's well-known poem *Būy-i jūy-i Mūliyān āyad hamī*, 'The fragrance of the River Mūliyān

flows hither', the same poem that was also imitated by Vaṣṣāf and others. I am afraid that Rūdakī's *dīvān* was all too soon lost.

20. The *Shāh-nāma* also bears witness to Rūdaki's version, ed. Tehran 1314:8, 3503; in addition Nafīsī, *Rūdak*, 583–92. A short survey of the versions of *Kalīla u Dimna*: Ishaque, 'Rūdakī', *Indo-Ir.*, 2/1, 1947, 6, note 2.

21. The credit for having established Rūdakī as the author of this epic poem must be given to Th. Nöldeke, cf. Asadī's New Persian dictionary, ed. P. Horn, 21; according to Nafīsī, *Rūdakī*, 2, 595, perhaps identical with the *mathnavī Daurān-i āftāb*, which the dictionary *Farhang-i Jahāngīrī* attributes to Rūdakī, Siyāqī, 'Rūdakī va Sindbād-nāma', *Yaghmā*, 8/5, 1334, 218–23 *et seq.*, has made important progress in the sifting of all doubtful 'Sindbād' verses.

22. The millenary celebrations of the poet's birth held at Dushanbe in the autumn of 1958 brought to light, among other things, beautiful editions of his *dīvān* and of the *Ash'ori hamasroni Rūdakī* (both being the work of the eminent Tajik scholar A. Mirzoyev), that of the *dīvān* also in Arabic script.

23. Also perhaps 'Barlam and Joasaf'? See below, n. 36.

24. *Pers. poez. v Bukhare* (B VIa), recently again IPTL, 125 *et seq.*

25. Ṣafā, 2, 536.

26. Barthold, 'Shu'ūb.', 262.

27. *Rūdakī*, 44 (Russian 40). Muhandis Nāṭiq takes Badī'u'z-zamān to be an Arab fully conscious of his nationality and with anti-Shu'ūbitic inclinations: *Yaghmā*, 7, 269 *et seq.*

28. Rev. translation (Bibl. B VIb, *s.v.* 'Niẓāmī 'Arūḍī'), 119.

29. Zarre, *Ocherk* (B V), 58.

30. *Op. cit.*, 55 *et seq.*

31. Thus Bertel's, cf. however p. 95.

32. Cf. his works enumerated in the Bibl. (D IIa).

33. Minorsky, *Early Documents* (B VIa), I, 183 *et seq.*; *Ḥudūdu'l-'ālam*, XII.

34. *BSOAS*, 20, 1957, 335–342.

35. Cf. Shafī'ī Kadkanī (M. Sirishk), RK, 6, 1342, 349 *et seq.*

36. See Bibl. under W. B. Henning.

37. On this treatise: Mahdī Bayānī, 'Yak namūna-i nathr-i fārsī az daura-i Rūdakī yā qadīmtarīn nathr-i fārsī-i maujūd', *MDAT*, 6/3-4, 1338, 57–70; *Yaghmā*, 16, 1342, 193–200. Earlier M. Mu'īn, *MDAT*, 2, 1333, 2_2; idem, *Jashn-nāma-i I.-Sīnā*, 2, 343 *et seq.*; A. N. Boldïrev, *Iz istorii* (B IV), 81. According to Arberry, *CPL*, 32, there are some grounds for thinking that a 'prose epic' already existed in the first half of the 8th century and that it related the revolt of Ḥamza b. 'Abdu'llāh against Hārūn ar-Rashīd. *

38. In two redactions, the second composed between 976 and the end of the 10th century, cf. Gryaznevich-Boldïrev in the bibliography (B VIb *s.v.* 'Ṭabarī'). *

39. Romaskevich, *Pers. tafsīr* (B VIb), 803 *et seq.* R. Levy, 'Tafsīr-i kuhan', *RK*, 4, 1340, 1078 *et seq.*: MS. 628/1231 from an original text, probably about 400/1006. *

40. Cf. *Gulistān*, ed. Garakānī, p. 'nz' and Mahdī Bayānī, *l.c.*, 60.

41. Cf. V. Minorsky, *Iranica* (B VIa), 327–32.

42. 'Svodï', 170, 182.

43. *Sabk*, 2, 24; Qazvīnī, *Bīst maqāla*, 2, 202–4.

44. Krause, *Al-Bīrūnī* (B VIb), 14 *et seq.* *

45. Ateş, *İA*, 2, 638a.

46. Acc. 'Abb. Iqbāl, *Jashn-nāma-i I.-Sīnā*, 2, 201 *et seq.*, more accurate: *Dānish-māya-i...*

47. *Sabk*, 2, 35 *et seq.*

48. In this connection the introduction to the Persian translation of the great commentary on the Koran deserves attention. When in about the year 963 A.D. the forty volumes of the Arabic original

by the Iranian Ṭabarī reached the Samanid court, it was soon realised that only with difficulty could the book be read and understood. Therefore Amīr Abū-Ṣāliḥ Manṣūr b. Nūḥ decreed that the work should be translated into Persian. The 'Ulamās gave legal permission based on the Koran, 14, 4: "And let no prophet be sent out except with the language of his people." Dating approximately from the same time are the first interlinear translations of the Koran (A. J. Arberry, *Class. Pers. Lit.*, 40 *et seq.*).

49. 'Abb. Iqbāl, 'Qadīmtarīn āthār-i mafqūd-i nathr-i fārsī', *Majalla-i Sharq*, 93–103; Dh. Ṣafā, *Ta'rīkh*, 1, 105; *GAL*, 1, 231; suppl. 1, 413. The most complete record that has appeared up to date of the earliest, no longer extant documents of literature is that of Madhī Bayānī, *op. cit.*, 58 *et seq.*, containing in all 17 titles dated between 132–401/749–1011.

50. See the recent standard work on the subject by M.-N. Osmanov, 'Svodï' (Bibl. B VIb). *

51. Rozen-Kirste: Bibl., see under 'Kirste'.

52. Barthold-Schaeder, *Zur Gesch. des pers. Epos*, 152.

53. *Op. cit.*, 176 *et seq.*

54. Chaykin, *Ferdousi*, 76.

55. Barthold-Schaeder (note 52), 122.

56. Cf. A. N. Boldïrev, *Novopersidskiye obrabotki* (B VIa), and idem in *Nauchnaya konferentsiyapo iranskoy filologii (tezisi dokladov)*, Leningrad 1962, p. 45. *

57. Minorsky, *Iran* (B II), 199 (2).

58. Barthold, *ibid.*, 153; Schaeder, 'War Daqīqī Zoroastrier?', *Jubilee Volume G. Jacob*, 1932; Ritter, 'Daqîqî', *İA*, 3, 463b.

59. Ritter, 'Firdevsî', *İA*, 4, 648b *et seq.*; from *GIPh*, 2, 148 it can be concluded that Bīrūnī's account was unknown to Nöldeke; Massé, *Firdousi*, 48.

60. Massé, *ibid.*, 50; Ritter, 'Daqîqî', *İA*, 3, 463a *et seq.*

61. Ritter, *ibid.*, 462b.

62. *Sabk*, 2, 24.

63. Barthold-Schaeder (see note 52), 143.

64. *Pers. poez. v Bukh.* (B VIa), 39 *et seq.*

65. 'Le texte du Draxt asūrīk et la versification pehlevie', *JA*, 1930, 224.

66. Incontestably to be interpreted thus: Ritter, 'Firdevsî', *İA*, 4, 644a; von Grunebaum, 'Firdausī', *Islam*, 168, thus on p. 156 only apparently in disagreement: *Shāh-nāma*, 21, 31, according to Wolff's glossary the only place – perhaps overlooked by Firdausī – where the Samanids are mentioned.

67. Bertel's, *Pers. poez. v Bukh.* (B VIa), 38, 40.

68. See below, note 82.

69. *Das iran. Nationalepos*, 151; Ritter, 'Firdevsî', *İA*, 4, 643a *et seq.*

70. 'Svodï', 188.

71. Cf. von Grunebaum, 'Firdausī', *Islam*, 170, 171.

72. Mīnuvī, *Kit. Hazāra-i Fird.*, 17 *et seq.*

73. Cf. however above, note 66.

74. In his interesting essay 'Şâh-nâme'nin yazılış tarihi', A. Ateş places the final redaction of the *Shāh-nāma* between 409–12/1019–22, these dates being based first of all and purely theoretically on accurately certifiable dates. The aged poet is said to have submitted this redaction to the sultan in 409/1019 or 410/1020, though without appearing in Ghazna himself. The familiar traditional story about the arrival of the gifts from Maḥmūd is maintained by Ateş with certain reservations, but the poet himself will not have lived to see it since he died in 411/1021. In his essay 'Otnositel'no nekotorïkh dat zhiznennogo puti Firdousi', *KS*, 65, 1964, 128–33, M.-N. Osmanov takes an opposite view to A. Ateş and puts forward the following very plausible dates: Firdausī born 329/940–1, commenced the *Shāh-nāma* 365/975–6, completed the first redaction 384/994–5, completed the second redaction 400/1009–10, though Osmanov admits that some passages may have been composed after this date.

75. Chaykin, *Ferdousi*, 83; Ateş, *op. cit.*, 164_2 (French 174_1); *ibid.*, 164 *et seq.* respect. 174 *et seq.* Ateş rejects the satire attributed to Firdausī altogether on the ground of convincing evidence.
76. Mīnuvī, *Kit. Hazāra-i Fird.*, 19 *et seq.*; Bibl. see under 'Khayyāmpūr', *Yūsuf u Zalīkhā*; Bibl., see under 'Nafīsī, 'Le "Yûsuf et Zalîkhâ".'
77. Muḥ. Qazvīnī, *Bīst maqāla* (Bibl. VIa), 2, 2, is not able to disclose any connection between Bāysunghur b. Shāh-rukh b. Tīmūr Gūrkān and the above-mentioned preface. A copy of Bāysunghur's redaction dating from 1425–6 has been preserved in the library of the Gulistān Palace in Tehran (Bertel's, IPTL, 170 note).
78. *Op. cit.*, 353.
79. See however M.-N. Osmanov, 'Svodï', 173_{90}, according to whom priority is already due to Abu'l-Mu'ayyad Balkhī (10th century).
80. Ritter, 'Firdevsî', *İA*, 4, 644 *et seq.*; Tagirdjanov, 338. It is quite possible that both have altered their opinions in the meantime. Bert., IPTL, 232 has no doubts whatsoever as to the authenticity.
81. M.-N. Osmanov does not reach a similar final conclusion in his 'Tekstologicheskiye zametki k "Shakh-name"', *KS*, 63, 1962, 136–8; Parts III and IV 1965.
82. 'Novoye izdaniye "Shah-name" Firdousi ot redaktsii "Kratkikh soobshcheniy"', *KS*, 13, 1955, 3–71. Meanwhile Part I has already appeared, see my review *ArOr.*, 29, 1961, 689; Part II in 1962 (up to and including 'Suhrāb').
83. To Firdausī we owe the definitive uniting of the Sistan and Zabulistan Saga with the main stream of Iranian tradition, cf. von Grunebaum, 'Firdausī', *Islam*, 170; Hansen, *Das iranische Königsbuch*, 70–72 (= Sep. 8–10).
84. Tardov, *Ferdousi i Mazdak*, 134 *et seq.*
85. Chaykin, 'Ferdousi', 86, 85.
86. Osmanov, 'O nar. tendentsiyakh', 42; cf. Ritter, *Das Meer der Seele*, 126.
87. From the military point of view: Aḥmad Bahār-mast (*q.v.*).
88. Osmanov, *Firdousi*, 155, 165.
89. Cf. von Grunebaum, 'Firdausī', *Islam* (B II), 170, b. 1–2.
90. Bibl. *s.v.* 'Kovalski, Les Turcs' – according to Bertel's, IPTL, 200_{43}, incorrect.
91. Bibl. *s.v.* 'Ptitsïn, K voprosu'.
92. Chaykin, 'Ferdousi', 76 *et seq.*
93. Osmanov, *Firdousi*, 149 *et seq.*: a detailed analysis of the creative work of Firdausī.
94. Cf. Dr. Rajā'ī, 'Madhhab-i Firdausī', *NDAT*, 11, 1338, 105–13: there can be no doubt of Firdausī's adherence to the Shī'a. Similarly Osmanov, *Firdousi*, 85.
95. 'Firdausî', *Islam*, 171, 172, 175 *et seq.*
96. A. Mirzoyev, *Sayyido Nasafī* (D IIb), 11_1.
97. Osmanov, *op. cit.*, 77 *et seq.*
98. *Kit. Hazāra-i Fird.*, 24b; Ṣafā, 'Tasalluṭ' (B II), 53 *et seq.*
99. Osmanov, *Firdousi*, 23 *et seq.* *
100. Ethé, *Firdûsî als Lyriker*, München 1872; further material: Shafaq, *Firdausī-nāma* (see Bibl. *s.v.* 'Firdausī'), 615 *et seq.* An unauthentic verse is referred to by 'Abb. Iqbāl, *ibid.*, 478.
101. Bibl. *s.v.* 'Ṣafā, *Ḥamāsa*' (B VIa); Bibl. *s.v.* 'Molé'.
102. *Op. cit.*, 309.
103. Molé (in a letter dated 30.4.54) with a reference to Wl. Ivanow, Conc. descr. Cat., 1924, 249 *et seq.*; cf. also Molé, 'L'épopée', 384; Ṣafā, *Ḥamāsa*, 335–40. A. J. Arberry sees a *mutaqārib* epic of this class in the *Humāy-nāma*, undoubtedly dating from before 1200 A.D. and dealing with an event that took place before 223/838: 'An Early Persian Epic', *Mél. Massé*, Teheran 1963, 11–16.
104. Massé, *Firdousi*, 263. The authors are enumerated by Ṣafā, *Ganj-i sukhan*, 1, 63 *et seq.*
105. Ad Massé, see Molé, 'L'épopée', 387 *et seq.*; cf. Molé, 'L'orthodoxie zoroastrienne'. *La nouv. Clio*, 1951, 312_3, 316.

106. The present author: Maulānā Muḥ. b. Ḥusām (d. 875/1470) from the mountainous regions of south Khurasan. Not a courtier but a husbandman who even wrote poetry in the fields. Not a distinguished talent. Both his *Khāvarān-nāma* (correct version, not *Khāvar-nāma*!) and his *qaṣīdas* in praise of the Prophet and the Imāms are favourite reading among the people (Krïmskiy, 3, 121; Ṣafā, *Ḥamāsa*, 356 et seq.) Ṣafā, *ibid.*, 357–65: other later epics of the same trend. See also Bibl. *s.v.* 'Rājī'.
107. Cf. J. Rypka–M. Borecký, 'Farrukhī', *ArOr.*, 16, 1947, 22. Ye. E. Bertel's, IPTL, 401, and all the others only mention 'Uthmān Mukhtārī (d. 544/1149–50 or 549/1154–5) as the author of the *Shahryār-nāma* which, according to Bertel's, *l.c.*, describes the struggle of the Muslims against the Indian heathens at the time of the Ghaznavids. The epic was composed in the space of three years, between 492–508/1098–1115. The small fragment preserved in the British Museum (add. 24,095) has now been completed by the MS 1718 acquired by the Foundation of Oriental MSS of the AN Taj. SSR. Cf. K. S. Ayni, *K izucheniyu* (B VIb). On the significance of the *Shahryār-nāma* (and other cyclic epics) for criticism of our *Shāh-nāma* text, see the extremely important explanations of Humā'ī in his *Dīvān-i Mukhtārī*, 747–95. *
108. Bibl. *s.v.* 'Chaykin, *Asadi*'. Unusually valuable and new is H. Massé, Introduction to *Le Livre de Gerchâsp*, 2, I–XXI.
109. *Sukhan va sukhanvarān*, 2/1: Asadī, 89–94.
110. Ye. E. Bertel's, 'Pyatoye munazare' (Bibl.) makes some very astute observations: his theory is that Asadī left Ṭūs on account of hunger and made his way across N. Iran to Nahjavān (78); necessity led him to become copyist of the *Kitābu'l-abniya* (*ibid.*; cf. p. 150). He was a *dihqān* and defender of the Iranian aristocracy against the Arab influence (79), but he was also critical of the former – their decadence could not escape his notice (88); a Shu'ūbī (78) but nevertheless true to the orthodoxy of Islam (92). Through a lack of humaneness and his failing to idealise the ancient heroes he came into collision with tradition (68), but through affectation and a straining after effect with the *Shāh-nāma* (67). His dictionary is closely related to his epic poem (86), being a preliminary study to the same.
111. Cf. above, p. 150; thus also *Muḥaṣṣil* in Kāve, 1921, Nr. 12, p. 28 (Chaykin, *Asadi*, 157).
112. J. Marquart and E. Herzfeld: Molé, 'Rustam', 269.
113. Ad Massé: cf. Molé, 'L'épopée', 388 *et seq.*; Molé, 'L'orthodoxie' (see note 105), 317.
114. For details on the separate historical epics, see Ṣafā, *Ḥamāsa*, 335–54.
115. Likewise the Georgian translations of the *Shāh-nāma*, cf. D. I. Kobidze, Bibl. B VIb; A. A. Gvakhariya, Bibl. B VIb, where, among other things, emendations to the epic *Vīs u Rāmīn*, derived from the Georgian version (p. 179) is specially drawn attention to.
116. See nevertheless p. 168₂₇.
117. Brunschvig–von Grunebaum, *Classicisme* (B II), 347.

IV. THE GHAZNAVID PERIOD

(5th/11th century)

A. YAMĪNU'D-DAULA SULṬĀN MAḤMŪD OF GHAZNA

The Samanid empire, outwardly so glorious, was inwardly however troubled by dissension and strife [1], and this accounted for its falling an easy prey to the rapacity of Sulṭān Maḥmūd and the Iligh-Khāns (Karakhānids, Āl-i Afrāsyāb). Sulṭān Maḥmūd too relied for support on a guard of slaves belonging to various tribes and on volunteers (*ghāzī* or *mutaṭavviʿ*). But whereas the Samanids had pursued a policy of peace, he kept his army engaged in a rapid succession of campaigns against India, not so much with a view to annexation or sincere propagation of the Islamic faith as in the first place for the sake of loot. It was on this that Maḥmūd himself lived and maintained his army and his court, and perhaps also the municipal guilds of artisans in as far as he employed part of the plundered goods for the embellishment of his residency. In this way he satisfied the ruling classes as well as the army, including the *ghāzīs*, who owing to the restlessness of the situation had no leisure in which to organise rebellions. Such was the nature of the Sulṭān's political wisdom. While the peasants were subject to high duties to cover the costs of the annual military campaigns, the Iranian *dihqāns* were systematically driven out of the army and the civil posts by a new Turkish 'nobility', drawn in the first place from the military ranks. The differences became more sharply pronounced than before, but Maḥmūd managed to keep all his opponents in check with his regiments and his officials. Although he was more far-sighted than the Samanids, he was nevertheless only able to suppress the outbursts of dissatisfaction and in no sense to remove the cause. His foreign policy had various objects in view. While he was of one mind with the Iranian world in its struggle against the Iligh-Khāns, his sympathy for Iran slackened when he started making advances to the Caliphs of Baghdad, a step on which he apparently set great store. The third period of his reign is characterised by the attempt to penetrate into Central Asia and Western

Persia, i.e. to form a great Iranian empire. A reflection of this last stage can be seen in the sentimental legend about an extremely generous gift to Firdausī who had just died (see pp. 157, 169). Whereas Maḥmūd himself managed to set bounds to the pressure of the Turkish tribes, his successors lacked sufficient talent, and so it came to pass that as early as the year 1040, thus ten years after Maḥmūd's death, comparatively small groups of Seljuq Turks succeeded in overthrowing the great kingdom, for all that was left to the dynasty consisted of a few scanty remnants.

B. MAḤMŪD'S ATTITUDE TO CULTURE

Although Sulṭān Maḥmūd undeniably possessed qualities as a warrior and a statesman, the fact that he was one of the most wicked despots must nevertheless not be ignored. With his domineering will he interfered with everything. As an avowed Sunnite and conqueror he naturally found no satisfaction in the Shīʿa and hated the Ismāʿīlī doctrine of whose liberating political tendencies he was quite conscious. He spent considerable sums on pompous display at his court, on the erection of various edifices and on the stimulation of poetry, for he was well aware that this in itself would help to establish his popularity and authority. He thus gained a reputation for being the greatest Maecenas ever known in the literature of Persia. He was surrounded by a large group of poets and scholars; for Ghazna now took on the leading part that had been played by Bukhara under the Samanids. Although it cannot be denied that Maḥmūd was a cultured man, the aureole of legends surrounding his person must be counted responsible for his being reported by some 'histories' of literature to have been actively engaged in the field of poetry himself.[2] These very legends prove that his faith in the effect of propaganda was not misplaced. In order to enhance the brilliance of his court he concentrated at Ghazna the plundered libraries and had no scruples about inducing the bearers of the most famous names among contemporary Islamic scholars, such as Abū-ʿAlī b. Sīnā (Avicenna) of Bukhara (b. 370/980, d. 428/1037) and Abu'r-Rayḥān al-Bīrūnī of Khvārazm (b. 362/973, d. 443/1051) to move from their home towns, that had recently been subjugated, and to take up their residence in Ghazna. The Ismāʿīlite Avicenna managed to escape, but not so al-Bīrūnī, who obeyed the command but nearly lost his life because he was suspected of Qarmatism. It was only thanks to his fame and the practical applicability of his extensive knowledge in the interests of the kingdom that he was treated leniently and was eventually even able to enjoy the high favour of the court at Ghazna. Maḥmūd introduced the office of *Maliku'sh-shuʿarā'*, 'King of Poets', the first to bear the title being ʿUnṣurī. There is no doubt that the establishing of this post implied a certain control on the poetry of the court.[3] It was only natural that under these circumstances panegyric

Notes on pp. 181–182

poetry should flourish most of all. And indeed poets and scholars took such pains to create a cloud of glory around the king that the figure of Maḥmūd was endowed for all time with the grotesque proportions of a hero of Iranian culture. The foresight with which he had conducted his propaganda was now in fact followed by great success.

C. THE PANEGYRIC POETS UNDER MAḤMŪD AND HIS SUCCESSORS

(Unṣurī and his circle; ʿAsjadī, Farrukhī; Manūchihrī)

In the *Shāh-nāma*, a true product of the Samanid period, the heroic epic reaches its climax, though the love-scenes already give it a certain tinge of romanticism. The poets surrounding Sulṭān Maḥmūd and his dynasty accomplish still more: the romantic epic, a manifestation of urban power, broadens and expands, contrary to works by the successors of Firdausī. The Turkish usurpers' need of popularity gives rise to a flowering of the *qaṣīda*, that glorifies them and is already highly embellished with tropes and figures. The *ghazal*, now becoming independent, as well as the fact of its increasing appearance, suit the wishes of Ṣūfism, a powerful and growing movement directed against the ruling classes. Whereas the epic, of whatever kind, adheres to the Iranian vocabulary as its basis, we find in the lyric a steady increase in arabising flourishes.

Feudalism calls for the nomination of a 'King of Poets' and regulates the relations of the masters of the profession and their pupils in the manner of the mediaeval guilds.

The central figure at court is Abu'l-Qāsim Ḥasan ʿUnṣurī (b. at the beginning of the second half of the 4th/10th century, d. 431/1039–40). Tradition maintains that he was born at Balkh as the son of a merchant and was intended to carry on the same occupation as his father. On one of his business journeys, however, he is said to have been robbed of all he possessed – of course a beggar-man's tale! He then, it is said, turned to study (typical of the attitude in respect of feudal poetry as a means of subsistence, which Firdausī was also familiar with) and won the favour of the Amīr Naṣr, a younger brother of the ruler. Through him he came into touch with Sulṭān Maḥmūd, who, as a result of his vanity and in the desire for publicity, was particularly pleased with the poet's aptitude for the panegyric. ʿUnṣurī was given the title 'King of Poets' and placed at the head of the 'four-hundred' members belonging to the court guild of poets. His *qaṣīdas*, embellished by a rhetoric hitherto unknown but which in no sense diminished the value of the contents, were considered both then and later as models of poetical perfection, as regards the lyrical introductions as well as the encomiums. For this reason, like his pupil Farrukhī, he was compared to the famous Arab poet al-Mutanabbī (d. 354/965). ʿUnṣurī's position at court – he was always a member of his master's retinue – brought him not only power but also riches and envy. Labībī, who was writing at about the same time, says quite openly: "When Farrukhī [see below] died, why did not 'Unṣurī also die? The old man went on living for a long time and the young man had to die prematurely."[4]

Of his lyrical *dīvān*, said to have contained 30000 distichs, only about 2500 have survived – panegyric poems written during the last period of his life. His romantic work is even less favourably represented, for we can gain only a slight idea of it from isolated lexicographic documents (about 200 verses, including a few dozen lyrical ones). The loss of his *Khizāna-i Yamīnu'd-daula*, 'Treasury of Yamīnu'd-daula' (viz. Maḥmūd), a collection of epics, robbed the history of literature of an important link in its development which is not compensated by Lāmi'ī's' (d. 937–8/1530–32) Turkish version of his epic *Vāmiq u 'Adhrā*. From the fragments preserved[5] we can ascertain that the above-mentioned epic, similarly to *Khing-but u Surkh-but*, 'White Idol and Red Idol' (the proper names of two lovers) – another romance of his and apparently an insipid story, as M. Bahār tells from the earliest Alexander Book in Persian prose[6] – is written in the *mutaqārib* measure, that was thus neither during the Ghaznavid period nor in earlier times confined to the heroic epic.[7] *Vāmiq u 'Adhrā* is an old tale of Alexander (see p. 132) already adapted to Arabic prose by Sahl b. Hārūn (215/830) and, more important, by 'Unṣurī's contemporary, the famous scholar al-Bīrūnī (b. 362/973, d. 443/1051), as well as a little later (in the middle of the 5th/11th century) by Faṣīḥī Jurjānī, again in *mutaqārib*. In none of these cases are the direct sources known to us nor are their mutual relationships; but the Greek origin of the material has been proved without reservation by Tarbiyat (1931), K. Chaykin (1935), and also by H. Ritter (1948)[8] from Greek geographical and proper names. On the other hand verses have been preserved from a *mathnavī* in *khafīf* measure, possibly from *Shād-bahr u 'Aynu'l-ḥayāt*, 'Happy One and Life Source' (again the names of a pair of lovers), or from another untraceable *mathnavī*. All these fragments at least permit the conclusion to be drawn that 'Unṣurī's narrative epics follow the paths of Iranian tradition in their content and form, as opposed to his lyric poetry, which is entirely dominated by the growing tendency towards arabising peculiar to the poetry of the court. His lyrics also transmit the thoughts of the Arab poets, thus signifying not only a continuation but also a further deepening of the cleft in the nature of the poet, such as is already to be seen in Firdausī. This applies in like manner to the form, ideology and themes. The music and emotional quality of Rūdakī's *qaṣīdas* are absent in those of his successor 'Unṣurī, who compensates for the lack of simple directness partly by virtuosity of expression[9] and partly by a distinct political orientation. And herein lies the importance of 'Unṣurī as regards subsequent development. The romantic tendency of his epics bears witness to the already descending line of Iranian chivalry.[10]

And the same feudal relationship that existed between 'Unṣurī and the Sulṭān prevailed also between the 'King of Poets' and the other poets, who in a certain sense constituted his retinue, were dependent on him and were expected to flatter him. Of the school of ʿUnṣurī we may mention Abū-Naẓar ʿAbdu'l-ʿAzīz b. Manṣūr ʿAsjadī of Merv (or Herat?, d. 432/1040–1), who also acquired wealth but of whose *dīvān* not very much has been preserved. This is a poet in whose work form dominates substance. Abu'l-Ḥasan ʿAlī b. Jūlūgh Farrukhī of Sistan (d. 429/1037–8)[11], the best among Maḥmūd's followers, has retained his charm up to the present day. The fact that more than 9000 verses of his *dīvān*, representing a considerable portion of his collected poetical works, have been preserved, testifies to his centuries-old popularity. From being in the service of a *dihqān* Farrukhī came via the court of Chaghāniyān to Ghazna, where he sang the praises of Maḥmūd, the latter's successors, princes and viziers, and gained both renown and riches. Characteristic of Farrukhī are a lucid, easily comprehensible and elegant style (he was also an accomplished singer and musician), charming, unforced metaphors and similes – although the poet was a master of rhetorical ornamentation, particularly in poems known as *qaṣīda-i maṣnūʿ* – wise maxims amidst high praise, expert exordia on such diverse subjects as natural scenery, parks, balconies, castles, traditional feasts, love and wine. Now and then he inserts a *ghazal* in the *qaṣīda*, a custom that was imitated by the poets of the 6th/12th century. Among the best known of Farrukhī's poems are the *qaṣīda-i dāgh-gāh* referring to the branding of horses in the presence of the Amīr, which marked the beginning of his public career as a poet; a long *qaṣīda* describing the military campaign of Sulṭān Maḥmūd against Somnāt (416/1025); the *marthiya* on the death of Sulṭān Maḥmūd, one of the finest elegies in Persian literature. In the whole gamut of emotions, joy is with him the most prominent, and it is for this reason that Anvarī praises him and Rashīd Vaṭvāṭ cherishes a real fondness for him. As he usually accompanied the Sulṭān on excursions and hunting expeditions, his descriptive *qaṣīdas* written on such occasions provide valuable cultural and historical details. A work on prosody entitled *Tarjumānu'l-balāghat*, 'The Dragoman of Eloquence', used later by Rashīdu'd-dīn Vaṭvāṭ (see p. 200) for his poetics, was erroneously attributed to Farrukhī, as Ahmed Ateş has pointed out. The work has been preserved and belongs in reality to Muḥammad b. ʿUmar Rādūyānī[12] (written between 481–507/1088–1114). Here and there the authorship of the *Shāhryār-nāma* is accredited to Farrukhī (see p. 164).

Among the poets at the court of Sulṭān Masʿūd, a son of Maḥmūd, must be included Abu'n-Najm Aḥmad b. Qūs (?, Yaʿqūb?) Manūchihrī from Dāmghān (d. about 432/1040–1). He was related to the Samanids and owed his *nom de plume* to his first master, the Ziyarid Prince Falaku'l-maʿālī Manūchihr b. Qābūs Vushmgīr, ruler of Tabaristan. He has unjustly been given the nickname of 'Shast-galla', Owner of Sixty Herds. He too learned that there was nothing that aroused jealousy like court favouritism. As a connoisseur and admirer of pre-Islamic Bedouin poetry (*jāhiliyya*) he emulates its descriptions of deserted places, adventurous wanderings, deserts, stars, camels, separation from the Beloved, etc., in addition to providing reminiscences of Arabic passages and expressions. As against the artificiality of others, he represents the conservative ancient Arabic school. Nevertheless he has a masterly command of the Persian language such as is seldom seen in others. His descriptions excel in plasticity and naturalistic conception. It is incorrect to regard him as a pupil of ʿUnṣurī; if he refers to the latter as his *ustād*, 'master', on chronological grounds only this must be taken as a form of flattery, for he did not go to Ghazna until of maturer age. But it is also evident from their differences of style – Manūchihrī dislikes rhetorical artificialities, his field of activity lies rather in similes and metaphors. His verses are imbued with the joy of living, especially in the highly esteemed *musammaṭs*, a form that he was the first to employ. He also knows how to use the riddle in brilliant manner for purposes of panegyrism. His *dīvān*, in the edition dating from the year 1338, contains 57 *qaṣīdas*, eleven *musammaṭs*, twenty *qiṭʿas* and small verses, altogether 2758 distichs. He was the first and only one of the ancient Ghazna panegyric poets to be edited and intensively studied by a European orientalist (A. de Biberstein-Kazimirski, 1886).

D. THE ROMANTIC EPIC

(ʿAyyūq and Fakhruʾd-dīn Asʿad Gurgānī)

Until recently *Vīs u Rāmīn* was considered to be the earliest romantic epic in existence, but it has had to cede its priority in favour of the extremely fortunate discovery made by Professor A. Ateş (Istanbul) of the epic poem *Varqa u Gul-shāh* by ʿAyyūqī[13], a poet who lived at the time of Sulṭān Maḥmūd of Ghazna. It is composed in *mutaqārib*, which fact again substantiates the theory that the use of this verse-metre was not confined to heroic subjects (see p. 98) but that it had been employed from olden times in romantic and other epics or long poems. It is well worth noticing that the monotony of the coupled rhymes is broken here and there by love songs in the form of *ghazals*. The plot itself is comparatively simple: two cousins fall in love with one another in early childhood. Death puts an end to the adversities of their unhappy love, just at the time of the appearance of Muḥammad. The Prophet raises both to new life and thenceforth they see all their hopes fulfilled. The story – in point of fact a eulogy of true love – is of Arabic origin and has parallels in the literatures of Spain and France in the 12th century ('Floire et Blancheflor'), where however the resurrection motif is absent. From two verses preserved in a lexicon it can be concluded that ʿAyyūqī wrote another epic (this time in the *ramal* metre) and also panegyric *qaṣīdas*.

Only slightly more recent is the romantic epic *Vīs u Rāmīn* by Fakhruʾd-dīn Asʿad Gurgānī, composed after 446/1054[14] by consent of ʿAmīd Abuʾl-fatḥ Muẓaffar b. Ḥusayn Nīshāpūrī, the governor of Isfahan.[15] It appears that the frivolity of the theme largely contributed to a popularity – on which the author himself lays stress – both in the 'artless Persian prose version' and also in the Middle Persian source of the latter, although it is an insult to Islamic morality and in fact to every other religion. The most eloquent proof of its popularity is the fact that the poem has remained intact through such a long space of time. (In view of the very small number of MSS preserved, some scholars hold the opposite opinion!) It is the oriental counterpart of Tristan and Isolde[16], a triangle composed as follows: the old king Mūbad Manīkān in Merv, his younger brother Rāmīn, who in his youth has been brought up with Vīs, the young wife of Mūbad. The old man is a ridiculous, pitiful figure in the hands of the two lovers, who never tire of inventing cunning and deceitful tricks at his expense. The chance death of the king leads the way to a happy ending. Whereas A. Christensen regards the fable as a pure phantasy, V. Minorsky[17] comes to the following conclusions on the ground of numerous reflections from the Parthian period: according to its geographical background, the story of Vīs and Rāmīn belongs to the Arsacid period. He thinks it very probably relates the adventures of a descendant of the house of Gūdarz but touches only indirectly on the main line of the Arsacids. Manīkān, patronymic of Mūbad, the King of Merv, may indicate descent from the Gūdarzid Bīzhan and his wife Manīzha. Vīs may be descended from the Kārēnids, one of the seven '*māh*' (Median) leading families under the Arsacids. Further identification would be rash, for Gurgānī's Pahlavi sources followed the customary course of the epic in altering the sequence of events and the personal relations of the heroes. If the origin of the epic is to be found at the time and in the atmosphere of the Parthians it is easy to understand that Gurgānī too retained many a feature of the emotional and social life of that epoch, which in this respect is difficult to fathom. As opposed to this opinion of V. Minorsky's, M. Molé[18] expresses the conviction that the historical references do not concern the epoch of Gotarzes Geopothros, but the period that immediately affected the poet, namely that of the Seljuq Ṭughril-Beg. Another differing point of view is expressed by 'Abdu'l-Ḥusayn Zarrīnkūb[19]; he rejects the theory that there is any connection with the history of the Arsacids as such an occurrence could not have survived the Sasanian era; *Vīs u Rāmīn* must be a fictitious story originating in the district of Fahla (ancient Media) and written in the local dialect (Pahlavi); possibly enriched with other elements, it may have been translated into verse much later by Fakhru'd-dīn Gurgānī in the Darī language. The Iranian critic does not consider Minorsky's proofs convincing and himself relies more on speculative arguments.

The Pahlavi original, together with its Persian version, is enveloped in many an obscure point that give rise to various surmises. Nevertheless there may be no doubt as to the existence of a Pahlavi original, especially as Gurgānī has retained a certain reference to the calendar which allows the genesis of the original tale to be placed in the 5th century A.D. (the middle of the Sasanian period).[20] I will not enter here into the question of the form of the Pahlavi original but should like to allude to the 'artless' Persian version. I think it may be concluded from Gurgānī's own words that we are here concerned with a regular poem written in metre, although he himself held a quite different and contrary opinion. It was evidently composed in syllabic metre with an appropriate style of rhyme and must therefore have appeared to Gurgānī and to his contemporaries, who were no longer familiar with these principles, as a product devoid of art, all the more so as the abundance of Pahlavi and obsolete expressions rendered comprehension more difficult. Yet it was already written in the Persian language, in a very early stage of its development, it is true, when indigenous prosody was still in force. Should all this be correct, then the date given by Minorsky[21] for the compilation of the Persian version, viz. 950 A.D., would be somewhat late. In that case a romantic epic of considerable length might have been expected already in the beginning stages of Persian poetry, a supposition consistent with the general popularity of the story. "Pio, devoto ai suoi mecenati, innamorato della sua patria e soprattutto del Ḫorāsān e di Merw, inzeppato di retorica eppure non incapace di sollevare di quando in quando la retorica a poesia, tale ci appare Fakhr ad-dīn Gurgānī. Il suo grosso poema, se non merita certo la stroncatura di Pizzi [e Nöldeke], altrettanto non merita le iperboliche lodi di ʿAwfī e la troppo benevola caratteristica di Ethé, che vi trovava inagguagliabile verità e profondità psicologica. Ma la sua importanza culturale non a torto è stata sempre proclamata."[22] Dihkhudā draws attention to the agreement in conception between the customary argumentation on the Oneness of God (*tauḥīd*) in the introductory songs of an epic poem and the ideas expressed in Avicenna's *Khuṭba*, 'Sermon'. The poem exhibits the same epical *hazaj* already used by Masʿūdī of Merv in his attempt at a *Shāh-nāma* and later by Niẓāmī in *Khusrau u Shīrīn*. Several surviving *mathnavī* fragments of Gurgānī (the earliest Address to the Cup-bearer) do not lead to any decisive conclusion as to the nature of the work as a whole.[23] *Vīs u Rāmīn* was already translated into Georgian at the turn of the 12th/13th century and certainly had an influence on the Georgian chivalric epic.[24]

E. AVICENNA – HIS IMPORTANCE AND HIS INFLUENCE

Amongst the greatest figures of the era of Maḥmūd and of Iranian, in fact of Moslem culture in general were the scholars Avicenna and Bīrūnī (see Ibn-Sīnā and Bīrūnī, above, p. 150). Whereas the polyhistor Bīrūnī belongs almost exclusively to the field of Arabic learning, the physician and philosopher – and last but not least the poet – Avicenna (b. 370/980) extended his activities to other domains as well. His father professed the Ismāʿīlī faith and he himself did not depart from his religion.[25] As a boy he already showed a talent bordering on the miraculous. At the age of sixteen he cured the Samanid Nūḥ b. Manṣūr, which achievement opened to him the doors of the magnificent library of the Samanids. He was accused by his rivals of being responsible for its being burnt down. Revolts of the feudal lords and the discontent of the oppressed peasant classes led to a crisis in the Samanid dynasty which was no longer able to resist the attacks of the Turkish Karakhānids and of Sulṭān Maḥmūd. All this, added to the obscurantism of the new rulers of Bukhara and the death of his father caused Avicenna to leave his native country. From now on begins his eventful but nevertheless highly prolific literary life. Although Sulṭān Maḥmūd did his best to retain him at his court, Avicenna would not and could not remain there where the Sunna and its dangerous narrow-minded priesthood reigned supreme. He fled first to Khvārazm and thence to the Ziyarids, but not until he reached the courts of the Buyids (first at Ray, ca. 1016–17, later at Hamadan and Isfahan, where he spent respectively six and thirteen years) did he succeed in escaping from the reach of Maḥmūd's power, and then not entirely, for the ruler of Ghazna was also more or less lord over Western Iran. In Hamadan particularly both joy and sorrow were his lot, for he was appointed vizier but was later imprisoned for high treason. He died there in 428/1037, by no means old, but exhausted by feverish work and lack of moderation in pleasure; he was buried at Hamadan where, on the occasion of the celebrations commemorating the millenium of his birth, a magnificent mausoleum was erected. His fame is based on the work *Kitābu'l-qānūn fi'ṭ-ṭibb*, 'Canon of Medicine', and the philosophical *Kitābu'sh-shifā'*, 'Book of Healing', compendiums that are equally famous in the East and in the mediaeval West, classical surveys of the scientific knowledge of his time (both works were written in Arabic, like everything that ever flowed from his pen, with but a few exceptions; see p. 150). Opinions on Avicenna vary to an incredible extent – from indisputable materialism[26] to a system that "not only is crowned by mystical aspiration but saturated with it".[27] But references to Avicenna in chapters dealing mainly with poetry are directed not so much to the truly very scanty surviving portions of his poetic oeuvre (all in all they consist of twelve quatrains, one *qiṭ'a*, one *ghazal* in Persian, and one *qaṣīda* on the soul written in Arabic; otherwise, M. Zand[28]) as to the influence he exerted on the whole of Persian mysticism by his Ṣūfistic writings. This influence was two-fold – partly ideological, partly thematical. In respect of the former, Ye. E. Bertel's[29] is thinking of Avicenna's almost monistic conception of the soul, that in substance resembles the spirit and in attributes the body (Maulavī, Jāmī), and of the notion of an evolution from mineral to man (Maulavī and his son, Sulṭān Valad, Bīdil). Regarding the latter, Avicenna enriches Ṣūfī epic poetry by introducing the theme of a conducted pilgrimage to the highest goal (after the manner of the *Divina Commedia*). This had already had a predecessor in Iran, namely the Middle Persian *Artāk-Virāz-nāmak*, 'The Book of Artāk-Virāz'. It furthermore constitutes a framework for different variations, as in Sanā'ī's *Sayru'l-'ibād ila'l-ma'ād*, 'The Way of the Servant of God to the Place of Return', in 'Aṭṭār's *Manṭiqu'ṭ-ṭayr*, 'The Language of Birds', and Abū-Ḥāmid Auḥadu'd-dīn Kirmānī's (?) *Miṣbāḥu'l-arvāḥ*, 'The Light of Souls', and finally in Bahā'u'llāh's *Haft vādī*, 'Seven Valleys'. But Bertel's' list of Avicenna's activities does not even end here; there is still Avicenna the philosopher who influenced the Ismā'īlite Nāṣir-i Khusrau and that originally-minded thinker Bābā Afḍalu'd-dīn of Kāshān; finally Avicenna the Ismā'īlite in his relation to Khayyām, that was no doubt affected by the disparity between a courtier such as Avicenna and Khayyām the man in despair, as also by the distance between the generations in their attitude towards one and the same problem.

NOTES

1. Yakubovskiy, *Machmud*, 64.
2. As an eminent jurist (!!) he is alleged to have written *Tafrīd fi'l-furū'*, 'The Submersion in the Deductions (from the Principles)' (Nafīsī, *Qābūs-nāma*, p. 28).
3. The Baramakid Yaḥyā b. Khālid appointed Abān al-Lāḥiqī head of the 'poetry department', even before the year 800. His duty was to examine the value of the panegyrics produced; cf. von Grunebaum, *Kritik* (B IV), 26. Not even the court poets were exempted from the attentions of Maḥmūd's secret service; Bert., IPTL, 302, 304.
4. *Tarjumānu'l-balāgha*, ed. A. Ateş, 32 (of the Persian text).
5. A considerable portion of it was recently discovered in India by Muḥ. Shafī'ī, cf. Dh. Ṣafā, *Ganj-i sukhan* (B VIa), I, 74, and M. J. Maḥjūb, *Mathnavī-sarā'ī* (B VIa), 200.
6. *Sabk*, 2, 130_1.
7. See p. 98.
8. Chaykin in the collective work "Khakani, Nizami etc.", M. 1935, 41–52; Bertel's, 'Lit. ... v Sr. Az.' (D IIa) 209; idem in his transl. 'Kabus-name', 260; Ritter, *Oriens*, I, 1948, 135; above all Tarbiyat, 'Vāmiq', *Arm.*, 12, 1931, 520 *et seq.*
9. A master of the *taqsīm* figure: *Tarjumānu'l-balāgha*, 68 (of the Persian text); Bertel's, 'Lit. ... v Sr. Az.' (D IIa) 208, IPTL, 323.
10. Idem, *Pers. Poez. v Bukh*, (B VIa) 40.
11. Labībī testifies to his premature death, cf. Ṣafā, *Ta'rīkh*, I, 538; see above, note 4.
12. Bibl. *s.v.* 'Muh. etc.', according to MS dating from 507/1114.
13. Cf. Bibl. *s.v.*; Ṣafā, *Ta'rīkh*, I, 604 *et seq.* and I. S. Braginskiy, *Iz istorii* (D IIa), 309 *et seq.* Also F. Bajraktarević, 'Dve arapske ljubavne pripovetke' (B VIa).
14. Scholars hold varying opinions as to this date! I follow M. J. Maḥjūb's lengthy preface to his edition, pp. 16–17.
15. According to 'Aṭṭār the poet was stimulated to compose his great epic poem by frantic grief on the death of his beloved slave in the flames (?!); cf. Ritter, *Das Meer der Seele*, 365.
16. O. Spies, *Der Orient*, 31_{23}.
17. *Vīs*, I, p. 5, where Christensen is quoted, and p. 35 (again 2, p. 31).
18. *Vīs u Rāmīn et l'histoire seldjoukide* (see Bibl.). V. Minorsky refutes this construction (in a letter dated 28.5.61). Cf. I. Braginskiy's important work *Ocherki iz istorii* (D Ib), 184 *et seq.*; treated exhaustively in his foreword to Lipkin's translation. Here we find the purport of the poem in a derision of the upper classes; similarly Bertel's, IPTL, 285.
19. *Sukhan*, 9/10, 1337, 1015–8. Prof. Minorsky perseveres steadfastly in his point of view (letters).
20. Minorsky, *Vīs*, 2, p. 34 (*ibid.*, dating according to Taqī-zāda).
21. *Ibid.*, I, p. 4_2.
22. Gabrieli, Note, 187; Nöldeke: Minorsky, *Vīs*, 2, p. 35. Concerning Gurgānī's influence on Niẓāmī see p. 212. On the extremely difficult and extensive problems concerning the epos, cf. the detailed foreword of M. J. Maḥjūb in his edition of the poem (1–105) and V. Minorsky, *Vīs u Rāmīn*, I–IV, now collected in his Iranica (B VIa), 151–99.

23. M. J. Maḥjūb, *op. cit.*, 271.
24. See p. 171, note 115.
25. Ṣafā, *Jashn-nāma-i Ibn-Sīnā*, I, 45 *et seq.* (French 46).
26. Bolotnikov, *Khayyam*, 20.
27. Gardet, *La pensée*: W. Caskel, *ZDMG*, 102, p. 361. Bausani, *Storia* (B v), 548 *et seq.* adopts the view of H. Corbin ('Avicenne', B vib), who sees in Avicenna a gnostic (*'ārif*) on the basis of rational philosophy: the whole of philosophy is for him only a preparation for a 'visione realizzatrice', that is quite unknown to modern philosophy.
28. Bibl. *s.v.* 'Avicenna' (B vib).
29. 'Avitsenna' (B vib), 82 *et seq.*, 90 *et seq.*

V. THE SELJUQ PERIOD

(5th/11th to 6th/12th century)

As a result of the overthrow of the Ghaznavids and Buyids, the Seljuqs were able to build up a new supremacy and thus to bring a further partition of the eastern Islamic world to a standstill. They did not lay stress on their Turkish origin but adopted the Moslem-Persian civilisation the more readily since they themselves were unlettered and thus obliged to depend on the existing Iranian governmental administration. A purely Turkish dynasty in whose power lay a vast complex of countries, the Seljuqs bore an uncommonly large contribution to the spread of Persian literature and Persian culture: in fact this period constitutes one of the peaks in the history and civilisation of Iran. This rise can be attributed to the progress of the towns, to excellent schools (e.g. the *Niẓāmiyya*), to the shifting of the civil administration from the hands of the old nobility into those of the intelligent bourgeoisie as well as to the penetrating though not apparent influence of the Ismāʿīlites. In contrast to the Buyids, the Seljuqs hoisted the flag of the Sunna and, like Sulṭān Maḥmūd, acknowledged the Caliph of Baghdad as their head. While western Islam became spiritualised through the reforms of al-Ghazālī (b. 450/1058–9 in Ṭūs, d. there in 505/1111), the course of eastern Islam was marked by the increasing influence of Ṣūfism which in the 5th/11th century spread out far and wide as a protest against oppression, religious and otherwise – a protest that was the more effective because of the close association that existed at this period between Ṣūfism and Ismāʿīlism.[1] Through the Seljuq universities with their pronounced Sunnite syllabus, the State gained control of all learning, as had been the case with poetry since the time of Sulṭān Maḥmūd. The reaction to this onerous pressure on learning and poetry is demonstrated by ʿOmar Khayyām and the Ismāʿīlite Nāṣir-i Khusrau. Strong oppositional currents were responsible particularly for throwing political life, that was being undermined by the Shīʿite Ismāʿīlī sect, into confusion. The latter, with its powerful propaganda, based on a socio-political anti-feudal programme and disseminated among the broad masses of the people, had become a real danger.[2] The most embittered opposition was offered by the Assassins[3], a tough, intransigeant, ingeniously thought-out organisation of Ismāʿīlī terrorists, in reality fighters for a state as conceived by the ancient Persian feudal nobility, the last representatives of the Shuʿūbiyya. This last residue of the age of chivalry, in its struggle against the victorious new epoch[4], defended Persian patriotism and their own influence against the Turkish or turkophile official and military aristocracy, but directed their activities also against the rising power of the towns. When the Seljuq empire collapsed there existed centrifugal tendencies in the west of the kingdom, namely in a number of lesser states ruled by Turkish Atabegs. Whereas the omnipotent hand of the great Seljuq rulers was able to foil these movements, their successors – Sanjar (512/1118–551 or 552/1157) not excepted – no longer possessed such power. A certain degree of hegemony then came into the hands of the Khvārazm-Shāhs, likewise of Turkish descent; but it was left to the Mongols to again build up a great power in the Persian districts of the former Seljuq empire, albeit at the cost of the most terrible atrocities from which western Islam was spared, thanks to the Mamelukes, the restorers of the state as conceived by the Seljuqs.[5]

A. THE RISE OF PANEGYRISM UNDER SULṬĀN SANJAR AND DURING THE DISINTEGRATION OF THE SELJUQ SUPREMACY

Political and economic events were responsible for poetry's having evolved as it did. After the defeat of Sanjar and the unprecedented devastation of Khurasan by the Turkish Ghuzz (Oghuz) the focal point of literary life was shifted to the western provinces. There was no lack of panegyrists at the court of the Great Seljuqs, but their number would have been greater still had it not been for the reluctance and niggardliness shown by the all-powerful vizier and realistic statesman, Niẓāmu'l-mulk (d. 485/1092) towards poets and poetry of this kind. He regarded panegyrists as good-for-nothings, perhaps just because he was a patron of learning, proof of which can be seen in the Niẓāmiyya University founded by him at Baghdad. Evidence of a more favourable attitude towards poets can however be found in the rise of panegyrism in the 12th century until its culmination under Sanjar (Muʿizzī, Anvarī, and Adīb Ṣābir, a poet and translator of Persian into Arabic who perished tragically for his master, drowned at the instigation of Atsïz, between the years 538-42/1143–48), and at the courts of the lesser princes, for whom propaganda was important in view of mutual rivalry. Despotism, lack of great exploits, court intrigues and the wealth extorted from the broad masses of the people on the one hand, parasitism and exorbitant flattery on the other – this was the soil that nourished the panegyric *qaṣīda*, which required a greater degree of arabisation of the Persian language and a more high-flown rhetoric in proportion as the merits to be exaggerated were slighter and the vices to be concealed greater. The greatest masters of panegyric poetry certainly set a bold front to this movement and introduced philosophical opinions, warnings and counsels into their verse. The real oppositional current was formed by Ṣūfism, which preached independence, the abandonment of the sink of corruption of the court and self-denial. The *ghazal* with its love-themes and hedonism found a ready response in the expanding towns and their cultured circles; particularly was this the case with the romantic *mathnavī* with its unheroic content, for the world of heroes inherent in Iranian chivalry had almost entirely vanished and the Iranian people become firmly established as a nation. Niẓāmī brought the romantic epic to its highest consummation by means of the fable, his narrative technique, the psychological background and the basically humane views he proclaimed in the spirit of social progress. Last but not least, this period can also boast of several excellent prose works.

B. NĀṢIR-I KHUSRAU

In order to mark more emphatically the intellectual and social revival of Iran at that time, the literature of the Seljuq period may well be ushered in by a figure who stands apart from the general literary trend. The complicated personality of the free-thinker, heretic and poet Abū-Muʿīn Nāṣir-i Khusrau al-Marvazī al-Qubādiyānī, whose biography suffers from a paucity of attested data and even more from a surplus of legends that appeared early on and even contained some mysterious features, has repeatedly attracted the attention of renowned scholars and experts. (Cf. recently A. A. Semenov, A. Ye. Bertel's, and W. Ivanow.) There is no doubt about the date of Nāṣir-i Khusrau's birth, namely 394/1004, for the poet mentions it himself explicitly in his 'Confessions' *qaṣīda.* His birthplace, Qubādiyān, a district in the province of Merv, is apparent in the two indications of his origin included in his name as quoted above. Up to the time of his 'exile', he resided in Balkh. While Ḥasan Taqī-zāda contests his descent from ʿAlī ("ʿAlavī'), Ivanow insists on his Sayyid origin, referring – as does Taqī-zāda – to quotations to be found in his *dīvān.*[6] Nāṣir-i Khusrau, offspring of a worthy family of officials, was of course sent to school in his youth, but his education does not appear to have been very thorough. This is particularly noticeable in regard to theological subjects, after all the backbone of all studies, for there are many omissions to be found in his works in this respect. Maybe he was premature in accepting an official post, though it is also possible that ambition and disposition drove the young man in another direction than that usually followed at school. His subsequent boasting about his erudition is seen by W. Ivanow rather as an expression of the indignation[7] that he, later as an autodidact, must have felt as a consequence of the lack of esteem accorded him by the learned profession. The natural sciences always had an attraction for him, as had alchemy and magic. In his youth he composed a frivolous kind of secular lyric poetry which enjoyed great popularity among his friends.

Nāṣir-i Khusrau's further career is veiled in an almost impenetrable obscurity. It is unlikely that he was ever in the service of a Ghaznavid prince, seeing that the seat of the Ghaznavids was Ghazna, where Nāṣir-i Khusrau never appears to have stayed[8], let alone occupied a high position, as legend will have it. The question is: Who was the amīr to whose train the poet belonged? Perhaps ʿAlī b. Asad al-Ḥārith, amīr of Badakhshan, at whose instigation Nāṣir-i Khusrau at the end of his life wrote *Jāmiʿuʾ l-ḥikmatayn*, 'The Union of Two Wisdoms'? Should this assumption prove to be true, it would explain much in the further course of his life. The time in the service of the amīr was spent in excesses and this affected the poet's lyrical composition, of which unfortunately nothing has been preserved. His real profession was that of *dabīr*, a government official.

An if possible still deeper obscurity envelops the religious convictions of Nāṣir in his pre-Cairo period. Up till then he had been regarded by orientalists as a searcher after truth, who undertook wanderings through the countries of eastern Islam[9] in order to gain an insight into their life and faith and thus to attain the only true knowledge. He is said to have returned unsatisfied and to have attempted to drown his despair in reckless living and conviviality. It is true that in his 'Confessions' *qaṣīda* he himself speaks about his investigation into matters of faith among followers of all kinds of religious doctrines. All this is partly invented by him for poetical purposes and partly fabricated by later writers. In fact all his assertions call for a careful and experienced interpretation. Thus the vision he recalls in the *Safar-nāma*, that – it is said – inspired him to make the pilgrimage to the sacred places, is in fact a motif for conversion frequently met with in biography and, as von Grunebaum[10] perspicaciously assumes, the outcome of a long spiritual process. This is remarkably consistent with the construction of W. Ivanow[11], according to whom Nāṣir-i Khusrau had already become a follower of Ismāʿīlī doctrine before the pilgrimage; having been for a long time a disciple of the Shīʿa he was far from happy under the Seljuqs who may have dismissed him from his office and persecuted him in other ways too. He sees salvation in the Ismāʿīlī doctrine and in its leader, the Imām of that time, the Egyptian Fatimid al-Mustanṣir biʾllāh (1035–94). His journey lasted more than seven lunar years (437–44/1045–52). There can be no question of a sudden conversion having taken place only after he had become acquainted with the economic and social progress in Egypt, but it may very well be that his convictions were strengthened by recently acquired experience. It is hardly to be believed that in Cairo he attained the fourth degree (*ḥujjat*) in the strict hierarchy of the Ismāʿīlī sect, for as *ḥujjat* he would not have spent his time from then on in such a forgotten place as Yumgān. Certainly from then on he takes the term Ḥujjat(-i Khurāsān) as his *takhalluṣ*, but of his own accord and for reasons which can only vaguely be surmised. He returned to Balkh as a trained missionary, unless it was that he went direct from Egypt to Mazandaran for missionary purposes. But when in due course a rumour went round in Balkh as to his real sentiments and his connection with the Fatimids, the great indignation of the masses, goaded on by the Seljuq officials, was aroused and an attempt was even made on his life, so that he was obliged to flee for safety. If the identification of the unnamed amīr with the amīr of Badakhshan be based on truth, then it is quite possible that in his distress Nāṣir-i Khusrau turned to the latter, likewise an Ismāʿīlī, who provided him with a hiding-place on his territory in Yumgān.[12] In this dismal hole among the impenetrable mountain ranges of Badakhshan he was doomed to remain until the end of his life. His persistent complaints about this – his 'prison' – were of no avail and no release was granted. Was it that the Ismāʿīlī centre in Cairo refused to let him leave the place? To carry out missionary work from there was of course out of the question. But how, in such a wild spot with its extremely primitive population, could he devote himself to his literary work, the greater part of which must have been produced there? Was he in communication with Egypt in order to obtain political and religious information, and material indispensable for his literary activities? Who provided for his daily needs? Unfortunately we do not know the answers to these questions; how else should this part of the life of Nāṣir-i Khusrau be more veiled in obscurity than any other? Despite all his complaints he does not enter more closely into his doings. There, in Yumgān, near Garm in Afghanistan, he died between 465–470/1072–7[13], and still today his grave can be seen in a region inhabited by fanatical Sunnites who profess to be Sayyids and at the same time descendants of Nāṣir-i Khusrau!

A chronological list of the authentic literary legacy of Nāṣir-i Khusrau, together with works attributed to him or forged, has been drawn up by W. Ivanow.[14] It is therefore unnecessary to enumerate his writings here, especially as I can only touch on the most important of them. Let us consider the cardinal point in Nāṣir-i Khusrau's philosophical works and those composed for purposes of propaganda. E. G. Browne, with his expert knowledge of theology, already perceived that a work like *Zādu'l-musāfirīn*, 'Sustenance for Travellers', contains practically nothing about Ismāʿīlism. And this is true of almost the whole of the poet's oeuvre. An explanation was first given in the edition of Nāṣir-i Khusrau's *Gushā'ish va rahā'ish* prepared by S. Nafīsī from a unique copy. The text, as the copyist himself admits, is divested of 'the Untrue', viz. Ismāʿīlī ideology. There is no doubt that this is the key to a correct evaluation of the preserved version of most of Nāṣir-i Khusrau's works: their Ismāʿīlī features were eliminated in the course of a later alien revision.

His literary output during the seven years of travel to the west of Iran was inevitably bound to be subjected to a similar revision. Nevertheless the description of the journey (*Safar-nāma*) gives an invaluable picture of culture on the Nile at that period and in Western Asia. The doubt that had arisen as to whether, considering the prevailing Sunnite attitude, it might have been the work of another Nāṣir-i Khusrau, had already been removed by scholars before the appearance of *Gushā'ish va rahā'ish*. The question whether the preserved text is not a later, alien redaction[15] can therefore be answered nowadays in the affirmative.

Among the speculative works (dealing with more or less similar problems in the fields of philosophy, religion and the natural sciences) the most prominent are *Zādu'l-musāfirīn*, 'Sustenance for Travellers' (453/1061) and *Vajh-i dīn*, 'The Countenance of Faith' (of unascertainable date). Their value is increased by the fact of their containing philosophical prose – in general rare in the Persian language and particularly so at this early stage. It may be remarked that the poet's philosophic prose is characterised by an attempt to replace the Arabic by a Persian nomenclature. As regards the substance the following opinion is expressed by A. A. Semenov[16]: "The author's rationalism appears in the guise of a polemical-philosophical treatise in which there is no declaration of the Ismāʿīlī faith and its esoteric doctrine, no justification and no explanation of its organisation and terminology. It rather brings forward, in addition to the opinions of the author, the reflections of Greek philosophers, sometimes with reference to their original works – reflections of natural scientists, materialistic philosophers and atheists of the 9th–10th century with whom the author carries on a polemic." A. A. Semënov rightly observes that the work has practically nothing whatever to do with Ismāʿīlī doctrine. With a greater sense of history H. H. Schaeder[17] expresses the following, to some extent divergent opinion: in these two treatises Nāṣir-i Khusrau presents a complete system of the Bāṭiniyya and identifies himself with the movement for spiritual enlightenment that from the 3rd/9th century onwards had been endeavouring to harmonise Islamic dogma with Greek philosophy and at the same time shows proof of being inspired to a high degree by the Manichaean gnosis. He regards *Zādu'l-musāfirīn* as nothing but a compendium of the corpus of the 'Pure Brothers' (*ikhvānu'ṣ-ṣafā*), a canon of the Bāṭiniyya, the doctrine of the hidden interpretation of the revelation, a compendium with an even more lucid arrangement and a more rigid train of thought. Nāṣir-i Khusrau, he says, accepted *ibdāʿ*, 'creatio ex nihilo', and turned particularly against the hypothesis of the eternity of matter.[18]

Among the later works of Nāṣir-i Khusrau we find *Jāmiʿu'l-ḥikmatayn*, 'Union of the Two Wisdoms' (462/1070), written at the command of the amīr of Badakhshan. The contents are characterised by the editor H. Corbin in the sub-title: 'Le Livre réunissant les deux Sagesses, ou Harmonie de la Philosophie grecque et la Théologie ismaélienne'. The amīr had put questions to him in the form of a *qaṣīda* by Abu'l-Haytham, which Nāṣir-i Khusrau answered by means of a popular encyclopaedia of useful knowledge, a typical feature of the early Middle Ages of Byzantium that had also spread to Islam.[19] As the amīr himself was a member of the Ismāʿīlī sect it was unnecessary for Nāṣir-i Khusrau to go very deeply into relevant questions, and this may have saved the work from censure on the part of fanatics.

One of the two *Rūshanā'ī-nāma's*[20] (very rare in the case of one and the same writer!) is composed in *mathnavī* form and is at the same time one of the master's earliest works (444/1053); it is a didactic poem of an ethical nature that puts forward a cosmographical-metaphysical system based on the philosophy of Aristotle in the light of Avicenna and al-Fārābī, but with the addition of Ṣūfī features. This work had a great influence on Persian literature.

Nāṣir-i Khusrau's important *dīvān* is said initially to have contained over 30,000 verses. In Sayyid Naṣru'llāh Taqavī's edition there are rather more than 11,000, all, except for a few fragments, *qaṣīdas* of a philosophical or theosophical character. It is not impossible that some foreign matter has crept in, for kindred spirits to Nāṣir-i Khusrau were fond of concealing their own productions under his wings. The lyric poetry preserved in the *dīvān* refers to the sojourn in Yumgān and is devoid of the customary hedonistic themes. It is not however so completely free of panegyric elements as was assumed until now, though with this difference that the praise is addressed to prominent Ismāʿīlīs, certainly not without hope of reward, which indeed the lonely poet certainly stood in great need of. Veiled Ismāʿīlī expressions, only familiar to members of the sects, and numerous references to religious and other questions are such serious obstacles to comprehension that a deeper interpretation and evaluation of the *dīvān* is still in its infancy. This is greatly to be regretted, for it is just in the *dīvān* that we find uncensured material eminently suited to an increase of our knowledge of the poet and his Ismāʿīlism. But for purposes of research on this subject a familiarity with Fatimid literature is required, as well as a new edition of the *dīvān*.[21]

Nāṣir-i Khusrau has an individuality all his own; he is no common poet but one with a straightforward personal style, a man to whom thought is pre-eminently important, a remarkable figure amidst the parrot-like talk of others, not least on account of his mental evolution. Remarkable, even original and in accordance with their function closely related to the philosophical substance of the *qaṣīda*, are his descriptions of nature in the *nasīb*.[22] Muḥammad Qazvīnī ranks him among the six greatest Persian poets (he omits Niẓāmī!) with the sole restriction that his personality is obscured by religion.[23] Shiblī, on the contrary, holds the blunt opinion that although Nāṣir was the first to introduce philosophy into Persian poetry, his verse is entirely lacking in 'poetry' (5, 152).[24]

C. ʿOMAR KHAYYĀM

It is not so very long ago that in his native country Ghiyāthu'd-dīn Abu'l-fatḥ ʿUmar b. Ibrāhīm al-Khayyāmī, known briefly as ʿOmar Khayyām, was not ranked among the most famous poets, thus sharing the fate of several others in the 16th–18th centuries, the appreciation of whom at home was far less than were their fame and influence abroad. As this comparison applies only to the effect his work produced it must be supplemented by a recognition of the difference in circumstances, for whereas the admiration accorded already during their lifetimes to ʿUrfī, Ṣā'ib and Shaukat was limited to India and Turkey, the quatrains of Khayyām, thanks to the masterly paraphrase of Edward Fitzgerald (1859) aroused, although not immediately, an almost idolatrous, even snobbish enthusiasm in the West, especially in the Anglo-Saxon countries – an attitude that for a long time remained incomprehensible to the Persians. In Europe and America he is in fact the most famous of oriental poets, with a reputation that, rightly or wrongly, throws into the shade the fame of other masters, such as a Ḥāfiẓ, whose praise was sung by Goethe, a Firdausī or a Niẓāmī, who gained recognition at home as well as abroad through their jubilee celebrations, and a Saʿdī who was already long known in the West – not to mention other, lesser poets. A. G. Potter's[25] Khayyām bibliography bears ample testimony to this. It was through the Khayyām cult in the West that he acquired or regained a reputation as poet in Iran as well. During his lifetime ʿOmar Khayyām was nevertheless unreservedly recognised in Iran as one of the most brilliant figures in Persian culture, albeit exclusively in the field of learning.

We possess but few details of his life, yet more is known about him than about other classical poets. This is thanks to his wide reputation as a scholar. Only the most important dates can be quoted here: he was born at the earliest in 412/1021–22 (?) at Nishapur and died at the same place most probably in the late winter or early spring of the year 515–6/1122.[26] If the former date be correctly estimated, there may after all be some truth in the legend regarding the friendship between the Seljuq vizier, Niẓāmu'l-mulk, the dreaded 'Master who lives on the Mountain' Ḥasan-i Ṣabbāḥ and * ʿOmar Khayyām, who are said to have sworn during their student days to stand by each other all their lives; admittedly there is no proof of the truth of this and it seems more likely that Ismāʿīlī tendencies account for the legend. A thorough education at Nishapur introduced Khayyām to 'all branches of learning', the humanities as well as the exact sciences. We even know the names of his teachers in geometry and astronomy. Outwardly a Sunnite – or he could not have been named ʿOmar! – of the Shāfiʿite rite, as philosopher he followed the same path as Avicenna, which bore a strong resemblance to the Ismāʿīlī doctrine and Ṣūfism. This may explain a great deal'.[27] From the widely-known theologian and grammarian Zamakhsharī (d. 538/1143–4, see p. 224) – to whom we owe the earliest data as the result of a personal meeting between the two men – we learn that Khayyām was familiar with the work of the Arab sceptic Abu'l-ʿAlā' al-Maʿarrī (d. 449/1057).[28] An important turning-point in Khayyām's life was the year 467/1074, when he was appointed by Sulṭān Malik-Shāh and his vizier Niẓāmu'l-mulk to be head of a council of scholars commissioned to reform the calendar. The success of this work (1079) made his name famous throughout all regions of the vast empire and thus gained for him the lasting respect of his ruler. When in 485/1092 Niẓāmu'l-mulk was murdered by an Ismāʿīlī extremist belonging to the group of Ḥasan-i Ṣabbāḥ (the Assassins) and – curiously enough – Malik-Shāh died almost immediately afterwards, the work of ʿOmar Khayyām at the court, where there was neither money for purposes of research nor much sympathy for the scholar, came to an end for the time being. The slander of his rivals and later on religious quarrels in Nishapur (1095) obliged the master to break off his pedagogical activities and – more out of fear for his fellowmen than for Allah – to set out on a pilgrimage to the holy places of the Prophet. On his return he resumed his teaching in Nishapur, carried on discussions on scientific problems with his colleagues, among whom even a man like Muḥammad al-Ghazālī was to be found, and even worked again for a time in the service of the court (outside Nishapur), where he was highly esteemed for his gift of predicting events to come. The records concerning the old age of this noble old man close with details of the last moments of his life.

He was a brilliant mathematician, physicist, astronomer, physician and philosopher, and though we are here not concerned with these aspects of his personality it should be noted that it is just on account of his scientific achievements that his name was held in such high esteem in the East. Nearly all his scholarly works, whether scientific or philosophical, were written in Arabic; only the shorter essays were written in Persian, including translations from Avicenna. (The *Naurūz-nāma*, 'On the New Year Feast', written in Persian, is undoubtedly apocryphal![29]) He was by no means a prolific writer; in the records he is even accused of 'niggardliness' regarding the imparting of his boundless knowledge. In the West his name was immortalised by his quatrains which in Iran were apparently being relegated to obscurity. This too requires further explanation. All things considered, Khayyām is one of the most complicated figures, both intrinsically and from the point of view of literary history. Though the earliest accounts represent him as a pious professor of Ṣūfism who "was praised and honoured until after the middle of the 12th century as one of the greatest luminaries in the whole of the learned circles of Islam"[30], this picture is completely reversed about the middle of the 13th century, without however the image of his Ṣūfī inclinations being modified. As a Persian poet he is not mentioned at all in the earliest sources. His contemporaries probably considered his poetry as the least of his accomplishments. This fact, together with the strange contradictions in the quatrains, led many orientalists to form a hypercritical opinion – even to the extent of a complete negation – of Khayyām's authorship of the quatrains circulating under his name. Such an attitude certainly went too far, for it overlooked the circumstance that in mediaeval Iran science and poetry went as it were hand in hand and that Iranian scholars in no way scorned the writing of verse – one needs only to think of Avicenna (p. 180), Mullā Muḥsin-i Fayḍ-i Kāshānī, Mīr Abu'l-Qāsim Findariskī, Ḥājjī Mullā Hādī Sabzavārī, and others.[31] The elucidation of the problem was not particularly easy. That Khayyām did write poetry is vouched for by a report dating from 572/1176 with a few specimen verses in Arabic and with further examples from the still earlier Bayhaqī. Regarding the most important factor of all, the Persian quatrains, it appeared that during the whole of the 7th/13th century (from 1223 onwards) there were not more than three examples known – as specimens therefore of small import. Added to the 53 examples in existence dating up to the year 1384, an increase of about 700 is registered at the end of the following century, after which the flow of new quatrains again mounts only gradually (Chr. Rempis).[32] This increase is remarkable. How can it be explained? There is also the Proteus-like diversity in ideas and manuscripts, which was so striking as to arouse feelings of uncertainty among the investigators and doubts as to the authenticity of the tradition. For in the earliest attested quatrains one already finds completely conflicting ideologies, a feature that becomes more and more marked. V. Zhukovskiy[33] has moreover remarked that the same quatrains can also be found elsewhere, notably under the name of earlier and later poets. Thanks to the further extension and improvement of methods of work in connection with the discovery of new manuscripts, efforts to free the original stock of quatrains from later additions has led to some remarkable results.[34]

Now that A. J. Arberry[35] has succeeded in identifying complete collections of Khayyām's quatrains, obviously selections from earlier, larger collections, in manuscripts dating from 604/1207–8, 613/1216–17 and 658/1259–60 (and this, as far as I can see, is the most recent decisive step forward), he has brought the hitherto existing basic stock of three pieces up to at least two-hundred and fifty, thereby finally putting an end to all doubts concerning ʿOmar Khayyām as a poet.[36]

From the earliest testimonies it is evident that conflicting trends of thought, however strange they may be, form no criterion for non-authenticity. "The simultaneous juxtaposition of doubt, agnosticism, criticism of God, insolence towards God and deep piety", states H. Ritter[37], "is also to be found in the work of ʿAṭṭār, of whose fundamentally mystic attitude there can be no doubt. And indeed he put these sceptical and insolent utterances into the mouths of the poorest of the poor, the 'fools' (*dīvānagān*). This attitude stems from the circles of the simple folk, thus strengthening my opinion that these thoughts were the common property of the people and that it was not ʿOmar who first introduced them, though it may have been he who gave them their classical form." Similarly this same scholar[38] dismisses the objections concerning the incompatibility of Khayyām's positive philosophical attitude with on the one hand scepticism and on the other mysticism. In one of his philosophical treatises "ʿOmar, just after having explained the ten intellectual stages according to the views of his master Ibn-i Sīnā, declares that the true way to the knowledge of God is the way of the Ṣūfīs! To his mind the way adopted by the dogmatists, philosophers and Ismāʿīlites is not the true one. Thus mysticism and peripatetic philosophy can go hand in hand just as mysticism is compatible with rebelliousness or insolence towards God." Perhaps Khayyām found support in the poetry of the people, whose opposition to the world-order, to fate, injustice, the impotence of religion arises from a feeling of oppression. It may even be that Khayyām himself was instrumental in forming this protest of the people. The striking similarity between Khayyām and Avicenna in their choice of the quatrain form may likewise be explained by their common point of departure, namely the poetry of the people. Yet it cannot be denied that many a free-thinker also poured out his heart in quatrains which he then sent out into the world under Khayyām's flag. Khayyām's own words give us the impression of a despondent scholar, as if he were either a swindler or an object of scorn and hatred to this treacherous environment.[39] The portrait, sketched in 1911 by I. P. Umov, of the poet and his period, quoted by A. Krïmskiy[40], certainly applies up to the present day: "Incomparable as regards form, his quatrains contain profound thoughts, sometimes philosophical, sometimes hedonistic, then again sad and pessimistic. As a sceptic and mystically-minded philosopher, absorbed in the mysteries of Fate, seeking in God an explanation for earthly suffering, supplicating 'Him', the Silent One, in vain – a man renouncing his past, without faith in the future, living only for the fleeting present, scourging with biting satire the hypocrisy and show of saintliness of his contemporaries – he lived and wrote at a time when the views of the Ṣūfī mystics appeared as it were to be like the result of life itself, in which everything was transient and doomed to perish, in which one kingdom after another collapsed, great and wise men fell victim to the hands of unknown murderers, old doctrines were exchanged for new and rough nomadic hordes from foreign regions swept away and destroyed the ancient culture of Iran."

And yet, though a rebel, he was unable to revolutionise the social conscience through his writings. "The social conditions in Iran at that time were too firmly consolidated for the class whose ideology 'Omar Khayyām in fact represented to venture to play a revolutionary part. The merchant class and the world of commerce and finance to which he looked for support were unable to put up a stand against the feudal system. Added to this were political oppression and incessant intrigues. The negativism of his philosophy can be attributed to this, the despairing scepticism that merges into a pessimism without hope."[41] This is certainly a more acceptable explanation of Khayyām's personality and its conflicting elements than "the hypothesis of a historical connection between Zervanism and the ideology of 'Omar Khayyām's quatrains" (M. Molé, and earlier A. Christensen).[42] And the cause of the unexpected spontaneous response to 'Omar Khayyām's quatrains in the western world? In them the European perceived his own despondency as though reflected in a mirror. And this is the reason why the eastern world of today is also beginning to rediscover 'Omar Khayyām. But his influence on the development of thought in Iran is exemplified by no less a poet than Ḥāfiẓ and a legion of others who raised their voices against the omnipotent but hollow and hypocritical obscurantism.

D. THE PANEGYRIC POETS

I. QAṬRĀN (AZERBAYJAN)

At the courts of Tabriz and Ganja lived Abū-Manṣūr Qaṭrān ʿAḍudī from Shādīābād near Tabriz (b. about 400–4/1009–14, d. after 465/1072 in Ganja), the most famous panegyric poet of his time from Azerbayjan. He squandered his patrimonial estate in youthful excesses, but the constant favour of the princes in consequence of the fame he attained by his verses procured for him new possessions to compensate for his losses. The gout of which he later complained may be an indication of good living. In his *dīvān*, which consists of 3000 to 10,000 couplets – and there is certainly a good deal of alien material in the larger of these assessments – he sings the praises of some thirty patrons. His work has aroused the interest of historians, for in many cases Qaṭrān has perpetuated the names of members of regional dynasties of Azerbayjan and the Caucasus regions that would have otherwise fallen into oblivion. His best *qaṣīdas* were written in his last period, when he expresses his gratitude to the prince of Ganja, the Shaddadid Faḍlūn, for the numerous gifts that were still recollected by the famous Jāmī (d. 898/1492). Qaṭrān's poetry follows in the wake of the poets of Khurasan and makes an unforced use of rhetorical embellishment. He is even one of the first after Farrukhī to try his hand at the *qaṣīda-i maṣnūʿ*, 'particularly artificial *qaṣīda*'. When Nāṣir-i Khusrau visited Azerbayjan in 438/1046, Qaṭrān requested him to explain some of the more difficult passages in the *dīvāns* of Munjīk and Daqīqī that were written in 'pārsī', i.e., according to Chr. Schefer[43], in the Persian of Khurasan, a language that he, as a Western Persian, might not be expected to understand, in contrast to the guest from Khurasan. Kasravī[44] is of the opinion that the text of the *Safar-nāma* (see p. 187) has here been corrupted because Qaṭrān, though he spoke Iranian *Ādharī*, was fully acquainted with 'pārsī', as his *dīvān* shows. Qaṭrān's *qaṣīda* on the earthquake in Tabriz in the year 434/1042 is regarded as a true masterpiece. In other passages too he shows himself to be an eminent portrayer of natural scenery. The *Qaus-nāma*, 'The Book of the Arch', attributed to him, is in fact the work of Qaṭrān of Tirmidh, a poet who lived a hundred years later and is otherwise unknown.[45] Our Qaṭrān must certainly have been an excellent poet for his verses – through an error or for other reasons – later on to have been taken for the *dīvān* of Rūdakī (see p. 144). He does indeed often resemble Rūdakī in the latter's authenticated verses, although Qaṭrān's use of rhetoric contrasts with the natural simplicity of the Samanid poet. Badīʿu'z-zamān Bushrūya'ī Khurāsānī (Furūzānfar[46]) characterises him as a poet who loves to spend his time in the enjoyment of pleasure; for that reason he is able to find consolation for the loss of a friend and seeks nothing other than personal and material success. That Qaṭrān's Persian lexicon[47] has not been preserved is not surprising, for Asadī already reproached him for having included only well-known expressions.

2. MUʿIZZĪ AND AZRAQĪ (AT THE SELJUQ COURT)

In the foremost ranks of masters of the panegyric *qaṣīda* must be included Amīr ʿAbdu'llāh Muḥammad Muʿizzī. He was born about 440/1048–9 (the family came originally from Nisā) and lived at the court of the Sulṭāns Malik-Shāh and Sanjar. He obtained the office of *Amīru'sh-shuʿarā*, 'Prince of Poets', not as heir to his father Burhānī (*c.* 409–465/1018–1073), who in his semi-frivolous songs in praise of wine had already in the early Seljuq period expressly assumed the same attitude towards devotion to the laws as did ʿOmar Khayyām and Ḥāfiẓ[48] later on, but in virtue of his own art which rightly brought him fame during his life and throughout all generations to come. He owed his wealth to his unlettered patrons but was obliged to comply with their strange whims. Thus we see that, for reasons that have never been explained, he was shot by the arrow of the king's son, Sanjar (511/1117–8). He was seriously wounded and after a long period of suffering died some time between 519–21/1125–7[49] – not, as tradition erroneously has it, in 542/1147–8. His great lyrical *dīvān* numbers more than 18,000 distichs. Its importance is due partly to its poetical value (Muʿizzī was a master of *vaṣf*, 'description') and partly to the elucidatory evidence it provides concerning contemporary events, persons and customs. As to themes and style, Muʿizzī follows the panegyric poets of Khurasan, ʿUnṣurī and Farrukhī (presumably also ʿAsjadī) and now and again we can hear Manūchihrī's tones as well. That Anvarī accused him of literary plagiarism cannot be proved with certainty, but it is sure that Anvarī himself made use of the verses of Muʿizzī.[50] He shows superiority in descriptions, *sahl-i mumtaniʿ*, 'inimitable facility', and naturalness of expression. Muʿizzī's work forms an important link in the development of the Persian *qaṣīda*.

Among the important poets of the 5th/11th century we may mention Azraqī, whose real name was Abu'l-maḥāsin Abū-Bakr Zaynu'd-dīn of Herat (d. some time before 465/1072–3).[51] Firdausī is said to have taken refuge in the house of Azraqī's father, Ismāʿīl Varrāq, 'the bookseller', on his flight from Ghazna to Ṭūs. As a consequence of his father's occupation, the son was brought up in a literary sphere. Some of his *qaṣīdas* testify to his particular affection for his elder and renowned compatriot, Anṣārī (p. 234). Among those whom he lauded in his *qaṣīdas*, the first in chronological order is Shamsu'd-daula Abu'l-favāris Ṭughān-Shāh, under his father Alp-Arslan governor of Khurasan, who cherished such an affection for Azraqī that he used to write to him when he was absent from Herat. Azraqī is an eminent panegyrist; among his characteristics are fanciful similes, which a hundred years later were unjustly censured by the poet and poetical scholar Rashīdu'd-dīn Vaṭvāṭ (d. 578/1182–3) (p. 200), but which came into their own at the time when the Indian style[52] was prevalent. Azraqī also versified the obscene book *Alfiyya u Shalfiyya* and is said to have introduced himself with it to Ṭughān-Shāh.[53] Neither this book nor his recasting of the *Sindbād-nāma* (see p. 223) have been preserved. He is not the original author of either of these works.

3. MASʿŪD-I SAʿD-I SALMĀN, ḤASAN GHAZNAVĪ AND ABU'L-FARAJ RŪNĪ (GHAZNAVID INDIA)

An important poet living during the later Ghaznavid period is Masʿūd-i Saʿd-i Salmān, born in 438/1046–7 in Lahore of wealthy parents who originally came from Hamadan. He had a very eventful life. Attached to the court of the prince of Ghazna and governor of India, Sayfu'd-daula Maḥmūd, he rose to wealth and honour thanks to his civil and military talents. He was about forty years of age when catastrophe overtook him: when attempting to save his patrimony in Ghazna from being seized, he was thrown into prison in connection with the affair of Prince Maḥmūd who was accused by the Sulṭān Ibrāhīm b. Masʿūd (451–92/1059–99) of being in treacherous league with the Seljuqs. The calumny of his enemies and the resentment of the Sulṭān proved stronger than any intervention or all the pleading and complaint contained in Masʿūd's *qaṣīdas*. For seven years the poet languished in the fortresses of Dahak and Sū and suffered subsequently even more greatly in the fortress of Nāy. He was not released until 490/1096–7, when he returned to Lahore and was appointed governor of Chalander. This appointment however lasted but a short time, for he was involved in the fall of his protector and incarcerated in the terrible fortress of Maranj (near Ghazna). Eight years elapsed before he was set free once more (about 500/1106–7). The last years of his life were spent in retirement and high favour, despite all the changes in public life. He died about 515/1121–2.

Both as man and poet, Masʿūd showed brilliant qualities and capacities. For this very reason he was not spared stubborn hostility when times were bad nor sycophancy when they were good. His knowledge included astrology (learnt in prison), hippology, military affairs, and even calligraphy. He was a great master of the *qaṣīda* in the style of ʿUnṣurī, but possessed too great a talent to simply imitate the latter or anyone else, as is implied by the criticism of Khāqānī. Sanā'ī bestows high praise on Masʿūds *sahl-i mumtaniʿ*. His *Tristia*, written in prison, are among the most charming achievements in Persian poetry. It has been said that no one understood as he did the art of introducing some wise maxim (*kalām-i jāmiʿ*) into his poems. His themes included eulogy, instruction, lament, derision and polemic, court and battle, and to a lesser extent nature, love and wine. Always the optimist, he believed that justice must ultimately prevail, even in the most acute crisis.[54] Muʿizzī and ʿUthmān Mukhtārī of Ghazna (d. 554/1159?) were not the only ones to appreciate him. Navā'ī refers to him as "the agile horseman on the racecourse of the *qaṣīda* and the incomparable creator of words", and Sanā'ī himself arranged his *dīvān*, albeit rather carelessly. To speak of an Arabic *dīvān* of Masʿūd's is to exaggerate the importance of a few Arabic verses. The report of a *dīvān* in Hindi belongs to the realm of fables, although the poet, an Indian by birth and habitation, must necessarily have known this language. His selection from the *Shāh-nāma* has not been preserved.

At the same court and contemporaneous with Masʿūd-i Saʿd lived and worked his friend Abu'l-Faraj Rūnī (born at Lahore, his family hailing originally from Rūna near Nishapur; died at the turn of the 5th–6th/11th–12th century). He was a writer of delicate panegyrics and was praised and imitated by no less a person than Anvarī. A satirical *mathnavī* directed against the 'Great Ones' at the court of Sulṭān Shīrzād b. Mas'ūd reflects approval as well as disapproval of the social order.[55]

A very remarkable poet, who lived somewhat later but is as yet less well known, is Ashrafu'd-dīn Abū-Muḥammad Ḥasan b. Muḥammad Ḥusaynī Ghaznavī, known in brief as Ashraf (d. 556/1160–1). His best period falls in the reign of Bahrām-Shāh of Ghazna at whose court he worked for a long time. Later on he travelled about in Khurasan and Iraq, singing the praises of Sulṭān Sanjar and lesser Seljuq princes. His *dīvān*, that contains among other things 83 *ghazals*, is of importance for the history of this form of poetry.

Ḥasan's *ghazal* poetry, occasionally signed with the *takhalluṣ* 'Ḥasan', although as a rule adhering to the lyrical style, frequently sings the praise of Bahrām-Shāh, occasionally however only in the closing verse. The panegyrism of his *qaṣīdas* alternates now and then with moralising and didactic passages. Though not insensitive to the influence of his predecessors and contemporaries, he strikes his own original note which is even powerful enough to affect the second half of the 6th/12th century. Simplicity and clarity are not the least of his merits.

4. ADĪB ṢĀBIR, ANVARĪ AND MAHSATĪ (AT THE COURT OF THE SELJUQS)

A good and cultured poet in the service of Sulṭān Sanjar was Shihābu'd-dīn Sharafu'l-udabā Ṣābir ('Adīb Ṣābir') of Tirmidh. It appears, however, that the Sultan employed him for other purposes as well, namely as a spy. Under pretence of a display of courtesy he stayed at the court of Sanjar's rival, Khvārazm-Shāh Atsïz, betrayed the assassins hired by the latter against Sanjar and was on that account drowned in the Oxus some time between 538–42/1143–8.[56] His verses are remarkable for their simplicity, fluency and refinement.[57] Proficient as he was in the Arabic language and literature, he translated Persian verse into Arabic.[58]

The honour of being the greatest master of panegyric verse, and an unusually abstruse master at that, must be accorded to Auḥadu'd-dīn 'Alī b. Vaḥīdu'd-dīn Muḥ. Anvarī, born *c.* 520/1126 in Abīvard in Dasht-i Khāvarān. The first *takhalluṣ* that has been handed down, namely Khāvarī, probably arose as a corruption of Anvarī.[59] After having acquired an uncommonly extensive knowledge of all the sciences cultivated at that time, including astrology – the most highly esteemed of all by feudal society – he devoted himself to poetry and was soon received at the court of Sanjar. His elegy, full of patriotic feeling, testifies to the violent emotion that shook him when the terrible Ghuzz invasion overtook Khurasan in the year 548/1153. He remained faithful to the Seljuqs also when the dynasty collapsed after the death of Sanjar (552/1157). There exists an almost incredible confusion as to the date of his death which usually, though erroneously, is connected with his tragi-comical prediction of a dreadful natural catastrophe, the date of which is also difficult to establish. Whereas A. Ateş, of whose article on Anvarī I gratefully make use, arrives at the year 563/1168 as the *terminus post quem*, M. Mīnuvī fixes 565/1169–70 as being the only possible year of his death.[60] But the most recent researches of S. Nafīsī and Raḍavī indicate the date as 585/1189–90.[61]

Anvarī lived at a time when literature was in full flower. The scholar and the poet in him strove for the upper hand, both equally brilliant and sincere. He decided on a poetical career only because he did not wish to suffer the penury of scholars, and the life of a court poet opened quite other perspectives. He boasted of his knowledge but did not hold poetry in very high regard, less in view of literary monstrosities as because he had in mind the niggardly spirit of the *qaṣīdas* and the extortionate blackmail expressed in the satires[62], and finally the compulsory service of the court panegyrists; he even regrets having dedicated himself to poetry, for he considers that the world has no need of poets and poetry. He vows he will never again use praise or slander, but it must be admitted that he did not keep his word, in fact it would have been impossible for him to do so, for his work shows as clearly as daylight that he was a genuinely inspired poet, probably one of the most brilliant figures in Persian literature. His work is pervaded by an exceedingly powerful scholarly element that takes the form of a superfluity of erudition, but he himself regards it as an indispensable ornament and even as an integral part of the substance of panegyric. It is this very erudition that makes him one of the most difficult poets to understand, together with Khāqānī, with whose nature and style he was familiar. Without some commentary Anvarī is barely comprehensible, and even with it he is still often unfathomable. He was well versed in the earlier and later masters as well as with Persian and Arabic literature. Thanks to his imagination, learning and sovereign mastery of language and rhetoric, he raised the *qaṣīda* to such a high level that a subsequent decline was inevitable. Jāmī[63] speaks of him as "almost a miracle" and is also right in another sense than he meant, for with all his linguistic peculiarities and Arabisms Anvarī is a master of *sahl-i mumtaniʿ*, if one interprets this professional term here as the 'inimitable facility' with which he composed his verse. He often begins his *qaṣīda* immediately with the eulogy, while descriptions of nature are only seldom to be found in the introductions; there is no excess of eroticism but on the other hand the dialogues with the Beloved, i.e. the object of his praise, are striking. In his pleadings he likes to include a touch of humour, a characteristic feature of his *qaṣīdas*. Anvarī separates his *ghazal* almost completely from the *qaṣīda*, an important step in the development of the *ghazal* before Saʿdī. The chief purpose of the *qaṣīda* is the eulogy, and this is achieved by the intensive use of every conceivable medium. He lets himself go in invective and libellous writings. His biting sarcasm must have been known throughout Iran or he would not have been dragged through the streets of Balkh on account of a pamphlet that in reality he had not written, despite all accusations to the contrary – an incident bearing a remarkable resemblance to that which befell Khāqānī! He was frequently called *ḥakīm*, 'the Sage'. Wisdom and an echo of the philosophy of Avicenna do indeed permeate his *qaṣīdas* and *qiṭʿas*. Two circumstances provide proof of Anvarī's relations with Avicenna: first his commentary named *Kitābu'l-bashārāt fī sharḥi'l-Ishārāt li'sh-shaykhi'r-ra'īs*, 'The Book of Good Annunciations for the Explanation of Avicenna's Ishārāt', and secondly a request in verse to return Avicenna's *ʿUyūnu'l-ḥikmat*, 'Sources of Wisdom', that had been transcribed by Anvarī himself for his own purposes, but in some inexplicable manner borrowed by one of his friends.[64] Anvarī raises his voice against certain stupidities prevailing amongst the rank and file, against fawning and irregularities in the social order, turns his satire even against women, perverse passions and the blindness of fate.[65] He only attained a state of sincere repentance when the life at court, that he had once longed for so intensely, had become intolerable. At the end of his life he was able to enjoy the quiet solitude of a scholar's life, such as he had formerly rejected. Incidentally we find in his works already a certain anticipation of the law of gravity.

A very misty figure is the beautiful and talented composer of quatrains, the poetess Mahsatī[66] Dabīra of Ganja[67], a contemporary of ʿOmar Khayyām and Niẓāmī, with both of whom she is said to have associated.[68] She is also alleged to have been the companion of Sulṭān Sanjar. It is hardly likely that she was already alive at the time of Maḥmūd of Ghazna; there is here evidently some confusion with Sulṭān Maḥmūd b. Muḥammad b. Malik-Shāh, Sanjar's governor in Azerbayjan. Her love-affairs are recounted in a work of fiction written by Jauharī[69] of Bukhara, embellished with numerous quatrains by the poetess herself and by her lover and later husband, Tāju'd-dīn ('Crown of Faith'!) Amīr Aḥmad, 'Son of the preacher of Ganja' (!). Unfortunately the authenticity of the quatrains attributed to her cannot be proved, however much her originality makes her stand out favorably above all the other insipid poetesses of the classical period. Quatrains that describe dallyings with young apprentices are patently constructed only on fantasy and word-play and are devoid of reality. Mahsatī's alleged free way of living and her peddled verses have stamped her as an Iranian Madame Sans-Gêne though both pieces of evidence may be unfounded. But she knows better than anyone else how to capture the pleasing tone of the quatrain.

5. ʿAMʿAQ (BUKHARA)

Shihābu'd-dīn ʿAmʿaq[70] of Bukhara (d. *c.* 543/1148–9) was a true *amīru'sh-shuʿarā*, 'prince of poets', not only in title but also in the feudal sense, for he enforced his claim to personal marks of respect on all the poets living at the court of the Iligh-Khāns in Bukhara. Through the favour of the prince, his master, he had come to possess both goods and slaves. An excellent panegyrist, he was even more renowned as a composer of elegies, and was praised by Anvarī as a master of the word. He wrote a *mathnavī*, unfortunately no longer in existence, that following on after Abu'l-Mu'ayyad Bakhtyārī (at the court of the Buyids of Iraq[71]) and Amānī, deals with the story of *Yūsuf u Zalīkhā*. It is written in an attempt at an over-artificial verse-technique, such that every verse could be read in two metres. His *qaṣīdas* also abound in samples of rhetorical skill; he knew, however, how to convert these artificialities into genuine poetry that was not lacking in emotional elements. He excelled in similes which on the one hand reveal his gift of observation, but on the other spring from his imagination.

6. RASHĪD VAṬVĀṬ (KHVĀRAZM)

At the court of the Khvārazm-Shāh Atsïz (521–51/1127–1156), the arch-enemy of Sanjar, and of his successors, there lived Rashīdu'd-dīn Muḥammad al-ʿUmarī (i.e. of the house of Caliph ʿUmar), panegyrist and epistolographer, known under the nickname of Rashīd-i Vaṭvāṭ, 'Rashīd the Bat', on account of his small insignificant figure with the bald head (b. *c.* 508–9/1114–6[72] at Balkh, d. 578/1182–3, though possibly as early as in 573/1177–8).[73] His vanity and arrogance had doubtless something to do with his outward appearance. Even less attractive are his religious fanaticism and his contempt of philosophy. Through his high position he was known in a wide circle and was thus in close contact with the poets of his time. His case demonstrates clearly how cautiously one must interpret the mutual praise and abuse of contemporaries, for his judgements express nothing other than purely personal sympathies and antipathies, those of his partners merely flattery addressed to their sovereign lord. Khāqānī, for instance, hated him. But Vaṭvāṭ also possessed good qualities: he was a passionate collector of manuscripts, comparing them one with another. He also endowed religious foundations (*vaqf*) and patronised men of letters. He even allowed the latter to live with him, providing he was permitted to help in correcting their poetry, etc. His *qaṣīdas* give evidence of learning but very seldom betray emotion; they almost invariably consist of pure panegyrism and descriptions of the wars of Atsïz, often overburdened with rhetorical artificiality. Flashes of sagacity are unable to lend warmth to his verse. His prose is of greater value; it includes both the Arabic and Persian correspondence (official and private) as well as the important rhetorical work *Ḥadā'iqu's-siḥr*, 'The Gardens of Magic', that was intended to discount the shortcomings of the *Tarjumānu'l-balāghat*, 'Interpreter of Eloquence' (see p. 176). Some parts of his works have not been preserved and of the rest certain portions are worthless. He also composed *qaṣīdas* in Arabic.[74]

E. THE SCHOOL OF AZERBAYJAN

The panegyric poets Abu'l-ʿAlā, Khāqānī, Mujīru'd-dīn, Falakī and their counterparts in eastern Iran, Athīr and Ẓahīr-i Fāryābī. – The epic poet Niẓāmī

In the 11th and 12th centuries there is a close association between the history and cultural life of the Caucasus region and those of Iran. Although the great Seljuq rulers endeavoured to bring Transcaucasia under the central administration of the kingdom, they did not succeed, despite their powerful governmental machinery, in definitively suppressing the native feudal forces, and in preventing the dissolution of the territory into independent princedoms. The feudal conditions prevalent in Transcaucasia far more closely resembled those in Europe. A proof of the high standard of culture is to be found in its poetry. It was not merely that there were in Caucasia and Azerbayjan men of letters and scholars in plenty; of even more importance was their individual character. Not the fact that they lived in one and the same century but this very individuality is the reason for including them in a separate group, which should, properly speaking, have begun already with Qaṭrān (see p. 194). In their style, choice and arrangement of words we discern certain characteristics that are either not present at all or only very occasionally among the eastern Iranian poets. This does not mean in the least that there was no connection between this school and the Khurasan poets of the 5th/11th century, as well as those from Bukhara in the 4th/10th century (the connection with Eastern Iran in the 6th/12th century is already looser). Even though all the movements sprang from one root, they were nevertheless subject to local influence. With the exception of Niẓāmī, the entire poetical output consists of lyrical poetry and in particular the *qaṣīda*, either panegyric or satirical. It was the courts alone that furnished the pecuniary reward for this poetry, that is only superficially tinged with Ṣūfism and with Ṣūfī criticism of feudal society, a criticism based on the point of view of those who have come within the sphere of influence of the rulers and for that very reason feel their deprivation all the more directly. Although there can be no real question here of a specific Ṣūfī literature, it is the very Ṣūfī mask that allows the poets to give utterance to criticism that under normal circumstances would be impossible. Under the influence of Ṣūfism, namely of the urban classes, the *ghazal* enjoys an increasing popularity (Khāqānī, Niẓāmī). A complicated technique is one of the most conspicuous qualities of the Transcaucasian school. Under the growing influence of the towns the themes occasionally escape from the sphere of the court. Archaisms are discarded but correspondingly more words are drawn from the Arabic vocabulary. Even indigenous folklore puts in an appearance. These distinctions have also been perceived by several Persian scholars of recent times[75], who have given a special place to the exponents. They have been examined with unusual care by Ye. E. Bertel's[76], to whom I am indebted for a series of observations as ingenious as they are original. Hence the Caucasian and Azerbayjanian panegyrists must be placed in a special chapter; they form a clearly defined group of three generations of teachers and pupils, one of whom, as grand master of the *qaṣīda*, had a powerful influence on the development of this form of poetry. To this group belonged the most brilliant poet of Azerbayjan, the romantic Niẓāmī. All the poets worked at court or at least within the realm of the Shirvān-Shāhs, who favoured literature written in the Persian tongue with their especial patronage, for the Shirvān-Shāhs traced their descent from Bahrām Chōbīn. Yet Persian was not their native language, though it predominated in works of literature; folk-poetry of course developed in consistence with local idiom.[77] It would nevertheless be erroneous to regard the Shirvān-Shāhs as ideal patrons of literature – the imprisonment of Khāqānī and Falakī, the ostracising of Abu'l-ʿAlā, for instance, give sufficient evidence of their attitude. The position of the court poets had deteriorated to such an extent that the caprices of the rulers had free play. Perhaps this is in some way connected with the financial crisis – clearly indicated by the coinage – that accompanied the fall and disintegration of the Seljuq supremacy.[78]

Foremost in this group stands the courtier Niẓāmu'd-dīn Abu'l-ʿAlā Ganjavī (b. 472–483/1080–90, d. 554/1159), the first notable figure from the Shirvān school, critic and teacher of the succeeding generations. Whether the fact that at the age of 55 he was divested of his court honours[79], albeit only for some time, is connected with Khāqānī (see p. 203). I cannot say. Little of this work has survived, yet the few remnants, dispersed as they are among various anthologies, provide evidence of the eloquent language of a by no means mediocre poet, distinguished by his vocabulary, his syntactical constructions and not in the last place by his lucidity.

A master of the panegyric *qaṣīda* and no less of the *ghazal*, and a poet to be ranked with Anvarī, is Afḍalu'd-dīn Badīl (Ibrāhīm) b. ʿAlī Khāqānī Shirvānī (b. 515/1121–2).[80] He was more closely attached to his native land Azerbayjan than any other poet and is therefore difficult of access for those unacquainted with the political and cultural life in Eastern Transcaucasia, the centre of the interwoven cultures and religions of Islam and Christendom.[81] O. L. Vil'chevskiy maintains[82] that Khāqānī was the offspring of an illegitimate liaison and that his 'uncle' and teacher, the physician Mīrzā Kāfī'd-dīn ʿUmar b. Uthmān, may in fact have been his father. It is certainly no mere coincidence that at one point in his *dīvān* he significantly refers to his parents and himself in the same mutual relationship as the figures of Mary, Joseph and Jesus. Khāqānī by no means ignores the carpenter ʿAlī, his father or guardian, and even devotes a whole *qaṣīda* to him. He writes with extreme tenderness of his mother, originally a slave of the Nestorian faith who later accepted Islam, but who no doubt instructed her son in the basic ideas of Christian doctrine and liturgy. Yet the poet owes his remarkable knowledge of matters concerning Christianity, so rare in the world of Persian literature, not to his mother but to the reciprocal penetration of these religions in his country, as we have already mentioned. Khāqānī's *dīvān* embraces a profusion of specifically Christian imagery and symbols, interwoven with equally characteristic images and symbols of Islam; quotations can also be found from the sacred books of

Christianity and from prayers.[83] Such a *dīvān* could only have been composed in Transcaucasia[84], where the two religions met and intermingled. We gather from it that Khāqānī also stayed at Tbilisi and was familiar with the language and culture of Georgia. His youth was spent in a period of oppression and want; as the son of an ordinary artisan he would have grown up as wild as the creatures of the forest had not his talent and exceptionally acute powers of observation attracted the attention of his 'uncle' who, as a physician and apothecary, was an educated man and gave him instruction in the Arabic language.[85] A thorough education in all the other branches of learning followed, leaving deep traces in the soul of Khāqānī. *Ghazals* and *na'ts*, written under the mystical *takhalluṣ* Ḥaqā'iqī, 'Seeker after Truth', already procured for the young student a name of some importance, at first naturally only in the immediate vicinity of his home. The *na'ts*, written at the time when his literary talent had reached its zenith, procured for him the title of Ḥassānu'l-'Ajam, 'the Persian Ḥassān'.[86] It seemed as if the fortunes of Khāqānī were assured when the poet Abu'l-'Alā Ganjavī, mentioned above, accepted him as a pupil and, as a mark of esteem, gave him his daughter in marriage – the same daughter whom another pupil of Abu'l-'Alā's, the poet Falakī (see p. 208), had been courting. In addition to this Abu'l-'Alā, in his capacity of *maliku'sh-shu'arā*, 'King of Poets' and *sayyidu'n-nudamā*, 'Chief of the King's Intimate Friends', introduced Khāqānī to the Shirvān-Shāh Abu'l-Muẓaffar Khāqān-i Akbar Manūchihr b. Farīdūn, on which occasion our poet requested permission to use the *takhalluṣ* Khāqānī. Unfortunately the father-in-law soon grew jealous and the high hopes of the young man were dashed. All prospects of a career came to an end when his father, the carpenter, was obliged to sell many of his household goods and chattels in order to feed and clothe his son and the latter's family. He would have preferred to tie him down to a trade. This was the true background of the violent quarrel that arose between the two poets, until finally Khāqānī even charged Abu'l-'Alā with entertaining sympathy for Ḥasan Ṣabbāh, the founder and leader of the Assassins, which in the eyes of a Sunnite prince was an extremely serious accusation. This was a period in which informers were rife. The poet Falakī, Khāqānī's rival as a suitor and consequently his life-long enemy, is said to have nearly lost his life in the atmosphere of calumny (Khāqānī however was not involved). The reproaches of ingratitude constantly levelled against Khāqānī must be regarded as unjustified. It was the hard struggle for a bare existence that obliged him to resort to self-defence. As regards the unfair accusation of heresy against Abu'l-Alā, this was probably caused not by hate only but also by firm Sunnite partiality. Khāqānī tried to gain a footing elsewhere, in particular with the famous Khvārazm-Shāh 'Alā'u'd-dīn Atsïz. But objections were raised by Rashīd Vaṭvāṭ (see p. 200). The otherwise friendly treatment on the part of the latter was repaid by Khāqānī in his agitation by a satire, of which he soon repented, without however improving his relations with Rashīd Vaṭvāṭ. When in 545/1150 his uncle, patron and teacher, the physician 'Umar, died, Khāqānī began to yearn for the life of an anchorite. These tendencies returned later, but may have been put into practice only at the end of his life. An attempt to be admitted to the court of Sanjar failed. Khāqānī got no further than Ray because the destruction of the great Seljuq empire by the Ghuzz tribes had in the meantime ruined his expectations for ever. Khāqānī went on his first pilgrimage (*ḥajj*) to the sacred cities of Islam in 551–2/1156–7; permission was probably granted him through the intercession of the King of Georgia, Dimitri I, to whom he had applied by means of a *qaṣīda*.[87] He broke his journey at Isfahan and Baghdad. His reception at Isfahan on the homeward route was extremely unpleasant. The town, in a mood of excessive agitation, rose up against Khāqānī because of a malicious satirical poem that had been launched by Mujīr Baylaqānī under the name of Khāqānī. The latter's reputation for biting satire left no room for doubt among the indignant citizens of Isfahan (see p. 208). In a long *qaṣīda* Khāqānī tried to mollify the population and to explain the fraud. The fruit of his pilgrimage consists mainly in *Tuḥfatu'l-ʿIrāqayn*, 'The Gift from the Two Iraqs', the first Persian book of travels in *mathnavī* form. Shortly after his return he was cast into prison (554/1159). This he complains of in the *Prison Qaṣīdas*. Whereas the *tadhkiras* throw the blame on Khāqānī, Ye. E. Bertel's and O. L. Vil'chevskiy ascribe it to the confusion that arose after the death of the Shirvān-Shāh Manūchihrī (554–7/1159–62). Possibly Khāqānī did not share the political views of Tamara, the widow of the deceased ruler, who wanted to secure the throne for her younger son Muḥammad Ruknu'd-dīn Ṭughān-Yozaq to the exclusion of the elder one, Akhsatān.

One definite piece of evidence is provided by a *qaṣīda* dating from the year 564/1168, addressed to the Byzantine emperor Manuel Komnenos (1143/1180), as O. L. Vil'chevskiy ingeniously points out, and in any case not to his cousin and rival, Andronikos Komnenos.[88] In it we read that Khāqānī went from Shirvan via Georgia to the court of the Byzantine emperor at Constantinople; he refers to the religious problem that at that time was causing a stir in Byzantium and its orthodox world, namely the interpretation of the words occurring in the Gospel of St. John (14, 28): "I go unto the Father, for my Father is greater than I." Khāqānī agreed with the opinion of the ecclesiastical council that stood under the influence of Manuel against Andronicus. From a Persian poet this is an unusual contribution to byzantology and was thus entirely misunderstood by the Moslem interpreters and was in fact quite beyond their grasp. An important factor later on is the relationship between Khāqānī and Andronikos Komnenos, who stopped at the court of the Georgian King Giorgi III (1156–84) during his wanderings in the east as an exile with his wife Theodora. He was received with honour and took part in the Georgian-Shirvan battles against the Russian army that was advancing towards Transcaucasia (569/1173). The poet, already thus associated with Byzantium, could not fail to respond to such an event, and in one of his *qaṣīdas* (it is the second poem addressed to the 'Byzantine emperor') he describes Andronikos as the only man capable of destroying the Russian army, even as the most capable pretender to the imperial throne (which indeed Andronikos had never ceased to strive for), and offers him his services. Thus a complete change took place in the attitude of Khāqānī, which, added to the fact of Andronikos' hostile feelings towards the Russians, was no doubt brought about by his dissatisfaction with Akhsatān and with Shirvan in general, so that his one aim was to get away. He could not very well foresee that the emperor would one day defend the interests of the peasants. He managed to disguise his departure by the *ḥajj* pilgrimage, which did actually take place (570/1175), apparently this time too through the intercession of a Christian, a member of the Byzantine dynasty, although Khāqānī had also requested the intermediation of Akhsatān's sister and of his wife. Under pretence of undertaking the sacred *ḥajj* and entrusted by Andronikos with some commission, he set out for Iraq. He spent some time in Baghdad but declined the offer of the Caliph to enter his service. It was probably during the second *ḥajj*[89] that he made the acquaintance of Sayfu'd-dīn Arslān Muẓaffar Muḥammad, prince of Darband, to whom after his return and while still staying in Shirvan he sent a *qaṣīda* in six parts, memorable on account of a verse directed against the tyrants[90]; only the addressee is exempted, but he makes caustic references to Akhsatān (presuming that we have dated the *qaṣīda* correctly). Shortly after his return he suffered a terrible loss in the death of his son Rashīdu'd-dīn (571/1176) which was followed by many other cares, for it is evident that the *qaṣīda* addressed to Qïzïl Arslan (in the year 576/1180) was written in a mood of despair. The constant desire to escape from the atmosphere of the court of Shirvan grew steadily stronger, but none of his hopes were fulfilled. Akhsatān disliked him but was nevertheless afraid to lose him. Khāqānī longed once more for Khurasan which by this time lay in the power of the Khvārazm-Shāh, with whom he had hoped to ingratiate himself after the death of Vaṭvāṭ (573/1177–8). In 580/1184 he went, or fled, to Tabriz, but got no further. From there he visited Baghdad and several places in the neighbourhood and further afield, though Tabriz remained his chief place of residence. A large number of the poems in the *dīvān* were composed during this period, but up till now it has not been ascertained how Khāqānī spent his time there, apart from writing. It was while staying at Tabriz that he composed eight elegies in memory of his wife, who had died in the meantime at Shirvan, and it was at Tabriz too that he ended his days, apparently far away from the bustle of the world, in 595/1199.[91]

As well as the *dīvān* Khāqānī left some letters and the lesser known *'Ajā'ibu* (or *Khatmu*)*'l-gharā'ib*, 'Curious Rarities'[92], but perhaps most important of all the *mathnavī Tuḥfatu'l-'Irāqayn*, 'The Gift from the two Iraqs', (viz. the Persian and the Arabic), which the poet himself called *Tuḥfatu'l-khavāṭir va zubdatu'ḍ-ḍamā'ir* (or *zubdatu'n-navāẓir*), 'The Gift of Memories and Choice of Thoughts'. It is an account in poetical form of Khāqānī's first pilgrimage (551–2/1156–7) to the sacred places.[93] The purposeful activities and sudden changes of fortune in the life of Khāqānī are all effectively and eloquently echoed in his *qaṣīdas*, which he never failed to send to the rulers and to persons in their environment, either at home or abroad, in order thus to provide for his own sustenance. The abundance of autobiographical elements is characteristic of Khāqānī. Credit is due to Muḥammad-ʿAlī Nāṣiḥ, Badīʿu'z-zamān Furūzānfar and A. Ateş[94] for being the first to lend a firmer foundation, based on material drawn from the *dīvān* as a whole, to the biography of the poet, as opposed to the prevailing distortions and inventions of tradition. Subsequently, however, the studies of K. Chaykin and Yu. N. Marr, and latterly those of V. Minorsky and O. L. Vil'chevskiy, have proved that even these theories do not represent the last word on the subject. They show, on the contrary, that we are still only at the first stages and that a further comprehensive study of the *dīvān* will raise a multitude of problems. An investigation into the eventful life of Khāqānī is, in fact, one of the most difficult tasks for the history of Persian literature. Fortunately his *dīvān* forms a rich mine of documentation, important not only for the information it contains concerning the poet's life but also for the history of the places and countries where he had acquaintances or where he used to stay. It is not very easy to draw on this source, for it is quite impossible to understand it rightly unless the history of Caucasia and both Islamic and Christian culture be taken into consideration, as well as the relationship of Khāqānī to Byzantium. Some help is given by the poet, not only in references but also in numerous chronograms which, in their turn, lead the way to the references, but – like so many of his verbal tricks – are so veiled that only now, thanks to O. L. Vil'chevskiy, can we find the key to them. Among the specialities of Khāqānī – and perhaps also of other poets belonging to the Azerbayjan school – are double chronograms, the determination of dates according to the Ḥijra and the Christian era simultaneously, though without any external indication that chronograms are involved. As an example we may take the famous *qaṣīda* on Madā'in (Ctesiphon, see below, p. 207): although up to now it has generally been assigned to the second pilgrimage, this is incorrect since a double chronogram establishes the year 561/1166 perfectly clearly as the date of its composition.[95] Khāqānī must therefore have composed this *qaṣīda* not from feelings of dismay * on the ruins of the famous metropolis, but ten years after his return from the pilgrimage, thereby even using a similar *qaṣīda* by the Arab poet Bukhturī (d. 284/897) as model.[96] Khāqānī's *qaṣīda* is entirely devoid of any patriotic sentiment or of any reflection of Iranian national ideals, for it contains nothing but the usual lamentation on the inconstancy of this world.

His self-undermining restlessness is evident in all the accounts of Khāqānī's life. He complains and laments without ceasing. But the fault lay not only in his environment – where, it is true, the moral standard was not any too high – but also in himself. It cannot be said that he did not participate in the gifts of the Shirvān-Shāhs or that he received no payment. Manūchihr in particular was well-disposed towards him and Akhsatān too eventually recalled him. Khāqānī lived constantly under the delusion that he was being unjustly treated and was therefore ever in search of something better. He was a poetic genius, but his conceit knew no bounds and he was easily slighted owing to his over-sensitiveness. All this provides the clue to a right understanding of his unstable, irregular way of living.

Khāqānī is a panegyric poet but not quite in the ordinary sense. He was not a craftsman in the art of poetry but possessed the true and genuine qualities peculiar to a poet's nature, one of the greatest geniuses in the literature of Persia. Outwardly he is characterised by the enormous difficulty of his verse which forms an obstruction to comprehension by any but the few. This very fact has given rise to a series of commentaries aiming at the interpretation of the works of the master. A brilliant scholar, Khāqānī employed all the knowledge and conceptions of contemporary learning and gave vent to them in a display of rhetorical virtuosity. His whole being is based on scholarship and poetry, but because he was in the first place a poet, knowledge had to be subservient to poetry. This explains the nature of the difficulties: they originate neither in ostentation nor in a desire for artifice, but in his superlatively rich intellect which, as it were, presupposes as a matter of course a certain congeniality in the reader. This same quality is noticeable in his panegyrics and in the emotional passages – of which there are no few! – and in spiritual elegies and dirges when he grieves for the death of his son or his wife, the murder of a scholar during the Ghuzz invasion, when he laments the transitory nature of the material world – the ruins of Ctesiphon (Madā'in) –, when he suffers from the lack of friends, from envy, betrayal or imprisonment. His descriptions of nature and scenery, especially of dawn and sunrise, are magnificent, influenced, no doubt, by the beauty of his native Caucasia. Amorous feeling is not lacking, though it is encountered but seldom. The conception of Allah as the Beloved was alien to him. In his panegyrics he did not seek to indulge in hollow encomium alone but also to give advice and instruction. But he knew too how to attack and to abuse with vehemence. He was more easily carried away by religious and Ṣūfī wisdom than by philosophy. Although he possessed a style of his own that provides evidence of his connections with the poets of Azerbayjan and Iraq, his *qaṣīdas* were first influenced by Sanā'ī[97]; he knew and admired the great poets of Khurasan, whom he also imitated (such as Manūchihrī), and attempted to outdo ʿUnṣurī in artifice. The short verse-metres which Khāqānī favoured most give a lively fluency to the long *qaṣīdas* and this is enhanced by the revival of the initial verse (*maṭlaʿ*) and of course by his supreme control over thought and form. By this revival of the *maṭlaʿ* his *qaṣīda* poetry approaches the strophic synthesis (*tarkīb-band*) that he likewise used. He delighted in *tarṣīʿ*, i.e. parallelism of the two hemistichs, and in long *radīfs*, 'refrains', which now and then however formed a danger to the meaning or the expression. The *ghazal* is used by him both for the actual *ghazal* themes and for the dirges. A. Ateş [98] is of the opinion that Khāqānī was the first in the literature of Persia to give the *ghazal* its final classical form, but to my mind this might also be said of his contemporaries Anvarī or Niẓāmī, possibly of others too.

A master of language, a poet possessing both intellect and heart, who fled from the outer world into the inner, a personality who did not conform to type – all this places him in the front ranks of Persian literature. His frequent and intentional self-praise does not sound vain in these circumstances. We realise to what heights a *qaṣīda* can attain in the hands of a real master – in the case in point a genius. Unfortunately an entirely exclusive art. Khāqānī's influence on the whole of panegyric poetry is beyond estimation. But it can be remarked in other fields as well, for it seems as if in a number of his *ghazals* Maulavī has made use of Khāqānī's exordia (*nasīb*) and *ghazals*; on the other hand the vagabond and roguish tone of some of Khāqānī's poems remind one of Ḥāfiẓ[99], who lived round about two centuries later.

Yet all this does not reflect Khāqānī's innermost feelings; his true nature is revealed elsewhere than in his panegyrics. In numerous lesser-known *qaṣīdas*, open letters and elegies in honour of relatives and friends, of craftsmen, market-drivers, poets and other simple people of Shirvan, in works not written for profit but springing from his inmost soul, imbued with his deep sympathy for the lower classes, there and in his purely lyrical *ghazals*, quatrains and *qiṭʿas*, often soaring to the heights of true humanism – in these works Khāqānī voices the thoughts and ideals of the mediaeval town of the Orient which carry force down to the present day.[100]

An outstanding figure among the pupils of Khāqānī is Mujīruʾd-dīn of Baylaqān (nowadays in ruins), though he is certainly least successful when attempting to follow in the steps of his master. But he resembles Khāqānī in that he turns against the latter just as Khāqānī had turned against his patron and father-in-law, Abu'l-ʿAlā Ganjavī. Mujīruʾd-dīn too is a panegyric poet, but in contrast to Khāqānī his style is mostly clearer and more natural; it approaches that of Farrukhī and possesses the melodiousness of Manūchihrī. He admonishes those whom he praises. His *qaṣīdas* tend rather towards a passion for fame than towards importunity. Mysticism also becomes audible but only on the surface, and more in the nature of an ascetic renunciation of the world. The remainder of his lyrics are of slight importance. Sometimes he basks in the favour of his patrons, the princes of Azerbayjan and Iraq, sometimes he falls into disgrace and is even imprisoned, as is shown by the 'prison poem', *ḥabsiyya*. This was frequently the fate of court poets, but in the case of Mujīruʾd-dīn it does seem as if the fault lay in his own quarrelsome and arrogant nature. There was perhaps not one poet in his vicinity with whom he did not quarrel. Because he imagined he was not received in Isfahan with the honour due to him, he flew into a rage against the men of letters there and even scoffed at the town. Khāqānī himself was drawn into the controversy and was obliged to clear himself of all blame by singing the praise of Isfahan. Later on the town was reported to have been the scene of Mujīr's violent end: he is said to have been beaten to death by obscure individuals about 594/1197–8. This makes the other date sometimes given (586/1190) practically untenable, since in 587/1191 he still wrote a dirge on the violent death of the Ildigizid ʿUthmān Qïzïl-Arslan (582–7/1186–91). His *dīvān* has survived. It is worth mentioning as a curious fact that Khusrau Dihlavī holds him in higher esteem than Khāqānī.

Abu'n-Niẓām Muḥammad Falakī[101] Shirvānī, a native of Shamākhī (b. circa 501/1107; he was still alive between 549–551/1154–7[102]) enjoyed a liberal education, especially in astronomy to which he devoted a learned treatise. His pseudonym too is evidently derived from that science. The report that he was a pupil of Abu'l-ʿAlā Ganjavī's (see p. 202) and teacher of Khāqānī is regarded by Hādī Ḥasan[103] as being more picturesque than true, and he considers it more likely that Falakī was a protégé than a teacher of his alleged pupil. Strangely enough Falakī deems none of the contemporary poets worth mentioning at all, whereas he places himself on a level with Abū-Tammām (d. 230/845) and Abū-Nuvās (d. 198/810) and that certainly not on account of the few verses in Arabic which he wove into his *qaṣīdas*. He spent all his life at the court of the famous Shirvān-Shāh Manūchihr II b. Farīdūn and unlike other poets during that time eulogised in his elegant *qaṣīdas* no one but his master. And yet the slander of his rivals led also to his imprisonment, just as in the cases of Khāqānī, Mujīr and possibly Abu'l-ʿAlā. This had a disastrous effect upon him. The *dīvān* shows that he did not survive Manūchihr, which is consistent with the reference to Falakī's short life in Khāqānī's elegy. For this reason dates such as 587/1191 or 577/1181 given for his death are untrustworthy. Of his poetic oeuvre, about 1510 scattered verses have been preserved. We are indebted to the excellent Indian scholar Hādī Ḥasan for having collected and evaluated them. They are comparatively simple even where they touch on science, just as if he were trying to emulate Masʿūd-i Saʿd, though this was hardly any longer feasible. *Taghazzuls* (purely lyrical portions) are placed only at the end of the *qaṣīdas*. He subscribed neither to hypocrisy nor to ostentation. The lines written in prison are those of a true poet or, as Badīʿu'z-zamān Bushrūya'ī[104] puts it, "the iron chains of the Shirvān-Shāhs released the hands and feet of his ideas from the bonds of artificiality". And yet it is not originality that is his most striking quality. ʿIṣmat of Bukhara (see p. 274). imitated him, as did Salmān Sāvajī, without however admitting it as did the former.

The courts of the princes of Azerbayjan evidently had a great power of attraction, for Eastern Iranians gravitated there. Among them was Athīr of Akhsīkat (Fergana; d. about 570/1174), the mention of whose name must suffice, and Ẓahīr Fāryābī.

Ẓahīru'd-dīn Abu'l-Faḍl of Fāryāb (near Balkh), in brief Ẓahīr-i Fāryābī (b. about 550/1156), who was an adept particularly in Arabic and in philosophy and astronomy, struggled along from court to court in Mazandaran, Nishapur and Azerbayjan, extolling and glorifying first one prince and then another in far-fetched panegyrics for which he was reproached by Saʿdī[105], until finally he retired into solitude (d. 598/1201–2 at Tabriz). His panegyric style, later often imitated by other poets, was itself an imitation of Anvarī and Khāqānī. It is distinguished for its metaphorical language. Majdu'd-dīn Hamgar (d. 678/1279) is guilty of gross exaggeration when he puts it on a level with that of an Anvarī, from whom it was that Ẓahīr derived the whole of his art of rhetoric. In relation to Khāqānī and Anvarī his style was simple but it lacked a comparable emotional impulse. He is a mediocre poet, a master only of excessive servile humility. Ḥāfiẓ' praise is based on a forged verse. But all the same it is true that even a Saʿdī imitated his lyrical introductions. *

F. THE EPIC POET NIẒĀMĪ AND HIS IMITATORS AMĪR KHUSRAU AND MAKTABĪ

The rise of the panegyric *qaṣīda* to its apogee does not provide the only claim to the place of honour held by the southern Caucasus in Persian literature; for that same Azerbayjan gave it and the whole world the most brilliant poet of the romantic epic – Ilyās b. Yūsuf Niẓāmī (b. in Ganja, now Kirovabad), a master 'hors concours' of thought and word whose freshness and vigour have not been effaced throughout the centuries. Very little is known about his life. We can only conclude that he was born in 535/1141 in urban surroundings. The Azerbayjan of today, extremely proud of its world-famous countryman, is not content with the mere fact of his being a compatriot but also considers him as belonging to its Turkish tribe.[106] His mother, whom the poet mentions as Ra'īsa in his *Laylī u Majnūn* and designates as a Kurdish woman[107], was at any rate of Iranian extraction. As to his youth we have no other information than that he became an orphan at an early age. Only in his work do we find irrefutable evidence of his excellent training in 'all' the then known branches of learning. It seems as if his birthplace, Ganja, laid a spell on him. Only once, about 581–2/1185–7, did he leave it, and then not of his own accord but because the prince of Azerbayjan, Qïzïl Arslan-Shāh, was passing by some thirty *farsakh* away and expressly requested a meeting. Did he live by and for poetry alone? A certain hint in this direction is again given in *Laylī u Majnūn*, an epic poem containing more than 4000 distichs, written by Niẓāmī in less than four months. He states that he would have completed it in fourteen nights if he had been freed from all other occupations.[108] There was nothing of the courtier about him, precluded as he was by his convictions. It is true that he dedicated his great epics, and now and then his *ghazals*, to princes. Such was the usual custom, in expectation of a gift, or properly speaking, a fee. The village of Ḥamdūniyān, which the prince had presented him with, appears to have been an object of ridicule on the part of his rivals rather than of any benefit to Niẓāmī himself. We may therefore assume that he was far from possessing an abundance of earthly goods. Tradition brings him into contact with persons belonging to the 'Akhīs', a kind of freemasonry at that time recruited from humbler circles, mainly craftsmen. He is generally supposed to have died in 600/1203, but according to Ye. E. Bertel's[109] there are grounds for favouring any date up to 1211. We owe the correct date to A. A. Alesker-zade[110], who discovered an old tomb-stone bearing the date 4 Ramaḍān 605/12 March 1209 on the actual spot. For hundreds of years pilgrims have visited Niẓāmī's mausoleum as if it were the tomb of a saint. It has now been restored by the Soviet authorities in Azerbayjan.

The epical works of Niẓāmī consist of five separate poems that have been assembled by later generations into a collection called a *Khamsa*, 'Five Poems'. Each epic has its own characteristic metre. In his first work, *Makhzanu'l-asrār*, 'Treasure-Chamber * of Mysteries', dating from 572/1176 (?) Niẓāmī creates an ethical-philosophical poem in the manner of Sanā'ī's *Ḥadīqa* (see p. 236), yet with an enormous power of poetic invention. Niẓāmī employs reflections, parables, allegories and every means of rhetorical ornamentation in order to master the stubborn material and to transform it into perfect poetry and a poetical whole. But he did not continue on this ascetic path. A fundamental turning-point occurred in his life – he experienced true love, its ecstasy and also, within a short time, its sorrow. As a token of gratitude, the prince of Darband had sent him the Kipchak slave-girl Āfāq, whom Niẓāmī grew to love so dearly that he married her. After living together happily for five or six years Āfāq died leaving a delicate little boy named Muḥammad whom the poet apostrophises in touching fashion in all his later epics. Anxiety on the boy's account induced him to remarry, but death broke up this second marriage as it did his third. He commemorates these two wives also in his verses. The second epic, *Khusrau u Shīrīn*, composed during the years 573–6/1177–81, is chiefly inspired by the happiness and tragedy of a young woman, for Shīrīn is none other than Āfāq herself (according to Ye. E. Bertel's actually in Turkish 'Apaq', meaning 'Snow-White').[111] It is the story of the love and sorrow of a princess as girl and wife, in its sincerity unequalled by any other work in Persian literature. Occurrences are depicted that demonstrate only too clearly the baseness of the ruling classes. The irresoluteness of the Shāh gives rise to a rebellion on the part of the feudal lords and leads to the downfall of all the principal personages. *Laylī u Majnūn* (584/1188) springs from quite a different source. It is the story of the * love between two children from the Arabian desert who owe their unhappy fate to the foolishness of the parents – actually a very old theme derived from folklore. Only with reluctance did Niẓāmī obey wishes from above, for he feared that this essentially simple popular theme or the *membra disjecta* of different episodes would not provide sufficient material for an epic. The result however showed great genius: in respect of structure and psychology a perfect picture, with the final result that Majnūn ('fool'), the composer of love-*ghazals*, is obliged to suffer so that mankind may find enjoyment in his heart-rending songs. J. Dunayevskiy[112], in a comparison with Romeo and Juliet, calls attention to the following fundamental difference: whereas the western conception is based on the personal enmity between two families, the oriental version proceeds from the premature love of Majnūn, his disobedience and outbreak of madness, factors in his attitude towards which the father concurs with the general opinion. Here a violation of the prevailing social order can be perceived and the impossibility of a marriage inferred.

Haft Paykar, 'Seven Portraits', dating from 593/1197, describes the education and deeds of an ideal ruler, representing, according to popular tradition, the idealised Sasanian king Bahrām Gōr. A number of episodes have been woven into this framework, culminating in the stories of the Seven Princesses, the most fervent but also the most serious declaration of the master's views on love. Because of the diverse nature of its art and emphasis the *Haft Paykar* certainly occupies the first place among

Niẓāmī's works, but in its social aspects it already anticipates his last epic poem, the Song of Alexander. This latter consists of two parts, the *Sharaf-nāma*, 'Book of Honour', and the *Iqbāl-nāma*, 'Book of Happiness', in which the portrait of Alexander as warrior, philosopher and prophet is successively developed. Here the poet works with a mass of images and episodes intended in different ways to elevate the individual, human society and the rulers. The opinion that the last epic of Niẓāmī signified his decline is a grievous error. The material itself does not admit any excessive rhetoric, but nevertheless in the hands of the master it attains such poetical and philosophical depths as are only granted to isolated geniuses in the literature of the world.

Niẓāmī stands out on account of his ideas and imagination, infinite religious feeling, precision of expression, superior technique, selection and arrangement of material, philosophical profundity, and social understanding. While *Khusrau u Shīrīn* abounds in imagery, a simpler form has been adopted for the later epics. As regards artistry the *Haft Paykar* stands supreme. The ideology of urbanism is making a peremptory bid for a hearing.

Great credit is due to Niẓāmī for having introduced the living language into the epic – the same vocabulary that had long before penetrated into the court lyric.[113] By so doing he delivered a decisive blow to the ancient epical tradition, particularly because it was no longer sufficiently comprehensible as a result of its negative attitude towards arabising trends. Even Gurgānī's *Vīs u Rāmīn* had not been able to avoid this entirely. The production of epics of chivalry had fallen off, not only in consequence of changes in the social strata and lack of interest on the part of the masses, but because this form of poetry was as it were incapable of shaking off the lingual purism that was symptomatic of it. Through the language of the lyric moreover, a hitherto more or less furtive element in the epic was reinforced: the lyrical attitude and the underlying psychology. Chivalric ideals died out, the personal factor forced its way to the front, the tragedy of the individual increased in range – all this in connection with the rise of the urban bourgeoisie, that in the meantime had driven all other classes far into the background. As against this, in none of his epic poems was Niẓāmī an innovator as regards versification, for all his metres are to be found in earlier epics. There is no doubt that the influence of Fakhru'd-dīn Gurgānī's *Vīs u Rāmīn* can be observed in certain passages of the *Khamsa*, notably in the conversations between Khusrau and Shīrīn[114], the description of the night in *Laylī u Majnūn*, etc. But one may not lose sight of the fact that all these bear the stamp of Niẓāmī's unique mind.

Niẓāmī's lyrical *dīvān* is said to have contained about 20,000 distichs but practically the whole of it has been lost. Tradition apparently exaggerates in no small measure in regard to the number. Yet even from the scanty vestiges we still possess (about 2000 distichs from *ghazals, qaṣīdas*, etc.) one can conclude that they were written by a great master of the *ghazal* at a time close to that of Sa'dī. The lyrical poems are in fact permeated with passionate emotion and transported into a state of constant ecstasy by an unusual distinction between Thou and I. It certainly occupied the master during the whole of his life, as M. Th. Houtsma[115] would also have said if he had had access to the material available and known to us today.[116]

Niẓāmī found an uncommonly large number of imitators in Iran and in the areas falling under the influence of Persian culture – in Turkey, Central Asia, India and so on.[117] They imitate his form, choice of material, treatment of analogous and sometimes like subjects, preferably in the same *Khamsa* form. Amīr Khusrau (see p. 258), the first in point of time, occupies a prominent place and he in his turn also influences his successors. Among these, as Vaḥīd Dastgirdī[118] repeatedly emphasised, Maktabī[119] of Shiraz approaches his model most nearly in his admirable epic poem *Laylī u Majnūn*, which dates from 895/1489–90 and is a work that even achieves new effects by means of lyrical *ghazal* insertions. Somewhat later it was imitated by Fuḍūlī (see p. 298) in a treatment of the same material in the language of Azerbayjan, one of the highest achievements in the poetry of that area. If Maktabī really did write a parallel to *Haft Paykar* as well, its loss is most regrettable, presuming that it reached the same high standard as *Laylī u Majnūn*. – Tremendous admiration of Niẓāmī is reflected also in the miniature and in the minor arts in general, where the themes are for the greater part taken from the *Khamsa*. In Persian and Turkish literature its figures (thus, for instance, Farhād) have become almost historical.[120]

G. THE ISFAHAN SCHOOL
JAMĀLU'D-DĪN, KAMĀLU'D-DĪN ISMĀʿĪL

Jamālu'd-dīn Muḥammad b. ʿAbdu'r-Razzāq of Isfahan (d. 588/1192), a goldsmith or at any rate descended from a goldsmith's family, is an important but relatively little known ʿIrāqī poet. He lived in his native town which he zealously defended against the attacks of others, though often censuring it himself. He sang the praises of the later ʿIrāqī Seljuqs but also, and to a greater extent, extolled two patrician families of Isfahan, the shāfiʿite Āl-i Khujand and the Ḥanafite Āl-i Ṣāʿid.[121] Although in his verses he gives free play to his knowledge of Arabic literature and theology, he distinguishes himself from his models, the poets Khāqānī and Anvarī, by his flowing and limpid style. For the rest he cannot hold a candle even to Masʿūd. In particular he is far inferior to Sanā'ī (see p. 236), although both were advocates of the idea of renunciation. His views are motivated neither by philosophy nor by Ṣūfī speculation but by material theological conceptions. He criticises contemporary conditions, the *madrasas* and the scholars. Doubts may arise as to whether his incessant praise of asceticism be altogether sincere, since he does not obey his own injunctions but constantly proclaims his longing for renunciation and solitude despite its never being realised. There is a lack of power in Jamāl's *qaṣīdas* which betray all the more potently the sensitive composer of *ghazals* that he really was, and even one of the best before Saʿdī. This is evident from the fact that the later poets, Saʿdī not excepted, often gladly adopted his ideas with only slight alterations. His poetry is conspicuous for its parables. "The *qaṣīda* known as *ashūb-i rūzgār*, 'Confusion of Time', sums up all the bitternesses of human life."[122]

Far more famous than Jamālu'd-dīn is his son Kamālu'd-dīn Ismāʿīl (b. about 568/1172–3). He is the last great poet of olden times from Isfahan. A comparison of the two poets is enlightening. Each expresses in his own way the love for his native town and each extols the same Isfahan families. If the father enlarges more theoretically on the excellence of renunciation, the son does likewise but rather from the standpoint of a good Ṣūfī (in appearance!), only to remove the mask at once in a positive attitude to such a non-mystical object as wine. This insincerity is still more sharply apparent in his striving after honour and luxury. On the other hand he was well-disposed towards the people, was not devoted to Mammon and – an uncommon characteristic of Persian men of letters – had never and nowhere done anyone any harm. The father died in penury, the son, following the example of many a panegyric writer, retired into solitude and perished in the Mongol invasion (635/1237). He had concealed gold from his fellows, and thus not even his monk's cowl could save him. His domain is that of panegyric poetry (at the early age of twenty he made a name for himself with a brilliant *qaṣīda*) but it differs from that of his father in that it is less emotional, being on the other hand highly polished and fabulously rich in original ideas. This is the reason for his being known as Khallāqu'l-maʿānī, 'Creator of Subtle Thoughts'. In his *qaṣīdas* we find no *taghazzul* but all the more frequently injunctions, mystical ponderings, laments on life and physical suffering, on the prevalent lack of appreciation of poetry and on a general degeneration. Circumstances compelled him to the composition of satires. His descriptions too are admirable. Kamālu'd-dīn created a model for the *qaṣīda* in the Iraqi style that thanks to Saʿdī – like his father's *ghazal* – rises to the summit of perfection. A *mathnavī* on mystical love from the hand of Kamālu'd-dīn[123] is also mentioned.

H. THE SATIRIST SŪZANĪ

Neither the career nor the poetry of Muḥammad b. ʿAlī Sūzanī of Nasaf (near Samarkand) follows the beaten track. His youthful wild spirits gave way to God-fearing behaviour in later years (d. 569/1173–74; according to Ye. E. Bertel's 1179).[124] The poet, a son of the people, is characterised by a genuine and rare simplicity that triumphed over even his *madrasa* erudition. Although he was accomplished in all he did, his fame was not due to the panegyric poetry that he clearly wrote only in order to earn a living, but to the satires and parodies in which he ridiculed and severely criticised his fellows. But he indulged in extravagance, often at the cost of propriety and unfortunately also of art. As documentary evidence for an assessment of his period and as a shrill discord amidst the cloying sweetness and fancies of his contemporaries, Sūzanī's work has certainly unusual value, and it is gratifying that his *dīvān* has thanks to its recent editing attracted some attention in present-day Persia. Sūzanī's style formed a precedent in Transoxania; he found a follower in the *dihqān* Abū-ʿAlī Shaṭranjī of Samarkand who composed a number of noteworthy *qiṭʿas*, and in Lāmiʿī of Bukhara.

NOTES

1. Bertel's, *Kabus-nama* (transl. B VIb), 246; idem, 'Lit. ... v Sr. Az.' (D IIa), 216.
2. Nafīsī, *Shāh-kārhā* (C), 5.
3. Bertel's, *Kabus-nama* (transl.), 243; Minorsky, *The Middle East*, 431.
4. Barthold, *Shuʿūb.*, 256; Minorsky, *Iran*, 188 (B II), holds a different view: the unification of the country or countries based on an organisation of all classes into a single social pyramid according to their degree of initiation.
5. Tschudi, *Vom Islam*, 453.
6. Taqī-zāda's preface to the *dīvān*, ed. Taqavī, p. 'ṭ'; Ivanow, *Problems*, 11; A. Ye. Bertel's, *Nāṣir-i Khosrov*, 169 *et seq.* acknowledges that Taqī-zāda is right; Muḥaqqiq, *Yaghmā*, 1340, I, 35 *et seq.* as well.
7. Ivanow, *op. cit.*, 12 *et seq.*
8. In *op. cit.*, p. 171 *et seq.*, A. Ye. Bertel's recalls that Balkh was the second capital of the Sultans Maḥmūd and Masʿūd and that it can be proved that they also resided there. It is thus not unlikely that the poet entered service at Maḥmūd's court, though not later than 417/1026. Bertel's corroborates this by referring to a passage in the *Safar-nāma*, the same that Ch. Schefer had in mind in his edition (*q.v.*), p. XIX. Yet unless there are other points of support the testimony of the *Safar-nāma* is dubious. Does not the passage just cited savour somewhat of the Sunna?
9. W. Ivanow, *Problems*, 26, contests the assumption of Nāṣir-i Khusrau's travels previous to his journey to Egypt, which he is said to have undertaken in order to gain an insight into the life and religion of different countries (Bertel's, *op. cit.*, 174 *et seq.*).
10. *Med. Islam*, 272.
11. *Op. cit.*, 17 *et seq.* Contradicted by Fritz Meier, *Oriens*, 9 (1956), 191.
12. According to A. Ye. Bertel's, *op. cit.*, 186 *et seq.*, Nāṣir-i Khusrau was obliged to flee from Khurasan for fear of the masses lashed into fury by the priesthood. Bertel's dates the flight some time between 1056 and 1063. Despite the natural beauty and wealth of Yumgān, the poet is said to have felt very lonely and deserted at first, though later on he managed to get together a number of companions. From there, still according to Bertel's, he carried out his propaganda and correspondence with Egypt and there too the greater part of his philosophical *qaṣīdas* and the works *Rūshanā'ī-nāma*, 'The Book of Enlightenment', *Jāmiʿu'l-ḥikmatayn*, 'Union of the Two Wisdoms' (462/1069–70) and probably *Zādu'l-musāfirīn*, 'Sustenance of the Traveller' (see however *ibid.*, 185!) originated. The exact date of his death cannot be ascertained. It can only be proved that he was still alive in 465/1072–3.

From one and the same source, the year 481/1088–9 is quoted repeatedly as the date of his death.
13. Ivanow, *op. cit.*, 47.
14. *Ibid.*, 54. A bold plagiarism under the name of Nāṣir-i Khusrau is *Kalām-i pīr* (or *Haft bāb-i Shāh Sayyid Nāṣir*): *ibid.*, 78 *et seq.*
15. Bertel's, 'Lit. ... v Sr. Az.' (D II a), 215; Gabrieli, *Il 'Sefer-Nāmeh'*, 557 *et seq.*; Bahār, *Sabk*, 2, 152. A. Ye. Bertel's points out in *op. cit.*, 163, that in the year 1426 the text of this work differed from the present version. One should therefore be constantly on one's guard against fortuitously added Sunnite co-efficients (cf. *ibid.*, 164 *et seq.*).
16. Recension of *Zādu'l-musāfirīn*, *Iran*, I, 229.
17. 'Die islam. Lehre' (B VI a), 228, 235; *ZMDG*, 1924, p. LXXVI.
18. Idem, 'Die islam. Lehre', 229.
19. Ivanow, *Problems*, 73.
20. The *Sa'ādat-nāma*, 'Book of Bliss', that resembles the *Rūshanā'ī-nāma*, has as its author Nāṣir-i Khusrau Sharīf-i Iṣfahānī (d. 753/1352) and is thus erroneously attributed to our poet; cf. Bahār, *Sabk*, 3, 189; Nafīsī, 'Dū kitāb-i tāza az Nāṣir-i Khusrau', *Sukhan*, I, 96, where even Nāṣir's authorship of the *Rūshanā'ī-nāma* is questioned. – "No specifically Ismā'īlī ideas": G. M. Wickens, *The Sa'ādatnāmeh*, 118.
21. The recently discovered, hitherto unknown works of Nāṣir-i Khusrau are listed in *ShS*, 1959/10, 158.
22. Cf. V. B. Nikitina, *Pejzaž* (*q.v.*).
23. Preface to Q. Ghanī's *Baḥth*, I, p. 'z'.
24. Bibliography dealing with the positive appreciation of the aesthetic elements in Nāṣir-i Khusrau and Sanā'ī by Persian and Tajik historians of literature as opposed to the western standpoint: V. B. Nikitina, *Iranskaya filologiya*, 111 $_3$. This same scholar connects the latter with a want of esteem for the oratorical tradition in didactics: *K probleme* (*q.v.*).
25. Bibl. *s.v.* 'Khayyām'.
26. Rempis, *Neue Beiträge*, 24. – 'A. Iqbāl: b. 437/1045, d. 508/1114.
27. Bertel's, 'Lit. ... v Sr. Az.' (D II a), 215.
28. Badī'u'z-zamān, *Qadīmtarīn iṭṭilā'*: cf. Ritter, *Oriens*, 5, 193.
29. Minovi-Minorsky, 'Naṣīr ad-Dīn Ṭūsī on Finance', *BSOAS*, 10 (1940–2), 766 $_3$.
30. Rempis, *'Omar Chajjām*, 50.
31. Muḥsin: Bibl. *s.v.* 'Bertel's'; Bibl. *s.v.* 'Findariskī'; Hādī: see below, p. 344, and LHP, 4, 431 *et seq.*
32. Rempis, *Beiträge*, 83 *et seq.*
33. *'Omar Chajjām*, 325 *et seq.*
34. Bibl. *s.v.* 'Rempis'; *s.v.* 'Ritter, *Zur Frage*'; *s.v.* 'Christensen'.
35. Bibl. *s.v.* 'Khayyām' and 'Arberry'.
36. Mīnuvī, in *Az khazā'in-i Turkiya* (see Bibl.), 74 *et seq.* prints a Persian *qaṣīda* by Khayyām. The same scholar regards the earliest MSS of quatrains alleged to be by Khayyām as forged (announcement made at the 25th International Congress of Orientalists, Moscow 1960); cf. further S. Nafīsī, *Qadīmtarīn nushkhahā* (*q.v.*).
37. *Oriens*, I, 362 (on Gabrieli's translation).
38. *Ibid.*
39. Bolotnikov, *Khayyam*, 195.
40. See Krïmskiy, II, in the section on 'Omar Khayyām.
41. Bolotnikov, 205.
42. Molé, 'L'épopée', 390, in which even Christensen is quoted.
43. *Relation* (Bibl. *s.v.* 'Nāṣir-i Khusrau'), p. XXIV, or 19.
44. E. D. Ross, *JRAS*, 1927, 149. It is probably only a matter of "certain ways of expression of the Khurasan poet", cf. H. Ritter, *Oriens*, 9 (1956), 367 *et seq.*

45. Ṣafā, 2, 442. *
46. *Sukhan va sukhanvarān* (B v), 2/1, 138.
47. Asadī, *Lughat*, ed. ʿAbb. Iqbāl, 1; S. Nafīsī, 'Qadīmtarīn kutub-i lughat dar Īrān', *Majalla-i Sharq*, 1, 399; C. Salemann, Bericht, *Mél. Asiat.*, 9 (1888), 507 *et seq.*
48. Ritter's notes on M. Muʿīn, Burhānī (*q.v.*), *Oriens*, 5, 192.
49. ʿAbb. Iqbāl, Preface to Muʿizzī's *dīvān*, p. 'l'. The poet himself states that a year after having been wounded he was again able to appear at the court of Sanjar (Hādī Ḥasan, *Researches*, 5). Similarly to Iqbāl, also S. Nafīsī, *Dīvān-i Anvarī*, 39*.
50. Iqbāl, *op. cit.*, p. 'm'.
51. The dates 526/1131–2 and 527/1132–3 are considered less accurate by E. G. Browne, *Chahār Maqāla*, 124, and Dh. Ṣafā, 2, 435 *et seq.*
52. Aless. Bausani, *Bedil* (D IIb), 192 footnote 2; cf. also *al-Muʿjam* (ed. 1314), 257.
53. Cf. M. J. Maḥjūb, *Mathnavī-sarā'ī* (B VIa), 284 *et seq.*
54. Bertel's, IPTL, 398.
55. M. J. Maḥjūb, *op. cit.*, 282 *et seq.*
56. Ṣafā, 2, 644, with the remark that the traditional date of his execution, *viz.* 546/1151–2, is erroneous.
57. Not so Ye. E. Bertel's, 'Lit. ... v. Sr. Az.' (D IIa) 212, according to whom the *qaṣīdas* of Ṣābir are characterised by their artificiality and a special preference for the figure *taqsīm.*
58. A. Abdulloyev, *Chand sukhan doyir ba nashri devoni Adib Sobiri Tirmizī. Akhborot AN Taj. SSR*, 2 (1964), refers to his prose, but this has been lost.
59. Thus S. Nafīsī in the substantial preface to his edition. Otherwise there are but few biographical data.
60. Ateş, 'Enverî', *İA*, 4, 280a; Mīnuvī, *Ijtimāʿ-i kavākib dar sāl-i 582*, p. 26. Nafīsī, *op. cit.*, 35, refutes this and asserts that Anvarī died in Balkh in the year 585/1189–90.
61. Anvarī, *Dīvān*, ed. Raḍavī 109*, Nafīsī 36*.
62. Yet he himself knew how to be impudent in his demands, cf. Ṣafā, 2, 350.
63. Bertel's, *Navoyi*, 153; Ḥikmat, *Jāmī*, 122, l. 16.
64. *Cf.* ʿAbb. Iqbāl in *Jashn-nāma-i Ibn-i Sīnā*, 2, 202 *et seq.* As regards the borrower cf. *Oriens*, 7 (1954), 202.
65. Krïmskiy, 2, 125.
66. Now very exhaustively treated in F. Meier's monograph (*q.v.*). M. Ishaque quotes in his treatise 'Mahsatī', *Indo-Iranica*, 3/4 (1949), 11, the pronunciation Mahastī, Mihastī, Mihsatī and various etymologies. In ʿAṭṭār's *Ilāhī-nāma* (ed. H. Ritter, p. 232 *et seq.*) Mahastī, Mahsatī, and Mahsattī.
67. Mention is also made of Nishapur, Badakhshān and according to *Arm.*, 10, 123 Khujand (Ishaque, *op. cit.*, p. 12).
68. It is even said that she was laid to rest in the mausoleum of Niẓāmī in Ganja: *Arm.*, 10, 127 *et seq.*
69. Bertel's, 'Lit. ... v Sr. Az.' (D IIa) 210 *et seq.*; idem, IPTL, 489. But we shall have to wait for the appearance of Volume II of F. Meier's *op. cit.*, which is to be devoted specially to this romance and its author.
70. Perhaps transmitted in error instead of the original ʿAqʿaq? Cf. Ṣafā, 2, 536 *et seq.*
71. Ṣafā, 2, 360.
72. O. L. Vil'chevskiy: in a letter, instead of the usual 480/1087–8.
73. Ṣafā, 2, 631. S. Nafīsī, Anvarī, 39* as well.
74. Rashīd's complete works annotated and discussed in detail: *Dīvān*, ed. S. Nafīsī, 28 *et seq.*
75. Shafaq, *Tā'rīkh-i adabiyyāt*, 204–46; Badīʿu'z-zamān, *Sukhan va sukhanvarān*, 2/1.
76. 'Lit. ep. Niz.', 42–57; idem, *Nizami* (1940), 20–6; idem, *Nizami* (1947), 29–55.
77. The turkicising of Azerbayjan by the Seljuqs: V. Minorsky, *Iran* (B II), 187; Azerbayjan was finally won over to Turkish *ethnos* under the Mongols, cf. B. Spuler, *Die Mongolen in Iran*², 458.

78. Sanaullah, *The Decline* (B II): rec. Minorsky, *BSOAS*, 10 (1940–2), 258; Ad. Grohmann, *Einführung und Chrest. zur arab. Papyruskunde*, I, Pr. 1955, 208.
79. Bertel's, 'Lit. ep. Niz.', 46; Badī'u'z-zamān, *Sukhan va sukhanvarān* (B V), II/I, 323 *et seq.*
80. Thus O. L. Vil'chevskiy in a letter dated 28.9.1959, more accurately than his article *Khakani*, 63: 514/1120–1. V. Minorsky, *Khāqānī*, 572, upholds emphatically approx. 519/1125 against K. Chaykin's 528/1133–4. V. Minorsky approaches A. Ateş, *Hâqânî*, 85, with the date [520] '1126?' Out of the question is LHP, 2, 391: 500/1106–7 in Ganja.
81. Vil'chevskiy, *Khakani*, 63.
82. Idem, *ibid.*, 74–5.
83. Idem, *ibid.*, 65 *et seq.*
84. Idem, *ibid.*, 74 *et seq.*
85. Khāqānī's virtuosity in the use of the Arabic language is demonstrated in ten Arabic *qaṣīdas*, pp. 711–24 in the *dīvān* ed. 'Amīr-i Kabīr'. The caliph also wanted him to enter his service.
86. Ḥassān b. Thābit (d. 54/674), the Prophet's own poet. In *Tuḥfatu'l-'Irāqayn* he states that this *laqab* was given him by his 'uncle'.
87. Vil'chevskiy, *ibid.*, 65.
88. Vil'chevskiy, *ibid.*, 67; for the latter see the observations brought forward in V. Minorsky's 'Khāqānī'.
89. Thus Vil'chevskiy, *op. cit.*, 71, whereas Ateş, *op. cit.*, 89, and Minorsky, *op. cit.*, 560, place the meeting of the poet and the prince in Mecca at the time of the first pilgrimage (Minorsky even gives 552/1157 as the date of the *qaṣīda*).
90. Ed. Amīr-i Kabīr, 175, 3 *infra.*
91. This date, ascertained philologically by A. Ateş, was confirmed by A. A. Alesker-Zade's epigraphical discovery, cf. M. D'yakonov, *VoIst.*, 1948, 9, 121.
92. Cf. *NAA*, 3, 1964, 169; Y. Qarīb, *Tuḥfa* 'm'.
93. Of another opinion is S. Ḥus. Āmūzgār (*q.v.*), who, after an exhaustive enquiry, reaches the conclusion that the *Tuḥfa* was composed in 549–50/1154–6 in Shirvan, thus before the first *ḥajj*. This makes it impossible for it to contain a description of the latter. As far as I know Āmūzgār is alone in this view. Since he assumes Khāqānī to have been born in 525/1130-1, the poem must be a youthful work, even perhaps an intentional companion poem to Sanā'ī's *Sayru'l-'ibād ila'l-ma'ād* (see below, p. 237). According to Āmūzgār, Sanā'ī and Khāqānī died in the same year. The *Tuḥfa* is said to be one of the most difficult texts in Persian literature.
94. Nāṣiḥ, see Bibl.; Badī'u'z-zamān, *Sukhan va sukhanvarān* (B V), 2/1, 300–349; Ateş, see *İA*.
95. O. L. Vil'chevskiy's letters of 22.7. and 26.9.1959.
96. Cf. Turjānī-zāda, *Ta'aththurāt-i Khāqānī* (Bibl.), 114 *et seq.*
97. Badī'u'z-zamān, *Sukhan va sukhanvarān*, 2/1, 308; likewise also in the *ghazal*, *ibid.*, 314.
98. Hâkânî, *İA*, 5, 95a.
99. *Ibid.*, 95b. Khāqānī's life as reflected in his works: *Oriens*, 7 (1954), 206 (reproducing *Yādgār*, 1325–26, fasc. 6 *et seq.*).
100. Vil'chevskiy, *op. cit.*, 76. *Dīvān-i Khāqānī*, ed. 'Amīr-i Kabīr', p. 15*, states that Khāqānī's *qaṣīda* 'Falak-i kažrau...' has been translated into French already by J. Chardin, though the poet's name is not mentioned.
101. The *laqab* is uncertain: Najmu'd-dīn, Afṣaḥu'd-dīn, Mu'ayyidu'd-dīn; cf. Badī'u'z-zamān, *op. cit.*, 2/1, 283.
102. Thus Hādī Ḥasan recently (1958) in *Researches*, 7 and *Majmū'a* (1956), 119–20.
103. *Falakī*, I, pp. 52, 53, 55.
104. *Op. cit.*, 285.
105. Krïmskiy, 2, 31.
106. On the turkisation of Azerbayjan cf. S. M. Aliyev, 'Rabotï Ahm. Kesravi po srednevekov'yu', *Blizhniy i Sredniy Vostok* (Sbornik in Memoriam B. N. Zachoder), M. 1962, 131 *et seq.*

107. Thus according to Vaḥīd, *Ganjīna* 'z', while S. Nafīsī, *Dīvān-i Niẓāmī*, 3, sees in the expression *ra'īsa-i kurd* literally 'the forewoman of the Kurds'.
108. *Laylī u Majnūn*, ed. Vaḥīd, 29, lines 10–11.
109. *Nizami* (1947), 278.
110. Cf. above, p. 218, note 91.
111. *Kak zvali* (*q.v.*). According to Nafīsī, *op. cit.*, 12, not a proper name but *āfāq*, 'the (quarters of the) world'. Not convincing!
112. *Nezami*, 263.
113. Bertel's, *Stil' 'Unṣurī*, 53.
114. *Ḥamāsa* (B VIa), 321 footnote. For details see M. J. Maḥjūb in his edition of *Vīs u Rāmīn*, 92 *et seq*. This same scholar demonstrates once again in *Mathnavī-sarā'ī* (B VIa), that Niẓāmī certainly had models.
115. *Some Remarks*, 225.
116. Nafīsī's edition of Niẓāmī's lyrical poetry (see *s.v.* 'Niẓāmī') ist the most comprehensive. *
117. Cf. Ye. E. Bertel's, *Jāmī*, 26–30. Deserving of special mention is the excellent translation of *Khusrau u Shīrīn* that Quṭb contributed to the Turkish literary language of the Golden Horde not later than 1342 and that has been preserved in a good MS dating from 1383. In view of these circumstances Quṭb's version becomes particularly valuable (apart from its importance for turkology) as an outstanding instrument for criticism of the Persian text, all the earliest MSS of which are more recent than this Turkish version (cf. Bibl. *s.v.* 'Niẓāmī' and 'Zajączkowski'). Regarding *Laylī u Majnūn* in Turkish literature: Bibl. *s.v.* 'A. S. Levend' and 'Araslī'.
118. *Ganjīna* (Bibl. *s.v.* 'Niẓāmī') p. 'mḥ', 'ṣv', etc.
119. According to 'Abdu'l-Ḥusayn Navā'ī d. probably in 916/1510–11, cf. *Oriens*, 7, 202 (*Yādgār* 2/5, 1324–25, 52–60).
120. H. W. Duda, *ZDMG*, 57, 234.
121. Cf. S. Nafīsī, 'Khāndān-i Ṣā'idiyyān', *Mél. Massé*, Tehran 1963, 85–101.
122. Abdullah, *The Value*, 5.
123. Ritter, *Philol.*, 7, 105, Nr. 20.
124. 'Lit. ... v Sr. Az.' (D IIa), 210; as against this, ditto, *Ocherk*, 50: 569/1173–4.

VI. THE PROSE OF THE SELJUQ PERIOD

(5th–6th/11th–12th century)

A. ON THE BORDER-LINE BETWEEN LEARNED LITERATURE (OR INSTRUCTION) AND BELLES-LETTRES

The prose of the Seljuq period is characterised in some parts by the same directness and simplicity as is that of the foregoing era, but in others it already shows signs of affectation, long sentences, accentuated Arabisms and so on, all of which phenomena gradually become more pronounced. Whereas the belletristic literature proper is more conspicuous for its quality than its quantity, there are several works in existence that, mainly on account of their style, can be placed on the border-line between learned (or at least instructional) and polite literature. To these ambivalent prose works belong especially those on (a) mystical, or (b) ethical topics, and (c) essays. As examples we may take the following:

(a) *Asrāru'ṭ-tauḥīd fī maqāmāti'sh-shaykh Abū-Sa'īd*, 'The Secrets of the Unity of God as revealed on the Stages of the Sheikh Abū-Sa'īd', dating from about 570–80/1174–85, a valuable account of the life of the famous mystic Abū-Sa'īd b. Abi'l-Khayr (see p. 233) written by his great-great-grandson Muḥammad b. al-Munavvar; 'Alī Hujvīrī's (d. 465/1072–3) *Kashfu'l-Maḥjūb*, 'The Revelation of That which is hidden', on the life and doctrines of the Ṣūfīs, probably one of the sources used by 'Aṭṭār; there are also several writings by Shihābu'd-dīn Suhravardī al-Maqtūl, viz. 'he who was executed' (d. 587/1191), who proclaimed the heretical monism of light (*ishrāq*) and was, as far as I know, the first to introduce allegorical tales into Persian literature; he wrote both in Arabic and Persian. Then there is 'Aṭṭār's *Vitae, Tadhkiratu'-auliyā* (see p. 239). Aḥmad al-Ghazālī (d. 517/1123–4), brother of the renowned reformer, wrote *Savāniḥ*, 'Notions', aphorisms on Love, "in which a highly subtle psychology of love is analysed by means of a (non-rhetorical) language of metaphor rather than of ideas".[1]

(b) Mirror for Princes:[2] *Naṣīḥat-nāma*, 'The Book of Counsels', generally called *Qābūs-nāma*, 'The Book in the Spirit of Qābūs' Wisdom', dating from the year 475/1082–3, and written by the Ziyarid 'Unsuru'l-ma'ālī Kay-Kā'ūs (b. 412/1021–2, d. 492/1098–99) for his son Gīlān-Shāh[3]; the author was a grandson of the prince of Tabaristan, Shamsu'l-ma'ālī Qābūs b. Vushmgīr (murdered in 403/1012) who was an epistolographer and poet writing in excellent Arabic, but a merciless despot. What a contrast between the two! True, they both belonged to the Shu'ūbiyya, but in the third generation the cult of Arabic had already come to an end in favour of Persian. The book presents a mixture of aristocratic feudal ethics and superficial Moslem piety, of common sense and cunning[4], and in addition some of the contradictions arising from the peculiar position of the writer: for although a descendant of a legendary Iranian family and a member of the recently fallen dynasty of Tabaristan, he toadies to the by no means high-born Turkish Ghaznavids, probably for fear of further degradation. Notwithstanding the fact that he was still at least a petty feudal land-owner, he no longer considered it beneath his dignity for his son to become a market-dealer, for Kay-Kā'ūs knew only too well what real life was like. The conjuncture of various interests or considerations in a person inevitably driven into a state of discord by the course of events will always lead to his finding singular solutions to his problems (A. Krïmskiy[5] speaks of a Pharisaic egoistical morale): the author, rooted as he was in the ancient native traditions, nevertheless endeavoured to appear a genuine Moslem, solely for the sake of his reputation. His admonishments to justice and the care of the ruler's subjects cover purely egoistic motives. This work gives a faithful reflection of the social conditions of the times, a picture such as is nowhere to be found in native chronicles, a "miscellany of Islamic culture in pre-Mongol times"[6], a proof that the art of story-telling, in which the masters of Sasanian prose excelled, had not died out in the 5th/11th century – in short it is a document of exceptional value in every respect. The *Siyāsat-nāma*, 'The Book of Statecraft', a work by the eminent Seljuq vizier Niẓāmu'l-mulk dating from 484/1091–2, was added to after the death of the author by the editor, the court writer Muḥammad Maghribī, or by someone else, round about the years 492–505/1098–1112.[7] Its style is less polished than that of the *Qābūs-nāma*, but it possesses a similar intrinsic importance and provides a like deep insight into the structure and opinions of contemporary society. It is a compendium said to have been written at the request of Malik-Shāh (465–85/1073–92) by Niẓāmu'l-mulk shortly before the latter was murdered by the Assassins (10th Ramaḍān 485/14th October 1092). Malik-Shāh wished to procure an account of the views of this brilliant statesman on the manner in which a feudal kingdom should be governed, with observations based on his long years of experience – and this despite the fact that Niẓāmu'l-mulk had shortly before fallen into disfavour.

(c) *Chahār maqāla*, 'Four Treatises', dating from 550–1/1155–7, by Aḥmad b. 'Umar b. 'Alī, commonly known by the name Niẓāmī 'Arūḍī of Samarkand, is a book of fundamental importance for the knowledge of contemporary and preceding trends in

Notes on pp. 224–225

literature. It should however be borne in mind that it was composed in the environment of the Ghurid dynasty and thus certainly reflects the intentions of the latter as well as opposition to everything related to the enemy, in particular the Ghaznavids.[8]

All of these works may be regarded as models of a prose as straightforward in substance as it is in style. Other works of the kind have already been mentioned (see Nāṣir-i Khusrau, ʿOmar Khayyām).

B. BELLES-LETTRES

The following works fall under the heading of belles-lettres:

(a) 'The Book of *Samak-i ʿAyyār*' by Ṣadaqa b. Abu'l-Qāsim Shīrāzī (in the version of Farāmurz Khudādād b. ʿAbdi'llāh al-Kātib al-Arrajānī, 585/1189), the earliest work of romantic fiction, full of the fantastic adventures of the knights in their attempts to win the daughter of the Emperor of China. Probably it contains also prototypes of other romances and tales.[9] *

(b) Collections of anecdotes within the framework of various unifying mottoes: *Javāmiʿu'l-ḥikāyāt va lavāmiʿu'r-rivāyāt*, 'Necklaces of Anecdotes and Splendours of Tales' (2113 stories) by Muḥammad ʿAufī, the author of the earliest preserved literary *tadhkira*, *Lubābu'l-albāb*, 'Quintessence of Hearts' (618/1221–2); *Al-faraj baʿda'sh-shidda*, 'Joy after Sorrow', adapted from the Arabic model by Muḥsin at-Tanūkhī (d. 384/994), first by the same ʿAufī about 620/1223 and some forty years later by Ḥusayn Asʿad Dahistānī Mu'ayyadī.[10] *

(c) Collections of moralising fables or tales within a tale; first and foremost *Kalīla u Dimna*, from time immemorial one of the books most valued by oriental and occidental peoples; it is also known by the name of 'Bidpay's Fables'. The appropriate point of departure for our purpose is the Arabic translation by the Persian ʿAbdu'llāh b. al-Muqaffaʿ, an eminent master of Arabic prose (put to death about 142/759), from Burzōē's Middle Persian version of the Indian text. (Al-Bīrūnī severely criticised the translation![11]) Ibn al-Muqaffaʿ's translation gave rise to several Persian versions but they were all surpassed by Abu'l-maʿālī Naṣru'llāh, probably a native of Shiraz, who was commissioned by the Ghaznavid Bahrām-Shāh (510-52/1117–57) to write a revised edition. Rūdakī's elaboration in verse form was lost. Neither did the work of Naṣru'llāh (538–9/1143–5), a masterpiece of Persian prose in virtue of its comparative simplicity, remain intact, even though it made concessions to contemporary taste by the inclusion of various rhetorical ornaments; even this embellishment did not suffice in the ensuing periods, which outdid each other in the bombastic style and eccentricity that had meanwhile taken root and that could not fail to have effect on such an exceptionally popular and treasured book. The elegance of Abu'l-maʿālī's style paled, the text was tampered with to such an extent that it will remain impossible to form any accurate idea of the original version until a critical reconstruction of the text has been made. In the meantime new versions continued to appear until Ḥusayn Vāʿiẓ Kāshifī (d. 910/1504–5) satisfied the baroque taste of the Timurid period with his absurdly high-flown *Anvār-i Suhaylī*, 'The Lights of Canopus', which for a long time enjoyed the reputation of being the loveliest Persian prose (see p. 313). A valuable imitation of *Kalīla u Dimna* is the *Marzbān-nāma*, originally composed in the Ṭabarī dialect by Ispahbad ('Prince') Marzbān b. Rustam b. Shahryār b. Sharvīn at the turn of the 10th–11th century. Only two Persian versions have been preserved: first, the *Rauḍatu'l-ʿuqūl*, 'The Garden of the Wise Spirits', written at the end of the 6th/12th century by the Rūm-Seljuq vizier, Muḥammad b. Ghāzī of Malaṭiyya, and second the *Marzbān-nāma* by Saʿdu'd-dīn Varāvīnī of Azerbayjan, dating from 607–622/1210–25. The style of both these works is over-profuse. The *Sindbād-nāma*, 'The Book of the Seven Viziers', and another work resembling it, the *Bakhtyār-nāma*, 'The Book of the Ten Viziers', further *Ṭūṭī-nāma*, 'The Parrot Book'[12], etc., were once extremely popular collections of stories within the framework of a certain 'moralising' theme. *Qiṣṣa-i chahār darvīsh*, 'The Story of the Four Dervishes', a fantastic story imbued with the spirit of erotic romanticism, contains no such common thread. There are frequent indications of the Indian and Sasanian-Iranian origin of all these books, though many and variegated developments are to be found in the text. Sooner or later they were revised in a loftier style of prose, e.g. *Ṭūṭī-nāma* by Ḍiyāʿu'd-dīn Nakhshabī, 730/1330, and an abridged version by Muḥammad Qādirī (11th/17th century). There also appeared transpositions into verse: *Sindbād-nāma*; (a) by the poet Azraqī (see p. 195) before 465/1072–3, based on the prose version by Khvāja ʿAmīdu'd-dīn Abu'l-favāris Qanārizī (339/950–51)[13], not indeed on the prose of Muḥammad aẓ-Ẓahīrī al-Kātib as-Samarqandī, that dates from 556–7/1160–1; (b) by an unknown poet in 777/1375–6[14]; *Bakhtyār-nāma*, by an otherwise unknown versifier, Panāhī, at the court of the Qara-Qoyunlu (851/1447), etc.[15]

Works on a higher level of rhetoric are the *maqāmas*, 'meetings', in rhymed prose – pure 'art for art's sake' – intermixed with verses, tales of the adventures of witty vagabonds, an 'attenuated' offshoot of the classical mimes.[16] The most representative specimens are Arabic works, although Badīʿu'z-zamān of Hamadan (d. 398/1007)[17] is regarded as the actual creator of the typical *maqāmas*. These were later on developed to the height of perfection by Ḥarīrī (d. 516/1122), unless priority is accorded to Abū-Bakr al-Khvārazmī (d. 383/993 or 393/1002). Both these main exponents were imitated in Persian by Qāḍī Ḥamīdu'd-dīn (d. 559/1163–4). He does not use such rare and far-fetched expressions as Ḥarīrī but rather resembles his compatriot Badīʿu'z-zamān. His style has neither the ease of Naṣru'llāh's *Kalīla u Dimna* nor the elegance of the *Gulistān*.

Notes on pp. 224–225

C. HISTORICAL WORKS IN PROSE

Works falling into this category belong to the field of learned literature and will therefore be discussed in Professor Tauer's section, 'Persian Learned Literature'.

D. IRANIAN WRITERS OF ARABIC (1000–1200 A.D.)

In conclusion we must at least mention in brief the unusually large number of scholars who although of Iranian descent wrote either entirely or mainly in Arabic. The most important of these are: the Shī'ite theologian Muḥammad Ṭūsī (d. 459/1076); the greatest Islamic theologian and at the same time influential reformer of orthodoxy, Muḥammad al-Ghazālī, 'Alghazel' (d. 505/1111); Maydānī (d. 518/1124–5), the collector of proverbs; the grammarian, lexicographer and Mu'tazilī theologian Zamakhsharī (d. 538/1143–4), together with 'Abdu'llāh al-Bayḍāvī (d. 685/1286), who later had to eliminate the false Mu'tazilitic doctrines in Zamakhsharī's commentary on the Koran; the theologian, jurist and philosopher Fakhru'd-dīn Rāzī (d. 606/1209–10) and many others.[18]

NOTES

1. Ritter, *Philol.*, 7, 93.
2. "The extent to which this literature (Mirror for Princes and books on statecraft) suited the opinions of classes interested in literature is shown by its wide circulation in the following centuries and its after-effects on didactic poetry, as in Sa'dī who raised such themes to the level of world literature"; B. Spuler, *Die histor. Literatur*, (B II), 278, in which ingenious analyses are also to be found.
3. Nafīsī, *Muntakhab-i Qābūs-nāma*, p. (24). Richard N. Frye's allegations (B VIb) are based on a MS forged after 1942, cf. M. Mīnuvī, *Kāpūs-nāma-i Frāy* (B VIb).
4. Gabrieli, *Oriens*, 5, 337 on R. Levy's edition; Bertel's *Kabus-nama* (transl.), 245.
5. A. Krïmskiy: Bertel's, *ibid.*, 239.
6. *Sabk*, 2, 113.
7. Zachoder, *Siaset-name* (transl.), 249; 'Abb. Iqbāl, ed. *Siyāsat-nāma*, p. 'b'.
8. Chaykin, *Ferdousi*, 82.
9. A detailed survey of all such tales and also often romances in many volumes: Ethé, 317.
10. Thus M. Qazvīnī, *Yaghmā*, 7 (1333), 250 *et seq.*, 296 *et seq.* in one of the years 651–663/1253–1265; acc. to M. Mīnuvī, *ibid.*, p. 302, before 656/1258. On 'Mu'ayyadī' (not e.g. Vazīrī) cf. S. Nafīsī, Preface to *Shāhkārhā* (C). On this document, with its superior style, cf. *Oriens*, 7 (1954), 215 (from *Yādgār*, 5/6–7, 1327–28, 49–62).

11. Cf. Denison Ross, *JRAS*, 1926, 505.
12. Detailed bibliography: Chauvin (B I), VIII; A. Krïmskiy, 3, 85–91.
13. Qanārizī: thus correctly *Yaghmā*, 8, 220. For the history of the text see CPL, 165 *et seq.*
14. Āzād?, cf. T. A. Gorelishvili, 'Neizvestnaya rukopis' stikhotvornoy versii "Sindbad-nama"', *Nauchnaya Konferentsiya* (B VIa), 47.
15. For further information see A. A. Gvakhariya, 'O poeticheskoy versii "Bakhtiar-name"', *Trudī tbil. gos. univ.*, 91 (1960), 125–131, based on another MS and on the Georgian translation. According to CPL, 170, another earlier version has been preserved, presumably from a Pahlavi source, composed by Shamsu'd-dīn Muḥ. Daqā'iqī (7th/13th century), to whom is also attributed a version of the *Sindbād-nāma.* *
16. von Grunebaum, *Med. Isl.*, 289; Brockelmann, *EI*, *s.v.* 'maqāma'.
17. Not a Persian but a patriotic Arab born in Hamadan!
18. See also Tughrā'ī (453/1061 – 515/1121–2), the poet of the famous *Lāmiyyat al-'Ajam*, cf. B VIb, *s.v.* 'Schabinger von Schowingen'.

VII. ṢŪFISM

The disturbances caused by the Ghuzz tribesmen and the constant wars and conflicts in which Iran was engaged in the 6th/12th Century, the terrible Mongol invasion, all the concomitant distress and despair – this was ideal soil for the nourishment of the most glorious products of Persian mysticism.

A. ORIGIN, DEVELOPMENT AND IDEOLOGY OF ṢŪFISM

As far as we can gather from the sparse vestiges still in existence, the earliest Persian poetry exhibits no special tendency towards religious subjects, not even towards Islam. This is particularly strange in view of the peculiar aptitude of the Persian psyche for spirituality and religious meditation, though there is no doubt that this was often a reaction to economic and social oppression. The phenomenon obviously bears some relation to the liberal ideology of the Samanid court and to the social classes associated under the motto *razm u bazm*, 'fighting and feasting'. A change set in when the aristocratic poets were gradually replaced by professionals recruited from the lower classes (see p. 142). At that time we find a manifestation of the orientation towards the irrational that is characteristic of the Iranian, not however in the light of strict Islamic doctrine but in that of Ṣūfī ideology, which in the meantime had become firmly anchored in the urban classes. An intrinsic expression of Iranian mentality, this basically liberal school of thought (this last factor should be especially borne in mind) not only continued to exist but increased in strength until it reached its zenith in the 12th to 13th century. Even then it did not decline but was more or less continuously dominant. It stamped the whole of Persian literature, first and foremost the poetry, with an indelible mark, the results of which, both in speech and thought, have not been obliterated up to the present day. *Taṣavvuf*, 'the mysticism of Islam', is the *Leitmotif* underlying – though often only outwardly – the greater part of the aesthetic literary manifestations of the Persian spirit, and this flourished with such beauty that its fruits are among the finest creations of the human mind. Unfortunately, however, this same mysticism also formed a handicap, being as it was prejudicial to a sense of reality, thus rendering a great deal of Persian poetry too one-sided, at any rate to the European mind.

It is nowadays generally recognised that the expression *Ṣūfī* – properly speaking the designation of those professing the *taṣavvuf* and originally a nickname – is derived from the Arabic word *ṣūf*, 'wool', because the first Ṣūfīs wore coarse woollen garments (according to A. J. Arberry mentioned perhaps for the first time in Europe at the end of the 16th century in Nicholay's *Voyages*[1]). The use of this expression to convey merely asceticism (*zuhd*) is however unacceptable because, except in the initial stages, Ṣūfism is not essentially analogous to asceticism. It is therefore necessary to touch on the origin, the first stages of development and the essence of this doctrine, at any rate as regards the most elementary features, for it is to Ṣūfism, according to L. Massignon[2], that Islam owes its growth into an international and universal religion. These are certainly among the most knotty problems in the science of Islam. Many of them are still unsolved and debatable. What follows gives only a general outline, indispensable however for an understanding of the history of Iranian literature.

Under the Omayyads an intensification of religious feeling had already begun to appear in the western parts of Islam as a reaction against the too mundane disposition of the Caliphs of Damascus and against the dull spirit of formalism, a reaction based partly on an exaggerated sense of sin and partly on the fear of God's reprisals.[3] But it can equally well be seen as an anti-feudal revolt[4] against those in authority on the part of the destitute classes among the urban population. The opposition's remote prospect of success promoted its very growth, expansion and pessimistic character.[5] The movement bore obvious ascetic-pessimistic features and spread from Syria and Iraq to the whole of the Islamic world. It met with especial response in Khurasan – in the first half of the 2nd/8th century a hot-bed of anti-Omayyad intrigue. While in Syria monks belonging to various Christian churches and sects, which frequently bore a gnostic tint, were bestirring themselves, Central Asia formed a centre of early-blossoming Buddhism. In Khurasan the echoes of Iranian doctrines of faith, such as fire-worship and Manichaeism could at least still be heard. Indian theosophy from the east and Nestorian Christianity advancing from the west had both spread as far as here. These circumstances were of course particularly favourable to asceticism but they also accounted for the introduction of new features, and in fact a kind of Persian school of Ṣūfism came into being. It may be mentioned here that even in one and the same region there was a lack of unity among the followers of the movement, because mysticism, unrestrained by any kind of dogmas, signifies the longing of one's heart for the Infinite and is nothing other than "a total disengagement of the mind from all temporal concerns and worldly pursuits; an entire throwing off not only of every superstition, doubt,

Notes on pp. 242–245

or the like, but of the practical mode of worship, ceremonies etc. laid down in every religion"[6], and bears the greatest possible consideration for individuality. Almost all the important mystics go their own way.

Especially later on we encounter a multitude of views and attitudes, including very mild as well as extreme varieties, and related to a greater or less extent to Islam. Thus in Baghdad, the international centre of Islamic culture, there appears al-Muḥāsibī (d. 243/857), "the first Sunnite mystic whose works betray a thorough theological training"[7], who exercises considerable influence on the further development of a moderate *taṣavvuf*. Of a different calibre was his contemporary Dhu'n-Nūn (d. 245/859) to whom the Ṣūfīs ascribed "the formulation of the doctrine of gnosis (*ma'rifa*) and the classification of mystical states and stages".[8] Bāyazīd (viz. Abū-Yazīd) Bisṭāmī (d. 260/874) stands out as a Ṣūfī of pronounced Iranian stamp, who laid emphasis on ecstasy to a greater extent than did any of his predecessors or contemporaries. To later generations, albeit not altogether rightly, he was known as the herald of pantheism, or rather of pantheistic monism which is based on the conception that everything that is outside God does not exist. "The most original and most penetrating intellect among the Ṣūfīs of his time" is al-Junayd of Baghdad (d. 298/910), who contrived 'with an artist's eye' to combine all mystical speculation into one unified system of Islamic theosophy, "the nucleus of all subsequent elaboration".[9] If al-Junayd regarded the 'supreme mystical experience' as lying in reunion with God, Ḥusayn b. Manṣūr al-Ḥallāj went further than this in some measure admissible limitation, and taught that the apotheosis of Man was the apotheosis of the incarnation of God. Although he laid no claim to divinity himself, yet his judges interpreted his dictum *ana'l-ḥaqq*, 'I am the Creative Truth'[10], in this sense and put this zealous preacher to death in most cruel fashion (d. 309/921). In the course of its further development Ṣūfism even went so far as to deify Ḥallāj and his dictum became one of the most frequently repeated apophthegms. On the other hand there was no lack of attempts to bring *taṣavvuf* into harmony with official doctrine. The most successful of these attempts was made by Muḥammad al-Ghazālī (d. 505/1111); his doctrine was adopted by the Sunna and is still held today. In consequence of the introduction of ideas and terminology from Aristotle's 'pseudo-theology', Plato's idealism and Plotinus' doctrine of emanation, Ṣūfism became alienated from orthodox theology as regards the form of some of its doctrines. The pantheistic movement reached its zenith in the 7th/13th century in the works of the Arab poet Ibnu'l-Fāriḍ of Cairo (d. 632/1235), the famous Jalālu'd-dīn Rūmī (see p. 240), a Persian poet, and in the Spanish-Arab theoretician Ibn al-'Arabī of Murcia (d. 638/1240); the latter's system, *vaḥdatu'l-vujūd*, 'unity of Being', monistic rather than pantheistic ("existential monism", according to L. Massignon), "marks a turning-point in the history of speculative Ṣūfism".[11]

The question of the origin and development of Ṣūfism has, as already noted in the introductory paragraph, not as yet been fully solved. Several scholars have voiced their opinions; many have modified their earlier convictions, and that not wantonly but on the grounds of new evaluations and new sources, whereby we may not forget the fact that there still remains a vast quantity of material as yet unpublished. General acceptance has been given to the view of Alfred von Kremer and Ignaz Goldziher[12], namely that the history of Ṣūfism should simply be divided into the original asceticism and the theosophical abstract speculation subsequently linked up with it. It is not possible to enter here into the labyrinth of scholarly suppositions, but the reader must nevertheless be referred to A. J. Arberry's excellent summary, *An Introduction to the History of Ṣūfism* (1942). It must suffice to quote in brief the opinions of those who in the last few decades have done especially meritorious work on this extremely difficult and almost unlimited subject. While R. A. Nicolson[13] drew attention above all to the Neo-Platonic philosophy of emanation as the origin of Ṣūfī speculations, towards the end of his life he regarded it as only one of the many different elements that had influenced this speculation. In the same way L. Massignon[14] modified his original opinion, notably that Ṣūfism was of purely Islamic origin, and became more and more convinced that Greek and particularly Christian influences had been at work. A. J. Arberry[15] also admits a liberal interchange of ideas between the Christian and Moslem ascetics of the 2nd/8th century and does not believe "that future research will overthrow the theory that Ṣūfism was influenced in its earliest period by Christian mysticism, and that all other Western influences – Neo-Platonist, Neopythagorean, Hermetic, and Gnostic – impinged on early Islam through this medium". A somewhat too far-going exponent of the Christian influence on the various aspects of Islamic philosophy and mysticism, in particular on that of al-Ghazālī and Ibn al-ʿArabī, is M. Asín Palacios[16], just as M. Horten[17] enthusiastically maintains the existence of influences from India. It would be entirely wrong to regard early or even later Ṣūfism as a purely Iranian phenomenon, for the Arabs have also had their share in this movement and way of thinking, though on the other hand there is no doubt that Persian poetry dedicated itself to it in the broadest and deepest sense.

It would be vain to attempt to present the doctrine of *taṣavvuf* in a concise summary. This would be impossible since Ṣūfism consists of a multitude of systems which though linked up with one another are lacking in unity both as regards philosophical conception and ethical details. Common to all of them is the basic elementary belief in the possibility of direct intuitive cognition of God.[18] The central conception of *taṣavvuf*[19] is *tauḥīd*, 'the substantial unity with God', "the perception of unity with God"[20], and it is in fact this conception that enables Ṣūfism to bridge the terrifyingly vast gulf between God and Man. Therefore *taṣavvuf* imparts another meaning to the conception of *tauḥīd* than does theology, which rests content with the dogma 'there is no other god but God'. To Ṣūfism *tauḥīd* means that Allah is the only Being with a real or absolute existence, compared with which all the rest is merely a fortuitous state of being or – going still further, wholly pantheistic – that there is no other god but God, but also that all else but God is nothing. Since the Ṣūfīs base their train of thought not on theological but on theosophical methods, poetry was and remained their chief instru-

Notes on pp. 242–245

ment. Disproportionately less use was made of the coherent discourse because it would have revealed too clearly the more audacious deviations from Islam, thus exposing the author to greater danger, whereas poetry dazzled by its constant play of metaphor, symbols and literal sense. There were orthodox Ṣūfīs, it is true, but there were also some who abandoned the fundamental elements of Islam and of every other religion and, by refusing to distinguish between Good and Evil, reached the supreme inferences of philosophy, however assiduously they manoeuvred with verses from the Koran and the Tradition. These they interpreted more or less arbitrarily and fantastically (*ta'vīl*), in fact in their own way, by referring in the same manner as the Shīʿa to ʿAlī, to whom Muḥammad was supposed to have entrusted the hidden meaning of the revelation.

B. GROUPS AND SCHOOLS. RITUAL

Already early on there had been groups or schools where the disciples (*murīd, shāgird*) gathered voluntarily around the revered teacher (*murshid, shaykh, pīr*) to be led by him along the immensely difficult path (*ṭarīqa*) of mysticism so that they might attain the state of ecstasy (*ḥāl, vajd*), the moment of most sublime experience, when the Ṣūfī is in communication with and united with the Beloved. Then from the 6th/12th century onwards we witness the foundation of innumerable congregations that were of great importance for the cultural life of the Islamic orient. These congregations had clearly-defined statutes (no celibacy or obligation on principle to dwell in monasteries) and a ritual peculiar to each order, with the aim of rendering possible, as it were, a communal attainment of the solemn moments of *unio mystica*. These rites were actually only a synthesis of those that had been customarily celebrated at the musical gatherings, known as *samāʿ*[21], since the earliest periods of theosophical Ṣūfism. It is in fact in connection with these gatherings, as being the most expressive demonstration of Ṣūfism, that Ye. E. Bertel's[22] has constructed the following picture of the origin of Ṣūfī poetry, which indeed forms an integral part of *taṣavvuf* as it actually evolved, for *samāʿ* presumably derived from the chanting of the Koran. The earliest Ṣūfīs, he states, must have grown aware of the psychological effect of singing and the overwhelming power of song on the emotions of the simplest Oriental, and have made use of this factor for arousing a state of ecstasy. *Samāʿ* held its own in spite of bitter opposition on the part of the orthodox theologians and puritans, at first with vocal and later on with instrumental music, finally accompanied by ecstatic dancing or, as at the beginning, merely by rhythmical movement. (H. Ritter[23] holds a different opinion, and not indeed without factual support, namely that *samāʿ* was originally "music with dancing as a form of social entertainment after a feast. Later reforms gave it the shape of a solemn ceremonial.") In Iraq Arabic love-songs, transmuted metaphorically into a mystical sphere, were employed for the singing. In Khurasan, where up till then poetry as an art had not existed, at any rate not to the extent and degree of perfection of Arabic poetry (we are now speaking of the second half of the 2nd/8th century; at the beginning of the 3rd/9th century the movement had already spread over the whole of Persia!), it may be that the same purpose was originally served by Persian folk-songs, filled of course with the fervour of love. The Persian lyric, particularly the mystical, retained its chant-like character. The folk-song was gradually replaced by the artistic, the original popular character made way for a complicated symbolism. Ye. E. Bertel's[24] sees the course of development of Ṣūfī poetry as follows: (1) profane poetry, mainly of an amorous nature, merely as a substitute for the attainment of ecstasy; (2) purely Ṣūfī poetry written with the same purpose, adopting the appropriate terminology from the former type; (3) erotic symbolism based on Ṣūfī philosophy; (4) didactic poetry which, though originating in Ṣūfī circles, does not on the whole deviate from the Islamic doctrine of faith. The Ṣūfī epic owes its origin in the first place to Sanā'ī.

C. ṢŪFĪ SYMBOLISM

Ṣūfī symbolism revolves around three main topics: love, wine and beauty. For immensurate love is the real foundation of the mystical relation to God and it is earthly love (*ʿishq-i majāzī*, 'metaphorical or allegorical love') that forms the bridge to this celestial love (*ʿishq-i ḥaqīqī*, viz. 'True Love'). "Mystical love is distinct from the profane in that in it a transcendental, absolute object is introduced into the sphere of the love-life. Through this kind of relationship with an absolute object, the value of love is enhanced to such an extent that it claims primacy, even supremacy over all other emotions of the soul. Hand in hand with this goes such a strong intensification, differentiation and refinement of the spiritual love-life, that love becomes a real spiritual art and those who master it understand how to exploit and to express the extreme possibilities of spiritual experience and the spiritual erotic state. If now love, religiously enhanced and deepened in this way, encounters a human object, then there arises that hybrid picture of mystical love towards human beauty that has found its most perfect vehicle of artistic expression in the mystical love-poetry of Persia."[25] Love as opposed to Reason, and vice versa – the value and insufficiency of which provide an inexhaustible supply of material for lyrical poetry – and the conflict between them form, as H. Ritter puts it[26], a separate branch of the literature on love, namely the allegorical tale. The intoxication caused by wine expresses ecstatic exaltation, the beauty of the juvenile body represents the absolute perfection of God. This is a language elaborated down to the finest detail; without a knowledge of it the uninitiated can form no conception of the hidden meaning. There is no doubt that mystic symbolism penetrated

Notes on pp. 242–245

deeply into the literature of Iran. Nevertheless it would be wrong to seek for mysticism and again mysticism in every poetical utterance and, conversely, never to see reality or *jeux de style*. Orientals construct a whole nomenclature of poetic metaphors from real or pseudo-mystics and apply these as it were lexicographically to metaphysical symbolism. It was this ambiguous aspect that proved an effective weapon for the liberal Ṣūfīs and non-Ṣūfīs against spying and searching orthodox believers, a weapon wielded either offensively or defensively, as is testified by Nāṣir-i Khusrau[27], when referring to the Arab free-thinker Abu'l-'Alā' al-Ma'arrī (b. 363/973, d. 449/1057). In this way all blasphemy is camouflaged and the forbidden enjoyment of wine transformed into a spiritual delight. Very often the true face of the poet is quite unrecognisable. This is without doubt the reflection of a certain already observed insincerity or hypocrisy, but also very likely the echo of monstrous oppression in the spiritual as well as the social sphere. The tolerance of the Ṣūfīs, a direct antipole of the attitude of the priesthood and allied classes, is nevertheless one of the most noble manifestations of the Iranian mind.

D. BENEFICIAL AND DELETERIOUS EFFECTS OF ṢŪFISM ON CULTURE *

The perfect harmony that existed between the Persian psyche and Ṣūfism is proved by the fact of their union having lasted so long and having been able to attract both the common people and the intelligentsia, though not the priesthood – at any rate those members who continued to hold a strictly theological opinion. Thought was impregnated to a great extent by Ṣūfism, expressing at first the opposition of the towns and guilds to the courts and feudalism, but ultimately serving the feudal lords as a means of retaining their power by deluding the people as a whole. On the other hand mysticism is known to be a phenomenon accompanying economic depression. This fact would seem to be fully corroborated by the Persian people, who suffered atrociously from continual invasions and were exploited and plundered most shamelessly by the ruling classes. True or not, we may not overlook the dark shadows cast by Ṣūfism on society in its widest sense and consequently also on literature: aversion to the world, an extravagant reliance upon God (*tavakkul*) lead to passivity, to quietism, to inertia among the masses, to vagrancy among the dervishes. Every reflection is tinged with a pessimism arising from the inconstancy of this life and of the world. The philosophy of 'Yonder side of Good and Evil', is demoralising. Contempt of intellect and of the knowledge thereby gained, and its substitution by the principle of intuition necessarily led to an indulgence in fantasy, absence of culture, an agnostic neglect of scientific research, the increasing superficiality in the dervish orders, and an incredible increase in the worship of saints. Belief in miracles and in the miraculous powers of saints dulls the masses; the conception of 'pure love' promotes homosexuality and the desire to attain a state of ecstasy leads to the use of intoxicating drugs. The unconditional obedience due to the *pīr* and the great number of followers that flocked around him, added to the affluence of the Ṣūfī institutions, together formed too important a factor for the ruling classes not to attempt to gain the favour of such powerful and influential feudal leaders in the common – but by no means idealistic – interest. We see more than once how dangerous the holy dervishes, ascetics and sheikhs could be for the public order, or at least for the ruling classes, for they electrified the common people to the point of political subversion.[28] (One has only to recall the rebellion of Andijan, 1899, in Central Asia, the Murīd Shāmil in the Caucasus, the rise of the Safavids.) Such is the reverse side of that exalted doctrine as it affected ordinary everyday life. And what was its effect on literature, which the Ṣūfīs appropriated and dominated in such elemental, outwardly as it were integral manner? Despite the glory of this poetry we cannot after all rid ourselves of the impression that it arouses of a certain uniformity, for it is founded partly on the too subtle variations on a few basic and perpetually repeated themes (*tauḥīd, vaḥdat-i vujūd*, 'He is everywhere and yet hidden', and the associated conception of the exile of the soul and its longing for return; the idea of asceticism) and partly on such an abstract treatment of the same thoughts as to banish from lyrical poetry all reality, clarity and unequivocalness. This impression is in no way modified by the non-Ṣūfī allegories, numerous as they were. The sentiments of the Oriental, of whom Shiblī Nuʿmānī may be considered as interpreter, may not be overlooked in this connection. A *ghazal*, untouched by *taṣavvuf*, may be a rose to him, but it is a rose without perfume! This is the effect on him of Khvājū and Salmān.[29]

For these reasons the opinion formed by B. G. Gafurov[30] is bound to be negative. According to him the Ṣūfī doctrine proved from the very beginning of its propagation to be an obstacle to the development of the profane sciences, blocking the way to economic and cultural progress. Later on, under the Timurids and the Khāns of Bukhara, Ṣūfism even took the lead in the struggle against all liberal thought, against the resistance movement in which the common people defended themselves against the oppression of the feudal lords and khāns.

E. THE QUATRAIN POETS: ABŪ-SAʿĪD B. ABIʾL-KHAYR, (BĀBĀ KŪHĪ), BĀBĀ ṬĀHIR ʿURYĀN, ANṢĀRĪ, BĀBĀ AFḌAL

The first Persian Ṣūfī poetry is usually associated with the name of Abū-Saʿīd b. Abiʾl-Khayr of Mihna or Mayhana (b. 357/967–8, d. 440/1049). He was the pupil of a series of profound mystics and became head of the Ṣūfī centre in Nishapur and an important proclaimer of the Ṣūfī doctrine. He is said to be the author of some dozens of *rubāʿīs* of a mystical nature, but this is an error for we can conclude with certainty from the biography written by his great-great-grandson, Muḥammad b. Munavvar b. Abī-Saʿd b. Abī-Ṭāhir b. Abī Saʿīd in 570–80/1174–85 that Abū-Saʿīd composed no poetry.[31] The poetical legacy ascribed to him is therefore the work of others, maybe already his forerunners.

Here we may touch on the *dīvān* supposed to have been composed by the contemporary searcher after truth in the Islamic countries, Ibn-i Bākūya, 'Bābā Kūhī'. This man was at one time principal (*pīr*) of the monastery at Nishapur. 'His' *dīvān* shows Ṣūfī terminology already at its fullest stage of development and employing the nomenclature of the later Ṣūfī poets. It was thought that from this point a link might be found with Abū-Saʿīd.[32] It can in any case be taken for granted that there must have been a stage of development previous to the quatrains ascribed to Abū-Saʿīd; however, we are not concerned to relate this in any way with a Bābā Kūhī or Ibn-i Bākūya, for in the first place the identification of Bābā Kūhī with Abū-ʿAbdi'llāh Muḥammad b. ʿAbdi'llāh b. ʿUbaydi'llāh b. Aḥmad b. Bākūya of Shiraz (d. 442–43/1050–52) is dubious and probably based on a misrepresentation or popular etymology of Ibn-i Bākūya→ Bābā Kūhī, whose grave is in Shiraz but about whom nothing further is known; secondly however – and this is decisive! – the *dīvān* attributed to Bābā Kūhī turns out to be a gross forgery dating from the time of Ḥāfiẓ.[33]

Among the earliest composers of quatrains, Bābā Ṭāhir ʿUryān is one of the most celebrated, but it is difficult to place him chronologically (according to Rashīd Yāsimī[34], who bases his conjectures on a chiliastic allusion, he was born about 390–1/1000 in Hamadan, or in the province of Luristan, and died later than 447/1055–6 in Hamadan). Unlike others, he does not make use of the customary *rubāʿī* metre but employs the *hazaj* (for this reason his quatrains are often called *du-baytī*, 'double distichs'), which H. S. Nyberg[35] regards as being obviously associated with Middle Persian poetry. Although the *risālas* he composed in Arabic give evidence of a thorough education, he wrote not only in the common idiom but even in dialect, but his quatrains have long since lost the concrete local colour that might be expected.[36] (Similarly the Lurs and Bakhtyaris adapt Fā'iḍ of Shiraz to their own linguistic peculiarities.) The Persian nomads regard him as one of themselves, the dervishes as a saint, while the simplest * Iranian sings his verses to this very day.[37] The Ṣūfī strains are accompanied by a deep sensitivity flowing from the heart; humility and absorption in things lying beyond the range of sensory perception resound in each and every distich and give expression to a sorrow which only a state of non-existence (*fanā'*) can hush. This absorption in sorrow constitutes the main difference between him and the later ʿOmar Khayyām, whose emotional qualities were of quite another calibre.

Among the earliest and most eminent composers of Ṣūfī quatrains must be included Shaykhu'l-Islām ʿAbdu'llāh Anṣārī of Herat (b. 396/1006, d. 481/1088) who used the *takhalluṣ* Pīr-i Anṣār. From the point of view of literary history, however, his main importance is due to his authorship of the first *risālas*, 'treatises', in rhymed prose (*nathr-i musajja'*), which strangely enough met with no appreciation until the 6th/12th century. It is from this circumstance that S. Nafīsī[38] draws the perhaps erroneous conclusion that this was the work of a writer of the same name living in India (d. 1006/1597–8). In Anṣārī's frequent use of eight-syllabic parallelism Bahār[39] sees an imitation of Sasanian verse and Arabic *rajaz*, by which this *saj'* in fact becomes a kind of metrical verse. The directness and euphony of the glowing and highly artistic *munājāt*, 'prayers', in which *saj'* and verse alternate, may have charmed even a Sa'dī to such an extent that he imitated them in his *Gulistān*. Anṣārī, highly cultured as he was, owes the idea of an intimate dialogue between the soul and God in the form of a monologue – for the *munājāt* are nothing other than this – to his *murshid*, Abu'l-Ḥasan Kharaqānī (d. 425/1033)[40], who was not a scholar but a simple man of the people. Anṣārī has the habit of enlivening the loosely connected theoretical reflections in the sermons by the constant insertion of legends and parables. In point of fact we are here dealing with prose, only alternating with verse, as is the case in particular with the so-called 'Pseudo-*Manāzilu's-sā'irīn*' (viz. 'Halting-places for Travellers', written in Persian, as opposed to the Arabic work of the same name but different contents by the same author). In this kind of prose Ye. E. Bertel's[41] sees the seed of later mystical-didactic epic poems, of which Sanā'ī was the first exponent (for another opinion see p. 165). Anṣārī himself aimed at composing speeches, as a rule in rhyme, intended to have a rapid, deep and lasting influence on the Ṣūfī audiences. Unfortunately he has been somewhat neglected as a poet until recently. His reputation was involuntarily weakened by the very men for whom he had paved the way. It is a matter for great satisfaction that four manuscripts of Anṣārī's translation of the *Ṭabaqāt-i ṣūfiyya*, 'Biographies of Ṣūfī Saints', from Abū-'Abdu'r-Raḥmān Sulamī's (d. 412/1021) Arabic original into the ancient dialect of Herat has been preserved[42] (Ritter, 1962). From the rendering of this work into written Persian and the additions to its contents, there originated Jāmī's *Nafaḥātu'l-uns*, 'Whispers of Confidence', in 881/1476. In connection with Jāmī it may be observed, and certainly not without grounds, that Anṣārī was the first to give form to the story of Yūsuf and Zalīkhā in Persian prose; he did this in the mystical didactic work *Anīsu'l-murīdīn va shamsu'l-majālis*, 'The Comrade of the Adepts and the Sun of the Sessions'. (R. Levy[43], though admitting the antiquity of the text, doubts the authorship of Anṣārī.) It need only be added that Anṣārī, a Ḥanbalite traditionalist, also wrote a great deal in the Arabic language.

Another poet, distinguished for his witty verse and pithy quatrains, is Afḍalu'd-dīn Muḥammad of Maraq near Kāshān, generally known as Bābā Afḍal. (S. Nafīsī[44] gives as his dates of birth and death respectively 582/1186–7 or 592/1195–6 and 654/1256 or 664/1265–6.) He is said to have been a nephew of Khvāja Naṣīru'd-dīn Ṭūsī (see p. 313). He is the author of numerous Persian and Arabic treatises on theosophical and metaphysical subjects, an excellent translator of the psychology of Aristotle (*Kitābu'n-nafs*, 'The Book of the Soul') from the Arabic, a stylist of the old, plain cast. In his prose he successfully makes use of Persian in place of Arabic terminology. E. H. Whinfield[45] already observed the rebellious notes in his quatrains – an echo of Avicenna and a foreshadowing of ʿOmar Khayyām.

F. THE GREAT ṢŪFĪS: SANĀʾĪ, ʿAṬṬĀR, MAULAVĪ

The first great poet of *taṣavvuf*[46] is Abu'l-Majd Majdūd Sanāʾī (b. in Ghazna or Balkh about the middle of the 5th/11th century, d. 525/1130–1)[47], a contemporary of the later Ghaznavids, whose praises, couched in an extremely affected style, ran all through his *qaṣīdas*. A spiritual conversion that does not lend itself to closer comprehension (ostensibly caused by a jester's ridicule of the futility of Sanāʾī's poetry and aspirations) led him to dedicate himself wholly to mysticism. He relinquished his court appointment and lived further the life of a dervish in complete retirement from the world. Of the 30,000 distichs originally attributed to him, his *dīvān* now only contains 13,346.[48] He himself confessed to a leaning towards philosophy. His panegyric writings were influenced by Manūchihrī, Farrukhī and Masʿūd-i Saʿd. Nevertheless the substance was of more importance to him than the form. As Bertel's has already remarked, his style is rendered extremely complicated by the use of brachylogy. He worked independently in the field of Ṣūfism, where there was nothing – either in the *qaṣīda*, the *ghazal* or the *mathnavī* – on which he could build. He was one of the first to make use of the *ghazal* for mystical meditation, thus creating a model for future generations. The occasional use of the *takhalluṣ* in this *ghazals* is merely a continuation of the practice of others.[49] Whether priority must be accorded to him or not is immaterial, but the fact remains that Sanāʾī's significance lies in his effective and decisive introduction of asceticism and mysticism as a philosophy of life into the longer or shorter didactic *mathnavī*. Here we find thematically free, vaguely defined, but rhymed sermons, in addition to inserted parables or anecdotes taken from the lives of the saints, combining with the simple, non-mystical didactic epic to constitute a new form. After Anṣārī only one more step was required – the verse-metre; all the rest had been provided (Ye. E. Bertel's, otherwise H. Massé, see p. 165[50]). The most famous of these epics (seven in all, and with the exception of the one quoted here, none of them very long) is *Ḥadīqatuʾl-ḥaqīqa va sharīʿatuʾṭ-ṭarīqa*, 'The Garden of Truth and the Law of the Way', which dates from 525/1130–1 and consists of approximately 10,000 couplets divided into ten chapters, differently arranged in different manuscripts, with varying titles and in any case without any intrinsic coherence; Sanāʾī speaks about God and the Prophet, about reason, gnosis, care-free trust, heaven, philosophy, love, his own circumstances, and finally about Sulṭān Bahrām-Shāh of Ghazna (512–52/1118–57), to whom the poem is dedicated. The manuscripts abound in variants and according to the reports that have reached us there are at least two recensions to choose from.[51] Numerous parables break the uniform sobriety of the system but are for the most part far too short and devoid of expression to enhance in any way the not very great poetical value of the whole. Such a judgment betrays obviously an unfair, European, and therefore not altogether accurate point of view if we bear in mind how eagerly the *Ḥadīqa* was read and how it cast its rays on contemporary as well as all subsequent generations and even reaped the praise of the genius Jalālu'd-dīn Rūmī. Another factor that should not escape mention is Sanā'ī's pungent criticism of society.[52] A kind of *Divina Commedia* in miniature is his *Sayru'l-'ibād ila'l-ma'ād*, 'Journey of the Servants of God to the Place of Return' (viz. the next world; 'Journey of the Human Spirit in Search of Enlightenment through all Regions of the Physical and Spiritual World').[53] An assessment of Sanā'ī's immense contribution to the development of Ṣūfī poetry cannot be made in a short survey, for it would require a study of the complicated phenomenon presented by the relationship of Ṣūfism to the broad masses of the people and a pursuance of the connection between Ṣūfī literature and the vast amount of material arising from popular legends and traditions, which more often than not have nothing in common with Islam.[54] Let us, like Khalīlu'llāh Khalīlī[55], lay stress on the social factor: in the eyes of Sanā'ī all Moslems are equal.

The second great Ṣūfī poet and thinker is Farīdu'd-dīn Abū-Ḥāmid Muḥammad 'Aṭṭār, whose life and work are however obscured by an incredibly dense layer of subsequently added fictitious material. He was born in Nishapur or in the neighbourhood, according to S. Nafīsī probably in 537/1142–3. In Nishapur he combined the profession of apothecary with a medical practice, which is implied in the name 'Aṭṭār.[56] *
He inherited the business from his father and was himself a well-to-do man. His double profession will probably have occupied most of his time and he is thus all the more to be admired for having managed to compose such a wealth of poetry while carrying on his daily work. Though not a true Ṣūfī[57], he cherished a great admiration for the saints and from his boyhood on found edification in stories of their lives and piety. On at least one occasion he paid a visit to Majdu'd-dīn Khvārazmī (d. 606/1209–10 or 616/1219–20).[58] Unfortunately nothing definite concerning important dates in his life can be obtained from 'Aṭṭār's own works[59], but they nevertheless bear conclusive evidence of his having been a man of extremely wide reading, which 'Aṭṭār supplemented in his shop by conversing with men of letters and Ṣūfīs.

Other biographical details must be ignored since they are derived from works wrongly attributed to him. A mist of uncertainty surrounds the date of his death. H. Ritter renounces his former conclusions, that were based on works since proved unauthentic, and is now more in favour of 617/1220, the year of the Mongol occupation of Nishapur[60], as the year of the poet's death, than of the traditional date 627/1229, maintained persistently by S. Nafīsī. Ritter supports his opinion by averring that an error in the figure is more probable than an error in the relatively ancient tradition, according to which 'Aṭṭār perished in a Mongol massacre. Other dates are also put forward, but the accuracy of none of these can be proved.[61]

Notes on pp. 242–245

Even if the traditional number of ʿAṭṭār's works (66) must be rejected as extravagant, there nevertheless remain eight poetical works containing 45,000 distichs and a voluminous work in prose. Besides these several authentic works may have been lost. Seeing that until recent times no distinction was made between his authentic works, those attributed to him and those that were forged, the vast size of the poetic output assumed to be his has obviously proved a hindrance to its publication. For the portion that has been printed, in whatever way, is relatively small and of this only a fragment has been critically edited. This lack of accessibility to his work, added to its profuseness, has resulted in its not having been accorded the attention it deserves, scholars having confined themselves to the best-known titles.[62]

In his first study on ʿAṭṭār, H. Ritter already reached the conclusion that two persons bearing the same name were involved, and S. Nafīsī voices the same opinion in a monograph on the subject.[63] Another question is whether Farīdu'd-dīn Muḥammad ʿAṭṭār Tūnī Mashhadī (9th/15th century) is the author of all the poems ascribed to him by Nafīsī[64], or whether some of these were the work of others.

ʿAṭṭār is a born story-teller, as is shown in the first place by the *Khusrau-nāma* (*Khusrau u Gul*)[65], a purely profane love and adventure story written in his youth, and in the second by his composition technique in other *mathnavīs*, which introduce a wealth of legends and anecdotes and form a very treasury of material for comparative folklore and history – a story-teller whose skill far surpasses that of Sanā'ī. If one excludes the early *Khusrau-nāma*, which stands apart, three periods can be distinguished in the 'whole' of ʿAṭṭār's oeuvre: in the first one finds mysticism in perfect balance with a finished story-teller's art that shows mastery over all stylistic media; in the second, pantheistic zeal gains the upper hand over the structure of the work and the literary interest as a whole; and in the third the 'ageing' poet falls a prey in his loquacity to a mystical idolising of ʿAlī and "not a trace is left of ordered thoughts or descriptive skill". Recent investigations confirm this former classification of H. Ritter's[66] to the effect that only the first group contains undoubtedly genuine works by ʿAṭṭār (viz. *Manṭiqu'ṭ-ṭayr*, 'The Language of Birds', *Ilāhī-nāma*, 'The Book of God', *Muṣībat-nāma*, 'The Book of Affliction', etc.) and that on the other hand the works belonging to the second group cannot with certainty be ascribed to him, though Jāmī himself and his contemporaries (9th/15th century) regarded them as authentic (e.g. *Ushtur-nāma*, 'The Book of the Camel', *Jauharu'dh-dhāt*, 'The Essence of Being'), whereas the works in the third group are undoubtedly either disguised or open falsifications (among these are *Maẓharu'l-ʿajā'ib*, 'The Theatre of Wonders', the main source of all errors; *Khayyāṭ-nāma*, 'Khayyāṭ's Book', i.e. someone who by name and by profession was *Khayyāṭ*, 'tailor', and who inspired the work).[67] The latest research however proves that the third group of works must be attributed to another ʿAṭṭār.

Only the most famous works in ʿAṭṭār's entire output can be briefly referred to here. Foremost among them is the *mathnavī* entitled *Manṭiqu'ṭ-ṭayr*, 'The Language of the Birds'[68]: the birds, led by the hoopoe, are on a pilgrimage to the phoenix Sīmurgh as their highest goal; thirty of them (*sī-murgh*) do in fact reach their aim by way of an inner perfection of self progressing to self-destruction, which ultimately is equivalent to self-annihilation, only to realise that all they have really attained is the Self (*Sīmurgh*, 'phoenix' = *sī-murgh*, 'thirty birds'). Muḥammad Ghazālī's 'Bird Risāla' in prose[69], which ʿAṭṭār amalgamated with the 'Language of the Birds' from the 'Conflict between Man and Beast', a well-known treatise by the Ikvānu'ṣ-ṣafā', 'Brethren of Purity', served him to a great extent as model. "This poem displays the author in his characteristic role of allegorist, introducing to Persian verse the mystical parable which Suhravardī at about the same time was acclimatising to Persian prose."[70] The *Muṣībat-nāma*, 'The Book of Affliction', relates the journey of the soul in mystical meditation during the forty stages of seclusion. The personified thought of the mystic passes through forty 'stations' in the mythical and physical cosmos and at each one converses with one of the mythical, cosmic and physical Beings, seeking their aid in his desperate bewilderment. All these Beings however are in a similar situation and are unable to help the suppliant. The only one who can help him is the Prophet Muḥammad, who points the way to liberation in the sea of the soul, whence the pilgrim enters upon the way to God. – In the *Ilāhī-nāma*, 'The Book of the Divinity', the king asks his six sons to name their dearest wishes. The first wishes to win the daughter of the Parī king, the second desires to possess the art of magic, the third the magic cup of Jamshīd, the fourth the water of life, the fifth Solomon's magic ring, the sixth the elixir of alchemy. The king of course shows them the folly of their wishes and persuades them to seek higher aims.

As a rule ʿAṭṭār's long poems consist of stories within a story, but an exception is the *Asrār-nāma*, 'The Book of Secrets', with its gnostic motif of the intermingling of the pre-existent soul with the lower material world. The *Pand-nāma*, 'The Book of Advice', enjoyed greater popularity and a wide circle of readers. It was published and translated many times.

In his lyrical *dīvān* (containing *ghazals* and *qaṣīdas*), devoid of any admixture of panegyrism and with an almost entire absence of natural description, the poet indulges in a fervent transport of ecstasy (often *rindī*, see p. 268). These poems were not without influence on Saʿdī and Ḥāfiẓ. The endless anaphoras in the works of ʿAṭṭār and other Ṣūfī poets, evidently a medium to promote intensified emotion (like the regular refrain, *radīf*, in *ghazals*), are considered by Ye. E. Bertel's to result rather in monotony, compared with the more effective method of repetition found in Mullā Muḥsin-i Fayḍ-i Kāshānī (d. 1090/1680).[71] A remarkable collection is the *Mukhtār-nāma*, 'The Book of Selections', containing 2010 quatrains, selected as the best from his complete oeuvre by the poet himself and arranged by him according to subject in fifty chapters.[72] Of the foremost importance is the *Tadhkiratu'l-auliyā*, ninety-seven biographies of ancient mystics, a model of simple ancient Persian prose. Twenty-three of them, it is true, revert to Aḥmad aṭ-Ṭūsī (13th century) and four to a later writer.[73]

ʿAṭṭār gives a deeper significance to the pantheistic *taṣavvuf* by a more exhaustive method of searching for the Absolute with the central conception of self-deification. The Way Man must follow in order to release entirely the divine substance in himself, to himself become God, is *fanā'*, non-existence. The power required to achieve this is Love prepared to endure extreme suffering.[74] Mystical speculation is accompanied by passionate tones. A man such as Jalālu'd-dīn Rūmī testifies to his respect for Sanā'ī, but in relation to 'Aṭṭār he regards himself as a mere slave (*ghulām*).

As also in other cases, it has been left to modern research to bring to light the untruthful and legendary features which have been woven around the life of Maulānā Jalālu'd-dīn Muḥammad Rūmī[75] during the course of time. (Rūmī is generally known to the Iranians as Maulavī.) It must however be admitted that his romantic fortune provoked such a development. He came from an ancient family of scholars in Balkh (b. 604/1207), where his father, Bahā'u'd-dīn Muḥammad Valad, was a well-known preacher, not unacquainted with mystic speculation. Fear of the Mongols and various controversies were the cause of his leaving the town with his family in about 616/1219–20, going first to the sacred places, thence via Damascus to Qonya (about 618/1221–2). After his father's death in 628/1230–1 Maulavī fell in with the mystic circle of Burhānu'd-dīn Muḥaqqiq of Tirmidh (d. 638/1240–1), who had been one of his father's pupils. This relationship prepared the ground for the outburst of passion to which he fell a prey when the wandering dervish Shamsu'd-dīn Muḥammad of Tabriz[76] appeared in Qonya (642/1244). It is not impossible that Jalālu'd-dīn had already met him some time before during his family's peregrinations. The physical beauty of the dervish[77] and his exorbitant mystical-narcissistic assertions on the more exalted spheres of the Beloved (*ma'shūq*) captivated Maulavī completely. Because this ecstatic love-relationship aroused the antipathy of the disciples, Shams in his indignation departed for Damascus; but he eventually allowed himself to be mollified by the imploring letters and messages from his pupil and finally consented to return to Qonya, only to arouse a fresh storm of protest that resulted in his being compelled to leave the place again (645/1247). No one knew where he had gone and Maulavī searched for him in vain. The latter's longings and anxiety on account of the Beloved made of him a great poet. By identifying himself with the vanished *Ma'shūq* he finds him again. It is not he himself who sings his songs but the teacher, personified in him, who writes under the *takhalluṣ* Shams-i Tabrīz, 'Sun of Tabriz'. Listening to music and the singing of passionate odes, as well as the dance, roused him to an equal state of emotional agitation as did a new mystical love-relationship with the unlettered Ṣalāḥu'd-dīn Farīdūn Zarkūb, the 'goldsmith', which absorbed him to such an extent that it once again excited the jealous anger of the other disciples (*murīds*) and a violent crisis in the Order ensued. On Ṣalāḥ's death (in 662/1263–4) the master transferred his affections to Ḥusāmu'd-dīn Ḥasan (d. 683/1284–5) who actually inspired Maulavī to write the *Mathnavī*. Jalālu'd-dīn died on Sunday, the 5th Jumādī II 672/7th December 1273; his funeral was attended by the whole population of Qonya, not only by Moslems but also by Christians and Jews, in recognition of the master's immense spirit of tolerance.[78]

The lyrical work *Kulliyyāt-i Shams-i Tabrīz*, 'The Collected (lesser) Poems of the Sun of Tabriz', numbers 36349 distichs plus 1983 quatrains in the six-part critical edition prepared by Professor Badī'u'z-zamān Furūzānfar (Tehran 1336–45), as * against the 50,000 contained in the Lucknow impression dated 1302/1885 – a reduction that was to be anticipated. This work is one of the most prodigious achievements in poetry. From beginning to end the undercurrent of the songs is formed by the mysticism of the identification of Subject and Object, flowing on the one hand into pantheism and on the other into self-deification, "with strong emphasis on the narcissistic motif of the identification of the Self with the Object of Love and of Mergence with Him".[79] In ecstatic vehemence of surging emotions and visions they surpass anything that has ever been written in Persian poetry. Moreover, they were actually dictated in a sort of trance. Although the verses show a straightforward style they are nevertheless not lacking in fine sculpture. Yet the grandeur of the underlying thoughts proves fatiguing by reason of its monotonous seriousness, while the lyrical variations, colourful and fervent as they are, are not sufficient to lend a more varied aspect to the whole. But variety, and this must be emphasised again and again, is certainly not one of the merits of Persian poetry. Against this, however, one can put to its credit the extreme subtlety of the spiritual processes it describes.

The most important work of Jalālu'd-dīn, an encyclopaedia, or rather the Bible of Ṣūfism, is the *Mathnavī-i ma'navī*, 'The Mathnavī devoted to the Intrinsic Meaning of all Things', in six books comprising 27,000 couplets (the 'seventh' book is unauthentic). It is less fervent than the *ghazals* but possesses great poetical beauties and artistic qualities, not to mention its significance for Ṣūfī philosophy and ethics. The poem does not begin with the customary opening hymns but with the lament of the Reed-pipe, suggested to Jalālu'd-dīn by 'Aṭṭār.[80] Our amazement at his vast power of imagination – the master dictated the work to its inspirer during a period lasting more than ten years, albeit with interruptions – is somewhat modified by the lack of balance in the material (resembling Sanā'ī in this respect) and by minor slips of style. Meditations alternate with parables and tales of the most varied kind[81], sometimes interrupting one another; emotion alternates with thoughts, erudition and rhetoric with simple directness, while the style is adapted to the content with admirable flexibility.[82] There is no doubt that in the anecdotal insertions the *Mathnavī* is an improvement on the technique of 'Aṭṭār. One difficulty in particular is the "peculiar looseness in the association of ideas, which almost resembles a flight of thought. The relationship between the tale and the accompanying moral is also very curious. The point in view is sometimes neither allegory nor moralising fable, but that the tales should simply arouse the interest of the listener for what is to come, though the degree of coherence is but slight. One expects to gather the moral from the essential point of the story, but this is by no means always the case."[83] Here too the influence of 'Aṭṭār can be felt. The epoch-making critical edition of R. A. Nicholson, the translation and commentary from the pen of the same scholar, have now for the first time made it possible to penetrate into the theological conceptions of Maulavī and to investigate the connection with Sanā'ī and particularly with 'Aṭṭār, as well as with others. H. Ritter[84] fears that in this respect the result, though of course not without importance, may be less than might be expected. He considers it therefore necessary to study Maulavī's philosophy first of all from other authentic sources. These are his letters and sermons, the discourses contained in the *Fīhi mā fīhi*, 'There is in it, what is in it', i.e. unsystematical miscellanies, his father's works, tradition such as it remained from his teacher Shams-i Tabrīzī, Aḥmad Aflākī's (d. 761/1360) memoirs, and in particular the works of Sulṭān Valad (b. 623/1226, d. 712/1312), his son, likewise a Ṣūfī poet. It is with him, properly speaking, that the history of the Maulavī Order begins. The foundation and propagation of the Order, the first ritualistic customs of its *samā'* must all be accredited to Valad.[85] He applied theophany to the saints and sheikhs and made famous persons of three hitherto unknown favourites of his father's. He wrote a *mathnavī* in three parts giving authentic information on his father and the latter's doctrine; the second 'volume' (*daftar*), usually known as *Rabāb-nāma*, 'Book of the Rebeck', contains two supplements, one in Seljuq Turkish and one in Greek, that are of great importance from a philological viewpoint. One also comes across occasional Turkish words or verses in Maulavī's works.[86]

NOTES

1. Arberry, *An Introduction* (B III), 6–7.
2. Massignon: Arberry, *ibid.*, 47.
3. Goldziher, *Vorlesungen*[1] (B III), 142 *et seq.*
4. *Ibid.*, 150.
5. Zarre, *Ocherk* (B V), 68.
6. Graham: Arberry, *ibid.*, 12.
7. Massignon, 'al-Muḥāsibī', *EI*, 3, 755a.
8. Arberry, *Handwörterbuch des Isl.*, *s.v.* 'Dhu'l-Nūn'.
9. Arberry, *Sufism*, 56–7.
10. *Ibid.*, 60.
11. Massignon: Arberry, *ibid.*, 101; Massignon, *EI*, 4, 740b.
12. von Kremer: Arberry, *An Introduction*, 21 *et seq.*; Goldziher, *Vorlesungen*[1], 30 *et seq.*
13. Nicholson: Arberry, *ibid.*, p. XX.
14. Massignon: *ibid.*, 51.
15. *Ibid.*, 64.
16. Asín Palacios: *ibid.*, 53–7.
17. Horten: *ibid.*, 38; a fervent opponent of Horten here is H.H. Schaeder, *OLZ*, 1927, 833–49.
18. Really a revolt against *lan tarānī*, 'never seest thou me' (Koran 7, 139): Bausani, *Storia*, 357.
19. Schaeder, *ibid.*, 845.
20. Goldziher, *Vorlesungen*[1], 164.
21. Cf. D. B. Macdonald, *EI*, *s.v.* 'Samā''.

22. *Osnov. momentī* (B VIa), 95 *et seq.*; *Poez. Muḥsin-i Fayḍ*, 17.
23. *Oriens*, 3, 145; 4, 182.
24. *Op. cit.*, 102–3.
25. Ritter, *Philol.*, 7, 89 *et seq.*
26. *Ibid.*, 107.
27. Schefer, *Relation* (Bibl. *s.v.* 'Nāṣir-i Khusrau' [B VIIb]), 35 *et seq.* or 10 (Persian text); cf. Klimovich, *Chrestom.* (D IIa), 776.
28. Krïmskiy, 2, 26.
29. Shiblī, 5, 30; Qazvīnī, "for whom the only poetry worth considering was the Ṣūfī poetry" (V. Minorsky, *Iran*, 206, with reference to LHP, 4, 27).
30. *Istor. tadzhikskogo naroda* (D Ia), [2]262, [3]289.
31. Zhukovskiy: Bertel's, *Kabus-nama* (transl.), 259; *Ocherk*, 55. The same standpoint is adopted by Fritz Meier in Brunschvig–von Grunebaum, *Classicisme* (B II), 237, who rejects S. Nafīsī's contrary allegations as lacking conviction; idem likewise in 'Mahsatī', 18.
32. Ye. E. Bertel's supported this conception in the years 1924–28, but now appears to have rejected it, see IPTL, 523. His original view is to be found in the following passages: 'Dva gazeli Bābā Kūkhī Shīrāzī', *DRAN-B*, 1924, 59–61; *Kosmich. mifī*, 1925; *Poez. Muḥsin-i Fayḍ-i Kāshānī*, 1926, 17; *Ocherk*, 1928, 53 *et seq.* – Cf. Ritter, *Das Meer*, 481 *et seq.*
33. Cf. M. Qazvīnī, *Yād-dāshthā*, 2, 3–9.
34. *Bābā Ṭāhir* (Bibl.).
35. 'Ein Hymnus auf Zervān', *ZDMG* 82 (1928), 25.
36. Cf. recently however Adīb Ṭūsī, *Fahlav. Lurī*, and especially the wording based on ancient MSS discovered by M. Mīnuvī: Ṣafā, 2, 384–6.
37. Romaskevich, *Pers. nar. chetverostishiya* (G), 13; Mīr Afḍalī, *Rūzgār-i nau*, 5/3, 53.
38. *Shāh-kārhā* (C), 6.
39. *Sabk*, 2, 241.
40. Bibl. *s.v.* 'Kharaqānī', ed. Bertel's, 159; Ritter, *Philol.*, 9, p. 63, no. 126.
41. *Grundlinien* (B VIa), 5.
42. Bibl. *s.v.* 'Anṣārī': Ivanow, *Tabaqat* (B VIb); Arabic text ed. J. Pedersen, Leiden 1960.
43. Levy, *A Prose Version.* *
44. J. Rypka, *EI*^{2}, 1, 838b.
45. LHP, 2, 109 *et seq.*
46. Bertel's, IPTL, 437, does not agree with the view of Sanā'ī as a Ṣūfī poet, except in a few isolated passages, and quotes a number of reasons for this, but he does not deny the ascetic touch.
47. Thus Jāmī and an inscription on a pillar, although according to Khalīlu'llāh Khalīlī (see Rahmat Ali's review *JA* 231, 1939, 144 *et seq.*) not the original one. According to Muḥ. b. 'Alī ar-Raqqā' (H. Ritter, *Oriens*, 5, 190: ar-Raffā') in the Preface to the *Ḥadīqa*, the poet died on 11 Sha'bān 525/18 July 1131, which Mudarris Raḍavī in his Preface to the *dīvān* sees as an erroneous annotation for the 'correct' date, viz. 535/1141. 'Abb. Iqbāl, basing his theory on the elegy in which Sanā'ī, an admirer of Mu'izzī and publisher of the latter's *dīvān*, mourns the death of the poet, fixes the date as 518–21/1124–7 in his foreword to Mu'izzī's *dīvān*, p. 'l'. In any case the commonly cited date 542/1147–8 or 545/1150–1 is improbable. Mīnuvī insists on the year 545 in *Dar bāra-i Taḥrīmatu'l-qalam*, 5, without paying any apparent attention to Khalīlī and Iqbāl. Cf. also Ṣafā, 2, 559 and 'Mahsatī', 49$_2$. *
48. According to Raḍavī's edition.
49. Arberry, *Pers. Lit.*, 210.
50. Bertel's, *Grundlinien* (B VIa), 15.
51. Ritter, *Oriens*, 5, 190–2, in the review on the edition prepared by Mudarris Raḍavī.
52. Worthy of note from the point of view of cultural history is Sanā'ī's satirical *Kārnāma-i Balkh*,

'The Book of the Heroic Deeds of Balkh' (ironical!), a small *mathnavī* dating from before 508/1114, the first of his 'Six', ed. Muḥ. Raẓavī, *FIZ*, III/4, 1334 (Ṣafā, *Ta'rīkh*, 2, 563).

53. Bertel's *loc. cit.*, 18 *et seq.*; Bertel's, *Odna iz melkikh poem Senai* where (p. 42) there is also a reference to the analogy with Dante's *Divina Commedia*; similarly in Avicenna's *Ḥayy b. Yaqẓān*, cf. Bertel's, *Avicenna i pers. literatura* (B VIb), 80 *et seq.* and H. Corbin, *Avicenne et le récit visionnaire* (B VIb), 1–3, Tehran 1952–4.

54. Bertel's, *Osnov. momentī* (B VIa), 103. A reliable, concise evaluation of the collected works of Sanā'ī is given by Ṣafā, 2, 565 *et seq.*; the fullest and most detailed by Bertel's, IPTL, 402–55.

55. Khalīlī (see note 47), 142.

56. Also derived from the surname of 'Aṭṭār's grandfather, cf. S. Nafīsī, *Justujū* (*q.v.*), 169.

57. Thus H. Ritter, *EI*[2], I, 752b, whereas S. Nafīsī regards the fact of 'Aṭṭār's having belonged to the Kubrāviyya Order as being beyond all doubt (*op. cit.*, 89). Opposed to this view is Badī'u'z-zamān Furūzānfar, who repudiates it in *Sharḥ-i aḥvāl etc.* (see below, note 62), 28, 11 *et seq.*

58. H. Ritter, *Philol.*, XIV: *'Aṭṭār*, II, 5.

59. H. Ritter, *EI*[2], I, 752b.

60. H. Ritter, *Philol.*, XIV, 7.

61. *Ibid.*, 6.

62. Cf. Bibl. In this respect S. Nafīsī's detailed study on 'Aṭṭār, *Justujū etc.* (*q.v.*) forms a tremendous step forwards. Prof. Badī'u'z-zamān Furūzānfar's voluminous work *Sharḥ-i aḥvāl etc.* (*q.v.*), which I have unfortunately been unable to peruse in detail, penetrates deeply into the subject.

63, Ritter, *Philol.*, X: *'Aṭṭār*, 157; Nafīsī, *op cit.*, 145 *et seq.*

64. Nafīsī, *op. cit.*, 167; Ritter, *Philol.*, XIV, *'Aṭṭār*, II, 3.

65. "... gehört ... einer literarischen Gattung an, die wahrscheinlich in letzter Linie auf hellenistische Vorbilder zurückgeht": Ritter, *Das Meer der Seele*, 1. Detailed contents: idem, *Philol.*, X: Attār, 160–72.

66. Ritter, *Philol.*, X: 'Aṭṭār, 143.

67. Bertel's, 'Farīduddīn 'Aṭṭārs Khayyāṭ-nāma', *IAN OGN*, 1929, 203, 25. Bertel's maintains that 'Aṭṭār's authorship stands beyond all doubt!

68. Koran 27, 16. A *qaṣīda* bearing the same name: *Khāqānī* ed. 'Amīr-i Kabīr', 37 *et seq.*

69. Before Ghazālī, Avicenna had already expounded his philosophical theories in a story about * birds. 'Aṭṭār's source is Ghazālī: thus Ritter, *Das Meer der Seele*, 8, where an analysis of the contents of the Bird-Risāla is also to be found. *Ibid.*, 8–30, analyses of the contents of the *Ilāhī-nāma*, *Manṭiqu'ṭ-ṭayr*, *Muṣībat-nāma*, and *Asrār-nāma.*

70. A. J. Arberry, *CPL*, 130.

71. Bertel's, *Poez. Muḥsin-i Fayẓ-i K.*, 21. For further characteristics of 'Aṭṭār's *ghazal* poetry: H. Ritter, *Philologika*, XV, 2.

72. Thus Ritter, 'Aṭṭār, IV/8, 195. This outdates the view that the *Mukhtār-nāma* was originally intended to contain 5000 quatrains but that this was not accomplished: Bertel's, IPTL, 521.

73. Cf. N. D. Miklukho-Maklay, *O proiskhozhdenii* (B VIb).

74. Ritter, 'Das Proömium', 179.

75. Viz. from Asia Minor, called by the Moslems *Bilād ar-Rūm*, the countries of Rūm, the land of the Byzantines, the Eastern Romans. For further information on the use of the term Rūm see P. Wittek, 'Le Sultan de Rūm', *Annuaire de l'Inst. de Philologie et d'Histoire Orientales et Slaves* (Bruxelles), 1938. Cf. H. W. Duda, *Die Seltschuken-Geschichte des Ibn Bībī*, Copenhagen 1959, 6, footnote 2.

76. According to a verbal communication from A. A. Semënov in 1946 a son of Khvarshāh, the last Grand Master of the Assassins: *Stroyeva, Unichtozheniye* (B II), 213. In his latest essay, *Mawlānā*, A. Gölpinarlı shows proof of Maulavī's having been 62 years old at the time of his meeting with Shams-i Tabrīzī, whereby the date of his birth would have to be put back to 580/1184. I am sceptical about the interpretation of the *ghazal* on which this theory is based.

77. Ritter, *Philol.*, XI, 121 *et seq.*

78. Badī'u'z-zamān, *Maulānā*, 123.
79. Ritter, *Philol.*, VII, 91.
80. Ritter, 'Das Proömium', 169 *et seq.*
81. Latterly closely examined by Badī'u'z-zamān Furūzānfar in the *Ma'ākhidh* (B VIb).
82. Cf. Arberry, *CPL*, 240.
83. Ritter, 'Zum Mesnewi-Text', *OLZ*, 1928, 8. Of a different opinion is G. Richter (*q.v.*).
84. Ritter, *op. cit.*, 9. The statements of R. Khorb (*q.v.*) on Maulavī's dialectics are interesting. The author reaches the conclusion that G. W. F. Hegel was acquainted with the work of the Persian poet.
85. Idem, *Philol.*, XI, 126.
86. Cf. *s.v.* 'Yaltkaya' (B VIb). *

VIII. THE MONGOLS

The Mongol invasion[1] began in the autumn of the year 1219. Devastating everything in its path, it brought the natural development of the lands it passed through to a halt for a long time. In the territories inhabited by Iranian peoples the conquest took place in two stages. The first, led by Chingiz-Khān, was directed towards the northern (Central Asiatic) districts which were defended with great courage but with little political forethought by the Khvārazm-Shāhs Muḥammad and Jalālu'd-dīn. The Mongols advanced victoriously as far as Tiflis. In unprecedented fashion they laid waste the countries that had been brought to such a flourishing state of cultivation. Unprecedented too was the butchery perpetrated among the native population; and this was no haphazard savagery, on the contrary it was all well thought out and organised. By their bestial behaviour Chingiz-Khān and his myrmidons intended to terrify the subjugated peoples and weaken them so radically as to prevent them from ever again being able to summon up the courage to effectively resist the invader. By about 1250 the Mongols were in control of Central Asia, Khurasan, Sistan, Mazandaran, the Persian districts of Iraq, Azerbayjan and other countries. The south and south-western lands were left intact because the Atabegs of Fars, the Karakhitaīs of Kirman and the rulers of Luristan lost no time in surrendering to the aggressor and becoming tributary subjects. Yet this Mongol invasion did not injure the strong hearth of resistance that the Ismāʿīlitic Alamūt proved to be. Central Asia with the adjacent territories and Iran were absorbed into the vast empire of the Great Khāns, whereby Central Asia fell to the share of Chaghatay, while Persia was allotted to the Golden Horde, although in point of fact Persia was ruled directly by the governors appointed by the Great Khān until the middle of the 13th century.

The second wave of aggression, under Hülägü-Khān, had as aim the consolidation and extension of the power of the Mongols in the Near East. It was above all Alamūt, the centre of the Ismāʿīlitic authority of the 'Mountain Chiefs' (the Assassins), and with it the numerous other strongholds belonging to the Order, that were now completely destroyed – destroyed as a political power and also, as it were, as a symbol of Iranian independence of foreign usurpation. This act removed the last obstacle on the way to a complete conquest of Persia, at the same time however bringing about its almost complete unification. It also cleared the path to the metropolis of Islam, Baghdad, which, although it only possessed a small feudal hinterland, was, in the person of the Caliph, nevertheless still the religious centre of orthodox Islam.

Baghdad was conquered at the beginning of the year 1258. The last of the Caliphs of the Abbasid dynasty was put to death in the most atrocious manner[2], and the town, the home of so many monuments of culture and art, plundered and destroyed. (Hülägü's third campaign, which was to have resulted in the conquest of Syria, was a failure.) Owing to all this and to all kinds of the most horrible incidents, not only the Persian districts but the whole of eastern Islam suffered to a degree that beggars description; the blows they experienced were so catastrophic that they were never able to regain their former greatness. Curiously enough however the development of western Islam also came to a standstill.

At the end of the campaign in Mesopotamia the dominion of Hülägü-Khān and his successors had reached its widest limits. The empire of the Īl-Khāns "became essentially an Iranian state, which after some time united once again the greater part of the nation. The importance of this for the development of the Persian people as a whole and for the further shaping of Iranian culture cannot be too highly estimated."[3] But the Mongols too did not escape the laws of history: numerically weak and with an infinitely lower standard of living, as political overlords they entered a land with a highly developed culture and were thus obliged to come to terms with their new environment as best they could. They could not avoid calling in the help of experienced native advisers to whom they ultimately entrusted the civil government. The uncivilised conqueror was obliged to adapt himself to the vanquished but civilised nation; he became so merged in it that he finally disappeared altogether. This is most obvious in the case of the Īl-Khān dynasty (1256–1335) which, under the pressure of the Persian environment, became civilised and assimilated soon enough and involuntarily tried to make amends for the cruel deeds perpetrated by the armies of Chingiz-Khān. Among the members of this dynasty there appeared not a single poet or writer, for which there were no doubt fundamental reasons.

The customary florid style of the Persian writers found no favour with the first Mongol rulers, beginning with Chingiz-Khān.[4] Of far-reaching significance, however, was the opening of a safe Central Asian trade route from the Far East to Europe, involving economic bonds between east and west that were bound to lead to a certain intellectual contact.

The Mongols overthrew the petty dynasties of the subjugated regions and drove the remaining Iranian nobles into the background.[5] Ghāzān-Khān (694–703/1295–1304) set to work more energetically to bring about reforms and together with his Mongol army adopted the faith of Islam. He seriously endeavoured to put an end to all kinds

Notes on pp. 274–278

of abuses because thereby the state was threatened with bankruptcy and a pauperising of the people; but at the same time he fettered the peasant to the soil and, in addition to the existing taxes and dues, obliged him to do forced labour for the owner of the *iqṭāʿ*, already a hereditary fief. Nothing could ward off a speedy ruin[6], caused – and this must be stressed – not by exorbitantly high taxation but by the random manner in which it was levied. Tax payments were constantly demanded anew[7] – an inveterate vice on the part of the rulers that spread throughout the whole domain of the Īl-Khāns and slowly but surely undermined economic life and ultimately brought about the decline and final ruin of the Mongol empire: the Īl-Khāns, like the Seljuqs before them, fell a prey to disintegration. Iran and Transoxania had to await the advent of the no less ruthless Tīmūr before they again became united, this time, it is true, not for very long but to a greater extent than before.

For the small group of people that remained in the smouldering ruins art could bear no attraction whatever. Scholars and men of letters fled for safety to less afflicted areas. The cultural goods and chattels they were unable to take with them were doomed to perish. Only the archives of the Assassins fell into the hands of historians at the time of the sack of the fortress of Alamūt. The culture of the north-eastern provinces shifted to the south-west and elsewhere. This accounts for the appearance of Jalālu'd-dīn Rūmī in the Seljuq town of Qonya, of Saʿdī in Shiraz and of Amīr Khusrau in India. When, under Hülägü, Tabriz (from 710/1311 onwards the newly-founded Sultaniyya) was promoted to capital city, political and intellectual life was transferred to this corner of the country. For 80 years Azerbayjan then remained the heart of the kingdom. In literature the style of Iraq became predominant and the first symptoms of the Indian style appeared. The old panegyric *qaṣīda* lost its position since there were no Iranian leading personages and the Mongols did not as yet understand Persian (see p. 282). The few *qaṣīdas* composed at this time are merely works constructed to a standard pattern by mediocre or insufficiently trained poets. This at any rate is the customary explanation, but it is a superficial one and not entirely correct at that. It must be opposed that as time went on the Īl-Khāns became more and more adapted to the Iranian way of life and that they were succeeded by smaller rival ruling families, so that it was impossible for the *qaṣīda* simply to sink into oblivion. We must remember that Saʿdī, Salmān Sāvajī, and others did indeed write panegyric poems which are certainly not among the worst of their kind. One must therefore go into the question more thoroughly and consider the development of the towns under the Mongols[8], for to the urban population the panegyric *qaṣīda* had now lost its significance. The *ghazal* and the *mathnavī* were the forms that could give expression to urban interests. And indeed the troubles that beset the towns were far from few. Unrest and oppression continued and this led to a further escape into Ṣūfism. The times demanded the mystical and didactic *qaṣīda* and above all the short *ghazal*, that had previously come into its own and now, first with Saʿdī and later with Ḥāfiẓ, reached its climax. That the mystic epical poem attains its zenith, that Ṣūfī doctrines appear in verse-form and that in general *taṣavvuf* comes more noticeably to the fore – all this is clear evidence of the desire to escape from gruesome reality. When the Īl-Khāns happen to show interest in any branch of learning, it only goes as far as their power of comprehension permits. Hülägü founds an observatory in Marāgha and entrusts it to the care of his favourite and counsellor, Naṣīru'd-dīn from Ṭūs (b. 597/1200–1, d. 672/1273–4). The latter was an eminent polyhistor and the author of a renowned work on ethics (see p. 313), but at the same time a somewhat unscrupulous man[9], who, as head of the Iranian Shīʿite oligarchy, managed to obtain from the Mongols a certain amount of indulgence towards the Shīʿa in virtue of his privileged position. As the observatory had not been built for scientific purposes but solely for reasons of astrological superstition, all the more respect is due to the Persian scholars for availing themselves of this opportunity for serious astronomical research. – A second branch of learning that flourished in this period, and indeed attained a remarkably high standard, is that of historiography. Chingiz-Khān and the Īl-Khāns set great store by having their deeds and the fame of the Mongols perpetuated. In the realm of historiography, however, several works appeared that carried the bombastic style and the use of Arabisms too far. They thus deviated from the general line which, though it showed an increasing tendency both to repress the pure Iranian vocabulary and to resort to a flowery method of expression, nevertheless made little headway in the traditional sense. A dreadful example – but for the world at that time regarded as an ideal model – is Vaṣṣāf's chronicle (see p. 314), a most extraordinary piece of work, coupling grotesqueness of language with a particularly reliable and valuable content.

The Mongols killed such a large portion of the population and destroyed so much that was of economic and cultural worth that the catastrophe thus caused could not but leave lasting traces behind it. The general and lasting moral corruption, which the poets complain of so bitterly, was not the least part of the total harm done. Although later on Iran rallied politically several times, the literary and scholarly output (with the exception of historiography)[10] never again reached the pitch it had formerly attained, in spite of a few outstanding figures and of a gradually increasing range of subjects. A change is particularly to be noticed in the characteı of learned pursuits even though the decline did not set in at once, but only later. Then, however, it lasted all the longer. The negligent Daulatshāh (see p. 316) is the standard example of a decadent scholar among the Timurids. This does not apply to the culture of Iran only but also to that of the whole of the eastern half of Islam, and even to western Islam. The latter region, although in no way affected by the Mongol incursion, fell into a decline similar to that in which the world of eastern Islam soon found itself. And here we must seriously consider whether it was in fact the Mongols, and they alone, who were responsible for the downfall of the culture of Islam or whether there may not have been other, more powerful and deeper causes at work which have hitherto not been brought to light.[11]

A. SAʿDĪ.[12] THE RISE OF THE *GHAZAL*

One of the most curious and captivating personalities, and a man who had a far-reaching influence in every respect, was Shaykh Abū-ʿAbdiʾllāh Musharrifuʾd-dīn b. Muṣliḥ Saʿdī of Shiraz.[13] Unfortunately there are but few incontestable dates and facts known about his life, considerably fewer than the biographies seem to offer, though much of the material they contain has been derived from the *tadhkiras* and from his own works, more especially the *Būstān* and the *Gulistān*. It should be borne in mind that these two works are of a belletristic nature, so that what the poet relates about himself need not be taken too literally. Many an anecdote and detail provide ample evidence of this. They are in appearance autobiographical, in themselves mostly not impossible but nevertheless improbable.[14] The right to poetic licence of course remains intact.

There are unfortunately no contemporary records concerning Saʿdī, and a critical edition of his works, into which a great deal of foreign material has certainly crept, is only in its initial stages.[15] Therefore, when re-constructing his biography, many a feature must be omitted that may well be interesting from a non-critical point of view. In other respects too various deviations from the prevalent version will be found. The poet was born into a cultured family some time between 610–5/1213–9 and was about twelve years old when his father died. He commenced his studies in his native town of Shiraz but was driven by the campaigns of the Khvārazm-Shāh and the Mongol raids to Baghdad, where he continued them at the famous Niẓāmiyya Academy. Compelled by his restless nature, he set out to see the world. He saw and experienced a great deal, but invented still more that might be entertaining or instructive. It may be taken as certain that he travelled through Mesopotamia, Asia Minor, Syria, Egypt and to Mecca, but the alleged journeys to Kashgar and India must be rejected. At that period he does not appear to have been known as a poet.[16] He achieved fame only after his return to Shiraz in 654–5/1256–7, when he composed the *Būstān*, 'Orchard' in honour of the local Salghurid ruler Abū-Bakr b. Saʿd b. Zangī, and a year later (656/1258) published his second renowned work, the *Gulistān*, 'Rose Garden'. The latter was dedicated to prince Saʿd b. Abī-Bakr b. Saʿd, the same whose name he chose as *takhalluṣ*. Neither need we take literally the short space of time during which these two works were composed (cf. the *Encomium Moriae* of Erasmus of Rotterdam!) but must regard the latter rather as the final versions of sketches already practically completed. These two works resulted in an increased general respect for the poet as well as the favour of the Atābegs of Shiraz. His meeting with the two Juvaynīs – ʿAlāʾuʾ-dīn ʿAṭā Malik (d. 681/1283), the author of the *Taʾrīkh-i Jahān-gushāy*, 'History of the World Conqueror' (Chingiz), and his brother Shamsuʾd-dīn Muḥammad Ṣāḥib-dīvān (executed 683/1284) – at Tabriz as well as with the Īl-Khān Abāqā can hardly be based on truth[17] as this information is derived from an apocryphal *risāla* ('treatise'). But he sings the praises of both brothers in his *qaṣīdas*. Saʿdī died in his monastery on 27 Dhi'l-Hijja 691/9 December 1292.[18] His monastery also granted him his last resting-place.

The literary output of Saʿdī is many-sided. Not only that, but everything he turned his hand to reveals the touch of the master. He is on the whole less interested in abstract mystical speculation than in its application to everyday life, viz. ethics and didactics, as, for the rest, he himself admits. Both the masterpieces mentioned above are actuated by this mental attitude. Whereas the *Būstān*, composed in the *mutaqārib* verse-metre, follows a more theoretical aim, the *Gulistān* consists almost entirely of anecdotes (not always of a didactic nature). The *Gulistān* is composed in rhymed prose (no misfortune for the development of Persian literary prose?) and is closely interspersed with ethical observations and deductions in verse[19], for which no doubt Anṣārī's (d. 481/1088) *Munājāt* served him as model. Superior narrative technique and subtle pointed observations betray the hand of the master even in the platitudes – of which there are many – in the same way that the realism, on the other hand, reveals the man with experience of life.

The social conditions of the period are mirrored in the *Gulistān* with all the specific virtues and vices of the Persian people. Oriental utilitarianism predominates, convincing proofs are given of the absurdity of the absolute axiom. In the controversy between wealth and poverty, Saʿdī ironically praises the rich man. The philosophy of 'human common sense' and its application – a universally acceptable morale – were, according to K. Chaykin[20], the real reasons for the continuous success of the book in the whole of the Near East throughout many centuries and even up to the present day. It was not (and here Chaykin brings forward a new idea) Saʿdī's mild scepticism, his contempt of property and of the possessive instinct that arose from a contemplation of world catastrophes, and it was not his humanitarianism and religious tolerance[21] – in short it was none of the qualities which raised Saʿdī above the common level that made the book famous. Even today constant quotations from the *Gulistān* add a zest to friendly gatherings and serious talk.

Chaykin[22] gives special attention to the metre of the *Būstān*. The *mutaqārib* is by no means only an heroic metre; this is demonstrated by the poet Sharīf's[23] *Pand-nāma-i Anūshīrvān*, that dates from the 5th/11th century, and by the still earlier *Āfarīn-nāma*, composed in 333–6/944–8 (see p. 144). The *Būstān* is also reminiscent of Sharīf in its equally stylised appeals to important persons to pronounce judgments. Thanks to this and to the practical, sensible way in which it approaches its aim the *Būstān* stands apart from the didactic works of the 6th/12th century and bears a greater affinity to the *Qābūs-nāma*.

A large portion of Saʿdī's works are lyrical, some of a panegyric and others of an amorous-mystical nature. His *qaṣīdas* and *ghazals* have been assembled in several collections, possibly compiled only later.[24] The *qaṣīdas*, whether written in Persian or in Arabic – Arabic scholars label Saʿdī's Arabic *qaṣīdas* as mediocre compositions![25] – and elegies, although not devoid of panegyric tendencies, differ from the customary types of hollow eulogy thanks to their didactic purport. Saʿdī himself says that he was driven by poverty to write panegyrics. But what must one think of a moralist who glorifies Hülägü-Khān, the man who had executed the Salghurid Seljūq-Shāh, the same man whose praises our poet had sung a few months previously; who, forgetting that after the terrible devastation of Baghdad he had written a long elegy mourning the Caliph al-Mustaʿṣim, who in his turn had been made to suffer a most cruel death at the hands of none other than the same Hülägü-Khān? Some of his *qaṣīdas* suffer from verbosity and repetition.

Saʿdī's *ghazals* are held in especially high esteem, nowadays perhaps more than ever before, although it should be emphasised that from the very first the innovations introduced in them were afforded due appreciation. The great Amīr Khusrau Dihlavī (d. 725/1325) describes himself as Saʿdī's successor in the *ghazal*, and even a Ḥāfiẓ makes use of Saʿdī's wording in certain passages, though without stating his source. It is natural that Saʿdī should also borrow to a large extent from his precursors[26], especially since he was thoroughly familiar with their works; but thanks to his ingenuity and his special fondness for the *ghazal* his work surpasses all previous achievements. While for a long time the poets had expressed their amorous and other emotions mainly in the introduction to the *qaṣīda* and had devoted but little attention to the independent *ghazal*, the Mongol period was to witness a change caused by the altered social conditions. With the rise of the towns the *ghazal* acquired more prominence and the cultivation of the panegyric *qaṣīda* gradually waned (see pp. 248, 282). The *ghazal* even obtained primacy, thanks to the genius of Saʿdī.

According to Alṭāf-Ḥusayn Ḥālī[27], the special features that characterise Saʿdī's *ghazals* are the following: (1) the melodious form, that so harmonises with the subject as to cause the 'lovers', listening to these *ghazals* in the *samāʿ*, to lose consciousness; (2) love predominant among the motifs, without affectation; (3) a plastic form arising from the genuine inward experiencing of real impressions and emotions; (4) effect enhanced by the use of metaphor; (5) graceful simplicity; (6) mystic love in the guise of earthly love; (7) contempt of the hypocritical priesthood and those in authority. Is there not something rather old-fashioned in these lines of Ḥālī's? We can detect nothing that was not present in one *ghazal* or another before Saʿdī's time, but such synthesis accompanied by such a total harmony has certainly never been met with before. With Ḥāfiẓ the composition is set to quite another key.

Another formulation of the revolution brought about in the *ghazal* by Saʿdī is given by M. F. Köprülü[28]: a mixture of love and Bacchic themes with *ʿirfān*, 'theosophy', and *ḥikmat*, 'wisdom'. A more accurate view is that of M. Bahār[29], who points out that in the work of Saʿdī, as in that of Ḥāfiẓ, in point of fact many *ghazals* almost, as it were, proclaim political opinions under cover of Wine and the Beloved. It is indeed not advisable to look for Ṣūfism always and everywhere – either in Saʿdī or in other poets. Saʿdī adheres to the opening theme throughout the whole *ghazal* until he has exhausted it.[30]

The traditional four *ghazal* cycles in Saʿdī's *Kulliyyāt*, 'Collected Writings', are followed by short aphoristic poems (taken from the collection *Ṣāḥibiyya*) that pass almost unnoticeably into *qiṭʿas*, *rubāʿīs*, and *mufradāt*. Whether all six of the *risālas*, 'treatises' in rhymed prose, are authentic appears to be extremely dubious in view of the *naiveté* that is here and there evident. A seventh has also been attached to them, a frivolous parody of the semi-mystical, semi-religious consessus (*majlis*), 'homilies', of the second *risāla*. Saʿdī was partial to such extravagances, as is proved conclusively by some witticisms in the *Gulistān*. The same can be said for the *Khabīthāt*, 'Monstrosities', obscene homosexual verses for which the poet apologises at the request of some high personage – unless it is that the obscenities were forged.

One of Saʿdī's special attractions is his partly natural, partly extremely subtle refinement; in any case the most brilliant *sahl-i mumtaniʿ*, 'inimitable facility', is in this case quite matchless, though many and frequent attempts have been made to emulate it. The whole work is imbued with a practical rather than a profound wisdom of life. Through his tolerance the poet ranks among the most noble of the Moslems. The social, ethical and didactic elements in his poetry are worthy of the greatest attention. Unlike the others, Saʿdī did not turn his back upon the world. The voice of nature is able to rouse him to intense emotion. Less praiseworthy is his all too flexible adaptability in theory and practice. The impact of his subject-matter and style was direct and is still so today. His last resting-place in Shiraz has rightly become a renowned and sacred spot; that he belonged to the Sunna has long been forgotten by the Shīʿa, who have also forgotten that Ḥāfiẓ too was an adherent of that doctrine.

The *Gulistān*, and to a lesser extent the *Būstān*, was an enticement to others to imitate it. The greatest fame was acquired by Jāmī's *Bahāristān*, 'Spring Garden' and Qā'ānī's *Kitāb-i parīshān*, 'Pell-mell' (or 'The Book of the Bewildered'), that furnish us with fascinating pictures of the period.

B. SAʿDĪ'S CONTEMPORARIES

Imāmī – Hamgar – Humām; Ṣūfī Theorists: Bābā Afḍal, Husaynī Sādāt, Maḥmūd Shabistarī; Didactic Poets: Auḥadī of Marāgha and Auḥadī of Kirman; the ecstatic poet ʿIrāqī

Khurasan and Azerbayjan had been so heavily hit by the Mongol invasion that it was a long time before poetry was able to recover. The great poets of the 13th century belong to the periphery that had been spared the shock, namely the south-west (Saʿdī), Asia Minor (Maulavī) and India (Amīr Khusrau Dihlavī). Living round about the same time as Saʿdī there were several lyrical poets of note, such as Imāmī of Herat (d. 676/1277–8), Majdu'd-dīn Hamgar of Shiraz (d. 686/1287) and Humām of Tabriz (d. 714/1314), an able imitator of Saʿdī's *ghazals*. Panegyrists of the Īl-Khāns soon

Notes on pp. 274–278

came forward, all of whom were epigones lacking a specific note of their own. For the influence of the Persian element was far too strong for the Mongol invaders to withstand. Concurrently with their iranisation, i.e. cultural assimilation, and with the national recovery – this refers to the last fifty years of the dynasty – a few more impressive figures make their appearance. One of these was Afḍalu'd-dīn Muḥammad Kāshī, generally known as Bābā Afḍal (see p. 235), a writer of seditious *rubā'īs* often ascribed to 'Omar Khayyām and besides this an interpreter of Ṣūfism in terse Persian prose. A poet bearing a certain resemblance to him is the theorist Mīr Ḥusaynī Sādāt (d. later than 718/1318)[31] who wrote his *Zādu'l-musāfirīn*, 'Provisions for Pilgrims', after the manner of the *Gulistān*. A remarkable figure, however, is Shaykh Maḥmūd Shabistarī (d. about 720/1320–21) whose *Gulshan-i rāz*, 'Rose-garden of Secrets', that appeared in 710/1311, attracted great attention in the east and gained a thoroughly deserved esteem in the west. It is a relatively short résumé of the symbolical terminology of the Ṣūfīs – one of the earliest of its kind – in a plain, lucid explanation that was actually a series of versified answers to versified enquiries by Mīr Ḥusaynī Sādāt. The author of this work was not a particularly eminent poet but he was an experienced Ṣūfī and a writer of prose[32] in the same trend. Auḥadu'd-dīn Auḥadī of Marāgha (b. about 670/1271–2, d. 738/1338 in Marāgha), born in Azerbayjan although his family came from Isfahan, made a name by his exposition of the same theories in artistic form, particularly in his most important work, the *mathnavī Jām-i Jam*, 'Jam's Goblet' (i.e. The Mirror of the Universe). It was written in 733/1332–3 and consists of about 5000 verses modelled on the lines of Sanā'ī's *Ḥadīqa*. But his work is not a blind imitation, particularly in the way he adapts it to the requirements of his time. More than to his mysticism he owes his importance to his social and pedagogical interests (such as human intercourse, town-planning, the education of children, censure of judges and of superficial interpretation of *taṣavvuf*[33], etc.), to which he devoted more of his pages than almost any other poet. Some of his *ghazals* even found their way into Ḥāfiẓ' *dīvān*. Muḥammad Bahār[34], himself a finely sensitive poet and critic, observes that Auḥadī's *ghazal* is in no sense inferior to that of Ḥāfiẓ! Auḥadī presumably owes his *takhalluṣ* to his *pīr*, Shaykh Abū-Ḥāmid Auḥadu'd-dīn of Kirman (d. 697/1298), author of the *mathnavī Miṣbāḥu'l-arvāḥ*, 'The Lantern of Souls'.[35] This is an allegorical pilgrimage through imaginary towns, bearing here and there a striking affinity to Dante's *Divina Commedia*, an affinity that surely can only be accounted for by the existence of a common basis.[36] Auḥadī of Kirman was suspected of heresy, which is not to be wondered at in a disciple of the most important expounder of pantheism, the Spanish Moor Muḥyi'd-dīn ibn al-'Arabī (d. 638/1240); he propounded the doctrine of deified Man[37], or "belongs with Aḥmad Ghazālī and 'Irāqī to that ... group of Ṣūfīs who worshipped celestial beauty in the terrestrial".[38]

A poet who was completely steeped in ecstasy was Fakhru'd-dīn Ibrāhīm 'Irāqī of Hamadan (d. in Damascus 8 Dhi'l-Qa'da 688/23 November 1289), a man whose spirit thirsted after higher, gnostic knowledge. It was for this reason that he pursued the holy shaykhs from India as far as Hijaz. Deeply impressed as he was by the lectures of the Shaykh Ṣadru'd-dīn in Qonya on the famous work *Fuṣūṣu'l-ḥikam*, 'Bezels of Wisdom', by the above-mentioned Arab ecstatic poet Muḥyi'd-dīn ibn al-ʿArabī, he committed to paper his most important work, *Lamaʿāt*, 'Lightnings', of small compass but profound and truly poetical, written in prose interspersed with Arabic and Persian verses. Of the various commentaries on the work, Jāmī's *Ashiʿʿa-i Lamaʿāt*, 'Flashes of Lightnings', dating from 886/1481, attained great fame. "ʿIrāqī's theoretical statements on mystical love are all the more important because we possess very accurate information on the mystical love-life of the poet thanks to the detailed biography that has been preserved – a rare occurrence in the case of a Persian poet."[39] ʿIrāqī's *dīvān* and the charming *ʿUshshāq-nāma*, 'Book of Lovers' (or *Dah faṣl*, 'Ten Chapters'), a *mathnavī* with *ghazal* interpolations, traverse the same erotic-mystical path as do the works of Maulavī.

The fact that in all these figures from one and the same period an intensive Ṣūfī speculation and mystical ecstasy constantly come to the fore goes to prove that the latter was all part of the general social decline at that time and a typical 'escapist' phenomenon.

C. NIZĀRĪ

Ḥakīm Saʿdu'd-dīn b. Shamsu'd-dīn b. Muḥammad Nizārī[40] Quhistānī (b. 645/1247–8 in Birjand, d. there in 720/1320–21)[41] stands out on account of his striking personality. From Borodin's most informative study we learn that the pseudonym 'Nizārī' is an old family *laqab*, which was at one time adopted in deference to the Caliph Nizār in view of the family's old association with the Ismāʿīlī doctrine.[42] Our poet was descended from an ancient but already impoverished family of landed aristocrats and his entire patrimony was lost during the Mongol occupation, so that he lived in penury. His early education was given him by his father, who also wrote poetry, and later he attended the schools in Birjand. He became acquainted with Persian and Arabic literature, the works of ʿOmar Khayyām in particular having a lasting and powerful influence upon him. In spite of his having Sunnite teachers he clung to the religion of his father, in form apparently Shīʿite but with a certain leaning towards Ismāʿīlism, especially in regard to the interpretation of the Koran and the external features of the commandments (e.g. the partaking of wine), the denial of the existence of Hell, etc. From his youth onwards he was in the service of the chancellery at the court of the Kurts, so that quite naturally he sang their praises in his *qaṣīdas*.[43] To a certain extent true to the tradition of the Ismāʿīlites he endeavoured to become acquainted with the country and its people as well as with their beliefs. He travelled widely both officially and privately in the immediate and further vicinity, and accompanied Tāju'd-dīn ʿAmīd

Notes on pp. 274–278

on a journey for the purpose of supervising the revenues and expenditure of Azerbayjan and Arrān, but he fell ill in Tabriz and joined the train of the Ṣāḥib-dīvān Shamsu'd-dīn Juvaynī, who was travelling to Georgia, Armenia and Baku for a similar reason. After his return he married and re-entered court service but was so grossly slandered that he suddenly found himself on the streets. He was now obliged to moderate his opinions. Thanks to a defence of himself, *Munāẓara-i shab u rūz*, 'The Conflict between Day and Night', which he composed in verse-form, he was once more taken into favour. The pleasure was however short-lived, for his enemies never wearied of trying to influence the prince against him. His fortune was even confiscated. The poet retired from the court and is alleged even to have taken a dislike to writing poetry. Finally he took up agriculture which had always held great fascination for him, as it did too for Ibn-i Yamīn.

As a poet Nizārī is known far too little and is certainly underestimated. The reason for this was of course his convictions, his opinions and the trend of his poems. Ye. E. Bertel's regards him as a confirmed free-thinker and blasphemer, who sought to undermine the foundations of orthodox religion. We can indeed find more or less superficial references to him in the *tadhkiras* (best of all in the *Tadhkira-i shuʿarā-i Qāʾināt*, dating from 1330/1912)[44], but the first to take a deeper interest in Nizārī were the Soviet scholars. To S. G. Borodin we are indebted for an authentic biography derived directly from the poet's own works, to J. Durrī for a valuable insight into his whole oeuvre, especially the *Safar-nāma*, 'Book of Travel', and to Ye. E. Bertel's who translated and published the *Dastūr-nāma*, 'Book of Rules'.

The *dīvān* consists of 15 parts, among them the great *mathnavī Aẓhar u Maẓhar* that deals with the fidelity of two lovers (it contains about 10,000 verses!) and dates from 700/1300. Nizārī's *ghazals* depart from the usual pattern but present all the more vividly a reflection of the embittered social sentiments aroused by the Mongol oppression. Of an entirely original nature is the *Dastūr-nāma* with its 576 verses – a kind of parody on the popular 'Books of Advice' – perfect as regards its language and poetic form. Though written for the poet's sons, it is in point of fact intended for "gluttons and wine-bibbers and is a manual that actually disavows the precepts of the Koran". Daulatshāh says that this is a book to be treasured by gifted and intellectual minds, but for the rest he makes no secret of the attitude of the priesthood towards the heretic poet.[45]

The *Safar-nāma*, 'Book of Travels', containing about 1200 verses, is the result of the poet's two years' wanderings (678–9/1280–1). Nizārī writes no banal accounts but describes life in the countries and districts he passes through, the characters he meets, and his experiences. In Baku he witnesses a revolt against the Mongols, and the death of a small group of heroes grieves him deeply.

The flavour of Ḥāfiẓ' poetry reminds Jāmī[46] of the *salīqa* of Nizārī, except that the latter apparently possesses much 'lean and fat', viz. good and bad, which Ḥāfiẓ does not. Nizārī certainly showed no great inclination towards the mystical allegory.

D. INDO-PERSIAN LITERATURE: AMĪR KHUSRAU, NAJMU'D-DĪN ḤASAN SANJARĪ

Indo-Persian literature, already mentioned without further comment (see p. 196), will be treated systematically in a separate portion of this book. For the present, within the framework of a history of Persian literature in the narrower sense, only the most prominent Indo-Persian figures can be discussed, namely those who have either acquired rights of citizenship in Iran and Transoxania so that they have become inseparable from native literature proper, or those who have influenced the latter. The following reasons are decisive for the non-inclusion of Indo-Persian writings as one of the elements which constitute Persian literature proper: the Indo-Persian poets and writers are an integrated group belonging to a foreign, ethnologically different tribe, as opposed to individuals who wrote in the Persian language, e.g. poets of Turkish origin; a considerable portion of the elements of Indian culture, as well as the difference of conditions of life in general, inevitably result in certain peculiarities that to the Iranians must seem un-Iranian and foreign. For the so-called Indian style in poetry does not entirely conform to the Persian taste when it is met with in poets of Iranian descent. A striking analogy can be drawn with Indo-Persian miniature paintings and architecture. Although obviously falling into the category of Persian art, they yet display intrinsic elements that are felt by all to be specifically Indian. Finally, the vastness of this material necessitates any study of it being taken up separately from that of Persian literature proper. Nevertheless it would be wrong to altogether exclude this undoubtedly remote branch of Iranian culture, since India has produced several figures whom no survey of Persian literature can afford to ignore. This is especially true of Yamīnu'd-dīn Abu'l-Ḥasan Amīr Khusrau Dihlavī (b. 651/1253 in Patyālī, d. 725/1325 in Delhi), and not only because he was the greatest Indo-Persian writer and moreover noteworthy for the vastness of his output, though the figure of 400,000 verses sometimes quoted may be only legendary. Nor is the reason to be sought in a purely Indian descent, for he was Indian only on his mother's side and by his place of birth. On the paternal side he was a Turk, his father having emigrated to India from Transoxania during the Mongol invasion with other members of the tribe of Hazāra-i Lāchīn. The decisive factor is rather his important influence on the Persian literature of the 8th–9th/14th–15th century, with the feudal interests and mentality of which he was evidently more in sympathy than was his famous model Niẓāmī. Throughout the whole of his literary career he took part in court life as a panegyric poet under successive rulers and dynasties, constantly adapting himself to contemporary trends. He did not give up his place at court when in 671/1272–3 he became *murīd* to the widely-renowned Holy One of Delhi, Muḥammad Niẓāmu'd-dīn Auliyā of the Chishtī Order. This relationship continued until the death of the latter (in 724/1324) whose most dearly-loved disciple he was, and he did not even relinquish his court appointment when the shaykh fell into

Notes on pp. 274–278

disfavour with the ruler. In five *dīvāns*, already classified during the poet's lifetime, *Ṭūṭī-i Hind*, 'The Parrot of India', sings the praises of his sulṭāns in a large number of *qaṣīdas*, in which he endeavoured to imitate Khāqānī and other old masters of this form, but without their abstruseness, and later on the highly modern Kamālu'd-dīn of Isfahan. The *ghazals* of Amīr Khusrau, whether as supplements to single *dīvāns* or as separate collections arranged by later editors, follow in the train of Sa'dī without departing from traditional themes. They were among the most popular *ghazals*, at least in India, as is convincingly testified by the abundance, variety and bulk of the collections. Without wishing to underestimate the poet's other works, Muhammad Wahid Mirza[47] considers the *ghazal* the most important of all that Amīr Khusrau ever wrote and lays stress on the simplicity, the inner coherence, the wealth of feeling and the harmony of these poems (which accounts for their popularity with the Ṣūfīs), as well as to a manifest subtlety of thought that was supposed to be absent in the works of the Persian poets proper, with the exception of Jāmī and Naẓīrī (d. 1021/1612–13). To my mind some doubt must be attached to the assertion that he must be regarded as the greatest lyric poet before Ḥāfiẓ.[48] How highly he was esteemed by Ḥāfiẓ is evident not only from the latter's self-written and preserved copy of Amīr Khusrau's *Khamsa* but also from the fact that the famous first verse of the first *ghazal* in Ḥāfiẓ *dīvān* was obviously inspired by Khusrau.[49] The significance of the Indian poet in relation to Persian literature rests in his suggestive romantic epic poetry and especially in his *Khamsa* which, as is shown already in the headings to the separate epics, adopts all Niẓāmī's themes, introducing greater or lesser alterations in the events, motivations and media of expression, with a considerable though inferior erudition. The sharp outlines characteristic of Niẓāmī give place to a certain haziness, and the latter's philosophical profundity and emphasis on social matters are absent in the work of Amīr Khusrau. But it was just this undeniable lowering of the standard as well as the baroqueness of his style that awakened response among his contemporaries. While Niẓāmī, genius as he was, and notwithstanding his tremendous skill and creative urge, spent half his life in composing his *Khamsa*, Amīr Khusrau accomplished the same feat in less than three years (698–701/1298–1301). It is indeed true that his *Khamsa* is only little more than half as long as Niẓāmī's, but the rapidity with which Khusrau committed his verses to paper suffices in itself to make it impossible for him to equal the master of Ganja, despite his brilliant gifts and lively imagination. One can quite well understand that his contemporary, the writer Maulānā (Qāḍī) Shihābu'd-dīn, not only read through the separate portions of the *Khamsa* but also touched them up here and there.[50] The best of them is considered by Muhammad Wahid to be the romantic epic *Majnūn u Laylī*; M. Habib on the other hand gives priority to *Hasht Bihisht*, 'The Eight Paradises'[51], into which the poet had interwoven several Indian tales. A new and very remarkable experiment are Khusrau's short stories in verse-form. They are derived from the most recent or contemporary history of the Sulṭāns of Delhi and describe the political, private and spiritual life of their heroes. The most striking of these is the *ʿAshīqa* or *ʿIshqiyya*, the tale – possibly also known by other names – of the tragic love of prince Khiḍr-Khān, a contemporary of the poet and object of his praise, for the beautiful princess Duval-Rānī[52]; likewise *Qirānuʾs-saʿdayn*, 'The Conjunction of the Two Lucky Stars', that dates from 688/1289 and deals with the struggle for the throne and the ultimate reconciliation between the son Kay-Qubād and his father Bughra-Khān. Among the formal innovations introduced by Amīr Khusrau may be mentioned the interspersion of *ghazals* into these historical tales, evidently intended to break the monotony of the double-rhymed verses (cf. p. 213); further the *abyāt-i silsila*, uniformly versified titles to the cantos of such epics (the poet treats the *qaṣīdas* in his *dīvāns* in similar manner).

As to his prose: *Tārīkh-i ʿAlāʾī*, 'The History of ʿAlā', or *Khazāʾinuʾl-futūḥ*, 'The Treasure-chambers of the Victories', is a short description of events that took place between the years 695–711/1296–1312, during the reign of ʿAlā'u'd-dīn Khaljī (695–715/1296–1315), written in a bombastic style; *Iʿjāz-i Khusravī*[53], 'Khusrau's Inimitability', is a famous and extensive work on stylistics and epistolography, remarkable in many ways, for it stresses the element of thought and offers much valuable information on the society of the time.[54] *Afḍaluʾl-favāʾid*, 'The Most Excellent of Moral Laws', contains logia by Niẓāmu'd-dīn Auliyā. – This is in no sense an exhaustive list of Khusrau's abundant output, but one must constantly bear in mind the unreliability of tradition. For instance *Qiṣṣa-i chahār darvīsh*, 'The Story of the Four Dervishes', and *Inshāʿ*, 'Guide to Letter-writing', are wrongly attributed to Amīr Khusrau; in other works again the authorship cannot be proved or is unauthentic. Judging by some of the quatrains, we may consider as probably a work by Khusrau *Shahr-āshūb*, * 'Disturbers of the Town', a collection of epigrams in praise of fair youths[55], and we may not overlook the observation to be found in the *tadhkira Tuḥfa-i Sāmī*[56] on the poet Āgahī of Khurasan (d. 932/1525–26) as the author of a satirical *qaṣīda* on Herat called *Shahr-āshūb*, allegedly the counterpart of Amīr Khusrau's *Daryā-i abrār*, 'The Sea of the Innocents'. It is only strange that such an excellent musician as was Amīr Khusrau should have written nothing about music. There is no clear information available about his poetry written in Hindi. Although he expressed himself in highly baroque fashion (Ye. E. Bertel's even speaks of 'powdered'[57]), which developed more and more into a specifically Indian style[58], he imitated in word and rhetoric the masters already referred to, including Sanā'ī. In one of his letters he even enumerated by name the models he made use of for the different genres of his literary work.

In the same line as Amīr Khusrau we may place his trusted friend Najmu'd-dīn Ḥasan Sanjarī (better Sijzī, d. 727/1327), who likewise had an influence on later Persian poetry. He was a master of a passionate tone such as is not even to be encountered in the works of Amīr Khusrau.[59]

E. PANEGYRIC POETS AT THE SMALLER COURTS: KHVĀJŪ, IBN-I YAMĪN, SALMĀN SĀVAJĪ

Kamālu'd-dīn (or Afḍalu'd-dīn) Abu'l-ʿAṭā Maḥmūd Murshidī (b. 679/1281), commonly known as Khvājū-i Kirmānī, 'the little master of Kirman', (probably originally the nickname for the son of a patrician family) spent a great part of his life wandering about from place to place, though most of his work was produced in the south-western part of Persia. While still a lad he made a name by writing a *Ta'rīkh-qaṣīda* on the baths at Yazd which was then perpetuated by being inscribed on the walls of the building. On his journeys through many towns and courts far into western Iran he composed panegyrics on dynasties and persons whom fate or chance had raised to high positions. He joined the Kāzarūniyya Order and testified to his adherence to the Ṣūfīs by the *qaṣīdas* written in the manner of Sanā'ī and also by *mathnavīs*. He died in 753/1352 or 762/1361[60] in Shiraz. His *dīvān*, *Sanāyiʿu'l-kamāl*, 'The Arts of Perfection' (alluding to his *laqab*) bears the marks characteristic of the average *dīvān* of the 8th/14th century, even to riddles and logographs; *qaṣīdas* on the Imāms, especially on ʿAlī, are numerically well represented. His lyrical poetry is clearly influenced by the Iraq school. In the *ghazal* he imitates Saʿdī though he avers that Ḥāfiẓ was his master. There may be some truth in this for Khvājū does indeed borrow many an inspiration and many a theme almost word for word from Ḥāfiẓ' lyrics, and the *ghazals* of one are frequently taken for the work of the other.[61] On the other hand Khvājū's repute cannot be substantiated otherwise than by a laudatory but unauthentic verse in Ḥāfiẓ' *dīvān*. But the fact that they lived in the same place and at the same time leads to the natural conclusion that they were acquainted with one another. M. F. Köprülü considers Khvājū to be an indispensable link between the two grand masters of the *ghazal*, Saʿdī and Ḥāfiẓ.[62] His *mathnavīs* are of a certain importance. Although in other ways he was influenced by such masters as Niẓāmī and Amīr Khusrau, his *Khamsa* is distinguished from theirs both in the selection of the romantic material and in the relationship of the epics to each other. He begins not with meditations but with the romances centred around the pairs of lovers *Humāy u Humāyūn*[63] (732/1331–2) and *Gul u Nau-rūz*, '"Rose" and "New Year"' (742/1341–2), priority sometimes being given to the one, sometimes to the other. The material for both these tales is derived from the Iranian saga-cycle. The incitement to write *Humāy u Humāyun* and the fable on which it is based he owed to Abu'l-fatḥ Majdu'd-dīn Maḥmūd, the chief judge under the Īl-Khān Abū-Saʿīd (716-36/1316-35). In *Gul u Nau-rūz* his model was an epic of the same name by Jalāl Ṭabīb of Shiraz (d. 795/1392–3) dating from 734/1334.[64] There now follow three Ṣūfī ethical *mathnavīs* (743–6/1342–5) inspired by his membership of the Order, though their outward form is based on the patterns of Niẓāmī and Sanā'ī. Two *risālas* in prose close the list of works indisputably written by Khvājū. In spite of his fame Khvājū was not a poet of outspoken personality, he excelled rather in imitating the great poets, whether it was in the lyric or in the romantic and contemplative *mathnavī*. This indeed went so far that a contemporary, Ḥaydar of Shiraz, accused him of plagiarism in a lampoon in verse-form (see p. 92), inspired apparently by no other motive than jealousy of the repute that Khvājū already enjoyed during his lifetime.

There must be few Persian poets who went through as many political upheavals as did the small land-owner of not very large means, Amīr Maḥmūd b. Amīr Yamīnu'd-dīn Ṭughrā'ī, briefly Ibn-i Yamīn (b. 685/1286 in Faryūmad in Khurasan, d. there in 769/1368). Having lost even the sole manuscript of his *dīvān* during the struggle between the Sarbadars and the Kurts in 743/1342, he was obliged to reconstruct it – the sum total of his literary output up to date – as well as he could from memory and with the aid of his friends. His strength lies in the 'fragments' (*qiṭ'a*) with their matter-of-fact philosophical, ethical, and Ṣūfī character. Among other things he here recommends diligence, independence, rural economy, but also renunciation of the world; and eventually he himself put all these admonitions into practice. As to the rest he is characterised by views so vague and flexible as to be contradictory. In this connection his *qaṣīdas* reveal a strange morale, for – although he was actually the panegyrist of the Sarbadars, rulers of Sabzavār, and incidentally *malgré lui* also of the Kurts (a dynasty in Herat) – he sings the praises of sixty-five different lords, whether or not they were worthy of such. Apparently he was driven to this by the political situation and by the miserable conditions under which he was obliged to live. That means that Ibn-i Yamīn was a typical representative of his age.[65] His *qaṣīdas* cannot be rated very highly, for they suffer from repetition and plagiarism. A Shī'ite by conviction, he belongs to those who early on sang the praises of the Imāms and Karbalā.

The country nobleman Jamālu'd-dīn Salmān Sāvajī (b. about 700/1300, d. 778/1376) was the last pre-Safavid panegyrist of repute. He eulogised the Jalā'irids, but had not the slightest scruples about even praising *en passant* their conquerors of the moment. As he was the poet laureate and confident of the ruler, there were many who strove to win his favour. He soon gained fame by his playful handling of the hyper-artificial *qaṣīda* (*qaṣīda-i maṣnū'*) after the manner of the panegyrist Sayyid Dhu'l-faqār Shirvānī (d. 689/1290). This was an art that had long been admired and that was raised to an ever-increasing degree of perfection[66], especially in the 9th/15th century when even the work of Salmān was cast into the shade. There is no doubt that compensation had to be sought for the lack of ideas and it was for this very reason that the principle of 'art for art's sake' was the more fervently pursued. Salmān was particularly clever in his treatment of amphibology (*īhām*).[67] But at the beginning of his poetical career all this was rather a kind of ostentation. Of greater literary value were the new themes and similes he invented. Nevertheless we can hear in his *qaṣīdas* echoes of Kamālu'd-dīn Ismā'īl, Ẓahīr Fāryābī, Anvarī and even of the old Manūchihrī. In his *ghazals* one * can recognise the masters of mysticism as his models. He composed hymns to the glory of God, the Prophet and the Imāms, particularly 'Alī – whose praises had not been sung to any great extent in Persia up till then – although on the other hand it cannot be said that Salmān was a pronounced adherent of the Shīʿa. Besides these and other lyrical poems that conform to the usual type he composed a *Sāqī-nāma*, 'Book of the Cup-bearer', that may be accounted among the first of its kind, being even earlier than Ḥāfiẓ'.[68] Then there is the romantic epic *Jamshīd u Khvarshīd* (written in 763/1361–2), a "re-striking of the old coin *Khusrau u Shīrīn*"[69] under another name, and the romantic tale *Firāq-nāma*, 'The Book of Separation', dating from 770/1368–9, written to console Sulṭān Uvays for the loss of his beloved; the separation was at first temporary but shortly after the reconciliation it became permanent when the beloved died. In taking a current topic as his theme Salmān was one of the first to follow the example of Amīr Khusrau. Broadly speaking his works give more evidence of culture than of genuine poetic inspiration. The praise traditionally bestowed upon him by Ḥāfiẓ in his *dīvān* is based on verses falsely attributed to Ḥāfiẓ, although the latter was certainly acquainted with Salmān's work, and vice versa. Altogether their styles bear such a resemblance to one another that several of Salmān's *ghazals* have found their way into Ḥāfiẓ' *dīvān*. Obscene verses ('witticisms') remind one of Saʿdī.[70] ʿUbayd Zākānī reproached him with the femininity of his idiom, asserting that he must have written his verses for his wife! They nevertheless became good friends.[71]

F. THE LYRIC POET KAMĀL KHUJANDĪ

and his friend, later his 'personal enemy'[72], *the mystic Moghribī*

Likewise in Tabriz, though somewhat later, there lived and died the poet and saint (according to a report[73] *Shaykhu'l-islām* of Tabriz) Kamālu'd-dīn Masʿūd Khujandī ('Shaykh Kamāl') (d. probably in 803/1400–1) and his friend Muḥammad Shīrīn Maghribī (d. 809/1406–7). Khujandī's modest *dīvān* slavishly follows the pantheistic current of Muḥyi'd-dīn b. al-ʿArabī, the concept of *vaḥdat-i vujūd*, 'unity of Being', becoming the one sole theme, albeit with innumerable variations.[74] According to Jāmī[75] the lyrical poetry of Kamāl is so strongly influenced by Ḥasan Dihlavī (d. 727/1327, see p. 259) that there were some who, though wrongly, accused him, Kamāl, of plagiarism. While ʿA. A. Ḥikmat[76] maintains that most of his *ghazals* presuppose a serious study of Saʿdī, Sūdī[77] considers him abstruse, in contrast to Ḥāfiẓ. This however, is in contradiction to the *sahl-i mumtaniʿ*, 'inimitable facility' which, as tradition will have it, was one of Kamāl's most characteristic features. The gentle writer of lyrics that was Kamāl preferred light and flowing verse-metres, but on the other hand he made use of complicated rhymes and *radīfs*. He was particularly fond of hyperbole and applied it in a manner perfectly in harmony with the emotional content. He left an unusually deep mark on the whole of the 9th/15th century.[78] To his school belong not only Muḥammad Shīrīn Maghribī, at first his companion, later his personal enemy, or Bisāṭī Samarqandī (p. 283), Hilālī (p. 285) and many another, but also the Uzbek poets ʿAṭā'ī, Luṭfī and others who were living during the first half of the 15th century. It is they who demonstrate the intrinsic qualities of their master.[79] Conversely Kamāl Khujandī draws from the great poets of the past and from Ḥāfiẓ, his contemporary, partly in passages reminiscent of their verses and partly in *istiqbāl* (cf. p. 97). Maulavī fascinated him.[80] I. S. Braginskiy[81] draws attention to him, as well as to Ḥāfiẓ and Nāṣir of Bukhara, as lyrical exponents of the protest against the ruling and ecclesiastical circles, an attitude very rare in one in such a high position as was the *shaykhu'l-islām*. Yet it is explainable when one considers that in that very capacity the poet was able to gain a deeper insight into the manners, customs and morals of these classes. The attitude of revolt and to an equal extent the folklore elements[82] in Kamāl's poetry account for its exceptionally great circulation among the Tajiks. Kamāl's *ghazals* (that usually consisted of seven verses, though often of six and sometimes only five), as I. S. Braginskiy points out, also resemble the folk-song in that the quantitative construction of the verses now and then gives the impression of the popular syllabic metre.[83] His themes are generally centred around Love (*ʿishq*) under which, according to the same Soviet scholar[84], he conceals "a grievance concerning the obligatory lack of personal liberty, a longing for life and a rapture inspired by all living things". But this can also be taken in the literal sense, for Kamāl's greatness as a poet also lies in his masterly handling of love.[85] According to the *tadhkiras* the mutual admiration between Ḥāfiẓ and Kamāl was so deep that they exchanged their freshly-written *ghazals* with each other.[86] But Kamāl differed from the poet of Shiraz in that he never sang the praises of those in power.[87] He was the first of the contemporary poets to mention Ḥāfiẓ by name.[88]

G. ḤĀFIẒ, THE *GHAZAL* AT ITS SUMMIT

Our knowledge of the life of Ḥāfiẓ[89], the most famous of the *ghazal*-lyricists, was until recently based upon a few unauthenticated anecdotes, and in fact it seemed that no other records existed and that apart from the already familiar passages there was nothing new to be obtained from the *dīvān*. Latterly, however, research carried out by a number of Persian scholars such as ʿAbdu'r-Raḥīm Khalkhālī, Muḥammad Muʿīn, Saʿīd Nafīsī, Qāsim Ghanī and Muḥammad Qazvīnī[90], has resulted in a number of excellent works, the final outcome of which – at any rate for the time being – may be seen in the studies of A. J. Arberry, Mary Boyce, R. Lescot, H. Ritter, H. R. Roemer, H. H. Schaeder and G. M. Wickens.[91] It may be said that thanks to them and to the acquisition of a more reliable edition of the text by ʿAbdu'r-Raḥīm Khalkhālī and

Notes on pp. 274–278

Muḥammad Qazvīnī our insight into the life and work of Ḥāfiẓ has undergone a fundamental change[92], though we may still only be on the point of unravelling the knots! – Khvāja Shamsu'd-dīn Muḥammad Ḥāfiẓ was born round about 726/1325–26 (Muʿīn; according to Ghanī as early as 717/1317–8, while A. J. Arberry gives 720/1320)[93] in Shiraz; there he lived, except for a brief intermission, and there he died in 792/1320.[94] It is true that the town was spared from the Mongol storm, but since the rival princes and dynasties were perforce continuously bringing about changes of government, there was no question of an idyllic calm. Ḥāfiẓ himself calls to mind the peaceful days under Shaykh Abū-Isḥāq Īnjū (743–54/1343–53). The latter was a patron of poets but as ruler he violated his agreements all too frequently and at the same time appeared enviably care-free! But finally he paid the penalty for his levity on the scaffold (757/1356) at the hand of Mubārizu'd-dīn Muḥammad (754–59/1353–8), the savage founder of the turbulent Muẓaffarid dynasty. When this cruel tyrant and bigoted zealot was forcibly deposed by his sons, one of them, Jalālu'd-dīn Abu'l-favāris Shāh Shujāʿ (759–86/1358–85), took possession of the throne. His long reign was marked by incessant wars against his brother Maḥmūd, Shāh of Isfahan, and against his neighbours. This led to such upheavals that he was obliged to leave Shiraz for a time (765–67/1363–66). At first a liberally-minded man, he yet returned from exile as a conqueror with weapons in his hand; but eventually he had to surrender to the priesthood. Three rulers followed whose reigns were but of short duration. Then, however, Tīmūr came and interfered in their affairs, twice ravaging Fars and the surrounding districts, terrorising the people by his cruelty and extirpating the Muẓaffarids in Shiraz as well as in other places. Such stirring times could not fail to affect Ḥāfiẓ as a citizen, and it would have been strange if, considering his relation to the court, whereby he was brought into close contact with these events, the poet had shown no reaction to the latter in his *dīvān*. It will presently be seen that the echoes to be found in Ḥāfiẓ' poetry are not confined to a few traditional specimens but that the whole of his *dīvān* is, as it were, their sounding-board.

The cultured milieu of Shiraz provided the poet with the opportunity for a good education. The direction taken by this education is evident from his title and also from his *takhalluṣ*, Ḥāfiẓ, viz. 'he who knows the Koran by heart', but even more so by the report that he wrote learned Arabistic and theological works in prose. (Some of these are even extant in his own hand-writing![95]) An autograph copy of the *Khamsa* of Amīr Khusrau, preserved in Tashkent, confirms a later account of the poor material circumstances under which Ḥāfiẓ spent his youth.[96] G. M. Wickens[97], by means of a microscopic analysis of one of the *ghazals* based on his focal theory (see p. 270), became convinced that Ḥāfiẓ also knew Turkish. (Turkish was certainly not unknown at court, particularly as the Shāh Shujāʿ was the son of a Turkish princess.) The brilliantly gifted young man later adopted the career of a Madrasa professor, as we are led to conclude from references in the *dīvān*. He was popular at court and honoured by the friendship of Shāh Shujāʿ, who was himself also a poet and at times even carried on his diplomatic correspondence in verse.[98] For a long time Ḥāfiẓ basked in the favour of the princely benevolence which, as a dutiful courtier, he repaid by panegyrics; he would have had no reason to seek a like good fortune elsewhere had he not tasted the inconsistency of the moods and favours of his masters. While most of the *tadhkiras* agree that Ḥāfiẓ fell into disfavour for a time, the *dīvān* reveals that the truth was worse than the legend. Round about the year 770/1368–9 the clerical clique contrived to influence Shāh Shujāʿ to such an extent that the poet was forbidden to enter the court. Ḥāfiẓ, spoilt as he was, complains in many of his *ghazals* of the unkindness of Fate, pleads for mercy and mediation but nowhere gives a clearer explanation of the actual cause of his fall. This degradation was not, as the *tadhkiras* would give us to suppose, of a temporary nature but was permanent; for although there were passing moments of reconciliation Ḥāfiẓ did not regain his former privileged status. All this must have made his position in Shiraz so thoroughly distasteful to him that, as the *dīvān* again discloses, he departed for Isfahan and in about 774–5/1372–4 turned his steps to Yazd. Finding no satisfaction there either – the avarice of the ruler of Yazd was in fact proverbial – he returned to Shiraz and renewed his supplications, imploring his patrons far and wide for assistance. These are the true facts of the case which led to the report that not even the most flattering invitations of foreign rulers were able to persuade him to leave his lovely native region, with its brook in Rukn-ābād and the delightful Muṣallā with its cooling breezes. But once, it is said, did the poet go away, only to return immediately. Yet it is indisputable that in the meantime the *ghazals* of Ḥāfiẓ have found their way into all the countries where Iranian culture has taken root. How he stood in relation to Shāh Shujāʿ on his return from Yazd and subsequently until the latter's death cannot as yet be ascertained from the *dīvān*. Under Shāh Shujāʿ's successor, Zaynu'l-ʿĀbidīn (786–9/1384–7) he led a retired life, and also under Shāh Yaḥyā (789–90/1387–8). It was only under Shāh Shujāʿu'd-dīn Manṣūr (790–9/1388–92), viz. towards the end of Ḥāfiẓ' life, that the poet was granted the rehabilitation he had so passionately longed for.

Apart from a few 'fragments' (*qiṭʿa*) and quatrains, two *qaṣīdas*, two *mathnavīs* (one of them being *Sāqī-nāma*, 'Book of the Cupbearer')[99], Ḥāfiẓ' *dīvān* consists solely of *ghazals*. Steps are being taken to obtain an authentic text. Although not even the edition prepared by Muḥammad Qazvīnī and Qāsim Ghanī[100] comes up to what might be expected of a critical elaboration, these scholars and their predecessors – especially ʿAbdu'r-Raḥīm Khalkhālī – have nevertheless established the first hypotheses, thereby annulling many an earlier theory about the poet. For instance, most of the verses written in praise of individual poets have turned out to be spurious. Similarly the authenticity of hardly any of the 'Shīʿite' verses is confirmed by the earliest manuscripts, and any of them that remain should be subjected to a close scrutiny. (Whereas A. Krïmskiy sees Ḥāfiẓ as an avowed Shīʿite, Muḥammad Qazvīnī[101] is greatly distressed at the probability of his having had Sunnite convictions – basing his supposition on the fact that the Sunna was the official religion of Shiraz at that time.) First and foremost, however, the editions mentioned have given us a deeper insight into Ḥāfiẓ' works. The problems that confront us today culminate in two closely connected points: the chronological order of the *ghazals*, and the question as to how in fact Ḥāfiẓ' *ghazals* are to be understood. These points are of fundamental importance in *dīvān* poetry in general and will be illustrated here in the light of their foremost exponent, though he is to a certain extent an exception, at any rate in relation to his panegyrism. In order to establish the chronological order, serious research has been carried on in recent years in Iran and elsewhere; and it must be admitted that important progress has been made which has led to the chronological determination of a considerable number of the poems. The philological-historical method made it possible to obtain more certain results than did purely psychological speculative considerations, which take concrete evidential facts into account to a far less extent (Maḥmūd Hūman consciously opposed to Dr. Ghanī; Karl Stolz, refuted by H. H. Schaeder[102]). An all-embracing and perspicacious use of historical, stylistic and rhyme material did not, however, result solely in the establishment of the chronology but showed at the same time – at least in part – how Ḥāfiẓ should be understood, namely literally or in a mystical allegorical sense. While the orient interpreted Ḥāfiẓ in the mystical sense and, with few exceptions, still does so today, the west viewed him from the standpoint of a reality that practically ignored his mysticism altogether. And yet it may be observed that oriental conceptions were penetrating to the west through H. Wilberforce Clarke (1891) and Adalbert Merx (1893)[103] just as, conversely, the realistic opinions of the west were beginning to gain ground in the modern east. But even the earliest period was not entirely devoid of realism if we may interpret the excellent purely philological (Turkish) commentary of the Bosnian Sūdī (d. 1000/1591–92) in this light. The most recent investigations[104] prove above all that Ḥāfiẓ was a court poet who sang the praises of the rulers and high-placed persons of Shiraz in the same way as did the others but that he nevertheless differed from the customary panegyrists in several respects. This characteristic attitude is already conditioned by the form: he employs the *ghazal* instead of the *qaṣīda*, whereby the essence of this procedure is not to be sought in the smaller number of verses but in the reduction of the panegyric portion to one or two verses and in the use of the love and bacchantic elements in the *ghazal* to express in poetry the relationship to the Honoured One (*mamdūḥ*) and to external events. Thence it follows that the interpretation of Ḥāfiẓ has to consist in transposing the metaphors derived from the erotic and bacchantic convention of *ghazals* into a real environment: the 'Beloved' (*ma'shūq*) is the 'Celebrated One' (*mamdūḥ*). "Even if the poetry of Ḥāfiẓ is not a poetical description of experience in the occidental sense, the experiences in the poet's world penetrate nevertheless through the veil of the traditional form, sometimes only dimly, yet ... in many places clearly enough to make references to events and to persons quite recognisable. But if the circumstances of the poet's life can be gathered from his work, why then should not the ideas expressed be taken at their face-value?"[105] If it used to appear as though Ḥāfiẓ' lyrics reflected nothing of contemporary events and as if only the peace of God and an infinite heavenly bliss hung permanently over Shiraz, the reason for this was twofold: insufficient acquaintance with the metaphors applied to public life and, on the other hand, sublimation on principle of all erotic and bacchantic elements into mystic allegory. As early as 1941 H. Ritter[106] uttered a warning against this second modality (not only in relation to Ḥāfiẓ but also in general) in the words "that on principle one should not consider as an allegory anything that cannot be confirmed, either by the *ipsissima verba* of the poet, or by the failure of other methods of explanation, as being irrefutably intended as such. Exegesis of allegory by foreign commentators, especially by those who translate the several expressions of love poetry in lexicon fashion into mystical-theological concepts, casts an impenetrable veil over the countenance of the poet, behind which his vital personal traits disappear for ever. This applies especially to those passages in which the poem touches on the personal emotional life of the poet." Muḥammad Bahār[107] went still further; for in view of the current political convulsions, he holds the opinion that several of Saʿdī's and Ḥāfiẓ' *ghazals* simply cry out that the wine, the Beloved, the commissioner of police (*muḥtasib*) may not be understood otherwise than in a political sense. I. S. Braginskiy[108] goes even further still by asserting that in Ḥāfiẓ he can feel the horrors of the period. There are of course, says Bahār, numerous other *ghazals* of Ḥāfiẓ' that require a literal and certainly not a mystical interpretation. They must be judged according to the symptoms, case for case; only the mystical verses are easily recognised and of these there do not appear to be very many. From the very beginning of Ḥāfiẓ' poetical career they were unacceptable at the voluptuous court of Abū-Isḥāq Īnjū. When later on Ḥāfiẓ employed mysticism, either in images derived from Ṣūfism or in complete thoughts, he did so mainly in order to give a mystical flavour to the whole and, by means of an explanation projected into mysticism, to gain an opportunity of escaping blame for his antinomies and blasphemies. During the first half of the reign of Shāh Shujāʿ mystical tones are rare and only become more frequent when Ḥāfiẓ falls into disgrace. But there too in the images drawn from mysticism we detect tricks of style rather than mysticism itself. If his protector cherishes a disposition for mysticism, it is in this direction that Ḥāfiẓ tries to curry favour with him, as in the case of Shāh Shujāʿ's Grand Vizier, Jalālu'd-dīn Tūrān-Shāh (765–787/1363–86). "Ainsi, de même qu'il spiritualise le vin, Ḥāfiẓ spiritualise l'amour. Il recherche, dans l'un et dans l'autre, beaucoup plus qu'un oubli passager ou qu'un frisson de la chair. Le premier agit sur lui à la façon d'un stimulant moral, il lui procure cette exaltation de l'âme qui seule permet de soulever par moment le voile des réalités cachées. Quant au second, il constitue, sous toutes ses formes et presque en lui-même, l'idéal que se propose le poète au cours de sa vie terrestre; la voie que cette passion oblige à suivre, semée de peines autant que de joies, la *ṭarīqat* dont il est parlé dans le Divan, est la seule qui conduise à la pureté et au terme de laquelle on soit assuré de trouver la miséricorde divine. C'est là toute la mystique de Ḥāfiẓ: elle n'est faite que de son culte de l'amour et du vin, et des termes dans lesquels il l'exprime."[109] And

Notes on pp. 274–278

therein lies another characterisation of Ḥāfiẓ. Yet it cannot be denied that some of the *ghazals* are composed entirely in the spirit of mysticism – concessions to the prevailing fashion, experiments knowing only a 'today' and no 'tomorrow', because they did not come naturally to Ḥāfiẓ.

R. Lescot[110] singled out a few of the cycles which on the one side run parallel with the changes in political life or with the relationship to political personages, and on the other are connected with private affairs, such as, for example, 'The Poet in Disgrace', *Durr-Dāna*, 'The Pearl', viz. the Beloved (of either sex), this second cycle forming part of a larger group, 'The Distant Beloved' (sex again unspecified). The limits of the two latter cycles are less clearly defined than those of the others, but of their existence there is no doubt. Few verses have been preserved from the earliest years of Ḥāfiẓ' life (a *qiṭʿa* from the period of Masʿūd Īnjū dating from before 743/1343 is probably the earliest). Everywhere we find the familiar stock of motifs, the only variation being in the emphasis with regard to the predecessors and their mutual relationships in the course of the fifty years of Ḥāfiẓ' literary activity, as we have already seen in the sketch given of his 'mysticism'. From beginning to end he sings of wine, the joy of life, love and friendship, because the inconstancy and the vanity of the world can be forgotten only in these enjoyments. One should be content with little, a life of concentration is then all the sweeter. Pious verses alternate with scepticism, with heresies and even with slander. Ḥāfiẓ attacks the shaykhs, the Ṣūfīs of the Orders, hypocrites, zealots, preachers, professors at the Madrasas, the priesthood and the conniving police, for he observes and experiences in their conduct and deeds nothing but lies, hypocrisy, formalism, intrigues and stupidity. Ḥāfiẓ drinks wine and frees himself from the strict letter of the canon, but openly acknowledges his actions. As if the God of the Church were only there to mercifully forgive the sins He himself had preordained. This sounds like an echo of the thoughts of ʿOmar Khayyām, only with this difference, that Ḥāfiẓ does not stray into nihilism; for despite all he believes in God and honours the Koran – reason alone is not sufficient to explain the riddle of our existence, its beginning and its end. Is it not better to enjoy the pleasures of this world now than to resign oneself to the hope of unknown delights in the world to come? And his whole life long these questions never ceased to cause him anxiety and agitation. While it may appear that with increasing age he shows indications of piety and good resolutions, there are from the same period other poems immediately following on the first category that demonstrate the frailty of human intention and the transitory nature of piety. All in all, Ḥāfiẓ never ceases to proclaim *rindī*, a philosophy of life that had been developing ever since the second half of the 5th/11th century, largely thanks to the Qalandarī dervishes: under the fundamental assumption of 'goodness of heart' (*ṭību'l-qalb*), the *sharīʿa* (the canonical law of Islam) is only valid within certain limits. One may even disregard it altogether and drink wine as a symbol of contempt for the world and the law, even boasting about it[111] just as if a kind of drunkards' order had been established as a rival to the Ṣūfī Order, with a *pīr-i mughān*, 'chief of the Magi', at its head. In this sense

Ḥāfiẓ, like ʿAṭṭār, lets the *pīr* go straight from the mosque to the wine tavern, the Ṣūfī all at once detests the *khirqa*, 'cowl', and pawns it at the inn; mention is made of the ceremonial of a drunkards' order, etc. But what characterises Ḥāfiẓ is his mental lucidity and the disarming optimism that permeates all his work.[112]

In this connection it would not be right to overlook the opinion of a Soviet expert. I. S. Braginskiy[113] lays stress on Ḥāfiẓ' criticism of society and his revolt against social customs, for it is in just such a critical verse that we find the true meaning and the real object of a *ghazal*. He interprets Ḥāfiẓ' love poetry in similar fashion: real human love with a humane tendency is opposed to the recognised ideology. It is the longing for personal liberty, for life, for enthusiasm for every living thing; it is the release from compulsory service under temporal and spiritual rulers. Yet the bacchic poetry of Ḥāfiẓ is marked even more strongly by a spirit of rebellion; the 'vagrant' (*rind*) represents the personification of his imagined heroism. Thus Braginskiy.

There can be no doubt that in spite of all the mystical camouflage the ancients rightly scented the infidel in Ḥāfiẓ. This is attested by the anecdotes concerning the refusal of a ritual funeral and the threatened destruction of his grave under the Safavids. These accounts were certainly invented, though in essence founded on truth. No less significant is the euphemism of the assiduous Jāmī[114], who lived soon after, to the effect that it was impossible to ascertain to which Order Ḥāfiẓ did belong. But the extraordinary beauty of his verse had such a powerful effect that neither the Ṣūfīs nor the pious were willing to yield him up, and both begrudged him to the freethinkers. The customary interpretation, in conjunction with Safavid hypocrisy, made him out to be a perfect man of God and a saint, so that Sunnites and Shīʿites alike were able to accept him without having to expose themselves. They named him *lisānu'l-ghayb*, 'the tongue of secrets'[115], referring to his alleged mysticism. Others take this expression to mean that his verses are free from artificialities[116] or that his *dīvān*, like the sacred Koran, can be consulted to interprete the future.[117] But these explanations are more ingenious than plausible. Some of his verses are obviously duplicates of verses taken from the *dīvāns* of his forerunners or contemporaries.[118] Ḥāfiẓ did not invent his material but managed nonetheless within the limits imposed by the conventional stock to give expression to a criticism of the period and of society, as well as to his feelings and needs; he understood the art of panegyrism and did all this in the highest perfection of form with the media common to lyrical *ghazal* poetry. Every verse is a true masterpiece in miniature, from whatever viewpoint one regards it. His thoughts are aphoristically concentrated, elegantly pointed, his style fittingly embellished with tropes and figures[119], often – though not always – simple and natural, in fact a song containing numerous idioms taken from colloquial language, always however with charm and a personal touch[120] that reflects the poet's inner life and his relation to the world at large.[121] From olden times the opinion had taken root both in east and west that Ḥāfiẓ' *ghazal* was disconnected and that it lacked logical continuity. The first scholar to express a divergent view, namely his conviction that it possessed unity of thought, was Friedrich Veit (1908), followed later and more emphatically by H. H. Schaeder (1942). R. Lescot (1944)[122] came to the same conclusion: "Pour ne s'attacher qu'au sens logique du texte, la plupart des pièces du Divan apparaissent comme admirablement construites. Tout s'y enchaîne avec une perfection rarement égalée ... Tout poème de Ḥāfiẓ comporte donc un fil directeur qui commande le sens, amoureux, mystique ou bacchique, qu'il convient d'accorder à chacun des vers qui le composent. Lorsqu'on éprouve des difficultés à dégager cette idée maîtresse, c'est presque toujours que l'ordonnance de la pièce a été dérangée par un copiste négligent, ou encore que l'on commet quelque faute d'interprétation." Surely a more radical reversal in the estimation of a poet is hardly conceivable!

A. J. Arberry[123] also pleads the coherence of the *ghazals*, but in a manner different from that of R. Lescot. To him Ḥāfiẓ' *ghazal* is an artistic unity consisting of a combination of conventional subjects, in word and sound analogous to Iranian mosaics or miniatures. The mono-thematic principle of the *ghazal* reached the summit of perfection in Saʿdī. Ḥāfiẓ increased the number of themes to two or even more, gathering them it is true from the traditional inventory. As a young man he still followed in the wake of Saʿdī, giving as yet no utterance to his subsequent philosophy but standing firmly rooted in reality and not providing the subjects of Love and Wine with a subtle undertone of Ṣūfī allegory. Though the mature Ḥāfiẓ no longer adhered to the mono-thematic principle, this only meant a break with tradition and in no case destroyed the artistic unity of the poem – quite the contrary – for he wove the themes in and out of one another as in counterpoint and constructed 'thematic patterns', thereby faithfully following a course parallel to the masters of the Iranian miniature and mosaic. His philosophy is 'doctrine of unreason': ignoramus, ignorabimus. Events teach him that it is impossible to believe in a 'rational universe' and lead him to a pessimistic estimation of the individual purpose in life, an estimation which for that very reason is hedonistic only in appearance. Yet in spite of all he regards with a clear mind and even indifference the confused and irrational world in which Fate has placed him. – The third and last period in the poet's development is characterised, according to A. J. Arberry, by a growing austerity of style together with a tendency, that increased as time went on, to obscurity and allusions. G. M. Wickens[124] rightly points out that the western conception of the unity of a poem may not be confused with that of the east, and that in the *ghazal* the dramatic impetus is entirely absent. He amplifies Arberry's idea of counterpoint in the themes by introducing the image of radiation and demonstrates the astounding technique by which Ḥāfiẓ as it were brings into focus the rays issuing from the words and pictures within the framework of the selected themes. It may indeed be true that the theory of the focal themes is more in sympathy with the Iranian mentality than with the general European demand for logical combination and a dramatic climax in the poem. In this way too the fluctuating arrangement of the single verses in the *ghazal* may perhaps be explained. But a further elucidation will require more detailed research, not only in relation to Ḥāfiẓ but to all the main exponents of this form – an unusually promising and gratifying object for future scholars and investigators.

In conjunction with his study of Goethe's *West-östlicher Divan*, among other subjects, the late H. H. Schaeder[125], a brilliant scholar, made a thorough examination of the problems surrounding Ḥāfiẓ. He was presumably familiar with the opinion of H. Ritter quoted above, which is all the more reason why his point of view should not be ignored. He draws a distinction between firstly "verses in which Love, Wine and Spring are celebrated in words belonging to profane poetry, then those dealing with religious, ethical and mystical things wherein he introduces words from the technical language of theologians and mystics, and finally – and these are the most important and most characteristic of Ḥāfiẓ – those in which the profane and the sacred, terrestrial and celestial love, sensuality and spirit are intermingled. The question – which since Goethe is or should no longer be a question – amounts to whether the verses in the first and third categories are to be understood according to the then prevailing meaning of the words or are first to be 'translated' in such a way that by 'friend' the attainment of mystical unity is everywhere to be understood, and by 'wine', mystical knowledge. Seen in this light, the question answers itself." "The main thing now is to recognize that religious and especially mystical motifs were introduced by the poet in this apparently playful and ingenious manner for purposes of style and that in fact this was perhaps the conception of style that was dominant in him. It becomes dimmed and destroyed when the balance it has established between the two spheres, the sensual and the metaphysical, is disturbed in favour of one of the two elements."

H. ḤĀFIẒ' ENVIRONMENT IN SHIRAZ

Imād. The Satirists: ʿUbayd-i Zākānī, Bushāq, (later on) Qārī.
Echoes of Ḥāfiẓ in Transoxania: Nāṣir, ʿIṣmat

Ḥāfiẓ' environment was by no means tranquil; indeed Shiraz, his birthplace, experienced many a political revolution from which it suffered deeply. Especially in the latter half of the 8th/14th century there were often stormy periods which however never seriously endangered the rich cultural life and the ancient tradition. As already stated, these parts of the country were hardly affected by the Mongol invasion. Thus we find in Shiraz older and younger generations of eminent scholars, men of letters and poets, with whom Ḥāfiẓ must naturally have entertained more or less cordial relations. Not only Rukn-ābād and Muṣallā but also these ties of friendship account for Ḥāfiẓ' love towards his native town. He had admirers far and wide – everywhere where Persian culture and language had spread. Yet for his part too he knew how to appreciate the contemporary poets, not to mention the older masters such as Saʿdī. This is incontestably proved by the numerous motifs from their *dīvāns* used by Ḥāfiẓ in varying rhetorical combinations and the no less frequent 'parallels' (*istiqbāl*, Turkish *naẓīre*) to their *ghazals* (see p. 97).

He must of course also have had adversaries, rivals and enemies. Among them, so far as the testimony of some of the *tadhkiras* can be trusted, was Khvāja 'Imādu'd-dīn Faqīh of Kirman (d. 773/1371–2)[126], the head of the local monastery. He was a panegyrist of the Muẓaffarids, a writer of lyrics and in addition the author of five Ṣūfī *mathnavīs*, the first of which is the delightful *Maḥabbat-nāma-i ṣāḥib-dilān*, 'The Book of Love of the Pure in Heart', dating from 722/1322. His *ghazal* style is that of Khvājū, i.e. the same employed by Ḥāfiẓ, Salmān, and Kamāl. It is therefore not surprising that, in spite of the existing hostility – and this may be taken for granted in view of 'Imād's position as jurist and head of the monastery – Ḥāfiẓ' *dīvān* shows many points of resemblance with 'Imād. This does not necessarily imply a direct relationship between the latter and Ḥāfiẓ, for the possibility of common sources – Salmān, Kamāl and others – would be sufficient explanation.

In the case of Khvāja Niẓāmu'd-dīn 'Ubaydu'llāh, in brief 'Ubayd-i Zākānī of Qazvīn, a scion of a distinguished family of Arab descent, it is true that there is no record of his having been in any way associated with Ḥāfiẓ, but the fact that a man of his individuality (d. 772/1371) lived and worked for a time at the same court as Ḥāfiẓ in Shiraz surely justifies such an assumption. Probably Ḥāfiẓ was even influenced by the satirical tone of Zākānī.[127] For the latter's attitude was just the reverse of Ḥāfiẓ' serious world of thought. It must also be remarked that if there is any one in Persian literature who can really be termed a satirist, then it is he – the Iranian P. Aretino. Ḥāfiẓ too was critical, but only of those of the same class at himself, whereas Zākānī – unlike the sensitive lyric poet – persecuted everyone by giving free play to mockery and ridicule, sometimes even venturing as far as crudeness and obscenity. Notwithstanding that, however, works such as *Akhlāqu'l-ashrāf*, 'Ethics of Nobles', and others, however modest their proportions, place their author in the foremost ranks. Their high artistic value is incontestable and from both sociological and folkloristic points of view they are unparalleled. Verses in Arabic testify to Zākānī's thorough education. As well as a number of frolicsome anecdotes in Persian and Arabic he wrote more serious things, e.g. *'Ushshāq-nāma*, 'The Book of Lovers', and panegyrical *qaṣīdas*. *'Ushshāq-nāma* is a *mathnavī* containing more than 700 couplets with *ghazal* insertions (see p. 213). It dates from the year 751/1350–51. It is evidently inspired by the *mathnavī* of the same name by 'Irāqī (p. 255), but in contrast to the latter is written in a mundane mood: we find the customary amorous yearning, finally the visit of the Beloved to the Lover (the poet), separation and thenceforth only yearning for evermore. But the burden of his works lies in his unequivocal censure of the social order. In the 'Ethics of Nobles' he compares the 'ancient' moral ideals with morality as it really was. Jokes, humour, sarcasm and censure are the instruments he uses. Minute, but pithy are the *Ta'rīfāt*, 'Definitions', where with a single appropriate word or in a short phrase he lays his finger on the characteristic shortcomings of each class. As far as up-to-dateness and aesthetic qualities are concerned the verse and prose of Zākānī have not suffered from the ravages of time. They are extremely valuable poetical documents for obtaining a closer acquaintance with the Iran of that period. Like Ḥāfiẓ he envelops the precarious passages in Ṣūfī terminology. How deeply he was rooted in the minds of the people is evident from his semi-satirical, semi-comical miniature epic poem *Mūsh u gurba*, 'Mouse and Cat', that probably had a highly political significance.[128] This work is still being widely read in primitive lithographs today. – Less attention has been accorded to his lyric poetry which, though comparatively small in bulk (*qaṣīdas*, *ghazals* and comic poems – in all about 3500 couplets), are most fascinating and in surprising contrast to the majority of Zākānī's works. These poems are worthy of attention not only on their own account but also because here the author obviously bridges the gap between Saʿdī and Ḥāfiẓ and introduces new elements into the *ghazal* that certainly influences his younger contemporary, who moved in the same court circle.[129] A. J. Arberry shows that Ḥāfiẓ' 'doctrine of unreason' (see p. 270) is to be found already fully developed in Zākānī, likewise his 'carpe diem' and evidently also his satirical innuendoes. Zākānī's *ghazals* do not as a rule exceed seven distichs in length.[130]

One might be inclined to think that the element of ridicule could play no part in the works of Busḥāq al-Aṭʿima, 'Foods', whose real name was Fakhru'd-dīn Aḥmad Ḥallāj, 'wool-carder', a somewhat younger contemporary (d. 827/1424 or 830/1427 or 860/1456) of Zākānī's and likewise from Shiraz. At a superficial glance he is no more than a simple humorist, whose peculiarity consists in including one or another term from the rich culinary vocabulary of Iran into each of his verses, no matter what literary form he happens to be engaged in. Thus the whole of his *dīvān* is devoted to the subject of food – the Jos. de Berchoux of Iran.[131] Though his *dīvān* was published several times, it was received so far as we know with a minimum of interest. Food and humour were not considered worthy to dwell under the roof of Persian literature. Yet I doubt whether Busḥāq was guided by gastronomy alone. In the first place his work is a protest against the colourless species of Persian poetry prevalent at the time and which our poet ridiculed in his parodies on the leading poets. But its significance lies deeper: Busḥāq makes fun of the lofty character of the classical literature together with the high-flown flattery of the rulers and the never-ending transcendental meditation.[132]

There is still a third member of this group, namely Niẓāmu'd-dīn Maḥmūd Qārī of Yazd, who lived during the second half of the 9th/15th century[133], and whose works may be described as a decoction from Busḥāq. The fact that his *dīvān* is on the subject of clothes and not of food is immaterial. For the rest, excepting the question of his poetical talent, the foregoing may be repeated. He enhances the comic effect, as does Busḥāq, by introducing dialect here and there (*fahlaviyyāt, shīrāziyyāt*). Is it possible that political factors played a part in such cases?

In substance, though not in style, a resemblance to Ḥāfiẓ can be found in his contemporaries Nāṣir (d. 779/1377–8), a friend of Salmān Sāvajī, and Khvāja 'Iṣmat (d. 829/1425–6 or 840/1436–7), both of whom came from Bukhara. Their bold protests prove that the voice of Ḥāfiẓ did not fade away into the void, in as much as it is not to be regarded as an expression of the spirit of the times. 'Iṣmat, one of the panegyrists of Tīmūr and court poet of Sulṭān Khalīl, beseeches God at the end of his life for forgiveness for the poetry he has written. In the *ghazal* he follows in the train of Amīr Khusrau.

NOTES

1. The description of this cataclysm is very vividly given in *Istoriya Irana* (B II), 175–192, excellent also in other respects.
2. Cf. J. A. Boyle, 'The Death of the Last 'Abbasid Caliph: a Contemporary Muslim Account', *Journal of Semitic Studies*, 6/2 (1961), 145–161.
3. Spuler, *Die Mongolen in Iran*², 59.
4. *Sabk*, 3, 168.
5. Bertel's, *Navoyi*, 39.
6. Ivanow, *Ocherk*, 51, 54; Petrushevskiy, *K voprosu* (B II).
7. Spuler, *Die Mongolen in Iran*², 310 *et seq.*; Barthold-Hinz (B II), *Die pers. Inschrift*, 257, 247.
8. Barthold, *Shu'ūb.*, 256.
9. 'the moral dichotomy of the time': Minorsky, *Iran*, 190 (B II).
10. On the decline cf. M. Murtaḍavī's quotation from M. Qazvīnī in *NDAT*, 13 (1340), 31–2.
11. 'Uṭārid, 'Maẓāhir' (B VIa), 14 *et seq.*, though his expositions are not altogether satisfactory, cf. Ritter, *Oriens*, 5, 193.
12. Special bibliography: Krïmskiy, 3, 416–69.
13. Bahār, *Sabk*, 3, 161 (derived from an old *risāla*) and Shiblī, 2, 34. Otherwise and more detailed S. Nafīsī in his edition of the *Dīvān-i Anvarī*, 28* below. Regarding his *takhalluṣ* see Qazvīnī's foreword to Shams-i Qays' *al-Mu'jam* (B IV), p. 'v' *et seq.*
14. Garakānī, ed. *Gulistān* (Bibl. *s.v.* 'Sa'dī') p. 'jḥ', as against H. Massé.
15. Recently (1959) the indeed critical edition of the *Gulistān* made by R. M. Aliyev and the editions by M. 'A. Furūghī, cf. our Bibl. *s.v.* 'Sa'dī'.
16. 'Abb. Iqbāl, *Zamān-i tavallud*, 632.
17. Cf. also Juvaynī, *Jahāngushāy*, ed. M. Qazvīnī (B VIb), Vol. I, p. LIII. Cf. A. Ye. Bertel's, *Nasir-i Khosrov*, 159_{44}, on the fondness for anecdotes dealing with meetings between great contemporaries.
18. Cf. S. Nafīsī, 'Ta'rīkh-i durust' (Bibl.). Similarly *Arm.*, 17, 122–3: Friday (wrong!) 10th Shavvāl 691/24 September 1292. Tradition gives also other dates within the period 690–4/1291–95.
19. One third of the *Gulistān*, see R. M. Aliyev, 'Gulistan', *UZIV*, 19, 140.
20. *Sa'di*, 318; idem, *Bustan* (transl.), p. VIII.
21. But occasionally also differently, see Krïmskiy, 3, 197.
22. *Bustan* (transl.), p. XIX *et seq.*
23. Bibl. *s.v.* 'Sharīf', *Pand-nāma-i Anūshīrvān*'.
24. Furūghī, ed. *Ghazaliyyāt-i Sa'dī*, Preface, 2.
25. *LHP*, 2, 533.

26. On the influence of Mutanabbī see Bausani, *Storia* (B v), 412 according to H. A. Maḥfūẓ, *Mutanabbī va Sa'dī*, Tehran 1336.
27. *Ḥayāt-i Sa'dī*, 96 *et seq.*
28. 'Hâcû', *İA*, 5, 400.
29. *Baḥth* (B VIa), 186. Similarly A. M. Mirzoyev, *Rūdakī*, 57 (Russian 52); *ibid.*, 57–61 (Russian 53–7), a comprehensive analysis of the *ghazals* of Sa'dī from a formal viewpoint.
30. Cf. *Arm.*, 19, 421.
31. According to an old list of dates of the death of several poets, *Arm.*, 17, 122–23: 6 Shavvāl 728/14 August 1328.
32. "... the fact that an Agha Khan interested himself in the publication of the *Gulshan-i rāz* accentuates the problem whether Shabistarī (if he was indeed the author of these tracts) may not himself have had Ismā'īlī leanings" (Arberry, *Class. Pers. Lit.*, 304 *et seq.*); cf. W. Ivanow, *Ismaili Lit.* (B III), 190.
33. Cf. Man. Murtaḍavī, *Taṣavvuf dar daura-i Īl-Khānān* (B III), 306 *et seq.*
34. Baḥār, *Baḥth*, 184.
35. 'Abb. Iqbāl, 'Dhayl-i Sayru'l-'ibād ila'l-ma'ād az Ḥakīm Auḥadu'd-dīn Ṭabīb-i Rāzī', *MDAT*, 2 (1334), 8: *Miṣbāḥ* is said to be a work by Muḥ. b. Īl-Ṭughān Bardasīrī and only attributed to Auḥadī-i Kirmānī.
36. Bertel's, *Ocherk*, 63.
37. Idem, *Fuḍūlī*, 60.
38. Ritter, *Philol.*, 9, 60.
39. Idem, *Philol.*, 7, 95.
40. Thus 'Bārādīn' (*q.v.*), 181 and 183; erroneously Bertel's, *Ocherk*, 63; similarly *Destūr-nāma*, ed. Bertel's (Bibl. *s.v.* 'Nizārī'), 43 and Durrī, *Ba'ze ma'lumot* (*q.v.*), 140 etc.: Na'īmu'd-dīn b. Jamālu'd-dīn Nizārī.
41. His tomb was re-erected in 1344/1925, but when later the graveyard was closed down the tomb was left to decay: *Sukhan*, 14 (1343), 850–1.
42. The explanation given later that he was thin, viz. *nizār*, was due to ignorance.
43. The *qaṣīdas* are by no means numerous so far as can be judged from the *Kulliyyāt*, described by Bertel's in the *Destūr-nāma*, 37.
44. See under Bertel's, B VIa
45. Ed. Leiden 231, 24; 233, 7 *et seq.*; *Destūr-nāme*, 44 *et seq.*
46. *Bahāristān*, ed. Schlechta-Wssehrd, p. 100 (Persian) and p. 116 (transl.).
47. Wahid, *Khusrau*, 207.
48. Krïmskiy, 3, 84.
49. Bertel's, 'Lit. ... v Sr. Az.' (D IIa) 2012. – *SV*, 1957/6, 149a. Bertel's allows the possibility of a common source, i.e. the *ghazal* of Caliph Yazīd. *
50. Shiblī, 2, 104 *et seq.*
51. Wahid, *Khusrau*, 199; Habib, *Khusrau*, 76.
52. See Bibl. *s.v.* 'Baqoyev'. – A. L. Srivastava, 'Historicity of Devalrani-Khizr-Khan', *Isl. Cult.*, 30 (1956), 24–30: "substantially true" and "rejecting it as a piece of poetic fancy".
53. *i'jāz*, 'inimitability of the language of the Koran, its uniqueness' (a rhetorical term).
54. Wahid, *Khusrau*, 202.
55. *Ibid.*, 214. See above, Mahsatī, p. 199, and Bert., IPTL, 520.
56. *Tuḥfa-i Sāmī*, ed. Vaḥīd Dastgirdī, 117.
57. *Ocherk*, 41; idem, *Navoyi i Nizami*, 81.
58. Bahār, *Bāz-gasht* (B VIa), 446.
59. Shiblī, 2, 97.
60. 753: *LHP*, 3, 223; 762: Nafīsī in Köprülü, 'Hâcû', *İA*, 5, 37b.
61. Ḥāfiẓ imitates some of Khvājū's *ghazals*, cf. Yār-Shāṭir, *Shi'r*, 103.

62. Köprülü, *ibid.*, 40a.
63. Cf. above, p. 163.
64. *GIPh*, 2, 249.
65. A different opinion is held by Mullojonovi Shakhristonī (Bibl.), who depicts Ibn-i Yamīn as a progressive poet of even materialistic views (p. 137) and anti-feudal leanings (*ibid.*, and p. 139). He also mentions the high esteem in which he held women (p. 138) and his attitude towards the poor (p. 139; cf. also Daulatshāh 275, 17), etc. His *dīvān* thus provides us with most valuable documentary evidence of the social and historical conditions of his period (pp. 135, 139). The author also draws attention to a hitherto unnoticed Leningrad MS of the *dīvān* dating from 757/1356 (Dorn 403) containing 16,120 verses, although even this cannot embrace everything written by Ibn-i Yamīn in the course of his long life.
66. Cf. pp. 176, 194, 281, and the list in *Arm.*, 11, 892 *et seq.*
67. *LHP*, 3, 271. Shiblī, 2, 162. A great and organic function must be attached to this figure in the works of Ḥāfiẓ, see footnote 119 below.
68. According to 'Tadhkira-i maykhāna', *RK*, 4/2 (1340), 159 l. 4, priority must be given to Ḥāfiẓ.
69. Krïmskiy, 3, 99.
70. Idem, 3, 106.
71. Idem, 3, 106 *et seq.* and footnote.
72. Braginskiy, *Zum Studium des Schaffens Kamol Hudshandis*, 6.
73. Īraj Afshār in his comprehensive and thorough criticism of Daulat-ābādī's edition of the *dīvān*, *Rāhnamā* 2/1 (1338), 101. These and other lines of Afshār's compel one to reflect on how rash the literary historians of Iran can be in practice when editing the monuments of classical literature.
74. Shiblī, 5, 116.
75. Jāmī (see above, note 46), 101, 116 resp.
76. Ḥikmat's translation of *LHP*, 3, 348₃.
77. Sūdī, *Sharḥ-i Ḥāfiẓ*, ed. Būlāq, 3, 84.
78. Bertel's, 'Lit. .... v Sr. Az.' (D IIa), 217.
79. I. S. Braginskiy, *Zum Studium*, 6; idem, *K izucheniyu*, 86.
80. Īr. Afshār, *loc. cit.*, 103.
81. Antol.[1], 14; I. S. Braginskiy, *Iz istorii* (D IIa), 363a, and Sh. Husayn-zoda in the foreword to the Muntakhabot (B VIb).
82. A series of ancient proverbs is quoted by Īr. Afshār, *loc. cit.*, 104 *et seq.*, who draws special attention to the peculiar nature of Kamāl's language and recommends it for thorough study, though otherwise he shows no great enthusiasm for this poet (*ibid.*).
83. *Zum Studium*, 7.
84. Antol.[1], 16.
85. I. S. Braginskiy, *Iz istorii* (D IIa), 365.
86. Bertel's, 'Lit. ... v Sr. Az.' (D IIa) 201, 217; Mu'īn, *Ḥāfiẓ*, 211 *et seq.*
87. 'Aynī, *Namūna* (D IIa), 80, No. 31; Braginskiy, *Ocherki* (D IIa), 251.
88. Ḥikmat's transl. of *LHP*, 3, 350 footnote; Ghanī, *Baḥth*, 1, 356.
89. 'A. A. Ḥikmat (see Bibl.) draws our attention to two MSS which would appear to be of fundamental importance for research on Ḥāfiẓ. Very briefly, the main points are as follows: (1) from a *majmū'a*, composed by the famous Maulānā Jalālu'd-dīn Muḥ. b. As'ad aṣ-Ṣiddīqī ad-Davvānī (830–908/1426–1502, see our Index): a certain Shaykh Maḥmūd ('Aṭṭār) is said to have been Ḥāfiẓ' Ṣūfī mentor; Ḥāfiẓ' poetry should be understood in a Ṣūfī sense; one hundred years after his death his *dīvān* already enjoyed popularity in all the countries that fell within the sphere of Iranian culture; (2) from *Laṭā'if-i Ashraf*, in which Shaykh Niẓāmu'd-dīn Gharīb Yamanī faithfully wrote down accounts of the travels and axioms of his *murshid*, the Sayyid Ashrafu'd-dīn Jahāngīr as-Simnānī (d. 808/1405–6, being thus the earliest source on Ḥāfiẓ); their meeting with the poet took place in

Shiraz, probably in the year 782/1380–1; Ḥāfiẓ belonged to the Uvaysiyya Order, he had Shaykh Qivāmu'd-dīn 'Abdu'llāh as *pīr* ('A. A. Ḥikmat hereby corrects an obvious error on the part of the author) and already during his lifetime bore the honorary name of *lisānu'l-ghayb*; his death took place in 792/1389–90. There are a great many of the poet's verses scattered about in the MS. – According to the *Tadhkira-i Maykada* Ḥāfiẓ was 25 years old in 750/1349–50, and would thus have been born in 725/1324–5.

90. See Bibl. *s.v.* 'Khalkhālī etc.,' and *s.v.* 'Ḥāfiẓ'.

91. Bibl. under the actual names.

92. A very important step forwards is Professor P. N. Khānlarī's recently published edition of a MS dating from 813–14/1410–12 (thus 22 or 23 years after the poet's death!), containing 152 *ghazals* in an excellent text, cf. idem, 'Chand nukta dar taṣḥīḥ-i dīvān-i Ḥāfiẓ', 1337, offprint from *Yaghmā*. On the basis of this extensive and largely new material, Professor Khānlarī is now engaged in preparing a really critical edition.

93. Mu'īn, *Ḥāfiẓ*, 83; Ghanī, *Baḥth*, 1, 354; Arberry, *Ḥāfiẓ* (both editions), 2; idem, *CPL*, 1958, 330, yet "most probably" 1326.

94. Qazvīnī, *NDAT*, 2, 41 *et seq.*

95. Krïmskïy, *Khafïz*, 31.

96. Bertel's, 'Lit. ... v Sr. Az.' (D IIa), 201.

97. *An Analysis*, 627з.

98. Lescot, *Hafiz*, 58 (= 2 offprint); Ghanī, *Baḥth*, 1, 301.

99. Cf. Muḥ. Ja'far Maḥjūb: 'Sāqī-nāma – Mughannī-nāma', *Sukhan*, 11/1 (1339), 67–79 and above, footnote 68.

100. Bibl. *s.v.* 'Ḥāfiẓ'.

101. Krïms'kïy, *Khafïz*, 13 *et seq.*, 125 *et seq.*, 137; Qazvīnī, *Bīst Maqāla* (B VIa), 2, 73 *et seq.*

102. Bibl.: *s.v.* 'Hūman, *Ḥāfiẓ*'; *s.v.* 'Ghanī, *Baḥth*' (B VIa), 1; *s.v.* 'Stolz, *Die seel. Entwicklung*'; *s.v.* Schaeder, *Lässt sich...?*

103. Bibl. Wilberforce Clarke *s.v.* 'Ḥāfiẓ'; *s.v.* 'Merx' (B III).

104. Lescot, 'Hafiz', 59 (= 3 offprint).

105. Roemer, 'Probleme', 133 (= 13 offprint).

106. *OLZ*, 1941, 249: review of R. A. Nicholson's *The Mathnawí* (Bibl. *s.v.* 'Jalālu'd-dīn Rūmī').

107. *Baḥth* (B VIa), 186.

108. Braginskiy, *Khafiz, Pjat'desyat gazeley* (1949; Bibl. *s.v.* Ḥāfiẓ), 40

109. Lescot, 'Hafiz', 96 *et seq.* (= 40 *et seq.* offprint).

110. *Ibid.*, 67 (= 11 offprint), 73 (= 17 offprint), etc.

111. *Yādgār*, 2/7, 78; Ritter, 'Ḥāfiẓ', *İA*, 5, 70a; Shiblī, 5, 43 *et seq.*; *Sabk*, 3, 80; recently H. Ritter, *Philologika*, XV: "Aṭṭār, *Der Dīwān*'; *Oriens*, XII (1960), 14 *et seq.* ('Qalandarīyāt').

112. Ritter, *İA*, *loc. cit.*; similarly Shiblī, 2, 188 line 8 from under.

113. Criticism of society: antol. (D IIa) 15 *et seq.*; Braginskiy, *Khafiz* (see above, note 108), 38: "the rebellious lyric poet"; likewise V. V. Kotetishvili, 'K voprosu poezii Khafeze' (Georgian with summary in Russian), *Trudī Tbilisskogo univ.*, 99 (1962), 101–126; The Protest Function of the Ghazal in the 14th century: Braginskiy, *op. cit.*, 47.

114. Jāmī: Lescot, 'Hafiz', 97 (= 41 offprint).

115. The earliest evidence is given by Maykhāna (see above, footnote 68), 162, where a great deal of new material on Ḥāfiẓ is to be found.

116. Jāmī, *Bahāristān* (see above, note 46), 100, 116 resp.

117. Schaeder, *Goethe*, 120. – 'Fāl-i Ḥāfiẓ', e.g. *Sukhan*, 6/11 (1334), 1045.

118. List of the poets quoted or imitated by Ḥāfiẓ: A. J. Arberry, *CPL*, 352.

119. For details see M. Murtaḍavī, *Īhām* (*q.v.*).

120. Shiblī, 2, 230; Yār-Shāṭir, *Shi'r*, 127.

121. To translate Ḥāfiẓ into a foreign language is an exceptionally difficult task. On the translations of Ḥāfiẓ into English and the problems arising therefrom: A. J. Arberry, *loc. cit.*, 332–355, and also the same author's *Fifty Poems of Ḥāfiẓ*, 1953, 33 *et seq.* Indeed, a translator finds himself placed before more or less similar problems in practically the whole of Persian literature.
122. Veit, *Platen*, 4, 149; Schaeder, 'Lässt sich...?', 209 *et seq.* Lescot, 'Hafiz', 61 (= 5 offprint).
123. 'Orient Pearls', 704 *et seq.*; idem, *Ḥāfiẓ*, 29 *et seq.*
124. 'The Pers. Conception', 239 *et seq.*
125. 'Lässt sich...?', 204; idem, *Goethe*, 120. Most recent and fundamental: Wolfg. Lentz, *Goethes Noten ... zum W.-Östl. Divan (q.v.)*.
126. This is refuted in *Maykhāna* (see above, footnote 68), 163: it was not 'Imād Faqīh who was hostilely disposed towards Ḥāfiẓ but the shaykh Zaynu'd-dīn 'Alī Galāh Shīrāzī (d. 780/1378–9).
127. Mu'īn, *Ḥāfiẓ*, 203.
128. Thus according to the view of my late lamented friend R. Šálek. So also Arberry, *CPL*, 296 *et seq.* 'A. Iqbāl is thinking of the Muẓaffarid Mubārizu'd-dīn (see p. 264), a perfidious and cruel tyrant, but to outward appearances an irreproachable church-goer. On the genealogy of the subject cf. M. Mīnuvī, *Qiṣṣa-i mūsh u gurba* (q.v.).
129. *CPL*, 297.
130. Cf. p. 95. An analysis of the work of the poet: M. Rajabov, *Mirovozzreniye* (*q.v.*), summarized *ibid.*, 108–9.
131. On culinary poetry after the Baghdad caliphate see Krïmskiy, 3, 109 *et seq.* and the appropriate footnotes.
132. Likewise A. Mirzoyev, *Sayyido Nasafi* (Russian, D 11a), 120.
133. Thus Ghanī (*q.v.*), 1, 'mt'. According to *LHP*, 3, 352 *et seq.*, round about 866/1461 still alive; according to Ethé, 304, and A. Khayyāmpūr, *Farhang*, 462, he died in 993/1585!

IX. TĪMŪR AND HIS SUCCESSORS

A. CULTURAL AND LITERARY LIFE

A new scourge for the country now appears on the scene in the person of the formidable warrior Tīmūr (b. 736/1336; in power 771–807/1370–1405). He was a Moslem who, solely for political reasons, feigned subservience to the theologians and Ṣūfī Shaykhs. It may have been with Tīmūr in mind that Ḥāfiẓ coined the phrase *ṣūfī-i dajjāl-fi'l-i mulḥid-shakl*, 'Ṣūfī with the deeds of the anti-Christ and in the shape of an infidel'[1], for in bestial cruelty Tīmūr even managed to outdo the Mongols of unhappy memory. He spoke Turkish and Mongolian, knew Persian but no Arabic. On his military campaigns he had Persian books read aloud to him, but for the rest he must be regarded as a primitive being. It would be impossible to explain his behaviour otherwise than by the assumption that he succeeded in winning over the population of Transoxania because his aims and means suited it: Transoxania most probably sanctioned his attempts to bring about the political unification of a dismembered Iran mainly by means of plundering expeditions. While the southern regions had on the whole been spared the Mongol storm, the whole of Iran now fell a prey to Tīmūr. All the regional dynasties into which post-Īl-Khān Persia had been split up were now swept away. Whether or not they deserved credit for promoting culture, either in their own kingdoms or in Iran as a whole, was immaterial. The old country of the Samanids once again came to the fore, this time with Samarkand, the town so dear to the Amīr, as metropolis. There too the gravitational centre of cultural activity was transferred – for the most part automatically but in some cases by force, such as when Tīmūr ordered craftsmen and artists from Fars and Iraq to settle there – an ancient oriental custom of which the Sasanians had already made use.[2] The new glory of Samarkand and Bukhara is echoed in the well-known verse of Ḥāfiẓ':

Notes on pp. 289–290

'f that unkindly Shiraz Turk would take my heart within her hand
I'd give Bukhara for the mole upon her cheek, or Samarkand!
(trans. E. G. Browne)

Samarkand also flourished under the progressive rule of Ulugh-beg, a scholar on the throne (850–3/1447–9). As governor of Turkestan he had already done much to further the development of the town. Besides encouraging the fine arts, he turned his attention to astronomy and mathematics, these being independent of religion and nationality. But his success was only temporary; ultimately the winner turned out to be Khvāja Aḥrār "who stood at the head of the Central Asian dervishes and of the religious opposition to Ulugh-beg and his system of government".[3] At this time too we witness the rise of Herat, for the clerical Sulṭān Shāh-rukh (807–50/1405–47), who after a brief struggle became the successor to Tīmūr and was both politically and culturally a mediocre personality, had made the town his residence. Under Sulṭān Ḥusayn Bāyqarā (872–911/1468–1506) Herat became in fact the centre of the newly-revived Persian culture, although after the death of Shāh-rukh, who had held together Tīmūr's heritage as well as he could, Iran disintegrated altogether. In the east the Timurids were quarrelling among themselves, a direct consequence of the curious policy of Shāh-rukh that consisted of dividing the fiefs among his sons and grandsons. In the west there appeared the Turkoman Qara-Qoyunlu, 'Those of the Black Sheep' (totem), who were soon succeeded by a related tribe, the Aq-Qoyunlu, 'Those of the White Sheep'. The situation can now be described as a struggle between separatist feudal forces against any progressive attempt to assemble the various districts into one great, even though feudal, domain. The rulers certainly strove to uphold their military authority, but they did not possess Tīmūr's genius and energy, although it is true that the latter was more of a warrior and conqueror than the founder of a state. The temporary cessation of hostilities increased their riches at the expense of the agricultural and artisan classes, who are always the ones to suffer in peace as well as in war. The small land-owners groaned under the taxes levied by the central government as well as under the tributes and dues imposed by their feudal lords. Together with the manual workers they were obliged to do forced labour on the building of canals, fortifications, courts, mosques, etc. None of these burdens weighed on the large property owners, in particular the numerous Timurid families. Neither did they hit the members of the court, the Sayyids or the higher ranks of the priesthood, with the result that these classes alone were able to enjoy the whole of the common revenue and the power. Religious ferment can only serve to cloak the dissatisfaction and misery of the people – it is the fitting form of revolt on the part of the unpropertied against the propertied and of the oppressed against the oppressors. But it must be admitted that some of the Timurids did not spend their wealth on pleasure only but that they also devoted it to cultural objects. This action reached its culmination in the Herat of Ḥusayn.[4] We refer to the minor forms of art, particularly bibliophilism, to the Herat school of poets represented by the great Jāmī (d. 898/1492) and Ḥusayn's famous vizier, the noble philanthropist, maecenas and patron of every form of beauty, Mīr 'Alī-Shīr Navā'ī (d. 906/1501), though he did not always see eye to eye with his master. Jāmī's brilliance lies in the field of Persian, Navā'ī – a man supremely conscious of his Turkish origin – shone in that of the Chaghatay language ('ancient Uzbek')[5], the importance of which, thanks to the patronage of the cultured Chaghatay nobility, was on the increase.[6] Even the court of Shiraz had its Turkish poets. We must not omit to mention one of the most cultured bibliophiles, namely Bāysunghur (d. 837/1433), the son of Shāh-rukh, because it was under his patronage that, among other things, the vulgata of the *Shāh-nāma* was produced (Muḥ. Qazvīnī[7] however is doubtful about this). Now that the development of culture in Herat began to take a different course from that in Samarkand, the exact sciences became neglected. As far as the humanities are concerned, mention should be made of the histories written by such men as Ḥāfiẓ-i Abrū, 'Abdu'r-Razzāq Samarqandī, Mīrkhvānd, Khvāndamīr and others. It is thanks to the Timurids that Persian culture and the Persian language gained a still firmer footing in India as a consequence of the founding of the Mogul empire, which was established in Delhi by the Timurid Bābur (932–7/1525–30), though only after the extinction of the dynasty in the homeland. This was the same Bābur who made a lasting name for himself as a Chaghatay writer by his memoirs. He was succeeded by a line of rulers all of whom bore a similar attitude towards the spirit of Iranian culture.

The 15th century, the age of the Timurids, gives no great cause for satisfaction if one considers the disproportion between the quantity of literary works that appeared and their quality. It is hardly possible to assume that in such stormy and restless times the wounds inflicted by the Mongols and renewed by Tīmūr would heal rapidly. The historiography of this epoch is not to be compared with the masterpieces of the previous century and the poetry degenerates into the decadent cult of an affected artificiality. The growing importance of the middle class of the population explains why the action radius and the range of the poetry did not become narrowed down to the point of exclusiveness but that, on the contrary, an active and passive participation in the art of poetry is to be witnessed among all classes, with the exception of the agricultural population. In place of the panegyric *qaṣīda* which had faded away at the same time as the last remnants of the Iranian feudal nobility – destroyed by the Mongol catastrophe – there now appears the philosophical *qaṣīda* which, though already introduced by Nāṣir-i Khusrau (see p. 189), had had but little success with the following generations on account of his Ismā'īlitic way of thinking. The meditative *qaṣīda* was later adopted by the brilliant poet Khāqānī (see p. 207) whose art had just then reached a dazzling height. The Timurid era was one of literary gourmets in high social positions who set more store by a refined artificiality than by eulogism. The poets in Herat, Ahlī of Shiraz (d. 942/1535–6) for instance, were able to continue on the lines of the *qaṣīda-i maṣnū'* of Salmān Sāvajī (d. 778/1376, see p. 261), but they surpassed the latter in breakneck acrobatic tricks. Vahmī's *qaṣīda* in honour of the marriage of the Indian prince Dārā Shikūh (1043/1633–4) proves that, in the era of the Great Moguls too, linguistical jugglery was not despised.

Compared with the philosophical *qaṣīda* the content of these poems became a prey to the technique. In fact this period is chiefly characterised by a disregard of the substance in favour of the form. *Ghazals*, strictly limited as to theme, were composed almost according to prescription; chronograms (*taʾrīkh*) and letter- or word-riddles (*muʿammā*, logogriphs) enjoyed great popularity and were cultivated extensively, the two latter being held in as high esteem as though they belonged to the most valuable species of poetry. In face of such rivals the *qaṣīda* was obliged to be content with a humbler place in every *dīvān*.

The Soviet scholar I. Braginskiy[8] rejects the theory that the importance of the panegyric *qaṣīda* diminished from the Mongol period onwards because the Mongol lords did not understand the language, while on the other hand that of the *ghazal* increased. He rejects this explanation as being merely conjunctural and for the rest points to a figure like Salmān Sāvajī whose work contradicts the foregoing hypothesis. He considers the root of this change to lie in the protest of the urban classes, whose special instrument he considers to have been the *ghazal*. It was hard for the population of the towns to endure the violent seizure by the rulers of their private property and produce, for it was just this that was bound to hamper the most industrious and culturally most highstanding section of mediaeval society in its development. Freedom in the management of their affairs, economic independence, the limitation of feudal arbitrariness – these were the most pressing demands in the towns. Ideologically this protestation was given expression in the cult of freedom, personal autonomy, the proclamation of the right to happiness in life, and free thinking. All this was expressed in the *ghazal* by such paragons as Ḥāfiẓ, Kamāl of Khujand, Nāṣir of Bukhara and others as the 'educated' form of protest, and indeed expressed so well that the motifs of protestation and humanism grew into an intrinsic part of the *ghazal* and gradually came to form the standard pattern. Thus Braginskiy.

A. Mirzoyev calls attention to a very important feature of the *ghazal* at that time by demonstrating that the concrete treatment of the contents in Bināʾī's *ghazal* poetry (p. 497) leads to an enhanced coherence of the verses in the poem as a whole. This is also one of the distinctive features of Jāmī, Navāʾī ('Fānī') etc. and particularly of Sayfī Bukhārāʾī. In the opinion of the eminent Tajik critic, who shows that the splitting up of the content of the *ghazal* is one of the characteristics of the development of this form[9], the increasing coherence may not be regarded as a sign of decadence in the lyricism of the *ghazal*. A proof of this is that the philosophical, ethical, meditative and anti-feudal thematic material experiences a parallel enrichment, thus the *ghazal* undergoes a further development that is continued in the works of important poets of the 16th and 17th centuries, among them being Sayyid Nasafī (see p. 509).[10]

Occasionally we find attempts being made to compose several *dīvāns*, since a single one was not considered sufficient. The romantic epic, fairly characteristic of this epoch, is also saturated with superfluous affectation. Kātibī Turshīzī (d. 838–9/1434–6) composed a *mathnavī Dah bāb*, 'Ten Chapters', also called *Tajnīsāt*, 'Homonyms', throughout which the rhymes end in homonyms; another *mathnavī* by the same poet can be read in two metres at the same time. A hundred years later Ahlī of Shiraz even surpasses him (see p. 281).

Accordingly we see an unusual increase in the formal elements, presumably for the purpose of concealing lack of originality and poverty of thought. Conventionality predominates both in the application of subjective standards to everything and in the purpose pursued. To this it may be added that in times of terror a tendency towards mysticism is nothing new in Persian literature. What is now new is a deeper absorption in allegory, which dominates both lyric poetry and the romantic epic. These allegories however are not bold Ṣūfī conceptions but pantheistic ideas brought down to the level of the orthodox Sunna or Shī'a.

Although ancient literary tradition is still held in high honour, the *Khamsa* of an Amīr Khusrau is preferred to that of Niẓāmī. Here again is an example of the degeneration of thought and of the decadent taste of the period, which was incapable of rightly comprehending the art of Niẓāmī, this unique master, and his philosophical and social opinions. The influence of the Indian poet is especially evident in short versified tales of which, in point of fact, he was the creator. His *ghazal* proved attractive to a large number of the Iranian poets. The 'Indian' style takes root in Herat.[11]

Prose-writings on the Prophet, his family and his companions enjoyed popularity at this time. They were obviously written at the instigation of Navā'ī, as for example Jāmī's *Shavāhidu'n-nubuvva*, 'Witnesses of Muḥammad's Prophetic Mission', etc.[12]

The picture of an animated, eventful life of creativity may be completed by reference to the criticism passed by the members at the sessions of the numerous literary circles that were in existence at this time.

B. LYRIC AND EPIC POETRY UNDER THE TIMURIDS

Of the lyric poets brief mention must at least be made of the following: the flowery and extremely affected Khvāja 'Iṣmat of Bukhara (see p. 274) and his pupil Bisāṭī of Samarkand (d. 815/1412–3), who even ventured to enter into competition with the old Kamāl Khujandī (see p. 262); Shāh Ni'matu'llāh Valī (d. 834/1431) – from the 8th/14th century onwards the saints were called 'Shāh'[13] – Sayyid of Aleppo, the famous founder of an Order, author of more then 300 Arabic and Persian treatises on mystical subjects; for the rest he was a mediocre, dull poet with distinct pantheistic leanings in the manner of Maghribī. Resembling him there is his friend, the Azerbayjan saint Shāh Qāsimu'l-anvār (d. 837/1433–4), who was suspected of sympathising with the Safavid party as well as of Ḥurūfī heresy (Jāmī[14] maintains that the disciples of Qāsim scorned the customs of Islam and proclaimed a kind of communism). Among other things he wrote the *mathnavī Anīsu'l-'ārifīn*, 'The Mystics' Companion', an explanation of Ṣūfī terminology. Amīr Shāhī of Sabzavār (d. 857/1453), a descendant of the democratic Sarbadārs, was a composer of such melodious verses that even the Ottoman Sulṭān Selīm I (1512–20)[15] imitated him; then there was the highly esteemed Āṣafī of Herat (d. 923/1517); Kamālu'd-dīn Binā'ī (Bannā'ī) of Herat (see p. 497), who was put to death on account of his Sunnite convictions in 918/1512–3, was the same type of poet as Ḥāfiẓ and further the author of a romantic epic entitled *Bahrām u Bihrūz* or *Bāgh-i Iram*, 'The Garden of Iram', a story consisting of some 5000 verses in which, among other things, he expounds his social and ethical views[16]; he was also a historian. "'Alī Shīr Navā'ī depicts Binā'ī as an exceptionally clever and cultured man, thoroughly adept in all branches of learning but very arrogant and suspicious. As a consequence he is said to have been almost reduced to poverty."[17] He contrived to quarrel with Navā'ī on two occasions.

There was a whole series of poets who strove to acquire fame by composing a *khamsa*, but they seldom got further than writing one or two poems. The fact that so few of these have been preserved – and even then often in single copies – undoubtedly goes to prove their weakness. We must moreover remember that the harvest of epical works surpasses that of the lyrical in quality. More numerous and at the same time more successful are the poetical tales of smaller compass. Kātibī Turshīzī, already mentioned above, stayed in several towns and courts and tried his hand at both genres: of his *khamsa* he seems only to have composed *Gulshan-i abrār*, 'Flower-garden of the Saints', and *Laylī u Majnūn*, but there are a few works of his in existence, among them being *Sī-nāma*, 'Thirty Letters', an oriental analogy to Ovid's *Heroides*.[18] One continually comes across play on words and ideas. Navā'ī[19] regards him, together with Amīr Shāhī (d. 857/1453), as the greatest master of the *ghazal* in the 9th/15th century.

In the *Ḥāl-nāma*, 'Book of Ecstasy', 'Ārifī of Herat (d. about 853/1449) depicts the tragic passion of a dervish for a prince and at the same time symbolises the relationship between them by the ball and the mallet (*Gūy u Chaugān*, as the poem is generally called) in the game of polo that the prince was fond of playing. The quarrelling-song (tenzon) 'Earth and Heaven', contained in the introduction, is particularly beautiful. Jāmī considers it the best of 'Ārifī's *mathnavīs*, symbolising as it does languishing love and boundless cruelty.[20] The advantage it possesses in containing a new theme is however prejudiced by the inclusion of insertions, verbosity and extravagance.[21]

The charming allegory *Ḥusn u dil*, 'Beauty and Heart', was received with eager enthusiasm both at home and in Turkey. It was composed by Fattāḥī (whose real name was Muḥammad Yaḥyā b. Sībak of Nishapur, d. 852/1448–9) and is actually a short summary of the long allegorical epic *Dastūr-i 'Ushshāq*, 'Handbook for Lovers' dating from 840/1436–7. It is a semi-psychological, semi-symbolical work of fiction and is written in easily comprehended prose, interspersed with verse. It deals with the profound problems of mysticism by personifying parts of the human body and various human qualities, a true "Index of the Methaphorical Language of Oriental Erotics".[22] He earned even greater renown by his *Shabistān-i khiyāl*, 'Bedchamber of Phantasy', viz. *Shabistān-i nikāt va gulistān-i lughāt*, 'Bedchamber of Subtleties and the Flower-garden of Expressions', that dates from the year 843/1439–40. The poet himself says that new forms will have to be found, which suggests that at that time the ancient feudal poetry with its traditional cycle of themes was beginning to breathe its last. General attention was focussed on Fattāḥī's work, as is proved by the large number of commentaries it evoked; things even went so far that to be able to understand and interpret the *Shabistān* was regarded as a criterion of poetical competence (just as was the case later on in Transoxania with Bīdil). The title *Shabistān-i khiyāl* and some details from the work were even included in the inventory of poetical expressions. Fattāḥī thus created strains that proved agreeable to the taste of the times, and their effect lasted for centuries. His mastery lies in his never-ceasing allegorising, his constant play on words, his flourishes, hidden meanings, etc.[23] It would almost seem as if juggling with words, in prose and verse, that had been driven to extremes in the *Shabistān-i khiyāl* particularly, was the main constituent of Fattāḥī's poetry. It was to the spirit of the time that he paid tribute also in his *Taʿbīr-nāma*, 'Book of Dreams', that was composed in verse-form. And we have not yet touched on all that Fattāḥī wrote. The *tadhkiras* also mention the little-known *Kitāb-i asrārī va khumārī*, which was probably nothing more than a quarrel between a hashish-smoker and an alcoholic (like the later tenzon *Bang u bāda*, 'Hashish and Wine', written in the Azerbayjan language by Fuḍūlī) with insertions (*taḍmīn*) from the works of great poets. R. S. Greenshields[24] mentions further the treatise *Tajnīsāt*, 'Homonyms' (as rhetorical puns) which are truly characteristic of the author of the *Shabistān*. The sources point to his culture and calligraphic skill, but also show that he would have acquired far more fame, according to his deserts, if he had not led the solitary retired life of a dervish.

As may be gathered from dates already mentioned here and there, there were poets who, though they lived until after the end of the Timurid era, were in point of fact rooted in it, as for instance ʿAbdu'llāh Hātifī of Kharjird (d. 927/1520), a nephew of Jāmī's, and the 'Chaghatayan' Badru'd-dīn Hilālī (put to death 936/1529 on the grounds of his Shīʿite faith and a libellous verse on ʿUbaydu'llāh-Khān).[25] The former departed from the customary Alexander-song of the *khamsa* in so far that he replaced it by an extensive epic on Tīmūr which, as he himself boasts, represented the true state of affairs. In the unfinished epic on Shāh Ismāʿīl he found a continuer in Muḥammad Qāsim, 'Qāsimī', of Gun-ābād (d. after 989/1581), the same who in two further *Shāh-nāmas* sang of Ṭahmāsp and Shāh-rukh and was, like Hātifī[26], the composer of a *khamsa* in his own style. – Hilālī, also held in esteem as a lyric poet, won fame by his somewhat exalted story of *Shāh u gadā*, 'King and Beggar', that is written entirely after the fashion of ʿĀrifī. It may be mentioned that Bābur[27] disapproved of the alleged homosexual

Notes on pp. 289–290

tone (which incidentally can also be felt in Jāmī), however innocent and idealistic the intentions may have been. The essence of Bābur's criticism naturally lies in the aversion of an aristocrat to the idea of the beggar approaching the king. Hilālī wrote three *mathnavīs* in all of which he lays emphasis on humanity. K. Ayni[28] regards *Laylī u Majnūn* as the best of the three (it has a happy ending, thus differing from Niẓāmī's version). In the *ghazals*, which the poet considers the most exacting genre of poetry, he turns grief, caused by the contemporary situation, allegorically into lovesickness.

Here we must also refer to Muḥammad Ahlī of Shiraz who lived somewhat later (d. 942/1535–6) and has already been mentioned above. We may add that in his mystical erotic *mathnavī Sham' u parvāna*, 'Candle and Moth', and especially in *Siḥr-i ḥalāl*, 'Permissible Magic', he delights so much in the use of rhetorical puns that he even surpasses Kātibī in that respect. His *ghazals* on the other hand are remarkably simple.[29]

It was the extreme subjectivism, the would-be wittiness and the artificiality of this and the following period that made it necessary for every epic poet to turn his hand to lyrical poetry to a greater extent than ever before. This is proved above all by the greatest figure of this illusory decline, who constituted as it were an epilogue to classicism but was at the same time a typical reflector of his period – Jāmī.

C. JĀMĪ

Maulānā Nūru'd-dīn 'Abdu'r-Raḥmān Jāmī (b. 817/1414, d. 898/1492) was an outstanding man and poet. Close relations with the court at Herat and the sincere friendship of the vizier 'Alī-Shīr Navā'ī did not affect his independence. His object was neither wealth nor success, though the general respect paid him at home and abroad did perhaps stir his vanity. His attachment to the Order of Naqshbandīs was genuine; a dervish without pose, he did not live aloof from the world and its tumult. On the other hand he gave the title *Tuḥfatu'l-aḥrār*, 'Gift of [or 'to'] the Free', to one of his didactic *mathnavīs* in honour of the Naqshbandī Shaykh 'Ubaydu'llāh-Aḥrār, and professed the faith of the Order in another, called *Silsilatu'dh-dhahab*, 'The Golden Chain', taking the title from the terminology of the Order. Though an orthodox Sunnite, he supplemented his philosophical views from those of Muḥyi'd-dīn ibn al-'Arabī.[30] He thus grew into an unusually prolific poet and scholar in both movements. Whereas 'A. A. Ḥikmat[31] enumerates only 45 authenticated works, earlier biographers recorded as many as 99. There is no genre of classical poetry in which he was not at one time or another engaged. He even turned his attention to the logigraph. In addition we find erudite works on theology, mysticism, biography, poetics and rhetoric, grammar, epistolography, literary exegesis and music, some of them written in Arabic. The most famous is the group containing his poetical works: (a) three lyrical *dīvāns* composed in youth, middle age, and old age; (b) *Haft aurang*, 'Seven Thrones' (also 'The Constellation of the Great Bear') containing three themes taken from Niẓāmī's *Khamsa* (*Tuḥfatu'l-aḥrār*, 'Gift of [or 'to'] the Free', *Laylī u Majnūn*, *Khirad-nāma-i Sikandarī*, 'The Book of the Wisdom of Alexander'). Neither these nor two other poems of religious, mystical and ethical nature found a wide circulation, although, contrary to the opinion of E. G. Browne[32], native critics considered *Subḥatu'l-abrār*, 'The Rosary of the Pious', to be one of the best works of its kind. But *Yūsuf u Zalīkhā* is one of the most widely read *mathnavīs*, and rightly so, for it is the best of all the epic poems of this name. The mystical allegory *Salāmān u Absāl* takes its subject from the commentary of Naṣīru'd-dīn Ṭūsī (see p. 313) on Avicenna's *Ishārāt*, 'Hints'[33], a story presumably of Greek origin and in the Arabic version obviously of a hermetic nature[34] that Avicenna himself had already made use of in a separate allegory of the same name. In relation to Naṣīru'd-dīn, Jāmī – or maybe already his unknown source – exhibits some variations[35], but without depriving the fable of its grotesqueness (the motherless birth of the boy Salāmān, on the contrary, appealed to Jāmī in view of his misogyny, just as did the fact that Absāl, Salāmān's nurse, gets burned while the boy emerges from the same fire unharmed); (c) The *Bahāristān*, 'The Spring Garden', a masterly but affected imitation of the *Gulistān* with an excellent chapter (the seventh) on the history of literature. Among his learned prose works mention should be made of *Nafaḥātu'l-uns*, 'Breaths of Familiarity', which consists of biographies of 616 scholars, saints and poets regarded as mystics (of which Ḥāfiẓ was one), and is a revision and continuation of Anṣārī's *Ṭabaqātu'ṣ-ṣūfiyya*, 'Classes of the Ṣūfīs' (see p. 235).

This universality must be understood correctly: "It was not by chance that Jāmī tried his skill at all genres of poetry, but in order to prove his basic theory that a work lives not by its form, as was commonly thought at that time, but by the profundity of its content. Jāmī demonstrated that not a single one of the classical forms has died out definitively but that it was possible to revive them if the poet were capable of lending them a deep and significant meaning. Instead of bringing superfastidious forms into play, his *qaṣīdas* speak of the urgency of acting justly and further insist that those in power have not the right to indulge in the joys of life while the masses are obliged to beg and suffer violence."[36] He took Ḥāfiẓ and Niẓāmī (sometimes Amīr Khusrau) as his models, though without equalling them on their own grounds. To quote his own words, he "put old stories to new tunes", but he was nevertheless accused of having more likely stolen old and new verses from Sa'dī, Anvarī, and Khusrau.[37] His main virtues are a relative lucidity and simplicity as compared with the pomposity and perverseness of the 9th/15th century. Yet Jāmī too knows when to open all the registers of an extravagant style. As a brilliant epigone he knows how to bring the available material elegantly into harmony with the demands of the period. Through his great genius he was able to influence the literature of Central Asia and Persia, Turkey and India, besides the Chaghatay poetry, embodied at that time in 'Alī-Shīr Navā'ī

(b. 844/1441, d. 906/1501)[38], the admirable vizier and Jāmī's friend and patron. It only remains to add that the vast fame enjoyed by Jāmī in his homeland and abroad during his lifetime faded considerably later on, especially in the Shīʿite Persia of the Safavids, and that it ultimately became confined to a few of his works.

As late as the 11th/17th century Herat, as provincial literary centre, under the Begler Begs of the Shāmlū dynasty, still lived on this early fame.[39]

D. OUTSIDE HERAT. BĀBĀ FIGHĀNĪ AND HIS INFLUENCE. LISĀNĪ

The poets so far discussed did not all live and work in Herat. Those for whom Herat was too remote geographically, or uncongenial on account of its sympathies, frequently turned their steps to the liberal court of the Aq-Qoyunlus at Tabriz. It was there, at the rival court to Herat, that there lived for seventeen years, at the time of the eminent Sulṭān Yaʿqūb Aq-Qoyunlu, the poet Bābā Fighānī (b. during the latter half of the 9th/15th century in Shiraz), the 'little Ḥāfiẓ'[40], a sensitive, kind-hearted man, an altruistic Bohemian, a melancholy drinker and ardent lover. He was never able to forget Tabriz, and with it the happiest part of his life, and although his already arranged *dīvān* was lost there in the confusion caused by the war, his poems ceaselessly give expression to his longing for this metropolis after his return to Shiraz when the first of the Safavids ascended the throne. Later on he moved to Abīvard, where he spent the greater part of his time in taverns. Bābā Fighānī died in 925/1519 in Mashhad where towards the end of his life he did penance at the grave of the Imām Riḍā, to whom he dedicated a *qaṣīda* that subsequently became famous.

Heart-rending passionate lamentation is the underlying tone in his *ghazals*. "Fughānī, on his arrival in Herat" (where he spent some time before going to Tabriz) "could not find much support for his new type of lyrics. He contacted Maulānā Jāmī also but no tangible result came out of it. Rather he was condemned as a frivolous writer, singing of the pleasure of the flesh so much that his obscene (??) writings were dubbed as 'Fughāniyyah'. This naturally disheartened Fughānī and he decided to move to Tabriz."[41] His style influenced such poets as Sharaf Qazvīnī, Ḥālatī Turkmān, Vaḥshī, Ḍamīrī, and Shifāʾī[42]; the language of Qasamī even approached the popular idiom.[43] This is particularly significant since otherwise the 10th/16th century suffered from a hypertrophy of affectation.

On partly similar and partly dissimilar lines to the career of Bābā Fighānī ran that of his contemporary and compatriot Lisānī, likewise an emulator of Ḥāfiẓ. He lived in Baghdad and Tabriz, but led the consecrated life of a dervish. He is said to have composed about one hundred thousand verses in honour of the Twelve Imāms, and his influence on Muḥtasham (see p. 298) and others is evident. He lost his life at the hands of Osman aggressors in Tabriz in 940/1534. This is the same Lisānī who wrote a *Shahr-āshūb*, 'Pasquinade sur la Ville de Tébriz'[44] in sixty-four quatrains as a counterpart to Maḥsatī's similar quatrains on the craftsman's apprentices (see pp. 199, 259).

NOTES

1. Ghanī, *Baḥth*, 1, 400$_1$.
2. Ivanow, *Ocherk*, 31; Barthold, *Shu'ūb.*, 253; likewise the Mongols, cf. Spuler, *Die Mongolen in Iran*^{2}, 437 *et seq.*
3. Barthold, *12 Vorlesungen*, 231.
4. The last Timurid, Sulṭān Ḥusayn Bāyqarā (1469–1506), was not only a patron of literature and art but himself the author of a *dīvān* in the Chaghatay language. The *tadhkira Majālisu'l-'ushshāq*, 'The Meetings of the Lovers' (i.e. of the poets, shaykhs, and scholars), written in Persian, is, according to Bābur (see p. 281), wrongly ascribed to him (it is in fact by Kamālu'd-dīn Gāzurgāhī) and is incidentally sharply condemned by the same Bābur (cf. Al. Bombaci, *Storia della lett. turca*, 130–2.) On Bābur and his memoires see Al. Bombaci, *loc. cit.*, 156–78 and Bibl. *ibid.*, 500 *et seq.*
5. For the two terms, cf. Bertel's, *Navoyi* (D 11b) 54, where the term 'old Uzbeg' is preferred, although the ethnical term 'Uzbeg' means another Turkish tribe.
6. Cf. Al. Bombaci, *loc. cit.* 122 *et seq.*
7. See above, p. 170, note 77.
8. Antol.^{1}, (D 11a) 15.
9. Cf. above, p. 122, note 75.
10. Mirzoyev, *Binoyī* (1957; D 11b), 51; a brief résumé on the *ghazal* seen from this point of view, *ibid.*, 49 *et seq.*; idem, *Rūdakī*, 70 (Russ. 66).
11. *Sabk*, 3, 186.
12. Ḥikmat's transl. of *LHP*, 3, 471–72 footnote.
13. Mu'īn, *Ḥāfiẓ*, 139; an unfriendly, even hostile attitude towards Shāh Ni'matu'llāh, his disciples and their still active followers is taken by *Sukhan*, 7 (1335), 928b; otherwise, according to this periodical, neither the poet nor his successors in the Order were of any importance whatsoever to the development of Iranian thought!
14. *LHP*, 3, 475; Yār-Shāṭir, *Shi'r*, 24. – Shāh-rukh's apprehensions on account of the numerically great band of adherents: Mu'īn, *Ḥāfiẓ*, 194.
15. Krïmskiy, 3, 118; Horn, *Gesch. der pers. Lit.*, 123.
16. Cf. Mirzoyev, *Binoyī*, 184. The author refutes (175 *et seq.*) the dedication of the epic to the Aq-Qoyunlu Sulṭān Ya'qūb in Tabriz.
17. Barthold-Hinz, *Herat*, 85; Bertel's, *Navoyi* (D 11b), 229 *et seq.* Regarding the alternatives Binā'ī-Bannā'ī cf. Storey, *Pers. Lit.*, 2/2, 301$_2$ (and 371 *et seq.*); Mirzoyev, *loc. cit.*, 91 *et seq.*
18. Bertel's, *ibid.*, 35. Eleven love-letters in *Vīs u Rāmīn*: cf. Massé, 19, where a reference is also made to thirty love-letters in 'Aṭṭār's *Gul u Hurmuz*. Ye. E. Bertel's, *IPTL*, 518, suggests that the 'Hundred Love-*ghazals*' of 'Alī b. Aḥm. Sayfī Nīshāpūrī (second half of the 6th/12th century: Ṣafā, 2, 626), written by the lover to the beloved, were perhaps composed under the influence of *Vīs u Rāmīn*.
19. Bert., *ibid.*, 30 (91); the opposite opinion, Horn, *Gesch. der pers. Lit.*, 123.

20. Krïmskiy, 3, 119.
21. Yār-Shāṭir, *Shi'r*, 179 *et seq.* On the dissimilarity to Hilālī's *Shāh u darvīsh*, cf. K. Aynī, *Khiloli*, 112₂.
22. *Ḥusn u Dil*, ed. R. Dvořák (Bibl. *s.v.* 'Fattāḥī'), 21.
23. A. Mirzoyev, *Sayyido Nasafi* (Russ.; D IIb), 31 *et seq.*, 37, 121, 185.
24. *Dastūr-i 'Ushshāq*, ed. R. S. Greenshields (Bibl. *s.v.* 'Fattāḥī'), Preface 2.
25. For an account of his execution and his grave see Aḥm. Gulchīn-i ma'ānī, *Yaghmā*, 16 (1342), 157–60. – Cf. K. Aynī, *op. cit.*, 81 *et seq.*
26. On Hātifī's 'Quintet' cf. K. Aynī, *op. cit.*, 77₂.
27. Krïmskiy, 3, 132. On the subject: Ritter, *Das Meer*, 128. With regard to the *mathnavī Ṣifātu'l-'āshiqīn*, cf. below, p. 500–1.
28. *Loc. cit.*, 126–46.
29. Krïmskiy, 3, 129.
30. On his religious views cf. Ḥikmat, *Jāmī*, 135 *et seq.*; concerning his dependence on Ibn al-'Arabī cf. Ritter, *Das Meer*, 477. I. Braginskiy devotes a valuable essay in *Ocherki* (D IIa), 264–80, to the contradictions evident between Jāmī's views and the social Utopia in his *Khirad-nāma-i Sikandarī*.
31. Ḥikmat, *op. cit.*, 161.
32. *LHP*, 3, 528, and, a contradictory view, Ḥikmat's transl. 584₂. – Chapter XVII sings the praise of fair youths.
33. Full title: *Kitāb al-Ishārāt va't-Tanbīhāt*. A.-M. Goichon (Paris 1951): *Le livre des directives et remarques*.
34. Ritter, *Philol.*, IX, 47 *et seq.*
35. Ḥikmat, *Jāmī*, 193, 190 *et seq.*; Ritter, *Philol.*, IX, 48. – According to R. Yāsimī, *Salāmān u Absāl*, Tehran 1319, or M. Zand (in a letter) and others directly from a shorter version of Avicenna's *Salāmān u Absāl*; cf. Corbin, *Avicenne* (B VIb), 2, 236 *et seq.* – For contents of the separate epics, cf. Bausani, *Storia* (B V), 752–74.
36. Bertel's, *Navoyi* (D IIb), 158.
37. Krïmskiy, 3, 123.
38. For a summary on him see Al. Bombaci, *loc. cit.*, 133–5 with an expert up-to-date bibliography, *ibid.*, 500. Cf. also 'Index', *s.v.* 'Navā'ī'.
39. Krïmskiy, 3, 156.
40. *Ibid.*, 3, 126. Sakkākī, 'belonging to the cutlers', was the pseudonym he used in his youth, cf. *LHP*, IV, 230; nothing has been preserved from this period, unless it was the original *dīvān* that subsequently got lost. It may also be that the adoption of a new *takhalluṣ* wiped out the trail.
41. Kausar, *Journal of the Pakistan Hist. Soc.*, 10 (1962), 54. For a different opinion see Ye. E. Bertel's, *Char. Orient.*, 56, an essay focussed on Fighānī: contemporaries used to call abstruse verses lacking in good taste and intelligibility 'Fighāniyyāt'. Cf. *Arm.*, 17, 532 (Bibl. *s.v.* 'Suhaylī').
42. Köprülü, 'Fighânî', *İA*, 4, 629b.
43. Qasamī: *Arm.*, 17, 782 (Bibl.: see above, note 41). Shiblī, 5, 48₃ too is not unconscious of Fighānī's influence on later generations, but in his opinion its effect was mainly to be seen in the compression that was one of the chief marks of his style. Shiblī even holds Fighānī responsible for the increasing deterioration of this quality that ultimately became dangerously enigmatical, but Bertel's (*loc. cit.*, 58) emphatically disagrees with this view.
44. Ed. by Aug. Bricteux in *Mélanges de Phil. Or.*, Univ. de Liège, 1932. For more information on *shahr-āshūb* cf. A. Mirzoyev, *Sayyido Nasafi* (Russ.; D IIb), 143 *et seq.*, 161.

X. THE SAFAVIDS

In many respects the Safavids (907–1148/1501–1736) continued to pursue the policy of their predecessors, the Turkomans Aq-Qoyunlu, but unlike the latter they professed the Shīʿa. This Shīʿa, it is true, was not the original faith of their ancestors, the shaykhs of the family of the sacred Shaykh Ṣafiyyu'd-dīn from Ardabīl (650–735/1252–1334). These latter gathered the Murīds around them and from the turn of the 8th–9th/14th–15th century onwards spread militant Shīʿa opinions which found a ready response among the population. To put it in another way, the successors to the sacred shaykh took advantage of the situation by letting the general discontent serve their own purpose. Thus the holy family obtained a steadily increasing temporal power. During the second half of the 9th/15th century the lesser and middle feudal rulers joined forces with the belligerent saints in their resistance to the Turkomans. Their example was followed by a part of the merchant class, to whom the idea of a united Iran must have been more acceptable than long drawn-out struggles between and within the dysnasties.[1] Fanatical followers and several Turkish nomadic tribes in the south of Azerbayjan placed the 13-year-old Ismāʿīl on the throne (905/1499–1500; d. 930/1523–4). The Safavids united Persia, established a theocratic state, extended their dominion and engaged in violent struggles with their Sunnite neighbours under the proudly waving banner of the Shīʿa as the one and only state religion. At the same time this was a struggle for political and economic supremacy. But the Safavids of the 10th/16th century must not be regarded as a kind of Persian national dynasty. They were a Turkish dynasty, just as were their predecessors Qara-Qoyonlu and Aq-Qoyunlu. But the Shaybanids in Central Asia were also Turks. Here, just as there, power was in the hands of the military nomadic nobility – in Persia the Qïzïlbash, in Transoxania the Uzbeks, both of whom spoke Turkic languages. These two dynasties soon began to quarrel over Khurasan, a quarrel that lasted throughout the whole of the 10th/16th century. This too must not be seen as a combat between Iranians and Turks but as a conflict between two Turkish feudal dynasties. The Safavids gained possession of the whole of Khurasan, except the region of Balkh, and converted it to the Shīʿa. Ṭūs, Mashhad and especially Herat had to suffer terribly from the continual invasions of the Uzbeks during the reign of Ṭahmāsp I. And the final result? – the isolation both of Central Asia and Iran, the breaking-off of economic and cultural relations, and the downfall of Khurasan.[2] The Safavids can certainly not be spared blame for this. On the other hand it must not be forgotten that, although they were Azerbayjanians and could rely for support on the Turkish Qïzïlbashes, they nevertheless prevented a further turkisation of Persia, which would inevitably have taken place if there had been an influx of Turks from Central Asia.[3] They restricted the disproportionately great power of the nomadic military Qïzïlbash aristocracy and the Qïzïlbash leaders by patronising the towns; thus as early as 1565 Shāh Ṭahmāsp I (930–84/1524–76) lifted all taxes on trade.[4] Other measures levelled by the rulers against the Qïzïlbash consisted in siding with the purely Iranian bureaucracy and in taking even more radical steps, like ʿAbbās I (995–1038/1587–1629) who organised the corporation of the *Shāh-seven*, 'Followers of the Shāh', which was now formed not of members of one tribe but of individuals belonging to several who were personally devoted to the ruler.

A. THE LITERATURE OF THIS EPOCH

The literature of the Safavid period is usually regarded as a literature of decline. Let us now examine in how far this judgment is justified. Even when the Timurid supremacy became weaker and weaker and eventually fell to pieces, this did not at all imply that the flow of literature diminished. In point of fact the 10th/16th century benefited from this situation because the first Safavids had other things to occupy themselves with than only the fostering of poetry. Their 'cultural' interest was concentrated on propaganda and on the consolidation of the state religion. This was effected partly by encouraging the study of theology and partly by stimulating the composition of religious poetry, both of course in the spirit of the Shīʿa. We must not ignore the fact that until this dynasty came into power a by no means inconsiderable portion of the population adhered to the Sunna. Of course the Shīʿite standardisation of literature, a necessary consequence of the harsh Shīʿite policy, could not be accepted by Central Asia or by Afghanistan and India, all of which were and remained Sunnite countries; or, to put it differently, Iranian literature was deprived of the flow of force from these lands, ceased to be international and started to become a purely Persian concern. The interchange of poets with India certainly continued for a time, but this too finally became dormant; on the other hand contact between Safavid Iran and its immediate Central Asian neighbours, with which it was on a footing of violent hostility, became more difficult. Central Asia entered upon a course which it had in common above all with India. With the exception of occasional local peculiarities the same language remained in use in affairs of state and in literature, but it did not form a link strong enough to prevent a schism. Besides this Iran itself showed little understanding of poetry imported from the north and east. Thus for instance Shaukat of Bukhara and the Indian Bīdil are practically unknown in Iran.

Although Turkish was the language spoken by the Safavids in their homes, Persian did not lose its importance. On the contrary! Thanks to the fact that the rulers did all in their power to promote the spread of the Shīʿa throughout the empire and even beyond the frontiers, in order that it might pervade the population rapidly and effectively, the Persian language also gained ground in matters of religion that had hitherto been dealt with exclusively in Arabic. In other respects Safavid prose followed the patterns of the foregoing period. Secular panegyric and lyric poetry is replaced by hymns in honour of the Prophet and ʿAlī, or threnodies on the Imāms, but otherwise there is a palpable lack of interest in the poets, their works and their burial-places. All the more striking is therefore the interest in the *Imām-zādas*, 'descendants of the (sacred, almost deified) Imāms' and in their mausoleums, also known as '*Imām-zādas*', though the latter are not always authentic. But here too one must not ignore the fact that at any rate the members of this polycephalous dynasty, if not the rulers themselves, gave support to literary activities, and in some cases were themselves actively engaged as poets, as for instance Ismāʿīl I, with a *dīvān* written in the Turkoman language, and his son Sām Mīrzā with an important *tadhkira* on contemporary Persian poets. In the field of poetry we even find an endless number of names. The works of these poets have unfortunately not yet been thoroughly studied so that for the present the names remain practically without significance. Only a few isolated milestones indicate the course of literary development. The main difference between the literature of this period and that of the past lies in the greater wealth of substance in the average work of earlier times. This can only be assessed as a symptom of decadence. Nevertheless it is not impossible that more detailed research, and especially a lesser degree of prejudice – of which there is evidence from post-Safavid times up to the present day – against a movement that in some measure replaced both the Khurasanian and the Iraqian styles, will serve to modify prevalent opinion in favour of the new trend.

If a further explanation be sought for this lack of prominent figures – actually an intensification of their disproportionate distribution in Timurid times – in the first place it can be advanced that from the 10th/16th century onwards an economic decline took place in the Near East as a result of the disappearance of the Italian colonies on the Black Sea and the discovery of the sea passage to India by the Portuguese.[5] This inevitably led to a general cultural depression. But there were still other causes. The history of Iran demonstrates that decentralisation was favourable to the blossoming of feudal literature. The Safavids however introduced a more rigid centralisation in conjunction with a dogmatising and levelling of public opinion. Hand in hand with this went a tightening of the regulations for study and education as a whole. The study

Notes on pp. 302–304

of theology provided the most tempting perspectives, for to become an all-powerful *mujtahid*, 'authoritative exponent of the articles of faith and of the law', was the ideal of youth in the Safavid epoch. V. Minorsky[6] explains the dearth of great poets by the fact that mysticism – after all an intrinsic feature of Persian literature – is usually a reverberation of wretched and necessitous circumstances, whereas under the Safavids the Iranians were first of all engaged in upholding their own position, then in expanding their property and in pursuing other aims of a practical nature. The religious orders died out under the pressure of Safavid policy and with them the Ṣūfī conceptions and speculations, which were contested and suspected by the *mujtahids* with the most intense hatred. To keep Maulavī's *mathnavī* in one's house involved constant danger. Moreover, Ṭahmāsp I (930–84/1524–76) had already driven the Maulavīs from Persia. The Ṣūfīs were persecuted in an even more cruel manner by the last real Shāh of the Safavid dynasty, the grossly degenerate Ḥusayn (1106–35/1694–1722; d. 1139/1726), who bore the nickname 'Mullā Ḥusayn' and was a mere puppet in the hands of the unbridled Mullās.[7] This animosity towards the extravagances of Ṣūfism might very well be considered as a beneficent characteristic of the vigorous Safavids, but unfortunately the result was that one evil was substituted for another. The whole of cultural life was delivered over to obscurantism, and there are only a few luminous points, such as the philosopher Mullā Ṣadrā of Shiraz (d. 1050/1640–1) and his pupils Mullā Muḥsin-i Fayḍ of Kāshān (d. 1091/1680)[8] and 'Abdu'r-Razzāq Fayyāḍ of Lāhijān (d. later than 1072/1661–2). These latter were, it is true, seeking to bring the doctrines of their master into harmony with religion. During the two hundred years and more that the dynasty was in power, one can barely count four capable rulers. Under 'Abbās I a certain amount of goodwill towards secular poets can be discerned for the first time. During his reign the country reached the zenith of its power and received a great economic impetus partly by a skilful home and foreign policy and partly by an efficient administration of revenues. The strengthening of the bureaucracy and of Iranian elements among the ruling classes was to the advantage of the Iranian portion of the population.[9] But here again the financial resources of the people were exhausted by costly building enterprises, the construction of roads and endless wars. How different was the effect of the reputation for munificence of the court at Delhi! It was for this reason that the more important poets betook themselves thither, where better material advantages awaited them and where there was also sometimes a greater liberty of conscience. But the poets did not always feel at their ease in India. Willingly or unwillingly they were obliged to adapt themselves to the Indian environment and as a result became more and more estranged from the old Persian masters. Thus literary life was partially transferred to India, where poets of the greatest eminence were working. It is for this reason that Indo-Persian historians and critics of literature are not inclined to give support to the unfavourable opinion of the Persians in relation to the poetry of the Safavid period, an attitude that has been maintained in Indo-Persian literature up to modern times. But although the so-called 'Indian' style in poetry (this designation is of very recent origin) does not enjoy any special popularity in present-day Persia, the opinions of Persian scholars in this respect are far from being unanimous.

I. THE 'INDIAN' STYLE

What are the essential features of the 'Indian' style[10], that under the influence of men like ʿUrfī, Fayḍī, Faṣīḥī, Ṣā'ib, Shaukat, Bīdil and others gained supremacy in poetry? It is a movement that adopted several characteristics of the Timurid epoch (signs of this appear already in the works of Amīr Khusrau[11]). But it added several other features, enjoyed great popularity and became widespread, particularly in India, on whose special climate it came into being under certain definite, political, socio-economic and cultural circumstances. It is however necessary to emphasise that its masters were for the most part of Persian birth and that this same manner of writing not only flourished in India but that it also found its way to Persia and Transoxania and especially to the Tajik people. The change-over to this movement must be placed at the end of the 10th/16th century. The foregoing years however served to prepare the way. The affected and artificial elements are a legacy from Herat; the Indian style expanded these traits and made them even more baroque.[12] In substance and form the verses are true labyrinths, riddles that often make the impression of being soluble only with the aid of geomancy and the astrolabe. Niceties of style become strained, thus excluding the expression of emotion. The Indian elements owe their effect to their novelty and result in an alienation of the poets from the old established masters. The effects of this were the greater and more lasting because Shīʿite fanaticism excludes philosophy and all subjects not directly connected with the theological disciplines, while we must remember that the pursuance of the latter was also accompanied by personal advantage. Philosophical theorems (or rather ethical axioms) and Ṣūfī conceptions, with which poets so frequently display their talents, are nothing but aphoristic platitudes accompanied by an explanatory parallel taken from experience. And this presupposes observations from daily life, which must be counted as a genuine contribution and a positive gain to the credit of this movement. The bondage of conscience, fostered by Safavid centralising tendencies, is demonstrated in the vast distance between the poles, when the Lover writhes before the Beloved like a cur, whether in a literal or an allegorical sense. For the ruler himself wishes nothing more than to be "a cur on the threshold of the immaculate Imāms".[13] Such a manner of expression is even employed by an extreme autocrat like the Ottoman Sulṭān Selīm I (918–26/1512–20) in relation to the Beloved![14] Whilst Kamāl of Khujand (d. 803/1400–1) already made use of the image of a cur belonging to the Beloved[15], time in due course supplied the foundation and substance for such a train of thought. This is nothing other than what Manuel Philes wrote in Europe as early as 1330: "I wish to be a dog, to submit faithfully to my master and to watch for the scraps that fall from his table."[16] Zaynu'l-ʿābidīn Mu'taman con-

Notes on pp. 302–304

tests the importance of this phenomenon and sees in it no greater self-abasement than is to be found in other periods.[17]

It is the Golden Age for the figure *irsāl-i mathal*, 'application of a simile or allegoric expression' (Faṣīḥī, Abū-Ṭālib, Kalīm, Ṣā'ib, etc.); the poets revel in proverbs and figures of speech, witty sayings and paradoxes. In one *miṣrā'* a thesis is set up, in another it is demonstrated by means of an example. Deduction and induction are constantly involved. This clear division of the *bayt* into two – albeit parallel – parts is as an isolated phenomenon nothing new. Its novelty lies only in the consistent, intentional and constant use of the figure mentioned. An intensified complicated 'harmony of images' (*murā'āt-i naẓīr*) is in full flower, the 'imaginative argument' (*ḥusn-i ta'līl*) is frequently encountered. The poets have no qualms about enriching their vocabulary with non-literary and even vulgar expressions, as for instance Mīr 'Abdu'l-'Alī Najāt (d. 1122/1710–1) of Isfahan[18], whose *dīvān* aroused criticism on account of the baseness of its style and generally vulgar mode of expression. Yet it is worth noting that his *mathnavī, Gul-i kushtī*, 'The Rose as a Challenge to Battle', composed mainly on amorous subjects, has obtained a remarkable popularity. The subject-matter is expanded to include accounts of daily happenings, new experiences and observations, without however in any way dispensing with the old stock. In literature we are confronted with the same phenomenon that was witnessed by E. K. Kverfel'dt[19] in regard to textiles from the Safavid period: a certain realism is gaining ground. A favourite subject is *qaḍā u qadar*, 'Fate'[20], namely some remarkable incident contained in the form of a short story in verse. Attempts at originality, supported on too narrow a foundation that was derived from centuries-old conventions, very often lead to the grotesque, to a lack of good taste and unity. The *ghazal* suffers from disintegration. The triangle consisting of 'the Beloved', the Lover (i.e. the poet), and the Rival becomes the rule.[21] But that there must have been something inspiring, something admirable, something fascinating in it can be concluded from the fact that this style appealed to the poets on Persian soil in the same way as on Indian and that Turkestan and Turkey also succumbed to it. In the *qaṣīda* Ottoman lyric poetry follows the lead of 'Urfī. This is even more markedly the case in the *ghazal*, for this form of poetry as represented by Fayḍī, Ṣā'ib and Shaukat constitutes the Ottoman transitional period. It is a well-known fact that literary vices can also have a dazzling and overmastering effect. Was this so in the case in point? This new technique demanded a higher poetical standard than had ever been required before. A galaxy of insignificant poets appeared, whose talents were clearly not equal to the task. But besides these we find good and even superior figures. Whereas during the first half of the 10th/16th century the stars of the foregoing period still shone in the firmament – thus concealing the inevitable consequences of the great political upheaval in Persia – the second half can boast a Muḥtasham, an 'Urfī and the Indian Fayḍī. The 17th century was to go further still.

2. THE CLASSICISTS

The theory that even the most dramatically new and attractive fashion is incapable of entirely supplanting loyalty to older forms is here indisputably confirmed. Thus at the time when the good and bad elements from India were at their peak we still find fanciers and even very loyal followers of the classical style, such as Āqā Ḥusayn Khvānsārī, who lived at the time of ʿAbbās II, and Mīr Abu'l-Qāsim Findariskī (d. *c.* 1050/1640–1).[22]

B. POETS OF THE SAFAVID PERIOD

Ḍamīrī and the possible repercussion from Turkish literature ('Shahr-angīz'); Muḥtasham, the lampoonist Ḥayratī, ʿUrfī, etc. Shifāʾī and his circle

Of the poets belonging entirely to the Safavid period I select only those most worthy of notice. I should probably make no mention at all of Ḥusayn Ḍamīrī of Isfahan (d. shortly after 985/1578), the author of yet another of the numerous *Laylī u Majnūn* epics, were it not that A. Krïmskiy[23] saw in Ḍamīrī's *Vāmiq u ʿAdhrā* a reflection from the Ottoman-Turkish epic of the same name by Lāmiʿī (d. 937–8/1531–2), although certain doubts can be entertained as to whether the Isfahanian understood Turkish at all. A. Krïmskiy puts forward other evidence of an echo from Ottoman literature: *Shahr-angīz*, 'City-thriller', from the pen of Vaḥīdī of Qum (d. 942/1535) depicts the juvenile masculine beauties of Tabriz[24] in *mathnavī* form, just as the Ottoman Mesīḥī, who lived earlier (d. 918/1512), describes the fair apprentices of Edirne. A. Mirzoyev, on the contrary, asserts that the originator of such medallions portraying young artisans – at any rate in the *ghazal* form – was the celebrated writer Sayfī of Bukhara (d. 1504) and that in all probability Mesīḥī wrote the *Shahr-angīz* under his influence round about 1510.[25] An entirely different type from this is exhibited by two satirical *qaṣīdas* composed under the name of *Shahr-āshūb*[26], 'The Disturber of the Town', one of which, by Āgahī Khurāsānī (d. 932/1525–26, see p. 259) was directed against Herat, the other, by Ḥarfī, against Gilan.

Mullā Vaḥshī of Bāfq (d. 991/1583) was in his time an esteemed writer of love lyrics and bears affinity to Bābā Fighānī (and Fuḍūlī) by his directness, sincerity of emotion, and lamentations. If his panegyrics are of no great importance when compared with those of the ancient poets, he did not depart from the general lines prevalent at that time in this form of verse. He was also a didactic poet (*Khuld-i barīn*, 'Highest Paradise') and a mystic (*Nāẓir u Manẓūr*, 'The Seer and the Seen') and was particularly successful as a romantic poet, for otherwise Viṣāl would certainly not have taken the trouble to complete the torso of Vaḥshī's *Farhād u Shīrīn* during the first half of the 19th century. Vaḥshī's *musammaṭ* has the reputation of being a real *chef-d'oeuvre*.

Even up till now the twelve-strophic elegy of Maulānā Muḥtasham of Kāshān (d. 996/1587–8 at the age of 91 lunar years[27]) has not lost its charm of genuine sincerity and intimacy. It is a moving dirge on the tragedy of Karbalā and has been frequently imitated but never surpassed. Although the Shīʿite theme so truly characterises this period of tense fanaticism, the author of the celebrated threnody was nonetheless no fanatical zealot. Another well-known poem is the eleven-strophic elegy on the death of his brother ʿAbdu'l-Ghanī, who negotiated the poet's connection with the Indian court. Muḥtasham also distinguished himself in other kinds of lyric poetry, but the same cannot be said of him in private life, for as a silk merchant he went bankrupt. In view of the three *dīvāns*[28] that stand to his name this would be quite possible. His *qaṣīdas* on the king's sons (*Shāh-zāda*) were received with favour even by the dull-minded Shāh Ṭahmāsp, who for religious reasons was otherwise not wont to regard panegyric poetry with sympathy. The eternal 'lover' (*ʿāshiq*) gave free rein to this emotion in his works, as is particularly clearly demonstrated in the *Jalāliyya*, 64 *ghazals* interposed into lyrical prose with descriptions of his love for Shāṭir-Jalāl, a singer (*muṭrib*) belonging to an itinerant troupe that had stopped at Kāshān. He displays an incredible dexterity in the art of *ta'rīkh* by managing to squeeze 1128 (??) chronograms into six *rubāʿīs* composed in honour of the accession to the throne of the contemptible Ismāʿīl II (984/1576)[29] – a versatility of language that had already attained a high pitch under the Timurids (see pp. 281 *et seq.*).

The trilingual poet Muḥammad b. Sulaymān Fuḍūlī (b. before 900/1495 in Karbalā, d. 963/1556)[30], the most sensitive of the lyrical and romantic poets in the Azerbayjanian-Turkic language[31], is not of the same importance to Persian literature despite the fact that he began his literary career in its arena. He wrote the customary *Sāqī-nāma*, 'Book of the Cup-bearer', and *Rind u zāhid*, 'Vagrant and Hypocrite', where prose is intermingled with verse. The rest of Fuḍūlī's Persian lyric poetry consists of the following works: a Persian *dīvān* similar to the one he composed in Azerbayjanian; the *qaṣīda Anīsu'l-qalb*, 'The Confidant of the Heart', a parallel (*javāb*) to Khāqānī's *qaṣīda Mir'ātu'ṣ-ṣafā*, written in the manner of Khusrau-i Dihlavī's and Jāmī's earlier imitations; *Ṣiḥḥat va maraḍ*, 'Health and Sickness'. All these works are steeped in liberal and social ideas. But his greatest work is the epic *Leylī ve Mejnūn*, composed in the Azerbayjanian language.

There is no dearth of satires during this epoch: Muḥammad Taqiyyu'd-dīn Ḥayratī of Tūn (in Khurasan; d. 961/1553–4; according to Nakhjavānī: 970/1562–3) would certainly have fared badly on account of his libellous writings had he not been assured of the protection of Shāh Ṭahmāsp thanks to his religious odes, an epic on the twelve Imāms entitled *Kitāb-i muʿjizāt*, 'Book of Miracles'[32], and finally also his panegyrics. A purely literary work such as the imitation of the *Gulistān* in the *Gulzār*, 'The Rosebed', would scarcely have produced the same effect on the bigoted ruler. But the death of Ḥayratī was nevertheless somewhat mysterious – he is said to have fallen off a roof in Kāshān, where he may have been resting. But it is also possible that he was murdered.[33]

The 10th/16th century closes with the death of one of the most prominent figures of this age, though it is true he is today but little known in Persia. Muḥammad ʿUrfī * (b. 963/1555–6) set off for India immediately after the completion of his studies in his native town Shiraz. The favour accorded him in court circles and later on even with Akbar himself caused him to become disagreeably conceited. He died in the year 999/1590–1 at the age of 36. It is difficult to believe the rumour that he was poisoned on account of jealousy or in connection with a love-affair. In two *mathnavīs* he emulates the first and second epics of Niẓāmī's *Khamsa*.[34] His fame however is founded neither on these nor on the Ṣūfī tract *Nafsiyya* – ʿUrfī was no more a Ṣūfī than were his contemporaries – but on his *dīvān*, for the hitherto unheard-of pomposity of style, the grandeur of the language and the sublimity of his *qaṣīdas* transported India and Turkey into ecstasy. The greatest Ottoman panegyrist, Nefʿī (strangled 1044/1634–5) follows closely in his footsteps. ʿUrfī does not strive after play on words, but he is nevertheless a consummate master of language. He embellishes his verses both with new stylistic features and fresh metaphors and motifs; moreover he pays great attention to coherence and harmony. His *ghazals* on the other hand are so weak that it often seems impossible that their author could be a poet of ʿUrfī's stature.[35] It must nevertheless be accorded that a mastery of one form of poetry does not necessarily imply equal genius in another. Many examples are to be found in Persian poetry. ʿUrfī too composed a *Sāqī-nāma*, 'The Book of the Cup-bearer'. His Ṣūfī conceptions do not reach the standard of his philosophical ideas.[36] He reaches supreme heights in the praise of self (*fakhriyya*).

His patron was the free-thinker Abu'l-Fayḍ Fayḍī (Fayyāḍī) (d. 1004/1595), brother of Akbar's famous minister Abu'l-Faḍl, himself one of the most prominent Indo-Persian poets. An Indian by birth, he includes in his *Khamsa*, under the title of *Nal u* * *Daman*, a recast of the well-known episode of Nala and Damayantī from the *Mahābhārata*, and draws both here and elsewhere on Indian sources for his subjects. His influence on Ottoman lyric poetry was considerable. In this context it should also be mentioned that translations of the most celebrated Sanskrit works form an important part of the political activities of the emperor Akbar (963–1014/1556–1605) and his immediate successors. Their aim was to bring about a rapprochement between the two irreconcilably hostile religions.

The Indian style reached its zenith in the 17th century, in the course of which there appeared several excellent poets including one who may be ranked among the very best, namely Ṣā'ib. But even at that time not all the poets subscribed to the Indian movement. Among those who remained aloof was Bahā'ī (d. 1030/1620–1), an extraordinarily prolific scholar, man of letters and, under certain circumstances, poet. Of his works the following may be mentioned: *Kashkūl*, 'The Beggar's Bowl', a varied

Notes on pp. 302–304

collection of Arabic anecdotes and Persian verses; *Pand-i ahl-i dānish u hūsh ba-zabān-i gurba u mūsh*, 'Advice of the Learned and Clever in the Speech of Cat and Mouse', stories within a story and linked by a common framework, of the same kind as *Kalīla u Dimna*; but above all short didactic and religious *mathnavīs* bearing symbolical titles such as *Nān u ḥalvā*, 'Bread and Ḥalvā-sweetmeats', *Nān u panīr*, 'Bread and Cheese' and *Shīr u Shakar*, 'Milk and Sugar', and containing numerous Arabic verses, *ḥadīths*, expressions etc. – obviously the work of a scholar, but of no particular value as poetry. The wide field of activity of Bahā'ī (viz. Bahā'u'd-dīn Muḥammad 'Āmilī) included Shī'ite theology, law and the exact sciences. The majority of his works are written in Arabic. S. Nafīsī regards his endeavour to bring Ṣūfism into harmony with the official dogma of faith as Bahā'ī's greatest merit.[37] – It is equally difficult to speak of the Indian style with regard to the poet Saḥābī, chiefly a writer of quatrains, who came from Astarabad (d. 1010/1601–2) and spent twenty years in Najaf. This poet professed pantheism; and even if for this reason Shiblī[38] places him in one line with Maghribī (see p. 262) one must not lose sight of the respective circumstances under which the two poets lived. – One of the best poets of the Safavid epoch, the 'Poet Laureate', physician and companion of 'Abbās I, Sharafu'd-dīn Ḥasan Shifā'ī (d. 1037/1628) says of his *qaṣīdas* that they are modelled on those of Khāqānī. In relation to the *ghazal* he avers that he is adopting a new course but in reality this is only a somewhat modified Bābā Fighānī. His famous *mathnavī Namakdān-i ḥaqīqat*, 'Salt-cellar of Truth', is such a close imitation of Sanā'ī that many people have taken it to be a work from the pen of the latter. Khāqānī's poetical account of his travels, *Tuḥfatu'l-'Irāqayn* (pp. 204–5), is also the model employed by Shifā'ī in his *mathnavī Maṭla'u'l-anvār*, 'Rising of the Lights', which we occasionally find bearing the title *Majma'u'l-baḥrayn*, 'Confluence of the Two Seas'. There are also other *mathnavīs* of his in existence. He appears predominantly as a satirist and a polemic with a sharp personal tone; sensitive, easily insulted, violent as he was, he reacted correspondingly to ungracious behaviour and unkindness on the part of others; he nevertheless despised non-essential things and would bow to no one, not even to Shāh 'Abbās I, who had a high regard for him in spite of his whims. In old age he grew weary of the struggle. He lived on friendly terms with Jalāl Asīr of Isfahan (d. 1049/1639–40) though not because the latter was a son-in-law of Shāh 'Abbās I but because he was a cheerful, sometimes even wanton carouser and poet. Among Shifā'ī's friends were also Faṣīḥī Anṣārī of Herat (d. 1046/1636–7)[39], a sensitive writer of lyrics who exploited the customary love themes to the point of melancholy and also anticipated the sententiousness of Ṣā'ib. Faṣīḥī also had his imitators, as for instance in lyrical poetry Nāẓim of Herat (d. about 1080/1670) who, in *Yūsuf u Zalīkhā*, is the only one to incline *expressis verbis* to Firdausī's version – a testimony which came too late and is therefore insignificant.

C. SUBSEQUENT DEVELOPMENT OF THE INDIAN STYLE

Naẓīrī, Ẓuhūrī, Ṭālib, Kalīm, etc.; the epic poet Zulālī

The following poets all worked in India and made contributions to the Indian style: Naẓīrī of Nishapur (d. 1021/1612–3[40]), who even wrote verses in praise of tobacco; the *bel esprit* Ẓuhūrī of Khujand near Turshīz (killed in a brawl 1024/1615), a writer of high-flown prose much admired in India, but practically unknown in Persia; Ṭālib of Amul (d. 1036/1626–7), Jahāngīr's 'King of Poets' and highly esteemed in India; Shāh Jahān's 'King of Poets', Abū-Ṭālib Kalīm of Hamadan (d. 1061/1651–2), a precursor of Ṣā'ib in regard to his apophthegms who showed moreover great originality in his choice of themes; he was the author of the *Shāh-Jahān-nāma* that, in the manner of the *Shāh-nāma*, sings the praises of Tīmūr and the Timurids up to Shāh Jahān (Ye. E. Bertel's[41] also cites Ṭālib and Kalīm as masters of the miniature adventure novel in verse-form); last but not least, Ruknā Masīḥ of Kāshān (d. 1066/1655 or 1070/1659–60). Sceptical, now and then cynical, he was Ṣā'ib's tutor, calligrapher and physician and the author of some 100,000 verses.[42]

Many of these poets left *mathnavīs*. This genre was at that time in full flower and, in so far as its contents were of a romantic nature, it embodied material that was unknown to the classical period and was frequently given a symbolical point. First place must be accorded to Maulānā Ḥakīm Zulālī of Khvānsār (d. 1024/1615), the 'King of Poets' of ʿAbbās I. Of his *Sabʿ sayyāra*, 'Seven Planets', the part entitled *Maḥmūd u Ayāz* acquired fame. This was a *mathnavī* on which the poet had worked for the last twenty-two years of his life; it indeed put into the shade both the earlier poet Fakhru'd-dīn ʿAlī Ṣafī (d. 939/1532–3), son of the famous Ḥusayn Vāʿiẓ, as well as Ṣā'ib and others, all of whom came after him.

D. ṢĀ'IB, SHAUKAT, BĪDIL

A poet of the first order in the Safavid and Indian style and a great master of Persian poetry in all its aspects is Mīrzā Muḥammad ʿAlī Ṣā'ib of Tabriz (b. 1010/1601–2, d. 1088/1677–8) – often known as 'Isfahānī' with reference to the place where he was educated. Finding no recognition at home, he went to India in about 1036/1626–7 where he earned an outstanding reputation at the court of the emperor Shāh Jahān. When after six years' absence, during which he had lived for a considerable time in Kabul and Kashmir, he returned to his native land at the request of his aged father, who even went to Aghra to meet him, he was granted the favour of ʿAbbās II and even

Notes on pp. 302–304

the honour of 'King of Poets'. His fame was based on his *ghazals*. Ṣā'ib greatly admired Ḥāfiẓ and was well versed in Persian poetry as a whole. To his knowledge, accompanied as it was by the good taste of a well-read poet, we owe an excellent anthology from which later poets have borrowed in large measure. In his lyrics he transmits into verse philosophical problems and axioms of greater or less profundity – sometimes almost trivial. His *ghazals* are thus characterised not so much by emotion as by ingenuity, flashes of wit, practical knowledge and concrete observation in incessant combination with parallelism of ideas. This accounts for a certain aridity which one finds adhering to his poetry. The range of subjects is broadened, the object of his poetry consists in the subtlety of the choice of words. With Ṣā'ib the Indian style reaches its greatest deployment. His output borders on the incredible: 300,000 couplets, 12,000 of which are contained in *qaṣīdas*, 130,000 in a *mathnavī* entitled *Qandahār-nāma*, 'The Campaign against Qandahar'; the rest consists of *ghazals* which despite Ṣā'ib's great genius are nevertheless of varying quality.[43] Most astounding of all – Ṣā'ib also wrote verse in Turkish! From this *embarras de richesse* numerous selections have been made. Ṣā'ib exercised a fascinating influence on the Indo-Persian and Ottoman poets (Nābī, Thābit and their school). In the Persia of today he unfortunately does not get the appreciation he deserves, although latterly there has been no lack of attempts to make good this neglect.

Shaukat of Bukhara (d. 1107/1695–6) and the 'Indian' Bīdil (d. 1133/1720), the last great exponent of this movement, went to still further lengths in their realisation of the Indian style. It is true that Shaukat spent the last years of his life in the very heart of Safavid Iran, yet there is no evidence of his having aroused any notable response there. Bīdil found no echo in Persia at all, for as a consequence of his ideology he inevitably kept aloof from a country that was sinking deeper and deeper into retrogressive currents and was heading for ruin.[44]

NOTES

1. Ivanow, *Ocherk* (B II), 57 *et seq.*
2. Miklukho-Maklay, 'K istorii' (B II); Mirzoyev, *Sayyido* (Russ.), 21 *et seq.*, 162.
3. Minorsky, *The Middle East* (B II), 451; idem, *Unity* (B II), 195.
4. Hinz, *Steuerinschriften* (B II), 758 *et seq.*
5. Sykes, *Hist. of Persia*[3] (B II), 2, 184 *et seq.*; Bouvat, (B II), 'Essai', 287; Bertel's, 'Lit. ... v Sr. Az.' (D II a), 227.
6. 'Iran' (B II), 196.
7. Krïmskiy, 2, 93.
8. Mullā Muḥsin was a rigorous adherent of the theological school of Akhbārī, that repudiates analogy in juridical thinking, thus undermining the authority of the all-powerful Mujtahids. Muḥsin was at the same time a poet who well knew how to give expression to the Ṣūfī tone. His *ghazals* are

conspicuous for their affinity to folklore and their suitability for singing. His Ṣūfism did not pander to quietism (Bertel's, *Poez. Muḥsin-i Fayḍ*, 15, 14, 18).

9. Miklukho-Maklay, 'K voprosu' (B II), 354.

10. For more details see Mirzoyev, *Sayyido Nasafi* (D IIb), 34–56; Ye. E. Bertel's, 'K voprosu ob "indiyskom stile"', *Char. Orient. (Rypka)*, 56–9; Bahār, *Bāz-gasht* (B VIa), 714. See the two following notes. For the prose: *Sabk*, 3, 186 and 259 *et seq.* *

11. Al. Bausani, *Contributo* (B IV), 168, quotes Fighānī in this context by referring to Shiblī-Nu'mānī.

12. A. Bausani, *op. cit.*, 176 and *Storia della letteratura del Pakistan* (E IV), 63 *et seq.* deduces from a series of quotations two trends as being characteristic of the Indian style: (1) collapse of the old-established 'armonia formale', and (2) 'concetti puramente astratti'. With these two basic characteristics Bausani throws light on several apparent contradictions in the Indian style. Thus the observation has frequently been made that a great many of these poets introduce the terminology of the bazaar and other popular expressions into their verses. Bertel's and other Soviet experts regard this as principally a social phenomenon. When these poets (especially Bīdil) disclose a strong predisposition for detailed descriptions of natural phenomena, plants and animals, it is interpreted as evidence of a progressive or scientific tendency, for such subjects are seldom or never mentioned or described in works composed in the classical style. According to Bausani this is nothing other than the logical consequence of the two basic characteristics already quoted, it is merely an extension of the terminology in the poetical vocabulary; for as soon as the classical harmony of form is violated, the number of subjects that can be employed for poetical purposes increases. At the same time, says Bausani, the second of the two characteristic features (the concretising of abstract things) evokes an intellectual game of semi-personified images that – more or less by chance – is able to express a profound philosophical thought, but may not be confused with actual philosophy.

13. *LHP*, 4, 354.

14. Horn, *Gesch. der pers. Literatur*, 115.

15. Bertel's, 'Lit. ... v Sr. Az.' (D IIa), 217; a still earlier proof of this I find in the Seljuq period (Bert., *IPTL*, 518) and in Auḥadī Marāghī (see p. 254); Shiblī, 5, 29 l. 17. Mīnuvī produces a large number of quotations from Jāmī, *Khākpāy* (Bibl.). The conception of *sagiyya* is quite general during the first half of the 9th/15th century: Yār Shāṭir, *Shi'r*, 147, 117, etc.

16. E. Stemplinger, *Horaz im Urteil der Jahrhunderte*, Leipzig 1921, 66.

17. Bibl. *s.v.* 'Ṣā'ib': *Mu'taman, Ash'ār* 62 *et seq.* Certainly not correct, cf. V. Minorsky, 'Iran' (B II), 195: "When the travellers of Safavid times declared that the shahs were worshipped as God, these statements were interpreted figuratively, but they should rather be taken literally." As early as the time of Shaykh Junayd the Safavids' claim (that it was unlawful is demonstrated by Z. V. Togan, 'Sur l'origine etc.' [B II] and already earlier by A. Kasravī) to descent from the Prophet had grown to "a living embodiment of the line of Imams" (*ibid.*, 194).

18. Cf. Aḥm. Gulchīn-i ma'ānī, 'Mīr Najāt-i Iṣfahānī', *Māhnāma-i Vaḥīd*, 1/3 (1342), 32 *et seq.*

19. *Tkani*, 263 *et seq.*

20. See Bibl. B VIa, *s.v.* 'qaḍā'; Bertel's, 'Lit. ... v Sr. Az.' (D IIa), 226; Avicenna, *Risāla-i qaḍā u qadar, Jashn-nāma* 2, 240.

21. 'Uṭārid, *Maẓāhir* (B VIa), 24 *et seq.*

22. Vaḥīd, 'Rahbarān', *Arm.*, 18, 162 (B VIa).

23. Ḍamīrī: Krïmskiy, 3, 150; Vaḥīdī: *Tuḥfa-i Sāmī*, 126 *et seq.*; Mesīḥī: *HOP*, 2, 226 *et seq.*; Āgahī: Krïmskiy, 3, 144 and *Tuḥfa-i Sāmī*, 117 *et seq.*; Ḥarfī: *Tuḥfa-i Sāmī*, 153.

24. Cf. above, p. 289. – Ritter, *Philol.*, XI, 245. – Cf. A. S. Levend, *Türk edebiyatinda şehr-engizler* (İstanbul 1958).

25. *Sayyido Nasafi* (Russ.; D IIb), 143 *et seq.* Yet in view of the dissimilarity of the form I am somewhat in doubt, if I see it rightly.

26. A. Mirzoyev, *Sayyido Nasafi* (Russ.), 143 *et seq.*, makes a distinction in practice between small

'artisan medallions', called above *Shahr-angīz*, and satirical poems in *qaṣīda* form, *Shahr-āshūb*, but designates both types by the term *Shahr-āshūb*. The terms appear to be used indiscriminately. In relation to the satirical poem he quotes Mīr Muḥ. Hāshim (against the grandees and courtiers of Herat) and Maulānā Jalālu'd-dīn Muḥ. Ilāhī in the year 920/1514–5 (against the temporal and spiritual leaders of Herat). Continuous love-strophes (*mukhammas*), each containing five semi-distichs, rhymed according to a fixed pattern, were also called *Shahr-āshūb* (*ibid.*, 144).

27. According to Abū-Ṭālib's *tadhkira* d. 1000/1591–2 (E. G. Browne–R. Yāsimī, p. 183, 2).

28. Thus R. Yāsimī in his translation of *LHP*, 4, p. 183_{3}, as opposed to Krïmskiy, 3, 148_{3}, who even established seven lyrical *dīvāns*. – When compared with a Naẓīrī or an 'Urfī, a very mediocre poet (Shiblī, 5, 49).

29. Bibl. *s.v.* 'Muḥtasham': *Arm.*, 11, 271–72; *s.v.* 'Vaqār': *Arm.*, 15, 231 *et seq.*

30. Thus according to Abdülkadir Karahan, *Fuzûlî*, 67 *et seq.*, 72 *et seq.*; 109 *et seq.* Other dates: according to Abū-Ṭālib's *tadhkira* 976/1568–9 (E. G. Browne–R. Yāsimī, p. 180_{1}); Qinālizāde: 970/1562–3 (*HOP*, 3, 72 *et seq.*). On Fuḍūlī's ethnical extraction cf. Karahan, *loc. cit.*, 115.

31. Cemil Yener, 'Fuzulî'ye ve aşkına dair', *Türk Dili*, 8/94 (1959), 558–65. With regard to Niẓāmī see Bibl. *s.v.* 'Araslï', to whom we owe an excellent monograph on the poet and a series of editions (see Bibl.). For a clear survey of Fuḍūlī's life and work, see M. F. Köprülü, *İA*, 4, 686–99. *

32. Ḥus. Nakhjavānī, 'Ḥamāsa-sarā'ī dar Īrān', *NDAT*, 3/8 (1329), 39.

33. Krïmskiy, 3, 147; Ethé, *GIPh*, 2, 297; Nakhjavānī, as in note 32.

34. H. W. Duda (*WZKM*, 57, 234) states that 'Urfī's *Farhād u Shīrīn* possesses a preponderantly lyrical strain. *

35. Muḥ. 'Alī, *'Urfī*, 327 *et seq.*

36. Shiblī, 3, 17; 102.

37. Nafīsī, *Shaykh Bahā'ī*, 50 *et seq.* On Bahā'ī's birthplace see Ḥasan al-Amīn, 'Juba', zādgāh-i shaykh Bahā'ī', *Ad-dirāsāt al-adabiyya*, 2/4 (1961), 367–73.

38. Shiblī, 5, 50.

39. Krïmskiy, 3, 155; in Suhaylī's 'Shifā'ī', *Arm.*, 18, 426, the relationship appears less friendly.

40. By Shiblī, 5, 96, even preferred above Shifā'ī!

41. Bertel's, 'Lit. ... v Sr. Az.' (D IIa), 226.

42. *Calligraphers and Painters* by Qāḍī Aḥmad, son of Mīr-Munshī, transl. by V. Minorsky, Washington 1959, 169 n.

43. On the subject of his epic poem *Maḥmūd u Ayāz* I have no further information at my disposal.

44. For further information on these two writers, see p. 515 *et seq.*

XI. THE TURBULENT 12TH/18TH CENTURY

Nādir-Shāh, Karīm-Khān, Āqā Muḥammad

The internal oppositional currents that had developed within the Safavid empire eventually became so acute that the dynasty was no longer able to keep the situation under control. The all-powerful upper ranks of the Shīʿite priesthood were at strife with the secular feudal lords, which latter were also engaged in quarrels among themselves. As if this state of affairs alone were not enough to greatly weaken the influence of the ruling circles, the opposition of the peasant population to the secular and ecclesiastical feudal rulers did the rest. Besides this, the religious, or rather national, feud between the subjugated Sunnite districts and the intolerant Shīʿa, the state religion, became more and more difficult to check. The logical conclusion of this struggle for supremacy was the Afghan revolt, the results of which were a rapid overrunning of Persia, a sudden downfall of the dynasty and – most serious of all – an atrocious laying waste of the countryside; for the Afghan rising, that in itself was understandable, soon degenerated into a marauding campaign. The reign of terror of its leaders and the lust for plunder on the part of neighbouring states were put an end to in 1730 by Nādir-Khān, who had first come to the fore as Ṭahmāsp-qulī-Khān, 'Ṭahmāsp II's slave', under the pretence of being a submissive disinterested servant to the later Safavids. The general hatred of the almost incredible desire for robbery and murder on the part of the Afghan leaders came most opportunely for this undoubtedly competent upstart. But within a short time he ripped off the mask, drove the last of the Safavids from the throne (1736) and soon proclaimed himself the sole holder of power in Persia. Nādir-Shāh was a warrior of the Napoleonic type.

The Afghan invasion, which imparted severe and long-lasting wounds on cultural life, was followed by immense decline. The reign of the warlike Nādir-Shāh (*de facto* 1143–60/1730–47) was hardly conducive to a revival of literature, moreover it was of relatively short duration and, as it were, only an interlude in the midst of anarchistic periods, quite apart from the fact that Nādir had no understanding of literature. The only poet to enjoy his esteem was a relative of the Safavid dynasty, Mīrzā Mahdī-

Notes on pp. 309–310

Khān 'Fighānī' of Astarabad[1], his secretary and historiographer and an eminent authority on the Chagatay language (see p. 315). Nonetheless this epoch maintains its place in the history of Persian literature. The military triumphs of Nādir and his generals were so brilliant that they inevitably provided inspiration for the writing of panegyrics. The *qaṣīda,* transformed during the Safavid period into pious hymns in praise of the Imāms, now regained its former designation. In the healing process the newly-powerful Isfahan and the period of Karīm-Khān Zand played a conspicuous part. The way was prepared for a renaissance of Persian literature when, as successor to the new unifier of Persia, the Qajar Āqā Muḥammad-Khān, severe to the point of cruelty, Fatḥ-'Alī-Shāh ascended the throne (1212/1797). He was fond of culture and splendour, and himself dabbled in poetry; amidst his wives and female slaves, of whom he possessed several hundred, he cooed tenderly and amorously like a cock-pigeon.

A. SHIRAZ, POLITICAL CENTRE IN THE SECOND HALF OF THE 12TH/18TH CENTURY; 'RETURN' (*BAZ-GĀSHT*) IN ISFAHAN

The decline and dramatic end of the Safavid dynasty shook Iran to its foundations. The material condition of the country was not improved by Nādir's marauding campaign in India and to an even lesser extent by his subsequent policy of war. In order to find support for his despotism he conferred certain privileges on the Khāns of Khurasan, who thus came to occupy a special position. It was the estrangement from them that later on led to Nādir's fall.[2] Though he had succeeded in restoring unity to Persia, his assassination resulted in further disintegration and a state of unrest that lasted until nearly the end of the century. There was but one peaceful interlude that, with a view to what had gone before as well as to what followed, was alas all too short. We refer to the reign of Karīm-Khān Zand (1173–93/1760–79), a Kurd of humble birth, but an unusually humane man in relation to Persian standards as a whole and especially to those of his time. Although he ruled over the whole of Persia with the exception of Khurasan (with Shiraz as the metropolis, situated as it was among the pasturing lands of the tribes on which he relied for support[3]), he nevertheless adopted no other title for himself than that of a simple *Vakīl*, 'Regent', of the imaginary Safavids. Up to the time of his advent there existed such a state of chaos that by many it is compared with the destruction brought about by the Mongol invasion and with the era of Tīmūr. Karīm-Khān took several precautionary measures to raise the impoverished state of agriculture, handicrafts and trade. In order to increase foreign trade he granted certain privileges to England and Holland. All this could not fail to have favourable repercussions on the general state of the country. But he had also given permission for the Capitulations, a fact which must not be overlooked. The main object of the Vakīl's care was Shiraz, which under the Zands was to become a sort of miniature Paris, where under peaceful conditions the wealth plundered previously in India and subsequently dispersed at the time of Nādir's assassination, was now again assembled. It was Karīm-Khān's aim to concentrate in his metropolis the Indian artisans who had been brought into the country by Nādir and who after his death had scattered over the whole of Iran. Magnificent buildings sprang up in Shiraz, but with poets and poetry Karīm-Khān did not stand in any particularly close relationship; it was ʿAlī-Murād-Khān (1195–9/1782–5) who first showed interest in them by commissioning Shihāb of Turshīz to write a history in verse of the Zand dynasty after the manner of the *Shāh-nāma*. On the whole the gay life in Shiraz was not very conducive to a thriving of literature.

It stands to reason that the reign of the incompetent Shāh Ḥusayn, the tragic end of the Safavid dynasty and the atrocities of Nādir were accompanied by a flagging of literary activity. The subtleties of the Indian style could only prosper in the death-like calm and decline of a Safavid regime, dependent materially on agricultural and professional labour, with its hyper-cultivated upper classes and its all-powerful priesthood, but not in the midst of the greater and lesser disturbances which left such deep marks on the 12th/18th century. The new spark now ignited was to be found, strangely enough, in Isfahan, which meanwhile had gradually recovered from the effects of the terrible Afghan massacres. There is no doubt that here the traditions of the erstwhile capital also played a part. At the head of the movement we find a number of men whose talent was not outstanding. But that their efforts were nevertheless rewarded by a decisive success shows that they rightly understood the spirit of the time. Themselves possessing a sense of discrimination and good taste, they recognised the way in which the Indian style had gone astray. The absence of relations with India and Transoxania was likewise favourable for the renunciation of former models. As the power of attraction of the Indian style waned the conviction grew that it was necessary to turn back to the healthy traditions of the old masters of Persian poetry. The latter half of the 18th century witnessed the departure from the school of the two preceding centuries and a return to the ancient poets. This 'return' (*baz-gāsht*) signifies the liberation of poetry, a hundred years before that of prose. *From then on*, according to Muḥammad Bahār[4], and not roughly speaking from the time of the accession of the Qajars – more accurately with Fatḥ-ʿAlī-Shāh, because his predecessor Āqā Muḥammad-Khān was a barbarian with no interest at all in literature – *we must date the new epoch in poetry, the epoch of the 13th/19th century*, that lasted up to the assassination of Nāṣiru'd-dīn-Shāh. In the course of this period of 'return' the paths of Iran and India finally diverge. Iran goes its own way, but Turkestan and Afghanistan henceforth maintain their adherence to India. In the vanguard of this renaissance stand Sayyid Muḥammad Shuʿla (d. 1160/1747) and Mīr Sayyid ʿAlī Mushtāq (d. 1171/1757–8, both of whom came from Isfahan and

Notes on pp. 309–310

were well acquainted with the ancient poetry. To these names may be added that of Mīrzā Muḥammad Naṣīr of Isfahan (d. 1191/1777), a physician and scholar who worked in Shiraz. The most meritorious of them all is the master of the *ghazal*, Mushtāq, who brought new life into the old style and also trained his younger contemporaries in the same way (e.g. the melancholy Āqā Muḥammad ʿĀshiq of Isfahan, d. 1181/1767–8), thereby also extending his influence to the new generation, as for instance Mullā Ḥuṣayn Rafīq of Isfahan (d. 1215/1800–1), the predecessor of the circle of poets around Fatḥ-ʿAlī-Shāh. Among his exceedingly numerous pupils were Sayyid Aḥmad Hātif of Isfahan (d. 1198/1783–4) with his inseparable friends, the poets Ḥājjī Luṭf-ʿAlī-Beg Ādhar (d. 1195/1780–1), a master of the *qaṣīda* and author of the *tadhkira-i Ātash-kada*, 'The Fire Temple', and Ḥājjī Sulaymān Ṣabaḥī (d. 1218/1803–4).[5] Hātif won fame by his unsurpassed *Tarjīʿ-band*, a work that sings of a mystical vision, albeit with all the conventional erotic and wine-house accessories, but in an uncommonly straightforward style, in a lucidly arranged metaphorical language intensified to the highest degree of perception, free of the euphuisms and obscurities of the foregoing period. Here we have one of the best examples of Persian poetry in the 12th/18th century and one that at the same time stands on an incomparably higher level than anything else this poet produced.

B. ḤAZĪN

An important writer on the fringe of the 'return' movement is Shaykh Muḥammad ʿAlī Ḥazīn (b. 1103/1692, d. 1180/1766–7).[6] After escaping from Isfahan, that was being besieged by the Afghans, he roved about Persia for ten years until in 1734 he arrived in India. Although well received there he did not tire of producing pamphlets in which he aired his displeasure regarding this hospitable country; but he remained there nevertheless. He describes the dire distress which he witnessed on his travels in his memoirs *Tadhkiratuʾl-aḥvāl*, 'Description of the Conditions', which was written in 1154/1741–2 and is a valuable source of knowledge on contemporary social and literary life. It is to be regretted that this acute observer did not also include India in his survey. But the omission is due to the fact that his sojourn there was not agreeable to him, as was the case with most of the Persian poets who escaped to India. Of his numerous prose works[7] we may mention two small historical writings, a *tadhkira* on contemporary men of letters, and treatises on hippology and zoology. Although in no sense a poor poet, he was not very scrupulous either in the correct use of language or with ideas borrowed from others. With his four *dīvāns* he certainly exhibited an exceptional productivity. His broad-minded attitude towards other people, no matter what their creed or nationality, deserves particular mention.

C. SHIHĀB

To the Isfahan group we may add Mīrzā ʿAbdu'llāh Shihāb of Turshīz (b. 1167/1753–4, d. 1215/1800–1), a panegyrist at the western and eastern courts of Iran. During the years 1197–1202/1782–8 he witnessed the glory and fall of the Zand dynasty in Shiraz and Isfahan. He stayed longest in Herat and enjoyed the favour of the Afghan governor, prince Maḥmud Durrānī. He turned away from the Indian style and followed the patterns of the ancient poets, especially Anvarī, with whom he has in common a freshness of subject-matter in his *qaṣīdas* and particularly in his *qiṭʿas*. He also touches on daily life and shares with Anvarī a lucid and flowing style, as well as humour when reciting his petitions, and the latter's antipathy to literary importunity. With a like predilection he, too, alludes to mathematics and astronomy, but will have nothing to do with astrology. In accordance with the spirit of his times, Shihāb is a straightforward poet, void of abstract philosophy and mysticism. But he regards life as a struggle and shows great skill in the depiction of temporal things and popular customs. The infrequent appearance of the *taghazzul* is compensated by a greater naturalness as compared with other poets. In the *ghazal* he takes an independent course, often employing new verse-metres of his own. In addition Shihāb wrote several romantic and historical *mathnavīs*, but he did not always complete everything he embarked on. His speciality was the satirical *mathnavī* and in fact the satire in general. He sought out and criticised shortcomings, for he had witnessed and experienced many things. A certain love of dispute must have been firmly rooted in him, for there is scarcely a single contemporary poet whom he spared from his invective. It may be that he thus gave vent to the feelings of a Khurasanian who found no recognition in Iraq. This phenomenon can be regularly encountered at that period as a result of the political separation of Khurasan from Iraq and the accompanying social and literary divergation. Shihāb was without a doubt several decades ahead of his compatriots. His satirical verse is counted among the best of its kind in Iran. M. Bahār does not hesitate in designating him *durr-i yatīm*, "the unique pearl" of his age.[8]

NOTES

1. Bahār, 'Bāz-gasht' (B VIa), 521.
2. Ashrafyan, 'Antifeod. dvizheniya' (B II), 204.
3. Ivanow, *Ocherk* (B II), 107–8.
4. Bahār, *loc. cit.*, 715.
5. Thus according to Bayḍā'ī's essay (see B VIb), 116; erroneously 1206/1791–2 Riḍā-qulī Hidāyat,

Majma', 2, 263, and *LHP*, 4, 521. The poet's full name is Ḥājjī Sulaymān-Beg Ṣabāḥī Bīdgulī Kāshānī.
6. Latterly L. Lockhart, *The Fall of the Ṣafavī Dynasty etc.* (B II), Cambridge 1958, 500–4.
7. They are enumerated in full by Khatak (B VIb), *s.v.* 'Ḥazīn', 156–234.
8. 'Shihāb', *Arm.*, 13, 125b.

XII. LITERARY AND ASSOCIATED SPECIES OF PROSE DURING THE 7TH–12TH/13TH–18TH CENTURIES

In the category of belletristic prose in Persian literature we may include not only the literary but also in due course – and by virtue of its language – a considerable portion of the scholarly literature. One might therefore reasonably expect the present chapter to be of great length, especially since there has been a continual increase in the production of prose works. But there are certain deterrent factors that will serve to counteract any undue expansion of this survey. In the first place there is the inadequate recognition hitherto accorded to a great deal of the prose belles-lettres that not even M. Bahār's classic *Sabk-shināsī* 2–3 can remedy. In the second place there is the impossibility of enumerating more than the most characteristic scholarly works because, despite all their artistic or semi-artistic drapery, they belong beyond doubt to the category of instructional and on occasions actually to that of learned literature in the fields of history, religion, ethics, and literary theory. As such they will be dealt with in a separate portion of the present work by the eminent expert Dr. Felix Tauer (p. 419–82). Moreover, the output of genuine belletristic prose was disproportionately smaller than that of poetry, and with the exception of a few masterpieces it never reached the high standard that distinguishes the verse. An explanation for this is not difficult to find: men of letters ascribed full aesthetic value only to writing in verse-form. At the back of this there lies, of course, the great artistic talent of the Iranian and the ancient tradition in this direction. How loth a poet was to relinquish the metrical form in favour of prose is to be seen in the fact that he employed every conceivable method of embellishing the latter and of interweaving it with verse.

For these and other reasons this chapter can offer no more than a superficial survey in which only a selection of the achievements spread over the enormous period of six centuries requires mention, since some of the prose works have already been discussed in connection with the verse productions of the author under consideration.

JAN RYPKA

A. TWO TRENDS IN STYLE: EXTRAVAGANCE AND SIMPLICITY

By mentioning Sa'dī's *Gulistān* and Jāmī's *Bahāristān*, 'Irāqī's *Lama'āt*, 'Ubayd Zākānī's *Akhlāqu'l-ashrāf* and other works, we have already drawn attention to the best specimens of literary prose. We shall discuss now mainly those authors whose achievements lie pre-eminently in the field of belletristic prose (e.g. Ḥusayn Vā'iẓ). During the centuries under review, however, there appeared works on scholarly subjects which, apart from the arabising that went parallel with it, are written in such a decorative style that they can be classed as works of art. A similar tendency took effect in the pre-Mongol era, and each subsequent period contributed its share in a more exuberant embellishment and affectation both in belletristic and scholarly prose. Yet this development was not direct – on the contrary, it was decidedly complicated. For a detailed and apt exposition of the evolution of prose we are indebted to Muḥammad Bahār[1], that incomparable master of modern classical poetry. Although it cannot be contested that the basic line shows a rising degree of artificiality – even if there were occasional exceptions which, taken separately, may be quite important – this was not the only trend in the development of prose. Numerous authors, whose names are cited by S. Nafīsī[2], showed preference for a straightforward style even during periods when poetically modelled prose was at its height. There were thus two contiguous currents – the constantly increasing tendency towards artificiality and the less presumptuous movement; and of these the former was not without influence on the latter. A few special works strike the eye (e.g. Vaṣṣāf's *History* in the field of historical prose, and Ḥusayn Vā'iẓ' *Anvār-i Suhaylī* in that of belles-lettres), which excited admiration and led to imitation, and to even further extravagance (e.g. Mīrzā Mahdī-Khān's *Durra-i nādira*, 'Rare Pearl', see p. 315). Present-day Iranian scholars emphasise with remarkable, though unspoken apologetic vigour the existence of a succession of authors who used the simple straightforward style. I fancy however, that when assessing the simplicity of style of a given author European observers will frequently entertain a different view. There is a tremendous difference between the directness of the first prose works and that of Jāmī's *Bahāristān*. Undoubtedly this is only a question of relative simplicity. It must also be borne in mind that differing kinds of prose follow different courses. But it should be remarked that arabising alone, be it ever so hypertrophied, is in itself still not a sign of stylistic extravagance. This is proved by works on philosophy, theology, law, and the natural sciences. While historical works employ all possible varieties of style, including the most pretentious, Ṣūfism generally makes use of a simpler key. The subjects most susceptible to bombast are essays, history and epistolography. Of course belletristic prose is in similar case. One finds a flowery, dallying, bombastic, often superfluously garrulous style, trifling and often even empty in substance. This causes an increase in the use of Arabic words in Persian to the utmost possible limits, so that only professional *beaux-esprits* are capable of understanding such literature. No regard is paid to the necessities of everyday life. This manner, or rather ill-manner, was in use up to the time of Qā'im-maqām (d. 1251/1835) who was the first to begin to conquer it in the state epistolography. India embraced the florid style even more convincedly and for a longer period of time. Not for nothing was a knowledge of the surfeited *Anvār-i Suhaylī* (see below) made compulsory for the higher examinations of the British Civil Service in India. This manner of writing became very widespread and was in use for 600 years, with the result that in Europe it came to be regarded as the genuine Persian style. In the following survey we can only mention the most prominent names.

B. ḤUSAYN VĀʿIẒ; THE MORAL PHILOSOPHERS

A prose writer *par excellence* is the extraordinarily prolific Kamālu'd-dīn Ḥusayn Vāʿiẓ Kāshifī of Sabzavar (d. 910/1504–05), a preacher (*vāʿiẓ*) in Herat. He became known mainly for his recasting of the collection of fables *Kalīla u Dimna* (see p. 222) under the title of *Anvār-i Suhaylī*, 'The Lights of Canopus', or rather 'The Lights of Suhaylī', after the *takhalluṣ* of his patron. This was the poet Niẓāmu'd-dīn Amīr Shaykh Aḥmad (d. 907/1501–2). The motive underlying the work was that the relatively simple style of the classic translation by Abu'l-maʿālī Naṣru'llāh did not appeal to current taste, which demanded a high-flown style. And this requirement was more than met by Ḥusayn Vāʿiẓ. Written in the same exaggerated manner we find the Ottoman-Turkish version *Hümāyūn-nāme*, 'The Imperial Book', by ʿAlī-Chelebi (d. 950/1543–4), which is based on the much-admired *Anvār*. In itself extremely popular and used moreover as a school-book, the *Anvār-i Suhaylī* left an ineffaceable and unfortunately calamitous mark on Persian literary style. Surprisingly enough it was in India that it became simplified and also integrated (996/1588): with his *ʿIyār-i dānish*, 'The Right Measure of Knowledge', Abu'l-Faḍl b. Mubārak, a renowned historian and minister under Akbar, complied with the wise command of his ruler, to whom the *Anvār* evidently appeared unbearably bombastic. Ḥusayn Vāʿiẓ wrote among other things *Rauḍatu'sh-shuhadā*, 'Garden of the Martyrs', which he devoted largely to the martyrology of the Imām Ḥusayn, younger grandson of the Prophet; but above all mention should be made of the treatise on moral philosophy, *Akhlāq-i Muḥsinī*, that dates from 900/1494–5. This is the third of a series of famous treatises on ethics, the first of which, *Akhlāq-i Nāṣirī* (633/1235–6) is from the hand of Naṣīru'd-dīn Ṭūsī (b. 597/1201, d. 672/1274), the influential adviser of Hülägü. Naṣīru'd-dīn was an eminent astronomer and the author of numerous scientific works in Arabic and Persian. But he was also an extremely unusual moralist[3], who managed simultaneously to make himself of use to the Assassins and to their Mongol enemies, and to play a part in the fall of the last of the Abbasids, ostensibly driven by his Shīʿite convictions. It is known that his book, especially the introduction, was written originally in the spirit and according to the wishes of his lords and masters, the rulers of Alamūt, but that later on it was subjected to a thorough revision[4] under Hülāgü, the destroyer of the Assassin Order. Naṣīru'd-dīn argues himself out of the restrictions to which, at the period of the first edition, he had been exposed as their prisoner. It was of course an object of concern with him to veil his past as far as possible under the new regime. On his theory of ethics, which for the rest drew on Arabic sources, the philosopher Jalālu'd-dīn Muḥammad Dav(v)ānī (d. 908/1502–3) based his *Akhlāq-i Jalālī*, actually *Lavāmiʿu'l-ashrāq fī makārimi'l-akhlāq*, 'The Splendour of the Rising Sun on Lofty Morals' (872–82/1467–77), that contains the most florid ethics of all. To what psychological source can we trace a letter which the same scholar couched in an entirely 'pure' Persian style?[5]

C. VAṢṢĀF (8TH/14TH CENTURY) AND HIS IMITATOR MAHDĪ-KHĀN (12TH/18TH CENTURY)

In the series of excellent historical works that marked the Mongol period, there is one that far surpasses even the already stylistically exuberant *Ta'rīkh-i Jahān-gushāy*, 'History of the World Conqueror' (Chingiz) by ʿAlā'u'd-dīn ʿAṭā Malik Juvaynī and serves as a warning against the excessive embellishment of historical prose. It is *Ta'rīkh-i Vaṣṣāf*, actually *Tajziyatu'l-amṣār va tazjiyatu'l-aʿṣār*, 'The Division of Land and the Passing of the Ages', a picture of events from 655–728/1257–1328 (Hülāgü to Abū-Saʿīd), the author being Sharafu'd-dīn ʿAbdu'llāh[6], known as Vaṣṣāfu'l-haḍrat, 'the panegyrist of His Majesty', who hailed from Shiraz (b. 663/1264, d. 735/1334). In point of fact it is a vast exercise in style, for the author himself admits that he has style particularly in view, the historical events merely serving him as a foundation on which to build. With his excessive tendency to arabising, his monstrous bombast, unbearable floridness and dallying, Vaṣṣāf did tremendous harm to Persian prose, on which he exercised a lastingly bad influence. (A similar fabulous 'mastery' is exhibited also in his *qaṣīda* on prosody and poetics.) It is almost comical that from the practical point of view his historical work contains a great deal of extremely valuable material that can only be reached after struggling through a vast and indigestible mass of exaggeration and superfluities.[7] The height to which Persian historiography had risen in the Mongol period can be seen from the fact that it did not confine itself merely to foreign affairs but that it describes the internal situation of the country in minute detail during the reign of each of the Īl-Khāns. This is done the most meticulously by Rashīd'ud-dīn Faḍlu'llāh (put to death 718/1318) in his *Jāmi'u't-tavārīkh*, 'The Sum of Histories'.[8] But a different attitude is taken by the historiographers of the period of decline; it appears as if they had lost sight of the real aim of their writings. It is true that under the later Safavids a baroque phraseology was required to counteract the deadly dullness of these times. One of the most high-flown stylists is Niẓāmu'd-dīn Muḥammad Hādī al-Ḥusaynī aṣ-Ṣafavī, known as Mahdī-Khān (see p. 305), the secretary (*munshi'u'l-mamālik*) and historiographer of Nādir-Shāh, epistolographer, eminent grammarian of the Chagatay language[9] and even a physicist. He wrote about his lord and master in *Tā'rīkh-i Jahān-gushā-i Nādirī*, 'History of Nādir, the World Conqueror' (revised by Mīrzā 'Alī'-Askar), and in *Durra-i nādira*, 'Rare Pearl' (containing the obvious pun: *nādir*=rare→Nādir). With regard to its contents, the *Durra* coincides pretty well with the *Tā'rīkh*, but the affectation of its style is unprecedented. Mahdī was commissioned to co-operate with Christian priests in translating the Gospels into Persian, and this participation in Nādir's plans for religious reform earned for him the accusation of atheism after the murder of his patron. His *Mabānī'l-lughat*, 'Foundations of Language', a Chagatay grammar written in Persian, owes its existence to material he had collected in an attempt to make as penetrating a study as possible of his favourite poet Navā'ī, whom he had read from his youth onwards.

I. INDIAN ESSAY-WRITING; 'INSHĀ', 'LETTER-WRITING', 'MODEL LETTERS'; 'TADHKIRAS', ETC.

The essay was grist to the Indian mill, for it offered opportunity for extravagance of expression in the most brilliant form, both in word and in thought. Leading figures are Nūru'd-dīn Muḥammad Ẓuhūrī (see p. 301) and Mullā Ṭughrā in the 11th/17th century, Ni'mat-Khān 'Alī (d. approx. 1122/1710) and above all the highly gifted Bīdil (see p. 515).

In the same florid style epistolography, likewise a scion on which Iranian, Indian and Turkish progenitors bestowed unceasing care also finds its element. The early Mongols had certainly taken up an averse attitude to this manner of writing (see p. 247), but they were nevertheless unable to prevent it and were eventually obliged to give it free rein. Methodical instruction in letter-writing and models of this art bear the common name of *inshā*. The Iranian *inshā* frequently oversteps the boundaries set by our guide to letter-writing, dealing as it does not only with the whole of private correspondence, including social affairs and those of the heart, but also letters of a public and diplomatic nature. The model letters can have been composed *ad hoc* or extracted from correspondence that had actually taken place, no matter from what section of society or of state politics. In the latter case they are not without importance in connection with the biographical and historical aspects, although it must be admitted that their factual contents stand in inverse ratio to their verbosity. There is an enormous number of such guides and collections of letters[10], belletristic or otherwise, and it is significant of the attitude of the later classical writers that a man like Jāmī did not disdain to enrich literature by a guide to letter-writing. It must also be assumed that the poets and men of letters kept up a lively correspondence with each other. The periodical *Armaghān*, and occasionally others as well, were in the habit of publishing specimens from the pens of the most important personalities of classical literature.

There is a long series of *tadhkiras*, collections of biographies and anthologies which can really be regarded as first indigenous attempts at a history of literature and which form an invaluable source of information despite their primitive nature and lack of accuracy. Typical of its period is the *tadhkira* of Amīr Daulat-Shāh of Samarkand (d. 900/1494–5?) that for a long time was virtually the sole handbook of Persian literature for Europe. It embraces literary figures from the Arab invasion onwards up to 892/1486–7. Daulat-Shāh knows how to communicate a great deal in an interesting fashion, but his work is unfortunately not without errors which are to be met with at every turn.[11] The *tadhkiras* are sometimes general, sometimes regional in content, now and then again confined to contemporary poets; the arrangement is either chronological, alphabetical, geographical, according to class or otherwise. The choice of examples is not always equally felicitous. In this connection an exception is formed (according to an oral communication from professor S. Nafīsī) by *Khulāṣatu'l-ash'ār*, 'Selection of Poems', by Taqī of Kashan dating from 1016/1607–8 (in the second, enlarged redaction). We are indebted to the poet Ṣā'ib for an excellent anthology, of which later compilers have made willing use. The no small number of already known *tadhkiras* and anthologies increases steadily as a result of recent finds. The following, picked at random, may be cited: *Mu'nisu'l-aḥrār fī daqā'iqi'l-ash'ār*, 'The Companion of the Free on the Subtleties of Poesy', by Muḥammad b. Badr Jājarmī, dating from 741/1340–1[12]; the *tadhkira* of Ḥasan Nithārī, important with regard to cultural life in Central Asia in the 10th/16th century; the anthology of the poets of Qā'ināt from the 13th/19th century[13], etc. There is also a wealth of literature dealing with poetics, prosody and rhyme. Here too Jāmī demonstrates his universality.

2. BELLES-LETTRES

Despite its pomposity, prose of an exclusively narrative character, devoid of all symbolism, allegory and philosophy, does not cease to arouse interest. It can be divided into the customary categories, which have already been discussed (see p. 220). Folk literature will be dealt with in a separate portion of this book. A few words here will suffice by way of a summary. Lengthy romances, mostly written anonymously, find their material as in former times in the realms of fancy, chivalry and the life of the Bedouins; occasionally too in religious legends. In the same category can be placed the shorter tales – almost always anonymous and complete in themselves – of a romantic or fairy-tale nature. These enjoyed great popularity. Here too humour comes into its own, notably in the form of amusing tales from the life of jugglers and tramps, finally in the cultivated form of *maqāmas* (see p. 223). The *Ṭūṭī-nāma* has already been referred to as a typical example of a collection of fairy-tales and anecdotes within the framework of a story (see p. 223), likewise the book of fables, *Kalīla u Dimna*, the most important of them all (p. 222). Among the books containing tales, adventures and anecdotes around specific subjects must be included the imitations of the *Gulistān*, on the whole not so numerous as one might expect. The most important of them is Jāmī's *Bahāristān* (see p. 287). Finally, with H. Ethé[14], whom I follow in abridged form, we can class here the legends of the prophets (under the general title *Qiṣaṣu'l-anbiyā'*) and hagiographical collections in general. ʿAlī b. Ḥusayn Vāʿiẓ Kāshifī, son of the famous author of *Anvār-i Suhaylī* (see p. 313), writing under the pseudonym Ṣafī (see p. 301), produced a collection of anecdotes and funny stories called *Laṭā'ifu'ṭ-ṭavā'if* (or *Laṭā'ifu'ẓ-ẓarā'if*), arranged according to the social classes. But there are also some collections that contain no particular aspect by which they can be classified. Among the allegories invested with mystical speculation, the symbolical story *Ḥusn u ʿIshq*, 'Beauty and Love', or *Ḥusn u Dil*, 'Beauty and Heart', stands out. It has been adapted by various authors – Fattāḥī's arrangement (see p. 284) being especially deserving of attention and thrice paraphrased in Ottoman-Turkish.

3. SCHOLARLY WORKS

Within the given plan the foregoing lines aim merely at completing the previous chapters with relation to belles-lettres. More information on the subject will be found in a separate portion of the present book in Dr. F. Tauer's systematic discussion of writings with a scholarly or didactic content.

As a result of the collapse of the Baghdad caliphate the political influence of the Arabic language finally came to an end. The same, however, was not true of its cultural influence, although this too gradually waned, in the same manner as did the one-time preponderance of Latin in Europe. The number of Iranian poets writing in Arabic was reduced to a minimum, but the language still held its own in the realms of physics, mathematics and some of the humanities. Its firmest hold was on theology, jurisprudence and philosophy. But in these disciplines too Persian came more and more to the fore, particularly in the first two, when under the Safavids the powerful and blustering propaganda of the Shī'a as state religion began to exercise an influence on the masses. For the rest, it would not be correct to apply pre-Mongol standards when judging the post-Mongol learning of Eastern Islam. Perhaps nowhere does the difference between the situation before and after Chinghiz-Khān come to light so clearly as just in the output of scientific works. Great thoughts and aims have disappeared completely and in their stead an uninspired band of compilers and priests seems to have settled in. It is as if an echo of former times becomes audible when in the field of Arabic lexicography an Iranian scholar appears in the person of the philologist Muḥammad Fīrūz-ābādī (d. 817/1414). He is the author of *Qāmūs*, the largest Arabic dictionary after Jauharī's (d. 392/1002) *Ṣiḥāḥ*, also the work of an Iranian.

Let us close this chapter by mentioning two distinguished figures: Sa'du'd-dīn Mas'ūd at-Taftazānī (d. 791/1389), one of the greatest of Islamic scholars, and his friend and rival 'Alī al-Jurjānī (d. 816/1413). Both delivered lectures – not altogether voluntarily – in Timurid Samarkand and composed their works almost entirely in Arabic. (Taftazānī's alleged authorship of an Ottoman-Turkish translation of the *Būstān* at the beginning of Ottoman literature is grounded on his being taken erroneously for another person bearing the same name.)

NOTES

1. *Sabk*, Vols. 2 and 3.
2. Preface to *Shāh-kārhā* (C), 8–14.
3. "on whom Professor Levy remarks that the verdict of history is a most unfavourable one": Arberry, *CPL*, 253.
4. Cf. Jalālu'd-dīn Humā'ī, 'Muqaddima-i qadīm-i Akhlāq-i Nāṣirī,' *MDAT*, 3/3 (1335), 17–25. – The edition of *Akhlāq-i Nāṣirī* dated 1339 bears the title *Akhlāq-i Muḥtashamī*, in both cases in honour of one and the same person, namely Khvāja Nāṣiru'd-dīn 'Abdu'r-Raḥīm b. 'Alī-Manṣūr Muḥtasham of Quhistān which was one of the centres of Ismā'īlism. Naṣīru'd-dīn Ṭūsī also stayed there for some time and dedicated his writings to prominent persons who subscribed to this heresy. Cf. *RK*, 3/6 (1339), 726 *et seq.*
5. *Arm.*, 22, 14 *et seq.*
6. Storey: *Shihābu'd-dīn 'Abdu'llāh 'Sharaf'*.
7. Works bearing the same bombastic stamp which, if one may judge by the considerable number of preserved manuscripts, were highly popular, are: Mu'īnu'd-dīn Yazdī's History of the Muzaffarids under the title *Mavāhib-i ilāhī*, 'Gifts of God' (!) dating from 757–67/1356–66; Sharafu'd-dīn 'Alī Yazdī's History of Tīmūr, entitled *Ẓafar-nāma*, 'The Book of Victories', composed in 828/1424–25, and perhaps also Iskandar Munshī's *Ta'rīkh-i 'ālam-ārā-i 'Abbāsī*, 'The World-adorning History of 'Abbās II'. For further details see the appropriate portion of the present book, by Felix Tauer.
8. Barthold-Hinz, *Die pers. Inschrift*, 249 *et seq.*; Krïmskiy, 3, 47, refers to the work as the fruit of a collective effort; Spuler, *Die Mongolen in Iran*², 249: contains a reproach on account of plagiarism. – Krïmskiy, 3, 51: *Criticism of the Īlkhān Historiographers*.

9. See Bibl. (B VIb), *s.v.* 'Mahdī'.
10. See Krïmskiy, 3, 135. Even today such primers exist: cf. e.g. *Sukhan*, 12 (1340), 469b. *
11. For a positively destructive verdict see *Sabk*, 3, 186 *et seq.*
12. Bibl. *s.v.* 'Qazvīnī, *An Account of the Mu'nis*'. – Vol. 1, ed. Mīr Ṣāliḥ Ṭabībī, 1337.
13. Bibl. *s.v.* 'Boldïrev' (D IIb), and Bertel's (B VIa), or Āyatī (B VI). A whole series of MSS of *tadhkiras* unknown to western scholars are cited by Kamol Aynī, Abdulgani Mirzoyev, and other Soviet historians of literature. The *tadhkira* by Muḥ. Sharīf Malīḥā Samarqandī (b. 1053/1643–4) entitled *Mudhakkiru'l-aṣḥāb* was the subject of a lecture delivered by A. Mirzoyev at the 25th International Congress of Orientalists at Moscow in 1960 under the title 'Novïy istochnik po literature Irana sefevidskogo perioda' (*Trudï kongr.*, II, 1963, 269–75); cf. *ShS*, 1961/7, 148 *et seq.* A number of *tadhkiras* are quoted by Fritz Meier, *Die schöne Mahsatī*, 117–24. – A *Majma'u'sh-shu'arā* was also composed by Qāḍī Aḥmad, author of a *tadhkira* on calligraphers etc., translated by V. Minorsky (see above, p. 304), p. VIII. *
14. *GIPh*, 2, 317 *et seq.*

XIII. THE 13TH/19TH CENTURY

A. GENERAL CHARACTERISTICS OF THE CENTURY

The Unification of Persia under the Qajars. Torpor of Ancient Institutions. Interference by the Great Powers.

Iran in the 19th century is the Iran of the Qajars and of Tehran. This must however not be regarded either as laudatory or as derogatory, for the country now finds itself in a situation to which it had repeatedly fallen a prey in greater or less degree at each former change of dynasty: namely either an automatic transformation if the new rulers fell in with the nation's longing for a renaissance, or a compulsory accommodation when power was transferred to the assailants and usurpers. Thus the Qajars gave its specific character to their epoch just as all other ruling dynasties had done before them. Nevertheless it is an irrefutable fact that it was not always they who formed the driving force. Actually only one of them was conspicuous for the energy he brought into play, namely the 'founder' of the dynasty, Āqā Muḥammad-Khān, a remorseless tyrant and man of violence who – in virtue of just these qualities – succeeded in bringing about the unification of Persia. Chronologically he belongs to the previous century, but the effect of his deeds was such as to determine in large measure the course of Iranian history in the 13th/19th century, whereas for his successors – irrespective of their strength or weakness – it only remained to carry out his ideas. Not one of them was really aware of the actual needs of the country. Nevertheless it can be stated emphatically that the century under Qajar rule differed essentially from the foregoing epochs. Compared to the decline of Iran in the 12th/18th century it presents a fundamentally constant picture, with the exception, roughly speaking, of Azerbayjan. This picture was such as Āqā Muḥammad-Khān had created it (Afghanistan, and still earlier Turkestan, were already irretrievably lost and were henceforth to go their own way). Unlike comparable moments of time when confusion had dominated the scene, on the whole there was now peace and security. Several small campaigns did take place, but whenever – as an exception to the rule – any of these were victorious (as for instance the one against Herat) they were none-theless without lasting success and generally involved considerable territorial losses (Georgia, Southern Caucasus). But there were other, more fundamental differences compared with the past. Shaken up out of its torpor by Napoleon, the Iran of Fatḥ-'Alī-Shāh – up till then independent and self-supporting – made its entry upon the world stage. But the pleasure was to be short-lived, for this step, as well as those that followed, were all based on nothing but vague promises that were never kept. Add to this Iran's astounding lack of information on conditions in Europe[1], and it will be evident that the attempt was bound to turn out a failure so that Iran lost the place it thought to have attained as an equal partner on the chess-board of world politics, where England and Russia were steadily becoming more and more unbridled rivals. While Iran now ceased for a long while to exert its will in the political sphere, even though at the same time the ruler continued to boast the title of *Shāhanshāh*, 'King of Kings', great and momentous changes were taking place within the nation and among the population, that ultimately turned into a complete revolution: contact with Europe, that had died out after the Safavid period, was now revived. But this contact, that had hitherto been somewhat superficial, resulted in the 13th/19th century in a European influence on Iran that was to be lasting, for it caused the overthrow of the old feudal structure of the country. The close of the struggle over Iran between the rival foreign powers in the first quarter of the century was in fact more disastrous for Iran itself than was the mere loss of the Caucasian provinces, for the country became involved in foreign economic interests and in this way sank to a semi-colonial position, independent only in name. The incompetent Fatḥ-'Alī-Shāh (1212–50/1797–1834) was unable to utilise to the full the heritage of his uncle, namely the actual re-unification of the empire. It is true that this unity was preserved on the surface, but nothing was done to prevent an extension into the 13th/19th century of the interior disintegration that had taken place during the 12th/18th and that was enhanced by the economic rise of Europe. This paved the way for the penetration of European capital into Iran and to an increase in the establishment of European industries in the country. Under such pressure – and this is the most important factor – feudal economy was being transformed into financial economy, viz. economic and social conditions in Iran took on a completely new aspect as compared with the past. The feudal system underwent an irremediable crisis that was exploited by the bour-geoisie, for the latter had grown wealthy thanks to trade and to the new social conditions and now occupied the position of the former feudal lords, having achieved this both by buying up the lands and properties belonging to the peasants and by seizing political power. With the continued transformation of its basis, cultural life slowly but surely underwent a metamorphosis. In Iran too the 19th century sailed along in the wake of the bourgeoisie. This situation is symbolised by the Qajar

Notes on pp. 348–351

dynasty itself, especially after the accession to the throne of Nāṣiru'd-dīn-Shāh, who brought about several reforms, inadequate though they were. But the Iranians had already long been aware that the cause of their military failures and loss of prestige was to be sought in their backwardness. Already in ʿAbbās-Mīrzā, the son and heir-apparent to Fatḥ-ʿAlī-Shāh, a man as full of promise as he was hard, who died prematurely (1249/1833), we find a convinced adherent to the movement for reform and europeanisation. The training of model regiments in Tabriz; the introduction of book-printing and lithography; the sending of thirsters after knowledge to Europe (London)[2] for purposes of study, which began in the first decade of the century; the selection of men like Qā'im-maqām, the founder of a relatively plainer prose style – are all achievements of ʿAbbās-Mīrzā. At first the results were of no great consequence, and indeed they could not have been otherwise, for all these undertakings represented alien grafts on to an inadequate socio-economic foundation. But it is a fact that endeavours to bring about a renaissance were unremitting once they had found their way to Iran. The execution of the enlightened Qā'im-maqām at the behest of Muḥammad-Shāh (1250–64/1834–48), a rough and foolish despot, proves that the path of revival in Iran was strewn with thorns. Ḥājjī Mīrzā Āqāsī, Qā'im-maqām's rival and enemy, and the omnipotent premier and *murshid* (Ṣūfī leader) to the Shāh, is the very personification of a futile reaction and almost comical militarism. It was to the growing hatred of his opponents that Amīr-i Kabīr (d. 1852), prime minister and brother-in-law to Nāṣiru'd-dīn Shāh (1264–1313/1848–96), a reformer and one of the very greatest statesmen of Iran, fell a victim. Nonetheless the idea of progress everywhere made itself felt. During the primacy of Amīr-i Kabīr we witness the appearance of the first serious newspapers and the foundation of the polytechnic institute Dāru'l-funūn, for which European instructors were engaged. From then on the wave of European civilisation discharged itself over Iran. The Shāh's three journeys to Europe contributed only in slight degree to this development. Yet they left a lasting trace behind them, namely the diaries of Nāṣiru'd-dīn. These constitute an important preliminary stage to modern literature thanks to the unique simplicity of style, closeness of observation and dispassionate pertinence of description revealed therein, though at the bottom of it all there is certainly a large dose of naïveté. Though the first signs of 'journalism' can be traced back to the latter years of Fatḥ-ʿAlī-Shāh's reign, the newspaper founded in the year 1851 on the initiative of the above-mentioned Amīr-i Kabīr aroused a more active response in the form of a gradually increasing succession of imitators. These and other constructive acts of Nāṣiru'd-dīn were more than counterbalanced by the darker aspects of his reign: a deaf ear to the most urgently needed reforms in the social, economic and popular educational fields; a complete lack of sympathy for the requirements of agriculture; despotic arbitrariness in the still prevalent mediaeval system of administration; cruelty towards the adherents of Bāb; the granting of important concessions to foreigners that rebounded to his own advantage, and in general unscrupulous indulgence towards the penetration of rapacious capital. The reforms he did introduce into the administration and in the army could only be superficial and consequently had little result, for they left the feudal foundations just as intact as had the earlier attempt of ʿAbbās-Mīrzā to bring about a europeanisation.[3] When on 18 *dhiʾl-qaʿde* 1313/1st May 1896 the shot rang out that brought the life of Nāṣiru'd-dīn-Shāh to an end on the eve of his 50-years' jubilee celebrations, there disappeared the last tolerably important personality of the Qajar dynasty, in fact it meant the end of the dynasty and its absolutist regime. A shot from the hand of a follower of the Sayyid Jamālu'd-dīn, generally known as 'Afghānī', brought the Middle Ages in Asia to an end. Sayyid Jamālu'd-dīn, though a Utopean pan-Islamist, was also a patriot with progressive views, a man with whom Nāṣiru'd-dīn had never been able to come to an understanding.

A new epoch now set in in Iran, an epoch that, though it did not lack vicissitudes and setbacks, ultimately ended with the victory of the constitutional bourgeoisie.

B. CONTINUATION OF THE EPIGONE 'RETURN' MOVEMENT WITH ITS TENDENCY TOWARDS SIMPLICITY

In its literary aspects the 13th/19th century continues the renaissance movement of the 12th/18th, when the old style again became the new, when the simple manner of thought in poetry again came to the fore, as opposed to what had been in demand during the two previous centuries. Once more we witness a decadence in literature, especially at the beginning of the reign of Fatḥ-ʿAlī-Shāh, that nevertheless gradually acquires a degree of refinement that is truly admirable (Mijmar, Viṣāl). In all this we can perceive a certain progress. In other words, the economic basis remains the same, but unlike the 12th/18th century peace prevails under the severe hand of the Qajars; moreover, an interest in Europe, that is also reciprocated, begins to emerge. The poetry reaches a perfection of style, in the *qaṣīda* as well as in the *ghazal*.[4] Simplicity of expression goes hand in hand with transparency of substance and with a purging of the language from immoderate arabising, that in the case of Yaghmā leads to purism (here necessity became to some extent a virtue). A progressive differentiation, both general and individual, marks the further course. Not even panegyrists such as Qāʾānī or Surūsh are quite deaf to everyday life, and even less so is the plebeian Yaghmā, who had ample personal experience of penury due to the social order. In contrast to the pomp and splendour of the court, Yaghmā is conscious of the wrongs, the sore places in society. He differs from the writers of earlier periods in that his censure is not directed at individuals but aims at pronouncing judgement, albeit for the time being only tentatively, on the public institutions. But his criticism is naïve and fails entirely to get to the bottom of the underlying evils. In as far as reforms were envisaged at all, they lay only within the framework of the current religious Ṣūfī or ethical maxims. Even more emphatic are several figures who appeared during the second half of the 13th/19th century, when a severe criticism of society raised its voice. The followers of Sayyid ʿAlī-Muḥammad Bāb, it is true, found a solution in revolution, but though it brought forth one poetess of exceptional worth (Qurratu'l-ʿAyn, b. 1233/1817–8, tortured to death in 1268/1852)[5] and several other minor figures, this movement had no effect whatsoever on literature, and thus had a disproportionately smaller result in this sphere than in public life, where it at least attracted attention to general shortcomings. Yet it did not succeed in bringing about a reform of public morality in Iran. Bāb appealed to the *petite bourgeoisie* who at the beginning of the 13th/19th century were suffering under an economic crisis.[6]

Despite the fact that the poets were closely associated with current events, there appeared but few – and then almost fortuitous – echoes in poetry and never a powerful voice of national consciousness, a voice that might have been regarded as a real reaction to actual life and not merely as a reverberation of court chatter on interesting events. On the whole the poetry of the 13th/19th century cannot be said to have attained a profound harmony with the life of the nation and the country. At the most there were a few exceptions and not until the end of the century do we witness the beginnings of a change. The poets lived at, or at any rate on the court, or were mere parasites on those in high positions, but in all cases were in a state of dependence on the feudal lords.

In the case of prose, however, it was a different matter. Here too, as in poetry, we find a constant recourse to simpler forms, but the development was far slower. Whereas poets continued to draw on the traditional stock of subjects, from the middle of the 13th/19th century onwards prose-writers began to seek a broader sphere of interest in their work and to cater for a steadily growing public. There was certainly good reason for this: contact with Europe gave form to or enforced the political and social development of the country, which was synonymous with the gradual dissolution of the old feudalism and absolutism. To the extent that the reforms proved to be inadequate, patriotism – that in the course of its growth took up a stand against the antiquated regime and was also kindled by the smuggling in of revolutionary newspapers and reviews – waxed in strength. Although at first newspapers – for the production of which lithography or printing is essential – were only for the use of the court, during the last decades of the 13th/19th century the tide turned and periodicals began to penetrate into the provinces also. Translations from European literature formed an important element.

C. 1800–1830

Panegyrists at the glittering court of Fatḥ-ʿAlī-Shāh: Saḥāb, Ṣabā, Nashāṭ, Mijmar

The group of men of letters at Isfahan had already prepared the ground when Fatḥ-ʿAlī-Shāh ascended the throne. As a politician he cannot stand comparison with his uncle. An unparalleled erotomaniac, he was yet a man who possessed a sort of culture of his own. He was acquainted with the history of Iran and had probably read the *Shāh-nāma*, composed poems himself[7] and cherished a sympathy for poets. But he thought that by the pomp and circumstance of his court he would be able to earn for himself the renown of a Sulṭān Maḥmūd of Ghazna. Just as around the latter there had grown up a Round Table of poets, a kind of academy of *beaux-esprits* also came into being with the name of *Anjuman-i khāqān*, 'The Emperor's (literary) Society', that held its meetings in the presence of Fatḥ-ʿAlī-Shāh. The leading light of this company was the poet laureate Ṣabā. To this period belong poets such as Mijmar, Nashāṭ, Saḥāb, ʿAbdu'r-Razzāq-Beg Dunbulī who bore the *takhalluṣ* Maftūn (b. 1176/1762–3 in Tabriz; d. there 1243/1827–8), Asīrī of Isfahan, etc., and men of letters such as Qā'im-maqām, Fāḍil-Khān Garrūsī[8] (b. 1196/1781–2, d. 1254/1838–9), the author of the *Tadhkira-i Anjuman-i khāqān*, that he dedicated to the panegyrists of this group, and a number of others. The panegyric *qaṣīda* underwent a revival. Beside it the *ghazal* bloomed in manifold variations. The stabilising of the political situation gave to poetry a new lease of life.

The chief aim of Fatḥ-ʿAlī's son and successor-elect ʿAbbās-Mīrzā was to appropriate the achievements of European civilisation as quickly and completely as possible. He was not too well disposed toward poetry at his court at Tabriz. The prosaic Qā'im-maqām, who was the first to begin to demolish bombastic excesses in prose, was a man after his own heart. Prose was faced with more difficulties in its struggle against pompousness than was poetry, and therefore the results became apparent only far later. Nonetheless the court at Tabriz also possessed good poets, such as Ṣabūr of Kāshān (d. 1228/1813) and others.

Hātif's son, Mīrzā Sayyid Muḥammad Saḥāb (d. 1222/1807–8) of Isfahan, was one of the panegyrists of Fatḥ-ʿAlī-Shāh, who held him in great respect. His *tadhkira Rashaḥāt-i Saḥāb*, 'The Drops of Saḥāb', viz. of the cloud (referring to Ṣafī's *Rashaḥāt-i ʿaynul-ḥayāt*, 'Drops from the Source of Life' [see p. 301] with Khvāja Aḥrār as central figure)[9] was never completed. His careful upbringing in the principles of the old scholastic school, paternal tradition and the influence of his native town leave no room for doubt as to his belonging to the Isfahan school. The tone of his poems is simple and straightforward but captivating. His *dīvān* contains 5000 verses.

After Mushtāq's Isfahan group there follows that of Tehran with Ṣabā at the head. The advancement brought about by this man, both in form and in substance, is nonetheless closely connected with Isfahan, being contemporaneous and having the same roots; for we know that Ṣabāḥī of Kāshān (see p. 308), who belonged to a younger generation of this school, was Ṣabā's teacher. Though both schools have their foundations in the old tradition, Tehran showed greater advancement because it could put to use the experience of Isfahan and besides this had the advantage of support from the side of the ruler and of leading personages. Ṣabā's talent made itself master of all these hypotheses and created the second, Tehran stage, that likewise adopted the 'Khurasan' movement. His attitude resembles that of the poet with whom he shows the closest affinity: like 'Unsurī he was also 'King of Poets' and was likewise able to influence his contemporaries.

When the star of Luṭf-'Alī-Khān Zand had set, Fatḥ-'Alī-Khān Ṣabā of Kāshān (b. 1179/1765), a descendant in the 31st degree of Khālid the Barmakid, remained – as a follower and panegyrist of the Zands – for a long time in hiding from Muḥammad-Khān Qājār, who had previously killed his elder brother, the vizier of Luṭf-'Alī. But Fate was kind to him, for the governor of Fars, who later on became the ruler Fatḥ-'Alī-Shāh and was a patron of the arts, took him under his protection. He earned the gratitude of his new master by composing a chronogrammatic *qaṣīda* of welcome on the occasion of the latter's accession to the throne, with the result that he was promptly appointed *Maliku'sh-shu'arā*, 'King of Poets', at his court and was henceforth amply rewarded for his eulogies. And this was not all: the 'King of Poets' (this title remained in the family until the time of his grandson)[10] was held in such high esteem that for some time he administered the provinces of Qum and Kāshān as governor, was guardian of the key to the mausoleums of Qum, and bore the honorary title *Iḥtisābu'l-mamālik*, 'Police of the Provinces'. In times of famine he did all in his power to help, and saw to it that the grants of money assigned by the ruler to relieve the distress were spent in full where they were most needed. He lavished paternal care on the poets and utilised his privileged position with the Shāh for the purpose. Finally he devoted himself entirely to poetry. He died in 1238/1822–3.

Ṣabā is a true panegyrist. Not only are his *qaṣīdas* written to serve encomiastic purposes but in his epic poem, *Shāhanshāh-nāma*, 'The Book of the King of Kings', that embraces some 40,000 verses, he also sings the praises of his imperial master and of a 'victory' over the Russians won by the Shāh's son, 'Abbās-Mīrzā.[11] Less well-known are two other epic poems, *Khudāvand-nāma*, 'The Book of the Lord' (on the Prophet)[12] and *'Ibrat-nāma*, 'The Book of Instruction'. M. Bahār[13] notes with some astonishment that a large number of verses known under the title *Gulshan-i Ṣabā*, 'Ṣabā's Rose-garden', are to be found in the collection *Kitāb-i anjuman-ārā-i Aḥmad-Beg Akhtar*, 'Ahmed-Beg Akhtar's Book that embellishes the Society', under the name of the poet Asīrī of Isfahan.

Ṣabā's *Shāhanshāh-nāma* was in its time regarded more highly than the *Shāh-nāma*, and the author himself remained convinced of the superiority of his epic until on his deathbed his eyes are supposed to have been opened. His work cannot be classed as a chronicle because its contents are not in keeping with the truth. The poet departs from the truth in blindly imitating the *Shāh-nāma*; for instance, military equipment and battles that took place in the 19th century are depicted in the ancient manner and from the standpoint of Firdausī in the chivalric feudal epoch! Moreover, his ultimate aim is the glorification of the hero. The concise economy of his model gives place here to a panegyrical verbosity and rhetoric, but in the absence of any disparagement of the enemy the great teacher and his minor pupil exhibit a similar nobility. – Ṣabā's *qaṣīdas* constitute an important part of his output. Though they undoubtedly possess great qualities they are nevertheless not lacking in defects: next to a superb mastery of language and poetical technique, we find forced and coarse expressions. They still however served as patterns for the poets of the Qajar period, not in the last place for his sons ʿAndalīb (d. *c.* 1264/1848) and Furūgh (d. 1290/1873) and his nephew Ṣabūr. And the generation of poets that lived half a century later still looked back admiringly on Ṣabā. Riḍā-qulī-Khān[14] states that a poet of Ṣabā's greatness had not appeared for nearly 700 years, but even after reducing such an obviously monstrous exaggeration to reasonable proportions, it is still not necessary to regard such a verdict as being equal to the customary encomium. At any rate he is said to have composed 300,000 distichs! In addition he was an excellent painter and a most versatile artist.

Mīrzā ʿAbdu'l-Vahhāb Nashāṭ of Isfahan (b. 1175/1761–2, d. 1244/1828–9) was descended from a wealthy family of part Jewish, part Sayyid extraction. Out of sheer generosity he squandered his inherited fortune so completely that in a very short time there was nothing left. This highly talented and cultured poet, whose life was shipwrecked, found a means of alleviating his pecuniary embarrassment by writing panegyric verses that won him favour at court. A further result was his appointment as 'mayor' (*kalāntar*) and later governor of Isfahan, where he gave special attention to the local literary life. Still later, in Tehran, he was entrusted with important missions, such as that of emissary to Napoleon in Paris, the pacification of Ghuriyan and Bakharz in East Khurasan in 1233/1818, the quelling of a revolt on the part of certain Afghan tribes in 1237/1821–2. He acquitted himself well of these tasks and proved himself worthy of his sobriquet *Muʿtamadu'd-daula*, 'The Reliable Man of the Empire'. He conducted the state correspondence, drew up important documents and drafted the Shāh's letters, but despite his large income he was always in debt. In the literary circle of the Shāh he was one of the leading figures. He wrote prose in Persian, Arabic, and Turkish. His Persian prose follows in the tracks of the later classical masters. His *qaṣīdas* find their inspiration in the school of Ṣabā, but are somewhat simpler in form. He rose to great heights in the *ghazal*, and in fact we see him at his best in this genre, for as emulator of Ḥāfiẓ he is alleged to have approached very nearly the standard of his model.[15] Whether his *ghazals* do in fact show personal elements, as Riḍā-qulī-Khān maintains, is open to doubt. We are more inclined to agree with M. Bahār[16], who is of the opinion that Nashāṭ produced nothing of any

Notes on pp. 348–351

novelty, either in prose or verse. At the command of Nāṣiru'd-dīn-Shāh, Nashāṭ's verse and prose were collected and published in a lithographed edition under the title *Ganjīna*, 'Treasure'. Ibr. Ṣafā'ī calls special attention to his liberality, which indeed bordered on waste, and on the other hand to his strongly ascetic traits.[17]

A most tragic figure is Nashāṭ's protégé and friend Sayyid Ḥusayn Ṭabāṭabā'ī Mijmar (b. 1190/1776–7 in Zavāra near Ardistan). He studied in Isfahan, but as it went against the grain with him to be indebted to anyone for favours, he earned his bread-and-butter exclusively by illustrating manuscripts. Even at this point he attracted the attention of the governor of the town, the poet Nashāṭ, who was so fascinated by him that he took his young friend with him when he moved to Tehran. Here he introduced him to Fatḥ-ʿAlī-Shāh, who gave him material security and, on the death of Saḥāb (d. 1222/1807–8) conferred on him the honour of a *Mujtahidu'sh-shuʿarā*, 'Legislator of the Poets'. Mijmar died unmarried and at a very early age, according to some in 1225/1810, to others even ten years earlier. There are also varying accounts as to the cause of his premature death. Either he was poisoned by his enviers (maybe there were amorous motives involved) or he perished as the result of debauchery, in which he had indulged to excess in Tehran. There is also an account stating that gossips had finally succeeded in troubling his relationship to the good Nashāṭ, so that the latter is said to have uttered his malediction over the ungrateful fellow. The lithographed edition of his *dīvān* contains more than 3000 verses, nearly all of them composed during the Tehran period. The character of Mijmar's poetry was determined by his rank, but even so as a panegyrist he surpassed all his contemporaries. He took Rafīq (d. 1215/1800–1) as his model, in fact the Isfahan group as a whole, to which Nashāṭ had given an enormous impulse during his period of office in the erstwhile capital. It is of course imitation of the old poets, pure and simple. Mijmar himself followed Muʿizzī, Anvarī, ʿAbdu'l-Vasīʿ Jabalī (d. 555/1160) in the *qaṣīda*, and in the *ghazal* Saʿdī, whose *Gulistān* he copied on a small scale. One special feature of Mijmar's is his emotional life, which is of a sombre tint; it is just for this reason that in the *ghazal* he achieves a far more original note. Further hopes were frustrated by his early death.

D. 1830–1850

I. PANEGYRISTS: QĀ'ĀNĪ, VIṢĀL, FURŪGHĪ

Fatḥ-ʿAlī-Shāh was succeeded by his grandson Muḥammad-Shāh (1250–64/1834–48), the son of ʿAbbās-Mīrzā. When reviewing the panegyrists of this period mention must at least be made of Mīrzā Muḥammad-ʿAlī Mufliq of Tehran with the *laqab*

Ṣadru'sh-shu'arā, 'Chief of the Poets'. This title was conferred on him by the ruler, the predicate *Fakhru'l-udabā*, 'Pride of the Men of Letters', on the other hand, he obtained from the all-powerful minister Ḥājjī Mīrzā Āqāsī.

But the brightest star of Muḥammad-Shāh's court, and in fact of the Qajar period as a whole, is Qā'ānī. Ḥabību'llāh Fārsī Qā'ānī[18] (b. 29 *sha'bān* 1223/20 October 1808 in Shiraz) was the son of the poet Gulshan. He lost his father at the age of eleven and the family fell into distressed circumstances. That he was still able to attend school was thanks to a small stipendium he received from the governor of Fars as a reward for some laudatory verses he had written. At an unusually early age he showed a talent for poetry. He first studied in his native town, later on in Isfahan where he took up mathematics and metaphysics. Then he returned to Shiraz, turned his attention to metrics and wrote commentaries on the works of the panegyrists Khāqānī and Anvarī, a pursuit that for him, the most brilliant panegyrist of the last century, was certainly significant. His verse attracted the attention of Ḥasan-'Alī-Mīrzā Shujā'u's-salṭana (1239/1823) who was just taking up his position as governor and who conferred on the poet, hitherto known as 'Ḥabīb', the name of Qā'ānī after his own son Ogotāy-Qā'ān. The governor also took him under his protection and relieved him from penury. He became in fact so attached to the young poet that he took him with him to Khurasan, where Qā'ānī continued his studies, composed poetry and collected old manuscripts. On the journeys to Yazd, Kirman, later on to Rasht, in Gilan, Mazandaran and Azerbayjan, he consorted with poets and scholars and strove constantly to broaden his education. About this time he made the acquaintance of Furūghī (see p. 332) an eminent writer of *ghazals*. When in 1250/1834 Muḥammad-Shāh ascended the throne, he was greeted with verses composed by Qā'ānī, who in turn received the honorary title *Ḥassānu'l-'Ajam*, 'Ḥassān of the Persians'.[19] Thenceforth the poet divided his time between Shiraz and Tehran, and was to have accompanied his master on the latter's Afghan campaign. But he was obliged to return home as he fell ill in Bistam. In Tehran Qā'ānī fell into a life of luxury and revelry. He got into debt and had to be helped out by Muḥammad-Shāh. Shortly before the accession to power of Nāṣiru'd-dīn the poet moved permanently to Tehran. But together with the new Shāh several mutations took place in the leading circles. One of those who now came to the fore was the all-powerful Amīr-i Kabīr (see p. 336), who was not kindly disposed to poets in general and to Qā'ānī in particular. He is even said to have inflicted corporal chastisement (?!) on him when Qā'ānī protested against a reduction in salary.[20] But Qā'ānī found a protector in Prince 'Alī-qulī-Mīrzā I'tiḍādu's-salṭana, 'Support of the Sultanate', and in the ruler himself who knew the poet from former times and who now showed his appreciation by appointing him *maliku'sh-shu'arā*, 'King of Poets'.[21] He thus became the official court poet and composed *qaṣā'id-i salām*, 'Panegyrics of Greeting', for special occasions. But he did not remain in this position for long: alcohol and opium, truly pernicious drugs that he may have used in an attempt to dispel bouts of melancholy, had a disastrous effect on his health. He died on the 3rd or 4th of *sha'bān* 1270/1st or 2nd May 1854 and was buried in Shāh 'Abdu'l-'Aẓīm. *

His output amounted to at least 23,000 verses[22], a very considerable achievement when one takes into account the shortness of Qā'ānī's life. Some editions of his *dīvān* include the *Kitāb-i parīshān*, 'Pêle-Mêle' (or 'The Book of the Confused'), a parallel to the *Gulistān*. The unusually high rewards he received, added to the fact that he was many times imitated, bear witness to the magic effect of his words. And that the spell has lost none of its power is proved by the large number of lithographed editions of his works. Even Europeans living in Tehran at the time, though assumedly none too susceptible in this respect, asserted that there was no more inspired poet in Iran than Qā'ānī. Vaḥīd Dastgirdī[23] praises his *taghazzul*, others his talent for composing strophes. But, viewed from a critical standpoint, with him the word outweighs the thought and his images are superficial. He is content with outward show.[24] His best *qaṣīdas* are those written in glorification of victories and battles.

Qā'ānī was the first of his contemporaries to be acquainted with European languages, especially French – from which he translated a text-book on botany[25] – and to a smaller extent English. Perhaps this was not without a certain effect on his works. Particularly in the tales and anecdotes in the *Kitāb-i parīshān* we find, in addition to perfect copies of Sa'dī, passages from which it is clear that he was attempting to find themes in the reality of everyday occurrences and to expose faults and defects in the social order of the time (hypocrisy of the priesthood and magistrates, corruption of the police, swindling on the part of artisans, etc.). Besides this, Qā'ānī delights in describing various kinds of abnormal individuals – drunkards, pederasts, unfaithful women – often depicted in the most lascivious scenes and with such detail that it is difficult to understand what right he had to censure his contemporary Yaghmā (see below). As in the case of the latter, we find vulgar trends in Qā'ānī too; true, they are wittier and do not possess the coarse bluntness that is especially typical of Yaghmā. In immediate proximity to this there are challenges to lead a moral life, to practise renunciation, virtue and piety; or there appear sentimental elegies on the sufferings of Shī'ite saints and sometimes too outbursts of boundless pessimism. One is confronted with a split personality, both as poet and as human being – a true mirror of his time when the old was moribund and the new as yet unborn. Qā'ānī was a poet who led the formal mastery of traditional poetry to its peak, at the same time gropingly seeking for new methods of expression; a man of pleasure, yet also capable of renouncement; an official panegyrist who also gave utterance to thought on the evil conditions prevailing in contemporary society; a man in the grip of world-weariness to which sensitive souls were bound to fall a prey in the face of an accumulation of seemingly overpowering events. Often we are in doubt as to whether Qā'ānī means his words to be taken seriously or not. An innovator in the true sense of the word, or even a pioneer, he never was. None of the western knowledge he had acquired had any deep influence on his work. Shiblī even goes so far as to regard all of Qā'ānī's *qaṣīdas* as parallels to Farrukhī, Manūchihrī, Sanā'ī, and Khāqānī.[26] His clarity and directness are enchanting, his humour delicious. But his output was so great that he inevitably incurs blame for occasional offences against good taste, language and rhythm. He was nevertheless held to be the best poet of the 13th/19th century, equal in rank to the greatest classical masters.[27] He was the Voltaire of the Iranians.

Living away in Shiraz was Viṣāl, whose official name was Mīrzā Muḥammad Shafīʿ, and whose nickname Mīrzā Kūchuk (b. 1193/1779, d. 1262/1846). He drove the imitation of the old masters to extremes. An unusually cultured man with a fascinating personality, attractive appearance and a melodious voice, he was an eminent calligrapher and musician. His life was influenced to such a high degree by the Ṣūfī Mīrzā Abu'l-Qāsim Sukūt of Shiraz, a *pīr* of the Dhahabiyya order, that finally to Viṣāl too was attributed the mystical nimbus of a miracle-working saint. Twice a week he gave instruction to the people, according priority to none and excluding no one. Contemporary writers of literary history were not sparing of their praise and gave him a place among poets of the first rank. Nowadays we realise that Viṣāl was merely an adept at reconstructing the classical traditional forms. Neither in form nor in substance did he introduce any innovations, yet he is capable of reproducing each and any of the old masters to perfection, as if reflected in a mirror. The reading of his verses affords great artistic enjoyment but almost every line reminds the connoisseur of some passage from the ancient poets.[28] Large portions of the *dīvān* are direct parallels to the *ghazals* of Saʿdī and Ḥāfiẓ. He wrote approximately 25,000 distichs, contained in ordinary lyric poems including two *mathnavīs* (*Bazm-i Viṣāl*, 'The Feast of Viṣāl' or 'The Feast of the Meeting', a moralising description in poetry of an excursion undertaken in 1246/1830 with Muṣṭafā-qulī-Khān[29], and the completion of Vaḥshī's *Farhād u Shīrīn*, see p. 298). This grafting on to a romantic epic of the 10th/18th century is characteristic. Though he enters entirely into the spirit of Vaḥshī's style, contrary to the classical tradition he does not let the poem end in tragedy, as this would have shown lack of respect towards the governor of Fars, the Qajar prince Farhād-Mīrzā, had he allowed the Farhād in the epic to die. For the rest he here shows a conception of love that is distinctly original; for him love is not a grief that weakens human beings, rather does the lover become stronger and better capable of resistance.[30] Otherwise Viṣāl is on the side of the classical tradition and its mystical tint. But still we frequently find reflections of actual events in his *qaṣīdas*. Viṣāl's elegies are regarded as marking the apogee of this literary accomplishment. He was associated in a close and sincere friendship with his compatriot Qā'ānī, though the latter's poetry exhibits a different mood. Their divergent trends are also betrayed in another way: while Qā'ānī, likewise from Shiraz, translates from the French, Viṣāl renders into Persian Zamakhsharī's (d. 538/1143) difficult work *Aṭvāqu'dh-dhahab*, 'Golden Necklaces'[31], from the Arabic. One thing they had in common was the struggle to obtain payment of the fees due to them, a complaint that was still raised by Viṣāl's sons.

Viṣāl's six sons grew up in an atmosphere of classical scholarship. All inherited the poetical talent and calligraphic skill of their father. The most gifted of them is the third son, Muḥammad Dāvarī: Navābī[32] places him on the same level as his father in respect of his poetical talent. He too reacts to several current events. Of lesser importance are Ismā'īl Tauḥīd and 'Abdu'l-Vahhāb Yazdānī, the two youngest sons, although they too appear to have introduced new motifs now and then; thus Tauḥīd sings the praise of a silver watch from Europe with the studied finesses of the love lyric. Abu'l-Qāsim Farhang, the fourth son, wrote a *qaṣīda* in honour of Paris. The French expressions introduced – for the first time in a Persian poem – must have made a curious impression. It is interesting to note that at the end of the poem Farhang refers to the republican regime in France and censures it severely. It is open to doubt as to whether this really reflects the opinion of the poet or whether it was dissimulation out of loyalty to the Qajars. The latter explanation is the more likely, for the *qaṣīda* written in honour of the English Queen Victoria gives evidence of Farhang's admiration of everything European, though his field of vision and his education can scarcely have made him capable of a truly critical verdict[33]; apart from two visits to Tehran he had not travelled at all! Maḥmūd Ḥakīm, the 'doctor' (and an excellent one at that!) did not subscribe to the panegyrism of the other brothers but adhered on the whole to the style of Nāṣir-i Khusrau. Aḥmad Vaqār, the eldest, was extremely prolific and versatile.[34]

A leaning towards mysticism is displayed by Mīrzā 'Abbās b. Āqā Mūsā Bisṭāmī (b. 1213/1798–9 in Karbalā or Najaf, d. 1274/1857 in Tehran), who first wrote under the pen-name Miskīn, later as Furūghī in honour of Furūghu'd-daula, son of the governor of Khurasan and Kirman, Shujā'u's-salṭana Ḥasan-'Alī-Mīrzā, whose praises he sang like Qā'ānī. Even at that time he had active intercourse with the Ṣūfī world and was initiated (*irādat*) by Mīrzā Amīn of Shiraz. He was panegyrist to three consecutive Shāhs, but relinquished his post after moving to Tehran where he dedicated himself to contemplation. In all probability this withdrawal from the world has something to do with Furūghī's having very closely associated himself with the extremist movement of the famous mystic saints, Bāyazīd Bisṭāmī and Manṣūr Ḥallāj. But it is recorded that he had to defend himself before Nāṣiru'd-dīn-Shāh on a charge of atheism. Nonetheless it must be emphasised that Nāṣiru'd-dīn-Shāh was extremely well disposed towards him. Once every month Furūghī came out of his isolation to pay his respects to the Shāh, reading his *ghazals* to him, listening to the latter's verses, and occasionally suggesting improvements. Nobility was his most conspicuous characteristic. He was buried in Shāh-'Abdu'l-'Aẓīm, but the locality of his grave is not known. As a poet he is one of the greatest masters of the *ghazal* in the Qajar period – a gentle poet, imbued with ecstatic warmth. His printed *dīvān* contains about 20,000 verses.

2. THE REACTION TO THE DEGENERATION OF THE SOCIAL ORDER. THE SATIRIST YAGHMĀ

That a new era had now set in is more clearly evident in the books of the poet Yaghmā (='Plundering') than in the classical school of Ṣabā with the inclusion of Qā'ānī. Yaghmā's life is in itself unusual, which fact is clearly reflected in his work: ups and downs and varying contrasts are typical of his fate and also of his verse. Mīrzā Abu'l-Ḥasan (b. *c.* 1196/1782 in Khūr-i Biyābānak near Jandaq in Dasht-i Kavir to the north of Yazd) grew up in very poor circumstances. But as a camel-herd he could certainly breathe more freely than was the case later on, for after the failure of a rising on the part of his patron (1216/1802), to whom he was secretary, he had to resist compulsory enlistment in the army, subsequently to be chased hither and thither in the service of the newly-appointed general (*sardār*) whose unremitting abusive language he had to endure for six long years. This period of his life ended with ignominious corporal punishment, imprisonment and the sequestration of his possessions, for which, as usual, enviers and informants were responsible. When six months later he was released he exchanged the *takhalluṣ* he had hitherto employed, namely *Majnūn*, 'The Insane', for Yaghmā, took up the dervish's staff and wandered for years from town to town, even as far as Karbalā and Baghdad, to return only after having received the news of the *sardār's* death. But he cannot have felt very happy at home, for after a short time he proceeded to Tehran. Here he won the favour of the premier Ḥājjī Mīrzā Āqāsī, the vizier who, besides strong worldly tendencies, also showed a certain inclination towards Ṣūfism. Yaghmā was appointed his spiritual guide, and despite the high position he had now attained he never abused his influence over the all-powerful ruler of Iran. For some time he resided in Kāshān as provincial vizier until a satire he had written on a family scandal caused the downfall, not of the censured aristocrat but of the moralising preacher himself. It is characteristic of the moral standard of the priesthood that Yaghmā was violently attacked on this account by one *mullā*, while another – though in vain – took him under his protection. Yaghmā was obliged to leave Kāshān. We know that he again set out on his travels and accompanied Muḥammad-Shāh to Herat. Otherwise this last part of his life is veiled in obscurity. He died in his birthplace at the age of eighty in 1276/1859. Just as in the case of Viṣāl, in the Yaghmā family too the father's talent for poetry was transmitted to his children.

The fact that Yaghmā is one of the most important poets of the first half of the 19th century is certainly not due to his *ghazals*, for though they can boast of sensitive, melodious language, in other respects they follow the well-worn paths of classicism. He can only be regarded as a neologist in his 'Laments with beatings of the breast', as in the well-known Muharram processions (*nauḥa-i sīna-zanī*). Their subjects are religious or philosophical, always in a mood of extreme unworldly pessimism. Their language often exhibits the simplicity of popular idiom. It is quite possible that the

Notes on pp. 348–351

form (*mustazād*, see p. 96) of these 'laments', that was derived from folk-poetry, was used as a model by the satirists of the stormy years between 1906 and 1912. His elegies in honour of the Shīʿite Imāms were of course of a serious nature.

At the base of Yaghmā's fame are his satires and small *Hazaliyyāt*, 'Dirty Jokes'. The satires are cast in the form of *ghazals*, combined into larger wholes, such as the *Sardāriyya*, attacks on the general referred to above and entitled *Khulāṣatu'l-iftiḍāḥ*, 'Short Description of the Ignominy', in connection with the occurrence in Kāshān, and three others. The verses cannot exactly be called dainty and are full of obscenities, mostly coarse and not particularly witty. Yaghmā closely follows the 'satirists' of the old school, viz. he pours out the vials of his wrath in unseemly words over the heads of his personal enemies. His brother poets gave him the nickname of *qaḥba-zan*, 'whore', after his favourite and most complimentary term, the sole legacy of the *sardār*. Yet there is a difference between him and his precursors, for in his blunt fashion he lays a finger on the open wounds of contemporary society. Yaghmā speaks from the heart of the suffering nation in comprehensible language and in perfect poetic style. Thence his popularity. To all appearances not even court circles took offence at his abusive writings. It would probably have gone worse with him if he had known and named the remedy, but neither he nor anyone else was capable of doing so. Meanwhile Yaghmā became a pioneer, in whose footsteps others were to follow later on.

It was probably due to his mediocre education that Yaghmā, unlike other important poets, was not well acquainted with Arabic. He even showed a distinct aversion to this language and maintained that Perisan could very well manage without it. But this opinion is erroneous – both in theory and practice – and is completely at variance with that held by the conservatively critical Riḍā-qulī-Khān (see p. 340).[35] It appears as if Yaghmā had wished to disprove the latter's theory by means of several letters that he wrote in pure Persian (*fārsī-nigārī*). But what is more important is that he avoided Arabic expressions even when writing in normal language, being thus a predecessor of the purists who later on, borne by a powerful wave of nationalism, attempted to effect a too radical purging of the Persian language, without realising that thereby on the one hand an impoverishment of expressive media and on the other clumsiness and incomprehensibility were bound to result. (A forbidding example of the absurdities in which this linguistic zeal can get itself entangled is brought forward by M. Bahār[36] in a 'purged' version of the *Gulistān*, written by somebody or other in *pārsī-i sara*, 'pure Persian' in the 13th/19th century.) Yaghmā was a man of great talent and socially his importance was no less than it was linguistically. He freed poetical language from rhetorical excrescences and used popular expressions. For himself he made a copy of the well-known Persian dictionary *Burhān-i qāṭiʿ* and constantly added new entries. As regards the subjects of his poems, we find here an obvious bipolarity: he strives after a purging of society; but as he meets only with failure he escapes into the sphere of philosophic mystical pessimism and renunciation of the world.

3. THE FIRST PROSE-REFORMER: QĀ'IM-MAQĀM. THE DIARIES OF NĀṢIRU'D-DĪN AND THEIR IMPORTANCE

Mīrzā Abu'l-Qāsim Qā'im-maqām Farāhānī (b. about 1193/1799 in Tehran), descended from an old family of viziers, showed poetic talent at an early age and put this into practice by writing sound *qaṣīdas* under the pseudonym of Thanā'ī. But his real importance lies in another sphere. Though his education had followed the old traditional course – he also composed *qaṣīdas* and *qiṭ'as* in Arabic – this uncommonly intelligent young man was attracted by the personality of the enlightened and progressive crown-prince and governor of Azerbayjan, 'Abbās-Mīrzā, in whose service we already find Mīrzā Buzurg, the father of Abu'l-Qāsim and himself a poet, in the quality of a *Qā'im-maqām*, 'Deputy'. The attractive force of the prince made itself felt throughout his immediate surroundings. After the death of Mīrzā Buzurg (1237/1822) the young man was appointed to his father's post where he became the companion to the heir to the throne and his right hand. But as he became suspicious of the friendship with Russia, he was obliged to retire from public life in 1239–41/1823–5. He was rehabilitated but soon fell into disfavour with Fatḥ-'Alī-Shāh because he opposed an adventurous war with Russia and was in fact banished to Mashhad for the duration of the war (1242–43/1826–7). But events very soon justified his attitude; he was recalled and in 1828 Qā'im-maqām signed a peace with Russia at Turkmanchay. Later, after the death of 'Abbās-Mīrzā, he was charged with the raising of the siege of Herat (1249/1834). An incorruptible, noble and loyal man, he, true to his promise, was responsible for making prince Muḥammad, who was hostilely inclined towards him, what he indeed became, namely the successor to Fatḥ-'Alī-Shāh (d. 1250/1834). His loyalty could not have been more evilly rewarded, for before a year had passed the seemingly all-powerful Qā'im-maqām was strangled at the command of the Shāh in his palace Nigāristān (1251/1835). The back-biting of former rivals, at the head of them the Shāh's tutor, the reactionary and obscurantist Ḥājjī Mīrzā Āqāsī, had achieved its aim, but the result was that progress in this very backward country was held up for a long time. The activity of Qā'im-maqām manifested itself in many directions. There were reforms in the army after the European pattern, and in conjunction with this the establishment of a war and textile industry. Then there was introduced an accurate budgeting of court expenditure, which was one of the main reasons for the hostility towards this far-seeing man on the part of higher court dignitaries. In the cultural field he pleaded for the introduction of a suitable letter-type, abolition of the roll in state correspondence and – a reform of eminent importance for the history of Persian culture and literature – the freeing of official epistolography from the arrant bombast and rhetorical jugglery that made it sound so ridiculous. Though he was not able to eradicate the old mannerisms of style entirely, he did achieve a considerable simplification and a greater objectivity. A parallel course in epistolary prose was followed by Mīrzā Muḥammad Taqī 'Alīābādī,

Notes on pp. 348–351

'Ṣāḥib-dīvān' (d. 1256/1840). A man who went still further was Amīr-Niẓām, 'Amīr of the Army'[37], also known as Amīr-i Kabīr, 'the great Amīr', in point of fact Mīrzā Taqī-Khān, the prime minister of Nāṣiru'd-dīn, a broad-minded statesman who was subjected to the same token of 'gratitude' on the part of the Qajars (d. 1268/1852) as had earlier on brought Qā'im-maqām to his end. In this context Nāṣiru'd-dīn himself must also be mentioned, for he wrote diaries on his three journeys to Europe in 1873, 1878 and 1889, as well as on two to Karbalā and Mazandaran respectively, that in all their aspects are of the greatest interest. His son and successor Muẓaffaru'd-dīn Shāh (1896–1907) also took up the same course, though without attaining his father's standard.

The diaries of the Shāh contributed in large measure to the simplification of the modern Persian style, but that is not the only reason for their importance. There is a certain irony in the circumstance that the form of the two undoubtedly progressive works *Masāliku'l-muḥsinīn*, 'The Ways of the Charitable' (see p. 343) and *Siyāḥat-nāma-i Ibrāhīm-Beg*, 'Travel Diary of Ibrahim-Beg' (see p. 369), that sharply criticise the incompetent administration and corrupt society of the Qajar epoch, should have been founded on an account of the travels of the typical Qajar despot that Nāṣiru'd-dīn-Shāh actually was. Into the same stylistic category must be included Muḥammad Ja'far Qarāja-Dāghī's excellent translations of the equally excellent Azerbayjanian comedies of Fatḥ-'Alī Ākhund-zāda[38], that were composed in the middle of the 19th century under Russian influence. But now we are running too far ahead.

E. SECOND HALF OF THE 13TH/19TH CENTURY

The Epoch of Nāṣiru'd-dīn, the Last of the Despots. Reforms

The second half of the 19th century is included almost entirely in the reign of Nāṣiru'd-dīn-Shāh and is characterised mainly by the fact that Qajar society, intentionally or unintentionally, was obliged to become europeanised on account of the economic and political pressure exerted by the rival powers, Russia and England. This period forms a logical sequence to the foregoing one and an indispensable premise to the development of Iran in the 20th century. In literature the newly-awakened life of the country is reflected in a series of highly remarkable phenomena: the foundation of the Polytechnic College, Dāru'l-funūn; the translation of European fictional and scientific works; the increased spread of ancient and modern literature thanks to the medium of lithography. We may further mention a greater orientation towards reality on the part of certain poets; a strongly marked and significant simplification in prose style, which resulted in a large numerical increase in the circle of readers; and, last but not least, a greater density in the network of newspapers. All these positive achievements are of the utmost importance and they may not be overlooked when judging the apparent passivity that prevailed at the time. If the poetry of the previous period had become more flexible here and there, in the second half of the 19th century an even more effective relaxation was brought about by the increasingly intensive changes in the economic system of the country.

1. BOOK-PRINTING

All endeavours towards further cultural development would have been unavailing, in fact impossible, if it had not been for that most important tool, namely book-printing. It says much for the uncommonly great circumspection and energy of ʿAbbās-Mīrzā, governor of Azerbayjan, who has already been referred to several times, that he recognised the cultural and political importance of this fact. As early as the first half of the 17th century the Armenians had attempted to introduce book-printing into Isfahan, but their efforts were unsuccessful. On the initiative of ʿAbbās-Mīrzā a delegation was sent to London to become acquainted with the art of printing and to take the necessary steps for its introduction into Iran. The first printing-press was opened at Tabriz in 1232/1816–7, followed shortly afterwards by one at Tehran. ʿAbbās-Mīrzā sent his men to St. Petersburg to be trained in lithography, while Tehran followed his example only later. The first printing business in Iran was set up in 1240/1824–5 in Tabriz, and in Tehran one was opened round about 1253/1837–8 (the first lithographed book produced in Tehran was the *Kulliyyāt-i Ḥāfiẓ*, 'Collected Poems of Ḥāfiẓ'). But the number of printing-houses did not remain confined to the first ones nor to the towns in which these were established. The striking preference for lithography was such as to completely overshadow printing with leaded type (*surbī* as distinguished from *sangī*) for some time. The printing-works in Tabriz and Tehran disappeared in 1250/1834–5 and 1263/1846–7 respectively, and it was not until 1290/1873–4 in Tehran and 1316/1898–9 in Tabriz that typography was revived. Not only books of all kinds but also newspapers were lithographed and it is not so very long ago that printing won the day throughout the country, except for the *Koran* and popular reading matter.

2. THE PRESS

By the introduction and spread of printing one of the essential conditions for an effective policy of enlightenment in Iran was fulfilled, and that in two directions, namely in the field of the press and in the foundation of the Dāru'l-funūn.

K. Chaykin[39] remarks that the Iranians would not even have known anything about their first newspaper had it not been for a reproduction in the *Journal of the*

Notes on pp. 348–351

Royal Asiatic Society in 1839; the paper appeared as two sheets under the title of *Rūz-nāma-i akhbār-i vaqāyiʿ*, 'Journal of Reports on Events', in an anopisthographical lithograph about once a month and, under the editorship of minister Mīrzā Ṣāliḥ, contained only reports on events in court circles. Nothing more than this is known about it. Not a single copy of the original paper has been preserved, let alone any sort of collection. Our conception of a newspaper is more nearly approached by *Rūz-nāma-i vaqāyiʿ-i ittifāqiyya*, 'Journal of Current Events' (the first number appeared under another title), a weekly containing four to eight pages, that was founded in 1267/1851 – thus at the beginning of Nāṣiru'd-dīn-Shāh's reign, and instigated thanks to his "care for the education of the people of Iran and for information on home and foreign affairs".[40] This paper was no doubt founded on the initiative of the enlightened prime minister Mīrzā Taqī-Khān Amīr-Niẓām ('Amīr-i Kabīr'), who himself contributed articles on politics. The editor was Mīrzā Jabbār Tadhkirachī. In 1277/1860–1 the paper was renamed *Rūz-nāma-i daulat-i ʿaliyya-i Īrān*, 'Journal of the Exalted Empire of Iran', and Mīrzā Abu'l-Ḥasan-Khān Naqqāsh-bāshī ('The chief painter') Ṣanīʿu'l-mulk appointed editor. An admirable maker of lithographed portraits who had received a European training, he provided the paper with valuable illustrations in the form of pictures of the Shāh and leading figures in court and public life. From 1288/1871 onwards there appeared a publication entitled *Īrān* three times weekly, under the editorship of the 'Minister for Printing' (*ra'īs-i dāru'ṭ-ṭibāʿa*), Muḥammad Ḥasan-Khān Ṣanīʿu'd-daula (see p. 341). Besides court news on the Shāh's hunting expeditions and the gifts presented to him by the people for his good shots, it published tolerably interesting articles of an instructive and literary nature.[41] One of the idiosyncrasies of the Shāh was to take lithographic equipment with him on his journey in 1287/1870, by means of which he published a one-page bulletin, *Mir'ātu's-safar va mishkātu'l-ḥaḍar*, 'Mirror of the Journey and Niche for the Lamp at Home'. M. Bahār[42] calls special attention to the fine lay-out of the illustrated monthly *Sharaf*, 'Honour', that appeared for the first time in 1300/1882. It is true that it became dormant after the death of the energetic Muḥammad Ḥasan-Khān Iʿtimādu's-salṭana, but it was revived in 1314/1896–7 under the title *Sharāfat*, 'Sublimity', and continued to appear until 1320/1902, though it never again reached its former standard.

These publications were followed by other official and semi-official professional and provincial papers (of the latter sort the first one appeared in Tabriz, as capital city of Azerbayjan, in 1275/1858[43]), all of which were reproduced lithographically. Some were destined to be but short-lived, others subsisted longer, but a striking point about them is their frequent change of title. The first real daily newspaper is *Khulāṣatu'l-ḥavādith*, 'Summary of Events', that was first published in 1898. The periodical press dit not reach its zenith until the years of revolution between 1906 and 1911, because it then became not only the exponent of the new national policy but also of the revolutionary – in fact the only real literature of the period. It shook off the oppressive bonds of censorship and placed itself entirely at the service of the new ideology. The importance of foreign papers, published in Persian and introduced illegally into Iran, cannot be estimated too highly, for they contributed to the greatest possible dissemination of the principles of the Constitution and even of revolution, with which the thoughts of the middle classes, the bourgeoisie and the priesthood were intensely occupied. Of these we may mention *Akhtar*, 'The Star', in Istanbul 1875 till 1895–6; *Qānūn*, 'The Law', published in London in 1891–2 which was the most influential; further *Ḥablu'l-matīn*, 'The Strong Cord', in Calcutta from 1893 onwards and a few in Cairo. Occasionally they possessed literary qualities.

3. DĀRU'L-FUNŪN AND ITS FIRST DIRECTOR, RIḌĀ-QULĪ-KHĀN HIDĀYAT

The basis of Iranian culture in modern times was laid by the Polytechnic College *Dāru'l-funūn*, 'The House of Knowledge', that was founded in 1852 with the very promising coöperation of the young Nāṣiru'd-dīn-Shāh who had recently come to the throne, and his prime minister Mīrzā Taqī-Khān Amīr-Niẓām, a man who was kindly disposed towards reforms. It was to be an institution for higher education and was to include army affairs, technology, medicine, natural sciences, the humanities (also music) in its curriculum – the instruction in all subjects to be based on the achievements of western learning. It was impossible to realise this programme without the aid of European teachers, although in view of an inimical attitude towards foreigners that prevailed in certain circles it was considered opportune and necessary to appoint a few Iranian teachers as well and even, as an exception, exponents of traditional knowledge. It is true that Europe did not place any great authorities at the disposal of the Dāru'l-funūn, but this was not necessary. It was more important that the institution should be entrusted to a number of good, conscientious European specialists and educators, whose cultural activity and undisputed success are deserving of the sincere gratitude of the awakening nation. Among them was the physician dr. med. Jakob Eduard Polak (1818–1891), from 1855 on physician-in-ordinary to the Shāh and author of one of the best books on Persia (publ. Leipzig 1865) that have appeared up till now. He taught European medicine from 1852 to 1860. These men wrote the first text-books in Persian, each in his own subject. This work, difficult as it was, was from the very beginning rendered more so by the reactionary Mīrzā Āghā-Khān Nūrī, who was successor to Amīr-Niẓām (executed 1852). Yet the school acquitted itself of its task in full measure and became one of the essential elements in the endeavour to liberate the country from its backwardness.

No small part of its success was due to the felicitous choice of Riḍā-qulī-Khān, who, as the school's first principal, had a powerful influence on the deployment of the whole of cultural life in Iran. On account of his fruitful activity, as well as his own

Notes on pp. 348–351

excellent scholarly publications, he deserves more esteem than he would otherwise have acquired merely as a poet, though he took great delight in writing. Riḍā-qulī-Khān Hidāyat, known also as Lālā-bāshī, 'Educator in the Family of the Ruler', was born in Tehran into a family of higher officials in 1215/1800. Among his ancestors was the admirable poet Kamāl of Khujand (see p. 262). He received a thorough education at Shiraz where he entered the service of the Qajar princes (at the onset of his poetical activity, in which he showed conspicuous energy at an early age, he adopted the *takhalluṣ Chākar*, 'Servant'). When Fatḥ-'Alī-Shāh visited Shiraz in 1829, Riḍā-qulī-Khān was introduced to him and was granted the *laqab Amīru'sh-shu'arā*, 'Prince of Poets', for a panegyric *qaṣīda*. From 1254/1838 onwards we find him at the court of Tehran in various functions. He reached the summit of his development under Nāṣiru'd-dīn-Shāh, especially after he was appointed assistant to the Minister for Public Instruction and Principal of the recently founded Dāru'l-funūn. In the interests of progress in a thoroughly under-developed country the choice could not have fallen on a more suitable person. After fifteen years of successful work as head of the institution he was summoned to Tabriz, the residence of the heirs to the throne as nominal governors of Azerbayjan, in order to take charge of the education of the young crown prince Muẓaffaru'd-dīn. But this office was beyond the power of Riḍā-qulī, the more so as he appears to have always suffered from ill-health. He went into retirement and died after a severe illness in 1288/1871.

Though he produced a *dīvān* containing 50,000 distichs and six *mathnavīs*, among them being a great romantic epic poem entitled *Gulistān-i Iram*, 'The Rose-garden of Iram', or *Baktāsh-nāma*, that sings of the love of the young hero Baktāsh (the material is taken from the *Ilāhī-nāma* of 'Aṭṭār[44]), as poet Riḍā-qulī-Khān has no significance at all for the further development of the art. All that we find in his work are the utterances of a highly cultivated man, a passionate and devoted admirer of the classics and a faithful follower of the old masters who, partly as a result of these characteristics and partly in a striving after originality, in a preciosity that bordered on bad taste and grotesqueness, attempted to compensate his inadequate poetic talent. But this by no means diminishes his greatness as a scholar. For as such he was engaged in the field of history (continuation of the work of Mīrkhvānd, see p. 441), in an account of his diplomatic mission to Khiva (1267/1851), in the history of literature and lexicography, on all of which subjects he produced works of extreme value. We are particularly interested in the printed *tadhkiras*: *Majma'u'l-fuṣaḥā*, 'The Meeting-place of the Eloquent', and *Riyāḍu'l-'ārifīn*, 'The Gardens of the Mystics'; the former is a summary in two volumes of earlier *tadhkiras*, with supplements bringing it up to the time of the author; the latter, a much smaller volume, is devoted entirely to real or supposed Ṣūfism. These are works of the greatest importance, containing as they do an abundance of names and accounts, accounts moreover taken from sources often inaccessible to us. The dictionary *Farhang-i anjuman-ārā-i Nāṣirī*, 'Nāṣir's Dictionary that Embellishes Society', was likewise published, but to my mind it hardly deserves the esteem in which it is held by Ye. E. Bertel's, for I cannot recollect having found anything essentially new in it when compared with the dictionaries generally known and used in Europe; at the most, examples of text variants are quoted here and there.[45]

4. THE DEVELOPMENT OF LEARNED PROSE. TRANSLATIONS FROM LITERATURE OF THE WEST

Among the students at the Dāru'l-funūn, Muḥammad Ḥasan-Khān stands out as the most competent. His first honorary title, *Ṣanī'u'd-daula*, 'The Skilled One of the Empire', was followed by *Mu'tamanu's-sulṭān*, 'The Reliable One of the Sulṭān', and finally by *I'timādu's-salṭana*, 'The Confidence of the Sultanate'. He came from a wealthy Marāgha family, served in the army, in the diplomatic corps, at court, and from 1288/1871–2 was head of the interpreters' corps and of the press. He died in 1313/1896. His writings mainly consist of the history and topography of Iran, accounts of travels, biographies of the men and women of Islam, thus exclusively with learned subjects. The truly enormous compass of these books forces us to the conclusion that they were the result of collective work, apparently taken in hand by Ṣanī'u'd-daula during the long tenure of his last post. The fact that he was able to provide stimulus for a series of works (lithographs dating from 1290–1323/1873–1906) possessing great scholarly or utilitarian value, to organise their composition and to publish them, cannot do otherwise than fill us with admiration for a man of such energy and intelligence.

There is no doubt that in the first place the task of the Dāru'l-funūn was educational, but this in its turn stimulated other activities that were equally far-reaching. These consisted especially in the publication of text-books and other expedients, the need for which had already been experienced by the first teachers at the institution who with the aid of their Iranian assistants published handbooks written in Persian, thus laying the foundation of a modern Persian scholarly prose and terminology. The historian of literature is more closely concerned with translations of a belletristic nature, at first almost entirely from the French (an exception is J. Moriers' *The Adventures of Haji Baba of Ispahan*), or with French, as the predominant European language in the Near East and taught at the Dāru'l-funūn, as intermediary. These translations were intended to provide instruction and entertainment – in both cases something entirely new. But, as we shall soon see, they provided far more. European fictional literature demanded quite a different style from that which the Persian language at that time was able to offer, although by the reforms of Qā'im-maqām the latter had already undergone a simplification. All the antiquated conventions, melismas and pomposities had to be done away with and an attempt made to accommodate the language to the demands of the original texts. Some time it would be well worthwhile to trace the struggle of these pioneers of modern fictional literature in Persian from the beginning. This transformation of the language was certainly a task that was neither easy nor realisable in a short time. But it was these translators who paved the way to a simple and thereby easily comprehensible manner of expression. The Persian written language of today is their progeny. For this reason it is well to pay some attention to the prose works with which a beginning was made. Firstly we find Voltaire the historian (*Pitr-i Kabīr*, 'Peter the Great', *Shārl-i Davāz-dahum*, 'Charles XII', *Iskandar-i Kabīr*, 'Alexander the Great'; lithographed in Tehran 1263/1846–7) and John Malcolm, author of the *History of Persia*. In these works the influence of the scholars of Dāru'l-funūn is unmistakable. When the turn came for the novel, the choice was not so fortuitous as many people imagine. Names of established repute in Europe were given priority: Dumas the Elder, Fénelon, Daniel Defoe, A.-R. Le Sage, the excellent translation of J. Morier's *Haji Baba* from the pen of Mīrzā Ḥabīb Iṣfahānī[46] (put to death 1314/1897), Bernardin de Saint-Pierre, Jules Verne (see p. 364).[47] Under the influence of Aḥmed Vefīq's Turkish translation of Molière, there appeared in Istanbul in 1286/1869 a Persian translation of *Le Misanthrope*, that was given the title of *Guzārish-i mardum-gurīz*, 'The Adventure of One who Flees from his Fellow-men', by Ḥabīb Iṣfahānī. But the play met with no response at all in Iran, although Ḥabīb did his best to adapt it to Persian taste and circumstances (proper names included).[48] This was certainly a bold venture, but it was doomed to frustation as a result of the general lack of interest. Molière did not appeal to Iranian society at that time, whereas works of the above-mentioned novelists met with full acclaim because they reflected the inborn inclination of the Persian towards adventure, frivolity, elegance, humour, good advice. They thus formed up to a certain point a continuation of his own literary creations, as expressed in the romantic epic and in folk-literature, the didactic epic and ethical writings – henceforth in an entirely new garb that was obviously to his taste.

Let us not judge the Iranians too haughtily for translating P.-Al. Ponson du Terrail (1829–71), for did not the Turks translate Paul de Kock? In fact many more parallels between the Iranians and the Turks might be found in relation to the first works translated from European literatures.

In a more effective manner than anything else light trashy novels were to reveal new worlds to a credulous circle of readers athirst for novelty. This is a phenomenon that can still be witnessed today in the orient in the effect of the film on the masses. However it may be, we must admit that the translations accomplished a great task. For many people they provided an inducement to read, they helped in the clearance of antiquated rubbish and led the language into a new course. All these are important services that could only with difficulty have been rendered by translations of other, more exacting works – European poetry for instance – even if the most famous names had been involved. Without these translations Persian belles-lettres and the prose of the 20th century as a whole is difficult to imagine.

5. TRENDS TOWARDS POPULARISATION AND PRO-RUSSIAN REACTION TO THE OCCIDENTAL CULT. ṬĀLIBŪF

The Dāru'l-funūn had trained Persian specialists of European orientation and had brought a European influence to bear on scientific literature, when a movement aiming at popularisation began to assert itself. Actually it cannot be proved that there was any direct connection between this tendency and the Dāru'l-funūn. Nor do the antecedents of the authors in the movement towards enlightenment indicate such. But one cannot overlook the time-factor and especially the probability that the new educational system would ultimately bear fruit of this kind. These results could certainly not have been predicted and they cannot have been agreeable to the government.

Ḥājjī Mīrzā ʿAbdu'r-Raḥīm, son of Abū-Ṭālib Najjār of Tabriz, known as Ṭālibūf (viz. Talibov, b. *c.* 1260/1844)[49], studied at the Madrasa Ṭālibiyya in Tabriz. At the age of about thirty he went to Baku and settled down as a merchant in Tamir-Khān-Shūra; he died there in 1328/1910. He was elected to the first parliament (*majlis*) by Tabriz but declined the appointment owing to ill-health. He made a name for himself as pioneer in the popularisation of scientific and political knowledge by a series of writings that for their period were certainly progressive. In *Masāliku'l-muḥsinīn*, 'The Ways of the Charitable', he describes a journey to the top of the Damavand undertaken by five professional men, giving an account of their conversations on various cultural subjects with the inhabitants of the districts they passed through, whereby he does not shun expressing criticism of the existing order. *Kitāb-i Aḥmad yā Safīna-i Ṭālibī*, 'Aḥmad's Book of the Album of Ṭālibī', consists of a dialogue in two volumes between the author and (chiefly) Aḥmad, the eldest of his children (three sons and two daughters), dealing with new discoveries and giving all kinds of useful instructions. Several of his works, such as *Masā'ilu'l-ḥayāt*, 'Problems of Life', or *Āzādī chi chīzast*, 'What is Liberty?' are concerned with political subjects, others deal with questions of natural science. The scenes of country life present pleasant pictures even today, but the meditations – the essential parts of Ṭālibūf's work – do not rise above a certain primitiveness. Yet they fulfilled their social and literary purpose. Ṭālibūf's native language was Azerbayjanian, which had an obvious influence on his Persian. Notwithstanding this, the very simplicity of his manner of expression and style form an important stage in the development of modern prose. Contrary to the Dāru'l-funūn, with its western orientation, Ṭālibūf sought rather association with the language and civilisation of Russia.[50]

6. THE SOLE PHILOSOPHER OF THE 13TH/19TH CENTURY: HĀDĪ SABZAVĀRĪ

Quite apart from this movement stands Ḥājjī Mullā Hādī of Sabzavār (b. 1212/1797, d. there 1295/1878), a man who brought new life into Iranian philosophy, that had sunk into a state of torpor in the 18th century. For this very reason he certainly deserves mention in a survey of the prose of the 19th century. "He is in no sense an imitator of the philosophers of the classical epoch. His work is founded on their investigations and there is no lack of coherence, but the consequences he draws are entirely original and merit the serious attention of western thinkers."[51] He wrote a great philosophical work in Persian entitled *Asrāru'l-ḥikam*, 'The Secrets of the Wisdoms' (he also signed his *ghazals* with the *takhalluṣ Asrār*), and a commentary on Maulavī's *Mathnavī*; in Arabic he composed, among other things, glosses to several of Mullā Ṣadrā's works (see p. 294), a scholarly poem on logic, etc.

7. CLASSICISM IN POETRY, OCCASIONALLY WITH CONTEMPORARY THEMES: SIPIHR, HUMĀ, SURŪSH, SHAYBĀNĪ, SHŪRĪDA, ADĪB NĪSHĀPŪRĪ

During the second half of the 13th/19th century too, the poets of the classical movement continued to cherish the classical tradition, adhering to its principles more or less closely as the case might be but without violating either its form or its substance. They have followed this course right up to the present day, even though their number has gradually diminished, both in the capital and in the provinces, in favour of those who took up a more modern attitude. It was not a violent transformation. Slowly, almost imperceptibly, just in the same way as the economic revolution took place, the poet underwent a metamorphosis, began to take notice of the world and the things around him and to subject the state and society to criticism.

Not only by verbal enthusiasm but also by including copious selections from the works of Mīrzā Muḥammad Taqī Sipihr (d. 1297/1880) (*Lisānu'l-mulk*, 'The Tongue of the Kingdom') in his anthology did Riḍā-qulī Hidāyat[52] draw attention to the friendship that existed between himself and Sipihr, who was historian and panegyrist to the Qajars. Carried away by his feelings, Hidāyat classed this poet too highly. Sipihr's *dīvān* contains *ghazals* in the spirit of 'Unṣurī and Mas'ūd-i Sa'd, *musammaṭs* after the pattern of Manūchihrī and finally a *mathnavī* after the manner of Sanā'ī. His 'universal' history in eight volumes bears the presumptuous title *Nāsikhu't-tavārīkh*, literally 'Abrogation of Histories', but the work is incomplete and his description of the course of events from the fall of Adam up to the Imām Huṣayn is worthless – as could hardly otherwise be expected! It was continued by his son 'Abbās-qulī Sipihr up to the Imām Mūsā b. Ja'far in twelve volumes. M.-T. Sipihr took up the history again with the Qajar period up to 1281/1864 (?) in four volumes, and this is the only part of any importance. In order to revive the practice of rhyming, that had fallen into disuse, Sipihr wrote an excellent book entitled *Barāhīnu'l-'Ajam fī qavānīni'l-Mu'jam*, 'The Arguments of the Persians with regard to the Rules of the al-Mu'jam (Book on Poetics)'[53], in 1251/1835–6 (edited in 1272/1855).

A figure such as one does not come across every day is Muḥammad Riḍā-qulī-Khān Humā of Shiraz (b. 1212/1797–8, d. 1290/1873–4 in Isfahan). He often recalled the poverty against which he had had to struggle during his time as a student in Najaf. The consciousness of this fact remained with him all through his life; as a result he had great sympathy for the poor and gave evidence of great generosity. He never strove after wealth. His descent from a nomadic family ever betrayed itself – roaming was for him a vital necessity. Whenever the desire seized him he disappeared, often for long periods at a time, without having taken leave of his family or friends. His journey to Iraq is described in a *qaṣīda*. He never ceased to obey the dervish rules in spirit but ultimately he alienated himself entirely from the outward observances of the Order. The lithographed edition of his *dīvān* numbers some 18,000 verses. He composed *qaṣīdas* in honour of the Imāms, persons in high positions and sulṭāns, but some of them also contain wise counsel. He is important chiefly however on account of his *ghazals*, which he endowed with *sahl-i mumtaniʿ*, 'inimitable facility', and the true straightforwardness and sincerity of Saʿdī, throughout opposed to the poets of the Indian style. Humā adhered strictly to the traditional rhymes and all the other time-honoured rules. His talent was inherited by his three sons, of whom ʿAnqā even obtained the title of *maliku'sh-shuʿarā*.

Mīrzā Muḥammad ʿAlī 'Surūsh' (b. 1228/1813 in Sidih near Isfahan, d. 1285/1868–9 in Tehran) gave evidence of a disposition for poetry in his early youth, but did not find the recognition he desired in his native town. This induced him to roam about Iran until he gained a firm footing in Tabriz, where he found patrons of high rank and at last was introduced to the heir to the throne, Nāṣiru'd-dīn. The latter cherished such a predilection for the poet that after his accession he summoned him to Tehran and, in addition to giving him generous gifts, bequeathed on him the *laqab Shamsu'sh-shuʿarā*, 'Sun of the Poets', and raised him to the rank of Khān. Riḍā-qulī Hidāyat[54] notes that Surūsh was constantly perfecting himself by studying the old masters, especially Farrukhī and Muʿizzī. Like Qā'ānī, after whom he took over the duty of composing ceremonial proclamations on feast-days, he was a characteristic court panegyrist of his period. From his *qaṣīdas*, that were occasionally written in *mathnavī* form, we learn what took place in court circles, and also news concerning the country at large, for instance the introduction of the telegraph, etc. He composed *qaṣīdas* in honour of ʿAlī, further a *Sāqī-nāma*, 'Book of the Cupbearers', *Ilāhī-nāma*, 'The Divine Book', and the unfinished epic *Urdībihisht-nāma*, that only deals with the Prophet and does not include the twelve Imāms.[55] Surūsh's similes are usually original, but often to the extent of affectation; his thoughts are clear and precise. Ye. E. Bertel's[56] designates many a line from the introductions to the *qaṣīdas* as pearls of poetry. Vaḥīd Dastgirdī[57] places him in the immediate proximity of Qā'ānī and a few other poets of the literary revival. To the translation of the 'Thousand and One Nights' into Persian, executed by Mullā ʿAbdu'l-Laṭīf Ṭasūjī at the bidding of Prince Bahman-Mīrzā, governor of Azerbayjan, Surūsh contributed the metrical insertions. This he did either by interpreting the Arabic texts or, in cases where the latter proved unsuitable, by replacing them by verses taken from the old masters, thereby even improving on the original texts.[58]

Abū-Naṣr Fatḥu'llāh-Khān Shaybānī distinguished himself from the average epigones of his time by the audacity with which he translated his experiences into poetry and by his criticism of a society that was in the course of disintegration. He was born into a military aristocratic family in Kāshān about 1246/1830. Curiously enough he later on regarded the excellent and cultured education he had been privileged to enjoy as the cause of his misfortunes. After the death of his father, a warrior who fought against the Turkomans, he took over the management of the properties he had inherited in Kāshān but lost the whole of his fortune as a result of the encroachments of the officials. He therefore betook himself to the court in order to claim compensation, but "justice in Persia was dormant" and he failed in his purpose, though not through lack of connections. Disappointment and worry then forced him to a decision to retire and write verse. The rest of his wealth he devoted to the founding of a monastery. In an adjacent garden he had a vault built for himself bearing an inscription that would constantly remind him that this was all that was left to him. Shaybānī professed the *taṣavvuf*. For a long time he wore the dervish's garb and was constantly in touch with the poor and the dervishes, as can be seen in a large number of his verses.[59] He spent some time in Istanbul, but there too he held himself apart from his fellow-men. He died in Tehran in 1308/1891. Throughout Shaybānī's work we find a harsh, pessimistic tone, whether he is complaining about his education and training, about the lack of faith in this world or whether he is fulminating against his profession as a poet, ostensibly one of the most vexatious that exist, for he considers it better to be as dumb as a beast since the great and the powerful have little esteem for poetry. He exposed the abuses and infringements of the law of an absolutism represented by the corruptible and dissipated officialdom and looked for reforms from the side of the Shāh. The latter, however, he considered should not be surrounded by babblers. In his panegyric poetry he reproached the Shāh of looking on passively at the unsatisfactory state of affairs. Elsewhere again he uttered a warning that the soldiers would revolt and turn against their own Sulṭāns if they remained without clothing and bread, and he censured the fact that actions were concealed and delayed under cover of fair words. To strike such an embittered note in a *qaṣīda* was hitherto unheard-of.[60] Shaybānī must be accorded the first place among those who anticipated the development of poetry both in form and substance. His best verses are devoid of affected preciosity; he simplified the language and subordinated it to the subject-matter. Two collections of his works may be found in the Bibliography. In addition to these he himself mentions *Fatḥ u ẓafar*, 'Conquest and Victory', and *Ganj-i gauhar*, 'Treasure-chamber of the Jewels', composed in honour of the Shāh's sons, but unfortunately without tangible result for the poet himself; his *Kāmrāniyya*, 'The Successful' (in honour of Kāmrān-Mīrzā) also remained no more than a title without reward.[61]

Approximately the same period was covered by the life of Farhād-Mīrzā (d. 1305/1888), a son of the erstwhile heir to the throne (*valī-'ahd*) 'Abbās-Mīrzā. Notorious for his inconsiderate severity, he restored order to Fars, over which he was twice appointed governor, for a considerable time. In all his offices he proved himself to be the true *Mu'tamadu'd-daula*, 'The Trustworthy Man of the Kingdom'.[62] Finally he became the court poet with all the customary duties. These he was able to fulfil with ease: a cultured man and master of a perfect poetic technique, though for all his routine he never showed a spark of inspiration. The gifts he did possess however were sufficient to enable him to perform with success all his obligations as the official poet. But at the time that the Dāru'l-funūn was at the height of its importance he was provided with yet another task. Farhād translated Bahā'ī's book on arithmetic (see p. 300) from the Arabic, rendered into verse a small English-Persian dictionary entitled *Niṣāb-i ingilīsī*, 'Basic Stock of English Words'[63], and edited a geography book by W. Pinnock under the title *Jām-i Jam*, 'The Mirror of Jam'. Ye. E. Bertel's[64] adds to this that the period of enlightenment is beginning to supersede that of a decaying panegyrism.

A true master of the classical form is Ḥājjī Muḥammad Taqī Shūrīda Faṣīḥu'l-mulk, 'The Eloquent One of the Kingdom' (b. 1280/1863–4 or 1274/1857–8 in Shiraz[65], died there in 1345/1926). Any other man might have been ruined by fate if, like our poet, he had been stricken blind at the age of seven as the result of smallpox and had lost his father when he was ten. This latter event meant a heavy blow for the family of small artisans, if not dire distress. But Shūrīda was endowed with brilliant gifts and thanks to his exceptional intelligence and good memory managed to master all the traditional doctrines or theories of poetry, for which he had shown a strong disposition in his very early youth. Throughout his life he constantly aimed at adding to his knowledge, especially of history. He was engaged in textual criticism and interpretation of the works of Niẓāmī, Sa'dī, Farrukhī and others. His prose writings were never published. Characteristic of these is *Nāma-i rūshan-dilān*, 'Book of the Clear-minded', a work of consolation for the blind. Shūrīda's voluminous lyrical works are permeated with an optimism and energy that border on cheerfulness and mockery. He has a great admiration for the classical masters and writes in their style and form. But political events too, such as the parliamentary elections, the First World War, etc., are capable of arousing deep emotion in him. He occupied himself with literary questions, for instance the defence of Sa'dī; in short, his serious physical handicap was unable to cut him off from the bustle of life. He wrote songs (*taṣnīf*) in the folklore spirit and also put them to music.

A younger contemporary, Mīrzā 'Abdu'l-Javād Adīb Nīshāpūrī (b. 1281/1864–5 or 1284/1867–8[66], d. 1344/1926) has many things in common with Shūrīda. Unlike the poet from Shiraz, he came from a family of middle-class farmers. In another respect too fate was kinder to him, for small-pox left Adīb with one, albeit half-blind eye. It was by no means easy for him to acquire the profundity of knowledge that was his and that is thus all the more to be wondered at. He went through life a lonely man, but associated himself in a sincere friendship with the poet Īraj (see p. 384). He humbled himself for no one, had no scruples in criticising the great and extolling the mean, and continued his studies uninterruptedly.

At first he followed on in the steps of Qā'ānī, later on in those of Ṣafā of Isfahan (d. 1309/1891), and finally the old masters such as Farrukhī and others. Despite the high esteem in which he was held, he did not introduce much that was new, while current events interested him less than they did Shūrīda. His *dīvān Laʿālī-i maknūna*, 'Hidden Pearls', was published. Adīb was well versed in Arabic literature and also composed poetry in that language. He was fruitfully engaged in teaching and trained whole generations in Khurasan, not limiting himself only to the interpretation of Arabic and Persian texts but also subjecting them to scholarly criticism.

8. ADĪBU'L-MAMĀLIK

Amīru'sh-shuʿarā, 'Prince of Poets', later known as Adību'l-mamālik, 'Man of Letters of the Regions', Mīrzā Ṣādiq-Khān Farāhānī, has his roots in the classical tradition as regards form, but the substance of his works reflects modern times. He has been described as "primary among his contemporaries, if one omits Qā'ānī, Surūsh and one or two others in the modern movement in literature, a movement that began with Nashāṭ and ends with himself – a poet whose most essential deployment was evoked by political events, a master whose *dīvān* far surpasses those of the older poets, with the exception of six or seven".[67] He will be dealt with in greater detail in the following section of this book (see p. 375).

Finally it should be remarked that in the 13th/19th century there was a large number of more or less well-known poets, of many of whose works we possess lithographed editions. There is no doubt that the classical, archaic movement enjoys their preference. Only a few of these poets found recognition, in the main – as far as I can see – in the papers *Armaghān*, *Yādgār*, *Yaghmā*, *Mihr*, *Sukhan*, etc.

Summer 1967

NOTES

1. Cf. Qā'im-maqām's *Dīvān* (ed. *Arm.*), Preface, 38.
2. Bahār, *Sabk*, 3, 340 *et seq.*
3. Ivanov, *Ocherk*, 191.
4. Bahār, 'Bāz-gasht' (B VIa), 717.
5. M. L. Root, *Ṭāhirih*, 62 *et seq.*

6. V. Minorsky, *Iran* (B II), 198.
7. See Ibr. Ṣafā'ī, *Yak shāh* (Bibl.).
8. His pseudonym was Rāvī (specimina to be found in Riḍā-qulī Hidāyat, *Majma'*, 2, 142), but his verse does not attain the level of his prose (the letters). Cf. Ṣafā'ī, *Nahḍat* (B VIa), 57 *et seq.* – *Sukhan*, 8/9 (1336), 932a, refers to his biography in *Arm.*, 26, nos. 6–7. Though in high office, he was – characteristically – deeply in debt, as were many of his contemporaries.
9. Krïmskiy, 3, 132.
10. These were: Muḥ. Ḥusayn 'Andalīb, 'the Nightingale', Ṣabā's son, *maliku'sh-shu'arā*, 'King of Poets', to Fatḥ-'Alī-Shāh and Muḥammad Shāh, and Maḥmūd-Khān (d. 1311/1893), son of 'Andalīb and *maliku'sh-shu'arā* to Nāṣiru'd-dīn-Shāh. He was an all-round scholar and artist, like his grandfather Ṣabā, and in particular a fine painter, one of the best of his period. The *qaṣīdas* composed in his last period are truly vivid pictures. In other respects he followed the masters of the pre-Mongol age. Maḥmūd-Khān used no pseudonyms and signed his *qaṣīdas* simply with the name Maḥmūd. From the same family are descended Furūgh (d. 1290/1873), son of Ṣabā, and Muḥammad-Khān Nadīm-bāshī, 'the chief confidant of the Shāh', who used the pseudonym Khujista and was Maḥmūd-Khān's brother.
11. Ṣafā, *Ḥamāsa* (B VIa), 351 *et seq.*
12. *Ibid.*, 385.
13. 'Bāz-gasht', 717.
14. *Riyāḍ*, 264.
15. Bahār, 'Bāz-gasht', 716, 752.
16. Riḍā-qulī Hidāyat, *Majma'*, 2, 510; Bahār, 'Bāz-gasht', 752.
17. *Nahḍat*, 17–23.
18. The above biographical sketch is based mainly on Bertel's' *Avtobiografiya Ḳā'ānī* (DAN, 1927, 13 *et seq.*) and on his *Ocherk*, 90 *et seq.*, as well as on the monograph by Mrs. V. Kubíčková, the latter also drawing on other sources. More detailed is Ṣafā'ī, *Nahḍat*, 63–92, but it shows considerable deviations and alas gives no documentary evidence. The biography with which M. J. Maḥjūb precedes his excellent edition also shows variations. I give here a short résumé according to Maḥjūb, who bases his views on Mīrzā Ṭāhir, a contemporary of Qā'ānī's, as well as on the *dīvān*: Qā'ānī (b. 1222/1807–8 in Shiraz), was descended from a family that included poets and scholars among its members. He remained only seven or eight years in Shiraz, namely until his father's death; having drawn attention to himself by his verses when still a lad, he was introduced to the governor of Khurasan, Shujā'u's-salṭana Ḥasan-'Alī-Mīrzā, in Mashhad, whither he had gone to study. The grants given him by the prince relieved him of pecuniary worry. Qā'ānī distinguished himself in the mastering of sciences and languages, in the latter to such a degree that he composed poems not only in Persian but also in Arabic and Turkish. During the reign of Muḥammad-Shāh, at whose court he occupied the position of *mujtahidu'sh-shu'arā* with the honorary name of Ḥassānu'l-'Ajam, he acquired an excellent knowledge of French, which he also taught to his son Muḥammad Ḥasan Sāmānī, who was three years old when Qā'ānī returned to Shiraz in 1259/1843. When, after the death of his friend, the poet Viṣāl (d. 1262/1846), he moved to Tehran with his son, he found a new Shāh, in the person of Nāṣiru'd-dīn, and a new situation at court with Amīr-Niẓām occupying the foremost position. The latter was not favourably disposed towards poets, whom he regarded one and all as parasites. Nevertheless Qā'ānī continued his activities as court poet by winning the favour of the Shāh and of the Minister of Public Instructions, 'Alī-qulī-Mirzā. He died in Tehran in 1270/1854. – His family life was unsatisfactory, for he was notoriously addicted to alcohol, which of course no wife could put up with. He even wrote his poems when he was in his cups! That only one-fifth of Qā'ānī's incredibly large output (allegedly nearly 100,000 verses) is now in existence may be explained by his gross carelessness with regard to his own work. The poems composed in Khurasanian-Afghan dialectical expressions must also have been known, but although they are said to have numbered several thousand, these too have

been lost. Maḥjūb subjects the work of this poet to an extensive and all-round analysis and sharp criticism, but finally joins in the praise accorded him by M. Bahār.
19. See above, p. 203.
20. Ṣafā'ī, *loc. cit.*, 75 *et seq.*
21. Muḥ. Kāẓ. Shīrāzī's foreword to the *Selections from Qā'ānī*, Calcutta 1907, 3.
22. Thus far ed. Bombay 1277; *ibid.*, Introduction, fol. 2r., l.2 *infra*: "more than 100,000 (verses)"; according to "Abbās' (see Bertel's, *Avtobiografiya Q.*, 17) as many as 120,000!
23. 'Rahbarān' (B VIa), *Arm.*, 18, 87.
24. Bahār, 'Bāz-gasht', *Arm.*, 14, 57.
25. Ibr. Ṣafā'ī, *Nahḍat*, 70; according to Maḥjūb (see note 18), p. 8, it was a book dealing with agriculture.
26. Shiblī, 5, 13.
27. Cf. 'Ash'ar-i shu'arā'-i du qarn-i akhīr kīst?', a series of articles by various authors, *Arm.*, Vols. 15 and 16. – The preface to the lithographed edition 1274 A.H. fol. 2b, in margin below, and that to the lithographed edition 1277 A.H. fol. 2b, l. 2 *infra*, make mention of numerous essays (*rasā'il*) and amicable letters (*ikhvāniyyāt*). *Sabk*, 3, 334 quotes Qā'ānī's foreword to the *Dīvān-i Farīdūn-Mīrzā-i Qājār*, treatises or essays on *ilm-i shānabīnī*, 'fortune-telling from the shoulder-blades', on exorcism and on the new geometry (!).
28. Bertel's, *Ocherk*, 87.
29. Navābī (Bibl.), 232 *et seq.*
30. von Kégl, 'Viṣāl', 123.
31. A catalogue of Viṣāl's work in Navābī, p. 225 *et seq.*
32. Navābī, 419.
33. Bertel's, *Ocherk*, 87 *et seq.*
34. Navābī (*q.v.*) gives a detailed and reliable account of Viṣāl's family.
35. von Kégl, 'Riḍâ Kulî', 64 *et seq.*
36. *Sabk*, 3, 293.
37. Or 'Amīr of the order', cf. Ivanov, *Ocherk* (B II), 172.
38. Chaykin, *Kratkiy ocherk* (C), 12. Cf. *s.v.* 'A. T. Tagirjanov "C"'.
39. *Loc. cit.*, 14. 'Alī Mushīrī's essay, 'Avvalīn rūznāma-i īrānī', *Sukhan*, 14 (1342), 609–11, offers nothing essentially new.
40. *Sabk*, 3, 345.
41. Chaykin, *Kratkiy ocherk*, 16.
42. *Sabk*, 3, 346.
43. In detail: Chaykin, *Kratkiy ocherk*, 15; Bibl. B VII *s.v.* 'Tarbiyat' and *s.v.* 'E. G. Browne'.
44. Ritter, 'Attâr', *İA*, 2, 9b. Contents: F. Meier, *Die schöne Mahsatī*, 28–30.
45. Bertel's, *Ocherk*, 113.
46. Thus Nikki R. Keddie, 'Religion and Irreligion in Early Iranian Nationalism', *Compar. Studies in Society and History*, 4 (1962), 285, and B. Alavi, *Geschichte und Entwicklung der modernen persischen Literatur*, Berlin 1964, 31.
47. Bertel's, *ibid.*, 116.
48. A similar trend is shown in Molière's *Le Médicin malgré lui*, in the lithographical edition Tehran 1322/1904, signed by Muḥammad Ḥaṣan-Khān I'timādu's-salṭana. But in view of the custom of this encyclopaedist (see p. 341) of publishing work written by his colleagues as his own, there is no guarantee that the adaptation did in fact flow from his pen. A comparison of the French with the Persian text shows "how profoundly Persian psychology had appropriated western comedy" (Bertel's, *Pers. Teatr.*, L. 1924, 73; Krīms'kïy, *Pers'kīy teatr*, Kiev 1925, 87). My copy of *Ḥikāyat-i ṭabīb-i ijbārī*, Tehran 1306 (?)/1888 only states that the lithographed MS is the work of 'Abdu'l-'Alī Mashhadī at the behest of I'timādu's-salṭana. Bertel's (*Ocherk*, 129) also announces a new translation of *Le Tartuffe*.

49. For more information about him see B. Alavi, *Geschichte und Entwicklung der modernen persischen Literatur*, Berlin 1964, 76–7; Bertel's, *Ocherk*, 117–8. *
50. On the influence of Transcaucasia see Tagirjanov, *Istor. korni* (B VIa).
51. Bertel's, *Ocherk*, 107.
52. Riḍā-qulī-Hidāyat, *Majma'*, 2, 156–81; cf. Storey, *Pers. Lit.*, II/I, 152 *et seq.* and Vol. I/2, 1247 *et seq.*
53. See Bibl. *s.v.* 'Shamsu'd-dīn etc.' (B IV).
54. Riḍā-qulī Hidāyat, *Majma'*, 2, 184.
55. Ṣafā, *Ḥamāsa*, 387 *et seq.*
56. *Ocherk*, 89.
57. *Arm.*, 15, 610 *et seq.*; 784.
58. Qazvīnī, 'Vafāyāt-i mu'āṣirīn', *Yādgār*, 5/1–2, 102; *Sabk*, 3, 370. M. J. Maḥjūb holds him in higher estimation than the famous Qā'ānī.
59. Qazvīnī, *loc. cit.*, 5/3, 67.
60. Bertel's, *Ocherk*, 101.
61. *Ibid.*, 100.
62. This public activity is dealt with in the series of articles 'Farhād-Mīrzā' by Murt. Mud. Chahār-dihī, *Arm.*, 29, 257–61 *et seq.* Idem, *Arm.* 30, 11–13 on Farhād's prose and translations, nowhere however on his poetical works; on his buildings etc. *ibid.*, 65–7. Farhād demonstrated his verse technique in the autobiography dedicated to his father. This consists of approx. 200 couplets in 28 sections, each one being constructed with intentional suppression of the respective letter in alphabetical order (see Riḍā-qulī, *Majma'*, 1, 47 *et seq.*).
63. *Niṣāb* originally means a vocabulary intended to be committed to memory (A. Sprenger, *ZDMG*, 16, 311), as for instance the well-known Arabic-Persian *Niṣābu'ṣ-ṣibyān*, 'Basic Stock of Words for Boys', written in verse in the 8th/14th century by Abū-Naṣr al-Farāhī.
64. *Ocherk*, 102.
65. 1280 A.H.: *Arm.*, 9, 80; 1274 A.H.: Qazvīnī, 'Vafāyāt-i mu'āṣirīn', *Yādgār*, 5/3, 64.
66. 1281 A.H.: *Arm.*, 7, 45; 1284 A.H.: Qazvīnī, *Yādgār*, 5/6–7, 133 *et seq.*
67. *Dīvān*, ed. Vaḥīd Dastgirdī, Preface, p. 'yḥ'.

VĚRA KUBÍČKOVÁ

PERSIAN LITERATURE OF THE 20TH CENTURY

When in 1959 this article appeared in J. Rypka's *Iranische Literaturgeschichte* (Harrassowitz, Leipzig, 341–389), it constituted the first attempt to present a summary of modern Persian literature up to the middle of the 1950s. Bearing this in mind, the present, slightly revised English version may be justified, though modifications of some of the views expressed are really called for as a consequence of the continued development of Persian literature on the one hand, and on the other because of the considerable growth of interest recently displayed in the subject by researchers at home and abroad.

V.K.

I. BRIEF SURVEY OF THE ECONOMICO-POLITICAL SITUATION IN IRAN AFTER 1896

A. STRUGGLE FOR A CONSTITUTION AND FALL OF THE QAJARS IN THE PERIOD 1896–1921

It has already been explained in the preceding sections how the policies of the second Qajar, Fatḥ-ʿAlī-Shāh, which totally lacked the broader conceptions of statesmanship and clung to the empty show of oriental pomp, opened the door to European capital and also to a change in the feudal economy such as it had so far existed. The rivalry of British and Russian imperialism throughout the 19th century accelerated this process, during which the first signs of a modernisation of Iranian life made their appearance, notably a few of the technical advantages of European civilisation, and an occasional waft of western thought. Later Nāṣiru'd-dīn supported the trend by introducing various reforms and European novelties – such as official newspapers, high-school education of a polytechnic character with European teachers, travel grants for studies in Europe, and so on – but he could no longer set limits to the trends he himself had helped to initiate. Dāru'l-funūn, the centre of modern education (see p. 322), brought up a new intelligentsia, acquainted with modern science, with European economic and political systems, and thus equipped with the premises for a critical view of the situation of its own country and people. Echoes of European revolutions and the consciousness of social changes which followed in their wake, joined with the lessons learned from the patriotic struggles of their more advanced Islamic neighbours (the success of the reformist movement in Turkey with the proclamation of a Constitution in 1876; the revolution of ʿArābī Pāshā in Egypt in 1881–2), inspired far-reaching analogies. Terms hitherto more of a religious or narrowly local character (*vaṭan, millat*) acquired a new political content and a more universal connotation: native country, nation, freedom.[1] Basic changes of view are apparent also in the new evaluation of supposedly immutable truths; now it is realised that the will of the

Notes on p. 361

nation and its true interests are not always identical with the will and interests of the ruler and that the nation has the right to make its will felt with more effective means than the fireworks of Saʿdī's invective against the tyrants.

"The powerful stream of regeneration is rolling towards the East, despotic rule is nearing its fall. Summon all your forces and destroy the foundations of this despotism." This challenge – and certainly not the only one – of the famous reformer and feared revolutionary Sayyid Jamālu'd-dīn Asadābādī Afghānī[2], characterises the situation and points to its solution.

And at the instigation of Sayyid Jamālu'd-dīn, the first blow was delivered at Qajar despotism: one of his pupils shot Nāṣiru'd-dīn Shāh on May Day 1896 (18 Dhi'l-qaʿda 1313), at the time of the preparations for the festive celebrations of the fiftieth anniversary of his accession.

With the advent of Muẓaffaru'd-dīn Shāh, who succeeded his assassinated father, the Persian throne was still occupied by the Qajar dynasty – but from then on the Court was no longer the only, or even the decisive force controlling the course of events. The Shāh's policy, leading to a growing dependence of Iran on the financial assistance of Russia and Great Britain, only helped to speed the designs of the Persian patriots and hasten the more precise formulation of their demands. Every error of judgement, every move of the Shāh or his court, dictated by selfish interests and the consciousness of absolute power – the long-term concessions by which the country's wealth was sold out to foreigners, costly journeys to Europe, the calling in of foreign experts into the internal administration of the empire, and so on – were analysed and criticised in the patriotic press, in pamphlets, in satirical verses and songs, and all this literature found its way, in word and song, among the broad masses of the people (p. 363, n. 5). This work soon bore fruit. Now in this part, now in another part of the country, disorders and revolts broke out which then merged into a spontaneous movement of resistance.[3] In this situation the final impetus was provided by the Russian Revolution of 1905, and the Persian patriots came out openly with their demands for the promulgation of a Constitution and the setting up of a Parliament. A valuable contribution to the successful realisation of these demands was made by the higher ranks of the priesthood; the top representatives of the spiritual power supported the demand for a Constitution with all the weight of their authority, and by an effective use of religious orders and prohibitions enabled the patriotic intelligentsia to bring home to the nation the errors of court policy (for instance, when the Shāh was negotiating the matter of tobacco trade concessions, they published a religious prohibition of smoking on a nation-wide scale which, along with the removal of the smallest speck of tobacco, undoubtedly caused the Shāh and his court considerable chagrin). And again, in the decisive moments of the final stages of the talks between the patriots and the Shāh, the high religious dignitaries, by a demonstrative departure from the capital (which meant for the believers of Islam the practically complete paralysis of normal life) induced the Shāh to hasten his decision in favour of national demands.[4] The Constitution was proclaimed and on August 19th, 1906 (28 Jumādā II 1324) the Shāh opened the inaugural session of Parliament (*majlis*).

The struggles of the Persian patriots were not, however, thereby at an end. The Shāh died the following year and his successor, Muḥammad ʿAlī, showed himself from the first to be a sworn enemy of the Constitution, the enactments of which he tried to limit in every possible way.[5] And so a stubborn struggle was waged between the ruler and Parliament or, in other words, between the Qajar court and the nation, the first phase of which ended with a victory for reaction – the *coup d'état* of the 23rd June, 1908, and the prorogation of Parliament. The patriots, however, were far from giving up the fight. Despite all the means of terror at the disposal of the Shāh, despite his artillery divisions and Cossack cavalry, the nationalists finally won the victory with the entry of the patriotic divisions into the capital on July 16th, 1909, (known as the *Fatḥ-i millī*).[6]

The Shāh, who had sought asylum at the Russian Legation, abdicated; he was succeeded by his scarcely twelve-year-old son, Aḥmad, and a regent was appointed in the person of the senior member of the Qajar House, ʿAḍudu'l-mulk. The Constitution was again proclaimed and a new Parliament (the *Second majlis*)[7] opened on the 15th November, 1909.

The liberally orientated government appointed by the Revolutionary National Council occupied a difficult position. Various groups with widely differing radical trends held up the consolidation of the country, which provided Great Britain and Russia with a welcome pretext for intervention.[8] Both powers made use of every possible means to further their imperialistic interest and, after the accession of a new reactionary regent – the ex-Shāh is said to have had a finger in it –, succeeded in bringing about the dissolution of the *Second majlis* in December 1911. Russian aggression followed in December and in January of the next year[9]; thereupon, in March, both powers forced the Persian government to make the official declaration that it would conduct its home and foreign policy in conformity with their interests, on the basis of the agreement of August 1907.[10]

The *Third majlis* was opened on the 14th December, 1914, really only in order to declare Iran's neutrality in the First World War. The democratic parliamentary majority, which made no secret of its dislike of Iran's official allies, Great Britain and Russia, hastened rather than delayed its re-dismissal.[11] Soon the country, important for its allies both strategically and for its mineral wealth, was occupied by their forces. The behaviour of the occupying forces made still worse an already miserable situation; national pride cultivated in the patriotic struggles led to ever new revolts against the occupying forces, and the former antipathy to the two imperialist powers changed into open hatred which in some patriots led to a convinced Germanophilism (cf. Adīb Pīshāvarī, Vaḥīd Dastgirdī) or Turcophilism (cf. ʿĀrif Qazvīnī).

The First World War ran its course in a context of sharply antagonistic views and inner and outer unrest. The October Revolution, which preceded its conclusion, was

Notes on p. 361

enthusiastically welcomed by many Persian patriots, nor were there lacking poetical appeals to follow its example (see pp. 376, 387). When the victory of the Allied Powers was proclaimed and Great Britain hastened to strengthen its economic position in Iran by means of a new treaty, the patriots condemned it all the more resolutely, having before their eyes the completely contrary attitude of the young Soviet-Union, which on its own initiative annulled the imperialistically tendentious treaty concluded between Iran and tsarist Russia.[12]

B. THE RISE OF RIḌĀ KHĀN AND HIS PATH TO POWER

The struggles in the country, already in their second decade and waged with words and arms, broke out anew with even greater intensity. This time, unlike the first phase of the patriotic struggle when the nation stood united behind the demand for a Constitution, various political groups contested the field, whereby the programme of the journalist, poet and politician, Sayyid Ḍiyā'u'd-dīn finally won supremacy. In the name of this programme, the old government was overthrown on the night of February 21st, 1921 (3 Isfand 1299); the uprising was planned and carried out by young officers, supporters of Sayyid Ḍiyā'u'd-dīn, under the command of Colonel Riḍā Khān, who came with his Cossacks from Qazvīn and occupied the government building.[13]

The majority of the people accepted the resolute action of Riḍā Khān with enthusiasm, and politicians of various tinges placed their hopes in his rise to power: the Liberals hoped that he would curtail the power of the ruling dynasty and not countenance too great deviations to the left; the Democrats expected him to proclaim a Republic; the Left wing supported him in the conviction that, not belonging to the governing caste, he would be in favour of social reforms; the Nationalists believed that he would build a strong state, independent of foreign powers. And the whole nation was sure that he would consolidate conditions in the country and at last create order. In the given situation, however, this was no simple matter. The nomad tribes began to revolt, being opposed in their conservatism to any more radical political changes, especially when news began to come through of Riḍā's intention to transform the monarchy into a republic, after the example of the neighbouring Turkey. The younger generation of politicians and intelligentsia, on the contrary, brought up in European ways of thought, were keen advocates of this form of government and, in the spring of 1924, stormy pro-Republican demonstrations took place in Tehran.

Through continual changes of ministries Riḍā Khān remained Minister of War, from the autumn of 1923 also Prime Minister, and his power in the State continued to grow. The Qajar Shāh remained in Europe through this time of unrest and did not return even at repeated requests from the governments; so, on October 31st, 1925 the Shāh was deposed and the Qajar dynasty came to an end by decree of Parliament, which at the same time entrusted Riḍā with the interim government of the country. Proof of the political aplomb of the new Regent was the expedition with which a law was passed relating to new parliamentary elections – the old Parliament had a decidedly Republican orientation – and the promptness with which these were carried out, so that the opening session of Parliament took place already on the 6th December, the first task Riḍā set it being to resolve on the new form of State administration. Surprisingly, the little short of twenty years of struggle on the part of Persian patriots for the democratisation of the country ended in the election of a Parliament which made Riḍā Khān the first member of a new hereditary imperial dynasty, the Pahlavi, on December 13th, 1925.[14]

The severe régime of military dictatorship, which Riḍā Shāh tightened up from year to year, was characterised above all by a strong admiration for European civilisation, in the name of which a feverish reconstruction of the whole country was entered upon; transport and industry were developed, European architecture made rapid headway and changed the physical character of the capital, European novelties in dress and manners were prescribed, and many traditional customs connected with the Islamic faith were done away with.[15] In foreign policy, which in the first years showed a striking turning away from Great Britain and a growing friendliness with the Soviet-Union, there set in from the 'thirties ever closer political and economic ties with Nazi Germany, with which country almost half of Persia's foreign trade was carried on.

C. CHANGES IN HOME AND FOREIGN POLICY AFTER 1941

This circumstance was one of the main reasons why in the middle of the Second World War, on October 16th, 1941, Riḍā Shāh was forced to abdicate and leave Iran. His son, Muḥammad Riḍā, ascended the throne and the Allies again occupied the country with British and Soviet forces. This time the occupation was not the occupation of a semi-colonial country, as in the First World War (which fact, with all due reserve, must be placed to the credit of Riḍā Shāh and his policy), so that the departure of the dictator was immediately observable in both political and cultural life. We see a renewal of democratic orientation: numerous political parties spring up with a wide variety of programmes, from radical right-wingers to those of the extreme left, each of them contributing assiduously to the enlivenment of political journalism. In the economic field efforts are made to abolish survivals of semi-colonial dependence – as in the liquidation of the Anglo-Iranian Petroleum Company – and similarly in the

Notes on p. 361

wide domain of culture there is evidence of endeavours to create a modern national individuality. This widespread effort to set up new forms of national life often runs its course against a background of sharp ideological conflicts of which we are eye-witnesses and which are as yet far from being fought to a finish.[16]

As will be clear even from this brief survey, Iranian events of the 20th century fall into three periods, each of which has so specific a character that it stamps to a considerable extent the literary production of the years that compose it. These three epochs therefore form the basis for our division of the Iranian literary output of the 20th century into three chapters, always with the reservation that no periodisation is more than a methodological aid, making no claim to confine strictly within its dividing lines the living organism that is creative art. As the whole period under review covers little more than half a century, it is to be expected that many a literary personality will produce work in all three periods. The question then arises as to what criteria should be applied when placing an author in this or that period, or when deciding whether his work should be treated in all three. After excluding the latter system, which would lead to undesirable repetition, and other more or less mechanical points of view, we have chosen as our guiding line the endeavour to deal with the poet in that period during which he most fully stood for the ideas and forms of a progressive and revolutionary character. With this explanation, we subjoin the periodisation which will be observed in our article:

(1) the struggle for a Constitution, from the period of preparation following the assassination of Nāṣiru'd-dīn in 1896 to the Riḍā Shāh Rising of 1921; here the poets are at once the leaders of a national awakening, the propagators of new ideas, the teachers of the nation; journalism is an important domain of literary activity, of topical patriotic and nationalist poetry and of political pamphlets in verse and prose; the rise of the first historical novels;

(2) the *coup d'état* and the path to Riḍā's founding of a new dynasty and military dictatorship up to his abdication (1921–41); the new conditions lead to a turning away from topical events in poetry, and attention is directed to the solving of problems related to the formal character of the new poetry and the new style; the significance of literary prose is recognised and critically evaluated; the subject-matter includes new social themes coloured with romantic sentimentality;

(3) endeavours at democratisation after Riḍā Shāh's abdication in 1941, struggle for a modern style of life; a world orientation in literature, an increase in the number of periodicals with a cultural mission, the first attempts at the documentation of all native literary output; a perceptible 'new wave' in poetry, a promising upward trend in literary prose, especially the shorter forms of the short story and the long short story or *novella*.

NOTES

1. On conditions in the Near East at this time cf. E. Kedourie, *Afghani and Abduh* (London 1966) and N. R. Keddie, *Religion and Rebellion in Iran* (London 1966).
2. Jamālu'd-dīn's national awakening work as a journalist and a public speaker was of great importance too in defining the content of modern political terms, which he was able to do from a philosophical point of view, close to Islamic thought, cf. Jamāl-al-dīn al-Afghānī, *Orient*, 6 (1958), 123 *et seq.*; A. M. Goichon, *Réfutation des matérialistes* (translations of important speeches by Jamālu'd-dīn from the Arabic); *Maqālāt-i Jamāliyya*, collection of his less-known Persian speeches.
3. Cf. Ivanov, *Iranskaya revolutsiya*, 8–66, to which a bibliography has been added.
4. Cf. Browne, *Persian Revolution*, 121 *et seq.*; on the basis of new documents Bihzād, *Inqilāb-i mashrūṭiyya-i Īrān*, 201 *et seq.*
5. Shafaq, *MEJ*, 6 (1952), 421, believes that it was the aggressive conduct of several of the patriots that provoked the Shāh to attacks on the Majlis.
6. The important role of the Bakhtiyars in connexion with the Fatḥ-i millī is dealt with by N. Dānishvar (see Bibl.).
7. The chronology of the Second Constitution is given by Browne in *Press and Poetry*, 318–36.
8. Ivanov, *op. cit.*, 409 *et seq.*, 414 *et seq.*
9. Shuster, *Strangling of Persia*, 199 *et seq.*; Ivanov, *op. cit.*, 501.
10. On this see Browne, *Persian Revolution*, 127; Kasravī, *Inqilāb-i mashrūṭiyya*, 460 *et seq.*; Litten, *Persien*, 14 *et seq.*
11. Musil, *Země Arijců* [*The Land of the Aryans*], 126.
12. Hurewitz, *Diplomacy...*, 90 *et seq.*; Lenczowski, *Russia and the West in Iran* 1918–1948; Kuznetsov, *SV*, 1957, 5, 100 *et seq.*
13. A chronicle of events is given in *Oriente Moderno*, from 1921 onwards.
14. Cf. (C), especially Aubin, Artzt, Hesse, Tahmasp.
15. Cf. (C), Armayānī, Doroshenko.
16. On this see (C), especially H. C. Atyeo, A. B. Bashkirov, Elwell-Sutton, Ch. Farmanfarmanian, N. S. Fatemi, ʻA. A. Ḥikmat, F. Laurent, A. K. Lavrentiyev, L. Massignon, A. Michaelis, G. M. Petrov, *Sovremenniy Iran*; for chronicle of events from 1954, see *MEJ* and *MEA*.

II. CHARACTER OF THE LITERARY RENAISSANCE

Economic and cultural contact with the occident, which since the middle of the 19th century has increased in width and intensity, was one of the main factors in initiating the transformation of many countries of the orient, among them Iran, from the traditional to the modern way of life. Literature was also affected by this trend. The knowledge of European languages and literatures, western education, with its opening up of new possibilities in technology, natural science, and the social sciences, and the reflection of all this in everyday life, is for Iranian literature a discovery in the light of which truths accepted as immutable for thousands of years collapse and the existing social order appears as what it is – a mediaeval survival. The critical attitude towards national reality, once awakened, is further cultivated and reveals inadequacies of a fundamental character, investigates their causes and thinks out ways of removing them. This forms the main stream of the literature of this period – a literature that is tendentious and militant, addressed to the broad masses of the nation, with the aim of educating, instructing and awakening them from their backwardness and passivity. The best poets of the country, where from time immemorial the masters of the word had composed *qaṣīdas* in praise of the ruling dynasty and court and sent them with enthusiastic dedications to their monarchs, now placed all their art in the service of the struggle to limit and finally overthrow the monarchal power, and of the enlightenment and liberation of their fellow-citizens. This is the first *novum* forming the dividing-line between modern and traditional literature, and pointing to the new trend in which the poet no longer aims to create for a small aristocratic circle, but for the broad masses of the nation.

The greater part of the literary production of this period tends to be associated in its content with political events; care for the formal aspects of the art is at first only superficial and consists mainly in the negation of the often almost unintelligible literary language of the previous centuries, and in the jettisoning of the most blatant examples of clichés and empty rhetorical embellishments. Classical poetry is submitted to strict revision: the patriots declare the only truly noble art to be the heroic epic of Firdausī, where they find the perfect expression of national pride, an important component of modern patriotism. There is a turning away from Ṣūfī mysticism, and lyrical panegyrics are rare. The Qajar court still has its court poets, but none of them surpass the average of professional versifiers, as the outstanding ones among them, such as Īraj and Bahār, voluntarily gave up the honours formerly so coveted by poets. In his shaɪp condemnation of the poetical eulogies of the past, the poet and publicist Mīrzā Āqā-Khān Kirmānī (see p. 365) most aptly expresses the attitude of the time when he says: "The result of the praises and flatteries of those poets was that the monarchs and their ministers were stimulated to carry out the most impossibly crazy and eccentric actions... etc."[1]

Satire occupies the foreground; formerly narrowly personal in content (see *Prolegomena*, p. 333), it now becomes a topical political poem in the broadest sense of the term[2], as is at once evident from a reading of the texts gathered in Browne's monograph. This modern satire documents best certain important changes in poetic diction: expressions and turns of speech taken from the colloquial language, various onomatopoeic plays on words proper to folk-poetry, dialect words and slang.[3] Metric principles are less strictly observed and, together with *mathnavī, qaṣīda* and *ghazal*, strophic song forms are popular.[4]

The literary output of the period of the Constitution, for the main part still poetry, is thus of a didactic and political character and serves its time and its topical problems, while the so-called 'eternal problems' of classical poetry no longer occupy the foreground of interest. If such poetry is to have the intended effect, if it is to fulfil the didactic mission with which the poet and the time have endowed it, it must impress the reader at once. And so the poets reach out for the medium which modern technology places at their disposal, namely the daily press, journalism, which thus becomes the first arena of the literary activities of the time. The best poets are at the same time journalists, editors and newspaper publishers; the papers thereby reach an excellent level and achieve wide popularity.

This popularity is an interesting factor in a country with such a large percentage of illiterates. Musil[5] explains it as being due to the fact that in a time of such general interest in political events, people, not only in the towns but also in the country districts, gathered round anyone who could read, listened to the newspapers being read aloud and then started lively discussions on topical problems. After the dissolution of the 'Third majlis' and the occupation of the country (p. 357), many of the foremost poets were obliged to emigrate and a strict censorship was exercised over the daily press, with the result that its quality deteriorated and interest on the part of the readers and literati decreased. At that time and also later in the more recent history of Iran, whenever a similar political situation recurred, the active participation in politics of creative workers declined and they turned their attention to formal problems connected with their art.

Notes on pp. 377–378

A new phenomenon in the literary art of the first two decades of our century is the development of belletristic prose in the European sense of the term. Traditional Persian prose had always endeavoured to come as close as possible to real art, namely, poetry; from poetry it took over rhyme and rhythm (often even in scientific treatises, see *Prolegomena*, p. 341) and was frequently only an accompaniment to verse, as in the classic, *Gulistān*. Such prose, together with various more popular forms were the legacy of historical prose forms, so that here the creators of new prose had practically no domestic models. The first modern prose, like the first modern poetry, had a predominantly topical political content and its best examples were newspaper articles, the authors of which were Malkum Khān, Ṭālibūf, Dihkhudā.[6] The school in which these first prose writers learnt their craft were European belles-lettres – mostly French – which reached Iran and were translated into Persian.[7] They included Morier's *Haji Baba*, the prose of Cervantes, Molière, Jules Verne, Chateaubriand, Victor Hugo, and a number of novels by Dumas Père.[8] In this more or less haphazard selection, the literati chose as patterns above all what was nearest to their aesthetic sensibility: undaunted heroes, heedful of honour and glory, intricate plots, in which the ruling dynasty or nobility played a part and which contained a grain of historical truth, high standards of chivalry and plenty of adventure – in short, the atmosphere and trappings of the heroic epic, the beloved *Shāh-nāma*. All this the Persian reader found in modern prose form in the adventure novels of Dumas Père. These were the main source on which the Persian novelist drew, a source which gave the first Persian novels their strongly marked, if not always the most desirable, traits.

Similarly, the work of translation was itself to a certain extent a school for the Persian literati; for if they were to express the relatively simple style of European prose, they had to create a new literary Persian as its medium. The literary language as it then existed, bound for centuries by a system of rhetorical rules, cluttered up with phrases which no longer had any real meaning, had so estranged itself from the spoken language that it was no longer suited to the translation of a western novel and still less a stage play. Thus here translation was, in the true sense of the term, creative work, an important factor in the forming of a modern literary expressive medium; sometimes the translation was so successful that it became an integral part of the native literature, as in the case of *Haji Baba* or the comedies of Ākhund-zāda.

The endeavour to create a new literary Persian – one of the many endeavours characterising this period of a universal search after a modern way of life in Iran – was at the same time the first step towards the rise of a modern literary language. In this field, there came to the assistance of the national awakeners certain sociological realities, such as the growth of a compact administrative class in the capital and in the larger provincial centres, together with modern communication media – railways, telephone and telegraph, and especially the press and journalism.

A. THE PRESS AND ITS ROLE IN THE LITERATURE OF THE CONSTITUTIONAL PERIOD

During the time of the constitutional struggles Persian literature – in the main political and openly tendentious – was presented to the reader not in books or *dīvāns*, but in newspapers and magazines. For this reason journalism is still the best literary mirror of that time.

Some ninety different periodicals, mostly of a high literary standard, flooded the country – a truly remarkable number, particularly when we remember that the press only arrived in Iran during the first half of the 19th century and that the first official journals quietly vegetated at a level which could offer no inspiration for future development (pp. 322, 337–9). It was not these, however, but several unofficial, semi-illegal pamphlets of a revolutionary and critical nature which appeared here and there in the country long before the revolution, that were the real precursors of constitutional journalism.

The first centre of this national awakening was Tabriz, whose writers had direct connections with the Russian revolutionary intelligentsia.[9] Nāṣiru'd-dīn was still on the throne when a paper appeared in Tabriz, called *Talqīn-nāma-i Īrān*, 'Instruction Sheet for Iran', a necrology of Iran in pamphlet form, and also the illustrated satirical newspaper *Shab-nāma*, 'Night-Paper'.[10] Later a circle of revolutionary writers and journalists was formed also in Tehran; it produced similar publications and even set about organising their distribution. These included, among others, *Ghayrat*, 'Zeal', and *Lisānu'l-ghayb*, 'Tongue of the Unseen'.

This work at home was supported by Persian poets and journalists of repute abroad. They attempted, in a good literary style, to draw the attention of their contemporaries to the unhappy situation of their country. Thus in Istanbul a circle of outstanding poets and journalists worked on the newspaper *Akhtar*, 'Star', which was founded in 1292/1875. The two chief editors, the poet Mīrzā Āqā-Khān Kirmānī and Shaykh Aḥmad-i Rūḥī, were executed in Tabriz after the murder of Nāṣiru'd-dīn (p. 363). Witty, ironic criticisms of conditions in Persia, published in the form of popular pamphlets called *Shāh-seven* after a semi-nomadic Turkish tribe, were also the work of these writers.

In Cairo the work was centred around the paper *Thurayyā*, 'The Pleiades', founded in 1316/1898 by Mīrzā 'Alī Muḥammad-Khān Kāshānī. The Calcutta paper *Ḥablu'l-matīn*, 'The Firm Cord', which first appeared in 1311/1893, maintained a very high standard; during the constitutional period Ḥasan-Khān Kāshānī, brother of the Calcutta publisher, founded a paper of the same name in Tehran, and this became one of the best periodicals of the time.

Undoubtedly the best and most influential of all the pre-revolutionary papers was the London *Qānūn*, 'The Law', founded in 1890, which Browne holds to be one of the main stimuli of the political and literary renaissance, of the revolutionary revival of Persia.[11] Its founder and publisher, Mīrzā Malkum-Khān Nāẓimu'd-daula, former Persian ambassador in London (recalled for his revolutionary views), an educated man and ardent patriot, regarded contemporary reality from the point of view of the future. This enabled him to create a paper which for fifteen years was a model for the journalists of the Constitution. A lucid modern style, enriched with felicitous new formations, is combined in Malkum-Khān's articles with a thorough knowledge of the problems of which they treat and with a revolutionary spirit which occasional collaboration with Jamālu'd-dīn Afghānī (p. 356) in the pages of *Qānūn* happily reinforced.[12]

The patriotic literary work of Malkum-Khān was not confined to journalism. Linked with the awakening of Iran was, in his view, the reformation of Arabic script, which he simplified on the basis of Latin script. He himself published several books (e.g. Saʿdī's *Gulistān*), in order to demonstrate to the public the advantages of the reform.[13] Here, however, his endeavours suffered defeat. Of great importance in the forming of a new prose style were his political pamphlets which, although originally intended only for the educated reader, were soon secretly circulated throughout the country, because they expressed in a comprehensible way all that the nation lived and hoped for. Finally, Persian drama, too, found an innovator in the versatile personality of Prince Malkum: he was the author of satirical comedies with themes treated from the angle of social criticism.[14]

We then see how, not only in the capital but also in the larger provincial towns, a great number of periodicals shoots up after the declaration of the Constitution and the introduction of a free press, and how the circulation of those that had already been in existence increased, sometimes even tenfold.

During the period of revolutionary enthusiasm, the papers did not represent any particular party. They fought, united, for the Constitution. At this time almost every poet of any importance published his own periodical, and this explains the high standard of newspapers, in both their literary and informative aspects, since the spontaneous joy with which poets and writers offered their services to the nation was evident in every article.

ʿAlī Nau-rūz, H. L. Rabino, Muḥ. ʿAlī-Khān (in Browne's *Press and Poetry*) and S. Hāshimī, amongst others, compiled a bibliography of the revolutionary press (see Bibliography, VII, for further information). Here we can only mention those papers that were important in the development of literature, either because of their subject-matter or because they enjoyed the cooperation of some noteworthy contemporary poets.

Among the daily newspapers, the consistently liberal-democratic *Īrān-i nau*, 'New Iran', enjoyed the greatest popularity. This paper is of interest from a literary point of view in that it published the first poems of the poets Maliku'sh-shuʿarā Bahār (pp. 373–4) and Lāhūtī Kirmānshāhī (p. 376). It also published translations of

Krïlov's Fables, especially those embodying allegories that reminded the reader of the blunders of the contemporary government or of the administration.

Otherwise the majority of the daily papers were only of secondary literary importance, as articles of an artistic nature were more frequently to be found in weekly papers and in various magazines. The leading weekly was *Sūr-i Isrāfīl*, 'The Trumpet of Israfil', founded in Tehran in 1325/1907. Ideologically it was known for the polemics by which it sought to prove the responsibility of the Islamic priesthood for the decline of Islamic nations. The satirical column of the paper, designated 'Charand-Parand', was particularly popular. In it the poet Mīrzā ʿAlī Akbar-Khān Dihkhudā, one of the most important personalities of the time, created a new and in Persia previously unknown type of literary satire. In the measure that it was popular with its readers, it was hated by the opponents of the Constitution. Its publisher, Mīrzā Jahāngīr-Khān Shīrāzī was executed after the accession of Muḥammad ʿAlī (p. 357)[15], and Dihkhudā had to take refuge abroad, whence he continued his literary activities.

As regards the standard and number of good and interesting articles – and particularly poems – the paper *Nasīm-i shimāl*, 'The Breeze of the North', founded in 1325/1907, in Rasht, was of the same quality as the Tehran *Sūr-i Isrāfīl*. It appeared somewhat irregularly until 1911. Its editor and publisher, Sayyid Ashraf Gīlānī, was a capable poet and a brave fighter for a better future for his country. The journalists' magazine in Rasht, *Khayru'l-kalām*, 'The Best of Discourses', which from its first appearance in 1325/1907 was directed by its editor Afṣaḥu'l-mutakallimīn, was conspicuous for its effective and sharply pointed satire.

Tabriz also remained true to its pre-revolutionary tradition during the period of struggle for the Constitution, particularly as regards good humorous periodicals[16], for example *Ḥasharātu'l-arḍ*, 'The Reptiles of the Earth', that was founded in 1326/1908 by Ḥājjī Mīrzā Āqā Billūrī and contained witty articles and colourful caricatures. *Ṣuḥbat*, 'Conversation', was lithographed first in 1327/1909 in Azerbayjāni Turkish and was attacked, mainly by the Islamic theologians, on account of its articles against the veiling of women and on the question of emancipation. *Ādharbayjān*, published since 1325/1907 in Persian and Azerbayjāni Turkish and edited by the well-known ʿAlī Qulī-Khān Safarof, was also famous for its caricatures.[17]

The poet Mīrzā Ṣādiq-Khān Adību'l-mamālik (pp. 375–6), a descendant of the famous Qā'im-maqām, was also the publisher and editor of a good periodical, *Adab*, 'Culture', which started to appear before the Revolution. In addition to poems by the editor, the paper published serious items of a popular nature on science by the physician Mīrzā Najaf-Qulī-Khān Qā'im-maqāmī, and sometimes translations, mainly from the French. These items gave information on world literature and science, and were accompanied by portraits of world-famous writers and scientists. The liberal-democratic intelligentsia of Tabriz centred around the magazine *Āzād*, 'Free', published by the bookseller Tarbiyat.

Among the papers published in Mashhad the best known was the consistently democratic *Nau-Bahār*, 'New Spring', founded in 1328/1910 under the leadership of the poet Bahār. The Russian Legation in Tehran protested against the paper's attacks on the aggressive policy of Russia and its publication was suspended. It appeared again under the name *Tāza-Bahār* 'Fresh Spring', without, however, changing its policy to any great extent.

At this time Sayyid Ḍiyā'u'd-dīn Ṭabāṭabā'ī attained great popularity on account of the revolutionary ideas he proclaimed in his paper *Sharq*, 'The East', (founded in 1327/1909). Later, after repeated suspension, its name was changed to *Barq*, 'Lightning'. For this same reason he fell into disfavour with government circles. His *Sharq* included a column entitled, 'Adabiyyāt – Literature', in which, in particular, the poems of Lāhūtī Kirmānshāhī appeared.

Amongst the various ideological problems discussed, that of the status of women, which has already been mentioned, soon came to the fore. Contemporary poetry often included in its themes the need of education for women on an equal basis with men, and the necessity for the emancipation of women from their unsatisfactory social position.[18] Under the influence of this school of thought there appeared magazines for women, even edited by women. The first of these, *Dānish*, 'Knowledge', was founded in 1328/1910 in Tehran. It is interesting to note, however, that basic problems which were often raised in other papers were never discussed in its pages. It was only after the First World War that women's magazines representing more progressive trends began to appear.

After the dissolution of the 'Second majlis' (December 1910) literary life gradually died out. Many poets and revolutionaries were executed, others lived in exile.[19] The papers which continued to appear preferred to follow official policy. Their style is consequently arid and their literary value negligible.[20]

When therefore the 'Third majlis' met under these unfavorable circumstances and voted in favour of Iran's neutrality, the democrats and nationalists withdrew. Shortly afterwards the *majlis* was dissolved and England and Russia occupied the country. This intervention strengthened the pro-German movement among Persian patriots, which soon acquired a skilful advocate in the paper *Kāva*, under its editor Ḥasan Taqī-zāda. *Kāva* was established in Berlin in 1335/1916. At first it was a purely political paper, but from January 1920 onwards (the so-called *Daura-i jadīd*) *Kāva* turned its attention to literature, to which subject and to science it finally devoted itself entirely. It published noteworthy essays on the history of Iranian literature, to which young research scholars, among others M. 'A. Jamāl-zāda, applied European scientific methods. *Kāva* also founded its own publishing house (Kaviani-Press) and upheld Persian culture outside the borders of the country, so that it became at this time one of the important focal points of the Persian literary renaissance.

B. THE BEGINNINGS OF MODERN PROSE

Even were there no other argument against the claim of some Persian patriots that *Haji Baba* was the work of a Persian author, a critical survey of the then prevailing situation in Persian belles-lettres would be sufficient to prove this to be wrong. Even today there are but few novels possessing a similar degree of artistic homogeneity in style and composition which, while being in full accord with the spirit of the times, still has an important message for later generations. It seems therefore all the more impossible to aver that such a novel could have been written at a time when modern Persian prose was still in its infancy.

One thing however can rightly be maintained, namely that the first Persian novel may have been inspired by the work of Morier, among other sources[21], both as regards its form – that of an itinerary – and its satirical conception.

This first novel was the *Siyāḥat-nāma-i Ibrāhīm Beg*, 'Travels of Ibrahim Beg', by Ḥājjī Zaynu'l-ʿĀbidīn from Marāgha. The author had a keen eye and his criticisms were pertinent and comprehensible, as was proved by the popularity which the work attained. Composed about 1880, the work first appeared in 1888 in Istanbul; the second edition was printed in Calcutta in 1890, others in 1905–6 in Bombay and in 1910 again in Calcutta.[22] In 1903 the work was translated into German, and in 1963 into Russian.

The book contains a great deal of autobiographical detail. We meet the hero, a young Persian brought up in Egypt, who returns to his native country to study the social and political life there. The conditions with which he is confronted correspond to those in Persia at the end of the 19th century, thus providing the author with an opportunity for bitter satire on the backward state of his country. That is the first part of the novel. In the second part the plot develops with the somewhat sentimental love story of the hero and ends with his death, caused by a pining for his country and grief over its pitiable condition. The third part is a kind of Persian *Divina Commedia*: the hero's teacher, Ibrāhīm Yūsuf ʿAmū, has a dream about the Persian Inferno and the Persian Paradise, again with numerous allusions to contemporary events.

Zaynu'l-ʿĀbidīn not only influenced later generations of prose writers, he also deserves credit for having invariably encouraged criticism of the unsatisfactory conditions in Iran.

Through his life and his work, the author was among the first active workers of the revolutionary generation. He was born into the family of a well-to-do merchant, but when still young broke with his family whose mode of living he found insupportable. He fled from the country and lived in Yalta in the Crimea, where he earned a good living and even acquired the rights of citizenship. He gave all this up, however, and in order to work for a better national future emigrated to Istanbul where

Notes on pp. 377–378

he collaborated with Persian democrats on the paper *Akhtar*, 'Star' (p. 365). He died in 1910.

If we examine any given branch of Persian literature during the period of the Constitution, we can see how closely this literature is bound up with the contemporary life of the nation and its burning problems (frequently this tendency pushes artistic questions into the background). So it was with the novel: the patriotic duty of presenting their splendid history to the people leads novelists to work up themes from Iran's distant past. Such a subject is chosen by the most prolific Persian novelist, Ṣanʿatī-zāda Kirmānī, for his first novel, which is thus the first work in Persian belles-lettres to treat of a historical theme.

The plot takes the reader to the court of the last Sasanian, Yazdgird III (632–51), and the novel bears the title: *Dām-gustarān yā intiqām-khvāhān-i Mazdak*, 'The Plotters or the Avengers of Mazdak'. The Sasanian ruler is shown surrounded by traitorous Zoroastrian priests, and threatened on the one hand by the supporters of the revolutionary, Mazdak (pp. 59, 127), on the other by the danger of an Arab invasion. Under the pressure of these two forces the kingdom collapses. The novel ends with the assassination of the fleeing Yazdgird by a supporter of Mazdak, and with the murder of the Caliph ʿUmar, whereby Yazdgird's son Hurmuzān avenges the fall of his father's kingdom.

The author used historical events in a somewhat arbitrary manner. There are many anachronisms and the intricate plots of adventure remind one of Dumas. Not even in his characterisation does the author observe historical veracity. As in the naïve world of fairy-tales, the heroes are of unblemished virtue while the villains are painted completely black; the setting is reduced to sketchy backdrops – in short, the novel shows all the signs of a literature in a new, not yet fully explored world. As with all the other works of the period, Kirmānī's novel pursues didactic aims: to show the causes of Iran's loss of independence in such a light as would serve as a warning. From this point of view, the work has undoubted value. It was written about 1900, but was first published 20 years later in Bombay and five years after that in Tehran.[23]

Ṣanʿatī-zāda kept to the same trend in his later novels. He did not engage in historical studies; nor does he show any intensive development on the artistic side. *Dāstān-i Mānī-i naqqāsh*, 'The Story of the Painter Mānī', is the romantic story of Mānī's life and love and takes place in the 3rd century, at the time of Shāpūr's battles against the Roman emperor Valerian. It was published in 1346/1927 in Tehran. *Silāḥ-shūr*, 'The Knight', which appeared in 1934 in Tehran, draws for its subject-matter on the time of the first Sasanians; *Siyāh-pūshān*, 'Men in Black Armour', describes the fight of the Persian element, personified by Abū-Muslim, against the Arab; another of his novels has its setting in the time of the Safavids.

Ṣanʿatī-zāda, who in addition to his literary work ran a successful commission agency in Tehran, did not confine himself exclusively to historical material. Persian prose is indebted to him for the first Utopian novel, *Majmaʿ-i dīvānagān*, 'Assembly of Fools', which took its motto from Saʿdī: "All men are fools and the fool is the only normal (rational) person." The novel is a framework composition. A group of people fall into a hypnotic sleep during which they are transported 2000 years into the future, into an epoch called the 'Age of Reason'. Here, because of their previous life, the group experiences strange and surprising adventures; still stranger and more surprising are the adventures they meet with on a further pilgrimage into the Sun Age. This novel dates from 1343/1924–5 and the author promised to write a sequel which, so far as I know, has not yet appeared, despite the success enjoyed by the work.

Among the foremost story-tellers is Mīrzā Muḥammad Bāqir Khusravī of Kirmanshah, a descendant of the old aristocracy, who, like so many others in his situation, joined the Constitutional movement. During the battles against the reactionary Muḥammad ʿAlī (p. 357), he retired to the country where, "in deepest sorrow and sympathy for the misfortunes of his people and comrades"[24], he wrote a chronicle of a Persian family at the time of the Īl-Khāns, a trilogy under the titles *Shams u Ṭughrā*, 'Shams and Ṭughrā', *Mārī-i Venīsī*, 'Mary of Venice', and *Ṭughril u Humāy*, 'Ṭughril and Humāy'.[25]

The story is presumably set in the reigns of Abaqā-Khān and Aḥmad Takūdar – but historical events are modestly relegated to the background. The main themes are romantic episodes, battles and wars, intrigue and love, tragedies and victories, built around the hero Shams, a handsome knight of irreproachable character: his love for the beautiful aristocrat Ṭughrā, which, after almost inconceivable difficulties have been overcome, ends in their marriage; the passion of a Christian girl, Mary of Venice, for Shams, which also ends happily; and finally the story of the love of Shams' son for the young girl Humāy. This synthesis of the Persian heroic epic with the French adventure-story also contains the necessary didactic note: it shows the immorality and treachery of feudal elements. In his detailed analysis of Bāqir's work, mentioned above, Machalski underlines the ideological and social values and holds the work in great esteem.

Chronologically, the third historical novel was *ʿIshq u salṭana*, 'Love and Power', written during the second year of the First World War by the Director of the Madrasa in Hamadan, Shaykh Mūsā (it appeared in Hamadan for the first time in 1338/1919 and in 1343/1924–5 in Bombay). This novel is a trilogy, the second part being entitled *Sitāra-i Līdī*, 'The Star of Lydia', and the third *Sarguzasht-i shāhzāda-khānum-i Bābilī*, 'Story of a Babylonian Princess'. In the introduction the author states that he wishes to inform the reader about the life and times of Cyrus the Great and mentions that this is the first historical work in Persian written in European style.

In the developing of his heroes' characters, Shaykh Mūsā's work suffers – as do most of the prose literary experiments of this period – from the stereotyped heroes, *sans peur et sans reproche*, and their ignoble opponents, from the sentimental motivation of all their actions and from the lack of understanding of the psychological background to human behaviour. The slight advance that can be seen in this book is in its language. His heroes talk simply and naturally – even if one cannot yet speak of an individualising of the language – and the description of nature is truer to life and has more human appeal than the traditional clichés.[26]

C. IMPORTANT POETS OF THE CONSTITUTIONAL PERIOD

The first bard of the revolutionary period, "the man to whom the whole nation listened", was the poet 'Ārif Qazvīnī (1312/1882).[27] Mīrzā Abu'l-Qāsim, which was his real name, was born in Qazvin. His father, Mullā Hādī Vakīl Qazvīnī, gave him a sound education, taught him calligraphy – the most highly prized of the decorative arts – and also recitation, singing and music, for he recognised the declamatory and musical talents of his son and wanted him to become a *rauḍa-khvān*, a public singer and reciter who depicts the lives and sufferings of Islamic saints. 'Ārif did not fulfil his father's pious hopes and, at the end of the century, in 1316/1898–9, he was firmly ensconced in the circles of the Tehran *jeunesse dorée*. In this company he soon began to drink, smoke hashish and indulge in all the usual vices. He married at the age of 17, but the marriage ended in divorce and he never repeated the experiment.[28] Thanks to the popularity he achieved as a singer, 'Ārif was soon accepted into court circles where he could have established his position. However, disgusted with the intrigues that went on there and with the empty pleasures and dull pastimes of Tehran higher society, he departed and cut himself off completely from this class. He went over to the supporters of the revolutionary movement and here at last he found something that gave meaning and purpose to his work. He tended to the democratic left wing, to whose ideas he dedicated his entire poetic art and vocal talent. During the First World War he became for a time a Turcophile – as did many nationalists out of opposition to England and Russia – and in 1334/1915 he emigrated to Istanbul, where he remained until 1338/1919. The policy of Turkey, however, particularly in relation to Azerbayjan, caused a change of heart and later, at one of his famous concerts, he was particularly ironical about Turkey and the Persian turcophile.

After his return to Persia, 'Ārif roamed the country as an itinerant bard, joined the republican rising of Muḥammad Taqī-Khān in Khurasan and sang songs inciting the people to march against Tehran. After the tragic death of Taqī-Khān, the poet went to Kurdistan where, in the depths of the country, he led the life of a dervish and devoted himself to his poetry. As a man with a strong love for his country and interest in its destiny he could not long continue in this isolation and once more he organised a series of his famous vocal concerts, with even more success than before, making use of his own pamphlets and satirical poems. In the last years of his life, 'Ārif, like so many of his contemporaries and former republicans, wrote poems glorifying the Zoroastrian faith. He died in 1934.[29]

ʿĀrif's *dīvān* was first published in Berlin in 1343/1924, with a foreword by Riḍā-zāda Shafaq and an incomplete autobiography in the style of Rousseau's *Confessions*. The *dīvān* contained his famous ballads, *taṣnīfs* and *ghazals*, that were known throughout the country thanks to the poet's outstanding musical interpretations. ʿĀrif is the type of a minstrel, a mediaeval bard, a Persian Villon, who follows an inner compulsion to sing and to write verses; a popular figure who appears unexpectedly, sings, entertains his friends and then as suddenly disappears. He was not a profound original thinker, only a poet who knew how to combine his inspiration with a spontaneous revolutionary pathos and a tunefulness peculiar to folk-song, all of which made him the most popular singer of his time.[30]

The poet Mīrzā Muḥammad Taqī, better known as Maliku'sh-shuʿarā Bahār (1880–1951), was the famous son of a famous father, the Khurasan court poet and miniaturist Ṣabūrī Maliku'sh-shuʿarā (King of Poets). Bahār received an excellent training for the profession of court poet from his father, an appointment he actually obtained on the latter's death.

But the King of Poets was carried away by the pathos of the revolutionary patriots; he threw up his court career and, with profound conviction, entered the service of the revolution. His poems and satires, full of pithy comment on the existing situation and enthusiastic praise for the Constitution, were so successful that the poet, who now wrote under the pseudonym Bahār, soon came to the forefront of the democratic party. He became a journalist (after 1910 he edited a democratic paper *Nau-Bahār*, 'New Spring', in Mashhad), politician, poet and member of Parliament. When in 1916, during the Occupation, the younger poets formed a literary circle, Bahār was called upon to lead it in virtue of his literary merits. Under his leadership, this circle, *Jarga-i dānishvarī*, received a new name, *Dānish-kada*, 'Place of Knowledge', and published a literary review under the same title, in which Bahār upheld the classical tradition against the excesses of the modernists.[31]

After the War, Bahār devoted himself to a wide range of cultural activities. For some time he directed his own literary magazine, called *Nau-Bahār* (pp. 382–3); he wrote articles dealing with literary problems, an excellent manual on Persian stylistics, *Sabk-shināsī* (see B VI a) edited a number of classical works, etc.

Bahār was educated in the classical tradition of Persian poetry and often uses extremely complex art forms: only rarely is he influenced by European poetry, and this applies particularly to the arrangement of the rhymes, which affects only the external form. In theme his poems were closely associated with contemporary events.[33] He supported the Constitution, criticised the policies of the court, was sarcastic about the lack of state organisation (perhaps the garbage-strewn streets of Mashhad) and in the *ghazal* we even find him using social and political instead of the traditional themes. Thus Bahār achieved a homogeneous personal poetic style, intended for a wide public. His poetry was explicitly didactic in aim, but he succeeded in finding the appropriate poetic form for his teaching so that his poems rarely seem dry or pedantic.

After his death, Bahār's poetry was collected and published in a *dīvān*[34]; one of his friends, ʿA. ʿIrfānī wrote a biography, the second part of which contains a selection of poems made by the poet himself.[35]

One of the members of the European school of revolutionary poets was Mīrzā Yaḥyā Daulatābādī (1864–1939). He joined the constitutional movement when it was in its first phase, now as editor, now as propagandist, translator, poet or member of Parliament (he represented the Socialist Party in 1924).

Yahyā Daulatābādī's work shows great versatility. We have poems of his, collected in *Nihāl-i adab*, 'Shoot of Knowledge', and *Urdī-bihisht*, which are written not only in Persian but also in French. Besides this he wrote a comprehensive autobiography–*Ḥayāt-i Yaḥyā* – which contains references to contemporary political events; in addition there are several novels, and translations from French (Leconte de Lisle, Sully Prudhomme). His novel *Dāstān-i ʿishqī-i Shahrnāz*, 'Story of the Love of Shahrnāz', is characteristic of his philosophy. It was written in Istanbul about 1335/1916 and appeared ten years later in Tehran. The author, in telling the story of the beautiful and cultured heroine Shahrnāz, seeks to solve one of the urgent problems of contemporary Iran, the problem of the emancipation of Persian women. Perhaps the poet's membership of the Bahā'ī sect led him to seek for an improvement of relations with women and of their position in society within a somewhat naïve natural philosophy. "Nature is the eternal fount of happiness and bliss for the human race." He makes this statement in the introduction and the entire mental concept of the work is shaped by this attitude. Yet he does not offer anything very concrete in the way of a solution to the problem of women. The significance of the novel lies in something quite different from that intended by the author: it brought to light an extraordinary amount of ethnographic information from all regions of Iran.[36]

The whole of his output bears witness to the fact that Yaḥyā Daulatābādī was not a *poeta natus*. He had decided to serve the ideas of freedom and a better future for his people and it was this idea that spurred on his pen.

Shafaq[37] describes the poet Sayyid Aḥmad Adīb Pīshāvarī as "the herald of modern awakening". The learned historian Sayyid Aḥmad Adīb Pīshāvarī, a descendant of the eminent Shaykh Shihābu'd-dīn Suhravardī, was born in 1260/1844. His childhood was spent among the nomads in the Pishavar district. He constantly listened to the famous savants – among them the only Persian philosopher of the 19th century, Mullā Hādī Sabzavārī – and travelled through a large part of Afghanistan and Persia until he settled in Tehran about 1300/1882–3. He was first and foremost an expert on the history of eastern Islam; among other works he prepared an edition of the well-known history *Ta'rīkh-i Bayhaqī*. Although in age he belonged to an older generation, his poetical works are characteristic of the way of thinking of the Persian patriots during the period of the Constitutional struggles. He was a dedicated nationalist, a zealous enemy of western imperialism and, above all, such a strong Anglophobe that he became a convinced Germanophile in the idealistic fashion of the Berlin paper *Kāva* (p. 368).

A reflection in poetry of this attitude was the epic *Qayṣar-nāma*, 'The Emperor's Book', which, in 14,000 couplets composed in the manner of the *Shāh-nāma*, glorified the struggle of the German Emperor William II and his generals who, the author believed, were fighting for freedom for all nations. The background to the story is the First World War, and it is interesting that the author describes the German heroes as having lances, swords and spears, as in Rustam's time. The *Qayṣar-nāma* remained in manuscript. Pīshāvarī's verses, however – dispersed in various periodicals and characterised by the same trends of thought as his epic – were collected and published in a *dīvān*. They are interesting evidence of the ideas of a whole group of Persian patriots, to which the well-known Vaḥīd Dastgirdī belonged on account of his admiration for Hindenburg.

Adīb Pīshāvarī died in 1349/1930. He was an educated man of noble character with a remarkable memory, who remained single and without possessions all his life, dedicating himself to the pursuit of knowledge, philosophy and poetry, and renouncing all worldly pleasures. As such he was a new type of the old *adībs*. He differs from them in having a passionate love for his country and being in touch with political events.

A poet and patriot of the same type, but with a more marked interest in poetry as an art and in its future, was Mīrzā Ṣādiq-Khān Farāhānī Amīru'sh-shu'arā, better known under the pen-name of Adību'l-mamālik. He was born in the village of Kāzarān, near Sulṭānābād, of parents related on both sides to Qā'im-maqām (p. 335); the slights he suffered from his rich relations after the premature death of his father he has described in a fascinating autobiography which goes back, however, no further than to his seventeenth year. He began his career as a court poet in the service of Amīr-niẓām Ḥasan 'Alī-Khān Garrūsī, in Tabriz, where he changed his original *nom de plume*, Parvāna, to Amīrī. He travelled a great deal in the entourage of Amīr-niẓām and on his own, changed his abode and profession more than once, was teacher and government official, but chiefly editor, journalist and poet, one of the foremost propagators of the Constitution and of modern enlightenment of the people. He died in 1336/1917 shortly after having been appointed Judge of the Supreme Court in Yazd.

The output of Adību'l-mamālik covered a wide range of subject-matter. He wrote scientific articles (being acquainted with western culture and languages) on astronomy, prosody, geography, etc., travel books, *maqāms* and was possibly the compiler of a rhyming dictionary – but of this work not much seems to have been preserved. His *Dīvān* was first collected and published in 1312 *sh.*, by Vaḥīd Dastgirdī, after prolonged transactions with the poet's heirs. Adību'l-mamālik composed poems in all the classical forms except the *ghazal*; his particular domain, however, was the *qaṣīda*. In it was mirrored all the political activity in which the poet took such a keen part: criticism of public life and persons, appeals to fight for freedom and the Constitution, the propagation of a new and effective patriotism, and so on. All this had never hitherto been expressed with such noble pathos and in such

Notes on pp. 377–378

artistic form. In harmony with his progressive ideas was his poetic diction, his inner engagement imbuing it with an expressive freshness and vigour. He consistently followed the path which he unceasingly encouraged young poets to enter: "It is necessary to find something new! And if you wish to write verses, dedicate them to your country. Perhaps you are fond of love poetry. But what purer love is there than that which we feel for our native land?"[38]

A different trend is represented by the revolutionary pathos of the poet Abu'l-Qāsim Lāhūtī (1887–1957). He began his career as a poet with contributions to the daily press. His poems in the newspapers of the revolutionary period point along the path of militant nationalism, with strong anti-British tendencies, and a growing inclination towards socialist ideas. This brought him into conflict with official opinion to such an extent that he was taken to court and, in 1920, sentenced to death. He fled to Istanbul where, under particularly difficult circumstances, he published jointly with ʿAlī Naurūz a Persian-French periodical entitled *Pārs* (from 1921). Not long after he returned to his native country and took part, along with many other revolutionaries, in the unfortunate February Rising in Tabriz in 1922.[39] After its defeat and the occupation of the city by government troops Lāhūtī fled, this time to the Soviet-Union, where a new epoch of his life began: he became the leading poet of Soviet Tajikistan. He wrote lyrical poetry, epics in which he sings the praises of modern national reawakening as embodied in the enthusiastic activities of enlightened patriots; he translated works from world literature and took an active part in the nation's cultural and political life.[40]

On the occasion of the poet's sixtieth birthday in 1946 his *dīvān* was published in Moscow. This is a comprehensive selection comprising 440 pages and containing examples of both his lyrical and his political poems, *ghazals*, of which several can well bear comparison in their poetical fragility and simple beauty with the *ghazals* of the classical poets.[41] As a man with a clearly defined philosophical outlook, Lāhūtī has the gift of clear-cut formulation of his poetical thoughts. The disputes so dear to his contemporaries about the old and the new style leave him indifferent.[42] In keeping with the subject-matter, he chooses now traditional, now modern forms, and his classical *rubāʿī* rank, according to Bertel's, "among the most progressive verses ever to have been written in the Persian language".[43]

Other poet-personalities. – A quite different type of poet from any that we have so far mentioned is Jaʿfar Khamnā'ī, a native of Tabriz. In opposition to the will of his father, a reactionary Tabriz merchant, prejudiced against poetry and particularly against the study of foreign languages, Khamnā'ī acquired a good command of French and an extensive knowledge of European literatures. The verses in which he wittily glossed contemporary events in the revolutionary newspapers of Tabriz, are written in rhymed stanza form. This consistent formal disregard for prosodic tradition distinguishes Khamnā'ī's lyric and especially his nature poetry. In this respect he is a poet-pioneer and a model for the youngest generation of poets.

From the large number of poets who took part in the literary life of Iran in the period of national enlightenment, we have here presented only a few, and these belonged to various artistic and human types. But by no means all of the most outstanding, who impressed the hallmark of their personality on contemporary life, have found mention here. Such a one, for instance, is the famous editor of the paper *Nasīm-i shimāl* (p. 367), Sayyid Ashrafu'd-dīn (Ashraf) Gīlānī, with his satires[44] – in which he made use of colloquial expressions and found scope for his sparkling wit – and his melodious ballads, *taṣnīfs*.

An abundant contribution to the development of political satire was made by the founder of a modern prose style, ʿAlī Akbar Dihkhudā (p. 367); notable for the formal novelty and lyrical charm of his work is the poet Niẓāmī-i Vafā. A share in the poetry of the time falls also to the admirable authority on and editor of classical poetry, Vaḥīd Dastgirdī[45] (p. 382); even at this time Farrukhī Yazdī documented his socialist convictions in his work (see pp. 387–8), among many others. Specimens of the poetry of these writers are contained in the anthologies compiled by M. Ishaque; some works have been edited in *Dīvāns*.

NOTES

1. Cf. F. Machalski, *La littérature de l'Iran contemporain* (1965), 34–5.
2. Cf. Tagiryanov, *Vest. Leningrads. Univ.*, 1952,8, 93 *et seq.*
3. Specimens of texts in Browne, *Press and Poetry*, 168–306; Machalski, *op. cit.*, ad 1.
4. Cf. on this, Klyashtorina, *KS*, 1956,22, 56 *et seq.*
5. Cf. Musil, *op. cit.*, 126.
6. Specimens, with English translations, by Browne, *LHP*, 4, 469-82.
7. The influence of the French novel is analysed by Bertel's, *TMIV*, 1932,1, 111-126, on economic grounds, to which Nikitine, in *JA*, 1933, 321 *et seq.*, has certain critical objections.
8. A list of the first translations of belles-lettres into Persian is given by Browne, *Press and Poetry*, 156 *et seq.*
9. Cf. Browne, *Persian Revolution*, p. 121 *et seq*; Shoytov, *KS*, 9 (1953), 58 *et seq.*
10. Regarding the nature of the illustrations, cf. Browne, *Press and Poetry*, 16, 21, 26, etc.
11. *Press and Poetry*, 19.
12. Cf. p. 361, note 1.
13. For a fuller account see Bertel's, *Kul'tura i pis'mennost' Vostoka*, 3 (1928), 10–17.
14. Also translated into French (A. Bricteux) and into Danish (A. Christensen), cf. Bibl. (C); on the influence of Akhundov on Malkum-Khān, cf. Shoytov, *KS*, 9 (1953), 62; Ibragimov and Mamedzade consider Malkum-Khān's authorship doubtful in the case of several plays, cf. (C).
15. Chaykin, *Ocherk*, 54, mentions Dihkhudā's elegy on this occasion as one of the first strophic poems in European style.
16. Cf. Nicolas, *RMM*, 4 (1908), 261 *et seq.*; 5 (1908), 297 *et seq.*
17. For relations between Persian and Azerbayjani revolutionary journalism cf. Klyashtorina, *KS*, 27 (1958), 31 *et seq.*; Sharīf, *KS*, 27 (1958), 23 *et seq.*

18. Cf. Vorozheykina, *O tvorchestve Iradzh-mirzī*, 76.
19. E. G. Browne, *The Reign of Terror in Tabriz; England's Responsibility* (London 1912).
20. G. Bouvat, 'La presse à Téhéran en 1915', *RMM*, 30 (1915), 274 *et seq.*
21. For further information see Shoytov, *op cit.*, p. 62.
22. Cf. the Introduction to the Calcutta edition 1910 by Muḥ. Karīm Shīrāzī included in the Russian translation of the work by G. P. Michalevitsch.
23. For further information see Nikitine, *op. cit.*, 330 *et seq.*
24. This appears in the introduction to the work; see further, Machalski, *Charisteria Orientalia (Joanni Rypka)*, 151.
25. A new edition of all three parts appeared in Tehran, in 1950–1.
26. Further see Machalski, *Historyczna powieść*, 44–9.
27. Chaykin, in his *Ocherk*, p. 59, puts his date of birth as 1878–9.
28. Further see Bombaci, *OM*, 25 (1954), 42–53.
29. Cf. Shafaq, *MEJ*, 6 (1952), 427.
30. See B. Alavi, *Geschichte und Entwicklung der modernen persischen Literatur* (B. 1964), 36–44.
31. Further see Yāsimī, *La poésie iranienne contemporaine*, 207, 209.
32. For further information on his scientific works see Peysikov, *KS*, 37 (1959), 9–22.
33. Cf. also Browne, *Press and Poetry*, pp. 260 *et seq.*; Ishaque, *Indo-Iranica*, 1946–7, 41 *et seq.* and Alavi, *op. cit.*, ad 30, pp. 56–8.
34. *Dīvān-i Bahār*, I (Tehran 1335), II (1336).
35. 'Abdu'l-Ḥamid 'Irfānī, *Aḥvāl va āthār-i Maliku'sh-shu'arā Muḥammad Taqī Bahār*, Tehran 1335.
36. See Chaykin, *Ocherk*, 106, 131 *et seq.*
37. Cf. *MEJ*, 6 (1952), 421; *Yādgār*, 8 (1924–5), 62 *et seq.*
38. Yāsimī, *op. cit.*, 208.
39. For a fuller account see Lenczowski, *Russia and the West in Iran 1918–1948*, 63.
40. For more on this, see M. Zand, *Abulqasim, Lakhuti*, M. 1957, and especially *Ocherk istorii Tajikskoy sovietskoy literaturī*, M. 1961, 274–336.
41. A more detailed analysis of the work is given by Osmanova, *SV*, 6 (1957), 74 *et seq.*
42. Cf. Lakhuti, *Lit. Gazeta*, 31.8.1954.
43. *Ocherk*, 171.
44. Cf. Shafaq, *MEJ*, 6 (1952), 424.
45. See Bertel's, *Ocherk*, 169–70.

III. LITERARY LIFE IN THE YEARS 1921–1941

The literature of the Constitutional period was, as we have seen, mainly of a topical political character; it aimed at communicating a content that should be comprehensible and give pointed expression to the ideas of the patriotic struggle then being waged. As regards form, of first importance was always the clarity of the formulation of the thought and its comprehensibility for the broad masses and an inclination to use folk-literature as a medium of expression. And even though it might seem at a first glance that, in a literature bound by the tradition of very strict rhetorical principles, such a situation was indicative of a clear break with the past, this was in reality not the case. It was merely that the revolutionary wave had for a time forced its will upon all artistic activities; a basic change in the literary attitude had not so far taken place, as the further course of development was to show when Riḍā-Shāh began to rule the country according to strictly defined conceptions and when conditions in public life ceased to be favourable for the active participation of free-thinking men of literature.

It then became evident that the formal aspects of their work were constantly in the minds of men of letters. Many theoretical studies on the new poetical and prose styles, criticism of the classical heritage and still more of what had spontaneously arisen in recent years, evoked at this time no less interest than the actual literary production. Literary periodicals were founded (pp. 382–3) and literary circles and societies came into being, the members of which worked out and justified their creative programmes and propagated their conceptions of the path along which modern Persian literature should advance. In this whirl of thoughts and views two main streams began to form: the conservatives (*kuhna-parastān*) and the modernists (*mutajaddidūn*, *inqilābiyyūn*). In questions of Persian poetry, both proceeded from the same presumption, namely the need for its revival, resuscitation, rejuvenation. With regard to the means to be employed to gain this end they differed fundamentally. The conservatives sought salvation in a return to the simpler pre-Mongolian styles (p. 115)

Notes on pp. 395–396

which they tried to revive and link up with, taking Firdausī, Niẓāmī and Sa'dī as their models. The modernists, in their most radical theories, thought to find a solution, on the contrary, in a complete departure from all classical tradition, whose rhetorical prescriptions and laws they considered to be so much dead weight preventing the poet from letting his thoughts soar untrammelled; as for the fixed metaphors of the classical lyric (figure=cypress, waist=sugar-cane, eyebrows=bow, etc.)[1], these they ridiculed in parodies in order to support their arguments. They declared the European poetry – especially French romantic poetry, which thanks to its freedom of form and simplicity of diction can, they believe, best express the modern world – to be their pattern. In support of the correctness of their views they cited contemporary Turkish poetry which had adopted this course with good results (only in Turkey the situation was somewhat different, especially in the attitude to classical poetry). The most intensive theoretical thought cannot, however, lead to any generally valid conclusions, for here we are concerned with a matter of art, the new orientation of which cannot be laid down by theorists, but only by the poets themselves in their works.

The poetical production of this period shows clearly that only in the choice of themes is a departure from traditional canons observable on a larger scale. Here the door is opened to a modern view of nation and native land[2], of social and societarian problems, of human relations and also of Nature, not seldom with a philosophical undertone betraying a predilection for French romanticism. Social themes are frequently employed, often charged with a sentimental sympathy for the suffering and oppressed, for hardship and poverty, and accompanied by the expression of moral indignation at such a state of affairs and a call for remedy (cf. Parvīn).

These thematic innovations are only seldom linked up with any substantial modernisation of form; we come across the traditional metres and rhyme patterns; we read *mathnavīs*, *rubā'iyyāt*, *ghazals*, *qiṭ'as*, and sometimes variations of stanza forms just as in the period of the Constitution. The European stanza, free rhyme and metre, are much less common than might be expected judging by the radical theories held by these writers – and even poets belonging to the modernist group still write occasional verses in classical style (cf. 'Ishqī).

Another fundamental question that is a matter of dispute between the conservatives and the modernists is the role of literary prose in the modern literature of Iran. The few novels, mostly historical, which had so far represented this genre, did not contribute much to the solution of the question, if only because they were frequently ranked as scientific in the traditional use of the term, that is, as based on historical facts. It was the modernists who came forward in defence of prose as a literary genre. They boldly proclaimed that it was of greater merit to write good straightforward, non-bombastic prose than a few lines of rhyming verse, and supported their view with examples from the prose of western nations. In this field the decisive word – in respect of both the theoretical and practical aspects of the matter – was spoken by Muḥammad 'Alī Jamāl-zāda (pp. 389–91). His article on the social, cultural and instructive significance of literary prose is rightly cited and from his first book of short stories, *Yakī būd yakī nabūd*, with which he illustrated his theory, the new generation of prose writers learnt their craft.[3] The short story or *novella* thus occupied the ground plan in the development of modern prose and achieved a much higher level than the novel, despite the fact that an occasional outstanding work was to be found, especially as regards the choice of theme.

The strong nationalist character of Riḍā's régime explains to a considerable extent an access of interest in folklore production. In Tehran, a Museum of Folklore was installed and the Ministry of Culture appealed for the collection of folk-songs, fairy-tales, music, etc. Many notable poets, several of whom were also excellent theorists in the domain of folklore, took part in this work, among them being S. Hidāyat (pp. 410–2), with his *Nayrangistān* and studies on folk-song, of which he was a collector. Another of the collectors of songs, texts and melodies, who was the great pioneer in this field, was Ḥ. Kūhī Kirmānī[4]; a comprehensive collection of proverbs and sayings was edited by the versatile ʿA. A. Dihkhudā (p. 377)[5]; an assiduous collector of proverbs being also professor Aḥmad-Khān Bahmanyār[6]; fairy-tales were collected, published and related on the Tehran Radio by F. Muhtadī Ṣubḥī (d. 1962).[7]

Besides providing the impetus for a more thorough study of folklore, the nationalism of this period – though on the whole a step back as compared with the liberalism of the Constitutional period – produced some other tendencies which favourably influenced contemporary prose literature: such were a scholarly interest in national history, in language and its purity, in extensive archaeological excavations, etc.

An important contribution to the evolving of a modern literary style were, in this period too, translations from western literatures. As many of the literati of this time had a good knowledge of foreign languages and themselves did translation work, both the selection of translated works and their quality are on a high level. Thus not only Dumas Fils, Victor Hugo and Daudet enter Persian literature, but also Plutarch, Anatole France, Voltaire, Goethe, Pushkin, Tolstoy, and many[8] of the best representatives of the short story – Chekhov, Maupassant, Poe, Wilde, in translations by Falsafī, Jamāl-zāda, Hidāyat, Hunarī, Yāsimī, Nafīsī, and other masters of Persian prose.

The daily press, as follows from the contemporary situation described above, had no longer the importance for the literary world that the newspapers had had in the revolutionary period. Nevertheless it took over their didactic role and in time even enlarged it, so that public opinion was very skilfully directed into the channel dictated by the central will. It is interesting that Lescot[9], in his evaluation of the Persian press of this period, underlines the positive aspects, showing how a wide variety of problems of daily life, questions of health and hygiene, of human relations, of political importance, etc., were solved in its pages, in open discussion and in relatively modern fashion. Similarly magazines for women served above all educational aims, confining themselves, however, to the narrower circle of women's interests –

the home and the upbringing of children; the more fundamental questions of the emancipation of Iranian women, their education and so on, were not touched upon. In spite of the vigilance of the censorship, papers did appear now and again that criticised existing conditions and propagated the revolutionary ideas of democratic or socialist trends.[10]

A. LITERARY REVIEWS BETWEEN 1921 AND 1941

The main scene of the literary battles, which became sharper as time went on in an attempt to curb the excesses of the modernists, was the monthly paper *Armaghān*, 'The Gift', the first volume of which appeared in 1298 *sh*. In 1926 it was the rallying point of one of the more important of Tehran's literary societies, 'Anjuman-i adabī-i Īrān'. At its head were Ḥusayn Ṣanīʿī, Mīrzā Nāʿimī and Vaḥīd Dastgirdī, the latter being the editor of the review. In *Armaghān* we find the most important polemical treatises on aesthetic problems, experiments in contemporary poetry and prose and translations.[11] In 1923 the paper *Bahār*, 'Spring', directed by the poet-journalist Iʿtiṣāmu'l-mulk, competed for a short time with *Armaghān*. The standard of this paper was equally high but since it appeared for such a short time its influence on literary development was not comparable with that of *Armaghān*. The poetry it published consisted mainly of work by its editor, the first essays into poetry of his daughter Parvīn (p. 387), and the verses of Rashīd Yāsimī (p. 388). Among the many translations which appeared in its pages was a remarkable Persian paraphrase of Lermontov's *Demon*. In 1342/1923 the poet Niẓām-i Vafā started to publish his magazine *Vafā*.[12] This paper had no definite programme and its contents were very mixed in quality. It contained more translations from French and German than original Persian work, among the latter being mainly poems by the editor – sentimental in character and closely linked in theme with the western romantic lyric. Their value lies in their simple, comprehensible and completely unaffected language. The poet also wrote an autobiography in verse, entitled *Mathnavī*.

The paper of progressive Persian youth, the so-called 'Young Iranians', brought up in western ways, was the monthly *Āyanda*, 'The Future', which was edited by Maḥmūd Afshār. Samples of both the European style and the conservative form appeared in its pages. One of the most talented poets working for the paper was Badīʿu'z-zamān Bushrūya'ī, now Furūzānfar Khurāsānī. He excelled first and foremost as a scholar, as an admirer of and a distinguished authority on Ṣūfī poetry. In this field he wrote several valuable books and a series of outstanding studies.

A literary-political review was also published for a short time by Maliku'sh-shuʿarā Bahār. Its title, *Nau-bahār*, 'New Spring', was taken from the journal which he had directed during the Constitutional period in Mashhad (p. 368). The tradition of the satirical supplement of *Sūri-i Isrāfīl* (p. 367) was continued, as far as censorship permitted, about six years later by the weekly *Nāhīd*, edited by Mīrzā Ibrāhīm-Khān.[13]

Round about 1929 the linguistic purists of Tehran also founded several periodicals devoted to the problems of 'pure Persian'.[14] They not only aimed at substituting Persian for Arabic words, but they also endeavoured to eliminate the European words that had crept into the native vocabulary with technical civilisation and the industrialisation of the country. What they in fact strove after was the use of a pure, vigorous language. Such purist trends were already evident during the second half of the previous century (see, for example, the poet Yaghmā, pp. 333–4). They were characteristic of the pre-revolutionary era, exemplified by the essays of Malkum-Khān with their lucid modern style (pp. 365–6). Now and again papers appeared propagating the revolutionary ideas of democratic or socialist trends, but they were short-lived. Of these, *Tūfān*, 'The Whirlwind', founded in 1921 by the poet Farrukhī (pp. 387–8), had the longest life, in spite of continual persecution by the censorship. The group of poets and journalists that gathered around *Tūfān* helped to solve the problems of modern literature by means of their theoretical articles on the importance of realistic prose; and it is also to their credit that they spread a knowledge of Russian and Soviet literature (*Tūfān* published translations of Pushkin, Tolstoy, Bielinsky and contemporary authors) and of the Russian contemporary scene (thanks to *Safar-nāma-i Farrukhī* – a report of the poet's visit to the U.S.S.R. in 1927, where he attended the celebrations of the tenth anniversary of the October Revolution).[15]

During this period too the Persian periodicals published abroad were not without importance, for in many respects they were in a better position to express opinions freely. The best of them was the Berlin paper *Irānshahr*, founded in 1341/1922 and, from the point of view of literary history, the successor to the former *Kāva* (p. 368). It must be admitted that it did not always possess sufficiently accurate information – in 1924 it celebrated somewhat prematurely the establishment of a republic in Persia – but that did not diminish its significance. Kāẓim-zāda was the editor and his regular collaborators included Ḥusayn-Khān Dānish, a poet from Isfahan, bi-lingual in Turkish and Persian, who lived permanently in Istanbul, and the poet Ghanī-zāda, amongst others. The review helped to spread Persian culture by carrying on the publishing-house Kaviani-Press (p. 368).[16] Of rather less importance was a second Persian magazine published in Berlin, the monthly *Farangistān*, directed by the youngest generation of Persians. They had grown up in Berlin, were somewhat germanophile and tended in several respects to overestimate the value of western civilisation. Although only six or seven numbers of the bi-monthly *Pārs* appeared, it was of a high literary standard. It was published in French and Persian in Istanbul under the editorship of the poets Lāhūtī (p. 376) and 'Alī Naurūz (also known under the name of Ḥasan-Khān Muqaddam).

Notes on pp. 395–396

VĚRA KUBÍČKOVÁ

B. THE MAIN TRENDS IN POETRY

According to Arberry, the last of the classical poets and the first of the moderns was Mīrzā Īraj Jalālu'l-mamālik. His life, almost untouched by the tumultuous times in which he lived, was essentially different from that of his contemporaries. He was born in 1291/1874. His father, Ghulām Ḥusayn Mīrzā, a great-grandson of Fatḥ-'Alī-Shāh, gave him a thorough and systematic education. He learned Arabic, Turkish, Russian and French, which he mastered completely. At an early age he entered the service of the court and at 19 was made court poet by the Qajar Shāh Muẓaffaru'd-dīn on account of his undoubted poetic talent. This appointment with its duties became increasingly burdensome to him, as he was exceptionally broadminded and very independent in his thought and judgement. He therefore left the court and became secretary to the governor of Tabriz. When the latter became Prime Minister he accompanied him on a journey to Europe. During the Constitutional revolution and counter-revolution, he was employed at the Ministry of Education and later at the Ministry of Finance. During the upheavals following the First World War, he was confidential adviser to the American financial mission, which he accompanied on numerous tours of inspection throughout the country. He returned to Tehran a sick man and died relatively young in March 1345/1926.[17]

Just as political events had no disturbing effect on the life of Īraj Mīrzā, so his poetry was only indirectly affected by them. His attitude was that of a sympathising intellectual, who, although accepting the need for many reforms, was not touched emotionally by revolutionary happenings, because as a Qajar prince their pathos was alien to him. Among the new ideas which abounded at that time, the one which interested the poet most was the problem of women.[18] He wrote a very popular satire on the hypocrisy of covering the face called *Ḥijāb-nāma*, 'Book on the Veil', a poem which produced such a strong response that the pupils of a Tehran girls' school welcomed the poet with gifts and a letter of greeting when he returned to Tehran from Mashhad shortly after its publication. Numerous beautiful verses on the theme of motherhood and maternal love, springing from deep feeling and written in simple, tender poetic language, were quite a novelty in contemporary poetry – and apart from this they influenced the modern attitude to the pressing problem of the status of women.

The fable was a suitable vehicle for the poet's intellect and sense of humour. He made verse translations of a series of Lafontaine's Fables and also wrote some himself. Social and political questions are the subject-matter of the poems in his *'Ārif-nāma*, 'Book of 'Ārif'. It contains venomous satires on the poet 'Ārif and he makes critical mention of other poets as well (Kamālī, Dihkhudā, Bahār, etc.) who, in his opinion, were following in the wake of various political objectives (Īraj brands all politicians as charlatans). Vorozheykina maintains that his pamphlet – which also contains attacks on the reactionary views of Islam on the question of women – increased the poet's popularity.[19]

Most of Īraj's work was collected into a *dīvān* by his son Khusrau, who added an affectionate introduction. No criticism, however justified, can diminish the value and significance of this poet who, during a period of trial and error, succeeded in finding a method of expression in poetry which strove towards the future.

Although the social position of poets has undergone fundamental changes in recent times, one of its remarkable peculiarities remains; for even in present-day Iran statesmen and politicians, court officials, university teachers and scholars all write poetry. Typical of the latter is the poet Pūr-i Dāvūd who, in his admiration of Zoroastrianism, is also characteristic of a certain circle of contemporary progressive patriots.

Mīrzā Ibrāhīm-Khān Pūr-i Dāvūd was born in Rasht in 1303/1885; he studied Islamic languages and literature at home and French in Beirut and Paris. Later he went to Berlin, where he studied law. Even then he was interested in literary events in his own country and with some of his friends founded the 'Literary Society of Persians in Paris'.[20] During the revolutionary period, he enthusiastically praised the Constitution in his poetry and wrote poems on Persia's glorious past in a spirit of romantic patriotism. Some of his poems were written in a pure Persian, purged of all Arabic words. He was, however, neither a rigid purist nor a literary conservative, for on other occasions he turned to European models and then used normal Persian. Later on the poet was one of the collaborators on the Berlin paper *Kāva* (p. 368) and *Īrān-shahr* (p. 383). Like many other writers living abroad, he too was premature in celebrating in verse the establishment of a republican constitution in Persia that proved to be a false report. Pūr-i Dāvūd's joy at this event resulted in an outburst of poetry and led to his speedy return to Persia. For some time he devoted himself to journalism on the Tehran *Rastākhīz*, 'The Resurrection', but soon returned to Berlin, where he studied Zoroastrianism and translated texts from the *Avesta* (for example, he published a translation and commentary on the Book of Yasht). Later he visited India several times and finally settled in Bombay among the Parsee community.[21] In 1345/1926 he gave a vivid description of their cultural life in a well-documented book. He soon felt at home there and published a *dīvān* – consisting mainly of patriotic poems in classical style – entitled *Pūrāndukht-nāma*, with appended English translations.[22]

It was from distinctly patriotic motives that the short-lived poet 'Ishqī also paid homage in verse to Zoroastrianism. The romantic love he bore towards his native land was the cause of constant modification in his convictions, and this finally cost him his life. Muḥammad Riḍā, whose *nom de plume* was 'Ishqī, was born in Hamadan in 1312/1894 and was descended from the family of Sayyid Abu'l-Qāsim Kurdistānī. He studied Arabic and French and for a time even worked as a commercial interpreter in Hamadan – but he was soon swept into the stormy course of events. His opposition to the intervention of the Great Powers during the First World War forced him into the circle of the most radical nationalists. During 1334/1915 he fought in the Nationalist Home Army (p. 393), after the defeat of which by the British he emigrated to Istanbul. After the end of the First World War, he returned to Persia and once more entered politics on the Nationalist side. As an outspoken opponent of the Anglo-Persian agreement of 1338/1919, he was even imprisoned for a short time. It was during this period that the vehement poems appeared in which he poured out his disgust at the representatives of the Qajar government. During the troubled post-war period he tended towards the views of Ḍiyā'u'd-dīn (p. 358) and supported the review *Qarn-i bīstum*. For some time he edited the radical paper *Shafaq-i surkh*, 'Red Sky', and wrote essays with revolutionary titles, which however contained no very lucid ideas. He launched bitter satires against the members of the 'third majlis' and particularly the poet Bahār (pp. 373–4) whom, as a former revolutionary, he reproached for having accepted a seat in the majlis.[23] At the time when the democratic supporters of Riḍā-Khān believed that his revolt (see above) would lead to the establishment of a republic, ʿIshqī also wrote poems expressing his enthusiasm for the latter. When however it became clear that Riḍā-Khān had other aims in view, the poet went to the opposite extreme and in July 1342/1924 expressed his opposition to Riḍā-Khān by publishing caricatures of the latter and a satire written from the point of view of a devoted supporter of the Qajar dynasty. The publication of the paper was immediately suspended and the poet treacherously assassinated several days later. His funeral turned into a royalist manifestation encouraged by the Qajar court.

ʿIshqī's work was collected and published in a *dīvān*; the first edition appeared at the end of the 1920's and another in 1324 *sh.* under the redaction of ʿAlī Akbar Sulaymī. Machalski[24], in his detailed analysis of ʿIshqī's poetry, draws particular attention to those of his poems which, on account of the novelty of their thought and form (highly ingenious variations in the strophic form of the *musammaṭ*, new rhymes, experiments with syllabic verse, etc.), can be considered significant for the moulding of the new style. Among these are the *Kafan-i siyāh*, 'The Black Shroud', a phantasy among the ruins of Ctesiphon, with an emphatic call to the fight against the veiling of women; the poem *Īdeāl* 'The Ideal', the story of a father who loses his three children in tragic fashion and now hopes for a 'Leninist' revolution to bring about an improvement in the terrible political and social conditions that were largely responsible for his misfortune; the tender early work *Naurūz-nāma*, 'New Year Book'; and several political satires. ʿIshqī's works include a play, which served as libretto for the first Persian opera, called *Rastākhīz-i-salāṭīn-i Īrān*, 'The Rise of the Sulṭāns of Iran'. (The poet himself took part in the performance.) It is full of patriotic pathos and the final scene introduces the Prophet Zoroaster. The play is still performed.

During his short life ʿIshqī wrote more than 5000 couplets. Many were written around topical events and disappeared with their subject-matter. Yet among his lyric poems – and particularly in his nature lyrics – are to be found some of the finest examples that we possess in the new Persian style.

The most important poetess of this time, Parvīn Iʿtiṣāmī, belonged in years to the younger generation, and her work is entirely untouched, even at the beginning, by the revolution. Daughter of the journalist and poet Yūsuf Iʿtiṣāmu'l-mulk (p. 382), Parvīn was born in 1328/1910 and received a modern education at the American girls' college in Tehran as well as a classical training, above all in Persian and Arabic poetry, at home from her father. Her first poems, doubtless written under her father's guidance, appeared in the second volume of Iʿtiṣāmu'l-mulk's review *Bahār*. Examples of her work are also to be found in modern anthologies.[25] Parvīn's *dīvān* was published in Tehran in 1344 *sh.* and shows clearly that the poetess stood aloof from the theoretical controversies of her time and from the then disputed forms. She composed according to the rules of classical poetry – albeit in simple language – often consciously imitating the 'Art of the Ancients'.[26] Just as did classical authors, she enjoyed using philosophical and moralising themes with pointed reference to contemporary events. Unfortunately, however, she hardly grazed the surface of the really urgent problems, even in the poems on social themes. She chose her subject-matter from the lives of the pauperised members of the lower classes, and had sympathy for their misery and suffering. She did not, however, attempt to find a solution or to penetrate more deeply into the social context, but lapsed into sentimental and affected melancholy.

The novelty of the themes treated by Parvīn is, however, undisputed[27], and one might venture to suggest that, had she lived longer, she would have attained a greater depth of philosophy and feeling in her work than was evident when she died at the age of 30, in 1320 *sh.*

Mīrzā Muḥammad Farrukhī of Yazd (b. 1306/1889), poet-journalist, was the antipode of ʿIshqī as regards consistency of views. From the beginning of the revolutionary struggles he had stood on the left wing of the Democrat-Socialists. He began writing poetry when still at school. At the age of fifteen he recited a revolutionary and patriotic *musammaṭ* of his own composition at a New Year's celebration of the Democratic Party in Yazd; he was arrested, imprisoned and his mouth sewn up as a punishment.[28] After some time he managed to escape from prison and in 1910 reached Tehran where he worked with other patriotic poets on revolutionary papers. His views acquired an increasingly strong bias towards socialism; of this he made no secret even during the First World War when it was particularly dangerous, and he welcomed the October Revolution with enthusiastic verses.[29] As a result he awakened the suspicion and displeasure of official circles, which was apparent later in the continual persecution and ultimate confiscation of the newspaper *Tūfān*, which he edited from 1921.

Farrukhī remained an enthusiastic supporter of socialist views even as a member of the majlis, in 1930–31, indeed so openly that, because of the disfavour of government circles, he was obliged to emigrate to Berlin. Not even then did he give up his work as a poet and journalist, and immediately joined the editorial board of the newspaper *Paykār*, 'The Struggle', which came out there. After some time he was given official permission to return to Tehran, but shortly afterwards he was accused of insulting the ruling house and sentenced to imprisonment. He died in the prison hospital in 1939.

"In my heart there was no other passion than the longing for the freedom of Iran" – this confession might serve as the most fitting motto for his lifework. A fearless fighter for social justice and freedom, in his verses he never ceased to rouse the nation to fight against all the forces that held the people in subjection; at the same time he proclaimed his conviction that Iran had the strength to free herself without any foreign aid.[30] In respect of poetic form, Farrukhī – as the title of his *dīvān* also indicates – was an upholder of classical poetry, which, considering Iranian conservatism in these matters, is undoubtedly one of the reasons why his poems are still so assiduously read.[31]

The Iʿtiṣāmu'l-mulk review, *Bahār*, published the verses of Rashīd Yāsimī (b. 1314/1896 in Kirmānshāh), literary historian – in the view of native critics one of the best – and well known for his monographs on Ibn-i Yamīn, Salmān of Sāva, and many smaller literary studies. From his pen comes the translation of Browne's *Literary History of Persia*, IV, as well as of a number of works from world literature, such as Bourget's *Disciple*, Goethe's *Die Leiden des jungen Werthers*, and many Persian versions of French poetry. Yāsimī was among the youngest founders of the first modernist literary circle, 'Jarga-i dānishvarī' (p. 373), yet he was never a radical modernist. His reflective lyrics, the best part of his poetry, remain within the limits of the classical canon.

"A great master of the word", is Chaykin's[32] designation for the poet Badīʿu'z-zamān Bushrūya'ī (now Furūzānfar), who is a typical exponent of the trend to write about topical matters (Iran Yesterday and Today, Praise of Railways, etc.) in classical form.[33] By profession this poet is a historian of literature, and occupies a chair in the Literary Faculty at Tehran University. Here he lectures on Persian literature and is first and foremost an authority on mystical poetry.

A poet who was persecuted at times for his verses and whose critical orientation was determined by the conscious socialism of his political views, was Mīrzā Yaḥyā-Khān Rayḥān. At the opposite pole in respect of his opinions was the pan-Islamist Aḥmad-Khān Bahmanyār, who used the *takhalluṣ Dihqān*, and was also a professor at the University of Tehran. In addition he made a study of folk-art (p. 381). A disciple of the poet Īraj Mīrzā was the jurist Sayyid Ṣādiq-Khān. Couched in modern untraditional style and in European forms are the verses of Mīrzā Luṭf ʿAlī-Khān Ṣūratgar and Mīrzā ʿAbdu'l-Qāsim-Khān Iʿtiṣām-zāda Niyāzī, editor of the bilingual Tehran daily *Sitāra-i Īrān*, 'Star of Iran'. Vice-President of the majlis and for a time Chairman of the literary society 'Anjuman-i adabī' (p. 382), M. Hāshim-Mīrzā Shaykhu'r-ra'īs is known for his didactic verses which are well spiced with humour. A composer of good *ghazals* is the woman miniature-painter Jannat.

From this handful of names, which could easily be multiplied a number of times, as Ishaque's and other anthologies confirm, the truth of what was pointed out above can be seen. Among the Persian intelligentsia which belonged to a wide variety of social groups and occupations, it was still a matter of honour to cultivate the art of poetry. This extensive amateurism, which naturally was mainly imitative and conservative in character, helped to create a milieu that was almost positively hostile to attempts to introduce modern expression.[34] To this too must be attributed the fact that no few Persian literary works – the foundation stones of the new style – achieved recognition abroad sooner than at home, and that modern poetry has made much slower headway than might be expected in a nation with such a rare poetical genius as has the Persian.

C. PERSIAN PROSE AND THE RISE OF THE MODERN SHORT STORY

A literary event of the 1920's that was to be of historical importance for the development of the new prose was the publication of a slim book of short stories (*novella*) under the title *Yakī būd-yakī nabūd*. The work appeared in 1340/1921–22, the publishers being *Kāva*, Berlin, and the author the young historian Muḥammad ʿAlī Jamāl-zāda. When the stories first reached Iran they were very unfavourably received; nor were condemnatory demonstrations lacking against the writer who had dared so to criticise his compatriots, and in some places the book was actually publicly burned.[35] All of this only serves as proof that the stories of Jamāl-zāda were, in their way, a literary revolution. The further development of prose and the role of the short story in it confirmed such a view.

Sayyid Muḥammad ʿAlī Jamāl-zāda was born in Isfahan as the son of Sayyid Muḥammad Iṣfahānī, the well-known public speaker and journalist of the period of the Revolution and one of the tragic victims of patriotic aspirations.[36] Jamāl-zāda's education was predominantly European in character: the French lycée in Beirut, law studies in Lausanne and then in Dijon. After the First World War he lived in Berlin for some time and collaborated with members of the Persian progressive intelligentsia on the staff of the periodical *Kāva*. There his first stories were published, as well as several scientific works dealing with history and sociology.

With the six stories of his first book[37], Jamāl-zāda laid the foundations of Persian satirical prose. The stories reveal a remarkably fresh approach and a fearless militancy, and from the formal point of view a true mastery of poetical hyperbole. As a trained historian and sociologist the author saw things and relations in their wider implications – thus not only corrupt politicians, shameless career-hunters, a hypo-

Notes on pp. 395–396

critical priesthood, but also the social system and the social conditions which allowed such people to exist. But his erudition never weighs down the wings of his poetical flight. And even though in the author's philosophical attitude and especially in his rare humour, there is still perceptible a gleam of Saʿdī's humanism, his means of expression, his style and diction are consistently modern. They are brought into closer conformity with the spoken language and often enlivened with expressive vulgarisms.[38] Of fundamental importance, too, was the Introduction with which the author prefaced the stories. In it he treats of the role of prose in literature. The article designates prose as the most democratic of the literary genres and stresses, in addition to its artistic significance, its important function as a medium of instruction and enlightenment. Hereby Jamāl-zāda took his place among the foremost pioneers of modern literary views in opposition to the conservatives, who declined to recognise prose as an art at all.

The artist continued his literary activities as a writer of short stories (seven stories were published in 1321 *sh.* under the title *ʿAmū Ḥusayn ʿAlī*, and many more are scattered about in various periodicals), but his novels constitute the main and most voluminous part of his oeuvre. These comprise the satire *Dāruʾl-majānīn*, 'The Madhouse', from the year 1320, along with *Qiṣṣa-i qiṣṣa-hā*, 'The Story of Stories'; then a fantasy abounding in wit and originality, *Ṣaḥrā-i maḥshar*, 'The Plateau of the Last Judgement', in which the writer's young Iranian biographer M. Vasīghī discerns his subject's basic philosophical attitude, namely the demand for absolute freedom of the individual – almost reminiscent of Ismāʿīlī radicalism.[39] The sad end of human cunning and greed is the theme of *Rāh-i āb-nāma*, 'Story of the Water-Channel', in a story with the inhabitants of a little street in Tehran as its actors. Among the best of Jamāl-zāda's novels is *Qultashan-i dīvān*, 'Custodian of the Dīvān', where, against the background of an excellently drawn Tehran of the first two decades of the century, he unfolds the story of a career-hunter, whom society rewards for all his swindles and trickery with success and general esteem.[40] Jamāl-zāda's social criticism gives way to reminiscences of his youth in the last of his novels, *Sar u tah-i yak karbās yā Iṣfahān-nāma*, 'Beginning and End of a Web or Book of Isfahan', where he returns to the countryside setting where he spent his childhood.[41]

Of the first importance for Iranian modern prose are also Jamāl-zāda's translations from French, English and German (Bernardin de St. Pierre, Daudet, his special favourite Anatole France, then Wilde, Schiller and others). Significant work, too, for the raising of the cultural level of the nation – an aim which this outstanding artist never ceased to follow – are Jamāl-zāda's historical, socio-political and economic works, beginning with his *Mazdak* (*Kāva*, 1920) and ending with his 'Survey of the Social and Economic Situation in Iran' (*Revue Internationale du Travail*, 1949–51).

From the 'twenties onwards, following Jamāl-zāda's example, Persian writers began to introduce social criticism into their novels, but so far none can equal him in the penetration and non-sentimentality of his view of life. A favourite theme among these authors, brought up with a knowledge of western views of society, was the problem of the Persian woman and her social status, practically still untouched by modern emancipation. For the artistic treatment of these themes many of the novelists found their most congenial models in the sentimental, moralising French authors of the 19th century, foremost among whom was Dumas Fils.

The first work of this type appeared under the title *Tihrān-i makhūf*, 'Dreadful Tehran'. It was published in the paper *Sitāra-i Īrān* in 1341/1922 and in book-form in 1343. The author was the young poet Murtaḍā Mushfiq Kāẓimī, a collaborator on the Berlin papers *Īrān-shahr* and *Farangistān* (p. 383). He later joined the Tehran *Īrān-i javān*, in which he published mainly translations from the French. This greatly influenced his style of writing. The novel attempted to describe in realistic fashion the unhappy situation of Persian women, the rottenness of society and the social circumstances which forced women to descend to the very lowest of social levels – the brothel. From conversations with prostitutes the reader becomes acquainted with the life-stories of a number of these women, and the devious ways that have led to their fall. The main theme of the story is the unhappy love of the young hero Farrukh and his mistress Mihīn and the adventures in which they become involved. Indeed the romantic story of Farrukh often recalls whole passages of Dumas' *Count of Monte Christo*. From an artistic viewpoint the novel is of slight significance. However, thanks to its vivid narrative style and its attractive theme, the book met with extraordinary success among a wide audience and ran to several editions. Its particular importance lies in the fact that in this form it drew the attention of contemporary Iranian society to the pressing need for finding a solution to the problem of women.[42]

'Abbās Khalīlī, a journalist who was born in Irak, tackled similar problems in his novels *Rūzgār-i siyāh*, 'Black Destiny'[43], which appeared in 1925, *Asrār-i shab*, 'Secret of the Night', *Intiqām*, 'Revenge', and *Insān*, 'Man'. In the story of *Rūzgār-i siyāh*, the author, tired of city pleasures, is living in the country and meets a young woman. She turns out to be a prostitute who is there to be cured of tuberculosis. The two young people get to know each other and out of friendship the author looks after her, but her condition becomes steadily worse. At last she feels that she is dying and decides to tell her new friend the chain of events that led her to the brothel.[44] Her life-story is the real nucleus of the work, and its close resemblance to Dumas Fils' *La Dame aux Camélias* is immediately obvious. In *Intiqām* Khalīlī likewise describes an unhappy woman who tells her son of her sad fate. Khalīlī too is concerned to describe a social milieu which, until then, was hardly known in Persian literature. The adventurous intrigues which he describes also reveal a certain dependence on his model Dumas. The flow of the narrative is held up by long sentimental passages interspersed with affected rhetorical exclamations. Characteristic of Kahlīlī is his negative attitude to the situation in the country in which the tragic

Notes on pp. 395–396

position of women is but one of an infinite number of evils and injustices. The poet frequently denounces this situation, but in his hopeless pessimism he sees no solution that can bring relief.

The popular prose-writer of the upper classes, the intellectual M. Ḥijāzī, deals with the problem of women from a slightly different point of view (pp. 409–10). Half-way through the 'thirties Muḥammad Masʿūd Dihātī appeared with trenchant criticism of social conditions from the philosophical standpoint of an avowed pessimist. His first works, *Tafrīḥāt-i shab*, 'Entertainments of the Night' and *Ashraf-i makhlūqāt*, 'The Most Sublime of Creations', to a certain extent follow a new track and will therefore be dealt with more thoroughly in a following chapter (pp. 408–9).

Subjects taken from Persian history have always been popular with prose-writers. Apart from artistic aims, they serve the patriotic purpose of firing the national pride by recalling the country's glorious past.

Among the best works of this kind are the historical novels of Ḥasan-Khān Nuṣratu'l-vizāra Badīʿ, which clearly show that the Persian novel is gradually throwing off European influence and starting to fashion its own forms. Badīʿ wrote two novels: *Dāstān-i bāstān yā Sargudhasht-i Kūrūsh* 'An old Legend or The History of Cyrus', and *Shamsu'd-dīn u Kumar*. The former appeared in Tehran in 1340/1921. The story takes place, as do the earlier novels of Shaykh Mūsā (pp. 371–2), at the time of the Achaemenids. Unlike the latter, who displayed his knowledge of European historians by introducing passages from their works into the plots of his own novels, Badīʿ studied Western European sources solely to gain a thorough knowledge of the facts. This proved useful to his work. His picture of the time has considerable plasticity and he seldom introduces anachronisms. The plot is associated with native tradition through the lovers Bīzhan and Manīzha, well-known from Firdausī's *Shāh-nāma*. The novels ends, as does Shaykh Mūsā's, with the conquest of Babylon. There can hardly be any question of mutual influence. The similarity lies rather in the endeavour at that time to arouse patriotic feeling by spreading a knowledge of Persia's past. Apart from this tendency, the two works have little in common. Badīʿ's work does not possess the sensational adventurousness by which Shaykh Mūsā shows his dependence on Dumas. His novel is well constructed and for the first time the personages are distinguished by their way of speech. Nor is his characterisation limited to a description of the outward appearance of his heroes. The author attempts to demonstrate the correct principles of government in the person of Cyrus, whom he depicts as an ideal ruler, as regards both his personal qualities and his social and economic opinions. Cyrus is taught the sound basic principles of administration by his father; he is urged to encourage his subjects to cultivate handicrafts, but not to oppose free trading and to ensure that imports do not exceed exports, etc.[45]

A curious work, which openly rejects all European influences (although the author cannot completely evade them in prose; the vocabulary too, particularly in its military terminology, contains many europeanisms) is ʿAlī Aṣghar Sharīf's *Khūn-bahā-i*

Īrān, 'The Blood Feud of Iran', published in Tehran in 1345/1926. The story takes place in the recent past, during the First World War. It describes the occupation of the country, the founding of the Home Army, the desperate battles and the complete political breakdown. The central figures are two young patriots, the lovers Īraj and Mihrangīz, besides whom there is a group of well-drawn subsidiary characters. Less successful are the last chapters of the novel, in which we find passages quoted verbatim from Persian and foreign journals and diplomatic documents, so that the thread of the story is lost. Sharīf also wrote another successful novel, *Maktab-i ʿishq*, 'The School for Love'. He is a deeply pious Shīʿite Moslem and this, together with strong conservatism and a rejection of everything European, permeates his whole work. His opposition to the radical europeanisation of the country is in fact explained by this attitude.

The literary output of Raḥīm-zāda Ṣafavī betrays the scholarly accuracy of a philologist and historian. He intended to relate the whole history of his country in novels but to date has only completed a small part of it. From his book *Dāstān-i Shahrbānū*, 'The Legend of Shahrbānū' (the second edition appeared in Tehran in 1948–9; the subject was taken from the period of the collapse of the Sasanian kingdom) it is possible to trace the development of the novel at that time, for this one was written ten years after Ṣanʿatī-zāda (p. 370) had handled the same theme. Above all it is based on a reliable knowledge of historical facts, from the social structure and the position of women in contemporary society to architecture and popular customs and habits. This knowledge is passed on to the reader not by copious references to historical works and documents, as was frequently the case in some previous novels, but by detailed and faithful descriptions of the background to the plot. The characters show individuality and their manner of speech is appropriate to their social rank. Only the psychological development of the heroes and the motivation of their actions still remain weak. The style of the novel is straightforward and simple. In contrast to Ṣanʿatī-zāda, the optimistic ending of the work is particularly effective. The beautiful Sasanian daughter, Shahrbānū, the heroine of the novel, marries ʿAlī's son Ḥusayn. In this way, on the ruins of the disintegrated Middle Iranian kingdom, the illustrious past is joined to the promise of the future.[46] Well versed as he is in history, the author recognises the power of survival of Persian culture, which in the long run has always proved superior to all invaders of Iran.

Also during the 'thirties there appeared two novels by the poet Ḥaydar ʿAlī Kamālī. He was a manual worker and illiterate up to the age of 23. Having taught himself to read and write, he soon began to compose poems, which were considered very promising. At the end of the 19th century he went to Tehran, where he devoted himself mainly to business, and started a teahouse that became the meeting place for Tehran's literary and journalistic circles. As a member of the democratic wing, he took part in the political life of his time.

Kamālī's *dīvān* was published in Istanbul in 1922. It cannot, however, be numbered

Notes on pp. 395–396

among the most outstanding literary works because the author wrote too easily and too fast and imitated the most diverse styles and patterns. Yet Kamālī was the author of several successful historical novels and must be counted among the innovators. His first novel, *Maẓālim-i Turkān-Khātūn*, 'Tyranny of Turkan-Khatun', bears the name of the famous Queen-Regent at the time of the Mongol invasion of Iran; it appeared in Tehran in 1348/1929–30. A fine style and an exciting plot, which is dramatically well constructed without deteriorating into sensationalism, together with well-drawn characters, are merits of the first as well as of the second of the poet's works. The second novel appeared two years after the first, also in Tehran. Its title *Lāzīkā*, 'Colchis', indicates that the story is placed at the time of the struggles between the Sasanians and the Romans in the former province of Colchis on the shores of the Black Sea. The historical side is true to fact, while a completely new feature in the construction is formed by the main plot in which, contrary to custom, not the sovereign's court and its members, but the patriotic gentry is placed in the foreground.[47] This concept is entirely in keeping with the new militant patriotism, which also constitutes the underlying idea of the work. The fact, too, that the border-line between patriotism and chauvinism is often not drawn with any precision is a reflection of the contemporary ideological situation.

Another good prose writer of this epoch is Zaynu'l-ʿĀbidīn Mu'taman, with his historical novel *Āshyāna-i ʿUqāb*, 'Eagle's Nest'. This work was written between 1352–8/1933–9 and describes the rivalry between the Saljuq vizier Niẓāmu'l-mulk and the chief of the Assassins, Ḥasan Sabbāḥ. In ideological respects, the author is on the side of the oppressed and proclaims the necessity of freeing the enslaved classes in human society. For the first time in the history of the Persian historical novel, Mu'taman was not satisfied with describing court circles – which until then had been depicted with idealistic patriotic pathos – but placed them within the framework of the whole social set-up.[48]

A literary experiment of quite unique character is the novel *ʿIshq u adab*, 'Love and Literature', in which the president of the Literary Society in Hamadan, Mīrzā ʿAlī Muḥammad-Khān Āzād, made an attempt at a biography of the poet Firdausī in the form of a novel. It appeared in Tehran in 1353/1934 (ten years later the same material was used by H. Mīrzā Sālūr in his novel *Juft-i pāk*).

During this interesting experimental period works also occur which show no trace of artistic 'research'. The two novels of Yaḥyā Qarīb, *Yaʿqūb-i Layth* (1936) and *Khūn-i Siyāvush* (1937), make the impression that their author has slept through almost twenty years of development. We can discern a palpable ignorance of facts and numerous anachronisms, the characters are either blameless or thoroughly vicious. Yet they contain a strange experiment: the author interweaves a number of verses, partly quotations from the *Shāh-nāma*, partly his own.[49] It is an experiment which not only upsets the development of the plot but which, in view of the situation of Persian prose at the time, has the effect of an almost hybrid anachronism. Another work, the novel *ʿArūs-i Mādī*, 'The Bride of the Medes' (Tehran 1349/1930) by the Persian translator of Sienkiewicz' *Quo Vadis?*, ʿAbbās Aryān Pūr-i Kāshānī, is patently inferior in quality in view of its lack both of artistic mastery and historical accuracy, its style and its language. The main development in Persian belles-lettres tends more and more towards the shorter forms, tales and short stories; the future will show whether this has any connection with the general inclination towards shorter forms in world literature or whether it is a purely Persian phenomenon. The short story is also the best literary mirror of contemporary events, with the problems and uncertainties to which they give rise. After the successful début of Jamāl-zāda, there appeared during the 'thirties Ṣ. Hidāyat (pp. 410–2), with his fantastic and introspective tales, B. ʿAlavī, whose tragic, shipwrecked lives are seen from a Freudian psycho-analytical viewpoint (pp. 414–5); later Ṣ. Chūbak (p. 415), and others, who even in their first works follow the new trends in Persian prose.

NOTES

1. Cf. Yāsimī, *op. cit.*, 207; *Armaghān*, 17 (1315), 60.
2. Shafaq, *op.cit.*, 417 *et seq.*
3. Nafīsī, *Shāh-kārhā*, is of the opinion that in his *novella* Jamāl-zāda only set the crown on what his predecessors, Tālibūf and Dihkhudā, had begun.
4. These have been published in several collections, such as *Tarānahā-i millī*, Tehran 1310; *Afsānahā-i rustā'ī-i Īrān*, Tehran 1332; *Haftṣad tarānahā-i rustā'ī-i Īrān*, Tehran n.d.
5. Under the title *Kitāb-i amthāl u ḥikam*, Tehran n.d.
6. *Majmaʿu'l-amthāl*, Tehran n.d.
7. E.g., *Afsānahā-i kuhan*, Tehran 1336.
8. Cf. Massé, *REI*, A (1938), 107–8.
9. *REI*, 1938, 261 *et seq.*
10. Cf. Chaykin, *Ocherk*, 139 *et seq.*
11. On the history of this review, see F. Machalski, 'Vaḥīd Dastgirdī and his Armaghān', *Folia Orientalia*, 4 (1962), 81–104.
12. Cf. Ishaque, *Sukhanvarān....*, II, 363 *et seq.*
13. Fore more detailed information cf. Chaykin, *Ocherk*, 167.
14. E.g. *Namakdān*, edited from 1929 by A. Kasravī Tabrīzī.
15. Cf. Osmanova, *KS*, 27 (1958), 68.
16. See Browne, *LHP*, IV, 490.
17. For more detailed information see E. Rossi, *OM*, 23 (1943), 208 *et seq.* For an analysis of Iraj's work cf. Z.N. Vorozheykina, *Iraj Mirza*, Moscow 1961.
18. More on this: Yaukacheva, *KS*, 27 (1958), 45 *et seq.*
19. *KS*, 17 (1955), 76, 77.
20. Cf. Browne, *Press and Poetry...*, XVIII.
21. See a note in Duchesne-Guillemin, *La religion de l'Iran ancien*, Paris 1962, 381.
22. More on this cf. Ishaque, *Sukhanvarān...*, I, 52.
23. See Chaykin, *Ocherk*, 116 *et seq.*

24. *Folia Orientalia*, I (1959), 66 *et seq*.
25. Ishaque, *Sukhanvarān...*, I, 38 *et seq*., II, 92 *et seq*., and others.
26. Cf. J. Rypka, 'Parvín, novodobá básnířka perská', *Český časopis filologický*, I (1943), 187 *et seq*.
27. Cf. Bertel's, *Ocherk*, 163.
28. Cf. Ishaque, *Sukhanvarān...*, II, 311 *et seq*.
29. More on this, Shafaq 'Patriotic poetry', *MEJ*, 1952,6, 425 *et seq*.
30. Ishaque, *Sukhanvarān...*, II, 323; *Dīvān-i Farrukhī*, 11 *et seq*.
31. *Dīvān-i Farrukhī – Ghazaliyyāt va qaṣā'id va qiṭa'āt va rubā'iyyāt bā taṣḥīḥ va muqaddima dar sharḥ va aḥvāl-i shā'ir ba qalam-i Ḥusayn-i Makkī*, Tehran 1328; for an analysis of the work, cf. Osmanova, *KS*, 27 (1958), 67 *et seq*.
32. Cf. *Ocherk*, 114.
33. Ishaque, *Sukhanvarān...*, I, 33 *et seq*.
34. On this see also 'Alavī, *Das Land der Rosen und Nachtigallen*, 110 *et seq*.
35. Cf. Amū Ḥusayn 'Alī, *Introduction*; Vasīghī, *Jamāl-zāda*, 26.
36. See Browne, *Press and Poetry*, 70; *Yaghmā*, (1933).
37. *Fārsī shakar ast*, 'Persian is Sugar'; *Rajul-i siyāsī*, 'The Politician'; *Dūstī-i khāla Khirsa*, 'The Friendship of Uncle Bruin'; *Dard-i dil-i Mulla Qurbān-'Alī*, 'The Troubles of Mullah Qurban Ali'; *Bīla dīg – bīla chukundar*, 'Every man to his deserts'; *Vilānu'd-daula*, 'Loafer of the Empire'.
38. As these language peculiarities were incomprehensible to the average educated Persian, the author appended a Glossary of these terms – 'Kalimāt-i 'avāmmāna' – to the book.
39. Vasīghī, *op. cit*., 26; Borecký, *MEJ*, 7 (1953), 238, rightly comments that this book presumes an extensive knowledge of Shī'ite theology on the part of the reader.
40. Cf. Borecký, *op. cit*., 238.
41. For a more comprehensive review of the work, see B. 'Alavī, in *OLZ*,54 (1959), 52 *et seq*.; Komissarov, *SV*, 3 (1958), sees in Jamāl-zāda a certain bias towards naturalism.
42. Further see Chaykin, *Ocherk*, 154 *et seq*.
43. A. A. Khudādāda is the author of a work of the same name; he described the wretched life in the Iranian countryside.
44. Further see Bertel's, *Ocherk*, 149 *et seq*; Chaykin, *Ocherk*, 128 *et seq*.
45. Machalski, *Historyczna powieść*, 54.
46. Machalski, *Historyczna powieść*, 72 *et seq*.
47. Machalski, *Historyczna powieść*, 70 *et seq*.
48. Zaynu'l-'Ābidīn is also a good theorist in his work *Shi'r va adab-i fārsī*; cf. Machalski, *Folia Orientalia*, I (1959), 154 *et seq*. and 3 (1962), 335 *et seq*.
49. Machalski, *Historyczna powieść*, 127 *et seq*.

IV. THE MAIN LITERARY TRENDS AFTER 1941

In the middle of the Second World War, in the autumn of 1941, Riḍā Shāh Pahlavī was obliged to abdicate in favour of his son, Muḥammad Riḍā (p. 359). Immediately after this the territory of Iran was occupied by British and Soviet armed forces; the occupation, however, had a very different character from that of the First World War, so that in cultural life too democratic tendencies soon began to make themselves felt. New world-orientated branches of science were cultivated; the number of translations from western literature increased; Persian literary production broadened its horizons and obtained greater opportunities for publication, thanks to the better organisation of the publishing trade; and later, when all literary output was systematically documented, the situation was ripe for the appearance of the synoptical surveys and literary evaluations that now flowed from the pens of those engaged in the study of literature. The numerous reviews and periodicals were not confined solely to the literary field; the specific problems of every domain of cultural activity, even the youngest – cinematography, for instance – were catered for in special magazines.

The efforts aiming at a general modernisation of the language, which already with the founding of the Farhangistān-i Īrān in 1935 acquired an official character, were extended more and more to the domain of a scientific language. The reviews of the literary faculties of the universities (e.g. those of Tehran, Tabriz and others, p. 402) reflect this activity in articles by the foremost literary historians and in good translations of foreign scientific studies (following the initiator, ʿA. Furūghī[1], the most notable names associated with these trends are M. Qazvīnī, Q. Ghanī, Badīʿu'z-zamān, P. N. Khānlarī, R. Yāsimī, S. Nafīsī and others). And even in articles not directly connected with literary research, where linguistic considerations came naturally less to the foreground, a distinct advance is to be observed in the direction of simplification and clarity of expression.

An event of great importance for Iranian literary production and its representatives, from the artistic point of view as well as from a purely practical standpoint, was the

Notes on pp. 416–418

First Congress of Iranian Writers held in 1946. The publication reporting its sessions[2] gives a good survey of modern literature up to the 1940's, and from the Congress resolutions it is clear that the artists who adopted them had as their aim above all the dissemination of the ideas of enlightened humanism and peaceful co-operation.

Translation from foreign literatures began to extend its range; in the early phase of this activity, directed at that time by Dāru'l-funūn (p. 322), the chief emphasis was laid on its educative function. Now many other considerations became operative – aesthetic, social, political and commercial – in determining the choice; a conscious endeavour to supplement the home book market with the important works of world literature was not, however, as yet evident. On the contrary, first place as regards number was occupied in the field of translated fiction by detective and crime novels (*dāstān-i pūlīsī va jinā'ī*) which, from the time more accurate data relating to book production became available, comprise more than half (about 60 %) of all translations.[3] Of the more serious works, the first place is occupied by French literature, followed by English and American, Russian, German and, only occasionally, others (e.g. Karel Čapek, Julius Fučík from Czech and H. Sienkiewicz from Polish literature). Here too selection was more a matter of chance than of a guided cultural policy (Rolland's *Jean-Christophe*, the exotic novels of Claude Farrère, Hemingway and Longfellow, F. Sagan, Pasternak's *Doktor Zhivago* and Gogol's *Taras Bulba*, are all to be found side by side), and if we consider that in the world production of books Iran is near the bottom of the list[4], it is evident how much still remains to be done in this field. A similar situation exists in regard to the artistic fidelity of the translations, which show a very uneven level. Considerably better, both in respect of choice and of the quality of translation, are those which appear in literary periodicals.[5]

A bias towards stories of adventure of a lighter genre also continues to be a feature of original writing. Many novels show a strong predilection for exciting plots, often regardless of the bounds of possibility, sickly sentimental stories from the lives of prostitutes, illicit loves, illegitimate children, murders and suicides – not seldom under the serious title of an historical or social novel (p. 406). Nevertheless, there are also works which show a real advance, both in their wider thematic range and in their artistic value.[6]

New themes derive mainly from a marked effort to comprehend contemporary social reality in all its complexity, in attempts to elucidate various social problems arising out of changes in the social and economic structure of the country: modern woman and her status in life and society; the clash between traditional ways of thought and life and those of western civilisation, which permeates every page; the problems of youth and its upbringing; changes in the life of the Iranian countryside; the condition of the lowest social classes, etc.[7] In the treatment of historical themes a new light is shed upon certain periods and certain personalities in Iranian history, even the most recent.

The manner in which these themes are approached and artistically worked out naturally depends very much on the author's view of the world and, inseparable from his philosophical attitude, also on his conception of the writer's role in national life. In the period of the Constitution the image of the writer-awakener, the teacher of the nation became deeply impressed in the general consciousness. This conception of the writer's role often comes out very clearly in contemporary prose. It appears in novels and short stories with historical themes (sometimes in the somewhat strained seeking after analogies between situations in the nation's past and the present) and still more markedly in prose with social and socially critical themes. A preacher's moralising is sometimes coloured with a superficial sentimentality, which the average western reader would look upon as an artistic shortcoming, whereas the Persian critic sees it with quite different eyes: not only does he completely identify himself with the writer's educational role, but he is in this respect often unconsciously influenced by the distinguished tradition of native didactic poetry. These tendencies do not, however, affect all modern prose. In it we find – though in much smaller measure – a stream more or less opposed to the first, and linking up to a certain extent with Western European literary-philosophical thought: in the works representing this trend the central theme is modern man, his individual experience, feelings and mental world, his confrontation with his fellow-beings, the world around him, the fact of death. These problems conform in the main with modern existentialistic thought, correspond to some extent with the native tradition of Ṣūfī poetry and have reached the highest degree of artistic mastery in the works of Ṣ. Hidāyat (p. 410).

Persian prose-writers produce novels, short stories, reports, etc. The medium of the main line of artistic development in prose would seem to be the shorter prose forms.[8] In the novel a firm structure, a logically worked-out development in the course of the plot, and other requirements of the genre as a literary form, are so far the weaker side of modern prose. Similarly, as regards language the short story is more enterprising and inventive than the novel. Its literary language shows a greater approximation to the spoken language, and it enriches its vocabulary from the fund of old, forgotten words, for centuries supplanted by Arabic expressions, and then, following in the footsteps of Jamāl-zāda's innovation, by the use of folk turns of phrase and of expressions taken over from dialect and slang. Differentiation of character, social or occupational status by means of linguistic elements in the dialogue, which at the beginnings of modern prose was something quite unprecedented, later becomes a matter of course in good prose-writing.

If, in accordance with Professor Khānlarī, we have designated the period of modern Persian literature 'an Age of Prose', that is not to say that the Persians have by any means lost their innate love of poetry. Despite all the seeking after new forms and all the experimentation of the literati, there is still alive in all classes of the nation a knowledge of classical poetry and the tendency to compose poems in the traditional forms. With this fact is connected a remarkable Iranian peculiarity: in anthologies of poetry, even today, there still appear the names of contemporary scholars and scientists, university professors, statesmen, lawyers and doctors, who contribute as poets to the literary life of their country. The curious fact, too, that this culturally very admirable trait may and does operate as a brake on every effort at revolutionary changes in the art of poetry has been pointed out above (p. 389); and so modern poetry is still in a much more difficult situation than prose, which is not bound by any such universally recognised tradition.[9] This also explains why it is that almost fifty years after the appearance of the first theoretically founded programmes and manifestos, announcing the discarding of the classical canon (p. 378 *et seq.*), much verse is still written (and assiduously read) in the old style.

Nevertheless, in spite of all these circumstances, which unfortunately also prevailed in the domain of literary criticism, the stream of modern poetry has grown in breadth and strength. This was natural if only because changing life itself, in face of all conservative opposition, called for modern poetical expression. For lack of a better term we have called this modernity Persian romanticism, because in a number of basic points its programme is in agreement with European romanticism: such are a manifest turning away from the objective intellectual poetry of classicism and its abstract rational ideal of beauty, and protest against the formalistic view of poetry as expressed by Ibn Khaldūn, who declared that the art of writing poetry is concerned only with words and not with thoughts; a passionate striving to seize the reality of life and nature; a love for folk-art, music, poetry; finally, the search for individual expression of the feelings and emotions of one's inner life. A deeper analysis of certain of the characteristic traits of modern Persian poetry in this sense would perhaps help to explain why its exponents, when they seek their models in European poetry, incline more towards the romantic poets (Hugo, Vigny, Lamartine, Musset, and others) than to those representing the more objective and formalistic trends of a later time.

As in prose, we find among representatives of the modern stream in Persian poetry several who follow the course taken by left-wing literature of the present day, the course of socialist realism, with stress on its basic component: the creation for the reader of a human and social ideal. But since here the educative and enlightening role that is the characteristic feature of this poetry is often combined with the Iranian love of didactic verse, the cumulative effect is unfortunately closer to rhymed advertisement with a copy-book tendentiousness than to true poetry.

In studies on modern Persian literature, of which there are still too few, we come across attempts at a classification of the trends in contemporary poetry. The first to do so was the Indian literary historian, M. Ishaque, in his monograph on the 1930's, in which from the point of view of content and form he divided the poets into three main groups: those writing verses classical in form and content; those preserving the old form, but filling it with topical themes; and lastly those who, both as regards subject-matter and form, are non-traditional.[10] Similarly, ʿA. A. Ḥikmat, in the publication issued on the occasion of the First Congress of Iranian Writers, deals with this question and supplements Ishaque's classification with a more detailed division according to subject-matter.[11] More recently, M. Ṭabāṭabā'ī bases his first two groups on considerations of style (form), while in determining others he applies the criteria of content (theme).[12] In the present article an endeavour has been made to find a philosophical basis for contemporary poetical trends, for we believe that in such a basis are implicit the different points of departure from which these trends start out to shape reality in their verse; the three main streams from which they derive are discussed more fully in the chapter on poetry.

A. IMPORTANT LITERARY AND CULTURAL PERIODICALS OF RECENT YEARS

Even though after Riḍā Shāh's abdication the daily press quickly expanded and numerically fell little short of the peak reached during the period of the Constitution, it no longer possessed the national revivalist character as far as collaboration with contemporary poets was concerned, nor was it any longer the poetical chronicle of the time, as it had been then. Literature had other interests and stimuli besides political ideas and events and we learn of its life from special periodicals and from literary and art reviews.

Continuing along the lines of a well-founded tradition, which conscientiously guarded the classical heritage and barred all exaggerated modernist eccentricities, the review *Armaghān*, after the death of its founder, the literary scholar and poet, Vaḥīd Dastgirdī (d. 1942), preserved its character under the editorship of Vaḥīd's son, Nasīm. The occasionally over-conservative character of the periodical is counterbalanced by several studies on classical poetry, based on new literary-historical finds and manuscript sources.

A group of literary modernists founded the review *Sukhan*, 'The Word', in 1322 *sh.*, with P. N. Khānlarī as chief editor. *Sukhan* publishes the latest output of modern poets and prose-writers, including the work of the best – Ṣ. Hidāyat, M. 'A. Jamāl-zāda, Ṣ. Chūbak, B. 'Alavī, M. Farzād and others. Only rarely does it publish less well known or newly discovered verses of the classics, as in *Armaghān*. *Sukhan* devotes considerable space to translations from western literatures, notably modern work, well selected and often admirably interpreted (such as translations of F. Kafka by Ṣ. Hidāyat). In the domain of literary theory, there are essays on the problems of modern Persian literature (especially poetry and numerous articles of a programmatic character by the chief editor), as well as informative studies taken from the histories of western literatures and articles on other branches of the arts, as for instance contributions on occidental painting, etc. Speaking generally we may characterise this review as one of the most representative of that section of the Persian intelligentsia that aims at a world orientation of Persian culture.

Notes on pp. 416–418

Its junior by five years is the review *Yaghmā*, 'Spoil', the first volume of which came out in 1327 *sh.* The title is an allusion to the name of the first Persian satirist of the preceding century, whose grandson Yaghmā'ī, a poet, is also the chief editor of the magazine. Its sub-title – *adabī, ʿilmī, taʾrīkhī, ijtimāʿī* ('On literature, science, history, and sociology') – indicates that its wide range of interest is extended to scientific rather than to artistic problems. It provides the general public with information on the situation in modern science and deals with questions of modern sociology, ethnography, linguistics, etc. (Here, for instance, appeared a sharp criticism of western Iranian studies, especially in respect of lexicography, from the pen of Persian philologists.) Among the contributors to the review are such well-known names as R. Shafaq, M. Mīnuvī, L. Ṣūratgar, Mahdī Ḥamīdī, Īraj Afshār and others.

Occasionally modern literary work appears in the pages of scholarly journals, such as those of the Literary Faculties of the Universities in Tehran and Tabriz, *Majalla-i dānishkada-i adabiyyāt-i Tihrān* and *Nashriyya-i dānishkada-i adabiyyāt-i Tabrīz* respectively, that are otherwise devoted to the problems of the humanities in the works of Iranian and foreign scholars; or of *Farhang-i Īrān-zamīn*, 'The Culture of Iran', which deals mainly with linguistic questions, but also with matters of wider cultural interest.

The official literary periodical of the Tūda Party was the literary-aesthetic review *Mardum*, 'The People', which first came out in 1325 *sh.* under the editorship of M. Rādmanish. Its leading journalist was the politician and poet, I. Ṭabarī (p. 405). Among its poet-contributors were M. Shaybānī, Nīmā Yūshīj, Sāya, B. ʿAlavī, as well as many left-wing poets of the youngest generation. In its theoretical articles, *Mardum* acquainted its readers with the Marxist view of problems of literature and art (as, for instance, in the articles contributed by M. Shakī on Marxist aesthetics, and in literary studies by I. Ṭabarī).

The excellent literary magazine *Mihr*, 'The Sun', has had as its editor since its foundation Īraj Afshār, noted amongst other things for his valuable work in the field of bibliographical documentation of contemporary literary production in Iran. *Yādgār*, 'Memorial', founded by ʿA. Iqbāl Āshtiyānī (d. 1334 *sh.*), is devoted not only to literature but also to historical studies. *Āyanda*, 'The Future', edited by Maḥmūd Afshār, deals with social and political questions.

The Iranian Committee of the World Peace Council brings out a magazine to which especially the younger progressive generation of Iranian writers contributes; here we may read translations of the works of the foremost world fighters for peace, such as L. Aragon, Ilya Ehrenburg and others, as well as theoretical studies aimed at propagating peaceful collaboration among the nations. The title of the periodical was originally *Kabūtar-i ṣulḥ*, 'The Dove of Peace', later *Payk-i ṣulḥ*, 'The Messenger of Peace'. In connection with the magazine a series of translations was initiated, with a publishing programme of titles from world literature that have contributed to the struggle for peace and social progress. In this edition have been published, for instance, Gorky's *Mother*, Barbusse's *The Fire*, Fučík's *Report from the Gallows* and others.

The literary organ of the Society of Iranian-Soviet Friendship, entitled originally *Payām-i nau*, later, *Payām-i navīn*, gives priority to the work of writers who are interested in topical problems of a social character and aim to solve them in the spirit of a progressive socialist ideology (B. ʿAlavī, Bihādhīn, S. Nafīsī, and others); here, too, we find studies in literary criticism, while a particularly valuable contribution to Iranian letters are good translations of Russian classics and of Soviet literature.[13]

REVIEWS FROM OTHER SPHERES OF CULTURE

We also find work of contemporary poets and writers in journals dealing with other aspects of culture, for instance in *Naqsh u nigār*, 'Picture and Print', *Numāyish*, 'The Theatre', *Sīnimā va zindagī*, 'The Cinema and Life', *Majalla-i mūsīqī*, 'Musical Review' *Mardum-shināsī*, 'Anthropology', and in periodicals devoted to ethnographical questions, folk-art, etc.

The number of magazines for women is growing and their level is improving thanks to the collaboration of members of the young generation of Iranian women, brought up in ideas of freedom and democracy. *Bīdārī-i mā*, 'Our Awakening', *Tashkīlāt-i zanān*, 'Organisation of Women', *ʿĀlam-i nisvān*, 'Women's World' are some of the titles of these reviews, which are reminiscent of the early phases of the European emancipation of women.

BIBLIOGRAPHICAL JOURNALS

With the growth in the volume of literary production, the need arises for a systematic documentation. The first attempt at such was made in 1332 *sh.* by Īraj Afshār in a bibliography entitled *Kitāb-shināsī-i Īrān*. Two years later this task was taken over by the Publishers' Association in the bibliographical monthly *Kitābhā-i māh*, 'Books of the Month', and though this monthly at the same time serves the purposes of advertisement and propaganda, it is nevertheless a valuable aid for the survey it gives of contemporary literary life.[14] Occasionally the journal publishes reviews or readers' opinions, more comprehensive surveys of the book market in some special domain (children's literature, for example), arranges or gives information about literary competitions, and so on. Finally, in 1336 *sh.*, a bibliographical bulletin began to appear under the title *Rāhnamā-i kitāb*, 'A Guide to Books', edited by Ī. Afshār. Each number contains in its close on 200 pages a critical bibliography of all the new books published, classified according to subject-matter; included are also articles of a programmatic character, public opinion polls (for instance, on the problem of textbooks), and finally full reviews – taking up, as a rule, almost half the issue – of more important publications in the domains of scientific works and belles-lettres by native authors, and also

Notes on pp. 416–418

of books of interest for the Iranian reading public published abroad. The bulletin numbers among its contributors the names of Iran's foremost scientific and literary personalities. It further confirms the importance of this publication, which will undoubtedly become the chief source of information on the book market.

B. BRIEF SURVEY OF CONTEMPORARY PERSIAN POETRY

Following the division into the three main currents indicated above (p. 400), we find in present-day Persian poetry first of all a group of poets who carry on the classical tradition of lyrico-philosophical verse. Their bias is towards the so-called 'eternal' problems of philosophy, ethics and love, and they write verse on these themes in the cool spheres of abstract rhetoric. This poetry is of an expressly imitative and formalistic character and is doomed, as a glasshouse plant, to perish. The poets themselves, who are upholders of the classicising tendency, realise this–whence the attempts at rejuvenation by giving artistic expression to their own experiences and feelings, of conjuring up the moods of Nature, and so on. This is true, however, only of the best of them, of those whose passion for classical poetry has not stifled their own creative powers. Such are Rashīd Yāsimī[15], whose reputation is founded on his reflective lyrical poetry, Mahdī Ḥamīdī[16], another lyric poet, the sovereign master of the *ghazal*, M. Ḥ. Shahriyār of Tabriz[17], and one of the younger generation of classicists, Rāhī Mu'āyirī, to mention a few.

Another trend is represented by political poetry, mostly strongly tendentious, whether the didactic 'point' rouses to revolution or patriotism, or to criticism of existing conditions. It arose out of the needs of the revolutionary epoch; since then it has been a prominent component of Persian poetry and the mirror of a certain aspect of the most recent national history, namely that of its unceasing efforts to improve living conditions. In periods when these efforts were most intense almost all contemporary poets wrote political poetry (p. 363); in the case of some it formed then the main body of their work.[18] Representative of this trend is a growing group of poet-socialists, whose forerunners were Farrukhī Yazdī (p. 387) and A. Q. Lāhūtī (p. 376) both of whom show a characteristic attitude to the formal questions of poetry, which they consider a matter of secondary importance – a trait distinguishing this group up to the present day. One of their number, in respect of his poetry, is the journalist and sometime editor (1951–53) of *Chalangar*, 'The Smith', M. 'A. Afrāshta (d. 1958), also well known as the author of short prose forms. As a poet he tends to follow the satirical line in Persian political verse. His popularity owes not a little to his excellent knowledge of pithy folk-expressions, the use of which enables his militant and critical verses to reach a wide public. Another journalist (the combination of journalism and poetry is as typical of these poets as it ever was), the chief editor of the review *Mardum* (p. 402), I. Ṭabarī – one of B. ʿAlavī's 53 men – engages in literary criticism, writes short stories with social themes, and political poetry which Shoytov has aptly characterised in the following words: "His programme poems show that Ṭabarī sees in his poetry above all a weapon in the struggle of his nation to throw off the yoke of dependence."[19] To a progressive, militant poetry the poet Sāya makes his way from a romantic compassionate view of the world and its suffering[20]; a similar path is followed in her verse by the poetess Zhāla Sulṭānī. Of the younger generation belonging to this group we may mention here the poets Daryā and ʿAlī Jalālī.[21]

The third group of modernist poets, pioneers of a new style and of free verse, has to a greater extent than the two previous groups the character of a school. Its leader was the resolute opponent of the conservators of classicism, Nīmā Yūshīj (1895–1960). At one time a friend of and collaborator with the poet ʿIshqī on the review *Qarn-i bīstum* (p. 386), he inclined in his early work as a poet to the romantic school of European poetry (for instance, in his longer poem *Afsāna*, 'Romance', written in the early twenties), but his erotic lyrics lacked primary emotional experience. Even then, however, his artistic programme contained the striving after a new poetical form, essentially free verse grouped in strophic forms, with irregular rhymes or unrhymed; often in the course of a single poem Nīmā changes the rhythmic pattern and the strophic structure (cf. ʿIshqī), to the disgust of conservative readers and critics. In the period of his artistic maturity Nīmā achieved a notable individuality of expression in his nature (the best!), love and social lyrics. Thanks to his endeavours to create a new style, which he propagated in a number of theoretical articles (published mainly in the review *Majalla-i mūsīqī*, p. 403), he had many followers, conscious and unconscious. A selection from his poetry was published in 1334 *sh.*, edited by A. Jannatī ʿAtā'ī, who wrote an Introduction dealing with the poet's personality, life, and poetry; the second part of the Introduction contains something of the poet's credo and theoretical views: "The new style is really another kind of classical *ʿarūḍ* – only the poetical method is quite the opposite: here form must adapt itself to content, and never the other way about!"[22]

Representatives of the younger generation of poets now making their impact in the new style are Nādir Nādirpūr (b. 1929), A. Ṣubḥ, Ṣ. Sarmad, F. Tavallalī and others. In his collection of poems entitled *Rahā* ('Liberation', published in Tehran, in 1333 *sh.*), Farīdūn Tavallalī (b. 1917) showed himself to be a good theorist of the new style: he calls for independence of classical poetry, for poetical expression of individual feeling, for a new literary expression to serve as the mirror of changing moods. In his own poetry, however, he is more successful in my view in his love and nature lyrics (for example, in the charming *Maryam*) than in his pessimistically keyed reflective verse.[23] Of the modernists expressly pessimistic in tone there is the lyric poet Islāmī, the Persian disciple of 'les poètes maudits'. The European-educated physician Fakhrā'ī, under his *nom de plume* Gulchīn, belongs to the group of writers who wage war on the classical 'nightingale and roses' school, in the name of his enchantment with modern western civilisation[24] (admiration for technical achievement is no novelty in Persian poetry, where it figured already in the last century, for example, in the poetry of the Viṣāl family (p. 331)); among contemporary writers, there are also those, however, who look upon western civilisation with disdain, and even with positive condemnation (cf. p. 407).[25] In connection with Gulchīn's poetical oeuvre, it would be well to call to mind the words of the poet Nādir Nādirpūr, who said that to write about the atom or aircraft did not suffice to make poetry modern – for in truth these verses of Gulchīn's on modern scientific topics are, as poetry, weaker than those which express simply, and without *ad hoc* theorising, the poet's feelings and the freshness of his talent (as in several of this wartime poems). To the modernists also belong the excellent translator of Shakespeare, Masʿūd Farzād, together with many poets of the younger and youngest generations whose names crop up in periodicals and literary reviews. To assign them their place in the renaissance of Persian poetry will be the task of the future, which alone can provide the proper criteria.[26]

C. PERSIAN PROSE AFTER 1941

I. THE NOVEL AND THE SHORT STORY WITH HISTORICAL THEMES

Interest in the national past, stimulated by the modern conception of the nation evolved before and during the struggles for a Constitution and later by the still proud nationalism of Riḍā-Shāh – an interest often strongly tinged with romanticism – has inspired many Persian prose-writers to handle historical themes. Among the works of this kind there are very substantial differences in artistic quality; many make use of historical material merely as a pretext for giving rein to their partiality for exciting adventure and sensation. This is the case, for instance, in the novel, *ʿIshq u Khūn*, 'Love and Blood', from the pen of the very prolific writer Javād Fāḍil; he draws on the time of the Constitutional struggle for his material, but the simple title indicates its true content. The same can be said of many of the other novels by this author, such as, *ʿIshq u ashk*, 'Love and Tears', *Taqdīm ba tu*, 'Only for You', *Dukhtar-i hamsāya*, 'The Neighbour's Daughter', and others. Borecký notes that this author, whose novels are typically exciting stories written in a light, accessible style and with sentimental motivation, enjoys great popularity among Persian women readers.[27]

Not unlike these works in character are the historical novels of L. Taraqqī: the bloodstained history of the Barmacids and the horrifying revenge of their adherents in *Shabhā-i Baghdād* ('Bagdad Nights', 1952) or the earlier *ʿIshq-bāzīhā-i Nāṣiru'd-dīn shāh*, 'The Love-Making of Shāh Nāṣiru'd-dīn', with its unconcealed delight in lasciviousness. Somewhat better is an attempt at bringing to life the time of Cyrus the Great and of his son, Cambyses, by ʿA. Jalālī, under the title *Shabhā-i Bābil*, 'Babylonian Nights', composed more as a crime novel.[28] A much happier excursion into history is made by Jalālī in his book of historical tales, *Dāstānhā-i tāʾrīkhī yā hazārdāstān-i Jalālī*, 'Historical Tales or The Nightingale of Jalālī', and his two historical plays, *Shāh ʿAbbās*, 'Abbās the Great' and *Rustam u Suhrāb*, are relatively successful. The latter has been translated into French.[29]

Ḥusayn Ruknzāda Ādamiyyat renounced the popular adventurous plot in his book *Dilīrān-i Tangistān*, 'The Heroes of Tangistan'. He took his material from the time of the occupation of Iran during the First World War and described the uprising of the people, with the Tangistanīs at their head, against the domination of the occupying powers. As regards composition, the writer is closely linked to the novelists of the old school, for example Shaykh Mūsā (p. 371), particularly in the way he often swamps the story with long quotations from documents in an endeavour to give it an air of historical authenticity. However, Persian critics, whose views may not be disregarded in the evaluation of contemporary work, gave this novel a spontaneous welcome (these critics included S. Nafīsī, R. Ṣafavī, etc.) on account of its ideas, its noble patriotism, and its bitter criticism of the doubtful significance of western civilisation which "with bombs and armies oppresses the people of Asia."[30] This attitude on the part of the critics bears witness to the fact that the duties imposed on poets by the present situation in Iran still often go beyond mere literary and aesthetic considerations. The second novel by Ādamiyyat, *Fārs u jang-i baynaʾl-milal*, 'Fars and the First World War', takes place during the First World War and exhibits the same ideas.

Pahlavān-i Zand, 'The Hero of the Zands', by Shīrāz-pūr Partau, also found favour with the critics. It describes the period after the death of the noble regent Karīm-Khān of the house of Zand, when his descendants Jaʿfar and Luṭf-ʿAlī (between 1785 and 1796) strove to follow his example through the enlightenment and justice of their rule over Shiraz. After a short interlude of peace in which Shiraz experienced the beginnings of an economic and cultural revival, the country was attacked by the eunuch Āqā Muḥammad, a member of the Turkish tribe of Qajar. He usurped the throne, persecuted the people with massacres of incredible barbarity and destroyed the cities that dared to come to the help of the beloved ruler Luṭf-ʿAlī. In this book Shīrāz-pūr Partau developed the idea of the struggle between the indigenous population and the foreign elements, the Turkish Qajars, and purposely stressed the idea of a patriotism that was ready to oppose the interference of foreigners in the internal affairs of Iran. We notice this tendency manifested again and again in ever-differing variations in conformity with the changing political situation. The eventful history of Iran, that from ancient times up to the present day has been repeatedly invaded by foreigners, does indeed offer ample evidence of this.

From an artistic viewpoint, the novel *Pahlavān-i Zand* is a good work, written in a lively style. The enthusiasm with which it was received by native critics – even ʿA. Ḥ.

Notes on pp. 416–418

Maykada, in the introduction to the book, is generous in his praise – is evoked by the ideological facets mentioned above rather than by its poetic qualities; a more thorough analysis can be found in Machalski.[31] Shīrāz-pūr Partau also wrote a few novels of a sentimental character, such as *Kū ʿisq-i man*, 'Where is my Love?', *Kām-i shīr*, 'The Revenge of the Lion', *Vīdā* and other tales. Muḥammad ʿAlī Khalīlī, the prose-writer, also composes novels, short stories and reportages. His novel *Dukhtar-i Kūrūsh*, 'The Daughter of Cyrus the Great', is a picture of Achaemenid times, in which the author describes the adventures of the fair heroine of the ancient Persian story on the basis of his knowledge of historical facts. The theme chosen by Khalīlī for a novel dealing with the recent past is worthy of note. Somewhat unusually, it is written in the first person. Its title is *Parīvash yā qiyām-i 1314 dar Khurāsān*, 'Parīvash or The Rising of 1314 in Khurasan'; it describes the reaction of the people in the province of Khurasan to the European innovations introduced by Riḍā-Shāh, often by force (the wearing of European hats, the removal of the veil, etc.). The rising was ruthlessly suppressed and this event gives the author scope for criticism. He accepts only those innovations that are supported and dignified by local tradition.

Several outstanding authors, of whose work we have already made mention, point the new path along which the Persian historical novel was to advance. This course is characterised, first and foremost, by an endeavour to give all-round instruction in historical matters (now it can draw on native studies in the domains of history, archaeology, etc.), by individualisation of stylistic and linguistic expression, and, finally, by emancipation from the often unfavourable influence of A. Dumas *père*. Besides the above-mentioned authors, we may include in this group Ḥ. Masrūr, with a novel which has its setting in Qazvīn under the Safavid Ṭahmāsp, published under the title *Dah nafar Qizil-bāsh*, 'The Ten Qizilbashes', M. Taqī Kardānī, whose novel *Dilīrān-i Khvārazm*, 'The Heroes of Khorezm', deals with the time of the Mongol invasion of Iran, and others.

2. SOCIAL THEMES IN MODERN PROSE

Another prominent group of themes engaging the interest of novelists of the present time are those connected with Iranian society and its problems, seen very often through highly critical eyes. A pioneer in this domain was Muḥammad Masʿūd Dihātī, prose-writer and journalist, whose promising talent was prevented from developing to its full extent by his premature and violent death. His view of Tehran society is of a pessimism that sees no gleam of light or hope. In his first work, *Tafrīḥāt-i shab*, 'Night Entertainments', which came out already in the 1930's, his *dramatis personae* are a group of youths of different occupations (a government clerk, a printer, a shop assistant, etc.), who have no other aim in life than to earn a little money and squander it on amusements of a shady character. They are without moral scruples, cynical and without consideration for others – for them the dividing line between good and evil is lost.[32] The social undercurrent of the novel is a bitter accusation of a society unable to give young people either a solid education or the prospect of a happy life. In his two later novels, Masʿūd does not change his view. *Ashraf-i makhlūqāt*, 'The Noblest Creation', is the ironical title of a work whose rough invective is directed against the whole race of women, as being one of the chief causes of the unhappy state of modern society. *Dar talāsh-i maʿāyish*, 'Seeking a Livelihood', shows the tragedy of young people whom society is unable to provide with suitable employment.[33] Of Masʿūd's last work, a critical picture of Iranian life under Riḍā-Shāh, planned to comprise several volumes, only the first was published, its title being *Gulhā-i ki dar jahannam mīrūyand*, 'Flowers of Hell', as in 1948 the author fell a victim to assassination. M. Masʿūd has sometimes been compared to Zola for his sharp criticism of social evils.[34] In my opinion, however, he lacks the rationalist objectivity, the unbiased view, so characteristic of the French novelist.

A tendency to an unadorned naturalism is apparent in the prose of Abu'l-Qāsim Partav-i Aʿẓam. In his novel *Kāj-i kaj*, 'The Crooked Pine', he draws a sharply delineated portrait of the hero, an old hypocritical Mulla, whose twisted character is projected against the critically observed life of the holy city of Mashhad. Another of the author's works, *Mardī ki rafīq-i Asrāʾīl shud*, 'The Man Who Was Asrael's Friend', is a naturalistic picture of the Iranian countryside at a time when the demoralising influence of the city was beginning to reach it. In conformity with the general trend of Iranian prose, in the work of Partav-i Aʿẓam too the short stories and sketches stand artistically higher. Meanwhile he has collected them in the book *Ādamhā-i mā*, 'Our People'. Partav also made an excursion into Iranian history in the tragedy *Bābak*. From the point of view of literary history, his pamphlet on Ṣādiq Hidāyat, entitled *Sāda*, 'The Simpleton', is not without interest.

An analyst of the emotional life of the Iranian woman of higher society might serve as a description of the novelist Muḥammad Ḥijāzī. The main core of his work comprises three novels, bearing as titles the names of their respective heroines; thus the novel *Humā* is the story of a rich and charming girl, but at the same time an unconcealed defence of europeanising education and feminine emancipation in the form of frequent eulogies on this theme inserted into the plot of the novel. The second novel, *Parīchihr*, is intended to be a psychological analysis of a young marriage relationship, the partners being an adventure-loving and flirtatious woman and a man who endures all her faithlessness and whims with a devotion that is hard to comprehend. The novel is full of pessimism and ends tragically. The third, *Zībā* (1948), is the story of an inexperienced young man of considerable promise whose acquaintance with an attractive but completely amoral and over-experienced young woman helps him to a career, but is at the same time a source of much unpleasantness and personal suffering.[35] This work, too, is permeated by a pessimistic outlook on contemporary society, just as is Ḥijāzī's political comedy, *Maḥmūd Āqā-rā vakīl kunīd!*, 'Make Mr. Mahmud a Deputy!', which gives an unflattering picture of political life.

Notes on pp. 416–418

Muḥammad Ḥijāzī is also a fertile writer of *novella* and the author of numerous short prose pieces in essay style. They have appeared in a number of collections: *Āyīna*, 'The Mirror', *Sāghar*, 'The Chalice', *Āhang*, 'Melody', and others. Ḥijāzī too chooses themes from the life of the lowest social classes, but he still remains the cold observer, the intellectual with an almost scientific interest in the human species, without emotional participation in the fate of his characters and without a real understanding of their world (very different in this respect from Hidāyat).[36] This approach, typical of higher society, undoubtedly contributes not a little to his popularity. Similarly, the author's style, aiming at poetical and witty (in the intellectual sense) expression, with a miniaturist's precision and wealth of detail, is certainly more congenial to readers who cling to tradition than the language of common speech, spiced with folk-idioms, to be found in many modern works.[37] Their point of view is also shared by official circles: in 1957 Ḥijāzī was awarded a State Prize for prose. We come across the view, nevertheless – and a correct one, in my opinion – that the work of Ḥijāzī is so remote from the stream of modern Persian prose that it can exercise no influence on the further development of the latter.[38]

A sensation in literary circles was caused by the appearance of the social novel, *Shauhar-i Āhū-Khānum*, 'Āhū-Khānum's Husband'. The author, an ex-officer, 'Alī Muḥammad Afghānī by name, published it at the end of 1961 at his own expense, and with it made his literary début. A year later the Tehran publishing house, Amīr-i Kabīr, brought out a second edition of this voluminous work of 887 pages – something quite exceptional in the literary life of Iran and itself proof of the stir the novel aroused. The main theme of the work is the situation of woman in contemporary Iranian society as portrayed in the principal characters, the master baker Sayyid Mīrān and his two legitimate wives, Āhū-Khānum and Humā. Together with a number of children, these three form a common household, the complex problems of which are seen by the author in a wider social context that embraces a crowd of subsidiary characters. Many situations in the novel, which seem to us like episodes from the dark Middle Ages, are still quite common in Iranian life, as B. 'Alavī reminds us in his exhaustive review of the book[39]; he has certain justified criticisms to make, especially as regards the technique of its structure and the language. Other critics, however, received this novel with enthusiasm and without serious reservations.[40]

3. THE CHIEF REPRESENTATIVES OF THE SHORT STORY

It has been pointed out above that modern Persian prose has achieved its highest artistic level in the shorter genres, the short story and the *novella*. Among the authors of this order of literature first place must be accorded to Ṣ. Hidāyat, who today may be ranked among the leading figures of world literature. Ṣādiq Hidāyat (b. Feb. 17th, 1903, d. April 4th, 1951) came of an aristocratic family from Tehran, among his ancestors being the celebrated Lālā-bāshī (p. 340). He continued his studies, begun in Tehran, in Belgium and France (Paris and Besançon) from 1926 to 1930, at which time he had not yet decided what vocation to follow; he was attracted by various professions, among them that of dental surgery![41] Finally, however, he decided to devote himself to literature, to which he had felt drawn at an early age. He was prepared for it by extensive reading of his native and of world literature. He acquired a special liking for the outstanding French masters of the *novella*; Stefan Zweig, Chekhov and Dostoyevski were also highly congenial to him, but his greatest favourites were Poe, Maupassant and Kafka. From their works he learnt much that was of value for his art, while they provided him with the inspiration for original work. Yet he never adopted the method of facile imitation. He himself translated several of Kafka's short stories[42] and prefaced his translation of the story *Gurūh-i maḥkūmīn*, 'In the Penal Colony', with a comprehensive Introduction entitled 'Payām-i Kāfkā – Kafka's Message', where he elucidates his view of Franz Kafka's rôle in modern world literature (1327 *sh.*).[43]

Hidāyat wrote his first stories while studying in France; later they appeared in two volumes under the titles *Zinda ba gūr*, 'Buried Alive', and *Si qaṭr-i khūn*, 'Three Drops of Blood'. Belonging to his French period, too, are the historical drama *Parvīn dukhtar-i Sāsān*, 'Parvīn – Daughter of the Sasanians', and several essays of a more or less philosophical character which nevertheless overstepped the limits of belles-lettres (for instance, on the advantages of vegetarianism, a study on Man and Animals, etc.).[44]

After his return from Europe at the beginning of the 'thirties, Hidāyat lived in Tehran and devoted himself mainly to literary work and cultural activities in the circle of his poet friends. (Literature, however, could not provide him with a sufficient livelihood, and so he occupied various unimportant official positions.) He took part in the well-known literary group *Rabʿa*, 'The Four', the three other founding members being M. Farzād, M. Mīnuvī and B. ʿAlavī. Later they were joined by others – writers, artists, theatre people, theorists in the fields of art and literature. Of these, mention must be made of P. N. Khānlarī, who later became chief editor of the periodical *Sukhan* (p. 401), to the founding of which the *Rabʿa* group gave the impulse.

A modern conception of patriotism led Hidāyat to a thorough study of Iranian history. The Sasanian period had such a fascination for him that he mastered Pahlavi and even translated from it into Neo-Persian.[45] (His knowledge of the history, institutions, life and language of this period were a source on which he drew for his fiction, for instance, *Takht-i Abū-Naṣr, Ātash-parast* and other stories.) In the years 1936–7 he carried his studies of Pahlavi and Zoroastrianism still further during his stay among the Parsees of Bombay. Two tales which he composed at this time are inspired by a purely Indian milieu, and even by Hindu philosophy, which is agreeable proof that patriotism and scholarly interests never supplanted in Hidāyat the perceptive and receptive artist.[46]

Another of Hidāyat's pursuits, in which he rose to be an acknowledged authority, was his interest in folklore, which included both the practical and theoretical aspects.

He collected folk-songs, wrote studies on folk-customs, Persian magic, and folklore in general.[47] Connected to a certain extent with his wide knowledge of this subject were his innovations in the field of language. He is a master of modern Persian, and his work is a treasury of expressions, idioms, sayings and turns of speech taken from the folk-vocabulary. It is true that these unusual linguistic elements often make the reading of Hidāyat's works more difficult; for the enriching of modern Persian prose, however, this trait is of outstanding importance; equally so is the influence it exercises on the younger generation of prose-writers.

In his choice of themes too Hidāyat introduces much that is new. For his social material he ventures into the milieu of the dregs of society and among the most untutored people: casual workers, mule-drivers, etc. Kākā Rostam, a cunning and boastful loafer, the pious Ābjī-Khānum, always with an eye to her own interests, the popular hero, Dāsh Ākol, primitive Zarrīn Kolāh, craving for a man who would show his love by beating her, the mule-driver, Gul Babū – a whole gallery of portraits testify to Hidāyat's literary mastery, and also to the fact that, in the milieu he explored, he sought and found not only interesting characters, but living people. And this because he, unlike many other Iranian literati, did not assume the cool aloofness of the intellectual: he knew all the sorrows and joys and hardships of these people down to the smallest detail; he was able to get inside their thoughts and to express them in their language. Not all Hidāyat's *novellae* are set in this milieu: sometimes he lets the wings of his imagination take flight into a world of Poe-like fantasy (yet never denying his Iranian poetic upbringing); at times, again, he makes excursions into the complex psychology of modern people. He describes the problems, tragedies and misery of their lives, into which dark forces inexplicably intrude, he portrays life's unfortunates and life's misfits. He can be realistic and satirical, fantastic and decadent, this "lonely seeker of the meaning of human existence, who tries to discover the nameless absolute, an artist whose endeavour it was to destroy all illusions that people have about their past, their present and their future."[48]

Hidāyat's quest of Man, as is evident from his poetry, was motivated by a much deeper interest than in the case of many of his literary contemporaries. What attracts him is not the newly discovered milieu or the external plot, but people's inner life, psychological stimuli and reactions in their effects on human conduct and complex mutual relations, man's commentary on the experiences of his temporal existence. This personal confession on the meaning of life he seeks both among educated people and among the least cultured; he poses his question not only to present-day man but also to the man of the past and even of the future – and almost always he finds the recurring motif of the vanity of human existence, of its uselessness and absurdity, from which the most certain escape is voluntary death.[49] Nor did the author himself find any other way out; in the spring of 1951 he left his native country for Paris and there, in a hotel room, he committed suicide. He is buried in the Paris cemetery of Père Lachaise.[50]

Saʿīd Nafīsī (1897–1966), university professor of the history of literature, devoted himself first and foremost to scholarly activities (his numerous studies on literary history and the problems of Persian classical poetry are listed in the Bibliography). In the domain of belles-lettres, he figures as a poet, as a translator, and as a very popular writer of prose. Proof are the ever new editions of his novel, *Farangīs*, a love story in the form of letters, inspired by Goethe's *Werther*, and his collection of *novellae* under the title *Sitāragān-i siyāh*, 'Black Stars', with humerous sketches from the life of people whom the changing style of life brings face to face with unexpected situations (for instance, the abolishing of the veil, clean-shaven faces instead of beards, etc.). The most recent collection of prose by this author, entitled *Māh-i Nakhshab*, 'Moon from Nakhshab', contains historical tales, the life-stories of historical personalities living in the first century after the Arab Conquest. Nafīsī, too, initiated the publication of collections of modern Persian short stories; he himself compiled one such anthology[51] and wrote for it a study on Persian literature, seeking among other things to find in the historical development of Persian poetry parallels with the philosophical currents in European literature.

A prose-writer who occasionally approaches Hidāyat's mastery in his social insight is Muḥammad Iʿtimād-zāda, whose *non de plume* is Bihādhīn. He is a native of Rasht. He graduated from the Naval College in France and was formerly a naval officer attached to the Caspian fleet.[52] He made his entry into literature as a story-teller, with a warm interest in ordinary poor folk and their everyday lives. The psychological motivation of his prose works is sometimes forced (as, for instance, in the novel *Dukhtar-i raʿiyyat*), but the motifs of social criticism are presented in a very original and realistic fashion. Artistically valuable, too, is his expressive language, which owes much of its inspiration to the folk-idiom. In philosophical outlook, however, Bihādhīn differs very considerably from his master, Hidāyat. He is no pessimist but believes in Man and in the positive side of human nature, and also in a better future for the lowly and oppressed of whom he writes. In his stories, collected in *Parā-kanda*, 'Pêle-mêle', and *Ba-sūyi mardum*, 'Closer to the People', he often portrays people who realise that they live in the bonds of social, religious or other prejudices and find enough strength of will to throw off these bonds and fight for a better future. Sometimes the author succeeds in achieving a perfect artistic effect, as in the story *Ghurūb-i Ramaḍān*, 'On the Eve of Ramazān', when a young woman, at a time of the greatest anguish, pain and fear, disregards a religious injunction.

The social tendency is also underlined in a novel that Bihādhīn set in the surroundings of Rasht in his native Gilan. The time of the action is the very disturbed period at the beginning of the 1930's, and the title of the novel is *Dukhtar-i raʿiyyat*, 'The Country Girl'. The heroine is a poor girl who grew up in the family of a rich merchant where she was later to be a servant; the more she grows up the more she suffers from the coarse and degrading treatment with which she meets; finally, she is seduced by the son of the house and driven by shame to suicide. On the whole, however, the novel does not reach the artistic level of the author's tales.

Notes on pp. 416–418

Bidādhīn's most recently published work is a slim volume of poetical prose, with the title *Naqsh-i parand*, 'Drawing on Silk'. This little work – quite different from anything he has so far brought out – testifies to its author's creative maturity in its disciplined respect for form and in its individual and manly lyricism, in its view of the world and of people.

Buzurg 'Alavī, who adopted Hidāyat as a model when writing his first stories in prose, followed a directly opposite course of development to that of his friend and master, both as writer and as man. From a pessimistic view, coloured with romantic individualism, he has worked his way to a socialist outlook, from which the optimistic undertone of his later works derives.

'Alavī (b. Feb. 2nd, 1904) studied in Iran and later in Berlin, where he acquired an excellent knowledge of German. This enabled him to translate and recast in Persian verse Schiller's *Maid of Orleans*, Th. Nöldeke's study *Das Iranische Nationalepos*[53], and other works. He made his literary début with a collection of six *novellae*, published under the title *Chamadān*, 'Baggage'. For his stories the author here selects exceptional people, often eccentric in character and in their predilections, and from their lives he weaves plots showing considerable invention and romantic fantasy.[54] Here, too, there is evidence of a deeper interest in Freudian psychoanalysis, as in the tragic relationship between a common servant and a sexually abnormal intellectual, in the story *Sarbāz-i surbī*, 'The Tin Soldier', and in the rivalry of father and son in their love for the same girl in the tale from which the collection takes its title.

As a teacher on the staff of an industrial college in Tehran, 'Alavī's convictions brought him into touch with a group of young socialists, headed by Dr Īrānī. Riḍā's police declared these persons to be dangerous to the State and arrested them in 1937, whereupon they were sentenced to four years' imprisonment, and 'Alavī along with them. His literary output at this time is represented by two works: first *Panjāh u si nafar*, 'Fifty-three People', an autobiographical description of the stories of the 53 members of the socialist group from the time of their arrest, through all the police investigations and imprisonment, to their release following Riḍā's abdication, imbued throughout with a firm belief in the victory of the socialist idea; and then the collection of short stories, *Varaq-pārahā-i zindān*, 'Notes from Prison', artistically worked-out stories of the fates of several of 'Alavī's fellow-prisoners, in which it is possible to observe the author's growth in the transition from the portraying of individual traits to the seizing of typical features of Iranian life.

After the Second World War 'Alavī remained true to his socialist convictions; he worked untiringly in cultural life for an improvement of social conditions, propagated the idea of world peace and international co-operation, contributed to progressive periodicals (p. 401), and translated anew from English (G. B. Shaw) and Russian.[55] As a notable member of the Iranian-Soviet Friendship Society, he made a journey to Soviet Uzbekistan, publishing his impressions and experiences in an optimistic and lightly sketched travel diary, *The Uzbeks*. This was followed shortly afterwards

(1951–2) by another collection of tales, some of which had already appeared in periodicals, more especially in *Mardum* (p. 402), under the title *Nāmahā va dāstānhā-i dīgar*, 'Letters and Other Stories'. For this collection the author was awarded the Gold Medal of the World Peace Council in the autumn of 1953. In it attention is focussed on various aspects of contemporary life in Iran, with a strongly critical bias against bureaucracy, bribery and social injustice.

ʿAlavī shows himself to be a cultivated artist also in his first novel, *Chashmhāyash*, 'Her Eyes'.[56] This is a story of a Persian painter, a convinced socialist and worker in an illegal group, and a young girl from the highest bourgeois circles. Love for the painter and the longing it inspires to get closer to him, brings her among left-wing Persian intellectuals, both at home and in Paris, where she studies. The hero does not trust her love nor her ideological conversion – and this conviction he embodies in a picture in which she is portrayed with a curiously hard expression in her eyes, hence the title of the novel. He is persecuted unceasingly for his political views, thrown into jail and finally meets a tragic end.[57]

In recent years ʿAlavī has lived in Berlin, where he holds a professorship of Persian Language and Literature at the Humboldt University. Besides his educational work he is engaged on research on the problems of Persian literature, especially modern literature and is editor of the German translations of the works of Hidāyat, etc. He writes his new prose-works in German. Thus, his *Kämpfendes Iran* was published in Berlin in 1945. It is a picture of the recent history of Iran in which the author condemns existing conditions with a severity that sometimes borders on lack of objectivity. Altogether delightful is the book *Das Land der Rosen und der Nachtigallen* (Berlin 1957), a shrewdly observed account of the cultural and social life of the Iran of yesterday and today.

Hidāyat's legacy is most consistently inherited by Ṣādiq Chūbak (b. 1918, Bushir). He too began as a writer of short stories, his first collection, *Khayma-i Shab-bāzī*, 'Puppet Theatre', being very favourably received by the literary public; among the critics who expressed their praise was Hidāyat himself. In this first collection Chūbak already showed himself to be an original story-teller with an excellent feeling for his native tongue and a sharp insight into the inner motives of human behaviour, which is somewhat rare in modern Persian literature. Another of Chūbak's works is the book entitled *ʿAntarī ki luṭiyash murda būd*, 'The Monkey Whose Master Died', written in 1327 *sh.* The title tale and the second of the three stories, which bears the title *Qafas*, 'The Cage', are notable too as revealing the author's rare understanding of the world of animals and of their special psychology. Included in the second edition of this collection (Tehran 1341 *sh.*) is Chūbak's one-act satirical play *Tūp-i lāstīkī*, 'The Rubber Ball'. It is a play about the panic of fear with which the family and close circle of friends of a high-ranking official are seized when they mistakenly suppose themselves to be under observation by the State Police. Here the author demonstrates his outstanding mastery of psychological short-circuiting. The above-mentioned edition lists

Notes on pp. 416–418

in the author's bibliography two novels, *Tangsīr* and *Sang-i ṣabūr*. Besides his original work as a writer, Chūbak also translates from English (e.g., the excellent translation of Lewis Carroll's classics *Alice in Wonderland* and *Alice through the Looking-glass*).

Another writer and journalist who has written a widely read book, which has reached many editions, is 'Alī Dashtī. This is an account of his experiences in jail, *Ayyām-i maḥbas*, 'Days in Jail'. The author has, however, gained still greater popularity with a collection of *novellae* bearing the name of one of its heroines, *Fitna*. Here he deals chiefly with the psychological state of mind of Persian women in higher circles, in whom modern education has created inner contradictions and intellectual and emotional demands which their environment can neither resolve nor satisfy. Another of Dashtī's works, *Sāya*, 'The Shadow', is again a collection of tales and essays, which critics rank among the foremost works of contemporary prose, thanks to its modern style and ideas.

Jalāl Āl-i Aḥmad started his literary career with the publication of touching stories about the victims of political persecution, the title being *Az ranjī ki mībarīm*, 'Our Suffering'.[58] Among other good story-tellers, to judge from their contributions to anthologies and periodicals, and in several cases on the basis of work published in book form, are 'Alī Aṣghar Ṣadr Ḥājj Sayyid Jawādī, Jamāl Shahrān, M. N. Khurāzī (under the *nom de plume* of Nūrī), 'Alī Sharī'atmadārī (under the *nom de plume* of Dārvish)[59], Aḥmad Ṣādiq, I. Ṭabarī, M. Ḥamīdī, and the satirist Afrāshta.

In this section on new and recent literary works that have appeared in Iran, certain names have been mentioned, certain evaluations expressed; yet we fully realise that no enumeration is or can be complete and that any evaluation, especially that relating to the younger authors, is only of temporary validity and must depend on the course of their future artistic development. This is true of every literature of whose birth we are witnesses and which has to struggle for a new poetical shaping of reality: what counts today as absolute is tomorrow surpassed or rejected. This is pre-eminently true of Iran, where the last five decades have been an epoch of revolutionary changes reaching to the very core of the social structure and undermining its thousand-year-old traditions in all domains – including those of culture, art and literature. It is a period of struggle, uncertainty and groping, a period of unwearying search and experiment, which bears within it all the negative and positive traits of a period in which "the old is moribund and the new has not yet been born".

Summer 1967

NOTES

1. On the occasion of the sixth anniversary of his death, cf. *Yaghmā*, 1 (1337), 417 *et seq.*
2. Under the title *Nukhustīn kongre-i navīsandagān-i Īrān* (Tehran 1325).
3. Cf. *RK*, 1338, 1–4, Bibliograph. Section *Adabiyyāt-i khārijī.*

4. Cf. *SV*, 6 (1958), 158.
5. On the artistic aspect of the translation, see Rozenfel'd, L. 1958, 77.
6. A good survey of modern prose is compiled by D. S. Komissarov, in *Ocherk sovremennoy persidskoy prosï* (Moscow 1960); original observations on this problem are contained in R. Gelpke's Introduction to the anthology of translation from the modern Persian *novellae*, entitled, *Persische Meistererzähler der Gegenwart* (Zürich 1961), 7–17.
7. Cf. also Nikitine, *OM*, 34 (1954), 225 *et seq.*; Yaukacheva, *KS*, 27 (1958), 42 *et seq.*; Komissarov, *KS*, 17 (1955), 53 *et seq.*, and others.
8. Avery, in *MW*, 45 (1955), 319, is of the opinion that the popularity of short prose forms derives from the traditional *Ḥikāyats*.
9. How shackled native criticism is by this conservatism is shown by Machalski in *Folia Orientalia*, 1 (1959), 66, and 2 (1960), 56–7.
10. *Sukhanvarān...*, 1 (4) *et seq.*
11. *Kongre-i navīsandagān-i Īrān*, 11–39.
12. *Indo-Iranica*, 1951,2, 21.
13. Cf. Rozenfel'd, L. 1958, 75.
14. Cf. Zachoder, *SV*, 1957,1, 3 *et seq.*
15. Cf. 'Dīvān-i Rashīd-i Yāsimī', *Sukhan*, 1337,10, 103.
16. In the Introduction to the anthology, *Sovremennaya persidskaya poeziya*, 14–15, Shoytov too speaks of the realistic poems of Mahdī Ḥamīdī.
17. Cf. *Sukhan*, 1336,7, 607–8.
18. On this see Shafaq, *MEJ*, 1952,6, 417 *et seq.*
19. *Op cit.*, p. 13; for more detailed information on Ṭabarī see Shamukhamedov, *Ekhsan Tabari* (Tashkent 1959).
20. An analysis of Sāya's poetry is given by Klyashtorina, *KS*, 1959,36, 33 *et seq.*
21. Other poets showing a similar trend are listed by Rizayev in his study *Revolyutsionno-demokraticheskaya poeziya Irana.*
22. A. Jannatī 'Aṭā'ī, *Nīmā, Zindagānī va āthār-i ū* (Tehran 1334), 11 *et seq.*; some notes on the poetry of Nīmā Yūshīj are in the article by Komissarov, *SV*, 1958,3, 61 *et seq.*; for an analysis of the work, see F. Machalski, *Folia Orientalia*, 2 (1960), 53–82, and M. Rahman, *Ar. Or.*, 1961, 53–63.
23. Borecký, *MEJ*, 1953,7, 241 makes mention of the prose work of Tavallalī (b. 1917), which is satirical and aphoristic in character; accessible in the collections *At-tafāṣīl*, 'Definitions', and *Kārvān*, 'Caravan' (1952).
24. On this, cf. Law, *Persian Symposium*, 311.
25. On the attitude of Persian intellectuals to European civilization, cf. Nikitine, *Charisteria Orientalia Ioanni Rypka*, 210 *et seq.*
26. An excellent small anthology of the poets of the new style is that compiled by Parvīz Dāryūsh, and published under the title *Numūnahā-i shi'r-i āzād* 'Specimens of Poetry in Free Verse' (Tehran 1340 *sh.*); a contribution to a knowledge of contemporary Persian lyrical poetry of the old and the new style is the Soviet anthology compiled by V. Klyashtorina and Dj. Dorri, *Sovremennaya persidskaya lirika* (Moscow 1961), with an authoritative Introduction by the two authors.
27. *Op. cit.*, 242.
28. A number of other prose-works of a similar literary standard are enumerated by Borecký, *op. cit.*, 242 *et seq.*
29. For more detailed information on Jalālī, see Machalski, *Historyczna powieść*, 93 *et seq.*
30. For an analysis of this novel see Machalski, *Historyczna powieść* p. 136.
31. *Historyczna powieść*, 112 *et seq.*
32. The plot of the novel is summarized by R. Lescot, *BEO*, 1943,9, 95 *et seq.*
33. For Mas'ūd's literary profile, cf. Nikitine, *OM*, 1954,34, 231, 233.

34. Avery, *op. cit.*, 321.
35. Comments on the work of Ḥijāzī occur in the studies of Lescot, *BEO*, 1943,9, 95 *et seq.*; Nikitine, *OM*, 1954,34, 230 *et seq.* Komissarov, *KS*, 1955,17, 56 *et seq.*, and *KS*, 1958,27, 73–81.
36. Komissarov in his monographic article, *KS*, 1958,27, 79, notes in this respect a favourable change in Ḥijāzī's most recent works.
37. Borecký, *op. cit.*, 239, mentions native critical notices which, on account of its style, describe this novel as a truly Persian work; it only remains to add that such a verdict confirms anew the well-known conservatism of Persian literary criticism.
38. Avery, *op. cit.*, 322.
39. *Wissenschaftliche Zeitschrift der Humboldt-Universität Berlin*, 12 (1963), 717–21.
40. M. ʿA. Islāmī Nidūshanī, *Yaghmā*, 14,11, 525; S. Parham, *Rāhnamā-i Kitāb*, 4,10, 970; N. Daryā Bandārī, *Sukhan*, 12,8.
41. For more detailed material on Hidāyat's biography, see especially Monteil, *Sādeq Hidāyat*; Rozenfel'd, *KS*, 1955,17, 66 *et seq.*; Komissarov, Introduction to the Soviet selection from Hidāyat's works; B. Alawi, *Die Prophetentochter* (Berlin 1960), 271–95 and *Hadshi Agha* (Berlin 1963), 149–152, recently, *Modern Persian Prose* (Cambridge 1966), 137–201.
42. *Sukhan*, 1 (1332), 59, 121, 187, 281, 350, etc.
43. Republished in book-form in Tehran 1337; Kafka's translator is Ḥ. Qā'imiān.
44. Republished in *Nuvishtahā-i parākanda-i Ṣādiq Hidāyat* (Tehran 1334 *sh.*), 290–64.
45. *Ibid.*, 436 *et seq.*, 526 *et seq.*
46. Originally written in French under the title *Lunatique et Sampingué,* now published in a Persian translation in the collection of shorter prose works cited above, in note 44, 565–625.
47. For instance the collection of folk-songs entitled *Ausāna*, with a theoretical study, 'Folklor yā Farhang-i tūda – Folklore or Folk Culture', in *Sukhan* 1324,2–4; study of folk-customs, under the title *Nayrangistān*, and others.
48. Monteil, *op. cit.*, 47, note 1.
49. For an analysis of Hidāyat's work, see D. S. Komissarov, *op. cit.*, in Notes 6, 7, 22, 36, 41, pp. 417–8; G. Scarcia, *Annali (Napoli)*, Nuova serie, 1958,9, 103–23; V. Kubíčková, *Charisteria Orientalia Ioanni Rypka* (Praha 1956), 142–8; *Mélanges d'orientalisme (H. Massé)* (Tehran 1963), 198–205, etc.
50. Hidāyat's short stories are accessible in the collections: *Zinda ba gūr*, 'Buried Alive' (1309 *sh.*); *Si qaṭra khūn*, 'Three Drops of Blood' (1332 *sh.*); *ʿAlaviyya Khānum*, 'Madame Alaviyye' (1312 *sh.*); *Sāya-raushan*, 'Twilight' (1312 *sh.*); *Vagh-vagh sāhāb*, 'The Clapper' (1313 *sh.*) (satirical lashes and fables, in collaboration with M. Farzād); *Būf-i-kūr*, 'The Blind Owl' (1315 *sh.*); *Sag-i vilgard*, 'The Stray Dog' (1321); *Vilangārī*, 'Criss-Cross' (1323 *sh.*); *Ḥājjī Āqā* (1324 *sh.*), then the stage play *Parvīn dukhtar-i Sāsān*, 'Parvin, Daughter of the Sasanians' (1309 *sh.*); *Māziyār* (in collaboration with M. Mīnuvī (1312 *sh.*); *Afsāna-i āfarīnish*, 'Legend of the Creation' (1325 *sh.*); other works are contained in the collection cited in note 44 above.
51. The work in question is the anthology *Shāh-kārhā-i nathr-i fārsī-i muʿāṣir* (Tehran 1951).
52. Further material in the biography of Bihādhīn contained in L. Peysikov's Introduction to the Russian translation of his selected short stories, *Uzorī na sholku* (Moscow 1961), 5–11.
53. Published in 1930, in Tehran, with an Introduction by Ṣ. Hidāyat.
54. An exhaustive analysis of *Chamadān* is given by Rypka, *Ar.Or.*, 1935,7, 312 *et seq.*
55. On his translations of Chekhov, see Rozenfel'd, L. 1958, 77.
56. The novel has been translated into Polish by J. Bielawski and F. Machalski, with an Introduction by the latter. Published in Warsaw 1955; into German by H. Melzig (Berlin 1961).
57. Analysis of the work by Shoytov, *KS*, 159, 36, 23.
58. See further Borecký, *op. cit.*, 240 *et seq.*
59. Brief biographical and bibliographical data on the four last-mentioned writers are given by Farīdūn Kār, in his anthology *Shuʿlahā-i Javīd* (Tehran 1336).

FELIX TAUER

PERSIAN LEARNED LITERATURE FROM ITS BEGINNINGS UP TO THE END OF THE 18TH CENTURY

I. INTRODUCTION

The literary history of recent times usually deals only with those realms where artistic creative force comes to the fore, above all poetry, belles-lettres and drama, and thus only turns its attention to works on learned subjects on those rare occasions when, from the point of view of cultural history, these have a special significance for the literary development of a nation. This is perfectly justifiable, because specialised literature dealing with single fields of knowledge, the output of which has latterly increased enormously, can but seldom stand up to judgement by artistic standards. The application of such a criterion is nevertheless unfounded when we are concerned with research into earlier periods of the literature of any nation, because on the one hand artistic qualities cannot be denied to a much larger number of learned scripts than is the case today, and on the other hand erudite literature was then much more important to the general cultural development of the nation concerned than it is now – technical development is not the same thing as culture. This is the aspect from which the learned literature of the Persians must also be seen.

From the point of view of cultural history, Persian learned writing has a peculiar character in that it represents in fact only one component of Islamic erudition. In many ways the latter can be said to form a whole in which the linguistic media of expression, Arabic, Persian and Turkish, intermingle. Quite naturally too, the national characteristics of these three, ethnically different, peoples now and then predominate to a greater or less degree.

The beginnings of Islamic learned literature date from Umayyad times, but it only came into full flower during the first two centuries of the Abbasid age. At that time Arabic was its only medium of expression, and this language was also used by the Iranians, who contributed in no small measure to its development. It was not until the 4th/10th century that, as a result of the political emancipation of the Iranians, their mother-tongue underwent a literary revival and this, as is testified by the earliest creations of poetry and scholarly prose, with a capacity for expression which cannot

Notes on pp. 422–424

be explained without the supposition of a link, barely detectable today, with Pahlavi literature and of a continuous use of Persian during this dark age.

During the nine centuries here depicted, Persian learned literature passed through various momentous revolutions which deeply influenced its potential development as well as the individuality of its style. Being subject to political influences, it followed closely the general development of Islamic culture, which during this long period went through times of rise and fall and on which changing opinions and standards of taste, different methods of working and stylistic idioms all left their mark. All this can be observed in the relevant chapters dealing with separate branches of knowledge, and it would thus be superfluous to discuss it in detail here.

Although Persian has not become an international language of scholars, and scholarly works in Persian never acquired the character and bulk of Arabic writings in the circle of Islamic culture, or of Latin in western Christendom, it has nevertheless occupied a significant place in Islamic erudition and attained very large proportions. As a medium of expression the Persian language also traversed the borders of Persia; to the East it spread as far as India, to the north-east to Central Asia and in the west into the empire of the Seljuqs of Asia Minor and the Ottoman empire. In the west it was a question of a relatively short period, but in the east of many centuries.

In this sketch it has of course only been possible to indicate the most important and most interesting phenomena in the development of the literature on various branches of learning.[1] For the close of my essay I have chosen approximately the year 1800. This I have done for a number of reasons, the main one being that the already mentioned gap between polite literature and specialised learned literature began to manifest itself in Persia too, if not in the 19th then certainly in the course of the first sixty years of the present century.[2]

NOTES

1. When some time ago I was requested by the publisher to write a summary of about 50 pages on Persian learned literature, I was quite unable to imagine how much space a relatively satisfactory description of this subject would encompass. When I began to work on the material assembled from catalogues, bibliographies, histories of literature and various edited works, the number of written pages took on such proportions under my hand that eventually from the compendium, that already covered some 200 pages, I was obliged to make a selection consisting of only about one quarter of the whole, for an extract would merely have given a list of authors and their works. Owing to the limited space at my disposal I moreover had to omit two complete chapters on 'Theology and Theory of Mysticism' and 'Miscellaneous – Music, Weights and Measures, Warfare, Games, Superstitions, Magic, etc. etc.' respectively. Summaries of these two chapters have meanwhile been published in Czech (*Dějiny perské a tádžické literatury*, 2nd ed., Prague 1963, 369–74 and 407–10). Even in the

footnotes I have been able to do no more than refer to other important works dealing with a particular subject and to draw attention to recent publications and editions not mentioned elsewhere. Even so I am by no means certain of not having overlooked other works of importance, the reason being that owing to the present circumstances it has not been possible to obtain much of the necessary literature in Prague, and private travel abroad for purposes of study is practically impossible.

2. The first attempt to describe Persian learned literature was made about sixty years ago by Hermann Ethé in the final chapters of his New Persian Literature in the second volume of the *Grundriss der Iranischen Philologie* (abbr.: *GIPh*) (Strasbourg 1896–1904), 346–368. His work is still of value today, although it dealt disproportionately with the various fields of knowledge. Since then the subject has been included in an integral part of the more comprehensive treatises on Persian literature; or, alternatively, special works, mainly of a more bibliographical character, have been devoted to the separate sciences. Of the first category, the following have been of great value to me: E. G. Browne, *A Literary History of Persia*, I–IV (Cambridge 1902–1924) (abbr.: *LHP*); A. J. Arberry, *Classical Persian Literature* (London 1958) (abbr.: *CPL*); Dhabīḥu'llāh Ṣafā, *Ta'rīkh-i adabiyyāt dar Īrān*, I–III (Tehran 1332 *et seq.*) (abbr.: Ṣafā); Muḥammad Taqī Bahār, *Sabkshināsī*, I–III (Tehran 1321 *et seq.*) (abbr.: *SSH*). E. Sarton, *Introduction to the History of Science* (Baltimore 1927 *et seq.*) (abbr.: Sarton) offers rather less to the literary historian. C. A. Storey, *Persian Literature*, I, II/I (London 1927–1958) (abbr.: *PL*), is a really excellent bibliographic aid. The volumes which have already appeared include the literature of the Koran, historiography and biography, mathematics, astronomy, as well as astrology and geography. Copious additions and amendments: I, 1189–1355; II, IX–L. In view of the close connection with Arabic literature, C. Brockelmann's *Geschichte der Arabischen Litteratur*, 2 volumes, Weimar-Berlin, 1898–1902 and three supplementary volumes, Leiden, 1937–1942 (Abbr.: *GAL*) is very informative. In addition, the relevant articles in the *Encyclopaedia of Islam* (Abbr.: *EI*) and in the *İslâm Ansiklopedisi* (Abbr.: *İA*) should be considered. Of the catalogues of Persian manuscripts, those in Berlin (abbr.: Pertsch), London (British Museum, abbr.: Rieu; India Office, abbr.: *IO*), Oxford (Bodleian L., Additional Persian MSS, abbr.: Beeston), Paris (abbr.: Blochet), Vienna (abbr.: Flügel) and the catalogue of the collection of E. G. Browne (by R. A. Nicholson, abbr.: Browne Cat.) are of value. As far as the separate subjects are concerned, philology is dealt with in Jalālu'd-dīn Humā'ī, 'Dastūr-i zabān-i fārsī', *Lughat-nāma*, 40 (1337), 110–47; H. Blochman, 'Contributions to Persian Lexicography', *Journal of the Asiatic Society of Bengal*, 37 (1868), 1–72 (abbr.: Blochman); de Lagarde, *Persische Studien* (Göttingen 1884) (abbr.: Lagarde); C. Salemann, 'Chronologisches Verzeichnis der Farhange', *Mélanges Asiatiques*, 9 (1880–1888), 505–94 (abbr.: Salemann); further 'Alī Munzavī, *Farhanghā-i 'arabī ba-farsī* (Tehran 1337) (abbr.: Munzavī); Sa'īd Nafīsī, *Qadīmtarīn kutub-i lughat dar Īrān* (*Sharq* 1310–11), 393–405 (abbr.: Nafīsī), and Farhanghā-i fārsī, *Lughat-nāma*, 40 (*Muqaddima*), 1337, 178–86; Shahriyār Naqavī, *Farhangnavīsī-i fārsī dar Hind u Pakistān* (Tehran 1341) (unavailable to me). Important articles on the development of Persian historiography are the following: B. Spuler, 'Die historische Literatur Persiens bis zum 13. Jahrhundert als Spiegel seiner geistigen Entwicklung', *Saeculum*, 8 (1957), 267–84 (abbr.: Spuler) and 'The Evolution of Persian Historiography', in *Historians of the Middle East*, by Lewis-Holt (London 1962), 126–37; Cl. Cahen, 'The Historiography of the Saljuqid Period', *ibid.*, 59–78 (abbr.: Cahen); Ann K. S. Lambton, 'Persian Biographical Literature', *ibid.*, 141–51, and K. Jahn, 'Study on supplementary Persian sources for the Mongol History of Iran', *UAS*, 23 (1963), 197–204. Sayyid 'Alī Riḍā Naqavī's *Tadhkiranavīsī-i fārsī dar Hind u Pākistān* (Tehran 1343) brings a detailed specification of the *tadhkiras* written in India. Persian geographical literature is reviewed by I. Y. Krachkovskiy in 'Arabskaya geograficheskaya literatura', in *Collected Works*, IV (Moscow 1957), 514–46. M. Krause, *Stambuler Handschriften islamischer Mathematiker* (Quellen und Studien zur Geschichte der Mathematik, Astronomie und Physik, Abt. B, 3) (1936), 437–532) is important on the exact sciences. Medical and pharmacological literature is indexed bibliographically in A. Fonahn, *Zur Quellenkunde der persischen Medizin* (Leipzig 1910) (abbr.: Fonahn) and treated by E. Elgood, *A Medical History of Persia and the Eastern Caliphate*

from the Earliest Times until the Year A. D. 1932 (Cambridge 1951) (abbr.: Elgood), by M. Siddiqi, *Studies in Arabic and Persian Medical Literature* (Calcutta 1959), and Maḥmūd Najmābādī, *Ta'rīkh-i ṭibb dar Īrān* (Tehran 1341). – Some information on Persian learned books is to be found in the extensive work *adh-Dharī'a ilā taṣānīf ash-Shī'a* (in Arabic) by Muḥammad Muḥsin Āqā Buzurg aṭ-Ṭihrānī (some of the volumes improved by 'Alī Munzavī), 13 volumes up till now, Najaf 1355–1380/1936–1962. The books are arranged alphabetically according to their titles, the last one being: *Sharḥ qaṣīdat Ibn Sīnā al-'Aynīya.*

II. PHILOSOPHY

In the Islamic world of learning, the concept of philosophy cannot be precisely defined. On the one hand, following the pattern of the ancient Greeks, it embraces mathematics (*riyāḍiyyāt*), natural sciences (*ṭabī'iyyāt*) and even music (*mūsīqī*), besides logic, psychology and metaphysics; on the other hand the metaphysical branch passes unnoticeably into theology, because the Islamic *kalām* played the same sort of rôle as scholasticism in the Christian Middle Ages. According to their character the philosophical subjects are divided into two groups: the theoretical (*naẓarī*), already mentioned, and the practical (*'amalī*), i.e. ethics and politics.[1]

The purely theoretical disciplines are very rarely represented in the philosophical literature written in the Persian language, whereas the practical branch, ethics, occasionally associated with politics, has borne remarkable fruit. The causes of this phenomenon are not difficult to fathom. During the period when scientific works were first written in Persian, the full flowering of Islamic philosophy was already over. The writings of the great Aristotelians of the Islamic countries were therefore composed in Arabic. Even their last representative of any significance in the east, Avicenna, although of Persian origin, wrote very little in Persian. In later times theoretical philosophy was confined almost entirely to logic; compendious works on this subject were very important for the formal education of students of dogmatics and law at the madrasas. Because these studies were among the last into which the Persian language penetrated, it was easier for theologists and jurists to study dialectics also in Arabic and to make use of the compendia written in Arabic, including those by Persians. Occasionally one also finds a Persian commentary or a concise extract of such a work. The only notable books on logic written in Persian were the small *Risāla dar manṭiq*, 'Treatise on Logic', by Ibn Sīnā (d.428/1037)[2] and the more detailed *Asāsu'l-iqtibās dar 'ilm-i manṭiq*, 'The Basis of Acquiring the Science of Logic', by the polymath Naṣīru'd-dīn Ṭūsī (d.672/1274)[3], who also wrote a book, originally in Persian, on metaphysics called *Fuṣūl*, 'Chapters'.[4] Another rather voluminous work is the *Tabṣira*,

Notes on p. 428

'Demonstration', which, among other Arabic and Persian treatises on Logic, was written by 'Umar b. Sahlān Sāvī (Sāvajī), who lived in the 6th/12th century.[5] The *Risāla-i nafs*, 'Treatise on the Soul', by Ibn Sīnā deals with psychology, the Persian adaptation being attributed to the author himself.[6] Furthermore there are old translations of his writings on logic, psychology and metaphysics.

Three distinct types of works devoted to practical philosophy can be distinguished. First, those on ethics in general; second, those concerned with politics, i.e. works in the manner of 'mirrors of princes', designed to present the latter with a picture of the ideal ruler and his officials; and finally, works which unite both types.

The earliest of the general works on ethics, and at the same time one of the best examples of this type of Islamic writing, is the *Akhlāq-i Nāṣirī*, 'The Ethics of Nāṣir', which Naṣīru'd-dīn Ṭūsī wrote for Nāṣiru'd-dīn 'Abdu'r-Raḥīm b. Abī-Manṣūr, the governor of the two last Grand Masters of the Assassins in Kūhistān.[7] The second of the three well-known Persian works on general ethics is *Lavāmi'u'l-ishrāq fī makārimi'l-akhlāq*, 'Rays of Light on Distinguished Character Traits', usually called *Akhlāq-i Jalālī*, 'The Ethics of Jalāl', after its author, Jalālu'd-dīn Muḥammad b. As'ad aṣ-Ṣiddīqī ad-Dauvānī (d. 908/1502–3). His work, dedicated to the Aqqoyunlu Sulṭān Uzun Ḥasan, is strongly influenced by the *Akhlāq-i Nāṣirī*.[8] The last of the three is the *Akhlāq-i Muḥsinī*, 'The Ethics of Muḥsin', by Ḥusayn b. 'Alī Vā'iẓ Kāshifī (d. 910/1504–5). This is called after Abu'l-Muḥsin, one of the sons of the Timurid Ḥusayn-i Bāyqarā, and in forty chapters deals with the various excellent qualities and virtues of Man.[9] Later on several other works of similar content appeared, inspired mainly by the *Akhlāq-i Muḥsinī*.

Interest in ethics for princes goes back to pre-Islamic times in Iran. The earliest works of this type are associated with this tradition and contain, for the most part, the sayings of ancient Persian kings renowned for their wisdom, the Greek philosophers, and the Prophets. Their origin is surrounded by fantastic, highly suspect legend. This type of concoction does not seem ever to have lost its power of attraction, for several new editions of such ostensibly ancient works appeared in India in the 11th/17th century.[10] Among the works written originally in Persian, there are three particularly famous 'Mirrors for Princes' dating from the 5th/11th century. One of these, under the title *at-Tibru'l-masbūk fī naṣīḥati'l-mulūk*, 'Gold poured into a Mould for the Sincere Exhortation of Kings', was written by the renowned theologian Abū-Ḥāmid al-Ghazālī (d. 505/1111). Several manuscripts of this Persian work have survived; there are however many more of its Arabic translation in existence.[11] The second, the *Qābūs-nāma*, 'Book of Qābūs', a manual on ethics for princes, was written in the second half of the 5th/11th century for the edification of his son Gīlānshāh by Kaykā'ūs b. Iskandar, the grandson of the famous poet Shamsu'l-ma'ālī Qābūs b. Vushmgīr, who was murdered in the year 403/1012. In it the author lays down a series of extremely interesting observations, illustrated by examples from the lives of historical personages, on the way of life and duties of rulers and their officials and courtiers, and gives a revealing insight into the disposition and methods of the ruling circles, and particularly into the state of culture at that time.[12] The third work, the *Siyāsat-nāma*, 'The Book of Government', alternatively known as the *Siyaru'l-mulūk*, 'The Qualities of Kings', is supposed to be the result of a competition proclaimed by Malikshāh and won by the author, Malikhshāh's minister Niẓāmu'l-mulk (d. 485/1092). This book, entirely devoted to the art of ruling a great kingdom, contains much historical information and many anecdotes, as well as descriptions of happenings taken from the author's own life, and is written in a lucid, simple style. Only after the murder of the vizier was it finally edited by Muḥammad Maghribī, the copyist of the court chancellery (*nāsikh*), who himself added several chapters.[13] Of a different type is the *Chahār maqāla*, 'The Four Discourses', by the poet Niẓāmī 'Arūḍī, which was written between 550–1/1155–6. He completely disregards the ruler and devotes his attention to the four classes of advisers most necessary to the latter: ministers, poets, astrologers and doctors, giving his opinion on ten eminent representatives of each of these professions. This work contains much biographical, cultural and historical material.[14] The content of the *Dhakhīratu'l-mulūk*, 'The Provision of Kings', is built on a far wider basis and was written by the wandering dervish and Holy One of Kashmir, Sayyid 'Alī b. Shihābu'd-dīn al-Hamadānī (d. 786/1385).[15] In the year 813/1411 Jalālu'd-dīn Zakariyyā' b. Muḥammad al-Qāyinī wrote a book of ethics for kings for the son of Tīmūr, Sulṭān Shāhrukh, based on the commandments of the Koran and on the Tradition, called *Naṣā'iḥ-i Shāhrukhī*, 'Sincere Counsels for Shāhrukh'.[16] Of similar content and written in a strongly orthodox spirit is the *Sulūku'l-mulūk*, 'The Behaviour of Kings', by the historian Faḍlu'llāh b. Rūzbihān Khunjī Iṣfahānī.[17] It was composed at the command of 'Ubaydu'llāh, the nephew of Muḥammad ash-Shaybānī.[18] For the Sulṭān Bābur, or rather for his son Humāyūn, Ikhtiyār al-Ḥusaynī wrote his *Akhlāq-i Humāyūn*, 'The Ethics of Humāyūn', in 912/1506–7, which was a book on ethics for kings based on ancient Arabic writings. Another book of advice for princes, the *Tuḥfa-i Quṭbshāhī*, 'A Present for Quṭbshāh', appeared in India in the 11th/17th century. It was written by 'Alī b. Ṭayfūr al-Bisṭāmī, who dedicated it to the Quṭbshāh Sulṭān 'Abdu'llāh.[19] As a curiosity, though nevertheless characteristic of religious conditions at that time, may be regarded a work called *Ādāb-i salṭanat*, 'The Morals of the Sultanate', written in 1609 by Jerôme Xavier S.J. (d. 1617), the grandson of the sister of St. Francis Xavier and Archbishop-Coadjutor of Cranganore, which was dedicated to the Emperor Jahāngīr.[20] Apart from general ethical writings and advice to princes, works of a miscellaneous character combining both types appeared particularly in India. An example might be *Mau'iẓa-i Jahāngīrī*, 'Admonition for Jahāngīr', which Muḥammad Bāqir wrote in 1021/1612–3 for the same Jahāngīr.[21]

A good deal of moral exhortation is contained in many biographies, as also in collections of stories in the manner of Sa'dī's *Gulistān*. This will be discussed in the chapters on biography and belles-lettres.

Notes on p. 428

NOTES

1. Cf. *LHP*, IV, 423–7.
2. *Jashn-nāma-i Ibn-i Sīnā* (Tehran 1331), I, 61. – See *İA*, *s.v.* 'İbn Sînâ'.
3. Ed. by M. Taqī Mudarris Riḍavī (Tehran 1326). – M. Taqī Dānish-Pazhūh, 'Payvastagī-i manṭiq u riyāḍī nazd-i Khvāja Ṭūsī', *Yādnāma-i Khvāja Naṣīr*, I (Tehran 1336), 166–75.
4. *GAL*, I, 509; S. I, 927. Ed. by M. Taqī Dānish-Pazhūh (Tehran 1335).
5. *GAL*, S. I, 830. Ed. by M. Taqī Dānish-Pazhūh, *Tabṣira u du risāla-i dīgar dar manṭiq* (Tehran 1337).
6. *Jashn-nāma-i Ibn-i Sīnā* (Tehran 1331), I, 60. Ed. by Maḥmūd Shihābī (Tehran 1315), and Dr. Mūsā 'Amīd (Tehran 1331).
7. *GIPh*, II, 348–9. *CPL*, 254, 256–7. *GAL*, S. I, 928 footnote. Ed. by M. Taqī Dānish-Pazhūh, *Akhlāq-i muḥtashamī u si risāla-i dīgar* (Tehran 1339). *The Nasirean Ethics*. Transl. by G. M. Wickens (London 1964). – Concerning Ṭūsī see M. Taqī Riḍavī, *Aḥvāl u āthār-i Khvāja Naṣīr-i Ṭūsī* (Tehran 1334).
8. *GIPh*, II, 348–9. *CPL*, 396–8, 401–2, 457. *EI*, *s.v.* 'al-Dawwānī'. *İA*, *s.v.* 'Devvânî'.
9. *GIPh*, II, 349. *CPL*, 401–2. *EI*, *s.v.* 'Kāshifī'.
10. *GIPh*, II, 346–7.
11. *GAL*, I, 423; S. I, 750. Ed. by Jalāl Humā'ī (Tehran 1315–7). Transl. by F. R. C. Ragley (1964).
12. *GIPh*, II, 347, 349. Ed. by Munshī Khalīlu'r-Raḥmān (Bombay 1916), Sa'īd Nafīsī, 2nd ed. (Tehran 1343), Amīn 'Abdu'l-Majīd Badavī (Tehran 1342), and R. Levy (London 1951). English translation by M. A. Shaikh (Bombay 1910), by P. B. Vachba (Bombay 1916), and R. Levy (London 1951), Russian translation by Jevg. E. Bertel's (Moscow 1958). – 'Abdu'l-Majīd Badavī, *Qābūs-nāma u baḥthī dar bāra-i Qābūs-nāma* (Tehran 1334–5). Mujtabā Mīnuvī, 'Kapūs-nāma-i Fray. Tamrīnī dar fann-i tazvīrshināsī', *Yaghmā*, 9 (1335), 448–65, 481–93. R. N. Frye, 'The Andarz Nāme of Kāyūs b. Iskandar b. Kāpūs b. Vušmgīr', *Serta Cantabrigiensia*, 1954, 7–21. R. N. Frye, 'The manuscript of the Andarznāme in New Persian', *JAOS*, 1955, 24–6. 'Abdu'l-Majīd Amīn Badavī, 'Qābūs-nāma', *Mardumshināsī*, 3 (1338), 106–18. 'Alī Aṣghar Ḥikmat, 'Qābūs-nāma', *Ta'līm u tarbiyat*, 2 (1305), 355–66. Parvīz Nātil Khānlarī, 'Andarz-nāma-i Kāyūs', *Sukhan*, 7 (1335–6), 336–40. M. Mu'īn, "Ibāratī az Qābūs-nāma', *Yaghmā*, I (1327), 180–5. M. Minovi, 'Qābūs-nāma'nin yeni nüshası hakkında', *ŞM*, 2 (1958), 105–30.
13. *GIPh*, II, 347–9. *EI*, *s.v.* 'Niẓām-al-Mulk'. *İA* *s.v.* 'Niẓâm-ül-mülk'. Ed. by 'Abdu'r-Raḥīm Khalkhālī (Tehran 1310), by Murtaḍā Chahārdihī (Tehran 1334), and by H. Darke (Tehran 1341). English transl. by H. Darke (London 1960), German transl. by K. E. Schabinger (München 1960), Turkish transl. by M. Şerif Çavdaroğlu (İstanbul 1954), Russian transl. by B. N. Zachoder (Moscow 1949). – Faiz Ul-Hasan Faizi, 'A Peep into Wasaya and Siyasat-Nama of Nizam ul-mulk', *Islamic Culture*, 20 (1946), 351–407.
14. *EI*, *s.v.* 'Niẓāmī 'Arūḍī'; *SSH*, II, 297–318; Spuler 279–80. Reprint of M. Qazvīnī's edition in *Gāh-nāma* (Tehran 1311), rev. text by M. Mu'īn (Tehran 1334; 6th ed. 1341). Russian translation by S. I. Bayevskiy and A. N. Vorozheykinova (Moscow 1964).
15. *GIPh*, II, 349–50. Rieu 447 – 'Alī Aṣghar Ḥikmat, 'Dhakhīratu'l-mulūk az nafā'is-i āthār-i manthūr-i fārsī dar qarn-i hashtum', *Yaghmā*, 4 (1330), 241–9.
16. Flügel, Nr. 1858.
17. See p. 445.
18. *GIPh*, II, 350. Rieu 448. – M. Amīn Khunjī, 'Faḍlu'llāh b. Rūzbihān Khunjī', *FIZ*, 4 (1335), 173–84.
19. *GIPh*, II, 350.
20. *PL*, I, 163.
21. *GIPh*, II, 351. *IO*, Nr. 2205.

III. PHILOLOGY

(Including the Theory of Style and Epistolography)

It is indeed remarkable that although it was the Persian Sībavayhi who created the Arabic system of grammar and that later on important works on this subject flowed from the pens of learned men of Persian origin, the Iranians left the field of the grammatical treatment of their own language almost untouched. It cannot of course be denied that the extremely simple grammatical structure of Persian contributed to this and that an impressive system could not be developed on the basis of Aristotelian dialectics, as was possible in Arabic, and that it was just these facts that forced Persian philologists to turn their attention to other branches of their subject, namely to lexicography, the theory of style, poetics and epistolography, which they studied far more zealously than did the Arabs. In the preface or epilogue to their dictionaries the philologists thus usually found an opportunity to deal shortly with the grammatical rules of Persian, the arrangement of which is certainly very confused and the conception often seemingly very odd, and this they apparently considered to be sufficient.

Independent works on grammar are limited to small treatises of a few pages on single grammatical problems, and here too the lexical tendency is more evident. It is only in the second half of the 12th/18th century that a Persian grammar appears, viz. the *Mīzān-i fārsī*, 'The Scales of Persian', by Jamālu'd-dīn Ḥusayn b. Nūru'llāh al-Mar'ashī ash-Shushtarī[1] and the *Qavā'id-i fārsī*, 'The Rules of Persian', by Raushan 'Alī Anṣārī of Jaunpūr (d. 1225/1810).[2] In the same way, grammars of foreign languages written in Persian are also comparatively rare. Even for Arabic there are only very small summaries, such as the much used *Ṣarf-i Mīr*, 'Mīr's Inflection', by Mīr Sayyid Sharīf Jurjānī (d. 816/1413–4)[3] or the *Zubdatu'ṣ-ṣarf*, 'The Cream of Inflection', by Ẓāhir b. Maḥmūd al-'Alavī.[4] The *Mabānī'l-lughāt*, 'The Foundations of Language', an Eastern Turkish grammar book written by Mahdī Khān Astarābādī in the 12th/18th century is worth mentioning.[5]

As regards lexicography, little was produced actually on Persian soil; the many valuable dictionaries that do exist originated in India. In earlier times the compilation of dictionaries seems to have been mainly dear to the hearts of poets. The oldest known dictionary, at least by name, was one compiled by the poet Abū-Ḥafṣ Sughdī, who lived most probably in the 3rd/9th century.[6] This was not an extensive work but was still accessible to Indian philologists in the 11th/17th century. The only dictionary to have survived is the *Lughat-i Furs*, 'Dictionary of the Persians', by Asadī.[7] An imitation of the Arabic dictionary by al-Jauharī called *Ṣiḥāḥu'l-Furs*, 'Correct Expressions of the Persians', was compiled in 728/1327–8 by Shamsu'd-dīn Muḥammad b. Fakhru'd-dīn Hindūshāh Nakhjuvānī, known as Shams-i Munshī, who was later secretary to the Jalā'irid Sulṭān Shaykh Uvays.[8] The last dictionary compiled in Persia, and at the same time the most important of all, is the *Majma'u'l-Furs*, 'Collection of the Words of the Persians', usually known as *Farhang-i Surūrī*, 'Dictionary of Surūrī', after the pseudonym of the author Muḥammad Qāsim b. Ḥājjī Muḥammad of Kāshān. Surūrī, the son of a shoemaker, displayed a phenomenal memory and was said to know by heart over 30,000 verses. After a long study of Persian literature, he chose sixty prominent works on different subjects and codified their vocabulary, from which he segregated the common Persian words as well as all the Arabic words. The first edition, in 1008/1599–1600, was dedicated to 'Abbās the Great. When later the *Farhang-i Jahāngīrī* fell into his hands, he produced a second edition (in 1038/1628–9), which included many more words and definitions. The importance of Surūrī's work lies in its containing the Iranian pronunciation of Persian, which shows certain deviations from that used in India and Turkestan.[9]

At an advanced age Surūrī himself went to India, which henceforth became the home of Persian lexicography. This was promoted in particular by the Indian Timurids, and the number of dictionaries produced in that country is so considerable that we can here only mention the most important. Before the Timurids came to power in India, four dictionaries appeared there, written in the course of the 9th/15th and the first half of the 10th/16th century. The earliest of these is the *Adātu'l-fuḍalā'*, 'The Tool of the Excellent', by Qāḍī Khān Badr Muḥammad Dihlavī, known as Dhārvāl, who was living in Dhār, the capital of the Mālvā line of the Ghurid dynasty, at the beginning of the 9th/15th century. It is a book of modest proportions, in the first part describing individual words and in the second their usage, all taken from classical poetry but without quotations.[10] About twice as large is the *Sharaf-nāma-i Ibrāhīmī*, 'Ibrāhīm's Book of Honour', also called *Sharaf-nāma-i Aḥmad-i Munayrī*, 'Aḥmad Munayrī's Book of Honour', compiled by Ibrāhīm Qivām Fārūqī in the second half of the 9th/15th century. This dictionary gives quotations from the poets from Firdausī to Ḥāfiẓ and also from the works of the author.[11] The *Tuḥfatu's-sa'ādat*, 'Gift of Happiness', by Maḥmūd b. Shaykh Ḍiyā'u'd-dīn Muḥammad which was completed in 916/1510 during the reign of Sikandar Lōdī, contains no quotations. In two volumes it records the simple words (*mufradāt*) and then the compound words and modes of speech (*murakkabāt*).[12] The fourth of these dictionaries is the *Mu'ayyidu'l-fuḍalā'*, 'The Helper of the Excellent Ones', by Shaykh Muḥammad b. Shaykh Lād from Dihlī, probably compiled in 925/1519. It cites separately words of Persian, Arabic and Turkish origin and ends with a short grammar of the Persian language.[13] The emperor Akbar seems to have taken a particularly lively interest in the work of compiling dictionaries. Jamālu'd-dīn Ḥusayn Īnjū, a member of an old Shirazian Sayyid family, came to Akbar's court from Persia and held high offices in his new homeland. He had studied Persian poetry since his youth and for thirty years had collected its vocabulary from original texts as well as from dictionaries already in existence. In the year 1005/1596–7 he was commissioned by Akbar to collate all this material in a dictionary. He had not yet finished the work when the emperor died and only in 1032/1623, after frequent revision, did he hand over a finished copy to the latter's successor Jahāngīr, after whom the work was named the *Farhang-i Jahāngīrī*, 'Jahāngīr's Dictionary'. The introduction contains an essay on the Persian language and its dialects, a summary of the grammar and a list of forty-four more ancient dictionaries which he had used in his work. He records all the words of Persian origin and illustrates their meanings by a large number of verses.[14] Two more very important lexicons appeared in the middle of the 11th/17th century. The first is the much-used *Burhān-i qāṭi'*, 'The Decisive Argument', by Muḥammad Ḥusayn b. Khalaf Tabrīzī, produced in 1062/1652 and dedicated to Quṭbshāh 'Abdu'llāh of Gulkunda. The author's aim in this book was to produce a practical dictionary based mainly on the *Farhang-i Jahāngīrī*, but without quotations, and in this he was successful, in view of the favour his book has enjoyed ever since.[15] The second one, completed in 1064/1654, is the equally well-known *Farhang-i Rashīdī*, by 'Abdu'r-Rashīd b. 'Abdu'l-Ghafūr al-Ḥusaynī at-Tattavī, who belonged to a Sayyid family from Medina and is numbered among the great scholars of India. The author says in the Preface, which also offers a short summary of the grammar, that his intention was to produce a new edition of the two older dictionaries, the *Farhang-i Jahāngīrī* and the *Farhang-i Surūrī*, in which he discarded the superfluous verses and non-Persian words and on the other hand tried to give more precise definitions of the words. His work constitutes the first essay of a critical nature in Persian philology.[16] From the beginning of the 12th/18th century onwards Persian lexicography in India took a new turn. Whereas hitherto the authors of dictionaries had always turned their attention exclusively to classical literature and the ancient poets (*al-mutaqaddimūn*), now later, post-classical poetry (*al-muta-'akhkhirūn*), composed in the period that started with the year of Jāmī's death, was included. Both trends are united in the two complementary dictionaries written by the well-known poet Sirāju'd-dīn 'Alī Khān, who used the pseudonym Ārzū (d. 1169/1756). On the one hand there is the *Sirāju'l-lughāt*, 'The Lamp of Words', a kind of critique, copiously illustrated by quotations, of the *Burhān-i qāṭi'* – the serious use of which is inconceivable without the *Sirāj* – in which moreover various items have been corrected in accordance with the *Farhang-i Rashīdī*. This is the last dictionary produced on Indian soil, and entirely devoted to the ancient language, that is worthy of consideration. His second work, in verse, the *Chirāgh-i hidāyat*, 'The Torch of

Notes on pp. 435–437

Leadership', deals with those words and turns of speech used by the more recent poets that had not already been dealt with in the earlier dictionaries.[17] Several decades later came the *Bahār-i 'Ajam*, 'The Springtime of the Persians', by a pupil of 'Alī Khān Ārzū, the Indian Rāy Tēkchand, whose pen-name was Bahār. He started it in the middle of the 12th/18th century and revised it many times up to the year of his death. It is an enormous dictionary, dealing equally with ancient and more recent words and phrases.[18]

Special glossaries relating to well-known works were very popular, such as those to Firdausī's *Shāh-nāma*, Jalālu'd-dīn Rūmī's *Mathnavī*, Sa'dī's *Gulistān* and others, and as regards prose-works mainly to the *History* of Vaṣṣāf, as well as indexes to specialised works on certain branches of knowledge.

The large number of Arabic-Persian dictionaries is not surprising when we consider the importance acquired by Arabic in the whole cultural life of the Moslem Persians. In the 5th/11th century the historian Abu'l-Faḍl Bayhaqī, among others, had already compiled an Arabic-Persian vocabulary.[19] The *Muqaddimatu'l-adab*, 'Introduction to Literature', by Abu'l-Qāsim Maḥmūd b. 'Umar az-Zamakhsharī (d. 538/1143), dedicated to the Khvārizmshāh Atsïz, dates from the 6th/12th century.[20] Better known was the *aṣ-Ṣurāḥ mina'ṣ-Ṣiḥāḥ*, 'Clarity from Correct Words', by Abu'l-Faḍl Muḥammad b. 'Umar, known as Jamālu'l-Qurashī, about whom nothing more is known than that he came from Transoxania. This is an extract from the famous Arabic dictionary *aṣ-Ṣiḥāḥ fi'l-lugha* by al-Jauharī, with the addition of Persian equivalents, and was completed in 681/1282–3.[21] During the first half of the 7th/13th century Abū-Naṣr Farāhī compiled the *Niṣābu'ṣ-ṣibyān*, 'The Capital Stock for Children', an Arabic-Persian vocabulary in verse for use in schools.[22] In India the *Muntakhabu'l-lughāt-i Shāhjahānī*, 'Shāhjahān's Selection of Words', was the one most commonly used and was written by 'Abdu'r-Rashīd at-Tattavī, already mentioned above, in the year 1046/1636. It is commonly called the *Rashīdī-i 'arabī*, as opposed to the *Rashīdī-i pārsī*.[23] The *Tarjumānu'l-Qur'ān*, 'The Interpreter of the Koran', by Abū-'Abdu'llāh al-Ḥusayn b. 'Alī Zauzanī (d. 486/1093), the well-known interpreter of the *Mu'allaqāt*, and another of the same name by 'Alī b. Muḥammad (Mīr Sayyid Sharīf) Jurjānī (d. 816/1413) are special glossaries to the Koran.[24] Mahdī Khān compiled an Eastern Turkish-Persian dictionary called *Sanglākh*, 'Stony Place'.[25]

As we have already noted, a great deal of attention has been devoted since the earliest times to the theory of poetry, versification and rhyme. Two books on the subject which have not survived were already being referred to in the 4th/10th century. At the beginning of the 5th/11th century the poet Abu'l-Ḥasan 'Alī Bahrāmī, panegyrist of Sabuktagīn and Maḥmūd, wrote the *Khujasta-nāma*, 'The Book of Happiness'[26], which has since been lost, further between 481–507/1088–1114 Muḥammad b. 'Umar Rādūyānī wrote the *Tarjumānu'l-balāgha*, 'The Interpreter of Eloquence', which has been preserved and was until recently usually ascribed to the poet Farrukhī.[27] The aim of Rashīdu'd-dīn Vaṭvāṭ, a poet writing in both Persian and Arabic during the second half of the 6th/12th century, was to correct the shortcomings of this script. His *Ḥadā'iqu's-siḥr*, 'The Gardens of Magic', is a standard work on Persian versification, rhyming and the beauties, or flaws, of the poems[28], a new edition having been undertaken in the second half of the 8th/14th century by Sharafu'd-dīn Ḥasan Rāmī for the Jalā'irid Sulṭān Shaykh Uvays and called *Ḥaqā'iqu'l-ḥadā'iq*, 'The Truths of the Gardens'.[29] Even earlier, in the first half of the 7th/13th century, Shamsu'd-dīn Muḥammad b. Qays ar-Rāzī wrote a treatise on poetry in Arabic, which he also produced in Persian under the title *al-Mu'jam fī ma'āyīr ash'āri'l-'Ajam*, 'Enlightening Book on the Tests of Persian Poetry', at the request of the scholars of Shiraz.[30] Naṣīru'd-dīn Ṭūsī is also supposed to have written a *Mi'yāru'l-ash'ār*, 'Touchstone of Poems'.[31] In 745/1344 Shamsu'd-dīn Muḥammad b. Sa'īd-i Fakhr Iṣfahānī, known briefly as Shams-i Fakhrī, wrote the *Mi'yār-i Jamālī*, 'The Touchstone of Jamāl', which he presented to the illustrious Jamālu'd-dīn Shaykh Abū-Isḥāq Īnjū. It is divided into four parts: the first three deal with poetry and prosody while the fourth, by contrast, is a glossary of rare and archaic words with quotations from the poets.[32] At the beginning of the 9th/15th century Vaḥīd Tabrīzī wrote two * treatises on versification, rhyme and poetics for his nephew Ṣafī'u'd-dīn. The first bears the name of *Miftāḥu'l-badā'i'*, 'The Key of Wonders', and the second *Jam'-i mukhtaṣar*, 'Short Summary'.[33] During the second half of the 9th/15th century the poet Jāmī wrote two treatises on our theme.[34] At about the same time, 896/1491, Maulānā Sayfī 'Arūḍī produced the *'Arūḍ-i Sayfī*, 'Sayfī's Versification'[35], and Ḥusayn Vā'iẓ Kāshifī the *Badā'i'u'l-afkār fī ṣanā'i'i'l-ash'ār*, 'The Wonders of Thoughts on the Arts of Poems', which dealt with tropes and figures of speech as well as poetic tricks and faults made in the latter.[36] There are many theoretical treatises on the composition and solution of riddles (*mu'ammā*) and logogriphs (*lughz*). Four such works were written by Jāmī[37], and a most highly valued book, *Risāla fi'l-mu'ammā*, 'Treatise on Riddles', was compiled by the famous riddle-maker Muḥammad Ḥusayn al-Ḥusaynī (d. 904/1499) and later attracted many commentators.[38]

From the earliest times the Persians have taken great pains with the composition of letters and official documents, which were written with the same artistry as so many a piece of learned prose. Their drafting thus became an object of profound study and scholarly treatment. Works on *Inshā'*, or epistolography, are of two types, as were also their prototypes written in Arabic: one being more of a theoretical introduction to good style and the other an actual guide to letter-writing, containing collections of sample letters and deeds; but it is hard to define the exact boundary between the two groups. The samples were either written by the authors themselves merely as models, or, as happened most frequently, were actual letters and official papers written by good stylists, so that these collections have an undeniable value, both as literary documents and as sources of historical information. Of special interest are the collections of letters written by certain outstanding personages.

The earliest work of this sort – one which has not been preserved – is probably the

Notes on pp. 435–437

Zīnatu'l-kuttāb, 'The Ornament of Writers', written by the historian of the Ghaznavid period, Abu'l-Faḍl al-Bayhaqī (d. 470/1077).[39] We possess two extremely important collections of letters and documents from the 6th/12th century. One is the *'Atabatu'l-kataba*, 'The Writers' Threshold', by Muntajabu'd-dīn Badī' al-Kātib al-Juvaynī, who was Munshī to the Seljuq Sulṭān Sanjar and director of his chancellery.[40] The second is the *at-Tavassul ila't-tarassul*, 'Introduction to the Art of Letter-Writing', containing documents dating from the years 578–9/1182–4 and composed by Bahā'u'd-dīn Muḥammad al-Baghdādī.[41] Of a different kind are old collections of letters by prominent people such as al-Ghazālī[42], Naṣīru'd-dīn Ṭūsī[43] and the vizier Rashīdu'd-dīn.[44] The *I'jāz-i Khusravī*, 'The Miracle of Khusrau', written in 719/1319 by the Indian poet Amīr Khusrau, is more concerned with theory, and among other official and private letters it also contains some by the author.[45] In the middle of the 8th/14th century Muḥammad b. Hindūshāh Nakhjuvānī, who has already been mentioned, wrote the *Dastūru'l-kātib fī ta'yīni'l-marātib*, 'A Canon for the Clerk on the Appointing of Ranks'. This collection offers basic instruction on state and cultural relations in the time of the Mongols, containing as it does a very varied selection from letters of different social classes and official documents of all kinds.[46] From the 9th/15th century onwards the stream of sample collections begins to flow in abundance though among these the number of predominantly theoretical works written intentionally as such is slight. We have many more works on Inshā in Iran dating from Timurid times. There are the collections of the historians Sharafu'd-dīn 'Alī Yazdī[47], Mu'īnu'd-dīn Isfizārī[48] and of the poet Jāmī.[49] Ḥusayn Vā'iẓ Kāshifī edited two books of this type at the beginning of the 10th/16th century.[50] At the same time there appeared the *Sharaf-nāma*, 'The Book of Honour', by 'Abdu'llāh b. Muḥammad Marvārīd, a collection of official papers of particular importance as a source of historical information[51], and the *Nāma-i nāmī*, 'The Renowned Book', by the historian Khvāndamīr[52], which bears rather the character of a guide to letter-writing.[53] A few years later came the *Badī'u'l-inshā'*, 'The Wonderful Art of Letter-Writing', by the Munshī of the Emperor Humāyūn, Maulānā Yūsufī, which enjoyed great popularity.[54] A valuable collection of letters and documents, drafted on behalf of the emperor and addressed to various dignitaries by the famous minister and historiographer of Akbar, Abu'l-Faḍl 'Allāmī[55], was made by his nephew 'Abdu'ṣ-Ṣamad after the latter's assassination and published in 1015/1606–7 under the title *Mukātabāt-i 'Allāmī*, ''Allāmī's Correspondence'.[56] The *Inshā'-i Harkarn*, 'Harkarn's Art of Letter-Writing', written by Harkarn b. Mathurādā Kanbū of Multān, originated about the same time and became a formal book of instruction on letter-writing in India.[57] We have a great many similar collections from the time of 'Ālamgīr. Among the collections originating in Iran in the 11th/17th century, there are two of particular importance from the time of 'Abbās II. One is by the poet and historian Ṭāhir Vaḥīd Qazvīnī[58], the other by Abu'l-Qāsim Ḥaydar Īvāghlī[59], who was executed in the year 1075/1664–5. The best known collection of the 12th/18th century is that of Mahdī Khān.[60]

NOTES

1. Pertsch, Nr. 106.
2. *IO*, Nr. 2520–1.
3. *IO*, Nr. 2406–9. Pertsch, Nr. 108. Many lithographs.
4. *IO*, Nr. 2420.
5. *EI*, *s.v.* 'Mahdī Khān'. *İA*, *s.v.* 'Mehdî Han'. *The Mabáni'l-lughat being a Grammar of the Turki Language in Persian.* Ed. by E. Denison Ross (Calcutta 1910). – A. N. Samoylovich, *Persidskiy turkolog XVIII v. Mirza Mekhdi-Chan* (Izv. Obshch. obsledovaniye i izucheniya Azerb., Nr. v) (Baku 1927). J. Eckmann, 'Mirza Mehdis Darstellung der tschagataischen Sprache', *Anal. Or.* (Budapest), 1942–7, 157–222. K. H. Menges, 'Das Čagataische in der persischen Darstellung von Mīrzā Mahdī Xān', *Ak. der W. und der L. Mainz. Abh. der Geistes- und Sozialw. Kl.*, 1956,9, 623–730.
6. Blochmann, 4. Salemann, 506. Nafīsī, 395–8.
7. Blochmann, 4. Lagarde 38–40. Salemann, 507. Nafīsī, 401–5. *EI*, *s.v.* 'Asadī'. Ed. by 'Abbās Iqbāl (Tehran 1319), and M. Dabīr Siyāqī (Tehran 1336). Ṣādiq Kiyā, 'Kuhnatarīn dastnavīs-i Lughat-i Furs', *MDAT*, 3 (1335), 1–9. Sa'īd Nafīsī, 'Lughat-i Furs-i Asadī', *Lughat-nāma*, 40 (*Muqaddima*) (1337), 186. Ṣādiq Hidāyat, 'Dar pīrāmūn-i Lughat-i Furs-i Asadī', *Mūsīqī*, 2 (1319), 31–5.
8. Lagarde, 44–5. Salemann, 510. Ed. by 'Abdu'l-'Alī Ṭā'atī (Tehran 1341). – 'Abdu'l-'Alī Ṭā'atī, 'Ṣiḥāḥu'l-Furs', *Lughat-nāma*, 40 (*Muqaddima*) (1337), 187–8.
9. Blochmann, 12, 16–8. Lagarde, 50. Rieu, 498–9. Ed. by M. Dabīr Siyāqī (Tehran 1338–1341). – 'Alī Aṣghar Ḥikmat, 'Majma'u'l-Furs-i Surūrī-i Kāshānī', *Lughat-nāma*, 40 (*Muqaddima*) (1337), 198–9.
10. Blochmann, 7. Lagarde, 15–6. Salemann, 513.
11. Blochmann, 7–9. Lagarde, 43–4. Salemann, 514.
12. Lagarde, 28–9. Salemann, 520. S. I. Bayevskiy, 'Redkaya rukopis persidskogo tolkovogo slovarya "Tuhfat as-saadat"', *KS*, 67 (1963), 160–3. S. I. Bayevskiy, 'Rukopis rannego persidskogo tolkovogo slovarya "Tuhfat as-sa'adat"', *Iranskaya Filologiya*, 1964, 144–8.
13. Blochmann, 9. Lagarde, 55–6. Salemann, 522.
14. Blochmann, 65–70. Lagarde, 45–9. Salemann, 537–41. (Lith. Lucknow 1293). 'Alī Aṣghar Ḥikmat, 'Farhang-i Jahāngīrī', *Lughat-nāma*, 40 (*Muqaddima*) (1337), 196–7.
15. Blochmann, 18–20. Lagarde, 24–6. Salemann, 546. Ed. M. Mu'īn (Tehran 1330–42), and M. 'Abbāsī (Tehran 1336). – 'Alī Aṣghar Ḥikmat, 'Burhān-i qāṭi'', *Lughat-nāma*, 40 (*Muqaddima*) (1337), 199–217, and 'Sīsadumīn sāl-i ta'līf-i kitāb-i Burhān-i qāṭi'', *Nāma-i Farhangistān*, 3 (1324), 1–24.
16. Blochmann, 20–4. Lagarde, 49–50. Salemann, 546. Ed. M. 'Abbāsī (Tehran 1337). – M. 'Ali Dā'i'l-islām, 'Farhang-i Rashīdī', *Lughat-nāma*, 40 (*Muqaddima*) (1337), 218–9.
17. Blochmann, 25–8. Lagarde, 33–6. Salemann, 556. *Chirāgh-i hidāyat*, ed. by M. Dabīr Siyāqī (Tehran 1338).
18. Blochmann, 12–5, 28–30. Lagarde, 26–7. Salemann, 559.
19. Munzavī, 7–8. Sa'īd Nafīsī, *Āthār-i gum shuda-i Abu'l-Faḍl-i Bayhaqī* (Tehran 1315).
20. *GAL*, I, 291–2; S. I, 511. Munzavī, 40–7. Ed. by Maḥmūd Kāẓim Imām I (Tehran 1342). *Horezmce Tercümeli Muqaddimat al-adab* [Khorezmian Glossary of the Muqaddimat al-adab]. Ed. (facs.) by Zeki Velidi Togan (İstanbul 1951).
21. *GAL*, I, 128; S. I, 196. Munzavī, 142–9.
22. *GAL*, II, 193; S. II, 258. *EI*, *s.v.* 'Farāhī'. Munzavī, 84–121. Ed. by 'Abdu'sh-Shakūr Tabrīzī (Berlin 1341/1922). – M. Ibrāhīm Khalīl, 'Abū Naṣr Farāhī', *Āriyānā*, 13 (1333–4), 21–6. 'Abbās Iqbāl, 'Kitāb-i Niṣābu'ṣ-ṣibyān', *Āmūzish u parvarish*, 9 (1318), 16–9. M. Nakhjuvānī, 'Niṣābu'ṣ-ṣibyān', *Yaghmā*, 10 (1336), 218–20.
23. *GAL*, S. II, 598. Munzavī, 221–5.

24. Concerning Zauzanī see *GAL*, I, 288. Munzavī, 16–8. His *Kitābu'l-maṣādir* 'The Book of Infinitives', was edited by Taqī Bīnish (Mashhad 1340). Concerning Jurjānī's work see Munzavī, 171–4. Ed. by M. Dabīr Siyāqī (Tehran 1333).

25. See p. 429. *A Persian Guide to the Turkish Language. Facsimile text with Introduction and Indices* by Sir Gerard Clauson (London 1960). – J. Eckmann, 'Mirza Mehdi'nin "Senglâh" adlĭ Çagatayca sözlüğü', in *VIII. Türk Dil Kurultayĭnda okunan Bilimsel Bildiriler, 1957* (Ankara 1960), 37–40.

26. *GIPh*, II, 226, 343.

27. *GIPh*, II, 343. Ed. by Ahmed Ateş (İstanbul 1949). – A. Ateş, 'Dar ḥaqq-i matn-i Tarjumānu'l-balāgha', *Yaghmā*, 3 (1329), 67–9. A. Ateş, 'Dar ḥaqq-i matn-i Tarjumānu'l-balāgha', *Dānish*, I (1328), 582–4. A. Ateş, 'Muqaddima bar Tarjumānu'l-balāgha', *Dānish*, I (1328), 279–86. 'Abdu'l-Ḥayy Ḥabībī, 'Tarjumānu'l-balāgha va kashf-i ma'khadh-i Vaṭvāṭ', *Āriyāna*, 8,2 (1328–9), 1–14; 8,3, 1–11.

28. *GIPh*, II, 225. Ed. by 'Abbās Iqbāl (Tehran 1308), and (with the *dīvān*) by Sa'īd Nafīsī (Tehran 1339). *Nāmahā-i Rashīdu'd-dīn Vaṭvāṭ*, ed. Qāsim Tuysarkānī (Tehran 1338). – 'Abbās Iqbāl, 'Sharḥ-i ḥāl-i Rashīd-i Vaṭvāṭ', *Armaghān*, 11 (1308), 398–400, 453–62, 518–26, 600–8, 690–703, 724–5, 820–33. 'Abbās Iqbāl, 'Abkaru'l-afkār-i Rashīdu'd-dīn-i Vaṭvāṭ', *Yādgār*, 4-1/2 (1326–7), 43–54. 'Yak risāla dar 'arūḍ ta'līf-i Rashīdu'd-dīn-i Vaṭvāṭ', ed. 'Abbās Iqbāl, *Yādgār*, 1,10 (1323–4), 67–71.

29. *GIPh*, II, 343. Ed. by Sayyid N. Kāẓim Imām (Tehran 1341).

30. *CPL*, 242–4, 455. Ed. by M. Qazvīnī and M. Taqī Mudarris Raḍavī (Tehran, 4th ed., 1342).

31. *GIPh*, II, 344–5. Lith. (Tehran 1325; Lucknow 1927).

32. Lagarde, 62. Salemann, 417–505. *LHP*, 358–9. *EI*, *s.v.* 'Fakhrī'. Ṣādiq Kiyā, 'Mi'yār-i Jamālī', *Lughat-nāma*, 40 (*Muqaddima*) (1337), 189–95. *Vazha-nāma-i fārsī. Bakhsh-i chahārum-i Mi'yār-i Jamālī*. Ed. Ṣādiq Kiyā (Tehran 1337).

33. *GIPh*, II, 344. Vakhid Tabrīzī. *Dzham'-i mukhtaṣar. Traktat o poetike. Kriticheskiy tekst, perevod i primechaniya A. B. Bertel'sa* (Moscow 1959).

34. *GIPh*, II, 344–5. 'Alī Aṣghar Ḥikmat, *Jāmī* (Tehran 1320), 162, 166–8.

35. *EI*, *s.v.* 'Saifī'. Rieu, 525–6.

36. *GIPh*, II, 344. See p. 426.

37. 'Alī Aṣghar Ḥikmat, *Jāmī*, 166–8.

38. *GIPh*, II, 345.

39. *PL*, I, 253.

40. *PL*, Nr. 339 (1). Ṣafā, II, 969–72. M. Qazvīnī, "Atabatu'l-kataba', *Bīst maqāla*, 2 (1313), 156–66. M. Qazvīnī, 'Majmū'a-i Munsha'āt-i Muntajabu'd-dīn Badī' Atābak Juvaynī dabīr-i sulṭān Sanjar mausūm ba 'Atabatu'l-kataba', *Yādnāma-i dīnshāh-i īrānī*, 1943, 1–16.

41. *PL*, I, Nr. 339 (2).

42. Ed. by 'Abbās Iqbāl (Tehran 1333). – 'Abbās Iqbāl, 'Majmū'a-i makātīb-i fārsī-i Ghazzālī', *MDAT*, 1,2 (1332), 1–11.

43. *SSH*, III, 163.

44. *HPL*, III, 80–7. Browne Cat. 146–7. *PL*, I, 1230. Vaḥīd Dastgirdī, 'Maktūb(-i Rashīdu'd-dīn Faḍlu'llāh bā muqaddimaī dar aḥvāl-i ū)', *Armaghān*, 6 (1303–4), 241–53. 'Maktūb-i ta'rīkhī(-i Rashīdu'd-dīn Faḍlu'llāh)', *ibid.*, 518–22. 'Makātīb-i tā'rīkhī (ba-qalam-i Khvāja Rashīdu'd-dīn)', *ibid.*, 7 (1304–6), 125–41. 'Makātīb-i ta'rīkhī (-i Khvāja Rashīdu'd-dīn ki ba-farzand-i khvud nigāshta ast)', *ibid.*, 9 (1307), 159–64. 'Maktūb-i ta'rīkhī (Ruq'a ki Khvāja Rashīdu'd-dīn ba-Mavlānā-i Rūm nivishta būdand)', *ibid.*, 22 (1320), 230–1. Mahdī Bayānī, 'Rasā'il-i fārsī-i Rashīdu'd-dīn Faḍlu'llāh', *Mihr*, 8 (1321–2), 549–52. 'Abbās Iqbāl, 'Maktūb-i Khvāja Rashīdu'd-dīn Faḍlu'llāh ba-Ṣadru'd-dīn Muḥammad Turka', *Yādgār*, 1,4 (1323–4), 6–8.

45. *GIPh*, II, 243, 338. Pertsch, Nr. 1055.

46. See p. 430. Flügel, Nr. 244. *Kriticheskiy tekst, predislovie i ukazateli A. A. Ali-zade*, vol. I (Moscow 1964).

47. Browne Cat., 107–9. Pertsch, Nr. 1059.

48. *GIPh*, II, 339. *IO*, Nr. 2041.
49. *GIPh*, II, 339. Flügel, Nr. 285–6. 'Alī Aṣghar Ḥikmat, *Jāmī*, 205–7.
50. *GIPh*, II, 339. See pp. 426 and 433.
51. Ed. and transl. by R. H. Roemer, *Staatsschreiben der Timuridenzeit* (Wiesbaden 1952). A few letters in *Asnād u makātīb-i ta'rīkhī-i Īrān* by 'Abdu'l-Ḥusayn Navā'ī (Tehran 1341). – Īraj Afshār, 'Sharaf-nāma. Inshā'-i Marvārīd', *Mihr*, 8 (1321–2), 640–4.
52. See p. 441.
53. *IO*, Nr. 2055. Blochet, Nr. 2337.
54. *EI*, *s.v.* 'Yūsufī'. Rieu, 529. Pertsch, Nr. 1065.
55. See p. 449.
56. *GIPh*, II, 341, 343. Pertsch, Nr. 1062.
57. *GIPh*, II, 341, 343. *EI*, *s.v.* 'Harkarn'.
58. *PL*, I, 315.
59. *PL*, I, Nr. 394. About fifty letters published by 'Abdu'l-Ḥusayn Navā'ī in *Asnād u makātib-i ta'rīkhī-i Iran* (Tehran 1341).
60. *PL*, I, 322. Lith. (Bombay 1346).

IV. HISTORY AND BIOGRAPHY

Though practised to but a modest extent until the Mongol invasion, historiography has since then become the most exuberant branch of Persian learned literature. The number of historical works is uncommonly large, and even though a high percentage of them are inferior as sources of objective information, there still remain a great number that offer considerable profit to the historian.

Persian historiography developed from the Arabic and during the early years of Islamic learning also made use of the Arabic language. Thus historians of Persian origin, writing in Arabic – aṭ-Ṭabarī, Abū-Ḥanīfa ad-Dīnavarī, Ḥamza al-Iṣfahānī to name only a few – though they were in no way inferior to the native Arab writers, found very little stimulus for their work at home. They were on the contrary obliged to apply the specific method handed down by Islamic tradition, and only in later times, when the Persian language and mentality had won their position in literature, was Persian historiography able to a certain extent to pursue its own course.

As far as the contents are concerned, this very rich branch of literature can be divided into three groups. The first embraces the histories of the world, usually starting with the creation of the world and subsequently describing general history, above all of the Islamic countries. Of these works sometimes only the last part is of any value to historians. In this category there exist lengthy works running to many volumes as well as some very concise summaries. Of far greater importance are the monographs, which are sometimes devoted to certain periods of time, to dynasties or to single historical figures, and sometimes deal with the history of certain countries or cities. The dividing-line between the last two groups cannot of course be drawn exactly, as will subsequently be seen when we consider this division into three groups. In the majority of historical works there is a great deal of biographical material; this is particularly so in the first and third groups, where extensive sections are frequently to be found on the life history of prominent persons, poets, scholars and saints of different eras or countries.

As with most of the other narrative types of Persian learned literature, we find, in respect of the outward form of the histories, works in the simple, strictly objective style of the old Arabic histories standing next to books in which artificiality is carried to its extremes and rhetoric stretched to its uttermost limits. This mode of writing developed gradually from the 7th/13th century and has remained very popular ever since. The poetic treatment of historical material started at about the same time and reached its peak in the 10th/16th century.

The most outstanding work in the first group is also the earliest and best known history in the Persian language. It is the abridged translation of the Arabic chronicle by aṭ-Ṭabarī, which was made in the middle of the 4th/10th century by Abū-ʿAlī Muḥammad b. Muḥammad Balʿamī, vizier to the Samanid Prince Manṣūr I b. Nūḥ, at the latter's command. This translation possesses great significance both as a cultural and philological document as it is one of the oldest prose works in New Persian.[1] About a hundred years later an original text appeared entitled *Zaynu'l-akhbār*, 'The Adorning of History', dedicated by ʿAbdu'l-Ḥayy b. aḍ-Ḍaḥḥāk Gardīzī to the Ghaznavid Sulṭān ʿAbdu'r-Rashīd b. Maḥmūd. It is a short but very valuable general history describing the mythology of ancient Iran, the life of Muḥammad and the history of the Islamic countries with particular reference to Iran up to the year 432/1041.[2] Minhāj b. Sirāj Muḥammad Jūzjānī, who held various offices first in the service of the Ghurid Sulṭāns and later, after the Mongol invasion, of the Mamlūk Sulṭāns of Dihlī, wrote a larger general history during the middle of the 7th/13th century. His *Ṭabaqāt-i Nāṣirī*, 'The Generations of Nāṣir', called after the Sulṭān Nāṣiru'd-dīn Maḥmūd Shāh, deals in 23 chapters (*ṭabaqāt*) with the patriarchs and prophets, the caliphs, the ancient kings of Persia and southern Arabia, the various Moslem dynasties in Iran and India; it ends with a description of the disaster which the Mongol invasion brought upon Islam.[3]

Thus we enter the Mongol period of Iran. After the terrible wounds inflicted on Iran by the ravaging hordes of Chingiz-Khān, to some extent healed by his successor Hulagu, a new epoch of Persian historical writing set in with a new quality of style. This is less noticeable in the general works of history than in the specialised books, which will be dealt with later. The *Jāmiʿu't-tavārīkh*, 'Collector of Chronicles', one of the most important works of the Mongol times, is nevertheless written in a simple fashion. The career of the author, Rashīdu'd-dīn Faḍlu'llāh Ṭabīb, who was first personal physician to the Īlkhān Abaqa and ended his life on the gallows, after having been deposed as vizier in 718/1318, belongs more to political than to literary history.[4] His comprehensive history of the world, which must be regarded as one of the most important accomplishments of oriental chronicling, was originally divided into three parts, but of the third part ('Geography') no manuscript is known. The first contains priceless information about the Turkish and Mongolian races, the history of Chingiz-Khān, his predecessors and successors, particularly of the Persian Īlkhāns up to Ghāzān; the second part, following the contemporary example of Islamic world chronicles, gives the histories of the patriarchs, prophets and kings of ancient Iran, the life of Muḥammad and the history of the caliphs and dynasties that ruled until the Mongol invasion. In addition he included the history of the Chinese, the Jews, the Franks and Indians, with a long section on Buddha.[5] Of the seven extant shorter histories of the world dating from the time of the Īlkhāns and the disintegration of their empire, the *Ta'rīkh-i guzīda*, 'Selected History', has met with particular approval and been widely circulated. The author, Ḥamdu'llāh Mustaufī Qazvīnī, completed this work in 730/1329–30.[6]

Extensive world histories came into being during the reign of Tamerlane's successors. The first is the *Majmaʿu't-tavārīkh*, 'Compendium of History', by ʿAbdu'llāh b. Luṭfu'llāh b. ʿAbdu'r-Rashīd Bihdādīnī (d. 833/1430), who was better known as Ḥāfiẓ-i Abrū. Even before the publication of this history of the world, the author was commissioned by Shāhrukh, the son of Tīmūr, whose court historian he was, to produce a comprehensive historical work, a sort of historical library, the main components of which were to be the three most famous works of Persian historical literature, namely the translation of aṭ-Ṭabarī by Balʿamī, the *Jāmiʿu't-tavārīkh* of Rashīdu'd-dīn and the *Ẓafar-nāma* by Niẓāmu'd-dīn Shāmī.[7] The portions linking up these three works, as well as the additions bringing it up to the year 819/1416, were written by Ḥāfiẓ-i Abrū. This work, the *Majmūʿa*, 'Collected Work', was the outcome of the plan and Ḥāfiẓ-i Abrū's additions are often very important as sources. The above-mentioned *Majmaʿu't-tavārīkh* is divided into four voluminous *Arbāʿ* ('quarters'); of them the first is devoted to the pre-Islamic prophets, the legends and stories of ancient Iran up to the Arab conquest; the second deals with the life of Muḥammad and the history of the Caliphate until the year 656/1258; the third describes the history of Iran during the Seljuq and Mongol periods. The fourth book, which has the independent title *Zubdatu't-tavārīkh-i Bāysunghurī*, 'Bāysunghur's Cream of History', because it was dedicated to Prince Bāysunghur, the son of Shāhrukh, is divided into two parts. The first is in fact a partially amended or supplemented copy of the *Ẓafar-nāma* by Shāmī, to which copies of certain parts of the *Majmūʿa* were added, dealing with the history of Iran during the lifetime of Tīmūr (736–807/1336–1405). All this material is divided up chronologically into separate years. The second part describes the reign of Shāhrukh until the year 830/1427 and forms the third and largest edition of the same material, the first of which (up to 576/1413) exists separately, while the second is really the last part of the *Majmūʿa*[8]. From the time of Shāhrukh we still have several smaller world chronicles, the closing sections of which are valuable as sources. To these belong the chronicle of Muʿīnu'd-dīn Naṭanzī, the second edition of which was dedicated to Shāhrukh in the year 816/1413[9], the *Ta'rīkh-i khayrāt*, 'History of God's Gifts', by Muḥammad b. Faḍlu'llāh Mūsavī[10], the *Ta'rīkh-i anbiyā' va'l-mulūk*, 'History of the Prophets and Kings', by Jaʿfarī b. Muḥammad al-Ḥusaynī[11] and the *Jāmiʿu't-tavārīkh-i Ḥasanī*, 'Ḥasan's Compendium of History', by Ḥasan b. Shihābu'd-dīn Yazdī[12], which was dedicated to prince Ghiyāthu'd-dīn

Abu'l-Muẓaffar Muḥammad b. Bāysunghur. The *Mujmal-i Faṣīḥī*, 'Faṣīḥī's Summary', by Faṣīḥu'd-dīn Aḥmad b. Muḥammad Khvāfī, is a historical vademecum which gives in short sketches the most important historical and biographical dates from Adam until the year 845/1441–2.[13]

After the brilliant period under Shāhrukh, Herat again developed into an important literary centre towards the end of the rule of the Timurids in Iran, when in the year 873/1469 it was seized by Sulṭān Ḥusayn-i Bāyqarā, among whose associates was the learned poet Amīr 'Alīshīr Navā'ī. This period and the protection of 'Alīshīr gave Persian historical literature two comprehensive world histories, which in the succeeding ages outshone all earlier works of this kind and became almost the only sources of information for the Iranians between the 11th/17th and 13th/19th centuries about the history of their country. These two chronicles were the *Rauḍatu'ṣ-ṣafā'*, 'The Garden of Purity', by Muḥammad b. Khāvandshāh, best known as Mīrkhvānd (d. 903/1498), and the *Ḥabību's-siyar*, 'The Friend of Biographies', by his daughter's son Ghiyāthu'd-dīn Muḥammad, known as Khvāndamīr. The first chronicle is composed of seven voluminous sections, the last of which, about the Sulṭān Ḥusayn and his sons, was most probably completed and continued up to the year 929/1522–3 by his grandson only after the author's death.[14] Khvāndamīr was first a favourite of Amīr 'Alīshīr, but later, after the fall of the Persian Timurid dynasty, he, like many of his contemporaries among the Persian scholars and poets, went to India to seek interest in their work among the heirs to the Timurid traditions. He remained in the service of Bābur and Humāyūn until his death, in 941–2/1534–6. His chronicle ends with the year 930/1524.[15]

It is true that numerically the period between the 10th/16th and the 12th/18th century was far richer in world histories than the previous era. Few of these works however rose above the level of mediocrity. During the second half of the 10th/16th century Ḥasan Beg Rūmlū produced a plan for a comprehensive general history. His *Aḥsanu't-tavārīkh*, 'The Most Beautiful History' was to be in twelve volumes, only two of which are known; the others were probably never written. These two are Volume 11, which begins with Shāhrukh's accession to the throne in 807/1405 and ends in 900/1494–5, and Volume 12, which describes the reigns of the first three Safavid shāhs up to the year 985/1577. The latter forms one of the most important sources of information on the first decades of the Safavid dynasty.[16]. A second immense work is the *Khuld-i barīn*, 'The Highest Paradise', completed in 1078/1667–8 by Muḥammad Yūsuf Vālih. In this case too it is doubtful whether the work ever existed in its entirety; fortunately the most important section has survived.[17] The third of these world chronicles, the completion of which is also dubious, is the *Khulāṣatu't-tavārīkh*, 'Quintessence of History', by Qāḍī Aḥmad Ibrāhīmī, the son of Mīr Munshī Sharafu'd-dīn Ḥusayn. The most important part of this work, namely that dealing with the earlier period of the Safavid supremacy, has been preserved.[18]

An extremely large number of general histories appeared during these centuries in

Notes on pp. 455–459

India, only two however are worth mentioning. The first appeared during the second half of the 10th/16th century and is generally known as *Ta'rīkh-i īlchī-i Niẓāmshāhī*, 'The History of the Ambassador of Niẓāmshāh', because it was written by Khvurshāh b. Qubād al-Ḥusaynī, who spent many years at the court of Shāh Ṭahmāsp as the ambassador of Burhān I b. Niẓāmshāh of Aḥmadnagar. He was thus enabled to set down very valuable information on the Safavid and smaller Persian dynasties of this time in a book that covered the years up to 970/1562–3.[19] The second is the *Ta'rīkh-i alfī*, 'The History of the Millenium', which was to have appeared at the command of the Emperor Akbar to celebrate the year 1000 of the Hijra (1591–2). It is a collective work by more than ten authors, among whom Aḥmad Tattavī, Āṣaf Khān Ja'far Beg and 'Abdu'l-Qādir Badā'ūnī wrote the greatest part.[20]

Of far more importance than these general histories, both as sources of information and frequently also as literary documents, are the specialised works.

The lives of Sabuktagīn, founder of the Ghaznavid empire, and of Yamīnud-daula Maḥmūd up to the year 411/1020–1 were recorded in Arabic by their contemporary Abū-Naṣr Muḥammad al-'Utbī in the *al-Kitāb al-Yamīnī*, 'The Book of Yamīn'. The extreme importance of these two men for knowledge concerning the history of Iran gave rise to an old edition of the work in Persian, written at the beginning of the 7th/13th century by Abu'sh-Sharaf Nāṣiḥ b. Ẓafar al-Jarbādhaqānī and known in brief as *Tarjama-i Yamīnī*, 'The Translation of the Yamīnī'.[21] Several decades after the composition of the Arabic work by al-'Utbī, a Persian work appeared on the history of the Ghaznavid Sulṭāns from the pen of Abu'l-Faḍl Muḥammad al-Bayhaqī (d. 470/1077), who was for many years an official at the court chancellery. His work, called *Ta'rīkh-i Āl-i Sabuktagīn*, 'History of the House of Sabuktagīn', or, in brief, *Ta'rīkh-i Bayhaqī*, is, as the author himself stresses, not really a history of the empire, but rather resembles a memoir, mentioning every conceivable kind of activity at court and describing in detail the conditions of government. It was said to be composed of more than thirty volumes, but of these only one part has survived. This deals with the reign of the Sulṭān Mas'ūd from his accession in 421/1030 until Ṣafar 432/October 1040, and is thus generally called *Ta'rīkh-i Mas'ūdī*, 'The History of Mas'ūd'.[22] Of the lost historical works of the Seljuq age, originally written in Persian, only the Arabic versions by 'Imādu'd-dīn al-Kātib al-Iṣfahānī and Muḥammad al-Bundārī have been preserved. This was a kind of memoir called *Futūr zamāni'ṣ-ṣudūr va ṣudūr zamāni'l-futūr*, 'Relaxation of the Time of the Leaders and the Leaders of the Time of Relaxation' by Sharafu'd-dīn Abū Naṣr Anūshirvān b. Khālid al-Kāshānī (d. 532/1138)[23], which dealt in a somewhat tendentious manner with events during the years 464–529/1072–1134. On the other hand we still have the original of the *Rāḥatu'ṣ-ṣudūr va āyatu's-surūr*, 'Recreation of the Breast and Symbol of Joy', written by Abū-Bakr Najmu'd-dīn Muḥammad b. 'Alī ar-Rāvandī, which describes the history of the Seljuq Sulṭāns of Iran and Iraq up to 595/1199 and is based on the lost *Saljuq-nāma* of Ẓahīru'd-dīn Nīshāpūrī.[24]

As soon as the situation had become more or less consolidated after the Mongol invasion and its horrors, the writing of historical works flourished above all other types of literature, for rich material was to be found in the events of the Mongol invasion and the epoch of the Īlkhāns. At the same time not only had the florid style triumphed in historical prose but history had even become a subject for poetic treatment. Even the earliest history of Mongol times, the *Ta'rīkh-i Jahāngushāy*, 'History of the World Conqueror', by 'Alā'u'd-dīn 'Aṭā Malik al-Juvaynī (d. 681/1283), was enveloped in such affected trappings. This extremely important work, completed in 658/1260, relates the history of the Mongols and ends with the campaign of Hulagu against the Assassins in the year 654/1256.[25] Among the historical prose writings of the Mongol period, a work that appeared towards the end of the Īlkhān epoch marks the culmination of such stylistic excesses. This was by Shihābu'd-dīn 'Abdu'llāh Sharaf Shīrāzī, who is better known by his honorary title of Vaṣṣāf (u'l-ḥaḍrat), i.e. the panegryrist (of His Majesty). His history was called *Tajziyatu'l-amṣār u tazjiyatu'l-a'ṣār*, 'The Partition of Places and the Pushing Forward of the Epochs of Time', the punning title sufficiently revealing the nature of his bombastic style. The factual content, although of great value to the historian, is almost lost amongst the rhyming torrent of words, larded with long Arabic quotations as well as with fragments of Arabic and Persian poetry and verses. In five volumes it describes the times of the Īlkhān dynasty up to the year 723/1323.[26] With the death of the last of the Īlkhāns, Abū Sa'īd, in the year 735/1335, the decline of the Persian Mongol empire set in. From the ruins arose several mutually hostile kingdoms, of which the kingdom of the Muẓaffarids in Fars, Kirman and Isfahan and that of the Jalā'irids in Azerbayjan and Mesopotamia were the most important, whilst in Khurasan the Kurtids, who formerly ruled under the dominion of the Īlkhāns, became completely independent. At all three of these courts literary centres were established where, in addition to poetry and the other branches of learned literature, history was also studied. Here we should mention at least two works: the *Ta'rīkh-nāma-i Harāt*, 'Book of the History of Herat', by Sayf b. Muḥammad al-Haravī, which describes the history of the Kurtid dynasty up to the year 721/1321[27], and the *Mavāhib-i ilāhī*, 'The Gifts of God', by Mu'īnu'd-dīn Yazdī (d. 789/1387). The latter is a history of the Muẓaffarid dynasty up to the year 767/1365, written at the request of Shāh Shujā', the greatest ruler of this house, and among the most famous pompously written historical works it is second only to Vaṣṣāf's history of the Īlkhāns.[28] Two monographs on the Muẓaffarids dating from the first half of the 9th/15th century go as far as the fall of the dynasty. One of them, by Ḥāfiẓ-i Abrū, forms part of his *Majmū'a*[29]; the second, by Maḥmūd Kutubī, exists in some manuscripts of Qazvīnī's *Ta'rīkh-i guzīda*.[30]

At the end of the 8th/14th century disintegrated Iran was reunited by Tīmūr. Despite his atrocities, which often equalled those perpetrated by Chingiz-Khān, it cannot be entirely denied that the new invader from the north-east had some feeling for the achievements of culture. Among other things he had a preference for history, and during his campaigns was accompanied by Turkish and Persian scribes, whose duty it was to record every important event. These reports were later revised by practised stylists. Two of these works have survived. One is an account of Tīmūr's Indian campaign by Ghiyāthu'd-dīn 'Alī[31], the second is a much larger historical work by Niẓāmu'd-dīn Shāmī, who in the year 804/1402 received Tīmūr's command to describe his deeds of war, using older material, which in its original form had not found favour with the conqueror, and to do this in such a way that it would be easily understood by any reader and not only by ten out of a hundred. In the year 806/1404 he presented Tīmūr with his version, a work written in a not particularly simple style although the author stated in the Preface that he had tried to use a style such as ordinary people could understand but which would not offend the aesthetic feelings of the educated. This was the first time that the book appeared under the title *Ẓafar-nāma*, 'Book of Victory'.[32] Shāmī's book did not of course cover the period up to the death of Tīmūr, whose son and successor Shāhrukh consequently saw to it that the *Ẓafar-nāma* was continued. Ḥāfiẓ-i Abrū, who wrote a sequel up to the time of Tīmūr's death[33], and Tāj as-Salmānī, whose supplement describes the first four years of Shāhrukh's reign, were commissioned with this work.[34] In 828/1424–5 another work appeared about Tīmūr, also called *Ẓafar-nāma*. This deals not only with the whole life of the Conqueror but also with the fate of his grandson, Prince Khalīl Sulṭān, who as Shāhrukh's rival held sway for some time in certain areas of the kingdom. Shāhrukh's son, Prince Ibrāhīm Sulṭān, the governor of Fars, was interested in historical studies and collected a great deal of original material on Tīmūr's life which he entrusted for revision to Sharafu'd-dīn 'Alī Yazdī, famous on account of the elegance of his style (d. 858/1454). This second *Ẓafar-nāma* far outshone the first, from which it had nevertheless borrowed very liberally. For Sharafu'd-dīn was able to give free rein to his florid imagination and for this very reason his book was sought after, frequently copied and considered as the third of the historical works famous for the affectation of their style. The contents of this book, as of the two earlier ones, are very valuable.[35] The two greatest personalities of Timurid times, the Conqueror himself and his son and successor, Shāhrukh, became the heroes of epic poems, although not until after the decline of the kingdom. 'Abdu'llāh Jāmī, whose pseudonym was Hātifī (d. 927/1521), cousin of the last Persian classicist 'Abdu'r-Raḥmān Jāmī, produced an epic called *Tīmūr-nāma*, 'The Book of Tīmūr' during the reign of Shāh Ismā'īl, which is thought to have taken the place of the traditional *Iskandar-nāma* in the *Khamsa* which he had prepared.[36] The son of Ṭaraghāy was thus placed alongside the greatest conqueror of ancient times. The history of Shāhrukh was transformed into a poetic narrative called *Shāhrukh-nāma*, 'The Book of Shāhrukh', by Muḥammad Qāsim Junābādī, as poet Qāsimī.[37] The life-time of Tīmūr and almost the whole reign of his house in Iran is described in a lengthy work by 'Abdu'r-Razzāq b. Isḥāq Samarqandī (d. 887/1482). It is known as *Maṭla'u's-sa'dayn u majma'u'l-baḥrayn*, 'The Rising of the Two Stars of Fortune and the Confluence of the Two Seas', the two Stars of Fortune and the two Seas representing two rulers of the same name, the last of the Īlkhāns Abū-Saʿīd, with whose accession the book begins, and the authors' patron, the Timurid, Abū-Saʿīd, with whose death it ends. Although up to the year 830/1427 it is simply an extract of Ḥāfiẓ-i Abrū's *Zubdatu't-tavārīkh*, the work was very popular and outshone its source, a fate which befell this book in its turn on the appearance of the works of Mīrkhvānd and Khvāndamīr.[38]

A history of the Aqqoyunlu dynasty from its beginning is the *Kitāb-i Diyārbakrīyya*, 'Book on Diyārbakr's (Dynasty)', by Abū-Bakr-i Ṭihrānī, written in the 'seventies of the 9th/15th century[39], to which the *Ta'rīkh-i ʿālamārā-i Amīnī*, 'The World-adorning History of Amīn', by Faḍlu'llāh b. Rūzbihān Khunjī Iṣfahānī, completed during the reign of Bāysunghur (896–7/1490–1), the grandson of Uzun Ḥasan, forms a continuation.[40]

With the rise of the Safavids, Persian literature, as is well known, suffered a severe setback. This, it is true, cannot be said of historical writings, at least if the number of such works produced at that time is considered, although here again only the best known can be mentioned. The life and deeds of the first two Safavids were narrated in poetry; the life of Ismāʿīl I was recounted by Hātifī, whom we have already mentioned, in the unfinished *Shāh-nāma*, 'Book of the King', or *Ismāʿīl-nāma*, 'Book of Ismāʿīl'[41], and by Qāsimī in the *Shāh-nāma-i Ismāʿīl*, 'Book of King Ismāʿīl'; and the life of Ṭahmāsp also by Qāsimī in the *Shāh-nāma-i Ṭahmāsp*, 'Book of King Ṭahmāsp'.[42] An interesting document comes from Shāh Ṭahmāsp himself. In the summer of 969/1562 a great embassy came to Tabriz from the Ottoman Sulṭān Süleymān the Great to request the delivering up of prince Bāyezīd who had taken refuge at the Safavid court. The Shāh made a long speech to the ambassadors in which he sought to justify his policy, particularly with regard to the Ottoman empire. We still have this speech in its original text and also in a revision carried out by the Shāh himself which became famous under the title *Tadhkira-i Shāh Ṭahmāsp*, 'The Memoir of Shāh Ṭahmāsp'.[43] The fourth of the very famous Persian historical works in the artificial style – and at the same time the most important as regards content – is the *Ta'rīkh-i ʿālamārā-i ʿAbbāsī*, 'The World-adorning History of ʿAbbās', by Iskandar Munshī (d. probably 1038/1628–9). This much-read book deals in the introduction with the beginnings of the Safavid dynasty and the reigns of Ismāʿīl I and Ṭahmāsp and in the book itself with events, of which the author was frequently an eye-witness, during the reign of ʿAbbās the Great until his death.[44] The first fifteen years of the reign of Shāh ʿAbbās II were described in the most bombastic style by the greatest contemporary stylist, ʿImādu'd-daula Muḥammad Ṭāhir Vaḥīd Qazvīnī, in his *ʿAbbās-nāma*, 'Book of ʿAbbās'.[45]

Among the books about Nādir Shāh, the best known are two works by his secretary Muḥammad Mahdī Khān Astarābādī; these are preserved in many manuscripts and were printed several times in the east. They are the *Ta'rīkh-i (Jahāngushā-i) Nādirī*, 'The History of (the World Conqueror) Nādir', and the *Durra-i Nādira*, 'The rare

Pearl or the Pearl of Nādir', which is very similar in style to Vaṣṣāf's work.[46] *

The Persian language was also most often used by historians in the kingdom of the Seljuqids in Asia Minor, and in earlier times in the Ottoman empire. We possess two important histories about the Seljuqids of Asia Minor. The first is the *al-Avāmiru'l-'Alā'īya fi'l-umūri'l-'Alā'īya*, 'The 'Alā'id Commands on 'Alā'id affairs', by Ḥusayn b. Muḥammad al-Ja'farī, called after his mother Ibn Bībī (d. 670/1272); at the suggestion of 'Alā'u'd-dīn 'Aṭā' Malik Juvaynī, he describes the history of the dynasty, in particular of the reign of 'Alā'ud dīn Kayqubād I in the first half of the 7th/13th century.[47] The second is the *Musāmaratu'l-akhbār va musāyaratu'l-akhyār*, 'The Communication of Information and Acquaintance with the Elect', by Karīmu'd-dīn Maḥmūd b. Muḥammad al-Aqsarā'ī, which dates from the year 723/1323 and deals mainly with the history of the Seljuqids in Asia Minor and their overlords, the Persian Īlkhāns.[48] From the long list of books written in the Ottoman empire in the Persian language on historical themes let us mention only the two most prominent ones. These are the *Bazm u razm*, 'Feasting and Fighting', by 'Azīz b. Ardashīr al-Astarābādī, written in the year 800/1397–8, which recounts the life of the prince of Sivas, Qāḍī Burhānu'd-dīn Aḥmad[49], and the *Hasht bihisht*, 'The Eight Paradises', in which Ḥakīmu'd-dīn Idrīs b. Ḥusāmu'd-dīn 'Alī al-Bidlīsī (d. 926/1520) describes the history of the first eight Ottoman Sulṭāns.[50]

No less important than these works on the history of particular periods or dynasties are those which deal with the history of special provinces or towns. One extremely interesting history of Kurdistan dating from the year 1005/1596 we owe to Sharafu'd-dīn Khān Bidlīsī, of the old Kurdish dynasty of the Sharafkhāns who ruled the area of Bidlīs. His *Sharaf-nāma*, 'Book of Sharaf or Book of Honour', contains an introduction on the origin and customs of the Kurds and four chapters on the history of Kurdistan, the last of which is devoted to the house of the Sharafkhāns.[51] We also have some special histories on the provinces to the south of the Caspian Sea. The oldest of these is the *Ta'rīkh-i Ṭabaristān*, 'History of Tabaristan', by Muḥammad b. al-Ḥasan b. Isfandiyār at the beginning of the 7th/13th century.[52] Two more works on the history of this part of Iran have been preserved; one on the history of Tabaristan, Ruyan and Mazandaran up to the year 881/1476–7, and the other on the history of Gilan and Daylamistan up to 894/1489, both by Ẓahīru'd-dīn Mar'ashī.[53] Another history of Gilan, called *Ta'rīkh-i khānī*, 'History of the Khāns', which describes the history of Gilan between 880/1475–6 and 920/1514, was written during the first half of the 10th/16th century by 'Alī b. Shamsu'd-dīn Lāhijī.[54] The events of 923–1038/1517–1628 are told in the *Ta'rīkh-i Gīlān*, 'History of Gilan', by 'Abdu'l-Fūmanī[55] about a hundred years later.

About Isfahan and its history al-Mufaḍḍal b. Sa'd al-Māfarrūkhī wrote a monograph in Arabic in 421/1030 which was somewhat enlarged by Ḥusayn b. Muḥammad al-Ḥusaynī al-'Alavī in his translation into Persian, probably about the year 729/1329, under the title *Tarjama-i Maḥāsin-i Iṣfahān*, 'Translation of "The Beauties of Isfahan"'.[56]

The history of Fars is described in the *Fārs-nāma*, 'The Book about Fars', written by Ibnu'l-Balkhī[57] for the Seljuq Sulṭān Ghiyāthu'd-dīn Muḥammad at the beginning of the 6th/12th century, and in the *Shīrāz-nāma*, 'The Book about Shiraz' by Aḥmad b. Abi'l-Khayr Shīrāzī, known as Ibn-i Zarkūb, in the 8th/14th century. Apart from the purely historical section, this book also contains biographies of the Shaykhs, Imāms and saints of Shiraz.[58] A monograph on the history of Yazd, its famous buildings and renowned places (mosques, madrasas, shrines, baths, gardens and springs) entitled *Ta'rīkh-i Yazd*, 'History of Yazd', was written in the first half of the 9th/15th century by Ja'far b. Muḥammad b. Ḥasan Ja'farī.[59] On this work is based the *Ta'rīkh-i jadīd-i Yazd*, 'The New History of Yazd', by Aḥmad b. Ḥusayn b. 'Alī al-Kātib dating from the second half of the same century.[60]

Between 1082/1671 and 1090/1679 Muḥammad Mufīd Mustaufī Bāfqī Yazdī wrote his *Jāmi'-i Mufīdī*, 'The Compendium of Mufīd', which is a history of Yazd from Alexander the Great to the Safavid Shāh Sulaymān, with additional topographical and biographical notes about the city, including an autobiography of its author.[61]

The two earliest books on the subject of Kirman from the 6th/12th century are by Afḍalu'd-dīn Aḥmad b. Ḥāmid Kirmānī. These are the *'Iqdu'l-'ulā li'l-mauqifi'l-a'lā*, 'Necklet of Pearls of Eminence for the Highest Position' which, in a highly artificial style, describes the conquest of Kirman by the Chief of the Ghuzz, Malik Dīnār, in the years 581–3/1185–7, and the *Badā'i'u'l-azmān fi vaqā'i' Kirmān*, 'The Miracles of Time in the Events of Kirman', which is preserved almost word for word in a later world chronicle.[62] Still later, in the year 716/1316–7, the Munshī Nāṣiru'd-dīn Kirmānī completed his *Simṭu'l-'ulā li'l-ḥaḍrati'l-'ulyā*, 'String of Pearls of Eminence for the Highest Majesty', a history of the Qutluqkhāns (Qarakhitāy) of Kirman.[63]

An anonymous *History of Sīstān*, notable for its ancient origin, although for the main part consisting only of a list of events, appeared in the middle of the 5th/11th century.[64] Of the cities of Khurasan, the histories of two have been preserved in monographs. The first deals with Bayhaq and is from the pen of Ẓahīru'd-dīn Abu'l-Ḥasan 'Alī b. Zayd al-Bayhaqī, known as Ibn-i Funduq (d. 565/1169–70); it also contains biographies of well-known men who had lived there.[65] The second concerns Herat and is called *Rauḍātu'l-jannāt fī auṣāf madīnat Harāt*, 'The Paradise Gardens on the Properties of the City of Herat'. It was written in the year 897/1491–2 by Mu'īnu'd-dīn Muḥammad Zamajī Isfizārī.[66]

There are many histories of Afghanistan, the majority of which naturally date only from the last century, since from a historical point of view that country first began to develop independently in the 12th/18th century. Its ancient history and the genealogy of the Afghans are dealt with in the *Ta'rīkh-i Khānjahānī u Makhzan-i Afghānī*, 'The History of Khānjahān and the Storehouse of the Afghans', by Khvāja Ni'matu'llāh al-Haravī, who was first court historian of the emperors Akbar and Jahāngīr, but, in 1017/1608–9, entered the service of general Khānjahān Lōdī, whose name he gave to the book which appeared in 1021/1613.[67]

Notes on pp. 455–459

Most of the histories of Transoxania are similarly of a later date. The history of Bukhara, written in Arabic by an-Narshakhī in the 4th/10th century, was translated into Persian (*Ta'rīkh-i Bukhārā*) during the first half of the 6th/12th century by Abū-Naṣr Aḥmad al-Qubāvī, with a short sequel up to the year 365/976. Both works have been lost and only a Persian extract from the latter, by Muḥammad b. Zufar, also dating from the 6th/12th century, has been preserved.[68] After a long interval, specialised works on the history of Transoxania first appear under the Shaybanids. The poet Binā'ī (d. 918/1512) wrote a *Shaybānī-nāma*, 'Book of Shaybānī', in verse, on the founder of the dynasty, Muḥammad Shaybānī[69], and his third campaign against the Qazaqs in the year 914/1508–9 was described in the *Mihmān-nāma-i Bukhārā*, 'The Guest-book of Bukhara', by Faḍlu'llāh b. Rūzbihān Khunjī Iṣfahānī.[70] A detailed history of Transoxania under the Jānid Sulṭāns of Ashtarkhān during the years 1006–1050/1597–1641 is contained in the *Baḥru'l-asrār fī manāqibi'l-akhyār*, 'The Sea of Secrets about the Glorious Deeds of the Elect', by Maḥmūd b. Amīr Valī.[71]

Just as we were forced to note that a large number of the works on general history were written on Indian soil, so it is also true to say that an immense number of works appeared especially in the field of Indian history. These can be divided into two groups: collective works on the history of Islamic India, relatively few in number, and local histories, of which there are many more. Only the most important ones in each group can of course be cited here, namely those most important either as literary histories or as sources of information on the more ancient history of India.

The earliest work in the first group is an epic poem, *Futūḥu's-salāṭīn* 'The Conquests of the Sulṭāns', written in 750/1349–50 by a certain 'Iṣāmī for 'Alā'u'd-dīn Abu'l-Muẓaffar, the first ruler of the Bahmanid dynasty in the Deccan, and describing the history of Islamic India from the Ghaznavids up to the middle of the 8th/14th century.[72] Some 150 years later came the much better known *Ṭabaqāt-i Akbarī*, 'The Generations of Akbar', by Niẓāmu'd-dīn Aḥmad al-Haravī (d. 1003/1594), who was for many years in the service of the Emperor Akbar. This book contains an introduction on the history of the Ghaznavids and nine chapters dealing with the dynasties which ruled in India both before and occasionally at the same time as the Great Moghuls.[73] Chronologically the next work, which borrowed extensively from the previous one, is the *Muntakhabu't-tavārīkh*, 'Selection from History', frequently referred to just as the *Ta'rīkh-i Badā'ūnī* after its author 'Abdu'l-Qādir Badā'ūnī who came to the court of Akbar in 981/1574. There he was appointed to a religious office and given some property that enabled him to continue his literary work, which for the most part consisted of writing history and translating the *Mahābhārata* and *Rāmāyana* into Persian. His historical work covers the history of India from Sabuktagīn to the fortieth year of the reign of Akbar (1004/1595–6) and gives at the end short biographies of contemporary theologians, scholars and poets.[74] The third well-known history of the whole of India was written by Muḥammad Qāsim Hindūshāh, called Firishta, for the ruler of Bījāpūr, 'Ādilshāh Ibrāhīm II. His work is called

Gulshan-i Ibrāhīmī, 'The Rosebed of Ibrāhīm', or *Ta'rīkh-i Firishta*, 'The History of Firishta', and is preserved in two versions, the second of which, dating from the year 1018/1609–10, received a new title, *Nauras-nāma*, 'The New Book'.[75]

Among the specialised historical works on India, several deal above all with the history of Dilhī in pre-Moghul times. The reign of the Mamlūk Sulṭān Quṭbu'd-dīn Aybak and the first years of the reign of his son Īltutmish (587/1191–614/1217) are described by Ḥasan Niẓāmī in his *Tāju'l-ma'āthir*, 'The Crown of Exploits', which ranks among the most bombastic histories written in prose and verse and contains very little of any value.[76] The well-known poet of India, Amīr Khusrau Dihlavī (d. 725/1325), wrote amongst other things poems and prose-works on history in which he mainly glorified the victories of the Khaljī Sulṭāns of Delhi.[77] A longer period, namely the history of the Sulṭāns of Delhi from the accession of Ghiyāthu'd-dīn Balbān in 664/1265–6 to the sixth year of the reign of Fīrūzshāh III (758/1357), is described by Ḍiyā'u'd-dīn Baranī in his *Ta'rīkh-i Fīrūzshāhī* 'History of Fīrūzshāh'.[78] Shams-i Sirāj 'Afīf devoted his book, probably of the same name, to the whole of the reign of Fīrūzshāh.[79] The age of the Grand Moghul has attracted the attention of many historians. The *Memoirs of Bābur* were edited in Persian three times during the 10th/16th century.[80] The governmental institutions and buildings of his son and successor have been described by Khvāndamīr, already known to us, in his *Humāyūn-nāma*, 'Humāyūn's Book', which was probably his last work.[81] The two most important works on the Emperor Akbar are the *Akbar-nāma* 'Akbar's Book', dealing with his life and the first forty-six years of his reign, and the *Āyīn-i Akbarī*, 'The Law of Akbar', on the administration of his empire. These works flowed from the pen of Abu'l-Faḍl 'Allāmī (d. 1011/1602), the younger brother of the poet Fayḍī and close friend of the emperor's.[82] Akbar's son and successor, Jahāngīr, himself worked on a history, a kind of memoir, of his own reign, which he wrote in two versions up to the 17th year. From then on it was continued, under the sovereign's supervision, by his private secretary Muḥammad Sharīf b. Dūst-Muḥammad, better known by his honorary title Mu'tamad Khān. In 1029/1619–20, under Jahānshāh, Mu'tamad Khān himself composed the *Iqbāl-nāma-i Jahāngīrī*, 'Jahāngīr's Book of Happiness', a history of Jahāngīr and his three predecessors.[83] A great number of historians and poets have described the reign of Shāhjahān, among them being his favourite poet Kalīm (d. 1062/1652).[84] About fifty historical works have been written on the history of the Indian Timurids of the 12th/18th century and among these the best known and most useful is probably the *Siyaru'l-muta'akhkhirīn*, 'Biographies of the Later Ones', by Ghulām-Ḥusayn Khān Ṭabāṭabā'ī. This covers the period from the death of Aurangzīb in 1118/1707 up to the year 1195/1781.[85]

Persian biographical literature is particularly abundant. As in Arabic literature, biographical collective works predominate whilst biographies of individual persons and autobiographies are rarer.

The life of the Prophet of course excited a lively interest amongst the Moslem

Persians. This is most clearly demonstrated by the certainly imposing series of biographies of Muḥammad, translations from Arabic as well as original works. The *Ma'āriju'n-nubūva fī madāriji'l-futūva*, 'The Stages of Prophecy on the Paths to Magnanimity', by Mu'īnu'd-dīn Farāhī (d. 907/1501–2)[86] and the *Madāriju'n-nubūva*, 'The Paths of Prophecy', by the Indian scholar 'Abdu'l-Ḥaqq Dihlavī (d. 1052/1642), enjoyed the greatest popularity among original works in Persian.[87]

In addition to works dealing solely with the life of Muḥammad, there are some that also include legends on the pre-Islamic and other prophets. We also find works in which either the lives of Muḥammad's companions, and in most cases those of the rightly guided caliphs as well, or those of the Imāms are added to the first theme. Works belonging to the first type, most of which bear the stereotyped title *Qiṣaṣu'l-anbiyā'*, 'Stories of the Prophets', are extremely numerous and take their material from Arabic works of the same name. Abū-Isḥāq Ibrāhīm b. Manṣūr b. Khalaf an-Naysābūrī, who lived in the 5th/11th century, produced the most popular original work in Persian.[88] Similar works also appear in verse form and there are also a few legendary tales about single ancient prophets, especially Mūsā (Moses), Sulaymān (Solomon), and Iskandar Dhu'l-qarnayn (Alexander the Great). Among works of the second type, the *Shavāhidu'n-nubūva*, 'The Proofs of Prophecy', is the most famous. The fact that it was written by the renowned poet Jāmī in 885/1480 may be one of the reasons for this.[89] The Amīr Jamālu'd-dīn al-Ḥusaynī (d. 926/1520), a well-known theologian and preacher of the time of Ḥusayn-i Bāyqarā, had finished another work of similar content in the year 900/1494–5 called *Rauḍatu'l-aḥbāb fī siyari'n-nabī va'l-āl va'l-aṣḥāb*, 'The Garden of the Amateurs on the Life-history of the Prophet, (his) Family and Companions'.[90] The great Shī'a theologian, Muḥammad Bāqir Majlisī (d. 1110/1698–9 or 1111/1699–1700) wrote about the pre-Islamic prophets, Muḥammad and the Twelve Imāms in his *Ḥayātu'l-qulūb*, 'The Life of Hearts'.[91]

A work dealing with the orthodox caliphs and the first Umayyads, with particular reference to the great conquests made under their rule, is the novel-like but nevertheless very popular *Futūḥ-i Ibn-i A'tham*, 'The Conquests of Ibn A'tham', which appeared at the end of the 6th/12th century. Its authors, Muḥammad b. Aḥmad al-Mustaufī al-Haravī and Muḥammad b. Aḥmad al-Kātib al-Mābarnābādī, who continued the work[92], used the very rare Arabic book *Kitāb al-futūḥ*, 'The Book of Conquests', by Muḥammad b. Aḥmad b. A'tham al Kūfī (d. 314/926).[93] There are other works about the first caliphs, and in particular about 'Alī, his son al-Ḥusayn and the Imāms of the Shī'a, some of which are in verse and of a more or less legendary character. We may here mention the most popular of these, a work describing the martyrdom of 'Alī and al-Ḥusayn in a truly fantastic fashion and in an affected style. This work bears the title *Rauḍatu'sh-shuhadā'*, 'The Garden of the Martyrs', and was composed at the beginning of the 10th/16th century by Ḥusayn Vā'iẓ Kāshifī.[94] The story of Mukhtār, the adventurous champion of the Shī'a in the second half of the 1st/7th century, in whom the Persians saw the first fighter for the rights of Persian against Arab, has been immortalised and popularised in the same way in several works, all called *Mukhtār-nāma*, 'Book of Mukhtār'.[95]

Many saints of later times have found biographers who likewise adorned their lives and works with legend. In spite of this, these accounts are of unmistakable value because they allow more insight into the social relations of wider classes of the population, whose leaders and trusted advisors these shaykhs were, than can be gained from most of the official histories. Only one anonymous selection, made before the year 698/1299, has been preserved from the *Nūru'l-'ulūm*, 'The Light of Knowledge', a likewise anonymous biography of the saint Abu'l-Ḥasan al-Kharaqānī (d. 425/1033) that has since disappeared.[96] The life of the famous Abū-Sa'īd b. Abi'l-Khayr (d. 440/1049) was described by his great-great-grandson Muḥammad b. Abi'r-Rauḥ Luṭfu'llāh b. Abī-Sa'īd in a book entitled *Ḥālāt u sukhanān-i Shaykh Abū-Sa'īd*, 'Ecstatic States and Sayings of Shaykh Abū-Sa'īd'.[97] At about the same time, in the 6th/12th century, his other great-great-grandson, Muḥammad b. Munauvar, using this and other sources, wrote the *Asrāru't-tauḥīd*, 'The Secrets of Divine Unity'.[98] During the first half of the 8th/14th century Shamsu'd-dīn Aḥmad Aflākī wrote the *Manāqibu'l-'ārifīn*, 'Virtues of the mystic Sages', containing biographies of the great mystic and founder of the Maulavī order, Maulānā Jalālu'd-dīn Rūmī, of his father, his friends and descendants, at the request of Maulānā's grandson, Jalālu'd-dīn al-'Ārif, the author's teacher. This is the finest of his biographies.[99] The life of Shaykh Ṣafī, the ancestor of the Safavids (d. 735/1334), his sayings and miracles, form the theme of the *Ṣafvatu'ṣ-ṣafā'*, 'The Purest of the Pure', by Tavakkulī b. Ismā'īl al-Ardabīlī, known as Ibn-i Bazzāz, who knew the holy man personally and wrote this work twenty-four years after the latter's death.[100] The famous saint of Turkestan, Shaykh of the Naqshbandī order, Nāṣiru'd-dīn 'Ubaydu'llāh b. Maḥmūd Shāshī, known as Khvāja Aḥrār (d. 895/1490) found a biographer in 'Alī, son of the well-known Ḥusayn Vā'iẓ Kāshifī, whose book on him and some of his pupils is called *Rashaḥāt-i 'ayni'l-ḥayāt*, 'The Drops of the Spring of Life', and was composed in the year 909/1503–4.[101]

Biographies of other personalities are far fewer in number than those of the saints. Apart from historical works on ruling figures, already mentioned elsewhere, a panegyric on the Amīr 'Alīshīr Navā'ī by the historian Khvāndamīr[102] under the title *Makārimu'l-akhlāq*, 'The Noble Qualities', is in some sort worthy of our attention.[103]

Autobiographies in the true sense are just as rare. The only work really worthy of note is the *Tadhkiratu'l-aḥvāl*, 'Memoirs of Life Situations', by Shaykh Ḥazīn, whose real name was Muḥammad 'Alī b. Abī-Ṭālib Gīlānī. He was born as a descendant of the Shaykh Zāhid Gīlānī, the teacher of Shaykh Ṣafī, in 1103/1692 in Isfahan. At the age of 30 he fled from his native city which was threatened by the Afghans. Many years later, after having lived in different cities in Iran and made a pilgrimage to Mecca, he returned to Isfahan, only to find it laid waste and deserted by all his friends and acquaintances. Shocked by the tragic situation in Iran, he left it for ever and,

Notes on pp. 455–459

following in the footsteps of so many of his compatriots, in 1146/1734 he went to India, where he spent the remaining years of his life. He died in Benares in 1180/1766, never having become accustomed to living in a foreign country and unable to curb his derision of the land where he had received hospitality. The autobiography, written in 1154/1742, offers valuable information on the political, economic, social, cultural and above all literary conditions in Iran during the first half of the 12th/18th century.[104]

A work that resembles a memoir or travel report is the *Badā'i'u'l-vaqā'i'*, 'The Wonder of the Events', in which Zaynu'd-dīn Maḥmūd Vāṣifī gives valuable information on contemporary events in Transoxania during the first half of the 10th/16th century with backward glances to its history and culture.[105]

Collective biographies are far more numerous. Collections of a general character, in which statesmen appear next to theologians, saints, poets and learned men, are comparatively rare. There are several such works in Arabic, and of these the *Vafayāt al-a'yān* 'The Deaths of Prominent Men', by Ibn Khallikān (d. 681/1282) was translated into Persian.[106] An original Persian work is the *Ṭabaqāt-i Shāhjahānī*, 'The Classes of Shāhjahān', by Muḥammad Ṣādiq Hamadānī, dating from the first half of the 11th/17th century. It is divided according to the reigns of the Timurids in Iran and India and contains biographies of 871 famous men who lived from the time of Tīmūr up to that of Shāhjahān, i.e. between about 770/1370 and 1046/1636–7.[107] Some time before, between the years 993/1585 and 1010/1602, Sayyid Nūru'llāh b. Sayyid Sharīf Shushtarī wrote in Lahore the *Majālisu'l-mu'minīn*, 'Meetings of the Faithful', which describes the lives of eminent Shī'ites, ranging from saints to rulers.[108] The copious collection by Amīn Rāzī, bearing the title *Haft iqlīm*, 'Seven Regions', was completed in the year 1002/1593–4 and is arranged geographically. It contains about 1560 biographies.[109]

Among specialised collections there are a great number that deal with the lives of eminent mystics, ascetics and saints, with particular reference to their pious exercises, their parapsychological abilities and miracles. They of course contain many legends and anecdotes. The earliest is probably the *Ṭabaqātu'ṣ-ṣūfīya*, 'The Ranks of the Mystics', which was written down in the ancient dialect of Herat from the dictation of the famous mystic 'Abdu'llāh b. Muḥammad al-Anṣārī (d. 481/1089) by one of his pupils. It deals with 120 saints and is based on an Arabic work by Muḥammad b. al-Ḥusayn as-Sulamī (d. 412/1021) of very similar title.[110] Far better known is the *Tadhkiratu'l-auliyā'*, 'Memoirs of the Saints', by the poet Farīdu'd-dīn 'Aṭṭār (d. 627/1230), which for the greatest part tells edifying tales about some 70 holy men of the first three centuries of the Hijra (7th–9th A.D.) and records their sayings. An appendix on some later saints has also been added.[111] About 300 years later, between 881/1476–7 and 883/1478–9, comes the *Nafaḥātu'l-uns*, 'The Inspirations of Confidence', written by the poet Jāmī at the request of the Amīr 'Alīshīr Navā'ī. It is in fact a modernised and greatly expanded version of al-Anṣārī's *Ṭabaqāt*.[112] The *Majā-*

lisu'l-'ushshāq, 'The Lovers' Meetings', is frequently attributed to the last important Timurid Sulṭān of Iran, Ḥusayn-i Bāyqarā (d. 911/1506), although in fact it stemmed from Ḥusayn's Ṣadr, Kamālu'd-dīn Ḥusayn Kāzargāhī. It contains romantic accounts written in pompous style, plentifully interwoven with verses, of 76 great mystics, unhappy lovers and kings, starting with Ja'far aṣ-Ṣādiq and ending with Ḥusayn-i Bāyqarā.[113] The *Akhbāru'l-akhyār fī asrāri'l-abrār*, 'Stories of the Chosen, concerning the Secret of the Pious', compiled at the end of the 10th/16th century by 'Abdu'l-Ḥaqq Dihlavī, is devoted to the Indian saints, 255 in number.[114] The *Gulzār-i abrār*, 'Rosebed of the Pious', by Muḥammad Ghauthī, composed at about the same time in an extremely affected style, is dedicated to the Emperor Jahāngīr. It deals with almost twice as many Indian saints and gives valuable, most detailed and otherwise unknown information.[115] The *Safīnatu'l-auliyā'*, 'The Ship of the Saints', by Prince Dārā Shikūh, is written on a wider scale. It was completed in 1049/1640.[116] Apart from these * general hagiographic collections, there are also some in which we find descriptions of the members, and in particular the shaykhs, of certain dervish orders. Many such works are concerned especially with the Naqshbandī and Chishtī orders.

Particularly numerous are collections which deal with poets, describing their lives and giving larger or smaller selections from their verse. These are known briefly as *Tadhkira*, 'Memoirs', which is in fact the name given to many of them, unless the author preferred a more florid title. We must here distinguish between two types: the general ones, dealing with the lives and works of the poets up to the lifetime of the author, and the specialised ones, which cite only poets of a particular period or type. As for the arrangement of these works, they are divided either chronologically or geographically, according to the native country or country of domicile, then according to family, type of poetry, and so on. If alphabetical division is used, we get a formal dictionary of poets.[117] The earliest of the general collections is the *Lubābu'l-albāb*, 'Quintessence of Hearts', compiled by the poet 'Aufī probably in 618/1221–2. It contains biographies of nearly 300 poets.[118] It has been surpassed in popularity however by the *Tadhkiratu'sh-shu'arā'*, 'Memoirs on Poets', by Daulatshāh as-Samarqandī, dating from the year 892/1487.[119] An excellent selection of quotations and precise biographical details, beginning with the earliest times and including contemporary poets, is given in the *Khulāṣatu'l-ash'ār va zubdatu'l-afkār*, 'Quintessence of Poetry and the Cream of Thought', by Taqī'u'd-dīn Muḥammad Dhikrī, known as Taqī Kāshī, who finished writing this work in the year 993/1585.[120] Of the other general *tadhkiras*, only the *Ātashkada*, 'Temple of Fire', by Ḥājjī Luṭf-'Alī Beg Ādhar, which appeared about two centuries later, in the second half of the 12th/18th century, is worth mentioning.[121] Amongst the *tadhkiras* limited to particular periods of time, usually that of the author himself, we find one compiled by Sām Mīrzā (d. 974/1566–7), son of Shāh Ismā'īl I. This is a collection of biographies of poets living during the first half of the 10th/16th century and is entitled *Tuḥfa-i Sāmī*, 'The Gift of Sām'.[122] Muḥammad Ṭāhir Naṣrābādī's *Tadhkira*, dating from the last quarter of the 11th/17th

Notes on pp. 455–459

century and containing more than a thousand observations on contemporary poets[123], is likewise worthy of note, as is the *Tadhkiratu'l-mu'āṣirīn*, 'Memoirs on Contemporaries', which deals with about one hundred poets and was written in 1165/1752 by Shaykh Ḥazīn, of whom we have already heard.[124] The greatest of the alphabetically arranged works is the *'Arafātu'l-'ārifīn va 'araṣātu'l-'āshiqīn*, 'The Vigils of the Learned and Scenery of Lovers', by Taqī Auḥadī, who first enjoyed the favour of 'Abbās the Great but then went to India, where he completed this work in 1024/1615. It contains about 3000 key-words.[125] A later, similar dictionary of poets, containing about 2500 names, is the *Riyāḍu'sh-shu'arā'*, 'The Gardens of the Poets', by 'Alī-Qulī Khān Vālih Dāghistānī, who went to India after the Afghan invasion and died there in 1169/1756.[126] Many of these works pass into the category of anthologies which now and then also contain biographical notes. Some of them are discussed among the belles-lettres.

In view of the exceptional part played by book-craft among the Persians, it is hardly surprising that attention has been paid to the history of calligraphy and book-craft and, above all, to the lives of calligraphers and painters of miniatures. In 953/1546 Dūst-Muḥammad al-Kātib produced a summary of the history of Moslem calligraphy and book-craft as introduction to a magnificent album of early and later splendid book illustrations which he had collected for Abu'l-Fatḥ Bahrām Mīrzā, a younger brother of Shāh Ṭahmāsp.[127] About the year 1000/1600, Qāḍī Aḥmad Ibrāhīmī b. Mīr Munshī Sharafu'd-dīn Ḥusayn wrote a *tadhkira* on calligraphers, which was divided according to the three main groups of Arabic writing, i.e. the Thuluth, Ta'līq, and Nasta'līq. In the epilogue he discusses the origin of writing and book-craft with reference to the most important artists in both fields.[128]

Far rarer are collections of biographies of scholars. The most important of these are written in Arabic but in time some of them were made available to the Persians in their own language. The first work we possess of this nature, written originally in Persian, dates from the 10th/16th century and is entitled *Khulāṣatu'l-ḥayāt*, 'The Quintessence of Life', by Aḥmad Tattavī.[129] Nor are there many biographies of dignitaries. Famous viziers are written about in the *Nasā'imu'l-asḥār*, 'Breezes of the Day-break', completed in 725/1325 by Nāṣiru'd-dīn Munshī Kirmānī[130], the *Āthāru'l-vuzarā'*, 'The Paths of the Viziers', by Sayfu'd-dīn Ḥājjī b. Niẓām 'Uqaylī, written in 883/1478–9[131], and the *Dastūru'l-vuzarā'*, 'The Pattern of the Viziers', by Khvāndamīr, which dates from the year 915/1509–10.[132] The lives of dignitaries under the Indian Timurids, from Akbar up to the time of the author, were collected by 'Abdu'r-Razzāq Aurangābādī, better known as Shāhnavāz Khān (d. 1171/1758), in his *Ma'āthiru'l-umarā'*, 'Exploits of the Amirs', the two versions of which reached their final form only after the author's death.[133]

There is also a great deal of biographical material in many other works on history, geography and other topics. This can be found in other chapters.

NOTES

1. *PL*, I, Nr, 101. *Tarjama-i Ta'rīkh-i Ṭabarī*. Ed. by M. Taqī Bahār and M. Parvīn Gūnābādī, I (Tehran 1341). *Qismat marbūṭ ba Īrān*. Ed. by M. Javād Mashkūr (Tehran 1337). *Chāp-i 'aksī* (the years 15–132/636–750) bā muqaddima-i Mujtabā Mīnuvī (Tehran 1345). – Bahār M. Taqī, 'Tarjama-i Ta'rīkh-i Ṭabarī', *Nāma-i tamaddun*, I (1309–10), 133–44. P. A. Gryaznevich i A. N. Boldīrev, 'O dvukh redaktsiyakh "Ta'rīkh-i Ṭabarī" Bal'amī', *Sovyetskoye vostokovedeniye* 1957,3, 46–59.
2. *PL*, I, Nr. 102; 1229; II, X. *Faṣl-i Sāsāniyān az Kitāb-i Zaynu'l-akhbār*. Ed. Sa'īd Nafīsī, *Payām-i nau*, III (1325–6); IV (1327–30), in several articles. – M. Qazvīnī, 'Zaynu'l-akhbār', *Bīst maqāla*, I (1313), 196–201.
3. *PL*, I, Nr. 104; 1229–30; II, X–XI. *İA*, *s.v.* 'Cûzcânî'.
4. Cf. *EI*, *s.v.* 'Rashīd-al-Dīn Ṭabīb'. *İA*, *s.v.* 'Reşîd-üd-Dîn Tabîb'. Muḥammad Qazvīnī, 'Nuktahāī dar bāra-i Rashīdu'd-dīn Faḍlu'llāh. Gird āvarī-i Īraj Afshār', *MDAT*, 3,2 (1334–5), 44–51. Muḥammad Murtaḍavī, 'Jāmi'u't-tavārīkh u mu'allif-i vāqi'ī-i ān', *NDAT*, 13 (1340), 31–92, 311–50, 516–26. Muḥammad Taqī, ''Ilm dar 'ahd-i Mughūl', *Bākhtar*, I (1312–3), 119–25.
5. *PL*, I, Nr. 106; 1230–2; II, XI. Ed. by M. Taqī Dānish-Pazhūh and M. Mudarrisī Zanjānī (Tehran 1338). Ed. by Bahman Karīmī (Tehran 1338). *Cāmi' al-Tavārīḫ: Metin*. II/4: *Sultan Mahmud ve devrinin tarihi*. II/5: *Selçuklular Tarihi*. Ed. by Ahmed Ateş (Ankara 1957, 1960). *Faṣlī az Jāmi'u't-tavārīkh (Dar firaq-i rafīqān u Ismā'īliyyān-i Ālamūt)*. Ed. by M. Dabīr Siyāqī (Tehran 1337). *Jāmi'u't-tavārīkh (Qismat-i Ismā'īlīyān u Fāṭimīyān u Nizāriyyān u dā'iyān u rafīqān)*. Ed. by M. Taqī Dānish-Pazhūh and M. Mudarrisī Zanjānī (Tehran 1339). *Faṣlī az Jāmi'u't-tavārīkh (Ghaznavids, Būyids, Sāmānids)*. Ed. by M. Dabīr Siyāqī (Tehran 1338). *Tārīkh-i ijtimā'ī-i Mughūl (Bakhsh-i sivum az Ta'rīkh-i Ghāzān Khān u muqaddima-i Jāmi'u't-tavārīkh u risāla-i avval az Kitāb-i laṭā'if az Khvāja Rashīdu'd-dīn Ṭabīb)*. Ed. by Amīr Ḥusayn Jahānbaghlu (Tehran 1337). *Sbornik letopisey*, T. 1,1 per. L. A. Chetagurov; 1,2 per. O. I. Smirnov. T. 2 per. J. P. Verkhovskiy. T. 3 per. A. K. Arends (Leningrad-Moscow 1946–60). – M. Şemseddin Günaltay, 'Türk tarihinin ana kaynaklarīndan Camiüttevarikh', *TTC*, Bel. 1 (1937), 165–79. K. Jahn, *Rashīd al-Dīn's 'History of India'*. Collected Essays with facsimiles and indices (The Hague 1965). Īraj Afshār, 'Jāmi'u't-tavārīkh', *Rāhnamā-i kitāb*, I (1337), 70–2. Ahmet Ateş, 'Dar bāb-i naqd-i Jāmi'u't-tavārīkh', *MDAT*, 8,3 (1340), 58–93. K. Jahn, 'The still missing Works of Rashīd al-Dīn', *CAJ*, 9 (1965), 113–22. Kriticheskiy tekst A. A. Romaskevicha, A. A. Khetagurova, A. A. Ali-zade, 1/1 (Moscow 1965). K. Jahn, 'Rashīd al-Dīn as a world historian', *Yádnáme-ye Jan Rypka* (Prague 1967), 79–87; idem, 'Zu Rašīd al-Dīn's "Geschichte der Oğuzen und Türken" ', *JAH*, I,1 (Wiesbaden 1967). *PL*, I, Nr. 111; 1233. *İA*, *s.v.* 'Hamdullah Müstevfî'. Ed. by Dr. 'Abdu'l Ḥusayn Navā'ī (Tehran 1339). – J. P. Petrushevskiy, 'Khamdulla Kazvini kak istochnik ... vostochnago Zakavkazya', *Izv. AN. SSSR*, 1937, 873–90.
7. See p. 444.
8. *PL*, I, Nr. 117; 1235–6. *Cinq opuscules de Ḥāfiẓ-i Abrū concernant l'histoire de l'Iran au temps de Tamerlan*. Ed. crit. par F. Tauer (Prague 1959). – F. Tauer, 'Beiträge zur Kenntnis der Geschichtswerke Ḥāfiẓ-i Abrūs', in *Akten des XXIV. Intern. Orientalisten-Kongresses* (München 1957), 328–30. F. Tauer, 'Beiträge zur Kenntnis der Geschichtswerke Ḥāfiẓ-i Abrūs', *BIO*, 15 (1958), 146–8. F. Tauer, 'Analyse des matières de la première moitié du Zubdatu-t-tawārīḫ de Ḥāfiẓ-i Abrū', in *Charisteria Orientalia* (Prague 1956), 345–73. F. Tauer, 'Le Ẕail-i Ǧāmi'u-t-tawārīḫ-i Rašīdī de Ḥāfiẓ-i Abrū et son édition par K. Bayani', *AOr*, 20 (1952), 39–52; 21 (1953), 206–17; 22 (1954), 88–98, 531–43; 23 (1955), 99–108. F. Tauer, 'Ḥafīz-i Abrū sur l'historiographie', in *Mélanges d'Orientalisme offerts à Henri Massé* (Tehran 1963), 10–25. *EI*, new ed., s.v. 'Ḥāfiẓ-i Abrū'.
9. *PL*, I, Nr. 115. *Muntakhabu't-tavārīkh-i Mu'īnī mansūb ba Mu'īnu'd-dīn Naṭanzī*. Ed. by Jean Aubin (Tehran 1336).
10. *PL*, I, Nr. 118; 1236.

11. *PL*, Nr. 116; 1234–5.
12. *PL*, I, Nr. 121; 1236. See p. 462.
13. *PL*, I, Nr. 120. Ed. by Maḥmūd Farrukh (Mashhad 1339–41). – Maḥmūd Farrukh, 'Mujmal-i Faṣīḥī-i Khvāfī', *Rāhnamā-i kitāb*, 4 (1340), 473–6.
14. *PL*, I, Nr. 123; 1236–7. *İA, s.v.* 'Mirhond'. Published (Muqaddima by 'Abbās Parvīz) (Tehran 1338–40).
15. *PL*, Nr. 125; 1237–8; II, XII. *İA, s.v.* 'Hândmîr'. 'Abdu'l-Ḥusayn Navā'ī, *Rijāl-i Kitāb-i Ḥabību's-siyar* (Tehran 1324).
16. *PL*, I, Nr. 381; 1279.
17. *PL*, Nr. 149; 1243.
18. *PL*, I, 1279–80. See p. 454. Publ. and transl. by H. Müller (Wiesbaden 1964).
19. *PL*, I, Nr. 131.
20. *PL*, I, Nr. 135; 1240–1.
21. *PL*, I, Nr. 333; II, XIV. *Khātima-i Tarjama-i Ta'rīkh-i Yamīnī*. Ed. by 'Abdu'l-Ḥusayn Navā'ī, *Yādgār* 1,4 (1323–4), 58–76. 'Alī Qavīm, 'Dar pīrāmūn-i Ta'rīkh-i Yamīnī', *Dānish*, 3 (1331–2), 456–9. Ed. (with the Khātima) by Ja'far Shi'ār (Tehran 1345).
22. *PL*, I, Nr. 334; 1271–2. *EI, s.v.* 'Bayhaḳī'. See p. 432. 'Abbās Iqbāl, 'Ta'rīkh-i Bayhaqī. Yak ṣafḥia az mujalladāt-i mafqūda-i Tārīkh-i Bayhaqī', *Armaghān*, 13 (1311), 25–35. Riḍāzāda Ṣādiq Shafaq, 'Abu'l-Faḍl Bayhaqī u Tārīkh-i Bayhaqī', *Armaghān*, 11 (1309), 859–65; 12 (1310), 70–8, 84–96; 26 (1336), 97–102, 145–52, 199–208. Abu-l-Fazl Beichaki, *Istoriya Mas'uda* 1030–1041. *Vstupitelnaya statya, perevod i primechaniya A. K. Arendsa* (Tashkent 1962). K. I. Kozlov, *Abu-l-Fazl Baihaki* (*Kratkiye soobshcheniya Instituta narodov Asii*, XXX) (Moscov 1961). Mujtaba Minovi, 'The Persian Historian Bayhaqi', in *Historians of the Middle East* (Lewis-Holt) (London 1962), 138–40. Sa'īd Nafīsī, *Dar pīrāmūn-i Ta'rīkh-i Bayhaqī* (Tehran 1343).
23. *PL*, I, Nr. 335; 1272. See Cahen, 67 *et seq*.
24. *PL*, I, 336; II, XIV. Cahen 73 *et seq*. Īraj Ismā'īl, 'Saljūqnāma-i Ẓahīrī Nīshāpūrī va Rāḥatu'ṣ-ṣudūr-i Rāvandī', *Mihr*, 1 (1312–3), 26–30, 157–61, 241–5. Partav Bayḍā'ī, 'Ash'ār-i Rāvandī mu'allif-i Rāḥatu'ṣ-ṣudūr', *Yādgār* 2,6 (1324), 8–12. Turkish transl. by Ahmed Ateş (Ankara 1957).
25. *PL*, I, Nr. 340; 1272. *İA, s.v.* 'Cüveynî'. *The History of the World-Conqueror by 'Ala-ad-Din Ata-Malik Juvaini*. Transl. by J. A. Boyle (Manchester 1958). – J. A. Boyle, 'Juvayni and Rashīd al-Dīn as sources on the History of the Mongols', in *Historians of the Middle East* (Lewis-Holt) (London 1962), 133–7.
26. *PL*, I, Nr. 344; 1272–3. Anastat (of the Lith. of Bombay 1269) (Tehran 1338). – Shādān Bilgrāmī Aulād-i Ḥusayn, 'Taṣḥīḥ-i Ta'rīkh-i Vaṣṣāf', *OCM*, 4,2 (1928), 73–80.
27. *PL*, I, Nr. 467; 1296; II, XVII. Sarvar Gūyā I'timādī, 'Sayfī-i Haravī', *Āriyāna*, 1,10 (1321–2), 16–20.
28. *PL*, I, Nr. 351; 1273.
29. See p. 440.
30. *PL*, I, Nr. 352. Ed. by 'Abdu'l-Ḥusayn Navā'ī (Tehran 1335). – 'Abbās Iqbāl, 'Āyā ṣāḥib-ii Ta'rīkh-i Āl-i Muẓaffar Maḥmūd Gītī ast yā Maḥmūd Kutubī?', *Yādgār*, 5,1–2 (1327–8), 135–40.
31. *PL*, I, Nr. 353; 1273. *Giyāsaddīn 'Alī: Dnevnik pokhoda Tīmūra v Indiyu. Perevod s persidskogo, predisloviye i primechaniya A. A. Semenova* (Moscow 1958).
32. *PL*, I, Nr. 354; 1273; II, XIV. Nizamüddin Şâmî, *Zafernâme. Farçadan çeviren Necati Lugal* (Ankara 1949).
33. *PL*, I, 279, 1235. See p. 440.
34. *PL*, I, Nr. 361; 1275–6; II, XV.
35. *PL*, I, Nr. 356; 1274. Ed. by M. 'Abbāsī (Tehran 1336). – 'Alī Aṣghar Ḥikmat, 'Sharafuddīn 'Alī Yazdī', *Āyanda*, 3 (1323–4), 169–80.
36. *PL*, I, Nr. 358; 1274–5. Ed. by Abū-Hāshim Sayyid Yūsha' (Madrās 1958). – Sarvar Gūyā I'timādī, 'Hātifī Jāmī u shu'arā-i muta'akhkhirīn', *Kābul*, 2 (1311–2), 32–7.

37. *PL*, I, Nr. 362.
38. *PL*, I, Nr. 363; 1276–7; II, XV.
39. Ed. by Necati Lugal and Faruk Sümer (Ankara 1962–4).
40. *PL*, I, Nr. 370; 1278; II, XV. See p. 427.
41. *PL*, I, Nr. 373; 1278.
42. *PL*, I, Nr. 379; 1279.
43. *PL*, I, Nr. 380; 1279.
44. *PL*, I, Nr. 387; 1280; II, XV. *İA*, *s.v.* 'İskender Bey Münşî'. A. Rahmani, *Tarikh-i Alam arai Abbasi kak istochnik po istorii Azerbaydzhana* (Baku 1960).
45. *PL*, I, Nr. 392; 1282; II, XV.
46. *PL*, I, Nr. 407; 1283. *Ta'rīkh-i jahāngushā-i Nādirī*. Ed. by Sayyid 'Abdu'llāh Anvār (Tehran 1341). *Durra-i Nādira*. Ed. Sayyid Ja'far Shahīdī (Tehran 1341).
47. *PL*, I, Nr. 578, 1305; II, XX. *İA*, *s.v.* 'Ibn Bîbî'. Ibn-i Bībī, *El-Evāmirü'l-'Alā'iyye fī'l-Umūri'l-'Alā'iyye*, I: Tıpkıbasım (Ankara 1956). Ed. by Necati Lugal and Adnan Sadik Erzi, I (Ankara 1957). H. W. Duda, *Die Seltschukengeschichte des Ibn Bībī* (Kopenhagen 1959).
48. *PL*, I, Nr. 580; 1305–6.
49. *PL*, I, Nr. 581.
50. *PL*, I, Nr. 587; 1306.
51. *PL*, I, Nr. 490. Arabic transl. by M. Jamīl Band-i Rūzbayānī (Baghdad 1372).
52. *PL*, I, Nr. 477; 1298. See *Rāhnamā-i Kitab*, 5 (1342), 752–6.
53. *PL*, I, Nr. 479; II, XVII. Shihāb Ṭāhirī, 'Sayyid Ẓahīru'd-dīn Mar'ashī mu'allif-i Ta'rīkh-i Māzandarān u Daylamistān', *Sāl-nāma-i dunyā*, 8 (1330), 99–102.
54. *PL*, I, Nr. 482.
55. *PL*, I, Nr. 483.
56. *PL*, I, Nr. 455; 1292.
57. *PL*. I, Nr. 458; II, XVII. Ed. Sayyid Jalāl Ṭihrānī (Tehran 1313) and 'Alī Naqī Bihrūzī (Shiraz 1343). – Aḥmad Manṣūrī, 'Taḥqīq dar bāra-i Fārs-nāma-i Ibnu'l-Balkhī va mu'allif-i ān', *MDASh* I,I (1336), 44–9.
58. *PL*, I, Nr. 459; 1294.
59. Ed. by Īraj Afshār (Tehran 1338).
60. *PL*, I, 1293. Ed. by Īraj Afshār (Tehran 1345).
61. *PL*, I, Nr. 461. Vols. I and III, ed. by İraj Afshār (Tehran 1340–42). J. Aubin, *Matériaux pour la biographie de Shah Ni'matullāh Wali* (Tehran-Paris 1956). 'Juz'ī az jild-i duvvum-i Jāmi'-i Mufīdī' (ed. by Īraj Afshār), *FIZ*, II (1342), 193–228.
62. In the *Jāmi'u'-t-tavārīkh-i Ḥasanī* of Ḥasan b. Shihābu'd-dīn Yazdī. See p. 440. *PL*, I, Nr. 472; 1297. *Al-Muḍāf ilā Badā'i'i'l-azmān fī vaqā'i'Kirmān*. Ed. 'Abbās Iqbāl (Tehran 1335).
63. *PL*, I, Nr. 473; 1297.
64. *PL*, I, Nr. 484. 2nd ed. of M. Bahār (Tehran 1339).
65. *PL*, I, Nr. 466; 1296. 'Iqtibās az Ta'rīkh-i Bayhaq (Khāndān-i Sayyidi'l-vuzarā Niẓāmu'l-mulk)', *OCM*, 5,2 (1929), 85–94. '(Khāndān-i Ḥākimiyyān)', *OCM*, 9,2 (1934–5), 107–20. – Kalimullah Husayni, 'Life and Works of Zahiruddin al-Bayhaqi, the Author of the Ta'rikh-i-Bayhaq', *Islamic Culture*, 20,1 (1954), 297–318. M. Qazvīnī, 'Ta'rīkh-i Bayhaq', *Mihr*, I (1312–3), 656–62, 729–33, 831–7. *Bīst maqāla*, 2 (1313), 76–86.
66. *PL*, I, Nr. 468. Ed. by Sayyid M. Kāẓim Imām (Tehran 1338), and Muḥ. Isḥāq I (Aligarh 1961).
67. *PL*, I, Nr. 544; 1302.
68. *PL*, I, Nr. 495; 1300.
69. *PL*, I, Nr. 497. – A. Mirzoyev, *Binoyi* (Stalinabad 1957), 152–6, 357–75. A. Samoylovich, 'Sheybani-name. Persidskiy unicum biblioteki Khivinskago khana', *ZVO*, 19 (1909), 164–176.
70. *PL*, I, Nr. 499; II, XVII. Ed. by Mīnūchihr Sitūda (Tehran 1341). See pp. 427 and 445.

71. *PL*, I, Nr. 505.
72. *PL*, I, Nr. 612. Ḥusayn Mahdī, 'The Firdausī of India', *Indo-Iranica*, I (1947), 23–8.
73. *PL*, I, Nr. 613.
74. *PL*, I, Nr. 614; 1309. See p. 442.
75. *PL*, I, Nr. 617.
76. *PL*, I, Nr. 664; 1310.
77. *PL*, I, Nr. 665; 1311. *Khazā'inu'l-futūḥ*. Ed. by M. Vaḥīd Mīrzā (Calcutta 1953).
78. *PL*, I, Nr. 666; 1311.
79. *PL*, I, Nr. 669; 1313.
80. *PL*, I, Nr. 698; 1313. Gazi Zahirüddin Muhammed Babur. *Vekayi. Babur'un hâtîratî. Doğu türkçesinden çeviren Reşit Rahmeti Arat. Önsözü ve tarihî özeti yazan Y. Hikmet Bayur* (Ankara 1943–6). *Babur-name*. Per. M. Sal'ye (AN UzbSSR, Tashkent, 1958).
81. *PL*, I, Nr. 700. See p. 441.
82. *PL*, I, Nr. 709; 1313–5.
83. *PL*, I, Nr. 715, 717.
84. *PL*, I, Nr. 731; 1317. *Ḥayāt u taṣnīfāt-i Mīrzā Abū-Ṭālib Kalīm Hamadānī Maliku'sh-shu'arā-i darbār-i shāhanshāh-i Shāhjahān. Taṣḥīḥ u muqaddima (ba-Urdū) az Dr. Sharīfu'n-nisā Bēgum Anṣārī* (Ḥaydarābād 1961).
85. *PL*, I, Nr. 802. 'Qushūnkashī-i Nādir Shāh ba Hind. Ma'khūdh az Siyaru'l-muta'akhkhirīn' (ed. by Ḥusayn Nakhjuvānī), *FIZ*, II (1342), 175–92.
86. *PL*, I, Nr. 235; 1254.
87. *PL*, I, Nr. 243; 1255–6.
88. *PL*, I, Nr. 197. Ed. by Ḥabīb Yaghmā'ī (Tehran 1340).
89. *PL*, I, Nr. 234; 1254. 'Alī Aṣghar Ḥikmat, *Jāmī*, 179–81.
90. *PL*, I, Nr. 236; 1254–5.
91. *PL*, I, Nr. 247; 1256.
92. *PL*, I, Nr. 261; 1260. Publ. Tehran 1338 (Anast. reprint of Bombay 1300).
93. *GAL*, S. I, 220. *İA, s.v.* 'İbn A'semülkûfî'.
94. *PL*, I, Nr. 268. Ed. Muḥammad Ramaḍānī (Tehran 1341). See pp. 426 and 434.
95. *PL*, I, Nr. 271, 282, 311 (31, 34–42, 52, 56, 63); 1267.
96. *PL*, I, Nr. 1247.
97. *PL*, I, Nr. 1248.
98. *PL*. I, Nr. 1249. Ed. Dhabīḥu'llāh Ṣafā (Tehran 1332). – Aḥmad Bahmanyār, *Muntakhab-i Asrāru't-tauḥīd* (Tehran 1320). Īraj Afshār, 'Asrāru't-tauḥīd', *Jahān-i nau*, 8 (1332), 249–50. Riḍāzāda-i Shafaq, 'Kitāb-i Asrāru't-tauḥīd', *Mihr*, 4 (1315–6), 325–34, 473–82.
99. *PL*, I, Nr. 1256; II, XXVI–XXVII. Ed. by Taḥsin Yazîcî, 2 vols. (Ankara 1959–61). Turkish transl. *Âriflerin menkibeleri* by Tahsin Yazîcî (Ankara 1953).
100. *PL*, I, Nr. 1257. B. Nikitine, 'Essai d'analyse du Ṣafvatuṣ-ṣafā', *JA*, 245 (1957), 285–94.
101. *PL*, I, Nr. 1277.
102. See pp. 441 and 449.
103. *PL*, I, Nr. 1096. Khayyāmpūr 'Abdu'r-Rasūl, 'Mukhtaṣar-i Makārimu'l-akhlāq', *NDAT*, 3,7 (1329), 68–70.
104. *PL*, I, Nr. 1150/1; 1336. *Ta'rīkh-i Ḥazīn* (Iṣfahān, 2nd ed. 1332). 'Safarnāma-i Ḥazīn', *Paymān*, 4 (1316–7), 49–66, 121–37, 193–216, 265–88. Syed Hasan Askari, 'Fresh Light on Shaikh Ali Hazin and his Tours in Eastern Hindustan', in *Proc. 2nd Ind. Hist. Congr.* (1938), 382–8. Idem, 'The Political Significance of Hazin's Career in Eastern India', *Bengal Past and Present*, 63 (1949), 1–10. Sarfaraz Khan Khatak, *Shaikh Muḥammad Ali Hazin. His Life, Times and Works* (Lahore 1944).
105. *PL*, I, Nr. 501; 1301. *Badāi' al-vakāi'. Kriticheskiy tekst, vvedenie i ukazateli A. N. Boldïreva*, 2 vols. (Moscow 1961). – A. N. Boldïrev, 'Memuarï Zain-ad-dina Vosifi kak istochnik dlya izucheniya

kulturnoy zhizni Sredney Azii i Khorasana na rubezhe XV–XVI vv', *Trudï Otdela Vostoka Ermitazha*, 2 (1940), 203–74. Idem, *Zainaddin Vosifi, tadzhikskiy pisatel' XVI v.* (Stalinabad 1957). Idem, 'Vāṣifī shā'ir-i Harātī u Badā'i'u'l-vaqā'i'', *Āriyānā*, 3 (1323–4), 431–5. A. Mirzoyev, 'Ibni Sino va "Badoye'-ul-vakoye'"-i Muḥammad Vosifi', *Sharki surkh*, 1952,8,9,10,11.

106. *GAL*, I, 325; S. I, 561. *PL*, I, Nr. 1645.
107. *PL*, I, Nr. 1650.
108. *PL*, I, Nr. 1574; 1354.
109. *PL*, I, Nr. 1649; 1355. Ed. by Javād Fāḍil, 3 vols. (Tehran 1340).
110. *PL*, I, Nr. 1245; II, XXVI. Ed. 'Abdu'l-Ḥayy Ḥabībī (Kabul 1341). – Mujtabā Mīnuvī, 'Kitāb-i Ṭabaqāt-i ṣūfiyya-i Anṣārī', *Yaghmā*, 8 (1334), 135–7.
111. *PL*, I, Nr. 1250; II, XXVI. *İA, s.v.* 'Attâr'. N. D. Miklukho-Maklay, 'O proiskhozhdenii "Dopolneniya" k "Tazkirat al-Avliyā" 'Aṭṭāra', *Kratkiye soobshcheniya*, IV, 22 (1956), 19–27. *Moslem Saints and Mystics*. Transl. by A. J. Arberry (London 1966).
112. *PL*, I, Nr. 1274; 1344; II, XXVII. 'Alī Aṣghar Ḥikmat, *Jāmī*, 173–7. Ed. by Mahdī Tauḥīdīpūr (Tehran 1337). 'Abdu'r-Ra'uf Bīnavā, 'Nafaḥātu'l-uns-i Maulānā Jāmī ba-qalam-i khvud-i Maulānā', *Āriyāna*, 1,9 (1321–2), 44–9.
113. *PL*, I, Nr. 1276; II, XXVII–XXVIII.
114. *PL*, I, Nr. 1298; 1344.
115. *PL*, I, Nr. 1310; II, XXVIII.
116. *PL*, I, Nr. 1321 (1).
117. See *GIPh*, II, 212–7.
118. *PL*, I, Nr. 1088. *İA, s.v.* 'Avfî'. Ed. by Sa'īd Nafīsī, *Matn-i kāmil-i Lubābu'l-albāb* (Tehran 1334–5).
119. *PL*, I, Nr. 1093. *İA, s.v.* 'Devlet-Şah'. Ed. by Muḥammad 'Abbāsī (Tehran 1337).
120. *PL*, I, Nr. 1105.
121. *PL*, I, Nr. 1170; 1337. Anast. reprint *ba muqaddima u fihrist u ta'līqāt-i Sayyid Ja'far Shahīdī* (Tehran 1337). Ed. Ḥasan Sādāt Nāṣirī, 3 vols. (Tehran 1337–41).
122. *PL*, I, Nr. 1100; 1335. M. J. Kazi, 'Sám Mírzá and the Tuhfa-i-Sámí', *Indo-Iranica*, 15 (1960), 68–89.
123. *PL*, I, Nr. 1130. Ed. by Vaḥīd Dastgirdī (Tehran 1317). – Aḥmad Suhaylī Khvānsārī, 'Tadhkira-i Mīrzā Ṭāhir Naṣrābādī', *Armaghān*, 18 (1316), 69–74. Vaḥīd Dastgirdī, 'Mīrzā Muḥammad Naṣrābādī mutakhallaṣ ba-Ṭāhir', *Armaghān*, 19 (1317), 217–23. Ibrāhīm Burhānāzād, 'Tadhkira-i Naṣrābādī chi zamān ta'līf shuda ast?', *Amūzish u parvarish*, 26 (1331–2), 560–4.
124. *PL*, I, Nr. 1150 (2); 1336; II, XXV. See p. 451–2.
125. *PL*, I, Nr. 1113 (1). 'Tarjama-i 'Urfī az 'Arafātu'l-'ārifīn-i Taqī Auḥadī', *OCM*, 7,3 (1931), 68–70.
126. *PL*, I, Nr. 1147; II, XXV. 'Burhānu'l-mulk Bahādur Mūsavī mutakhallaṣ ba-Amīn (Naql az Riyāḍu'sh-shu'arā'-i Vālih-i Daghistānī)', *Armaghān*, 9 (1307), 289–306. 'Shaykh Muḥammad 'Alī Ḥazīn (Naql az Tadhkira-i Riyāḍu'sh-shu'arā')', *Armaghān*, 9 (1307), 417–29, 513–27. 'Fāji'a-i Afghān dar Iṣfahān (ba-naql az Vālih-i Daghistānī)', *Sāl-nāma-i dabīristān-i adab-i Iṣfahān*, 1329–30, 18–39.
127. *PL*, I, Nr. 1427.
128. *PL*, I, Nr. 1431. *Calligraphers and Painters. A Treatise by Qāḍī Aḥmad, son of Mīr-Munshī (circa A.H. 1015/A.D. 1606)*. Translated from the Persian by V. Minorsky. With an Introduction by B. N. Zakhoder. Translated from Russian by T. Minorsky (Washington 1959). 'Zahrā Ḥasanī (Dā'īzāda), Gulistān-i hunar', *Naqsh u nigār*, 5 (1337), 23–4. Ḥusayn Nakhchuvānī, 'Mu'arrafī-i Kitāb-i Gulistān-i hunar', *NDAT*, 9 (1336), 1–16. See p. 441.
129. *PL*, I, Nr. 1489. See p. 442.
130. *PL*, I, Nr. 1460. Ed. by Mīr Jalālu'd-dīn Ḥusaynī Urumavī (Tehran 1338). See p. 447.
131. *PL*, I, Nr. 1461. Ed. by Mīr Jalālu'd-dīn Ḥusaynī Urumavī (Tehran 1337).
132. *PL*, I, Nr. 1462. See pp. 441, 449 and 451.
133. *PL*, I, Nr. 1471.

V. GEOGRAPHY

Geographical literature written in the Persian language does not bear comparison with that written in Arabic, either as regards its quantity or its quality. It is however a notable and undeniable fact that the majority of the earliest Islamic geographers writing in Arabic in the 3rd/9th and 4th/10th centuries were of Persian origin.

Of the general geographical works written in Persian, the earliest is most probably the *Ḥudūdu'l-'ālam mina'l-mashriq ila'l-maghrib*, 'The Regions of the World from East to West', written during the second half of the 4th/10th century, by an author whose name has been lost, for the Farīghūnid Abu'l-Ḥārith Muḥammad b. Aḥmad, a local prince of the city of Jūzjānān in Khurasan. It deals in the traditional manner of Islamic geographies with the earth in general, then the seas, islands, mountains, rivers and deserts, after which follow descriptions of single countries, starting with China and ending with Europe.[1] The *Jahān-nāma*, 'Book of the World', dating from the beginning of the 7th/13th century, is a much smaller volume, in which Muḥammad b. Najīb Bakrān sketched in twenty short paragraphs a picture of the world as it was then known for the Khvārazmshāh 'Alā'u'd-dīn Muḥammad b. Takash.[2] Not until more than a hundred years later do we again encounter a general geographical work, written in 748/1347–8 at the time of the first Muẓaffarid ruler, Mubārizu'd-dīn Muḥammad Muẓaffar. The author is unknown and even its title, *Ṣuvaru'l-aqālīm*, 'Pictures of the Regions of the Earth', is uncertain. The first chapter contains a description of the globe, its nature and dimensions, as well as a picture of the southern hemisphere; the second describes the seven *iqlīms* – both chapters being interwoven with mythical tales and excursions into legend.[3] We possess two such works dating from Timurid times. One, which has most probably remained unfinished and has no definite title, is a book on geography by the court historian of Shāhrukh whom we already know, Ḥāfiẓ-i Abrū.[4] At his master's injunction he began to work on it in 817/1414 and was occupied with it for at least six years. This work too betrays the historian, for his descriptions of the Iranian provinces, which apart from any other considerations are of value for the contemporary topography of Iran, contain very extensive historical digressions, which for the most part correspond to certain sections of his historical writings, either word for word or in summary.[5] The second work dating from the latter half of the 9th/15th century was compiled by Sā'id b. 'Alī Jurjānī and may have borne the title *Masāliku'l-mamālik*, 'The Travel Routes of the Countries'. In contrast to the historical interest to be found in Ḥāfiẓ-i Abrū, this author turned his attention more to physical peculiarities, and showed a special liking for myths and legends.[6]

Under geographical literature of the Islamic countries must be included a species which was very popular there and which can be summarised under the title of cosmography. Its chief constituent is the description of the 'oikumene', to which however extensive sections on natural science, ethnography, astronomy and mythology are added with particular stress on everything mysterious, a tendency which is already clearly shown by the titles of such books: 'Wonders' and 'Curiosities' (*'ajā'ib, gharā-'ib*). The earliest work of this type is thought to be the *'Ajā'ibu'l-buldān*, 'The Wonders of the Countries', or *'Ajā'ibu'l-barr va'l-baḥr*, 'The Wonders of Land and Sea', which the poet Abu'l-Mu'ayyad al-Balkhī wrote in the 4th/10th century for the Samanid prince Nūḥ b. Manṣūr. Unfortunately it has only been preserved in a later, incomplete version dating from the beginning of the 7th/13th century.[7] The *'Ajā'ibu'l-makhlūqāt va gharā'ibu'l-maujūdāt*, 'The Wonders of Creatures and the Curiosities of Things', which was dedicated to the Seljuq Sulṭān Ṭughril II and whose author was probably a certain Najīb Hamadānī, dates from the last years of the 6th/12th century. It deals in ten sections with: (1) celestial bodies; (2) atmospheric phenomena; (3) the earth's surface; (4) topography; (5) plants; (6) talismans; hidden treasures and the graves of famous kings and prophets; (7) psychology, the human species and all kinds of mysterious things, particularly in the fields of natural science, alchemy and medicine; (8) jinn and other demonic creatures; (9) miraculous birds; (10) fabulous beasts. This work was also one of the sources for the above-mentioned later recast of the *'Ajā'ibu'l-buldān* by Balkhī.[8] The Persians cherished a particular fondness for an Arabic work on cosmography by Zakariyyā b. Muḥammad al-Qazvīnī (d. 682/1283) of which there are several translations and adaptations in Persian.[9] The most famous and best work in Persian on cosmography was produced by a namesake of the Arabic cosmographer just mentioned, Ḥamdu'llāh Mustaufī Qazvīnī, who is already known to us as a historian.[10] His cosmographic opus bears the title *Nuzhatu'l-qulūb*, 'The Pleasure of the Hearts'. It was completed in 740/1339–40 and contains three chapters. The first is devoted to the mineral, vegetable and animal kingdoms, the second to Man. Of particular importance to the historical topography of Iran is the third chapter which, according to the usual method employed in geographical works, first describes the three holy cities – Mecca, Medina and Jerusalem –, then Iran and foreign countries.[11] From the second half of the 10th/16th century we possess the *Majma'u'l-gharā'ib*, 'Collections of Curiosities', by Sulṭān-Muḥammad b. Darvīsh-Muḥammad al-Balkhī, which has been preserved in two redactions. These in turn

Notes on p. 463

were dedicated to two Shaybanid Khāns. The book is said to have been very popular in Central Asia until recent times.[12]

To the rare specialised geographical works belongs primarily the Geography of Persia with historical notes, mainly on the Imāms and the Safavids, entitled *Mukhtaṣar*, 'Compendium', which was completed in Lahore in 1091/1680–1 by Muḥammad Mufīd Mustaufī Bāfqī Yazdī.[13] A topography and history of Medina called *Jadhbu'l-qulūb ilā diyāri'l-Maḥbūb*, 'The Attraction of Hearts to the Land of the Beloved', was begun in that city by 'Abdu'l-Ḥaqq Dihlavī[14] in the year 998/1589–90 and completed in Dihlī in 1001/1592–3.[15] A very interesting *Risāla*[16] on the manners and customs of the inhabitants of Tabriz was written in 992/1584 or 993/1585 by Rūḥī Anārjānī. The *Ta'rīkh-i Khitāy u Khutan*, 'History of China and Khotan', dedicated to the Ottoman Sulṭān Süleymān the Great, contains a description of China and was written by 'Alī-Akbar Khitāyī, a man probably originally hailing from Turkestan, who spent many years as a merchant in Peking and later settled in Constantinople.[17]

The most excellent of Persian books of travel is the very informative *Safar-nāma*, 'Book of Travel', of Nāṣir-i Khusrau (d. between 465–70/1072–7), stylistically distinguished by its simple and lucid prose. In it he describes his seven years of wandering – during which he undertook four pilgrimages to Mecca – from Khurasan through Persia, Azerbayjan, Syria and Palestine to Egypt and thence back to his native land. The book gives not only valuable topographical details but also remarkable information about the political, social, economic and cultural conditions in the countries he visited during those politically and religiously turbulent times.[18]

A summary of an interesting diary of a journey to China and of a stay there during the years 822/1419 to 825/1422 was written by Khvāja Ghiyāthu'd-dīn Naqqāsh, one of the leaders of an embassy of the Timurid Shāhrukh and his son Bāysunghur to the court of the Emperor of China. This work was included in his great chronicle by Ḥāfiẓ-i Abrū. In a newly abridged form this narrative is to be found in the historical work of 'Abdu'r-Razzāq Samarqandī and as such is mentioned by later historians.[19] Apart from these, only two travel books from the latter half of the 12th/18th century are worth noting and both are of Indian origin. One is the account by the merchant Muḥammad 'Abdu'llāh of his journeys to Khurasan, Central Asia, Russia, China, Tibet and Kashmir[20], the other being the *Sayru'l bilād*, 'Travelling through the Countries', in which Mughul Beg b. Muḥammad Beg describes his travels in Punjab and the neighbouring areas of Iran in the service of Lt.-Col. Francis Wilford.[21]

Handbooks for pilgrims, a form of literature of geographic and religious content much loved in Islamic countries, are represented in Persian literature by the *Futūḥu'l-Ḥaramayn*, 'The Unlocking of the Two Holy Cities', written down in 911/1505–6 by Muḥyi'd-dīn Lārī (d. 933/1526–7), and containing a description of Mecca and Medina in verse[22], and by the *Manāzilu'l-ḥajj*, 'Stations of Pilgrimage', compiled in 1214/1799–1800 by Band-i 'Ālī b. Mīrzā Khayrāt-'Alī. This work describes two pilgrims' routes from Baghdad through the Shammar region and Syria.[23]

A practice that became prevalent among Persian historians was to include a section on geography in their historical works. Apart from the detailed geographical Khātimas in the World Chronicles of Mīrkhvānd and Khvāndamīr, other historical and biographical works, memoirs and books on astronomy and the natural sciences contained much geographical material. This fact is also mentioned in the other chapters of the present work.

NOTES

1. *PL*, II, Nr 181. Ed. by Minūchihr Sitūda (Tehran 1340). – 'Abdu'l-Ḥayy Ḥabībī, 'Yak nafar-i jughrāfiyānigār andar hazār sāl pīsh az īn 'aṣr (Ḥudūdu'l-'ālam)', *Kābul*, 10,11 (1318–9), 29–31. V. Minorsky, 'Ibn Farīghūn and the Ḥudūd al-'Ālam', in *Studia in honour of S. H. Taqizadeh* (London 1962), 189–96 (= 'Mu'allif-i Ḥudūdu'l-'ālam kīst. Ibn Farīghūn va Ḥudūdu'l-'ālam', *Adab*, 11, 1342, 1–10).
2. *PL*, II, Nr. 185. Ṣafā, I, 625–6. *Dzhahān-nāme (Kniga o mire). Izdanie teksta, vvedenie i ukazateli Yu. E. Borshchevskovo* (Moscow 1960). Ed. by Muḥammad Amīn Riyāḥī (Tehran 1341).
3. *PL*, II, Nr. 191.
4. See p. 440.
5. *PL*, II, Nr. 192.
6. *PL*, II, Nr. 195.
7. *PL*, II, Nr. 187. Sa'īd Nafīsī, 'Abu'l-Mu'ayyad Balkhī', *Sharq*, 1,3 (1309), 129–36.
8. *PL*, II, Nr. 183.
9. *GAL*, I, 481–2; S. I, 882–3. *PL*, II, Nr. 188. Persian translation ed. by Naṣru'llāh Ṣabūḥī (Tehran 1340).
10. See p. 440.
11. *PL*, II, Nr. 190. Ed. by Muḥammad Dabīr Siyāqī (Tehran 1336–7). – Aḥmad Kasravī, 'Ta'rīkh-i ta'līf-i Nuzhatu'l-qulūb', *Āyanda*, 2 (1305–6), 324–5.
12. *PL*, II, Nr. 199.
13. *PL*, II, Nr. 210. Jean Aubin, 'Quelques Notices du Mukhtaṣar-i Mufīd', *FIZ*, 6 (1337), 164–77. See p. 447.
14. See p. 450.
15. *PL*, I, Nr. 607; 1307.
16. 'Risāla-i Rūḥī Anārjānī. Ba-taṣḥīḥ u muqaddima-i Sa'īd Nafīsī', *FIZ*, 2 (1333), 329–72.
17. *PL*, I, Nr. 610; 1308. *İA, s.v.* 'Ali Ekber'.
18. *PL*, I, Nr. 1589. Spuler 272–3 *SSH*, II, 152. Ed. by Maḥmūd Ghanīzāda (Berlin 1341/1923; anast. reprint Tehran 1339). Ed. by Muḥammad Dabīr Siyāqī (Tehran 1335). – Īraj Afshār, 'Safar-nāma-i Ḥakīm Nāṣir-i Khusrau Qubādiyānī', *Jahān-i nau*, 6 (1330), 207–8. Tajribakār Nuṣrat, 'Safar-nāma-i Ḥakīm Nāṣir-i Khusrau', *Mardumshināsī*, I (1335), 112–7. F. Gabrieli, 'Il "Sefer-Nāmeh" e la crisi religiosa di Nāṣir-i Ḫusraw', *Atti del XIX Congr. Intern. degli Orient.* (Roma 1935), 556–9. G. M. Wickens, 'The Chronology of Nāṣir-i Khusrau's Safarnāma', *Islamic Quarterly*, 4 (1957), 66–77.
19. *PL*, I, 295–6; 1276. Turkish transl., see *GOR*, 295–6.
20. *PL*, II, Nr. 218.
21. *PL*, II, Nr. 224.
22. *GIPh*, II, 306–7. Rieu, 655.
23. *PL*, II, Nr. 225.

VI. THE EXACT SCIENCES

The exact sciences of the Moslems are derived from the writings of Greek scholars.[1] As far as mathematics and geometry are concerned, Naṣīru'd-dīn Ṭūsī (d. 672/1274) translated the Greek basic manuals of these sciences, Euclid's *Elements* and Theodosius' *Spherica*, into Arabic, and from these translations several Persian versions were made.[2] He was also interested in Indian arithmetic and wrote at least two treatises on the subject.[3] As in all other fields, the first Moslem mathematicians, including those of Persian origin, wrote in Arabic. Some of their works were then also translated into Persian.

The first works written in Persian belonging to this category appear to have been the *Risāla dar handasa*, 'Treatise on Geometry', in which Abū-'Ubayd 'Abdu'l-Vāḥid b. Muḥammad Jūzjānī, a pupil of Avicenna's, collected some of his master's notes on geometry[4], and the *Miftāḥu'l-mu'āmalāt*, 'The Key to Commercial Arithmetic', by Muḥammad b. Ayyūb aṭ-Ṭabarī, who lived in the 5th/11th century. The latter is intended as an aid to merchants and executors.[5]

Mathematics and geometry, in company with astronomy, received a powerful impetus during the first half of the 9th/15th century, thanks to the interest shown in these studies by Ulughbeg, the scholarly grandson of Tamerlane. A member of his circle of scholars, Ṣalāḥu'd-dīn Mūsā, known as Qāḍīzāda-i Rūmī, wrote a Persian treatise on arithmetic called simply *Risāla dar ḥisāb*, 'Treatise on Arithmetic'.[6] Apparently more widely read, more frequently annotated and also translated into Turkish, was the *Risāla dar 'ilm-i ḥisāb*, 'Treatise on the Science of Arithmetic', a treatise on arithmetic and geometry, also known as *Fārsī ḥisāb*, 'Persian Arithmetic', written by one of his pupils, 'Alī Qūshjī. After the death of Ulughbeg he first went to Uzun Ḥasan, but he ended his life in the service of the Ottoman Sulṭān Muḥammad Fātiḥ as professor at the Aya Ṣofya Madrasa in the year 879/1474–5.[7] The only important work in this field that dates from the 11th/17th century is the *Khulāṣatu'l-ḥisāb*, 'Quintessence of Arithmetic', by Bahā'u'd-dīn Muḥammad b. Ḥusayn 'Āmilī (d.

1031/1622). The book was written in Arabic but was translated into Persian more than once and was the subject of many commentaries.[8]

In India, two Sanskrit works by Bhāskara (12th century), the Līlāvatī (*Tarjama-i Līlāvatī*) on arithmetic and geometry and the Vīja-Ganita (*Tarjama-i Bīj ganit*) on algebra, were translated into Persian in the years 995/1587 and 1044/1634–5 respectively, the first book at the desire of Akbar.[9] Apart from these, some ten works on mathematics appeared in India, but of these only the *Risāla dar jabr u muqābala*, 'Treatise on Algebra', by Najmu'd-dīn Khān Kākūravī (d. 1229/1814) seems to have met with any great approval.[10]

Astronomy, closely and in practice inextricably linked with astrology – which in the east was regarded as a science and highly esteemed – is also based on the researches of Greek scholars. Persian astronomers apparently used the Arabic translations of the Greeks, as Persian versions of the latter are somewhat rare and of recent date. Only the hundred astrological judgements of Claudius Ptolemy (*Karpos, Centiloquium*) had been already translated and explained by Naṣīru'd-dīn Ṭūsī. His work is known under the name *Tarjama-i Thamara-i Baṭlamyūs*, 'The Translation of the Fruit of Ptolemy', or *Ṣad kalima-i Baṭlamyūs*, 'The Hundred Sayings of Ptolemy'.[11] The Indian work on astronomy by Varāha-mihira (d. 587) was translated into Persian in India at the request of the Sulṭān Fīrūzshāh III of Dihlī (752–90/1351–8) by 'Abdu'l-'Azīz b. Shams b. Bahā' Nūrī Dihlavī.[12]

Works written originally in Arabic were frequently translated into Persian, but occasionally too the reverse took place. Sometimes the author wrote his book in both languages. Thus the Arabic work *Mafātīḥu'l-qaḍā'*, 'The Keys of Destiny', an astrological treatise on the signs of the zodiac by the Indian Māshā'a'llāh al-Ḥakīm, who was famous as an astrologer in the second half of the 2nd/8th century and the first half of the 3rd/9th under the first Abbasids[13], as well as several works by Abū-Ma'shar al-Balkhī (d. 272/886)[14], and the *Ṣuvaru'l-kavākib*, 'The Patterns of the Stars', by 'Abdu'r-Raḥmān b. 'Umar aṣ-Ṣūfī ar-Rāzī (d. 376/986)[15], were translated into Persian. In the 4th/10th century, Abū-Naṣr al-Ḥasan al-Qummī wrote the *al-Bāri' fī aḥkāmi'n-nujūm va't-tavāli'*, 'The Thorough (Book) on the Decisions of the Stars and Horoscopes'[16], and Abu'l-Ḥasan Kūshyār b. Labbān (or Labār?) al-Jīlī produced the *al-Madkhal fī ṣinā'at aḥkāmi'n-nujūm*, 'Introduction to the Art of Interpretation of the Stars', a compendium on astrology, in the two languages, Arabic and Persian, at the same time.[17] Al-Bīrūnī (d. 440/1048) also wrote his elements of astrology in both languages and called it *at-Tafhīm li-avā'il ṣinā'ati't-tanjīm*, 'Instruction on the Basic Principles of the Art of Astrology'.[18]

Several astrological treatises by Muḥammad b. Ayyūb aṭ-Ṭabarī from the 5th/11th century are written in Persian only.[19] The *Rauḍatu'l-munajjimīn*, 'The Garden of the Astrologists', by Shāhmardān b. Abi'l-Khayr Rāzī, dates from the end of the 5th/11th century and is a detailed introduction to astrology for beginners.[20] In the 6th/12th century the polyhistor Fakhru'd-dīn Rāzī (d. 606/1209) wrote his *al-Aḥkāmu'l-'Alā'īya*

Notes on pp. 468–469

fi'l-a'lāmi's-samā'īya, 'Definitions for 'Alā('u'd-dīn) on the Signs of the Zodiac', or *al-Ikhtiyārātu'l-'Alā'īya fi'l-ikhtiyārāti's-samā'īya*, 'Selected Things for 'Alā('u'd-dīn) on the Choice of the Celestial Signs', a book on the hours and days favourable for various undertakings, composed for the Khvārazmshāh 'Alā'u'd-dīn Muḥammad b. Takash.[21] Apart from the works of Naṣīru'd-dīn Ṭūsī devoted to special subjects, which will be discussed later, we possess his handbook on astronomy that bears the title *Risāla-i Mu'īnīya*, 'The Mu'īnic Treatise', after Mu'īnu'd-dīn Abu'sh-Shams, the son of his former patron, Nāṣiru'd-dīn b. Abī Manṣūr.[22] The author himself later added explanations of the more difficult sections of this work, which is among his finest.[23] In the Ottoman empire, 'Alī Qūshjī, whom we have already mentioned, composed an outline of astronomy for the Sulṭān Muḥammad Fātiḥ, which is known under the name *Risāla dar hay'at*, 'Treatise on Astronomy', or *Fārsī hay'at*, 'Persian Astronomy'. This enjoyed great popularity, was often the subject of commentaries and was also translated into Turkish.[24] In Persia Ḥusayn Vā'iẓ Kāshifī, the author of the *Rauḍatu'sh-shuhadā'*, wrote the *Lavā'iḥu'l-qamar*, 'The Signs of the Moon', about this time. It discusses the establishment of favourable hours, days and months according to the different phases of the moon.[25] There are also books on astrology and astronomy in verse form. One such work, *Madkhal-i manẓūm*, 'Introduction in Verse', has been attributed to Naṣīru'd-dīn Ṭūsī.[26]

Meteorology is the subject of the *Risāla-i Sanjarīya fi'l-kā'ināti'l-'unṣurīya*, 'Treatise for Sanjar on the Events concerning the Elements', by 'Umar b. Sahlān Sāvī (Sāvajī)[27], written for the Sulṭān Sanjar (511–552/1117–1157), son of Malikshāh[28], and the *Risāla dar āthār-i 'ulvī*, 'Treatise on Sublime Impressions', by the astronomer Muḥammad b. Mas'ūd Mas'ūdī Marvazī, completed in the middle of the 7th/13th century.[29]

An indispensable aid to astronomers were astronomic tables. In Islamic countries they were known by the name *Zīj*, which originally meant a mason's rule and was already being used in this sense in the time of the Sasanians. As far as is known, the earliest Persian work of this type was a translation from Arabic, namely of a work dating from the 4th/10th century, the *az-Zīj al-Jāmi'*, 'The Comprehensive Tables', by Abu'l-Ḥasan Kūshyār b. Labbān[30], which was completed in the year 483/1090 by Muḥammad b. 'Umar al-Munajjim at-Tabrīzī.[31] The *az-Zīju'l-mufrad*, 'The Unique Tables', by Muḥammad b. Ayyūb aṭ-Ṭabarī[32] and the *Zīj-i Nāṣirī*, 'Nāṣir's Tables', by Maḥmūd b. 'Umar, which took its name from the Sulṭān of Dihlī, Nāṣiru'd-dīn Maḥmūd (644–64/1246–65), were both works originally composed in Persian.[33]

All earlier works were however put into the shade by two astronomical tables that have enjoyed extreme popularity ever since they were written and in 1652 became known in Europe too, thanks to a translation by the Oxford professor, John Greaves.[34] These are the famous tables of Naṣīru'd-dīn Ṭūsī and of Ulughbeg. The first, *Zīj-i Īlkhānī*, 'The Īlkhānic Tables', were undertaken at the behest of Hulagu (654–63/1256–65) and completed during the reign of his son, Abaqa (663–80/1265–82), to whom they were dedicated. These were annotated and expanded several times and also translated into Arabic.[35] The second, *Zīj-i (jadīd-i) sulṭānī (-i Gūrkānī)*, 'The (new) Tables of Sulṭān (Gūrkān)', is a thorough revision of the first, based on direct observations, and produced in the middle of the 9th/15th century under the supervision of Ulughbeg by his learned assistants Qāḍīzāda-i Rūmī, Ghiyāthu'd-dīn Jamshīd, and 'Alī Qūshjī. As the last significant work on Moslem astronomy it was highly prized in the period that followed; it was supplied with explanatory notes and translated into Arabic.[36]

Closely associated with astronomy and astrology were calendars (*taqvīm*). These were moreover of great importance in Islamic countries for the purpose of the accurate calculation of canonical times of prayer, fasting and feast days. Persian literature is also indebted to the versatile Naṣīru'd-dīn Ṭūsī for the earliest and most important work on the compilation of almanacs. It is called *Sī faṣl dar taqvīm*, 'Thirty Chapters on the Calendar'.[37]

Among later works the *Bīst bāb dar ma'rifati't-taqvīm*, 'Twenty Chapters concerning the Knowledge of the Calendar', written by Niẓāmu'd-dīn 'Abdu'l-'Alī b. Muḥammad Bīrjandī (d. 934/1527–8)[38] was very popular and several times annotated. The reform of the ancient Persian calendar, which is associated with the names of the Seljuq Sulṭān Malikshāh (465–485/1072–1092) and the famous mathematician and astronomer 'Umar Khayyām, was little in harmony with Islam. 'Umar Khayyām did not, however, write any of his treatises on mathematics or astronomy in Persian.[39] The *Naurūz-nāma*, 'Book of the New Year', an otherwise very interesting treatise on the Iranian New Year's feast, appears to be wrongly ascribed to him.[40]

Astronomers and astrologers needed instruments for their observations and measurements. The only instrument the Moslems knew, and which they had also taken over from the Greeks and improved in several ways, was the astrolabe (*asṭurlāb*)[41], a convenient piece of hand-apparatus. On the other hand gigantic astrolabes were set up in the two observatories, one of which was built in Maragha by Hulagu for Naṣīru'd-dīn Ṭūsī, and the second about two centuries later in Samarkand by Ulughbeg. We possess several Persian writings on the varieties, nature and use of the astrolabe. The oldest is probably the *Kitāb ma'rifati'l-asṭurlāb*, 'The Book of Information on the Astrolabe', or *Shash faṣl*, 'Six Sections', by Muḥammad b. Ayyūb aṭ-Ṭabarī, written in the 5th/11th century.[42] The best known however is the *Bīst bāb dar asṭurlāb*, 'Twenty Chapters on the Astrolabe', by Naṣīru'd-dīn Ṭūṣī.[43] In the following centuries, apart from commentaries on Ṭūsī's work, several similar treatises were written; the *Panjāh bāb-i sulṭānī*, 'Fifty Chapters for the Sultan (Bābur b. Bāysunghur)', by Ruknu'd-dīn al-Āmulī, dating from the 9th/15th century[44], and two works, the *Bīst u chahār bāb*, 'Twenty-four Chapters', and the *Risāla-i asṭurlāb*, 'Treatise on the Astrolabe', by Abu'l-Khayr al-Fārisī from the 10th/16th century[45] should be mentioned. The well-known assistant of Ulughbeg, Ghiyāthu'd-dīn Jamshīd, also wrote two special treatises on astronomical instruments.[46]

Notes on pp. 468–469

NOTES

1. See. p. 425, and Sarton, II, 1001–13.
2. *PL*, II, Nr. 1, 2.
3. *PL*, II, Nr. 10 (1, 2).
4. *PL*, II, Nr. 4.
5. *PL*, II, Nr. 5 (1). His *Shumār-nāma* was edited by Taqī Bīnish (Tehran 1345).
6. *PL*, II, Nr. 16.
7. *PL*, II, Nr. 20. *İA, s.v.* 'Ali Kuşçu'.
8. *GAL*, II, 414; S. II, 595. *PL*, II, Nr. 24.
9. *PL*, II, Nr. 6.
10. *PL*, II, Nr. 38.
11. *PL*, II, Nr. 70.
12. *PL*, II, Nr. 71.
13. *PL*, II, Nr. 72.
14. *PL*, II, Nr. 73.
15. *PL*, II, Nr. 75.
16. *PL*, II, Nr. 74.
17. *PL*, II, Nr. 77 (1).
18. *PL*, II, Nr. 80. *İA, s.v.* 'Bîrûnî'. – M. Krause, 'Al-Biruni, ein iranischer Forscher des Mittelalters', *Isl.*, 26 (1924), 1–15. S.P. Tolstov, 'Biruni i yego vremya', *Vestn. AN SSSR*, 1949,4, 177–96. Sayĭlì Aydĭn, 'Biruni. Hayatĭ, milliyeti ve şahsiyeti', *TTK Belleten*, 13 (1949), 53–88. V. J. Zakhoder i dr., *Biruni – velikiy uzbekskiy uchenĭy srednovekov'ya* (Tashkent 1950). *Biruni. Sbornik statey.* Pod red. S. P. Tolstova (Moscow-Leningrad 1950). V. Courtois, *Al-Biruni, a Life Sketch* (Calcutta 1952).
19. *PL*, II, Nr. 79 (1, 3, 4).
20. *PL*, II, Nr. 81.
21. *PL*, II, Nr. 87.
22. See p. 426.
23. *PL*, II, Nr. 91 (7). *Ar-Risāla al-Mu'īnīya.* Ed. by Muḥammad Taqī Dānish-Pazhūh (Tehran 1335). *Ḥall-i mushkilāt-i Mu'īnīya.* Ed. by Muḥammad Taqī Dānish-Pazhūh (Tehran 1335).
24. *PL*, II, Nr. 112 (1).
25. *PL*, II, Nr. 116. See pp. 426, 434 and 450.
26. *PL*, II, Nr. 91 (4).
27. See p. 426.
28. Ed. by Muḥammad Taqī Dānish-Pazhūh (*Du risāla dar bāra-i āthār-i 'ulvī*, 1–56) (Tehran 1337).
29. *PL*, II, 52. Ed. by Muḥammad Taqī Dānish-Pazhūh (*Du risāla dar bāra-i āthār-i 'ulvī*, 58–128) (Tehran 1337). – 'Risāla dar ma'rifat-i 'anāṣir u kā'ināt'l-jauv. Ba-ihtimām-i Muḥammad Shafī'', *OCM*, 4,3 (1928), 31–91.
30. *GAL*, I, 222; S. I, 397.
31. *PL*, II, Nr. 77 (2).
32. *PL*, II, Nr. 79 (5).
33. *PL*, II, Nr. 90.
34. *Binae tabulae geographicae una Nassir Eddini Persae altera Ulug Beigi Tatari opera et studio J. Gravii ... publicatae* (London 1652).
35. *PL*, II, Nr. 91 (14). Maljā'ī, 'Raṣad-i Marāgha u Zīj-i Hulagū', *Māhtāb*, I (1316–7), 122–6. J. A. Boyle, 'The longer Introduction to the "Zij-i-ilkhani" of Nasir-ad-din Tusi', *Journal of Sem. St.*, 8,2 (1963), 244–54.

36. *PL*, II, Nr. 104 (2). Taqī Bīnish, 'Zīj-i Ulugh Beg', *Nashriyya-i Farhang-i Khurāsān*, 1,4–5 (1336), 20–40. T. N. Karï-Niyazof, *Astronomicheskaya shkola Ulugbeka* (Moscow 1950). Aydın Sayıl, *Ulug Bey ve Semerkanddeki ilim faaliyeti hakkĭnda Gĭyasüddin-i Kâşî'nin mektubu* (Ankara 1960). E. S. Kennedy, 'A Letter of Jamshîd al Kâshî to his Father', *Orientalia*, 29 (1960), 191–213.

37. *PL*, II, Nr. 91 (10).

38. *PL*, II, Nr. 121.

39. *Kulliyyāt-i āthār-i pārsī-i Ḥakīm 'Umar Khayyām. Ba-taḥqīq u ihtimām-i Muḥammad 'Abbāsī* (Tehran 1337). *Rasā'il-i Khayyām. Ba-ihtimām-i Avistā* (Tehran s.a.). 'Omar Khayyām, *Traktati. Perevod B. A. Rozenfel'da. Vstupitel'naya stat'ya i kommentarii B. A. Rozenfel'da i A. P. Yushkevicha* (Moscow 1961). Reprint of the *Naurūz-nāma*, zīr-i naẓar-i 'Alī Ḥuṣūrī (Tehran 1343). Ghulām-i Ḥusayn Muṣāḥib, *Ḥakīm 'Umar Khayyām ba 'unvān-i 'ālim-i jabr* (Tehran 1339).

40. *CPL*, 85–8. *Omar Khayyâm, Nowrūz Nāmah. A Treatise on the Origin, History, & the Ceremonies of the Persian New-year Festival.* Ed. by M. Mojtabâ Minovi (Tehran 1933). See also the three books mentioned in the preceding note. – Fr. Gabrieli, 'Il "Nawruz-nameh" e Omar Hayyam', *Annali* (Napoli), 8 (1936), sep. Muḥammad Iqbāl, 'Naurūznāma-i Khayyām', *OCM* 9,1 (1934), 104–115. Muḥīṭ Ṭabāṭabā'ī, *Naurūz u Naurūz-nāma* (Tehran 1343).

41. *EI, s.v.* 'Asṭurlāb'.

42. *PL*, II, Nr. 79.

43. *PL*, II, Nr. 91 (1). Ed. by Mudarris Riḍavī (Tehran 1335).

44. *PL*, II, Nr. 108 (1).

45. *PL*, II, Nr. 123 (2, 4).

46. *PL*, II, Nr. 105 (2, 3).

VII. THE NATURAL SCIENCES

In Islamic literature, natural science has the peculiar characteristic of almost exclusively pursuing various kinds of practical aims.

As far as zoology is concerned, the titles of general works already betray this utilitarian attitude. Apart from two earlier Persian versions of Arabic works, dating from the 7th/13th and the 11th/17th centuries, a handbook by the already often-quoted Shaykh Ḥazīn [1], called the *Khavāṣṣu'l-ḥayavān*, 'The (useful) Properties of Animals', is an original Persian work. In the first chapter it describes the best known animals in alphabetical order, and in the other two their habits, faculties and abilities, with an introduction on the hunting and slaughter of animals.[2]

In research into the utility of animals, medical and veterinary interests come especially to the fore, the latter particularly in the two associated specialist branches, hippology and falconry.

Most of the *Faras-nāma, Khayl-nāma*, 'Book of Horses', or similarly entitled handbooks on hippology, contain in two separate sections discussions on the properties of the horse, its training and maladies together with their treatment. It is believed that some are based on Greek works, others have been translated from Sanskrit.[3] There are of course also translations from Arabic. The following two are probably the most important among the original Persian works: the *Miḍmār-i dānish*, 'The Race-course of Knowledge', published in 1071/1660–1 at the command of 'Abbās II (1052–77/1642–66) by Niẓāmu'd-dīn Aḥmad Ṣādir, who was probably the son of Mullā Ṣadrā [4]; and the small *Faras-nāma* by Shaykh Ḥazīn, which seems to be only a scanty list of contents of an earlier and larger work that he had already written in Isfahan and could not take with him to India.[5]

The specialised writings on falconry are also of a practical nature and contain a wealth of detail on maladies and their treatment as well as descriptions of sporting birds and other animals of the chase. These too are apparently based on ancient texts which may have been written, for example, for Alexander the Great or for Jamshīd.

One such book, written for the latter, is said to have been put into Persian by Naṣīru-'d-dīn Ṭūsī from an Arabic translation and adapted in verse in the year 896/1491 by 'Alī Ḥaydar Tabrīzī, chief falconer (*qūshchī bāshī*) to the Aqqoyunlu Sulṭān Ya'qūb Khān (884–96/1479–91), in his *Bāz-nāma*, 'Book of Falcons'. According to later information, such *Bāz-nāmas* are believed to have already existed at the time of the Samanids. Moreover, mention is made of a *Ṣayd-nāma-i Malikshāhī*, 'The Hunting Book of Malikshāh', written for Sulṭān Malikshāh, which became a model for the *Shikār-nāma-i Īlkhānī* of 'Alī b. Manṣūr, written at the command of the Sulṭān Ṭoghāytīmūr in the 8th/14th century[6], as well as for other works dealing with the same subject. Two larger *Bāz-nāmas* appeared in India. One, dedicated to the emperor Akbar, is by Muḥibb 'Alī Khān Khāṣṣmaḥallī b. Niẓāmu'd-dīn 'Alī Marghulānī (d. 989/1581), who in the foreword boasts of great experience in hunting[7]; the other was written by a certain Bahādur under Aurangzīb 'Ālamgīr.[8]

Botany was studied side by side with pharmacology; moreover it was of benefit to agriculture and horticulture, which in the Islamic east were highly developed and were steadily progressing as a result of experience and experiments. Works on pharmacology will be mentioned elsewhere.[9] The famous vizier Rashīdu'd-dīn Faḍlu'llāh[10] wrote the *Kitābu'l-akhbār va'l-āthār*(?), 'Book of Counsels and Traditions', only one extract of which however is extant. This deals with agriculture and its associated fields of knowledge, meteorology, irrigation, the combating of plant diseases, etc.[11] Another book of similar content is the *Irshādu'z-zirā'a*, 'Directions for Agriculture', written in the year 921/1515 by Fāḍil Haravī.[12] In India appeared the *Risāla-i nakhlbandiyya*, 'Treatise on the Cultivation of Plants.' This is a handbook based on Indian methods of cultivating fruit trees, flowers and various vegetables, by Aḥmad 'Alī b. Muḥammad Khalīl of Jaunpūr, and is an extract from an older work by Amānu'llāh al-Ḥusaynī (d. 1046/1636–7).[13]

Among the minerals, the Islamic natural scientists were most interested in precious stones and precious metals. We possess several books of modest proportions dealing, for the most part in two sections, with precious stones and metals, pearls, corals, as well as several organic substances such as musk, amber, camphor etc. The earliest work in Persian of this type that has come down to us is the *Tansūkh-nāma-i Īlkhāni*, 'The Īlkhānic Book of Precious Things', which Naṣīru'd-dīn Ṭūsī wrote for the Īlkhān Hulagu.[14] The *'Arā'isu'l-javāhir va nafā'isu'l-aṭā'ib*, 'The Brides of Jewels and the Best of Precious Things', written by Abu'l-Qāsim 'Abdu'llāh b. 'Alī b. Muḥammad al-Qāshānī in the year 700/1300–1, is to a great extent derived from that book. Of importance, however, is the last chapter, which deals with the glazing of ceramics and the techniques of fine pottery.[15] From the 9th/15th century originates the *Javāhir-nāma* (*Gauhar-nāma*) 'Book of Precious Stones', which Muḥammad b. Manṣūr Shīrāzī wrote for the Aqqoyunlu Sulṭān Khalīl Bahādur Khān (883–4/1478–79), the son of Uzun Ḥasan.[16] Two such treatises, the names of which are not positively known, appeared during the first quarter of the 10th/16th century; one was written in

Notes on p. 472

India by Muḥammad b. Ashraf al-Ḥasanī ar-Rustamdārī during the reign of Bābur[17], the other by Muḥammad b. al-Mubārak Qazvīnī for the Ottoman Sulṭān Selīm I (918–26/1512–20).[18] We possess a treatise on pearls by Shaykh Ḥazīn.[19] It is not known exactly when and where the small 'Book of Stones' appeared that was composed by Aḥmad b. 'Abdu'l-'Azīz Jauharī, who was already familiar with European jewelcraft and regretted the decline of oriental mines and the introduction of European stones.[20]

NOTES

1. See p. 451.
2. Rieu, 483.
3. See Elgood, 319–23.
4. Fonahn, Nr. 343. Rieu, 482–3. Pertsch, Nr. 630.
5. Rieu, 483.
6. Kilisli Rifat Bilge, 'İstanbul kütüphanelerinde bulunan bâznâmeler', *TM*, 7–8,2 (1945), 165–82.
7. Rieu, 485.
8. Rieu, 485.
9. See pp. 476–7.
10. See p. 439.
11. *SSH*, III, 176. Ed. by 'Abdu'l-Ghaffār Najmu'd-daula (*'Ilm-i falāḥat-i daura-i Mughūl*) (Tehran 1324).
12. Ed. in the preceding book.
13. Rieu, 489.
14. H. Ritter, *Orientalische Steinbücher und persische Fayencetechnik* (Istanbul 1935), 4–8.
15. Ritter, *loc. cit.*, 14–15. The final chapter is here (pp. 16–48) edited and translated by H. Ritter, J. Ruska and R. Winderlich, *Eine persische Beschreibung der Fayencetechnik von Kaschan aus dem Jahre 700h/1301d.* 'Abbās Iqbāl, "'Arā'isu'l-javāhir va nafā'isu'l-aṭā'ib', *FIZ*, 8 (1339), 153–60. The whole book has recently been edited anew by Īraj Afshār (Tehran 1345).
16. Ritter, *loc. cit.*, 9. Ed. by Minūchihr Sitūda, *FIZ*, 4, 185–302. – The chapter on Lājvard ed. and translated by H. Ritter, 'Das Kapitel über den Lâǧward im Steinbuch des Muḥammad b. Manṣûr', *loc. cit.*, 49–56.
17. Pertsch, Nr. 51 (1).
18. Browne Cat., 190.
19. *The Treatise on the Nature of Pearls*. Ed. and transl. by Sarfaraz Khan Khatak and O. Spies (Walldorf-Hessen 1954).
20. Ritter, *loc. cit.*, 10.

VIII. MEDICINE AND PHARMACOLOGY

Greek medicine had already found its way into Persia in pre-Islamic times, and during the Sasanian period it was being practised in the clinic at Gundīshāpūr. Moreover, it had absorbed certain Persian practices and was to some extent influenced by India as well. The Indian book on medicine written by Chanākiya (*Shānāq*), dating from the end of the third century B.C., is believed to have been translated into Persian during the latter half of the 2nd/8th century.[1] Islamic medicine, that exhibits more or less the same theory and practice among the Arabs as among the Persians, grew from this basis. Only since the 10th/16th century, and in fact on Indian soil, did it once again become more strongly stimulated by Indian medicine, whence it be gan to differ from the contemporary Arab system – then already to some extent on the decline.

The first Persian physicians naturally wrote in Arabic. Even the great Avicenna did not apparently write any great medical work originally in Persian.[2] The earliest medical work in the Persian language we possess is the *Hidāyatu'l-muta'allimīn fi-ṭ-ṭibb*, 'The Students' Guide to Medicine', by Abū-Bakr (or Abū-Ḥakīm) Rabī' b. Aḥmad al-Akhavayn al-Bukhārī, dating from the middle of the 5th/11th century. It is an encyclopaedic work, in which, after a lengthy general introduction, the treatment of various diseases is described.[3] About fifty years later appeared the *Dhakhīra-i Khvārazmshāhī*, 'The Treasure of Khvārazmshāh', which was composed at the court of the Khvārazmshāh Quṭbu'd-dīn Muḥammad (491–522/1098–1128). It derives largely from Avicenna's *Qānūn* and, except for a more intelligible treatment of the subject-matter, it brings us only a few novelties, based on the experience of the author, a famous doctor of his day called Zaynu'd-dīn Ismā'īl b. Ḥasan al-Jurjānī.[4] This book comprises the whole of contemporary medicine and is important linguistically because in it the Persian medical terminology was created. It falls into ten parts. The first deals with the conception and use of medicine, anatomy of the human body, the humours and their relative proportions; the second with health and disease, and further

Notes on pp. 478–479

with the causes and symptoms of illnesses; the third with hygiene; and the fourth with the diagnosis and prognosis of diseases. The next four books discuss in detail the treatment of individual diseases, arranged in order from the head to the foot. The ninth deals with poisons and antidotes, types of theriaca and the curing of bites from snakes and other animals, the uses of which are also mentioned one by one. The tenth part contains pharmaceutics.[5] The second and later work of our author is entitled *Aghrāḍu'ṭ-ṭibb*, 'The Aims of Medicine'. It appeared during the second quarter of the 6th/12th century during the reign of the Sulṭān 'Alā'u'd-daula Atsïz (522–51/1128–56), the son of his former patron, and was written at the request of his vizier Majdu'd-dīn al-Bukhārī. It is a revision of the *Dhakhīra*.[6] Before this work, he wrote a short extract from the *Dhakhīra* for the same Atsïz, when the latter was crown prince. This small book bears the name *Khafī-i 'Alā'ī*, 'The Secrets of 'Alā', because the original manuscript consisted of two oblong volumes which could easily be carried about everywhere in the boots.[7]

From the following period we possess only smaller systematic works that do not appear to have gained much response or popularity. One of the two such works preserved from the 9th/15th century seems to have been better known, namely the compendium entitled *Kifāya-i Manṣūrī*, 'The Sufficiency of Manṣūr', and probably dedicated to Zaynu'l-'ābidīn, the ruler of Kashmir (820–72/1417–67). The book, consisting of two parts, was composed at the beginning of that century by Manṣūr b. Muḥammad b. Aḥmad b. Yūsuf b. Faqīh Ilyās[8], already well known for his specialised work on anatomy. The subject of the first part is theoretical (*ṭibb-i naẓarī*) and practical (*ṭibb-i 'amalī*) medicine and of the second the enumeration of simple and compound foods and medicines.[9]

In the year 907/1501–2, in Ray in northern Persia, Bahā'ud-daula Qivāmu'd-dīn Qāsim b. Nūrbakhsh ar-Rāzī wrote the *Khulāṣatu't-tajārib*, 'The Quintessence of Experiments', a general work on medicine, written in traditional form; at the end a special chapter is added on foreign medical technical expressions and on medical weights.[10] It contains much that is noteworthy, such as the writings of the famous physician and scholar living in the 10th/16th century, 'Imādu'd-dīn Maḥmūd b. Mas'ūd of Shiraz[11], who in addition to several specialised works wrote a general work under the title of *Yanbū' fī 'ilmi'ṭ-ṭibb*, 'Source of Medical Science'.[12] His other work, *Risāla-i mujarrabāt*, 'Treatise on Tested (Curatives)'[13], is an example of several similarly entitled writings, in which the authors used to describe their practical experiences to the wide circle of their professional colleagues.

After the second half of the 10th/16th century the Indian Moghul empire became practically the only area in which medical science was at all intensively cultivated in literature, just as were many other branches of Persian learning, with the result that it was influenced even more strongly than hitherto by the knowledge of the Indians.

Even before the foundation of the Indian Timurid kingdom, also at the beginning of the 10th/16th century, one of his greatest Amīrs, Bhūva b. Khavāṣṣkhān[14], declared to the Sikandar Shāh Lōdī that Greek medicine was not suitable for the Indians, and he received permission to write a book on medicine in Persian which was to be based on Sanskrit sources. This work was completed in the year 918/1512 and bore the title *Ma'dinu'sh-shifā-i Sikandarshāhī*, 'Shāh Sikandar's Mine of Information on Healing'. The book, which has enjoyed the greatest authority in India ever since, is composed of an introduction containing a definition of medicine and a discussion of its value and basic principles, and three sections consisting of carefully prepared translations from the Sanskrit: (1) Introduction to therapy (*sūtrasthāna*); (2) Anatomy (*sharīrasthāna*); (3) Symptomatology and therapy (*sūdanasthāna* and *chikitsāsthāna*).[15] Muḥammad Qāsim Hindūshāh, already mentioned as a historian and known under the pseudonym Firishta[16], also used Indian sources as well as the older Islamic ones for his general work on therapeutics which appeared at the beginning of the 11th/17th century and which bears the title *Dastūru'l-aṭibbā'*, 'Memorandum for Doctors', or alternatively *Ikhtiyārāt-i Qāsimī*, 'Selections after Qāsim'. This work too has three chapters, the first two dealing with pharmacology while the third describes therapy in 160 sections. The whole is prefaced by an introduction on the constituent elements of the human body and the humours.[17] The *Ṭibb-i Dārā Shikūhī*, 'The Medicine of Dārā Shikūh', a large, copiously illustrated work in three volumes on the system of medicine, came from the pen of 'Aynu'l-mulk Nūru'd-dīn Muḥammad Shīrāzī.[18] It was written at the instigation of the scholarly prince Dārā Shikūh, and is based on the writings of forty earlier authors. The first volume treats of anatomy, external agents, i.e. climate, living conditions, etc., the pulse, symptoms of diseases, urine and excrements; the second deals with physical exercise and feeding, as well as the simple and compound medicaments; the third, which constitutes half of the whole work, describes pathology and the treatment of all diseases, giving the necessary prescriptions for each.[19] Mīr Muḥammad Akbar Arzānī[20], who studied for a long time in Shiraz where the study of medicine was an ancient tradition, worked as a famous doctor and technical writer under the Great Moghul Aurangzīb 'Ālamgīr. Three of his writings are systematic in character. The greatest is the *Ṭibb-i Akbarī*, 'Medicine of Akbar', dating from the year 1112/1700. In 27 chapters it deals with each disease separately and ends with a list of medicaments and medical terms.[21] The second, *Mujarrabāt (Tajribāt)-i Akbarī*, 'The tested (Prescriptions) of Akbar', is a collection of prescriptions.[22] His third work, the much used *Mīzānu'ṭ-ṭibb*, 'The Scales of Medicine', is a manual he originally wrote for his children and pupils. It contains the following three sections: (1) on the four basic qualities (heat, cold, damp, dryness); (2) on simple and compound remedies; (3) on diseases and their treatment.[23] Translations of European medical writings appear in India as early as the 12th/18th century.

Apart from the systematic works, the most important of which have just been enumerated, there are a great many specialised writings in Persian medical literature. Distinguished amongst those on anatomy is the *at-Tashrīḥ bi't-taṣvīr*, 'Anatomy in Pictures', or *Tashrīḥ-i Manṣūrī*, 'Manṣūr's Anatomy', that was popular on account

Notes on pp. 478–479

of its anatomical diagrams (the skeleton, nervous system, muscles, veins, arteries, intestines, occasionally also the genitals of a pregnant woman), written by Manṣūr b. Muḥammad, whom we have already mentioned, and dedicated to Prince Pīr Muḥammad-i Jahāngīr, the grandson of Tamerlane. The divisions of the human body are sketched in the introduction, and the book itself deals in five sections with the bones, nerves, muscles, veins and arteries. The compound organs (e.g. brain, eyes, heart, etc.) and the development of the embryo are described in the concluding chapter.[24]

A famous work on ophthalmology in the Persian language is the *Nūru'l-'uyūn*, 'Light of the Eyes', which was written by Muḥammad b. Manṣūr of Jurjān, known as Zarrīndast, 'Golden Hand', and completed in the year 480/1087–8 in the reign of the Seljuq Sulṭān Malikshāh. Linguistically the book is of value, for it is written in a clear question-and-answer form, but as regards the content it is based largely on the Arabic *Tadhkirat al-kaḥḥālīn*, 'Admonition to Oculists', by 'Alī b. 'Īsā [25], although it gives much that is noteworthy from the author's practice, particularly in the sphere of ophthalmic operations.[26] 'Imādu'd-dīn Maḥmūd b. Mas'ūd Shīrāzī, a physician we have already come across, wrote a separate *Risāla-i ātishak*, 'Treatise on Syphilis' during the second half of the 10th/16th century[27], after this disease, which was new at that time, had already been described by Bahā'u'd-daula. In catalogues of manuscripts one finds numerous specialised works on single diseases, as well as on the pulse, blood-letting, testing of urine, anaesthetics, etc., but these are mostly small works, usually anonymous and undated and thus of little value for the historian of literature.

Much loved by Persian physicians were handbooks on hygiene, of which there are many. They are generally divided into six chapters: (1) advantages and disadvantages of climate and living conditions; (2) food and drink; (3) exercise and rest; (4) sleep and being awake; (5) evacuation and constipation; (6) mental conditions.[28]

There are of course medical books written in verse and also single poems on the subject. The *Dānish-nāma*, 'The Book of Knowledge', a medical handbook by Maysarī[29], appeared in an early period of Persian literature, viz. during the second half of the 4th/10th century. The best known works of this type are those by Yūsuf b. Muḥammad, a doctor and poet born in Herat, who used the pseudonym Yūsufī and lived during the reigns of Bābur (932–37/1526–30) and Humāyūn (937–63/1531–56). His works embrace all branches of medicine.[30]

The Persians attached great importance to pharmacology, which thus forms a very profusely documented branch of medical literature; and although it was based for the most part on the Greek herbaria, the Persians added several new drugs. The earliest Persian work on the subject exists in only one ancient manuscript, which was written in 447/1056 by the poet Asadī. It is called *Kitābu'l-abniya 'an ḥaqā'iqi'l-adviya*, 'Book of Fundamental Principles on the True Nature of Medicines'. It was probably dedicated to the Sāmānid prince Manṣūr I b. Nūḥ, or, at the latest, written a hundred years later, that is during the second half of the 4th/10th century or the first half of the 5th/11th, by Muvaffaqu'd-dīn Abū-Manṣūr b. 'Alī al-Haravī. It describes 585 drugs according to Greek, Syrian, Arabic, Indian and Persian sources.[31] The next pharmaceutical work is the translation made during the first quarter of the 7th/13th century by Abū-Bakr b. ʿAlī b. ʿUthmān al-Aṣfar al-Kāshānī[32] of the Arabic *Kitāb aṣ-ṣaydala fi'ṭ-ṭibb*, 'Book of Materia Medica', which was edited by the famous al-Bīrūnī towards the end of his life with the assistance of a physician named Aḥmad b. Muḥammad an-Nakhsha'ī.[33] From the 8th/14th century we have two works from the pen of the Shirazian doctor, ʿAlī b. Ḥusayn Anṣārī, better known as Zaynu'l-ʿAṭṭār (d. 806/1403–4)[34], of whom the Muzaffarid Shāh Shujāʿ (759–86/1358–84) thought very highly. One, *Miftāḥu'l-khazā'in*, 'The Key to the Treasures', completed in 767/1366, deals in the first and third chapters with the simple and compound medicaments and in the second with their substitutes and correctives.[35] Three years later he revised this book and named it *Ikhtiyārāt-i Badīʿī*, 'Selections of Badīʿ', in honour of Shāh Shujāʿ's step-mother, Badīʿu'l-jamāl; its two chapters deal in alphabetical order first with the simple and then with the compound medicaments.[36] In the first half of the 10th/16th century, Muẓaffar b. Muḥammad al-Ḥusaynī ash-Shifā'ī (d. 963/1555–6)[37] composed an alphabetical list of medicaments known under the title *Ṭibb-i Shifā'ī*, 'The Medicine of Shifā'ī', or *Qarābādhīn-i Shifā'ī*, 'Shifā'ī's Pharmacopoeia'.[38] A Latin translation by the Carmelite Father Mattheus was printed in Paris in 1681 by his colleague Father Angelus of St. Joseph (de la Brosse), who falsely called it his own, as a handbook for missionaries, merchants and other travellers.[39] From the second half of the 11th/17th century comes the famous *Tuḥfatu'l-mu'minīn*, 'The Gift of the Faithful', which was begun by Muḥammad Zamān Tunakābunī and completed by his son, Muḥammad Mu'min Ḥusaynī[40] for the Safavid Ṣafī II Sulaymān (1077–1105/1666–94). This book was very popular and was printed several times in Persia and India during the last century.[41]

There are also pharmaceutical dictionaries, of which only the *Alfāẓu'l-adviya*, 'Vocabulary of Medicines', need be mentioned. It was compiled by Nūru'd-dīn Muḥammad ʿAbdu'llāh, son of ʿAynu'l-mulk of Shiraz, whom we already know, and dedicated to Shāhjahān in 1038/1628–9.[42]

Only the most important and best known general pharmaceutical writings have been mentioned here, but there is a long list of lesser known works of this type, most of them anonymous or difficult to date. From the 10th/16th century onwards we also find shorter specialised treatises – mostly consisting only of a few pages – on poisons and antidotes, perfumes, opium, bezoar stone (*pāzahr*), China-root (*chūb* (*bīkh*)-*i Chīnī*, Smilax), zedoary roots (*jāduvār*), bitumen (*mūmiyā*), and especially coffee, tea and tobacco.

Notes on pp. 478–479

NOTES

1. 'Abbās Iqbāl, *Sharq*, 1 (1309–10), 99.
2. See *Jashn-nāma-i Ibn-i Sīnā*, 1, 58, 61.
3. Beeston, Nr. 2841. Mujtabā Mīnuvī, 'Hidāyatu'l-muta'allimīn dar ṭibb', *Yaghmā*, 3 (1329), 497–510. Gilbert Lazard, 'Du risolayi tibbiyi asri X dar forsi dari', *Sharqi Surkh*, 1958,10, 129–38.
4. Fonahn, 129.
5. Fonahn, Nr. 15. *GAL*, 1, 487; S. 1, 889–90. Elgood, 216–8. *GIPh*, 11, 367. P. Horn, 'Der Schatz des Khvārezmšāh', *WZKM*, 4 (1890), 131–43. Dr. Abbas Nafisy, *La médicine en Perse des origines à nos jours. Ses fondements théoriques d'après l'Encyclopédie de Gorgani* (Paris 1933), 65–135. Maḥmúd Najmābādī, 'Dhakhīra-i Khvārazm-šāhī', *Jihān-i puzishkī*, 1,4 (1326), 37–42, and *Sāl-nāma-i dunyā*, 6 (1329), 198–201. – Ed. by Muḥammad Taqī Dānish-Pajūh, 1 (Tehran 1344).
6. Fonahn, Nr. 16. *Kitābu'l-aghrāḍi'ṭ-ṭibbīya va'l-mabāḥithi'l-'Alā'īya.* Facsimile of a MS dated 789/1387 (Tehran 1345).
7. Fonahn, Nr. 39. Lith. (Agra 1268). Maḥmūd Najmābādī, 'Khafī-i 'Alā'ī', *Jihān-i puzishkī*, 1,2 (1326), 38–40.
8. Fonahn, 129.
9. Fonahn, Nr. 18. Elgood, 347. Lith. (Lucknow 1290, 1303).
10. Fonahn, Nr. 28. Elgood, 278, 353–5. Lith. (Lucknow 1283).
11. Fonahn, 132.
12. Fonahn, Nr. 38.
13. Fonahn, Nr. 167.
14. Fonahn, 133.
15. Fonahn, Nr. 21. Lith. (Lucknow 1294, 1877, 1889).
16. See pp. 448–9 .
17. Fonahn, Nr. 22. Lith. (India 1901).
18. Fonahn, 131, 133.
19. Fonahn, Nr. 140. Elgood, 373–4. Leclerq, 11, 332–4.
20. Fonahn, 130–1.
21. Fonahn, Nr. 24. Lith. in India several times.
22. Fonahn, Nr. 27. Lith. in India several times.
23. Fonahn, Nr. 26. Lith. in India several times.
24. Fonahn, Nr. 1. Elgood, 332–5. Lith. in India several times. – K. Sudhoff, *Ein Beitrag zur Geschichte der Anatomie im Mittelalter speziell der anatomischen Graphik nach Handschriften des 9. bis 15. Jahrhunderts* (Leipzig 1908).
25. *GAL*, 1, 236; S. 1, 884–5. Elgood, 140–2.
26. Fonahn, Nr. 50. *GIPh*, 11, 367. Elgood, 142–3.
27. Fonahn, Nr. 103, Elgood, 379–81. C. Elgood, 'Translation of a Persian Monograph on Syphilis entitled Risála-i Átishak, the author being Imád-ul-dín Mahmúd Bin Mas' úd Bin Mahmúd-ul-Tabíb', *Annals of Medical History*, NS, 3 (1931), 465–86. Sayyid Ḥusayn Āmūzgār, 'Mu'arrafī-i yak athar-i nafīs az 'Imādu'd-dīn Maḥmūd b. Mas'ūd Shīrāzī (Manāfi'u't-tashrīḥ)', *Nashriyya-i Farhang-i Khurāsān*, 2,8 (1336), 13–6.
28. Fonahn, Nr. 36, 55, 64–6, 69, 76, 77, 83.
29. Blochet, Nr. 818. See Gilbert Lazar, *Du risolayi tibbi...*, Note 3.
30. Fonahn, Nr. 86, 206–11, 302. Elgood, 378–9. *Ṭibb-i Yūsufī.* Lith. in India several times. *'Ilāju'l-amrāḍ*, Lith. (Cawnpore 1288). Most likely the same as Yūsufī mentioned on p. 434. – 'Abdu'l-Ḥayy Ḥabībī, 'Ḥakīm Yūsufī Haravī ṭabīb u munshī darbār-i Bābur u Humāyūn', *Āriyāna*, 7,3 (1327–8), 1–4.

31. Fonahn, Nr. 224. Elgood, 363. *GIPh*, II, 367. A. Achundow, *Commentar zum sogenannten Liber fundamentorum pharmacologiae des Abu Mansur Muwaffak* (Dorpat 1892). A. Mieli, 'Entre los medicamentes y los venenos de Abu Mansur Muwaffaq', *Archeion*, 22 (1940), 398–406. Muḥammad Qazvīnī, 'Kitābu'l-abniya 'an ḥaqā'iqi'l-adviya', *Bīst maqāla*, 2, (1313), 202–4; *Mihr*, 7 (1321–2), 327–31. Facsimile with preface by Mujtabā Mīnuvī (Tehran 1344).
32. Fonahn, Nr. 268.
33. *GAL*, S. I, 874–5.
34. Fonahn, 129.
35. Fonahn, Nr. 230. Elgood, 363. Lith. in India.
36. Fonahn, Nr. 229. Elgood, 364. Lith. (Cawnpore 1305.)
37. Fonahn, 130.
38. Fonahn, Nr. 227. Elgood, 366. Lith. (Dihlī 1851, 1869) (on the margin of the Qarābādhīn-i Dhakā'ī). – Mīr Muḥammad 'Alī Āzād Kābulī, 'Ḥakīm Shifā'ī', *Armaghān*, 8 (1306), 553–7; *Jihān-i puzishkī*, 12 (1337), 157–9.
39. *Pharmacopoea Persica ex idiomate persico in latinum conversa* (Lutetiae Parisiorum 1681).
40. Fonahn, 130.
41. Fonahn, Nr. 228. Elgood, 366–8. Lith. in Persia and India several times. Ed. by Maḥmūd Najmābādī (Tehran 1338). Aḥmad Tafaḍḍulī, 'Vāzhahā-i guyishī dar Tuḥfatu'l-mu'minīn', *Intishārāt-i idāra-i Farhang-i 'āmma*, 2 (1341), 95–149. – Ṣādiq Kiyā, 'Chand vāzhahā', *ibidem*, 151–61.
42. Fonahn, Nr. 231. *Ulfáz udwiyeh, or, The Materia Medica, in the Arabic, Persian and Hindewy languages. Compiled by Noureddeen Mohammed Abdullah Shirázy* ... with English translation by F. Gladwin (Calcutta 1793). Lith. in India several times.

IX. ENCYCLOPAEDIAS

During the centuries discussed in this summary the various sciences formed a fairly well-defined whole and their basic principles could be mastered without difficulty. It is therefore not surprising that polyhistors were nothing exceptional, as can easily be seen from the frequent recurrence of the same names in many of the foregoing chapters. This also explains the frequent appearance and popularity of works planned on an encyclopaedic scale, of larger or smaller scope as the case might be. Most of them are concerned only with the philosophical and exact disciplines, other branches of learning being more rarely included.

The earliest Persian encyclopaedia of the philosophical and exact sciences is the *Dānish-nāma-i 'Alā'ī*, 'The Book of Wisdom of 'Alā', which was begun by Avicenna shortly before his death (428/1037) for the Kākūyid prince 'Alā'u'd-daula Abū-Ja'far Muḥammad b. Dushmanziyār (398–434/1007–41) at the latter's court in Isfahan. But his untimely death interrupted the work, which was then completed by his pupil Jūzjānī[1] after other Arabic writings of the master. The work owes its special importance to the fact that with it the Persian terminology of the philosophical and exact sciences was established.[2] A work of similar content, bearing the title *Nuzhat-nāma-i 'Alā'ī*, 'The Book of Pleasure of 'Alā', dates from about half a century later. It was written by the famous philosopher Sahmu'd-dīn b. Abi'l-Khayr for 'Alā'u'd-daula Abū-Kalījār Khāṣṣbeg Ḥusām, the prince of Tabaristan.[3] The *Ḥadā'iqu'l-anvār fī ḥaqā'iqi'l-asrār*, 'The Gardens of Lights on the Truths of Secrets', by Fakhru'd-dīn Muḥammad b. 'Umar b. al-Ḥusayn ar-Rāzī (d. 606/1209) is of much wider scope and more generally comprehensible. It was written at the command of the Khvārazmshāh 'Alā'u'd-dīn Takash (568–96/1172–1200). The work has been preserved in three redactions, the last of which, completed in 575/1179, contains short summaries of sixty sciences, whereas the two earlier ones deal with only forty and fifty-seven respectively.[4] The *Faraḥ-nāma-Jamālī*, 'Jamāl's Book of Joy', completed in 580/1184 by Abū-Bakr al-Muṭahhar b. Abi'l-Qāsim al-Jamāl al-Yazdī, with the *makhlaṣ* Jamālī, is concerned to a greater extent with the natural sciences. It deals with the properties of the human and animal body, plants, minerals, drugs, oils, poisons and antidotes, as well as divination and various curiosities.[5]

From the 7th/13th century comes the *Durratu't-tāj li-ghurrati'd-Dubāj*, 'The Pearl of the Crown for the Brow of Dubāj', which Quṭbu'd-dīn Maḥmūd b. Mas'ūd Shīrāzī (d. 710/1311–2), the most talented pupil of Naṣīru'd-dīn Ṭūsī and author of many Arabic writings in the fields of astronomy and medicine, wrote for the prince of Gilan, Dubāj b. Fīlshāh. The contents of the book proper are very similar to the above-mentioned encyclopaedias of Avicenna and Sahmu'd-dīn; in a postscript the author also discusses theology, ethics, politics, and mysticism.[6] Muḥammad b. Maḥmūd al-Āmulī, who was mudarris in Sulṭāniyya under Uljāytū (703–16/1304–16), wrote in about 740/1340 the *Nafā'isu'l-funūn fī 'arā'isi'l-'uyūn*, 'Treasures of the Sciences in the Brides of the Springs', for a vizier, whose name is unknown, of the Īnjū prince Abū-Isḥāq (d. 758/1357). This work falls into two parts: the first is concerned with the 'new sciences' (philology, theology, Ṣūfism, history, etc.); the second with the 'sciences of the ancients' (philosophy, the exact and natural sciences, medicine, etc.).[7]

In 879/1474–5 Ghiyāthu'd-dīn 'Alī 'Alī b. Amīrān Ḥusaynī Iṣfahānī wrote the very easily comprehensible *Dānish-nāma-i jahān*, 'The Book of Wisdom of the World', for the great-grandson of Tīmūr, Sulṭān Maḥmūd. This is a compendium of natural sciences dealing with celestial phenomena, minerals, plants, animals and Man.[8] The *Riyāḍu'l-abrār*, 'The Gardens of the Pious', by Ḥusayn 'Āqilī Rustamdārī, dating from 979/1571, is very widely conceived. The author boasted that, as against the sixty sciences of his predecessor ar-Rāzī, his book deals with ninety fields of study.[9] Similar in character is the *Shāhid-i ṣādiq*, 'The Upright Witness', from the middle of the 11th/17th century, by the historian Mīrzā Muḥammad Ṣādiq Iṣfahānī.[10] It is a rich mine of information of various kinds, anecdotes, quotations etc., set out in five chapters. The first is concerned with divine matters, the second with government, the third with comprehension and knowledge, the fourth with love, friendship, wealth and poverty, the fifth with the world and time, life and death. The concluding essay discusses celestial things.[11] The *Jām-i jahānnumā*, 'The Mirror Reflecting the World', completed in 1180/1766–7 by Mahārat Khān, deals in five chapters with ethics, history, geography, angels and earthly beings, and philology.[12] An encyclopaedic curiosity, in fact a medley of everything imaginable, is the *Ḥadīqa-i ḥādiq-i ganjīna-i Ṣādiq*, 'The Garden surrounding the Treasure of Ṣādiq', written by the historian Shākir Khān b. Ṣādiq in the year 1174/1760–1.[13]

Notes on p. 482

NOTES

1. See p. 464.
2. For a contrary opinion Ḥikmat-i 'Alā'ī. *GIPh*, II, 363. *Jashn-nāma-i Ibn-i Sīnā I*, 57–8. Ed. by Aḥmad Khurāsānī (Tehran 1315). Editions of certain parts: *Tabī'iyyāt*, ed. by Muḥammad Mishkāt (1331); *Ilāhiyyāt*, ed. by Muḥammad Mu'īn (Tehran 1331), *Risāla-i manṭiq*, ed. by Muḥammad Mu'īn and Muḥammad Mishkāt (Tehran 1331). *Le Livre de Science. I: Logique, Métaphysique. II: Physique, Mathématiques*. Traduit par Moh. Achena et Henri Massé (Paris 1955–8).
3. *GIPh*, II, 363. Fonahn, Nr. 191. Ṣafā, II, 909–11. A. N. Boldïrev, 'Datirovka "Nuzhatnama"', *Pamyati Ign. Yul. Krachkovskogo* (Leningrad 1958), 44–6.
4. *GIPh*, II, 363. Rieu, Suppl., 102–3. Pertsch, Nr. 92–3.
5. Rieu, 465–6. Pertsch, Nr. 607. Flügel, 1449.
6. *GAL*, II, 211–2; S. II, 296–7. Rieu, 434–5. *IO*, Nr. 2219. Flügel, Nr. 24. Ed. by Muḥammad Mishkāt (Tehran 1317).
7. Rieu, 435–7. *IO*, Nr. 2221–3. Pertsch, Nr. 94. Flügel, Nr. 25. Fonahn, Nr. 351. Ed. by Ḥājj Mīrzā Abu'l-Ḥasan Sha'rānī and Sayyid Ibrāhīm Miyānajī, 3 vols. (Tehran 1337–9). *Ta'bīr-i khvāb (Qismatī az Nafā'isu'l-funūn)*, Lith. (Tehran 1320).
8. Rieu, 439–40. *IO*, Nr. 2173–4. Lith. (Bombay 1291). – W. Ivanov, 'The Date of the Danish Nama-i Jahan', *JRAS*, 1927, 94–6.
9. *GIPh*, II, 364. Rieu, Suppl. 103–5.
10. *PL*, I, 125–6.
11. Rieu, 775. Pertsch, Nr. 96. Extracts by 'Abbās Iqbāl in *Yādgār*, 2 (1324–5): Nr. 4, 19–36; Nr. 25, 27–33; Nr. 6, 20–3; Nr. 7, 19–27; Nr. 8, 29–40; Nr. 9, 27–37; Nr. 10, 23–32. 'Alī Naqī Munzavī, 'Ganjafa-i Shāhid-i Ṣādiq' and 'Amthāl-i fārsī az Kitāb-i Shāhid-i Ṣādiq', *Dānish*, 3 (1331–4), 459–60, 517–22, 560–8. Ṣādiq Kiyā, 'Mathalhā-i fārsī az Kitāb-i Shāhid-i Ṣādiq', *Intishārāt-i idāra-i Farhang-i 'āmma*, 2 (1341), 15–44.
12. *PL*, I, Nr. 166.
13. *PL*, I, Nr. 795; 1321. *IO*, 2228.

JIŘÍ BEČKA

TAJIK LITERATURE FROM THE 16TH CENTURY TO THE PRESENT

I. BEFORE THE REVOLUTION

A. INTRODUCTION

The predecessors of the present-day Tajiks (Tojik)[1], the Soghdians and the Baktrians, had their own state and their own culture as early as the first millenium B.C. In the 6th century B.C. they resisted attacks by the armies of Cyrus and Darius, while in the 4th century B.C. they stood up against raids staged by the forces of Alexander the Great. They withstood attempts to bring about their arabisation following the Arab invasion in the 7th century A.D., and soon afterwards, at the end of the 9th century, they formed the powerful Samanid state, which lasted for a century and which brought Tajik culture to an unprecedented height. Throughout that period, the political, economic and cultural history of the Tajiks was closely linked with the history of Western Iran. The flourishing of Tajik literature between the 10th and 15th centuries started in fact under Samanid rule, and the founder of its greatness was undoubtedly Rūdakī, a native of Panjrūd, which was not far from Panjikent in present-day Tajikistan; the noted Iranian literary historian Saʿīd Nafīsī calls Transoxania the cradle of poetry in the Persian language. However, besides the Tajiks, contribution was made to the continued development of this literature by members of Turkic tribes in Central Asia, writing in Persian (in the *darī* language)[2], as well as authors from Afghanistan, northern India, Azerbayjan and, of course, primarily from Iran, which contributed such great literary figures as Saʿdī and Ḥāfiẓ. This literature, originating between the 10th and 15th centuries, should therefore be viewed as Persian-Tajik literature, forming part of the cultural heritage of both the Tajiks and the West Iranians, as well as of the Eastern Turks, and consequently also part of the Uzbek, Afghan, Indian (Urdu), and Azerbayjani cultural tradition.

Notes on pp. 536–545

B. THE PARTING OF IRAN AND CENTRAL ASIA

The end of the 15th century is a milestone in the history of Central Asia because it was then that the political ties with Western Iran were definitely broken. Political and economic independence was linked with a steady separation of the culture and literature of this north-eastern region. A gradual differentiation took place, which was intensified still further by the ideological split due to the fact that the Safavid dynasty had adopted Shī'a as the state religion. Quite naturally, it influenced both culture and literature. Transoxania, the Sunnite bastion in the east, sought allies in Ottoman Turkey, in Afghanistan and in northern India. It was especially with the latter that it maintained lively economic and cultural contacts in the 16th and 17th centuries. However, the influence of the split on the continued development of Persian and Tajik literatures has thus far been overestimated. The two continued to affect each other, especially as regards the influence exerted by the classical writers of Western Iran on Central Asian poetry; *tadhkiras* (anthology) on both sides of the Amu Darya often list authors from both banks and history shows that there had also been personal contacts between the poets of both regions.

However, as Central Asia became politically independent of Western Iran, it was affected by the growing political, economic and cultural influence of the nomadic Turkic tribes coming from the north. The Uzbeks who had fought among themselves eventually formed a union under the leadership of a member of the Chingiz-Khān dynasty, Abulkhaĭrkhon of the Shaĭbonī family, whose grandson set out in the 15th century to conquer the south.

Turkic-speaking tribes had already previously been living in Central Asia side by side with the Tajiks, but when the Uzbeks seized power many additional Turkic nomads settled down and the Uzbeks[3] finally penetrated into all the strata of the population, eventually gaining predominance. As early as the 14th century we find the appearance of the first authors, who wrote in Chighatoĭ (Old Uzbek), and in the 15th century the foundations were laid for the ethnic division of Central Asia, a division which has survived until our days. A cultural rapprochement took place between the Tajik and Turkic populations, the latter gradually attaining the cultural level of the former.[4] An outstanding personality was the founder of Old Uzbek literature, Alisher Navoī, who was however at the same time a typical representative of bilingual, i.e. Uzbek and Tajik, writers. Under the pen-name Fonī he wrote a large number of good Tajik poems, as did practically all the other Uzbek writers after him for the next five centuries[5], including the best of them, like Turdī, Umarkhon, Muqimī, and Furqat. The influence worked both ways, of course. The leading contemporary Uzbek poet, Ghafur Ghulom, has said that "one learns from the other, one is the other's teacher". Braginskiy is of the opinion that the relationship between Tajik and Uzbek literature, as well as the personal relations between the writers of both nations, had become so close that the two literatures cannot be studied separately, in isolation.[6] Every ethnic group in Central Asia underwent a specific historical development, but at the same time participated in the overall cultural development of the whole region.[7]

The 15th century was characterised by the decline of the Timurid empire. Its western part, Iran, fell under the rule of the Qaraqoyunlu dynasty, and the rest of its territory gradually split into ever smaller units. The small feudal lords tried to imitate the rulers in Samarkand and Herat, which placed an additional economic burden on the populace. In the second half of the 15th century also the Central Asian part of the Timurid empire was split into two parts: in 1469 Transoxania passed to the descendants of Abū-Saʿīd, while Khurasan with Herat went to the sons of ʿUmar Shaykh. The constant raids by the nomads brought about a shift of the cultural centre to the southern part of Herat. It was there that Central Asia had reached a peak of cultural development in the second half of the 15th century, during the lifetime and creative periods of two great friends, the Tajik Jomī (see p. 286) and the Uzbek Navoī.[8] The large library of Sulṭān Husayn Boïqaro[9] in Herat had 40 employees, calligraphers and painters of miniatures, including Bihzod (who died in 1526), and it was there that the historian Mirkhond, his grandson Khondamir and others had worked. Herat overshadowed even Samarkand which had been made famous in the first half of the 15th century by Ulughbek through his astronomical school and observatory; however, the fame of Samarkand waned after Ulughbek's assassination in 1449, when reactionary religious leaders seized power.

C. CHARACTERISTICS OF TAJIK LITERATURE FROM THE 16TH TO THE EARLY 20TH CENTURIES

Following the traditions of Persian-Tajik literature and proceeding from the best works written either in Central Asia (e.g. Rūdakī, Daqiqī, Kamol Khujandī), Iran (Saʿdī, Ḥāfiẓ), Afghanistan (Jomī) or northern India (Amir Khusrav Dehlavī, Bedil), there gradually emerged from Central Asia and Khurasan a literature marked with certain specific features not found in the past and contemporary literature of the neighbouring regions. This process culminated after the Great October Socialist Revolution in the creation of a standard literary language through the adoption of a new, vocalic script, and in particular by transition to the methods of socialist realism and integration into the multinational Soviet literature.

The similarity between the Eastern Tajik and Western Iranian languages continues to be considerable, and consequently the two cultures are very close to each other. Until the revolution there existed, in fact, only one common written language for

Notes on pp. 536–545

both Tajik and Persian literature, and only some expressions from local dialects penetrated into the Tajik writings. After the revolution the vernacular was elevated to a literary language; the difference was underlined by the adoption of the new script and its position was strengthened by the creation of a linguistic standard. However, this does not mean that the Tajik language becomes more or less Tajik simply by how much it does or does not differ from Persian. What is important, is the fact that it does exist and that all the factors which have evolved in the course of history as the requisites of a separate nation include the linguistic community of the Tajiks both in the vernacular and the literary language.

What then are the characteristic features of Tajik literature from the 16th to the early 20th centuries? This literature was certainly not ideologically uniform. It reflects two distinct trends: the anti-feudal ideology of the common folk on the one hand, and, on the other hand, the ideology of the courtiers and the priesthood which expressed the interests of the ruling classes. The former trend was first manifest in the works of such great literary figures as Rūdakī, Firdausī and Sa'dī, and very strongly in folk-poetry which, however, has not been preserved to any considerable extent. The anti-feudal trend appears more markedly from the end of the 15th century; poetry was being increasingly written also by members of the middle classes, urban artisans, who worked outside the ruler's court, as noted by Bartol'd with respect to 15th-century Herat. A typical representative of these groups was the 17th-century poet Saĭido. The decline of feudalism brought about a decline of the literature connected with it. This does not mean, however, that in the course of the centuries there had not been periods of relative peaks of literary creation, as indicated in the subsequent chapters. Neither was the development straightforward, for both the aforementioned trends would appear in the same author or even in a single work. It is erroneous, however, to claim that culture and literature went into complete decline in Central Asia; there had always been forces among the people, who upheld the best traditions and passed them on to the succeeding generations.

From the 16th century on, ties between Tajik and Uzbek literatures grew stronger[10], personal contacts between writers of the two nations increased, just as did the number of bilingual poets, and at the turn of the 18th century a whole new school was formed by a large group of poets at the court at Qūqand, where 'shiru shakar' poems, alternating Tajik and Uzbek verse, became quite frequent.

Folk-trends in the Tajik literature of the 16th to 19th centuries were apparent primarily in its content, in that humanistic and democratic ideas found their way into the works of various authors – opposing exploitation of man, religious fanaticism and ignorance, panegyrism, etc. Questions of morality and education also played an important role, proceeding from the old traditions. However, folk trends were also manifest in the literary forms. *Ghazals* were predominant (but with new themes), there was realistic description, and satire was used much more frequently. By the end of the 19th century these features marked increasingly the enlightened literature of Ahmad Donish, Shohin and other writers, who also promoted the idea of universal education in a new, enlightened spirit. On the other hand, the feudal-religious literature continued to support the ideology of the ruling classes, mysticism, and submission to the rulers and the powerful, which was formally manifest in the further development of the *qaṣīda* and highly complicated metaphors which bordered on the unintelligible. Jadid literature (p. 523) of the early 20th century, too, even though it put on a cloak of liberalism, in fact only toyed with very timid reforms to save the amīr on the throne, and tried to make peace between science and Islam. A special role was played in Tajik literature by the 'Indian style', which appeared as early as the late 16th century but which did not prevail until the second half of the 17th and the early part of the 18th centuries, culminating in 'bedilism'. These trends are discussed in separate chapters.

As in the past centuries, the basic literary type continued to be poetry with the traditional genres, such as the *qaṣīda, ghazal, mathnavī, ruboī, qiṭ'a, tarqībband*, etc., and tradition was also observed in the organisation of the individual genres: the *qaṣīdas* contained, as a rule, highly complicated, unreal parables and had an opening part – the *nasīb* – while the *ghazals* continued to have a uniform rhyme and scope, usually containing a prominent opening *baĭt* (*maṭla'*) and a concluding *baĭt* (*maqṭa'*), which included the author's name. A certain progress can be traced in that the best authors tried very hard to further increase the logical and substantial relationship between the individual *baĭts*, which trend may be already noted to a lesser degree in the works of Jomī, Navoī, and some of the other earlier poets.

Prose traditionally trailed behind poetry in its importance and was the exclusive affair of a narrow circle of intellectuals. It includes the memoires of Vosifī and Saĭido, while a new type of prose was introduced by Donish. In addition there is a number of historical writings, composed as a rule in a highly bombastic style.

Very few women writers appear in this outline of older Tajik literature. Nevertheless, there had been many more than those who are listed. Among the poetesses cited by Tojī Usmon in his small volume[11], sixteen had lived between the 16th and 19th centuries, while he lists others in another article[12]; women also composed folk-poetry, but they have remained anonymous because of the social status of women in the Islamic Middle Ages, as so poignantly described by Zebunniso.

D. THE STUDY OF TAJIK LITERATURE

Until recently literature of the 16th to 19th centuries was practically unknown outside Central Asia. Ethé, Browne and other literary historians ended the history of 'true' literature with Jomī and considered the subsequent period as one of decline and not

Notes on pp. 536–545

worth studying. It was only Soviet historians of literature and primarily Tajik scholars themselves who – through the study of the works of such authors as Binoī, Vosifī, Mushfiqī, Saĭido, Donish and others, as well as of the *tadhkiras* written in that period – have recently shown that the literature of the 16th to the 19th centuries not only was not a "rehash of the old" as even some prominent scholars had maintained[13], but that it was often an original literature with many new features, one which was definitely worth studying and deserving of being known.

One of the great merits of Rypka's *History of Persian and Tajik Literature*, first published in 1956, was that in contrast to previous works on the subject it covered the whole range of Persian and Tajik literature. Owing to a lack of material at that time, however, the first edition included only a brief outline of Tajik literature from the 16th century on; I was happy to have been asked to enlarge that section of the book to match the scope of its other chapters. I have done so even though I realise that my evaluation is necessarily premature. Much remains to be done in order to study thoroughly the works of hundreds of authors whose manuscripts lie undiscovered in various libraries, mainly, of course, in Tashkent, Leningrad and Dushanbe, and in private collections. The conclusions I have reached are necessarily incomplete and in some cases may even be erroneous because there are long periods, especially the second half of the 16th century, the whole of the 18th century, and the first half of the 19th century, which have as yet hardly been studied at all[14], and the works of very few Tajik authors from those periods have been published. It is only in the early 1960's that some studies, primarily by Tajik authors, have been published to fill these gaps.[15] Nevertheless, I have taken up the task of writing this brief history in order to acquaint the public at least approximately with the literature of this culturally advanced nation of the Soviet-Union, and also to make it known to the world where quite erroneous views prevail, even among literary historians, on the values of Tajik literature and its relationship to Persian literature. These erroneous views will no doubt eventually be disproved in a much better way by the Tajik historians of literature themselves, but until then the present treatise may, I hope, serve this purpose at least partially.

E. PERIODISATION

Artistic literature constitutes one of the forms of social ideology whose development is linked with the development of society and which reflects the social struggle just as any other component part of the ideological superstructure. Thus literature too is affected by the universal rules of progress based on the economic and political development of society, but these rules are realised in it specifically, which means, in other words, that literature has its own, specific rules of development. A truly scientific periodisation of literature must proceed from an analysis, it must be based on literary development, as has become the rule in the case of the modern history of European literatures (which is divided into periods of classicism, romanticism, realism, symbolism, etc.). Periodisation done on this basis cannot run counter to the general periodisation of history, but need not necessarily be identical with it. "Disagreement between a milestone in literary development and a milestone of social development need not indicate an aesthete's approach to literary science."[16]

We may only approach the application of these principles, however, after having acquired a thorough understanding of all the elements of literature and the whole course of literary development; and this point, as already indicated, has not yet been reached in Tajik literature, particularly as regards the pre-revolutionary period.

In the present treatise, literature from the 16th century up to the present has been divided into two parts, though these differ considerably as to the length of time they cover: the period prior to the October Revolution, and the Soviet period. There is certainly no doubt that there are many more common features between Tajik literature of the 16th century and the literature of the 19th century, than between the 19th century and our present era. As for the pre-revolutionary period, we were unwilling * to use the common but, in the case of Tajik literature, unsuitable periodisation according to the individual dynasties – the Shaĭbon, Ashtarkhon and Manghit dynasties – and for the time being have thus used a division according to the several centuries, with the exception of the last two divisions – the Russian occupation of Central Asia and the Great October Socialist Revolution –, which both undoubtedly constitute great milestones in the history of Tajik literature. The periodisation of Soviet Tajik literature is discussed in detail in the introductory chapter to the post-revolutionary period (p. 553).

F. THE 16TH CENTURY

I. POLITICAL AND ECONOMIC SURVEY

Since the 16th century the history of the Tajik people had centered in the realm of the Khān of Bukhara[17] and it was on this territory that most of the works covered by the term Tajik literature were written.

The conquest of Central Asia by Shaĭbonikhon at the beginning of the 16th century (1499–1500)[18] and the fall of Herat in 1507 ended the southern drive of the nomadic tribes.

Muhammad Shaĭbonī proclaimed his campaign a war against the infidel Timurid dynasty (the members of which were, of course, also Moslems), thereby gaining the support of Bukhara's religious leaders[19] and thus winning a relatively quick victory. But very soon the Shaĭbonī dynasty, that gradually conquered the whole east, had to face a new and very powerful enemy. This was Ismāʿīl, the founder of the Safavid dynasty which thenceforth ruled in Iran for almost 250 years. Under the banner of the 'true religion', namely Islam of the Shīʿite rite, Ismāʿīl defeated Muhammad Shaĭbonī at Merv as early as 1510, and then seized all of Khurasan, including present-day Turkmenistan, as well as Khwarazm with the whole of Afghan Turkistan. In Transoxania, in the 'Land Beyond the River Oxus', that is beyond the Amu Darya, the Persians helped back to power Bābur of Tīmūr's dynasty[20], who conquered Samarkand; but the Sunnite religious leaders of Bukhara launched a campaign against Bābur, accusing him of having accepted Ismāʿīl's help and thereby becoming a 'henchman of the Shīʿites'. This helped Ubaĭdullo Shaĭbonī to recapture Bukhara and Samarkand in 1512, and gradually other members of the Shaĭbonī dynasty also reconquered their lands from the Iranians, thereby placing Central Asia definitely under their rule for a century. The Iranian Shīʿite rulers were driven out of Khvarazm in 1511 by another Uzbek khān, Ilbars, whose dynasty ruled there independently of the Shaĭbonī dynasty for 200 years. Thus, beginning in the second decade of the 16th century, entire Central Asia found itself under the domination of Uzbek khāns, with the sole exception of eastern Khurasan, which continued to form a part of Iran for quite a long time.

The first half of the 16th century was taken up by constant wars between Transoxania and Iran. This, however, did not involve a struggle between Shīʿa and Sunna, as is often stated, but a struggle between the Shaĭbonī and Safavid dynasties for the domination of Khurasan.[21] This was true of the whole period of the rule of Ubaĭdullokhon (1533–1539), but as soon as the war with Persia stopped for a moment, a no less vicious struggle for the throne went on within the Shaĭbonī dynasty. The situation quietened down in 1559, when Abdullokhon of the Shaĭbonī dynasty took Bukhara and placed his father Iskandarkhon on the throne (1561–1583). He then consolidated the whole of Transoxania, with Khvarazm and Khurasan, around a single centre for which he chose Bukhara. Since that time the khanate has been called the Khanate of Bukhara.[22]

A characteristic feature of the Shaĭbonī period is a weak central rule[23], and only the energetic ruler Abdulloh (1583–1598) changed the situation to some extent. In 1584 the armies of Bukhara conquered Badakhshon, which had until then been under the rule of members of the Timurid dynasty, and at the same time seized Kūlob.[24] However, only one year after Abdullo's death, the rule of the Shaĭbonī dynasty came to an end and was replaced by that of the Ashtarkhon (Janid).

The 16th century marks the beginning of the decline of feudalism in Central Asia. Endless wars hampered economic progress, prevented the construction of new irrigation systems and destroyed the old ones. At the same time economic progress was obstructed by the rupture of contacts with the west due to the discovery of sea routes to India and the Far East – whereby Central Asia lost its position as a crossroads of trade routes[25] – as well as to a complicated customs system related to the feudal system, and the lack of safety on the routes linking the west and Central Asia.[26]

Some of the once cultivated land was turned into pastures used by the nomads from the north. On the other hand there was some development of the crafts and trade with India began to grow, just as with Siberia and, in the second half of the 16th century, also with Russia. Much of the latter was due to an Englishman, Anthony Jenkinson.[27] At the same time, however, commercial contacts with Iran had sharply dropped.[28] The influx of new population, the nomadic Uzbeks, and the development of crafts brought about a growth of towns. This process is aptly described by Vosifī in his *Badoe'-ul-vaqoe'*, where he indicates that Bukhara, Samarkand and Tashkent had grown into densely populated cities, true centres of lively economic and cultural activities. This period is also characterised by the considerable growth of the political and economic power of the priesthood, especially the Islamic Dervish shaykhs who often amassed great wealth and power in their hands; this was the case, for example, with Khoja Islom Jūĭborī, a contemporary of Abdullokhon.

The concentration of large estates in the hands of secular and ecclesiastical feudal lords was another cause of the impoverishment of the rural population. The acreage of land owned by the peasants steadily decreased and the peasants worked mostly as sharecroppers on the large estates. The feudal lords also used slave labour on their fields.

Culturally, 16th-century Central Asia followed the Herat tradition of the late 15th century, which had reached its peak in the poets Jomī and Navoī, the miniature painter Bihzod, various calligraphers, etc., and was one of the highest cultures in Central Asia. The revival of cultural life in this region was also spurred on by the * persecution of Sunnites under Shāh Ismā'īl in Iran and Herat. Poets and scholars emigrated in large numbers to Bukhara and other urban centres in Central Asia, among them, for example, Vosifī. Architecture, too, flourished. Bukhara was embellished by a number of new structures, which have survived the centuries until our days; they include such architectural gems as the Masjidi Kalon as well as a number of *madrasas*, such as the Miri Arab, the Madrasai Kūqaltosh and others; in Samarkand it is the well-known Shaĭbonī Bridge across the Zarafshon River. Caravan routes and postal services between important centres in Central Asia were also restored. Bukhara became an important cultural and religious centre, from which Moslem missionaries were sent to present-day Kazakhstan and Siberia, while under the Shaĭbonī dynasty it also became the Islamic centre of the Volga Tatars.

Some historians wrongly interpret the history of Central Asia as an "eternal struggle between the steppe and the oasis", that is between the nomads and the settled farmer, or between the Uzbeks and the Tajiks. Although it is true that the khāns of the nomadic tribes raided the farmers and robbed them, and the feudal landowners

Notes on pp. 536–545

robbed the nomadic tribes, this should not be interpreted as enmity between the simple farmers and the nomads.[29] On the contrary, we may say that during the 16th century contacts grew between the Tajik- and Turkic-speaking population, and the foundations were laid for a close economic and cultural cooperation between them that has lasted until today.

2. LITERATURE

Sixteenth-century literature, especially the work of the two friends – the Tajik Jomī and the Uzbek Navoī[30] – continued the tradition established in Ulughbek's Samarkand in the first half of the 15th century, and in Herat in the second half of that century. However, soon after its occupation by the Safavid dynasty early in the 16th century, Herat itself lost its importance as a centre of culture; its poets, scholars, painters and calligraphers (including Vosifī, Mir Alī[31], and many others) left, mostly for Central Asia. The centre of literary life shifted to the north of the Amu Darya, especially to the court of the Shaĭbonī rulers who, like the rulers of the Timurid dynasty, invited outstanding scholars and poets to their court. As early as the 1520's and 1530's, Bukhara the was centre of official court poetry and learning. Shaĭbonikhon's successor, Ubaĭdullokhon (1553–39) himself wrote Tajik, Uzbek and Arabic poetry[32] under the pseudonym Ubaĭdī; in his anthology, Aĭnī includes a short example of the writings of another member of the Shaĭbonī dynasty, Khon Abdullo II (1583–98).

What was important was the fact that besides Bukhara, another cultural centre developed in Samarkand, as indicated by Vosifī's *Badoe'-ul-vaqoe'*; there, unofficial, so-called urban or artisan poetry developed, and this flourished still further in the 17th century.[33]

Even though it lived off older traditions, the 16th-century period in literature should not be considered as one of decadence.[34] In addition to a number of lesser authors[35], three important representatives of the Herat school were still writing in the first quarter of that century: Binoī, Hilolī, and Vosifī. The second half of their life-time coincided with the period of upheaval during the struggle for Herat and power in Central Asia between the Timurid, Shaĭbonī and Safavid dynasties. Binoī and Vosifī were forced to leave Khurasan and seek haven in the north, while the former of the two poets and Hilolī died violent deaths. A period of relative peace was instituted under the firm rule of Khon Abdullo, who for some time reunited almost all of Central Asia and under whose rule literature to some extent flourished. During that same period, another important representative of 16th-century literature, the poet Mushfiqī, was active at the Shaĭbonī court in Bukhara. However, the poetry of the second half of the 16th century did not attain the level of that of the Herat group.[36]

The second half of the 16th century witnessed intensive cultural contacts between Central Asia and Mogul India. Many poets left for India while others came from

India to Bukhara. There was also extensive correspondence between the poets of the two areas.[37]

The basic source for the study of Central Asian Tajik literature of that period is provided by *Muzakkir-ul-ahbob*, 'A Note to Friends', written in 974/1566 by Saiid Khoja Hasani Bukhorī Nisorī, which is of the same importance for the literature of the first half of the 16th century as Navoī's *tadhkira* is for the second half of the 15th.[38] Other important sources are the *Tuhfai Somī*, by the literary historian Prince Sommirzo of the Safavid dynasty (born in 923/1517), the geographical and biographical encyclopaedia *Haft iqlīm*, 'The Seven Zones of the Earth', written in 1002/1593 by Amin Ahmad Rozī[39], as well as *Mehmonnomai Bukhoro*, 'The Book of the Guest of Bukhara', by Fazlullo b. Rūzbihon Isfahonī, an immigrant from Iran who lived at Shaibonikhon's court.[40] The rulers and princes who wrote poetry are discussed in *Tazkirat-ush-shuaro*, 'Anthology of Poets', in written 1013/1604–5 by Mutribī[41], while *Habībus-siyar*, 'Friend of Biographies' of 1521 by the Central Asian historian Khondamir, is of considerable importance especially for Hilolī's work. However, these are only the basic sources. There exist a number of *tadhkiras* of lesser importance, and we must also bear in mind various works on other topics, for example Darvesh 'Alī's *Risolai musiqī*, 'A Treatise on Music', which contains the elsewhere unpreserved text of Hilolī's *qaṣīda* on Ubaidullokhon.[42]

The great majority of poets whose names and works are included in the aforesaid and other *tadhkiras* are court writers living at various types of feudal courts, ranging from the khān's court in Bukhara to those of the small feudal lords who were more or less dependent on the khān. Their main duty was to sing the praises of their master, which they did mostly with the help of old poetical clichés. The growing importance of the clergy and theology was paralleled by a growth of religious literature – religious and mystical poems, morality tales, biographies of Moslem saints, etc. Both types of literature were anti-popular and artistically did not contribute anything novel. They praised the *status quo* and steadily strengthened formalism, artificiality and a lack of ideas, in all of this reflecting the decadence of feudalism.[43]

Only a few writers, all of them having close ties with the common folk and all men who saw social injustice and criticised it, stand out on account of their quest for new literary ways, new themes and new forms. It is not surprising that it was precisely the names and works of these authors, rather than the often worthless eulogies in verse written by the court panegyrists, that have been preserved in the memories of the people until our day.

Sixteenth-century prose attained its peak in Vosifī's *Badoe'-ul-vaqoe'*, 'Remarkable Tales'. The book was written in the form of memoirs and contains fairy-tales; but in conformity with the views and customs of the day it also includes letters and official decrees, in which at that time a high literary standard was required. This of course corresponded to the contemporary taste, namely for a style overabundant in figures of speech and epithets which were often in bad taste and unintelligible.

Besides the aforementioned great personalities of the 16th century, such as Binoī, Hilolī, Vosifī and Mushfiqī, whose lives and works are discussed separately in subsequent chapters, the names of other authors may at least be mentioned. However, in view of the lack of background material, they can serve only as examples, for there is no possibility of offering a reliable characterisation of these authors. Of the group active at Shaĭbonikhon's court we can mention the mystic poet Husamī Qaraqulī (died 1505 or 1516)[44], or, of the more important ones, Kamoluddin Husaĭn Voʻiz Koshifī of Sabzavār (died 910/1504–5), who re-wrote the collection of fables *Kalila va Dimna* under the title *Anvori Suhaĭlī* 'The Lights of Canopus'; according to Braginskiĭ, this book is an example of an inappropriate treatment of a folk-theme in a highly artificial form.[45] Among the early 16th-century writers we may mention Khojakii Kasanī, known as Makhdumi Aʻzam of Farghona (he died in 1512), the head of the Khojagon order, who is the author of 29 Ṣūfī treatises.[46] The group also includes the son of Jomī's sister, Mavlono Abdullo Hotifī (died in 927/1522), whose *Timurnoma* (a part of an unfinished *khamsa*, the traditional set of five great poems) is, according to Horn, the most important epos after the *Shāh-nāma*.[47] His *Laĭlī va Majnun* is remarkable for its plastic description of the lowly status of women in the society of his days. Hotifī is said to have been a rival of Hilolī[48], as was another of his contemporaries, Nargisī. The better known authors finally include Ahlī of Khurasan (died in 934/1527–28)[49] and the highly productive poet from the second half of the 16th and the first half of the 17th century, Hofizi Tanish binni Mirmuhammadi Bukhoroī, known as Nakhlī (956/1549 – ca. 1051/1645). Some 8000 *baĭts* and the historical treatise *Abdullonoma*[50] have been preserved from his extensive writings.

a. '*Sabki hindi*'

Eastern and western literary learning has not yet agreed on when, where and how the so-called 'Indian style' in Tajik and Persian literature originated, or even on where to seek its substance.[51]

The economic and political decline at the end of the 15th and the beginning of the 16th century was reflected in literature in an increased formalism, a highly contrived form in poetry and prose, marked by a still stronger Arab influence.[52] Poems were composed in excessively complicated metres, often in such a way that they could be read in four different dimensions. According to Kh. S. Aĭnī, this was a similar trend to that marking 17th-century French literature.[53]

This refined style of writing already contained elements of the later 'Indian style'; some of them are characteristic of the Herat literary school, but they still do not constitute the true 'Indian style' that was finally created on Indian soil in the works of poets of Tajik and Persian origin, such as Urfī Shīrāzī, Nazmī, Soib, and many others. It was created under specific social and natural conditions, which differed from the situation then prevailing in Iran and Central Asia. Beginning in the 13th century, many people from Central Asia and Iran emigrated to India, including for example Badri Chochī, the father of Khusrav Dehlavī, Aufī, and others.

This 'Indian style' however did not penetrate into Central Asia in the 16th century to any great extent. This took place only at the beginning of the 17th century, when contacts with India were once again made easier. At that time the 'Indian style' firmly dominated the work of all Tajik writers. There was not a single writer in 17th-century Central Asia and India who was not influenced by it[54], even though he may not have admitted such.

By the end of the 17th century the contrived form of writing reached its peak. The artificiality and complexity of form were the heritage of Herat, but the 'Indian style' developed them still further in a baroque manner. Verse written in this style is a true maze of ideas, a semantic puzzle which can often be deciphered only, as it were, with the help of 'geomancy' and an astrolabe.[55] The devotees of this style expressed their ideas in complex symbols and hints, obscuring the meaning of their poetry. The leading representatives, like Soib, Shavkat or Bedil, were, however, at the same time great thinkers, who garbed their profound ideas in an extremely complicated form. On the other hand, their numerous imitators produced only obscure words and unintelligible turns of speech without any true inner meaning.

This lack of intelligibility was further enhanced in poetry by Ṣūfī themes, the number of which grew as religious fanaticism increased. This formalism in poetry was also intensified by individual poets who tried to surpass each other in their mastery of the verse by writing 'answers' to *ghazals* of other poets, and the writing of *mukhammas* became far more popular.[56]

This situation evoked a negative reaction in some poets. Maleho, in particular, opposed these excesses in his *Muzokir-ul-ashob*, 'Remembering Friends'. He wrote, for example, that the verse of Kosimbek Devona, one of the representatives of the 'Indian style' of the late 17th century, could appeal only to its author, and only after he had smoked a powerful dose of opium.[57]

The 'Indian style' reached its pinnacle in Bedil's work, and this complex literary style consequently is often called 'bedilism'. But this topic will be discussed in the chapter dealing with this author of the 17th to 18th centuries.

b. *Binoī*

Although the early authors of *tadhkiras* all recognised Binoī's genius and the poet's work had already been greatly appreciated during his lifetime, European literary history has thus far devoted little attention to this remarkable author. Especially after the publication of Mirzoev's thorough study[58], Kamoliddin Binoī must be viewed as one of the leading Tajik poets of the end of the 15th and beginning of the

Notes on pp. 536–545

16th centuries. He is ranked as such also by Ghafurov in the chapter on 16th-century Tajik literature of his history of the Tajik people.[59]

In his study, Mirzoev also corrected the erroneous views held on Binoī by European literary historians[60] as regards his character. He throws light on the relationship between Binoī and Navoī; the bad relations between the two poets were described as the consequence of Binoī's disrespect for the Uzbek language and the emerging Uzbek poetry, and this, in turn, was wrongly interpreted as reflecting the relationship between the Tajiks and the Uzbeks. By analyzing Navoī's Uzbek work *Muhokamat-ul-lughataīn*[61], 'The Estimation of Two Languages', i.e. Uzbek and Tajik, Mirzoev demonstrates not only that Binoī had not been a "leader of a movement against the Uzbek language" but also that such a movement had never existed. Binoī highly appreciated Navoī's Uzbek and Tajik poetry in his work *Behrūzu Bahrom* (II, 188), written after Navoī's death, that is at a time when he could no longer feel threatened by the Uzbek poet. The rumour that Binoī hated everything Uzbek is entirely unsubstantiated. His work contains not a single indication of such an attitude and, in fact, Binoī himself had written poetry in Uzbek.[62]

In his work *Chordevon*, Navoī calls Binoī his friend, just as the only preserved *qaṣīda* written by Binoī, which is dedicated in fact to Navoī, reflects the great respect the Tajik poet had for the great Uzbek. They had certainly had differences of opinion but no hatred existed between them. Binoī did not leave Herat for Tabriz only under Navoī's pressure, but primarily because he was in disfavour at the court.

Kamoliddin (Sher) Alī Binoī[63] binni Ustod Muhammadkhon was born at Herat in 1453; in his early youth he accompanied his father when the latter spent three years in Shiraz. As a man of 34 he left his native town – probably also because of his differences with Navoī – to settle first in Tabriz, at the court of Sulṭān Ya'qūb, after whose death in 1491 he returned to Herat. The disfavour and envy shown by the courtiers to the extremely talented poet, who was of low birth, once again forced Binoī into exile, this time to Central Asia – to Samarkand, where he arrived in 1494/5. In Samarkand he witnessed the violent struggle for the throne between the last of the Timurids and the founder of the Shaibonī dynasty. He entered the service of Muhammad Shaibonī (1499–1510) with whose victorious army he entered his native Herat in 1507. After Muhammad's death and the occupation of Herat by the Safavid troops, he left his native town for the third time to settle in Qarshī, in the north, where he perished in 1512 during the massacre of the local population by the Shī'ite army.

Binoī was a poet as well as a prose-writer. His talent for music was praised by Navoī in *Majolis-un-nafois*, 'A Session of Remarkable Things', by Bobur in *Boburnoma*, by Sommirzo[64] and other writers, and he is highly appreciated by many authors of *tadhkiras*.[65] At the same time his work serves as an important source for the study of history.

Of Binoī's extensive work we must first mention the *mathnavī, Behrūzu Bahrom*, which the author himself sometimes calls *Boghi Iram*, 'The Garden of Iram'.[66] It consists of 6000 to 8000 *baĭts*. It is a didactic poem based on Binoī's ethical views. Like some of his outstanding predecessors, he condemns various human weaknesses and social ills, but at the same time also points to the importance of knowledge, believing that human character is formed by his environment, that is by education. It is remarkable that he believes knowledge to be of importance only if it is combined with concrete human activity. The poem contains a number of critical views and ideas. The poet sees the source of all evil in the bad character of the rich and the mighty, and he points to the moral decay of religious notables. His Behrūz is not intended to be a *qozī*, a judge, or a *muftī*, a priest, because they oppress and deceive the people and think only of amassing more property.[67] Although this *mathnavī* is a continuation of the traditional, moralistic *andarzes* and *pandnomas* of the Sasanian scholars and Islamic authors from Rūdakī to Jomī, it contains new ideas and develops the old ones. Also preserved is a part of Binoī's *qaṣīda Majma'-ul-gharoib*, 'A Collection of Remarkable Things', which is interesting in that its introductory chapter was written in the Herat dialect and contains verse dedicated to Navoī. It is not known, however, to whom the whole *qaṣīda* was dedicated.

Binoī's lyrical *ghazals* do not go beyond the scope and traditions of 15th-century poetry of this type, but in them, too, the poet presents new ideas. They include, in particular, scenes from the poet's life and even some critical notes.

Of Binoī's historical treatises, note should be taken of *Shaĭboninoma*, 'The Book on Shaĭbonī'[68], and its enlarged and rewritten variation *Futūhoti khonī*, 'The Khān's Victorious Campaigns', written between 1504 and 1510. Both books describe in prose intermingled with verse the most important events from Shaĭbonikhon's youth to the disintegration of the Timurid empire. They differ from other historical writings in that Binoī included in them a large number of moralistic principles that were apparently designed to influence the ruling class to whom the work was dedicated. On the other hand, Mirzoev shows convincingly that Binoī was not the author of the eulogy on Shāh Ismā'īl Ṣafavī, *Shohinshohnoma*[69], 'The Book on the King of Kings', which led Horn[70] and Ethé[71] to describe Binoī as a second-rate writer. Finally, Vosifī's *Badoe'-ul-vaqoe'* contains Binoī's travelogue called *Hikoyati safari Binoī*, 'A Tale of Binoī's Travels', which is especially of biographical value and contains valuable information about the Persian poet Darvesh Dehakī, who lived at the end of the 15th century. In addition, Binoī wrote two other *mathnavīs*, three *dīvāns* and many *qaṣīdas*. Unfortunately these works have not survived the centuries, neither have the aforesaid treatises on music.

Binoī was a representative of middle-class burghers[72], and we should therefore not be surprised by his non-conformist views and consequently by his lack of popularity among those close to the court. All his work is characterised by one feature: his fight against the evils prevalent in the ruling circles and his criticism of these evils. It is there that lay Binoī's extraordinary importance – he knew how to continue the best traditions of Persian and Tajik poetry and at the same time to include in his works new ideas reflecting the state of society at the turn of the 15th and 16th centuries.

c. *Hilolī*

Another of the outstanding Tajik authors of the end of the 15th and the beginning of the 16th centuries was Badriddin (sometimes called Nūriddin) Hilolī[73], who was and is almost unknown on the territory of present-day Iran, but who has always been respected by the peoples of Central Asia and Afghanistan. His *ghazals* can still be heard performed by folk singers – *hofizes* – and are often broadcast by Radio Dushanbe. They have also influenced the national Tajik music – *shashmaqom*. Like Binoī, Hilolī too belonged to the group of Herat poets. He struck the attention of Navoī, who mentioned him as a promising young poet in his *tadhkira Majolis-unnafois*.

Hilolī was born in Astarobod in Khurasan and was – according to Navoī – of Chighatoĭ origin. The exact year of his birth is unknown, but round about the age of twenty – in 1491 – he came to Herat to continue his education. He lived in Herat for the rest of his life, and it was there that he was put to death in 936/1529 – according to the chronogram of the mullo of Bukhara, Mirak Husaĭn – under the pretence of his being a member of the Shīʿa sect, but most probably because he had written verse criticising Ubaĭdullokhon.[74] The said chronogram also indicates that already earlier Hilolī had been considered a revolutionary.[75] Hilolī's gravestone is now located in the square in front of the Bālā Ḥiṣār in Herat.

Hilolī was not a court panegyrist as were the great majority of his fellow-poets at that time. He expressed quite frankly his dislike of court poetry at the end of his *Laĭlī va Majnun*, where he criticised those poets "who praise fools as wise men...". An important place in his work is held by an extensive *dīvān* of lyrical *ghazals*, most of which have love as their theme. They were considered by the author to represent the pinnacle of the art of poetry. However, besides love, his *ghazals* also contain – in contrast to tradition – some critical themes and biographical data, as does Binoī's work. Hilolī considered the aim of all endeavour to be man freed of all poverty, and appealed to the powerful and rich to be just and generous. The simplicity of his speech, the artistic perfection and song-like quality of his verse have made a large number of his *ghazals* survive five centuries by folk-tradition.

Hilolī also wrote three long poems: *Laĭlī va Majnun*, 'Laĭlī and Majnun', *Sifot-ul-oshiqin*, 'Description of My Darlings', and *Shohu darvesh*, 'The Shāh and the Dervish'. The longest and most valuable of the three is *Laĭlī va Majnun*, which has more than 3500 verses. In this poem, Hilolī presents a new conception of an old theme: his principal heroine is Laĭlī, a determined woman who has the courage to reject the man she is being forced to marry. Second, as far as its length is concerned, is *Sifot-ul-oshiqin*, a poem undoubtedly written under the influence of Niẓāmī's *Makhzanu'l-asrār*[76] (p. 210); each of its twenty chapters describes a certain human characteristic. Considering that it was written in the 16th century, the poem presents many remarkable ideas; for example, the author says that a good infidel is better than a bad Moslem, and criticises tyrants who oppress the poor. Hilolī's last *mathnavī*, *Shohu darvesh*, sometimes also called *Shohu gado*, 'The Shāh and the Beggar', which contains 1114 verses, has a mystical character and a strong didactic trend, and expresses the belief that the barriers of social inequality may be overcome. Because of this idea, the poem was sharply denounced by Boburmirzo, a spokesman of the ruling circles, in his *Boburnoma*.[77] This *mathnavī* describes the tragic love of a dervish for his ruler; it is a symbol of the desire of a simple human soul for God. The poem was translated metrically into German by H. Ethé (see the Bibliography).

d. *Vosifī*

Vosifī's extensive work *Badoe'-ul-vaqoe'*, 'Remarkable Tales' was studied by Russian scholars as a historical source as early as the middle of the 19th century, but the value of Vosifī's work in general was discovered for the first time by Sadriddin Aĭnī in his Anthology of Tajik Literature.[78] A thorough study was then made by A. N. Boldïrev.[79]

Zaĭniddin Mahmud ibn Abduljalil Vosifī was one of a group of outstanding literary figures of Herat living at the end of the 15th and the beginning of the 16th century. He was born in Herat in 890/1485 and was said to have written poems ever since his 13th year. Incredible stories are told of his physical strength and endurance. Vosifī's teacher of poetry was Husaĭn Vo'iz Koshifī (he died in 910/1504–5), who said that his pupil was much more talented than himself. For some time Vosifī was a tutor at the court of Husaĭn Boĭqaro but from 1505 onwards his life was one of adventurous travels through northern Iran and Central Asia. He paid several visits to Samarkand, Bukhara, Tashkent and other cities. He stayed in *madrasas*, often in great poverty, living with the common folk, while at other times he stayed as a tutor at the court of the ruler of Tashkent. In 1529 he took part in Abdullokhon's campaign against the members of the Safavid dynasty. No other details of the author's life are known, but we may assume from his writings that he lived at least until the beginning of the second half of the 16th century. Boldïrev estimates (*Zaynaddin Vasifi*, 243) that he died some time between 1551 and 1566.

Vosifī, a Central Asian Benvenuto Cellini, as Boldïrev calls him, was a universal writer. He was a master of poetry and its techniques arising from the traditions of his times. He composed *qaṣīdas*, lyrical *ghazals*, *chiston* (puzzle) and *mu'ammo* (verbal rebus), very popular in those days and highly praised also by Navoī; he wrote poems that could be read in four different metres[80], etc. Note should be taken of the *qaṣīda* he wrote in Samarkand during a period of famine, as well as of his critical *qaṣīdas*.

However, Vosifī's main achievement was not poetry. He must be praised primarily as the author of the afore-mentioned important document of his times, the voluminous 900-page *Badoeʿ-ul-vaqoeʿ*, 'Remarkable Tales'.[81] It is a book written in prose but includes much verse, according to tradition, and is remarkable for its comparatively clear and simple language – in contrast to other classical works. The book contains a great number of short stories about different people and events; we can find there important information on the life of the great Uzbek and Tajik poet and thinker Alisher Navoī, on Jomī, Hilolī, and many other poets and writers. It also includes, for example, fifteen fairy-tales about Abū ʿAlī ibn Sīnā (Avicenna). The book presents an excellent picture of the life of poets living at the feudal courts of Central Asia, and also contains a wealth of important autobiographical data up to 1518. Thus we may reconstruct the author's life almost perfectly up to that year. The various parts of the book were written at different times. Aĭnī already pointed to the fact that, compared with other books of this type, Vosifī's work described events and life quite frankly, without any embellishment.[82] However, the book is at the same time a kind of Vosifī's *dīvān*, containing not only much poetry (including poems by other writers), but also the texts of various documents, orations, gravestone inscriptions composed by the author, etc. Vosifī was outstanding also in this sphere, which had once belonged to literature.

It should be pointed out that the value of Vosifī's work does not lie in its historical exactness or in its information about various personages, but mainly in the fact that it shows how the serious political events of the day were reflected in the minds of the people.[83] In particular the book provides an insight into the cultural life of the craftsmen and artisans living in towns. Its progressive nature also lies in the fact that the author included in it a number of folk-tales, as in the case of the afore-mentioned folk legends about Avicenna, as well as in the fact that he considered Avicenna to have been an outstanding scientist, an opinion running counter to the official views of the religious circles.[84] Finally, Vosifī criticised the society of his times in a manner unparalleled among his contemporaries. Boldïrev further shows that Vosifī succeeded in developing a new literary style corresponding to the needs of the newly emerging social ideology of the townspeople.[85] It should still be added that the language of *Badoeʿ-ul-vaqoeʿ* goes beyond the standard of 'porsii darī', as Vosifī already used purely Tajik words.[86]

e. *Mushfiqī*

P. P. Ivanov considers Mushfiqī to have been the greatest Tajik poet of the 16th century[87], while Mirzoev views him as the last good panegyric poet of Central Asia.[88] But in point of fact Mushfiqī's work and life have not yet been thoroughly studied.

Z. Ahrorī deserves thanks for the publication of Mushfiqī's selected works[89], but Western scholars have ignored this poet almost completely.

In Central Asia, however, Mullo Mushfiqī is universally known among the people, who regard him as a folk-jester, a Tajik variety of Nasreddin Hoja, who is some, times called Afandī by the Tajiks. Aĭnī writes in his Anthology that Mushfiqī became so famous for his satirical writings that his serious works have been overshadowed[90], although they, too, are numerous and valuable.

The poet Abdurahmon Mushfiqī was born in Bukhara about 1538, but he also sometimes used the *nisba* (a name denoting local origin) Marvī after his father, who had come to Bukhara from Merv. Mushfiqī lived in his native town until 1561–2, when he left for Samarkand, where he stayed for six years, working at one time as the librarian of Sulton Saʿid, thereby gaining access to the court circles. Apparently he was not very successful because in 1567–8 he left for Delhi to join the court of Akbar the Great[91], whom he praised in two *qaṣīdas*. But he failed in Dehli too, and one year later returned to Bukhara where he won some recognition at the court of Abdullokhon (1583–1598) who, it is said, did nothing without first consulting the poet.[92] It was there that Mushfiqī became *malik-ush-shuaro*, the King of Poets. He died in Bukhara in 996/1587–8.

Mushfiqī was primarily a lyrical poet. He wrote *ghazals* and *qiṭʿas* in traditional form and with traditional content, but he brought the theme of love closer to real life than had been customary. He also wrote a number of magnificent *ruboīs*. The language of his poetry is flowing and easily understandable, and his work reflects the influence of folk-poetry. Mushfiqī also composed a number of *qaṣīdas* in the old style and spirit, which have been preserved mainly in the historical work of his younger contemporary, the historian of Abdullokhon's court, Hofiz Tanish Nakhlī, *Sharaf-nomai shohī*, 'The Royal Book of Honour', known also as *Abdullonoma*, 'The Book of Abdullo'. These *qaṣīdas* were mostly addressed to Abdullokhon, but also to a number of other prominent personalities. This whole *dīvān* of *qaṣīdas* contains some 3000 *baĭts*. Most outstanding among them is a *qaṣīda* called *Shikoyat az zulm*, 'Complaint Against Tyranny', dedicated to Abdullokhon and pointing to the misery and poverty of the common folk; Mushfiqī puts the blame on an irresponsible vizier who ignores the welfare of the people and devotes himself only to gluttony.[93] An important place in Mushfiqī's work is held by his *Devoni hajviët* or *Devoni mutoibot*, 'A *Dīvān* of Satire', written, according to the chronogram, in 1557–8. The verse contained in this book passed outside the court circles and thereby Mushfiqī entered into folklore as a folk-jester, a hero of *latifas* (anecdotes), although most of his work runs counter to this position. Khoja Hasan Nisorī called him in his *tadhkira* a remarkable writer of satire, the like of whom could not be found.

Mushfiqī was primarily a court poet who did not serve the people by his work, as did for example Hilolī or, later, Saĭido Nasafī. His satirical *dīvān* has some 1500 *baĭts* and also contains some prose. But it is mostly made up of critical poems aimed against various persons, mainly poets. The importance of this work also rests in the fact that Mushfiqī had used the vernacular, thereby making his poetry understandable to the common folk.[94] He also taught the art of poetry[95], and his daughter Munira is said – according to folk-tradition – to have been a good poetess; but only very short fragments of her poetry have been preserved.[96]

G. THE 17TH CENTURY

I. HISTORICAL SURVEY

There was a certain economic and cultural development under the rule of Abdullokhon (1583–1593) of the Shaĭbonī dynasty, who consolidated the central government and the prestige of his court by maintaining good relations with the Turkish sulṭān against their common enemy, Shīʿite Iran. He accepted gifts even from the outstanding Indian ruler Akbar the Great of the Great Mogul dynasty. However, after his death his empire again fell apart, and the whole of the 17th and 18th centuries were characterised by the general growth of power of the various local feudal lords and the decline of power of the khān of Bukhara.[97]

Abdullokhon's son, Abdulmuʿmin, was removed by his vassals after a rule of six months; the Shāh of Iran, ʿAbbās, exploited this situation and reconquered Herat and the whole of Khurasan. Khvārazm separated itself, and in the resulting confusion and tumult the Northern Kazakhs went into action and temporarily occupied Samarkand.

The amīrs decided to offer the vacant throne to the husband of one of Abdullokhon's daughters, whose family came from Astrakhan. He turned down the offer, but eventually it was accepted by his relative, Boqī Muhammad, who founded a new dynasty – of the Ashtarkhon family – which then ruled, rather ignominiously, until the second half of the 18th century. Imomqulikhon (1611–1642) first waged bloody battles with the individual feudal lords and the nomadic tribes in the north, and in the end consolidated his position. After the central government had been strengthened, there was a certain revival of trade and the crafts. In his *Shahroshub*, Saĭido notes that in Bukhara there were 250 different crafts. This was connected with a certain growth of the towns and trade with other lands, especially India and Russia.[98]

During this period there were, in fact, two political centres in the Khanate of Bukhara: Bukhara itself, which was the seat of the khān – who was, as a rule, rather restricted in his power – and Balkh in which the rule was held either by the successor to the throne or an outstanding military leader, the *ataliq*.

This relative prosperity did not last long, however. Under the rule of Imomqulikhon's successors new fratricidal strife took place. For some time the Great Moguls occupied Balkh, and the khān of Khiva waged a campaign against Bukhara during the entire second half of the 17th century, causing great material damage and impoverishment of the population. Abdulazizkhon (1645–1680) failed to terminate the unceasing struggle and eventually abdicated in favour of his brother Subhonqulikhon. These changes on the throne and in the rule of the lesser feudal lords were usually accompanied by unbelievable brutality. Fathers used to subject their sons, who aspired or might aspire to seize power, to bestial torture, while, on the other hand, the sons had their fathers mercilessly beheaded. Under the rule of Subhonqulikhon the local feudal lords exploited the dissatisfaction of the people and gradually made themselves independent. Subhonqulikhon's rule was a chain of aggressive and defensive campaigns which brought only suffering to the population.

This, of course, caused a considerable deterioration of the economic situation in the second half of the 17th century, following the relative growth in the first half. Corruption ran rampant throughout the administration of the country. Maleho notes that much money was needed to obtain an official appointment. In order to acquire sufficient funds for the upkeep of his court and for financing his wars, Subhonqulikhon, under whose rule the crisis reached its peak, had taxes collected seven years in advance. Irrigation facilities fell into disrepair and the concentration of farmland in the hands of the large feudal lords and influential shaykhs continued. The urban population, as noted by Saĭido, fled to the countryside, while the peasants were forced by high taxation to leave the land, so that the streets of the towns were crowded with beggars.[99] An important source for the study of the history of Central Asia in the second half of the 17th century is provided by *Dastūr-ul-mulūk*, 'A Handbook of Rulers', written by Khoja Samandar Tirmizī.

The grave political and economic situation was not, of course, conducive to cultural development. The end of the 17th century is a period of decline in literature, particularly of court poetry. Many writers left Central Asia to find a haven especially in northern India.[100]

2. LITERATURE

The 'Indian style' spread to Central Asia in the 1620's and 1630's, and did not reach its full extent there until the middle of the 17th century. Earlier penetration was prevented by the hostility between the Ashtarkhon dynasty and the Great Moguls, during which the Shāh of Iran occupied Herat and northern Afghanistan for a long period of time.

Many poets worked at the courts of the Ashtarkhon dynasty in both cultural centres of those days – Bukhara and Balkh (there were some thirty poets at the court of Abdulazizkhon alone), and poetry was also, according to tradition, written by some of the rulers and members of their families.[101]

Notes on pp. 536–545

The basic source of understanding of 17th-century literature – apart from the works of individual authors – is provided by the *tadhkira Muzokir-ul-ashob*, 'Remembering Friends', written in 1692 by Maleho Samarqandī[102], who lists some 150 Central Asian and Iranian authors of his times, and the *tadhkira* of Mutribī (written in 1604–1605), in which the majority of the poets represented come from craftsman families, such as Boqī Qaffosh (who was a shoemaker), Zarkhī Turkistonī (a jeweller), or poets who were blacksmiths, weavers, tent-makers, etc. Other important works are *Ubaĭdullonoma*, 'The Book of Ubaĭdullo', and the historical work of Mir Muhammad Amin Bukhorī.[103] Important information is also supplied by other historical writings, such as *Abdullonoma*, 'The Book of Abdullo', by Hofiz Tanish Bukhorī. This book is also called *Sharafnomai shohī*, 'The Royal Book of Honour', and contains the history of the rule of Abdullokhon. Other leading historical works are *Ta'rikhi Muqimkhonī*, 'Muqimkhon's History', written in 1116/1704–5 by Muhammad Yusuf Munshī[104], and *Saĭid Roqim* (written in 1113/1701–2) by Mir Saĭid Sharif Roqim Samarqandī.[105]

Under the rule of Imomqulikhon (1611–1642), when the local feudal wars were limited and conditions for economic prosperity were created, some cultural advance was also made. This is ascribed by Mirzoev in particular to the fact that Central Asia had expanded its cultural contacts with Iran.[106] However, this cultural growth did not last longer than until the 1690's.

Seventeenth-century literature in Central Asia is characterised by two parallel trends – the growth of urban craftsman poetry reached its peak, and the 'Indian style' fully dominated the work of all authors.

All the works left from the literary heritage of the 17th century (which is, as a rule, identical with what was worth being preserved) come almost entirely from authors who had not been connected with the court, from craftsmen and simple *madrasa* students, such as Saĭido, Fitrat, Muhammadamin Sarafroz, Maleho, Shokir, Sodot, and others. Besides Tajik poets there were also Uzbeks, like Mashrab Namangonī, who sharply criticised the Islamic priesthood (which cost him his life)[107], or Turdī Faroghī, who condemned the khān's injustice and carefree life, and called for his overthrow.[108]

In the 17th century literature divided itself still more markedly into progressive literature of the urban craftsmen, and reactionary court literature of which nothing of any true value has been preserved.[109] The same was true of dervish poetry.

Among the town poets we must rank along with Saĭido (p. 509) the little-known Fitrat Zarduzi Samarqandī (1660 – early 18th century), a tape-maker of Bukhara (he had moved to Bukhara from Samarkand between 1685 and 1688), whose real name was Saĭidkamol.[110] Ubaĭdullonoma states that "he never tried to visit the ruler's court".[111] His preserved works include the Ṣūfī-romantic *mathnavī Kozurpisar*, 'The Washerwoman's Son', known also under the title *Tolibu matlub*, 'The Seeking and the Sought', which is very closely related with folklore, as stated in the preface by the author himself. Also preserved are a satire, listed by Maleho in his *tadhkira*, and individual *ghazals* found in various anthologies.[112] Fitrat's works clearly reflect the ideology of the small craftsmen and their attitude towards the ruling classes. His writings were aimed against Islamic priests[113] and his themes were often anti-feudal – in his poem he describes the ruler as a merciless and stupid man, while the son of the washerwoman is a very pleasant character. His *dīvān* was published in Tashkent in 1917.

Of the many other authors we should take note of Muhammadbadeʿ Maleho Samarqandī (born in 1649), who is said to have been allowed by his father to write poetry only after he had promised not to compose *qaṣīdas* in honour of highly placed persons. Maleho was also a poet, but he is important mainly as the author of a most valuable *tadhkira* which contains information on Saĭido and a number of other authors from the lower ranks who are ignored – obviously on purpose – in other *tadhkiras*. Maleho undertook the task of writing an anthology of the literature of his times and intended to meet every author personally. He therefore left for Bukhara and from there went to Iran where he spent three years as a member of the khān's mission. He completed his *tadhkira, Muzokir-ul-ashob*, in 1692. It contains information on 166 17th-century poets living in Central Asia and Iran, and there is brief information on an additional 17 poets in the supplements. Maleho criticises imitators and plagiarism in poetry, and praises particularly those authors who came up to his ideal of a poet. The great value of his *tadhkira* lies also in the fact that it contains much information obtained directly from the authors he discusses.

Another 17th-century writer who should be mentioned is Muhammadamin Sarafroz (died in 1688–9), a poet of whom Maleho says that he had the memory of a genius. Unfortunately, his *dīvān* has not yet been discovered, but the good quality of his verse is apparent from his *ghazals* included in numerous 17th- and 18th-century anthologies.[114] Other outstanding poets and universal scholars include the teacher of Maleho Samarqandī, Lutfullo Shokir[115], while Khoja Sameʿ Sodot (who died at the end of the 17th century) was a very fertile poet whose talent can be judged only from a small number of preserved verses.[116] The work of Mir Muhammad Sharif (he died in 1697–8) has been preserved, but his importance lay in his scholarly writings rather than in his poetry, which contributed nothing novel either in form or content.[117] In his Anthology, Aĭnī also devotes considerable attention to Shavkat Muhammadishoq Bukhoroī, who was one of the town poets but whose poetry did not reflect the life of the common folk.[118] He left Bukhara for Isfahan where he died at the end of the 17th century. He was the last model of the Ottoman poets, in particular of Qoja-Rāghib Pasha (died 1176/1763) and his contemporaries, in so far as these poets still sought their ideal in Persian literature (see p. 328, 1st ed., Prague 1956).

a. *Poetry of the town craftsmen*

It was Ye. E. Bertel's who pointed to the interesting fact that, beginning in the 15th century, representatives of the middle classes, individual craftsmen, wandering singers, etc., were entering the literary world, and Ṣūfī poetry was not always involved.[119]

This theme was further developed by Boldïrev in his monograph on Vosifī[120] and by Mirzoev in his book on Saĭido.[121] In his *Badoe'-ul-vaqoe'*[122] Vosifī offered most valuable evidence of this development, and it was precisely Vosifī and Saĭido who best manifested the active participation of the ordinary townspeople in literary work.

Mirzoev notes that, from the 15th century on, anti-feudal trends are increasingly apparent among the craftsmen and members of other lower classes.[123] From that century, too, we learn from scanty reports something about authors of craftsman origin, such as Muflisī or Zorī, who used new themes, showing, in particular, the poverty suffered by the broad masses of the population. According to Khondamir and Navoī, this new craftsman poetry was supposedly founded by Saĭfii Bukhoroī (died in 1495 or 1503–4), who was the first to write poems devoted to individual crafts.[124] Vosifī's *Badoe'-ul-vaqoe'* clearly describes the development of town poetry in Samarkand. The poets gathered not at the court of the feudal lord but in the bazaars, in their shops, or in their cells in the *madrasas*. This is also indicated in the *tadhkiras* of Jomī, Navoī and Davlatshoh, even though these authors, as spokesmen of the ruling classes, took a negative view of the 'town illiterates'.[125]

Binoī, too, writes about the growing cultural level of the broad masses of townspeople; he was, after all, one of them. This literature is closely linked with the traditions of Tajik and Persian literature, primarily poetry, but it has some specific features of its own – in particular new themes in the *ghazals*, as in the case of the poets Saĭfī (15th century), Vosifī (16th century), and especially Saĭido.

The poetry of these authors is permeated with the ideology of the middle urban classes, which determines such stylistic qualities as a trend towards a realistic reflection of the world in the themes and poetic images, abandonment of the rhetorical verse of the court poets, and simplicity of language. This is shown, for example, by a lexical analysis of Vosifī's work.[126]

A further growth of town poetry took place in the 17th century[127], the period of the supreme representative and perfecter of this genre, Saĭido, himself a craftsman. Another outstanding representative of this period was the craftsman Mulham, whose many favourable attributes, according to Mir Muhammad Amin Bukhorī, included the fact that he "did not seek service with the ruler and the amīrs ... and did not engage in the sale of his verse".[128] Court poetry had completely lost its significance. The only poets living at the courts were panegyrists who knew nothing else but to laud their masters in fantastically overwrought metaphors. Moreover, even these songs of praise went into further decline and this type of poetry almost disappeared in the

1680's when many poets left the court because of the unsettled political and economic situation, and went abroad, usually to India.[129]

b. *Saĭido*

The greatest poet of the 17th century[130] – recognised as such already by his contemporaries[131] – was Mirobid Saĭido Nasafī, who was the first to stand up uncompromisingly to defend the oppressed people and to oppose the feudal regime.[132] This was, of course, a good reason for being ignored by many writers of *tadhkiras*, most of whom were connected with the ruling circles. He was discovered by Sadriddin Aĭnī, who devoted considerable space to him in his 1926 Anthology.[133] A more detailed study of Saĭido's life and work was made by Mirzozoda and, in a separate monograph, by Mirzoev.[134]

Saĭido was, above all, the representative and perfector of the best traditions of 'craftsman poetry', of poetry characterised by social themes, written for the broad masses of townspeople among whom he was extremely popular. In this respect he was the successor to the poet Saĭfī Bukhoroī[135], who "did not strive to visit the homes of the amīrs and the khān's court, being content with the piece of bread which was his destiny..."[136], and was greatly influenced by the poet Soib (see pp. 301 *et seq.*) who, however, only noted while Saĭido protested.

Saĭido was born in Nasaf – present-day Qarshī – but lived in Bukhara. There is little information available about his life. Proceeding from various data, Mirzoev assumes that he was born late in the first half of the 17th century.[137] He produced most of his work in the relatively peaceful period until the 1670's when he lived and studied with the support of the craftsmen of Bukhara. Then he visited the homes of some members of the ruling circles in order to find a 'patron', and wrote verse for them, but his poems did not have the mendicant and panegyric nature of the usual *qaṣīdas*. Nevertheless, Saĭido thought least of this part of his work. However, the poet soon learned that he did not need the favours of the feudal lords if he relied on the common people, and in his later years he recalled bitterly the indignities he had had to suffer. In order to make a living, he was forced to work as a weaver – probably in his more advanced age – but he was a free man. He died in poverty under the rule of Ubaĭdullokhon of the Ashtarkhon dynasty, i.e. between 1707 and 1711.[138]

Saĭido's work differs in many respects from the traditional poetry of his days. It is characterised by a folk-spirit, its language is close to the vernacular, and in the *ghazals* we often find folk-proverbs, while other proverbs were created by the poet himself. Typical of Saĭido's verse are social themes which until then had never been used to such an extent. Thus, for example, his *doston Bahoriët*, 'Songs of Spring', known also as *Haĭvonotnoma*, 'The Book of Animals', an animal fable, most successfully reflects the thinking of the various social classes of that period. The poem is remarkable also from the formal point of view, as in all its 184 *baĭts* the same rhyme is used. *Bahoriët* was often imitated by other poets.[139] Saĭido expressed his views of society very frankly also in his numerous *ghazals*. There, too, he often showed that the working people formed the basis of society and that the ruler should respect this fact. He pointed to the disunity of the country and to the true culprits – members of the ruling classes. He was greatly saddened by the division of the country into a large number of semi-independent areas and demanded a strong, central government which in the past had always resulted in economic prosperity. He speaks with bitterness about the fact that the bad economic and political situation in Central Asia forced the most talented people, outstanding artists and scholars, to go abroad. These are the main topics of Saĭido's poetry, and he also includes social themes in his lyrical love poems. His *ghazals* are rather long – having up to 26 *baĭts* – and their perfection was recognised by contemporary experts. Among them, Mir Muhammad Amini Bukhorī wrote in his *Ubaĭdullonoma* that Saĭido was the prince of the poets of Bukhara.[140]

An important place is held in Saĭido's work by the *mathnavīs* devoted to individual crafts: to the butcher, the baker, the carpenter, *et al.*; they best reflect the poet's respect for the common working people. It is also interesting that he used the form of a *mathnavī* for the contents of a *qaṣīda*, but one written not in praise of the ruler or a leading courtier, but in praise of a craftsman. The poems are also striking because in each of them Saĭido used the terminology of the respective craft and because he actually described in considerable detail the process used by the individual craftsmen in their work.[141]

Finally, note should be taken of Saĭido's *mukhammases*, a special form of a very difficult imitation (see note 56 on p. 538) popular in Tajik poetry. He wrote them in imitation of the poetry of Ḥāfiẓ, Jomī, his contemporary Bedil[142] (p. 515) and others.

Traditional didactics, too, holds an important place in Saĭido's work. He condemned corruption, which was rampant in the country, praised the importance of work and diligence for man's development, and greatly cherished friendship, the family, the family upbringing of children, truth, and the keeping of promises.

According to Maleho, Saĭido was already very popular in his lifetime – everybody, he says, knew his poems – and he had many pupils and followers. Although he proceeded from tradition, he introduced much that was new, in particular changing the meaning of previously much repeated poetic images. His language, which reflects the influence of the Bukhara dialect, is close to the vernacular. In his verse Saĭido was careful not to disturb the common syntax for the sake of the rhyme, and he liked to use live idiom. He deserves credit for having developed town literature; he gave it certain specific features and thereby created a literary school.

H. THE 18TH CENTURY UP TO THE RUSSIAN OCCUPATION OF CENTRAL ASIA

I. HISTORICAL SURVEY

This was one of the worst periods for Central Asia. Ubaĭdullokhon (1702–1711) failed to concentrate power in his hands and was eventually deposed by the feudal lords. His successor was no more fortunate. The Shāh of Persia, Nādir (1736–1747), exploited the weakness of khān Abulfaĭz (1711–1747)[143], invaded Central Asia in 1740, and without meeting any opposition turned the khanate of Bukhara into vassal territory under Iranian domination. At Nādir's behest, the throne was seized by *atalīk* Muhammad Rahim (1753–1759), a member of the Uzbek tribe of Manghits, who had the khān and his two sons executed in 1747, and took over the rule with the title of amīr. Through him the khanate of Bukhara came under the rule of the Manghit dynasty, which stayed in power until 1920, when the revolution deposed its last member. This dynasty did not produce a single ruler of any ability[144], except Shohmurod[145] (1785–1800). This amīr had at least some energy and introduced certain reforms, also deserving credit for some extension of the irrigated land and for abolishing various taxes, the number of which had become unprecedented, especially under his father Doniël-biĭ. He also achieved some political consolidation in that three central, despotic, feudal entities were formed in Central Asia: the amirate of Bukhara and the khanates of Khiva and Qūqand.[146] Although there still existed some small, independent and semi-independent territories, like Shahri Sabz and the territory of present-day Badakhshon, the situation was more favourable than under the predecessors of Shoh Murod. On the other hand, it was under his rule that the amirate of Bukhara lost for all practical purposes the territory on the left bank of the Amu Darya with a number of semi-independent Uzbek khanates, such as Andkhoĭ, Maĭmana, Ākcha, and others, which gradually submitted to the growing central power of Afghanistan. However, the relatively large princedom of Qundūz was not conquered by the Afghans until the middle of the 19th century. Murod's successor, Saĭid Amir Haĭdar (1800–1826), was unable to continue the centralist policy of his predecessor.

The first half of the 19th century was characterised by a violent and persistent struggle between the three khanates. Thus, for example, Nasrullo (1826–1860) invaded Shahri Sabz 32 times, until he finally conquered it in 1856. This ruler, who was called *amiri qassob* (amīr-the-butcher) also became notorious for having reached the throne over the corpses of his two brothers; after his accession he had 50 to 100 people executed every day for a period of one month.[147]

This whole period is also marked by a further growth of feudal oppression and by the continued growth of the power of the priesthood. As the latter increased its influence, cultivated land was gradually transferred into *vaqf* and placed under the ownership of landlords. According to Vambéry, in the second half of the 19th century there were still some 20,000 slaves in Bukhara, but slave labour did not play a major role in Central Asia. Production was based on the work of feudally dependent peasants and free craftsmen.[148] On the other hand, the second half of the 18th century was economically fairly prosperous: productive forces were growing, life in the towns was being consolidated, and economic contacts between the individual regions were progressing, just as the influence of the international market was being increasingly felt.[149] Trade was growing, especially with Russia. As early as 1716, Abulfaïzkhon sent a mission to Moscow to conclude a trade agreement, while Peter the Great dispatched his ambassador, Florio Beneveni, to Bukhara. However, a true growth of contact between Central Asia and Russia did not take place until the last decades of the 18th century, when capitalist relations began to develop in the Russian economy.[150]

All the three main Central Asian khanates had Uzbek populations, which were in the majority, as well as a Tajik minority that lived especially in the towns[151] as craftsmen and merchants, and in the mountain areas of present-day Tajikistan. The population also included some Turkoman, Kazakh and Kirghiz tribes.

In cultural life the Tajik language – which was also the official language – predominated next to Arabic, which ruled supreme in the *madrasas*. The cultural decline continued in general – nothing new was achieved in the field of learning and old religious customs were banished.[152] Only theology was allowed to develop – a casuistic study of commentaries on the 'Holy Books' – and in the schools, too, only scholastic, theological disciplines were being taught. The ignorance of the 'scientists' of those days is indicated by the then official thesis that "although it is true that in the whole world sunlight falls on the earth from above, in Bukhara it emanates from the earth because there are so many holy men buried in it."[153] Cultural traditions were not broken completely[154], but were preserved especially in the works of the most outstanding Tajik and Persian classical authors. These were popular among the broadest masses of the population, being passed on from generation to generation in the interpretation of folk-singers; this tradition was also continued in folk-poetry, which was quite different from the official panegyric court poetry and from the mystical poems then in vogue in official circles.

2. LITERATURE

Although the period of the 18th and the first half of the 19th centuries is one of the least studied in Tajik literature[155], we may say that it was characterised by a continued decline due to the adverse economic situation, the ceaseless wars, and religious fanaticism. There was practically not a single outstanding author deserving mention in Central Asia in that period, which does not mean, of course, that Tajik literature had disappeared completely; there were still many poets pursuing their art, as indicated by various *tadhkiras* and by Aīnī's Anthology of Tajik literature. However, the overwhelming majority of the poets served the interests of the ruling classes, turning mystical ideas into verse to keep the population in submission and ignorance. Ṣūfī poetry had completely lost its original meaning as a protest against religious fanaticism, and, on the contrary, had become its promotor. It was given expression in mystical, unintelligible *ghazals* and songs of prayer. At the same time, however, the poets associated with the court produced many pornographic poems for the entertainment of the amīr and his courtiers.[156] Poets of folk origin had no opportunity to exercise their talent, and their poems thus had no wider impact – but there is no doubt that during this period too there existed some progressive literature[157], which unfortunately has not been preserved.

Ranking first among the poets writing during this period are those who were active in India, primarily the poetess Zebunniso and the outstanding poet Mirzo Abdulqodir Bedil, whose work left a deep imprint on the whole of 18th- and 19th-century Tajik literature.

The poetess Zebunniso, whom already Ethé considered to have been of outstanding talent[158], was the daughter of Aurangzeb of the Mogul dynasty. She was a princess who was forced to live in seclusion and was devoted to the reading of Arabic and Tajik poetry. She herself is the author of a *dīvān*, which she wrote under the pseudonym Mahfī; it contains many progressive ideas, opposing the oppression of the common people and pointing to their poverty and starvation, condemning the dishonesty of the priesthood and in particular the enslavement of women. She had a remarkably progressive view on the necessity of maintaining harmony between the form of a literary work and its contents. In one of her *qaṣīdas* she said that no matter how polished the form might be, it could not make the work perfect if the content were weak. Zebunniso's name rarely appeared in *tadhkiras* but, thanks to the humanistic content of her work, her poems have been kept alive among the people.[159] She is usually said to have lived between 1639 and 1702, but Aīnī[160] believes that more exact information is provided by the *tadhkira Siyar-ul-muta'akhirin*, 'Biographies of Our Antecedents', which gives the year of her birth as 1643 and that of her death as 1721. Zebunniso wrote Tajik and Arabic lyrical poems, an anthology of which was published by S. Javharizoda in 1940, and by the same editor in co-operation with A. Sidqī again in 1958.[161] Her *dīvān* contains some 7000 verses.

The work of Bedil forms the subject of a separate chapter (pp. 515 *et seq.*).

The names of only relatively few authors have been preserved from the first half of the 18th century, for this period seems to have been exceptionally sterile. A prominent representative of dervish poetry was the rather prolific and formally outstanding Sūfi Olloër (Allāh-Yār) Kattaqurghonī (died in 1136/1723–4). In Tajik and Uzbek mystical poems he preached the abandonment of earthly life and set himself the goal of subjecting Islam inwardly and outwardly to Ṣūfism. Of the Ṣūfī poets note should also be taken of Eshon-Mullo (died in 1212/1798), the *okhund* i.e. professor at a *madrasa* of Bukhara.

A somewhat different situation developed in the second half of this period, when a second centre of Tajik poetry in Central Asia grew up at the court of the khān in Qūqand. During the first quarter of the 19th century, under Umarkhon's rule, there were some hundred poets living at the khān's court.[162] For some time Bukhara lost its importance as the only cultural centre and fell to the second place after Qūqand, which had become the haven even of some Bukhara poets, such as Hoziq, Mujrim, Koshif and others. The poets of the Qūqand group were characterised by the fact that they wrote in both Tajik and Uzbek, sometimes using both languages in one poem (*shiru shakar* – 'milk and sugar'). Some poets outside Farghona, too, were bilingual in their poetry, as, for example, the afore-mentioned Olloër. Since there was political hostility between Bukhara and Qūqand, one of the important themes which court poets were expected to treat was not only eulogy of their benefactor but also deprecation of his opponent; they wrote about his brutality and avarice, the deterioration of his realm, the poverty of his subjects and so on, all of which gave some democratically-minded poets the opportunity to describe the degenerate nature of the khān's regime and to express their sympathies with the suffering populace. The poetry of this period is well outlined in the important *tadhkira Majmūat-ush-shuaro* (1822) of Fazlī Namangonī, who himself was a poet at Umarkhon's court and in his work as well as in his anthology was a prominent advocate of the existing regime. Other sources are Aĭnī's *Namūnai adabiëti tojik* (see p. 561) and Vozeh's *tadhkira Tūhfat-ul-ahbob fī tazkirat-ul-ashob* (see p. 526).

The group of Bukhara poets of this period includes Mirzo Muhammad Sodiq Jondorī, the court poet of amīr Haĭdar (1800–1826), a follower of the 'Indian style', whose principal work is the *mathnavī Dakhmai shohon*, 'The Mausoleum of Shāhs', written in 1785, and marked by a certain originality. The poet lets the 18th-century amīrs of Bukhara speak from their tombs. Each ruler talks about his life, which Sodiq depicts as useless, as a life bringing nothing but upheaval and bloodshed. This work also attained a relatively high level from the point of view of form.

Of the Qūqand group of authors, note should be taken of Hoziq, Makhmur, Gulkhanī, Lisonī, Irsī, Ma'dan, and to some extent also of Bedil's devoted follower Sultonkhoja Ado (died in 1252/1836–7). There were also some good poetesses, especially Nodira, who left a Tajik and Uzbek *dīvān*.[163]

Junaĭdullo Makhdum Hoziq, who is considered by R. Hoshim[164] to have been one of the best poets of the period of amīr Nasrullo's reign (1826–1860), came to Bukhara from Herat at the beginning of the 19th century. According to other sources, he originally came from Karkh.[165] He soon left Bukhara for Umarkhon's court, but after the khān's death returned to Bukhara. There he wrote a poem which offended amīr Nasrullo and had to flee to Shahri Sabz. He did not escape punishment even there – he was murdered by assassins hired by the amīr in 1259/1843, judging by a *ta'rīkh* (words the letters of which denote a date) which he allegedly wrote shortly before his death.[166] Hoziq's principal work is the *doston Yusuf va Zulaïkho* (1239/1823–4) which is of a rather high quality and contains some progressive ideas. It was published in Tashkent in 1905. Hoziq also wrote *qaṣīdas* and *ghazals*, but did not leave a *dīvān*.

The bilingual poets of Farghona included Mahmud Makhmur, who is reported to have been still alive in 1845. He was outstanding as an author of *mukhammases*, in which he occasionally alternated Tajik and Uzbek verses, but he became popular especially as an author of satires and as a critic of various evils of his times. Well known among his works is a satirical poem on Fazlī, a representative of the feudal class.[167] Makhmur was a master of complicated poetical forms and his principal work is the poem *Khafalak*, in which he depicts the sorry fate of the inhabitants of a fictitious *kishlok Khafalak* (*khafa* = 'sad', 'somber'). His views are best indicated by the fact that in the *ta'rīkh* of Khān Olim of Qūqand the year of death was marked by the words '*zolimi mardud*', meaning 'damned tyrant'. Another author of similar character was Muhammad Sharif Gulkhanī Namangonī, who lived until the 1820's, when – according to *Ta'rikhi Khūqand* and *Ta'rikhi jahonnamo* – he was drowned in the Syr Darya by order of Umarkhon's son and successor.[168] Gulkhanī's verse may be considered as the first example of civil and social poetry.[169] According to Fazlī's *tadhkira*, Gulkhanī was a 'village poet' who "not once during his lifetime had eaten from a whole loaf or sat at a sumptuous feast" and who wrote poetry in his own dialect. Gulkhanī's important work, *Zarbulmasal*, 'Proverb', was written in prose and in Uzbek.

Another Qūqand poet of this period, Odina Muhammad Ma'dan (1762–1838)[170], wrote poems mainly in Uzbek, but he also contributed considerably to Tajik poetry. He is said to have refused an invitation to become a court poet, and lived as a peasant in his native village of Ponghoz. He was outstanding as an author of *mukhammases*, but he also wrote satire and lyrical poems.

Many other authors from this period are listed by Hodizoda in his monograph on 19th-century *tadhkiras*[171], and also by Ma'sumī.[172]

a. *Bedil and Bedilism*

Political disunity and social discord in north-western India, especially on the territory of present-day Pakistan, made it possible for Maḥmūd of Ghazna to seize power for his family and his Moslem chieftains as early as the 11th century. The final result was the emergence of the sultanate of Delhi, whose rulers were ethnically, religiously and linguistically quite alien to the local population. This situation was exploited by the ruler of Kābul, Bābur Mīrzā of the Timurid dynasty, who himself had been driven out of Central Asia by the Shaïbonī dynasty. He conquered Delhi after his

Notes on pp. 536–545

victory in the battle of Panīpat (1526), and within a very short time occupied most of northern India. He founded a new dynasty of the Great Moguls, which remained in power for the greater part of two centuries. The most outstanding of the Mogul rulers was Akbar (1556–1605) who realised that a vast empire could not be successfully built upon the rule of a limited number of Moslem conquerors and accordingly initiated a policy of including Indians in the administration and the army. However, this policy came to an end on Akbar's death. Under his successors, Jahāngīr (1605–1627) and Shāhjahān (1627–1658), a reaction set in against Akbar's political ideas, and at the same time the empire fell into a deep economic decline. Shāhjahān brought his realm to the brink of disaster by such expensive ventures as the building of the Taj Mahal in Agra and the palace with the Peacock Throne in Delhi, which was "the most magnificent of all and more luxurious than Versailles, but just like Versailles was maintained by the impoverishment and exploitation of the people. At that time a terrible famine was ravaging Gujrat and Dakhin."[173] The religious fanatic Aurangzeb (1658–1707), who was the last member of the Mogul dynasty and reigned over the whole empire, completed the disintegration of the realm by his reactionary policy.[174] For example, he reintroduced the capitation tax which was paid only by non-Moslems. This brought the masses of the Indian population to the side of the old Indian nobility, who declared a religious war against the Moslem intruders. There were numerous uprisings, such as those of the Marathas or Sikhs, which led to the fall of the Great Mogul empire after Aurangzeb's death and the establishment of British colonial rule in India. This was also the time when the first European factories were established on Indian territory (the British established a factory in Delhi and other places as early as 1613).

Throughout the rule of the Great Moguls India maintained close contacts with Central Asia.[175]

Bedil lived in the period of the decline of Mogul rule.[176] He was born in Azīmābād, present-day Putna, in 1644 (during the reign of Shāhjahān). His family was of Uzbek descent. His mother tongue was apparently Bengali but he also knew Urdu and Sanskrit. He learned to speak and write Persian at school. He soon lost his father and was raised by his uncles. He wrote his first verse at the age of ten. Already as a youth he was influenced by Ṣūfī dervishes and in his later years went several times into seclusion to live with them. For some time – probably in keeping with his family's tradition – he served in the army of prince A'ẓam, but left the prince's services on being asked to write *qaṣīdas* in praise of his master.[177] He always refused to accept the fate of a court poet and detested those poets who lent their talents to such service. Eventually he had a group of pupils, some of them important men, who supported him. Bedil travelled through most of India, meeting its Moslem and Hindu population, and was well acquainted with Brahmin philosophy. He rejected the doctrine of life after death, fairy-tales of paradise and hell, etc.[178] He died in Delhi in 1133/1721, at the time of India's complete disintegration. His tomb in that city was for a long time a place of annual pilgrimage for his admirers on the anniversary of his death. These meetings were called *rūzi arsi Mirzo*, and excerpts from his *Kulliyët*, 'Collected Works', were read on such occasions.[179]

Although by virtue of the region where most of his work was accomplished Mirzo Abdulqodir Bedil belongs to North-Indian Tajik-Persian literature, special attention must be paid to him in this part of the present study, because his works had a major impact on Central Asian Tajik (and Uzbek) literature[180], which was influenced by it until the 1920's.[181] In Mā-varā 'a'n-nahr and in Afghanistan a Bedil cult came into being under the name 'bedilkhonī'; the poet's verses and philosophical writings were read and analysed at weekly meetings. On the other hand, in northern India itself, Bedil's work did not greatly influence literature, and it made no impact at all on Iran.

Western literature has thus far paid very little attention to Bedil. Garcin de Tassy[182] devoted a short article to him in a book that appeared in 1870; Browne mentioned him very briefly, and in more recent times A. Bausani has shown some interest in him.[183] Among eastern authors, the Urdu literary historian Shiblī Nu'mānī speaks of Bedil quite critically, while another Urdu author, Ḥājjī 'Ibādu'llāh Akhtar wrote a remarkable study on the poet in 1952. Until quite recently Bedil was completely ignored in Iran and was unknown even in literary circles; now, however, historians of literature – Shafaq, to name one of them – are beginning to show interest in him. A number of studies on Bedil and his work has been published in the Soviet-Union, which was the first country to devote serious attention to this poet. First among the Soviet literary historians to study Bedil and his work are, quite obviously, Tajiks. A long chapter on Bedil was included by S. Aĭnī in his Anthology.[184] Bertel's studied him as early as 1945, Muminov's monograph was published in 1946[185], while at the same time S. Aĭnī published a series of articles on Bedil and his work in *Sharqi Surkh*[186]; in 1947 Mirzoev dealt with Bedil in his book on Saĭido Nasafī, in 1954 S. Aĭnī published an edition of Bedil's poetry with a 100-page preface, and, finally, Kh. Aĭnī published a small book on Bedil's principal work, *Irfon*, 'Discovery', in 1956.[187]

Bedil is rightly characterised as a poet-philosopher. He turned his attention to the basic problems of man's life, just as did other outstanding classical poets (mainly Sa'dī), trying to discover the truth of life through independent thinking. Philosophy also permeates his lyrical poems. He was not satisfied with the answers offered by Islam and studied the principles of the highly developed Indian philosophy, whereby he arrived at a rather progressive outlook on life and the world, combining features of both Islam and Hinduism. He did not differentiate between Moslems and Hindus[188] and often sided with the non-Moslem population, which suffered under dual oppression. Typical of Bedil were his anti-feudal views and philosophical scepticism, which constitute a progressive feature and positively influenced his contemporaries and subsequent followers and imitators. In his studies and writings he did not avoid even the most difficult problems, such as the origin of man, the origin of the world, etc. In one of his *ghazals* he says that "before acquiring his present shape, man was a monkey" and that in the world there were first minerals, then plants, and finally animals. He considered air to be the foundation of the world and the 'spirit' a form of air. All that was material, people and things, were the products of nature and the world was eternal and in constant motion. This should not be interpreted, of course, as meaning that Bedil had found the way out of the fetters of mediaeval thinking; he only envisaged many things and took up a progressive, humanistic position.

Bedil points in his work to the hypocrisy of the priesthood and voices his sympathy with the common folk. He resents sycophancy in eulogies praising the mighty of the world, saying that "no matter how good art may be, it deserves the heaviest condemnation if it is linked with a base idea".[189]

Bedil's work is exceptionally voluminous and has been preserved complete. His *Kulliët*, published in Bombay in 1299/1881–2, consists of 16 books of 147,000 verses[190] in addition to prose. One of his most important works is *Tilismi haïrat*, 'Talisman of Surprise', a *mathnavī* of 7500 *misra'*, written when he was 25 years old. It is a poetically advanced work dealing with the problem of man's physical and spiritual existence. When he was 37, Bedil wrote *Muhiti a'zam*, 'The Great Ocean', a *mathnavī* of 9000 *misra'* using the *mutaqorib* metre, which he composed entirely in the spirit of Ṣūfī poetry – *soqinoma*. His next work, the *mathnavī Tūri ma'rifat* 'Sinai of Learning', which he wrote at the age of 43, is a complete contrast to the preceding *mathnavī* as regards its content. The poet departed from religious meditation and described his impressions of the places he had seen on his travels, depicting nature and voicing his views on the usefulness of science and learning. Of his other works note should be taken of *Ishorot va hikoët*, 'Aphorisms and Tales', a *mathnavī* of varied contents, the individual parts of which must have been written in different periods, just as was *Nuqot*, 'Statements', which contains *ruboīs*[191], *qiṭ'as*, *ghazals*, *mathnavīs* and *mukhammases*. This is indicated by the fact that the collection includes poems with Ṣūfī themes as well as social and anti-religious poetry. Bedil's prose-work (traditionally interspersed with poetry, of course) includes *Chor unsur* 'The Four Elements', written between 1680 and 1694, which contains the author's biographical notes and reminiscences in addition to his philosophical views. It is in this book that he also writes about Central Asia, the Oxus, Turkestan and the fellow-countrymen of his ancestors who had come to India from Samarkand.[192] There is also *Tarkibot va tarjeot*, 'Compositions and Echoes' on religious topics, which he wrote in his youth, and a collection of letters he had written at various times, called simply *Ruqaot*, 'Collection of Letters'.

Bedil's most important work is undoubtedly his last *mathnavī* of 11,000 *baïts*, called *Irfon* 'Discovery'[193], which the poet wrote at the age of 68. It contains various stories, fairy-tales and historical notes, as well as some Ṣūfī essays. This work most tellingly bears witness to the philosophical, social and ethical views of its author.

An important part of *Irfon* is the poem *Komde va Madan*, which has been thoroughly studied particularly by Soviet scholars.[194] It is a highly artistic *doston*, the theme being based on an Indian fairy-tale. This fact alone is quite remarkable. The theme of strong, unselfish love between two young people, love free of the tragedy found in the classical themes of Farhod and Shirin, or Laĭlī and Majnūn, is new in Tajik-Persian literature. This is one of the few *dostons* written in the Middle East in which love prevails over death. In *Irfon* Bedil expressed his most progressive ideas. He points, for example, to the importance of irrigation and to losses due to constant feudal wars, comparing the feudal lords to insect pests that destroy the peasants' crops, leaving behind only straw.[195]

Bedil's style in poetry is difficult – his metaphors and sentence structure are very complex and often obscure the meaning, although the language itself is simple and the poet uses even vernacular expressions. On the other hand, the language of his prose is very difficult, even in the poet's letters, so that the argument that Bedil used complex form only for the purpose of obscuring his ideas is untenable. The special character of Bedil's style was already noted by his contemporaries, for example by Ghulomalikhon Ozod in his *Khizonai Omira*, 'The Treasure of the Amīrs'.

In his *Namunai adabiëti tojik*, 'The Picture of Tajik Literature', S. Aĭnī writes that in the period following the year 1200 of the Hijra (1785–6 A. D.) imitation of Bedil in poetry and prose was widespread in Bukhara and throughout Transoxania. Whosoever took the pen in his hand, writes Aĭnī, deemed it necessary to write something like Bedil.[196] Mirzoev however points out correctly that Bedil was not the founder of the new style[197] – *sabki hindī* – but merely brought it to culmination. As early as the middle of the 18th century Bedil's work spread throughout northern India, Afghanistan[198] and especially Central Asia. It was in the latter area, too, the home of Bedil's ancestors, that the poet's writings gained the greatest respect and became most widespread. His works were included among the basic textbooks in the *maktabs*[199] (elementary schools), his poems found their way into folk-poetry and were often sung by the *hofizes*. Practically all poets and prose-writers imitated his style, but it should be said that until the beginning of the 20th century none of the imitators had attained the mastery of their model. A struggle around Bedil's school developed especially after the middle of the 19th century; imitators who belonged to the upper classes copied only Bedil's literary form – the complex style so hard to understand – but their works lacked the humanistic and realistic features of his subjects. They discarded all that was progressive in Bedil's ideas and in their poetry promoted ascetism, mysticism and pessimism.[200] They included mainly the already mentioned Sultonkhoja Ado[201], in parts Mirzo Sodiq, Qone', and others. They claimed that Bedil had been a mystic and a staunch Moslem. On the other hand, some of Bedil's followers – members of the educated middle classes – who were aware of the rapid decline of their country, championed Bedil's progressive ideas. They called for better education in the *madrasas* and for the economic development of Central Asia, while some opposed the priesthood as the force holding back social progress and as being mainly responsible for the backwardness and ignorance of the people. They

Notes on pp. 536–545

were the advocates of enlightened ideas which gained greater influence in the second half of the 19th century and penetrated into Central Asia in the wake of the Russian occupation.

J. FROM THE RUSSIAN OCCUPATION TO THE OCTOBER REVOLUTION

I. HISTORICAL SURVEY

The second half of the 19th century brought a fundamental turn to the history of Central Asia. Tsarist Russia, where the capitalist development was gaining momentum, set out with great energy to seek new markets and new sources of raw materials; it continued its annexation of eastern territories – the major part of what was called Russian Turkestan fell easily and quickly under Russia's direct domination –, while the rest was under Russian control, which was not far removed from full dependence. While the tsarist government did help the amīr of Bukhara to put down the resistance of rebellious *begs* in the outlying regions, at the same time it installed its political agent in Kagan (Kogon), a town only several kilometres from Bukhara; no measure of any serious nature could be put into effect in the country without the agent's knowledge. Besides the amirate of Bukhara, the khanate of Khiva west of Bukhara and the khanate of Qūqand to the north-east consolidated their territories for some time. It was in the interest of Russia at that time to maintain these puppet states: their existence was to win the sympathies of the neighbouring countries[202] and also to pacify Great-Britain, that jealously followed the developments in Central Asia, to the domination of which – lying as it did so dangerously close to the Indian frontier – she herself aspired.

According to Ahmad Donish, a very small but much better armed number of Russian soldiers was able to defeat a large army of amīr Muzaffar (1860–1886), which before the decisive battle fought in 1868, was ordered to "chase the enemy all the way to Petrograd". This order well reflects the decay of the Manghit empire; its ruler did not show the least sign of statesmanship, he never had the support of his people, and until the last moment waged a war with Qūqand, which greatly weakened both Bukhara and Qūqand.

Nevertheless, the development of the two parts of Turkestan followed somewhat different paths. Russian Turkestan, which was under the almost absolute rule of a Russian governor, was subject to direct colonial exploitation and the tsarist government quite obviously followed the policy of forced assimilation of the local population.[203] On the other hand, in 'independent' Bukhara, the tsarist government did not intervene in the internal affairs of the amirate; with the exception of a ban on slavery[204], which was not observed, practically no change took place in the mediaeval conditions prevailing in Central Asia. Feudal religious ideology still ruled unchecked in Bukhara, the country continued to live in isolation from the rest of the world, even from Russia [205], and new ideas penetrated it only under extremely difficult conditions. Amīr Abdullahad (1885–1910) in particular closed Bukhara to any outside influence and maintained mediaeval ceremonial at his court [206], but at the same time he well understood the advantages of European civilisation; as he himself said, he held third place in the world as supplier of Persian lamb-skins and had 34 million gold rubles deposited in Russian banks. The backward khanate of Bukhara could be divided into two parts – the west with a rather well-developed monetary and marketing system, and the east which until the 1870's had been ruled by local dynasties and where subsistence economy prevailed.[207]

In this period we can distinguish roughly two stages: the period between 1864 and approximately 1895, when Russian capital showed no interest in Central Asia, and the period from 1895 up to the Russian Revolution, which was a period of expanding tsarist imperialism.[208] Nevertheless, the socio-economic system in Turkestan and Bukhara remained basically feudal until the beginning of the 20th century.[209] There was no financial system, nor were there any annual budgets in Bukhara, and regular and permanent salaries for government officials and clerks were introduced only by Olimkhon (1911–1920) who, however, abolished them again within a short period of time.

On the other hand, beginning in the 1880's, a disintegration of the mediaeval economic forms set in, the population grew, the first industrial enterprises appeared [210], banks were established in the 1890's, and Russian capital began to flow in. Trade with India and Afghanistan was restricted, the goods sold at Central Asian bazaars were mostly of Russian origin, as indicated by European travellers in Central Asia [211], and the cheaper industrial articles quite naturally forced the products of the local craftsmen off the market. For example, in Kūlob there were three caravanserais at the end of the 19th century, where only Russian products were sold.[212] The cultivation of quality cotton was introduced on a large scale, often to the detriment of cereals, of which there was then a shortage on the market.[213] A major factor in Central Asian economic development was the construction of the Trans-Caspian Railway, which linked Bukhara with the outside world and definitely brought it within the sphere of world trade. The consolidation and expansion of economic relations between Bukhara and Russia, the construction of the railway, industrial development (shortly before the outbreak of World War I there were 50 capitalist, mostly Russian-owned, enterprises in the amirate of Bukhara), the growth of the towns, and the active intervention of Russian capital in agricultural production – all these factors initiated a growth of capitalism in the amirate.

The situation was, quite naturally, very complicated. The economic oppression exerted by the local feudal lords was joined by tsarist colonial oppression [214], which, however, mostly affected the ruling classes, which resented their loss of power to a stronger rival. On the other hand, the broad masses of the population often felt friend-

Notes on pp. 536–545

ly towards Russia.[215] The situation was further complicated by the fact that Uzbeks were always given preference in the Bukhara administration, while Tajiks had very little chance of appointment to a higher office.[216]

The political progress of Central Asia was deeply affected by the first Russian revolution (1905–7), which played an important role in the east in general. However, the local working class was still too weak to be able to seize hegemony in the revolutionary movement; the major role in the movement was played by the Russian proletariat, especially the employees of the Trans-Caspian Railway. Strike committees were formed, mainly in Turkestan but also on the territory of Bukhara, in Kogon, Chorjūī, Tirmiz, and elsewhere, and eventually Russian troops had to be called in against the strikers. Banned political literature was distributed among the workers, and the Social Democrats published their periodicals and established local organisations in a number of towns.

The khanate of Bukhara gradually lost its independence. Russian troops were stationed in the country, especially in the frontier districts; in 1915 Bukhara was joined with Russia in a customs union, and the amīr could mint coins only with the permission of the Russian governor-general in Tashkent.

The situation did not improve under the rule of Olimkhon, the last member of the Manghit dynasty. Even the mild reforms called for by the jadids were strongly opposed by the amīr and his court. The mediaeval regime was maintained by force, the result being a number of popular uprisings which, as they were poorly prepared and organised, were always put down by bloodshed. In Turkestan especially, but also to a lesser extent in Bukhara, individual revolutionaries appeared from the ranks of the local population, and the first cells of the working-class movement were formed in the industrial centres. The amīr tried in vain to separate the people of Bukhara from the outside world. They left to work in Tashkent, Tirmiz, Samarkand, Kogon and other places and returned with new ideas. This movement, spurred on by the October Revolution in Russia, culminated in the revolution in Bukhara and the liberation of the whole of Central Asia.

Until the Russians arrived, Central Asia was culturally quite backward. In the land of Avicenna people were treated by exorcism and prayer; the land of Ulughbek, the great astronomer, believed that the sun rotated around the earth. There was almost absolute illiteracy. In the period between 1904 and 1917, which was the most productive in the literary field, only 21 Tajik books were published in the whole of Central Asia, in a total edition of some 20,000 copies.[217]

At that time Central Asia came into contact with two Russias. It is obvious that the oppressed people of this area could not be helped by the Russia of the tsar and his reactionary representatives in Tashkent or Kogon, but the people of Central Asia, including some members of the intelligentsia, also came into contact with the progressive Russian culture of such democrats as Gertsen, Belinskiy, or Chernïshevskiy, and through Russia also with western European culture. In addition, even the slow growth of agriculture[218] and industry resulted in the formation of a working class which was subsequently able – together with the progressive intelligentsia – to promote and realise the ideas of emancipation from mediaeval oppression. The first to appear on the scene – in the 1870's – was the democratic, enlightened movement led by Ahmad Donish (p. 529) and his pupils and followers Savdo, Shohin, Haĭrat, Muztarib, Somī, Aĭnī and others. These enlightened men fought for their ideals under extremely difficult conditions and their opposition to feudalism was consequently not always strictly defined. They often had to fight clandestinely against the distortion of science by the priesthood and the keeping in ignorance[219] of the people as well as against the absolutism of the ruler, while the same situation governed their striving for knowledge of Russian and western European culture and technology and for the education of the broad masses of the population. An important role was played by the promotion of the 'new school', a school using a curriculum patterned on the western model. This applied only to Turkestan, while in Bukhara the new schools were banned because the priesthood wanted to preserve the mediaeval educational methods. An edict said that "... the Prophet did not decree that European culture should spread in Asia".[220]

a. *Jadidism*

After the first Russian revolution a national bourgeois movement was formed in Central Asia along the lines of the New Turk movement founded by Gasprinskiy (Ismail Gaspir Alī, 1851–1914). It was called 'jadidism', and, since 1916, also 'the Young Bukhara movement'. It was a loose association without a firm organisation and had won primarily the sympathies of some intellectuals and members of the commercial circles. From its very beginning, the movement was linked with the ideas of Pan-Islamism and Pan-Turkism, which characterised to a greater or less degree its advocates individually. The jadids – the progressives – differed from the qadīms – the conservatives – in that they tried to realise some educational and administrative reforms, but their true aim was to create favourable conditions for competition with Russian capital, which was increasingly penetrating into Central Asia. But when the revolutionary atmosphere and mood increased, fear of their own people made the jadids seek the protection of the tsar.[221] This contrast was also reflected in the different views held by individual members of the movement, which, moreover, had many other reactionary features: hatred of foreigners, especially Jews and Armenians, contempt of the Tajiks[222] (some Tajik jadids ostentatiously spoke Ottoman Turkish)[223], opposition to the 1905 revolution, reconciliation of science and Islam, etc.

The leading ideologists of the movement included Behbudī[224] in Central Asia and Fitrat, both of whom later openly turned against their own people.

Since, however, before the October Russian Revolution, the jadid movement constituted the only opposition in the amirate of Bukhara, it was also joined by some of the

Notes on pp. 536–545

truly progressive intellectuals, like Sadriddin Aĭnī, who later, after the October Revolution, realised where they should really stand. On the other hand, a majority of the jadids formed the backbone of the counter-revolutionary forces in Central Asia and provided support to the *basmachi* bands which fought against the interests of the common people and for the interests of the amīr and the Islamic priesthood.

Originally, the jadid movement sprang in some respects from the movement of enlightenment at the end of the 19th century and from the ideas of Ahmad Donish, but when society progressed after the 1905 revolution, it represented a step backwards. Donish sharply criticised the ruling dynasty, and especially in his *Navodir-ul-vaqoe'* and *Risola* gave expression to democratic ideas[225] and a higher ideology; but the jadids tried to ingratiate themselves with the amīr, begged him for mild reforms, and interpreted the situation by claiming that the amīr was 'kind' but those around him prevented him from properly demonstrating his 'kindness'. In spite of all their subservience and desperate endeavour not to offend the feelings of the Islamic hierarchy, the jadids were still too progressive for the amīr and the priesthood, and so even they often experienced the wrath of reaction.[226]

b. *The Effect of the Russian Occupation of Central Asia*

While it is obvious that the tsarist generals did not occupy Central Asia with the intent of helping the local population, the Russian occupation was – from the objective point of view – a progressive factor. It put a stop to the endless feudal wars between the local rulers which had brought tremendous suffering to the peasants and the common folk; it led to the radical abolition of slavery, which had flourished until the second half of the 19th century[227], and the establishment of a few schools using the European educational system, which, though it could not eliminate the cultural backwardness of the area, could – and did – at least educate some progressively-minded people (including Paĭrav Sulaĭmonī, p. 567). During the Russian occupation the foundations were also laid for a better cultivation of cotton (by introducing better varieties) and for local industry (thereby making possible the growth of a working class). Another result was the prevention of the annexation of Central Asia by Great-Britain, which had planned such a move throughout the 19th century. Finally, the Russian occupation made it possible for the people of Central Asia to take part in the revolutionary struggle of the nations of tsarist Russia for emancipation, and the formation of economically and culturally flourishing republics. A leading Tajik historian, Zarif Rajabov, says that the importance of the Russian occupation lay not in any generosity or kindness on the part of the imperial Russian eagle, but in the fact that Russia was on the eve of revolution.

2. LITERATURE

Since the period under discussion is of great importance for the development of post-revolutionary Tajik literature, increased attention must be paid particularly to the end of the 19th and the beginning of the 20th centuries. Most authors from this period left no *dīvāns* and it is usually necessary to collect fragments of poems and verses from the various *tadhkiras* and *bayozes* (notebooks kept by poets, calligraphers etc., for writing notes and drafts), a task that involves considerable difficulty.

The important political changes and the growing ideological struggle of the 1870's and 1880's were naturally reflected in literature. The great majority of authors – again primarily poets – continued to write in traditional forms and still further developed the ideas dominating dervish and religious poetry.[228]

But although this official court poetry[229] was given every possible support, it sank to the lowest depths of imitative writing, while literature reflecting folk-trends developed and produced new ideas.[230] On the other hand, it is true that the 450 authors listed in the *tadhkiras* covering this period[231] include only a few who proceeded from the progressive traditions of classical literature and town poetry of the preceding centuries and the most positive aspects of Bedil's work, or who were receptive to the new ideas penetrating into Central Asia after the Russian occupation. But it was precisely these few authors who made a step forward for Tajik literature.

Under the changed conditions – the continued decline of the feudal system, which was also manifest in Bukhara's submission to tsarist Russia, the penetration of democratic ideas into Central Asia, usually through Moslem nations living in the west (the Azerbayjanis, the Tatars, the Uzbeks) as well as through the legal and illegal press (e.g. the Tatar *Tarjuman* or the Persian *Ḥablu'l-matīn* from Calcutta) – the progressive trends acquired new forms. Another progressive factor was the spread of the first novel written in the Persian language, the *Siyāḥatnāme-i Ibrāhīm Beg* of Zaynu'l-ʿĀbidīn (see p. 369 *et seq.*), as described by Aīnī in his *Bukhoro inqilobi taʿrikhi uchun materiallar*. The novel criticised the conditions existing in Persia, but the situation in Bukhara was even worse. Under the spiritual leadership of Ahmad Donish the progressive intelligentsia of Central Asia embraced the enlightened ideas. The works of authors belonging to this movement are usually devoid of Ṣūfī motives and themes of ascetic pessimism, their *ghazals* have a profound lyrical quality and are characterised by the endeavour to approach the spirit of folk-poetry.

Democratic trends are reflected in literature mainly by the contents of the works. Members of the enlightened movement fought against the mediaeval conservatism of the court and the religious circles and *madrasas*, and strove for education, pointing to the importance of science and technology, writing travelogues (Vozeh, Mirzo Siroji Hakim, and others), criticising the existing regime and the amīr himself, even though they often did so cautiously and in a veiled manner. All of this was of course very important, in spite of its limited scope owing to the brutal regime, for the very fact that an author had used other than religious themes was in itself revolutionary. Such an author was, as a rule, subjected to all kinds of chicanery by the ruling circles, and branded as a heretic and rebel by the influential religious hierarchy. Many poets had to pay for their writings with their lives: this was true, for example, of Hoziq[232]; Simo and Eso Makhdum had to flee from Muzaffar's court, many authors died at an early age as victims of court intrigue (Dilkash, Shohin), while others became the victims of the reign of terror instituted by the amīr in 1918, when Sahbo, Foiz, Saidkhon and others were executed.

The poetry of this period is marked by a greater simplicity of language and style[233], especially typical of the works of Donish[234] and Vozeh. These authors used grammatical forms close to the spoken language and occasionally also folk-sayings and proverbs; on the other hand, the devotees of feudal and dervish literature tried to use as fancy a language as possible, so that their verse, full of satirical distortions and grammatical errors, is often unintelligible. Only in pornographic literature, a considerable quantity of which was produced with the special purpose of entertaining the amīr and his courtiers, do we sometimes find expressions from the vernacular.

An important feature characterising the period under discussion was the link established between democratic Tajik authors and such Uzbek progressives as Muqimī, Furqat and Hakimzoda (whose works were marked by pointedly social themes) and the ideological leaders of other neighbouring nations, such as the Kazakh Abaĭ Kunanbaev and the Azerbayjani Mīrzā Fatḥ-ʿĀlī Ākhundov (pp. 336, 692). In any event, most of the enlightened Uzbek authors traditionally wrote in Tajik, for example – in the Qūqand group – Muqimī (1850–1903).

The list of enlightened writers as a rule includes the encyclopaedist and author of a valuable *tadhkira* and a travelogue on the Ḥijāz, Rahmatullo Vozeh (1817–1894), a most productive poet who wrote in one of his poems that the court, to which he was summoned by prince Muzaffar, was a jail in which he found himself innocent. Later he was banned from the court and earned his living by copying books. His poem *Koni lazzat va khoni neʿmat* reflects his close ties with the craftsman group.[235] Another enlightened author was Abdulvohid Sadri Sarir (1810–1886), who valued the progressive ideas expressed in Bedil's work, and under Donish's influence later changed over to a simpler style. There were also Savdo, an outstanding poet, who will be discussed separately (p. 532) and Eso Makhdum (1826–1898), who was forced to flee from Bukhara because of his beliefs, and after his return earned his living by copying books. Eventually, however, his poetry culminated in mysticism.[236] An eminent figure among the poets of Khujand (present-day Leninobod) was Muhammadaminkhoja Koshif (1825–1888), whose selected works were published recently on the basis of a fortunately discovered *dīvān*. Koshif's *dīvān* contains mainly *ghazals* written in the traditional spirit, but some of them also have a social theme. Koshif was one of the teachers of Asiri (see p. 534).

Abdulmajid Zufunun (b. 1903), a friend of Aĭnī, of whose work unfortunately only fragments have been preserved, was one of Donish's younger pupils, like Mirzo Azim Somī (died 1907), who as an enlightened author introduced new ideas into his poetry which was composed in the spirit of Donish. He criticised the amīr's regime and expressed dislike of the treatment of the common people; he was persecuted for his views in his old age and died blind and a pauper.[237] At the same time, however, he may serve as an example of how progressive ideas and reactionary themes can be found in the work of one and the same author. Somī (his original pen-name was Himmat) was also the author of a pornographic work which is a prime example of the decadence of official court poetry.[238] There was also a woman – the Bukhara poetess Miskin –, who voiced progressive ideas in her Tajik and Uzbek *dīvān* at the end of the 19th and the beginning of the 20th century.[239] The group of enlightened writers further includes Sharifjon Makhdum, known under the *takhalluṣ* Sadri Ziё (1865–1931). At the time of the October Revolution, the amīr appointed him *qozikalon* (supreme judge) to carry out some democratic reforms, but he was soon deprived of this office. His 'literary salon' (*mahfil*), in which the young Aĭnī also made his debut, played a relatively important role in the development of Tajik literature. Of great importance in this respect is his *tadhkira* in verse and the satirical *Tazkirat-ul-humaqo*, 'Anthology of Idiots', which forms a part of *Navodiri Ziёiya*, 'The Flower of the Intelligentsia', in which the author mercilessly laughs at all those who pretend to be wise. The language he uses – according to Aĭnī – is simpler than that of Donish. However, he lagged even behind Donish where his democratic beliefs were concerned[240], although he lived and worked under conditions more favourable for the growth of progressive ideas. A voluminous work of poetry was produced by Muhammadhusaĭn Khatlonī Hojī (1880–1922), who was also a painter and an outstanding calligrapher. He wrote a volume on this art, entitled *Khututi ashkoli islomiya*, 'Scripts of Islamic Forms'. He also left a *dīvān*, which was published in Tashkent in 1913, but the major part of his output has not yet been discovered. Remarkable among his works is the *mathnavī Komde va Madan*, written in Bedil's style, in which he describes the struggle between good and evil and the struggle for man's freedom.[241] The most outstanding among Donish's pupils are Shohin, Haĭrat and Asirī, who are discussed separately below.[242]

On the other hand it should be pointed out that the enlightened movement affected only the intelligentsia and had a limited impact. There were only a few enlightened authors and their activities were limited almost exclusively to Bukhara. It was consequently a movement far removed from the people[243] and one that benefited them only indirectly. The broad masses of the population knew nothing of Donish's enlightened ideas or of the revolutionary spirit[244] with which Shohin's poems were imbued.

Typical of the period under discussion was the very strong influence of bedilism, for it deeply affected both the work of authors who were not his followers and the poetry of some of the enlightened writers. Donish himself was an authority on Bedil and respected his work, although, quite correctly, he did not recommend imitation of him. Older bedilists such as Eso Makhdum and Sarir wrote some fine poetry in Bedil's style, but the themes of their poems were still of the old, feudal and clerical character. Shohin, Savdo and Vozeh, who had also been influenced by Bedil, especially in their earlier period, were not attracted by Bedil's mysticism but rather by the courage with which he opposed the oppressors, by his compassion with the common people, and by his close sympathy for science and learning in general. A new trend came into being during that period. Poets abandoned the complicated 'Indian style' and preferred the linguistic simplicity of the classics. This was true, for example, of Hairat and the group of poets in which the young Sadriddin Aĭnī made his debut. In this last period before the revolution, too, poetry predominated over prose. Nevertheless, we can speak of a certain turning point. Donish's most serious works, *Navodir-ul-vaqoe'*, 'Rare Events' and *Risola*, 'Treatises', as well as Shohin's *Badoe'-us-sanoe'*, 'Miracles of Art', were written in prose, the number of travel books, especially on European countries, was growing, and, finally, some jadid authors tried to write simple novels after the European pattern.

Jadidism failed to contribute anything new to Tajik literature, it was a 'fruitless tree' from the literary point of view.[245] Jadid literature promoted ideas which were far below the ideological level of the enlightened writers. It called for national intolerance and tried to reconcile Islam with modern technology; the quest for knowledge was claimed to be good only for helping 'our own people' to learn the skills required for widespread trading and for defeating Russian competition, and the tsarist regime was highly praised and admired. All these are features characterising the works of such jadid authors as Ajzī, Mirzo Siroj Hakim, known as Duktur Sobir, and Behbudī. Said Ahmadjon Siddiqī Ajzī (1860–1927) wrote, for example, of the poverty and colonial status of Turkestan, but did not believe in revolution and was convinced that education could eliminate all difficulties. The court is criticised in his *mathnavī Anjumani arvoh*, 'An Assembly of Souls', which was clearly influenced by Sodiq's *Dakhmai shohon* (see p. 514). It should also be noted that in view of the pan-Turkish character of the jadid movement, the jadid press and drama were almost exclusively Uzbek, while poetry continued to be written in Tajik.

A certain positive role was played by the few schools established by the jadids to "acquire educated people for commerce and the administration of the country". Their staff included some progressive teachers – propagators of new teaching methods – who wrote new text-books, quite unlike the old ones. These include, for example, the text-book written by the Samarkand teacher Abdulqodir Shakurī in 1909, which contained prose-tales by Tolstoy and Krylov translated into Tajik[246]; and, in particular, *Tahzib-us-sib'ën*, 'Education of Youth' (1st edition 1909; 2nd edition 1917), whose author, Sadriddin Aĭnī, was later to become one of the greatest Tajik revolutionaries. The language of early 20th-century prose was characterised by two trends: the conservative court circles maintained the old, highly artificial style, including many arabisms, while the democratic authors, including those who advocated the interests of the local bourgeoisie, followed Donish's example of using a simpler language.[247]

a. *Folk-Poetry*

Throughout the whole period of existence of artistic poetry, which did not penetrate beyond the middle, urban classes, there was also a rich folk-poetry, produced by anonymous professional and amateur – often illiterate – poets and singers. No records of any importance have been preserved about these poets, but a small portion[248] of their work has survived in several *tadhkiras* or has been handed down by oral tradition through folk-singers – *hofizes*.

Thanks to the fact that, beginning in the 1940's, Tajik folklorists recorded songs which the *hofizes* had learnt from the older generations, it has been possible to preserve longer poems produced not earlier than the 19th century, when incidentally folk-poetry underwent an extensive development. In his Anthology, Aĭni already mentions Mirzoolimjon Hasrat of Hisor (who lived at the beginning of the 13th/19th century), while *Namunahoi adabiëti tojik* contains some additional names, such as Mullo Rajab Parī, about whom it is only known that he was alive in 1854.[249] A well-known personality in the Badakhshon Mountains was Qudratullobek (1824–1914), who left a considerable number of *ghazals*, mostly lyrical in nature, and also satires with an atheistic content aimed against the priesthood.[250] He was the author of a number of *ruboīs* written both in Tajik and in the Shughnon language.[251] An outstanding poet of the second half of the 19th century was Fakhrii Rumonī (he was born in the Shaikhburhon *qishloq* in 1840 and died in 1914), a weaver, who became famous for his sharp satire directed mainly against the ruling circles.[252] Another native of Badakhshon was the popular author of satires, Nazarsho (about 1850–1910), whose writings indicate that the attitude of the simple mountaineers of Badakhshon to the Russians at the time the tsarist army occupied their area was better than their attitude towards their former masters who had fled to Afghanistan.[253] Among the leading folk-poets in the Hisor region just before the revolution in Bukhara we should also mention Karim Devona (1878–1916), a weaver by profession, who cleverly exploited the rumour that he was 'devona' – an idiot – and very sharply attacked the *begs*, the local moneylenders and the amīr's followers.[254]

There were obviously many more authors, today unknown, some of whom produced great and serious poems. These include, in particular, a long song about the popular uprising of 1885, which had been led by a simple peasant, Vose'. The poem reflects the remarkable courage shown by the unknown author in endowing the folk-hero with the right to stand up against the oppressors as well as with the belief that eventually the people would prevail.

b. *Donish*

Enlightened ideas first appeared in Central Asia as early as the middle of the 19th century, and their main propagator was Ahmad Makhdum Donish, known also as

Notes on pp. 536–545

Kalla, who founded a school of writing that deeply affected the growth of Tajik literature and developments in Bukhara and Central Asia in general. We must again thank Sadriddin Aînī for discovering this progressive author; Aînī writes in his *Namunai adabiëti tojik* (pp. 287–301) that if detailed biographical data were listed for no one else, they would still have to be given in the case of Ahmad Makhdum Kalla, and calls Donish "a brilliant star on the dark skies of Bukhara". Hodizoda regards Donish as the most progressive thinker in Tajik literature since the 15th century.[255]

Donish also wrote poetry: *ghazals*, *ruboīs* and *qaṣīdas*, but since they were not collected in a *dīvān* only a few of his poems have been preserved. One reason for this was undoubtedly the significance of his extensive prose-works which are by far the most important among his writings. Donish's prose provides an excellent picture of the material and cultural standard of Central Asia during the author's lifetime, and contains many progressive ideas on which his followers and successors built their own work. His prose is in keeping with Tajik tradition, consisting mainly of memoirs, descriptions of travel and nature, and all of this interspersed with the author's views on various vital problems. Donish, too, occasionally included verse in his prose, but to a lesser extent than did his predecessors.

Ahmad Donish was born in Bukhara in 1242/1827.[256] He acquired a very broad education, concerning himself with calligraphy and the copying of books[257], architecture, medicine and music. For some time too he was employed as court astrologer.[258] Though he was not very popular at the court on account of his free thinking, and though the priesthood, who realised that his writings were undermining the fundamental dogmas of Islam, considered him a heretic[259], the amīr had to appoint Donish – whose encyclopaedic knowledge he found indispensable – three times on missions to the tsar at Petrograd. These journeys convinced Donish still further of the backwardness of Central Asia and of the necessity of doing all that was possible to make radical changes. He did great service in the cause of the advancement of his people by founding his own school and assembling around himself enlightened men such as Shohin, Savdo, Asirī and others.

Donish's views were often remarkably progressive. He declared, for instance, that the amīr was a servant of the people and looked forward to a time when the mighty would no longer make guns and would stop conquering other lands, showing that "oppression is the cause of the decline of prosperity, of death and poverty".[260] He demanded education for everybody – modern education – and criticised the scholastic religious system of education prevalent in his time. He recommended that Russian should be taught as a means of learning a higher culture, and was the first in Tajik history to introduce to literature the theme of Tajik-Russian friendship.[261] One of the basic demands he raised was for the universal applicability of laws, instead of arbitrary rule. Quite obviously Donish could not go farther in his thinking than his times allowed.

He did not learn the true state of Russian society and believed that reforms had to be introduced 'from above'. He believed in an 'enlightened ruler' but at the same time showed that no progress could be achieved unless the ruling Manghit dynasty left the throne. Works written in his old age have overtones of pessimism. Ahmad Donish died in Bukhara in 1897.

Donish's principal work is his political and philosophical treatise *Navodir-ul-vaqoe'*, 'Rare Events', a voluminous book of about 750 pages, on which Shohin composed a *qaṣīda*. It contains most of its author's progressive ideas, as indicated above, and touches on most of the then current problems, such as the importance of education, culture and technology, which constitute the essential features of enlightenment. The book was written between 1875 and 1882, and was quite obviously addressed to the amīr and the ruling circles whom Donish tried – in vain, of course – to convince of the necessity of instituting reforms. The book is evidently based on older traditions, particularly Vosifī's *Badoe'-ul-vaqoe'*, but proceeds on a higher level, in the period when some knowledge of Russian and western culture, as well as certain enlightened ideas, had penetrated into Central Asia.

In *Navodir-ul-vaqoe'*, Donish also proposed to amīr Muzaffar (1860–1885) that a large irrigation canal should be built to provide water for all the Bukhara territory, a project which was realised under the Soviet government. He recommended that Russian should be taught and that ideas and things which could help the country should be taken over from the Russians. In his book he described elements of Russian life, the theatre, for example, which Bukhara then did not have, and the importance attached to science in Russia; he compared the broad, paved avenues of Petrograd with the narrow, dusty streets of Bukhara, etc. This must have had quite an impact on some members of the intelligentsia, who realised that the isolationist policy pursued by the amīr and the priesthood was disastrous for Central Asia. Understandably enough, the priesthood of Bukhara put *Navodir-ul-vaqoe'* on the Index.[262]

Another ideologically prominent work written by Donish is the so-called *Tarjimai holi amironi Bukhoroi sharif*, 'Biographies of the Amīrs of Holy Bukhara', a book to which the author himself did not give a title and which is also known under the names *Risola*, 'A Treatise' and *Ta'rikhcha*, 'Small History'. Donish wrote this book in the last period of his life. It hits hard at the Bukhara regime and at the work of the whole Manghit dynasty. He almost laughs at all its rulers, despising them and pointing to their incompetence and thirst for blood. This book was circulated in secret only – for quite obvious reasons.

However, in spite of his progressive views, Donish remained the prisoner of most of the then prevalent ideas, and especially in the sphere of philosophy he remained an idealist with a universal religious outlook, which led to an inner conflict within the author himself. In the last years of his life Donish wrote two books of a purely religious nature, *Nomus-ul-a'zam*, 'The Supreme Book of Laws', and *Me'ër-ut-tadaïyun*, 'A Measure of Piety', besides the afore-mentioned progressive treatise *Risola*.

Donish's views on Bedil and his attitude to bedilism are quite remarkable. He thought highly of Bedil and reserved a place of honour for him in the history of Tajik literature,

Notes on pp. 536–545

but at the same opposed a slavish imitation of his style.[263] Donish's poems excel in their lyrical quality and in their praise of nature and man; typical in this respect is his *ghazal* composed in Petrograd in honour of the actress Adelina Patti. Donish's style was simple, compared with the older authors, and he also tried to impress simplicity on his pupils. However, his new style did not at first find general recognition and did not come into its own until after the Russian revolution of 1905, when the first newspapers published in Tajik appeared in Bukhara and Turkestan.[264]

Donish did not even avoid writing *qaṣīdas*, but his *qaṣīda* dedicated to amīr Muzaffar, rather than praising the ruler, points to the sorry state of education in the country, and the author tries to convince the ruler of the importance of science and public education.[265]

c. *Savdo*

Another important 19th-century author was Abdulqodirkhoja Savdo, who – according to the *Namunahoi adabiëti tojik*[266] – was one of the most talented poets of his time. He is also highly praised in most of the *tadhkiras* written at the end of the 19th and the beginning of the 20th centuries. He was forced to serve at the amīr's court[267] where he successively occupied various posts, but as an enlightened intellectual he saw well the disorder in Bukhara, criticised the activities of certain officials, and also pointed to dishonest priests.

Savdo was primarily a lyrical poet and a satirist. No *dīvān* of his is available, but recently an anthology of his poetry was published on the basis of *tadhkiras* and the poet's own notes (*bayozes*), which contains *ghazals*, *qaṣīdas*, *ruboīs*, and other types of poems, as well as examples of his prose.[268] Savdo was at first an adherent of Bedil and wrote in his complicated style, but later, just like other authors of his time, he abandoned it and wrote his poetry and prose in a language full of vernacular phrases. In his satirical poems he uses – perhaps to indicate his parting from Bedil – the *takhalluṣ* Bepul, meaning 'Penniless'. His ideas did not attain the breadth or depth of those of Donish, but he was nevertheless one of the very first authors to criticise – even though often timidly – the disorder in the country and the slavish imitation of Bedil.

Savdo was born in Bukhara in 1823, and died about 1873 – by drowning in the Vakhsh River, according to Aĭnī, when he was about fifty. Savdo possessed an all-round talent; he was not only a writer but also an expert on the Central Asian musical system *shashmaqom* and a painter; he also did some book gilding. His work has yet to be fully collected and thoroughly studied and analysed.

Savdo is a leading representative of the satirical literature of the feudal period. Especially remarkable is the folk-character of his poetry and the freshness of his humour. He approaches folklore both in the selection of his themes and the method of their treatment.[269] He also wrote some pornography, probably by order of the amīr.

d. *Shohin*

The poets whose works were re-discovered and evaluated by Sadriddin Aĭnī[270] also include Shamsiddin Makhdum, known under the *takhalluṣ* Shohin. He was one of Ahmad Donish's pupils and admirers. He was born in Bukhara in 1859. He lost both his parents at an early age and was brought up by the blind poet Zariri Jūĭborī, with whose help he studied at a *madrasa*. In about 1889 he was invited to the amīr's court as an already well-known poet. He was ill, however, and the life at the court killed him. He died of tuberculosis in 1894 at the age of 35.

Shohin may be considered as one of the leading representatives of progressive thought of the late 19th century[271], and were it not for his untimely death, he would have undoubtedly produced works of great significance. Even so, his literary heritage includes more than 12,000 verses full of vitality. He is also the author of *Badoe'-us-sanoe'*, 'Miracles of Art', a voluminous piece of prose written in the last years of his life. This important work contains all of Shohin's ideas on the world and at the same time represents a new literary genre: it is a collection of proverbs, sayings, aphorisms, short satirical stories and advice. In about 1888 he wrote the *mathnavī Laĭlī va Majnūn*, following in the footsteps of his many predecessors, but his Laĭlī does not meet the mediaeval views on the position of women in society, which still prevailed during Shohin's lifetime. This poem, too, expresses his enlightened ideas, and his protest against the existing regime. He composed the poem to honour his prematurely deceased wife, with whom he had lived only one year. The poem reflects the poet's sorrow over the loss of his beloved. Another of his works is the *mathnavī Tūhfai dūston*, 'A Gift to Friends', written in 1890. It is a parallel to Sa'dī's *Būstān*; unfortunately only the introduction and one story from the first chapter have been preserved. Shohin either failed to complete the poem or the rest was lost.

In addition, Shohin wrote many *qaṣīdas* and lyrical as well as politically orientated *ghazals*. His poems include many ideas which place Shohin among the best poets. In disguised form he especially criticised life at court with all its intrigues, and included the amīr himself, sometimes using the form of apparent praise. He was an outstanding satirist and raised this genre to a new height by applying it against the evils of his times. In Mirzozoda's opinion, he was second only to Ahmad Donish in his ability to express the progressive ideas of his period.[272] He opposed bedilism and tried to write intelligibly, also making use of the vernacular.

Shohin's mastery was noticed already by Hashmat in his *tadhkira Tazkirat-ush-shuaro*, 'An Anthology of Poets'[273], and it was reluctantly admitted by the author of another *tadhkira*, Afzal, who had close ties with the court of amīr Abdulahad.[274]

e. *Haĭrat*

A promising writer at the turn of the century was Muhammad Siddiq Haĭrat (1295/1878–1320/1902), Sadriddin Aĭnī's colleague as a student at the *madrassa* and, as Aĭnī said, also his teacher in the art of poetry.[275] Being poor[276], he contracted tuberculosis and died at an early age. Haĭrat was a writer of lyrical poetry who was not satisfied with the old themes and forms, and as one of Donish's followers expressed enlightened ideas in his poems. His poetry is secular and the language he uses is simple, since he rejected unnatural and banal metaphors adopted from previous poets. Haĭrat was one of the first poets to use Russian words[277] and was also the first to point to the avarice of the newly emerging class – the *boĭs*, the rich merchants and landowners. In his poems he promoted friendship among nations, which was a courageous thing to do in the mediaeval atmosphere of the Central Asia of his times. Haĭrat wrote *ghazals*, *qaṣīdas* and *ruboiët* (short poems of four verses), and left altogether some 4000 verses – two *dīvāns* assembled after the poet's death by Sadriddin Aĭnī and Munzim. According to Aĭnī, the two *dīvāns* were destroyed in the stormy events of 1918, but fortunately one of Haĭrat's notebooks was found and R. Hodizoda was thus enabled to publish his *dīvān* of 2900 *miṣra'*.

f. *Asirī*

An outstanding literary personality of the early 20th century was the folk-poet and humanist of Khujand, Toshkhoja Asirī[278] (1864–1916), who was a stonemason by trade. His quest for knowledge helped him to acquire a good education, especially in Qūqand, where he also learned Russian. However, later he turned down an appointment as *qozī*, a judge. In his writings Asirī underlines the importance of knowing foreign languages. He wrote Tajik and Uzbek poetry, and maintained friendly contacts with progressive Uzbek poets like Furqat and Muqimī, and with their Tajik colleagues, especially Zufarkhon Javharī (p. 571) and Tojalī.

His style makes him an imitator of Bedil, but he used it to disguise ideas aimed against the priesthood, the feudal lords and the Russian colonisers. The priests therefore branded him a heretic and lunatic. In one of his poems Asirī praised technical progress, describing the construction of an irrigation canal in the 'Hungry Steppe' in 1913, the opening of which he attended. In his poem *Odamiyat chist*, 'What Is Humanity?', Asirī expressed his dislike of the *mullos*, defended secular culture and modern teaching methods against the scholastic methods of the *maktabs* and *madrasas*, and fought against the rivalry incited by some chauvinists between the Tajiks and the Uzbeks. In his moralistic *mathnavī Khitob ba musulmon*, 'Appeal to Moslems', he praised science and learning, but spoke with contempt of the study of theology.

Asirī was one of the spiritual pupils of Ahmad Donish; his poetry was exceptionally popular among the common people, and many of his poems became part of folklore.

g. *Aĭnī*

Sadriddin Aĭnī (1878–1954) was primarily a literary figure of the Soviet period of Tajikistan. He himself said that under the amirate in Bukhara he was unable to produce anything of value and that only the revolution had made him a writer. Naturally, his post-revolutionary literary success had its roots already at the beginning of the 20th century, when he had played a certain role as a progressive writer.

Aĭnī's activity developed fully after he had acquainted himself with Donish's work[279] and then mainly under the impact of the first Russian Revolution. He abandoned traditional and imitative, lyrical and love poetry, written sometimes in Bedil's style, for social themes and satire. In his poem *Mozī va hol*, 'The Past and the Present', written in 1913, Aĭnī rejected his older writings as individualistic. The literary talent of this poet is indicated by the facts that his poems had been included with praise in several *tadhkiras* published at the beginning of the century and that an attempt was made to persuade him to join the court, which he refused to do.[280] Even before the Revolution, Aĭnī's work included some social themes; for example, he wrote the poem *Zaminro mafurushed!*, 'Don't Sell Your Land!', in the form of a letter in which a son warns his father against selling his field to the usurers.

However, Aĭni's main importance in the pre-revolutionary period lay in his activities as a teacher. He taught in the modern schools (*maktabhoi usūli nav*), having acquired the necessary experience by eavesdropping in Tatar schools, as he later wrote in his Materials on the History of the Bukhara Revolution. On the basis of his teaching experience, he wrote the reader *Tahzib-us-sib'ën*, 'Education of Youth' (published in 1909 and 1917), in which he pointed to the importance of learning. In spite of certain shortcomings, the book was of great importance, for until then there had been only religious and Arabic text-books. From the very beginning Aĭnī opposed corporal punishment in schools, which up to that time had formed part and parcel of the educational system.[281]

From 1912 onwards, when the first Tajik periodical, *Bukhoroi Sharif*, 'Gracious Bukhara', was founded, Aĭnī published there his poems on moderately enlightened themes, and later he published in the magazine *Oina*, 'The Mirror', the poem *Nido ba javonon*, 'An Appeal to Youth', in which he urged youth to work for the whole, for society.

Being a teacher at the new jadid schools, in 1907 Aĭnī linked his enlightened activities with the jadids.[282] He soon realised his mistake and detached himself from them before the Revolution. When after the latter the jadids as a whole proved themselves to be the open enemies of the Tajik people, he sharply condemned Jadidism on several occasions.

However, as already indicated, Aĭnī, as the founder of Soviet realistic literature in Tajikistan, belongs mainly to the post-revolutionary period and will be discussed in that context later on (pp. 559 *et seq.*).

NOTES

1. See 'Guide to Pronunciation, p. XXV.
2. The majority of Soviet Iranists hold that the spoken Tajik, *darī (fārsī)*, first came into existence in Central Asia and became a literary language there in the 9th century. From there it spread to present-day Iran and eventually became the language in which poetry was written in a large part of the Islamic Middle East.
3. In the eastern part of the once Mongol realm of the White Horde (north of Syr Darya, between the rivers Ural, Irtysh and Chu), Mongolian tribes intermarried with the local Turkic tribes and adopted their language. The terms Uzbeks and Kazakhs cover many Turkic tribes which have been stabilized since the 16th century (Ivanov, *Ocherki*, 41).
4. A. I. Yakubovskiy, *K voprosu ob etnogeneze uzbegskogo naroda* (T. 1941), 15. For complete bibliographical data see the Bibliography on p. 814.
5. Radzhabov, *Iz istorii obshchestvenno-politicheskoy mīsli*, 296.
6. I. S. Braginskiy, *K izucheniyu uzbeksko-tadzhikskikh literaturnīkh svyazey*, 27; in the annals *Vzaimosvyazī literatur Vostoka i Zapada* (Moscow 1961).
7. Radzhabov, *op.cit.*, 7.
8. Mirzoev, *Binoī*, 9.
9. His rule has often been wrongly idealised, as if he had been an enlightened ruler (Mirzoyev, *Binoī*, 18).
10. Cf. I. S. Braginskiy, 'K izucheniyu uzbeksko-tadzhikskikh literaturnīkh svyazey', in *Vzaimosvyazī literatur Vostoka i Zapada* (Moscow 1961), 7–56.
11. Tojī Usmon, *Bistu se adiba*.
12. T. Usmon, 'Dar borai shoirahoi gumnom', *Tojikistoni Sovetī*, 1960, 43, 3.
13. A. Mirzoev in his speech at the 4th Congress of Tajik Writers in 1959, *SS*, 1959,4, 45. This outdated view is unfortunately expressed also in *Storia della letteratura persiana* by the Italian Iranists Pagliaro and Bausani in 1960 (p. 153).
14. Mirzoev, *op. cit.*, 53.
15. Note should be taken of a small synthetic study by N. Maʿsumī, *Adabiëti tojik dar asri XVIII va nimai avval asri XIX* (Dushanbe 1962).
16. J. B. Čapek in the magazine *Slovesná věda*, 4 (1951), 21.
17. B. G. Gafurov, *Istoriya tadzhikskogo naroda*, Vol. I (Moscow 1955), 360.
18. Which is at the same time very important for the history of the conquerors. – P. P. Ivanov, *Ocherki po istorii*, 49.
19. Gafurov, *op.cit.*, 364.
20. The subsequent founder of the Great Mogul empire in northern India (in 1526).
21. K. Aĭnī, *Badriddin Khiloli*, 57.
22. Gafurov, *op.cit.*, 367.
23. *Ibid.*, 367.
24. Ivanov, *op.cit.*, 65.
25. Gafurov, *op.cit.*, 359 and 360.
26. O. Majlisov, 'Voqeai taʿrikhī', *Tojikistoni Sovetī*, 1959,51, 3–4.
27. Anthony Jenkinson, a merchant and traveller, journeyed from Moscow to Bukhara and Iran (1558–1559), and along the Volga River back to Europe. As a representative of the Moscow Company he was instructed by Ivan the Terrible to negotiate with the Central Asian khanates on trade contacts (*Istoriya Uzbekskoy SSR* [in further references abbrev. to *Ist.Uzb.*], vol. 1, 434; *Encyclopaedia Britannica*, 1926, vol. XI, 627b; vol. XVI, 804a).
28. Gafurov, *op.cit.*, 374.

29. Cf. Gafurov, *op.cit.*, 361.
30. Their relationship is discussed in A. Maniëzov's 'Ëdgorii dūstī', *Sharqi Surkh*, 1958,6, 116–134.
31. Mir Alī, calligrapher and poet (died in Bukhara in 1558), originally from Herat.
32. The collections of the Institut vostokovedeniya in Tashkent include a marvellous 16th-century manuscript, 'Kulliëti Ubaĭdullokhon', No. 8931 (*Sobr.vost.rukop.*, II, 9).
33. A. N. Boldïrev, *Zaynaddin Vasifī*, 129 *et seq.*
34. A. Mirzoev, *Binoī*, 37. On the other hand, Kh.S. Aĭnī does consider this period to have been one of decadence, in his work *Bedil...* (p. 34). However, Browne's view that only Jomī, Hotifī and Hilolī were of any importance as poets is no longer valid (E. G. Browne, *A Literary History of Persia*, vol. IV, 25).
35. Nisorī lists 250 in his *tadhkira*. See p. 495.
36. Gafurov, *op.cit.*, 378.
37. Cf. Abdulgani Mirzoyev, *Iz istorii literaturnïkh svyazey Maverannakhra i Indii vo vtoroy polovine XVI – nachala XVII v.* (Moscow 1963). (A paper read at the 26th International Orientalist Congress in Delhi, 1964.)
38. Kh. S. Aĭnī, 'Tazkirai Hasani Nisorī va nuskhahoi on', *Izvestiya otdeleniya obshchestvennïkh nauk, Akademia Nauk Tadzhikskoy SSR* (Dushanbe) [in further references abbrev. to *Izv.Tadzh.*], 1956,9, 37–42.
39. *Sobr. vost. ruk. AN UzSSR*, vol. I, 298–299.
40. *Istoria Uzbekskoĭ SSR*, vol. I, 447.
41. *Sobr.vost.ruk. AN UzSSR*, vol. I, 131. From the year 1604/5. A pupil of Nisorī.
42. K. Aĭnī, *Badriddin Khiloli*, 37.
43. Cf. Gafurov, *op.cit.*, 378.
44. A. A. Semenov, *Kurzer Abriss der neuen mittelasiatisch-persischen (tadschikischen) Literatur (1500–1900)*, 3; *Namuna*, 113.
45. I. S. Braginskiy, *Ocherki iz istorii tadzhikskoy literaturï* [in further references abbrev. to *OITL*], 328.
46. Semenov, *op.cit.*, 3.
47. Horn, 192.
48. K. Aĭnī, *Khiloli*, 76.
49. *LHP*, III, 438; IV, 233.
50. Cf. N. Saĭfiev, 'Nakhlī va fikrhoi ijtimoī-siësī dar ejodiëti ū', *Sharqi Surkh*, 1963,8, 118–132.
51. Mirzoev explains (in *Saĭido*, 34 *et seq.*) the substance of the complicated nature and incomprehensibility of works written in the 'Indian style' by the fact that many themes linked with Indian culture and philosophy, which were not understood by people outside India, had been used in literature, as well as by the flowery character and artificiality of poetic imagery, and by the increased influence of Ṣūfī ideas. Bertel's shows in his article 'K voprosu ob "indiyskom stile" v persidskoy poezii' (in *Charisteria Orientalia*, published in honour of the 70th birthday of Professor J. Rypka, Prague 1956, 59) that this was neither a national nor a geographical phenomenon, as might appear from its name, but rather a social one. Bausani (in 'Contributo a una definizione dello "stile indiano" della poesia persiana'. *Annali*, NS, 7, 167–178), who considers A. Mirzoev to be the greatest expert on the 'Indian style', raises a number of interesting ideas and offers a "more precise stylistic definition": The 'Indian style' destroys the law of 'formal harmony'; that is why in the imagery abstract terms are used and even verbs in the infinitive; there is also a terminological expansion of the vocabulary. See also Pagliaro-Bausani, *Storia della letteratura persiana*, 478 *et seq.*
52. Note should be taken of Engels's view of Mirkhond's style as being full of images but devoid of content. (From Engels's letter to Karl Marx, Manchester, June 6, 1853.)
53. Kh.S. Aĭnī, *Bedil*, 35, footnote 3.
54. *Ibid.*, 39. However, the author points out that the 'Indian style' had been widespread in Central Asia as early as the 16th century.

55. See above, p. 295 *et seq.*
56. *Mukhammas* is, as a rule, a special type of *nazira*, a parallel to the poem of another author. The poet adds to the *ghazal* of another poet three additional *misra‘* with the same metre, rhyme, contents and other properties. Occasionally poets also wrote separate *mukhammas.*
57. A. M. Mirzoev, *Saïido Nasafī*, 45.
58. Abdulghanī Mirzoev, *Binoī* (St. 1957), 491. A basic monograph on Binoī.
59. Gafurov, *op.cit.*, 378.
60. Bartol'd, Semenov, Bertel's, Sal'e, and some Uzbek authors.
61. The Uzbek aristocracy itself was opposed to the Uzbek language. It was a similar situation to that in mediaeval England, when the court spoke French almost exclusively .
62. Examples of his Uzbek poems may be found in Khondamir's *Habib-us-siyar.*
63. Binoī (The Builder) is a *takhallus*, probably taken from the poet's father, who was a builder. In some sources he is referred to as Bannā'ī. See C. A. Storey, *Persian Literature*, vol. I, 1278. In two of his *dīvāns* he used the pseudonym Holī.
64. In *Tuhfai Somī*, 'Somī's Gift', he speaks of several treatises on music written by Binoī.
65. In *Badoe‘-ul-vaqoe‘*, Vosifī mentions Binoī in 25 places and also includes some examples of his work (Mirzoev, *Binoī*, 142 *et seq.*).
66. In his monograph on Binoī (p. 167), Mirzoev shows how wrong it was to ascribe this work to Sāno'ī, as had been done by some authors.
67. Mirzoev, *Binoī*, 191.
68. A work of the same title was also written by the 16th-century poet Muḥammad Solih (it has been published twice in Chighatoĭ), and yet another *Shaïboninoma* was written by an unknown author.
69. Mirzoev, *Binoī*, 146. In his article 'Eshche raz ob avtore "Shakhanshakh-name" he shows that its author was amīr Sadr-ad-dīn Sulton Ibrohim al-Amirī (*Probl. Vost.*, 1960,4, 111–112).
70. Horn, *Geschichte*, 192.
71. *GIPh*, 586, 587.
72. Navoī, *Majolis....*, 66 (Boldïrev, 258).
73. The major credit for discovering the value of Hilolī's work belongs to the Tajik historian of literature Kamol Aïnī, who, besides several shorter studies, wrote a detailed monograph, *Badriddin Khiloli* (St. 1957, 206 pp.), and also published a selection from Hilolī's work with an introduction, explanatory notes and a vocabulary (see Bibliography, D IIb).
74. Tojī Usmon, 'Hiloli charo kushta shuda bud', *Tojikistoni Sovetī*, 1957,225, 3.
75. Boldïrev, *Zainaddin Vosifi*, 280.
76. K. Aïnī, *Khiloli*, 107.
77. *Ibid.*, 30.
78. *Namuna*, 105–112. In 1946 S. Aïnī published a representative selection from *Badoe‘-ul-vaqoe‘* in a shortened version, intelligible to the contemporary reader; it is a classical example of how the work of an earlier author should be edited for lay readers. The book was published under the title *Vosifī va khulosai Badoe‘-ul-vaqoe‘* after the author's death in Dushanbe in 1956.
79. A. N. Boldïrev, *Zaynaddin Vasifi* (St. 1957), 354 pp.
80. *Namuna*, 107.
81. A complete critical edition of this work was prepared by A. N. Boldïrev (see Bibliography D IIb). A characterisation of the work is available in Boldïrev's article 'The 16th Century Tajik Writer Zainiddin Vosifi and His "Remarkable Tales" (*Badai' al-vaqai'*)'. *New Orient Bimonthly* (Prague), 1962,3, 75–78.
82. *Namuna*, 112.
83. Boldïrev, *Zaynaddin Vasifi*, 117.
84. A. Mirzoyev, 'Ibni Sino va "Badoe‘-ul-vaqoe‘"-i Muhammad Vosifī', *Sharqi Surkh*, 1952,8, 9, 10, 11.

85. Boldïrev, *Zaynaddin Vasifi*, 301.
86. *Ibid.*, 302.
87. P. P. Ivanov, *Ocherki*, 82.
88. A. Mirzoev, *Abū Abdullo Rūdakī*, 247.
89. Mushfiqī, *Muntakhabot* (on p. 7 of the bibliography; a review of the book was published in *Sharqi Surkh*, 1958,7, 146–8).
90. *Namuna*, 141.
91. According to *Nishtari ishq*, 'The Point of Love' – a valuable *tadhkira* by Husaĭn Qulikhon dating from the early 19th century – Mushfiqī was twice at Akbar's court (*Obshchestvennïye nauki v Uzbekistane*, 1961,6, p. 31).
92. A. A. Semenov, *Ocherk ustroystva*, 52.
93. *Adabiёti tojik. Kitobi darsī* (St. 1956), 88 *et seq.*
94. J. E. Bertel's speaks in his article 'Persidskaya literatura v Sredney Azii' (*Sov.vost.*, Moscow-Leningrad, 1948, 225) of the greatly reduced vocabulary of the poems.
95. In *Namuna*, Aĭnī mentions, for example, *Marhumii Bukhoroī* (p. 151).
96. Tojī Usmon, *Bistu se adiba*, 60–61.
97. Gafurov, in his *Istoriya tadzhikskogo naroda*, characterises the period of Ashtarkhon rule as the culmination of feudal wars (p. 381).
98. In 1620, the tsar's envoy Khokhlov came to Central Asia, while Odambiĭ, the envoy of Bukhara, was dispatched to Russia.
99. Gafurov, *op.cit.*, 387.
100. Mirzoev, *Saĭido*, 69.
101. In Aĭnī's *Namuna Imomqulikhon* (p. 146), *Qosimkhon* (pp. 146–148), *Abdulazizkhon* (p. 147), *Subbhonqulikhon* (pp. 156–158).
102. R. Khadi-Zade, *Istochniki*, 10.
103. A Russian translation with notes was published by A. A. Semenov (Tashkent 1957).
104. *Namuna*, 166–168.
105. *Ibid.*, 161–166.
106. Mirzoev, *Saĭido*, 22.
107. He also wrote in Tajik as did most Uzbek poets. See *Namuna*, 169, and *Namunaho*, XVII.
108. *Ist.Uzb.*, vol. I, 450.
109. This poetry may be characterised by the words of the poet M. Tursunzoda, the chairman of the Union of Tajik Writers, who said in 1959: "As regards the 17th and 18th centuries, the hostility existing among the feudal lords never ceased owing to the fact that the country had often been attacked from the outside and divided into small parts, into tiny feudal domains; at that time the *ghazal* passed into the hands of court eulogists and writers of *qaṣīdas*. The content of this poetic form gradually lost all meaning, and the *ghazal* itself changed into a tool of *radifs* and play on words, a single theme being repeated over and over again, a thousand times, to absurdity, by hundreds of poets. In such a situation it was not possible to speak of poetry but only of bombastic oratory and play with rhymes" (quoted from *Sharqi Surkh*, 1959,3, 115).
110. *Fitrat* is a *takhalluṣ*, a pseudonym, while *Zardūz* is a *laqab*, a nickname.
111. Mir Mukhammad Amin-i Bukhari, *Ubaydulla-nama* (Russian translation) (Tashkent 1951), 306.
112. Mirzoev, *Saĭido*, 186.
113. *Namunaho*, 197, 199–213.
114. Mirzoev, *Saĭido*, 182 *et seq.*
115. An example of his poetry is included in Aĭnī's *Namuna*, 156.
116. Mirzoev, *Saĭido*, 183.
117. *Ibid.*, 171.
118. *Adabiёti tojik* (St. 1956), 100.

119. Bertels', *Persidskaya literatura*, 219.
120. Boldïrev, *Zaynaddin Vasifi*, 129, 253, *et seq.*, 301 *et seq.*
121. Mirzoev, *Saïido*, 25 *et seq.*, 33.
122. Vosifī, *Badoe'-ul-vaqoe'*, 199 *et seq.* (S. Aīnī, *Vosifī va khulosai "Badoe'-ul-vaqoe'"*).
123. Mirzoev, 'Saïfii Bukhorī...', *Izv.Tadzh.*, 7 (1955), 3.
124. *Ibid.*
125. Daulatshāh, *Tadhkiratu'shu'arā* [of 1488], ed. E. G. Browne.
126. Boldïrev, *Zaynaddin Vasifi*, 301.
127. Mirzoev explains this phenomenon by the influx of landless peasants into the towns; this movement was linked with the growth of the crafts and the number of craftsmen, specialisation and increase in the number of crafts.
128. Mir Mukhammad Amin-i Bukhari, *Ubaydulla-nama* (Russian translation) (Tashkent 1957), 307.
129. Mirzoev, *Saïido*, 30.
130. Gafurov, *op.cit.*, 386; Ivanov, *Ocherki*, 83.
131. *Ubaydulla-nama*, 303.
132. *Ibid.*
133. *Namuna*, 176–181.
134. Bibliography D IIb.
135. Boldïrev, *Zaynaddin Vasifi*, 273; Mirzoyev, *Binoi*, 53; Mirzoyev, *Saïido*, 144.
136. *Ubaydulla-nama*, 303.
137. Mirzoyev, *Saïido*, 62.
138. *Ubaydulla-nama*, 303.
139. Mirzoyev, *Saïido*, 138.
140. *Ubaydulla-nama*, 303.
141. Mirzoev, *Saïido*, 122.
142. Kh.S. Aīnī, *Bedil*, 9; on the other hand, Mirzoyev writes in *Saïido* (pp. 49 *et seq.*) that the poet did not write *mukhammases* on the *ghazals* of the last representatives of the 'Indian style' or on Bedil himself.
143. According to P. P. Ivanov, Abulfaïz's domain did not extend beyond the limits of Bukhara – the town – and even there his power was limited (*Ocherki*, 90).
144. The whole dynasty was sharply criticised by Ahmad Donish in his *Risola*, and by S. Aīnī in *Ta'rikhi amironi manghitiai Bukhoro*.
145. Semenov, *Ocherk ustroystva*, 3.
146. The khanate of Qūqand was in Farghona. In the 1750's Farghona was annexed by China for a short time.
147. Semenov, *Ocherk ustroystva*, 4. Also see A. Burnes, *Voyages*, Vol. III, 275 *et seq.*
148. P. P. Ivanov, *Ocherki*, 126.
149. *Ibid.*, 112.
150. I. A. Remez, *Vneshnaya torgovlya Bukharī do mirovoī voīnī.*
151. At that time the town of Bukhara had 70,000 inhabitants and three quarters of them were Tajiks (P. P. Ivanov, *Ocherki*, 120).
152. Gafurov, *op.cit.*, 311.
153. Semenov, *Ocherk ustroïstva*, 5.
154. Ivanov, *Ocherki*, 215.
155. A. Mirzoev in his speech at the 4th Congress of Tajik Writers (*Sharqi Surkh*, 1959,4, 54). Since then N. Ma'sumī has published a treatise (see Bibliography D IIb).
156. Khadi-Zade, *Istochniki*, 98.
157. Hodizoda in the postscript of the edited work of Ahmad Donish, *Porchaho az...*, 179.
158. *GIPh*, 310.

159. *Namunaho*, 184.
160. *Bedil*, 43, footnote.
161. See Bibliography D IIb.
162. Valikhojaev, *Iz istorii*, 19.
163. *Namuna*, 185. Nodira was the wife of the amīr of Qūqand, Umarkhon. After her husband's death and the fall of Qūqand in 1842 amīr Nasrullokhon of Bukhara ordered Nodira to be hanged because she had engaged in debates on poetry with men and because she had managed state affairs (B. Hayit, 'Die jüngste özbekische Literatur', *Central Asiatic Journal*, 7,2, 1962, 123).
164. *Sharqi Surkh*, 1961,4, 100.
165. Khalīlī Afghān, *Āthāri Harāt*, III, 37.
166. See also Aziz Qayumov, *Hoziq* (Tashkent 1957), 53, (In Uzbek.).
167. *Sharqi Surkh*, 1959,3, text, 149. See also B. Hayit, *op.cit.*, 123.
168. *Ibid.*, 146.
169. N. Ma'sumī, *Adabiëti tojik dar asri XVIII va nimai avvali asri XIX* (St. 1962), 45. He was a soldier at Umarkhon's court and refused to become a court poet (B. Hayit, *op.cit.*, 123).
170. *M. va M.* of May 22, 1962, p. 2, noted the 200th anniversary of the poet's death. On the other hand, *Sharqi Surkh*, 1957,2, 61, notes that the poet lived between 1788 and 1856.
171. Khadi-Zade, *Istochiniki*, 117–131.
172. N. Ma'sumī, *Adabiëti tojik*, 5, 7, 74 *et al.*
173. Jawaharlal Nehru, *The Discovery of India* (London 1951), 248.
174. Cf. K. Marx, 'British Rule in India', in *Karl Marx, Articles on India*, 2nd Edition (Bombay 1951).
175. Nehru, *op.cit.*, 242, footnote.
176. Bedil's biography is comparatively well known thanks to the writings of the author himself (*Chor unsur*), as well as to reports written by his friends and by writers of *tadhkiras*, in particular Ghulomalikhon Ozod, who was 17 years old when Bedil died. He wrote *Khizonai omira.*
177. Ozod, *Khizonai omira* (S. Aĭnī, *Bedil*, 38).
178. S. Aĭnī, *Mirzo Abdulqodiri Bedil*, 40.
179. *Ibid.*, 57.
180. After his return from Central Asia in 1920, Dr. Josef Aul described the respect enjoyed in Bukhara by the poet Bedil, who until then had been unknown to European Iranists.
181. In his speech at the 4th Congress of Tajik Writers, Tursunzoda pointed to the fact that even some contemporary poets sought to imitate Bedil, and warned aginst such a trend (*Sharqi Surkh*, 1959,3, 119). The Tajik poet Muhammadjon Rahimī and his Uzbek colleague Ghafur Ghulom consider Bedil their 'very own writer'. I. S. Braginskiy, 'K izucheniyu uzbeksko-tadzhikskikh literaturnīkh svyazey', in *Vzaimosvyazī literatur Vostoka i Zapada* (Moscow 1961), 36.
182. In *Histoire de la littérature.*
183. *Annali*, NS, 6 (1954–1956), 163–199.
184. *Namuna*, 186–191.
185. See Bibliography D IIb.
186. *Sharqi Surkh*, 1946, 7; 1947, 1–2–3 ('Mirzo Abdulqodiri Bedil va ejodiëti ū').
187. *Bedil i ego poema "Irfon".*
188. S. Aĭnī, *Bedil*, 63.
189. *Ibid.*, 69.
190. 'Az ruboiëti Mirzo Abdulqodiri Bedil', *Sharqi Surkh*, 1958,8, 137; Kh. Aĭnī in her work on Irfon (p. 57) writes, however, of 200,000 verses, while the *tazkira Khizonai omira* lists the number as 90,000–100,000.
191. *Ruboī* was Bedil's favourite form; there are some 3500 of them in his work.
192. Muminov, 'Izucheniye tvorchestva Mirzī Bedilya v Uzbekskoy i Tadzhikskoy SSR', *Izv. Uzb.*, 1958,1, 14.

193. A basic study on this work was written by Kh. Aĭnī.
194. It was translated into Russian in 1946 (by L. M. Penkovskiy and not by S. Aĭnī, as listed by A. Bausani in *Annali*, 6, 182), and was published with a long preface written by S. Aĭnī; see also Klimovich, 'Bedil i ego poema "Komde i Modan"', in *Iz istorii literaturī Sovetskogo vostoka* (Moscow 1959); the contemporary poet Abdusalom Dehotī (see p. 583) used the theme for his drama *Komde va Madan*, etc.
195. K. M. Mirzaev, *K voprosu ob ekonomicheskikh vozzreniakh Mirzī Bedilya.*
196. *Namuna*, 289.
197. Mirzoev points in *Saĭido* (p. 35) to the wrong assertion made in this respect in *Namunahoi adabiëti tojik*, 186.
198. In Afghanistan Bedil is appreciated much more than Ḥāfiz (Bausani, *Annali*, 6, 163, footnote 2). In the 18th century the Afghan poet Abdulḥamīd was called the 'Afghan Bedil'. Bedil's influence is still very strong in Afghanistan, and most Afghan poets are still following in his footsteps (see the introduction to the publication *Namūna-i ashʿār-i shāʿirān-i Afghān* [St. 1959], p. 5, and the anthology by M. H. Bihrūz in Afghānistān [Kabul 1955], e.g. pp. 218, 306).
199. Cf. e.g. Fait, *Středoasijští národové*, 181.
200. Khadi-Zade, *Istochniki*, 109.
201. *Namuna*, 197–200.
202. B. I. Iskandarov, *Iz istorii bukharskogo emirata*, 9.
203. Radzhabov, *Poet-prosvetitel tadzhikskogo naroda Asiri*, 10.
204. See R. A. Pierce, *Russian Central Asia 1867–1917*, 32 *et seq.*
205. Khadi-Zade, *Istochniki*, 102.
206. Semenov, *Materialī po istorii*, 21; N. A. Kislyakov, *Les rapports de féodalité patriarcale* (see Bibliography D IIb), 1 *et seq.* The head of the Moslem representatives in the Russian Duma, the Tatar S. Maksudov, said after his visit to Bukhara in 1910 that the situation there was intolerable (S. A. Zenkovsky, *Panturkism and Islam in Russia*, 87).
207. N. A. Kislyakov, *Patriarkhalno-feudal'noye otnosheniye u osedlogo naseleniya Bukharskogo khanata* (Moscow 1960), 2.
208. Semenov, *Materialī po istorii*, 9.
209. Radzhabov, *Iz istorii*, 147.
210. Gafurov, *op.cit.*, 432.
211. M. Fait, *Ruská Střední Asie* (1901), 53 *et seq.*; M. Fait, *Středoasijští národové* (1910), 165, and others. These publications of the Czech ethnographer offer a good source of information on life in Central Asia at the close of the 19th century.
212. Radzhabov, *Iz istorii obshchestvenno-politicheskoy myslī tadzhikskogo naroda*, 44.
213. A. P. Fomchenko, *Russkie poseleniya v bukharskom emirate*, 23.
214. Lenin wrote in 1899: Central Asia serves Russian capitalism as a colony (*V. I. Lenin o Sredney Azii*, 11).
215. Bozorg Sharifzoda, 'Harakati ozodikhohī dar Rossiya va ahamiyati on baroi Bukhoroi Sharqī', *Sharqi Surkh*, 1959,2, 48.
216. Semenov, *Materialī po istorii*, 14.
217. I. S. Braginskiy, 'Nazare ba...', *Sharqi Surkh*, 1947, 4-5-7.
218. It is safe to say that Central Asian agriculture underwent a considerable advance in nearly all fields during the period of imperial rule (Richard A. Pierce, *Russian Central Asia 1867–1917*, 174).
219. As late as in the middle 1890's the shariat still prohibited the use of kerosene lamps (Aĭnī, *Ëddoshtho*, III, 162).
220. Radzhabov, *Iz istorii*, 367.
221. Gafurov, *op.cit.*, 474.
222. Radzhabov, *Iz istorii*, 390. 401.

223. S. Aĭnī, 'Mukhtasari tarjimai holi khudam', *Sharqi Surkh*, 1955,8, 30.

224. Mahmudkhūja Behbudī (1874–1919) was the leader of the Turkestan jadids and the publisher of several Uzbek periodicals in Samarkand (*Shūhrat*, 1907–1908, *Samarqand*, 1914, and *Oina*, 1913–1915). As a jadid he was sentenced to death by the amīr in 1918, but escaped. Under the Provisional Government in Russia, he was a member of the so-called National Centre. Behbudī was a typical representative of the nationalist bourgeoisie of Turkestan and an admirer of the Constitutional Democrats in Russia as well as of the tsarist regime in general. He believed that the amirate of Bukhara should be annexed by Russia (Olzscha, 370; see Bibliography D 1a) and was a great enemy of the Social Democrats. In 1913 he wrote a play, *Padarkush*, 'Patricide', which has no literary value but reflects the jadid ideology, urging religious and secular education as a means of acquiring a good position in commerce and of becoming rich (see E. Allworth, 'The Early Reformist Theatre', *Central Asian Review*, 12,2, 1964, 87 *et seq.*). According to B. Hayit ('Die jüngste özbekische Literatur', 134) Behbudī was stoned to death on the amīr's orders at Qarshi in 1919.

225. Braginskiy, 'Unsurhoi ejodiëti badeii khalq dar osori khattii qadim va asrimiënagii tojik', *Sharqi Surkh*, 1955,3, 95.

226. Cf. George Lenczowski, *Russia and the West in Iran 1918–1948*, 30 (see Bibliography C).

227. Semenov states that in 1868 there were 10,000 slaves in the Samarkand region alone (*Ocherki ustroystva*, 13).

228. An excellent example is provided by the poet Ojiz, which *takhalluṣ* hides none other than the amīr Abdullahad himself; in his worthless poetry he writes about the uselessness of human life, the burden of wealth and the happiness of ascetics. The others continue to eulogise the amīr, although he had no positive traits whatsoever. The leading representatives of the reactionary circles in Bukhara at the end of the 19th century also included Afzal Makhdum Pirmastī, the author of a satire aimed at Donish – which had been ordered by the amīr, – and of a *tadhkira*, written in 1904, which is directed against all that was not downright reactionary. For example, he also criticised Shohin for lack of gratefulness. It is a book of little value, just as is the *tadhkira* written by Abdī in 1906, which also advocates the feudal-clerical regime in the amirate of Bukhara.

229. Kh. Mirzozoda, *Shohin*, 206.

230. Under clerical pressure court poetry almost disappeared in the middle of the 19th century, in that poets were no longer directly linked with the court. However, we can still speak of court poetry because some poets continued to be in close contact with the court and depended on it for their living.

231. The *tadhkiras* of Vozeh, Hashmat, Afzal, Abdī, Mūhtaram, and Sadri Zië (see, in particular, Khadi-Zade, *Istochniki*). However, the *tadhkiras* list only the best-known authors from Bukhara and some larger towns, and obviously reflect the reactionary views of their authors. E.g. G. Galimova gives in her article 'Dastnavisi ...' (*Sharqi Surkh*, 1957,9, 116) the names and examples of the work of fifteen Darvoz poets who also wrote their poems in the local dialect.

232. He was murdered in Qunduz by order of the amīr Nasrullokhon (M. H. Bihrūz, *Adabiyyāt az Abu 'l-Faraj Sagzī ba-baʿd*, Kābul, Afghānistān, 1334/1955, 312).

233. Khadi-Zade, *Istochniki*, 106.

234. It is of course only a relative simplification. Compared to present-day language, Donish's manner of expression is still too complicated and involved.

235. T.Neʿmatzoda, 'Koni lazzat va khoni neʿmat'-i Vozeh', *Majmūai ilmī* (Universiteti Davlatii Tojikiston, St.), 26,2 (1959).

236. Braginskiy, *Ocherki*, 391.

237. *Namuna*, 338.

238. Khadi-Zade, *Istochniki*, 91.

239. Najmī Saĭfiev, 'Shoira Miskin va namunai ashʿori ū', *Sharqi Surkh*, 1959,9, 116 *et seq.*

240. Braginskiy, *Sharqi Surkh*, 1955,1, 45; Khadi-Zade, *Istochniki*, 63.

241. In 1962 the poet's *Asarhoi muntakhab*, 'Selected Works', containing 348 pages, were published in Dushanbe; the book was prepared and prefaced by Sayidumar Sulton.

242. The enlightened atmosphere and the characters of the individual authors were masterfully depicted by S. Aīnī in the third volume of his memoirs *Ëddoshtho*.

243. Braginskiy, *Ocherki*, 376.

244. Khadi-Zade, *Istochniki*, 108.

245. *Namunaho*, p. XXII, footnote 1. See also R. M. Khashimov (Hoshim), *Nekotorïye voprosï stanovleniya tadzhikskoy sovetskoy literaturï* (St. 1963), 4. (The author's report on his own dissertation.)

246. R. Hoshim, 'Chand sukhan dar borai yake az tarjimonhoi avvalini adabiëti badeii rus va kitobi ū', *Sharqi Surkh*, 1959,1. This is one of the first translations from Russian into Tajik.

247. Maʿsumī, *Ocherkho oyid ba...*, 7.

248. Maleho speaks in his *Muzokir-ul-ashob* (1692) of several such mountaineer poets, but unfortunately offers very few examples of their work.

249. *Namunaho*, 218 *et seq.*

250. Nodir Shanbezoda, 'Shoiri khalqii Kūhiston Qudratullobek va asari ū', *Sharqi Surkh*, 1958,12, 112 *et seq.*

251. T. Pūlodī, 'Nazare ba ruboiëti pesh az revolyutsiyagii Badakhshon', *Majmūai ilmī* (Inst. Davl. pedagog., Stalinabad), 4 (1954), 83.

252. His poetry was collected by Rahim Jalil, who was also the first to write about Fakhrī in *Tojikistoni Sovetī* on November 12, 1938. Fakhrī's *Majmūai sheʿrho*, collected by R. Jalil and R. Toshmatov, was published in 1964.

253. A. Habibov, 'Baʿze maʿlumotho dar borai shoir Nazarsho', *Sharqi Surkh*, 1957,12, 80.

254. The journey in search of reports on the *hofiz* and his poems was well described by Habibullo Nazarov (himself a poet and expert on classical literature, see p. 587) in his book *Dar justujūi Karim-Devona*, 'The Search for Karim-Devona'. In 1961 a collection of Devona's poems with a long introduction by H. Nazarov, *Satrhoi otashin*, 'The Fiery Verse', was published in Dushanbe. However, an extensive debate arose in the Tajik press on the value and even the authenticity of Devona's poetry, which ended in a decision to send a new ethnographic expedition to the Hisor region.

255. Hodizoda, in an extensive postscript to the book of Ahmad Donish, *Porchaho az "Navodir-ul-vaqoe"*, 171. See also G. Scarcia, 'Note su alcuni motivi della cultura tagica e su Ahmad Dāniš', *Annali* (Napoli), NS, 11 (1961), 63–103.

256. In 1960 the 150th anniversary of Donish's birth was celebrated on a grand scale and the occasion was used for the publication of a number of studies. See J. Bečka, 'Soviet Studies on Ahmad Donish', *Archiv Orientální*, 1963, 483–487.

257. The collection of manuscripts in Tashkent contains Donish's copy of Hilolī's *mathnavī*, *Shohu darvesh*, which he copied in 1849 at the age of 22.

258. He wrote the astronomical study *Ar-risola fī a'mol-ul-kura*, 'A Discourse on the Use of the Globe', dealing with the use of the globe and various astronomical problems based on the observation of two globes given to him in Petrograd by a certain Stramakhov (Mirzoev, 'Yak fakti muhimi...', *Trudï Tadzh.*, 29, 67–74.)

259. Radzhabov, *Iz istorii*, 155.

260. Donish, *Risola ë mukhtasare...*, ed. A. Mirzoev (St. 1960), 5.

261. Avezboeva, R., 'Ahmadi Donish dar borai kharakteri progressivii madaniyati rus', *Madaniyati Tojikiston*, 58,1, 13–14.

262. *Sbornik statey* (St. 1957), 151–161.

263. *Namuna*, 289, and Khadi-Zade, *Istochniki*, 111.

264. *Namuna*, 529.

265. Khadi-Zade, *Istochniki*, 105.

266. See p. 529.

267. S. Aĭnī, *Ëddoshtho* (St. 1955), vol. II, 93.
268. Savdo, *Muntakhabot*, 'Selected Works'. Selected and arranged by Gulsum Galimova.
269. V. Asrorī, 'Hajv va mazhaka dar adabiëti tojik', *Sharqi Surkh*, 1957,6, 95.
270. *Namuna*, 352–373. The first monograph dealing with this poet, entitled *Shamsiddin Shohin*, was written by Kh. Mirzozoda. See Bibliography D11b.
271. Radzhabov, *Iz istorii*, 207.
272. Mirzozoda, *Shamsiddin Shohin*, 208.
273. Khadi-Zade, *Istochniki*, 58.
274. *Ibid.*, 77.
275. *Namuna*, 271.
276. Aĭnī, *Ëddoshtho*, III (St. 1955), 214. In his Memoirs Aĭnī devotes considerable space to Haĭrat, discussing him in the third volume on pp. 204–221, and mentioning him often in other chapters as well.
277. Sodiqkhoja Gulshanī (died 1328/1910), one of Donish's pupils, is said to have also composed Russian verse (Radzhabov, *Iz istorii*, 247). See also *Central Asian Review*, 8,4 (1960), 351.
278. The first to write about Asirī was Aĭnī in his *Namuna* (pp. 210–217); attention was also paid to this poet by Gafurov in his *History* (p. 471), and he was discussed in greater detail by Z. Radzhabov in his study *Poet-prosvetitel' tadzhikskogo naroda Asiri* (St. 1951).
279. S. Aĭnī, 'Mukhtasari tarjimai holi khudam', *Sharqi Surkh*, 1955,8, 17.
280. *Namuna*, 369.
281. M. Orifī, 'S. Aĭnī hamchun pedagog', *Maktabi sovetī*, 1950,3, 9–12.
282. Braginskiy, *Ocherki*, 411 *et seq.*

II. AFTER THE REVOLUTION

A. INTRODUCTION

This chapter covers literature produced from 1917 until the present (1966) in Central Asia, particularly in Tajikistan, on territory which had developed between 1920 and 1929 within the framework of the Soviet-Union as a new state formation inhabited mainly by a Tajik-speaking population.[1] A national literature, written in Tajik, came into being in this area, differing considerably in its form and content from the old Tajik literature that had existed before the Revolution, roughly on the territory of the extinct amirate of Bukhara.

The differences between Persian and Tajik have already been explained, but it should yet be added that the differentiation between the two languages progressed more intensively precisely in the post-revolutionary period, when the formation of the Tajik nation led to a conscious and purposeful creation of a new, literary Tajik language, based on the language of the classical literature and making extensive use of the grammatical forms and vocabulary of the spoken language. The newly formed language was greatly consolidated by the introduction of the Latin script (in 1928), later replaced by the Russian (in 1940), instead of the older Arabic script. When compared with modern-day Persian, the new literary Tajik language is characterised by considerable differences in phonetics, some differences in the grammar, and a considerable number of Russian words as well as international expressions adopted through Russian. The Persian language, on the other hand, has taken over words for new concepts and things chiefly from the western languages, which have also been the source of the international terms introduced into Persian. The Tajik language is moreover characterised by a marked Uzbek influence.

Emphasis however should undoubtedly be laid on the common features rather than on the differences between the two languages, and it is certainly wrong to create artificial differences. The most prominent among the modern Tajik literary personalities, Sadriddin Aĭnī, writes about the older literature: "Just as both Tajiks and Iranians understand and like to read the works of Saʿdī, Hofiz, Nizomī *et al.*, they also understand and like to read Rūdakī, Kamol Khujandī, Ismat Bukhoroī, Saĭfī Isfaragī and others. A Tajik reader may find it difficult to understand the meaning of words used by Firdavsī from the old vocabulary, but an Iranian may run into the same trouble."[2] It is perhaps symbolical that Soviet Tajik literature was founded by the Tajik Sadriddin Aĭnī and the Iranian Abulkāsim Lohūtī. One of the most outstanding current Tajik prose-writers, Sotim Ulughzoda, writes in an open letter to young authors that in order to polish their style and language they must "study their mother tongue very deeply", and advises them that for this purpose "it may be recommended to read from the old literature the prose of Saʿdī, Ahmad Donish, Chordarvesh, the Persian *Thousand and One Nights, Anvoru Suhaĭlī,* etc."[3]

B. POLITICAL DEVELOPMENT

The period following the Russian Revolution of 1917 brought a drastic turn in the political, economic and social development of the peoples of Central Asia, who basically belong to two ethnic groups – the Iranian and the Turkic. The already previously undermined feudal relations disintegrated completely, the mediaeval conditions represented by the amīr and his court disappeared, the Islamic priesthood gradually lost its political and economic power, and an era of a broad political and cultural democratisation was initiated. Quite naturally these revolutionary changes were not realised smoothly; the first period especially was characterised by a vicious ideological struggle, which resulted in the loss of numerous values. Central Asia is one of the few areas in the world where feudalism was directly transformed into socialism without an intermediate period of capitalist development.

After its victory in Russia, the Revolution also reached the peripheral areas. As early as November 1917, Soviet government was proclaimed in Tashkent, and in April 1918 an autonomous republic was created in that part of northern Central Asia within the framework of the Russian Soviet Republic. In the meantime anti-Soviet forces were concentrating with foreign assistance[4] on the territory of Bukhara and Khiva, but at the same time the peoples of both these countries began to realise that here was an opportunity for ridding themselves of the centuries-old rule of usurpers of power – the Manghit dynasty in Bukhara. The anti-feudal and anti-imperialist revolution which broke out in Bukhara and Khiva[5] in August 1920 was thus a continuation of the Russian Revolution. The feudal regime was overthrown with the help of the Soviet army[6]; soon afterwards the Republic of Khiva was formed and in August 1920 the

Notes on pp. 601–605

People's Soviet Republic of Bukhara was proclaimed by the *kurultaĭ* of Bukhara.

Fighting continued, however, especially in the outlying regions of Central Asia and the mountains of eastern Bukhara. It was there that, with the help of the Central Asian jadids, the deposed amīr, who had fled to Kabul in neighbouring Afghanistan, formed *basmachi* units, which had sworn to destroy the new regime in a 'holy war' and to restore the power to the old ruler. At the end of 1921 the command of the *basmachi*[7] troops was taken over by the adventurous Enver Pasha[8], the former Turkish Minister of War, who had been forced by Kemal Pasha to flee from his homeland. He issued a proclamation in which he presented himself as the "supreme commander of all Islamic armed forces, the son-in-law of the *khalifa*, and the representative of the Prophet", who would create a vast Islamic empire in Central Asia. Fighting between the government of Bukhara and the *basmachi* went on until 1926, when it subsided for some time, only to resume in the period between 1929 and 1931. In 1931 all the rallying points and centres of the *basmachi* were destroyed once and for all, and the commander of the *basmachi* bands, Ibrohimbek, was killed.

Specifically Tajik affairs are very hard to trace in the first post-revolutionary years in the ethnic caleidoscope of Central Asia. The struggle going on was one between the old and the new world, and very little attention was paid to the language either side was using. However, as the overall situation gradually stabilised and economy and culture[9] began to develop slowly, the question of nationality also began to grow in importance and the Tajik nation was formed – besides a number of Turkic nations, the Uzbeks, Turkomans, Kirghizes and Karakalpaks – a nation speaking Tajik and other Iranian languages, and inhabiting eastern Bukhara and the Pamir Range. This nation was granted the right of independent existence on October 28, 1924, when the Autonomous Tajik Soviet Socialist Republic was established in the sweeping national division of Central Asia, when the Uzbek Soviet Socialist Republic was also formed. This development culminated in the transformation of the Autonomous Republic into a Union Republic in 1929, when Stalinobod[10] was made its capital. The development was not, of course, straightforward. Initially the Tajiks faced the stubborn opposition of Turkic nationalists, who denied the right of the Tajiks to their own national identity, claiming that the Tajik-speaking inhabitants of Central Asia were Turkish, which assertion seemed to have been supported by the fact that most Tajiks living in urban areas were bilingual, speaking also Uzbek. The struggle for Tajik national identity was extremely sharp; for example, after the revolution in Bukhara the pan-Turkic elements did not permit the opening of Tajik schools, and pressure was also put on the founder of Soviet Tajik literature, Sadriddin Aĭnī, who joined other writers to oppose these pan-Turkic trends in the article 'Tojiklar mas'alasi', 'The Tajik Problem', published in the magazine *Mehnatkashlar tovushi*, 1923–24.[11] He did a great service to the aspirations of his nation in 1925, when he wrote a voluminous anthology of Tajik literature to demonstrate through literary history the millenial culture of the Tajik nation and its right to an existence of its own. The pan-Turkic elements tried to prevent the publication of this book under the pretext that it included a thousand-year old *qaṣīda* praising the shāh. For this reason this work of the foremost Tajik fighter for a new life was marked as anti-revolutionary. Eventually, however, Aĭnī won, just as did the whole concept of a new Tajik state. The subsequent development may then be characterised as peaceful economic and cultural progress which was, however, disturbed – especially in the second half of the 1930's – by an atmosphere of distrust, dogmatism, false accusations and trials, followed by the elimination – and in some cases also physical liquidation – of many prominent and honest people. World War II affected the life and development of Central Asia in that the economic importance of these areas, sheltered from the horrors of war, had grown through the transfer of many economic centres to the eastern parts of the Soviet-Union. There was a growth of industry and exploitation of mineral resources, but agriculture, especially cotton-growing, continued to be the major economic factor affecting the development of Central Asia. The revolutionary political changes and economic progress were accompanied by a growth of Tajik culture – scientific advancement, profound changes in Tajik art and, in particular, Tajik literature, which closely reflected every change in the life of the nation.

C. INFLUENCES

As already indicated, modern Tajik literature developed primarily under the influence of Russian literature. The latter had already made its way to Central Asia before the Revolution through Azerbayjani, Tatar, Uzbek and a few Tajik translations of Tolstoy, Gogol, Pushkin and other Russian authors, and partly too by translations from other European literatures. A major influence was subsequently wielded by Gorky, who affected individual Tajik writers both by his works and by personal contacts, his theoretical treatises and speeches, as well as by his organisational activities. Thus, for example, the founder of Soviet Tajik literature, S. Aĭnī, often referred to himself as Gorky's disciple. Ikromī and a number of other writers and poets began their literary career by translating Russian classics. Initially Russian tradition was adopted mechanically, as, for example, in the case of the poet Sulaĭmonī, who at one stage of his development used Mayakovsky's forms without any substantial reason, and only later did the Tajik writers approach their models in a creative way. On the other hand, however, there is no doubt that sometimes the Russian influence was overestimated. Until 1929 there had been practically no Tajik translations from Russian prose and until then Aĭnī, for example, knew very little Russian; in fact, as late as 1941, he wrote in a letter addressed to Rahmatzoda: "Haĭf kī man zaboni rusiro namedonam..." (It's a pity that I don't know Russian...).[12] Nevertheless, by 1928 he had written several works in prose, including the novel *Dokhunda*. There is no doubt that prose also was considerably influenced by Vosifī's *Badoeʿ-ul-vaqoeʿ*, Donish's *Navodir-ul-vaqoeʿ*, by classical Afghan and Indian literature, etc. Finally it is most probable that in the initial period there was also a limited influence by the new literature of the geographically and culturally close Iran. A thorough study has yet to be made of the relationship of Tajik literature to Uzbek literature, which had played an important role especially in dramatic writing, but it should not be forgotten that Aĭnī, for example, had also founded modern Uzbek prose. There is considerable difference in this respect, however, compared with the previous situation. Although "now [i.e., in 1957] there is practically no Tajik writer and poet in Central Asia who does not know Uzbek and does not read Uzbek literature in the original"[13], a great change has taken place in that every author writes only in one language[14], such as, for example, Fotih Niëzī, who originally wrote Uzbek poetry and now writes only Tajik prose, while Ashirmat Nazarov wrote only Uzbek poetry although he lived in Tajikistan.

D. CHARACTERISTICS OF SOVIET TAJIK LITERATURE

It should first be said that Soviet Tajik literature came into being and has developed as a part of Soviet literature in general, that is literature produced by all the nations inhabiting the Soviet-Union, with Russian literature in the lead. Like all Soviet literature, Tajik literature too expresses in its entirety a belief in man, in his strength and his ability to overcome his internal problems as well as outside difficulties; it expresses man's assurance, which arises from his understanding of reality. As regards its content and to a lesser extent its form, post-revolutionary Tajik literature adopted the aesthetic views promoted by Marx and Engels, by the Russian democrats of the second half of the 19th century, by Soviet scholars of literature, and, in particular, by the founders of Soviet prose and poetry, Gorky and Mayakovsky. We should not, however, deduce from this fact any uniformity or subservience to Russian literature. The influence applies * rather to the content of the literary works, which are expected, in particular, to educate the reader. The purpose of literature is to fight for a better future of mankind, which, under the conditions prevailing in Central Asia after the Revolution, meant a struggle for the ideals of socialism, for the emancipation of women, for the elimination of illiteracy, etc.; the whole period of Soviet Tajik literature has also been characterised by the frequent use of themes taken from the civil war in Central Asia.[15] Because it was urgent in the 1920's to show the historical necessity of the fall of the amīr's regime, Aĭnī wrote his satirical pamphlet *Jallodoni Bukhoro*, 'The Executioners of Bukhara'. In the 1930's Tajik authors wrote works directed against the *basmachi*, while the writers of the World War II period recalled the courage of the mythological and historical Tajik heroes, like

Rustam and Muqanna'. But Tajik literature has also drawn heavily on the millenial classical Tajik and Persian literature. Experts in contemporary Tajik literature are urging writers to draw on the classics for their best imagery, to accept their humanistic ideas and especially their supreme artistic form. The course of development of post-revolutionary Tajik literature was marked by frequent clashes of opinion and serious ideological conflicts. From the very beginning, the authors who had chosen realism in keeping with the progress of time had to overcome strong opposition by reactionary forces, usually of jadid origin, such as Abdurrauf Fitrat, Bektosh and others, who claimed – under the slogan of defending the classical heritage – that the subjects for poetry were only the rose, the moon and a beautiful woman, that poetry was a synonym for allegory, play of words and graceful turns of speech. They forgot the fact that the classical authors had reflected in their works the development and the knowledge of their times, and that their allegories often had a hidden meaning. These trends centered in the literary society 'Chighatoĭ gurungī', established by Fitrat in 1919. Its members asserted that the only literary language of all Central Asia should be Chighatoĭ, the artificial, archaic Turki language. These trends continued until the 1930's, when nationalist tendencies, this time led by Bektosh and Komilī (1933), once again came to the fore; this spurred Tursunzoda to write the play *Hukm*, 'The Verdict', the first play with the ideological struggle as its theme. The struggle also went on on the other front against the followers of the 'proletkult', which rejected the classical literary heritage and denied the need of poetic metre. They criticised the poetry of 'the rose and nightingales', but went to the other extreme by appealing to the poets to abandon poetic images and metre and to praise work written in a schematic manner. Some literary genres like the *qaṣīda* disappeared from post-revolutionary poetry, and the scope of the *ghazal* (which was considered to be a dead form by some poets) and other strophic forms (e.g. the *mukhammas*) was restricted because most poets sought new poetic forms more suited for depicting modern life. Tajik scholars of literature no longer considered tenable such poetic images as comparing braids with snakes, the face with the moon, eyelashes with spears, eyebrows with the bow, etc. Very few of the old rules governing the use of rhyme were preserved. Today rhyme in Tajik poetry is based on consonance rather than on identity of letters as in classical poetry, and even assonance (the word *rang*, for instance, may rhyme with the word *pand*) is admitted. Similar rhymes can be found in the poems of practically all poets, including those who cling most to the old forms. However, the classical metre *arūz* still prevails in poetry, including folk and children's poems, and in Soviet prose too we may find remnants of some traditional elements; thus, for example, we find rhyme (*saj'*), though in a very limited number of cases, in the works of S. Aĭnī, Rahim Jalil, and others.

Another source of creative inspiration was, to a greater extent, folklore, folk-literature, which had already inspired the works of the literary giants in the classical period. In view of the democratisation of literature it became a still more important factor in the new Tajik literature, manifesting itself in the choice of poetic images, themes and

Notes on pp. 601–605

figures of speech. A major role has been played especially by the old epic ballads and legends, stories of historical heroes, various tales, as well as *latifas*, anecdotes, proverbs and sayings, lyrical poems and songs, which for centuries had been the products of folk-culture, reflecting the thinking and the aspirations of the broad masses of the common people. We may list as a typical, but far from unique example in this respect the poem *Qishloqi tilloī*, 'The Golden Qishloq', by Mirshakar. The theme is based on a folk-legend from Pamir. The influence of folklore is also manifest in the enrichment of literary works with folk-sayings, proverbs and humour, and in general in the use of the vernacular, which replaced the highly embellished, pre-revolutionary literary language. *Doston*, a type of folk poetry used by folk-singers, became a popular poetic form. *Dostons* are used as a rule to describe important historical and social events. It is certainly not by chance that many Tajik literary figures, including the most prominent ones, such as Tursunzoda, Dehotī, Mirshakar, or Rahimzoda, collected folklore. The new literary language has drawn on classical as well as on folk-literature, thereby helping modern Tajik literature to acquire a specifically national character. This close link with folk-tradition is one of the national characteristics of Soviet Tajik literature.[16]

In the past decade Tajik literature has logically developed from minor to more complex forms and from poetry to prose. In the first period there were mostly only marches welcoming the new life, such as Aĭnī's *Marshi hurriyat*, 'Freedom March', written in 1918, or short poems praising the Revolution, such as for example *Tillokamaron*, 'People with the Golden Belts', composed by Muhammad Rahimī, a journeyman shoemaker. It was only in the late 1920's that Ikromī, Rahim Jalil, Hakim Karim and Azizī wrote their first short stories; Aĭnī was an exception, for he wrote his first short story in 1920, and his first novel, as already mentioned, appeared in 1928. The first poems and stories were published in newly established magazines, first Uzbek and later purely Tajik (the first appeared in 1925), in particular those of a satirical nature, the most important of which was the magazine *Mushfiqī*, founded in 1926. As the years went by Tajik literature grew in stature not only by the number of new authors but mainly by the value and scope of their works. Aĭnī produced additional novels and was joined by younger story- and novel-writers, mostly his disciples, like Ulughzoda, Hakim Karim, Niëzī, and others, while poets began to write longer poems, and the first more serious plays appeared. During World War II, there was a temporary return to smaller forms, but in the 1940's and 1950's a number of great prose and poetic works were produced. Prose, which was one of the oldest genres, stood far in the background in the classical period and in fact until the late 1920's. The old literature did not produce any realistic prose or a literary prose language. Thus the first prose-writers in Tajik literature were in fact the translators of Russian stories. Prose, however, quickly won the favour of readers and gradually became the leading genre in Tajik literature; this is true especially of longer prose-works – the novel, which offers the greatest opportunity to depict man's inner life. Memoirs and autobiographies have played an important role in Soviet Tajik literature, and have greatly influenced its progress towards realism. These genres occupy an important place in Aĭnī's work, and also include, for example, Ulughzoda's *Subhi javonii mo*, 'The Dawn of Our Youth', and Tursunzoda's poem *Hasani arobakash*, 'Hasan the Cart-Driver'. *

E. DIVISION INTO PERIODS

Tajik scholars of literature have generally accepted the following division into periods, which is also recognized by other Soviet Iranists:

1. From the Revolution up to the consolidation of Soviet power, i.e. the formation of the Tajik Soviet Socialist Republic (1917–1929);
2. The period of the peaceful development of the country up to the outbreak of World War II (1929–1941);
3. Soviet Tajik literature during World War II (1941–1945);
4. Post-war literature, from 1945 up to the present.

This division is based on the history of the time but does not match it entirely. For example, in the history of Tajikistan the first period must be subdivided into two parts – from the Revolution up to the formation of the Autonomous Tajik Republic (1917–1924) and the period until the formation of the Union Republic (1925–1929). However, this division is not necessary for purposes of literary development. The first two periods did not affect Tajik drama. On the other hand the second one is sometimes divided into the years from 1929 to 1933, as being the time of the birth of Tajik drama, and the period of its flowering from 1933 to 1941.

Before we discuss individual authors and their works, we shall first briefly characterise the literature produced in the separate periods, except where this has already been done above.

I. DEVELOPMENT FROM 1917 TO 1929

It was during this period that a new realistic literature written in the Tajik language came into being in Central Asia. Only two writers of the older generation – Aĭnī and Lohutī – left a deep imprint on it. But it was only in this period that they fully developed their genius. The stormy events of those years favoured poetry rather than prose – small and especially propaganda poetry – which was typical of all national literatures on Soviet territory. The first poems with new form and content appeared. Outstanding among the poets of this period were Aĭnī, Hamdī, Lohutī, Munzim and in the second half of the period also Paĭrav, Rahimī, Lutfī, Aminzoda, and Suhaĭlī

Notes on pp. 601–605

Javharizoda. The literary output of this period appeared mainly in magazines and periodicals, especially in the first Tajik magazine *Shūʿlai inqilob*, which was published in Samarkand in the years 1919–1921, in *Ovozi tojik* (Samarkand, 1924–1930) and others, as well as in school books. In 1924 Aĭnī wrote his first short novel *Odina* – that was also the first to be composed in the Tajik language – and in 1927–8 his first full-length novel (*Dokhunda*). Ikromī began to write short stories with the direct support of Aĭnī. This period was the beginning of a great revolutionary epoch, and thus literature too centered its attention on the essential and socially most pressing problems and tasks, even at the price of having to sink to a lower level, compared with the literature connected with the feudal period, and even though it was often reduced to expressing general proclamations. All that had been linked with the old society was firmly rejected.

The first half of this period was characterised by a search for a realistic method and eventually the method of socialist realism in literature, the historical novelty of which lay in the fact that it excluded any inner ideological contradiction and was ideologically uniform. Neither Aĭnī nor Lohutī found the way immediately. Another important feature of this period was the ideological struggle against such proponents of the pan-Turkic movement as Fitrat, who denied the justification of the existence of a Tajik literature and urged a return to the old extinct Turki language, Chighatoĭ. The struggle was also directed against the nationalists, who tried to make of the Tajiks a superior nation, in obvious reaction to the previous pan-Turkic pressure. Such leading Uzbek writers as Hamza Hakimzoda, Ghafur Ghulom and others worked in close fraternal co-operation with the Tajik writers against pan-Turkic chauvinism. In spite of the existing great difficulties and obstacles, such new genres in Tajik literature as the short story, the novelette, the novel, and, by the end of the period, the drama and children's literature came into being, and the foundations were laid for literary criticism.

2. FROM 1929 TO 1941

Like the other Soviet literatures, Tajik literature experienced an unprecedented development in the 1930's. The improvisation typical of the 1920's disappeared, the number of published works increased, as did the number of literary genres. Prose was already dominant, with its highest form, the novel, as the most important; in poetry there appeared an increasing number of longer poems – *dostons* – and two new genres were introduced: the drama (Ulughzoda, in particular) and children's literature (Mirshakar and others). This development ran parallel to the political and economic consolidation of the country. The themes were chosen mostly from revolutionary events and from the fight against the *basmachi*, the collectivisation drive, the struggle for the emancipation of women; work and Soviet patriotism were praised and the evils of the old and defunct world were depicted, just as in other Soviet literatures, especially the Russian, the main works from which were translated into Tajik, thus serving as an example to Tajik writers. Collections of short stories were published by Hakim Karim and Rahim Jalil, who switched over to prose after having published a collection of poems in 1936, and in 1938 wrote the first volume of his novel *Gulrū*, devoted to the emancipation of women.

In this period too there was, quite naturally, no uniform opinion on the line Tajik literature should follow and the young generation waged a successful battle against the advocates of tradition, who tried to idealise the distant past by using old forms, laid a barrier between the literary language and the vernacular, and refused to treat contemporary themes. This group was led by Bektosh.

In prose-writing, Sadriddin Aĭnī continued to lead as the author of several novels, in particular *Ghulomon*, 'The Slaves', with which he completed his great trilogy on the life of the Tajik people. As a poet Aĭnī withdrew into the background, but instead gained prominence as the teacher of the young generation of writers, which included for example Jalil and Ikromī.

In poetry there was a certain stabilisation due to the growing influence of the classical heritage accompanied by a study of Russian poetry. The most revolutionary writer in this sphere was Lohutī, whose themes ranged far beyond the borders of his second homeland, Tajikistan and the Soviet-Union. In his poetry Lohutī fought against fascism and endeavoured to promote understanding among people. He also translated the works of such universal classical authors as Shakespeare and Lope de Vega. The great influence of Mayakovsky is especially apparent in the poetry of Paĭrav, while such poets as Rahimī, Suhaĭlī Javharizoda, Aminzoda, Lutfī and others continued their progress. This period was characterised by the appearance on the literary scene of the young, so-called Komsomol generation, which had been educated at post-revolutionary schools; it was a generation that still remembered the feudal regime but was dedicated to socialism. This group included in particular Tursunzoda, Ulughzoda, Dehotī, Mirshakar and Yusufī. All these writers were born in the decade preceding the Revolution, all had had similar experiences and all had used a similar form in their first works. Differentiation came only in the course of their further development. All were proclaimed disciples of Mayakovsky, but at the same time they tended towards the conventional method of allegorical expression. Tursunzoda was one of the first to rid himself of this convention.[17]

Among other poets of this period we should mention H. Obidī, N. Ma'sumī, T. Pūlodī and Boqī Rahimzoda. About this time too the works of the folk-poets, the *hofizes*, were first published, in particular those of Yusuf Vafo, Boboyunus Khudoĭdodzoda and Saidalī Valizoda.

In the 1930's there was a tremendous growth in the number of readers of Tajik literature, which of course greatly spurred on literary production. There was also a great advance in literary theory, especially literary criticism. This development was considerably promoted by the adoption of the Latin script in 1928 and of the new script, based on the Russian alphabet, which was introduced in 1940 and which cor-

Notes on pp. 601–605

rected some of the errors of the 1928 script. Important in this respect were also the 1930 Decree on Compulsory Education and the measures taken to speed up the elimination of illiteracy among the adult population. While only 0.5 percent of the total population could read in 1917, by 1940 most Tajiks were literate and practically all children attended school. The Union of Tajik Writers was established in 1933, and the first Tajik literary magazine, *Baroi adabiëti sotsialistī*, 'For Socialist Literature', was first published one year earlier; it was devoted mainly to literary theory, literary history and criticism. The highly valuable literary magazine *Sharqi Surkh*, 'The Red East', began publication in 1938. Considerable damage was caused to Tajik literature, especially in the second half of the 1930's, by a period of extreme distrust, which culminated in the years 1937 and 1938 in the arrest and trial of a number of Tajik intellectuals who were accused of nationalism and disloyalty.[18] Some were soon rehabilitated, including Hakim Karim and Ikromī, other writers had to wait long years for reinstatement, while still others, like Rashid Abdullo and Hamdī, did not live to see justice done.

3. FROM 1941 TO 1945

The war years were characterised in Tajik literature by a return to smaller forms, such as short and serial stories and reports, and the fact that poetry predominated. Not a single novel was published during the war, but drama developed rapidly. The stormy events restricted the choice of themes to some extent, with war themes in praise of heroism at the frontlines and on the home front prevailing in order to inspire the masses to fight the vicious aggressor. In this period too Tajik writers took another step towards using themes and images from folklore known to the broadest masses of the people, such as the heroes Rustam and Kova the Blacksmith, or such symbols of evil as Zahhok. They also wrote about the heroes of Tajik history, like Muqanna' or Temurmalik, or persons hated by the Tajiks, such as Changhiz-Khon, who was compared to Hitler. Satire was also widespread, especially short stories with heroes like Mushfiqī or Afandī, both figures popular in Central Asian folklore just as was Nasreddin Khoja in the folk-literature of the Turkic nations. In this period Tajik authors followed two trends in their writings: either they created vast pictures using symbols and allegories, and turned to old legends, about Rustam for example, as the symbol of strength and patriotism, or about Zahhok, symbolising the enemy, which was typical of Lohutī; or they tried to influence the reader with a realistic depiction of the heroism of the ordinary common man (Braginskiy).

On the other hand, lyrical poetry too developed, also love poetry, often in the form of a soldier's letter from the front to his beloved (e.g. Ma'sumī). Many writers, including Ulughzoda, Niëzī, Rahimzoda, Nazarov, Yusufī, Pirmuhammadzoda, H. Karim, and Buzurgzoda, were directly involved in the fighting, and the last four were killed in action. The works produced in this period were published mostly in magazines and newspapers rather than in book form.

The war events made the 82-year old poet Javharī take up writing once again after a silence of twenty-five years, and inspired the 50-year old Roziya Ozod to write her first verse and patriotic poems teaching the reader to hate the aggressor. New young poets like Farhat, Shukūhī, Qahhorī and others entered the literary scene. The older poets continued writing, especially Dehotī, Mirshakar – who produced the outstanding *doston Qishloqi tilloī* – and Tursunzoda, who wrote the libretto *Tohir va Zuhra* (both these works are based on well-known Tajik fairy-tales). The active writers also included Suhaĭlī Javharizoda, Aĭnī, who continued writing both poetry and prose, and the folk-poets. Commentaries from the frontlines were written by Ikromī, Rahim Jalil, Ulughzoda and others, while R. Jalil and Samad Ghanī wrote satirical stories. Although the war period covered only four years, it played an important part in the development of Tajik literature, having contributed to progress in patriotic and heroic lyrical poetry and in the drama.

4. FROM 1945 TO THE PRESENT

Post-war Tajik literature, which continued the development of the pre-war years and drew from the experience gained during the war, progressed in all genres. Once again, prose prevailed over poetry and the greatest advance was made in the most demanding prose form – the novel. Sadriddin Aĭnī lost his monopoly position as novel-writer, but he continued to occupy his leading position in Tajik literature. An important event for the development of Tajik literature was the second congress of Tajik writers, in 1945, at which authors were again asked to establish close links between their works and the life of the country. The congress also stressed the role of literature as one of the most important factors influencing man's education. It demanded that the works of Tajik authors should be national in their form and socialistic in their content. Literature must serve the great objectives set by Soviet society. In this respect, Tajik literature forms a part of the united, multi-national Soviet literature. Writers like Niëzī, Ikromī and Ulughzoda depicted the great history of the war in their works, while in the subsequent development novels dealing with life on the collective farms gained in importance. The latter include Ulughzoda's *Navobod* and Ikromī's novel *Shodī*. The post-war period is also characterised by the quantitative and qualitative growth of Tajik short stories using subjects from various spheres of life. Poetry is characterised by optimism and poetic pathos, by a broadening of its themes and by more varied form. However, the question of form still remains open. In poetry too there is an apparent trend towards larger works, epic *dostons*, so popular among Tajik readers, although lyrical poetry continues to predominate. Most successful among the poets is Tursunzoda with his series of poems devoted to the oppressed nations of Asia. Tajik poets increasingly seek their subjects beyond the borders of their country and the Soviet-Union.

Tajik literature began to outgrow the local boundaries also through being shared by other nations. Its best works have been translated into more than twenty languages (mostly through Russian translations) spoken in the Soviet-Union, as well as into other languages, such as Czech, Chinese, Persian, Hindi, Bengali, Polish, English, French, German, Spanish and Portuguese. The post-war period too has not been without an ideological struggle (as was the case throughout the Soviet-Union). Some writers idealised the old feudal system, as in the play *Tahmosi khujandī* by M. Qosimov while in the early 1950's a struggle was waged to overcome the harmful 'theory of no conflict' which had for some time negatively affected Soviet art and greatly harmed Tajik literature, in particular the short story in which "life was depicted as a holiday, all happiness and laughter, without struggle and without contradictions"[19]; it also resulted in a decline of satire. New young writers of prose and poetry have appeared. Considerable advance has been made, especially in short-story writing, where Tolis and Muhammadiev are the most successful authors, and the satirist Rahim Jalil continues writing; but the authors turn mostly to the past, to remnants of the past, and contemporary themes are rather rare. New themes, on the other hand, prevail in such journalistic genres as commentaries, where Ikromī, Bahorī, Niëzī, Sidqī and some others are outstanding. Satire is most advanced, especially when directed against backwardness and superstition, things that hinder development, and those who disturb peace. Literary critics, however, are not satisfied with this genre, although there has been a certain turn for the better since 1953, when the satirical magazine *Khorpushtak*, 'The Hedgehog', began publication.

It is undoubtedly encouraging that in recent years Tajik literature has been enriched by several large works, such as five novels (the second volume of Niëzī's *Vafo*, *Shūrob* by R. Jalil, and Ikromī's *Man gunahgoram*, *Tori ankabut*, and *Dukhtari otash*), Tolis's *Tobiston*, several new dramas, and several new *dostons* written by young authors.

Up till now it has been impossible to estimate the contribution made to Tajik literature by the elimination of the personality cult after the 20th and 22nd Congresses of the Communist Party of the Soviet-Union. As early as the second half of the 1950's some writers and literary figures, victims of the persecution of the late 1930's, were rehabilitated. Some of them resumed their positions in public life and have continued writing, while anthologies of other writers, whose very names had been suppressed, like Hamdī, for example, have been published. We may also mention the publication of Abdurauf Fitrat's story *Qiëmat*, 'The Last Judgment', although this fact does not involve a rehabilitation of the views held by this writer. A few authors, like Shukūhī, Mirzō and Qanoat, have already expressed their views on this unfortunate period, but no larger work of prose dealing with it has yet been published.

It is perhaps fitting to conclude this part of the present study with the opinion expressed on contemporary Tajik literature by the outstanding literary scholar and writer of Iran, Saʿīd Nafīsī. Speaking at the second congress of Soviet writers, which he attended as a delegate, Nafīsī said: "For us it is instructive to see in particular the path followed by the Central Asian Soviet republics which are historically close to us and which have greatly developed their culture within a short period of time. The works of such outstanding Tajik writers as Sadriddin Aĭnī, Tursunzoda, Mirshakar, Ulughzoda and Ikromī ... serve as an excellent example for our youth in creating a national and truly democratic culture."

F. THE FOUNDERS OF SOVIET TAJIK LITERATURE

I. SADRIDDIN AĬNĪ

Sadriddin Aĭnī (1878–1954) is one of the authors who form a link between pre-revolutionary literature and the literature of Soviet Tajikistan. He occupies the special position of a Father of the Nation in Tajik history – of the nation's teacher – and is undoubtedly the greatest personality in the last centuries of Tajik history. His influence will be felt in Tajik cultural development for many years to come. Aĭnī spent half of his lifetime in the mediaeval atmosphere of the amirate of Bukhara, and devoted the rest of his life to the building up of the new Tajikistan, which took great strides in overcoming its economic and cultural backwardness.

The literary work produced during the first half of his life, as described in the preceding chapter (p. 535), was certainly not without importance, but there is no doubt that it was only after the Revolution, thus during his second phase, that Aĭnī reached the stature of a writer whose significance exceeded the boundaries of his native country.[20]

The biography of *Ustod* – the Master – as Aĭnī is universally known in Tajikistan, is identical with the history of his nation, according to the poet Tursunzoda.[21] Aĭnī was born on April 15, 1878, in the *qishloq* Soktarī in the former *tuman* of Ghijduvon of the Bukhara Viloyat. His father was a small farmer and occasional craftsman, but at the same time a village man of letters, well versed in literature and writing, which was a rarity in Central Asia of those days. Being interested in learning, he tried to give his children a good education too. Aĭnī described his life in the village *maktab* in his memoir *Maktabi kūhna*, 'The Old School' (1936) and in his short autobiography, *Mukhtasari tarjimai holi khudam*, 'My Short Biography' (1940).[22] Aĭnī lost both his parents when he was eleven and remained all alone with his two younger brothers. Thanks to the talent which he showed already as a boy, and with the help of his grandparents, he went to Bukhara in 1890 after his elder brother, to get higher education. He had a hard time studying at various *madrasas* in Bukhara, often making his living as the servant of his rich fellow-students, but his talent and perseverance eventually helped him attain his goal. He devoted himself to poetry, getting valuable advice from his friend, the prematurely deceased poet Haĭrat (p. 534), and finally adopted the *takhalluṣ* Aĭnī after having previously tried out several others. A great change in Aĭnī's life took place at the turn of the century, when he read for the first time Ahmad Donish's *Navodir-ul-vaqoe'*. His previous beliefs were shattered: he saw in quite a different light the 'head of all believers', the amīr and all the other 'pillars' of contemporary society, whom he and the other students of theology had until then viewed as destined by God to rule the country. Aĭnī also broadened his views by reading foreign Persian newspapers like *Ḥablu'l-matīn*, 'The Strong Rope', *Chihranamā*, 'The Mirror', and the Tatar newspaper *Tarjuman*, 'The Interpreter'.

Like most progressive intellectuals of those days, Aĭnī became a jadid, advocated progress in education and, after the so-called modern schools were banned, joined the illegal society 'Education of Children' which supported secret schools using modern educational methods; for the time being, however, that was the limit of Aĭnī's aspirations. In 1916 the amīr appointed Aĭnī *mudarris*, professor, at the Khiëbon *madrasa* in Bukhara, because he realised that Aĭnī was a strong enemy who had to be won over to his side by a well-paid position. Aĭnī did not accept the appointment, using bad health as an excuse; he left Bukhara as a precautionary measure, and worked as a weight-controller in a cotton-cleaning establishment. After some time he returned to Bukhara and was arrested in 1917, as were many other people known to be in favour of new things. On the day he was arrested, he was almost whipped to death without trial at the amīr's court. He was saved by Russian soldiers who had heard of the amīr's bestial treatment of prisoners, and was taken to the hospital in Kogon. After having spent some time there, he left in the middle of 1918 for Samarkand and later for Tashkent, having been warned by his friends that the reactionary Islamic organisation 'Shuroi islom' (The Islamic Council) planned to assassinate him on the amīr's order. He offered his services to the Soviet government in Turkestan to fight for the overthrow of the amīr's regime in Bukhara, the bastion of mediaeval reaction in Central Asia.

Aĭnī did not hesitate to work for the establishment of a democratic state. He wrote for the Tajik magazine *Shū'lai inqilob*, 'The Ray of the Revolution', and the Uzbek *Mehnatkashlar tovushi*, 'The Voice of the Workers'. It was there that he published his first prosework, *Ta'rikhi amironi manghitiyai Bukhoro*, 'A History of the Manghit Amīrs of Bukhara' (1920), in which he showed the anti-democratic nature of the old regime. An outstanding contribution to Aĭnī's struggle against mediaeval tyranny was his *marthiya* – an obituary poem – on his murdered brother (1918), one of the best poems of Soviet Tajik literature.[23] In the conclusion the poet predicted the ignoble fall of the murderous regime. At that time Aĭnī also wrote one of the very first poems dealing with events abroad – *Marshi rahovard*, in praise of the heroic struggle of the Afghans. All of Aĭnī's subsequent activities were closely linked with the birth and growth of Tajikistan; his first revolutionary poems were published under the title *Akhgari inqilob*, 'The Spark of the Revolution' (1923). Between 1918 and 1924 Aĭnī worked chiefly as a journalist[24] and contributed to a number of periodicals.

As early as 1920 Aĭnī wrote another prose work, a booklet of memoirs entitled *Jallodoni Bukhoro*, 'The Executioners of Bukhara', which was published first in Uzbek (in 1922) in the magazine *Inqilob*, 'The Revolution', while its Tajik edition was not printed until 1935. In this booklet the author tells the readers – in the form of a conversation between the amīr's executioners – of the intrigues prevalent at the court. It reflects the influence of such classical stories as *Tūtinoma*, *Chahor darvesh*, and others. At the same time, Aĭnī began writing a historical documentary work in Uzbek, called *Bukhoro inqilobi ta'rikhi uchun materiallar*, 'Historic material on the Bukhara Revolution', which was published incomplete in Moscow in 1926, and has not yet been translated into Tajik.

In his articles Aĭnī criticised in particular the claims put forward by some Turki chauvinists, such as Fitrat and other jadids, that there was no Tajik nation and that the whole of Central Asia was inhabited only by Turkis. In this connection we should point to Aĭnī's anthology *Namunai adabiёti tojik*, 'A Picture of Tajik literature'[25] (1926), in which the author shows that the Tajiks possess an ancient and rich culture and that they have the same right to a separate national existence as the other nations of Central Asia. In compiling this anthology, Aĭnī made good use in particular of Mūhtaram's *Tazkirat-ush-shuaro*, 'An Anthology of Poets', written in the first years of this century (p. 544).[26] It is remarkable that Aĭnī did not succumb to Tajik chauvinism and, on the contrary, greatly contributed to the emerging Soviet Uzbek literature by writing articles for Uzbek periodicals and by producing literary works in the Uzbek language. He was one of the staunchest advocates of friendship between the Tajiks and the Uzbeks, together with his friend, the progressive Uzbek writer H. Hakimzoda.[27] Aĭnī was, in fact, the founder of the Uzbek novel.[28]

Aĭnī turned from poetry[29] to prose – a genre practically unknown in Tajik literature – and soon achieved considerable success. Aĭnī had already wanted to write prose before the Revolution – after having read Donish's *Navodir-ul-vaqoe'* – "but he only realised his desire after the October Revolution, when he had acquainted himself with the works of Russian writers..."[30] Prose, however, forms only one part of Aĭnī's work. He continued to write poetry, but his progress in prose-writing best reflects the course of his literary development. The next stage was the first Tajik novelette *Odina ё sarguzashti Tojikii kambaghal*, 'Odina or the Fate of the Poor Tajik' (1924–1927), in which, just as in his first novel – and the first Tajik novel ever – *Dokhunda*[31] (1927–1928), he depicts the life of simple Tajiks and the changes brought into their life by the great social transformation of the late 1920's. While Odina, the hero of Aĭnī's first artistic prose, was merely a sentimental witness of the events leading to the liberation of Central Asia, the novel *Dokhunda* is as regards content a logical continuation of the novelette *Odina*, and its hero becomes a revolutionary. As an author of novels, Aĭnī reached his peak in the monumental epical novel *Ghulomon*, 'The Slaves' (1934 – the book was simultaneously published in Uzbek under the title *Qullar*). This remarkable work covers the history of the Tajik people from the early 19th century onwards, and tells in a highly artistic form the story of three generations of simple folk, originally slaves, of the disintegration of the feudal regime, the initial progress of capitalism, and the growth of the new social order in Central Asia.

After this monumental novel, Aĭnī produced a number of lesser works, such as *Ahmadi devband*, 'Ahmad the Magician' (1928), which initiated his series of autobiographical works, the satirical novel *Margi sudkhūr*, 'The Usurer's Death' (1937)[32], a profound psychological study of a usurer and money changer, in which the hero can well stand comparison with similar characters depicted in world literature. In this novel Aĭnī shows his expert knowledge of the social and economic conditions prevailing in 19th-century Central Asia.

In 1939, after some lapse of time, Aĭnī again wrote poetry – 2000 *baĭts* of his *doston Jangi odamu ob*, 'Man's Struggle With Water', dedicated to the construction of a dam on the river Vakhsh. Shortly before the outbreak of the war he also published another novel, *Yatim*, 'The Orphan' (1940).

During World War II, Aĭnī did not publish any major work, but devoted himself to journalism and the writing of poetry. Thus, for example in 1944 he wrote a story of the Muqanna uprising, *Is'ëni Muqanna'*[33], and in 1945 *Qasidai jang va zafar*, '*Qaṣīda* on the War and Victory'; he also wrote lyrical poetry, especially at the beginning of the war, when he published *Marshi intiqom*, 'The March of Vengeance' (1941). Aĭnī ended his literary activities after his 70th birthday by publishing the voluminous *Ëddoshto*[34], 'Memories' (1949–1954). The series of Aĭnī's autobiographical works culminates in these memoirs. In the form of short stories the author depicts the period of his youth up to the beginning of the 20th century. In the first volume he describes the village of his boyhood, the second volume shows life in the *madrasas* of Bukhara at the turn of the century, the third volume describes urban life and contains valuable information on the literary personalities in the Bukhara of those days, while the fourth volume tells of various events at the beginning of this century, indicating the growing discontent with the amīr's regime. This quite original work also shows traces of the influence of such classics as Niẓāmī 'Arūḍī's *Chahār maqāla* (p. 221), Sa'dī's *Gulistān*, Vosifī's *Badoe'-ul-vaqoe'*, and Ahmad Donish's *Navodir ul-vaqoe'*. It also reflects the strong influence of folklore and Gorkiĭ (Aĭnī said of himself that he was Gorky's disciple). This work is a true treasure chest of the Tajik language, proverbs and sayings, folk-idiom and expressions, and was translated into a number of languages, including French.[35] Aĭnī is also the author of a number of short stories, short poems and many short narratives published in various Tajik and Uzbek periodicals.

Another of Aĭnī's characteristics is his encyclopaedic knowledge, typical of the early stages of literature. He greatly contributed to the history of the Tajik nation. He pointed to factors that had led the Tajiks to progress and to those that had hindered their advance. He gave the history of his people a progressive concept, and depicted mainly the most important and contradictory period in the history of the Tajiks – the 19th century. Aĭnī was also very active in the field of Tajik linguistics. He created a new literary language, which was intelligible to all Tajiks, and also developed a new Tajik literary style. An opponent of writers of the old school, who wanted to adhere to the form used by Firdavsī and Rūdakī, he saw to it that the new literary language was based on the living language, enriched by all that was useful and beautiful in the old and in the various dialects.[36] Finally, Aĭnī was also very successful as a literary historian and critic. Beginning in the 1930's, he published a number of monographs on such classical authors as Firdausī, Abū Alī Sino, Rūdakī, Sa'dī, Navoī, Bedil and Vosifī[37], besides the large anthology of Tajik literature already mentioned. In his works on the history of literature, which were highly praised by the contemporary Iranian literary historian Sa'īd Nafīsī[38] among others, Aĭnī usually presented a novel view of the classics. Aĭnī was also a great music lover and was deeply interested in the classical mediaeval musical genre *shashmaqom*, on which he wrote a number of learned articles.[39]

Aĭnī introduced into Tajik literature a realistic description of events and characters and thereby pointed the way for the younger generation of Tajik authors; he also introduced the dialogue, until then almost unknown in Tajik literature. He was a master in describing the landscape. His characters deeply influenced the broad masses of Tajik people. Gulnor and Ëdgor, the heroes of his novel *Dokhunda* have replaced the traditional Laĭlī and Majnūn. Aĭnī also created the first realistic pictures of Tajik women; besides the aforementioned Gulnor, they include especially Muhabbat, the heroine of his novel *Ghulomon*.[40] Typical of Aĭnī's writing is that his characters have been taken from real life and many of them actually lived – for example his Rahimi Qand and Qorī Ishqamba from the novelette *Margi sūdkhūr*, 'The Usurer's Death'.[41] That is why we may say of Aĭnī's work, as regards its contribution to the knowledge of Central Asia, what Engels said of the understanding of France through the works of Balzac. Aĭnī's minor historical works, such as *Is'ëni Muqanna'* and *Temurmalik*, reflect the author's profound love of his native land, and it is characteristic of him that they were both published during World War II. Aĭnī's entire work is permeated with his sense of humour and satire. He founded an Uzbek satirical magazine in Samarkand and contributed to several similar publications under various pen-names. In the 1920's Aĭnī poked fun at the uniform and 'novel' verses produced in Tajik and Uzbek poetry, and laughed at the futurists in poems written in the futuristic style.[42] Aĭnī's satirical sense is apparent in his other works as well, especially 'The Usurer's Death'. This is also true of his only play, written in Uzbek; it is a four-act play without a title and takes to task the jadid concern over property and depicts the bourgeois-nationalist character of the jadid leaders.

A Czechoslovak study on Aĭnī must not omit mentioning the friendship that existed between the Tajik writer and Czechoslovakia's national hero, Julius Fučík. At a meeting honouring Aĭnī, held in Dushanbe on November 26, 1935, Fučík said in his speech that Aĭnī was not only a Tajik but also a Czechoslovak writer and that his work was not only precious art but also a remarkable source of learning.[43]

Sadriddin Aĭnī was the teacher and adviser of almost all the other Tajik and some

Notes on pp. 601–605

Uzbek writers of the post-revolutionary period, not only through his work but also personally, and he has undoubtedly joined the ranks of the classical authors of Tajik literature. Like all great truths and beauty, the work of Sadriddin Aĭnī and his personality are great mainly because they are simple. Aĭnī reached the end of his most fruitful life on July 15, 1954.

2. ABULQOSIM LOHUTĪ

The life and work of this poet, who was born in Western Iran and was thus of Persian descent, have already been partly discussed in the chapter dealing with the leading poets of the Constitution (p. 376). Lohutī – the Tajik version of the Persian name Lāhūtī – placed his art fully at the service of Tajik culture from the middle of the 1920's and became one of the founders of Soviet Tajik poetry, although he never forgot his native Iran and its people, and considered his work as a part of the struggle for the liberation of the eastern nations. He is the author of the Tajik national anthem and of the Tajik translation of the Soviet national anthem.

Lohutī was born in the vicinity of Kirmanshah on December 4, 1887, as the son of a small shoemaker who was a lover of Ṣūfī poetry. Lohutī's own poetry, however, soon followed a different path. From his youth onwards he observed the situation in his country, writing for the relatively progressive newspaper *Ḥablu'l-matīn*, and in 1909 published his first poem, the *mathnavī Ay ranjbar*, 'Oh, Worker', which criticised social inequality. After the failure of the Iranian Revolution he was sentenced to death and fled to Baghdad. However, he returned in 1915 to take part in the popular movement against imperialism and in 1917 founded in Kirmanshah the *Firqa-i kārgar* (the Workers Party) which from its very beginning supported the Soviet Revolution and opposed the intervention against the new Soviet state. The party was disbanded after the British occupation of Iran in 1918, and Lohutī was forced to flee to Turkey where he founded the magazine *Pārs* in 1921. After the publication of the magazine was suspended he returned home, where the situation was tense following the unsuccessful Gīlān uprising. Lohutī made his way into the leadership of the revolutionary gendarmerie and in 1922 led the second Tabriz insurrection, known also as 'shūrish-i Lāhūtīkhān' (Lāhūtī's rebellion).[44] After ten days of democratic reforms Tabriz was recaptured by the armies of Riḍā Khān, and Lohutī, for whose head a reward had been offered, fled with other insurgents to the Soviet-Union.

Lohutī's poems written before his arrival in the Soviet-Union already reflect the poet's progressive views and are marked by the specific style which characterises the whole of his subsequent work. He gives new content to classical images – where 'Omar Khayyām writes of bricks made of the ashes of people of the past, Lohutī speaks of palaces constructed of the ashes of the poor. Similarly, in his poem *Sham' va parvāna*, 'The Candle and the Butterfly', he speaks of love of the motherland rather than of the traditional love of a woman or the mystical love of God.[45] But until 1922 his poetry laid stronger emphasis on the 'struggle against' than on the 'struggle for' – he had no clear-cut programme[46] and only in the Soviet-Union did he acquaint himself systematically with the ideas of socialism.

He wrote many poems, including twenty *dostons*, epic poems, which were published in several collections both in Tajik and Persian in Dushanbe, Moscow and Tabriz (in 1940: *Dīvān-i ash'ār*, 1944: *Mardistān*), and more than 150 of them were set to music.

Lohutī's most important works include the *qaṣīda Kreml*, published in 1923 and written in the style of classical *qaṣīdas* as a counterpart to Khāqānī's *Kharābahā-i Madā'in*, 'The Ruins of Ctesifon', written in the 12th century; it was the first poem in Tajik and Persian literature lauding the victory of the October Revolution.[47]

In 1925 Lohutī moved to Dushanbe (named Stalinobod between 1929 and 1961), became a friend of Sadriddin Aĭnī and was active in the cultural sphere. He published his poetry in Tajik periodicals, after 1933 especially in *Baroi adabiëti sotsialistī*. He was one of the first poets to introduce revolutionary political and social topics to Tajik poetry. At the same time, however, he wrote love *ghazals* according to classical models, which are very popular among the Tajiks. In his poetry he also fought against backwardness and superstition, for the emancipation of women, and for the socialist order; he was rightly called 'adibi surkh', the 'Red writer', by Aĭnī.[48]

As time progressed, Lohutī widened the scope of the topics with which he dealt in his poetry; his subjects included not only the burning issues of socialist construction in the Soviet-Union, the fight against the *basmachi* and the problems of the east, but also questions of wider importance, such as brotherhood among nations, the struggle for peace and against fascism, which was spreading in Europe between the two world wars. The latter theme is treated in one of his greatest poems, *Mo zafar khohem kard*, 'We Shall Prevail' (1930). Strengthening of the fraternal relations among the nations of the Soviet-Union is the topic of his poems *Boghbon*, 'The Gardener' (1932), aimed against the nationalists in Central Asia, and *Toj va baĭraq*, 'The Crown and the Flag' (1935), an epos from kolkhoz life, written with great courage and most successfully as a *nazira* on the *Shāhnāma*, even using the metre of the latter.[49]

During World War II Lohutī wrote the great poem *Hamsafaron*, 'Fellow-Travellers', on themes from Tajik and Persian folklore, as well as *Pahlavon Oshtī*, 'Peace, the Victor', and the *doston Mardiston*, dedicated to the heroes of the Panfilov Division who were killed in the Battle of Moscow in 1941. *Dostoni ghalabayi Tanya*, 'Doston on Tanya's Victory' (1942) is one of the best works of wartime Soviet poetry, praising the heroism of Zoya Kosmodemyanskaya, the young partisan hero who was executed by the Nazis. At the same time, however, he also wrote a number of lyrical poems in *ghazal* form, e.g. *Farzandi tojik natarsad az kas*, 'The Tajik's Son Fears Nobody', and *Ba mudofiyai Leningrad*, 'To the Defenders of Leningrad', and many others. A somewhat special position in Lohutī's work is held by the poem *Parii bakht*, 'The Fairy of

Notes on pp. 601–605

Happiness' (1948), dealing with Lenin's stay at Razliv in 1917, which was criticised for being too long and allegorical in some of its scenes.

Lohutī contributed greatly to Tajik drama; he is the author of the first original Tajik libretto – the very popular opera *Kovai ohangar*, 'Kova the Blacksmith' (1940), written on a theme from Firdavsī's *Shāhnāma*.

Lohutī's work since the 1930's has become popular throughout the Soviet-Union, where it has been published more than forty times. His poems have been translated into many languages, including those of the west. Lohutī used almost all the genres of classical poetry, from the *ghazal* and *ruboī* to the *mukhammas*, as well as all the metres of the classical *arūz*; but he also used non-traditional metres, often syllabic verse, and in his translations of Shakespeare introduced blank verse into Tajik poetry. Lohutī's work as a translator is of extreme importance, for he introduced to both Tajik and Persian literature the works of Pushkin, Gorky, Mayakovsky, Shakespeare and other famous western authors.

In 1954 Lohutī's enemies published abroad a false biography of the poet, which was designed to disparage his work. Though already a sick man, the old revolutionary answered this calumny in poems, newspaper and magazine articles and radio broadcasts, and eventually began writing his autobiography under the title *Sarguzashti man*, 'My Tales'[50], which unfortunately he did not live to finish. He died on March 16, 1957, but his work will continue to live for many years because it reflects vital problems which are still faced by many nations of the Orient.

3. OTHER MEMBERS OF THE FIRST GENERATION

Besides Aĭnī and Lohutī, who have joined the ranks of the classic writers of Tajik literature, there were some others, active since the 1920's, who belonged to the generation born before the end of the 19th century or shortly after 1900, viz. the generation who knew life under the amīr's regime from first-hand experience. Most of the progressive intellectuals associated themselves with the Soviet system, but there were some who needed several years to learn that the Soviet government was realising their old dreams. Particularly after 1924, when the Tajik Republic was formed, writers like Javharī, Pinaduz, Azizī, Sarvar, Noil Sherzoda and Paĭrav Sulaĭmonī again began to write. Others, like Sadri Zië or Ajzī, maintained their silence forever. Munzim, Tughral, Fakhriddin Rojī, Hamdī, Zehnī, Alizoda, Muinzoda and many others, however, continued writing from the very beginning.

The Bukhara revolutionaries before 1917, and Aĭnī's friends and pupils, included Mirzo Abdulvohid Munzim (1877–1934). In 1917 he left Bukhara for Samarkand and Tashkent, which were then already located in the liberated part of Central Asia, and through his revolutionary activities helped to overthrow the amīr's regime. While in exile he wrote a number of militant poems under the impact of Aĭnī's revolutionary song *Surudi ozod*, 'Free Song'; these include poems such as *Baëni hol*, 'Explaining the Situation' and *To ba kaĭ?*, 'How Long?' (1920), in which he calls on the people of Bukhara to overthrow the regime of the amīr and the mullahs. In the subsequent years he published in magazines poems directed against anachronisms, but often used uncritically the old forms and images of pre-revolutionary poetry, which were unsuitable for expressing the new ideas.[51] Of his later work, note should be taken of the poem *Dar borai alifboi navu kŭhna*, 'The Old and the New Alphabet', in which he convincingly showed the advantages of the newly adopted script on which he himself had also worked.

Another of Aĭnī's – and Haĭrat's and Munzim's – friends, Ahmadjon Hamdī (1875–1946), also wrote before and after the Revolution. In 1920 he appealed to the people of Bukhara to rebel in his poem *Khitob ba faqironi Bukhoro*, 'Appeal to the Proletariat of Bukhara', praised socialist literature and wrote patriotic poems. Outstanding among his poetry is his last great poem, the anti-religious satire *Karimboĭ ba (dar) khonai khudo*, 'Karimboĭ in the House of God', published in the magazine *Baroi adabiëti sotsialistī* in 1937. However, Hamdī was barred from literary activity during the period when public life was dominated by the atmosphere of distrust established by Stalin. Those poets who originally did not seem to trust the new government included Mir-Sarvar Mir-Haĭdarov who wrote under the *takhalluṣ* Sarvar (1883–1935). Since 1925 he had worked as editor of various Tajik magazines and one year earlier he produced his first post-revolutionary *ghazals* – somewhat suffering from rhetoric – first in praise of education and then of Lenin and the victory of socialism.

Aĭnī also included in his anthology *Namunai adabiëti tojik* the poems of the then unknown Paĭrav Sulaĭmonī (1899–1933), noting that "the garden of Tajik poetry will gain much from the talent of this young fellow".[52] Subsequent developments proved Aĭnī right in estimating the ability of the young poet. Paĭrav (a pseudonym) was an interesting character. The son of a rich merchant of Bukhara, he was raised in the old Central Asian tradition. However, he grew to like the Russian language and culture. Secretly he learned Russian, and when he was seventeen, he enrolled – again secretly – in the Russian school at Kogon, where he studied especially Russian literature. He was enthusiastic about the fall of the amirate in Bukhara and hailed the event in the poem *Ba munosibati inqilobi Bukhoro*, 'In Honour of the Bukhara Revolution', using Aĭnī's first revolutionary poems as his model. But Paĭrav's acceptance of the Revolution was somewhat abstract and he failed to understand the idea behind the Soviet government's New Economic Policy. In the first half of the 1920's he wrote only lyrical poetry, using the full range of the traditional and petrified allegories and comparisons, such as: your figure – a cypress, your face – a rose, your lips – water of life, etc. Paĭrav spent the whole of 1924 in Iran and Afghanistan, and it was his stay there, perhaps, that brought about a turning point in his work after his return home. He left his seclusion, wanting to participate actively in building up the new life whose early achievements had already become visible. He began to write poems like *Shukufai irfon*, 'The Growth of Education' (1926) or *Qalam*, 'The Pen' (1928), in which he backed the new ideals. His work acquired new values and his verse was full of excitement. Using the Russian model, Paĭrav began to apply new poetical forms without venturing beyond the scope of the *arūz*. He introduced live dialogue to his verse and, like Mayakovsky, used broken lines, but his themes remained specifically Tajik.

In the period 1926–1930, Paĭrav Sulaĭmonī was the only other Tajik poet – besides Lohutī – who concerned himself with international problems in his poetry, for example in the poem *Hinduston*, 'India' (1928), in which he severely censured colonial oppression, and *Ba militaristoni Yaponiya*, 'To Japanese Militarists' (1932).

Paĭrav's most successful poems date from the early 1930's. They include his great work *Takhti khunin*, 'The Bloody Throne' (1931) which allegorically depicts the amirate of Bukhara as a ruler's court, magnificent on the surface but abhorrent in its substance. The central image, a throne made of stone spattered with dried blood, symbolises violence and oppression. Unfortunately his second great work was never finished; it was the poem *Manorai marg*, 'The Minaret of Death' (1933) about the silent witness of the brutality of the ancient rulers, the Great Minaret of Bukhara, from which people who displeased the court were thrown to their death.

Sulaĭmonī also wrote satirical verse, often using the form of apparent praise.[53] He ridiculed formalism and the lack of ideas exhibited by those who denied the value of classical poetry and of left-wing trends of all kinds. He stood by Aĭnī in the struggle for the creation of a new literary language, its purity and clarity. He laughed derisively at the archaic and dialectic expressions unsuitably used by some writers. With his best militant poems, especially those written in the last period of his life, Paĭrav greatly contributed to the growth of the newly emerging life of Tajikistan.

The Czech writer and physician Josef Aul, who spent a considerable time in Central Asia, had amicable contact with Paĭrav during his stay in Bukhara between 1919 and 1920, and the poet dedicated some of his poems to him.[54]

Another of the fighters for new life in Central Asia who belonged to Paĭrav's generation was Lutfullo Obidkhūjaev (Lutfī) (1898–1957). He was born at Ūroteppa, fought as a volunteer against the *basmachi* in the first half of the 1920's, and wrote many *ghazals*. Most of these were of an imitative nature and were published in the collection *Satrhoi muhabbat*, 'Verses of Love' (1940). He also composed several *dostons*. In 1938 he published his great poem *Salim partizan*, 'Partisan Salim', which depicts the hard life of the Tajik people before the Revolution and their struggle for liberation. The poem *Najmunniso*, which realistically depicts the growth of Tajikistan's new generation, was published in 1941. At the end of the war and shortly after the Nazi surrender, Lutfī wrote one of the greatest Tajik *dostons*, describing the wartime heroism of Tajik soldiers fighting against fascism; it was published under the title *Nazar-pahlavon*, 'Poem of Nazar the Hero'. In some parts of this *doston* the poet was too subservient to the old traditions and some episodes emerged as too incredible. Lutfī's work also includes one drama – *Soli 1905*, 'The Year 1905' – depicting the struggle of the peasants against oppression after the Russian Revolution of 1905.[55]

The poets who founded the revolutionary literature include Suhaĭlī Javharizoda, who was born at Ūroteppa in 1900 and died in 1964. His father, Muhammad Zufarkhon Javharī (p. 571) was himself a poet (and the son of a poet), who gave his son a good education, and guided him towards poetry. Javharizoda published his first poem, *Khitob*, 'The Cry', in 1925 in the magazine *Ovozi tojik*, 'The Tajik Voice', in Samarkand; this was followed by many other poems, all directed against traitors of the country and the people, while the poet urged the strengthening of Soviet power and the collectivisation of the villages. He was criticised for being somewhat patronising in his first poems. His first collection, *Taronai zafar*, 'The Song of Victory', was published in 1933, followed by the *doston Kambaghal*, 'The Pauper' (1935), and several other collections. They include the poems written during the Second World War, *Dar kishvari amniyat*, 'In the Safe Country' (1955), containing in the first part poems dealing with work and progressive people, and in the second satirical poems, of which Javharizoda was a master.[56] In 1958 the poet published a large poem on the popular uprising in the old Hisor and on the civil war in southern Tajikistan, under the title *Qismati Karim*, 'Karim's Fate'. It was received by critics as a mature work. A voluminous collection, a selection from his work, was published in 1959 under the title *Gulshani afrūkhta*, 'The Burning Bed of Roses'. He also wrote poems for young people, including the collections *Nasli khushbakht*, 'The Happy Generation' (1955) and *Saĭqali fikr*, 'The Grindstone of Cleverness' (1961), which contains not only poems but also puzzles in verse (*chiston*) and humorous proverbs.

Literary and musical talent are combined in another fighter for the new order, Muhiddin Aminzoda (born in Leninobod, formerly Khujand, in 1904). He graduated from a school of music where he later became a teacher. His poems are characterised by a music-like quality and simplicity of language. They appeared in the Tajik press as early as 1924, and primarily laud the growth of the cultural level. Examples are *Donistam*, 'I Have Learned' (1926), which is still being recited by the folk-poets, the *hofizes*, and *Besavodī baloi jon dorad*, 'Illiteracy Is a Tragedy'. The equality of men and women also comes in for praise in these poems. His first collection, *Chaman*, 'The Meadow', was published in 1937, while another, *Bahori Vatan*, 'The Spring of My Country', appeared in 1940; a more recent collection, *Ba rafiqi pakhtakoram*, 'To My Friend, the Cotton Grower', contains his best poems from the post-war period. They are written in a double metre – in *arūz* and in the syllabic metre – and have been favourably received by the critics. In 1959 Aminzoda published a collection of satirical poems dating from various years, entitled *Az har jo yak shingil*, 'A Bit From Everywhere'. He feels at home in satire and consequently this collection contains many well-written poems.[57] Aminzoda is also considered in Tajikistan as one of the best translators of Russian and Uzbek literature: he has translated works by Pushkin, Lermontov, Ghafur Ghulom, Ashirmat Nazarov, and Navoī's great poem *Farhod va Shirin*, among others.[58] *

One of the poets who since 1918–19 have praised the new Soviet government and devoted themselves wholeheartedly to the fight against the rule of darkness in the amirate of Bukhara, is Muhammadjon Rahimī. He was born in the *qishloq* Foyiq, not far from Bukhara, in 1901, as the son of a poor musician. He had a hard time making a living in his youth and at the time of the Revolution worked as a shoemaker's assistant. He wrote his first poem, *Tillokamaron*, 'People With the Golden Belts', as early as 1919, expressing in it the hopes of the common folk and their hate of the tyrants; his poem *Dushanbe* (1929) sings of the newly born Tajikistan. Rahimī fought as a volunteer against the *basmachi* and then worked in various cultural institutions in Dushanbe. In 1940 he published a collection of lyrical poems written in the previous fifteen years. Other collections followed soon after, and in 1945 he published a *doston*, *Moskvajoni aziz*, 'Dear Moscow'. He preserves the old forms in his verse, but gives them new themes – only occasionally slipping into pure imitation. Many of Rahimī's poems have been set to music, including recently *Dostoni Mahiston*, 'Doston on Mahiston', written on a theme borrowed from a popular fairy-tale. Rahimī's war-time poetry in praise of heroism is included in the collection *Marg ba marg*, *khun ba khun*, 'Death For Death, Blood For Blood' (1943), while his best poems dedicated to cotton growing and the natural beauties of Tajikistan have been published under the title *Tilloi tojik*, 'Tajik Gold' (1958). Rahimī's recent work is contained in the collections *Mash'alai mehr*, 'The Torch of Love' (1960) and *Sabohi sukhan*, 'The Dawn of Words' (1963). Rahimī is also the author of several film scripts and has worked as a literary scholar and linguist. For example, he prepared a new edition of Bedil's *Ruboiët* (St. 1960), which is undoubtedly linked with the poet's affinity to the 'Indian style'. Earlier he had published the text of the *Shāhnāma* and the works of Jomī, and written down the tunes of numerous folk-songs.

The prose-writer Hakim Karim (1905–1941) had little opportunity to develop his talent; nevertheless, "whoever discusses Soviet Tajik literature, must not omit Karim".[59] He first served in the Red Army and fought against the *basmachi*, then worked in a local Soviet, and finally was employed in the editorial office of the magazine *Proletari Khujand*, 'The Proletarian of Khujand', in present-day Leninobod. He began to translate Russian authors, especially Chekhov and Gorky, whose works greatly influenced his style of writing. Karim is one of the founders of the Tajik short story, but he was also a dramatist and journalist. Particularly in the period 1922–1937, he wrote stories about the civil war, the liquidation of the *basmachi* bands, the consolidation of Soviet government in Tajikistan, and the emancipation of women from ancient bonds and Islamic prejudices, for the magazine *Baroi adabiëti sotsialistī*, 'For a Socialist Literature'. His style, especially in the initial stage of his work, was flowery and his language artificial; some of his later stories also indicate the author's search for a style of his own, but most of his work shows that Karim was a mature writer.[60] He wrote about fifty short stories, conspicuous for the attention devoted by their author to the character of the heroes. They have been published in four collections: *Sadoi rūzho*, 'The Voice of Days' (1933), *Hikoyahoi maĭda*, 'Short stories' (1935), *Oqshuda va hikoyahoi digar*, 'The Damned and Other Stories' (1936) and *Hikoyaho*, 'Stories' (1940). Finally, Hakim Karim edited a collection of folk-tales for children. In 1941 he volunteered for army service, in September left for the front, and soon after was killed in action near Leningrad.

Another prose-writer whose premature death cut short the full development of his talent, was Bahriddin Azizī (born at Ūroteppa in 1894, died in 1944). He wrote poetry already before the Revolution, then stopped writing for a decade, and between 1928 and 1932 reappeared on the literary scene as the author of short stories published in the magazine *Rohbari donish*, 'The Guide to Learning'; some of the stories were characterised by a pleasing and easily comprehensible language as well as by themes closely connected with real life[61], while others suffer from various shortcomings that were criticised by Aĭnī already in the late 1920's. His satirical writing was inspired by Zoshchenko. Azizī's best stories include *Dar khonai odami nav*, 'The House of a New Man' and *Gul*, 'The Rose'. He also took an active part in the debate on the form of the literary Tajik language.

Hasan Irfon, whose real name was Mamadkhonov (born in Samarkand in 1900) and who was a graduate of Shakurī's once modern school (see p. 523), is better known as a translator from Russian and Tatar. However, in recent years he has written some works of his own. He is the author of the novelette *Du ër az du diër*, 'Two Friends From Two Countries' (1961), which tells the story of a simple Tajik who left before the Revolution to find work abroad, but struck no roots and found no happiness anywhere, and finally returned home. Irfon's novel *Dar kulbayi kosibon* 'The Hut of Artisans' (*Sharqi Surkh*, 1962–63), too, is based on history, depicting life in Samarkand and the first, so-called modern, school at the beginning of this century.

4. JAVHARĪ AND THE POETESS OZOD

The poets Javharī and Roziya Ozod also belonged to the first generation of Soviet Tajik authors, but their literary development followed a different path.

Muhammad Zufarkhon Javharī (born at Ūroteppa in 1860, died in 1945) was a literary figure already known before the Revolution as an outstanding expert on Bedil and as his imitator, which he remained in his lyrical poetry until his death.[62] He was a typical lover of tradition – of imitative poetic canons. He failed to understand that the ossified and abstract turns of speech and images and the unintelligible language overflowing with arabisms could not express the revolutionary events taking place in Central Asia. Like other authors who persisted in this erroneous view, he remained on the sidelines and published his poems only rarely in various magazines; he was criticised for his pseudo-classical work. It should, however, be said that otherwise he did not oppose the newly developing society. He was especially pleased with the growing literacy of the people and the improving standard of culture. In the first post-revolutionary years he welcomed the new Tajik magazine *Ovozi tojik*, 'The Voice of the Tajik', expressed his joy over the formation of Tajikistan in 1924 in his poem *Qasida ba sharafi ta'sisi Jumhuriyati Tojikiston*, 'Qaṣīda In Honour of the Founding of the Tajik Republic', and appealed to women to throw away their veils. In the 1930's he stopped writing, but spoke up once again in the crucial years of World War II. When 82 years old, he published his great poem *Zafar*, 'Victory', an ideologically mature work describing the life of the Tajik people before the Revolution, their fight against the enemy and the years of progress of the Tajik Republic, as well as the heroic fight of Tajik soldiers at the front during World War II. The second large – and last – work of this poet is his *doston Muhammadjon*, 'Dear Muhammad', which depicts the heroism of a Tajik soldier in the Soviet Army – a real-life hero, the volunteer Muhammadjon Ibrohimov, one of the poet's neighbours. The language he used in both *dostons* differs considerably from his older poems in its simplicity and intelligibility.

Roziya Ozod (born in Khujand in 1893[63], died in 1957), too, was born in the past century, but, in contrast to Javharī, did not enter the literary scene until shortly before the Second World War, when she was almost fifty years of age. Then she wrote patriotic poems reminiscent of folk-poetry by reason of their simplicity and easy flow of verse; at the same time, however, they reflect classical tradition. The life of the poetess, as described in her poems, was most interesting. As a girl she did not venture farther than several street blocks away from her parents' house until her husband took her to his home, where she stayed until the Revolution, by which time she had not even seen the outskirts of her native town. Only the Revolution made her a free woman, which is precisely the meaning of her chosen *takhalluṣ* Ozod. This first talented poetess of Soviet Tajik literature published a number of collections of poems from 1944 onwards, including *Muhabbat va Vatan*, 'Love and Motherland' (1944), *Gulistoni ishq*, 'The Garden of Love' (1946), and *Zinda bod sulh*, 'Long Live Peace' (1954). Her post-war poetry contains especially poems dedicated to women – she shows the young generation how women lived before the Revolution – as well as poems for and about children. A large anthology of her poetry was published in 1959 under the title *Ash'ori muntakhab*, 'Selected Poems'.

G. THE SECOND GENERATION

I. PROSE

Among the prose-writers of Soviet Tajik literature a leading place is held by Sotim Ulughzoda, the author of short stories, novels, plays and literary essays. He was born in 1911 in the *qishloq* Varzik, in present-day Uzbekistan, as the son of a peasant. Until 1929 he studied in Tashkent and then devoted himself to literary work. He published his first writings in 1932. Of his pre-war work mention need be made only of his plays *Shodmon* (1939), depicting the life of cotton-growers, and *Kaltakdoroni surkh*, 'The Red Clubs' (1940), which describes the fight against the last *basmachi* invasion led by Ibrohimbek. Both plays rank among the most powerful in Tajik drama.

In 1944, Ulughzoda wrote a play entitled *Dar otash*, 'Under Fire', dealing with the war, in which members of the many nations living in the Soviet-Union fought side by side. He also wrote commentaries from the front-lines.

But it was not until after the war that Ulughzoda published a more extensive work in prose, *Ëroni bohimmat*, 'Noble Friends' (1947), that deals with the faithfulness of the wives of soldiers fighting in the war. This novelette is characterised by the author's endeavour to depict the birth and growth of his heroes' feelings, and to offer a deep and convincing psychological motivation of their behaviour.

Mention should be made of Ulughzoda's novel *Navobod*, 'The New Land'[64] (1953), one of the first to deal with *kolkhoz* life in Tajikistan, the new ways of farming on large fields, the construction of irrigation canals, the aspirations of Tajik women for higher education, and in general the struggle between the old and the new in the south of the country, in the Vakhsh Valley. The book was an object of wide discussion among Tajik and Russian critics. As this debate showed, in spite of its shortcomings the novel is a very good document of its times and from the artistic point of view too it contributed greatly to the development of young Tajik prose. In 1954 Ulughzoda published another work, the autobiographical novel *Subhi javonii mo*, 'The Dawn of Our Youth'. In this book the author followed in the footsteps of his teacher, Sadriddin Aĭnī; the opening part of the novel in particular has much in common with the first volume of Aĭnī's Memoirs, except that Aĭnī writes about village life before the Revolution, while Ulughzoda depicts the life of the rural Tajik population during the Revolution and in the post-revolutionary period up to 1926. Ulughzoda's novel, particularly its first half, represents an important phase in the writer's creative development, and its language, too, is far more advanced compared with his previous novel *Navobod*.[65] Every page of this novel is a page taken from the life of the writer's own generation, and the fate of its hero – the young Sobir – is the fate of thousands of Ulughzoda's contemporaries. The book describes the disintegration that preceded the end of the First World War and the upheaval of the first years of Soviet power, the famine, the *basmachi* raids, the backwardness of the country, etc.; at the same time, however, it describes the forces that brought about the great change. Like Aĭnī's *Ëddoshtho*, 'Memoirs', Ulughzoda's novel is, in fact, a series of short narratives which can exist separately but are linked through the character of Sobir.[66] *

Ulughzoda's comedy *Jūyandagon*, 'The Seekers', dealing with the work of Tajik geological surveyors and the help given them by the local population, also dates from the post-war period. It was very sharply criticised in the press during the period of the 'theory of no conflict', and unfortunately has never been produced on the stage. In recent years Ulughzoda has devoted himself exclusively to writing plays and film scripts, including that for the film *Ibni Sino*, 'Avicenna' (1954), written together with V. Vitkovich, and for the film *Qismati shoir*, 'The Poet's Fate' (1957), devoted to the first classical writer of Tajik poetry, Rūdakī. He also wrote the play *Rūdakī* (1958), the very first Tajik biographical drama, depicting the life of the 10th-century founder of Persian and Tajik poetry, who is so dear to all Tajiks. Ulughzoda's witty comedy *Gavhari shabchirogh*, 'The Precious Jewel' (1961) was proposed for the award of the 1962 Rūdakī Prize[67]; it has been very popular because it includes many new characters, has a truly humorous plot, and, in particular, is written in a beautiful language which perfectly fits every character and is spiced with folk-proverbs, turns of speech and wisdom.

Ulughzoda's language in general is most remarkable. He uses original expressions and phrases, while his diction reflects a positive influence of the Russian language. The author spares words in his descriptions, but does not thereby lessen the artistic impact of his writing.[68]

One of Sadriddin Aĭnī's most devoted disciples is the leading Tajik prose-writer Jalol Ikromī, the author of numerous short stories and of several novels and dramas. He was born in Bukhara in 1909 as the son of a judge, but lost both his parents at an early age. He graduated from a Soviet teachers' college and produced his first writings as early as the second half of the 1920's.

Ikromī's first short story, *Shabe dar Registoni Bukhoro*, 'Night at the Registan of Bukhara', was published with Aĭnī's support in the magazine *Rahbari donish*, in 1927. It contrasted the life of pre-revolutionary Bukhara with Soviet reality. In 1933, inspired by the story 'A Week' by the Russian author Y. N. Lubedinskiy, Ikromī produced his first novelette, *Du hafta*, 'Two Weeks', and some time later, his second, *Haët va ghalaba*, 'Life and Victory', both of which deal with the struggle against the *basmachi* bands. Another novelette, *Tirmor*, 'The Snake', is concerned with an interesting stage in the history of Soviet Tajikistan – that of agrarian reform. All these shorter pieces were a preparation for Ikromī's first novel, *Shodī*. The first volume of this novel was published in 1940 and deals with the beginnings of the collectivisation drive in Tajikistan. The author was obviously inspired by Sholokhov's *Virgin Soil Upturned*, but this does not in any way detract from the value of his own novel. After the war, Ikromī rewrote this first volume quite extensively and wrote a second volume, which describes life at the collective farm after Shodī's return from the front, thereby producing a work which ranks high in Tajik prose.[69] During the war Ikromī wrote short stories and commentaries on front-line heroes; outstanding among them is the story *Ocherki mardi tankshikan*, 'The Story of a Tank Destroyer' (1944), but in some other stories of this type he abandoned realism and wrote of unreal, fairy-tale heroes who are alien to modern times, as in the case of the story *Mekhtarobod*.[70] Ikromī also wrote a patriotic drama, *Dili modar*, 'The Mother's Heart' (1942), about a heroic mother, and a year later, in collaboration with A. Faĭko, produced a sequel, *Khonai Nodir*, 'Nodir's House', on the defenders of Stalingrad. Ikromī's post-war novelette *Javobi Muhabbat*, 'Muhabbat's Answer' (1947) and his comedy *Sitora* never became popular; the comedy especially was criticised for the schematic nature of its characters. This is also the fault of Ikromī's next play, *Rohi muhabbat*, 'The Road of Happiness', dealing with the construction of the railway line to Dushanbe in 1929. In 1954, Ikromī dramatised Aĭnī's novel *Dokhunda*; the play, bearing the same title, has been on the repertoire of Tajik theatres ever since. Ikromī also continued writing short stories. In 1955 he published the rather long story *Ghussa*, 'Grief'. His psychological novel *Man gunahgoram*, 'I Am Guilty', concerns the problems of family, love and morals; it was first published in instalments in the magazine *Sharqi Surkh* (1957) and later in book form; artistically it is one of the best novels in Tajik literature. It was criticised for shortcomings of an ideological nature, but this does not lessen the literary value of the work, the first in Tajik literature to deal with this theme. In 1960 Ikromī published another novelette, *Tori ankabut*, 'The Cobweb', describing the events of the Revolution in Bukhara when the enemy, according to their own words, worked like spiders, enveloping honest people in their cobweb of intrigue. The novelette contains basically the stories of three people – to a certain extent a parallel to the classical stories of *Chor darvesh*, 'The Four Dervishes', or the tales of the Arabian Nights. In 1960 Ikromī began publishing another novel, *Dukhtari otash*, 'The Daughter of Fire' in the magazine *Sharqi Surkh*. This appeared in book form in 1961. It is a three-volume historical work, one of the greatest achievements of Tajik prose after Aĭnī's novels. *Dukhtari otash* offers an excellent picture of the life of the common folk in Bukhara in the early part of the 20th century and their aspirations for freedom. For the first time in Tajik literature the novel includes * among its principal characters a beautiful type of woman. In recent years Ikromī also wrote two additional plays of which *Khor dar guliston*, 'A Thorn Among Roses', in particular was well received. Finally, Ikromī is the author of a number of successful biographical sketches, as well as articles on literature and art.

The teacher, and subsequently journalist and writer, Rahim Jalil was born in Khujand in 1909 as the son of a small artisan. He still lives in his native town, the present-day Leninobod, as a leading literary figure and the teacher of new literary talents. Like most Tajik writers, Jalil started his literary career as a poet and in 1933 published his first collection, *Mavjhoi muzaffariyat*, 'Waves of Victory', which contained poems about the new people of Soviet Tajikistan, the builders of a happy future. Soon, however, he devoted himself entirely to prose, and in 1936 published his first collection of short stories under the title *Orzu*, 'Desire', again concentrating on topical problems. His next collection of stories was published in 1939 under the title *She'rho va hikoyaho*, 'Poems and Stories', while the third one, *Hissa va qissa*, 'Tales', came out in the first year of the war; it contains mostly essay-type stories which are outstanding for their artistic form, fresh language and humour. Jalil laughs at senseless family quarrels, distrust, laziness, superstition, etc. He demonstrated his talent in the story *Margi*

Notes on pp. 601–605

Khushomadkhūja, 'Khushomadkhūja's Death', telling of the futile life and death of a formerly rich man, a covert enemy of the Soviet regime. Just before the war Jalil produced his first novel, *Gulrū* (1941), which shows a strong influence from Aĭnī's work. It contains one of the very first realistic portraits of the new Tajik woman. After the war Jalil re-wrote and completed his novel; it was published under a new title, *Odamoni jovid*, 'Immortal People', and undoubtedly ranks among the most successful post-war Tajik works of prose. The plot covers the revolutionary history of Tajikistan in the years 1926 and 1927. It depicts especially the political developments in northern Tajikistan, while Aĭnī, the only other prose-writer who dealt with this theme, concentrated on the revolution particularly in the southern and mountainous part of the country (especially in his novel *Yatim*, 'The Orphan'). During the war Jalil wrote essays on various heroes of the Red Army (e.g. *Pisarjon*, 'Sonny') and such successful short stories as *Komsomol*, *Bobo va nabera*, 'Grandfather and Grandson', *Hodisa dar front*, 'A Front-line Event', and others. He published them in the collection *Hikoyahoi zamoni jang*, 'Stories from the War Years' (1944), mostly again in essay form. Another collection of his is *Umri dubora*, 'Double Life', containing mainly stories on war themes and themes describing the fraternal relations of the various nations inhabiting the Soviet-Union. Jalil's next collection, *Hikoyaho*, 'Stories' (1954) was not well received because most of the tales it contains are unrealistic, just as his subsequent stories *Vasvasabonu*, 'The Temptress', and *Laĭlatulqadr* (1957). In 1956 Jalil began publishing in instalments his next long novel, *Angishtkanon*, 'The Miners', which was subsequently published in book form under the title *Shūrob* (1959). This is the first large Tajik literary work with a theme from working-class life. It covers the pre- and post-revolutionary period and describes the growing revolutionary consciousness of the people and their struggle against the feudal regime. The novel depicts the historical roots of the fraternal relations between the Tajiks, the Russians, the Uzbeks, and other nationals who worked at Shūrob, and was justly praised; it was criticised only for its language. After the novel *Shūrob*, Jalil wrote many short stories, the most outstanding among them being *Pushaĭmonī*, 'Sorrow' (1960); Shukurov believes that Rahim Jalil is the only author who has produced good short stories in recent years.[71] The publication in instalments of the second volume of the novel *Shūrob* began in 1964. Jalil also returned to play writing. In 1961 he rewrote his older musical drama *Subhi sahro*, 'The Dawn of Fields', and in 1963 produced the drama *Dili shoir*, 'The Heart of the Poet', dealing with the great poet of his native town, Kamol Khujandī.

Rahim Jalil is a talented prose-writer, whose work is characterised by optimism, a youthful spirit, sincerity, love of life and work[72], and who is at his best in humorous stories.[73] Even his serious short stories have distinct traces of humour, which gives them an optimistic character.

Foteh Niëzī (born in 1914), the son of a clerk from Samarkand, studied literature at the Uzbek Paedagogic Academy and has been actively engaged in literature ever since his youth. He first wrote poetry, also in Uzbek, but without much success. In

1938 he joined forces with Samad Ghanī in writing the play *Vatandūston*, 'The Patriots', depicting the life of the border guards in Tajikistan. He fought in the Second World War and his subsequent literary work was concentrated primarily on short stories and novels on war topics. He also wrote literary commentaries, rich in historical material. In 1947 he published a collection of short stories and commentaries under the title *Intiqomi tojik*, 'Tajik Vengeance'. Outstanding in this collection are the stories *Baĭraq*, 'The Flag' and *Rūmolcha*, 'The Scarf', both dealing with front-line heroes. His stories are characterised by the author's good knowledge of the subject-matter, truthfulness, sincerity and a lyrical tone.[74] Niëzī's work reached a peak with the two volumes of his novel *Vafo*, 'Loyalty', the first Tajik literary work devoted to the participation of the Tajik nation in the Second World War – in the defence of the Soviet-Union. The first volume was published in 1949. It describes rural life in Tajikistan at the outbreak of the war, and relates how the farmers send gifts to soldiers at the front and how they themselves leave to defend their country. It also tells of the hard fighting in the steppes along the Don River in 1942 and the defence of Stalingrad. The hero of the novel is Safar Odinaev, a young Tajik brought up under the Soviet government. The novel also depicts the friendship in battle of members of the various nations and nationalities living in the Soviet-Union. In 1957 Niëzī published the long-awaited second volume of his novel under the same title. It is a sequel to the events described in the first volume, and deals mainly with life behind the front-lines. It was criticised for some faults, especially a lack of pace in some parts.[75] In 1955 Niëzī published a successful novelette, *Dukhtari hamsoya*, 'The Girl From the Neighbourhood', which deals with the relationship between man and woman and the prejudices that still prevail in Tajik society in this respect. This novelette was published in a collection together with a number of short stories and journalistic essays written between 1950 and 1956 on various themes. Niëzi has also had success with another collection of stories of the events and heroic people of the Second World War, *Hissae az qissahoi jang*, 'Tales from the war' (1962) as well as with travel reports.

2. POETRY

The life and creative development of the second generation of Soviet Tajik poets were calmer and more balanced than those of the prose-writers. Outstanding among the second-generation poets is Mirzo Tursunzoda. He was educated in new Soviet schools and in the Komsomol, and is a member of a generation devoted to socialism and to service to the people. Tursunzoda was born in the *qishloq* Qarotoq, in the Shahrinav region, in 1911, as the son of a small artisan. Since his early youth he was interested in poetry to which, after completing, his studies he subsequently devoted his whole life. He did not begin, however, by imitating any of his predecessors, but entered poetry as a promoter of new ideas and a seeker of new ways.[76] From the first his work has

Notes on pp. 601–605

shown the poet's exceptional talent and has steadily improved; this is as true of his first small propaganda poems and the short tales included in his first collection, *Baïraqi zafar*, 'The Banner of Victory', as it is of his large *dostons* and opera librettos. Notwithstanding the wide scope of his themes and form, Tursunzoda is primarily a lyrical poet, and a lyrical excitement and passion mark all his works, as for example, his remarkable *doston Joni shirin*, 'Dear Soul' (1959). His poetry is characterised by the simplicity of its language and its folk-style, which is undoubtedly due to his love of folk-literature, of which he has been a devoted collector ever since the early 1930's. In 1940 he published a most valuable anthology of folk-poetry, *Namunai fol'klori tojik*, 'Samples of Tajik Folklore', which was later published in a new edition in co-operation with A. N. Boldïrev. Besides images taken from folklore, he has also used folklore motifs in his works; this is true, for example, of his great poem *Tohir va Zūhra*, 'Tohir and Zuhra'. Tursunzoda's work also reflects his profound knowledge of classical Tajik poetry, especially – as he himself notes – that of the master of Persian and Azerbayjani poetry, Niẓāmī Ganjavī (p. 210 *et seq.*).

Notable among Tursunzoda's pre-war works is the *doston Khazon va bahor*, 'Autumn and Spring' (1937), written in the traditional *mathnavī* form but on a contemporary theme. In 1933, Tursunzoda wrote one of the very first Tajik dramas – *Hukm*, 'The Verdict' – a play aimed against the nationalistic trends surviving in some groups of intellectuals. In the late 1930's Tursunzoda published a large collection of poems under the simple title *She'rho*, 'Poems', which show the poet's further progress both as regards the scope of his themes and the impact of his poetic images and means of expression. Noteworthy among these poems are one called *Vodii Hisor*, 'The Hisor Valley', in which the author compares old times with the present, combining lyrical and autobiographical elements, and *Ganjinai surūdho*, 'A Treasure Chest of Songs', a history of the Tajik people and their culture in verse. Another poem that should be noted is *Dildili Zaïnab*, 'As You Wish' (1939), which was dramatised after the war. The poet himself, however, is somewhat critical of this first stage of his work, admitting that his first poems contained too many 'mediaeval' allegories and outdated images. An important part of Tursunzoda's work before the war was the libretto written jointly with Dehotī for the first Tajik opera, *Shūrishi Vose'*, 'Vose's Uprising' (1939) on a theme taken from recent Tajik history.

During the period of the Second World War, Tursunzoda already ranked first among contemporary Tajik poets. He published the *doston Pisari vatan*, 'A Son of His Country' (1942), a *mathnavī* on the friendship of the Soviet nations and on Soviet patriotism.

As a mature poet he reached the summit of his creative talent and won the respect of his nation after the war, when he extended his themes and the problems dealt with in his poems beyond the borders of his country. He became famous for poems that sang of the struggle of the subjugated eastern nations against colonialism; these include two cycles written after the poet's journey to India, under the title *Qissai Hinduston*, 'The Indian Ballad' (1947), which were soon translated into other languages.

A *baït* from Tursunzoda's poem *Tojmahal* was engraved above the gate of the world-famous mausoleum in Agra. Another notable poem is *Arus az Moskva*, 'The Bride from Moscow' (1945), the story of the love between a Tajik girl and a Russian that blossomed during the war at the front-line; its theme was later used for the libretto of another Tajik opera, *Arus*, 'The Bride'. The poem is interesting on account of its containing a great number of such classical turns of speech as 'light-footed gazelles', 'discourse between the nightingale and the rose', etc., which no longer appear in Tursunzoda's poems about India.[77] The *doston Mavji tabrikho*, 'A Wave of Greetings' (1950) is remarkable for its changing forms (*mathnavī* and *murabba'*), rhyme and metre. Other outstanding works are the collections *Man az Sharqi ozod*, 'I, From the Free East' (1951) and *Sadoi Osië*, 'The Voice of Asia', that contain poems which are a logical sequel to the poems from India, being devoted to the current life of Asia, especially India. They include, for example, the great poem *Dukhtari muqaddas*, 'The Holy Girl', dedicated to India's new women and to friendship between the Soviet and the newly liberated Indian peoples. Tursunzoda sings of the people of his own country in a cycle of eight lyrical poems entitled *Dar kishvari tojik*, 'In Tajik Land' (1952). One of the poet's greatest post-war creative achievements is his exemplary synthesis of folk-poetry and classical literature[78], the *doston Hasani arobakash*, 'Hasan the Cart-Driver' (1954), which reflects some of the history of the post-revolutionary development of Tajikistan – the transition from the *aroba*, the Central Asian two-wheel cart, to the lorry – the idea of Russian–Tajik co-operation, as well as some autobiographical elements. The poem abounds in lyrical sidelights – the narrator's own reminiscences – and is written in a rich vernacular containing many proverbs and folk-sayings.

The two cycles, *Sadoi Osië* and *Hasani arobakash* earned the poet the 1960 Lenin Prize. In 1956 he published the epico-lyrical *doston Charoghi abadī*, 'Eternal Light', in which he tells of the birth of a child and recalls Bukhara's past, personified by Sadriddin Aïnī. The poem is full of philosophical thought. Tursunzoda's recent successes include the lyrical *doston Joni shirin*, 'Dear Soul' (1959) – a synthesis of the poet's love for his wife and family, of love for awakening Asia and Africa, and love of his native country. *

It should be said that Tajikistan's National Poet Tursunzoda is also intensively active in public life, holding as he does leading offices in the Union of Tajik Writers, being a member of the Tajik Academy of Sciences, as well as of the Supreme Soviet of the Tajik Socialist Republic, and engaged in the world peace movement. After the war he published a collection of journalistic articles dedicated to the cause of peace and progress under the title *Sulh bar jang ghalaba khohad kard*, 'Peace Shall Prevail Over War' (1950); they were written in the tradition of Gorky and Ehrenburg.

The poetry of Mirsaid Mirshakar occupies a special position among the works of Tajik poets. It is dedicated to the people of his native Pamir; in particular, his poems are written in a language and on themes close and readily intelligible to Tajik readers. On more than one occasion Mirshakar has been criticised for not having mastered

Notes on pp. 601–605

the technique of classical poetry – he does indeed draw mainly on folklore and has introduced metre used in folk-poetry, which is inadmissible in verse written according to the norms of classical poetry.

Mirshakar was born in 1912, in the small village of Sidnev, in the present-day Autonomous Badakhshon Mountain Region, "in a region which before the Revolution was less known than mysterious Tibet".[79] Mirshakar's father, a peasant, died soon after the poet's birth. The orphan boy attended the school in Khorūgh and from 1928 to 1930 studied in Dushanbe. Then he worked for some time as editor of the magazine *Komsomoli Tojikiston*, 'The Tajik Komsomol', and as secretary of the Komsomol organisation at the Vakhsh Hydro-electric Project and editor of the local newspaper. Since his early youth he enjoyed reading classical poetry, and poetry remained his hobby during his studies and work in the Komsomol organisation. Eventually it became his profession. As a young poet he was strongly influenced by Mayakovsky's inspiring verse (he met Mayakovsky personally at the Komsomol Congress in Moscow in 1929), and published his poems in the newspapers on which he worked. In 1934 he published his first longer poem, the *doston Livoi zafar*, 'The Banner of Victory', written in the classical *mutaqorib* metre and dedicated to the builders of the Vakhsh Dam. It is an immature work but already has some features that characterise Mirshakar's subsequent poetry – its wit, topical theme, youthful élan, simple language and simple form point to a promising talent. Mirshakar's second book is a collection entitled *Bahori javonī*, 'The Spring of Youth', published in 1940 and containing poems on various themes: *ruboīs* of a political nature, verse singing of the Red Army, poems directed against the traditional veil worn by women, as well as lyrical poems written in the style of classical *ghazals*. However, Mirshakar prefers to write longer poems – whole *dostons* rather than shorter forms. He reached the summit of his pre-war work with the great poem *Qishloqi tilloī*, 'The Golden Qishloq', which was subsequently, during the war, re-written into a work of high poetical standard and was set to music in 1964. The poem is based on an ancient folk-legend from the Pamir about a Happy Land, the age-long dream of the oppressed people. Ten young villagers set out on a long journey to find this Happy Land, but everywhere they go, they find oppression and poverty. The sole survivor of all the deprivations and suffering which they encounter on their way eventually returns home to discover that the Happy Land – the Golden Qishloq – is his native village, which had changed during his absence – under Soviet government – into a happy abode of free people. The poem is an interesting synthesis of an old legend and contemporary life. The poet did not preserve the original theme of the folk-tale but chose only its essence – the aspiration of the people for a happy future. He shows that the ancient dream of the Pamir mountaineers is being realised at the present time and that happiness should not be sought abroad; rather, it should be built at home. This ideologically and artistically outstanding work is written in classical metre (*hazaj*).

During the war, like other Tajik writers, Mirshakar wrote of heroism at the front and behind the lines, and the poems produced in this period were published in the collection *She'rho va poemaho*, 'Verses and Poems' (1945). The content of his war-time poetry is characterised by the poet's feelings towards the enemy – he does not condemn the German nation but only the fascist clique that drives the Germans to destruction. Mirshakar's other longer wartime poems include the *doston Odamoni az Bomi Jahon*, 'Men From the Roof of the World' (1943), dedicated to the work of miners; it is a *doston* written in the classical metres *ramal* and *khafif*, but with an irregular rhyme – a novelty in Tajik poetry. There is also *Qasami Teshaboĭ*, 'Teshaboĭ's Oath' (1942), a poem about a brave Tajik soldier and the friendship between the Soviet nations. Finally, during the war Mirshakar also wrote satirical poems in the form of anecdotes about the enemy; these are contained in particular in the cycle *Az daftari Afandī*, 'Afandī's Diary'.

After the war Mirshakar once again returned to poetry, mostly in praise of his country's happy life and peaceful coexistence. He has written several *dostons*, a number of shorter poems, as well as magazine articles and literary essays and criticism. One of the most important of his post-war works is the great poem *Kalidi bakht*, 'The Key to Happiness' (1947), another fairy-tale combined with real life, in which the poet shows that real life can be better than a fairy-tale. He tells of treasures in the Pamir Mountains, the legendary key to which has been acquired by the people of present-day Tajikistan. Between 1947 and 1949 Mirshakar wrote another *doston*, *Panji noorom*, 'Unfettered Panj', perhaps his greatest and best work. In it the poet describes the happy life of the Pamir villagers of our days and the hard service of the frontier guards on the river Panj who protect the frontier against foreign enemy agents. In 1951, after a longer interruption, Mirshakar produced another play, *Shahri man*, 'My Town', that was well received both by the public and the critics, especially in its second and improved version called *Fojiyai Usmonov*, 'Usmonov's Tragedy'. The play deals with the important problem of new urban construction. Among Mirshakar's more recent works note should be taken of the *doston Dashti Laband*, 'The Lazy Steppe' (1961), dedicated to the endeavour to reclaim new land and to the negative features of the period of the personality cult. *

An important section of Mirshakar's work is a number of short and long poems for children and young people. Mirshakar is, in fact, the most important of the founders of Tajik children's literature, to which he has devoted himself from the very beginning of his literary activity, both in practice and in theory; he has written a number of articles on this topic and presented many reports at international congresses. Note should be taken at least of the collection *Mo az Pomir omadem*, 'We Came from the Pamir' (1954) and the great poem *Lenin dar Pomir*, 'Lenin on the Pamir' (1955), which was highly praised and which again makes use of a folk-theme. Mirshakar's latest works for children include a collection of poems, songs and *dostons* published under the title *Bahori Tojikiston*, 'The Spring of Tajikistan' (1959), and *Bachagoni Hinduston*, 'Indian Children' (1961); some of the poems are completely free of the traditional norms, which fact has been criticised by some Tajik literary critics.

Notes on pp. 601–605

Habib Yusufī (1916–1945) of Samarkand was one of the prematurely deceased members of the Komsomol generation of Tajik poets. He studied to become a teacher and graduated in 1940. He published his first poem in 1936. He learned the art of poetry by translating Pushkin and especially Lermontov, who deeply influenced his original work.[80] Yusufī was a lyrical poet; his poetry was initially a simple play with words, but he soon improved.[81] His later work is characterised by its originality of thought, the depth of its themes, and the simplicity of its language. Yusufī's verse basically follows the rules of the *arūz*, more varied in form than in the case of other poets, but in his last works he used some elements of a new metre. He published his first collection of poems in 1939 under the title *Taronai Vatan*, 'Song of My Homeland'; it contains poems, translated verse, and more than a hundred quatrains. One of the most interesting among them is the poem *Tak'ya bar korat kunī*, 'Rely On Your Own Work' (1938), in which the poet presents quite a new conception of love, in contrast to the imitators of the ancient *ghazals*. He praises his beloved not for the beauty of her tresses but for her noble deeds and conduct. The poem is in the form of a *ghazal* and intentionally contains some traditional images in order to contrast them more intensively and with greater impact with the new system of Soviet poetry.[82] In 1938, Yusufī wrote the poem *In Vatan zinda dar jahon mebod*, 'Let This Homeland Live in the World', which condemned the surrender of Czechoslovakia to Hitler.

During the war Yusufī continued his creative progress, and his patriotic poem *Intiqom*, 'Vengeance' (1941) is one of the best of its kind. From 1942 onwards Yusufī fought at the front and was awarded the Order of the Red Star. In one of his letters to Sadriddin Aĭnī, Yusufī wrote: "I have heard that some of my friends are trying to arrange for my return to Stalinobod. I am very greatful to them for their concern, but please tell them that I shall return to Stalinobod only via Berlin." Unfortunately, Yusufī did not live to see his home again. He was killed in action shortly before the end of the war in the battle of Warsaw.

Another member of the Komsomol generation was the outstanding poet, writer, essayist, literary critic and folklore collector, Abdusalom Dehotī. He was born at Boghi Maĭdon in 1911. He first attended an old, Moslem school, but soon transferred to a new, Soviet school. After graduation he worked as editor on various Tajik newspapers and magazines and in publishing houses. He wrote his first verse and short stories as early as 1928, when he also published his first essays, *Hamidai siëhbakht*, 'The Unfortunate Hamida', and *Ajinaho*, 'Evil Spirits', which show a marked influence of Aĭnī's *Odina* and *Ahmadi devband*, 'Ahmad the Magician' (p. 562). However, Dehotī's main interest was poetry, and in 1934 he published his first collection, *Taronai mehnat*, 'Song of Labour', and soon after his only *doston*, *Manzarahoi segona*, 'Three Views'. He usually chose topical themes: the life of the socialist village, the struggle between socialism and capitalism, the emancipation of women, etc. He won great success with his lyrical quatrains which combine the simplicity and charm of folk *ruboīs* with new ideas and images. During the war he wrote poems praising the help provided by the people behind the front-lines to the Red Army and voicing their affection for and trust in the defenders of their homeland. Dehotī also wrote plays; his drama *Nur dar kūhiston*, 'Light in the Mountains' (1947) had as theme the history of the struggle against the enemies of Soviet government. He collaborated with B. Rahimzoda in writing the comedy *Qissayi Taʿrifkhūjaev*, 'Taʿrifkhūjaev's Story' (1953), which some critics did not like. His next play was *Komde va Madan*, 'Komde and Madan', for which he used one of the themes from Bedil's *Irfon*, the legend of love prevailing over death (p. 518). After the war Dehotī continued writing poems on socialistic themes. He published several collections; in 1949 it was *Asarhoi muntakhab*, 'Selected Works', while a new selection under the same title was published in 1957. In his last years Dehotī published a number of poems and essays from his travels abroad in Japan and Afghanistan, which appeared in various Tajik periodicals.

Dehotī held an important position in the Union of Tajik Writers. He was active in publishing classics of Tajik literature, was an outstanding collector of Tajik folklore (he published the book *Latifahoi tojikī*, 'Tajik Anecdotes'), played an important role in the publication of a large Russian-Tajik dictionary, and also wrote books for teen-agers as well as text-books. Dehotī died on January 31, 1962, soon after the publication of his latest poems, short stories, commentaries, and travel essays, entitled *Haët qadam mezanad* (Life Goes On, 1961) and after the celebrations marking his fiftieth birthday, which were held throughout Tajikistan.

Boqī Rahimzoda is a poet who worked mainly during and after the war. He was born in the village of Sorbogh, in the Gharm region, in 1910. Rahimzoda's work is characterised by his preference for *ruboīs*, which contemporary Tajik poets have not been using to any great extent. Rahimzoda artfully combined this folk and classical form with a new content, with praise of man who is transforming Nature and for whom work is a matter of honour. According to M. Tursunzoda's speech at the 1961 congress of the Union of Tajik Writers, Rahimzoda has mastered classical poetry but has not become its slave. Some of his poems are used as lyrics for songs performed by folk-singers throughout Tajikistan. Of his published works, note should be taken of the collection *Ba front*, 'At the Front' (1945), containing poems honouring the fighters against the invader, and of another collection, *Kūhistoni durakhshon*, 'The Brilliant Mountains', published in 1948 and dedicated to his socialist homeland, the friendship of the Soviet nations, to women, heroes of labour, etc. As already mentioned, he wrote with Dehotī the comedy *Qissayi Taʿrifkhūjaev*, 'Taʿrifkhūjaev's Story', which was criticised on account of some ideological shortcomings. He joined with his colleague Saidmurodov to write another play, from kolkhoz life, in the style of the pre-revolutionary folk-comedies, under the title *Chinori guë*, 'The Talking Plane Tree'. The poems written between 1960 and 1963, praising the achievements of the Tajik people and world progress, were published in the collection *Boli hunar*, 'The Wings of Art'. Boqī Rahimzoda actively encourages new poetic talent. *

Boltaqul Mahmudov, known under the *takhalluṣ* Diërī (he was born in Samarkand

Notes on pp. 601–605

in 1915), is one of the experienced poets who wrote modern poetry as early as the beginning of the 1930's. His first collection, *Navbahori mehnat*, 'The Spring of Work' (1933), as well as those he published subsequently, like *Shukufahoi haët*, 'The Blossoms of Life' (1934), contain poems chiefly dedicated to kolkhoz life, the Soviet army, and the struggle against religious superstition. After the war he published the collections *Kūli bulūrin*, 'The Crystal Lake' (1954) and *Zamburi asal*, 'The Bee' (1955), the verse in which has been criticised especially on account of shortcomings in the artistic treatment.

Just like many other Tajik poets, Tillo Pūlodī (born in 1912 in the *qishloq* Darmorakht in the Pamir Mountains) too was originally a teacher. This is due to the fact that, in the early years of Soviet Tajikistan, the primary objective was the elimination of the oppressive heritage of illiteracy and the earliest possible development of education for all the people. Pūlodī's first poems were written shortly before the war; they again praise his Soviet homeland and his native Tajikistan. In 1948 he published the collection *Badakhshoni ozod*, 'Free Badakhshon', containing poems about the great changes taking place in his native Pamir Mountains. Pūlodī has often published poems in various periodicals. In 1958 he published in book form a collection of poems dedicated to peace and his country under the title *Nomai bakht*, 'In the Name of Happiness', and in 1962 another collection, *Bahori shodī*, 'The Spring of Joy', containing poems on similar themes.

Although he writes in Uzbek, Ashūrmat Nazarov, an Uzbek born in 1913 in the *qishloq* Nov, in the Leninobod region, belongs to Tajik literature. This poet and essayist, who died in 1964, published from 1934 on several collections of poems, in most of which he praises the socialist construction of Tajikistan; his poems have often been translated into Tajik. His best works include the *doston Kofarnihon buida*, 'On the Banks of the Kofarnihon' (published under the Tajik title *Dar sohili Kofarnihon* in 1948), a hymn in praise of heroic work, a great poem depicting the struggle of Tajik women for higher cotton yields, the primary goal of Tajik economy. As a soldier who took part in the Soviet army's victorious advance and in the liberation of Cracow, Auschwitz and Prague, he wrote the *doston Mening ūlkam*, 'My Country' (published under the Tajik title *Kishvari man* in 1951), a dramatic poem devoted to a most interesting theme – the attitude of Soviet soldiers to the East-European nations that they liberated. Nazarov's *doston* also contains new formal elements – each story has an introduction briefly acquainting the reader with the depicted event. In 1958 Aminzoda translated into Tajik Nazarov's *doston Kheshovandon*, 'The Relatives', while in 1962 Nazarov published the excellent story *Chupon va Saïëd*, 'The Shepherd and the Hunter'.

Hamid Obidī (1911–1948) is one of the less known poets. He published his first poems as early as 1933, in the collection *Qadamhoi Komsomol*, 'The Steps of the Komsomol'. Subsequently he published several other collections and during the war produced the *doston Deputati qahramon*, 'The Brave Deputy' (1945).

Nosirjon Ma'sumī (born in the *qishloq* Qaratoq, in the Shahrinav region, in 1915) is primarily a literary historian and theorist, but he has also published several collections of poems and should therefore be mentioned among the poets as well. The most interesting of his poems is the autobiographical *Javonii man*, 'My Childhood', which depicts the Civil War in Qaratoq.

H. THE 'THIRD' AND 'FOURTH' GENERATIONS

I. POETRY

The Tajik people, like most other nations of Central Asia and Iran, have a great feeling for poetry. Even simple folk like to listen to recitations of verse and like to create poetry themselves. Poetry still holds sway among the broad masses of the Tajik people[83], as indicated by the relatively large editions of books of poetry. It is only natural that this wide base should produce many good poets. Besides those already mentioned there are many older, but mainly young, beginning authors who are trying to enter the literary scene and whose poems may be occasionally found in periodicals or even in first collections. Quite obviously, the present study cannot cover all these poets, but at least brief mention will be made of the most talented, poets who have already demonstrated their skill and some of whom will undoubtedly play an important part in Tajik literature. The endeavour to deal with the most important problems of their people, to present a vivid picture of the new Soviet man, inspires young authors to write epic *dostons*, a genre which is very popular among Tajik readers. The best works of the young poets, as well as prose-writers, are usually published in various anthologies. In recent years these have included *Qalamhoi purumed*, 'Promising Pens' (1957), containing the works of 20 young poets and 11 prose-writers, the collection *Iste'dodhoi javon*, 'Young Talents' (1961), with the works of young authors from the Leninobod region, and *Muzhda*, 'Good Tidings' (1962), a collection of verse by 34 young poets and stories by 14 new prose-writers.

The list of young poets must undoubtedly be headed by Ghaffor Mirzo (born in 1929), whose first verse, dating from the years 1948 and 1949, struck the attention of readers by its specific nature and high artistic standard. This young poet acquired his militant tone from Mayakovsky, while his models for style were Paĭrav Sulaĭmonī and Yusufī.[84] Some of his poems were published in the collection *Hazor rahmat*, 'A Thousand Thanks', in which every verse reflects the poet's gratitude to his socialist homeland. Another successful work was the autobiographical *doston Asror* (1956) containing almost 2500 verses. This was translated into Russian as early as 1957 and was awarded a high Soviet literary prize. Less successful was Mirzo's lyrical *doston Toji davlat*, 'Wreath of Happiness' (1958).[85] A passionate debate took place on his next *doston*, *Sesadu shastu shash pahlū*, '366 Degrees' (1962), which describes events taking

Notes on pp. 601–605

place on various days of the year and deals with the most burning problems facing the Soviet people. This *doston* reflects Mirzo's desire to seek new ways in poetry, one of the most dominant features of the poet's creative nature. Mirzo is one of the few Tajik poets who has abandoned the use of the *arūz*.

After publishing two rather weak collections, M. Farhat (Hasanov) – born in 1924 – published a collection of poems under the title *Nazmi ozodī*, 'Poetry of Freedom' (1955), which sings of the beauty of his homeland, the wealth of its towns and villages, peace, etc. Essentially he is a traditionalist, who also writes poetry for children. * Children's literature is also the forte of the young poet Abdumalik Bahorī (his real name is A. Rahmonov and he was born in 1927). The most outstanding among his published collections is the third, *Dar oghushi maktab*, 'In the School's Arms' (1955), and the very successful collection of poems and stories for children published in 1957 under the title *Qarzi jūragī*, 'A Debt to Friendship'. In 1958 he published yet another collection of poems and short stories entitled *Odamoni shinos*, 'Known People'. Finally, his latest collection of poems and prose-writings, *Dili bekaror*, 'The Uneasy Heart' (1962), demonstrates the poet's continued creative growth. Another of the successful * younger poets is Aminjon Shukūhī (Hojiboev, born in 1923), whose verse is full of lyrical inspiration and whose cycle *Muhabbat va oila*, 'Love and Family' deals with serious social problems. His collection *Sadoi dil*, 'Voice of the Heart' (1957) contains most of the poems written since 1947. Shukūhī is one of the best contemporary Tajik lyrical poets and his songs are extremely popular because of their national colour. It is therefore not surprising that the edition of his new poems, published under the title *Nafasi garm*, 'Hot Breath' (1964), ran to tens of thousands of copies. It also contains Shukūhī's first epic work, the opera libretto *Kūchaboghi oshiqon*, 'Lovers' Lane' (1962). This depicts the post-war confusion and contradictions in considering the cases of prisoners of war returning from Nazi camps and the eventual victory of sound reason over the distrust generated in the period of the personality cult. *

Several collections of poems have already been published by Abdujabbor Qahhorī (born at Koni Bodom in 1924). Note should be taken in particular of *Ovozi saodat*, 'The Song of Happiness' (1948), *Shuʿlai dil*, 'The Flaming Heart' (1948), and several other collections of poems with themes of love and peace, of war-time and peace-time heroism. His poems dedicated to Afghanistan, *Ohanghoi dūstī*, 'Voices of Friendship' (1964), abound in profound human feeling. As early as 1942, Qahhorī wrote a children's play, *Qahramoni javon*, 'The Young Hero'; he is also the author of several popular * songs. Faĭzullo Ansorī (born in 1931) is another of the better known younger poets. In 1954 he published his first collection written on the theme of a folk-tale, *Kalkhot va kabūtaron*, 'The Eagle and the Dove', while his second collection – also containing lyrical poems on his native land and love – was published under the title *Guldastai dūstī*, 'Flowers of Friendship' in 1957. In 1956 and 1957 he wrote several good *dostons* and surprised the critics in 1958 with his first drama, *Imtihon*, 'The Examination', the action of which takes place at a university. The young author has continued writing plays. In 1959 he produced *Haët va ishq*, 'Life and Love', again from the life of the intelligentsia, the same theme being used in a third play which appeared on the stage at Dushanbe in 1962, after having been re-written under the title *Hukmi modar*, 'Mother's Verdict'. This drama in verse deals with problems of the current young generation. *

The critics were favourable towards the collection of poems by Abdujalil Vositzoda, published in 1955 under the title *She'rho dar borai tabiyat*, 'Poems of Nature'; it describes the magnificent landscape of Tajikistan. His lyrical poems, written between 1947 and 1956, were included in another collection, *Dar sohili Sir*, 'On the Banks of the Syr Darya' (1957). Vositzoda's short stories, published in the collection *Diloro* (1964), are rather weak. The talented poets of the younger generation also include Hojī Bobo (born in 1928), who has been writing poetry ever since his student days; his first collection was published in 1956 under the title *Nasimi bahoron*, 'Spring Wind'. It contains poems describing the busy contemporary life of Tajikistan, as well as lyrical love poems. His other collection, *Izhori muhabbat*, 'An Expression of Love' (1961), demonstrates the poet's progress as an artist. The collection of poems by the young poetess of Iranian origin, Bade' Zhola, published in 1956 under the title *Modaron sulh mekhohand*, 'Mothers Demand Peace', was well received by the critics and the public. Her drama in verse, *Parastu* (1962), dealing with the life of workers at Ābādān, is * truly remarkable. The older poet, writer and former Minister of the Tajik Republic, Habibullo Nazarov (born 1907), published his first collection of poems, *Baroi sulh*, 'For Peace', in 1957. In 1958 he published a remarkable work, *Dar justujūi Karim-Devona*, 'In Search of Karim-Devona', which depicts in a most attractive manner the search for data concerning the life and the literary heritage of the folk-poet Karim Devona. However, in 1964 the book became the subject of a heated dispute when some folklore experts blamed the author for being insufficiently critical of the collected works of the folk-singer. *

There is yet a large group of poets of the youngest generation whose poems appear regularly in the press; some of them have already published collections in book form. We should list Mū'min Qanoat, whose collections *Sharora*, 'The Spark' (1960) and *Sitorahoi zamin*, 'Stars of Earth' (1963) show the young poet's talent. In his *Balladai sitorahoi Kreml*, 'Ballad of the Kremlin Stars', Qanoat touches on the disastrous consequences of the personality cult. Ubaĭd Rajab writes chiefly children's verse. The young lyrical poet Qutbī Kirom published the successful collection *Parvozi mehr*, 'Flight of Love' (1963), and the verse of the poetesses Gulchehra Sulaĭmonova and Mavjuda * Hakimova often appear in the press. The latter is the author of sincere poems on work and love published in the collection *Surudi sahar*, 'Song of the Field' (1964). Other talented and promising young poets are Akobir Sharifī, M. Haĭdarsho, Sheralī Maston, Alī Bobojon, and S. Halimsho Loiq, Ozod Aminova, Farrukh Burhon, to name only a few.

Notes on pp. 601–605

2. PROSE

Although prose has gained in importance in modern Tajik literature to an unprecedented extent and has gained in popularity among Tajik readers, strong tradition still makes it lag behind poetry in respect of both the number of authors and the number of published works. There are scores of talented young poets, but the number of young prose-writers is much smaller.

An already established figure in Tajik prose is the gifted story-writer Pūlod Tolis (whose real name was Tolstoĭ Pūlotov – he was born in Leninobod in 1929). He published his first story in 1946 and subsequently wrote a number of short stories on various themes: life and work on collective farms, friendship between the Soviet nations, the importance of culture, etc. Many of them, unfortunately, show a strong didactic trend. He was greatly influenced by Gorky in the selection and treatment of his subjects.[86] He published several collections of stories: *Charoghho*, 'Lights' (1948), *Dar sari rohi kalon*, 'On the Great Road' (1954), and *Hikoyahoi dah sol*, 'Stories of Ten Years' (1957). Tolis also published the novelette *Javonī*, 'Youth', dedicated to the young people who went to cultivate virgin lands in the eastern parts of the Soviet-Union. Many of Tolis's stories have been translated into Russian. He published another novelette, *Tobiston*, 'Summer', in instalments in the magazine *Sharqi Surkh* in 1958. It deals with the life of young people behind the front-lines in World War II. After it had been criticised for being too far removed from real life[87], the author rewrote it, and the result is an outstanding work remarkable for its content and its language. Tajik prose suffered a heavy blow when this talented writer died prematurely in 1961.

One of the story-writers whose names often appear in the Tajik press, and one of the great hopes of Tajik prose, is Fazliddin Muhammadiev (born in Samarkand in 1928), the author of a long story from military life, *Porchai ostin*, 'A Piece of Sleeve' (1956), and several long essays. His first book – a collection of essays and two longer stories – was published in 1959 under the title *Muhojiron*, 'The Settlers'. His novelette *Odamoni kūhna*, 'The Old People' (1962), about simple Tajiks, old in years but young in their zeal to build up a new life for themselves, deserves special mention, just as the fact that it was Muhammadiev who introduced into Tajik literature the detective or spy story – the novel *Tiri khokkhurda*, 'The Rotten Arrow' (1960), which, however, is not without its faults. Muhammadiev also translated into Tajik Aĭtmatov's *Jamila*. Hojī Sodiq, a journalist from Leninobod, is the author of short stories and theatrical plays. *

Rajabboĭ Amonov is the author – among others – of the short stories *Khatoi islohshuda*, 'The Corrected Error' (1955), *Zindagī*, 'Life' (1957), and the long story *Dar domanai kūhsori kabud*, 'At the Foot of the Blue Mountains'[88], about the life of the young Tajik intelligentsia. Amonov is primarily interested in folklore and has written several essays and articles on this topic. Usmon Tojī is an older, experienced writer, but he did not publish his first collection of short stories, *Kashfi asror*, 'Discovered

Secret', until 1959. Before that, in 1957, he published a small treatise on literary history, *Bistu se adiba*, 'Thirty-Three Poetesses', in which he briefly discusses the most important Tajik poetesses of the pre-revolutionary period (10th to 20th centuries). Qodir * Naimī is the author of the unassuming novelettes *Rohi durust*, 'The Proper Way' and *Rūzi ravshan*, 'Bright Day' (1957). He also wrote the drama *Soli 1916*, 'The Year 1916'. The most promising younger writers of Tajik prose include Yusufjon Akobirov, whose stories and essays were followed by the novelette *Ba'dē ki osiё bozmond...*, 'When the Mill Stopped Running...', (1963), describing, as do the works of most young authors, contemporary life in Tajikistan, and *Dukhtare ki justu-jūyash mekunam*, 'The Girl I * Seek' (1963), obviously inspired by Aĭtmatov's *Jamila*.

M. Boghirov occasionally publishes short stories, essays and especially children's stories in the press, just as B. Ortiqov, whose first novelette *Ta'til*, 'Vacations' (1959), * depicting the life of young people, was criticised both favourably and unfavourably by the leading Tajik literary experts. Other writers of the youngest generation include R. Haĭdarov, whose short stories deal with serious social problems, for example the changing attitude of men towards women. His first collection of short stories was published in 1964 under the title *Du dildoda*, 'Two Lovers'. There is also the journalist M. Najmiddinov, whose first collection of stories and essays, *Odamoni sarbaland*, 'Serious People', was published in 1963 and seems to promise more from the young author. M. Rustamova is a short-story writer who joined forces with her colleague, L. Qiēmova, to write in 1960 a play about workers with the title *Jūyanda-ёbanda*, 'He Who Seeks, Finds'. In recent years Lutfī Said published in particular a cycle of 'stories from real life' (*hikoyahoi voqeī*) under the title *Pesh az subh*, 'Before Dawn'. H. Askar has been writing short stories and plays, while A. Sharifī, M. Sharqī, Usman Usmanov, and others have produced successful stories for children. M. Khūjaev shows a promising talent, while stories from contemporary Iran are the favourites of Akbar Hamidī.

J. THE DRAMA

Tajik drama has been mainly identified with the poets and prose-writers mentioned in the previous sections – the names Ulughzoda, Tursunzoda and others will again appear on the following pages. Nevertheless, it is useful to review Tajik drama, even though only briefly and from the point of view of its basic features.[89]

Until 1929, the Tajiks had no professional theatre or a drama of their own as we understand it today, even though there was a certain tradition – performances by folk-singers, dancers, story tellers and folk humorists (known as *maskharabozī*). There was a popular marionette theatre (*zochabozī* or *lukhtabozī*), and old drawings seem to indicate that plays had been performed already in ancient Panjikent. But there were no written texts. The formation of Tajik drama was also influenced by the leading works of classical literature, in particular Firdavsī's *Shāhnāma,* which abounds in dramatic passages. To these traditional components we must add the great impact of Uzbek and Russian drama, which was introduced to Tajikistan by Azerbayjani, Tatar and Uzbek theatrical companies. Finally Shakespeare, whose plays have been produced by Tajik theatres ever since the 1930's, has also had some influence.[90] The jadid period contributed nothing to Tajik drama. While the jadids had written some seventeen plays by 1917, these were all written in Uzbek, quite in keeping with jadid pan-Turkism. The plays dealt mostly with problems which also predominated in the jadid press – religious reform, educational reform, and so on. Their heroes were *boĭs, domullahs,* journalists, etc.[91], and if a common man of the people ever appeared in them, he was depicted as a naïve simpleton. A typical example of this type of play was Behbudī's *Padarkush,* 'Parricide' (1913), a drama with no literary value, an extremely naïve plot, a highly artificial composition and a clumsy language.[92]

The cultural revolution in Tajikistan under the Soviet government urgently needed the theatre, for only the theatre could effectively communicate ideas to the mainly illiterate population. For this reason a Tajik national theatre was founded in Dushanbe between 1929 and 1930. Initially it staged chiefly Uzbek plays, but gradually Tajik authors began to supply it with their first dramatic works. The very first Tajik play produced in Dushanbe was Samadī's *Eshoni firebgar,* 'Ishan the Swindler' (1929). It was soon followed by Muinzoda's *Margi rūza,* 'Death of the Fast' (1929) and A. Aminzoda's *Navrūz va Gulchehra,* 'Navrūz and Gulchehra' (1929). These are all simple plays which have much in common with traditional folk-performances, but nevertheless constitute the first timid steps forward. The period from 1929 to 1933 may be considered as that of the birth of Tajik realistic drama, which also includes the plays of the young Rahim Jalil, *Muhabbat* (1932) and *Saodat* (1932). The first Tajik play which meets the standards of good play-writing is Abulhaq Usmonov's *Muboriza,* 'Struggle' (1932), which depicts the fight against the *basmachi* bands. Nor was the drama produced in this first period spared from the harmful influence of local nationalists of the type of Fitrat, whose activities were criticised especially by Tursunzoda in 1932. Even in this apprenticeship period, Tajik drama already possessed such important features as ideological consistency, folk-character and proximity to real life. The heroes of these early plays were people who struggled against everything that hindered progress. Of course, from the formal point of view, the plays were far from good.

I. FROM 1933 TO 1941

The success of the play *Muboriza* encouraged other authors to try their hand at play-writing, and with the help of Russian experts plays began to be produced which far surpassed the standard of the early attempts; Tajik drama, which was closely linked with the totality of Soviet dramatic production, was on the rise, both with respect to its quality and the number of plays written. One of the outstanding plays of this period is Mirzo Tursunzoda's drama *Hukm*, 'The Verdict', written in 1933 and directed against the nationalist trends prevailing among some of the intellectuals. Next was Jalol Ikromī's *Dushman*, 'The Enemy' (1933), the first play on a theme from factory life; all previous plays dealt with village situations. It was also the first of a series directed against saboteurs. A very important period for the development of Tajik drama was the second half of the 1930's. This was the time when most of the good dramatic works were produced, including comedies, opera librettos, and plays for children and young people. We may single out in particular Ikromī's *Tukhmi muhabbat*, 'A Grain of Love' (1936) dealing with the life of Tajik cotton-growers – a play that is considered one of the best ever written in Tajik – and the libretto for the opera *Shūrishi Vose'*, 'Vose's Uprising' (1939) written by Tursunzoda and Dehotī; this was the first national Tajik opera. Another good play, *Tūhmat*, 'Calumny' (1938), again based on kolkhoz life, was written by Sulton Saidmurodov and Ismat Ismoilov. Saidmurodov, a playwright, actor and stage director is one of the pioneers of Tajik theatre. Ulughzoda is the author of the drama *Shodmon* (1939), in which he deals with the conflict between the promoters of the new life and all the manifestations of backwardness at the time of the consolidation of the kolkhoz system in Tajik villages. Ulughzoda's next play, *Kaltakdoroni surkh*, 'Red Clubs' (1940), has as its principal theme the strengthening of Soviet patriotism which took place at the time Tajik volunteers, known as the *kaltakdoron* – 'people armed with clubs' – fought with the Soviet army against the *basmachi* under their leader Ibrohimbek, who invaded the southern part of Tajikistan in 1931. Another successful Tajik play is the first Tajik tragedy, *Rustam va Sūhrob*, 'Rustam and Sūhrob' (1936), written by the young Tajik playwright Abdushukur Pirmuhammadzoda (born at Boghi Maĭdon in 1914, killed in action on the battlefield in 1942), the brother of the poet Dehotī and one of the talented writers who unfortunately lost their lives in World War II. He wrote the play together with Ghanī Abdullo and later re-wrote it in collaboration with the Russian playwright Volkenshteyn.

A playwright of the Komsomol generation is Ghanī Abdullo (born in Samarkand in 1912). After graduating from a teachers' college, he entered the literary scene in 1932. First he wrote Uzbek poetry and in 1934–1935 produced his first Tajik play, *Vodii bakht*, 'The Valley of Happiness', about the building of the Vakhsh River hydro-electric project. Soon afterwards, he wrote the musical drama *Shūrishi Vose'*, 'Vose's Uprising' (1936), and subsequently produced a number of other plays. However, in 1937 he was forced out of literary life, which he resumed only after the elimination of the personality cult.[93]

During this period, too, Tajik writers produced a number of good plays on subjects reflecting the life and struggle of the Tajik people, the only exception being Pūlodī's *Dukhtari Eron*, 'The Girl from Iran' (1934), a less important play whose theme ranges beyond Tajikistan's borders. The other plays are concerned with various problems, following the aim of strengthening the ideas of humanism, Soviet patriotism, collectivism, etc. The authors use mainly a simple language, which is close to the vernacular and includes popular turns of speech and terms, as well as dialect – often in excess, as in the case of Ulughzoda's *Shodmon.*[94] Tajik critics usually consider as the best plays produced in this period *Shurishi Vose'* (Tursunzoda), *Shodmon* and *Kaltakdoroni Surkh* (Ulughzoda), and *Tūhmat* (Saidmurodov and Ismoilov).[95]

2. FROM 1941 TO 1945

The drama produced during the war, like all other literature, was based on themes believed to be of the utmost importance at a time when the whole country was geared to defence against the enemy, fight against traitors, and the heroism of Soviet people at the front and behind it. At the beginning mostly short one-act plays were written, to be followed, after 1942, by full-length, more powerful dramas. The war helped Tajik drama take another step forward. In 1942 and 1943 Jalol Ikromī wrote two plays based on real wartime events: *Dili modar*, 'Mother's Heart', dealing with the selfless endeavour of the civilian population to help the army in the field, and *Khonai Nodir*, 'Nodir's House' (1943), the best play of this period, with as subject the heroic defence of Stalingrad and the friendship of the Soviet nations fighting against the common enemy. A great cultural event was the production of the first Tajik opera *Kovai ohangar*, 'Kova the Blacksmith', on the stage of the newly opened Opera and Ballet Theatre in Dushanbe; the libretto for this opera was written by Lohutī. Other important works produced in this period include Ulughzoda's play *Dar otash*, 'Under Fire' (1944), depicting the heroism of the unknown soldiers of the Second World War. In 1943, Tursunzoda wrote the verse libretto for the opera *Tohir va Zūhra*, 'Tohir and Zuhra', based on a folk-tale and using the words of a number of folk-songs.

A musical drama called *Qishloqi tilloī*, 'The Golden Qishloq' (1944), written by Mirshakar on the basis of his famous *doston*, was produced in Khorūgh, while the theatre in Leninobod produced Rahim Jalil's musical play *Du vokhurī*, 'Two Meetings' (1942) about the participation of Tajiks in the partisan warfare behind the Nazi lines. But the play was too topical to survive the war and remain on the repertoire of Tajik theatres.

3. FROM 1945 UP TO THE PRESENT

Since the war the old and experienced playwrights and their younger colleagues have produced many plays, but essentially nothing has changed – Tajik drama continues to lag behind other literary genres and has not met with any response outside Tajikistan[96], in contrast to the best works of Tajik poetry and prose. Immediately after the war several plays appeared, written in the style of the fairy-tales of the Arabian Nights; they idealised the former feudal lords, and the critics rejected them as being ideologically worthless. They include the pseudo-historical play *Tahmosi Khujandī*, 'Tahmos of Khujand' by M. Qosimov and S. Saidmurodov, and *Shabi* 28-*ūm*, 'The Twenty-Eighth Night', and *Dukhtari nokom*, 'The Unfortunate Girl' by Jalol Ikromī, based on Aĭnī's *Ëddoshtho* and aimed at disclosing the dishonesty of the priesthood in dealing with believers.

The plays listed below are only those that have been most successful, for the total number produced by Tajik writers is much greater. A. Dehotī wrote *Nur dar kūhiston*, 'Light in the Mountains' (1947) which is devoted to an important event in Tajik revolutionary history – the heroic fight of a group of teachers from Gharm against the *basmachi* in 1929. M. Qosimov and J. Ikromī wrote the play *Rohi bakht*, 'The Road of Happiness' (1949) on the construction of the first railway line in Tajikistan and the fight against enemies of the Soviet government. Quite a different but no less important theme was chosen by M. Mirshakar for his play *Shahri man*, 'My Town' (1951), which he later re-wrote under the title *Fojiyai Usmonov*, 'Usmonov's Tragedy'. It deals with a conflict between two town planners concerning the architectural concept of building new towns and cities. The older architect advocates the so-called Moorish style as being national in character, while his younger colleague tries to promote a modern, sober style. In contrast to other literature, war themes have hardly appeared at all in recent Tajik drama.

The post-war period is also characterised by an increase in the number of comedies. This category includes Ulughzoda's *Jūyandagon*, 'The Seekers' (1951), about the work of Tajik geologists and the help given by local villagers in finding useful minerals. After this play Ulughzoda, like Rahim Jalil, stopped writing for the theatre for a long time. The next comedy to appear on Tajik stages was *Shodiëna*, 'Present for Happy News' (1950) by the young author Musokhon Zokirov; it is aimed against certain outdated customs. J. Ikromī wrote *Sitora* (1954), a comedy which takes to task some harmful practices in kolkhoz life; there was also a successful stage adaptation of Aĭnī's novel *Dokhunda*. Dehotī's and Rahimzoda's comedy on kolkhoz life, *Qissai Ta'rifkhūjaev*, 'Ta'rifkhūjaev's Story' (1953), has its shortcomings but it was popular with the audiences and Ansorī regrets that it is no longer being produced by the theatres.[97] The comedy *Dil-dili Zaĭnab*, 'As You Wish' (1956), written by the noted stage director and actor Shamsī Qiëmov and A. Moroz, has enjoyed great success for some time now; it is a light play without much ideological content, but skilfully written. It is one of the very first Tajik plays to have been translated into Uzbek and Turkmen and staged at theatres in those two Soviet republics. A play of a similar type is *Chinori guë*, 'The Talking Plane Tree' (1956) by B. Rahimzoda and S. Saidmurodov; it again is aimed against superstition and was produced for the first time on the stage of the Khorūgh theatre, but with little success. One of the good playwrights is M. Rabiev (born in

Notes on pp. 601–605

Samarkand in 1913) who joined S. Saidmurodov in 1948 to write the very successful drama *Saodat*; the play deals not only with family disputes arising out of outdated views on the position of women, but also with the question of introducing modern production methods in farming. In 1956 he wrote another play, *Nomi nek*, 'Good Reputation' which shows the responsibility borne by Communist Party officials at collective farms. In the 1950's, the experienced playwright Ghanī Abdullo again returned to the literary scene; his play *Surudi kūhsor*, 'Song of the Mountains' deals with the important current social question of national traditions, as does Mirshakar's *Fojiyai Usmonov*, by telling the story of a composer who departed from national traditions in his music and eventually lost the understanding of his own people. In 1957 Abdullo wrote another play, *Qarzi Vijdon*, 'A Pledge of Honour', on the life and work of Tajik intellectuals. Early in 1960 the theatre in Dushanbe staged the play *Vijdon*, 'Honour', written jointly by the young author Samad Ghanī and Y. Mitel'man. Some of Ghanī's earlier plays were unsuccessful and even this latest play, *Vijdon*, was criticised on account of the lifelessness of its heroes – that these young heroes, a boy and a girl, "never talk of anything but tractors".[98] One play that stands out above the average is Ulughzoda's *Rūdakī* (1958), the first biographical drama in Tajik literature, depicting the life of the great 10th-century poet.

One of the most promising authors of Tajik drama is F. Toshmuhammadov, even though his play *Darai dar'ëi kabud*, 'The Valley of the Blue River', is not quite up to standard.[99] Another talented young writer is the poet Faĭzullo Ansorī; his first play, *Imtihon*, 'The Examination', on a theme from university student life, was produced on the stage in Dushanbe in 1958 and was qualified by Ikromī as a promising beginning.[100] It has also been played in Uzbek theatres. Soon afterwards Ansorī wrote another play, *Ishq va haët*, 'Love and Life'. His latest dramatic works include the initially unsuccessful *Mebakhshed modar*, 'I Am Sorry, Mother', which he re-wrote under the new title *Hukmi modar*, 'Mother's Verdict'. This lyrical play in verse has as its heroine a mother and conscientious teacher whose children undergo serious moral crises. *Tūfon*, 'The Storm', a play written in 1958 jointly by Ghanī Abdullo and Shamsī Qiëmov, was negatively received by the critics.

At the third plenary session of the Union of Tajik Writers, in 1961, Tursunzoda complained that few plays were being written and that such experienced playwrights as Ulughzoda and others had turned away from the theatre. The situation soon changed and a number of plays have been written since. Many have been published and also staged. These plays were written by the older authors, but, what is more important, many have also been written by new young playwrights. Some of the latter have produced promising works. This is true, for example, of Safar Saĭfiddinov, Sidqī, Nosirov, and others. In 1961 Rahim Jalil published a new version of his older play *Sanavbar* (originally written in 1933) under the title *Subhi sahro*, 'The Dawn in the Fields', while Ikromī similarly adapted his older play *Sitora*, giving it the new title *Man – Fakhriddinov*, 'I am Fakhriddinov'. It condemns irresponsible and selfish hiding of arable land – a problem discussed shortly before by the Central Committee of Tajikistan's Communist Party.

However, many new plays have been written, the most important of these being Ulughzoda's comedy *Gavhari shabchirog*, 'The Dark Jewel' (1962) which was awarded the Rūdakī Prize. It takes to task various defects in human character as they manifest themselves in the daily life of a Tajik village, and its protagonist is masterfully depicted. Rahim Jalil produced a new historical drama in 1963 under the title *Dili shoir*, 'The Poet's Heart'. The author himself says he wanted to present the 14th-century poet Kamoli Khujandī not only as a lover of poetry but also as an advocate of truth and justice.[101]

Another experienced playwright, Jalol Ikromī, enriched the repertoire of Tajik theatres by his psychological drama from the life of Tajik intellectuals, *Khor dar guliston*, 'A Thorn Among Roses'.

Young authors, too, have enriched the repertoire of Tajik theatres with a number of new plays on current themes. For example, A'zam Sidqī's play *Irodai zan*, 'The Woman's Will' (1962), well depicts life on the virgin lands, and its heroine is a typical young Tajik woman. The critics liked Komil Nosirov's play *Tarma*, 'The Avalanche' (1961), which tells of the struggle between the old and selfish, and the new Communist morality. Of the other promising young Tajik playwrights, mention should be made of Muhiddin Saĭfiddinov and Sulton Safarov, to name only two. *

In Tajik opera, the outstanding work is M. Tursunzoda's libretto *Arūs*, 'The Bride' (1945), which he wrote on the basis of his great poem *Arūs az Moskva*, 'The Bride from Moscow'.

As already mentioned above, Tajik drama has been lagging behind other prose, and no truly great, serious and psychological play has yet been produced. Thus the repertoire of Tajik theatres is mostly made up of light comedies without any serious thought behind them.[102]

K. THE FOLK-POETS

Like all the other nations of Central Asia, the Tajiks, too, are very fond of folk-bards, singers and poets. Since time immemorial these itinerant singers have sung and often composed songs, *ghazals* and *dostons*, in which they expressed the aspirations of the common people at times when written literature was not accessible to the commoner. They greatly influenced the formation of new Tajik literature. The verses of these folk-poets, simple artisans and peasants, were however not as a rule recorded in writing, and only some of them have been preserved by oral tradition. Most of them unfortunately fell into oblivion.

The new literature, which came into being after the Revolution, a literature that was designed for the broad masses of the people, necessarily drew on folk-literature. Consequently considerable attention was paid to the folk-poets. Since the second half of the 1920's the periodic press has been publishing folk-poems, and since the 1930's collections of these poems have appeared in book form. The importance attached to folklore by Soviet Tajik literature is reflected in the fact that most Tajik writers have collected folklore and that this particular field has been the subject of increased attention in recent years. This is indicated by the large number of books and treatises published on the folklore of individual regions and on individual folk-poets.

The best products of the post-revolutionary folk-poets are being published in the press and in book form, and the survey of post-revolutionary Tajik poetry would not be complete without the mention, at least, of some of the oustanding *hofizes*, such as Valizoda, Bobo Yunus, Vafo, Kholzoda, and Rizo. Fragments of the works of several other folk-poets who had already died before the Bukhara Revolution have also been preserved – those of the satirist Karim Devona (1880–1918), Fakhrii Rumonī (born in 1840), and a few others (p. 529).

Certainly the most important of the living folk-poets is Saidalī Valizoda, who was born in Chuqurak in 1900. He inherited his talent for poetry from his father, who was also a *hofiz*. Valizoda himself worked as a peasant in his youth, and in his songs and verses he later promoted collectivisation of agriculture. Now he works for the theatre at Kūlob and since 1943 has been a member of the Union of Tajik Writers. In one of his earliest poems, *Dehqoni jabrdida*, 'The Oppressed Peasant' (1917), Valizoda told of the fate of a poor peasant before the Revolution. In 1922 he composed the first Tajik poem about Lenin, *Lenin barodar rahnamo*, 'Lenin, Brother and Leader'. Since the middle of the 1930's his poems have been published in various anthologies, and during the war his *dostons* appeared in book form, e.g. his *Dostoni Jangi Buzurgi Vatan*, 'Doston of the Great Patriotic War'. In 1953 the Dushanbe Publishing House published Valizoda's largest and most mature work, the *doston Nozimi Vatan*, 'Nozim, the Son of His Country' (1952), telling of the heroes of the Tajik nation. One of his latest collections is *Dar vodii mehnat*, 'In the Valley of Labour' (1955), which contains poems dedicated to his native land, praising the help of the Russian people, depicting his own youth in pre-revolutionary Bukhara, showing how emancipated women work as equals side by side with men, etc. The second part of the collection contains satirical poems criticising various shortcomings. On the occasion of Valizoda's sixtieth birthday, a small collection of his poetry was published under the title *Du dodaron*, 'Two Brothers' (1960). Valizoda has been publishing poems written for special occasions in the daily press, for example to mark Gagarin's space flight, the construction of the large dam in Norak, etc.

Valizoda is not the only folk-poet whose works have been published. Thus, in 1950, a collection of the poems of Hikmat Rizo (born in 1894) was published under the title *Surudi Vatan*, 'Song of the Homeland'. Rizo is a *hofiz*, known for his rendering of *Ghurughlī*, the well-known Central Asian epos, and in recent years has been writing poems of his own. He performed for the scholars who attended the XXVth International Orientalist Congress in Moscow in 1960, for which he also composed the song *Ba Moskva*, 'To Moscow'. Tajik readers received with acclaim an epic cycle written by the folk-poet Qurbon Jalil in the style of the epos *Ghurughlī*. In 1953 critics and public were surprised by the *doston Du haët*, 'Two Lives' written by the folk-poet and singer Said Kholzoda (born 1916) and published in the literary magazine *Sharqi Surkh*; in this *doston* Kholzoda compares the life of a common Tajik man before and after the Revolution. In lively language he recounts his own and his father's memories of the oppression suffered by the mountain villagers under the feudal regime.

Great attention is devoted to the study of the late folk-poet Bobo Yunus Khudoĭdodzoda (born in the *qishloq* Kosatarosh in 1870, died in 1945), a man who employed a flowery language and was endowed with great fantasy. From his youth Khudoĭdodzoda had been very popular as a folk-singer. His father was wounded during Vose's uprising (1885) and died soon afterwards. In his songs and poems written before the Revolution he already showed the poverty into which the common people were thrown and tried to rouse them against the oppression in such poems as *Firebgarii boĭ*, 'The Rich Man's Treachery', *Ushr*, 'The Tithe', *Zulm*, 'Tyranny', and others. He welcomed the Soviet government and in the 1920's wrote a *doston* directed against its enemies under the title *Taslim shudani bosmachiho*, 'Defeat of the Basmachi'. In another *doston*, *Pahlavonī*, 'Heroism', he praised those who conquered the Pamir by building a road into it. During the war a number of his *dostons* were published – *Dostoni Muhammadi Ibrohimov*, 'Doston about Muhammad Ibrohim', and *Intiqomgirandagoni khalq*, 'Avengers of the People' about war heroes, as well as other *dostons* on historical and mythological themes, like *Zahhoki moron*, 'Zahhok of the Snakes', *Kutaĭba ibn Muslim*, and *Alī Olimkhon*, which depicted the oppression of the people by the former feudal lords and the people's heroism. The poetry of Bobo Yunus is characterised by the fact that in his social and political poems he also used international expressions adopted from the Russian language, such as 'fabrika', 'traktor', 'gazeta', 'komandir', and others.

Another popular folk-poet was Yusuf Vafo (1888–1945). His work, too, was recorded to a large degree. Vafo had a hard life, having worked as a common labourer, but from his youth onwards he wrote poetry. He was a master of shorter poems, especially *ghazals* and *ruboīs*. His work is not extensive but extremely varied in its content. A selection of his pre- and post-revolutionary poems was published in 1956 under the title *Bo shumo zindaam*, 'I Live with You'.

One of the *hofizes* who writes his own songs is the composer of numerous *ruboiëts* – quatrains – Homid Said (born in Samarkand in 1892). He experienced considerable hardship as a farm labourer and in his verses voiced his admiration for the achievements of the Revolution and his condemnation of those who threatened these achievements. His work, mainly quatrains, was published under the title *Ruboiët*, 'Quatrains' in 1961.

Notes on pp. 601–605

There are also many so-called local poets living at various collective farms throughout Tajikistan, who – unlike the old folk-poets – know how to read and write and are greatly respected in their communities. They include such poets as Mirzo Khūja (1872–1942), Muhiddin Badriddinov (1900–1954), Hasan Sodiqzoda (1909–1958), and of those still alive, Davlat Abdullozoda, Mirzoniëz Huseĭnzoda, Safo Ziëev and many others. The work of these poets shows a strong classical influence.

L. THE STUDY OF TAJIK LITERATURE

The study of Tajik literature has grown from practically nothing. Before the Revolution there had been only *tadhkiras*, which were as a rule uncritical anthologies, and simple books on poetics. Today, with considerable Russian help, the study of Tajik literature, although young, has progressed quite far thanks to a number of highly qualified specialists in such fields as literary theory, history and criticism. It is now customary to subject every new literary work to thorough criticism, while monographs on Tajik literary classics and contemporary writers are being written, and great attention is being paid to the collection of Tajik folklore and publication of works of the folk-poets. Thus far, however, no detailed and systematic history of Tajik literature has been produced; there are only text-books of Tajik literature for secondary schools, and the *Ocherk taʿrikhi adabiëti sovetii tojik*, 'Outline of the History of Soviet Tajik Literature', the first volume of which was published in 1956 and the second in 1957, deals only with literature produced after the Revolution and is somewhat limited in scope. The most recent work of this type is the more voluminous product of a group of Tajik and Russian scholars (Braginskiy, Edel'man, Huseĭnzoda, Tabarov, Shukurov, Demidchik, Hodizoda, Zand, Boboev, Levkovskaya), *Ocherk istorii tadzhikskoy sovietskoy literaturï*, published in Moscow in 1961. Braginskiy's treatise on the whole of Tajik literature included in the book *Istoriya literatur narodov Sredney Azii i Kazakhstana*, that was published in 1960, is more limited in its scope. It should be remembered that the study of the history of Tajik literature from the 16th century onwards was practically initiated by Soviet scholars.

The Union of Tajik Writers plays an important role in raising the standard of Tajik literature. At its regular sessions the Union subjects to criticism the works of its members, still in manuscript[103], and recommends any rewriting that may be needed.[104] Other important institutions are the Decades of Art and Literature, which are held at specific intervals in Moscow (Tajik Decades were held in 1941, 1949, and 1957). Their purpose is to acquaint the Soviet capital with the progress made in the literature of other Soviet nations and, at joint meetings with the scholars of such other nations, to evaluate the achievements and point to the shortcomings. These Decades are preceded by an increased activity on the part of writers, translators and publishing houses because, as a rule, scores of new collections, almanacs and whole works are published in the original and in translation for these occasions. The Moscow Decades have become certain milestones in evaluating the progress of literature of the various Soviet nations. In recent years the Decades have also been held in other Soviet republics.

There seems to be no doubt that the study of Soviet Tajik literature was founded by Sadriddin Aĭnī. The chapter discussing his work listed a number of monographs, many of which contain previously unknown information and a new evaluation, and pointed to Aĭnī's unprecedented work, his first history of Tajik literature, *Namunai adabiëti tojik* (1926). An important subsequent achievement was the publication of a more thorough anthology, which was produced under Aĭnī's guidance by all the leading Tajik literary experts. This work, *Namunahoji adabiëti toçik*, 'Pictures of Tajik literature' (in Roman script), was published in 1940.

The study of Tajik literature is concentrated mainly in institutions of the Tajik Academy of Sciences – the 'Shuʿbai sharqshinosī va osori adab' (Cabinet of Oriental Studies and Literary Memorials) for classical literature, and the 'Instituti zabon va adabiët' (Institute of Linguistics and Literature) for modern and contemporary literature. The latter also possesses a special folklore department. In addition the study of literature is pursued at the Dushanbe University, the Paedagogical Institutes in Dushanbe and Leninobod, the universities in Samarkand and Tashkent, and elsewhere.

One of the oldest literary scholars is Bahrom Sirus (born in 1885) who is also the author of several collections of poems. He has studied classical literature, the *arūz*, published a selection of verses from the *Shāhnāma*, and is now doing research in Tajik folklore. Of the other founders of modern Tajik literary studies, mention should be made of Taraqul Zehnī (born in 1894) and Rahim Hoshim (b. 1908), and Obid Ismatī.

The outstanding literary historian Abdulghanī Mirzoev (born in 1907), who is a member of the Tajik Academy of Sciences, studies primarily classical literature of the 16th to 19th centuries (Saĭido, Binoī, Donish), but has also published many treatises and articles on older literature, especially Rūdakī. Other scholars who specialise mainly in pre-revolutionary literature include Rasul Hodizoda (19th century, Donish), Kamol Aĭnī (Hilolī and other writers), and M. Baqoev (Khusrav Dehlavī and others). Classical and contemporary literature are the subjects studied by Sharif Huseĭnzoda (born 1907), one of the authors of the afore-mentioned 'Outline of the History of Tajik Literature', published in 1956. His critical articles have been appearing in Tajik periodicals ever since 1930. Kholiq Mirzozoda (born 1911) is best known for his monograph on Shohin, and is the author of many critical articles and essays. Nosirjon Maʿsumī (born 1915), himself a poet, specialises in the linguistic analysis of contemporary literary works and of the works of Sadriddin Aĭnī. The latter are also studied by Muhammad Shukurov (born 1926), the author of a voluminous work on Aĭnī's *Ëddoshtho*. The leading younger literary historians and critics concentrating on modern literature include Sohib Tabarov (born 1924), who is professor at the Lenin University

Notes on pp. 601–605

in Dushanbe, and Assistant Professor Y. Boboev. Of the youngest generation, mention should be made, among others, of Atokhon Saĭfulloev, Mas'ud Mullojonov, S. Saloh, and Kh. Otakhonova. Most prominent among the scholars specialising in the theory * and history of drama and Tajik dramaturgy are N. Nurjonov and L. Demidchik, while folklore – a field to which increasing attention is being paid in Tajikistan – is the domain of Rajab Amonov, V. Asrorī and B. Tilavov, to name only three.

Quite naturally too, many Tajik authors write critical literary essays and articles, principally Tursunzoda, Ulughzoda, Rahimī and some members of the younger literary generation. Ikromī and Tabarov also appear in the press as drama critics, while Dehotī, Ulughzoda and many others collect and study folk-literature.

M. THE PRESS

Until the Revolution there was no printing industry on the territory of present-day Tajikistan, nor were any books or periodicals printed there. In the whole of Central Asia, only some 40 Tajik books were published between 1901 and 1917[105], mostly *dīvāns* of classical poets. The only Tajik periodical, *Bukhoroi sharif*, 'Gracious Bukhara', was published in Kogon from 1912 to 1913, when its publication was stopped. Another periodical, *Samarkand*, later called *Oina*, was published between 1913 and 1915, and brought out articles and poems written both in Uzbek and Tajik. All these periodicals were edited by jadids and their readers were mainly the liberally-minded rich merchants of Bukhara.

A tremendous development of the press took place after the Revolution. The first revolutionary Tajik periodical was the weekly *Shū'lai inqilob*, 'Flame of the Revolution'[106], which was published in Samarkand from 1919 to 1921 and devoted considerable space to literature. One of the most active contributors to and collaborators in this magazine was Sadriddin Aĭnī. It was there that he published his first prose work *Ta'rikhi amironi manghitiyai Bukhoro*, 'History of the Manghit Amīrs in Bukhara', and fought against the hostile nationalist ideology of Fitrat and his group. The first Tajik newspaper, *Ovozi tojik*, 'The Tajik Voice', was also published in Samarkand from 1924 to 1930. This newspaper too played an important part in helping the Soviet Tajik writers take their first steps in literature. It also first published Aĭnī's novelette *Odina*. An important moment in the growth of the Tajik press was the establishment in 1927 of the 'Nashriëti Davlatii Tojikiston' (the Tajik State Publishing House), which is still the major publisher of Tajik books. In 1928 the daily paper *Idi tojik*, 'Tajik Holiday', began publication in Dushanbe; it later changed its name to *Bedorii tojik*, 'Tajik Awakening'[107], then to *Tojikistoni Surkh*, 'Red Tajikistan', and finally, in 1955, to *Tojikistoni Sovetī* 'Soviet Tajikistan'. It is still being published under this name. The newspaper served from its very beginning as an outlet for the works of young realistic writers who formed a sort of literary club, the core of the future Union of Tajik Writers. Another periodical which had already earlier played an important role in the development of Tajik literature was the literary magazine *Rahbari donish*, 'Guide to Learning', which between 1927 and 1930 published the works of many a budding poet and writer. Its editorial staff included the talented short story-writer of the first half of the 1930's, Bahriddin Azizī. The satirical and humoristic magazine *Shirinkor*, 'The Jester', began publication in Samarkand in 1926; its successor was the magazine *Mushfiqī*. However it was not until 1953 that a more earnestly conceived satirical magazine was founded in Dushanbe under the name of *Khorpushtak*, 'The Hedgehog'. A magazine of the utmost importance for Tajik literature was *Baroi adabiëti sotsialistī*, published under the editorial guidance of Lohutī and Aĭnī between 1932 and 1937; it published not only a major part of the works of Tajik writers but also literary essays and critical articles. Another literary magazine, *Oktyabr*, appeared for four years between 1935 and 1938.[108] The two periodicals merged in 1938 to become the literary magazine of the Union of Tajik Writers, *Sharqi surkh*, 'The Red East', which again published the latest works of Tajik prose-writers and poets as well as literary essays and critical reviews of new works. In 1964, beginning with issue No. 5, the magazine was given the new name *Sadoi Sharq*, 'The Voice of the East'. Its standard has been steadily rising. A quarterly almanac was also published in Russian; in 1959 it was named *Guliston*, 'The Rose Garden', but it ceased publication in 1962. Important critical reviews, literary essays, articles and news, as well as new poems and short stories, are published in the magazine *Maorif va madaniyat*, 'Education and Culture'.

The growth of culture and the press is indicated by the fact that in the relatively small Tajik Republic, which in 1964 had 2,341,000 inhabitants (of whom 53.1 % were Tajiks, 23 % Uzbeks, and 13 % Russians), a large number of books and periodicals is published every year, and the size of their editions is steadily increasing.[109] Under the Soviet government in Tajikistan, more than 10,000 book titles had been published by 1958 in a total edition of almost 92 million copies, seven and a half million of which were belletristic works.[110]

Summer 1967

NOTES

1. Peoples speaking various Iranian languages and dialects but historically linked for a long period of time (Fārsī-speaking Tajiks, the peoples of the Pamir Range, the Yazghulems, Yaghnobs, *et al.*) consolidated into a single Tajik nation. Their common language is the contemporary literary Tajik language (Gafurov, *Nekotorīye voprosī natsionalnoy politiki KPSS*, Moscow 1959, 76).
2. *Rohbari Donish*, 1928, Nos. 4–5.
3. S. Ulughzoda, 'Maktubi kushod ba rafiq B. Ortiqov', *Sharqi Surkh*, 1961,1, 122.

4. "The British, in their readiness to help the anti-Communist insurgents in Tashkent in 1918, were motivated by the same reasons that had prompted them, in the same year, to undertake a hazardous intervention in Transcaucasia" (George Lenczowski, *Russia and the West in Iran, 1918 – 1948,* 31). See Bibliography C.

5. "Both emirs continued to live in a manner common to most oriental princes in the nineteenth century, trying to ignore the changes that were being produced in the outside world in the social, economic and political fields" (George Lenczowski, *op. cit.*, 29).

6. Cf. e.g. Yu. Aleskerov, *Interventsiya i grazhdanskaya voyna v Sredney Azii* (T. 1959).

7. The *basmachi* were regarded as bandits – see, e.g., *Oriente Moderno*, 2 (1922–1923), 114. G. Lenczowski writes in his book *Russia and the West in Iran, 1918–1948*: "These bands, known as Basmatchi, combined ordinary banditry with patriotism..." (p. 35).

8. "Enver Pasha made the mistake of fighting in Central Asia in the name of the exiled amir" (Olzscha, *Turkestan*, 392). G. Lenczowski states in his book (p. 37) that Enver Pasha maintained contacts with the former amīrs of Bukhara and Khiva in Afghanistan and that he was supported by Great-Britain.

9. Illiteracy among adults is being gradually eliminated. For example, as early as 1924, some 15,000 people were learning to read and write in 152 courses organised in the Bukhara Soviet Republic.

10. In 1961 its original name, Dushanbe, was restored to the city.

11. Cf. Kh. M. Mirzozoda, 'Adabiëti sovetii tojik dar solhoi bistūm', in the volume of articles by the same author, *Mulohizaho dar borai adabiyot* (Dushanbe 1963).

12. *Sharqi surkh*, 1957,4, 17.

13. Z. Rajabov, *Az ta'rikhi afkori...* (Stalinobod 1959), 242.

14. See I.S. Braginskiy, 'K izucheniyu uzbeksko-tadzhikskikh literaturnïkh svyazey', in the volume *Vzaimosvyazī literatur Vostoka i Zapada* (Moscow 1961), 52.

15. A. Saĭfulloev, 'In'ikosi jangi grazhdanī dar nazmi sovetii tojik', in the volume *Ocherkho oid ba filologiyai...*, 56–81.

16. R. Amonov, 'Qaidho dar borai munosibati adabiëti sovetii tojik bo ejodiëti dahanakii khalq', in *Haët va adabiët*, 223.

17. See Z. Usmonova, 'Shoiri muboriz', *Sharqi surkh*, 1960,6, 133.

18. In 1937, Ghanī and Rashid Abdullo, Alikhūsh, Hamdī, Obid Ismatī, Ikromī, Hakim Karim and Vaslī were expelled from the Union of Tajik Writers, and the cases of Rahim Jalil, Aminzoda, Suhaĭlī Javharizoda, and Rahimī were submitted to an investigating commission (*BSA*, 1937, 7-8,40).

19. Inna Levshina, 'Hikoya dar adabiëti sovetii tojik', in the volume *Haët va adabiët*, 205.

20. Many of Aĭnī's works have been translated into Russian and other languages spoken in the Soviet-Union, into most European languages and into Hindi, Arabic, *et al.*

21. *Sharqi surkh*, 1953,4, 8. In the *doston Charoghi abadī*, 'Eternal Light', Tursunzoda views Aĭnī's destiny as the destiny of all Asia.

22. *Sharqi surkh*, 1955,7-8-9; in 1958 it was published in Dushanbe in book form and also in a Russian translation under the title *Korotko o moyey zhizni*. See also *Central Asian Review*, 1,2 (1953), and the article 'Sadriddin Aini, Founder of Tajik Soviet Literature', *New Age Weekly*, 8,1 (1954), 11.

23. *Istoriya literatur narodov Sredney Azii i Kazakhstana* (Moscow 1960), 97.

24. See A. Maniëzov, 'Faoliyati zhurnalistii ustod S. Aĭnī', *Tojikistoni Sovetī*, 1958,89, 3.

25. Aĭnī included in his work more than 200 authors who had been active in Central Asia. He drew his material from some 70 to 80 sources. (S. Aĭnī, 'Javob ë inki musohibo', *Ovozi tojik*, 1927,138, 3; 1927, 139, 4).

26. R. Khadi-Zade, *Istochniki*, 7.

27. Radzhabov, *Iz istorii*, 380.

28. T. N. Kary-Niyazov, *Ocherki istorii kulturī sovetskogo Uzbekistana* (Moscow 1955), 289.
29. In his preface to the collection of poems, *Ëdgorī*, 'Memory' (1935), he states that the range of the metre and the rhyme had become too narrow for describing the achievements of the Revolution. And in his poem *Inqilobi surkh*, 'The Red Revolution' (1923), he writes:

Aĭnī ba yak ghazal natavon sharhi hol kard,
Boyad ba inqilob navishtan kitobi surkh.

(Aĭnī, the events cannot be described in a single *ghazal*/a red book must be written of the Revolution).
30. S. Aĭnī, *Ëddoshtho*, IV (St. 1955), 425.
31. *Dokhunda* was the name used for poor mountain villagers.
32. A Czech translation from Tajik was published in the publishing house *Svět sovětů*, in 1957. A French translation was published in Paris in 1958 under the tilte *La mort de l'usurier*. Jean Rousselot wrote in *Les Nouvelles littéraires* of June 26, 1958, 3, that this work "est une très remarquable nouvelle". It depicts, he writes, an Islamic Harpagon "auprès de qui l'avare de Molière est un monstre de prodigalité".
33. S. Aĭnī, *Is'ëni Muqanna'* (St. 1944).
34. For reviews of the Russian translation of this work in West-European periodicals see: A. Bausani in *Annali*, N.S., 11 (1961), 148–149, and M. Lorenz in *Orientalistische Literaturzeitung*, 1962, 7-8, 402–4. A part of the novel was published in French translation by Gallimard Publishers in Paris in 1957, under the title *Boukhara*. See also note 35.
35. French critics highly praised Aĭnī's Memoirs. Henri Wurmser compares the Memoirs with *The Great House* of the Algerian writer Muḥammad Dib (*(Lettres françaises*, No. 651, 1956, 72), and the review by Paul Grangeon in *Europe*, Nos. 142-143, (Oct.-Nov. 1957), 349–350, is also favourable. Several chapters of the Memoirs were published in an English translation in the *New Orient Bimonthly* (Prague), 1960,4, 20–22.
36. S. Ulughzoda, *Subhi javonii mo* (Dushanbe 1956), 311. (A Czech translation of the relevant chapter was published in the magazine *Nový Orient* [Prague], 1956, 76 *et seq.*)
37. *Dar borai Firdavsī va "Shohnoma"-i ū* (St. 1934); *Shaĭkhurrais Abūalī Sino* (Stalinobod–Leningrad 1941); Aĭnī's articles on Rūdakī in Russian translation were published in the volume: S. Aĭnī, *Ustod Rudaki*, edited by I. S. Braginskiy (Moscow 1959). Aĭnī also published an important article in *Sharqi surkh*, 1940,5, reviewing the results of his search for Rūdakī's birthplace and grave; *Shaĭkh Muslihiddin Sa'dii Sherozī* (St. 1942); *Alisher Navoī* (St. 1948); *Mirzo Abdulqodiri Bedil* (St. 1954); most valuable are such publications of Aĭnī's as *Vosifī va khulosai Badoe'-ul-vaqoe'*", 'Vosifī and Selections from "*Badoe'-ul-vaqoe'*", the text of which has been edited so as to be intelligible to the modern reader, or his edition of the folk tales *Chor darvesh*, 'The Four Dervishes', which he prefaced with valuable notes on the origin and contents of these tales. (For greater detail see R. Hodizoda's article 'Tadqiqoti ilmii Sadriddin Aĭnī oid ba ta'rikhi adabiëti tojik', *Sharqi surkh*, 1950,8, 98–114.)
38. Said Nafisī, 'Musohabat bo mardi buzurg', *Sharqi surkh*, 1963,4, 56–7.
39. S. Aĭnī, 'San'atkori buzurg', *Baroi adabiëti sotsialistī*, 1936,2, 9–12.
40. S. Aminova, *Zhenskie obrazī v tvorchestve S. Ayni*, report on a dissertation by a Candidate of Science (St. 1957), 10.
41. In his polemic with Bektosh, he lists the names of persons who had taken part in the events described in the novels *Odina* and *Dokhunda* (S. Aĭnī, 'Javobi man', *Baroi adabiëti sotsialistī*, 1933,4, 22–23).
42. B. Azizī, 'Ustodi hajvnavis', *Baroi adabiëti sotsialistī*, 1935,11-12, 25–26.
43. *Kommunist Tadzhikistana*, Nov. 28. 1935 ('Privetstvie cheshskogo pisatelya Yuliusa Fuchika').
44. Cf. George Lenczowski, *Russia and the West in Iran, 1918–1948* (New York 1949), 2, 63.
45. M. Zand, *Abulkosim Lakhuti* (St. 1957), 18, 13.
46. *Ibid.*, 33.

47. M. Ishaque in *Modern Persian Poetry* (Calcutta 1943, 146–147) considers *Kreml* and *Inqilobi surkh*, 'The Red Revolution', to be the best works expressing the anti-imperialistic idea.
48. *Namuna*, 586.
49. M. Zand, *Abulkosim Lakhuti* (St. 1957), 89 *et seq.*
50. Published in *Sharqi surkh*, 1961,11, 68-89.
51. *Ocherki ta'rikhi adabiëti sovetii tojik*, I, 49.
52. *Namuna*, 236.
53. See S. Aĭnī, *Vosifī va "Badoe'-ul-vaqoe'"*, 21.
54. *Nový život* (Prague 1954), 593–603. It includes several samples. The Tajik translation of the author's article with a preface by S. Tabarov was published in *Sharqi surkh*, 1964,3, 143–146; Jiří Bečka, 'Ëddoshti yak adib va olimi chekh dar borai Paĭrav Sulaĭmonī', *Sharqi surkh*, 1958,12, 120–123.
55. A large selection of his works was published in Stalinobod in 1959 – *Obidkhūjaev Lutfī, Asarhoi muntakhab*. It includes a preface about the author written by R. Abdullozoda.
56. A collection of satires in verse and in prose was published in 1957 under the title *She'rhoi hajvī*, 'Satirical Poems'.
57. See the reviews by A. Bobojonov, published in *Tojikistani Sovetī*, 1960,4, 2, and by S. Saloh in *Sharqi surkh*, 1960,9, 146–154.
58. Alisher Navoī, *Farhod va Shirin* (St. 1958), 256 pp.
59. Jalol Ikromī, *Sharqi surkh*, 1956,7, 78.
60. *Ocherki ta'rikhi adabiëti sovetii tojik*, I, 95.
61. Ulughzoda in *Baroi adabiëti sotsialistī*, 1935,5, 39–41, in the review of Azizī's collection of poems *Ghalaba*, 'Victory' (St. 1932).
62. S. Aĭnī, *Mirzo Abdulqodiri Bedil*, 109.
63. The year of his birth – 1898 – as listed by N. Nasrulloeva in *M. va M.*, 1962,127, 3, seems improbable.
64. Published in a Czech translation (from Russian) under the title *Vzkříšení země*, 'Resurrection of the Earth', in 1956.
65. See M. Najmiddinov, 'Dar borai povesti "Subhi javonii mo"', *Tojikistoni Sovetī*, 1954,244, 2.
66. A review with excerpts was published in the *New Orient Bimonthly* (Prague), 1960,5, 30–31.
67. Since 1962 the best works of art produced each year in Tajikistan are awarded the Rūdakī Prize.
68. *Ocherki ta'rikhi adabiëti sovetii tojik*, II, 393.
69. The novel, translated into Czech from Russian, was published in 1954 under the title *V gulistánském údolí*, 'In the Valley of Gulistan'.
70. *Ocherki ta'rikhi adabiëti sovetii tojik*, I, 158.
71. M. Shukurov, *An'ana, khalqiyat va mahorat* (St. 1964), 182.
72. N. Levshina, 'Qaĭdho oid ba ta'rikhi taraqqiëti hikoyai sovietii tojik', *Sharqi surkh*, 1955,12, 90.
73. *Ocherki ta'rikhi adabiëti sovetii tojik*, I, 197.
74. N. Levshina, *op. cit.*, 96.
75. M. Tursunzoda in his speech at the 4th congress of Tajik writers. *Sharqi surkh*, 1959,3, 108 *et seq.*
76. A. Saĭfulloev, 'Saroyandai ideyahoi kommunizm', *Tojikistoni Sovetī*, 1956,304, 2.
77. S. Kirsanov, 'Polet poezii' *Tadzhikskaya sovetskaya literatura*, 219.
78. See Y. Boboev, 'Oid ba mas'alai an'ana va navovarī dar ejodiëti Mirzo Tursunzoda', *Sharqi surkh*, 1957,6, 121. The same author wrote a detailed monograph on the occasion of Tursunzoda's fiftieth birthday, *Haët va ëjodiëti ū* (St. 1961).
79. M. Mirshakar, 'Zametki k moyey biografii', *Guliston*, 1959,1, 182.
80. *Ocherki ta'rikhi adabiëti sovetii tojik*, I ,116.
81. N. Ma'sumī, 'Poet – boets', *Tadzhikskaya sovetskaya literatura*, 277.
82. *Ocherki iz istorii tadzhikskoy literaturī*, 440.
83. R. Hoshim, 'Sūhbat bo rafiqoni javon', *Sharqi surkh*, 1962,1, 114.

84. M. Shukurov, 'Ba'ze mas'alahoi mahorati badeii shoironi javon', *Sharqi surkh*, 1955,8, 70.
85. Tursunzoda at the 4th congress of Tajik writers, *Sharqi surkh*, 1959,3, 101. Also, M. Shukurov, 'Dar khususi dostoni "Toji davlat"', *Sharqi surkh*, 1958,11, 120–128.
86. R. Khadi-Zade, 'Gor'kiy i tadzhikskaya literatura', *Tadzhikskaya sovetskaya literatura*, 25.
87. Tursunzoda at the 4th congress of Tajik writers. *Sharqi surkh*, 1959,3, 100.
88. *Sharqi surkh*, 1960,2-3-5 and 6.
89. See also 'The Stage in Central Asia', *Central Asia Review*, 3,2 (1955), 135–149.
90. Nizom Nurjonov, 'Shekspir dar sahnai tojik' [Shakespeare on the Tajik Stage], *Sharqi surkh*, 1964,4, 66–74.
91. Dungan, 'Dramaturgiyai jadidon', *Baroi adabiëti sotsialistī*, 1936,6, 27–30; 1936,7, 23–26.
92. Z. Radzhabov, *Az ta'rikhi* ..., 392 *et seq*. A satire on this play was written by Sadriddin Aĭnī, see *Tojikistoni Sovetī*, 1958,82, 2.
93. In his memoirs, entitled *Dar vodii bakht*, 'In the Valley of Happiness', he speaks of the profound impression made on him by Julius Fučík, a Czech journalist and national hero, during his visit to Tajikistan (*M. va M.*, 1964,55 and 58).
94. *Voprosī ist. tadzh. sov. dramaturgii i teatra*, 255. (See Bibliography D11b.)
95. *Ibid.*, 257.
96. S. Tabarov, 'Dramaturgiyai tojik ba'd az Dahrūzai adabiët va san'at', *Sharqi surkh*, 1958,6, 100.
97. *Haët va adabiët* (St. 1958), 267 and also 45.
98. Tursunzoda at the 3rd plenary session of the Union of Tajik Writers, *Sharqi surkh*, 1961,7, 28.
99. N. Nurjonov, L. Demidchik, 'Dramaturgiyai tojik dar davrai hozira', *Sharqi surkh*, 1957,8, 109.
100. *Tojikistoni Sovetī*, 1958,3, 3.
101. A. Saĭfulloev, 'Maktabi ejodii navisanda', *M. va M.*, 1964,59, 3–4.
102. Tursunzoda at the 4th congress of Tajik writers. *Sharqi surkh*, 1959,3, 124.
103. See, e.g., S. Aĭnī in his preface to *Margi sudkhūr*, 'The Usurer's Death'.
104. In 1960 the Union had 62 members; in the period between its 3rd and 4th congresses (i.e., between 1954 and 1959), it admitted 20 new members: six poets, five prose-writers, one playwright, three literary critics, three folklore specialists and two translators (*Sharqi surkh*, 1959,3, 126). The chairman of the Union has been for many years Mirzo Tursunzoda. The Union has a very active branch in Leninobod headed by the writer Rahim Jalil. *
105. *Ocherki iz istorii tadzhikskoy literaturī*, 392. The first printing works existed in Central Asia as early as 1868 (M. Holdworth, *Turkestan in the Nineteenth Century*, 35 *et seq.*) and their output was, of course, quite large, but most of it was in the Uzbek language.
106. See Z. Radzhabov, *K kharakteristike pervogo sovetskogo zhurnala na tadzhikskom yazīke "Plamya revolyutsii"* (St. 1959).
107. See 'Avvali gazetai tojikī', *Tojikistoni Sovetī*, 1959,44, 1.
108. Both magazines were printed in Latin script.
109. In 1963, 547 book titles were published in a total edition of 4,139,000 copies, of which 359 titles were Tajik, 25 Uzbek, and 161 Russian. 112 of the titles were belletristic works and their total edition amounted to 761,000 copies. In that same year, 29 newspapers were published with an annual edition of 102 million copies, as well as 43 magazines, of which two million copies were printed (Figures quoted from *Pechat' SSSR v 1963 g.*, Moscow 1964).
110. *Bolshaya sovetskaya encyklopediya*. Yezhegodnik 1960 (Moscow 1961).

JIŘÍ CEJPEK

IRANIAN FOLK-LITERATURE

General Remarks concerning the Terminology:

English usage prefers to say 'folk-literature', which in some cases is not entirely accurate. Only folk-books, folk-prints and some forms of religious folk-drama were composed and actually handed down in written form. On the other hand the folk-epics, both of the heroic and of the romantic type, of all sizes, have a long oral tradition. Their reduction to writing is only a result of collecting the folk-traditions in the course of folkloristic research. Therefore it is hardly adequate to speak of 'folk-literature' in the case of the above-mentioned orally transmitted forms. It is difficult to translate the German 'Volksdichtung' by 'folk-poetry' because of the ambiguity arising from the fact that 'folk-poetry' also means the verse forms of folk-literature (see Chapter IX) likewise transmitted in the oral form only.

As the terminological criteria applying to European and Oriental folkloristic research are divergent, I beg the reader to excuse the inevitable compromises.

By 'folk-tradition' must be understood all genres of folk-literature, whether handed down by word of mouth or in written form.

I. INTRODUCTION

A. CONTRASTS BETWEEN FOLK-LITERATURE AND POLITE LITERATURE

The boundaries between folk-literature and polite literature are neither definite nor clearly marked; on the contrary they intermingle freely and influence each other in such a manner that it is very often difficult to classify a work correctly.

The most decisive differences are those of style. Folk-tradition generally shows a distinct preference for a simpler style. Linguistically, works of folk-literature are characterised by the smaller number of Arabic words they contain compared with works of polite literature. Arabic loan words are used only to the extent that they are indispensable in the every-day speech of the least educated. Thus the Iranian element also predominates in the vocabulary.

Although in the case of most European nations, the fact that a certain work has been handed down in written form or orally can be seen as an important criterion for its classification for polite literature or folk-tradition respectively, this is not true for Iran. Some forms of Iranian folk-literature do not fit into the usual classification of European folk-literature, for a large number of Iranian folk-books have been handed down and given a definite shape in writing or in print. Dramatic folk-literature occupies an intermediate position as it makes use of written stage directions as well as orally transmitted models, while we also find a large measure of oral improvisation.

In general one might say that polite literature catered for the taste of the ruling classes and took their part against their enemies, and that folk-literature satisfied the cultural needs of the common people dominated by the comparatively small upper classes of society.

It is impossible to regard the folk-tradition as homogeneous in its ideology. Next

Notes on pp. 615–616

to undoubtedly progressive judgments on the faults and imperfections of society, there are also sentiments that are frankly unprogressive. An explanation might be that the ruling classes, aware of the value of literature, wrote small works (most often trashy and full of obscurantism) themselves or had them written by their literary hacks for the people, with the aim to discourage them – since they were uneducated and could seldom read and even more seldom write – from contemplating the burning problems of social antagonism. Apart from this, really worthwhile literature was for the most part accessible only to the nobility, the rich and the more educated among the priesthood, partly because of the scarcity of manuscripts and the high cost of copying or, in later years, of printing, and also because of the cultural and educational gulf between the common people and the upper classes. Folk-prints were therefore well suited, by idealising the way of life of the feudal upper classes of Iranian society, to dull the awareness of class differences and to disorganise the united front of the have-nots against the rich.

The area covered by Iranian culture is rich in linguistic variety[1], although nowadays the schools are beginning to level out these differences. But for a long time most of the language boundaries have formed no restriction for the subjects of either folk or polite literature. It is therefore rather difficult to separate Iranian subjects from those of Indian origin, and likewise to decide what is of East-Turkish derivation. Generally one can without exaggeration regard a considerable number of Iranian folklore elements as international in the best sense of the word, for in the area under discussion motifs and subjects were mixed frequently and with rich results. For the cause of this phenomenon one has to look to the historical circumstances of these regions – integration of various peoples happened more than once in Turkestan.[2] Consequently one cannot exclude the possibility of many themes, traditions and separate details having been transmitted from the original Iranian population to the nowadays East-Turkish-speaking inhabitants. Without going into the reasons, it is undoubtedly true to say that in most places the original Iranian population had for many centuries shown little resistance to turkization. Although the conquered had adopted the language of the conquerors, from a cultural point of view the former were at least a step ahead of the latter. It is understandable therefore that the disappearance of Iranian *ethnos* in Turkestan did not mean the disappearance of Iranian folklore subjects; on the contrary, an impressive number of these served as a foundation for countless developments in polite literature as well as folk-tradition, particularly among the East-Turkish peoples of Central Asia.[3]

B. DIRECTIONS OF DEVELOPMENT OF IRANIAN FOLK-LITERATURE

The real and decisive cause of the final separation, completed in the 16th century, of the Iranians – Persians in the west, Tajiks in the east – was their religious antagonism. From this time onwards, western Iran adhered to the Shīʿa and the inhabitants of the river basin of the Amu-Darya to the Sunna.[4]

The breach did not of course take place suddenly but was the result of a two-way linguistic development that had started very early on but began to be more productive only after the two cultural areas had become established as separate entities. These dividing influences have become particularly effective in recent years. When the Tajik written language was formed, its most natural sources were used, namely the colloquial language and local dialects.[5] Nevertheless the differences between modern Persian and the Tajik language are slighter than those between Low and High German; the most essential are the Tajik peculiarities regarding conjugation, verbal periphrasis, vocabulary, phraseology, and syntax.[6]

Far more conspicuous are the differences between specific folklore subjects, while opposing confessional principles, both in religious folk-literature and in the religious legends, are the most strongly marked of all.

These differences of faith come least to the fore in the heroic epics, where a great many pre-Islamic elements remain, and only exceptionally do we come across subjects that have been islamised, and then mostly only superficially. In the romantic epics Islamic or islamised motifs and subjects have become more common. The degree of religious colouring varies from case to case, so that often quite grotesque gradations of the same influence are to be found.

The principle of epic cyclisation has in any event proved to be an extremely effective stimulus to the arrangement of the most diverse epical subjects from Iranian folk-traditions and folk-literature in general.

Within the framework of the epic cycle there was abundant scope for imagination and creative liberty. We need not look far for examples – in some instances several themes had already found their way to neighbouring peoples, even before the final cyclisation had been achieved in the form of Firdausī's life-work. This explains the occurrence of differing versions or wordings of a common basic motif.

The impetus given by epic cyclisation stimulated not only the development of Iranian national traditions as established by Firdausī and his followers[7], although their works are undoubtedly the most important; its powerful effects can also be discerned in the Ossetian sagas about the Narts and in the Tajik epic cycle of Gūrughlī. The system of correlation, however, was not everywhere thought out and carried through as carefully and flawlessly as in the *Shāh-nāma*. It is precisely these disproportionate after-effects of epic cyclisation that teach us how the earlier stages of development were gradu-

Notes on pp. 615–616

ally reached, up to the composition of the *Shāh-nāma* and similar epic poems.

Romantic and erotic components are already to be found in the early epical poems. Here again many folklore subjects, usually of considerable antiquity, have been adapted in varying fashion in folk-tradition as well as in works of polite literature.

In the course of development of feudal society it was only logical that folk-romances of chivalry should also put in an appearance, and these bore unmistakable evidence of folklore influence. They were transmitted at first orally, later in written form, and even in print. The *dāstāns* can be seen as a transitional type between the epics, entertainment literature and fairy-tales.

Entertainment literature is often remarkable for its peculiar didactic aims. This genre always appealed to rulers and common people alike, and it did not really matter whether it took the form of fables (particularly *Kalīla u Dimna*), entertainment or didactic literature in a narrower sense (*Ṭūṭī-nāma*), or single motifs and subjects from the *Thousand and One Nights*. Even though they were laid down in writing, all of these remained very close to folk-literature despite many further developments, and quite apart from numerous recasts of single motifs. Of the greatest importance are further the many varieties of fairy-tales and anecdotes which would appear to be the chief sources of all types of folk-literature that have ever existed.

With a character of their own that is hard to account for are the folk-prints, possibly because this kind of folk-literature, as such not even of ancient origin, is really disappearing today after having developed under the most varied influences. This category of works is marked by an increasing imprint of both the main streams of Islamic orthodoxy, often conspicuous by glaring anachronisms (the legendary figure of Rustam, for instance, becomes islamised[8]).

The religious folk-literature of the Shīʿites served as the basis for religious mystery plays, which can be regarded as forerunners of the *taʿziyas*. In some respects the *taʿziya* may be said to be a kind of passion play. Several customs and ceremonies, mostly of a dramatic nature, are closely connected with them. To this category belongs also however the religious parody and farce, *ʿUmar-kushān*. This kind of religious drama does not occur in Tajik folk-literature – a logical consequence of the difference of religious denominations. And it is understandable that also the Tajik counting-out rhymes used by prize-fighters bear a different character, since in Persia proper they show a strong Shīʿite colour. This should not surprise us, for folk-customs are very closely linked with the general way of life, the culture and consequently the ideology of the society in question.

Folk-poetry, on the contrary, as long as it does not spring from a religious theme to begin with, generally remains unaffected by the religious differentiation we have just discussed.

Upon the whole it has to be remembered that the various forms of Iranian folk-literature are by no means isolated from one another. Many subjects have been treated in more than one way. Sometimes the different treatments are related to one another

(ʿAlī in religious legends and *taʿziyas*, later also in folk-tales; Rustam in epics, *dāstāns* and heroic folk-tales), but it also happened that one form served as model for a later one. In many cases, however, connections are more likely to be accidental. A singular and usually highly problematical group form those incidences where the names of famous heroes are connected with predominantly fantastic and romantic adventures. Such fabulous stories are to a great extent foreign to the epic cycles. What we meet here are very likely the last echoes of universally familiar motifs, while the hero's name (Rustam etc.) serves only to remind the audience of the traditional images and characteristics and of authentic heroic exploits and adventures, and to link up the new story with them. One may fairly suppose that in this way countless unhistorical episodes were accumulated around the historical core of a relatively small number of traditional sagas. In many cases such additions have obscured the original sagas and the prototypal characters of particular figures, sometimes even obliterating them completely.

C. THE IMPORTANCE OF FOLK-LITERATURE

Unfortunately it cannot be said that folk-literature has always been given its due rating. There have been periods during the development of human society when it was held in contempt. Belles-lettres were considered the only possible means of expression for the artistic impulse. How much it owed precisely to the inspiration of folk-literature was at the same time completely disregarded.

Since the number of tragic and other conflicts expressed in literature is fairly limited in any case, it is understandable that similar themes should appear in the literatures of different nations and ages. But this by no means implies that we should conclude without reserve that they were mutually influenced, or derived from the same primary sources. Schack[9] rightly observes that certain fundamental poetic archetypes never cease to repeat themselves.

However, it is a different matter when versions of the same motif issuing from different localities and different periods agree even in detail, in outward form, composition, sequence of events or in the presentation of the characters and the psychological make-up of personages. When this phenomenon can be witnessed among nations of common origin that were formerly in contact with one another, such similarities are of the greatest significance and importance.[10]

Folk-literature is by no means restricted to reproduction, its aim is always towards further development.[11] From the earliest times on and in its own particular manner, folk-literature has unceasingly formed an accompaniment to the history of Man. Maxim Gorky[12] made a striking observation on the significance of folk-tales handed down to us from ancient times when he said: Old folk-tales, myths and legends are of course

Notes on pp. 615–616

familiar to us, but it is essential that we become acquainted as thoroughly as possible with their original meaning. People living at the dawn of history were concerned with alleviating their toil, increasing its productivity and arming themselves against four-footed enemies. Further, they tried to influence the elements and natural phenomena inimical to mankind through the power of words and exorcism. This is very important since it shows how profound was man's belief in the power of words. At the same time Gorky points out that the conception of pessimism is quite alien to folk-literature, despite the fact that its creators must have experienced life as a constant struggle. He finally remarks that without a knowledge of folk-literature it is impossible to ascertain the true history of the working people.[13] In times of untroubled development folk-literature has the task of satisfying the cultural and artistic demands of the people, and in times of danger it has to instruct and guide them and inspire them with courage and endurance. The subjects of folk-literature, too, are suited to the circumstances: in dangerous times it is mainly concerned with concrete motifs, during periods of peace imagination and fancy take the upper hand.[14] Folk-literature forms part of the literary heritage of a people, it follows the laws that operate in the development of literature, it springs from the same society and consequently reflects the changes in the latter.[15]

Folklore subjects prove to be fertile for very long periods of time. Even today, for example, modern Tajik dramatists take their themes from folk-literature both for plays and opera librettos. Quite a number of folk-tales also prove their use as bearers of illustrative material in literary history, for there exist many anecdotes and tales about prominent men. Thus Firdausī, Nāṣir-i Khusrau, Mushfiqī, Navā'ī, among others have remained in the people's memory.[16] And even from the view of cultural history these tales are valuable and full of significance. Thus folk-literature, as a historical document and as an expression of the historical awareness of the people, must be considered of very great value.

Particularly is this so in the case of the very old epic story of King Sugdyn (Sughdak) and his daughter Queen Zarrīna that has so fortunately been preserved. To all appearances this must be a rare relic of Soghdian folk-tradition of great antiquity. Probably Zarrīna was in fact a historical figure, for her name is mentioned by Ctesias in a surviving fragment dated approximately 400 B.C.[17] Curiously enough no account was taken of this epic cycle when the *Shāh-nāma* was being composed.

Female characters in folk-literature appear in a position that is in crass contrast to the actual circumstances prevailing up to a few years ago, for it shows a reverence for women and gives them a social position such as they have not enjoyed since matriarchal times. This must not be seen as an anachronism, but as valuable historical evidence that once upon a time women also had their rights.[18]

Gorky is therefore right in insisting upon the collecting and studying of folk-literature.[19] As we have said already, folk-literature is a reflection of real life. And that is why modern Tajik literature consciously uses it as its starting-point.[20] The systematic work of investigation being done in this field in Tajikistan, Uzbekistan, Turkmenistan and elsewhere has encouraged Iranians too at last to pay some attention to their native folk-literature, which they had hitherto despised and considered backward. As a result of this activity the Ethnographic Museum of Tehran was founded in 1933. Among other things a considerable quantity of folklore material was brought together, but unfortunately in the copy that was made of it all peculiarities of origin and dialect were effaced, thus greatly diminishing the value of the collection. Ṣādiq Hidāyat made an attempt at sorting out the Iranian folklore[21] in his *Nayrangistān*. Another collector was Kūhī Kirmānī.

NOTES

1. Oranskiy, I.M., *Vvedeniye v iranskuyu filologiyu* (M. 1960), 22–53, 135–143, 212–221, 288–352; Oranskiy, I.M., *Iranskiye yazïki* (M. 1963); cf. also *Handbuch der Orientalistik*, I. Abt., IV. Bd.: *Iranistik*, I. Abschnitt: *Linguistik* (Leiden 1958).
2. Cf. Tolstov, S.P.–Zhdanko, T.A., 'Osnovnïye etapï etnicheskoy istorii narodov Sredney Azii i Kazakhstana', in *Narodï Sredney Azii i Kazakhstana*, I (M. 1962), 38–114.
3. Cf. Zhirmunskiy, V.M.–Zarifov, Kh. T., *Uzbekskiy narodnïy geroicheskiy epos* (M. 1947), especially 131–164, 278–301; Zhirmunskiy, V.M., 'Epicheskoe tvorchestvo narodov Sredney Azii', in *Narodnïy geroicheskiy epos* (M.-L. 1962), 195–240; cf. also *Istoriya literatur narodov Sredney Azii i Kazakhstana* (M. 1960).
4. Petrushevskiy, I.P., 'Iran v sostave gosudarstva Sefevidov', in *Istoriya Irana s drevneyshikh vremen do kontsa XVIII veka* (Leningrad 1958), 247–265; *Istoriya tadzhikskogo naroda*, II, kn. I (M. 1964), 364–420.
5. Cf. Rastorguyeva, V.S., *Opït sravnitel'nogo izucheniya tadzhikskikh govorov* (M. 1964).
6. Cf. Cejpek, J., 'Die verbale Periphrase als ein wichtiges Unterscheidungsmerkmal zwischen Neupersisch aund Tāǧikisch', *ArOr*, 24,2 (1956), 171–182; cf. also Lazard, G., *Caractères distinctifs de la langue tadjik* (Paris 1956)(=*BSL*, 52,1 117–186).
7. Cf. Bertel's Ye.E., *Istoriya persidsko-tadzhikskoy literaturï* (M. 1960), 169–286; cf. also Braginskiy, *Iz istorii...*, 307–323, *Ocherki*, 166–206; Zand, M.I., *Shest vekov slavï* (M. 1964), 79–95, 96–110.
8. Romaskevich, *Ocherki izucheniya Shakhname*, 45; Zhukovskiy, *Musul'manstvo Rustama*, 109, 116–117.
9. In his introduction to Firdausī's heroic epic tales.
10. Cf. Ethé, *Essays und Studien*, 256.
11. Zhirmunskiy, *Problema fol'klora*, 200.
12. Gor'kiy, Maxim, *O literature* (M. 1937); cf. also special anthology: *Pushkin i Gor'kiy o narodnom tvorchestve* (M. 1938), 27–98; cf. also an essay by Yu. N. Sidorova, 'A. M. Gor'kiy o narodnom tvorchestve', in *Rus. nar. poet. tvorchestvo*, ed. Bogatïrev, 138–156.
13. *Chuvashskiye skazki*, 10, 13, 15; *Skazki i legendï tatar Krïma*, 13.
14. Plotnikov, *Yangal maa*, 14–16.
15. *Sk. i leg. tatar Krïma*, 13.
16. Klimovich, L., *Khrestomatiya po literaturam narodov SSSR*, 23, 140, 108, 776 *et seq.*; cf. also Zand, *Shest vekov slavï*, *passim.*
17. *Antologiya tadzhikskoy poezii*, 1st ed., 23, 30, 579.

18. Klimovich, *op. cit.*, 789.
19. *Sk. i leg. tatar Krīma*, 9.
20. *Antologiya tadzh. poezii* 1st ed., 9, 21.
21. For Russian translation see *Peredneaziatskiy etnograficheskiy sbornik*, I, 259–336.

II. IRANIAN FOLK-EPICS

A. IRANIAN EPICAL SUBJECTS AS CONVEYED BY CLASSICAL AUTHORS[1]

The first classical author who consciously made use of Iranian tradition and brought it into play in his works was Herodotus.[2] The very nature of his work (the exposition of the causes and course of the Greco-Persian wars, and the explanation of all the circumstances which gave rise to them) provided the stimulus to make a start with the mythical history.

Herodotus had to content himself with second-hand information (using interpreters?). It is easy to imagine that the Father of Greek historiography based his accounts of ancient traditions and the earliest history of various classical and ancient oriental peoples upon their folk-tradition as it existed at his own time. This is true especially in the case of the historical traditions of the Persians and Medes. Apparently Herodotus was not familiar with the royal annals mentioned both by the ancient Greek author Ctesias[3] and by the Old Testament Book of Esther.[4] In any case he does not refer to them. He certainly had no archives at his disposal either when he wrote the history of Persia.

The Scythian traditions recorded by Herodotus in connection with the Scythian expedition of Darius[5] are of the greatest importance. Interesting too are his essays on the manners and customs of the Scythians.[6] Nevertheless it is clear that Herodotus was often at a loss to understand and explain specific points correctly. Value must also be attributed to his records concerning certain fragments of West-Iranian traditions.[7]

Xenophon's *Cyropaedia*[8] is another work that until now has not been duly esteemed. It is some hundred years younger than the *Histories* of Herodotus, having been composed approximately in the year 362 B.C., and should be regarded more as a historical novel than as a piece of authentic historiography. Iranian traditions are included in it

Notes on pp. 644–648

to a wide extent, though the author's own contribution, particularly from an ideological stand-point, is not to be underestimated. Nevertheless it appears that all those who have interpreted the works of Xenophon, from antiquity up till very recently, have attributed far too much to the imagination of the ancient writer. Of course he was responsible for rhetorical embellishments and for many additions in the sphere of composition, but he paid at least as much attention to the Iranian folk-traditions. Xenophon, after all, lived long enough among the Persians to become familiar with their traditional history.

A particularly important source for our knowledge of ancient traditions are the writings of Diodorus of Sicily.[9] It is true that he belongs to the age of Caesar and Augustus – considerably later therefore than his forerunners in this respect – but he consulted many documents that no longer exist, among them being the *Persika* of Ctesias.[10] Diodorus' practice of mixing authentic history with folk traditions somewhat uncritically has turned out to be our good fortune since in this way a number of ancient folk traditions have been preserved that would otherwise have remained unknown, other authors having passed them by as unsuitable for recording.

The rest of the classical authors do not contribute anything essential or new, apart from a few references, but we do find some fresh subjects in Justinus's *Excerpts from the Histories of Trogus Pompeius*.[11]

Of the late classical authors Athenaeus of Naucratis[12] should especially be mentioned. This grammarian of the 3rd century A.D. is mainly important for his *Deipnosophistai*, 'The Banquet of the Sages', which has been preserved. In this work, which in itself cannot lay claim to any great originality, the author provides an enormous mass of quotations from otherwise forgotten and unknown writers belonging to all manner of literary categories and trends. Among other material there is much that is valuable for the study of the old Iranian folk-traditions. Athenaeus gives us, for example, a most remarkable account by Chares of Mytilene[13], according to which the Persians already sang romances at the time of Alexander the Great. These romances gave a poetical rendering of legendary love stories. Chares mentions as an example a *Romance of Zariadres and Odatis*, Zariadres being of course none other than the Zairivairish of the *Avesta* or the Zarēr of Pahlavi literature.[14]

Very probably the influence of Iranian folk-tradition was much greater in the ancient world than the surviving evidence would have us believe. Greek influences, on the contrary, although they were very fertile during certain periods (at the time of Alexander and the Diadochi), had little lasting effect on Iranian folk-tradition and have disappeared almost without trace after contributing surprisingly little to its development or its store of subjects. An exception of course is the *Alexander Romance* by Pseudo-Callisthenes.[15] As for Greek philosophy in the 6th century A.D., it unfortunately lasted too short a time to have any effect on folk-tradition; such early Byzantine influences are to be found rather in Islamic philosophy.

It must be admitted, however, that the number of Iranian motifs we come across in ancient literature is comparatively small – limited in fact to fragments and relics. They nevertheless prove by their style and composition that the folk-literature of Iran can boast an ancient and richly developed tradition.

B. IRANIAN FOLK-EPICS IN PRE-ISLAMIC TIMES

The already discussed testimony of the classical authors as to the existence of Iranian folk-epics confirms that Iranian traditions had already at that time a long history of development behind them. This means that we have to place the beginning of these old folk-traditions in the pre-historic ages of Iran, which does not mean that they are unhistorical. Many a recollection in early folk-literature provides a tempting starting-point for historical investigation.

Analyses of the most ancient Iranian conceptions, especially their mythological components, would require the writing of special and extensive treatises. But we can surely prove true the syncretism in the conception of the world as seen by the ancient Iranians. Long before the reformation of the old religion by Zarathustra there probably existed completely worked-out cycles of cosmogonical myths[16], or else myths about animals containing obvious features of totemism[17], demonological myths[18] and others dealing with the first people and the first heroes[19] (Kayōmarth, Jamshēd, Garshāsp, Rustam and his clan, the Pēshdādiāns, Kayāniāns, etc.). A clear idea of the earliest form of Iranian mythology is hard to come by because Zoroastrian religious reform distorted old conceptions by means of dense strata of later and mostly syncretic innovations. Unfortunately we know the Avesta only from later versions, so that it is necessary to be very cautious in making categoric statements.

The ancient Iranian conception of the world is worth noting for the fact that the gods of the heavens were held to have become regents of the earth. In the Indian *Vedas* the heroes fight their battles in heaven, but in the Iranian Avesta these take place on earth. Ethical conflicts have arisen from the struggles between the natural phenomena. As far as its character goes, the Iranian heroic tradition has reached the threshold of true history.

The epical traditions of the Iranians go back very far indeed. This is borne out, among other things, by the fact that the Avesta presupposes an already richly developed system of mythical history. Even the continuity of the various episodes and single events had been fully worked out by the time the earliest parts of the Avesta were taking form. If we assume that Zarathustra was preaching in the 7th century B.C. (a very sober estimate) and that the Iranian plateau began to be inhabited by Iranian tribes around the 12th to the 10th century[20], we separate these two events by at least three-hundred years, which is the length of time usually necessary for memories of

Notes on pp. 644–648

historical events to turn into myths and legends. No doubt also these traditions were subjected to development, transformation and elaboration. In the Avesta, after all, there are many figures which Firdausī's *Shāh-nāma* does not mention; on the other hand there are entire cycles of traditions either not acknowledged in the Avesta or regarded as apocryphal and uncanonical.[21]

How abundant the Iranian folk-literature of pre-Islamic times was, can best be appreciated when one remembers that almost all Persian epics, Firdausī's as well as those of his followers, continue to build on pre-Islamic folk-motifs. And despite many hundreds of thousands of verses, it cannot be said that the wealth of motifs from folk-epics is altogether exhausted. It is characteristic of all Persian polite literature as well as of Iranian folk-literature that with few exceptions almost exclusively eastern Iranian subjects are used, local influences penetrating only occasionally. Western Iranian motifs have vanished completely, and the northern Iranian folk-traditions have gone their own way. The Ossetian sagas about the Narts show a very marked departure from the old Iranian tradition with which they used to be so closely linked. This was no doubt a result of the entirely different geographical and historical circumstances under which both developed. Firdausī's *Shāh-nāma* is invaluable as a source of information about Iranian folk-literature at the time of its transition from the pre-Islamic to the Islamic period. Nevertheless, it would be a serious mistake to suppose that the *Shāh-nāma*, or its model, the *Khvatāy-nāmak*, is anything but an epitome of the wealth of folk-traditions that existed at that time. Arabic historical texts (for the rest written by authors of Iranian descent, or at least dependent upon Iranian sources) prove that there existed also other versions of the ancient Iranian traditions that varied from those codified in the *Khvatāy-nāmak*.[22]

It is characteristic of the development of pre-Islamic Iranian traditions that the heroic motifs gradually became isolated. By the end of the Sasanian period we can therefore speak of two separate traditions existing side by side – the religious and the heroic. In a way the splitting up of the Iranian tradition was fortunate, for it is precisely due to this that so much of ancient Iranian folk-literature has come down to us. Only some of the most tangible signs of pre-Islamic religious thinking needed to be eliminated for Persian epic poetry founded on folk-literature to reach its greatest heights.

If comparatively little of the original Avesta has been preserved, Sasanian Pahlavi literature[23] fared hardly better; practically the only writings that have survived – and some of these are of a very late date – are religious and theological. We possess extremely little secular literature: the *Zhāmasp-nāmak*, *Artāk Virāz-nāmak*, *Kārnāmak-i Ardakhshēr*, *Chatrang-nāmak*, the *Āyātkār-i Zarērān*[24], and that just about sums it up. Although therefore almost nothing of the secular literature of the Sasanian era remains, one may safely suppose that a very considerable amount of entertainment literature was written in pre-Islamic Iran.

This is also borne out by the fact that the translators of the *Khvatāy-nāmak* into Arabic introduced several fragments from other Pahlavi books. There are a great many such Arabic translations, or rather adaptations, of single works of Iranian entertainment literature; moreover we must bear in mind that the translators selected their stories with great care, preserving in this way the best and most interesting samples from the Sasanian period. At the end of the pre-Islamic age there were therefore a great number of folk-books whose subjects were partly historical (or rather quasi-historical) stories, but were mostly based on folk-traditions and are indeed further developments of these. The *Kitābu'l-Fihrist* of Muḥammad b. Isḥāq an-Nadīm, dating from 377/988[25], records an imposing list of such Arabic translations from Iranian originals. Among these are also several local traditions, which are partly elaborations of some fragments of traditions. *Mazdak-nāmak*, *Anōsharvān-nāmak* and *Vahrām-Chōpēn-nāmak* are some of the titles mentioned.[26]

These works – to all appearances influenced largely by folk-literature, or in any case intended for the common people – are important also for the following reason, namely that some of them very probably survive not only in the cycle of *A Thousand and One Nights* (at least to the extent of certain motifs), but were still to be found resounding in early New Persian literature.[27]

A number of folk-books were adaptations of several legends about Sasanian kings. In addition to *Kārnāmak-i Ardakhshēr*, of which we possess the Pahlavi original, this category includes among others the *Book of Vahrām and Narsē*[28] that probably dealt with Vahrām V Gor and his brother Narsē. A certain Narsē is known to have been regent for his brother at the time of the campaign to the north, and later governor in Khurasan. Unfortunately we have no more precise information about the contents, but the work was probably based on one of the legends around Bahrām Gor, and was almost certainly of a later date. These legends were also in later days frequently used as a starting-point for numerous literary epics.

Another category is that of the love romances. One of the favourite subjects that is used again and again is *Vīs u Rāmīn*.[29] Although it is a typical love story it can also be regarded as a drama, notably the conflict between the generations, represented by an ageing king and a youth, ruthless in love. Repercussions of this cycle of motifs can be traced and found right up to the Middle Ages in Western Europe in the romance of Tristan and Isolde.[30]

But these are by no means all the epic subjects of the pre-Islamic period. Most of the sources of our knowledge about ancient Arabic and Persian chronicles and the *Khvatāy-nāmak* prove that there are many variants in existence that make it obvious that also other fountain-heads of folk-traditions need to be considered. At the same time these varying details reveal a distinctly Sasanian or even older, Arsacid stamp. This would explain the presence of a number of episodes in the *Shāh-nāma* for which it is impossible to find models. After all, we cannot expect Firdausī to have created out of his own imagination, without any previous patterns, so many of Rustam's deeds such as the conquering of the stronghold of Spand, or the seven adventures of Rustam, the battle between Rustam and the Dēv Akvān, the episodes about Rustam and Suhrāb,

Notes on pp. 644–648

Bīzhan and Manēzha, and others.[31] And the same is true when considering several motifs in the works of Niẓāmī.[32]

Neither these known stories, nor a fairly considerable quantity of traditional narratives, probably also shorter ones, which are unfortunately no longer known or have been lost, could meet the demand for ever new descriptions of likely and unlikely happenings. Writers were therefore obliged to borrow foreign, non-Iranian subject-matter as well.

The most important in this context is the *Alexander Romance* of Pseudo-Callisthenes. Although the Pahlavi version no longer exists, the thoroughly Iranian flavour of the place names and the allusions to Iranian conditions in the Syriac translation of the Pahlavi which we possess, prove its authenticity. In its turn, this Syriac version had a very strong influence on the Arabs, and from them the whole complex of the Alexander romance returned to Persian polite literature.[33]

This presumed Pahlavi version of the Alexander romance is of further importance because it made it possible for the figure of Alexander to be incorporated into the Iranian tradition, that had hitherto been hostile towards it. Ever since, Alexander has undisputedly retained his native right, also in Iranian folk-tradition.

C. IRANIAN SUBJECTS ADOPTED IN ARABIC LITERATURE

It has already been pointed out several times how many Arabic translations there existed of the most diverse Pahlavi texts, especially after the Arabs had subjugated the Iranians. This might suggest that Iranian subjects only reached Arabic literature and the Arabs themselves through the Iranians who had been converted to Islam and had begun to write in Arabic.

In a large number of cases this is indeed true, but it does not apply to the majority. After all, motifs from Iranian folk-literature had been known to the Arabs even before the appearance of Muḥammad. Largely responsible for this were the Lakhmids. The centre of their Arab vassal state, under the suzerainty of the Sasanians, was the Mesopotamian town of Ḥīra. Iranian cultural and literary influences began to be felt here first and Iranian traditions and folk-tales spread thence to the Bedouins. They appealed to these sons of the desert, who did much towards their further propagation.[34]

Among many other pieces of evidence there is a biographer of the Prophet[35] who relates that the merchant Naḍr b. al-Ḥārith al-Abdarī[36] had learnt many Iranian traditions – especially those on the fight between Rustam and Isfandyār – on the lower course of the Euphrates (about 620 A.D. in Ḥīra). By telling these tales Ḥārith had disturbed an audience held by Muḥammad, for which reason the Prophet reproved him (according to an ancient tradition registered by Muḥammad's interpreters).[37]

A particularly rich and fertile influx of Iranian subjects started however when the Iranians, then only recently converted to Islam, began to contribute to Arabic literature themselves. It need not surprise us that the Iranians, very often without conscious intention, simply retraced the old Iranian traditions. Sometimes this could not even be avoided as Arabic literature until this time had lacked many of the forms which did exist in the initially far more advanced Pahlavi literature. Shortly afterwards a systematic translation of Pahlavi literature was undertaken. Once again this was first and foremost the work of the islamised Iranians; of chief importance among them was Ibn al-Muqaffaʿ (executed about 143/760).[38]

A no less important result of this trend are the Arab Chronicles. Almost without exception these were written by Iranians in the Arabic language. It is not surprising therefore, that a very large proportion of the motifs and subjects are Iranian, for in those days history was a literary genre rather than a scientific discipline.

Unfortunately only the most important historians writing in Arabic can be mentioned here. They all, whether they were Dainavarī, Ibn Qutayba, Ṭabarī, Masʿūdī, Thaʿālibī or al-Bīrūnī[39], brought forward the old Iranian traditions as a source of knowledge of the history of their Iranian mother country. Of course we must not forget that they were all in the happy position of being able to draw from the Iranian folk-tradition which was considerably larger in those days, and also from many Pahlavi folk-books and other works which are now lost probably for ever. Certainly the *Khvatāy-nāmak* was not the only source that provided them with stories about the various events in ancient Iranian history, although we must not forget that the Arabic version of the *Khvatāy-nāmak* appeared relatively very early, in several different wordings and in various versions. We are not in a position to give further details of the circumstances under which all of this happened, or of the relationships between the different texts. Another question that will probably have to remain unanswered is at what time the changes were made and whether this was done in the Pahlavi original or not until the Arabic adaptation.[40] In any case there is no doubt that the Pahlavi version of the *Khvatāy-nāmak* really existed in the early days of Arabic rule in the Iranian countries. At the same time, however, this complicates considerably several questions concerning mutual relationships in this matter.[41] In any case the very ancient story on the Archer Ārash-i Shavātīr merits full attention. This subject is not to be found in the works of Firdausī but has been handed down in Arabic literature.[42]

It cannot be stressed too often how invaluable Arabic literature has been for the protection and preservation of pre-Islamic Iranian folk-literature which has been in existence for hundreds, even thousands of years. However paradoxical it may seem, besides using the ancient original recordings, the Persian writers of literary epic poems often turned to the Arabic adaptations of old prose folk-books of the Sasanian period when searching for inspiration for their mainly national heroic poems. Although they did not altogether ignore the suggestions that came to them from oral folk-traditions, the influence of the written sources was by far the largest and most penetrating. This need not surprise us, for as more and more of the Iranian countries adopted Islam the number of people able to read the Pahlavi books dwindled, if such did indeed still exist. Every year more and more of these old book fell victim to destruction because, being the products of a heretical way of thinking, they were not considered worth preserving. Eventually they became very rare indeed. In these circumstances it has proved providential and profitable that the Iranian tradition split up into two parts – the religious and the secular, or heroic as it might be called. During the Islamic period the old religious tradition inevitably had to lose its influence and die out. On the other hand, in the secular epic tradition it was enough to make a few small corrections, in themselves of slight consequence. When this had been done the old Iranian folk-stories could be translated into Arabic without any objection, while the Iranian characteristics and philosophical background remained untouched. It is only thanks to this process that the most important and valuable elements of Iranian folk-literature from the Sasanian period did not perish together with the Sasanian empire, but were preserved. After an interval during which the often incomplete and previously inconsistent tradition was able to crystallise and its details to become arranged, it returned by way of the Persian poets to the people from whom it had once originated. We must point out, however, that folk-traditions had been handed down both by word of mouth and by the already discussed means of Arabic versions and translations. It may be true that the material transmitted directly and orally constituted the smaller part and consisted of rather simpler stories, but there can be no doubt at all that even in the most difficult circumstances the Iranians held on to their folk-traditions. The result was that polite literature and folk-literature influenced each other extensively as far as subjects were concerned. However, since various subjects of folklore origin were remodelled to suit the style of belles-lettres and affected folk-literature anew only after this transformation; and since on the other hand it is possible that some works of polite literature may have been composed in a style resembling folklore even though they have in fact no folklore foundation, the solving of problems dealing with precise classification, origin, development and nature of a great many epical subjects has become extremely complicated. The immediate conclusion one reaches is of course that it would be a mistake, groundless and even useless, to try drawing artificial and exact dividing lines between folk-tradition and polite literature. Only the mutual link between the two categories can guarantee the vitality and lasting value of the latter.

D. FOLKLORE FOUNDATIONS OF IRANIAN EPICAL POETRY

It is typical of Iranian folk-tradition as well as of polite literature, particularly of the epics, that there are no single chief heroes. This feature is of course not limited to Iran, for we can find any number of examples in the folk- and polite literatures of other nations. Iranian folk-tradition and polite literature possess a whole group of heroes. Naturally we should not be surprised if at certain periods particular heroes such as Rustam are more prominent than others. It is rather that the entire people is raised to a heroic level, while the individual heroes must be seen as incarnations of the ideas and ideals of the people. This may quite well be the quintessence of the remarkable phenomenon that classical literary works based on folk-literature have even now lost none of their vitality.

There can be no doubt that the *Shāh-nāma*, as far as subject-matter goes, is based on elements borrowed from folk-literature, but the treatment bears the unmistakable signs of polite literature.[43] Firdausī's masterly work, however, can at the same time be regarded as the culmination of a long process of development which in fact continues today. After Firdausī's gigantic creation there can only be question of the completion or elaboration of certain subjects or situations. Some of the episodes were only intimated by Firdausī, or ignored altogether. The point we have just discussed proved fortunate for the authors of the classical Persian literary epics, because we can rightly consider the sources as well as the subjects of all these works written during the century following Firdausī's death as being based on folk-literature.[44]

It seems safe to assume that many multiform and extensive cycles of legends already existed in the days of Anōsharvān and Yazdgird III previous to the codifications known to us today. But the connections between them were perceptible only to a limited extent, in as far as they correspond with the common origin of all folk-tradition. The very carefully thought-out and close relationships between the various Iranian folk-epics which we find after the *Shāh-nāma* codification did not yet exist in the Sasanian period. There were of course a number of cycles of traditions, centred mostly round certain legendary figures who featured as protagonists. Only after the introduction and development of epic cyclisation can the Iranian system of traditions gradually have grown into the worked out multiplicity it has become today.[45]

A result of the composition and development of epic cycles was that epical biographies of individual heroes came into being. After the, mostly isolated, events had been collated and such contradictions as existed in different traditions had been eliminated, the portrait of the hero was further completed by the addition of tales about his birth, childhood, old age and death. But this did not generally take place until a very advanced stage in the development of epical biographies had been reached. Be that as it may, it is always the climax in the tradition that is to be regarded as the original

Notes on pp. 644–648

starting-point. All other episodes became centred round the nucleus of the epic at a later date. As to the drawing up of genealogical relationships, this is no doubt an even more recent development, for which historical or mythological motifs may be used as a basis. When once a cycle had been established around one of the heroes, this was complemented by degrees by the addition of traditions concerning his ancestors and descendants. It sometimes happens too that folk-tradition utilises previously independent and even non-contemporaneous incidents as rudiments for epic traditions, ignoring differences in time and adapting separate epical elements so as to fit each other. Not infrequently the result is that contradictions and inconsistencies occur in one and the same version and discrepancies between parallel versions.[46]

There is no better proof of the intense effect of the Iranian epic tradition than the fact that many originally epic elements and subjects penetrated also into the non-epic forms of folk-literature, embellished with fairy-tale motifs. Naturally the original character of the one-time epic subject undergoes considerable modification when this happens.[47]

However, the creative efficacy of the Iranian folk-epics was not to be sought only in a downward direction (i.e. in the smaller poetical forms), but also to a very considerable extent in the longer forms. There can hardly be any doubt that in the *Khvatāy-nāmak* many elements were lacking which we do find in the *Shāh-nāma* and which we must regard as being decidedly based on folk-literature. As examples only the most important incidences need be quoted. The entire cycle of epic traditions about Rustam, together with most of the episodes, may quite rightly be regarded as a Sistanian group of traditions; very likely these were once quite independent subjects, perhaps derived from a family chronicle of people who regarded themselves as the descendants of Rustam or at any rate as belonging to his clan.[48] In a similar way other regional subjects, or such as were confined to certain clans, also became part of the system of Iranian folk-tradition. The noble houses of the Arsacids who, as we know, retained their influential position during almost the entire Sasanian period, also contributed several episodes. Nowadays it is hard to find out whether local subjects were included in the traditions by Firdausī himself, or whether this had been done earlier in the oral tradition or in the prose folk-books, none of which exist today, though they were in circulation during the period between the late-Sasanian codification of Iranian traditions in the *Khvatāy-nāmak* and Firdausī's writing of the *Shāh-nāma*, and were even translated into Arabic on more than one occasion.

In any case many of the subjects of the *Shāh-nāma* do not derive from the same source. We must not forget that Firdausī himself was a member of the landed gentry. It is therefore hardly likely that the poet would remain entirely untouched by the ideas and opinions of his social milieu and class; on the contrary, he probably gave preference to a few aristocratic traditions above folk ones here and there, or at least rated them of equal value.

The part of the *Shāh-nāma* concerned with the oldest, mythological period in Iran was quite certainly founded on the earliest and decidedly popular traditions. In the section devoted to the Sasanians on the other hand, there is a lot of material affected by aristocratic and legitimistic tendencies. It should be noted that as far as is reported by tradition, there were no class conflicts yet up to the time of Ḍaḥḥāk. But as soon as Kāva the Blacksmith[49] (still one of the favourite personages in contemporary Tajik folk-poetry) makes his appearance, we get the first taste of social strife just because of this basic idea – a rising of the masses against tyranny and oppression. The conclusion of the story has distinct legitimistic overtones (and therefore probably expresses Firdausī's personal point of view), for Kāva voluntarily relinquishes to the legitimate ruler Farīdūn the real power he had won in battle, in the course of which he had brought about the overthrow and death of the tyrant. It is true that in the later period, in the history of the Sasanians, there are also many obvious folk-subjects and motifs with democratic leanings. Quite a surprising degree of objectivity is shown by the great poet in his description of the Mazdakite revolution, and only his attitude towards Mazdakite ideology reveals his aristocratic viewpoint. Other folk-traditions to be found in Firdausī are those dealing with the character and deeds of certain rulers. He renders the folk-traditions here in a form which, at the most, has been slightly elaborated and developed. Quite often ideas and desires come into play that are typically bound up with the common people, so that the legendary figure differs widely from historical reality and truth.[50] It is one of the peculiar ironies of Fate that a large number of historically important figures, even whole dynasties of rulers, have disappeared without leaving a trace in folk-tradition, while rulers who were in reality comparatively unimportant and had if anything less than average ability became the chief characters of numerous stories and sometimes even of a whole cycle of traditions. An example is Bahrām Gor, and we find something of a similar nature in the *Thousand and One Nights* (Caliph Hārūn ar-Rashīd). It would not be difficult to make an impressive list of other instances of this kind in the folk-tales of different nations.

From the earliest times there was a very strong romantic tendency in the Iranian epics, but for a long time it was only used to form episodes. The romantic element was seldom the starting-point for the main action. After the Seljuq invasion, however, there was a radical change of taste in literature – the horrors of real life made people turn away from the destitution of the present and seek solace in often extremely romantic subjects. Great popularity was enjoyed by tales like *Vāmiq and ʿAdhrā*, *Vīs and Rāmīn*[51], and others, which originally belonged to folk-literature but became more and more estranged from it through adaptation, interpretation and through the contents themselves. Finally they lost the last traces of and connections with folk-literature and were transferred completely into the sphere of polite literature, which for the common people remains a strange and remote realm.[52]

Although of course the epic poems composed during the period between the death of Firdausī and the heyday of the romantic epoch cannot generally speaking compete with that great model, the *Shāh-nāma*, either in popularity or in intrinsic quality, they

Notes on pp. 644–648

are of no less value for the study of Iranian folk-literature. As we have mentioned earlier, in the epic poems that appeared after Firdausī several motifs were further developed which he himself had merely indicated. A number of epic cycles now also came into use which Firdausī had either not known about or had deliberately ignored. It is not impossible either that authors who are no longer known today were able to make use of some ancient folk-books. The question whether such works, if they existed at all, were still written in the original Pahlavi or had already been translated into Arabic, is of comparatively little importance. In any case all these epics dating from the period after Firdausī's death prove that a new epic cycle was evolving. The fact that the means of expression of these poets already completely conformed to the requisites of high-aimed literary poetry, does not prove very much. The themes, as well as the way in which they were linked together, remain surprisingly close to the folk-style.[53]

It is a remarkable thing, however, that epic cyclisation retained its viability until comparatively recently. It is typical of the intellectual situation in late-feudal Iran in the 19th century that even figures like Rustam had to be islamised in order to make them acceptable for the narrow-minded and extremely fanatical Mullas. If one had opposed this absurd demand, one would have been in danger of being accused of heresy. Although the islamising of ancient Iranian heroes took place mainly in the smaller literary forms, this makes it no less interesting.[54]

One of the best, and at the same time richly documented examples of epic cyclisation in the field of epic folk-traditions are the various versions of the folk-traditions and legends about Alexander of Macedonia. These are particularly instructive, if only for the reason that we possess a great number of records illustrating very different stages in the development of these traditions. The same cannot be said, however, about the ancient Iranian epic traditions, as in most cases only the fully developed and 'final' versions of specific adaptations are available.

It must be pointed out that the oriental Alexander romances[55] are fundamentally different from the western, and especially the European versions. The Alexander romances of Europe are in the first place to be seen as typical examples of mediaeval romances of adventure and chivalry. What particularly distinguishes the oriental Alexander romances is the prominent position given in them to Alexander and Aristotle, with the result that philosophy and statesmanship become very important elements.

The peoples of the East had no clear notion of the actual events of which Alexander of Macedonia had been the central figure, and it was thus that traditions and legends came into being. Ignorance of the true happenings permitted new details to be added as required. The oriental Alexander romances thus acquired more and more the character of a 'mirror for princes' and may consequently be regarded up to a certain point as a collection of maxims. This increases their importance, for they rate not only as monuments of literature but also as an important source of information about the development of political conceptions.

The memory of Alexander lives on in works of various kinds. A biography proper, such as the one composed and written down by Cleitarch and Onesikritos[56], served as a model for Plutarch as well as for the Greek historiographers. In the East the real biography had a very limited effect. Of much greater appeal were numerous legends, which however bore little relation to the actual events.

The various traditions survived independently until the time of the later Roman emperors. As we know, it was the Roman rulers Caracalla and Alexander Severus who established the official Alexander cult that led to the systematic arrangement and completion of the Alexander traditions. The actual Alexander romance was at first attributed to Callisthenes, physician-in-ordinary to the famous king of the Macedonians, but it became evident that it must have been the work of some anonymous author – known therefore as Pseudo-Callisthenes. He may not even have been a Greek, but perhaps Egyptian by birth. The romance presents Alexander as a descendant of the Egyptian pharaohs, for according to the legend he was not the son of Philip of Macedon but of an Egyptian priest named Nektanebus – himself ultimately related to the kings. Thus Alexander appears not as an usurper, but as the legitimate heir to the royal power. The original Egyptian version would seem to be devoid of allusions to internal conditions and relationships in Macedonia, these having only been introduced in the Greek adaptation. In its turn this Greek version was the model for many an oriental redaction. Particularly important among these is the Middle-Persian Pahlavi version, and although it has not survived there is ample evidence that it must have existed, for there are Syriac, Coptic, Ethiopian and Armenian translations of the Alexander romance. The translators certainly handled their model in very free fashion; they inserted, altered and even omitted passages. In most cases, however, the main course of the story was preserved. The chief evidence that the versions we have just mentioned are founded on the Middle-Persian and not on the Greek translation of the romance, is contained in the ethnonymics etc. Among other peoples, mention is made of Turanians, Alans, Gubardebayis, Azerbayjanians, Tabaristanis and Gurganis. These names were well known to the Iranians in particular, and further show that the Persian translator, or rather adaptor, was well acquainted with Trans-Caucasia and the south coast of the Caspian Sea.

Initially the Zoroastrian priesthood was an arch-enemy of the memory of Alexander whom they regarded as a descendant of the infernal powers. This ancient belief and attitude is illustrated in the *Artāk-Virāz-nāmak*.

A change in the conception of the Alexander figure (already evident at the time of the Sasanians, but even more strongly pronounced during the hegemony of the caliphate) was motivated far more by political than by religious considerations. Because the authority of the *Farr*-theory was at stake, the high Iranian aristocracy could not rest content with this attitude of rejection. For political reasons they were forced to effect the transmission of the *Farr* in some acceptable manner. A starting-point in this direction was the romance of Pseudo-Callisthenes. The Middle-Persian

Notes on pp. 644–648

version – if not directly evoked for this purpose – enabled both the official historiographers and folk-tradition to place Alexander in an admissible genealogical relationship to the Achaemenids (as far as they were still remembered). Alexander thus became a legitimate heir to the throne. In the *Khvadāy-nāmak*, the official chronicle of the Sasanians, he is at any rate already portrayed as the evident legal successor to the Achaemenids. Arabic chronicles, as well as the *Shāh-nāma*, which have undoubted connections with some versions of the *Khvadāy-nāmak*, also give evidence of this new conception of Alexander.[57]

The ways and methods by which the Alexander traditions were introduced into Iranian folk-literature are also most instructive from other points of view. For since we have a pretty good knowledge of the true background of the legends, we are here able to assess how great can be the anachronisms that appear, as well as erroneous historical data, and how folk-traditions can be distorted. In this respect, the discrepancies between folk-traditions and historical facts are rightly to be seen as an instructive admonition that the evidence of folk-tradition should always be used with the greatest caution and even reserve as a source of true historical information. Although therefore the historical reliability of folk-traditions is obviously very slight, particularly as regards very early times, they are nevertheless of lasting value as one of the best sources of information on the cultural development of a nation and of its psychology.

Generally speaking we can nowadays distinguish the following groups of subjects in Iran itself: an ancient mythological group – obviously of folk-origin, strongly influenced by many and nowadays often obscure traditions of a religious and even partly pre-Zoroastrian nature; then a cycle with Alexander as central character – of a much later date and in several respects romantic and fantastic; and finally a Sasanian group, in itself very varied, since it embraces both folk and aristocratic traditions; next to heroic and epic elements we also find romantic ones. It frequently happens that a subject is productive in more than one way – it is remarkable enough that several typically Achaemenid subjects were transferred to the Sasanians. This would finally also justify the assumption that there was once a time when the so-called West-Iranian epic subjects were not confined to those recorded by the ancient Greek authors, but were also handed down in the folk-tradition, and were at least known to the ruling classes.

Another interesting fact is that numerous traditions, and even cycles of traditions, were also centred around real historical personages such as Rūdakī, Firdausī[58], Maḥmūd of Ghazna[59], and others. These are usually romantic and are often presented in the form of anecdotes. The *Gūrughlī* epic cycle will be discussed later. It seems appropriate, however, to point out here that throughout Iran there exists an immense number of local traditions and legends connected either with a particular building or neighbourhood.[60] In many countries, Afghanistan for instance, they were even to a certain extent cyclised.[61]

E. FOLKLORE FOUNDATIONS OF IRANIAN ROMANTIC EPICS

The increasing part played by romantic as compared to heroic elements in both polite and folk-literature was mainly conditioned by the political situation, ultimately also by the decline brought about by the Mongol invasion and the devastation it left in its train. Under such conditions heroic legends – which even now are still being related – must sometimes have appeared as bitter anachronisms. Indeed on occasions a poet or folk-singer would have been risking his life if he had dared to recount or record a new adaptation or conception of old traditional motifs. Such an undertaking might easily be seen as at attempt at allegory, and consequently as an incitement against the current oppressors or as an expression of confidence in their impermanence. This was why both literary and folk-poets preferred to steer clear of subjects uncongenial to the times and complied rather with the tastes of the moment. Moreover, it was not very difficult to find suitable subjects and motifs in the various folk-traditions which no one had hitherto exploited or which had only been used in a small way in episodes.

Thus one of the best loved and most widely known subjects is without doubt that of *Farhād and Shīrīn*. Almost all the Turkic peoples adopted this romantic subject from the Iranians, and in polite as well as folk-literature it has been used in a great variety of ways. Oddly enough it does not appear in Arabic literature, with the exception of a single shadow play (and then probably under Turkish influence).[62]

As early as the end of the Sasanian rule the romantic tradition of *Farhād and Shīrīn* was one of the most popular subjects in profane entertainment literature.[63] Strictly speaking this tale was only an episode in the popular cycle of traditions about Khusrau and Shīrīn, which in its turn is merely a fragment of the extensive traditional series about several of the Sasanian rulers. The two thematic groups – Farhād and Shīrīn, and Khusrau and Shīrīn – gradually moved apart until they eventually became almost independent of each other. It is characteristic of the attitude in folk-literature that tragic conflicts are so often brought to a happy ending.

The story of *Farhād and Shīrīn* is, however, far from being the only romantic subject in Iranian folk-literature. Particularly in Central Asia, where the sphere of influence of Iranian subjects reached far beyond its natural ethnic boundaries, other subjects were in evidence too, some of which we know from Persian polite literature.[64]

Judged as a whole, Iranian folk-literature of post-classical times shows a preference for erotic subjects in place of the earlier heroic ones. Tragic love stories in romantic style abound. Although the prevailing mood of nearly all the subjects of the period is tragic, this can hardly be regarded as an expression of general pessimism – we should see it rather as a sign of certain personal and, even more, social antagonisms of the time.

Notes on pp. 644–648

The subjects, which in the main do not differ very widely from those of the European versions of Romeo and Juliet or Tristan and Isolde, were treated to all kinds of variations and underwent many a metamorphosis. Of course in the East these tales became greatly popularised, even in adaptations for polite literature, which in their turn often re-affected folk-literature. Perhaps it is due to such counter-effects and mutual influences that these love-stories became such firm favourites in the East – much more so than in the European West where they were claimed almost exclusively by polite literature, although in the end here too they became the possessions of nearly all nations and national literatures.

One truly international story – for once not of Iranian but of Arabic origin – is that concerning the unhappy love of *Laylī and Majnūn*, which became very popular as early as the 11th century. The first ambitious version in polite literature comes from Niẓāmī. Until then the Arabs themselves evidently did not possess any major poetic versions of this tale. Although the subject most likely dates back to the end of the 7th century A.D. and at the time of Niẓāmī could look back on nearly 500 years of remarkable development, the history of its evolution even among the Arabs is somewhat obscure and enigmatical. This a is good example of how an unfortunate combination of circumstances can provide literary history with vexatious problems. In cases such as this, one is reduced to conjecture.[65]

Equally popular and widely known among the romantic-erotic folk-epics are the stories of *Ṭāhir and Zuhrā*[66] (about a predestined but undesired marriage), *Bahrām and Gulandām*[67] and of *Yūsuf and Zalīkhā*[68] (an old oriental theme, here according to the well-known Koran version). There are, however, vast numbers of other tales whose subjects are familiar among all Islamic nations of the East. The story of *Varqa and Gul-shāh*, written down by 'Ayyūqī, also belongs to this group. A parallel to this Iranian version of a non-Iranian subject is known in Europe too, notably in the old French mediaeval romance of *Floire et Blancheflor* (with many variants, even folk-books).[69]

An important circumstance worth remembering is that in the Near East mediaeval Iran held a similar position to mediaeval France in Europe. Both countries must be seen as the birth-places of romances of chivalry and chivalrous poetry (known in the West under such general terms as mediaeval German love-poetry, *Minnesang*, and troubadour and minstrel poetry).[70] Prose romances of chivalry started to be written in Iran as early as the 12th century.

In their early stages of development at any rate, Iranian romances of chivalry did not attempt to break away from folk-literature, despite the social circles they clearly portrayed. On the contrary, they made use of a lot of folklore material, particularly its imaginative and folk-tale elements. Individual subjects later developed independently along their own lines.[71]

It is always useful to pay some attention to at least some of the examples of Persian literary prose, since folk-literature has left its mark here too.

In Persian literary prose, unlike verse adaptations, we certainly find a fair medley of ancient Iranian epical elements, indisputably Arabic and Moslem chivalrous subjects, numerous legends (versions either taken from the Koran or related to the Jewish tradition), as well as romantic-erotic intrigues. The episodes are mostly strongly reminiscent of folk-tales with *dēvs, parīs,* demons, fairies, sorcerers and sorcereresses, and are thus not very far removed from folk-literature. These features can be found in the oldest known prose epic work of Iran, entitled *Kitāb-i Samak-i ʿAyyār.*[72] The ancient Iranian epic subjects were independently worked out by Abū Ṭāhir Ṭarsūsī. In any case it is interesting to note that he did not combine his romances into one epic cycle, as did Firdausī. Various kinds of folk-books seem to have originated in this genre of romantic epic. Not even the anonymous four-volume *Sikandar-nāma*[73] was without associations and subsequent influence.

A very important group of subjects is furnished by the *Hamza-nāma*. The Islamic romance of chivalry entitled *Qiṣṣa-i Shāh-i mardān ʿAlī*[74], with the fourth caliph as protagonist, is known in one single manuscript only. It is thus very hard to conjecture about its influence on religious folk-literature in the period that followed, but such a work was probably not the only one *sui generis* and was most likely influenced by the epic folk-tradition. It should also just be mentioned that there were some early and late prose versions of the *Shāh-nāma* in existence, and that these served partly as sources for folk-poets and folk-narrators.[75] There were also various versions of *Abū-Muslim-nāma*[76], especially in Central Asia.

Apart from the above-mentioned prose epics there are also several prose works of a didactic and historical content that must be taken into consideration as sources of Iranian folklore motifs and traditions. There is a whole wealth of tales recorded in the historical chronicles composed by Balʿamī, Narshakhī and other very famous authors. At least the fundamental motifs, and even in some cases complete tales, appear certainly to originate and to find their prototypes in folk-literature. Much interesting material for comparative studies may also be found in geographical literature, such as the *ʿAjāʾibuʾl-buldān* by Abuʾl-Muʿayyad Balkhī.[77]

Far greater approval and success than was met with by the mostly rambling and voluminous romances of chivalry, from which folk-literature could at the most re-borrow episodes only (although professional narrators probably took more from their literary models), we find given to the shorter compositions, which generally abounded in romantic motifs and fantasy. One of the best examples is the story of *Prince Sayfuʾl-mulūk and Princess Badīʿuʾl-jamāl.* It appears in many short rather than long versions. In this way many subjects that were most likely Iranian themes from *A Thousand and One Nights* returned to polite literature and folk-literature.[78] Here too there are many points of contact between polite and folk-literature, for one is sometimes tempted to suspect that written stories are really the recordings of old oral folk-traditions. In this respect it is certainly true that the study of the history of Persian literature is still in its first stages, and no doubt many problems remain to be solved.

Notes on pp. 644–648

Ascetic echoes of mediaeval European romances of chivalry (separations and heartbreak, great penances) are also not alien to the classical literary poetry of the Moslem east, especially when Ṣūfī mysticism comes into play. Many such incidences occur in the literary adaptations of *Laylī and Majnūn* and *Farhād and Shīrīn*. They are generally absent, however, in folk-literature and romances of chivalry as well as in the paraphrases of isolated Arabic motifs, since such sentiments are contrary to the general optimism of the common people with their inclination for a full and active life, no matter how hard conditions may be.[80]

Popular tendencies, specifically a true feeling for democracy and a clearly defined social attitude, are not always equally evident. Whereas in the heroic epics the personal opinions of the story-teller or poet are in most cases fairly clearly expressed, progressive tendencies are far less obvious in the romances, and particularly in the romances of chivalry and chivalrous tales – rather the reverse is true.

F. THE *GŪRUGHLĪ* EPIC CYCLE AND OTHER SUBJECTS OF IRANIAN FOLK-EPICS

Continual feudal conflicts, the complete decline of every form of state authority and the club-law of the strongest and most powerful were everywhere – also outside Central Asia – the real causes of rebellious movements.[81] The rebel groups were always more closely connected with the common people, from whom their ranks were recruited, than to the feudal and wealthy classes. On the whole the attitude expressed in folk-literature towards the rebels was not one of repudiation on principle, and it is therefore understandable how the latter soon came to be idealised in it. Impartial and critical opinions or objective judgments of rebellious disturbances are nowhere expressed.

In the first place one has to remember that the epic cycle of rebel traditions and tales, named after its chief hero Gūrughlī[82], is definitely East-Turkish, or to be more precise Turkmenian. Indeed the fact that Gūrughlī epic tales are to be found in Tajik folk-tradition is sufficient evidence that after the severing of connections with Western Iran, Tajik cultural life was closely linked with the cultural activities of the neighbouring East-Turkish peoples, especially the Uzbeks and the Turkmenians.

The folk-epics named after Gūrughlī were known in several versions in Tajikistan[83] – the North-Tajik one being in prose (probably under influence of the neighbouring Uzbek version) and the others in verse-form, in accordance with Iranian preference. The *Gūrughlī* verses are not metrical but quantitative. Like the *Shāh-nāma*, the *Gūrughlī* epics were recited or sung in a peculiar manner with the singer accompanying himself on a *dūtār*.[84] The audience, usually numbering twenty to thirty, were seated in a closed circle around the singer, and would on occasions listen to him for seven or eight hours without a pause. The recitative is sung in a fast rhythm, the plot is quickly unravelled and the singer's performance assumes an ecstatic quality – a typical case of improvisation.

It is interesting that Gūrughlī himself, just like Kaykā'ūs in the *Shāh-nāma*, or Vladimir in the Russian *Bīlinas*, does not usually take part in the actions, campaigns and battles. Generally Gūrughlī plays an active role only in the framing story which connects the separate episodes. The singer, *sāqī*, has an analogous function in an epic cycle.

In brief the basic plot of the *Gūrughlī* epic cycle is as follows: the existence of the imaginary land of justice and labour, known as Chambūl or Chambīl, is threatened by the attacks of a number of aggressors and royal tyrants, in particular by Kishvar Pādishāh, Turāb and Raiḥān-'arab (the last possibly recalls the erstwhile Arab invasion?). The foreign enemies are joined by traitors from the local nobility, as an example of whom Aḥmad-Khān is mentioned. These internal enemies are maybe also brought forward as a personification of class antagonisms. The people of Chambūl defend themselves, however, under the leadership of their heroes, repel the attack and preserve their liberty. Truth and justice triumph. An important figure in the epic cycle is Āvāz (sometimes called Āvāz-Khān), not a nobleman but the son of a butcher. The antagonism existing between the common people and the aristocracy is clearly expressed in a large number of episodes, whether we take for example the choice of a legitimate (viz. possessing the *farr*) king from among the peasants, or the many meetings in battle between Āvāz-Khān and Aḥmad-Khān. Another instance is when Aḥmad-Khān jeers at the 'lowly origin' of the Gūrughlī-sulṭān, who had formerly been a shepherd.

Owing to the fact that the recording of the *Gūrughlī* cycle has really only just been started, it is difficult to assess the size of the whole epic work and all its cycles. Neither are we yet certain of the number of songs (named *dāstān*), but in total there are undoubtedly many more than 100,000 verses. Some songs consist of 6000 verses, others of a mere thousand or less. As for the number of songs, some people guess at twenty, but an estimate of almost fifty also seems justifiable. Altogether we have here an enormous wealth of orally transmitted folk-literature. If we further add the various by no means small cycles of folk-traditions about Rustam, Siyāvush[85], Isfandyār and other heroes, the number of orally transmitted folk-epics of the Tajiks becomes quite amazing in its size and variety.

For all this the *Gūrughlī* epics should certainly not be regarded as a completed and terminated epic formation. Quite recently a new cycle came into being whose subject is the sketch of the *bāsmachī* movement and the resistance offered to it.[86] How very much alive the *Gūrughlī* epic cycle is from Azerbayjan to Tajikistan is proved, among other things, by the fact that Uzeyir Hajïbeyow[87] set to music a libretto by Mamed Seid Ordubadï for the opera *Köroghlï*, which became a great favourite with the people.

Notes on pp. 644–648

The *Köroghlï* epic traditions have indeed acquired a considerable degree of internationality throughout the Near East, despite differences of language, religion and cultural development of the various peoples.

Obviously the *Köroghlï* subjects, which are known to so many nations, are by no means identical everywhere. One can easily distinguish the different directions in which the same subjects developed.

The most ancient are the *Gūrughlī* subjects in Azerbayjan, especially those that originated in the Persian South-Azerbayjan. These appear still to reflect in parts the real historical background of the separate epical episodes.

In the Azerbayjan version Köroghlï is a rebel from Turkmenistan, therefore of nomadic origin. To the popular way of thinking the brave Jighit Köroghlï is not a brutal perpetrator of outrages but merely an enemy of the rich, the powerful and the high-born, and at the same time the protector of the poor.[88] Only in love does he behave aristocratically; his following, however, consists entirely of common folk. There are several details which the Azerbayjan version shares with the Ukrainian Ataman Mazeppa.[89] When Köroghlï was made into an epic personage, it is also very likely that the classical example of all Islamic heroes, the great Rustam, was not without influence. Nevertheless there are also pronounced differences. Rustam is presented as a loyal and devoted knight in the true feudal sense, Köroghlï on the other hand is a warrior who values his love of freedom and his word of honour above all else.[90]

The Azerbayjan variant of the *Köroghlï* traditions has very close connections with the other Trans-Caucasian and Near-Eastern versions, which differ from that of Azerbayjan only to the extent that they are less historical in character and already contain several fictitious episodes. This is particularly true of the Turkish version, in which the gradual transition from semi-historical account to folk-romance of chivalry has started.

The *Central Asian Goroghlï dāstāns* also have their own specific characteristics; they differ significantly from the first, Azerbayjan group. To this second, Central Asian, series belong the Turkmenian, Uzbek, Tajik and Kazakh versions. This last-named group has reached a very advanced stage in epic development, for, besides *dāstāns*, folk-tales with Köroghlï motifs have also become part of the tradition. The result is a complete disintegration of the epical texture. Despite, or perhaps because of this, the Köroghlï subjects cannot hold their own against the older epic cycles in Kazakhstan and never achieved the hegemony they customarily enjoy elsewhere.

The Azerbayjan and Uzbek *Köroghlï* versions (to mention the best-known) can thus be regarded as opposite examples of how a common model may be developed. Concerning the Uzbek version we have to remember, of course, that although it is cyclised to a high degree, it does not yet constitute a closed constructed system of epic traditions. Orally transmitted folk-epics never present a consistent biography. This is impossible from the outset because the subject-repertoires of the various folk-singers are never exactly the same, and do not agree on details but only in general outline and chief characteristics. Nothing else could be expected under the circumstances. Gradually, however, the epic biography is being pieced together, and here too genealogical cyclisation is gradually being achieved.

As we have already pointed out, the Uzbek cycle of *dāstāns* with Goroghlï as chief character has definitely travelled a long way in the development from tradition to epic cycle, or rather folk-romance of chivalry with many fictional features, especially if compared with the older and perhaps still semi-historical Azerbayjan version.

The Goroghlï of the Uzbek version is neither rebel nor singer, but of noble birth and excellent parentage, a Turkmenian or Uzbek *beg*. He is the lawful ruler of a country; under his wise leadership the people prosper and when occasion arises attacks from the enemy are repelled. Goroghlï thus becomes the model for rulers and leaders of the people. The creative imagination of the folk-singers made the brave Jighit Goroghlï into an epic hero similar in type to Charlemagne. His wives are no longer daughters of khāns and *begs,* but beautiful fairies from the imaginary land of Kuykōf. Goroghlï was even invested with magical powers. But even this did not satisfy the unbridled imagination, for an Uzbek religious legend declares that Goroghlï enjoyed the special protection of the Prophet Khiḍr and the Forty Saints. Finally, in another religious tradition he is identified with the holy caliph ʿAlī – he was held to be the sacred ʿAlī of his age. The whole Uzbek epic cycle therefore resembles much more a folk-romance of chivalry, often with mystical overtones and deformations, while sometimes even Shīʿite traits can be found.

This excessive idealisation of the Goroghlï figure started in Turkmenistan. At the same time several very ancient, even mythological elements became incorporated in the epic cycle – among other things a new interpretation of the name Goroghlï. The original Azerbayjan explanation was that the name Köroghlï meant 'Son of the Blind One', but in the Uzbek version another interpretation prevailed, namely that it should be understood as 'Son of the Grave'. One tradition, very well known throughout Central Asia, maintains that Goroghlï was born in a grave after his mother was already dead. In this context the Tajik view is distinctly strange. On the one hand Gūrughlī is interpreted as 'Son of the Grave', in agreement with the Uzbek tradition, but at the same time the older Azerbayjan explanation 'Son of the Blind One' is retained. In addition the two versions are linked together in Tajik tradition, so that they become parts of the same tradition. The Uzbeks have yet another legend about the childhood of Goroghlï – that the son of the dead mother was kept alive by being suckled by a mare from Rustam's stables.[91] Parallel motifs are not hard to find – out of the many we need only mention two specifically: Cyrus was suckled by a bitch[92], Romulus and Remus by a she-wolf.[93] That the Gūrughlī epic traditions were developed within the different peoples is shown by further peculiarities. While in the Azerbayjan group of versions Köroghlï's followers consisted entirely of adventurers (usually forty in number) who had turned their backs on an unsympathetic society, in the Uzbek

Notes on pp. 644–648

version he is surrounded by a retinue in entirely feudal and unromantic fashion which he had moreover inherited from his father. Generally speaking the Central Asian versions are less revolutionary in their ideology than are those of Azerbayjan. The attitude of the common people is also less evident in the East. However, the undoubtedly progressive leading idea of the entire *Gūrughlī* epic cycle – namely the struggle of the people against mainly foreign oppression – loses none of its force and is everywhere maintained.

From the point of view of form the various versions differ considerably. Prose predominates among the Azerbayjanis and Turkmenians, verse being used only for the occasional songs of the hero. The Uzbeks have mainly poetical adaptations, the Kazakhs almost exclusively so, and with the Tajiks it has become a hard and fast rule.

As we said earlier, most Central-Asian versions must be considered more recent – they date from the 18th and the first half of the 19th century. Single episodes that were possibly derived from other epic cycles, however, may be considered much older.[94]

Although *Gūrughlī* epic traditions play such an important part in Tajik folk-poetry, they are by no means its only product. Older by many centuries are the most diverse traditions about Rustam and Isfandyār, Ḍaḥḥāk, and Kāva the Blacksmith.[95]

All the types of epic subjects we have so far discussed can be divided into diverse categories. Folk-literature has a very stimulating influence on polite literature. Its motifs are ultimately linked into elaborated compositions and cyclisations, either in epic biographies of single heroes or in genealogical cyclisation and biographies of their ancestors and descendants. The *Gūrughlī* subjects form another, less rigidly cyclised group, in which single episodes sometimes retain a measure of independence although most of the contradictions and inconsistencies have already been smoothed out. The Rustam epic traditions, in so far as they still survive in folk-literature, display even more liberties in the linking together of separate motifs. Here it is often a case of epic traditions turning into a folk-tale. The epical texture became disintegrated.

Besides the epic traditions we have discussed, there are also other, minor forms. Often it is difficult to draw the line between folk-sagas and folk-tales.

These epical fragments vary considerably in character. Sometimes they are local traditions about the founding or fall of a city, or they consist of heroic traditions recalling the one-time inhabitants of some castle or other. There is hardly a bridge, tower, castle, bazaar, caravanserai, canal or any other structure that has not at least one legend connected with it. Similarly places of pilgrimage, mountains and caves (these last often served as hiding-places) and archeological sites (Bīsutūn among others) have their own traditions too, which moreover were formerly frequently misinterpreted.[96] Such folk-traditions connected with specific places can be divided into two groups: the first are old heroic, perhaps also totemic, traditions; the second are Islamic legends, the acting characters often being contemporaries of the story-teller, which makes the plot entirely topical.

The most diverse traditions appear side by side in motley profusion. Of very great age is certainly the Soghdian-Scythian tale of *King Sugdyn and his daughter Zarrīna* with its very remarkable counterpart, the Tajik heroic tale of *Bahādur and Zarrīna,* which is richly embellished with fantasy motifs. It is fitting to mention this Tajik version here[98], not only on account of a number of East-Iranian myths which were used in it very effectively, but also because it contains some very beautiful fragments indicative of an uncommonly high degree of reverence and respect for women. The Tajik version is of great importance because it has preserved such typical memories of matriarchal times (The Battle of the Women!), and has several points of contact with the – nowadays Qaraqalpaq – heroic tradition *Qïrq Qïz*, 'Forty Maidens', the origin of which is probably to be sought in very ancient times, in the days of Saka hegemony in Central Asia.[99] Further influence from the numerous Amazon traditions may not be excluded, though as such they appear in a very rudimentary form. Of great age are the ancient-Khvarazmian *Siyāvush-legends*, and others of a similar character.[100] A slightly different case form the many traditions of legendary character which centre around famous historical figures. Sometimes these have become anecdotes, but very often they have turned into genuine epic tales. There are legends about Muqanna'[101] and Navā'ī[102], while stories of the persecution of Nāṣir-i Khusrau[103] can also be found. No less popular, however, are the many legends about Firdausī and other poets of the classical period.[104] Sulṭān Maḥmūd of the Ghaznavids is another personage who turns up regularly in different traditions, the historical accuracy of which, however, leaves much to be desired. Among the Shī'ites there is an immense number of the most diverse and generally highly fantastic legends about the 'Alīids, which may have served to a certain extent as models for later dramatic adaptations. The Sunnites, on the other hand, are extremely fond of anecdotes and legends about the caliphs.

Finally it is difficult to imagine that not a little local tradition seeped into already completed epic cycles, particularly those of the later authors. This is indeed the case with the later versions of the Alexander romance. At any rate the poet cut his model into a fashionable shape and adapted it where necessary to contemporary conditions. Baluchi[105] and Kurd[106] folk-traditions – and the same goes for other Iranian peoples – are of some importance in so far as they reveal such phases in the development of Iranian folk-literature that have not been preserved elsewhere owing to the strong influence of the poet's individuality or because they were superseded by advanced and complicated systems of traditions. But here too the influence of the Persian literary language and polite literature proved stronger in the majority of cases, unfortunately even predominant, while at the same time folk-literature itself was held in such contempt that we have found quite a number of records in one dialect or another – though not all of them are new – of subjects which are unknown elsewhere.

Notes on pp. 644–648

JIŘÍ CEJPEK

G. THE OSSETIAN NART SAGAS AND THEIR IMPORTANCE

We have already mentioned a few Scythian traditions in ancient Greek records. Unfortunately neither the remaining early Scythian traditions nor their Middle Scythian versions have come down to us, so that it is extremely difficult to find out exactly how the Ossetian Nart epics developed.[107] These compositions may be seen as the latest phases of evolution in North-Iranian epics. Since up to a fairly late date the Ossetians possessed no written polite literature, the intellectual influence of folk-singers[108] was uncommonly great and the heroic epics dealing with the Narts were free to develop for centuries without interruption. The oldest traditions about the Narts are assumed to date back to the 8th century B.C., which already partially fills the gap in the tradition we have just mentioned. Most of the Ossetian sagas, however, are considerably younger, the most recent of them dating from around the 14th century A.D., although it is not impossible that in the later versions a lot of old traditions survived, even if in a more fully developed form. The Ossetian Nart sagas were of great importance for the Ossetian people: they took the place of literature and history and became the school for popular knowledge. It is owing to countless Ossetian bards that this veritable treasury of folk-tradition has survived the centuries, and what is more, retained such a surprisingly convincing artistic and inventive unity. Since the history of the Ossetians has not yet been fully investigated, it is impossible to be sure how faithfully the Ossetian sagas on the Narts relate the real history of this people, but the core at least is definitely historical. Social changes that took place over the many centuries of development of these traditions, are reflected clearly enough. The Nart folk-epics have preserved a fairly faithful description of the ideology and intellectual disposition of their creators up to the present time.

The earliest Nart sagas go back to matriarchal society. The tales that form the core of the epic contain memories of conditions as they were in early patriarchal society with very clear traces of the old matriarchy still present. In the oldest saga cycles (*Warkhag and his Sons, Shatana and Wryzmag*) we can still find reminiscences of the social, family and conjugal relationships which preceded patriarchal and monogamous family arrangements. In the Shatana sagas, for example, there are many allusions which can only be understood in relation to the matriarchal form of marriage. Shatana lived with her own kinsfolk, her brother Wryzmag was at the same time her husband; she was held in great respect and had great influence in public life, in fact she played a leading part among the Narts. No remotely comparable evidence of such ancient and remarkable customs is to be found in all of the other Iranian folk-epics put together.

Of course the Nart epics also reflect later stages of social development. The most recent subjects already show signs of antagonism to the growing feudal society of the

Ossetians. We hear about conflicts between the Narts and the Aldars (i.e. the nobility).[109] Economic relations within the bounds of concrete society also gradually changed. In this context we ought not to be surprised when mythology is often called in to explain professional specialisation and also certain branches of industry. Among others the Ossetians provide a charming myth that strongly reminds us of the well-known Prometheus legend.[110]

The Ossetian Nart sagas have reached us in the form of isolated traditions. These separate sagas, however, centre round individual heroes in cycles, while the heroes have been brought into relationship with one another. Despite their independence, all the sagas are linked together to make a perfect organic whole.

The following groups of sagas may be regarded as the chief cycles: *Warkhag and his Sons*, *Wryzmag and Shatana*, *Soslan*, *Syrdon*, *Khamyts and Batradz*, *Atsamaz*; as well as these there are some smaller cycles and even isolated subjects. The final song on the decline of the Narts declares emphatically that they chose death and everlasting glory above everlasting but inglorious life.

The Ossetian Nart epics are remarkable for their monumental descriptions, brief but penetrating characterisations, simple but clever presentations, effective dramatisation, and also humour. We have already mentioned the faithful presentation of the changes in ideology which occurred in the course of history. Indeed the Narts always had very definite and concrete ideas about both natural phenomena and social issues, and they never ceased to emphasise the importance of creative activity.

It is true that the Nart sagas are also to be found, in varying forms, among other Caucasian peoples, but nowhere else did they equal the Ossetian prototypes in their degree of perfection, in variety and sheer number.[111]

On the other hand it is not inconceivable that the Nart sagas played their part in the development of the heroic legends and cults in ancient Greece – still of course in some rudimentary form which disappeared long ago and was superseded in the course of history. The frequency with which Caucasian motifs turn up in Greek mythology seems to indicate such.[112]

The current dispute on the ethnological origin of the Caucasian Nart traditions is closely connected with an analysis of the ethnogenetical processes that have resulted in the present-day Ossetians. Of course the Scythian question is far from having been completely and satisfactorily solved. The Iranian character of the contemporary Ossetian ethnos is quite certain and beyond dispute, even the Caucasian substratum has been definitively established. Ossetian folk-tradition, moreover, was islamised only to a slight extent, a fact that is of great significance for the comparative study of Iranian folk-literature. The fact that the Scythians were ancestors to the present-day Ossetians as well as partially to the Tajiks is another reason for taking an interest in Ossetian folk-epics.

To summarise it may be stated that the Ossetian folk epics reached a degree of cyclisation comparable to that of the folk-epics in Iran proper at the time before the

Notes on pp. 644–648

Sasanian codification. It may be added that certain Ossetian subjects also found their way into smaller poetical forms as well as folk-tales. Modern Ossetian polite literature too very often makes use of them.

H. THE *DĀSTĀNS* – THEIR DEVELOPMENT AND CONNECTIONS

The *dāstāns* can properly be considered as an intermediate form between epics, narrative literature and folk-tales.

According to Romaskevich[113] the story-teller Juhūnvāz from Ardakān, near Shīrāz, used to hold sessions lasting several evenings during which he recited various tales, mostly related to each other through the main plot and common personages, interrupting the sequence with appropriate songs. This narrative style, in which the main story is interspersed with episodes and poetical interludes, is still alive and continues to be productive today not only among the Iranians but also among the Uzbeks and in other places in the Islamic east. The best example of this narrative technique for sheer size and number of variations, is really the *Book of a Thousand and One Nights*.

The element of imagination was developed in folk-romances of chivalry and particularly in the *dāstāns* under the direct influence of folk-tales. It is especially evident in *dāstāns* with a highly romantic subject. The exuberant fantasy to be found in the *dāstāns* is definitely not directly related to pre-Islamic superstitions and myths (though a few exceptions only prove the rule), nor to rites and customs of ancient times. As we have already said, most of it was derived from folk-tales, but in the *dāstāns* fantasy serves only as an attractive embellishment to the tale.[114] It is not determined by the earlier development of the subject, as in the case of fairy-tales.

The subjects of the *dāstāns* are noted for their very considerable variety. Besides the heroic epics we often find romantic epics with a substantial share of erotic subjects; sometimes they are penetrated by subjects of a novelistic character. These smaller epical forms are always full of exuberant imagination. The *dāstāns* very often used to be shaded with elegiac, sometimes even tragic tones.

A little tragedy in verse form is the *Tale of Mame and Ayshe*.[115] Kurdic *dāstāns* also contain other subjects.[116] Very well known is the *Tale of Aḥmad-Khān Lab-zerrīne*, the heroic defender of the fortress Dïm-dïm (with the Mukrī Kurds)[117], while the romantic tale of *Mamu and Zinē*[118] is generally popular. Apart from many other original subjects, no less in favour are the *dāstāns* on Rustam, influenced by the Persian *Shāh-nāma*, and those on Antar with subjects borrowed from the famous romance of chivalry of the same name.[119]

The Afghan *dāstāns* are of the heroic as well as the romantic type. They are written either in verse form or in prose, sometimes with verse interpolations. The latter are really of an intermediate type and form a transition to folk-tales. All categories of Afghan *dāstāns* are distinctly related to historical events and to the social development of the Afghan tribes. Besides the heroic tale on *Fātiḥ-Khān Baretsay*[120], the romantic story of the tender love between *Ādam-Khān and Durrkhāniy*[121] also enjoys popularity. The same applies to the tale on the gay *Dilyāy and his sweetheart Shahō*[122] and other similar subjects. Somewhat different are the historical songs, not only as regards their poetical form but also their content. They sing of concrete historical events and can be strictly dated as well as grouped into several cycles.[123] The songs on romantic subjects are closely connected with the prose-tales.[124]

The subjects of the Baluchi *dāstāns*[125] are either historical (e.g. the *Wanderings of the Rind-Baluchis*[126], the *Quarrel of Mīr Chākar and Gvaharām*[127]) or of the romantic type, for instance *Dōstēn and Shīrēn.*[128]

We can safely say that the *dāstāns* form the building material for more extensive epical compositions. Certainly the circumstances surrounding their development and the conditions under which this took place varied greatly, and evolution was mostly gradual and slow. Traces of this development have been relatively well preserved, although in the majority of cases we do not possess examples of all the phases. If we sum up all the facts mentioned here, we are bound to conclude that the great epic masterpieces of Persian polite literature are far more closely linked with folk-literature than was formerly supposed; the relationship between polite literature and folk-literature is far more profound, important and intense, the author's personal contribution to the composition, development and motivation much smaller, while the influence of folk-literature is far more extensive and penetrating than would appear at a first glance. Oddly enough the length of a story appears to be in inverse proportion to the number of motifs used. Minor poetical forms reveal a frankly prodigious wealth of the most heterogeneous motifs, while epic cycles pick out only the most suitable. One might put it this way: that the great epic works of polite literature canonised only a few of the 'classical' subjects ,whereas others were not used in epics until a considerable time later in the post-classical period, though even then only isolated non-classical motifs were incorporated. This may be very true of polite literature, but similar tendencies probably did not exist in folk-literature at all. Otherwise it would be hard to explain how so many undisputedly ancient motifs, which were never adopted by polite literature, have come down to us. By saying all this, we do not mean to belittle the part played by the poet in respect of his invention, talent or poetic skill. We only wish to give emphasis to the importance of folk-literature for the preservation and propagation of folk-traditions created by anonymous groups of poets.

Notes on pp. 644–648

NOTES

1. Cf. *Drevniye avtorї o Sredney Azii* (T. 1940); cf. also Christensen, *Les gestes*, 107–140.
2. Cf. Klinger, V.P., 'Skazochnїye motivї v istorii Gerodota', in *Izv. Kiev. univ., istor.-filol. fak.*, 1902, 111–202; cf. Lübker, *Reallexikon*, 459–460; Lur'ye, S. Ya., *Gerodot* (M.-L. 1947); Dovatur, A., *Povestvovatel'nїy i nauchnїy stil' Gerodota* (L. 1957); cf. also *Istoriya grecheskoy literaturї*, II, 28–68.
3. Cf. Lübker, *Reallexikon*, 567; Diodorus II, 32; *Ist.grecheskoy lit.*, II, 127–129.
4. *Est*, 2, 23; *Est*, 10, 2; Selin–Rost, *Einl. in das alte Testament*, 8th ed., 171–172; cf. also Cosquin, Emmanuel: *Le prologue-cadre des 1001 nuits – Les légendes perses et le Livre d'Ester* (Paris 1909).
5. Herodotus, IV, 1.–16.; also *Istoriya tadzh. naroda*, I (M. 1963), principally 189–211.
6. Herodotus, IV, 59.–82.
7. Herodotus, I, 96.–107, 108.–122.; with some restrictions also Herodotus, III, 67.–87.
8. Cf. *Ist. grech.lit.*, II, 101–126; Lübker, *Reallexikon*, 1129–1131.
9. Cf. *Ist. grech. lit.*, III, 153–156; Radtsig, *Ist. drevne-grech. lit.*, 495–497 *et passim*; the following chapters are based on old Iranian traditions: Diodorus, II, 24.–28., 32., 33., 43.–46.; IX., 32., 33.; cf. also Lübker, *Reallexikon*, 293.
10. Cf. Lübker, *Reallexikon*, 567; Diodorus, II, 1.–34., perhaps used directly.
11. Cf. Justinus, I, 1., 4.; II, 1., 3., 4.,; cf. Pompeius Trogus, *Fragmenta*, collegit Otto Seel (Bibl. Teubneriana)(Lipsiae 1956), *passim*: there are also important observations on textual criticism concerning Justinus, Pompeius Trogus, and other authors of antiquity; cf. also Teufel, *Gesch. der röm. Lit.*, 7th ed., II, 131–135.
12. Cf. Lübker, *Reallexikon*, 135.
13. Atheneus, XIII, 5., 75.; for German translation see *Griechische Märchen* (v. Bibl.!), 143–144.
14. Christensen, *Les gestes des rois*, 46, 51; Massé, *Firdousi et l'épopée nationale*, 23–24; Braginskiy, *Iz ist.*, 218–222; cf. also Zand, *Shest vekov slavї* (M. 1964), 17–18.
15. Cf. Lübker, *Reallexikon*, 135.
16. Cf. Braginskiy, *Iz ist.*, 91–97; for general information cf. also Nyberg, *Die Religionen des alten Iran* (Leipzig 1938), *passim.*
17. Cf. Braginskiy, *Iz ist.*, 97–101.
18. Cf. Braginskiy, *Iz ist.*, 101–120.
19. Cf. Braginskiy, *Iz ist.*, 120–144.
20. Cf. Just., I.1., II.1., III.3., and also Braginskiy, *Iz ist.*, 174–206; cf. also *Ist.tadzh.nar.*, I (M. 1963), 127–133; Masson–Romodin, *Istoriya Afganistana*, I (M. 1964), 41–45.
21. Cf. Christensen, *Les gestes*, 62; Osmanov, *Svodї*, *passim*; Braginskiy, *Iz ist.*, 174–206 *et passim*; also Molé, *L'épopée*, and Barthold, *ZDMG*, 1944, *ZVORAO*, 12 (1915); Inostrantsev, *Persidskaya literaturnaya traditsiya*; Darmesteter, James, *Etudes iraniennes*, II, 187–251; cf. also *Ist. tadzh. nar.*, I, 137–186.
22. Cf. Osmanov, *Svodї, passim*; Brockelmann, *Gesch. der arab. Lit.*, I, 123, 142, 284 *et passim*; see also Basset, *Mille et un contes arabes* (Paris 1924–1926), I–III, *passim.*
23. Cf. Christensen, *Les gestes*, 33.
24. Cf. Christensen, *Les gestes*, 50, 78–83; Braginskiy, *Iz ist.*, 189, 218–223.
25. Brockelmann, *GAL*, I, 147–148; Christensen, *Les gestes*, 56–60 *et passim.*
26. Christensen, *Les gestes*, 56–59; Fihrist, 305, 10; feudal transformation among others in the *Shāhnāma* and the *Siyāsat-nāma*; cf. also Firdausī, *Skazaniye o Bakhrome Chubine iz Shakhname* (St. 1953); cf. Czeglédy, K., '*Bahrām Čōbēn* and the Persian Apocalyptic Literature', *Acta Orientalia Acad. Sc. Hungaricae*, 8 (Budapest 1958), 21–43.

27. Christensen, *Les gestes*, 60; Molé, *L'épopée iranienne après Firdousi, passim*; Inostrantsev, *Persid. liter. traditsiya, passim.*
28. Christensen, *Les gestes*, 58, 78–83; Fihrist, 305, 12.
29. Nöldeke, 'Das Iranische Nationalepos', 139, 189, 197; Ethé, *Np. Lit.*, 240, 241, 267; Braginskiy, *Iz ist., passim; Ocherki*, 166–206; Baumgartner, *Gesch. der Weltlit.*, I, 535–539; Minorsky, *Vīs u Rāmīn, passim*; Zand, *Shest vekov slavī*, 107–110; cf. also Braginskiy's preface to the Russian translation of Gurgānī, *Vis i Ramin* (M. 1963), 3–20.
30. Cf. Ranke, Friedrich, *Tristan und Isold* (München 1925).
31. Christensen, *Les gestes*, 62; for a very interesting Kurdish adaptation of Bezhin and Manije cf. Mackenzie, *Kurdish Dialect Studies*, II, 92–107.
32. Cf. Rypka, 'Les sept princesses de Nizāmī', in *L'âme de l'Iran*, 99–125; Bertel's, *Nizami* (M. 1956); Shaginyan, *Etyudī o Nizami* (M. 190).
33. Bertel's, *Roman ob Aleksandre, passim*; cf. also Pfister, *Alexander..., passim.*
34. Cf. Pigulevskaya, N.V., *Arabī u granits Vizantii i Irana v IV–VI vv.* (M.-L. 1964), principally 57–123.
35. B. Hishām, ed. Wüstenfeld, 235–236.
36. Brockelmann, *GAL*, *v.s.* 'Amelang', 95.
37. *Qur'ān*, XXXI, 5.–6.
38. Cf. Khanna al'- Fakhūrī, *Istoriya arabskoy literaturī*, I (M. 1959), 334–363.
39. Cf. among others Basset, René, *Mille et un contes, récits et légendes arabes*, I–III (Paris 1924–1926).
40. But cf. also Osmanov, *Svodī.*
41. Christensen, *Les gestes*, 33, 34, 43; Massé, *Firdousi*, 28, 29, 32–34.
42. Braginskiy, *Ocherki*, 176; *Al-āthāru'l-bāqiya*, 220.
43. Cf. Nöldeke, 'Das iranische Nationalepos', *GIPh*, II, 130–211; Massé, *Firdousi et l'épopée iranienne* (Paris 1935); Bertel's, *Ist. pers.-tadzh. liter.*, 169–238.
44. Baumgartner, *Gesch. der Weltlit.*, I, 533; cf. in any case also Bertel's, *IPTL*, 169–286.
45. Older forms of Iranian folk-traditions are to be found in the Caucasus, cf. Miller, Vs., *Ekskursī v oblast' russkago narodnago eposa I–VIII* (M. 1892), 55–85, 117–152, 152–172, *Prilozheniya*, 1–69.
46. Cf. Zhirmunskiy–Zarifov, *Uzb. ger. epos*, 184, 185.
47. The best evidence of this process is to be found in several examples of after-effects produced by Iranian folk-traditions about Rustam as found among non-Iranian peoples in the Caucasus, cf. *Kaukasische Märchen* (Jena 1920), 210–236.
48. Cf. Massé, *Firdousi*, 195, but also Zhirmunskiy–Zarifov, *op. cit.*; also Braginskiy, *Iz ist.*
49. Kowalski, *Studia nad Š.–n.*, II, 4–7; Firdousi, *Kniga tsarey Shakhname* (M. 1934), 48–56; Firdousi, *Shakhname v dvukh knigakh* (m. 1964), 75–81.
50. Osmanov, *O nar. tendentsiyakh*, 39–42; *Literatura Irana X–XV vv.*, principally 126–156; Firdousi, *Shakhname v dvukh knigakh* (M. 1946), kn. 2, 705–712.
51. Cf. Braginskiy, *Ocherki*, 166–206, *Iz ist.*, 309, 396, 399; Ethé, *Np. Lit.*, 240, 246, 259, 310; Minorsky, *Vīs u Rāmīn;* Molé (cf. Bibl. B VI b); cf. Gurgani, *Vis i Ramin* (M. 1963), principally Braginskiy's Preface, 3–20.
52. But Braginskiy (*Ocherki*, 166–206) holds a different view.
53. Cf. Ethé, *Np. Lit.*, 233–234; Nöldeke, 'Iran. Nationalepos', 209–210; Massé, *Firdousi*, 263–268; Braginskiy, *Iz ist.*, 307–322; *Ocherki* 166–206.
54. Zhirmunskiy–Zarifov, *op. cit.*, 34; Zhukovskiy, *Musul'manstvo Rustama, passim.*
55. Cf. Pfister, *Alexander..., passim*; Bertel's, *Roman ob Aleksandre, passim*; Friedländer, J., *Die Chadhirlegende u.d. Alexanderroman* (Lpz. – B. 1913).
56. Cf. Lübker, *Reallexikon*, 534, 738.

57. Bertel's, *Roman ob Aleksandre*, 3, 4, 9–13.
58. Ayni, *Ustad Rudaki* (M. 1958); Braginskiy, *Ocherki*, 123–148; Osmanov, *Firdousi* (M. 1959); Massé, *Firdousi*, 53–97; Klimovich, *Khrestomatiya, passim*; cf. also Braginskiy, 'Okean "Shakh-name" i nekotorïye ego taynï', in Firdousi, *Shakh-name v dvukh knigakh* (M. 1964), I, 5–9.
59. E.g. *inter alia*: Morgenstierne, Georg, *Indo-Iranian Frontier-Languages*, II, 510–512 (Wakhan); Morgenstierne, *IIFL*, I, 165–171 (Parachi); Masson–Romodin, *Istoriya Afganistana*, I (M. 1964), 242–255; cf. also Mackenzie, *Kurdish Dialect Studies*, II (London 1962), 32–43.
60. Massé, *Croyances et coutumes*, 369–407 *et passim*; Hackin–Kohzad, *Légendes et coutumes afghanes, passim.*
61. Massé, *Firdousi*, 43, 95; Sirdar Ikbal Ali Shah, *Afghanistan of the Afghans*, 97, 114, 121–124, 136–148, 152–157; Hackin–Kohzad, *op. cit., passim.*
62. Duda, *Ferhād und Schīrīn*, 3; cf. also Aliyev, *Legenda o Khosrove i Shirin v liter. nar. Vostoka* (M. 1960).
63. Christensen, *Les gestes*, 66.
64. Cf. Zhirmunskiy–Zarifov, *op. cit.*
65. Cf. Bertel's, *Nizami*, 129–153; Krachkovskiy, *Rannyaya istoriya povesti o Madzhnune i Leyle...*, 31.
66. Zhirmunskiy–Zarifov, *op. cit.*, 294–301; *Tadzhikskiye nar. skazki*, 196–203.
67. An episode from *Seven planets* by Navā'ī.
68. Cf. Qur'ān, s. XII; among many other versions cf. also Mackenzie, *Kurdish Dialect Studies*, II, 180–201.
69. Braginskiy, *Ocherki*, 177–180; cf. *Der gehörnte Siegfried und andere Volksbücher* (B. 1956), 35–57; Huet, 'Sur l'origine de la Floire et Blancheflor', *Romania*, 27 (1899); Gröber, *Franz. Lit.* (Roman. Grdr.), 490, 527; ten Brink, Bernhard, *Geschichte der englischen Literatur*, 2.A (Strassburg 1899), 200, 273 (Middle-English romance of chivalry); Voretzsch, Carl, *Einführung in das Studium der altfranz. Literatur*, 2.A. (Halle 1913), 381 *et passim*
70. Petit de Julleville, *Histoire de la langue et de la littérature francaise*, I, 255–344; Vogt, *Mittelhochdeutsche Literatur* (Grdr. d. germ. Phil.), 2nd ed., II, 185–308.
71. Zhirmunskiy–Zarifov, *op. cit.*, 337, 449–450.
72. Cf. Baumgartner, *op. cit.*, I, 568–569; Ethé, *Np. Lit.*, 318; Zand, *Shest vekov slavï*, 162–164; cf. also *Plutovka iz Bagdada* (M. 1963), 14 (Borshchevskiy's excellent essay 'Persidskaya narodnaya literatura', 5–26).
73. Ethé, *Np. Lit.*, 318; Baumgartner, *op. cit.*, I, 568; cf. also Braginskiy, *Ocherki*, 298–301; Zand, *op, cit.*, 164.
74. Ethé, *Np. Lit.*, 318–320; Baumgartner, *op. cit.*, I, 569.
75. Cf. Braginskiy, *Ocherki*, 285–286.
76. Cf. Braginskiy, *Ocherki*, 286–289; Zand, *op. cit.*, 164.
77. Cf. Braginskiy, *Ocherki*, 338–360.
78. Cf. Ethé, *Np. Lit.*, 320–321; *Thousand and One Nights*, 756th–778th night; *Mille et un jours*, 99th–108th day; Zhirmunskiy–Zarifov, *op. cit.*, 281, 451.
79. Cf. Ethé, *Np. Lit.*, 317–323.
80. Zhirmunskiy–Zarifov, *op. cit.*, 340.
81. *Istoriya tadzh. naroda*, II, kniga 1-ya, 364–406; kn. 2-ya, 21–47, 57–66, 103–114 (M. 1964); cf. also Christina Hole, *English Folk Heroes*, 71–102 (Robin Hood!).
82. Several dialectal variants of the name exist.
83. Cf. Braginskiy, *Ocherki*, 88–119; 'O tadzh. epose "Gurguli" i ego khudozhestvennïkh osobenostyakh', in *Voprosï izucheniya eposa nar. SSSR*, 126–148; Klimovich, *Khrestomatiya*, 117–119, *Iz ist. literatur Sov. Vostoka*, 181–199; Zhirmunskiy–Zarifov, *op. cit.*, 164–279; Zhirmunskiy, 'Epich. tvorchestvo nar. Sred. Azii', in *Nar. ger.epos*, 195–240, mainly 203–204, 213–218.
84. Lenskiy, *Tadzhikskaya SSR*, *Muzïkal'naya kul'tura*, 2nd ed. (M. 1957) 25–26; Mironov, *Mu-*

zïka Tadzhikov (St. 1932); cf. also Zhirmunskiy, 'Sredneaziatskiye nar. skaziteli', in *Nar. ger. epos*, 241–281.

85. Zhirmunskiy–Zarifov, 34, 201, 282; Klimovich, *Khrestomatiya*, 23; Tolstov, *Po sledam drevnego Khorezma, passim*, v. indices!

86. Klimovich, *op. cit.*, 23.

87. *Sov. kompozitorï* (M. 1957), 126–128.

88. Zhirmunskiy–Zarifov, *op. cit.*, 165, 166, 177.

89. Cf. *Ukrayins'ka narodna poetïchna tvorchist*, I (Kïyiv 1958), 485; many texts in the anthology *Istorïchni pisni* (Kïyiv 1961), 306–330, annotations to texts 957–961.

90. Chodzko, *Specimens of Popular Poetry*, 7, 8.

91. Zhirmunskiy–Zarifov, *op. cit.*, 192–194.

92. Herodotus, I, 110.

93. Livius, I, 4.

94. Zhirmunskiy–Zarifov, *op. cit.*, 173, 174, 183, 184, 186–190, 191, 197, 199, 212.

95. Zhirmunskiy–Zarifov, *op. cit.*, 201; Zhukovskiy, *Musul'manstvo Rustama*, 109; Klimovich, *Khrestomatiya*, 23; cf. Kowalski, *Studia*, II, 4–7, 79–89; Firdousi, *Kniga tsarey, Shakhname* (M. 1934), 48–57; Lakhuti, *Kuznets Kova* (St. - L. 1941).

96. Massé, *Croyances*, 371–382, 390, 397, 409, 410, 413, 414; Hackin–Kohzad, *Légendes et coutumes afghanes, passim.*

97. Cf. *Antologiya tadzh. poezii*, 579; *Nar. poeziya Tadzhikistana*, 51–54; cf. also Diodorus, II, 34; III, 36; cf. Braginskiy, *Iz ist.*, 133.

98. *Tadzh. nar. skazki*, 178–182.

99. *Sorok devushek* (Klimovich, 'Predislovie'), 5, 12; Klimovich, *Iz ist. liter. nar. Sov. Vostoka*, 200–220; Zhdanko, *Karakalpak. poema Kïrk Kïz, passim*; cf. also *Istoriya tadzh. naroda* (M. 1963), I, principally 189–210.

100. Tolstov, *Po sledam drevnego Khorezma, passim.*

101. Cf. *Istoriya tadzh. nar.*, II, kn.I-ya, 115-119; Yakubovskiy, A. Yu., 'Vosstaniye Mukannï – dvizheniye lyudey v belïkh odezhdakh', *SV*, 5 (1948), 35–54

102. Bertel's, *Navoi, passim*; Klimovich, *Khrestomatiya*, 20, 776; Boldïrev, A. N., 'Alisher Navoi v rasskazakh sovremennikov', in *Alisher Navoi* (M.-L. 1946), 121–152.

103. Klimovich, *Khrestomatiya*, 20, 43, 776.

104. Cf. 'Aufī, *Lubābu'l-albāb, passim* (Bibl. B VIb); see also Braginskiy, *Ocherki*, 304–312.

105. Cf. Dames, *Sketch of the North Balochi Language*, 133–165.

106. Cf. Beidar, *Grammaire Kurde*; Makas, *Kurdische Texte, passim*; Mann, *Mukrī, Kurdskiye skazki, passim*; Mackenzie, *Kurdish Dialect Studies*, II (London 1962), *passim.*

107. Concise but excellent references to Ossetian folk-epics and folk-poetry are contained in: *Istoriya Osetinskoy ASSR*, I (M. 1959); for the most important passages see 36–37, 53–54, 68, 74–75, 78, 92–94, 96, 103, 107, 108, 113–116, 118, 128, 152–154, 172; an extremely important essay on the oldest heroic traditions of the Caucasian peoples was incorporated by E. M. Meletinskiy in his excellent book *Proiskhozhdeniye geroicheskogo eposa* (M. 1963), 156–246, mainly 156–206.

108. Cf. *Muzïkal'naya kul'tura avtonom. respublik RSFSR, Tskhurbayeva, Severo-oset. ASSR*, 245-262.

109. *Oset. nartskiy epos*, 7, 11, 95–116.

110. Dirr, *Kaukasische Märchen*, 247–248; cf. also Meletinskiy, *Proiskhozhdeniye ger. eposa*, 206-230.

111. *Nartskiye skazaniya* (Bitiyev, 'Predisloviye'); *Osetinskiye nartskiye skazaniya* (Kulov, 'Predislovie').

112. Semper, *Rassen und Religionen im alten Vorderasien*, 351; Meletinskiy, *Proiskhozhdeniye ger. eposa*, 156–246; Preller, *Griechische Mythologie*, I–II (Berlin 1872–1875), *passim*; v. Orelli, *Allg. Religionsgeschichte*, II, 187–259.

113. Romaskevich, *Persidskiye nar. skazki*, 32.
114. Zhirmunskiy–Zarifov, *op. cit.*, 379–402.
115. Kurdoyev–Tsukerman, *Kurdskiye tekstï*, 30–46.
116. Cf. *Kurdskiye skazki, passim*; Nikitine, *Les Kurdes*, 250–281; Vil'chevskiy, *Mukrinskiye Kurdï*, 218–222; Aristova, *Ocherki kul'turï i bïta kurd. krestyan Irana*, 256–258.
117. Mann, *Mukrī*, 12–24; cf. Vil'chevskiy, *Mukrinskiye kurdï*, 219.
118. Mann, *Mukrī*, 24–81; Makas, *Kurdische Texte*, 1–20; Vil'chevskiy, *Mukrinskiye kurdï*, 219.
119. Vil'chevskiy, *op. cit.*, 219; *Kurdskiye skazki*, 55–59.
120. *Afganskiye skazki*, 93–112.
121. *Afganskiye skazki*, 11–20; also Darmesteter, *Chants pop. des Afgh.*, 117–124.
122. *Afganskiye skazki*, 73–82.
123. Darmesteter, *Chants pop.*, 1–84.
124. Darmesteter, *Chants pop.*, 110–146.
125. Dames, *Sketch*, 133–171.
126. Dames, *Sketch*, 133–135.
127. Dames, *Sketch*, 137–140.
128. Dames, *Sketch*, 142–147.

III. INTRODUCTION TO FOLK-TALES

A. IRANIAN FOLK-TALES AND PROBLEMS ARISING FROM THEM

Iran is a country exceedingly rich in folk-tales. Some motifs from these tales are to be found only on their home ground, but most of them have spread to far-away places often beyond the domain of Iranian culture. Ingeniously devised and developed single fairy-tales or whole series of them grouped together according to the most diverse principles, form an essential part of Persian polite literature.[1] Until now, however, the study of folk-tales in Iran has been somewhat neglected.

It would be a mistake to regard and treat tales merely as a form of fiction. When studying them one has to find out about the way they were composed as well as about the social milieu in which they came into being.

The telling of folk-tales used to be, and is still in many cases, subject to a number of taboos. In the first place one was restricted to certain times of the day and often of the year. It was believed that if such rules were broken it might bring about the death of domestic animals or cause a pestilence. The use of musical instruments, with which it was the custom in many places to accompany the narrator, is also frequently limited. Winter nights were generally considered the most suitable time for telling folk-tales.[2]

In this context Zarubin[3] made an interesting observation among the Baluchis which confirms this: it is improper to tell folk-tales in the daytime. The practice has therefore been renounced and it is simply not done, even if people have the opportunity or the leisure. It is often said that the breaking of this rule will have serious repercussions on the house where a folk-tale was told at an unsuitable time, or that an accident may happen. Others are afraid lest there be unpleasant consequences for the narrator himself, particularly that he may be afflicted with irresoluteness, an effect of which might be the inability to take the necessary decisive action even in emer-

Notes on pp. 658–659

gencies. If in spite of all this the Baluchi do tell a folk-tale, they are careful to avoid ritual and other appurtenances connected with folk-tales.

The Tatis, a small Iranian tribe in the Caucasus, have a proverb about this which is quite amusing: If you tell a folk-tale in the daytime, a thief will steal your trousers!

Customs like these, so obviously bound up with taboos, can only be explained by conjecture: at night the cattle is safely asleep locked up in the stable and can be protected from evil spirits in many different ways, for instance with herbs. Also in winter the spirits of the forest and other demons are supposed to be asleep in the north, or at any rate so far away from man that they cannot possibly come near him, listen to him or harm him. Another tradition says that winter is just the only time when good spirits can listen to folk-tales, because in summer they are too busy attending to work and activities that are so beneficial to man.

Many nations have traditions to the effect that demons are fond of folk-tales. Very old examples are the Greek Sirens, the Old-German Lorelei, and various water sprites. The most varying kinds of spirits, too, are fond of listening to music.[4]

Folk-tales can also form a reliable and important source of information in an attempt to reconstruct the prehistoric form of a certain mythological subject; for Greek, Roman and to an equal extent Ancient-Iranian and Ancient-Indian myths in the form in which we have inherited them in religious texts, epics and edifying entertainment literature, are no more than relatively late and recent stylisations and adaptations of old traditions, myths, and folk-tales.

Of course folk-tales are not just simple poetical forms, on the contrary they are highly heterogeneous. This is not surprising if one considers for how long they have been evolving and how many different uses and functions they have served. In this respect social milieu and the purpose of this genre of folk-tradition were decisive.

Some tales were principally intended for the entertainment of the aristocracy or other ruling classes and consequently abound in princes and princesses. On the other hand we also know of folk-tales representing a very pronounced social and even democratic point of view; in these cases we find the principal characters are mostly peasants, craftsmen and other working people. One should not forget that when the folk-tales came to be cyclised in stories-within-a-framework, or in series, stories of dissimilar types – either completely contrasting or belonging to the intermediate type – could appear side by side.

Two main types that are diametrically opposed are the romantic and fairy-tales and the realistic tales of everyday life. In the first category fantasy and adventure play a very important part. They are often derived from legends, and certain motifs from this type of folk-tale have found their way into heroic epics, especially in more recent times. Characteristic of the more realistic folk-tales is the fact that fantasy is only seldom resorted to; they lack the demonic element and do not make use of canonised formulas for the plot or of stereotyped expressions. It must be strongly emphasised, however, that there are very few folk-tales belonging purely to one type – most of them are combinations of several categories.[5]

The gamut of folk-tale motifs is therefore extremely rich and varied. On the one hand there are the tales of magic with countless *dēvs*, *parīs,* giants and giantesses, sorcerers and sorceresses, miracles and people being transformed into animals or *vice versa;* on the other hand we find an enormous number of transitional forms, up to tales of everyday life that approach our idea of a short story – realistic in character with many details carefully observed from daily occurrences. These last are full of rogues and thieves, boasting and buffoonery (Seven in one Blow), wagers and tasks which, on condition they are brought to a satisfactory or successful end, are rewarded by a fortune or a wife. Stories about deceived husbands should also not be underestimated, for they are very much in vogue, though all too often these border on vulgarity and become almost pornographic. On the other hand, there is a very ancient group of animal folk-tales, mostly totemistic and at least partly aetiological (some properties of animals are explained). The distribution of these animal folk-tales is determined by zoological and geographical factors. And the division of animals into the deceitful and the deceived is understandable if one considers the popular psychology at the time when they came into being.[6]

The realistic folk-tales of everyday life are probably more recent than the animal and magic stories.

When studying Iranian folk-tales one must start with the Avesta.[7] In this respect the fact that the Sasanian part of the Avesta has been lost is not so distressing, for there were hardly any folk-tale subjects that we do not know of in the missing books. Valuable, however, are some episodes or even mere allusions which are to be found in the hymn-like Yashts. For the interpretation of these, a comparison with later texts is also necessary, otherwise much in them would be misunderstood. They are mostly Middle-Iranian works of a predominantly theological character; unfortunately, however, a large part of the original pattern has been destroyed by later additions. Very important therefore are the recordings of the ancient Greek authors, as they reflect earlier stages of development. However precious the old West-Iranian traditions may be, and particularly the epic and heroic ones that have been thus preserved, they remain somewhat isolated because we have no examples of subsequent developments. This will always give rise to considerable difficulties.

In the majority of cases collections of Iranian folk-tales were intended merely as entertainment and thus do not express any special trends. Many of these recordings of folk-tales are closely related to prose folk-books, and consequently served as model for folk-prints later on.[8]

Iran is a country in which the native culture very early became intermingled with Semitic influences. A very striking instance is the genesis of the *Thousand and One Nights*, as we shall see later, like other similar recorded collections of tales and stories rich in Iranian motifs. It makes no difference here whether these are literary or

Notes on pp. 658–659

popular adaptations. Indo-European features appear more often in tales that have been used in polite literature – mostly the products of popular narrators or harem women. Sometimes we find quite startling analogies to folk-tales of other Indo-European nations. Another important factor is that although Iranian folk-tales and fables were very frequently used as examples or parables in mystic literature, they were islamised only in form and very superficially at that, and in most cases remained completely untouched by later religious development. On the contrary, the philosophy of life as revealed in the folk-tales shows fundamental relics of original pre-Islamic religious ideas, especially in respect of the supernatural. The chief exponents of the supernatural in Iranian folk-tales are *dēvs* and *parīs,* sometimes also jinns and ghouls, which are of Arabic origin.

It is often very difficult to distinguish between adaptation for polite literature and popular tradition in folk-tales, since the latter are in fact frequently reflections of an earlier literary work of which the folk-literature model has long since been forgotten. It is worth noting that Semitic folk-tales most often came in for literary treatment in Iran, whereas the Indo-European type are only seldom to be found in polite literature and have consequently retained their original form fairly well.

We need not be surprised to find that Shī'ite philosophy is full of old Iranian ideas, for instance that the Twelfth Imām lives in hiding somewhere and will not appear until the day of the Last Judgment.[9]

The narrator is an exceedingly important person. He is usually known as *qiṣṣa-gū*, and his stories are mostly about animals and magic. His sphere of action is the *ma'rika*, i.e. a gathering of people in a public place. This custom was already mentioned at the beginning of the 16th century A.D. by Kāshifī.[10]

The profession of narrator of folk-tales is now dying out, but forty or fifty years ago it was by no means an exceptional occupation. Like the jugglers who used to come to annual fairs, the narrators generally brought along some pictures to which they could refer during the course of the story. As folk-tales were usually recited at a fairly high speed, this often caused considerable difficulties for the European scholar trying to write them down.[11]

Folk-tales, which are nearly always in prose, allow the narrator a large measure of initiative and the possibility of improvisation regarding the arrangement of details and performance. It is he who chooses it and adapts it to his own taste or to the company in question, and to his own relationship with other social classes.

Professional story-tellers were nearly always luckless beggars, often artisans who had come down in the world or small stall-holders at the market; some of them would do occasional jobs as carpenters or joiners, while others sold fruit in the town bazaar or knitted stockings. The social status of story-tellers in Iran was not bad, for the good ones among them enjoyed a fair measure of public esteem and even respect. A few managed to rise to the position of court narrator (*naqqāl-bāshī*), and became members of the Shāh's household. The better story-tellers were usually able to read and write and were relatively well-read, particularly in the field of folk-tales. This is why besides popular and orally transmitted folk-tales and stories, they would sometimes re–tell or quote from many a work of polite literature. Among samples of such works that were particularly popular with the public were several episodes from the *Shāh-nāma* – such as the adventures and heroic deeds of Rustam, Bīzhan and Manīzha[12] etc. – or parts of old Persian romances of chivalry.[13] Although many story-tellers had quite astounding memories, they recorded their repertory of tales in books (*Kitābcha,* also sometimes called *Tūmār*). In place of these manuscript memory-aids, recently cheap lithographs have been appearing – Iranian prose folk-prints.

The Iranians are passionately fond of listening to folk-tales while they are at work, but even more so after working-hours. That is how not only the *maʿrika* but also the Iranian coffee-houses and tea-shops (*qahva-khāna*) have become domains of activity for story-tellers. Particularly in summer they try to find a place shaded from the sun. The regular presence of a good story-teller helps to make a coffee-house popular. The coffee-brewers know this very well and often hire a narrator or story-teller or reader (who usually reads passages from the *Shāh-nāma*) to encourage business. Everything is carefully agreed upon: mutual obligations, wages, advances, the duration and hours of narrating or reading. They generally start after two o'clock or after sunset and go on until eleven.

The story-teller dramatises his recital and illustrates it with play of features and gesticulation. The audience also plays an active part, by responding in unison at appropriate points in the story. After all, they are not hearing it for the first time! When the climax of excitement is reached, however, the narration is suddenly interrupted, the interval providing an opportunity to collect the story-teller's fee. The main season for storytelling is the winter or the Ramaḍan, as soon as fasting is broken at sunset. Other festive occasions such as the Iranian New Year, weddings and births, also provide the storyteller with plenty of eager listeners. On all such occasions narrators are just as indispensable as musicians, but the former enjoy incomparably more respect and honour.

If a conversation on daily occurrences comes to a halt the moment has come to call upon the narrator. The same happens among the women; it is usually the eldest of them who remembers the folk-tales handed down for generations, captures thereby the imagination of the children and entertains the grown-ups with her stories. Not seldom, however, the women sit with the men and at such gatherings other types of folk-literature are also recited now and then.

Wandering and travelling story-tellers are also of great importance. It is they who spread local tales far and wide. Most of them are cattle-drovers (*chārvādārs*) and dervishes, both these categories of men being famous as professional narrators.

A further group of story-tellers, though a very small one, which deserves just as much attention, are the Persian Jews, among whom a great many stories have been preserved that have already completely disappeared from Moslem traditions.[14] This is also true of the even smaller minority formed by the Parsees.

Notes on pp. 658–659

It need not surprise us that until not so very long ago schools for story-tellers used to be set up. Often a group consisting of a strictly limited number of young men would gather round an old and experienced narrator of high repute, to learn the technique and practice of story-telling by repeated listening and watching. But all this is certainly a thing of the past now, apart from a very few exceptional cases.[15]

Owing to lack of space we can here mention only a few of the very many subjects and old traditions that have survived in such astonishing numbers in Iranian folk-tales. There are to all appearances extremely ancient folk-traditions about the sun and the moon, about eclipses of the sun, numerous legends about the origin of different animal species (monkeys, bears, elephants, toads, several birds – among them being the hoopoe –, boars, dogs, mules and camels), their evolution and characteristics, and also the reasons for mutual enmities (cats and dogs, dogs and jackals, crabs and asses, etc.). Often the issue of a story is an attempt to explain the longevity of certain animals. The belief that animals have their own language has given rise to several legends about men who were thought to understand this animal language (Solomon – Sulaymān, Muḥammad, etc.). A distinction is made between good and wicked animals and folk-tales attempt to explain this. At the same time there are numerous legends about plants and their power of speech and characteristics; among these we find some myths which are very old indeed, dealing with the sacredness of certain plants. Water, too, has been the subject of many folk-tales, traditions and superstitions since the very earliest times; there are stories of holy wells, lakes, and sacred springs. Supernatural beings (*dēvs, parīs, shayṭāns,* jinns, etc.) and the places inhabited or favoured by them have all given rise to romantic tales. The most diverse and fantastic traditions have also been woven around popular etymological explanations of place-names together with historical memories. There are a great many folk-tales to be found about the founding or destruction of cities, castles, bridges, canals and wells, towers, dams and dikes, and also caravanserais. Connected with castles there are highly fantastic tales about maidens, demons, secret treasures and heroic deeds, incredible adventures, etc. Ancient monuments, like Bīsutūn for instance, whose true history was either not known at all or only imperfectly, and places of pilgrimage, *Imām-zādas* and famous buildings all provided folk-tradition with a vast scope for the development of fantasies. One can thus easily understand that even such inhospitable places as the Iranian mountains, hills, crags and caves have their own folk-tales and that caves and mountain hide-outs are predominant features in them. To round off this by no means comprehensive list, it may be added that all the single tales used to be told either independently or in groups, which would seem to be the beginning of epic cyclisasation.[16]

Folk-tales very often reveal the social and ideological point of view of the narrator. We find a king or other influential person being contrasted with a poor fellow of the common people. More often than not the kings tend to be rather stupid and to depend on their viziers in everything, while their greatest worries are connected with adding more beautiful women to their harems. The poor man, on the other hand, is usually concerned about justice or happiness, and that is why, after overcoming a number of difficulties, he manages to attain his desire.

Differences between settled and nomadic ways of life also find expression in the folk-tales. One of the most obvious instances is the unequal status of women. Nomadic women, as is well-known, have an incomparably better position than wives in settled communities. Just for curiosity's sake it is worth mentioning that in Southern Azerbayjan (i.e. in the immediate proximity and clearly under the influence of Iranian culture) the theme of a wife choosing her husband by casting apples has been recorded – a motif that occurs also in West-Slavonic fairy-tales. A folk-tale on this subject has also been recorded in Tajikistan.[17]

Although by and large what has been said about the Persian folk-tales also applies to the Tajik ones, there are nonetheless a few differences and peculiarities. The heroes of Tajik folk-tales share many characteristics with those in the *Shāh-nāma*. And it should be added that in the East many a tradition has remained more alive than in the western part of the Iranian language area. It is important to remember in this connection that in the East popular motifs were never covered by Shī'ite influences, as happened in the West. In Tajik animal stories we are particularly struck by the energy of the animal heroes. The brave she-goat, for instance, punishes the wicked wolf herself and rescues her kids without outside assistance, instead of giving way to useless lamentations and waiting for help to appear. Common people always get far more sympathy among the Tajiks than gentlefolk. This is also the reason why in most Tajik folk-tales the principal character is a man or woman of the common people. Heroes have to satisfy strict moral demands: respect for their parents, a good reputation and unblemished honour, respect for labour, contempt for idlers and vagabonds, intrepidity in face of the menaces of nature, kindness and love for animals that serve man.[18]

Not infrequently we find the well-known epic motifs in Iranian folk-tales too. Farhād, in particular, makes his appearance in the West as well as in the East, and Majnūn also turns up quite often. It sometimes happens that the hero appears under another name, but the type is recognisable and unambiguous. There is, however, an even stranger phenomenon – new episodic tales continue to be attributed to a well-known name which has already become an institution in itself. The name serves merely to underline the connection with other deeds of the hero; this is the case in the countless stories of Rustam.[19] A special group in this respect is formed by several folk-tales and stories with historical persons as protagonists. The Talishes, for example possess tales about Shāh 'Abbās[20] (who has certainly been moulded to fit the scheme and strongly idealised as compared with his true historic personality), and in the East, among the Afghans, the Tajiks and the Iranians of the Pamir, the Ghaznavid Sulṭān Maḥmūd appears as principal hero. Among the Sunnites we find stories about caliphs, and the Shī'ites possess a great many tales about 'Alī and his family. It is usually quite

Notes on pp. 658–659

obvious that only in exceptional cases do the folk-tale heroes have anything more in common with their historical models than their name. Here we have very clear and convincing proof of how history has become legend and how the epic texture could develop. There can be no doubt that the integration of folk-tale episodes and their epic cyclisation on the one hand, and the breaking-up and dissolution of epic traditions on the other, caused many very widespread motifs from one category of folk-literature to be taken over by another.[21]

Even the folk-tales of other Iranian nations and peoples are worth systematical consideration. The relations between Persian, Afghan, Baluchi, Kurdish and Pamirian folk-tales are extremely complicated. In the non-Persian areas linguistically allied to Iran, these mutual influences penetrated indirectly by means of polite literature, records committed to writing, or folk-books.

The Kurdish folk-tales strikingly reflect the view of life of a heroic and hospitable but bitterly oppressed and afflicted people. A Kurd never attacks an unarmed man.[22] The obligation to hospitality is stronger than the blood-feud.[23] Among the Kurds women occupy an eminent position. They are not acquainted with *chadra* and possess rights equal to those of men. Frequently a woman has stood at the head of an army and has even ruled over a Kurd principality. From the moral point of view the picture of the Kurdish woman is most unusual, and this is borne out in many a work of Kurdish folk-literature (e.g. *Mamu and Zinē, Mame and Ayshe*).[24] Personal liberty comes first and foremost with the Kurds, and it stands to reason that this conception is also to be found in the folk-tales. The concretisation of this idea is the folk-tale relating to the Country of Freedom.[25] A pronounced feeling for justice is evident in the Kurdish folk-tale, in which foolishness, villainy, cowardice, infamy and above all avarice are despised. A much-loved hero is the Kurdish Naṣraddīn, named Bahlūli-zāna.[26] Numerous animal tales are also in vogue, and we find the bald-headed Kachal appearing very often.[27]

The folk-tales of Iranians who had settled in the Pamirs[28] exhibit many ancient features. The slight extent to which they have been islamised is another striking feature, and consequently important for ethnographical research. No less important is the fact that both Pamir and even Yaghnobi folk-tales[29] are rich in primitive elements, sometimes of a barbarous and almost savage character. But a detailed analysis of this phenomenon would require special study.

Ossetian folk-tales stand somewhat apart, as do the Ossetian Nart epics. Nevertheless they deserve more attention than they have hitherto been given, inasmuch as they have retained ancient motifs in a configuration that is but slightly deformed and also because until the last century the Ossetians had no polite literature, as a result of which their folk-tradition was able to develop practically undisturbed. Ossetian folk-tales bear great similarity to the Nart epics and deal mainly with supernatural beings. They quite clearly reflect the precarious situation of the common people. Thus it is quite reasonable to compare the Ossetian folk-tales with the Nart epics. Their epical motifs have often evolved in the form of prose, although in an independent manner.

Typical supernatural figures in the Ossetian folk-tales are giants and dragons, while the underground kingdom is also often mentioned. Social strife and the ideological standpoint of the narrator are invariably clearly demonstrated.[30]

As a rule the Ossetian folk-tales are more recent than the latest Nart epic cycles, which explains why the folk-tales reflect even more strongly the hard conditions of the women and of the common people than do the Nart epics.[31]

Up to the present only a start has been made in the study of Iranian folk-tales, and particularly their true folklore motifs and forms. But it is already quite clear that once we possess reliable information on all the folk-tales that have survived the years, many puzzling aspects of polite literature will be much easier to explain, if only because there is no better way of finding out about the mentality of a nation and its folk-literature than by studying its folk-tales.

B. IRANIAN FOLK-HUMOUR

There are few peoples that are fonder of short humorous stories than the Iranians. We are here confronted with two almost diametrically opposite forms. On the one hand we come across highly fantastic folk-tales, on the other scenes taken from every-day-life, often with satirical points. Political and social conditions accelerated the development of folk-satire in Iran, as it was the only weapon that could be used against the oppression of the ruling classes. It was very dangerous, however, to voice one's feelings or displeasure openly, so from the earliest times onwards fables were used. The animals that appear most often in the fables were a fairly safe protection against the anger and fatal criticism from more powerful classes. Zākānī too, was very well aware of this.[32]

Of course it was impossible to dispense with human characters for ever. Fairly early on therefore, a type of story evolved reminiscent of *Till Eulenspiegel,* in most cases highly spiced, even to an indelicate degree. This kind of poetry belongs mostly to the world of men, for women preferred the real folk-tales.

By and large it is immaterial whether the hero of these stories is called Naṣraddīn Khvāja or Mullā Mushfiqī, Apandī, Shaykh Bahlūl-i Dānā, Kamīna, Aldar Kosa, or whatever else it may be. Whether they are about Turks, Persians and Azer-bayjanians or Tajiks and Uzbeks, Lures or Turkmenians, Kazakhs and Kirgizes, in essence these tales are all more or less alike. We always find some priest of a lower rank, or often a preacher, even a judge, who all too often succeeds in fooling his neighbours and not infrequently his masters, which he does in none too choice a manner. Usually he is excused, even in circumstances that would otherwise provoke serious revenge. Of course the sneers and mockery of this odd figure very often conceal

Notes on pp. 658–659

bitter criticism and accusations levelled against existing conditions and abuses; sometimes, however, they are merely an effort to produce humour at any cost.

Yet another figure in Islamic folk-literature who, particularly in earlier days, may have influenced the development of the modern Naṣraddīn to a considerable extent, is Juḥ'ā, or Sī Juḥ'ā[33], very well known among the Arabs and Berbers of Northern Africa. His adventures and mischievous tricks are a West-Islamic parallel to the much better known pranks of Naṣraddīn. Juḥ'ā (generally, and especially in Persian literature, he is known as Jūḥī) also turns up in Southern Europe.

The jolly joker Giufà[34], or Giucca, is well known and loved in Sicily, Calabria, and even in Tuscany. According to Basset, the Arabs, as early as the 4th century A.H., possessed collections of stories which were not unlike the tales about Till Eulenspiegel, the stupid townspeople and the Seven Swabians, which later became widespread in Europe. Stories of a similar nature also existed in India many hundreds of years earlier.

Jūḥī is mentioned in earlier Persian literature several times, for instance by Anvarī (d. 565/1169–70) in his *dīvān,* and particularly by Rūmī (d. 672/1273), who includes three anecdotes about Jūḥī in his *mathnavī,* and finally by Jāmī in the *Bahāristān.*[35]

Neither must we omit to mention another well-known personage when dealing with Iranian folk-humour. This is the bald-headed Kachal, whom we find among the Kurds, the Persians and the Tajiks, while he is no less popular with the Yaghnobis.[36] He is the same figure who comes into puppet folk-drama.

An immensely widespread form of folk-humour are short anecdotes, called *laṭīfahā* or *ḥikāyāt,* not seldom satirically pointed. We find them among the Persians, the Tajiks, and even with the Afghans. In Afghanistan they are definitely recognised as a special genre of folk-literature.[37]

As to the anecdotes and jokes, there are genetic connections between folk-tradition and polite literature and their written records. These latter are very complex and often ambiguous.

NOTES

1. Cf. Ethé, *Np. Lit.*, 320–334.
2. Zelenin, *Religiozno-magicheskaya funktsiya fol'klornīkh skazok*, 215–217.
3. Zarubin, 'K izucheniyu beludzhskogo yazīka i fol'klora', *ZKV*, v, 663.
4. Zelenin, *op. cit.*, 218–223.
5. *Skazki i legendī tatar Krīma*, 18, 19, 24.
6. Huet, *Les contes populaires*, 6, 7, 11.
7. Darmesteter, *Etudes iraniennes*, II, 187–251; Braginskiy, *Iz ist.*, 80–206.
8. Christensen, *Märchen aus Iran*, 5-13; Romaskevich, *Persidskie skazki* (Predisloviye).

9. Christensen, *Märchen aus Iran*, 20–27.
10. Galunov, *Ma'rike girī*, 94, 95.
11. Christensen, *Märchen*, 17.
12. Kowalski, *Studia*, II, 25–28, 31–35, 57–60; Schack, *Heldensagen*, 156–187, 295–324.
13. Cf. Ethé, *Np.Lit.*, 318–320; Baumgartner, *op. cit.*, I, 568; Zand, *op. cit.*, 19–23, 94, 162–164.
14. Cf. Shohini Sherozī, 'Dostoni Ardasher va Ester', *ShS*, 1958,3, 86–106; 4, 105–128; for other subjects see also: Abrahamian, *Dialectes*.
15. Romaskevich, *Persid. nar. skazki*, 14–31; also Nikitine, *Les Kurdes*, 273–274.
16. Massé, *Croyances*, 171, 172, 186–190, 199, 200, 209, 213, 214, 219, 225, 226, 230, 235, 354–356, 359, 360, 365, 367, 371, 373, 374, 377, 378, 379–382, 385, 387, 399, 401, 410, 413, 414, 416, 439–489; Hackin–Kohzad, *Légendes et coutumes afghanes*.
17. *Azerbeydzhanskiye tyurkskiye skazki*, XVIII–XIX; *Tadzhik. nar. skazki*, 168–177; also Christensen, *Märchen*, 77–85.
18. Cf. *Tadzhik. nar. skazki, passim.*
19. Cf. Dirr, *Kaukasische Märchen*, 210–236.
20. *Azerb. tyurk. skazki*, VII; also cf. Romaskevich, *Persid. nar. skazki*, 67–70.
21. Sirdar Ikbal Ali Shah, *op. cit.*, *passim*; Morgenstierne, *IIFL*, I/II; Klimovich, *Khrestomatiya*, 794, 800.
22. *Kurdskiye skazki*, 84–94.
23. *Kurdskiye skazki*, 172–173.
24. Cf. Makas, *Kurdische Texte*, 1–20; Mann, *Mukri*, 28–81; Kurdoyev–Tsukerman, *op, cit.*, 30–46.
25. *Kurdskiye skazki*, 163–166, etc.
26. *Kurdskiye skazki*, 174–177, 123–126.
27. *Kurdskiye skazki*, 100–102.
28. Skjöld, *Materialien, passim; Oroshorskiye tekstī, passim*; Solokova, *Ocherki po fonetike iran. yazīkov*, I, II, cf. also Lentz, *Auf dem Dach der Welt* and *Pamirdialekte*.
29. Andreyev–Peshchereva, *Yagnobskiye tekstī*; Lentz, *Auf dem Dach der Welt*.
30. Britayev, *Oset. sk.; Oset. nar. skazki* (1951, Britayev, Kaloyev); cf. also Munkácsi, *Blüten der osset. Volksdichtung*.
31. Cf. *Osetinskaya literatura*, 7; Britayev, *Oset. skazki, Vvedeniye*.
32. Cf. Radzhabov, *Mirovozzreniye Ubayda Zokoni* (St. 1958).
33. Cf. *Les fourberies de Si Djeh'a, contes Kabyles, recueillis et traduits par August Mouliéras* (Paris 1892); cf.: René Basset, *Recherches sur Si Djoh'a et les anecdotes qui lui sont attribués*, 1–79.
34. *Ital'yanskiye skazki, obrabotannīye Italo Kal'vino* (M. 1959), 180–189.
35. Cf. Christensen, *Júhí in Pers. lit.*, 129–136; Ethé, *Essays*, 238–257; Klimovich, *Khrestomatiya*, *passim*; Christensen, *Märchen*, 13; Mann–Hadank, *Zâzâ*, 41; Mann–Hadank, *Khunsâr*, CIV; Mann, *Lur-Dial.*, XXX; Miller, *Talīshskiye tekstī*, V.
36. *Kurd.sk.*, 100–102; Romaskevich, *Persid. nar. sk.*, 267–272; *Persidskiye skazki* (1958), 75–84; Ivanova, 'Pyandzhikent. govor', *TIYa*, VI, 304–309; *Tadzhik. nar. sk.*, 363–367; Klimovich, *Khrestomatiya*, 125–127; Andreyev–Peshchereva, *Yagnob. tekstī*, 96–101, 149–153, 153–161, 184–186.
37. Cf. Hikāyāt, *Persische Schnurren; Tadzhik. nar. sk.*, 375–473; *Afg. sk.*, 7, 115–155.

IV. IRANIAN ENTERTAINMENT FOLK-LITERATURE

A. COLLECTIONS OF FABLES, PARTICULARLY *KALĪLA AND DIMNA*

Like the majority of oriental peoples, the Iranians are not fond of crude utterances, except in the case of proverbs. Instead of definitions, the Iranians prefer a concrete, though often fictitious story, which may take the form of a short narrative, a parable, or a fable. It is left to the audience to draw final conclusions from the indirectly implied truth. Perhaps this is a sign of true oriental courtesy, but without doubt the inborn urge to find the most elegant and pleasing way of expressing ideas plays a part.

It must not be forgotten that the Iranian passionately loves discussions back and forth, regardless of whether his part is that of an attentive and interested listener, or whether he has something to say himself. After all, most of the stories were intended to fulfil no mean task, notably to give advice to anyone willing to take it.

A favourite narrative form are fables in which the heroes are very often animals.

In the Islamic world two collections of fables have become particularly famous. These are the *Fables of Luqmān* and *Kalīla and Dimna*.[1] The *Fables of Luqmān* are essentially the fables of Aesop. Their alleged author is also mentioned in the Koran. By far the most popular, however, are the fables we know as *Kalīla and Dimma*. They are derived from a whole series of Buddhist Sanskrit texts. Nowadays it has already become very difficult to ascertain what the Indian model was like, since the Middle-Persian translator worked independently and adapted the stories so thoroughly to the conditions and taste of his own age and country, that it is more accurate to call his work a paraphrase or adaptation than a translation proper. A Pahlavi version, the existence of which stands beyond all doubt, was named after the two jackals of the frame-story. It dates from about 550 A.D., thus during the reign of Khusrau Anōsharvān. It is associated with the legendary physician Burzōē, and with the no less legendary figure of the vizier Buzurgmihr.[2]

About two hundred years later this Pahlavi source served as model for the Arabic version of ʿAbdu'llāh ibn al-Muqaffaʿ, and in this Arabic form the famous collection of fables returned to Iran.[3]

Rūdakī appears to be the first to have attempted a Persian translation.[4] He was succeeded by other adapters, some of whom completed, others abbreviated, while still others were tempted to do a complete recasting of the story. All such versions belong definitely to polite literature and have had little effect on folk-literature. Strangely enough, however, the Arabic version has had a comparatively wider influence. It would certainly seem true that this is a case where polite literature influenced folk-tales, rather than the other way round.

Two of the literary adaptations ought at least to be mentioned here, namely the *Marzbān-nāma*[5] by Ispahbad Marzbān b. Rustam b. Sharvīn (11th century A.D.) and the *Anvār-i Suhaylī* by Kāshifī (15th century A.D.). Kāshifī makes extensive additions to the original Indian core. The adaptation, which comprises a great deal of Iranian material, turned out to be such an affected affair that it appealed only to the educated classes – its effect on true folk-literature was slight and of no consequence.[6]

B. 'MIRRORS FOR PRINCES' AND OTHER ENTERTAINING AND INSTRUCTIVE LITERATURE

This branch of polite literature, which is very popular with the Iranians, was also noticeably influenced by motifs and subjects taken from folk-tradition. Little or no difference was made between real 'Mirrors for Princes' and literature intended to instruct and edify the rest of the population.

The important thing was to use parables that were familiar to the author's contemporaries so that the maxim or moral in view should be brought home and impressed upon the audience mnemonically. Again and again folk-tradition was found to be the richest source of short stories, of which it contains an endless supply. For all that, it certainly seems true to say that the popular flavour was somewhat diluted to suit the tastes of the upper classes.

Andarz, or *Pand-nāmak,* as this form of literature was called at the time of the Sasanians, was a great favourite with the Arabs of the early Islamic period and many translation were made, mainly by islamised Iranians. The need for Arabic versions was all the greater since the Iranians, newly converted to Islam, soon lost their ability to read Pahlavi characters and to understand the old language. The only remaining exceptions were a small number of *dihqāns,* petty country noblemen, who held on to their old

Notes on pp. 668–669

culture and customs for a time, though not all of them with the same tenacity. Another important factor was that besides holding most of the government posts in the service of their Arab rulers, the Iranian officials had to keep their capricious masters amused and sometimes even had to educate them.

The most important works of this genre are the *Qābūs-nāma* and the *Siyāsat-nāma*[7]. The former is richer in motifs borrowed from folk-literature (i.e. anecdotes and proverbs), but the *Siyāsat-nāma* also is not devoid of folklore narrative material. If we consider the story of Bahrām Gor and his vizier Rāst-Rāvish, or again that of Siyāvush[8], we see that the ideology of both works is based on explicitly feudal principles, and the same holds good for many more works in this genre.

Even writers preaching Ṣūfism liked to exploit folk-literature as a source of motifs and subjects, e.g. Farīdu'd-dīn 'Aṭṭār with his *Tadhkiratu'l-auliyā*, Jalālu'd-dīn Rūmī in his *Fīhi mā fīhi* and his *Mathnavī*.[9] A very large number of motifs and subjects from folk-tradition were recorded and elaborated by Muḥammad 'Aufī in his voluminous *Javāmi'u'l-ḥikāyāt*. The ideology of these works conforms to the orthodox view of the world and hardly ever allows the original milieu to manifest itself. Much the same applies to other works and authors, e.g. the *Gulistān* of Sa'dī, Jāmī's *Bahāristān*, and others.[10]

The countless small episodic tales about various Sasanian kings such as Anōsharvān and Bahrām[11], like the wealth of stories about other great persons of this world, the tales with Buzurgmihr as central character and the numerous legends describing the lives of poets and philosophers – all these were obviously of an instructive and moralising nature. Also the manner in which many figures were idealised (for instance Ḥusayn Bāyqarā in the Navā'ī stories[12]) seems to be determined by an attempt to make the rulers of the past, or their successors, conform, at any rate in the traditions, to the vain wishes of their subjects. It is possible, however, that the tales just mentioned were written to order for the ruling classes with the aim of levelling out and concealing social differences. The philosophy expressed in moralistic and didactic literature also has a strong 'popular' flavour, since it is primarily concerned with questions of practical ethics.[13]

Moralistic and didactic entertainment literature always clung firmly to one basic idea: no matter how difficult and ill-advised it was to oppose feudal abuses openly, moralistic and didactic literature of all ages has always tried to impress upon those in power that the ancient and praiseworthy models advocate a benevolent form of government. Such good counsel was presented in a humble, submissive, even servile manner. Any danger the author might risk was further lessened by a suitable choice of themes and universally known subjects from folk-literature, so that not he, the author, but the collective and anonymous creators of folk-tales and folk-literature would be responsible. When all is said and done, one has to admit the possibility that much of the material in books of this kind was quite intentionally cast in a popular tone in order to make it look like folk-literature.[14]

C. THE IRANIAN ELEMENT IN THE *BOOK OF A THOUSAND AND ONE NIGHTS* AND SIMILAR COLLECTIONS

There is another, very substantial group of works of an entertaining character (although the edifying purpose is here less noticeable and of secondary consideration) in which the Iranian element is much in evidence and of great importance. In these cyclic works, or framework compositions, of the type of the *Book of a Thousand and One Nights* and the *Ṭūṭī-nāma,* 'Parrot Book', etc. it matters little that many Arabic and Turkish elements have also been clustered round a definitely Iranian core. In fact this only increases the importance of the Iranian nucleus, for it proves that by using Iranian material and following an Iranian example, non-Iranian folk-literature was inspired to creative imitation. It remains somewhat doubtful to what extent there was also a direct Indian influence.

The old *Sindbād-nāmak,* 'The Book of the Seven Viziers', which subsequently became well known and very popular throughout the Islamic East, was certainly of Indian origin. Likewise the *Book of Bilauhar and Buddhasaf,* a remote forerunner of several West-European romances about Barlaam and Yosaphat, also sprang from Indian sources. Iranian versions always formed the connecting link, and it was also the Iranians who passed on the technique of telling a story within another story (framework technique)[15], which undoubtedly also came from India. There are nowadays few works of entertainment in existence in which this technique was not used. Later on the Iranians were no longer content to write simple frame stories – the latter became more and more complex, while further frame stories were built into some of the stories of the original frame. Even this was not enough and another series of small stories was inserted, so that the final product often turned into a four-fold frame. The question whether this was the result of trends which were also responsible for epic cyclisation, or whether it was a parallel development, is unimportant.

The core of the *Book of a Thousand and One Nights* is thus undoubtedly Iranian. It is modelled on the Middle-Persian prose folk-book *Hazār afsānak,* which was Iranian throughout in character, even if a few Indian motifs had crept in. Gradually several works that had previously existed independently were included in the *Book of a Thousand and One Nights.* Of Iranian origin are in the first place all the real fairy-tales, characterised by the intervention of good or evil forces or beings in the hero's fate. The question becomes less clear in the case of the jesting stories, for these contain a great deal of Indian material, although the contributions made by the Iranians are no less important.[16]

There is no doubt of the Iranian origin of the frame story of the royal brothers *Shahriyār and Shāhzamān* and their unfaithful wives or of the inserted episodic stories – the story of the woman shut up in a chest, The Merchant and his Wife, The

Notes on pp. 668–669

Ass and the Ox, The Cock and the Dog. Then there are the stories of the Merchant, the Ghost and the Three Old Men (an Iranian tale but maybe not a part of the original *Hazār afsānak*), The Fisherman and the Ghost, The Three Apples (modified to the extent that it takes place in the time of Hārūn ar-Rashīd), The Porter, The Three Ladies and the Three Qalandars (also altered and transferred to Hārūn ar-Rashīd), The Magic Horse, Ḥasan from Baṣra, Prince Badr and Princess Jauhar from Samandal, Ardashīr and Ḥayāt an-nufūs, Qamar az-zamān and Queen Budūr – all of which form part of the Iranian core in the *Book of a Thousand and One Nights,* i.e. the original *Hazār afsānak*.

More dubious are the stories about the hunchback and the various funny mishaps with the corpse, concerning which we cannot be altogether sure that they belonged to the original *Hazār afsānak*. The stories of the barber are in essence Iranian, but have been elaborated and interpolated with Arabic episodes to such an extent that it is already difficult nowadays to make out their original shape and size. Definitely Iranian too are the Tale about Aḥmad and the fairy Parībānū, and the Story of the Jealous Sisters. Whether they were part of the *Hazār afsānak* is doubtful and in fact unlikely, since these stories are to be found in one version only.

A great deal of Iranian material may also be concealed among the later stories that belong to the so-called Baghdad or even Egyptian group, but it is hard to recognise since it has been chopped and changed about so thoroughly. Among these are quite a number of repetitions, sometimes with different titles, as for instance the Story of Tāju'l-mulūk – a counterpart to the story of Ardashīr and Ḥayāt an-nufūs, or the Story of Jahānshāh – a counterpart to the tale of Ḥasan from Baṣra.

Finally there are in the *Book of a Thousand and One Nights* a number of formerly independent epic cycles, many of which are of Iranian derivation. The first of these are the various books about viziers (the number of viziers varies between seven, ten and forty). The best known are the *Sindbād-nāma* (about seven viziers) and the *Bakhtiyār-nāma* (ten viziers). Other stories which used to be independent are the one about *Shīmās and Kal'ād, Ḥāsib and the Snake-queen, Saifu'l-mulūk,* and a few other shorter ones. To discuss all this in detail would require a special study, for in many ways it would go beyond the scope of the present essay.

Proper names are a great help and rarely let one down when determining the origin of a story. If they are Persian it means they are original and prove the subject in question to be of Persian origin too. On the other hand, if one finds Arabic names in Iranian stories (which happens particularly in the magic fairy-tales), they have been invented and substituted for the Iranian ones later on. The classification of certain subjects may also reveal many things which appear to be Arabic but are in fact Iranian or Indo-Iranian. Similarly some very well-known Indo-European motifs appear here in circumstances which are tangibly Iranian in character and origin. We mention only a few: the exaggeration in numbers, the magic horse, the knowledge of animal language, people changing into animals, a spirit as principal character in a story, several snake stories, the motif of the discarded coat of swan feathers, the cloak of invisibility, and the rusty dagger signifying that the donor has died.[17]

Certain motifs in the ancient *Hazār afsānak,* including the possibly Indian models, are to be found in several works of Indian literature too. Thus Cosquin likes to regard the following works as the models for the frame story of the *Thousand and One Nights*: the Thirty-two Throne Stories (*Sinhāsana Dvatrinśatikā*), the Vampire Stories (*Vetālapañcavinśatikā*), The Seventy Parrot-stories (*Śukasaptati*), the Ocean of Stories (*Kathāsaritsāgara*), several Buddhist collections (From the Three Hampers – *Tripitaka*) and the 536th tale of the *Jātakas*. It is also thought possible that parts were derived from the *Pañcatantram*.[18] Meanwhile the Indian material was so completely iranised that there can be no question of the *Thousand and One Nights* being a direct descendant of an Indian model.

The influence of this work has always, and particularly in the Near East, been very strong. Many stories in different parts, for instance that of Sayfu'l-mulūk and others too, reverted to folk-literature. It is most remarkable that it was just the epic cycles, that had formerly been independent, that had the greatest effect in this direction. Quite often too, typically Arabic subjects from the *Book of the Thousand and One Nights* found their way into Iranian folk-literature. O. Mann, for example, recorded a version of the story about the butcher Vardān in Nayīn.[19] However, the influence of motifs and even complete subjects can be noticed much further afield, one might say throughout the whole domain of Iranian culture. To illustrate this we need only mention the Iranian influence in the Uzbek *dāstāns* (Seipulmelik among others), the Baluchi story of the Forty Thieves[20], or the Story of the Judge and his Wife among the Zāzā[21], to find examples in the east as well as the west.

In Western Europe there are many Old- and Middle-French *fabliaux* which seem to show considerable oriental influence. No doubt this can be attributed to the effect of subjects from the *Book of the Thousand and One Nights*, for they would have spread to the Christian West, particularly as a result of the crusades.[22]

Many famous collections of fairy-tales and short stories to be found in polite literature, parts of which at least are derived from folk-tradition, are linked up with each other either by a frame story or through a common basic idea that they are supposed to illustrate and explain, which they usually do very cleverly. To this category belongs the ancient *Bakhtiyār-nāma*[23], 'The Book of the Ten Viziers', already referred to. This is a frame story and taken as a whole a Moslem counterpart to the even older *Sindbād-nāma*[24], which appears to have been inspired by an Indian model. Still more obvious is the Indian origin of the *Ṭūṭī-nāma,* although many Iranian motifs were used in it too, especially outside the frame. The Persian version, containing several subjects borrowed from Iranian folk-literature, is however no more than a selection from the Indian collection *Śukasaptati,* for instead of the Indian seventy, there are here only fifty-two Iranian tales.

Actually there are a great number of other similar Persian collections of stories

Notes on pp. 668–669

whose titles mention varying numbers of viziers, dervishes and parrots, etc. Indian material replaces the Iranian more and more however, and it can be said of all this polite literature of entertainment that these works have lost all traces of their relation to folk-literature. Interesting as they may be from a point of view of cultural history, we cannot discuss them here.

D. *THE THOUSAND AND ONE DAYS*

This collection of fairy-tales and novel-like stories is an Iranian counterpart to the Arabian *Thousand and One Nights*. It is obviously a more recent imitation with a cognate frame story but with the difference that the latter and all the interspersions are addressed to a beautiful princess who is prejudiced against men. Over and over again the princess's nurse narrates stories about faithful lovers and husbands until ultimately she achieves her object, the princess renounces her prejudice and consents to be married. This principal frame story contains a number of secondary frame stories and in some cases even tertiary tales, so that some of the frame stories are interrupted again and again by the insertion of other narratives. The *Thousand and One Days* contains versions of many tales closely related to folk-literature, the subjects being common to the whole of the Islamic Near East. The majority of the subjects used is of Iranian provenance.[25]

The question as to whether the *Thousand and One Days* is of oriental origin – or a European imitation, falsification or paraphrase – is somewhat complicated. This problem would be hard to solve if we tried to investigate it from the position of literary history or philology. But from a folkloristic standpoint we can easily explain all difficulties. A hyper-critical philologist might be suspicious in view of the absence of a Persian manuscript, only a French translation by Pétis de la Croix (1653–1713) being available. This can be explained very simply. The original Persian work used by the translator (according to his own statement) did not fall into the category of polite literature, but was a unique folk-book in manuscript. It may also have been a *kitābcha,* i.e. an *aide-mémoire* for a professional story-teller. Mukhliṣ – Pétis says Moclès – was a dervish and these folk have always been propagators of folk-tales and other products of folk-literature; very often they were professional story-tellers. It is quite acceptable to suppose that Mukhliṣ neither would nor could relinquish his unique aid. The copy used by Pétis de la Croix was not considered by him to be worthy of preservation after he had translated it. Then there is no doubt about the authenticity of the translator's preface and it is useless to say that Pétis' statement on Mukhliṣ' authorship of the *Thousand and One Days* is fictitious. Pétis de la Croix was an eminent stylist, not only in his native tongue but also in oriental languages, and therefore it is quite probable that he smoothed out some unevennesses in the style and expression of the original work. Pétis may have kept the oriental features of his model untouched and made an accurate translation which is undoubtedly a masterpiece. The extremely high artistic quality of the *Thousand and One Days* is most remarkable even in a French adaptation and translation, but is not contradictory to the qualification of the model as a folk-book. Elegant and refined as it may be, the translation of the *Thousand and One Days* can be described as simple and free of baroque bombast and rococo affectation. If we tried to retranslate the Persian model from the French, we should see that such a reconstruction would differ very considerably from the torrent of words in the post-classical Persian literary prose of the period in question. And this is just the quintessence of the matter: folk-books arose as a reaction against the bombast of polite literature, both in the European West and the Asiatic East. We must also consider whether Pétis de la Croix (or anybody else of that period) had any reason to become the author of a mystification. Pétis de la Croix was certainly an eminent expert in oriental studies, he was thoroughly familiar with oriental life, customs, languages and literature as well as being a gifted artist; but it is extremely doubtful whether he would have intended and allowed his name to be connected with any mystification, for after all he occupied a high position and possessed great capacities, having first served in the French diplomatic service – where he proved his uncommon incorruptibility – and afterwards having been professor of oriental languages. It is beyond any doubt that he, as a *savant* and a man of diplomatic integrity, could not commit forgery, and indeed would not be likely to risk his prestige by doing so. Pétis de la Croix was certainly not a romanticist. And the romantic period, characterised as it was by numerous literary falsifications, forged historical documents and last but not least historical romances, began more than half a century later and culminated more than a whole century after Pétis de la Croix started to publish his translation of the *Thousand and One Days* (1710 A.D.).

On the basis of our present knowledge of the theory of oriental folk-tradition and polite literature, we may well declare that the *Thousand and One Days* is irrefutably of Persian origin on account of its content, colouring and composition, and that even at the present day a large group of orientalists and poets would be hard put to it to imitate this collection of tales. Consequently we can be sure of the absurdity of taking Pétis de la Croix as the author of the work. He was too much occupied with his official duties to have been in a position to spend much time is seeking and making use of the sources. He was not the person to enter into such a difficult investigation or to attempt to disguise his authorship by introducing a fictitious story about Mukhliṣ. *The Thousand and One Days* (the Persian title was probable *Hazār u yak rūz*, but other titles are not excluded) was arranged and recorded by a highly educated man, well versed in the realm of fairy-tales and stories from everyday life and moreover closely acquainted with polite literature. This can easily be proved, for instance, by the fact that the tale about Ibn Sīnā is a paraphrase of his biography. The author must have

Notes on pp. 668–669

been familiar with the oriental way of life, for he demonstrates an extensive knowledge and mastery of this subject, which forms an intrinsic part of the whole work. Under such conditions it is obvious that not a European man of letters but the Persian dervish Mukhliṣ was the only person fully capable of answering the requirements of authorship. The French translator may have not only improved the style in the French translation but may also have made various corrections in the wording for ethical reasons. We can well suppose that the title of *Thousand and One Days*, and consequently even the division of the whole book into days – often very short – may have been done by Pétis de la Croix. It is noteworthy that the 190th day is followed by the 960th without any break in continuity. The explanation may be simple, however. The numbers were of secondary importance and the text, as arranged by Pétis, may be merely an extract of a larger collection. It is possible that not only have some portions of the text of some of the stories, or of one day, been abbreviated, but even some substantial parts of the collection been omitted entirely. On the other hand the Pahlavi version of the *Thousand and One Nights* did not contain the full number of nights either, and the 'thousand' may perhaps be interpreted as 'a very large but unspecified number'.

The tales of Prince Kalaf and the Chinese princess Tūrāndukht[26] and that of Avicenna[27] are among the most interesting parts of the collection. But the other tales too possess great fascination owing to their ethical and artistic value. The stories from *Thousand and One Days* had a strong influence on European culture, especially Italian literature, above all the *Fiabe* by Carlo Gozzi,[28] and this applies not only to Turandot but also to some of the others. The epical subject of Turandot entered even into German literature through a translation and adaptation from the hand of Friedrich Schiller.[29]

NOTES

1. Ethé, *Np. Lit.*, 331, 346, 347; Carra de Vaux, *Les penseurs de l'Islam*, I (Paris 1921); 346; *Qur'ān*, s. XXXI; cf. Lübker, *Reallexikon*, 358–359; *Kalila i Dimna* (Krachkovskiy, Vvedeniye), 9–23; Ethé, *Np. Lit.*, 326; Schulthess, *Kalīla und Dimna* (B. 1911), 'Einleitung', p. IX.
2. Nöldeke, *Burzōēs Einleitung zu dem Buche Kalīla wa Dimna* (Strassburg 1922).
3. Ethé, *Np. Lit.*, 326; Brockelmann, *GAL*, I, 151, *GAL* ('Amelang'), 97; Massé, *Les versions persanes des contes d'animaux, passim*; cf. Khanna al'-Fakhuri, *Ist. arab. liter.*, I, 334–363, mainly 343–356 (very important!)
4. Aynī, *Ustod Rudaki, passim;* Braginskiy, *Ocherki*, 123–148.
5. Cf. *The Tales of Marzuban*, translated from the Persian by Reuben Levy (Bloomington 1959) (with an important preface!).
6. Ethé, *Np. Lit.*, 326–328; Braginskiy, *Ocherki*, 328–332; Schulthess, *op. cit.*, IX; *Kalila i Dimna* (Krachkovskiy, Vvedeniye), 12, 15, 16.

7. Braginskiy, *Ocherki*, 362–363; Ethé, *Np. Lit.*, 347, 349.
8. *Siyāsat-nāma*, 4th chapter, Russian translation 25–32, 43rd chapter, Russian transl. 180–181; Braginskiy, *Ocherki*, 363.
9. Braginskiy, *Ocherki*, 370–374; cf. also Rumi, *Pritchi, perevod s persid.* (M. 1963).
10. Braginskiy, *Ocherki*, 304–312, 327–328, 370–374.
11. *Siyāsat-nāma*, Russian transl., 35–43, 139–142, 173, 182, 186, 190–204, *et passim.*
12. Bertel's *Navoi*, 258–265.
13. Cf. Horten, *Philosophie des Islam*, 264–274.
14. Cf. Bertel's, *Roman ob Aleksandre, passim*; Pizzi, *Storia della Poesia Persiana*, chapter VII/1; Christensen, *L'Iran sous les Sassanides*, 431 *et seq.*
15. Cf. Grintser, P.A., *Drevneindiyskaya proza (Obramlennaya povest')* (M. 1963), a standard work with extensive bibliography; Grintser, 'Literaturnïe i fol'klornïye svyazi sanskritskoy obramlennoy povesti', in *Vzaimosvyazi literatur Vostoka i Zapada* (M. 1961), 182–234; cf. also Cosquin, E., *Le prologue-cadre des Mille et une nuits – Les légendes perses et le livre d'Esther* (Paris 1909).
16. Christensen, *Märchen*, 10, 12; cf. also B. Heller, in *Anm. zu KHM*, IV, 397–410.
17. Oestrup, *Studien über* 1001 *Nacht*, 106–109, *et passim.*
18. Cf. Lahy-Hollebecque, *Le féminisme de Schéhérazade*, 6; *Panchatantra* (M. 1958); *Dvadtsat'pyat' rasskazov vetalï* (M. 1958).
19. Mann–Hadank, *Khunsâr*, CVI.
20. Sokolova, *Ocherki po fonetike iran. yaz.*, I, 61–64.
21. Mann–Hadank, *Zâzâ*, 40.
22. Cf. Bédier, *Les Fabliaux*, 5th ed. (Paris 1925); Voretzsch, *Einf. in das Studium der altfranz. Literatur*, 2nd ed. (Halle 1913), 409–414, 455–457.
23. Cf. Braginskiy, *Ocherki*, 303–304.
24. Cf. Braginskiy, *Ocherki*, 301–303; cf. also Samarkandi, *Sindbadname* (M. 1960).
25. Cf. *Mille et un jours* (Paris 1838), 1–3.
26. *Mille et un jours*, 45th–47th, 60th–82nd day (pp. 69–73, 89–117).
27. *Mille et un jours*, 135th–141st day (pp. 180–186).
28. Gozzi, Carlo, *Skazki dlya teatra* (M. 1956), with an essay by Mokul'skiy, 'Karlo Gotstsi i ego skazki dlya teatra' (3–38) – a concise but excellent introduction.
29. Schiller, Friedrich, *Gedichte – Übersetzungen*, publ. by P. Merker (Lpz., Reclam, s.a.).

V. WRITTEN FORMS OF FOLK-LITERATURE*

A. FOLK-BOOKS – THE FORERUNNERS OF FOLK-PRINTS

The increasing penetration of Arabic elements into the late-classical and post-classical Persian literary language, which reached alarming proportions particularly during the decline at the end of the Safavid rule and continued until the middle of the 19th century, is probably chiefly responsible for the appearance of a great number of folk-books.

Any form of bombast has always been completely alien to the inborn artistic sense and feeling of the common Iranian, even when we bear in mind his preference for a flowery style and elegant ways of expression. In their tastes and interests the common townspeople had always been opposed in principle to the aristocratic and quasi-aristocratic aesthetes and their affectations. Not surprisingly, therefore, they looked around for other and more suitable sources of entertainment, amusement and edification, paying particular attention to lucidity in the expression of ideas as well as in style and language. These demands were as a rule only met by folk-books. The subject-matter of these cheap and generally unique little works depended almost entirely on polite literature; firm favourites were the old *Shāh-nāma* motifs, and episodes from the romantic epics of polite literature. A few of these folk-books, it is true, reached a higher level and measure of perfection than the mostly professional abstracts from larger works. One cannot deny them a certain independence where conception and development are concerned, but on the whole the role of the anonymous author is restricted to simplifying the extremely involved episodes and eliminating or at least partly replacing excessive janglings of words, whenever turns of phrase were incomprehensible to a common Persian.

The subjects used were mostly romantic, erotic and semi-romantic and semi-fictional. Some of the post-classical literary collections of fairy-tales, of which there is a fair number, really started their existence as prose folk-books. These became such favourites with the people that a need was felt to 'refine' the folk-character of the much-loved stories, at least as far as the style was concerned.

The number of folk-books that have been preserved is in itself not very large – in most cases we have only indirect evidence to go by. Their true importance, however, is incomparably greater, even if they never became so widespread as the products of polite literature. Iranian prose folk-books nevertheless played an impressive part in the spreading of Iranian subjects, particularly to Central Asia and among the Uzbeks.[1]

B. FOLK-PRINTS IN GENERAL

The folk-prints form an organic continuation of the earlier prose folk-books in manuscript form. Actually the transition from one to the other took place gradually. Folk-prints appear in the form of slender stitched booklets, printed on poor quality paper and provided with very primitive and naïve illustrations. The size is generally an eighth or sixteenth of a printed sheet. If the booklet contains more than two or three printed sheets, it is bound. In that case the cover is provided with drawings supposed to be reminiscent of the decorations on the covers of old manuscripts. A useful survey of folk-prints is given in the standard treatise on the subject – Bertel's' *Persidskaya lubochnaya literatura.*[2] Educated Persians, or those who consider themselves as such, have little respect for these books and even look down on them, leaving it to small craftsmen and traders in the towns and to individual, only partly literate villagers in the country to read and distribute the folk-prints. But this critical attitude should by no means mislead one as to the importance of the prints for folk-literature in Iran. It is enough to mention one small detail, namely that several story-tellers have so far moved with the times that instead of the manuscript *kitābcha,* they now use folk-prints to aid their memory and as a storehouse for their repertory.

C. FANTASTIC ROMANCES OF CHIVALRY IN FOLK-PRINT FORM

Fantastic romances of chivalry are the most common category of folk-prints. These booklets bear the most varied titles: *Nushāfarīn, Khusravī, Dīvzād*[3], and many more. The contents follow a fairly strict pattern and there are but few and insignificant deviations from the general scheme.

Notes on pp. 675–676

A handsome prince (*Shāh-zāda*) falls in love with a beautiful maiden (as a rule a princess) in a far distant land. A picture of her has been shown to him beforehand, or sometimes a report or a dream is enough to awaken his passion. The prince sets out to seek his bride and in the course of the journey has a number of extraordinary adventures. Frequently he is helped or hindered by supernatural powers, he overcomes all the adversaries and obstacles that cross his path and finally returns triumphantly to his native land with his fair prize. As in polite literature, the main story is interrupted by episodes in which subsidiary characters are introduced. Often these folk-romances of chivalry are adaptations of motifs from the *Shāh-nāma* or other classical heroic or romantic epics, and the universally familiar subjects are further richly elaborated. Not infrequently such folk-prints carry on with the plot where polite literature left off, describing a series of further happenings that are freely invented and probably not based on any model we know.

Connections with epics belonging to the field of polite literature are often very easy to establish. In some instances at least, it is a case of mutating relationships since sometimes the prototype is in verse and belongs to polite literature, or it may be the other way round, i.e. the model is in prose and finds its origin in folk-literature while the adaptation falls into the category of polite literature. The link in both directions will usually prove to be a prose folk-book in manuscript form.

There is not the slightest doubt that this type of folk-literature is a product of the feudal system. European equivalents, in subject-matter as well as treatment and artistic value, are the mediaeval folk-romances of chivalry.

These fantastic romances of chivalry in folk-print form are in most cases definitely not progressive – an interesting proof that the ruling classes of late feudal Iran, aware of the instability of their position, did not hesitate to make use of new technical advances in order to force their own ideology on their subjects.

It is nevertheless most correct, when classifying these works, to place them on the periphery of Persian feudal polite literature. Their social purpose is simply to penetrate to the masses.

It must certainly be admitted that it is not possible to find prototypes for all of the folk-prints. However, it would still be rash to assume on these grounds that any of them are quite original, for it is very likely that many of them consisted of contaminations of single motifs and were compiled from various sources. One should not expect high artistic qualities in these literary by-products – they were mostly of the shilling shocker variety. They were intended to gloss over the miseries brought about by the decline of feudalism and to divert public attention to trivial and harmless (from the upper-class viewpoint) matters. And this is precisely why this branch of folk-literature should be considered unprogressive and at the same time a symbol of decline, although there may be isolated exceptions about which one might say the opposite if if were possible to see them as anything more than exceptions.

Society and its actual political conditions sometimes even influence such subjects as one would expect to have been firmly canonised long ago. We have already discussed this peculiar fact in connection with the *dāstāns*. Here we find a further example of the strange things authors of folk-print romances were forced to do (even in the 19th century) by the obstinate and fanatical orthodoxy of the Moslem theologians. The figure of Rustam in particular had to suffer many adaptations and modifications that were quite unavoidable – Iran's greatest heroic figure had to be completely islamised. There is a short epic in folk-print form, written in classical *mutaqārib*, and entitled *Rustam-nāma*, which was printed in Tehran in 1298/1880. It contains a large number of anachronisms (the caliph ʿAlī is turned into a contemporary of Rustam's) and in a host of other ways too the subject-matter and its treatment are deformed.[4] The traditional figure of Rustam, shaped by many centuries, is now endowed with a new and far more modern trait – namely that of a religious man, showing that he had turned to Islam, for in this folk-print the champion of the fire-worshippers is defeated by ʿAlī in single combat and is converted to the Shīʿa.

D. SHORT STORIES IN FOLK-PRINTS

Another category of folk-prints are the short stories, which in their turn may be divided into three basic types. They either appear as single stories in which the whole plot is rounded off and brought to a conclusion, or as cycles of short stories (the separate stories being sequels to each other), or again as frame stories in which the individual tales are really episodes within the frame.[5] Fantasy now retires into the background and supernatural powers enter the plot only in exceptional cases, at any rate far less frequently than in the folk-print romances of chivalry.

The principal characters are recruited mainly from the middle and lower classes of the population – they tend to be merchants, *qāḍīs*, artisans or other townsfolk. The subjects are mostly taken from everyday life with the town as scene of action. Again it is difficult to make out whether these subjects are original or are derived from polite literature. They are either popular adaptations of short stories or tales from polite literature, or they may be orally transmitted folk-traditions which later found their way into the latter, albeit merely as a basis that by means of artificial mannerisms became elevated to a grander style.

In works of this kind the folk-prints do show unmistakably progressive elements, and not infrequently a critical view is taken of social abuses. It is usually the holders of temporal or spiritual power at whom criticism is specifically levelled, and they are reproached with various wicked and reprehensible qualities, the chief of which are avarice, voluptuousness and greed. We are no longer regaled with often foolish scuffles between knights and *dēvs* or monsters. Instead, preference is given to subjects

Notes on pp. 675–676

far closer to the everyday life of common people, arising from the continual encounters with their immediate oppressors.

Short stories in folk-print form too are known under varying titles: *Ra'nā u Zībā, Duzd u qāḍī*[6], often also *Laṭā'if, Ḥikāyat,* or something different again.[7]

The authors belong to the middle classes – as a rule they are townspeople, sometimes better-class artisans, humble citizens, just those whose lives were not characterised by luxury or by security from the various forms of oppression and the wilfulness of the aristocracy.

E. FOLK-TALES IN FOLK-PRINTS

Animal stories intended for children should be regarded as an introduction to animal fables of a more or less epical character. The mothers and grandmothers tell them to small children. For school-children there are folk-prints in which the anonymous authors have adapted the stories to their readers' power of comprehension. Little books of this kind are used in the schools as an introduction to folk-tale literature proper. The special juvenile literature known as *Bachcha-khvānī* really belongs to the people, and in many cases it makes up the entire mental nutriment of much older members of the uneducated peasant population. This explains why they are so widespread and have to be reprinted from time to time. Again there is a good variety of titles[8]: The Mice and the Cat, Auntie Frog, Aunt Ground-beetle, Mr. Sparrow, Wolf and Fox, etc. They are written in a very lively style, the language is concise, idiomatic and unadorned, and descriptions are mostly amusing, exciting and ingenious.

These editions cost very little and are illustrated with naïve folk-print pictures. The University Library at Leningrad has a large collection of them, brought together by V.A. Zhukovsky in the years between 1883 and 1886.[9] Professor Jan Rypka in Prague also possesses a fine collection of more recent publications in this genre.

For older children and also for adults, books of folk-prints are continually being reprinted. These exceedingly low-priced lithographs with their traditionally simple illustrations, which already formed part of the earliest folk-prints, often try to imitate literature proper in their choice of titles.

The way these and similar books are arranged is worth noting. The separate sections of these small anthologies deal successively with women, fools and judges. Very popular indeed are short anecdotes or funny stories. No matter how complicated these works are, they never lose the essential character of the folk-prints.[10]

Folk-print editions of separate folk-tales as mentioned by Romaskevich are much simpler.[11] Unfortunately it is very difficult to get any kind of thorough and reliable insight into this whole branch of folk-literature. There is no doubt, however, that an intimate acquaintance with these stories would be an enormous help in tracing the development of single subjects and also in the study of cultural history.

F. DREAM-BOOKS AND HANDBOOKS FOR ASTROLOGERS AND FORTUNE-TELLERS

A very important place in folk-print literature is occupied by the literary products of superstition, i.e. dream-books and handbooks for astrologers and fortune-tellers. The explanation is fairly simple: a deep-rooted preoccupation with the occult on the one hand, and the extremely hard living conditions of the petty citizens, minor tradesmen, shopkeepers and artisans in Iran on the other, provide an ideal climate for superstition to flourish, spread and penetrate the wide ranks of the middle and lower classes.

Fortune-telling is extremely widespread, and the most diverse methods are employed to probe the future. If a sacred text (Koran) is used, the practice is called *Istikhāra*, if it is a secular text or object, it is known as *Fāl*. Quite often fortune-telling is done by casting dice – this is called *Raml*. The interpreting of dreams is known as *Ta'bīr*.

The popularity of many of these works may be judged by the fact that the people use them to ensure success when forecasting the future. For this purpose the *dīvān* of Ḥāfiẓ is most often referred to, but sometimes also that of Sa'dī or the *Mathnavī* of Jalālu'd-dīn Rūmī. The procedure is largely the same as that employed in fortune-telling from the Koran: after an introductory formula or a short prayer, the book in question is opened, the person doing so having closed his eyes, in a special manner that is prescribed down to the smallest detail. These customs are minutely described by Massé.[12]

It is not surprising that there are so many handbooks for fortune-tellers and astrologers that for the most part belong to folk-print literature. Such popular works on astrology were almost certainly influenced up to a certain point by scientific literature on astronomy.

The same can be said of the dream-books in folk-print editions (though some of this material has been transmitted by word of mouth only). These too were probably based on more than one work of literature.

NOTES

* Cf. in general the excellent anthology of Persian folk-literature in Russian translation, published under the title *Plutovka iz Bagdada* (M. 1963), with a very instructive introduction by Yu. Borshchevskiy: 'Persidskaya narodnaya literatura' (5–26).

1. Cf. Zhirmunskiy–Zarifov, *op. cit.*, *passim*.
2. See *s.v.* 'Bertel's' in the Bibliography; see also note * on p. 675.
3. Cf. *Plutovka iz Bagdada*, 14.
4. Romaskevich, *Ocherki izucheniya Shakhname*, 45; Zhukovskiy, *Musul'manstvo Rustama*, 109, 116–117.
5. Cf. Grintser, *Drevneindiyskaya proza* (M,. 1963).
6. Cf. Plutovka, 387–399.
7. Cf. *Persidskiye anekdotĭ* (M. 1963)(with a good preface by N. Osmanov), a very useful and comprehensive anthology of anecdotes.
8. Cf. Romaskevich, *Persid. nar. skazki*, 134–136, 203–204, 327–330, 356–366, 367–376, etc; *Persidskiye skazki* (1958), 452–455, 494–496.
9. Zhukovskiy, *Kolĭbel'nĭye pesni*, 110.
10. Christensen, *Märchen*, 15.
11. Romaskevich, *Persid. nar. sk.*, 12–14.
12. Massé, *Croyances*, 243–246.

VI. THE INFLUENCE OF FOLK-LITERATURE IN MODERN PERSIAN AND TAJIK LITERATURE

The ways in which modern Persian and Tajik literature have used subjects and motifs from folk-literature differ greatly from one another. In this field, however, Tajik authors have indisputably been the most successful in their technique of adapting separate motifs, and it is also in Tajik literature that the folk-tales and their motifs and subjects have been most productive in the creation of various literary masterpieces.

The pioneer in this case, as in other basic issues, was Sadriddin Aynī, the founder of modern Tajik literature who nowadays already ranks as a classical author. He made wide use of popular stories and folk-tales and also of their composition techniqe, and was so successful that many of his characters have become part of folk-tradition. Aynī in his turn was influenced by an eminent master who taught him to love and value folk-literature and who was none other than Maxim Gorky.

Aynī became the leader of a group of authors who may rightly be described as a 'school'. Influences from folk-tradition came to be felt in many fields, and especially in modern drama and in film scenarios, a form of literature which of course had never existed before.

A masterly achievement by the Pamir poet Mīrsayyid Mīrshakar, is the poem *Golden Qishlāq*. It is true that he remodelled and developed an old Pamir legend, but in doing so he treated the motifs from folk-literature in a manner both superior and highly artistic. Other Tajik poets followed suit, and that is why modern Tajik song-writing in particular is distinguished by folk-traits to such an extent that 'artistic' songs very often become real folk-songs. In works of an epic nature again we find many ancient motifs from old epics and folk-tales being used, but it is significant that, although ancient folk-traditions are carefully preserved, in form and interpretation they show a strong sense of realism.[1]

In modern Persian prose, on the other hand, a different state of affairs can be witnessed. Let us examine first under what influences modern New Persian literature began to develop and take shape. Just as in the case of Turkey, there was in Iran the

Notes on p. 678

influence of French literature. Curiously enough it was not the most valuable and classical works that had the greatest effect on the developing embryo of Persian prose, but to a large extent those French novels that were most popular at the time, and these were not always artistically the most advanced. Later the Turkish novel *Millī* also left a deep impression.

The first French works to be tackled were Molière's plays, these being adapted for use in school theatres. Very often names, particular situations and even whole scenes were made to conform to Persian conditions, so that in many cases it is better to speak of an 'iranisation' than a straight translation. Next came the novels of Jules Verne, Bernardin de Saint Pierre, and especially Alexandre Dumas. Two of the latter's novels, *Le Comte de Monte Christo* and *Les Trois Mousquetaires*, had a great effect on modern historical novel writing in Persia, albeit in a somewhat negative sense. The subjects of *The Avengers of Mazdak*, by San'atīzāda Kirmānī, or *Shams u Ṭughrā* by Khusravī, for instance, are certainly partly historical or quasi-historical, but the treatment of the subjects reminds us very strongly of the Dumas novels just mentioned, which can hardly be regarded as an advantage.

Matters are made even worse by the fact that most modern Persian novelists use isolated motifs from folk-literature only haphazardly and superficially. Subjects from early Iranian history profit from the recent upsurge of nationalism. What is really surprising is that the Achaemenids in particular are so popular. There would be no objection to this if it were not for the gross anachronisms produced and – what is far worse – if the names of the *dramatis personae* were not rendered in the transliterations of the French Herodotus translation (cf. Astiāzh etc.). Actually the characteristics of the various personages in Herodotus' *History* are reproduced most faithfully and without inventions of the author himself, no attempt even being made to adapt French transliterations of Greek name renderings to real or supposed Persian forms. History thus becomes no more than a colourful background for the story. It will be clear that historical novel writing in modern Persia leaves much to be desired, especially as regards the use of motifs from folk-literature.

Apart from the odd occasion when a modern author makes use of a classical theme for a film scenario or a play (the most popular is the story of *Farhād and Shīrīn* or *Khusrau and Shīrīn*) – and in most cases he will turn to the literary and not to the folk-version – the whole treasury of motifs from Iranian folk-literature is ignored by literary currents in Iran itself, and is even despised rather than valued.[2]

NOTES

1. Cf. *Sovetskiye pisateli Tadzhikistana*, 9, 12, 38.
2. Cf. Machalski, *Historyczna powieść perska, passim*; *Sovremennÿy Iran, spravochnik* (M. 1957), 460–470; cf. also Komissarov, *Ocherki sovr. persid. prozï* (M. 1960).

VII. RELIGIOUS FOLK-LITERATURE

A. RELIGIOUS FOLK-LITERATURE AND ITS RELATIONS TO FOLK-TRADITION

When we consider how deeply the Iranian way of thinking has been influenced by Islam, and on the other hand how much the nation itself has contributed to its present form of literature from the treasures of its ancient culture and civilisation – an achievement that will never be equalled – it is not surprising to find that religious subjects have always played a prominent part in the development of both polite and folk-literature.

In this respect the question is nevertheless highly complex, chiefly because the thousand odd years during which Iranian, and particularly Persian, literature and culture developed saw so many changes in religious conceptions. The frequent changes of dynasty in the Middle Ages, with the accompanying vacillation between the Sunna and the Shī'a, meant that their subjects had – at any rate to outward appearances – to follow suit, for in the Moslem East the rule *cuius regio, eius religio* was also customarily observed. These are the reasons for the heterogeneous character of Persian literature devoted to religious subjects.[1] Only when the Shī'a finally triumphed after the Safavids had come into power was the direction determined in which later Persian religious polite literature was to develop.

As a contrast, religious folk-literature, in so far as it has come down to us at all, is not very old and therefore largely homogeneous. In Iran itself it is of an acknowledged and decided Shī'ite character.[2]

A very popular story among Shī'ite Iranians is that of the passion of 'Alī and his family; these themes are principally used in folk-drama, but there are also many adaptations in folk-book form. A logical result of this development, during which religious fanaticism increased, if anything, was the peculiar phenomenon that old

Notes on p. 681

Iranian epic subjects had to be islamised in order to make them conform to curre trends. At the same time several religious motifs were made into epic cycles. T illustrate many similar examples it is perhaps sufficient to mention the *Khāvar-nān* of Muḥammad b. Ḥusām (d. 875/1470).[3]

But of course religious folk-literature developed in another direction too. Bertel draws attention to the collection of folk-prints, *Jāmiʿu'l-ḥikāyāt*.[4] The purpose behin this collection is certainly a remarkable one – it was intended to vulgarise the mo important Shīʿite doctrines in a form that would be accessible to the masses. Howeve it would be fruitless to look for a consistent explanation or systematic discussion o the separate theological problems for, unlike Christian literature of similar natu and intention, this work is rather designed to deal with curiosities. The central ide emphasised is the characteristic common to all heroes, namely the determination t suffer every privation and torment without complaint with the sole aim of earning reward after death.

Judged purely objectively, this ideology – designed to divert the people from th real cause of their distress – as well as the folk-prints which propagate it, is by no mear a sign of progress, either in a literary sense or with regard to its effect on societ

B. RELIGIOUS FOLK-LITERATURE AS PRIMARY STAGE IN IRANIAN FOLK-DRAMA

An important figure, particularly from the point of view of cultural history, is th Iranian *parda-zan*, who in his performances glorifies the martyrdom of ʿAbbās. It i but a small step from alluding to simple pictures as accompaniment to a narrativ about a saint, to having his story actually dramatised by live persons.[5]

There was certainly no lack of subjects. There exist a large number of legends abou the Prophet's family and other martyrs who sacrificed their lives for their religiou ideals. These legends are known throughout the Moslem East, while there are als numerous figures of more local significance. All these together provided the orienta imagination with enormous scope for development in many directions.[6]

The Iranians have a natural aptitude for the theatre, but there were many difficultie in the way of dramatic performances, mainly owing to religious inhibitions. The onl dramatic forms that were acceptable to and not forbidden by the Moslem theologian were those that conformed to their philosophy. And this is why religious drama wa able to gain quite a respectable reputation, whereas the old traditional dramatic form were somewhat harshly condemned by the theologians. This, incidentally, did nothin to diminish their popularity with the broad masses of the people.

NOTES

1. Cf. Ethé, *Np. Lit.*, 329–331.
2. Cf. Ethé, *Np. Lit.*, 330–331; a counterpart to the work by Rudi Paret, *Die legendäre Maghāzi-Literatur* (Tübingen 1930), does not exist, although such a work would be very useful for analyzing motifs and epic subjects borrowed from folk-poetry by religious literature, as well as for comparative research.
3. Cf. Krïmskiy, *Ist. Persii i eyo liter.* (Bibl. Bv), III, 121.
4. Cf. Bertel's, *Persidskaya "lubochnaya" literatura*, 88, 89.
5. Cf. Galunov, *Narodnïy teatr Irana*, 67–69, also illustrations (73–75).
6. Cf. Ethé, *Np. Lit.*, 330–331; but see also Paret, *op. cit.*

VIII. DRAMATIC FOLK-LITERATURE IN IRAN

A. THE *TA'ZIYAS* AND OTHER RELIGIOUS FESTIVALS, AND THEIR DEVELOPMENT[1]

Among the Shī'ites, i.e. nowadays particularly among the Persians, in many parts of Mesopotamia and in the districts of India that fall under the cultural influence of Islam, annual dramatic performances are held (or at any rate used to be held until very recently) portraying the death of 'Alī and his sons Ḥasan and Ḥusayn. According to Shī'ite doctrine, of course, 'Alī is the only legitimate successor to the Prophet.

The difference between Christian passion plays and the *ta'ziyas* is mainly that the latter are versed paraphrases of Islamic traditions, whereas European passion plays reproduce texts taken from the Bible or at least from the Apocrypha.

The dramatic cycle of *ta'ziyas* is intended to glorify the memory of the Prophet's family. The principal characters are Ḥusayn and his brother Ḥasan. Besides these we also find, however, the Old Testament figures Jacob and Joseph, Eve and Rachel, and the New Testament Mary; but the most prominent are the Prophet's other relatives – in addition to Muḥammad himself we find 'Alī, Fāṭima, the other brothers and sisters of the two brothers and their children, as well as a host of further episodic figures and supernumeraries, all of whom serve only to set off the protagonist. The *ta'ziyas* are written in verse-form.

Two figures who play an important part are, first, the *vā'iẓ* (the preacher) who is usually a *mullā*, and secondly the *rauḍa-khvān* (prompter or narrator), whose task it is to recount the passion story of the Prophet's family. It often happens, however, that the *rauḍa-khvān* takes on the duties of the *vā'iẓ* as well, so that he first recites the prologue and then delivers the funeral sermon (*khuṭba*) during which he mentions the appropriate *ḥadīths*. Ranged around him is a boys' choir who do duty as women mourners. This is unavoidable since in the *taʿziyas* only men and boys are allowed to appear on the stage. Female parts have to be taken by dressed-up men with disguised voices, as for instance in the laments of widows and mothers. All this is highly reminiscent of the way in which classical Greek drama makes use of the chorus.

The dramatic effect of the *taʿziyas* is astonishingly great. They are performed practically everywhere: public squares, courtyards in caravanserais and mosques, temporarily erected platforms, but also permanent special buildings called *takyes* are all appropriate places for the performances. As a rule the plays are given during the first ten days of the month of Muḥarram, the climax of the festivities being reached on the tenth day. This is the anniversary of the Karbalā massacre in the year 61/680. Owing to a shortage of actors the plays are sometimes spread out over two months. On other occasions such complications are resolved ingeniously and simply by having different performances in the town start at different times. Actors who have finished their part on one stage, hurry to the next on horseback.

The acquisition of stage properties and scenery presents no difficulties. The most important requisites are the *tābūt*, Ḥusayn's catafalque, which has openings so that lanterns can be placed inside it, and Ḥusayn's arms and banner. Fitting out the supernumeraries is a simple matter too, for all participants have their own trappings and trimmings. As for armour, and especially the horses and camels essential to add splendour to the show, any Shīʿite would feel it an honour to be asked for the loan of his beasts. Everybody is pleased to contribute the best he has on these occasions. It goes without saying that the wealthy pay the expenses of the performance as well as the actors' wages. Admittance is free and it is even the custom for the audience to be offered free refreshments. An integral part of the *taʿziyas* are the street processions. Sometimes Ḥusayn's horse is led in the parade, sometimes it represents the bridal procession of Ḥasan's son Qāsim and Ḥusayn's daughter Fāṭima (II), but most important of all is the funeral cortège. In many cases the latter is held as sole ceremonial instead of the *taʿziyas*, if for any reason the plays themselves cannot be performed.

The *taʿziyas* reached their greatest height during the reign of the Qajars, i.e. the 19th and the first quarter of the 20th century, when Iran was at the lowest point of its decline. It was as if the people felt a need for real heroes and moral greatness, on the stage at least, and by taking part in the performances tried to escape to some extent from the depravity and corruption and impotence of contemporary life. From time to time the anonymous authors sacrificed veracity of representation to the idea. There are no intermediate shades or nuances, only light and dark, Shīʿa and Sunna. Contrasts are so absolute that one need not be incredulous of reports of actors having played the part of one of the Prophet's enemies too convincingly and thereafter having been lynched by the fanatically enraged audience. On the other hand the actors took good care to soften the effect of their theatrical prowess, if only for the sake of their personal safety, for instance by weeping over one of their own victims together with the bereaved. For all that it would not have been wise for a Sunnite to take part in the

Notes on pp. 692–693

ta'ziyas. A non-Moslem was more readily allowed to attend than someone known t be a Sunnite, for the latter were considered born opponents of the rightful claims c the Prophet's family – so fanatical were the emotions called forth by the memory c the martyrs' suffering.

As a rule the *ta'ziyas* consist of forty or fifty scenes, but the cycle is neither rounde off nor canonised, and there are several versions of the same numbers in existence It is thought that even today new variants are being added. Of course the texts of al these scenes should be seen as paraphrases of earlier versions, and so it is not sur prising that the folk-poets quote Koran verses and poems and even entire passage from the early poets, when it seems appropriate to include them in the story. Curses prayers and complete sermons that later appear in the *ta'ziyas* already existed in th earliest literature of the Shī'ites. Many of the songs are also of considerable age funeral choruses on the other hand are still being composed today.

Of course such an enormous number of scenes cannot be performed within th space of ten days. A selection therefore has to be made, and this is done in such a way that all the pieces appear in a sequence which forms a consistent cycle o scenes. It is not necessary here to discuss the contents of the various scenes[2], but th imagination of the versifiers and folk-poets was in no way restricted. Many scene suffer to a greater or less extent from diffuseness, critical situations usually being mad to last as long as possible. At the same time there are also a great many scenes whicl fulfil the highest dramatic demands, which fact is borne out by the tremendous effec they have on the audience.

The earliest and probably the original form of the *ta'ziyas* was the funeral sermon in honour of the martyrs of Karbalā. The contents of these sermons later inspired several works of poetry, really elegies (*marthiyyas*), of which the Shī'ites possess a great number. These lamentations, saturated with religious fanaticism as they are have even penetrated into Sindhi literature.[3]

The extent of the influence of the Arabic historical romance *On Ḥusayn's Death and Mukhtār's Revenge*, that was attributed to one of the earliest Arabic historio graphers, Abū Miḥnaf, remains a moot point.[4] Bearing in mind that this prose ro mance has retained its popularity until the present time, even among the Sunnites it seems safe to assume that at least Persians of average education (and among suc most of the *ta'ziya*-writers are to be found) were familiar with the content, if no with the romance itself. The various poets, however, did not simply write paraphrase or even translations, but they gave the subject an Iranian treatment, whereby man of the motifs were developed independently.

The dramatic form really evolved very slowly and gradually, in no way differentl from other similar developments. The sermons and narratives based on the passion story of the Prophet's family, whether in rhetorical or poetical form, were composed and delivered in such a way that they incensed the people to loud emotional outbursts the singing of refrains and wailing lamentations. In this way the solo recitals of th preachers and narrators were interrupted and dramatised. It is very difficult to ascertain to what extent the subjects and epic shaping of the Shīʿite *taʿziyas* were influenced by Arab or Persian legendary literature.[5] Some remote connection must at any rate be assumed. Later on processions were added to the original religious services on remembrance days. With the appearance of the *rauḍa-khvān*, these rudimentary dramatic scenes – which until then had stood loose from one another – became co-ordinated, for he served as director, playwright and narrator all in one. Gradually these productions ceased to be merely private enterprises. The people began to organise performances at their own expense so that also those who were not able to take an active part in the celebrations could at least fulfil their religious duties by attending the plays. The remarkable thing is that all these differing stages of development continued to exist quite happily side by side. It was only later that the scenes were put down in writing. These notes then served as stage directions and were universally put into use.[6]

All members of the Prophet's family appear in the *taʿziyas*, although Ḥasan and Ḥusayn remain the principal heroes throughout the cycle. Nevertheless, other persons too came to play important parts, so that it is more accurate to speak of them as being heroes collectively. This merely enhances the attraction of the plays since other figures from Shīʿite hagiography now also obtain appropriate recognition.

B. ʿ*UMAR-KUSHĀN*, RELIGIOUS PARODY, AND FARCE

If one thinks of the *taʿziyas* as a kind of counterpart to the Christian Passion Plays, the parallel does not end here. In mediaeval Europe it was a common practice to intersperse the tragic episodes of the passion plays with comic interludes, which often became quite outrageous and profane. In the same manner there evolved among the Shīʿites a special type of religous parody, or more accurately farce, directed against the second caliph, ʿUmar (634–644).

At first ʿUmar was cursed at every opportunity, an exercise the Shīʿite Iranians enjoyed passionately and vociferously. At the same time ʿUmar's murderer, the Persian artisan Abū Lūlū Firūz, was worshipped almost as a saint (he was given the honorary name of Shujāʿu'd-dīn, i.e. Hero of the Faith). The fanatical Shīʿites were not in the least worried by the fact that he was no Moslem at all, but a Christian.

The ʿ*Umar-kushān* day (also called *Qatl-i* ʿ*Umar*) is the ninth day of the month of *Rabīʿu'l-avval*. The ceremonies and rituals connected with it were kept up for three days. The substance and purport of the parody ʿ*Umar-kushān* as we know it today probably goes back no further than the very end of the 18th century.

The stage version of the ʿ*Umar-kushān* contains practically nothing but ridicule and

Notes on pp. 692–693

parody. Elegies are turned into songs of insult and malediction, the sermon is full of sneers, there is satire all the way, particularly during the procession. There is here certainly never any question of self-chastisement.

Like the *ta'ziyas*, the *'Umar-kushān* is intended to release passions in the audience, so that it is perhaps not unfortunate that since the beginning of the present century the *'Umar-kushān* in particular appears to have lost much of its popularity.[7]

C. FOLK-FARCES

In all probability the religious farce is no more than a relatively late development of very old traditions common to all peoples of the Near East. It is very likely, however, that there are certain connections between the mimes of ancient Greece and their oriental counterparts. The influence of the Greek mimes appears to have first become noticeable in the rather obscure times when the Diadoch realms were so strongly influenced by Hellenistic culture after the death of Alexander. Of course the gestures and facial expressions which form part of the mimes made them comprehensible even to an audience with a different language.

To a European spectator the Persian farce, *taqlīd*, must appear extremely primitive, in substance as well as plot. As a rule the subjects belong to everyday life. A favourite target for derision is the Iranian weakness for wine – a habit that has been frowned upon by religion for a long time but is as stubborn and ineradicable as ever, despite more than a thousand years of endeavour to stamp it out.

In their performances the Persian jesters expose the hypocrisy of Islamic sanctimoniousness and present life as it really is. They reveal publicly affairs which every one knows about, but anxiously keeps secret. It is here that one finds frequent glimpses of true art and clear evidence of a well-developed sense of reality. Whenever possible the spoken word is accompanied by singing, instrumental music and dancing. It need hardly be mentioned that all female parts are played by boys and men, the speeches and songs of course being rendered in falsetto.[8]

As we learn from Galunov[9], women too acted in performances at folk-theatres, though it is possible that the audience consisted of women only. This practice, however, seems to be on the decline.

As regards folk-farces from Tajikistan, it is quite sufficient to draw attention to the standard work published by Nizam Nurjanov. It also contains a selection of original texts with Russian translations of short farces and plays.[10]

D. IRANIAN BUFFOONS AND THEIR PRODUCTIONS[11]

Buffoons' shows are very closely related to folk-farces. Besides the many singers we know the Sasanian court employed, we can be quite sure that there were also large numbers of court jesters and jugglers.

After the victory of Islam there followed a long period during which there are no apparent traces of the old traditions, at any rate as far as we can tell. The early Islamic era with its outward asceticism and fanaticism was naturally opposed to all mundane affairs, and consequently negatively disposed towards dramatic performances.

With the decline of the centralised power of the caliphs, however, many things started to change. As soon as the feudal state began to disintegrate and the theocratic government grew weaker or disappeared completely, new courts formed around those in power and these became the centres of politics, culture and social life. It was now that jugglers and jesters made their appearance. They are already mentioned in the earliest Persian literature as *maskhara* or *maskhara-bāz*. They gave dramatic, acrobatic and dance performances.

The intrinsic dualism of Iran comes to light in dramatic folk-art also – on the one hand there are the pious *ta'ziyas*, deeply inspired by religion, and on the other the folk-farces with their personifications of sin and damnation. An actor playing the part of a saint in the *ta'ziyas* tries, through his performance, to approach this holy figure as closely as possible and this exercise earns him the right to a certain position of honour in the Moslem paradise. Farce actors, however, are predestined for hell and its tortures.

Actually the performances of the Persian *maskhara-bāz* have more in common with our circus productions than with theatrical performances as we know them in Europe. Persian jesters use no stage or theatrical appurtenances and they can put on a show anywhere and at any time.

During the performances amusing, usually satirical, couplets are sung and one is well advised not to get into the bad books of the travelling *lūṭī*. This intrepid vagabond fears not even the devil, let alone any local big-wig. Quite often it is the jesters who tackle the issues of the day in their own peculiar manner and give their racy comments on politics too.[12]

Favourable opportunities for the appearance of the *maskhara-bāz* are the various annual festivals, which are great occasions for masquerades and merry, even boisterous performances.[13]

In this connection it is interesting to recall what Nurjanov reports, namely that in Tajikistan too very varying customs are preserved at all kinds of festivities, and juggling shows are held with singing, music and dancing.[14] The texts of the farces, like other orally transmitted kinds of folk-literature, have no strictly fixed form. There

Notes on pp. 692–693

are several variants of the same subject, the result of improvisation, whole episodes being sometimes extemporised. In all these farces there is a strong element of social criticism, consequently we find many political allusions, in fact in some cases the subject itself may be some political issue.

The buffoons were really extremely versatile artists. They could act, dance, sing and play musical instruments, while their parodies and imitations were often highly realistic. A peculiar feature of their performances was that the audience was often drawn into the action.[15] It seems likely that much of the material found among the Tajiks is rather older than parallel developments in western Iran.[16]

E. SHADOW PLAYS

All the types of dramatic folk-poetry we have discussed so far, though they differ widely in many respects, have one thing in common – the characters are always portrayed by living persons. Equally popular, however, has always been the puppet theatre in its various forms. Only in recent years has there been a certain degree of competition from the cinema.

It is necessary to distinguish here between the true puppet theatre and the shadow theatre. The puppets are really an inheritance from ancient Greece and Rome, they are plastic and substantial. The shadow theatre, the favourite of the East, on the other hand, operates with flat figures and possesses an unreal, dreamlike character. Most likely it is one of the many acquisitions which came with the Mongol invasion from China and were brought far to the West. Of course the rotating magic lantern had already been known for a considerable time at least to a few people (*fānūs-i khayāl*). As ʿOmar Khayyām points out, the lantern was rotated by hot air generated by the light inside the lantern. The sides bore the images of various characters, the good ones in the form of people, the wicked in the form of devils. In Iran these images already had a real Iranian appearance.

If we try to explain how these shadow theatres have become so enormously widespread, we shall probably find that it is their very dream-like quality and their ability to create an illusion that attracts the Orientals so strongly. By clever manipulation a good performer can appear to control all natural forces and laws, particularly gravity, and he can turn palpable reality into a mere phantom.

Formerly it was absolutely essential to come to terms with certain of the dogmatic demands of Islam. For instance, it was undesirable to portray living creatures. This difficulty, however, was overcome by the manufacturers of the flat figures in an unexpected and most ingenious way. They punched holes in the figures through which rods could be stuck for moving them, and at the same time these holes, which usually went through the stomach, made it clear that the figures could not possibly be alive. In this way the strict rules of religion were obeyed.

The principal character in the shadow plays is 'Kachal pahlavān'. Much can be learnt merely from the different interpretations of this name. The old word *pahlavān* originally meant 'hero', but nowadays the meaning has weakened to 'artist' or 'athlete'. The second component, *kachal*, means 'bald head', 'scurfy head' or 'the scabrous one'. Kachal pahlavān has this bald-headedness in common with the Turkish 'Karagöz' and the Greek 'mimos'. Otherwise each of these related figures mirrors the different characteristics of its own nationality. Pahlavān kachal is actually closer to the Turkish 'Hajīavād'. Chodzko describes him aptly and briefly thus: "Kachal pahlavan is a hypocrite, he can read and write and is well-educated, he is even a poet. Most of all he likes to fool the *mullās* and make them look ridiculous, and he pays court to the ladies and sometimes even to the young boys."

It is very possible that the gipsies were at least partially responsible for the spreading of the puppet theatres, and especially the shadow theatres. Karagöz, after all, was a gipsy figure and even greeted people in the gipsy language.

It was however the religion of Islam that most influenced the shadow theatre and determined its present character. If we further reflect how much Islam owes to the Iranian temperament and Iranian culture, it appears only logical that the shadow plays must have preserved just as much that is essentially Iranian.

According to Islamic doctrine there is little man can do to influence his destiny, and this idea is widely upheld in the shadow plays. In appropriate ways and with the use of suitable dramatic devices they try to illustrate this basic law. To a Moslem the solving of personal ethical problems means little and makes no sense. He feels too much dependent on the will of Allah, and in following Allah's will he seeks redemption for his sins.

Other subjects too found their way into the shadow theatre. Sometimes folk-tales about *dēvs* provide the necessary variation in subject-matter – it goes without saying that the *dēvs* are always beaten by Kachal pahlavān. Very often the subjects of the shadow plays are taken from romantic or humorous tales and anecdotes. Whatever their source they are however always connected with folk-literature. Besides mythological subjects and motifs[17] we also find many of a heroic nature.

The classical subject of Farhād and Shīrīn, for example, occurs quite often, not of course in its literary form but in one derived from folk-tradition. The well-known prose folk-book about Ṭāhir and Zuhra has been used in the same way, although it has become badly distorted and corrupted. Parodies and imitations of speech and person (the technical term is *taqlīd*) have become as much a standard practice in the shadow plays as music, which is an important and essential part of them. The scripts of the shadow plays often remind us of librettos for musical plays.

Notes on pp. 692–693

F. GLOVE PUPPET THEATRES

Glove puppet shows are generally given during the day-time. The puppets are manipulated in the well-known way from below – they are worn like gloves and the head and arms are moved by the fingers. This makes it possible to perform without difficulty in daylight, when the gay colours of the puppets show up to their best advantage.

As early as the 15th century A.D. there were two kinds of puppet theatres in Iran – glove puppets and marionettes or string puppets, which we shall discuss next. The Iranian puppet theatre as a whole has a regrettable preference for coarse, crude and sometimes really vulgar modes of expression. Not infrequently we find blatant obscenities in some of the plays.

A glove puppet show is operated by two people. The proprietor stands outside the booth and takes part in the dialogue or directly in the action, while his assistant (*shāgird*) sits inside the booth and speaks the different parts. Both puppet players extemporise their lines, and they are often jugglers or professional story-tellers and reciters at the same time. Both these skills are of great service to a puppet player. The stage usually consists of a fairly small booth made out of four pieces of material attached to four poles (*khayma*).

The puppets (*ṣūrat*) are generally made by the owner himself. The head and neck are carved out of wood or modelled in *papier mâché*. A puppet is worn on each hand for performance. The thumb goes into one of the sleeves, the first and middle fingers into the head and the fourth and little fingers into the other sleeve. The man in the booth operates the puppets and speaks their parts, though usually not 'straight' but through a kind of decoy-trumpet (*sūt, sūtak*) which he holds between his lips.

Proprietors of puppet shows are often invited to give private performances in wealthy houses. Here they do not feel the restrictions and interferences of censorship. The way in which puppet players collect their money, particularly at public performances, is interesting, for in order to make a success of it they have to manage it with great cunning and tact. At the beginning of the show and several times during the course of it they try to get the audience into the proper spirit by reminding them frequently of 'Alī and how favourably he regards generosity. All this is done in very carefully chosen phrases. Were they to leave the collection until after the performance, there is no doubt that the result would be very poor.[18]

G. MARIONETTE THEATRES

The Persian designation *khayma shab bāzī* (i.e. evening booth show) indicates that the marionette shows are a form of dramatic art that is almost entirely confined to the evening hours and artificial light. The chief reason for this is that the strings that control the puppets are then less visible to the spectators.

The stage is arranged in the same way as for glove puppets, except that the actual platform is at ground level. A set of marionettes may number as many as sixty or eighty puppets. The properties and costumes follow current trends. In recent times, for instance, a toy motor-car has become one of the stage properties.

Quite often we find a small 'orchestra', consisting of a drummer (*ḍarb-gīr*), a fiddler (*kamāncha-kash*) and a castanet-player taking part in the performance.

Like the glove puppet shows, the marionette theatre is operated by two people. One of them stands in the booth and manipulates the puppets – a trumpet being used here too. The second man sits in front of the stall, beats a small cup-shaped drum (*dumbak*) and speaks the different parts, while he too often gets involved in the play himself.

The romances (*taṣnīf*)[19], which are sung by both puppet players during the show, vary a great deal. They may be folk-songs, historical *taṣnīfs*, or topical songs. The *taṣnīfs*, however, are not performed in their entirety, generally only their opening verses being given. Large portions of the text are improvised, and here again we come across many vulgarities and obscenities. The skill displayed by Persian marionette players during their shows in the way of dancing and acrobatics is remarkable and wins well-deserved praise from the audience. This can also be said of the artistic standard of their productions.

Marionette players too are often invited by the well-to-do to give performances in their homes. Especially in these marionette shows there is a strong ethnographic element: dances and processions connected with funerals or weddings are staged, and we also find performances of the rites appropriate to a birth, bastinadoes, etc. Less conspicuous here are the many anachronisms and modernisations, but equally important the more or less successful and subtle attempts to wheedle money out of the audience. It is collected under many pretexts: sometimes a cup of tea has to be provided for the driver of the car, otherwise he will remain stuck on the stage; another time it is to buy swaddling-bands for a new-born marionette baby. Because they are so closely connected with everyday life and the happenings are presented in such a realistic way, marionette theatres have become so popular that the shadow plays have to some extent disappeared into the background.[20]

H. MODERN DRAMA AND ITS CONNECTIONS WITH FOLK-LITERATURE

The fundamental difference between modern Tajik and Persian polite literature is clearly to be seen in dramatic literature.

Notes on pp. 692–693

What strikes one about the modern Persian theatre is that the amateur theatrical tradition is being abandoned only very slowly. Professional or even semi-professional enterprises are rare. The actors belong to spontaneously assembled groups and during the day-time they carry out their ordinary occupations, mostly as artisans, small shop-keepers or town-porters. They meet together in the evenings and play before a limited number of spectators, while they are often hired to perform in private houses. The chief person is the producer of the play, but the company of actors is constantly changing. Occasionally, however, a group may stay together for a longer period and put on performances in a particular part of the country, travelling from one place to another. Their books of words are more like scenarios or directions for the course of the plot, for the actors are allowed to improvise the details of the play, just as in the Italian *commedia dell'arte*. But of course this is no new development – the same occurs in the *ta'ziyas*.[21]

Tajik dramatic art is certainly more advanced. The once casually formed groups of amateur actors have become regular permanent theatres with professional artists, their own dramaturgy and their own acting schedule. This development was stimulated not only by European example but also by notable Tajik traditions.[22] But it is principally on account of its repertory and its strong connections with Tajik folk-literature that the modern Tajik theatre differs from the Persian. Mīrsayyid Mīrshakar, for example, dramatised the famous legend of *The Golden Qishlāq*, and Tursūnzāda, together with Dihātī, wrote in 1936 a musical drama in verse after Niẓāmī's *Khusrau and Shīrīn*, with the same title. These two authors again collaborated to write the libretto for the first national Tajik opera, *The Rising of the Vāsi'*, dealing with the popular revolt of 1885. In 1933 a play of this name had already been written by Sayyidsulṭān Sayyidmuradov.[23]

In marked contrast to this highly independent trend in Tajikistan is the development of Persian dramatic literature, the reason being that it is so largely derivative. Here the models are always foreign, whether one thinks of Fatḥ 'Alī Ākhundzāda (*Monsieur Jourdain*, etc. – in this case translations from the Azerbayjanian) or of European models. Initially it was mostly French works that were taken as models, Molière in particular. The Persian translators, however, had their own strange methods – they brought the events in the originals up to date and generally also adapted names and certain situations to Persian conditions. As a result these translations are really more like paraphrases or variations on a well-known theme. Through the intervention of its Persian editor such a play then becomes truly Persian in character.[24]

NOTES

1. Cf. Ethé, 'Das persische Passionsspiel', in *Morgenländische Studien* (Leipzig 1870), 174–194; Baumgartner, I, 577–584; Horn, *Pers. Lit.*, 201–212; recently published comprehensive catalogue of

ta'ziyas: Rossi–Bombaci, *Elenco di drammi religiosi persiani* (cf. Bibl.) is indispensable for any research in the domain of religious drama in Iran.

2. Cf. Horn, *Pers. Lit.*, 201–212; Chodzko, 'Théatre persan', in *Choix de téaziés* (Paris 1878); Baumgartner, *op. cit.*, I, 578–581; see also Rossi–Bombaci, *Elenco.*
3. Baumgartner, *op.cit.*, II, 289.
4. Baumgartner, *op. cit.*, I, 408 *et seq.*; II, 289; Wüstenfeld, *Der Tod des Husejn b. Ali und die Rache. Ein hist. Roman aus dem Arabischen* (S. B. der G. der W., Berlin, dated 3.8.1882 and 6.1.1883).
5. Cf. Paret, *op. cit.*, principally p. IV.
6. Litten–Rosen, *Das Drama in Persien*, III–XVII; Massé, *Croyances*, 120–136.
7. Krïmskïy, *Pers'kïy teatr*, 74–80.
8. Horovitz, *Spuren griechischer Mimen im Orient*, 12; Bertel's, *Persidskiy teatr*, 81, 82.
9. Galunov, *Nar. teatr Irana*, 69–74.
10. Nurdzhanov, *Tadzh. nar. teatr*, 197–326.
11. Cf. Galunov, *Nar. teatr. Irana*, 73–74.
12. Bertel's, *Persidkiy teatr*, 11, 12, 63–65.
13. Massé, *Croyances*, 146 *et seq.*
14. Cf. Nurdzhanov, *Tadzhikskiy narodnïy teatr*, principally 105–172.
15. Nurdzhanov, *Istoki nar. teatra u Tadzhikov*, 103 *et seq.*; see also his *Tadzhikskiy nar. teatr*, and other works of the same author.
16. Cf. also Galunov, *Nar. teatr Irana*, 55–83; see also Menzel, *Meddâḥ...*, *passim.*
17. Cf. Jacob, *Geschichte des Schattentheaters*, 10, 16, 31, 43, 44, 109, 132, 133, 137.
18. Galunov, *Pakhlavān-Kachal'*, 26–30.
19. A very representative collection was recently published under the title *Persidskie tesnifī* (M. 1964).
20. Galunov, *Kheyme shab-bāzī*, 1–3.
21. Chaykin, *Kr. ocherki noveyshey persid. liter.*, 134–137; cf. *Sovremennïy Iran, spravochnik* (M. 1957), 460–464.
22. Nurdzhanov, *Istoki*, 108; cf. also *Materialï k istorii zarozhdeniya tadzh. teatra, passim.*
23. *Sov. pisateli Tadzhikistana*, 12, 38, 52, 75, 93.
24. Bertel's, *Persid. teatr*, 72, 80–82.

IX. VERSE FORMS OF FOLK-LITERATURE

A. FOLK-QUATRAINS

One may safely say of Persian polite literature that nearly all major works are composed in verse, and that only very recently does this phenomenon appear to be undergoing a change. In Iranian folk-literature, on the other hand, the reverse is true – most types are composed and transmitted in prose, while a smaller proportion is in verse.

Among the various genres of rhythmical poetry the quatrain (*rubā'ī*) genuinely has its roots among the people. Each verse is usually made up of eleven syllables, though occasionally one finds twelve or fourteen. Not until later was the metric system of polite literature imposed upon the folk-quatrains (most common is the incomplete eleven-syllable *hazaj*). It is interesting to examine how these quatrains were designated by the people. Those written in dialect, in particular, are called *fahlaviyyāt* or *pahlaviyyāt*. It is significant that the Gīlakīs also give this name to their songs, which consist of several quatrains. Of course there are other names as well – *chōrbaytī*, *dūbaytī*, *sōrbūnī* (songs of the camel-drivers). In the province of Fars we find the names *shärve*, *shärbe*, *shälve*, and *shälvī*.

Quatrains are always recited in a monotonous and long drawn-out kind of chant which even by the Persian themselves is described as 'plaintive' and 'wailing' (*Āvāz-i mūya*, *Āvāz-i ḥazīn*). It is possible that the name used in the Fars dialects – *shärve* etc. – really refers to the way of singing and that this meaning has been forgotten elsewhere.

The quatrains do not always stand on their own but are sometimes incorporated into romances (*taṣnīf*), in which case both the romance and the quatrain continue to be recited in their own manner. The *shärve* is often given a refrain of one or two words. The rhyme pattern of the folk-quatrains is the same as that in literary poetry (*aaba*). So-called singing quatrains (*rubā'ī-i tarāna* with rhyme pattern *aaaa*) do not occur very often, but the rhyme formula *aabb* appears fairly frequently. The latter type of quatrain may easily be made up into *ghazals* and *mathnavīs*.[1]

B. LYRIC AND EPIC FOLK-SONGS

Chares of Mytilene[2] already mentioned that at the time of Alexander the Great the Persians sang romances such as the one on *Zariadres and Odatis*. The famous Pahlavi work *Ayātkār-i Zarērān* may originally have developed out of this romance. Benveniste is of the opinion that it first existed in verse form and that the pattern later became syllabic, i.e. syllable-counting.[3] Chares' observation is of the greatest importance since it proves that very early on there were lyric as well as epic folk-songs in Iran.

Folk-songs accompany the Iranian from the cradle to the grave. Lullabies are the first thing a child hears. In many respects the Iranian lullabies remind us of the Slavonic, partly on account of their refrains. In structure the lullabies are really *mathnavīs*, that is a series of rhymed couplets (*aa bb cc*, etc.), and strictly speaking an intermediary form between prose and poetry. The verses are syllabic, although sometimes again quantitative. Here too *hazaj* makes an appearance, but its popular modifications are relatively rare. Developments that remind us of polite literary forms give rise to the suspicion that there may have been a reciprocal – though maybe only partial – influence between the latter and folk-forms.

A study of the contents of the various lullabies is in many ways rewarding. As a rule these folk-songs give a very good picture of the true family relationships, social conditions and practical philosophy of the people (to a less extent of the ruling classes). Most lullabies were composed for a son, only rarely for a daughter, for to have a son was a blessing, to have several led to fame. In certain circumstances it was even considered a misfortune for a woman to have a daughter – one daughter was enough in any case.

The mother appeals to the saints to protect her child, 'Alī being most often invoked. Like mothers of all other nationalities, the Iranian woman likes to express tenderness in her song, for a lullaby is really a dialogue between mother and child. If the child misbehaves, however, the mother sometimes threatens or curses him.

We find a considerable difference between the lullabies sung by mothers leading a stationary life and those of nomadic women. The nomadic Bakhtiyaris consider the tribe to be of greater importance than the individual, a woman stands on an equal footing with the men of the tribe, so that a mother raises her child not for herself only but for the whole community. For all that, the lullabies bear witness to everything that is most dear to women as well as to their cares and worries. In these songs they

Notes on pp. 699–700

express their private thoughts and the joys and griefs of family life. It lies in the nature of things that the wife of the settled Persians has a much narrower outlook. Whereas a Bakhtiyari wife may sometimes complain about the trouble caused by guests, though also referring in her song to the stories she has enjoyed hearing in their company, the Persian woman languishes in loneliness since her men-folk tend to spend a large part of the year away from home to earn their living. Bakhtiyari women do not know the feeling of loneliness, and if they refer to an absence due to a journey or visit, there is no question of nostalgia because such partings are never for long. The Bakhtiyari lullabies are rich in motifs, subjects and inspiration – nature in its different seasons is described and so are the wanderings of the tribe, attacks by the enemy and the punishment of the latter. As a rule the story is told in a fairly impersonal manner. Persian women, on the other hand, complain mainly about domestic troubles and personal cares. If a Bakhtiyari woman occasionally mentions hard times this should not be taken as a personal utterance, but rather as an expression of regret for a misfortune that has befallen the whole tribe. Individual unhappiness is expressed only when a Bakhtiyari woman is unable to join her tribe on its journeyings. The total impression of the position of women obtained from the lullabies is that the Bakhtiyari wives have an incomparably better life and enjoy a relative measure of freedom and respect, in strong contrast to the sad lot of the women of the sedentary Persians, whose existence is hard and who are kept in a constant state of subjugation. The same is true of the mainly Central Asian Jewish women (the Central Asian and Persian Jews speak an extremely archaic Iranian dialect).[4]

Besides these lullabies, which are called *lālā'ī* and are popular everywhere, whether it be among dialect-speaking tribes who are mainly nomadic, or among the settled townspeople who speak the vulgar colloquial language known as *Bāzārī*[5], the folk-lyrics include a great number of love-songs. These may be in the form of *ghazals* or *qaṣīdas*. Structurally the love-songs are really identical with the lullabies, they differ only in subject-matter and content. Here too we find a typical characteristic of folk-tradition, namely that the verses are basically syllabic instead of quantitative[6], although there are also numerous regional variations. The number of syllables vacillates between seven and fifteen, while regular rhyme is sometimes represented merely by assonance. Be that as it may, an important factor appears to be the extent to which the folk-poet stood under the influence of polite poetry or allowed this influence to affect his work.

We can learn quite a lot from a short investigation into the folk-literature composed in verse-form by the Iranian tribes in Pamir. Some remarkable things come to light here, and since until recently the Pamir districts have been separated from other centres of Iranian culture, it is not at all impossible that peculiarities of folk-tradition that seem to have survived only here, have done so in a form which in other places has long since had to give way to the influence of polite literature.[7]

The versified folk-literature of the Shughnanians can be divided into the following types: the *dargīlīk* (songs of nostalgia) and its variants, though only as regards subject-matter, the *lālāīk* (lullaby) and the *shoīrä* (cf. Persian *shā'irī*, here however in the meaning of 'improvisation'). Whereas the *dargīlīk* and the *lālāīk* have a very rigid structural pattern, the *shoīrä* is rather a poem composed for a particular occasion and is more flexible in respect of poetic rules. There is notably a strongly marked contrast between the *shoīrä* and Persian or Tajik poetry (literary poetry and therefore sometimes referred to as *kitōb*). Persian or Tajik poems are here known as *sōz*, instead of the more familiar *bayt*.

In Shughnanian versified folk-literature the structural units are strophes rather than whole songs. Strophes may be joined together as required, so that new songs can be composed by combining them in different ways. Only thus can it be explained how several strophes re-appear in more than one poem. One might call them 'wandering strophes'. The rhymes are usually very pure, and the refrains never develop the ideas in the poem itself. A Chaghatay technical term for refrain is *qōshiq* ('connected').

As we have already said, there is also a formal difference between the *dargīlīk* and the *shoīrä*. A *shoīrä* is really composed of a number of quatrains (*chorbait*). The first three verses rhyme with one another, the fourth is the refrain and generally unrelated to the rhyme pattern. Each verse of a *shoīrä* consists of seven syllables without a caesura, but there are exceptions, although syllables are more often added to than substracted from the usual number. The refrain is sometimes in Persian. The subjects of the *shoīrä* vary a great deal. Sometimes they are love-songs, sometimes they are composed in praise of the beauty of some person, or they describe battle-scenes – even very recent ones – deplore social abuses or make fun of some locally known situation. It is a favourite form for poems written for special occasions or celebrations.

The *dargīlīks*, on the other hand, are of a more private nature. They are particularly suited to descriptions of intimate experiences or desires and are always composed in dialect. They are addressed to mothers or sweethearts by their sons or lovers, but sometimes also vice versa. They are not used at family celebrations, for they invariably possess a touch of melancholy and nostalgia. They consist of two rhyming four-footed verses, each of eight syllables, and one refrain that is not counted as part of the strophe. For this reason the latter is called *dubayt*. Each verse has a caesura after the fourth syllable, not only rhythmically but also semantically. Five- or three-footed verses are rare. The refrain consists of twice four syllables (each being one semi-verse) and the two halves, which are separated by two eight-syllable verses, rhyme with one another. The rhyme pattern thus becomes *aarbbr*. This symmetry is structural as well as semantic. As has been pointed out already, the *lālāīks* are really a special form of *dargīlīk*. The Pamir love-songs have a further peculiarity that is very interesting and worth noting – they pay tribute exclusively to married women. It is not permitted and thus impossible to approach an unmarried girl, but there is no objection to a relationship with the wife of another man. Perhaps this is an echo of ancient family relationships from pre-Islamic times.

Notes on pp. 699–700

As regards the music, it is curious that all *dargīlīks* are sung to the same melody, whereas for the *shoīrās* there are different ones. There are also of course intermediate forms between the two main types.[8]

Dargīlīks can be comparatively long; Skjöld for instance mentions one consisting of sixteen times two-and-a-half verses. The pairs of long verses rhyme with each other, while the refrains rhyme throughout the poem. This does not mean of course that there are no *ghazals* in the versified folk-literature of the Pamir Iranians.[9]

Tajik folk-songs are related to the *dargīlīks* of the Pamir Iranians, at least as far as their content is concerned. They are called *gharībī*[10] – 'songs from abroad' – and are moving expressions of the Tajiks' nostalgia for their home country from which they had been driven through sheer lack of a means of subsistence. Moreover the earlier folk-songs of the Tajiks give vent to an unconcealed opposition and animosity towards their oppressors. Folk-literature alone escaped the influence of the all-powerful upper class in the days before the Revolution. Social themes play an important part even in the love-songs and *ghazals*. Occasionally, for instance, the futility and utter hopelessness of a love affair between two people of unequal social classes have inspired really heart-breaking poems.[11] Modern Tajik folk-songs are entirely different in character. Many famous poets of the 'literary' school now write in such a 'folk' manner that their poems often become folk-songs surprisingly rapidly. We should mention here at least Sayyid-ʿAlī Valīzāda, Mīrsayyid Mīrshakar, Bāqī Raḥīmzāda, and Muḥīddīn Hasanovv Farḥat.[12]

It would be strange indeed if in a nation with a talent for epics like the Iranians, the epic element were to be missing from the folk-songs. Their epic folk-songs, however, are quite separate from the epics in polite and folk-literature. This emerges clearly from the material collected by Chodzko in his time. He also discovered that the Gilanians call poems written in their own dialect *pahlaviyyāt*, and those in Persian *taṣnīf*.[13]

For the sake of completeness it may be added that short folk-poems of an epic character – we have already discussed their contents – are usually in the form of *mathnavīs*. Rather than give a complete list, it will suffice to mention the Kurdic *dāstān*, *Mame and Aishe*[14], and the Balūchi texts of Dames.[15]

Afghan versified folk-literature on the whole resembles the average Iranian type. As far as it is possible to judge from the material supplied by Darmesteter, there appears to be a fairly strong influence from Persian polite poetry. The favourite form is *miṣraʿ*, and not *chahārbayt*, which is to be found mainly in ballads. It is curious to note that the Afghans recognise two different categories of poets. The first, called *shāʿir*, composers of literary poetry, are men of culture and have a distinguished position in high society. Although they rate so much higher than the folk-poets (*ḍum*) in a social sense, their popularity and influence with the common people is very small. The folk-poets (*ḍum*) on the other hand, have a great deal of authority because of their close ties with the people. They pay due attention to all current events in their songs. Reciprocal plagiarism is indulged in frequently, but is not taken very seriously. An interesting institution are the schools for folk-singers, where a group of young men gather around an experienced and famous *ḍum*. The apprenticeship is long[16], for the repertory of an Afghan folk-poet includes every current form of folk-literature, from love-songs to rebel songs.

C. FOLK-COUPLETS, COUNTING-OUT AND NURSERY RHYMES

Folk-poetry is an integral part of all varieties of dramatic art, either as the form chosen for particular passages or inserted in a prose text. Very often verse is used by jugglers and theatre proprietors when soliciting their reward from the audience and also for the counting-out of athletes. Apart from this, a few verses are frequently included in folk-tales which are themselves mainly in prose.

By far the most important and most common, however, are the lesser forms of folk-poetry like children's games or the games parents play with their children. It is significant that in these cases verse is preferred to prose, whereas in folk-literature the reverse is usually the case. The reason is of course that verse is more easily memorised, and further that there is less scope for improvisation, which is such an important factor in other types of folk-literature. Naturally each game requires a fixed shape and story, and it makes no difference whether it is a counting-out game, whether fixed questions are involved, or whether the particular verses are recited or sung to a special tune.

Of course we must not expect to find great artistic masterpieces among this kind of folk-poem. A more detailed discussion of the subject is provided by the French orientalist Massé.[17]

NOTES

1. Romaskevich, *Persid. nar. chetverostishiya*, 4–6; Eberman, *Persī sredi arab. poetov epokhi Omeyadov*, 119; Bertel's, *Persid. poeziya v Bukhare X veka*, 33; *Chetverostishiya, Iz tadzh. nar. liriki* (St. 1957); *Fol'klori tojik* (St. 1957).
2. Cf. *Griechische Märchen*, 143–144.
3. Massé, *Firdousi*, 23, 40.
4. Zhukovskiy, *Kolībel'nīye pesni, passim*; Lozovskaya, *Mat' i dit'ya u sredneaziatskikh yevreyev*, 206, 207.

5. Massé, *Croyances*, 491, 492, 494, 496; cf. also Kégl, *A persza népdal* (see Bibl.!).
6. Massé, *Croyances*, 491, 492; Minorsky, *Oriental Studies in the USSR*, 94; Miller, *O dialekte goroda Shustera*, 76.
7. Cf. also Lentz, *Auf dem Dach der Welt*, 139–142, 200–204 *et passim* this book contains a wealth of very useful information on ethnography and folklore; Lentz, *Pamir-Dialekte*, 57–67.
8. Lentz, *Auf dem Dach der Welt*, 200–204.
9. Skjöld, *Pamirsprachen*, 126–129.
10. Cf. *Fol'klori tojik*, 178–209.
11. *Nar. poeziya Tadzhikistana*, 4, 5; *Fol'klori tojik*, 164–397.
12. *Sov. pisateli Tadzhikistana*, 48, 75, 88, 108; *Fol'klori tojik*, 18–158.
13. Cf. Chodzko, *Specimens*, 418 *et seq.*, texts Nos. I, II, XLIII, XLVI, see also p. 474; cf. also *Persidskiye tesnifī* (M. 1964).
14. Kurdoyev–Tsukerman, *Kurdskiye tekstī*, 30–46; cf. also Nikitine, *Les Kurdes*, 259–281.
15. Dames, *Sketch*, 133–160.
16. Darmesteter, *Afghan Life in Afghan Songs*, 3; Darmesteter, *Chants populaires des Afghans*, CXCI, CXCIII, CXCIV; contemporary Afghan folk-poetry published by Lebedev, 'Afganskaya poeziya', in *Voprosī yaz. i liter. stran Vostoka*, pod red. Y. V. Rozhdestvenskogo (M. 1958), 258–273; Dvoryankov, N. A., 'Malang Dzhan – nar. poet Afganistana', *KSIA*, XXXVII (M. 1960), 60–75; cf. also Belyayev, V., *Afganskaya narodnaya muzīka* (M. 1960); Gerasimova, A.–Girs, G., *Literatura Afganistana* (M. 1963), 10–25; perhaps the Afghan *ḍums* are in some way connected with the gipsies in NW-India and Pakistan; similar schools also exist elsewhere, e.g. in Kurdistan, cf. Nikitine, *Les Kurdes*, 273–274.
17. Massé, *Croyances*, 419–438; cf. also Semenov, A.A., 'Detskie pozdravitel'nïye stishki v bukharskikh maktabakh', *Izv. Tadzh. AN*, 10–11 (St. 1956).

X. RIDDLES AND PROVERBS

The folk-literature of an oriental people like the Iranians would be unimaginable without riddles and proverbs. It is of prime importance for each utterance or proposition to be couched in elegant and ingenious, even rhetorical terms, and this just about sums up all that is to be said about these last two categories. The classical Italian adage, *si non è vero, è ben trovato*, could not be more appropriate.

Nevertheless, what has just been said cannot be taken without certain reservations, for it is difficult to be quite sure about what is really folk-literature and what has already been adapted to the rules of polite literature, or should be seen as a variation on a popular theme. Nowhere does the final form in which a particular thought is expressed depend so much on the poet – whether he be known or anonymous – as in the case of proverbs (*Gulistān !*). We have to rely on several collections falling into the category of polite literature, and even when European collectors believe to have struck a virgin source of folk-literature one cannot be certain beforehand that there has not been a secondary influence from written collections or at least from the sermons of a local *mullā*.

Iranian polite literature is almost unthinkable without proverbs. In each work at least one maxim or dictum must be included somewhere, and this may itself be a remnant of a proverb. The situation is summed up very well in the following comparison: just as classical prose and even scholarly treatises are rarely without a few quotations from the great poets, the latter in their turn are continously aided and guided by proverbs, riddles and allusions in their search for picturesque and elegant ways of expression.

It is not necessary to say anything more about the important part played both in the polite literature and the folk-literature of the Iranians by these two types of folklore. Like folk-tales, anecdotes and short stories, the riddles and proverbs are favourite building materials for more elaborate polite and folk-literature. Even in cultural epics and in theological writings, Islamic as well as pre-Islamic, there are clear instances of their use.

Notes on pp. 703–704

Even in the *Shāh-nāma* we find riddle-episodes. The most important is the episode from the story of Zāl and Rūdāba, in which Zāl has to answer six riddles put to him by the magi at the court of Mihrāb, whose daughter Rūdāba he wishes to marry.[1] It is worth noting that the riddles of the magi inspired Gozzi and Schiller, at any rate in a remote way, to create a similar situation in *Turandot*.[2] The collecting and interpreting of Iranian proverbs has been the work mainly of European orientalists, although native scholars have now started to make contributions. A good deal has moreover been published in India, and there are a number of Persian manuscripts. There is no doubt, however, that work in this field is most advanced in modern Turkey, though this is no reason to believe that Iran is less rich in proverbs than the latter country. Of course none of this implies that the Persians and their poets did not value proverbs or that they disdained them. On the contrary, as early as the 10th century A.D. there was a certain Abū'l Faḍl Sukkarī from Merv, who translated Persian proverbs into Arabic. Niẓāmī, too, was fond of using them and a few centuries later we find Sā'ib, an important poet who lived in the 17th century, using proverbs in his poems. One has to keep in mind that European influences penetrated here considerably later than in Turkey, which also explains why the methods and precepts of European folklore study have only in recent times had any effect in Iran. If one remembers the large number of other more urgent questions that still remain to be studied, it is easy to see why scholars have not as yet turned their attention to minor problems such as that of proverb investigation.

On account of their brevity Iranian proverbs can hardly be expected to record the Iranian practical philosophy of everyday life so extensively as does, for instance, the *Thousand and One Nights*. Nevertheless they are a good source of information on the moral concepts of the common Iranian. The fatalism so characteristic of them goes back to pre-Islamic ideology. Another interesting feature is the vast utilitarian outlook expressed in the proverbs, and the fact that they touch but superficially on the causes of concrete phenomena, never enquiring too deeply. Nonetheless, they often emphasise how important it is to control one's passions and to be just, moderate and unselfish. A man should be courageous, and also in a wider sense, self-denying and loyal to the accepted laws; also generous, although prodigality is heavily condemned.[3] It all adds up to that typical folk-wisdom which perfectly echoes the basic morals of fables and most folk-tales. This concordance is, of course, no coincidence but an organic and logical outcome of a long evolution.[4]

Horten rightly points out[5] that all collections of proverbs compiled and published so far are really no more than an assembling of material. A truly scientific investigation has yet to be made, and as things stand at the moment this is a difficult and even premature task. First it will be necessary to explore the cultural, social and economic situation of the society in question, and only on this basis will it be possible to attempt a classification.

An investigation along these lines would provide a valuable contribution to our knowledge of the practical philosophy of the peoples of the East, and at the same time give us an insight into the extent to which this branch of Islamic culture is indebted to Iranian sources and influences.

As to an examination and collection of the proverbs of other Iranian tribes, as yet only a start has been made. Unless real progress in this field is made, however, any study of proverbs based solely on Persian examples – which are generally strongly influenced by polite literature and have little to do with folk-literature – will be incomplete and premature.[6]

Our knowledge of Iranian proverbs is inadequate. No change in this state of affairs has been effected by the recently published large Russian anthology, though it contains a respectable proportion of Iranian proverbs (more than 2100).[7] Comparative research has a limited number of records at its disposal and these are of varying quality; wide areas of Iranian linguistic territory remain until now unexplored.[8] Unique as regards aims and content is the research into the application and use of Tajik proverbs to be found in the works of Sadriddin Aĭnī.[9]

Research on Iranian proverbs would have to include the following activities: (1) collection and publication of proverbs from dialectal records and the provision of literal translations; (2) study of the collected proverbs by means of accurate and thorough analyses from the standpoints of comparative research into their literary, historical, ethnographical and cultural values; (3) determination of genetical connections and affiliations of individual wordings; and finally (4) comparative juxtaposition with European proverbs. When studying wider contexts of proverbs it is important that the quality of any translation should be the best possible. Finally it will be important to find out whether proverbs have served to provide story-tellers with material on which to base their anecdotes and jokes.[10]

NOTES

1. Cf. Kowalski, *Studia*, I, 148–221; II, 16–17.
2. Cf. Schack, *Heldensagen des Firdousi*, I, 'Einleitung', 88; nevertheless not directly, the corresponding tale from *Mille et un jours* being intermediary; cf. also Niẓāmī, *Haft payikar* (ed. Ritter–Rypka), the tale of the Russian princess, 178 *et seq.*; see also Rypka, 'Les sept princesses de Niẓāmī', in *L'âme de l'Iran* (Paris 1951), 99–125; for the Tajik riddles and folk-tales with riddles as subjects see Chistonho (v. Bibl!).
3. Cf. Horten, *Philosophie des Islam*, 282, 283, 368, 369, note 248.
4. Carra de Vaux, *Les penseurs de l'Islam*, 337.
5. Horten, *Philosophie des Islam*, 282–285.
6. A Persian collection of great importance was published by 'Alī Akbar Dihkhudā, *Kitāb-i amthāl u ḥikam* I–IV (Tehran 1310).
7. *Poslovitsī i pogovorki narodov Vostoka*, red. I. S. Braginskiy, sostavitel' A. E. Bregel', predisloviye V. P. Anikina (M. 1961), with an excellent index (pp. 658–734).

8. Besides the recently published Soviet anthology only Phillott, *Persian Saws and Proverbs*; Beck, *Np. Konvers. Grammatik* (Heidelberg 1914), 210–212, and *Schlüssel z. np. Konversations-Gram.* (Heidelberg 1915), 52–54; St. Clair-Tisdall, *Modern Persian Grammar* (Heidelberg 1923), 208–214; cf. also Beidar, *Grammaire Kurde* (every § is followed by several proverbs); Miller, *Talïshskiye tekstï*, VII; Sirdar Ikbal Ali Shah, *op. cit.*, 119–120.
9. Abdullozoda, R., *Zarbulmasal va maqalho dar asarhoi Sadriddin Aynī* (St. 1958).
10. Cf. Gianbattista Basile, *Pentameron*, where each of the fifty tales is terminated by a proverb or saying; Archer Tylor, *The Proverb* (Cambr., Mass., 1931), 27 *et seq.*

XI. CONCLUSION

In the preceding chapters I have endeavoured to deal with at least the most important and most characteristic manifestations of Iranian folk-literature. It has been no simple task, not only on account of the vastness and complexity of the material, but even more so because until now questions pertaining to folk-literature have been tackled only as occasion offered and then not systematically.

Until quite recently problems to do with folk-literature have very often been passed over in silence, or at best some isolated details may have been glanced at. Reciprocal relationships have been overlooked and in most cases even historical and factual connections have not been given proper consideration. Synthesis is always difficult when there has been almost no analytical research and when comparative studies are still in a preliminary stage. The two standard works written by I.S. Braginskiy are the only exceptions in this respect.[1]

Under such circumstances it will be understood that the present essay, being the first of its kind, can be no more than an outline of Iranian folk-literature. May it serve as an introduction to a closer study of particular details.

The synthetical character, but mainly the limited extent, of the present work bars the inclusion of analyses of controversial questions. Consequently many very important problems remain still unsolved. Thus, for instance, questions concerning the influence of Iranian themes on other literatures have not been treated at all. In the same way an analysis of the mutual relations between the folk-literature of the Iranians and that of other peoples of the Near East has had to be omitted.

Each of these problems requires to be dealt with thoroughly and extensively in a separate monograph. Concise notes, explanations and references would not answer the purpose satisfactorily. An attractive object of discussion would be the connections between the Russian heroic folk-tale on Eruslan Lazarevich and the Iranian folk-epics[2], or the typological similarities between the *Gūrughlī* epics and the well-known English romances about the famous outlaw Robin Hood.[3] Just as im-

Notes on pp. 708–709

portant and interesting are the parallels between Celtic and Iranian folk-literature.[4] Analyses of such problems go beyond the scope of the present study, for they would provide sufficient material for several books. But the time for this is not yet ripe. The criteria used so far are in general no more than formal, being incomprehensive and insufficiently specific, while the material available for study is heterogeneous and inadequate.

The limits imposed on length are also the reason why the interpretation of the most ancient documents of Iranian folk-literature and their authors have not been discussed, for it was necessary to abstain from more detailed explanations and analyses of Iranian folk-tales and epic subjects. We have also had to refrain from giving ethnographical and folkloristic evaluations, despite the fact that many valuable documents have been found and edited in recent years.

Monographical research should be undertaken in a way similar to that used by Kahlo when analysing the folk-tales collected by the brothers Grimm.[5] A mechanical gathering together of material, such as we find in part in the work of Geissler[6], should be avoided. As to methods of analysing Iranian folk-epics (especially in regard to the smaller forms – *dāstāns*), the model established by Lambertz[7] certainly has its attractions. The analysis of Iranian folk-epics needs enlarging by the application of new procedures and principles, as defined by I.S. Braginskiy.[8]

The following steps should be taken when undertaking monographical research in the domain of Iranian folk-literature: first a descriptive inventory of subjects and motifs should be made, followed by genetical and typological analyses. Having accomplished these preliminary and fundamental enquiries we must attempt to reconstruct the historical continuity in the evolution of Iranian folk-literature, and to identify its sources and correlations. Again I.S. Braginskiy points the way, though comparative studies on the literatures of Islam should be executed still more extensively. Foremost in attention and interest should be those investigations dealing with the relations between Arab literature and the literatures of the Iranian peoples, on the levels of both polite and folk-literature. The mutual relations between the Iranian nations and those where substrata, adstrata and superstrata of Iranian influence may be expected, should be analysed, whether in the field of language, polite literature, or folk-tradition.

The excellent work of Zhirmunskiy and Zarifov[9], once a bone of contention and an object of unmerited doubts, should now serve as model and inspiration for investigations of a similar kind. Only a careful and universal research into the problems that were first discussed by the authors mentioned can lead us to the objective truth. One point is now quite certain: it has been proved true that a subject in folk- or polite literature may not be autochthonous, but this does not exclude the ethnical authenticity of the national version. It means that, for instance, the subjects of Uzbek *dāstāns*, Kuntugmïsh[10] and Orzigul[11] are certainly of Iranian origin, but the composition is beyond all doubt Uzbek. On the contrary, the *Gūrughlī*-epics, or

Alpamīsh[12], differ substantially in their Tajik presentations from other (Turkic) versions. The Tajik ethnical authenticity of concrete poetical formations is unquestionable, even though the eastern Turkish origin of the subjects cannot be denied.

It is unfortunately true that most of the specialists in Iranian dialectology have paid far too little attention to the theoretical aspect of folk-literature. Thus only a small proportion of the texts composed in Iranian dialects is of any importance, leaving aside their linguistic value, as documents of folk-literature.

An ignorance of folk-literature or insufficient enlightenment in this field has had deleterious effects on the study of polite literature too, for without a knowledge of folk-literature and its rules many fundamental questions in literary history cannot be understood; for example the problem as to why certain works of literature survive so much longer than others that enjoy but ephemeral popularity, or questions dealing with the individuality of literary productions.

The whole issue was put in a nutshell by Maxim Gorky[13] when he said: "Literature has its roots in folklore", and "An author with a poor knowledge of folk-literature is a poor author." And it is true that in Persian literature we find very good evidence for the validity of this statement. This explains why the *Shāh-nāma* has survived for so many centuries and is popular to this day, and also why it has remained comprehensible even to uneducated and analphabetic Persians. Firdausī took the trouble to examine and work out the best records of the Iranian folk-tradition.[14] The popularity of Saʿdī's *Gulistān*[15] and Ḥāfiẓ' *dīvān*[16] rests on the same basis. As opposed to these examples, the works of many other poets who deliberately ignored the rules and esthetic conventions of folk-literature were forgotten soon after the death of their authors, as might indeed be expected since even in their life-time the works were intended only for a very limited and select public, written in a context that was entirely alien to the common people.

Unless one is familiar with the laws of folk-literature therefore, it is hard to understand on what traditions Iranian culture as a whole is based. This also is why our main concern has been to define the lines along which specific monuments of literature have developed and to explain their nature and social relevance, and to determine at the same time the relationships between folk- and polite literature.

Because my space was limited I have been able to give only a very restricted interpretation of the earliest traces of Iranian folk-literature to be found in the work of Greek and Roman authors, and the same applies for any deeper enquiry into the subjects of Iranian folk-tales. In a monograph it would be possible to pay more attention to the questions I have had to pass by in the present essay.

The various genres of Iranian folk-literature do not all belong to the same phase of development. Next to genuinely alive and vital kinds of folk-literature we find examples that are now obsolete. Radical changes in the social structure of Iran itself, and the complete revolution in the political system of the Tajiks can only leave one gues-

Notes on pp. 708–709

sing at how folk-literature will develop in the years to come. The classical subjects will survive, as they have done in their long evolution up to now, irrespective of whether they belong to the categories of folk-epics, romantic epics, folk-stories of everyday life, folk-tales, both in prose and verse, or to folk-lyrics and proverbs. At the present moment it is impossible to forecast how soon and to what extent folk-literature will influence modern Persian polite literature, and contribute to its revival. In this respect Tajik polite literature is a long way ahead.[17]

It is equally hard to predict as yet how much the levelling out of language differences will effect folk-literature by spreading certain subjects that were formerly isolated in a smaller dialect area.

In Tajikistan as well as in Iran, new kinds of polite and folk-literature may be expected to develop. They will all owe their existence to the changing pattern of society. Whatever happens, however, we need not be afraid that folk-literature as such will disappear in the course of history. If we look at what has happened among the Tajiks, we have all the proof we need that the influence and importance of Iranian folk-literature is more likely to increase than to grow less. Everything will depend on whether modern writers know how to bring it into play in the right way, and to integrate it into their work.

Summer 1967

NOTES

1. Braginskiy, I.S., *Iz istorii tadzhikskoy narodnoy poezii. Elementï narodno-poeticheskogo tvorchestva v pamyatnikakh drevney i srednevekovoy pismennosti* (M. 1956); *Ocherki iz istorii tadzhikskoy literaturï.* (St. 1956).
2. Cf. *Russische Volksmärchen*, publ. by Erna Pomeranzewa (Berlin 1964), 390–417; cf. Zand, *Shest vekov slavï*, 95; cf. also Potanin, G. N., *Vostochnïe motivï v srednevekovom yevropeyskom epose* (M. 1899), 286–347; cf. Miller, Vsevolod, *Ekskursï* v *oblast' russkogo narodnago eposa* (M. 1892), *passim.*
3. Cf. Hole, Christina, *English Folk Heroes*, 71–102.
4. Cf. Coyajee, Sir J. C., *Studies in Shah-nameh* (Bombay (*c.* 1960)); Zenker, R., 'Die Tristansage und das persische Epos von Wîs und Râmîn', *Romanische Forschungen*, 29 (1910), 321–99; Suhtscheck, Fr. von, 'Wolfram von Eschenbach's Reimbearbeitung des Pārsivalnāmä', *Klio*, 25 (1932), 50 *et seq.*; Suhtscheck, Fr. von, 'Die iranischen Quellen in Wolframs Parzival', *ZDMG*, 82 (N.F. 7) (1928), LXXXII–LXXXIV, etc.
5. Cf. Kahlo, *Die Wahrheit des Märchens*; of course in any research the comparative and typological interpretation of folk-tales should be much more intensive and systematical; cf. also *Anmerkungen zu den KHM der Brüder Grimm*, von J. Bolte und G. Polívka, Bd. IV; *Zur Geschichte d. Märchen* (Leipzig 1930).
6. Geissler, Friedmar, *Die Brautwerbung in der Weltliteratur* (Halle 1955).
7. Lambertz, Max, *Die Volksepik der Albaner* (Halle 1958).
8. Braginskiy, *Iz istorii*, and *Ocherki.*

9. Zhirmunskiy–Zarifov, *Uzbekskiy narodnïy geroicheskiy epos* (M. 1947).
10. Zhirmunskij–Zarifov, *op.cit*, 136–143; *Uzbekskiye nar. poemï* (Tashkent 1958), 345–503.
11. Zhirmunskiy–Zarifov, *op.cit.*, 146–150; *Uzb. nar. poemï*, 683–780.
12. Cf. *Alpamïsh, Trudï Tadzh. AN*, 107 (St. 1959); cf. also Zhirmunskiy, *Skazaniye ob Alpamïshe i bogatyrskaya skazka, passim.*
13. Cf. the special anthology *Pushkin i Gor'kiy o narodnom tvorchestve* (M. 1938), 27–98.
14. Cf. Romaskevich, *Persid. nar skazki*, 34.
15. Cf. Braginskiy, *Iz ist.*, 339–351; *Ocherki*, 312.
16. Cf. Braginskiy, *Iz ist.*, 358–363; *Ocherki*, 207–238.
17. Cf. *Antol. tadzh. poezii*, 1st ed., 9, 21.

JAN MAREK

PERSIAN LITERATURE IN INDIA

Up to the present histories of Iranian literature have not as a rule included a comprehensive study of Indo-Persian literature, although many of the works produced by Persian authors in India are of considerable artistic importance.

The Iranians did not think of Indo-Persian literature as part of their national literature, but felt it to be an alien element. This is because Indo-Persian literature, that was mainly influenced by native Indian culture, shows several specific characteristics as the result of prevalent conditions peculiar to India. In respect to its form Persian literature was enriched in India by the development of the so-called 'Indian poetical style' (*sabk-i hindī*), with its abundance of ornaments and elaborate phraseology (see above pp. 295–6). All in all it is fair to say that Indo-Persian literature is an original creation with an individuality of its own.

A. FIRST CONTACTS BETWEEN IRAN AND INDIA IN THE FIELD OF LITERATURE. THE AGE OF MAḤMŪD GHAZNAVĪ AND MUḤAMMAD GHŌRĪ[1]

Islam was first brought to India in the 8th century by the Arab conquerors, but did not become firmly established until later. The real founders of Moslem supremacy in India were the Turks. The great ruler from Ghazna, Maḥmūd, invaded India for the first time in 1001, and in the last year of his life (1026) he added the Punjab to his territory. About 150 years later northern India was attacked by the army of Muḥammad of Ghōr (571/1175), who made his slave Quṭbu'd-dīn Aybak ruler over the Indian territory. During the years between 588/1192 and 595/1198 Aybak expanded his domain by conquering Gujarat and the adjoining countries, and in 1206 he ascended

Notes on pp. 733–734

the throne of Delhi as sovereign ruler and as the founder of the sultanate of Delhi.

It is not easy to ascertain exactly how the Persian language came to India. In spite of its being the mother tongue of the occupying power that ruled over India for several centuries, it was so popular with the rulers of the Timurid dynasty that it was preferred to Turkish and was generally used at their courts. The regular invasions by Persian and Turkish troops in India and their daily contact with the Indians had the inevitable result that Indian administrative officials also had to learn this language, which was after all the language of the court. The historian Bayhaqī[2] tells us that the Indian officers and soldiers serving in the armies of Maḥmūd of Ghazna had their own interpreters. Thanks to their natural talents the Indians soon acquired a good feeling for the language they had adopted. Professor Bausani rightly points out[3] that the strongest factor in the unity and coherence of the Indian Moslems ever since the time of the first Islamic invasion, was the Persian tradition.

In the field of New Persian literature contact between Iran and India dated from the time of the invasions of Maḥmūd's armies in India. The Hindu nobility of the conquered Punjab was in high esteem at the court of Maḥmūd and his successors, and we learn from the historian Firishta[4] that Ghazna had the appearance of an Indian city on account of the many Indians who lived there. On the other hand the town of Lahore, the centre of the Ghaznavid power, was beginning to be known as 'little Ghazna'.[5]

After the rulers had moved from Ghazna to Lahore, they did their best to uphold the cultural traditions of the court of Maḥmūd and gave their full support to art and literature. The generosity of the court attracted poets from Khurasan, Transoxania and other districts, so that the city of Lahore boasted eminent scholars and artists from many parts of the Islamic world. It was here that the first Indo-Persian poetry, that was to play such an important part in the further development of cultural life on the Indian subcontinent, was written.[6]

The first Indian poet to be born in India and write in Persian was Abū-ʿAbdu'llāh Nuqāṭī from Lahore. Of his life during the reign of Sulṭān Masʿūd we know practically nothing and of his works only a few verses have survived in biographies here and there.

Another poet who was born in India was Masʿūd-i Saʿd-i Salmān Jurjānī (b. 438/1046–7 in Lahore, d. about 515/1121–2 in Ghazna)[7], who spent part of his life in India as governor of Jallandar. He soon became so famous that many scholars came to him in Lahore. One of the best known of these was Muḥammad Rashīd Shihābu'd-dīn, whose lyrics are reminiscent of Rūdakī and Saʿdī. At the time of Salmān's long imprisonment (see p. 196), Badā'ūnī[8] tells us that a poet of no small merit was the panegyrist of the Sulṭān Ibrāhīm ibn Masʿūd (1059–1099) and his son Masʿūd III (1099–1115), the jealous and vain *ustād*, Abu'l-Faraj Rūnī, although it is not certain whether he came from Rune near Nishapur or from Rune (Ruin) near Lahore. He died at the beginning of the 6th/12th century.[9] A *dīvān* of 2000 verses by him still exists, written in a fluent and uncluttered style and later imitated by Anvarī (see p. 198).

At the time when the literature of Persia was first brought to India, it was already strongly coloured by mysticism. It is true that Abu'l-Ḥasan 'Alī ibn 'Uthmān al-Jullābī al-Hujvīrī, the author of the earliest treatise on the life and doctrine of the Ṣūfis – *Kashfu'l-maḥjūb*, 'The Discovery of the Hidden' – was born in Ghazna, but he spent all his life in Lahore and also died there (465/1072–3).

After the rulers of Ghazna had lost their power, instead of Lahore the centres of literary activity became Multan, ruled over by Nāṣiru'd-dīn Qabācha from Sindh, and Delhi, where Quṭbu'd-dīn Aybak, one of the generals of Shihābu'd-dīn Ghōrī, had proclaimed himself sulṭān. These two rulers vied with each other as supporters of art and literature. Scholars and poets from Khurasan, Ghōr and Ghazna emigrated to India, scared away by the violent attacks of the Tatars. At the court in Uch we find prolific poets like Shamsu'd-dīn Muḥammad Balkhī, Faḍlī Multānī and Ḍiyā'u'd-dīn Sanjarī at work. The Grand Vizier of Sulṭān Qabācha, 'Aynu'l-mulk, was himself a talented poet and a great patron of the arts. It was under his guidance that Muḥammad 'Aufī (see p. 222) completed his biographies of the poets, *Lubābu'l-albāb*, 'The Quintessence of the Hearts', while at the request of Nāṣiru'd-dīn Qabācha he embarked upon the immense work entitled *Javāmi'u'l-ḥikāyāt va lavāmi'u'r-rivāyāt*, 'Necklaces of Anecdotes and Rays of Stories'. He did not complete this, however, until he had joined the court of Sulṭān Iltutmish (607/1210–633/1236) in Delhi, who had conquered Uch in the meantime. In Delhi the vizier Qivāmu'd-dīn Niẓāmu'l-mulk Muḥammad b. 'Alī Sa'd al-Junaydī was 'Aufī's protector. In return 'Aufī dedicated his entire work to him, and he brought together numerous odes to his patron and to Sulṭān Iltutmish in the book *Kitāb-i madā'iḥu's-sulṭān*, 'The Book of Odes to the Sultan'.[10]

About the middle of the 13th century the shaykh Fakhru'd-dīn 'Irāqī (d. 688/1289, see p. 254) also came to Multan to see the mystic Bahā'u'd-dīn Zakarīyā, whose daughter he married. He further visited Delhi and Sōmnāth, but his stay in India does not seem to have been one of the happiest periods of his life. In the poems from this time he expresses a deep longing for his native country.[11]

B. LITERARY RELATIONS BECOME CLOSER. THE SULTANATE OF DELHI

When after the death of Muḥammad Ghōrī the feudal nobility had elected the former governor of the Indian territories, Quṭbu'd-dīn Aybak, as the first sulṭān to the throne of Delhi, the confused political situation gradually began to sort itself out. The establishment of a firm central power in Delhi created favourable conditions for the development of culture and education. The court of the sulṭāns of Delhi became the principal centre for Persian literature. Ten rulers of the so-called Slave Dynasty reigned there in succession during the 13th century and almost all of them evinced great interest in Persian poetry. Sulṭān Ruknu'd-dīn, Ghiyāthu'd-dīn Balban and his son Muḥammad made a choice collection of poems from the most celebrated authors, containing 20,000 couplets, which were adjudged the most select specimens then extant.[12]

The court of the generous Sulṭān Quṭbu'd-dīn Aybak (602/1206–607/1210) boasted a true galaxy of talented poets and prolific scholars. The most eminent of the poets was Ūshī, who composed delicate *ghazals* and was an all-round scholar. Jamālu'd-dīn Muḥammad and Ḥamīdu'd-dīn competed with him for the first place. During the reign of Aybak's successor, Shamsu'd-dīn Iltutmish (607/1210–633/1236) there was a new influx in India of scholars and poets from Central Asia. They were escaping from the horrors perpetrated by the Mongol tribes who, commanded by Chinghiz Khān, invaded Iran during the third decade of the 13th century and left a trail of destruction and desolation behind them. At this time Nāṣirī of Khurasan, the author of many flowery odes to Sulṭān Iltutmish[13], came to the court of Delhi and also Amīr Rūḥānī Samarqandī, who fled from Bukhara to escape Chinghiz-Khān and had been attracted by rumours that poets were liberally supported at the court of Iltutmish. It is believed that the sulṭān rewarded him magnificently for his *qaṣīdas* celebrating the conquests of Bihār, Ratnambhor and Mandūr.[14]

Famous among the poets who wrote Persian and had been born in India was the panegyric poet Tāju'd-dīn Riḍā (d. some time after 664/1265–6), whose ancestors came from Khurasan. He lived at the court of Sulṭān Iltutmish and the latter's successors as a professional panegyric poet and wrote charming and melodious *qaṣīdas* and eloquent quatrains (e.g. in celebration of the conquest of Gwalior). Outstanding qualities of his poems are sincerity of thought and simplicity of style. He ended by falling into disgrace and the sulṭān had him trampled to death by an elephant.[15]

In the 13th century Persian panegyric poetry written in the 'Indian style' began to develop to a greater extent. The sulṭāns had the poets accompany them on their campaigns so that they could describe battles, praise the heroic deeds of the soldiers and draw up chronograms laying down the dates when the most important strongholds had been conquered. The themes of the *qaṣīdas* were almost exclusively secular. The first to introduce more spiritual subjects was the court poet of Ruknu'd-dīn Fērōzshāh, the successor to Iltutmish, a man called Shihābu'd-dīn Muḥmara Badā'ūnī, also known as Shihāb-i Muḥmara[16], who is regarded as the innovator of a new, more florid style of writing *qaṣīdas*. He added a touch of spirituality and mysticism, since apart from those of his patron, Fērōzshāh, he mainly sang the praises of Allah and the prophets. His panegyric poetry does not depart from the usual scheme of the Indian style and is rich in rhetorical adornment, but it is remarkable for its integrity of experience and delicacy of expression. His pupil Amīr Khusrau (see p. 257), who called him "the nightingale in the garden of knowledge", attempted to imitate some of his *qaṣīdas*.

Until the middle of the 13th century *qaṣīdas* were almost the only form of poem written at the Indian court, while very few poets felt inclined towards the more melodious *ghazals*. This habit was first broken by Fakhru'l-mulk 'Amīdu'd-dīn Lūmakī, also known as 'Amīd Daylamī, who was born in Sannām and became a favourite panegyric poet of Sulṭān Nāṣiru'd-dīn Maḥmūd (644/1246–664/1266) and of Ghiyāthu'd-dīn Balban (664/1266–686/1287). He also used *qaṣīdas* to sing the praises of his patrons, but for his own pleasure he preferred *ghazals* which, though they resemble *qaṣīdas* in form, generally say things in a simpler and more natural way and are more musical and melodious. He was the first Indian poet to write so-called *munāẓara*, 'fights', in *ghazal* form, e.g. the fight between night and day (*munāẓara-i shab u rūz*), the fight between the sword and the pen, between hemp and wine.[17]

The sulṭāns of the Khaljī dynasty from Delhi and the governors of the provinces usually continued the tradition of encouraging and supporting literature and art. The founder of the dynasty, Jalālu'd-dīn Fērōzshāh Khaljī (689/1290–694/1295) who was himself no mean poet, had surrounded himself with a retinue of poets, six of whom had real genius, apart from the historian Firishta. Their names are the only thing we know about them, however.

Not until the reign of 'Alā'u'd-dīn Muḥammad Khaljī (695/1295–715/1315) did Persian literature in India reach one of its most brilliant periods. During his rule Delhi boasted a group of eminent scholars never equalled at the court of the Great Moguls. Scientific work was carried on in history, medicine, astronomy and astrology. Not only the sciences flourished, but also Persian literature in many forms. It was in the first place the steady and strong central power that ensured the general peace and prosperity of the country and made the development of Persian literature at the time of 'Alā'u'd-dīn possible. This general prosperity led to the development of a class that could devote itself to science and literature. Another factor that contributed to its rise was the gradually increasing number of immigrants from Iran who found a second home in northern India under its well-established, peace-loving government. The flourishing of Persian literature in India was first and foremost due to its most important and versatile poet, Amīr Khusrau Dihlavī (b. 651/1253 in Patiala, d. 725/1325 in Delhi), who lived at the court of Delhi during the reigns of several sulṭāns. For further details about him see p. 257 above.

1. ḤASAN OF DELHI

His close friend and schoolfellow was Amīr Najmu'd-dīn Ḥasan Sijzī Dihlavī, known by the name of 'Alā-i Sanjarī[18] (b. 651/1253 in Delhi, d. 729/1328 in Daulatabad, whither he was forced to move, together with the entire population of Delhi, by order of Sulṭān Muḥammad Tughluq; he could not endure the harsh climate of the Deccan, however, and died shortly afterwards). He belonged to one of the prominent families of the Sayyids, but nevertheless worked in a bakery as a youth. It was there that Amīr

Khusrau met him by coincidence and took him to the holy Niẓāmu'd-dīn Auliyā, who belonged to the Chishtī order. Later Ḥasan served at the court of the sulṭāns of Delhi. Being thus a court poet he had to honour his patron with panegyric poems. Besides these he had a talent for writing biting, satirical verse for which Khāqānī was famous, but he was careful to avoid obscure ambiguities. From the other panegyric poets he distinguishes himself by his honesty; he never agreed to extort money and he did not turn to satire when the results of his panegyric efforts were disappointing. The *qaṣīda* form apparently did not appeal to him very much; although he was in court service during most of his life, he wrote very few poems of this kind compared to the number of those he produced in other styles. It is possible that he owed this dislike to his tutor Niẓāmu'd-dīn, who considered songs of praise and flattery an abuse of the poetic creative force. Like his friend Khusrau, Ḥasan above all excelled in the *ghazal*, and indeed is counted among the greatest masters of this form. Most of his *ghazals* – about 800 in all – were influenced by Sa'dī, in style as well as thought; the chronicler Baranī remarks that because of this similarity his contemporaries referred to him as "Sa'dī from Hindustan".[19] The characteristic point about the *ghazals* of Ḥasan is that the entire poem is held together by one single conception, whereas it was usual for each line of a *ghazal* to be dominated by a different idea. Ḥasan's style is marked by simplicity and naturalness of language, emphasised by melodious, well-balanced rhyme. As he used short metres and words belonging to the colloquial language, his poems enjoyed a high degree of popularity during his lifetime as well as after his death, even beyond the boundaries of his own country.

Among his romantic and didactic *mathnavīs*, the romantic *'Ishq-nāma* or *Ḥikāyat-i 'Āshiq-i Nāgōrī*, 'The Story of the Lover from Nagor'[20] stands out. This is a short love poem comprising 606 couplets, written after the pattern of the romance of *Laylī and Majnūn*. Ḥasan derived his subject from the Rajasthani folk-tale about two Hindu lovers.

Apart from these poems Ḥasan's lyrical *dīvān*[21], collected together when he was 60 years old and consisting of more than 10,000 couplets dating from 1284 until 1314, also includes fragments (*qiṭ'a*) on the beauty of nature and quatrains on love.

The most important prose work by Ḥasan is a short *marthiya*. Here he describes the death of Prince Muḥammad Qā'ān Malik, eldest son of Sulṭān Balban, in the battle against the Mongol invaders. In the collection of prose works *Favā'idu'l-fu'ād*, 'Things Profitable to the Heart', Ḥasan records conversations with his tutor Niẓāmu'd-dīn Auliyā. They deal with various questions concerning religion and mysticism and are interwoven with maxims (*malfūẓāt*).

Like Khusrau, Ḥasan also had his imitators in Persian literature. His *ghazals* served as examples to Kamāl Khujandī (p. 263 above), and to Ḍamīrī from Isfahan.

Ḥasan's fate as an emigrant from Delhi to Daulatabad was shared by the poet 'Iṣāmī (b. 711/1311), who wrote a chronicle in verse[22] entitled *Futūḥu's-salāṭīn*, 'The Victories of the Sulṭāns', at the request of Sulṭān 'Alā'u'd-dīn Bahmanī.

The short duration of the reigns of Mubārakshāh Khaljī (716/1316–720/1320) and of his successor Khusrau-khān with their continuous unrest and disorder, certainly did not mean a period of progress in the history of Indian literature, but the founder of the Tughluq dynasty, Sulṭān Ghiyāthu'd-dīn (720/1320–725/1325) was quick to restore order to his country. He and his son Muḥammad (725/1325–752/1351) were, despite their peculiar excesses of temper, the most enlightened rulers who ever reigned in Delhi. The most outstanding of Muḥammad's court poets was the panegyrist Badru'd-dīn Chāchī (d. 747/1346), known under the name Badr-i Chāch, 'Moon of Tashkent'.[23] The sulṭān gave him the very honourable title of *Fakhr-i zamān*, which means 'Pride of the Age'. He wrote in an uncommonly difficult style, as is often the case among poets of Turkish origin working under Turkish influence.[24] It is very hard to understand his poems as they are full of astronomic terminology, astrological allusions and highly complicated parallels. On the other hand there are descriptions of a fascinating richness and detail, with dazzling vocabulary and non-trivial poetical embellishments. His voluminous *Shāh-nāma*, 'The Book of the Kings' (20,000 verses), is at the same time a valuable historical source, containing as it does a great deal of information about the reign of Sulṭān Muḥammad Tughluq. (H. Elliot, in his *History of India*, even gleaned some of this evidence from Badr's *qaṣīdas*.[25]) His lyrical poetry is contained in a *dīvān* of 2000 verses.

In the 14th century, during the reign of Sulṭān Muḥammad Tughluq and his successors, numerous biographies and 'Lives of the Saints' were written in Persian prose in western India. Generally popular were also collections of letters (*maktūbāt*) by mystics such as Shaykh Sharafu'd-dīn Yaḥyā Manērī (b. 662/1263, d. 782/1380)[26], a learned Ṣūfī and a poet of great originality who also wrote mixed Hindi-Persian verses according to the fast-spreading fashion of his day.

Among the religious treatises on the various Ṣūfī doctrines which deserve attention, there is also the fresh and original collection of 52 cyclic stories on morality and noble-mindedness written in the year 730/1330 by Ḍiyā'u'd-dīn Nakhshabī Badā'ūnī (d. 751/1350).[27] They were arranged according to Ṣūfī principles on the basis of a Sanskrit collection and called the 'Book of Parrots', *Ṭūṭī-nāma*, after it. Apart from this Nakhshabī wrote another work entitled *Gulrēz*, 'Scattering Roses'.

At the court of Fērōzshāh Tughluq (752/1351–790/1388), an enlightened and highly educated ruler who tried with all his might to re-establish the fame of the throne of Delhi and recalled the poets and scholars from Daulatabad, there lived in addition to the son of Khusrau, Malik Aḥmad, a panegyric poet named Muṭahhar-i Karā Dihlavī (d. at the end of the 8th/14th century), who wrote a *dīvān* of 16,000 verses. With their simplicity, natural and spontaneous way of expression and flowing rhythms, his *qaṣīdas* in praise of Sulṭān Fērōz Tughluq and his nobles are a marked contrast to the florid style and offensive complacency of Badr-i Chāchī. His *ghazals*, composed in short metres, are often satirical.[28] Another poet famous at the court of Tughluq was the panegyrist Qāḍī Ẓāhir from Delhi.[29]

Notes on pp. 733–734

As early as the first half of the 14th century the kingdom of the Bahmanids had become independent in the Deccan. Its many rulers, as for instance Muḥammad Bahmanī (1378–1397), were highly cultivated patrons of scholars and artists. The poet laureate at the court of the Bahmanids was Shaykh Ādharī of Isfarain who, in addition to a number of *qaṣīdas*, wrote at the request of his patron a verse chronicle of the Bahmanids entitled *Bahman-nāma*. This work was later completed by Naẓīrī and other poets.[30]

The strong central power of the sultanate of Delhi was of short duration. Intrigues at the court resulted in the throne being seized by unlawful rulers striving against each other; everywhere Hindu feudal lords revolted against the Moslem supremacy and governors in the provinces took power into their own hands. Such was the state of decline when Tīmūr invaded India in 1398–99. Although his invasion did not last long, it was the cause of Delhi's ceasing to be the spiritual and cultural centre of northern India for a full century. Before Tīmūr's arrival many scholars and poets had fled from Delhi to the smaller towns in the neighbourhood, and even to places as far away as the Deccan and Gujarat. The sources mention no literary or artistic activities during the period of Tīmūr's invasion either in Delhi or in Badā'ūn, whither the last ruler of the Sayyid dynasty, 'Alā'u'd-dīn 'Ālam Shāh, removed his seat. Only in Jaunpur did learning and art flourish. Sulṭān Ibrāhīm Shāh Sharqī (1401–1440)[31] was a generous patron of scholars and artists and summoned them to his court from far and wide. Jaunpur, now the cultural centre, was referred to as the 'Shiraz of India'.

When, after a considerable time of turmoil, social order was once again established by the Lōdī dynasty's taking the power in hand, Delhi again became the centre of culture, and at the same time also Agra, whither scholars began to migrate after the fall of the Sharqī empire in Jaunpur.

2. THE COURT OF SIKANDAR LŌDI

The rule of Sikandar Lōdī (894/1488–923/1518) became a mile-stone in the development of Persian literature in India. It signified the beginning of a new period in literary activity which developed further under the Great Moguls and corresponded in time with the age of Jāmī in the history of Persian literature in Iran. Sulṭān Sikandar Lōdī and his nobles were patrons of the arts and sciences. Scholars from all over the world came to the court at Delhi and settled in India.

The Indians began to study Persian more seriously at the time of Sikandar and they soon reached a high degree of perfection in it. Sikandar Lōdī was himself a poet and wrote in the old traditional style under the pseudonym of Gulrukh. He was a facile writer and his achievement in poetry was no less than his valour in the battle-field. He wrote a lyrical *dīvān* consisting of 8000 verses.[32]

The most important of the poets he invited to his court was Maulānā Jalāl Khān

Jamālī (d. 942/1535 in Gujarat)[33], a man who had travelled throughout the entire Moslem east. He was a pupil of the poet Jāmī whom he had met in Herat. According to the chronicle of Badā'ūnī his *dīvān* comprised about 9000 predominantly mystical poems. During his lifetime his lyrics were very popular as they could easily be put to music. Critics preferred his *qaṣīdas* to his *ghazals* and *mathnavīs* (best known is the tenzon *Mihr u māh*, 'The Sun and the Moon'). As to prose, Jamālī brought together the biographies of the saints in a book which he called *Siyaru'l-'ārifīn*, 'The Lives of the Sages', starting with Mu'īnu'd-dīn Chishtī and ending with his own spiritual master Samā'u'd-dīn Kambūh.

During the rule of Sikandar Lōdī many Indians took to the study of Persian. The fact that the Persian language was used daily by them made it necessary to have dependable dictionaries. In the course of the 15th century many such were written. In 1419 Badru'd-dīn Muḥammad from Delhi[34] composed a dictionary in two parts, *Adātu'l-fuḍalā*, 'The Scholars' Usage', containing Persian words in alphabetical order and selected phrases from the works of earlier Persian authors. In the year 1448 Ibrāhīm Qivāmu'd-dīn Fārūqī compiled the Persian dictionary *Farhang-i Ibrāhīmī* under the patronage of the Bengal ruler Bārbak-Shāh. It was also known as *Sharaf-nāma*, in memory of the first mystic of Bihar, Sharafu'd-dīn Manērī.

The writing of dictionaries was continued during the reign of the Lōdīs. In 1510 Maḥmūd ibn Ḍiyā'u-d-dīn Muḥammad completed the dictionary *Farhang-i sikandarī*, that contained 22 chapters and was also known as *Futūḥu's-sa'ādat*, 'The Victory of Bliss'. In the time of Ibrāhīm Lōdī another dictionary, *Mu'ayyidu'l-fuḍalā*, 'The Scholars' Assistant', was written by Shaykh Muḥammad. This was in three parts, divided according to the words of Arabic, Persian and Turkish derivation.

The foundations of learning and culture laid by Sikandar Lōdī remained intact during the reign of his son and successor Ibrāhīm Lōdī. He, however, was forced to devote more time and attention to the keeping at bay of foreign intruders and the suppression of revolts. The efforts of the feudal nobility to break loose from the central power gradually gained force and intellectual life was transferred from Delhi and Agra, which were in a state of turmoil, to the courts of the aristocracy in the provinces.

C. THE GOLDEN AGE OF INDO-PERSIAN LITERATURE. THE AGE OF THE MOGULS

The period of the Great Moguls witnessed the culmination of the development of all forms of Persian literature in India. It is true that his native Chagatay was the language in which the founder of the Timurid dynasty, Ẓahīru'd-dīn Muḥammad Bābur (he reigned in India from 932/1525 until 937/1530), wrote his excellent memoirs, but he

Notes on pp. 733–734

was nevertheless also an accomplished poet in Persian. By far the largest part of his Persian poetry bears the mark of Ṣūfī mysticism, of which Bābur was an ardent practiser, especially under the influence of his father, a keen reader of Jalālu'd-dīn Rūmī's *mathnavī*. Bābur derived the majority of the ideas in his quatrains and *ghazals* from Ḥāfiẓ and his contemporary Jāmī.[35]

Bābur's son and successor, Humāyūn (937/1530–964/1556) was also a poet of merit, who moreover possessed a wide knowledge of astronomy. To his inborn talent he added a systematic study of the Persian classical writers. His lyrical *dīvān*[36], which was discovered in Patna in the year 1940, contained 211 verses. They are full of perspicacity and humour, piety and erudition, historical references to events and persons, so that they provide a perfect reflection of the emperor's life and passions. Following the example of his father, he was a patron of the arts and favoured the Persian language above the Turkish.

Poets and scholars from various parts of Persia and Central Asia began to congregate in India. The Safavids in Iran did not reward their court poets as generously as did the powerful Mogul emperors and other Moslem rulers in India. Other factors that played an important part in the emigration of Persian poets to India were the severe centralisation of the Persian government and the Shī'ite oppression.

The Persian poets were welcome guests at the courts of India, for the continuous rivalry that existed between the empire, which was being consolidated by the Moguls, and the minor sultanates of the Deccan made the various monarchs feel the need of having their praises sung and they were willing to pay their panegyrists lavishly.[37]

For the first time in history we can thus speak of a large-scale emigration of Persian writers to India, whereas the earlier contacts between Iran and India had been brought about by the Ghaznavid invasions via Afghanistan and Turkestan. Consequently Indo-Persian literature went through a process of refinement, and with the remarkable poets from Persia the literary standard advanced.

The influx of Persian culture became even more concentrated after Humāyūn arrived in India for the second time. At that time Bayrām-Khān (b. 1559) came to the court of Delhi. He was a loyal friend of Humāyūn's, tutor to Akbar and author of a very notable *dīvān*.[38] With him came also the court poet of the emperor Akbar, Fayḍī (b. 954/1547, d. 1004/1595–6), who was one of the greatest Persian poets in India (see p. 299 for further details about him). Fayḍī regarded himself still as an upholder of the more simple style of Ḥasan Dihlavī. The later Persian poets, who arrived in India at the time of Akbar, started to write in the 'Indian style' proper.

I. THE AGE OF AKBAR

In the field of Persian literature the court of the intelligent and enlightened emperor Akbar the Great (963/1556–1014/1605) was far superior to Persia at the time of the

Safavids. This was no doubt partly due to a decree issued by Akbar's minister Tōdar Māl, dating from 1582, which made Persian the governmental language for the entire empire. Hereby Persian came to predominate throughout the whole of the Moslem east, from southern Europe as far as Bengal.

The best-known exponents of the Indian style of poetry from the time of Akbar were Muḥammad ʿUrfī (b. 963/1555–6, d. 999/1590–1), (see p. 299), Naẓīrī and Ẓuhūrī.

As well as these prominent persons there also came many poets of less importance but of Ṣūfī persuasions to India, mainly from Persia, where they had been unable to put up with the conditions prevailing during the reigns of both Shāh Ṭahmāsp (1524–1576) and ʿAbbās the Great (1587–1628). Among these we find coming to the fore Ghazzālī Mashhadī (b. 936/1530–31, d. 980/1572–3), for a short time Akbar's poet laureate, and the follower of the 'divine faith' of Akbar, Qāsim Kāhī (see further on), the poet laureate of Sulṭān Ibrāhīm ʿĀdilshāh II in Bijapur and father-in-law of Ẓuhūrī, Malik Qummī; then Mushfiqī of Bukhara (b. 945/1538, d. 994/1586), Rāfiʿī of Khurasan (b. 942/1535–6, d. 1009/1600–1), Ḥusayn Ṣanāʿī (d. 996/1588), Shakībī of Isfahan, Ḥayātī of Gīlān and others.

Muḥammad Ḥusayn Naẓīrī of Nishapur (d. 1013/1604)[39] was attracted to India by the rumours of the generous favours bestowed on poets at the court of the Moguls. Akbar, however, paid no special attention to him, and so Naẓīrī contented himself with the court of the former's minister, ʿAbdu'r-Raḥīm Khān-Khānān in Agra. The emperor Jahāngīr was the first to recognise the true quality of his *qaṣīdas*, and he gave him a rich fief as reward. Towards the end of his life the poet moved to Ahmadabad in Gujarat and devoted himself to the study of the Ṣūfī religion. He may be counted among the best poets of Akbar's period. His main importance lies in his *ghazals*, in which he was a disciple of Ḥāfiẓ. His verse is melodious and has an element of dark pathos (in particular the elegy on the death of the youngest son of Akbar, Murād). In the *ghazals* he always pursues a single line of thought throughout the poem. His popularity was further increased by his easily intelligible philosophical essays.

One of the most zealous of those who professed and propagated the religion of Akbar, '*dīn-i ilāhī*', was Najmu'd-dīn Muḥammad Abu'l-Qāsim Kāhī (b. about 868/1463–4 in Mīyānkāl in the mountainous country between Samarkand and Bukhara, died 988/1580 at Agra at the age of 120[40]). He remained unmarried all his life. From Kabul, where he lived for almost half a century, he went to India for the sake of the mystic Hāshim Kirmānī. During the years between 940/1533–4 and 956/1549 he stayed at the courts of Bahādur and Maḥmūd Ghāzī, the Sulṭāns of Gujarat, but then returned to his native land. In Kabul he sang the praise of the emperor Humāyūn in a beautiful ode on the astrolabe. For this he was made one of the courtiers of prince Akbar with whom he returned to India in the year 961/1554. The rest of his life was spent at the courts in Agra, Delhi, Jaunpur and Vārānasī. He deserves attention on account of his having ignored the campaigns and political activities of his patrons and having only been interested in civil life. Of his works a total of 1728 verses have been preserved. In his *qaṣīdas* he praises the prophet Muḥammad, the caliphs and the emperor Akbar. Although he is not conspicuous for originality of thought, his aphorisms and chronograms brought him fame at the court of Akbar among the most prominent poets.

One of the noblest patrons of the arts and sciences at the time of the emperor Akbar was ʿAbdu'r-Raḥīm Khān-Khānān (b. 965/1557–8, d. 1036/1626–7), the commander-in-chief of Akbar's army against Sulṭān Muẓaffar of Gujarat and at the same time a highly cultured man. His fame reached the court of the Persian Shāh ʿAbbās the Great, as is stated by the poet Kautharī who, in the introduction to his epic poem *Farhād and Shīrīn* (1606), bitterly complains that the market for poetry in Iran has shrunk and that he would do better to send his poem to the Khān-Khānān in India.[41] ʿAbdu'r-Raḥīm wrote Persian poetry under the name of Raḥīm. For his king he translated the memoirs of Bābur from the original Chaghatay into Persian under the title *Vāqiʿāt-i Bāburī*.

Of particular importance for the peaceful co-existence of adherents of the two religious faiths were the translations of Sanskrit works into Persian. Akbar and his successors encouraged these eagerly, and it was during the reign of Akbar that the most important Sanskrit works were translated.[42] Of these the most outstanding is *Razm-nāma*, 'The Book of the Battles', a Persian translation of the *Mahābhārata* by a group of scholars at the court of Akbar; further may be mentioned *Rāmāyana*, 'The Life of Rāma', *Ta'rīkh-i Krishnajī*, 'The Story of Krishna' (after the *Bhāgavatapurāna*), and also *Yoga Vāsishtha*, 'The Book of the Yoga Texts of Vāsishtha', all of them translations in which several scholars collaborated. Fayḍī (cf. p. 465 above) translated the treatise on algebra and geometry, *Līlāvatī*, 'The Playing One', from Sanskrit and he re-wrote the story of King Nala and Princess Damayantī from the *Mahābhārata* in the form of a *mathnavī*, giving it the title *Nal Daman*. He was probably also the translator of *Kathāsaritsāgara*, 'The Ocean from the Rivers of Story-telling', by the poet Sōmadēva from Kashmir.[43] To his brother Abu'l-Faḍl we owe the Persian adaptation of the *Bhagavadgīta*, 'The Song of the Sublime', and of other works in Sanskrit. Especially popular were *Singhāsan battīsī*, 'Thirty-two Throne Stories'[44], which were translated into Persian by Chaturbhūj Kāyasth at the time of Akbar, by Bihārī Māl Kshatrīy at the time of Jahāngīr, by Harkaran Dās during the reign of Shāhjahān, and by Kishan Dās Basudēv at the time of Aurangzēb.

The Deccan courts of the ʿĀdilshāhs in Bijapur, of the Quṭubshāhs in Golkonda and of the Valājāhs in Madras were also active in the fields of art and science and vied with each other in promoting Persian literature. Ibrāhīm ʿĀdilshāh II (1580–1626) was himself an able poet and a great patron of letters and music. But his Persian verses, which he composed under the name of Ibrāhīm, have not been preserved.

At the time of Akbar there lived at the court at Bijapur Nūru'd-dīn Muḥammad Ṭāhir Ẓuhūrī (d. 1024/1615), who originally came from a small town named Khujand in the Turshiz district of Khurasan.[45] In his youth he had studied literature and as a poet he lived at the courts of the nobles in Yazd and Shiraz. He also spent a short time at the court of Shāh 'Abbās the Great, but because he failed to procure suitable recognition and support he emigrated to India in 988/1580, where he became court poet to Shāh Burhān Niẓām in Ahmadnagar. In 1004/1596 he moved to Bijapur in southern India. He is noted for the flowery affected prose in which he wrote *Se nathr*, 'Three Essays', at the instigation of Sulṭān Ibrāhīm 'Ādilshāh II. The most valuable of these are the first essay, *Nauras*, 'The New Fruit', and 'Nine Styles'[46] which abounds in similes and metaphors derived from the world of music, being really an introduction to a book of songs bearing the same title and composed by Sulṭān Ibrāhīm in the Deccan language. The second essay *Gulzār-i Ibrāhīmī*, 'The Rose Garden of Ibrāhīm', sings the praises of the sulṭān, and the third, *Khān-i Khalīl*, 'The Table of the Friend of God (= Ibrāhīm)' is of historical importance as it discusses the court artists and their merits. These essays are named after the anthologies that were drawn up by Ẓuhūrī and Malik Qummī.[47] His graceful, poetical descriptions earned Ẓuhūrī fame as a poet, but in his *qaṣīdas* he never achieved the mastery of 'Urfī. His *mathnavīs* certainly deserve mention, the most outstanding of these being *Sāqī-nāma*, 'The Book of the Cup-bearer', written in praise of the magnate of Ahmadnagar. On the whole Ẓuhūrī is not a man of great ideas, he merely embellishes traditional subjects to the highest degree of formal perfection.

2. THE AGE OF JAHĀNGĪR

During the reigns of Akbar and his successors no changes in cultural policy took place at the court of the Moguls, who endeavoured to bring about a harmony between the Hindus and the Moslems. We find Hinduistic subjects penetrating Persian poetry more and more. A proof of this is shown in the poet Nau'ī (d. 1019/1610[48]). He wrote the small but moving epic poem *Sūz u gudāz*, 'Burning and Consuming', about the tragic death of a Hindu lady who, according to the Hindu custom *satī*, let herself be burnt to death on the funeral pyre of her deceased husband.

In the course of the same period 'Abdu'sh-Shakūr Bazmī of Kanauj (b. 1001/1592–3, d. 1073/1662–3[49]) composed a *mathnavī*, *Rat Padam*, after a folk-saga about Princess Padumāvatī and King Ratnasēna based on a Hindi version by Malik Muḥammad Jāyasī.

The influx of artists from Iran to India also continued after Akbar's death at the courts of his successors in the 17th century. Among the most moderate exponents of the Indian style at the court of Jahāngīr (1605–1627) must be counted, in addition to Rūḥu'l-āmīn of Isfahan (d. 1047/1637[50]), in particular Ṭālib 'Āmulī (d. 1036/1626–7 in Ahmadabad in approximately his thirty-fifth year). He started by writing poems in praise of the governors of his native region Mazandaran and those of Kashan and

Merv, but as the success he achieved was but small he migrated to India. He tried to find employment in the service of various notabilities in Agra, Delhi, Lahore and Gujarat, but was unsuccessful. It was not until he met the minister I'timādu'd-daula that he was introduced to the emperor Jahāngīr, by whom he was appointed poet laureate in the year 1028/1618–19. Of Ṭālib's works 27,547 verses have been preserved in manuscript.[51] They consist of *qaṣīdas* and *tarkīb-bands* in praise of the Prophet or the dignitaries of the court, and are highly esteemed in India; further the epical chronicle *Jahāngīr-nāma* and lyrical *ghazals*. In these we can trace Ṭālib's real intentions. They abound in unusual parallels and delicate metaphors, although their style is natural and far removed from the highly-coloured artifices of later generations.

Another prolific poet, prose-writer and author of *tadhkira* who blossomed out at the court of Jahāngīr was Ṭaqī Auḥadī (b. 973/1565–6 in Isfahan, d. about 1040/1630–1[52]), a favourite of Shāh 'Abbās II. In the company of some friends he set out for India in the year 1015/1606, where he arrived at the court of the emperor, whom he accompanied from Lahore to Delhi, Ahmadabad, and Agra. He wrote more than 3000 verses that have been collected into eleven *dīvāns*. The best known of these are *Nuṣratu'l-'ārifīn*, 'Refuge of the Gnostics', containing *qaṣīdas* in praise of the Imāms and satires directed against his contemporaries; then *Tadhkiratu'l-āshiqīn* 'Lives of the Lovers'. He also composed seven *mathnavīs*, of which *Safīnatu's-sakīna*, 'Boat of Peace', and *Ka'batu'l-ḥaramayn*, 'Shrine of two Sanctuaries', are the longest, as well as the Persian dictionary *Surma-i sulaymānī*, 'Solomon's collyrium', and several works in prose. But he achieved most fame with the *tadhkira 'Arafātu'l-āshiqīn*, 'Arafāt (a hill near Mecca) of Lovers', in which he collected biographies of 3186 Persian poets and quoted samples of their work. He made a selection from his own *tadhkira* under the title *Ka'ba-i 'irfān*, 'Sanctuary of Knowledge', which became a great favourite on account of its small compass and a source of many later *tadhkiras*.

3. THE COURT OF SHĀHJAHĀN

During the reign of Shāhjahān (1627–1659) the master of the Indian style, Muḥammad 'Alī Ṣā'ib of Isfahan (b. 1010/1601–2, d. 1087/1676-7), gained great repute, despite his short stay of only six years in India. His teacher was Ruknā Masīḥ of Kashan (d. 1066/1655–6), author of approximately 100,000 verses. After having been insulted by 'Abbās I he went to India to seek his fortune as a physician. (For further particulars of both see above, pp. 301–2).

An outstanding poet at the court of Shāhjahān was Abū-Ṭālib Kalīm from Hamadan (d. 1061/1651–2). He had come to India to serve in the army of Jahāngīr and became 'the King of Shāhjahān's poets'. It was he who wrote the romantic official chronicle *Shāhjahān-nāma* which, in an uncomplicated style, sings the praises of the Mogul rulers in Persian (see p. 301 above).

A similar kind of *mathnavī* entitled *Pādishāh-nāma*, 'The Imperial Book', was composed by the court panegyrist Mīr Muḥammad Yaḥyā of Kashan (d. 1064 1653–4).[53]

Another poet at the court of Shāhjahān was Ḥājjī Muḥammad Jān Qudsī (b. circa 991/1583 at Mashhad, d. 1056/1646 in Kashmir).[54] He was keeper of the treasure in the mausoleum of the Imām Riḍā in Mashhad and traded in drugs. He was fond of a free life and was not prepared to flatter the kings and amīrs, but he never descended to satire. He seems to have suffered many an insult from those in power on account of his outspokenness, and for that reason set out for India. At the court of Shāhjahān, where he arrived in the year 1041/1632, he was granted the title of khān. Altogether 22,432 verses of his work have survived. The chronicle *Ẓafarnāma-i Shāhjahānī*, 'Book of the Victories of Shāhjahān', a *mathnavī* in praise of Kashmir, and his *ghazals* are of a conventional nature and are not distinguished by any great originality. The mastery of Qudsī is shown by the dissimilarity between his *qaṣīdas* and those of the other court poets, for he made an attempt to introduce new thoughts into the prevalent rigid system of themes. He scoffed at those who continually made use of the old well-known subjects and passed them off as their own. His *qaṣīdas* in praise of the Prophet and the Imāms give expression to a sincere religious faith and an ardent desire towards universal peace.

One author who formed an exception by not writing in the elaborate Indian style was the personal secretary of the unlucky prince Dārā Shikōh, Chandar Bhān Brahman from Lahore (b. 982/1574–5, d. 1073/1662–3 in Vārānasī)[55], the greatest Hindu writer in Indo-Persian literature. Although he came from a Brahman family and never renounced his faith, he devoted himself to the study of Ṣūfī doctrines under the guidance of 'Abdu'l-Ḥakīm of Siyālkōt and the Mullā Shāh of Badakhshan. He was so proficient in Arabic and Persian that, although a non-believer, he gave lessons in these languages to the Moslems. He was first in the service of various amīrs, then in 1066/1656 the emperor Shāhjahān appointed him First Secretary to the State Chancellery, bestowed on him the titles *Rāy* and *Khvāja* together with the post of Commander of a Thousand, and entrusted him with the conducting of the imperial daily reports and chronicles. Brahman also stayed on in the service of Aurangzēb, but towards the end of his life he settled in Vārānasī, where he devoted himself to the religious duties of a Brahman. Of his *dīvān* 1543 verses have been preserved; in a simple and flowing style these express the emotions of the poet, in contrast to products of later times. A deeper Ṣūfī influence is apparent in his *ghazals* and quatrains. The main significance of Brahman, however, is to be found not in his poetry but in his prose, the most important of the latter works being *Chahār Chaman*, 'Four Meadows'. This is divided into four parts, the first describing events during the reign of Shāhjahān and giving particulars about the campaigns and about several viziers of the Mogul emperors. The second part deals with contemporary India, the third presents anecdotes from the author's personal life, while the last elucidates various religious and moral principles. The book also includes a chapter on Persian stylistics and syntax.

Notes on pp. 733–734

A sequel to *Chahār Chaman* is to be found in the prose work *Guldasta*, 'The Bouquet', which gives us a lively picture of the splendour and magnificence of the court. The merit of Brahman lies in the fact that he did not write an official systematic history of the times. He knew the emperor intimately and was thus witness of many an interesting detail which historiographers as a rule omit from mentioning. His reports on the everyday life at the court therefore form a valuable contribution to cultural history, just as do his letters, *Munsha'āt-i Brahman*, 'Brahman's Letters', and several other shorter prose works.

In India Islam never fused with Hinduism despite the efforts of one philosopher after another. Of these Prince Dārā Shikōh (b. 1024/1615 in Ajmer, executed 1068/1658) deserves to be mentioned. He was the eldest son of Shāhjahān and Queen Mumtāz Maḥal, for whom the Tāj Maḥal was built as a sepulchral monument, and the brother of Aurangzēb. Like his ancestor Akbar had done before him, he attempted to unite Hinduism and Islam into some kind of abstract monotheistic doctrine.[56] Being his father's favourite he was not sent out to the provinces as a governor, but remained in the capital and was able to apply himself to the study of Ṣūfī teachings. Biographies of the saints and a number of questions concerning Ṣūfism form the subjects of some of his Persian writings, e.g. *Safīnatu'l-auliyā*, 'The Ship of the Saints', and *Sakīnatu'l-auliyā*, 'The Tranquillity of the Saints', *Risāla-i Ḥaqqnumā*, 'The Compass of Truth', which is a short treatise on the ways by which ultimate spiritual fulfilment may be achieved, and *Shaṭḥiyyāt* or *Ḥasanātu'l-ʿĀrifīn*, 'The Noble Words of the Gnostics', a collection of Ṣūfī aphorisms and ecstatic proverbs.

His most important book is *Majmaʿu'l-baḥrayn*, 'The Mingling of the Two Oceans', a comparative study of Hinduism and Islam that attempted to demonstrate their various points of contact. To this purpose Dārā also translated from Sanskrit fifty chapters of the *Upanishads* into simple and easy-flowing Persian, to which he gave the title *Sirr-i akbar*. 'The Greatest Mystery', or 'The Mystery of Akbar'. His Persian *dīvān*, known as *Iksīr-i aʿẓam*, 'The Strongest Elixir', is a typical sample of the Persian poetry being written in India in his time. In its present incomplete form it includes 133 *ghazals* and 28 quatrains.[57] The principal theme of all the poems is Ṣūfism, the worshipping of the saints of the Qādiriyya sect, to which his spiritual tutor Mullā Shāh belonged, the praise of Kashmir, the Panjab and Lahore, and not in the last place Dārā's passionate desire for the throne, the feeling that he was superior to his brothers, and wrath towards his enemies. Dārā's poems failed to become generally popular because during the reign of Aurangzēb, who had had Shikōh put to death as a heretic, they were not allowed to be circulated.

Among the free-thinkers who gathered round Dārā Shikōh there was also a Jew named Saʿīd Sarmad from Kashan (put to death in Agra 1071/1661–2).[58] His parents, Armenian Jews, carried on a flourishing business and gave their gifted son a good education. Sarmad first became a rabbi, but later on continued his studies, particularly natural science and Christian as well as Islamic theology, under the guidance of

Ṣadru'd-dīn Shīrāzī and Abu'l-Qāsim Findariskī (see above, p. 297). Under the influence of his teachers he became a convert to Islam. After completing his studies he went into business and travelled by sea to India. During the reign of Emperor Shāhjahān he settled in Thatta, an important centre of trade in Sindh. He soon became wealthy, but, as the result of some mysterious happening (maybe a love intrigue)[59], from a well-to-do merchant he became a poor fakir who took his poverty literally and went about naked. He moved to Hyderabad where he got into touch with Mīrzā Fānī who has preserved a few of Sarmad's quatrains for us in the book *Dabistān-i Madhāhib*, 'School of Knowledge'. Sarmad again changed his place of abode, going this time to Delhi, but his friendship with Prince Dārā Shikōh, whose succession to the throne he had prophesied, made him a political suspect. After Emperor Aurangzēb had had the prince put to death, Sarmad was called before the council of the 'Ulamā as a heretic. He was accused of only having become converted to the negative part of the Islamic faith (*lā-ilāha*, 'there is no God') and of having gone about naked, and he was condemned to death. Several hundred mystical quatrains of Sarmad's have come down to us. With their pantheistic tendencies these verses resemble those of Abū-Sa'īd ibn Abī'l-Khayr (see above, pp. 233–4) and show an endeavour to bring about a rapprochement between Islam and Hinduism.

4. THE AGE OF AURANGZĒB. THE DECLINE OF THE MOGUL EMPIRE

During the reign of the Emperor Aurangzēb 'Ālamgīr (1659–1707) the reactionary theologians again acquired the upper hand and the orthodox puritan movement, which his three predecessors had tried to suppress, flourished. In matters of religion Aurangzēb knew no mercy. He made no exception for dignitaries of the realm nor for members of his own family. A proof of this is his daughter, the princess Zēbu'n-nisā (b. 1048/1638–9, d. 1114/1702–3)[60], known under the pseudonym Makhfī, 'The Hidden One', whom he tortured to death.

In her youth she had studied Arabic, mathematics and astronomy. She started writing poems in Arabic but later on changed over to Persian. She hated the cold orthodoxy of her father, but was greatly devoted to her teacher and uncle Dārā Shikōh, from whom she inherited her Ṣūfī ideas. Like her ancestor the emperor Akbar, she tried to weld together the two religions. Thirty-five years after her death her *dīvān* was compiled from sporadic notes. Even today it is much read. It shows some traces of Ṣūfī poetry, e.g. God in the shape of a handsome lover, but it also possesses a special Indian note in that it combines the ideas of Hinduism, Islam and the doctrines of Zoroaster.

At the time of Shāhjahān and Aurangzēb the florid Indian style reached a peak of formal refinement in the *ghazals* of Ghanī of Kashmir (d. 1661) and Nāṣir 'Alī Sirhindī

Notes on pp. 733–734

(d. 1697[61]). Their stylistic mastery was surpassed only by Mīrzā Bēdil (b. 1054/1644 in Patna, d. 1133/1720 in Delhi; cf. pp. 302 and 519 above).

In the 18th century a general decline of the Mogul empire began to manifest itself. The Marathas agitated against the weak central power, and incessant quarrels and intrigues among the feudal nobility hastened its fall. The badly organised army was unable to resist the invasions from Persia and Afghanistan. Nādirshāh's invasion of India in 1739 and the terrible massacre in Delhi were described in the memoirs of the last of the Persian poets of Iranian origin who went to the Indian court, Shaykh Muḥammad ʿAlī Ḥazīn (b. 1103/1692 in Isfahan, d. 1108/1766–7 in Vārānasī; cf. p. 308 above).

During this period Persian literature flourished most in the various provinces of the vast empire. Many Persian poets whose names, it is true, are no longer remembered today, came together at the courts of the minor feudal rulers. We shall mention only the most important exponents of Persian literature in the respective provinces. At the court of Quṭubshāh in Golkonda lived a learned Kshatrīy named Lakshmīnārāyan Shafīq from Aurangabad (b. 1158/1745[62]). His grandfather Bhavānīdās had accompanied the army of Aurangzēb to the Deccan and settled in Aurangabad. Shafīq was a poet of considerable talent, but he became more famous through his prose. He wrote in the first place the *tadhkira Gul-i raʿnā*, 'The Charming Rose', which deals with the lives of the Indian poets writing in Persian, and another with the title *Shamʿ-i gharībān*, 'The Candle of the Strangers', about poets of Persian origin who had settled in India.

Literature showed a steady decline. There were no new ideas – a masterly development of form, in which all the traditional subjects were repeated, became of prime importance. Poets lost themselves in 'poetising', which became an aim in itself. This made all kinds of text-books on poetry and dictionaries necessary. Niẓāmu'd-dīn Khān Fā'iq (d. 1165/1751[63]), for instance, wrote the *mathnavī Mir'ātu'l-ḥusn*, 'The Mirror of Beauty', which includes a detailed description of the Beloved from head to foot, exactly according to the literary fashion in India.

The literary taste of this period also made it necessary to have dictionaries of uncommon and seldom used words. And indeed the largest dictionary of the Persian, Arabic and Turkish languages was produced at this time in southern India, the author being Munshī Muḥammad Bādshāh.[64] He gave it the title *Farhang-i Ānandrāj*, 'The Dictionary of Ānandrāj', in honour of his patron, the Mahārāja Ānandrāj from Vijayanagar. At the provincial court of Jahāndār Shāh, Tēk Chand Bahār, whose proper name was Lāla Udai Bhān (d. 1189/1775), wrote the Persian dictionaries and manuals of idioms called *Bahār-i ʿajamī*, 'The Persian Spring', *Javāhiru'l-ḥurūf*, 'Gems of the Words' and *Navādiru'l-maṣādir*, 'Rarities of Infinitives'.[65]

At the court of the Valājāhs in Madras, the Rāja Makkhan Lāl Khirad (b. 1177/1763–4 in Venkatagiri) distinguished himself in another field – he was thoroughly versed in the Persian language, in astronomy and mathematics, and wrote excellent chronograms.

In Bengal[66] Persian literature flourished at the courts of the Moslem governors in Nadia and Bardvān. Murshid Qulī Khān (1707–1727) removed his government to Murshidabad, which became an important centre for Moslem culture and Persian literary activity. Many a Persian poet came here from Iran and Iraq. The most important among them were Aqdas, Makhmūr, and Barq, 'the parrot of Bengal'. After the battle of Palāsī (Plassey) in 1757, when the English East-Indian Company gained power over Bengal, the cultural centre was removed from Murshidabad to Calcutta. Here the Hindu reformer Rām Mōhan Rāy composed some of his important writings in Persian.

Among the Persian-writing poets in Bengal of the 19th century the following deserve mention: Nassākh from Calcutta, whose *dīvān* is of a high quality, further the Maulānā 'Ubaydu'llāh Suhravardī from Dacca, and Āzād who came from the same town.

D. THE RETROGRESSION OF PERSIAN AS THE LITERARY LANGUAGE OF INDIA. THE POETS AS BILINGUISTS

As a result of the constant advance of England's colonial power and at the same time the development of the native states, Persian literature in India gradually lost ground. Persian suffered a severe set-back when in 1260/1844 Urdu was proclaimed the official language. Many Indian poets, it is true, continued to write in both languages for a while, but it was inevitable that Persian should finally have to cede to Urdu.

One of the most important bilingual poets of the 19th century was Mīrzā Asadu'llāh Khān Ghālib (1796–1869)[67], who put only that section of his poetry into Persian that he himself considered to be most mature. He started as a follower of Mīrzā Bēdil and he never lost his preference for the involved style of this poet. So far as the content is concerned Ghālib's work is one uninterrupted elegy on the end of the Mogul power in India, and in all his poetry grief is the prevailing emotion. Ghālib's chief merit consists in his having introduced several realistic images into the world of Persian metaphors and allegories.

In the revolutionary periods of the first half of the present century the renaissance movement in Islamic ideology brought forth the last great poet in the history of Persian literature in India. This was Sir Muḥammad Iqbāl from Lahore (b. 1294/1877 in Siyalkot, d. 1357/1938)[68] who, like Ghālib, wrote in Urdu but used Persian for the most important works, to which he wished to give greater publicity. He came from a Moslem family of merchants[69], but his grandparents still belonged to the Kashmir Brahmans and were orthodox Hindus. He was sent by his father to study at the university of Lahore and later to the European universities of Cambridge, Heidelberg and Munich. Here Iqbāl became acquainted with English neo-Hegelism and with

Notes on pp. 733–734

German philosophy and literature. He reached the conclusion that the vitality of Islam was being undermined by the influence of Greek philosophy. The teachings of Plato in particular were changing Islam from a practical philosophy of life into one of passive meditation and submission to the will of fate. The present social situation, however, required that the Moslems should engage in active struggle. Thus Iqbāl felt it his duty to reject the influence of Greek philosophy and to revert to the original doctrine of the Koran, as the latter answered well to the requirements of the social class to which he himself belonged. This he did in the Persian philosophic *mathnavī*, *Asrār-i Khudī*, 'The Secrets of the Self'[70], in which he expounded his theory on individual personality and the stages of its spiritual development. At the same time he here repudiated the Ṣūfī doctrine and especially the concepts of Ḥāfiẓ. Some two years later he completed his philosophy in another *mathnavī*, *Rumūz-i bēkhudī*, 'The Mysteries of Selflessness', which investigates the relationship between the individual and the aims of the community. Goethe's *West-östlicher Diwan* inspired Iqbāl to a further Persian collection of quatrains and *ghazals, Payām-i mashriq*, 'The Message from the East', which reveals his return to Ṣūfī mysticism. For the message from the east is nothing more nor less than a conviction that the love of God is the only way to a complete revelation of truth. Iqbāl expanded this subject in the lyrical *ghazals* contained in the collection *Zabūr-i'ajam*, 'The Persian Psalms', which he wrote in 1927. His crowning work, however, is *Jāvēd-nāma*, 'The Book of Eternity', also known as 'The Book of Jāvēd' (Iqbāl's son), a *mathnavī* with inserted *ghazals*. Its theme is analogous to that of Dante's *Divina Commedia*. Instead of Beatrice, however, Jalālu'd-dīn Rūmī accompanies the author through the celestial spheres and discusses various mystical and philosophical questions with him. After an intermediary period during which he wrote in Urdu, Iqbāl returned to Persian towards the end of his life, notably in part of the collection *Armaghān-i Ḥijāz*, 'A Gift from Ḥijāz', which is philosophical as regards subject matter.

In all his works Iqbāl employed classical prosody and elaborated his verses with allusions to Islamic and world history, philosophy, religion etc., so that they demand a very high level of education on the part of the reader. Iqbāl's poetry reflects the philosophical insecurity and waverings of the Moslem middle classes, which had lost their bearings in the political developments between the two World Wars. They may be seen as part of the wave of romantic revolutionalism that had laid hold of Indian literature at the time.

All in all one may say that Persian literature has taken root in Indian soil; it would be hard to find any branch of science or art, any form of Persian poetry, didactic, lyrical, romantic, mystical or otherwise, or any Persian metre which has not in the course of history been adopted by the Indians, Moslems as well as Hindus. It might indeed be difficult to point out a comparable example in the history of world literature of a language being adopted, and to find another country having mastered a foreign language to such a degree as was the case with Persian in India. The Indians have contributed very really to the rise of Persian literature, and to them we owe many of its most brilliant pages.

Summer 1967

NOTES

1. The names and titles in this chapter are transliterated according to Indian pronunciation.
2. Cf. Abdulvahab Bukhari, *Persian in India*, 30.
3. Alessandro Bausani, *Storia delle letterature del Pakistan*, 65.
4. A. Bukhari, *op. cit.*, 30.
5. A. Bukhari, *op. cit.*, 65.
6. Cf. M. Z. Huda, *History of Persian Literature*, 87–93.
7. His destiny is described in *Majm'a'l-fuṣaḥā*, I, 514.
8. Badā'ūnī, *Muntakhabu't-tavārīkh*, I, 37; Engl. transl. by G.S.A. Ranking, I, 54.
9. His life and work are analysed in detail by Iqbāl Ḥusayn, *The Early Persian Poets of India*, 11–66.
10. Cf. Muḥammad Niẓāmu'd-dīn, Introduction to *Javāmi'u'l-ḥikāyāt* of 'Aufī, p. 14; quoted in M. Z. Huda, *History of Persian Literature*, 93.
11. Ahuja, *Iraqi in India*, 57 *et seq.*
12. N. S. Gorekar, *Persian Poets of India*, 69.
13. Huda, *op. cit.*, 170–71.
14. Badā'ūnī, *op. cit.*, 65; Ranking, 93.
15. Abdus Sattar Khan, *Tāj Rēzah*, 359. Cf. Badā'ūnī, 67; Ranking, 95.
16. Badā'ūnī, 71–83; Ranking, 99–119. Cf. *Majma'u'l-fuṣaḥā*, I, 304.
17. Huda, *op. cit.*, 174–5. Cf. Badā'ūnī, 96; Ranking, 138.
18. Cf. M. I. Borah, *The Life and Works of Amīr Hasan Dihlavī*, 1. Borah's assertion that the name Sanjari is very likely a misreading for Sijzī, i.e. inhabitant of Sīstān or Sijistān, seems to be justified.
19. Cf. Borah, *op.cit.*, 41.
20. Nāgōr is the name of an old town in the east of Rājasthān, the present part of Jodhpur. Cf. Borah, *op. cit.*, 54.
21. So far twenty-three of his manuscripts are known; none of his work was ever printed, however, apart from poor Indian lithographs.
22. Husain, *The Firdausi of India*, 23 *et seq.*
23. Cf. Huda, *op. cit.*, 275–6; *Majma'u'l-fuṣaḥā*, I, 169; Ranking, I, 296, note 6.
24. Cf. Browne, *A Literary History of Persia*, III, 110.
25. H. Elliot, *History of India as told by its own Historians*, III, 567–573.
26. A. Halim, *Growth of Urdu Language and Literature during the Sayyid-Lodi Period*, 54. Cf. also M. A. Ghani, *History of Persian Language and Literature at the Mughal Court*, I, 65–66.
27. *Ṭūṭīnāme*, translated into English by M. Gerrans (London 1792).
28. M. W. Mirzā, 'Muṭahhar-i Karā', *Oriental College Magazine*, 5 (1935). Shervānī, 'Qaṣā'id-i Muṭahhar-i Karā', *Ma'ārif*, 8 (1935).
29. A. Halim, *History of Persian Literature during the Sayyid-Lodi Period*, 14.
30. Huda, *op.cit.*, 284–5.
31. Stanley Lane-Poole, *Medieval India under Mohammedan Rule*, 169–171.
32. Gorekar, *Persian Poets of India*, 72.

33. A. Halim, *op. cit.*, 23.
34. *Ibid.*, 29 *et seq.*
35. M. A. Ghani, *History of Persian Literature*, I, 50 *et seq.*
36. Hadi Hasan, *The Unique Diwan of Humayun Badshah*, 212 *et seq.*
37. M. A. Ghani, *op. cit.*, I, 149 *et seq.*
38. A. Bausani, *Storia delle letterature del Pakistan*, 71.
39. M. A. Ghani, *op. cit.*, III, 67–103.
40. Hadi Hasan, *Qasim-i Kahi, His Life, Time and Works*, 103 *et seq.*
41. Krïmskiy, *Istoriya Persii*, III, 158. Cf. also Ghani, *op. cit.*, III, 224.
42. M. A. Ghani, *op., cit.*, III, 33–34.
43. Desai, *The Story of Nala-Damayantī as told by Faizī*, 84.
44. Roy Choudhury, *The Hindu Contribution to Persian Literature*, 125.
45. Ghani, *op. cit.*, III, 181. As his place of birth we also find mention of Turbat (Amīn Aḥmad Rāḍī in *Haft iqlīm*, 'The Seven Spheres') or Tehran (Bakhtāvar Khān in *Mir'ātu'l-'ālam*, 'The Mirror of the World').
46. *Ras*, in the Sanskrit language 'Sauce', signifies in Indian poetry and music a mood or a feeling that predominates in a work of art or a part thereof. There are nine basic moods. The song-book of Sulṭān Ibrāhīm contains songs in all of the nine moods.
47. Nazir Ahmad, *Kitab-i Nauras*, 338.
48. Ethé, *Die höfische und romantische Poesie der Perser*, 45. Cf. also Krïmskiy, *op.cit.*, III, 226.
49. Gai, *Development and Character of Persian Language and Literature,* 233.
50. Krïmskiy, *op. cit.*, III, 226.
51. S. A. H. Abidi, 'Talib-i Amuli, his Life and Poetry' (manuscript).
52. Nazir Ahmad, *Taqi Awhadi*, 276.
53. Hidayat Hosain, *Contemporary Historians during the Reign of the Emperor Shāh Jahān*, 64 *et seq.*
54. S. A. H. Abidi, 'Qudsi Mashhadi, his Life and Poetry' (manuscript).
55. S. A. H. Abidi, 'Chandra Bhan Brahman' (manuscript).
56. Cf. *Majma'u'l-baḥrayn*, ed. by Maḥfūẓu'l-ḥaqq, 1–30.
57. Zafar Hasan, *Manuscript Copy of the Dīvān of Dārā Shikūh*, 155 *et seq.*
58. Abdul Wali, *Sarmad, his Life and Execution*, 119 *et seq.*
59. Asīrī, *Sarmad-i shahīd*, 53 *et seq.*
60. Ishaque, *Four Eminent Poetesses of Iran*, 93. According to the *dīvān of Zēbu'n-nisā*, 7 *et seq.*, she died in 1689.
61. Bausani, *Storia...*, 73.
62. Bukhari, *Persian in India*, 35.
63. Gai, *Development and Character of Persian*, 234.
64. Bukhari, *Persian in India*, 38.
65. Choudhury, *The Hindu Contribution to Persian Literature*, 124.
66. Cf. Ikram, *Persian Literature in Bengal*, 30–31.
67. Cf. Pūlodova, *Shoiri mashhuri Gholib*, 131 *et seq.*; also Gilani, *Ghalib, his Life and Persian Poetry*' and Lakhanpal, *Ghalib, the Man and his Verse.*
68. Marek, *The Date of Muḥammad Iqbāl's Birth*, 620.
69. A good introduction to the life and work of Iqbāl is Iqbāl Singh's *The Ardent Pilgrim* (Bombay 1957).
70. In 1920 R. A. Nicholson translated it into English under the title of *The Secrets of the Self*, thus introducing Iqbāl into Europe.

JAN RYPKA

AN OUTLINE OF JUDEO-PERSIAN LITERATURE

Judeo-Persian literature is the product of a centuries-old co-existence between Jewish colonies and the Persian population. In the course of time these Jewish colonies adapted themselves to the language of their new environment, and it can also be said that up to a certain point there was a cultural rapprochement. The present summary deals only with the Islamic period, when the fact that intellectual association existed between the two groups is borne out by literary records. The language of this literature is Persian – most of it showing certain antiquated features – with a slight admixture of Hebrew words. It is written entirely in Hebrew script, this applying even to transliterations of texts taken from Persian classical literature. In the Orient, as is known, script was associated with religious sentiment, a fact that is also proved by the analogy of the Spanish Sefardim and the Turkish-speaking Armenians and Greeks, all of them living in Turkey. It is a curious coincidence that the earliest records in the Persian language are at the same time the earliest records of Judeo-Persian literature (cf. above, pp. 148 *et seq.*).

It can be shown that there were contacts between the Moslem world of learning and Jewish-Persian scholars as early as the 9th and 10th centuries A.D., for it was from the latter that Hamza Iṣfahānī and Bīrūnī obtained their knowledge of Jewish history, even though they wrote in Arabic. An even larger contribution was made by Ismāʿīlism whose followers showed a lively interest in Jewish affairs: Nāṣir-i Khusrau (see p. 187) wrote the first description of Palestine in the Persian language and al-Kirmānī (d. 1013) is only one of many who quoted and even transliterated passages from the Bible.

The first actual manifestations in Judeo-Persian literature date from the second half of the 13th century, when the financier Saʿdu'd-daula, together with the minister and famous historian Rashīdu'd-dīn Faḍlu'llāh – the former a Jew, the latter of Jewish extraction – held the reins of the Īlkhān empire in their hands. The earliest important work of this kind is a Judeo-Persian translation of the Pentateuch dating from the year 1319; this, however, may be only a copy of a still earlier translation by

Yōsēf b. Mōshē. There are also other manusripts, whose contents probably date back to the 13th century. A Jewish polyglot Bible printed in Istanbul in 1546 likewise contains a Judeo-Persian version of the Pentateuch, translated by Ya'qōv b. Yōsēf Tavas. This gave rise to a translation of the whole Bible as well as to commentaries and lexicographical works. Both historically and philologically these are valuable monuments, remarkable also because they bear marks of the influence of western rabbinical exegesis.

The blossoming of Persian literature could not fail to have its effect on the ghetto. Thus there appear transliterations in Hebrew script of works of the most important Persian poets (with the exception of 'Omar Khayyām), with a marked preference for those with Ṣūfī convictions. Persian Jews have already composed poems after these models, but their works are so constricted within the formal Judeo-Persian field of vision that they are practically beyond Moslem comprehension and even at this stage cannot be ranked among the treasures of Persian literature proper. A striking figure in the realms of original Judeo-Persian poetry is Maulānā Shāhīn of Shiraz[1], who lived during the first half of the 14th century. In the manner of Firdausī and Niẓāmī he composed poems in praise of Moses. He found a follower in 'Imrānī, who likewise came from Shiraz and whose *Fatḥ-nāma*, 'Book of Victories', goes back as far as Solomon; in this work the author reveals himself as a blind imitator of Shāhīn.

With the introduction of Shī'ism as the state religion of Safavid Persia, a policy of gross intolerance was adopted from which the Jews too had to suffer. Some relief was afforded by the government of 'Abbās I, but the oppression under 'Abbās II struck them all the more heavily, so that the Jews became obliged to resort to conversion, though in most cases only feigned. This servitude has been described in the poem *Kitāb-i Anūsī*, which gives a profound and poetically perfect insight into the life of Persian Jewry in the years 1617–1656. It was composed by Bābā'ī i. Luṭf of Kashan. His work was continued by his grandson Bābā'ī i. Farhād, who went through the terrors of the Afghan invasion (up to 1725). Other poets of the same type who lived during this period are Mashīakh b. Rāfāēl and Mullā Khizqīyāhū of Isfahan.

When the idea of a unification of the monotheistic religions was envisaged by the liberal Sunnite Nādir-Shāh (1736–1747), one of the things he arranged for was to have a translation of the Old Testament made into Persian. But apparently at that time no more than the Pentateuch and the Psalms were completed (Bābā b. Nūrīēl of Isfahan). Nādir-Shāh even ventured to remove the Jews from Qazvīn to the hitherto inviolable Mashhad, the most sacred place of the Shī'ites in Persia. Sīmān Tov Melamed became the representative of the new cultural centre of the Persian Jews, especially on account of his famous philosophico-religious book *Sēfer Ḥayāt ar-rūḥ*, a kind of commentary on the doctrine of Maymonides and influenced by Ṣūfī conceptions. When in 1839 the Jews in Mashhad were forced to become converted to Islam, they in fact only made a pretence of doing so; for out of the ranks of these 'Marraners' there emerged Mordekhay b. Rāfāēl Aklār ('Mullā Murād'), who later settled in Jerusalem and was the translator of numerous works from the Hebrew into the Judeo-Persian language.

The Qajar period meant a time of decline for the culture of Persian Jewry; propaganda on the part of Christian missionaries and of the Bahā'ī movement were to a large extent instrumental in bringing this about. As a reaction to this and at the same time as a method of defence there appeared in the year 1844 a translation of the *Tōledōt Yēshū'*, a political treatise aimed at Christianity. The attack launched by Christian elements became more serious when it received energetic support from an organisation as powerful as is the British and Foreign Bible Society. In the 19th century we witness very little creative activity among the Jews, but it began to revive at the beginning of the present century after the Constitution had taken form. The fertile climate thus created was taken advantage of by the Jews in Persia, for it was at this time that they set up schools and founded newspapers – in fact they had their own press, and this soon acquired such dimensions that Tehran became the centre of Jewish journalism and indeed of Judeo-Persian literature. But voices were also raised in favour of the Hebrew language. Head of the new movement is the blind but extremely energetic Rabbi Mullā Elīyāhū Khayyīm Mōrē, the author of several Persian-Jewish works on Jewish tradition, history and philosophy.

Judeo-Persian literature was not confined to Persia.The most important place where it was cultivated outside Persia proper was Bukhara, though with certain dialectical peculiarities. Though we possess some records of the Jews living there as early as the 12th century, they only come into the picture from the point of view of literature at the end of the 17th century. Eminent among them is the poet Maulānā Yūsuf Yahūdī (1688–1755), whose poems *Mukhammas*, written in glorification of Moses, and *Haft birādarān*, dealing with the martyrdom of the 'Seven Brothers' and their mother, are modelled on works by Shāhīn and 'Imrānī. Like his other poems these have remained the cultural property of the Persian Jews from Bukhara up to the present day. Other important names that may be mentioned are, for instance, the poet and translator Benyāmīn b. Mishal ('Amīna'), Elīsha' b. Shemūēl ('Mullā Rāghib'), and above all Ibn Abu'l-Khayr, who presents a vivid picture of the religious and political situation of the Jews in Bukhara during the second half of the 18th century in the tragical episode described in *Khudāydād*. It is not known how this movement subsequently developed; we only know that towards the end of the 19th century the Jews of Bukhara were actively engaged in the cultivation of Judeo-Persian literature, but by then as emigrants in Palestine. It is worth noting that from Bukhara Judeo-Persian literature spread to Afghanistan.

This literature blossomed as never before towards the end of the 19th century in Jerusalem, which at that time was the focal point of all its fields, both sacred and profane. Works belonging to the latter category are translations of the *Thousand and One Nights* and Shakespeare's *Comedy of Errors*. The upward surge in quality and quantity is the result of cooperation between the Judeo-Persian-speaking Jews from Persia, Transoxania and Afghanistan. Prominent place must be given to Shelōmō

Notes on p. 740

Bābājon b. Pinkhasov of Samarkand and Shim'ōn Khākhām (b. 1843 in Bukhara), both of whom became well known as editors of ancient documents and as writers and publishers. Khākhām's monumental translation of the Bible into Bukharan Persian earns for its author a place as one of the most eminent figures in the history of Judeo-Persian literature.

It is interesting to remark that Judeo-Persian influence has penetrated even into the liturgy of the Jewish colony in China.

Judeo-Persian literature may be regarded as lying near the periphery yet within the circumference of Persian literature. Nevertheless it is of extreme importance in its national and religious aspects for the Jewish colonies in the regions concerned, and linguistically for Iranian studies as a whole. The larger the collections of Judeo-Persian manuscripts become, and the more minutely they are subjected to expert investigation, the greater will be their value for Iranistic scholars. A great deal has already been achieved in both these aspects, but it is still far too little. It is quite possible that the ancient Judeo-Persian tranliterations will prove valuable in the preparation of critical editions of many a Persian text.[2]

NOTES

1. Cf. under 'G' *s.v.* 'Shohin'. – Asmussen, Jes P., 'Judaeo-Persica, I: Shāhīn-i Shīrāzī's *Ardashīr-nāma*', *Acta Orient.*, 28/3–4 (1965), 245–261; II: 'The Jewish-Persian Law Report from Ahvāz, A.D. 1020', *Ibid.*, 29/1–2 (1965), 49–60. – Shohin, Qissayi, 'Yusuf u Zulaykha', *ShS*, 1964,2, 101–13.

2. In the preparation of this extremely cursory survey I have made grateful use of the essay by Prof. Dr. Walter J. Fischel (University of California, Berkeley) entitled 'Israel in Iran. A Survey of Judeo-Persian Literature', reprinted from *The Jews. Their History, Culture and Religion*, ed. by J. Louis Finkelstein (New York 1949), 817–858, in which further details and an excellent bibliography are to be found. – Cf. further W. J. Fischel, 'The Beginnings...' (B VIa).

SURVEY OF DYNASTIES

ACHAEMENIDS (Hakhāmanishiyā)

ca. 700 B.C.	Achaemenes (Hakhāmanish)
559–529	Cyrus (Kūrush)
529–522	Cambyses (Kambūzhiya)
522–486	Darius I (Dārayavahush)
486–465	Xerxes (Khshayārshā)
465–424	Artaxerxes I (Artakhshathrā)
423–404	Darius II
404–359	Artaxerxes II Mnemon
359–338	Artaxerxes III Ochos
338–336	Arses (Arshā)
336–331	Darius III Codomannus

(Based on: Brandenstein-Mayrhofer, *Handbuch des Altpersischen*, p. 5.)

MACEDONIANS

331–323	Alexander the Great (Iskandar)

SELEUCIDS

311 – 2nd cent. B.C.

PARTHIANS-ARSACIDS

247 B.C. – ca. 225 A.D.

SASANIANS (Sāsānīyān)

ca. 225–240	Artakhshēr I (Ardashīr)
240–272	Shāhpuhr I (Shāpūr)
272–273	Ōhrmazd I (Hurmuzd, Hurmuz)
273–276	Varhrān I (Vahrām, Bahrām)
276–293	Varhrān II
293	Varhrān III
293–302	Narsē
302–309	Ōhrmazd II
309–379	Shāhpuhr II
379–383	Artakhshēr II
383–388	Shāhpuhr III
388–399	Varhrān IV
399–421	Yazdkart I (Yazdagird)
421–439	Varhrān V (Bahrām Gūr)
439–457	Yazdkart II
457–459	Ōhrmazd III
459–484	Pērōz (Fīrūz)
484–488	Valakhsh (Balāsh)
488–531	Kavāt I (Qubād)
531–579	Khusrō I Anōsharvān (Khusrau Anūshīrvān, Chosroes)
579–590	Ōhrmazd IV
590–591	Varhrān Chōbīn (usurper)
591–628	Khusrō II Aparvēz (Khusrau Parvīz)
628	Kavāt II Shērōē
628–629	Artakhshēr III

629–632	several kings
632–651	Yazdkart III

(Chronology according to R. N. Frye, *The Heritage of Persia*, p. 295.)

THE FOUR ORTHODOX CALIPHS (ar-Rāshidūn)

11/632–13/634	Abū-Bakr
13/634–23/644	ʿUmar I
23/644–35/656	ʿUthmān
35/656–41/661	ʿAlī

UMAYYAD CALIPHATE (Banū-Umayya)

41/661– 60/680	Muʿāviya I
60/680– 64/683	Yazīd I
64/683	Muʿāviya II
64/683– 65/685	Marvān I
65/685– 86/705	ʿAbduʾl-Malik
86/705– 96/715	al-Valīd I
96/715– 99/717	Sulaymān
99/717–101/720	ʿUmar II
101/720–105/724	Yazīd II
105/724–125/743	Hishām
125/743–126/744	al-Valīd II
126/744	Yazīd III
126/744	Ibrāhīm
126/744–132/749	Marvān II

ABBASID CALIPHATE (Banū-ʿAbbās)

132/ 749–136/ 754	Abuʾl-ʿAbbās aṣ-Ṣaffāḥ
136/ 754–158/ 775	al-Manṣūr
158/ 775–169/ 785	al-Mahdī
169/ 785–170/ 786	Mūsā al-Hādī
170/ 786–193/ 809	Hārūn ar-Rashīd
193/ 809–198/ 813	al-Amīn
198/ 813–218/ 833	al-Maʾmūn
218/ 833–227/ 842	al-Muʿtaṣim
227/ 842–232/ 847	al-Vāthiq
232/ 847–247/ 861	al-Mutavvakil
247/ 861–248/ 862	al-Muntaṣir
248/ 862–252/ 866	al-Mustaʿīn
252/ 866–255/ 869	al-Muʿtazz
255/ 869–256/ 870	al-Muhtadī
256/ 870–279/ 892	al-Muʿtamid
279/ 892–289/ 902	al-Muʿtaḍid
289/ 902–295/ 908	al-Muktafī
295/ 908–320/ 932	al-Muqtadir
320/ 932–322/ 934	al-Qāhir
322/ 934–329/ 940	ar-Rāḍī
329/ 940–333/ 944	al-Muttaqī
333/ 944–334/ 946	al-Mustakfī
334/ 946–363/ 974	al-Muṭīʿ
363/ 974–381/ 991	aṭ-Ṭāʾiʿ
381/ 991–422/1031	al-Qādir
422/1031–467/1075	al-Qāʾim
467/1075–487/1094	al-Muqtadī
487/1094–512/1118	al-Mustaẓhir
512/1118–529/1135	al-Mustarshid
529/1135–530/1136	ar-Rāshid
530/1136–555/1160	al-Muqtafī
555/1160–566/1170	al-Mustanjid
566/1170–575/1180	al-Mustaḍīʾ
575/1180–622/1225	an-Nāṣir
622/1225–623/1226	aẓ-Ẓāhir
623/1226–640/1242	al-Mustanṣir
640/1242–656/1258	al-Mustaʿṣim

TAHIRIDS (Ṭāhirīyān)

205/821–207/822	Abū-Ayyūb Ṭāhir I
207/822–213/828	Ṭalḥa
213/828–230/844	Abuʾl-ʿAbbās ʿAbduʾllāh
230/844–248/862	Ṭāhir II
248/862–259/873	Muḥammad
259/873–261/875	Ṭāhir III

SAFFARIDS (Ṣaffārīyān)

247/861–265/879	Abū-Yūsuf Yaʿqūb ibn Layth aṣ-Ṣaffār
265/879–287/900	ʿAmr b. Layth (executed 289/902)

SAMANIDS (Sāmānīyān)

250/ 864–279/ 892	Naṣr I
279/ 892–295/ 907	Abū-Ibrāhīm Ismāʿīl
295/ 907–301/ 914	Abū-Naṣr Aḥmad
301/ 914–331/ 942	Abuʾl-Ḥasan Naṣr II

331/ 942–343/ 954	Nūḥ I
343/ 954–350/ 961	ʻAbdu'l-Malik I
350/ 961–366/ 976	al-Manṣūr I
366/ 976–387/ 997	Nūḥ II
387/ 997–389/ 999	al-Manṣūr II
389/ 999–390/1000	ʻAbdu'l-Malik II
390/1000–395/1005	Ismāʻīl al-Muntaṣir

BUYIDS/BUVAYHIDS (Āl-i Būya)

d. 338/949	ʻAlī b. Būya, ʻImādu'd-daula
d. 366/976	al-Ḥasan b. Būya, Ruknu'd-daula

as *amīru'l-umarā'* in Baghdad:

334/ 945–356/ 967	Aḥmad b. Būya, Muʻizz-u'd-daula (from 324/936 in Kirmān)
356/ 967–367/ 978	ʻIzzu'd-daula Bakhtiyār
367/ 978–372/ 983	ʻAḍudu'd-daula (from 338/949 in Fars, Khuzistān, ʻUmān, and Kirmān)
372/ 983–376/ 987	Ṣamṣāmu'd-daula (in Fars and Kirmān till 388/998)
376/ 987–379/ 989	Sharafu'd-daula (from 372/983 in Fars and Khuzistān)
379/ 989–403/1012	Bahā'u'd-daula (from 388/998 also in Fars and Kirmān)
403/1012–412/1021	Sulṭānu'd-daula (also in Fars)
412/1021–416/1025	Musharrifu'd-daula (also in Fars)
416/1025–435/1044	Jalālu'd-daula
435/1044–440/1048	Abū-Kālījār ʻImādu'd-daula (from 415/1024 in Fars, from 419/1028 in Kirmān)
440/1048–447/1055	al-Malik ar-Raḥīm (also in Fars)

ZIYARIDS (Ziyārīyān)

316/ 928–323/ 935	Mardāvīj b. Ziyār
323/ 935–356/ 967	Vushmgīr b. Ziyār
356/ 967–366/ 976	Bīsutūn b. Vushmgīr
366/ 976–403/1012	Qābūs I b. Vushmgīr
403/1012–420/1029	Manūchihr b. Qābūs
420/1029–441/1049	Anūshīrvān b. Manūchihr
441/1049–462/1069	Qābūs II b. Dārā

GHAZNAVIDS (Ghaznavīyān)

367/ 977-8–387/ 997	Sabuktigīn
387/ 997 –389/ 999	Ismāʻīl
389/ 999 –421/1030	Maḥmūd Yamīnu'd-daula
421/1030 –433/1041	Masʻūd I
433/1041 –440/1048	Maudūd
440/1048 –440/1049	Masʻūd II
440/1049 –441/1049	ʻAlī b. Masʻūd I
441/1049 –443/1052	ʻAbdu'r-Rashīd b. Maḥmūd
443/1052	Ṭughril (usurper)
443/1052 –451/1059	Farrukhzād b. Masʻūd I
451/1059 –492/1099	Ibrāhīm b. Masʻūd I
492/1099 –508/1115	Masʻūd III
508/1115 –509/1116	Shīrzād
509/1116 –512/1118	Malik Arslān b. Masʻūd III
512/1118 –552/1157	Bahrāmshāh b. Masʻūd III
552/1157 –555/1160	Khusrau-Shāh
555/1160 –585/1190	Khusrau-Malik (only in Punjāb)

SELJUQS (Saljūqīyān)

A. The Great Seljuqs:

429/1038–455/1063	Ṭughril-Beg
455/1063–465/1073	Alp Arslān
465/1073–485/1092	Malikshāh I
485/1092–487/1094	Maḥmūd
487/1094–498/1105	Barkiyārūq
498/1105	Malikshāh II
498/1105–511/1118	Muḥammad
511/1118–552/1157	Sanjar (from 490/1096 ruler of Khurasan)

B. The Seljuqs of Kirman:

433/1042–466/1074	Qara Arslān
466/1074–467/1074	Kirmānshāh

467/1074–477/1085	Sulṭānshāh
477/1085–490/1097	Tūrānshāh I
490/1097–495/1101	Īrānshāh
495/1101–537/1142	Arslānshāh I
537/1142–551/1156	Muḥammad I
551/1156–565/1169	Ṭughrilshāh
565/1169–570/1174	Bahrāmshāh
570/1174–572/1176-7	Arslānshāh II
572/1176–579/1183	Tūrānshāh II
579/1183–582/1186	Muḥammad II

KHVĀRAZM-SHĀHS

470/1077-8–490/1098	Anūshtakīn
490/1098 –521/1127	Quṭbu'd-dīn Muḥammad
521/1127 –551/1156	Atsïz
551/1156 –568/1172	Īl-Arslān
568/1172 –589/1193	Sulṭānshāh
589/1193 –596/1200	Takash
596/1200 –617/1220	'Alā'u'd-dīn Muḥammad
617/1220 –628/1231	Jalālu'd-dīn Mankubartī (Mankubirnī)

MONGOLS

A. The Great Khans:

603/1206–624/1227	Chingiz-Khān
627/1229–639/1241	Ūgadāy (Ögedey)
639/1241–644/1246	Tūrākīnā (Töregene, widow of Ögedey)
644/1246–646/1248	Gūyūk (Göyük)
646/1248–649/1251	Oghul Qaymish (widow of Göyük)
649/1251–657/1259	Māngū (Möngke)
657/1259–693/1294	Qūbilāy

B. The Īl-Khāns:

654/1256–663/1265	Hūlāgū (Hülägü)
663/1265–680/1282	Abāqā
680/1282–683/1284	Aḥmad Takūdar
683/1284–690/1291	Arghūn
690/1291–694/1295	Gaykhātū
694/1295	Baydū
694/1295–703/1304	Ghāzān Maḥmūd
703/1304–716/1316	Uljāytū
716/1316–736/1336	Abū-Sa'īd

MUZAFFARIDS (Muẓaffarīyān)

713/1314–759/1358	Mubārizu'd-din Muḥammad b. al-Muẓaffar
759/1358–786/1384	Shāh Shujā'
759/1358–776/1375	Shāh Maḥmūd (in Iṣfahān)
786/1384–789/1387	Zaynu'l-'Ābidīn 'Alī

SARBADĀRS

737 /1337 –738 /1337-8	'Abdu'r-Razzāq b. Faḍli'llāh
738 /1337-8–745 /1344	Wajīhu'd-dīn Mas'ūd
745 /1344 –747-8/1346-8	Ay-Tīmūr Muḥammad
747-8/1346-8–748-9/1347-9	Kalwā (or Kulū) Isfandyār
749 /1348-9	Faḍlu'llāh
749 /1348-9–753-4/1352-3	Shamsu'd-dīn 'Alī
753-4/1352-3–759 /1358	Yaḥyā Karrābī
759 /1358 –760 /1359	Ẓahīru'd-dīn
760 /1359 –761 /1360	Ḥaydar al-Qaṣṣāb
761 /1360 –762 /1361	Luṭfu'llāh b. Mas'ūd
762 /1361 –766 /1364-5	Ḥasan Dāmghānī
766 /1364-5–781 /1379 or 783/1381	'Alī al-Mu'ayyad (died 788/1386-7)
778 /1376-7–780 /1378-9	Darwīsh Ruknu'd-dīn (usurper)

TIMURIDS (Tīmūrīyān)

771/1370–807/1405	Tīmūr
807/1405–850/1446	Shāhrukh
850/1446–853/1449	Ulūgh-Beg
853/1449–854/1450	'Abdu'l-Laṭīf
854/1450–855/1452	'Abdu'lāh
855/1452–872/1469	Abū-Sa'īd
872/1469–899/1494	Aḥmad
872/1468–911/1506	Ḥusayn b. Manṣūr b. Bāyqarā (Sulṭān of Herat)

QARA QOYUNLU

780/1378–790/1388	Qara Muḥammad Turmush

790/1388–822/1419	Qara Yūsuf
822/1419–841/1438	Iskandar
841/1438–872/1467	Jahānshāh
872/1467–873/1468	Ḥasan ʿAlī

AQ QOYUNLU

d. 839/1435	Qara Yoluq ʿUthmān
839/1435-6–842/1438	ʿAlī b. ʿUthmān
839/1435-6–848/1444	Ḥamza b. ʿUthmān
848/1444 –874/1469	Jihāngīr
857/1453 –882/1478	Uzun Ḥasan
883/1478 –884/1479	Khalīl
884/1479 –896/1491	Yaʿqūb
896/1491 –897/1492	Bāysunqur
897/1492 –902/1496-7	Rustam
902/1496-7–903/1497-8	Aḥmad Gevde
903/1497-8–908/1502	Murād

SAFAVIDS (Ṣafavīyān)

907/1501– 930/1524	Ismāʿīl I
930/1524– 984/1576	Ṭahmāsp I
984/1576– 985/1578	Ismāʿīl II
985/1578– 989/1581	Muḥammad Khudābanda
989/1581–1038/1629	ʿAbbās I the Great
1038/1629–1052/1642	Ṣafī I
1052/1642–1077/1666	ʿAbbās II
1077/1666–1105/1694	Sulaymān I (Ṣafī II)
1105/1694–1135/1722	Ḥusayn I
1135/1722–1144/1731	Ṭahmāsp II
1144/1731–1148/1736	ʿAbbās III

AFSHARS (Afshārīyān)

1148/1736–1160/1747	Nādir (Ṭahmāsp-Qulī-Khān)
1160/1747–1161/1748	ʿĀdil (ʿAlī-Qulī-Khān)
1161/1748–1210/1795	Shāhrukh

ZANDS (Zandīyān)

1163/1750–1193/1779	Muḥammad Karīm-Khān Zand
1193/1779–1195/1781	Ṣādiq
1195/1781–1199/1785	ʿAlī-Murād
1199/1785–1203/1788	Jaʿfar
1203/1788–1211/1796	Luṭf-ʿAlī

QAJARS (Qājārīyān)

1193/1779–1211/1797	Āqā Muḥammad
1211/1797–1250/1834	Fatḥ-ʿAlī
1250/1834–1264/1848	Muḥammad
1264/1848–1313/1896	Nāṣiru'd-dīn
1313/1896–1324/1907	Muẓaffaru'd-dīn
1324/1907–1327/1909	Muḥammad ʿAlī
1327/1909–1342/1924	Aḥmad

PAHLAVIS (Silsila-i Pahlavī)

1344/1925–1360/1941	Riḍā Shāh Pahlavī
1360/1941	Muḥammad Riḍā

DYNASTIES IN CENTRAL ASIA

SHAYBANIDS (Shaybānīyān)

905/1499– 916/1510	Muḥammad Shaybānī
916/1510– 937/1531	Köchkunju
937/1531– 940/1533	Abū-Saʿīd
940/1533– 946/1539	Abu'l-Ghāzī ʿUbaydu'llāh
946/1539– 947/1540	ʿAbdu'llāh I
947/1540– 959/1552	ʿAbdu'l-Laṭīf
959/1552– 963/1556	Naurūz Aḥmad
963/1556– 968/1561	Pīr Muḥammad I
968/1561– 991/1583	Iskandar
991/1583–1006/1598	ʿAbdu'llāh II
1006/1598–1007/1599	ʿAbdu'l-Mu'min
1007/1599–1008/1599	Pīr Muḥammad II

JĀNIDS/ASHTARKHĀNIDS (in Bukhara)

1006/1598–1014/1605	Bāqī Muḥammad

1014/1605–1017/1608	Valī Muḥammad
1017/1608–1052/1642	Imām-Qulī
1052/1642–1055/1645	Nādir Muḥammad
1055/1645–1091/1680	ʿAbdu'l-ʿAzīz
1091/1680–1114/1702	Subḥān-Qulī
1114/1702–1123/1711	ʿUbaydu'llāh
1123/1711–1160/1747	Abu'l-Fayḍ
1160/1747–1164/1751	ʿAbdu'l-Mu'min
1164/1751–1167/1754	ʿUbaydu'llāh
1167/1754–1171/1758	Muḥammad Raḥīm (of the Mangīt Dynasty)
1171/1758–1200/1786	Abu'l-Ghāzī

MANGĪTS (in Bukhara)

1199/1785–1215/1800	Mīr Maʿṣūm Shāh Murād
1215/1800–1242/1826	Ḥaydar Tora
1242/1826	Ḥusayn
1242/1826	ʿUmar
1242/1825–1277/1860	Naṣru'llāh
1277/1860–1303/1885	Muẓaffaru'd-dīn
1303/1885–1329/1910	ʿAbdu'l-Aḥad
1329/1910–1339/1920	ʿĀlim

DYNASTIES IN INDIA

GHŪRIDS

493/1100–540/1146	ʿIzzu'd-dīn Ḥusayn
540/1146–544/1149	Sayfu'd-dīn Sūrī
544/1149	Bahā'u'd-dīn
544/1149–556/1161	ʿAlā'u'd-dīn Ḥusayn Jihān-sūz
556/1161–558/1163	Sayfu'd-dīn Muḥammad
558/1163–599/1203	Shamsu'd-dīn (Ghiyāthu'd-dīn) Muḥammad
569/1173–602/1206	Shihābu'd-dīn (Muʿizzu'd-dīn) Muḥammad (in Ghazna)

SULṬĀNS OF DELHI

A. Turkish Slave Dynasty (Mamlūks):

602/1206–607/1210	Quṭbu'd-dīn Aybak
607/1210–633/1236	Shamsu'd-dīn Iltutmish (Iletmish)
633/1236–634/1236	Ruknu'd-dīn Fīrūz I
634/1236–637/1240	Raḍiyya-Begum
637/1240–639/1242	Muʿizzu'd-dīn Bahrām
639/1242–644/1246	ʿAlā'u'd-dīn Masʿūd
644/1246–664/1266	Nāṣiru'd-dīn Maḥmūd I
664/1266–686/1287	Ghiyāthu'd-dīn Balban
686/1287–689/1290	Muʿizzu'd-dīn Kay-Qubād
689/1290	Kayūmarth

B. Khaljī Dynasty:

689/1290–694/1295	Jalālu'd-dīn Fīrūz II
694/1295–695/1296	Ibrāhīm I
695/1296–715/1315	ʿAlā'u'd-dīn Muḥammad I
715/1315–716/1316	Shihābu'd-dīn ʿUmar
716/1316–720/1320	Quṭbu'd-dīn Mubārak-Shāh I
720/1320	Nāṣiru'd-dīn Khusrau (Barvārī)

C. Tughluq Dynasty:

720/1320–725/1325	Ghiyāthu'd-dīn Tughluq I
725/1325–752/1351	Muḥammad b. Tughluq
752/1351–790/1388	Fīrūz III
790/1388–791/1388	Tughluq II
791/1388–792/1389	Abū-Bakr
792/1389–795/1393	Muḥammad III
795/1393	Sikandar I
795/1393–797/1395	Maḥmūd II (first reign)
797/1395–801/1398	Nuṣrat-Khān
801/1398–815/1413	Maḥmūd II (second reign)

D. Sayyid Dynasty:

817/1414–824/1421	Khiḍr-Khān
824/1421–837/1434	Mubārak-Shāh II
837/1434–849/1445	Muḥammad IV
849/1445–883/1478	ʿĀlam-Shāh (from 855/1451 only in Badā'ūn)

E. Lōdī Dynasty:

855/1451–894/1489	Bahlūl Lōdī
894/1489–923/1517	Sikandar II Lōdī
923/1517–932/1526	Ibrāhīm II Lōdī

THE GREAT MOGULS

932/1526– 937/1530	Bābur
937/1531– 947/1540	Humāyūn (first reign)
947/1540– 962/1555	the Afghan Sūrī Dynasty
962/1555– 963/1556	Humāyūn (second reign)
963/1556–1014/1605	Akbar
1014/1605–1037/1627	Jahāngīr
1037/1627–1067/1657	Shāh-Jahān
1067/1657–1118/1707	Aurangzēb ʿĀlamgīr
1118/1707–1124/1712	Shāh-ʿĀlam I Bahādur-Shāh I
1124/1712–1125/1713	Jahāndār-Shāh
1125/1713–1131/1719	Farrukh-Siyar
1131/1719–1161/1748	Muḥammad Nāṣiru'd-dīn
1161/1748–1167/1754	Aḥmad Bahādur
1167/1754–1173/1759	ʿĀlamgīr
1173/1759–1221/1806	Shāh-ʿĀlam II
1221/1806–1253/1837	Muḥammad Akbar II
1253/1837–1274/1857	Bahādur-Shāh II

THE IMĀMS OF THE SHĪʿA

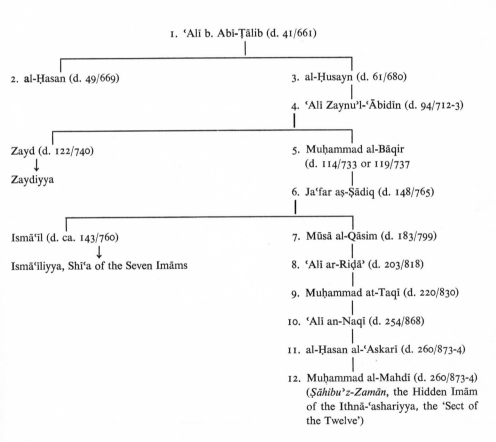

1. ʿAlī b. Abī-Ṭālib (d. 41/661)
   - 2. al-Ḥasan (d. 49/669)
   - 3. al-Ḥusayn (d. 61/680)
     - 4. ʿAlī Zaynu'l-ʿĀbidīn (d. 94/712-3)
       - Zayd (d. 122/740) → Zaydiyya
       - 5. Muḥammad al-Bāqir (d. 114/733 or 119/737
         - 6. Jaʿfar aṣ-Ṣādiq (d. 148/765)
           - Ismāʿīl (d. ca. 143/760) → Ismāʿīliyya, Shīʿa of the Seven Imāms
           - 7. Mūsā al-Qāsim (d. 183/799)
             - 8. ʿAlī ar-Riḍā' (d. 203/818)
             - 9. Muḥammad at-Taqī (d. 220/830)
             - 10. ʿAlī an-Naqī (d. 254/868)
             - 11. al-Ḥasan al-ʿAskarī (d. 260/873-4)
             - 12. Muḥammad al-Mahdī (d. 260/873-4) (*Ṣāḥibu'z-Zamān*, the Hidden Imām of the Ithnā-ʿashariyya, the 'Sect of the Twelve')

SELECTED BIBLIOGRAPHY

(For the abbreviations used here, see pp. XXI–XXIII)

A

OTAKAR KLÍMA: AVESTA. ANCIENT PERSIAN INSCRIPTIONS. MIDDLE PERSIAN LITERATURE

I

Spiegel, F., *Erânische Altertumskunde* (Leipzig 1871–8).
Geldner, K. F., *Avesta, die heiligen Bücher der Parsen* (Stuttgart 1886–95).
——, 'Avestaliteratur', in *GIPh*, II/2, 1–53.
Bartholomae, Ch., *Altiranisches Wörterbuch* (Strassburg 1904).
——, *Die Gathas des Avesta* (Strassburg 1905).
——, *Zum altiranischen Wörterbuch* (Strassburg 1906).
Reichelt, H., *Awestisches Elementarbuch* (Heidelberg 1909).
Nyberg, H. S., *Die Religionen des alten Iran* (Leipzig 1938).
Herzfeld, E., *Zoroaster and his World*, 2 vols. (Princeton 1947).
Duchesne-Guillemin, J., *Zoroastre. Étude critique avec une traduction commentée des Gathas* (Paris 1948).
——, *The Hymns of Zarathustra* (London 1952).
——, *La religion de l'Iran ancien* (Paris 1962).
Henning, W. B., *Zoroaster, Politician or Witch-Doctor?* (Oxford 1951).
Gershevitch, I., *The Avestan Hymn to Mithra* (Cambridge 1959).
Humbach, H., *Die Gathas des Zarathustra*, 2 vols. (Heidelberg 1959).
Struve, V. V., 'Rodina zoroastrizma', *SV*, 5 (1948), 5 *et seq.*
Klíma, O., 'Zarathuštra', *NO*, 13 (1958), 66 *et seq.*
——, 'The Date of Zoroaster', *ArOr.*, 27 (1959), 556–64.
——, *Zarathuštra* (Prague 1964).
Abayev, V. I., 'Skifskiy bït i reforma Zoroastra', *ArOr.*, 24 (1956), 23–56.
Molé, M., 'Rituel et eschatologie dans le mazdéisme', *Numen*, 7 (1960), 148 *et seq.*
——, *Culte, mythe et cosmologie dans l'Iran ancien* (Paris 1963).

II

Weissbach, F. H., 'Die altpersischen Inschriften', in *GIPh*, II/2, 54–74.
——, *Die Keilinschriften der Achämeniden* (Leipzig 1911).
Herzfeld, E., *Altpersische Inschriften* (Berlin 1938).

Meillet, A. and E. Benveniste, *Grammaire du vieux perse*, 2nd ed. (Paris 1931).
Kent, R. G., *Old Persian. Grammar, Texts, Lexicon*, 2nd ed. (Philadelphia 1953).
Brandenstein, W. and M. Mayrhofer, *Handbuch des Altpersischen* (Wiesbaden 1964).
Sykes, P., *A History of Persia*, 2 vols. (London 1930).
König, F. W., *Älteste Geschichte der Meder und Perser* (Leipzig 1934).
Cameron, G. G., *History of Early Iran* (Chicago 1936).
——, *Persepolis Treasury Tablets* (Chicago 1948).
Olmstead, A. T., *History of the Persian Empire*, 2nd ed. (Chicago 1959).
Herzfeld, E., *Archäologische Mitteilungen aus Iran*, 9 vols. (1929–38).
——, *Iran in the Ancient Archaeological Studies* (1941).
Ghirshman, R., *L'Iran dès origines à l'Islam* (Paris 1951). Engl. transl.: *Iran* (Pelican, 1954).
Klíma, O., 'Kyrové', *NO*, 15 (1960), 64 *et seq.*
——, 'Dareios Veliký', *Ibid.*, 180 *et seq.*
Frye, R. N., *The Heritage of Persia* (London 1963).

III

Nöldeke, Th., *Geschichte der Perser und Araber zur Zeit der Sasaniden. Aus der arabischen Chronik des Tabari...* (Leiden 1879).
Rozen, V. R., *K voprosu ob arabskikh perevodakh Khudây-Nâme* (St. Petersburg 1895).
Salemann, K., 'Mittelpersisch', in *GIPh*, I/I, 249–332. Engl. transl. by L. Bogdanov (Bombay 1930).
——, *Manichäische Studien* (Mémoires de l'Académie St. Pétersbourg) (1908).
——, 'Manichaica I', *Bulletin de l'Académie St. Pétersbourg* (1907).
——, 'III–IV', *Ibid.* (1912).
West, E. W., 'Pahlavi Literature', in *GIPh*, II/2, 75–129.
Müller, F. W. K., 'Handschriften-Reste in Estrangelo-Schrift aus Turfan, I', *Sitzungsber. der Preuss. Akad.* (1904);
——, 'II', *Abhandlungen der Preuss. Akad.* (1904).
Bartholomae, Ch., *Zum sasanidischen Recht*, 5 vols. (Heidelberg 1918–23).
——, *Zur Kenntnis der mitteliran. Mundarten*, 6 vols. (Heidelberg 1916–25).
Schaeder, H. H., 'Urform und Fortbildungen des manichäischen Systems', *Vorträge der Bibliothek Warburg 1924/1925* (Leipzig 1927).
——, 'Iranische Beiträge, I', *Schriften der Königsberger Gelehrten Gesellschaft*, Geisteswiss. Kl., VI (Halle 1930).
Andreas, F. C. and W. Henning, 'Mitteliranische Manichaica aus Chinesisch-Turkestan, I–III', *Sitzungsber. der Preuss. Akad.* (1932–4).
Andreas, F. C. and K. Barr, 'Bruchstücke einer Pehlevi-Übersetzung der Psalmen', *Sitzungsber. der Preuss. Akad.* (1933).
Hansen, O., *Die mittelpersischen Papyri der Papyrussammlung der Staatlichen Museen zu Berlin* (Berlin 1938).
——, *Mittelpersisches Lesebuch* (Berlin 1963).
Ghilain, A., *Essai sur la langue parthe* (Louvain 1939).
Henning, W. B., 'The Disintegration of the Avestic Studies', *Transactions of the Philological Society* (1942).
——, 'A Pahlavi Poem', *BSOAS*, 13 (1949–50), 641–8.
——, 'Mitteliranisch', in *Handbuch der Orientalistik*, ed. by B. Spuler and H. Kees, I/4-I (Leiden 1958), 20–129.
——, 'The Bactrian Inscription', *BSOAS*, 23 (1960), 47–55.

Altheim, F., *Weltgeschichte Asiens im griechischen Zeitalter*, 2 vols. (Halle 1947–8).
——, 'The most ancient Romance of Chivalry', *East and West*, N.S. 9/3 (Rome 1958).
——, *Ein asiatischer Staat. Feudalismus unter den Sasaniden und ihren Nachbarn* (Wiesbaden 1954).
——, *Geschichte der Hunnen*, 5 vols. (Berlin 1959–62).
——, *Die aramäische Sprache unter den Achaimeniden*, I (Frankfurt a. M. 1959–63).
Bailey, H. W., *Zoroastrian Problems in the Ninth-Century Books* (Oxford 1943).
——, 'The Persian Language', in *The Legacy of Persia*, ed. by A. J. Arberry (London 1953), 174–98.
Christensen, A., *L'Iran sous les Sassanides*, 2nd ed. (Copenhagen 1944).
Debevoise, N. C., *A Political History of Parthia* (Chicago 1938).
Sprengling, M., *Third Century Iran. Sapor and Kartir* (Chicago 1953).
Gershevitch, I., 'Iranian Literature', in *Literatures of the East* (London 1953).
Puech, H.-Ch., 'Le manichéisme, son fondateur, sa doctrine', *Musée Guimet, Bibl. de diffusion*, 56 (Paris 1949).
Tedesco, P., 'Dialektologie der westiranischen Turfantexte', *Le Monde oriental*, 15 (1921), 184–258.
Suhtscheck, Fr. von, 'Wolframs von Eschenbach Reimbearbeitung des Pārsīvalnāmä', *Klio*, 25 (1932), 50 *et seq.*
Pagliaro, A. and A. Bausani, *Storia della letteratura persiana* (Milano 1960) ('Letteratura della Persia preislamica', 7–147).
Widengren, G., *Iranisch-semitische Kulturbegegnung in parthischer Zeit* (Cologne-Opladen 1960).
——, *Mani und der Manichäismus* (Stuttgart 1961).
Tarn, W. W., *The Greeks in Bactria and India*, 2nd ed. (Cambridge 1951).
Tavadia, J. C., *Die mittelpersische Sprache und Literatur der Zarathustrier* (Iranische Texte und Hilfsbücher, 2) (Leipzig 1956).
Nyberg, H. S., *A Manual of Pahlavi*, Part I: *Texts* (Wiesbaden 1964).
Zaehner, R. C., *Zurvan, a Zoroastrian Dilemma* (Oxford 1955).
Klíma, O., *Mazdak. Geschichte einer sozialen Bewegung im sassanidischen Persien* (Prague 1957).
——, 'Povídka o Jóštu Frjánovci', *NO*, 2/8, 17 *et seq.*
——, 'Kniha činů Ardašíra, syna Pápakova', *NO*, 3/9, 217 *et seq.*
——, 'Měsíc v životě staroperského člověka', *NO*, 8 (1953), 151 *et seq.*
——, 'Výklad šachové hry a vynalezení név-artachšéru', *NO*, 11 (1956), 72 *et seq.*
——, 'Mání', *NO*, 14 (1959), 68 *et seq.*
——, 'Mazdak', *Ibid.*, 150 *et seq.*
——, 'Zur Chronologie von Mânîs Leben', *ArOr.*, 19 (1951), 393–403.
——, 'Iranische Miszellen', *ArOr.*, 26 (1958), 603–16; 28 (1960), 457.
——, *Manis Zeit und Leben* (Prague 1962).
Freyman, A. A., *Khorezmiyskiy yazïk* (Moscow 1951).
D'yakonov, Y. M., M. M. D'yakonov, and V. A. Livshits, *Dokumentï iz drevney Nisï* (Moscow-Leningrad 1951).
Pigulevskaya, N. V., *Goroda Irana v rannem srednevekov'ye* (Moscow-Leningrad 1956). French transl.: *Les villes de l'État iranien aux époques parthe et sassanide. Contribution à l'histoire sociale de la basse Antiquité* (Paris–The Hague 1963).
Braginskiy, I. S., *Iz istorii tadzhikskoy narodnoy poezii* (Moscow 1956).
Abayev, V. I., *Osetinskiy yazïk i fol'klor*, I (Moscow-Leningrad 1949).
Boyce, M., *The Manichaean Hymn Cycles in Parthian* (London 1954).
——, 'The Parthian *gōsān* and Iranian Minstrel Tradition', *JRAS*, 1957, 10–45.

IV

Inostrantsev, K. A., *Sasanidskiye etyudï* (St. Petersburg 1909).

Bailey, H. W., 'Persia. Language and Dialects', in *Encyclopaedia of Islam*, 1st ed., III (Leiden 1936), *s.v.*

Spuler, B., *Iran in früh-islamischer Zeit* (Wiesbaden 1952).

Daudpota, U. M., *The Influence of Arabic Poetry on the Development of Persian Poetry* (Bombay 1934).

Herzfeld, E., *Paikuli. Monument and Inscription of the Early History of the Sassanian Empire* (Berlin 1924).

Ibn an-Nadīm, *Kitāb al-fihrist*, ed. by G. Flügel (Leipzig 1871–2).

B

JAN RYPKA: HISTORY OF PERSIAN LITERATURE UP TO THE BEGINNING OF THE 20TH CENTURY

For works published before 1900, see: *Grundriss der iranischen Philologie*, hrsg. von W. Geiger und E. Kuhn, 3 vols. (Stuttgart 1891–1904).

I. BIBLIOGRAPHICA

(Catalogues of manuscripts are as a rule not listed; see below 'Preuss. Staatsbibliothek', 93–162. Several new catalogues of the Istanbul and Iranian libraries have since been published)

'Abstracta Islamica', in *REI* since 1927 (some special numbers on Iranian studies).

Afshār, Īraj, 'Kitāb-shināsī-i Īrān, I' (for 1333), in *Farhang-i Īrān-zamīn*, 2 (1333); II (for 1334, in book-form) (Tehran 1335); III (for 1335) (Tehran 1336); *Kitābhā-i Īrān*, IV (for 1336) (Tehran 1337); etc.

——, *Kitāb-shināsī-i fihristhā-i nuskhahā-i khaṭṭī-i fārsī dar kitāb-khānahā-i dunyā* (Tehran 1337) (Univ.).

——, *Fihrist-i maqālāt-i fārsī*, I: 1910–58 (Tehran 1340) (Univ.).

Arberry, A. J., *Persian Books, Catalogue of the Library of the India Office*, II/vi (London 1937).

Bābīs and Bahā'īs: see Bertel's, *Ocherk*, 200 *et seq.* (B V); List of Works in the New York Public Library (*q.v.*), 103–7.

Bahā'īs: see Āvāra (B III); *Isl.*, 19 (1930), 81–4; Esslemont (B III); Root (B VIb; till 1938).

Bertel's, Y. E., 'Bericht über die iranischen und turkologischen Studien in Russland 1914 bis 1920', *Islamica*, 3 (1927), 305–18.

——, *Ocherk* (B V), 178–203.

Bibliografia polskich prac orientalistycznych (1945–55), ed. by W. Kotański and B. Majewska (based on the material of Wł. Zajączkowski) (Warsaw 1957).

Bibliograficheskiy ukazatel' po Persii (Moscow 1928).

Bol'shaya sovetskaya entsiklopediya: on all matters of any importance.

Brockelmann, C., *GAL* (B V; with exhaustive bibliography).

Browne, E. G., *LHP* I, 481–96 (B V; survey of fundamental works).

Central Asia: see Gafurov (D Ia); Storey (*q.v.*).

Chauvin, Victor, *Bibliographie des ouvrages arabes ou relatifs aux Arabes, publiés dans l'Europe chrétienne de 1810 à 1885*, II (Liège 1897): 'Kalîlah'; VIII (1909): 'Syntipas' (Ṭūṭī-nāma etc.).

Critical bibliography: in *Der Islam*, from vol. IV (1913) onwards.

Edwards, E., *A Catalogue of the Persian Printed Books in the British Museum* (London 1922).
Encyclopaedia of Islam (Leiden-London 1913–34). *Supplement* (1934–8).
——, Turkish translation, resp. 'tâdil, ikmâl': *İslâm Ansiklopedisi*. (Istanbul, in progress since 1950). More up to date and often better than the original.
——, *The Encyclopaedia of Islam*, New Edition, in English and French (in progress since 1954).
Ethé, H., *Neupersische Literatur* (B v; bibliography up to 1904).
Fihrist-i kitāb-khāna-i ihdā'ī-i Āqā-i Sayyid Muḥ. Mishkāt ba-kitāb-khāna-i Dānishgāh-i Tihrān, I–II, ed. by 'A.-N. Munzavī (Tehran 1330–2) (Univ.); III, in 5 vols., ed. by Muḥ.-T. Dānish-puzhūh (Tehran 1332–8).
Gabeau-Thonet, Jeanne, 'Notes sur les ouvrages bibliographiques publiés pendant ces deux derniers siècles et relatifs aux Arabes, Persans et Turcs', in *Actes du XXe Congrès des Orientalistes (Bruxelles 1938)* (Louvain 1940), nr. 34.
Gabrieli, G., *Manuale di bibliografia musulmana*, I: *Bibliografia generale* (Roma 1916).
Ḥājjī Khalīfa, *Lexicon bibliographicum*, ed. by G. Flügel, 7 vols. ((Leipzig) London 1835–58).
Harrassowitz, Otto, *Das islamische Persien. Iran und seine Grenzländer. Kaukasus und Transkaukasien* (Leipzig 1931) (Bücher-Katalog 430).
Horn, P., 'Geschichte Irans in islamischer Zeit', in *GIPh*, II, 551–611 (historical bibliography up to 1904).
Iran, economy: bibliography of Soviet studies in *Bol'sh. sov. entsikl.*, 18 (1953), 404; history: *ibid.*, 421 *et seq.*
Jānā, 'A.-A., *Fihrist-i mauḍū'ī-i intishārāt-i Dānishgāh-i Tihrān, 1325–1342* (Tehran 1342) (Univ.).
Jewish-Persian literature up to 1915: extensive bibliogr. in *List of Works in the New York Public Library* (*q.v.*), 107–18.
Karatay, Fehmi Edhem, *İstanbul üniversitesi kütüphanesi farsça basmalar kataloğu* (Istanbul 1949) (gives many Istanbul editions and modern Turkish translations).
'Kitābhā-i māh', *Nashriyya-i Anjuman-i nāshirān-i kitāb* (Tehran, from 1334).
List of Works in the New York Public Library relating to Persia (New York 1915).
Mushār, Khān-bābā, *Kitābhā-i chāpī-i fārsī*, 2 vols. (Tehran 1337–42).
——, *Mu'allifīn-i kutub-i chāpī-i fārsī va 'arabī az āghāz-i chāp tā kunūn* (Tehran, in progress since 1340).
Nafīsī, Sa'īd [† Nov. 14th, 1966]: lists of his publications in *RK*, 9/5 (1345), 472–6 and Īr. Afshār (*q.v.*), *Fihrist-i maqālāt*.
Orientalische Bibliographie, hrsg. von L. Schermann (Berlin 1887–1915).
Pārsī: see *List of Works in the New York Public Library* (*q.v.*), 101–3.
Pearson, J. D. (with the assistance of Julia F. Ashton), *Index Islamicus 1906–1955. A Catalogue of Articles on Islamic Subjects in Periodicals and other Collective Publications* (Cambridge 1958).—*Supplement 1956–1960* (1962).
Persische Bibliographie. Zusammengestellt von dem Redaktionskomitee der persischen Zeitung Kaveh (Berlin 1920).
Preussische Staatsbibliothek: *Katalog der Handbibliothek der orientalischen Abteilung* (Leipzig 1929).
Rabino, H. L., *Ṣūrat-i jarā'id-i Īrān* (Rasht 1911). Bibliography of newspapers 1848–1911.
Rāh-namā-i kitāb, ed. by Īr. Afshār (since 1337; monthly, from 1340).
Saba, M., 'Bibliographie française de l'Iran', in *Bibliographie méthodique et raisonnée des ouvrages français parus depuis 1560 jusqu'à nos jours* (1936; 1951; Tehran 1345).
Ṣafā, Ibr., *Intishārāt-i Īrān dar sāl-i 1344* (Tehran 1345).
Salemann, C. – Shukovski, V., *Persische Grammatik* (Berlin 1889, and several unchanged reprints) ('Porta ling. orient.'; introductory bibliography, 105–18).
Schwab, Moïse, *Bibliographie de la Perse* (Paris 1875).
Social and economic history of Iran: see *Tadhkirat al-mulūk. A Manual of Safavid Administration.* Persian text in facs. Transl. and expl. by V. Minorsky (London 1943) (GMNS 16), 204–7.
Spuler, B. – Forrer, L., *Orientalistik*, III: *Der Vordere Orient in islamischer Zeit* (Bern 1954).

Storey, C. A.: see B v.
Tājīkistān: see Gafurov (D Ia).
Tal'man, R. O. and A. Yunusov, *Rudaki (ukazatel' literaturī)* (Dushanbe 1965) (an exhaustive Rūdakī-bibliography).
Tanaka, Otoya, *A Catalogue of Books relating to Persia, coll. by Shigeru Araki* (Tokyo 1934).
Ungarische Autoren über Asien und Afrika 1950–1962. Ausgewählte Bibliographie (Budapest 1963).
Vajda, G.: 'Publications iraniennes à l'occasion du millénaire d'Avicenne', *REI*, 22 (1954), A. 151–66.
Wilhelm, E. and Bomonji Byramji Patel, *Catalogue of Books on Iranian Literature publ. in Europe and India* (Bombay 1901) (English and Gujerati).
Wilson, A. T., *A Bibliography of Persia* (Oxford 1930).

II. POLITICAL, ECONOMIC AND CULTURAL HISTORY

Arasteh, A. Reza, *Man and Society in Iran*. In collaboration with Josephine Arasteh (Leiden 1964).
Arunova, M. R. and Ashrafyan, K. Z., *Gosudarstvo Nadir-shakha Afshara* (Ocherk obshchestvennīkh otnosheniy v Irane 30–40-kh godov XVIIIv.) (Moscow 1958).
Ashrafyan, K. Z., 'Antifeodal'nīye dvizheniya v imperii Nadir-shakha (1736–1747)', *UZIV*, 8 (1953), 166–204.
Azerbayjan: *Istoriya Azerbaydzhana. Kratkiy ocherk (s drevneyshikh vremen do XIX v.)* (Baku 1943).
——, *Istoriya Azerbaydzhana* (Coll. publ.) I (Baku 1958) (up to and including the 18th century).
Bartol'd, V. V. (Barthold, W.), 'Die persische Šu'ūbīja und die moderne Wissenschaft', *Zschr. für Assyr.*, 26 (1912), 249–66.
——, 'Die persische Inschrift an der Mauer der Manūčahr-Moschee zu Ani. Deutsche Bearb. von W. Hinz', *ZDMG*, 101 (1951), 241–69.
——, Th. Menzel, 'Versuch einer Barthold-Bibliographie', *Isl.*, 21 (1933), 236–42; 22 (1935), 144–62.
Bāstānī Pārīzī, Ibr., *Ya'qūb-i Layth-i Ṣaffārī* (1343).
Bausani, Aless., *I Persiani* (Firenze 1962). German transl.: *Die Perser* (Stuttgart 1965).
Belenitskiy, A. M., 'K voprosu o social'nīkh otnosheniyakh v Irane v Khulaguidskuyu epokhu', *SV*, 1948/5, 111–28.
Bellan, L.-L., *Chah Abbas I, sa vie, son histoire* (Paris 1932).
Bina, A. A., *La question iranienne au début du XIXe siècle. Les traités de Gulistan et de Turkman-Tschaï (1813–1828)* (1939).
Boldīrev, A. N., 'Ocherki iz zhizni geratskogo obshchestva na rubezhe XV–XVI. vv.', *TOV*, IV (1947).
Bosworth, Clifford Edmund, *The Ghaznavids, their Empire in Afghanistan and Eastern Iran (994–1040)* (Edinburgh 1963).
Bouvat, Lucien, *L'empire mongol, 2ème phase (Timurids)* (Paris 1927).
——, 'Essai sur la civilisation timouride', *JA*, 208 (1926), 193–299.
Bowen, H., 'The last Buwayhids', *JRAS*, 1929, 225–45.
Boyle, J. A., 'The Death of the Last 'Abbasid Caliph: a Contemporary Muslim Account', *Journ. of Semit. Studies*, 6/2 (1961), 145–61.
Brockelmann, C., *Geschichte der islamischen Völker und Staaten*, 2nd ed. (1943) (also published in English and French).
Browne, E. G., *A year amongst the Persians*. With a memoir by Sir E. Denison Ross and a foreword by Sir Ellis H. Minns, 3rd ed. (London 1950).
Brunschvig, R. et G. E. von Grunebaum, 'Classicisme et déclin culturel dans l'histoire de l'Islam', in *Actes du Symposium international d'histoire de la civilisation musulmane (Bordeaux 25–29 juin 1956)* (Paris 1957).

Cahen, Cl., 'Mouvements populaires et autonomisme urbain dans l'Asie musulmane du Moyen Âge', *Arabica*, v (1958), 225–50; vi (1959), 25–56, 223–65.

——, 'The Mongols and the Near East', in *A History of the Crusades*, ed. by K. M. Setton, R. L. Wolff and H. W. Hazard (Philadelphia 1959), ii, 715–32.

——, 'The Turks in Iran and Anatolia before the Mongol Invasions', *Ibid.*, 661–92.

Christensen, A., 'Fra Samanidernes Tid', *Studien fra Sprog- og Oldtidsforskning* (Copenhagen 1903).

——, 'Kadjarerne og deres Rige', *Tilskueren*, 1909, 2, 368–76.

——, 'Le règne du roi Kawādh I et le communisme mazdakite', *Hist.-filol. Medd.*, 9/6 (1925).

——, 'Les Kayanides', *Ibid.*, 19/2 (1932).

——, *L'Iran sous les Sassanides*, 2nd ed. (Copenhagen 1944).

Efendiyev, O. A., *Obrazovaniye azerbaydzhanskogo gosudarstva Sefevidov v nachale 16 v.* (Baku 1961).

Falsafī, N., *Zindagānī-i Shāh 'Abbās-i Avval*, i (Tehran 1332) (Univ.); ii (Tehran 1334); iii (Tehran 1340).

Gafurov, B. G., 'O prichinakh vozvïsheniya i padeniya Samanidov', *SV*, 1958/1, 51–5.

Gardet, L., *La cité musulmane. Vie sociale et politique* (Paris 1954).

Geschichte der islamischen Länder (*Handbuch der Orientalistik*, Leiden): 1. Spuler, B., *Die Chalifenzeit* (1952); 2. Spuler, B., *Die Mongolenzeit* (1953); 3. (coll. publ.): *Neuzeit* (incl.: 'Geschichte Irans seit 1500') (1959).

——, *The Muslim World*, i: *The Age of the Caliphs*; ii: *The Mongol Period*. Transl. by F. R. C. Bagley (Leiden 1960–1).

Gibb, H. A. R., 'The Social Significance of the shu'ūbīye', in *Studia orient. J. Pedersen dedicata* (Copenhagen 1953), 105–14.

——, *Studies on the Civilisation of Islam*, ed. by Stanford S. Shaw and Will R. Polk (London 1962) (on the Shu'ūbiyya pp. 62–73).

Gibb, H. A. R. and Bowen, H., *Islamic Society and the West. A Study of the Impact of Western Civilisation on Moslem Culture in the Near East*, Vol. i: *Islamic Society in the XVIIIth Century*, 2 vols. (Oxford Univ. Press, London 1950–7).

Gordlevskiy, V. A., *Kara-koyunlu* (Baku 1927).

Grunebaum, G. E. von, *Medieval Islam. A Study in Cultural Orientation* (Chicago 1946). French tr. by O. Mayot (1962).

——, *Islam. Essays on the Nature and Growth of a Cultural Tradition* (Comparative Studies of Cultures and Civilizations. The American Anthropological Association, 57/2) (1955).

——, 'Der Islam', off-print from the *Propyläen-Weltgeschichte*, 21–179.

Habib, Moh., *Sultan Mahmud of Ghaznin. A Study* (Bombay 1927; Delhi 1956).

Hazard, H. W., *Atlas of Islamic History*, 2nd ed. rev. and corr. (Princeton 1952).

Hidāyatī, Hādī, *Ta'rīkh-i Zandiyya*, i: *Karīm-khān (1165–93 h.)* (Tehran 1334) (Univ.).

Hinz, W., 'Shah Esma'īl II. Ein Beitrag zur Geschichte der Ṣafavīden', *MSOS*, 36 (1933), ii. Abt.

——, *Irans Aufstieg zum Nationalstaat im fünfzehnten Jahrhundert* (Berlin-Leipzig 1936).

——, 'Steuerinschriften aus dem mittelalterlichen Vorderen Asien', *Belleten*, 13 (1949), 745–69.

Huart, C., *Les Ziyarides* (Paris 1922).

Iqbāl, 'Abbās, *Ta'rīkh-i mufaṣṣal-i Īrān az istīlā-i Mughul tā i'lān-i Mashrūṭiyyat*, i (all published; Chingiz till the rise of the Timurid Empire) (Tehran 1312; 1341).

——, 'Bahrām-Shāh-i Saljūqī, mamdūḥ-i Makhzanu'l-asrār', *Arm.*, 19, 39–42.

——, *Mīrzā Taqī-Khān Amīr-i kabīr*, ed. by Īr. Afshār (Tehran 1340).

Istoriya Irana s drevneyshikh vremen do kontsa XVIII veka, ed. by N. V. Pigulevskaya, A. Y. Yakubovskiy, I. P. Petrushevskiy, L. V. Stroyeva and A. M. Belenitskiy (Leningrad 1958) (Univ.). Extensive bibliography, 373–85.

Ivanov, M. S., 'Babidskiye vosstaniya v Irane 1848–52', *TMIV*, 30 (1939).

——, *Ocherk istorii Irana* (Moscow 1952) (IVV).

Kasravī Tabrīzī, *Shahryārān-i gum-nām*, 3 vols. (Tehran 1307–8).

Kiknadze, R. K., 'Tamgoviye sbori v gosudarstve il'khanov', *Vost. sbornik*, 1, AN Gruz. SSR (1960), 93–120. (Georgian, with Russian and English summaries.)
Lambton, A. K. S., *Landlord and Peasant in Persia* (Oxford 1953). Persian tr. by Man. Amīrī, *Mālik va zāriʿ* (Tehran 1339).
Le Strange, G., *The Lands of the Eastern Caliphate ... from the Moslem Conquest to the Time of Timur* (Cambridge 1905).
Levy, Reuben, *An Introduction to the Sociology of Islam*, 2 vols. (London 1931–33). 2nd ed., with the title: *The Social Structure of Islam* (Cambridge 1957).
Lockhart, Laurence, 'Hasan-i Sabbah and the Assassins', *BSOS*, 5 (1928–30), 675–96.
——, *Nadir Shah. A Critical Study based mainly upon Contemporary Sources* (London 1938). Persian tr. by Mushfiq Tihrānī (Tehran 1331).
——, *The Fall of the Ṣafavī Dynasty and the Afghan Occupation of Persia* (Cambridge 1958) (bibliography, 545–64). Persian tr. by Muṣṭafā-qulī 'Imād (Tehran 1343).
Massignon, L., 'Valeur culturelle internationale de la coopération des penseurs iraniens du Moyen Âge à l'essor de la civilisation arabe', in *L'âme de l'Iran* (B VIa), 75–98.
Masson, V. M. and V. A. Romodin, *Istoriya Afganistana*, 2 vols. (Moscow 1965).
Mélikoff, Irène, *Abu Muslim, le "Porte-Hache" du Khorassan dans la tradition épique turco-iranienne* (Paris 1962).
Miklukho-Maklay, N. D., 'K istorii politicheskikh vzaimootnosheniy Irana so Sredney Aziyey v XVI veke', *KS*, 4 (1952), 11–18.
——, 'Iz istorii afganskogo vladïchestva v Irane (20-ye godï XVIII v.)', *Ucheniye Zapiski LGU*, No 179, 138–58.
Minorsky, V., *La domination des Daïlamites* (Publ. Soc. Ét. Iran., 3) (Paris 1932).
——, *Esquisse d'une histoire de Nader-Chah* (Publ. Soc. Ét. Iran., 10) (Paris 1934).
——, 'The Middle East in Western Politics in the 13th, 15th and 16th Centuries', *JRCentr. AS*, 27 (1940), 427–61.
——, 'Iran: Opposition, Martyrdom, and Revolt', in *Unity and Variety* (*q.v.*) (1955), 183–206.
——, *Persia in A.D. 1478–90* (London 1957).
——, Most of these studies also in his *Iranica* (B VIa).
Moscati, Sabatino, 'Studi su Abū Muslim', *RANL*, S. VIII, vol. IV (1949), 1–13; 474–95; vol. V (1950), 1–17.
Mustaufī, 'Abdu'llāh, *Sharḥ-i zindagānī-i man yā Ta'rīkh-i ijtimāʿī va idārī-i daura-i Qājāriyya*, 2nd ed. (Tehran 1343).
Nafīsī, S., 'Khāndān-i Ṣāʿidiyān', in *Mélanges Massé* (Tehran 1963), 85–101.
Najmī, Nāṣir, *Sharḥ-i zindagī-i 'Abbās-Mīrzā* (Tehran 1337).
Navā'ī, 'Abdu'l-Ḥusayn, *Karīm-Khān-i Zand* (1343).
Nāẓim, M., *The Life and Times of Sulṭān Maḥmūd of Ghazna* (Cambridge 1931).
Nūrī, Ḥus. Saʿādat, 'Ḥājj Mīrzā Āqāsī (1198–1265 q.)', *Yaghmā*, 16 (1342), 231–6, etc.
Pakravan, E., *Agha Mohammad Ghadjar. Essai biographique* (Tehran 1953).
——, *Abbas Mirza: Un Prince Réformateur* (Tehran 1958).
Petrushevskiy, I., 'K voprosu o prikreplenii krest'yan k zemle v Irane v epokhu mongol'skogo vladïchestva', *VoIst.*, 1947/4, 59–70 (Other literature also listed).
——, 'Gorodskaya znat' v gosudarstve Khulaguidov', *SV*, 1948/5, 85–110.
——, 'Dvizheniye Serbedarov v Khorasane', *UZIV*, 14 (1956), 91–162.
Pigulevskaya, N. V., *Vizantiya i Iran na rubezhe VI i VII vekov* (Moscow-Leningrad 1946).
——, 'Zarozhdeniye feodal'nïkh otnosheniy na Blizhnem Vostoke', *UZIV*, 1958/16, 5–30.
Raḥīm-zāda Ṣafavī, *Sharḥ-i janghā va ta'rīkh-i zindagānī-i Shāh Ismāʿīl-i Ṣafavī*, ed. by Yūsuf-pūr Ṣafavī (Tehran 1341).
Rāvandī, Murtaḍā, *Ta'rīkh-i ijtimāʿī-i Īrān*, 3 vols. (Tehran 1341–44).

Rāzī, ʿAbdu'llāh, *Taʾrīkh-i kāmil-i Īrān*, 3rd ed. (Tehran 1341).

Reychmann, Jan, 'Z nowszych badań nad dziejami stosunków agrarnych na Bliskim Wschodzie', *ROr.*, 19 (1954), 193–201.

——, *Orient w kulturze polskiego Oświecenia* (Wrocław–Warszawa–Kraków 1964).

Reysner, I., 'K voprosu ob otstavanii stran zarubezhnogo Vostoka k nachalu novogo vremeni', *VoIst*, 1951/6, 75–89.

Rippe, K. (= J. Rypka), 'Über den Sturz Nizām-ul-Mulks', in *Mélanges Köprülü* (Istanbul 1953), 423–35. (Cf. *Yādgār*, 1/3, 1323–4/1944–5, 62–6).

Roemer, H. R., *Der Niedergang Irans nach dem Tode Ismāʿīls des Grausamen, 1577–1581* (Würzburg 1939).

——, 'Die Safawiden. Ein orient. Bundesgenosse des Abendlandes im Türkenkampf', *Saeculum*, 4/1 (1953), 27–44.

Ṣafā, Dh., 'Tasalluṭ-i ghulāmān va qabāʾil-i zard-pūst az miyāna-i qarn-i panjum tā āghāz-i qarn-i haftum-i hijrī', *MDAT*, 4/1 (1335), 23–82.

Sanaullah, M. F., *The Decline of the Saljuqid Empire* (Calcutta 1938).

Sauvaget, J., *Introduction à l'histoire de l'Orient musulman. Éléments de bibliographie*, édition refondue et complétée par Cl. Cahen (Paris 1961). English translation: *Introduction to the History of the Muslim East. A Bibliographical Guide*. Based on the 2nd ed. as recast by C. Cahen. Transl. under the ausp. of the Near Eastern Center, Univ. of Calif. (1965).

Schabinger, Karl Emil, Freiherr von Schowingen, 'Zur Geschichte des Seldschuken-Reichskanzlers Nisāmu'l-Mulk', *Hist. Jahrb.* (Köln a. Rhein), 62-9 (1949), 250–83.

——, 'Nisāmulmulk und das Abbasidische Chalifat', *Ibid.*, 71 (1952), 91–136.

Semenov, A. A., 'Kul'turnïy uroven' pervïkh Sheybanidov', *SV*, 1956/3, 50–9.

Shamīm, ʿAlī-Aṣghar, *Īrān dar daura-i salṭanat-i Qājār (qarn-i sīzdahum va nīma-i avval-i qarn-i chahārdahum-i hijrī-i qamarī)* (Tehran 1343).

Shitov, G. V., *Persiya pod vlast'yu poslednikh Kadzharov* (Leningrad 1933).

Spuler, B., *Die Mongolen in Iran. Politik, Verwaltung und Kultur der Ilchanzeit 1220 bis 1350* (Leipzig 1939). 2nd enlarged ed. (Berlin 1955).

——, 'Iran und der Islam', *Welt als Geschichte*, 4 (1952), 227–32.

——, *Iran in frühislamischer Zeit. Politik, Kultur, Verwaltung und öffentliches Leben 633–1055* (Wiesbaden 1952).

——, 'Die historische Literatur Persiens bis zum 13. Jahrhundert als Spiegel seiner geistigen Entwicklung', *Saeculum*, 8/2-3 (1957), 267–84.

——, cf. p. 760, s.v. 'Geschichte der isl. Länder'.

Stroyeva, L. V., 'Unichtozheniye mongolami ismailitov v Iranu', *Ucheniye zapiski LGU*, 1954, No 179, 192–214.

——, 'Posledniy khorezmshakh i ismailitï Alamuta', in *Sb. Orbeli* (Moscow-Leningrad 1960), 451–63. Persian tr. *RK*, 6 (1342), 863–78.

Sykes, Sir Percy, *History of Persia*, 3rd ed., with Supplementary Essays, 2 vols. (London 1930; reprint 1951). Persian tr. by Sayyid Muḥ. Taqī Fakhr Dāʿī Gīlānī: *Taʾrīkh-i mufaṣṣal-i Īrān*, 2 vols.

——, *A History of Afghanistan*, 2 vols. (London 1940). (Bibliogr., II, 371–6).

Tājbakhsh, Aḥm., *Īrān dar zamān-i Ṣafaviyya* (Tabriz 1340).

Tauer, F., 'Dějiny a kultura islámu od poloviny VIII. do počátku XIII. století', in *Dějiny lidstva*, IV (1942), 1–60.

——, 'Malikšáh a Nizámulmulk', in *Tvůrcové dějin*, II (1934), 202–7.

——, 'Hulagu a Ghází́n', *ibid.*, 352–6.

——, 'Islám a jeho rozpětí do konce doby umajjovské', in *Dějiny lidstva*, III, 100–180.

Togan, Zeki Velidi, 'Sur l'origine des Safavides', in *Mélanges Massignon* (Damas 1957), 345–57.

Tschudi, R., 'Vom Islam zur Zeit der Kreuzzüge', *Asia Major*, 9 (1933), 441–54.

Turan, Osman, 'Iktâ', 'Iḳṭâ'', *İA*, 50. cüz (1951), 949–58.
Unity and Variety in Muslim Civilization, ed. by G. E. von Grunebaum (Chicago 1955).
Vil'chevskiy, O. L., 'Noviy istochnik dlya kharakteristiki mirovozzreniya gorodskogo naseleniya Irana v X–XI vekakh', *SV*, 1955/1, 96–103.
Vladimirtsov, B. Y., *Chingis-khan* (Berlin-Petrograd-Moscow 1922). French tr.: Paris 1948; Turkish tr.: Istanbul 1950.
Watson, Rob. Grant, *A History of Persia from the Beginning of the Nineteenth Century to 1858* (London 1866). Persian tr. by 'Abbās-qulī Ādharī (Tehran 1340).
Wittfogel, Karl, *Oriental Despotism: a Comparative Study of Total Power* (New Haven, 1957).
Yakubovskiy, A. Y., 'Makhmud Gaznevi. K voprosu o proiskhozhdenii i kharaktere gaznevidskogo gosudarstva', in *Ferdovsi* (see B VIb, *s.v.* 'Firdausī') (Leningrad 1934), 51–96.
Zakhoder, B. N., 'Khorasan i obrazovaniye gosudarstva Sel'dzhukov', *VoIst.*, 1945/5-6, 119–41.

III. RELIGION, MYSTICISM*, SECTS

Arberry, A. J., *An Introduction to the History of Ṣūfism* (London–New York–Toronto 1942?).
——, *Sufism. An Account of the Mystics of Islam* (London 1950). French tr.: *Le soufisme. Introduction à la mystique de l'Islam.* Trad. J. Gouillard (1952).
Āyatī (=Āvāra), 'Abdu'l-Ḥusayn, *Kashfu'l-ḥiyal*, 3 vols. (Tehran, several eds. since 1304) (anti-Bahā'ī).
——, *al-Kavākibu'd-durrīyah fī ma'āthiri'l-Bahā'īyah*, 2 vols. (Cairo 1924).
Barthold, Wilh., 'Der iranische Buddhismus und sein Verhältnis zum Islam', in *Oriental Studies of C. E. Pavry* (London 1933), 29–32.
Bausani, A., *Persia religiosa* (Milano 1959).
Belyayev, Y. A., *Musul'manskoye sektantstvo (Istorich. ocherki)* (Moscow 1957).
Bertel's, Ye. E., *Izbranniye trudi: Sufizm i sufiyskaya literatura* (Moscow 1965).
Boer, T. J. de, *Geschichte der Philosophie im Islam* (Stuttgart 1901). English tr.: *The History of Philosophy in Islam.* Transl. by Edw. R. Jones (London 1903).
Brakell Buys, R. van, *Gestalten uit de perzische mystiek, waarin opgenomen grondvormen der mystiek*, 2nd ed. (1951).
Browne, E. G., devoted several fundamental studies to the religious life of Iran, in particular to the Bābīs; see Wilson (B I). This interest is noticeable in all his works.
Burckhardt, T., *Vom Sufitum. Einführung in die Mystik des Islam* (München-Planegg 1953).
Corbin, H., *L'imagination créatrice dans le soufisme d'Ibn 'Arabi* (Paris 1958).
Donaldson, D. M., *The Shi'ite Religion. A History of Islam in Persia and Irak* (London 1933).
Esslemont, J. E., *Bahā'u'llāh and the New Era* (New York n.d. [about 1920]) (bibliography, 227–30). Transl. into several other languages.
Fidā'ī, *Kitāb bi-hidāyat al-mu'minīn aṭ-ṭālibīn (Istoriya ismailizma)*, ed. by A. A. Semenov (Moscow 1959).
Garcin de Tassy, *La poésie philosophique et religieuse d'après le Mantic Uttaïr de Farid-uddin Attar*, 4th ed. (Paris 1864).
Ghaffary, E. N., *Les soufis de l'Iran. Apologie d'une civilisation* (Tehran 1964).
——, *Farah. L'univers paradisiaque des soufis persans* (Tehran 1966).
Ghanī, Q.: see B VIb.
Goldziher, I., 'Islamisme et Parsisme', *Rev. hist. rel.*, 43 (1901), 1 *et seq.*
——, *Vorlesungen über den Islam* (Heidelberg 1910; 2nd ed. (Fr. Babinger), 1925).

* For literature on Ṣūfism not mentioned here, see A. J. Arberry, *An Introduction.... (q. v.)*

Gramlich, R., 'Die schiitischen Derwischorden Persiens, I: Die Affiliationen', *Abhandlungen für die Kunde des Morgenlandes*, 38/1 (1965).
Hartmann, Rich., *Die Religion des Islam* (Berlin 1944).
Hodgson, M. G.: *The Order of Assassins* (The Hague 1955).
Horovitz, Josef, 'Taqijja', *Isl.*, 3 (1912), 63–7.
Horten, Max, *Die Philosophie des Islam* (München 1924).
——, *Indische Strömungen in der islamischen Mystik* (Heidelberg, I: 1927; II: 1928). (Cf. H. H. Schaeder, *OLZ*, 1927, 833–49.)
Istakhrī, Iḥsānu'llāh, *Uṣūl-i taṣavvuf* (Tehran 1339).
Ivanow, W., *Studies in Early Persian Ismailism*, 2nd rev. ed. (Bombay 1955) (Ism. Soc. A 8).
——, *A Guide to Ismaili Literature* (London 1933). – *Ismaili Literature, a Bibliographical Survey* (A second enlarged edition ...) (Tehran 1963).
Kasravī, Aḥm., *Ṣūfīgarī*, 4th ed. (Tehran 1337).
——, *Shaykh Ṣafī va tabārash.* (Tehran 1324).
Lewis, Bernard, *The Origins of Ismā'īlism: A Study of the Historical Background of the Fatimid Caliphate* (Cambridge 1940).
Massignon, L., '"Ana al Ḥaqq". Étude historique et critique sur une formule dogmatique de théologie mystique', *Isl.*, 3, 248–57.
——, *Essai sur les origines du lexique technique de la mystique musulmane* (Paris 1922). Nouvelle éd. rev. et augmentée: Paris 1954.
Merx, Ad., *Idee und Grundlinien einer allgemeinen Geschichte der Mystik* (Heidelberg 1893).
Miklukho-Maklay, N. D., 'Shiizm i yego sotsial'noye litso v Irane na rubezhe XV–XVI vv.', in *Pamyati akad. I. Yul. Krachkovskogo* (Leningrad 1958) (Univ.), 221–34.
Minorsky, V., 'Persia: Religion and History', in *Iranica* (B VIa), 242–59.
Molé, Marijan, 'La danse extatique en Islam', in *Les danses sacrées* (Paris 1963), 147–280.
Muḥ. 'Abdu'l-Ghanī Ḥasan, *Abū Muslim-i Khurāsānī.* Transl. from Arabic by Shāfi'ī Kadkanī (Tehran 1344).
Murtaḍavī, Manūchihr, 'Dīn va madhhab dar 'ahd-i īlkhānān-i Īrān', *NDAT*, 10/1 (1337), 17–80; continued under the title 'Nabūdan-i ta'aṣṣub-i madhhabī dar daura-i Mughūl', *ibid.*, 11/2 (1338), 151–84.
——, 'Taṣavvuf dar daura-i īlkhānān', *ibid.*, 9/3, 297–337.
——, *Taḥqīq dar bāra-i īlkhānān-i Īrān (dīn va madhhab, taṣavvuf, ta'rīkh-navīsī, muqallidīn-i Shāhnāma)* (Tabriz 1341).
Nafīsī, Sa'īd, *Sar-chashma-i taṣavvuf dar Īrān* (Tehran 1345).
Nicholson, R. A., *The Mystics of Islam* (London 1914).
——, *The Idea of Personality in Sufism* (Cambridge 1923).
Nicolas, A. L. M., 'Les Béhahis et le Bâb', *JA*, 1933, 257–63.
——, *Qui est le successeur du Bāb?* (Paris 1933).
——, *Les massacres de Bābis en Perse* (Paris 1936).
Palmer, E. H., *Oriental Mysticism (Ibn 'Arabī in the interpr. of Nasafī)*, 2nd ed., with introd. by A. J. Arberry (London 1938).
Ritter, H., 'Der Reigen der "Tanzenden Derwische"', *Zeitschr. für vergleich. Musikwissenschaft*, I (1933), 28–40 (with "Notenanhang", 5–23).
Roemer, H., *Die Bābī-Behā'ī. Eine Studie zur Religionsgeschichte des Islams* (Tübingen 1911; Potsdam 1912).
Ṣafā, Dh., 'Firaq-i shī'a dar Īrān', *MDAT*, 4/2 (1335), 1–45.
Schimmel, A.-M., 'Alcuni aspetti del misticismo islamico', in *Aspetti spirituali dell' Islam* (Roma (1961), 35–60.
Siyāsī, 'A. A., 'Taṣavvuf va 'irfān', *MDAT*, 11 (1342), 82–6.

Smith, Marg., *Studies in Early Mysticism in the Near and Middle East* (London 1931).
——, *Readings from the Mystics of Islam. Translations from the Arabic and Persian, together with a short account of the history and doctrines of Ṣūfism* (London 1950).
——, *The Ṣūfī Path of Love. An Anthology of Ṣūfism* (London 1954).
Spooner, B. J., 'The Function of Religion in Persian Society', *Iran. Journal of the British Inst. of Persian Studies*, I (1963), 83–95.
Spuler, B., 'Der Verlauf der Islamisierung Persiens. Eine Skizze', *Isl.*, 29 (1950), 63–76.
——, 'Iran und der Islam', in *Welt als Geschichte*, 4 (1952), 227–32.
Wickens, G. M., 'Religion', in *The Legacy of Persia* (B VIa), 148–73.
Za'īmu'd-daula Tabrīzī, Muḥ. Mahdī, *Miftāḥ-i Bābu'l-abvāb yā ta'rīkh-i Bāb va Bahā*. Tr. by Ḥasan Farīd Gulpāyagānī, 2nd ed. (Tehran 1340).
Zarrīnkūb, 'A. Ḥ., 'Arzish-i mīrāth-i ṣūfiyya', *Yaghmā*, 16 (1342) and continuations.

IV. THEORY OF LITERATURE, STYLISTICS, ETC. LANGUAGE

Abdullah, S. M., 'The Value of Persian Poetry', *Isl. Research Ass., Miscellany*, I (Oxford 1949), 1–17.
Adīb-Ṭūsī, 'Shi'r va shā'irī dar Īrān. Qālib-i shi'r', *NDAT*, 4/1-2 (1330), 38–48. See also B VIb.
——, 'Yak pīshnihād-i tāza dar fann-i 'arūḍ', *NDAT*, 12/3 (1339), 360–95; 12/4, 461–502.
Āqā Sardār, Najaf-qulī-mīrzā, *Durra-i Najafī* (Bombay 1333/1915). (Poetics.)
Ateş, Ahmed, 'Gazel', *İA*, 37. cüz (1947), 730–3.
Bahār, Maliku'sh-shu'arā Muḥ. Taqī, *Sabk-shināsī yā taṭavvur-i nathr-i fārsī*, 3 vols. (Tehran 1321; 2nd ed. 1337–8).
——, *Ta'rīkh-i taṭavvur-i shi'r-i fārsī* (Mashhad 1334) (= Shi'r dar Īrān, Tehran n.d.).
——, *Sabk-shināsī* (IV/1) *yā ta'rīkh-i taṭavvur-i shi'r-i fārsī*, ed. by 'Alī-qulī Maḥmūdī Bakhtyārī (*s.l.*, 'ELMI', 1342).
Bahri, H., *Persian Influence on Hindi* (Allahabad 1960).
Bailey, H. W., 'The Persian Language', in *The Legacy of Persia* (B VIa), 174–98.
Bausani, Al., 'Alṭāf Ḥusain Ḥālī's Ideas on Ghazal', in *Charisteria* (B VIa), 38–56.
——,'Contributo a una definizione dello "stile indiano" della poesia persiana', *Annali* (Napoli), N.S. 7 (1958), 167–78.
Bertel's, Y. E., 'Zametki po poeticheskoy terminologii persidskikh sufiyev, I: Lokon i litso', in *Yazïk i Literatura* (Leningrad), I (1926), 261–86.
Blachère, R., 'Vue d'ensemble sur la poétique classique des Arabes', *RES*, 1938, 1–15.
——, *Les principaux thèmes de la poésie érotique au siècle des Umayyades* (Paris 1941).
Blochmann, H., *The Prosody of the Persians according to Saifi, Jami and Other Writers* (Calcutta 1872).
Boldïrev, A. N., 'Iz istorii razvitiya persidskogo literaturnogo yazïka', *Voprosï yazïkoznaniya*, 1955/5, 78–92.
Büchner, V. F., 'Stilfiguren in der panegyrischen Poesie der Perser', *Acta Orient.*, 2 (1924), 250–61.
Doerfer, Gerhard, *Türkische and mongolische Elemente im Neupersischen unter besonderer Berücksichtigung ältester neupersischer Geschichtsquellen, vor allem der Mongolen- und Timuridenzeit*, 3 vols. (Wiesbaden 1963–67, to be continued). (Cf. 'Prolegomena', *CAJ*, 5/1, 1959, 1–26.)
Freyman, A. A., 'Zadachi iranskoy filologii', *IAN OLY*, 5 (1946), 373–86.
Frye, R. N., 'The New-Persian Renaissance in Western Iran', in *Arabic and Islamic Studies in Honor of Hamilton A.R. Gibb* (Leiden 1965), 225–31.
Fück, J., 'Arabiya. Untersuchungen zur arabischen Sprach- und Stilgeschichte', *ASAW*, phil.-hist. XLV/1 (Leipzig 1950) (on: Ibn Mufarrigh, Ibnu'l-Muqaffa', Laylā wa Majnūn).
Furūghī, Muḥ. Ḥusayn "Dhukā'u'l-mulk" (d. 1325/1907), *'Ilm-i badī'* (124 pp.) together with a course on Persian literature (353 pp.), ed. by Muḥ.-'Alī Furūghī, lith. (*s.l.* 1335/1916).

Garakānī, Muḥ. Ḥus., *Abdaʿu'l-badāyiʿ dar fann-i badīʿ*, lith. (*s.l.* 1328/1910).
Garcin de Tassy, *Rhétorique et prosodie des langues de l'Orient musulman*, 2nd ed. (Paris 1873).
Goldziher, I., 'Hyperbolische Typen im Arabischen', *ZfA*, 7 (1892), 288–304; 17 (1902), 53–9.
Grunebaum, G. E. von, 'The Concept of Plagiarism in Arabic Theory', *Journal of Near Eastern Stud.*, 3 (1944), 234–53.
——, 'On the Origin and Early Development of Arabic *muzdawij*-Poetry', *ibid.*, 3 (1944), 9 *et seq.*
——, 'The Response to Nature in Arabic Poetry, *ibid.*, 4 (1945), 137–51.
——, 'The Aesthetic Foundation of Arabic Literature', *Comparative Literature*, 4 (1952), 323–40.
——, *A Tenth-century Document of Arabic Literary Theory and Criticism. The sections on poetry of al-Bâqillânî's Iʿjâz al-Qur'ân* (Chicago 1950).
——, Most of these studies also publ. in German: *Kritik und Dichtkunst* (Wiesbaden 1955).
Ḥālī, A. H., *Muqaddima-i shiʿr va shāʿirī.* With notes and introd. by V. Qurayshī (Lahore 1953).
Humā'ī, Jalālu'd-dīn, 'Ghazal va taḥavvul-i iṣṭilāḥī-i ān', *Yaghmā*, 13/2 (1339), 77–83.
Jhaveri, Krishnalal Mohanlal, *Outlines of Persian Prosody with Figures of Speech*, 2nd ed. (Bombay 1922).
al-Jurjānī, ʿAbdalqāhir, *Asrār al-balāgha. The Mysteries of Eloquence*, ed. by H. Ritter (Istanbul 1954) (Univ.).
——, *Die Geheimnisse der Wortkunst (Asrār al-balāġa) des ʿAbdalqāhir al-Curcānī.* Aus dem Arab. übers. von H. Ritter. (Bibl. Isl., 19) (Wiesbaden 1959). ("The most important and most original work on rhetorics and poetics that the Islamic Orient brought forth.")
Khānlarī, Parvīz Nātil, *Taḥqīq-i intiqādī dar ʿarūḍ-i fārsī va chigūnagī-i taḥavvul-i auzān-i ghazal* (Tehran 1327) (Univ.).
——, *Vazn-i shiʿr-i fārsī* (Tehran 1337; 1345) (Univ.).
Khānlarī, Mrs. Dr. Zahrā, *Rāhnamā-i adabiyyāt-i fārsī* (Tehran 1341).
Khaṭībī, Ḥusayn, *Ta'rīkh-i taṭavvur-i nathr-i fannī dar qarn-i shashum va haftum-i hijrī* (Tehran 1344) (Univ.).
Köprülü, M. Fuad, 'Yeni fârisîde türk unsurları', *TM*, 7–8 (1940-2), cüz 1, 1–16.
——, 'Arûz', *İA*, 1, 634b–653b.
Lazard, Gilb., 'Dialectologie de la langue persane d'après les textes des Xme et XIme siècles', *NDAT*, 13/2 (1340), 1–18 (=(Persian) *ibid.*, 129–45; =(Russian) *NAA*, 1961/4, 176–81).
——, *La langue des plus anciens monuments de la prose persane* (Paris 1963).
Maḥjūb, M. J., *Sabk-i Khurāsānī dar shiʿr-i fārsī* [Up to the 5th/11th cent.] (Tehran 1345).
Marr, Y. N., 'Vïrazheniye fonetiki stikha v persidskom pis'me', *IAN OON*, 1934, 137–78.
——, 'Stikhotvornïy razmer Shakh-nama', in *Stat'i* (B VIa *s.v.* 'Marr'), II (1939), 55–76.
Musul'mankov, R., *Sadzh' i yego istoricheskoye razvitiye v tadzhikskoy proze* (Autoreferat dissertatsii) (Dushanbe 1966).
Nashāṭ, S. Maḥm., *Zīb-i sukhan yā ʿilm-i badīʿ-i pārsī*, 1 (Tehran 1342).
Navā'ī, Māhyār, 'Lahja-i Shīrāzī tā qarn-i nuhum-i hijrī', *NDAT*, 17/1 (1344), 77–90.
Nikitina, V. B., 'K probleme stanovleniya didakticheskikh zhanrov v tadzhiksko-persidskom avtorskom pismennom tvorchestve', in *Iranskaya filologiya* (B VI a), 111–20.
Nöldeke, Th., 'Über den vokalischen Nachhall im Persischen', *Beitr. zur vergl. Sprachforschung*, 2 (1861), 494 *et seq.*
Oranskiy, I. M., *Vvedeniye v iranskuyu filologiyu*, red. A. A. Freyman (Moscow 1960).
——, *Iranskiye yazïki* (Moscow 1963).
ar-Rādūyānī, Muḥ. b. ʿUmar, *Kitāb Tarcumān al-balāġa*, ed. by Ahmed Ateş (Istanbul 1949).
Riḍā-qulī-Khān "Hidāyat", *Madāriju'l-balāgha dar ʿilm-i badīʿ*, lith. (Shiraz 1331/1912).
Rijā'ī, Muḥ. Khalīl, *Maʿālimu'l-balāgha dar ʿilm-i maʿānī u bayān u badīʿ* (Shiraz 1340).
Rückert, Friedr., *Grammatik, Poetik und Rhetorik der Perser*, neu hrsg. von W. Pertsch (Gotha 1874). Cf. Fleischer, *ZDMG*, 31, 563 *et seq.*; 32, 225 *et seq.*

Rypka, J., 'Über die Maʿrúf- und Mağhúl-Vokale im Reime von Niẓámís Haft Pajkar', in *Charisteria Guilelmo Mathesio ... oblata* (Prague 1932), 48–53.

——, 'La métrique du mutaqárib épique persan', *Travaux du Cercle Linguistique de Prague*, 6 (1936), 192–207. (Also Persian transl. in the periodical *Bākhtar*, Isfahan, 1334).

Shajīʿī Pūrān, *Sabk-i shiʿr-i pārsī dar advār-i mukhtalif*, 1': *Sabk-i Khurāsānī* (Shiraz 1340).

Shams-i Qays (Shamsu'd-dīn Muḥ. b. Qays ar-Rāzī), *al-Muʿjam fī maʿāyiri ashʿāri'l-ʿAjam*. "*A Treatise on the Prosody and Poetic Art of the Iranians*", ed. by Mīrzā Muḥ. Qazvīnī (1909) (*GMS*, 10). – Ed. by Mudarris Raḍavī (Tehran 1314; 2nd ed. 1338).

Sharafu'd-dīn Rāmī, *Anīsu'l-ʿushshāq*, ed. by 'Abb. Iqbāl (Tehran 1325). French tr.: *Traité des termes figurés relatifs à la description de la beauté*, trad. par Cl. Huart (Paris 1875).

Sipihr, Muḥ. Taqī, *Barāhīnu'l-ʿAjam fī qavānīni'l-Muʿjam*, lith. (Tehran 1272/1855).

Sirus, B. I., 'Rifma v tadzhikskoy poezii', *AN Tadzh. SSR, Inst. yaz. i lit. Trudī* (Stalinabad 1953) bibliography on poetics).

——, *Aruzi tojikī. (Tahqiqi intiqodī)* (Dushanbe 1963).

Umīd, M., 'Khusravānī va lāsakivī', *Yaghmā*, 13/10 (1339), 499–505.

Vaḥīd Tabrīzī, *Risāla-i jamʿ-i mukhtaṣar (Traktat o poetike)*, ed. by A. Ye. Bertel's (Moscow 1959) (Cf. *SV*, 1956/2, 77–82).

Zarrīnkūb, 'Abdu'l-Ḥusayn, *Naqd-i adabī* (Tehran 1338).

V. HISTORY OF LITERATURE

Arberry, A. J., 'Persian Literature', in *The Legacy of Persia* (B VIa), 199–229.

——, *Classical Persian Literature* (London 1958).

Badīʿu'z-zamān Bushrūya'ī (Furūzānfar), *Sukhan va sukhanvarān*, 2 vols. (Tehran 1308–12).

Bausani, Alessandro, *Storia delle letterature del Pakistan* (Milano 1958). (See also *s.v.* 'Pagliaro'.)

Bertel's, Y. E., *Ocherk istorii persidskoy literaturī* (1928) (Len. Vost. Inst.).

——, *Izbrannïye trudī: Istoriya persidsko-tadzhikskoy literaturī* (Moscow 1960) (until the end of the 12th cent. A.D.).

Bombaci, Alessio, *Storia della letteratura turca dall'antico impero di Mongolia all'odierna Turchia* (Milano 1956; 1962).

Braginskiy, I. and Komissarov, D., *Persidskaya literatura* (Moscow 1963).

Brockelmann, C., *Geschichte der arabischen Literatur*. 2., den Supplementbänden angepaßte Aufl., 2 vols. (Leiden 1943–44). Supplement-Bände 3 vols. (Leiden 1937–42).

Browne, E. G., *A Literary History of Persia*, I: *until Firdawsí* (London 1902); II: *to Saʿdí* (London 1906); III: *Tartar Dominion (1265–1502)* (Cambridge 1920); IV: *Modern Times (1500–1924)* (Cambridge 1924) (several reprints). In Persian: *Ta'rīkh-i adabiyyāt-i Īrān*, I, tr. by 'Alī-Pāshā Ṣāliḥ (Tehran 1334; 1342); II, tr. by Fatḥu'llāh Mujtabā'ī (Murvārīd) (Tehran 1341; 1342); III, tr. by 'A.-A. Ḥikmat (Tehran 1327); IV, *Gulzār-i adabiyyāt-i Īrān dar ʿaṣr-i salāṭīn-i Ṣafavī*, I, tr. by Sayfpūr Fāṭimī (Isfahan 1310); *Ta'rīkh-i adabiyyāt-i Īrān az āghāz-i ʿahd-i Ṣafaviyya tā zamān-i ḥāḍir*, tr. by Rashīd Yāsimī, 2nd ed. (Tehran 1329). In Arabic: II, tr. by Ibr. Amin Shawarby (Oxford 1954).

Ceadel, E. B. (ed.), *Literatures of the East. An Appreciation*. Intr. by A. J. Arberry (1953). (Among others: J. Gershevitch, 'Iranian Literature'.)

Ethé, Hermann, 'Neupersische Literatur', in *GIPh*, II, 212–368. Persian tr. by Riḍā-zāda Shafaq (Tehran 1337).

Gabrieli, Fr., 'Sguardo alla letteratura persiana', in *Storia e civiltà musulmana* (Napoli 1947), 128–45.

——, 'Letteratura persiana', in *Le civiltà dell'Oriente*, II (Roma 1957), 345–94.

Gibb, E. J. W., *A History of Ottoman Poetry*, 6 vols. (London 1900–9).

Hammer-Purgstall, J. von, *Geschichte der schönen Redekünste Persiens, mit e. Blütenlese aus 200 persischen Dichtern* (Wien 1818). (Antiquated, but by no means without value.)

Hāshimī, Muḥ. Ṣadr, *Shi'r va shā'irī dar 'aṣr-i Ṣafavī*, 3rd ed. (Isfahan 1341) (Univ.).

Horn, Paul, *Geschichte der persischen Literatur*, 2nd ed. (Leipzig 1909).

Humā'ī, Jalālu'd-dīn, *Ta'rīkh-i adabiyyāt-i Īrān*, 2 vols. (Tabriz 1348/1929); 2nd ed., in 1 vol. (Tehran 1340).

Iqbāl Āshtiyānī, 'Abbās, *Ta'rīkh-i adabī* (A series of articles) (Dānishkada 1297).

Kātibī, Ḥusayn-qulī, *Ta'rīkh-i mukhtaṣar-i nathr-i fārsī* (Tabriz 1327).

Kégl, S., 'Perzsia. A perzsa irodalom története' [History of Persian literature], in *Egyetemes Irodalomtörténet* [General History of Literature] (Budapest 1903), IV, 329–62.

Krïmskiy, A., *Istoriya Persii, yeyo literaturï i dervisheskoy teosofii*, I, 1-2, 4: 3rd ed. (Moscow 1909, 1916); II, lith. (1912); III, (1914–7) (Lazar. Inst., 16). A voluminous, "extremely valuable text-book" (Bertel's), particularly in the bibliographical sections, but unfinished.

Krïms'kïy, A., *Istoriya Persiyi ta yiyi pïs'menstva*, I: *IX. ta X. vv.* (Kiev 1923).

Levy, R., *Persian Literature, an Introduction* (London 1923).

Massé, H., '*Adabiyyāt-i fārsī*' tr. by 'A.-A. Ḥikmat, in *Mélanges Massé* (Tehran 1963), 35*–62*.

Nafīsī, S., 'Ta'rīkhcha-i mukhtaṣar-i adabiyyāt-i Īrān', *Sāl-nāma-i Pārs* (1321).

——, *Ta'rīkh-i naẓm u nathr dar Īrān va dar zabān-i fārsī tā pāyān-i qarn-i dahum-i hijrī*, 2 vols. (Tehran 1344).

Orient. Art et littérature en Iran (Paris 1964).

Osmanov, M. N., 'Iz istorii literaturï narodov Khorasana i Maverannakhra VIII–IX vv.', *SV*, 1956/2, 105–18.

Pagliaro, A. and Bausani, A., *Storia della letteratura persiana* (Milano 1960).

Pizzi, I., *Manuale di letteratura persiana* (Milano 1887).

——, *Storia della poesia persiana*, 2 vols. (Torino 1894).

Rypka, J., unter Mitarbeit von Ot. Klíma, V. Kubíčková, J. Bečka, J. Cejpek, Ivan Hrbek, *Iranische Literaturgeschichte* (Leipzig 1959).

——, *Dějiny perské a tádžické literatury*, 2nd, enlarged ed., ed. by J. Rypka, with the collaboration of the same and F. Tauer and J. Marek (Prague 1963).

Ṣafā, Dhabīḥu'llāh, *Ta'rīkh-i adabiyyāt dar Īrān*, I: *Az āghāz-i 'ahd-i islāmī tā daura-i Saljūqī* (Tehran 1332); II: *Az miyāna-i qarn-i panjum tā āghāz-i qarn-i haftum-i hijrī* (Tehran 1336; 1339); III/1: *Az avā'il-i qarn-i haftum tā avākhir-i qarn-i hashtum-i hijrī* (Tehran 1341).

Shafaq, Riḍā-zāda, *Ta'rīkh-i adabiyyāt-i Īrān barā-i dabīristānhā*, 2nd ed. (Tehran 1321).

Shiblī Nu'mānī, *Shi'ru'l-'Ajam* [in Urdu], 5 vols. (Lahore 1924). In Persian: tr. by Muḥ. Taqī Fakhr-i Dā'ī Gīlānī (Tehran, I: 1316, 1335; II: 1327, 1339; III: 1335; IV: 1314, 1337; V: 1318). III, tr. by Sarvar-Khān (Kabul 1315).

Storey, C. A., *Persian Literature. A Bio-Bibliographical Survey.* I/1: *Quran, History* (London 1927–39); I/2: *Biography, Additions and Corrections, Indices* (London 1953); II/1: *Mathematics*, etc. (London 1958).

Tarlan, A. N., *Iran edebiyatı* (Dünya edebiyatına toplu bakışlar, 4) (Istanbul 1944).

Zand, M. I., *Shest' vekov slavï. Ocherki persidsko-tadzhikskoy literaturï* (Moscow 1964).

Zarre, Abu-'l-Kasim, 'Ocherk literaturï Irana', in *Lit. Irana* (B VIa), 23–71.

VI. LITERATURE

a. *General Works*

Ādamiyyat, Muḥ. Ḥus. Rukn-zāda, *Dānishmandān va sukhan-sarāyān-i Fārs*, 4 vols. (Tehran 1337–40).

"'Ajab-nāma". *A Volume of Oriental Studies presented to E. G. Browne* (Cambridge 1922).
L'Ame de l'Iran, Sous la direction de R. Grousset, L. Massignon, H. Massé (Paris 1951).
Arberry, A. J., *Immortal Rose. An Anthology of Persian Lyrics* (London 1948).
Ateş, Ahm., 'Hicrî VI.–VIII. (XII.–XIV.) asırlarda Anadolu'da farsça eserler', *TM*, 7–8 (1945), cüz II, 94–135.
Bahār, Maliku'sh-shu'arā Muḥ. Taqī, 'Bāz-gasht-i adabī', *Arm.* 13 (1311), 441–8 and 3 continuations; 14 (1312), 57–69.
——, 'Baḥth-i intiqādī u adabī u ijtimā'ī', *Arm.*, 17 (1315), 181–8, 254-62.
Bajraktarević, F., 'Dve arapske ljubavne pripovetke i njichovi odjeci u svetskoj književnosti' [Two Arabic love-stories and their echo in world literature], *Zbornik fil. fak.*, IV-2 (Beograd 1959), 97–115.
Bašagić, Safvet Beg, *Bošnjaci i Hercegovci u islamskoj književnosti* (Sarajevo 1912).
Bashīr Ḥusayn, Muḥ., 'Tarjama-i manẓūm-i āthār-i fārsī ba-zabān-i urdū', *RK*, 6 (1342), 395–404; 7/2 (1343), 289–95.
Bertel's, Ye. E., 'Rukopisnaya antologiya poetov Kainata v Aziatskom Muzeye', *DAN-B* (1926), 63–6 (see B VIb, *s.v.* 'Āyatī').
——, 'Osnovnïye momentï v razvitii sufiyskoy poezii', *Or. Mem.*, I (*Sb. Ol'denburg*) (1927), 91–103.
——, 'Grundlinien der Entwicklungsgeschichte des ṣūfischen Lehrgedichts in Persien', *Islamica*, 3 (1927), 1–35.
——, *Persidskaya poeziya v Bukhare. X. vek.* (Moscow-Leningrad 1935).
——, 'K voprosu ob "indiyskom stile" v persidskoy poezii', in *Charisteria* (*q.v.*), 56–9.
Boldïrev, A. N., 'Novopersidskiye obrabotki epicheskikh predaniy v zapadnom Irane', *KS*, 67 (1963), 127–35.
Boldïrev, A. N. and I. S. Braginskiy, 'Soobrazheniya o periodizatsii persidsko-tadzhikskoy literaturï', *NAA*, 1965/2, 101–10.
Bowen, J. C. E., *Poems from the Persian.* With a pref. by S. H. Taqizadeh, 3rd ed. (1964).
Braginskiy, I. S., 'O vozniknovenii gazeli v tadzhikskoy i persidskoy literature', *SV*, 1958/2, 94–100.
——, 'K probleme periodizatsii istorii persidskoy i tadzhikskoy literatur', *Trudï XXV mezhdun. kongr. vostokovedov*, II (Moscow 1963), 349–56.
Browne, E. G., 'Some Notes on the Poets in the Persian Dialects', *JRAS*, 1895, 773–825.
Charisteria Orientalia praecipue ad Persiam pertinentia. Ioanni Rypka... hoc volumen sacrum. Edid. F. Tauer, V. Kubíčková, Iv. Hrbek (Prague 1956).
Christensen, A., *Hofdigtning og Digterhoffer hos Perserne* (Copenhagen 1905).
——, 'Lidt persisk Folkspsykologi', *Geogr. Tidskrift* (Copenhagen 1914).
Chukaszyan, B. L., *Armyano-iranskiye literarnïye svyazi (V.–XVIII. vv.)* (Yerevan 1963).
Dagher, J. A., *L'Orient dans la littérature française d'après guerre 1919–1933* (Beyrouth 1937).
Darmesteter, J., *Les origines de la poésie persane* (Paris 1887) (BOE, 53). Russian tr. by L. I. Zhirkov, *Proiskhozhdeniye persidskoy poezii* (Moscow 1924). English tr. by Nasarwandji Framji Tamboli (Bombay 1888).
Daudpota, Umar Muhammad, *The Influence of Arabic Poetry on the Development of Persian Poetry* (Bombay 1934).
Eberman, V. A., 'Persï sredi arabskikh poetov epokhi Omeyyadov', *ZKV*, 2 (1927), 113–53.
Falsafī, Naṣru'llāh, *Hasht maqāla-i ta'rīkhī va adabī* (Tehran 1330) (Univ.) From the contents: Zindagānī-i shā'irān-i darbārī. Chahār nāma-i tārīkhī: Malik-shāh – Ḥasan-i Ṣabbāh. Niẓāmu'l-mulk – Malik-shāh.
Fischel, W. J., 'The Bible Translation in Persian', *The Harvard Theol. Rev.*, 45 (1952), 1–45.
——, 'Tarjamahā-i fārsī-i taurāt va injīl', *RK*, 2/3 (1338), 674–80; 3/1 (1339), 17–23; 3/2 (1339), 168–75. See also B VIb, *s.v.* 'Dānish-puzhūh'.

——, 'The Beginnings of Judeo-Persian Literature', in *Mélanges Massé* (Tehran 1963), 141–50.

Frye, R. N., 'Die Wiedergeburt Persiens um die Jahrtausendwende', *Isl.*, 35 (1960), 42–51.

al-Furātī, Muḥ., *Rawā'i' min ash-shi'r al-fārsī.* [Arabic transl. from Ḥāfiẓ, Sa'dī and Rūmī by al-Furātī] (Damascus 1964).

Gabrieli, Fr., 'Problemi e forme della poesia mistica musulmana', in *Acad. Nazion. dei Lincei. XII convegno "Volta" (Oriente e Occidente nel medioevo)* (Rome 1957), 35–49.

Grünebaum, G. von, 'Eine Bemerkung zu den Anfängen neupersischer Dichtung', *WZKM*, 44 (1937), 226.

Grunebaum, G. E. von, 'The Spirit of Islam as shown in its Literature', in *Islam* (B II), 95–110. (= *Studia Islamica*, I/I, 1953, 101–19).

Gvakhariya, A. A., *Znacheniye gruzinskikh perevodov persidskikh pamyatnikov dlya osveshcheniya nekotorïkh voprosov persidsko-tadzhikskoy literaturï*, Inst. gruz. lit. AN Gruz. SSR (Tiflis 1960).

Hādī Ḥasan, *Studies in Persian Literature*, Series I (London-Aligarh 1924).

——, *Majmū'a-i maqālāt. (Khāqānī, Sām-nāma)*, with introd. by 'A. A. Ḥikmat (Hyderabad 1956).

——, *Researches in Persian Literature* (Hyderabad 1958).

Hekmat, A. A., *Glimpses of Persian Literature.* 7 lectures, Univ. of Delhi 1954/5 (1956).

Inostrantsev, K. A.: see F (= *Iranian Influence in Moslem Literature*, tr. by G. K. Nariman, Bombay 1918).

Iranskaya filologiya. Trudï nauchnoy konferentsii po iranskoy filologii (22–27 yanvarya 1962 g.) (Leningrad 1964) (Univ.).

——, *IV. vsesoyuznaya nauchnaya konferentsiya po iranskoy filologii* (*Tezisi dokladov*) (Dushanbe 1964).

——, *Iranskaya filologiya. Materialï IV. vsesoyuznoy mezhvuzovskoy nauchnoy konferentsii po iranskoy filologii (23–26 sentyabrya 1964 g.)* (Tashkent 1966).

——, *V. mezhvuzovskaya nauchnaya konferentsiya po iranskoy filologii* (*Tezisi dokladov*) (Dushanbe 1966).

Ivanow, W., 'Some Poems in the Sabzawari Dialect', *JRAS*, 1927, 1–41.

Kasravī, Aḥmad, *Maqālāt*, I, 2nd ed., ed. by Yaḥyā Dhukā (Tehran 1334) (Ṭarzī Afshār, Qaṭrān, etc.).

——, *Chihil maqāla*, ed. by Yaḥyā Dhukā (Tehran 1335).

——, *Dar pīrāmūn-i shi'r va shā'irī* (Tehran 1335) (collected and edited by someone other than Kasravī and after his assassination).

——, *Dar pīrāmūn-i adabiyyāt*, 3rd ed. (1340).

Kégl, Sándor (Alex. von Kegl), *Tanulmányok az ujabbkori perzsa irodalom történetéből* [Studies on the history of modern Persian literature] (MTA, Értekezések XV/II) (1892).

——, 'Zur Geschichte der Persischen Literatur des 19. Jahrhunderts', *ZDMG*, 47 (1893), 130–42.

al-Khalīlī, Ja'far, *Nafakhāt min khamā'il al-adab al-fārsī* (Beirut 1965). (Arabic transl. from Persian literature.)

Khānlarī, Mrs. Dr. Z., *Dāstānhā-i dil-angīz-i adabiyyāt-i fārsī* (Tehran 1337).

Khayyāmpūr, 'Abdu'r-Rasūl, *Farhang-i sukhanvarān* (Tabriz 1340).

Kishāvarz-i Ṣadr, *Az Rābi'a tā Parvīn. Zanānī ki ba-fārsī shi'r gufta and* (Tehran 1334).

Kowalski, T., *Na szlakach Islamu* (Krakow 1935).

Kuka, M. N., *The Wit and Humour of the Persians* (Bombay 1923; 1934).

Kverfel'dt, E. K. (E. Querfeldt), 'Chertï realizma v risunkakh na tkanyakh i kovrakh vremeni Sefevidov', *TOV*, 3 (1940), 263–73.

Lazard, Gilb., *Les premiers poètes persans (IXe–Xe siècles), fragments rassemblés, édités et traduits*, tome I: *Introd. et trad. française*; tome II: *Textes persans* (Tehran–Paris 1964).

Legacy of Persia, The, ed. by A. J. Arberry (Oxford 1953). Persian tr.: *Mīrāth-i Īrān* (Tehran 1337).

Levy, R., 'Persia and the Arabs', in *The Legacy of Persia* (*q.v.*), 60–88.

Literatura Irana X–XV vv. (*Vostok*, sbornik vtoroy) (Moscow-Leningrad 1935).

Maḥjūb, M. J., 'Mathnavī-sarā'ī dar zabān-i fārsī tā pāyān-i qarn-i panjum-i hijrī', *NDAT*, 15 (1342), 182–213, 261–85.

Majewska, Barbara, 'Tematyka polska w wydawnictwach irańskich', *Przegl. Or.*, 4 (8) (1953), 256–9.

Marr, Y. N., *Stat'i, soobshcheniya i rezyume dokladov* (Trudï Inst. yazïka i mïshleniya), 2 vols. (Moscow 1936–9).

Massé, Henri, *Anthologie Persane (XIe–XIXe siècles)* (Paris 1950).

Massignon, L., 'La nature dans la pensée islamique', *Eranos-Jahrbuch*, 14 (1946) (Zürich 1947), 144–8.

Minorsky, V., 'Some Early Documents in Persian', *JRAS*, 1942, Part 3, 181–94; 1943, Part 1, 86–99.

——, *Iranica. Twenty articles* (Tehran 1964).

Mudarrisī Chahārdihī, Murt., 'Ta'thīr-i 'ilmī va adabī-i Īrān dar tāzī', *Arm.*, 18, 41–51 and 7 continuations. (Cf. *ibid.*, 17, 389–99.)

Mu'īn, Muḥ., *Bar-guzīda-i shi'r-i fārsī*, I. (3rd – 4th cent. A.H.), 2nd ed. (Tehran 1334).

——, *Mazdayasnā va ta'thīr-i ān dar adabiyyāt-i pārsī* (Tehran 1326; 1338).

Mushīr-i Salīmī, 'Alī Akbar, *Zanān-i sukhanvar*, 3 vols. (Tehran 1337).

Mu'taman, Zaynu'l-'ābidīn, *Taḥavvul-i shi'r-i fārsī* (Tehran 1339).

Ojha, D., 'Studies in Romance', *Journal Jha*, 9, 2–4, 189–238. (Ḥāfiẓ, 'Urfī, Jāmī and 'Irāqī compared with European romantic poetry of the Middle Ages.)

Orlov, R., 'Vvedeniye', in *Lit. Irana* (*q.v.*), 3–22.

Polak, J. E., *Die österreichischen Lehrer in Persien* (Vienna, Österr. Museum, 1876).

'Qaḍā u qadar', *Arm.*, 8, 120; 10, 458 and 554.

Qazvīnī, Muḥ., *Bīst maqāla*, I, ed. by Pūr-i Dāvūd (Bombay 1928); II, ed. by 'Abbās Iqbāl (Tehran 1313) (partly copied from Vol. I); 2nd ed. in 2 vols. (1332).

——, *Yād-dāshthā*, ed. by Īr. Afshār, Vols. I–VII (Tehran, since 1332) (Univ.).

Rempis, Ch. H., 'Die ältesten Dichtungen in Neupersisch', *ZDMG*, 101 (1951), 220–40.

Remy, A. F. J., *The Influence of India and Persia on the Poetry of Germany* (New York 1901).

Richter, G., *Studien zur Geschichte der ältesten arab. Fürstenspiegel* (Leipzig 1932).

Ringgren, H., *Fatalism in Persian Epics* (Uppsala–Wiesbaden 1952).

Ritter, H., 'Philologika, VII: Arabische u. persische Schriften über die profane u. die mystische Liebe', *Isl.*, 21 (1933), 84–109.

——, 'Muslim Mystics' Strife with God', *Oriens*, 5 (1952), 1–15.

Ross, E. Denison, *La prose persane. La poésie persane* (Paris 1933) (Soc. Ét. Iran., 4). Engl. tr.: *Persian Prose* (1936–8), 8 pp. (Proceedings of the Iran Soc. 1).

Rückert, F., *Orientalische Dichtung. In der Übersetzung F. Rückerts.* Herausg. und eingeleitet von Annemarie Schimmel (Bremen 1963).

Rypka, Jan, 'Forma, jako jeden ze środków prowadzących do głębszego poznanija poezji nowoperskiej', *Przegl. Or.*, 29 (1959/1), 1–17.

Ṣafā, Dhabīḥu'llāh, *Ḥamāsa-sarā'ī dar Īrān* [History of heroic poetry in Iran from the oldest times till the present day] (Tehran 1324; 1333).

——, *Ganj-i sukhan*, 3 vols. (Tehran 1339–40) (Univ.-UNESCO); 2nd ed. *Ibn-i Sīnā* (Tehran 1339–40). French transl.: *Anthologie de la poésie persane (XI–XXième siècles)*, trad. par G. Lazard, R. Lescot et H. Massé (Paris 1964). The introduction on the history of literature in Arabic: *Ad-dirāsāt al-adabyīyah*, 3 (1340), 67–102, 147–83.

——, 'Maqām-i shi'r dar zabān-i fārsī', *MDAT*, 9 (1341), 17–27.

Ṣafā'ī, Ibrāhīm, *Nahḍat-i adabī-i Īrān dar 'aṣr-i Qājār*, 2nd ed. (Tehran 1333).

Sajjādī, S. Ja'f., *Farhang-i muṣṭalaḥāt-i 'urafā-i mutaṣavvifa va shu'arā* (Tehran 1339).

Samsani, N. D., *L'Iran dans la littérature française* (Paris 1936).

Schaeder, H. H., 'Die islamische Lehre vom vollkommenen Menschen, ihre Herkunft und ihre dichterische Gestaltung', *ZDMG*, 79 (1925), 192–268; cf. *ibid.*, 78 (1924), LXXVI *et seq.*

Schimmel, A.-M., 'Rose und Nachtigall', *Numen*, 5/2 (1958), 85–109.
Spies, O., *Der Orient in der deutschen Literatur*, I (Kevelaer 1950).
Spuler, B., 'Sahm-i Ālmān dar tatabbuʿāt-i rājiʿ ba-Īrān', *Sukhan*, 13 (1341), 409–15.
——, 'La contribution allemande aux études iraniennes', in *Mélanges Massé* (Tehran 1963), 375–82.
Studia Irańskie [Études Iraniennes]. Wydawnictwo Towarzystwa Studiów Irańskich, 3 vols. (Tehran 1943–5).
Ṣūratgar, Luṭf-ʿAlī, *Tajalliyyāt-i ʿirfān dar adabiyyāt-i fārsī* (Tehran 1345) (Univ.).
Szkice z dziejów polskiej orientalistyki. Joint publ. by J. Reychman, An. Zajączkowski, *et al.* (Warsaw 1957).
Taeschner, Fr., 'Nufūdh-i shiʿr-i kilāsīk-i Īrān dar adabiyyāt-i Ālmān', *MDAT*, 4/3 (1336), 1–10.
Taqavī, S.ʿAlī Riḍā, *Tadhkira-navīsī dar Hind va Pākistān* (Tehran 1344).
Tarlan, A. N., *Çağdaş Iran Şiiri* (*s.l.* 1938).
Turkzāda, Aḥmad, *Āthār-i adabī-i Īrān ba-tarjama-i Ingilīsī* (Tehran 1342).
ʿUṭārid, 'Maẓāhir-i tanazzul-i ʿilmī va adabī baʿd az ḥamla-i Mughūl', *NDAT*, I/10 (1327), 14–32.
Vaḥīd Dastgirdī, 'Muqāyasa-i shuʿarā-i fārsī bā tāzī', *Arm.*, 4, 401–28 and contin.; 5, 130–9 and contin.
——, 'Rahbarān-i sukhan', *Arm.*, 18, 81–7 and 2 contin.
Vambéry, H., 'Aus dem Geistesleben persischer Frauen', *ZDMG*, 45 (1891), 403–28.
Világirodalmi Antológia [Anthology of world-literature], Vol. II (Budapest 1952), 268–77; Vol. V (1958), 961–8.
Voprosï iranskoy filologii. Ed. by B. M. Huseynov (Baku 1966).
Vzaimosvyazi literatur Vostoka i Zapada, ed. by I. S. Braginskiy (Moscow 1961).
Wiener, Alfred, 'Farağ baʿd aš-šidda-Literatur', *Isl.*, 4 (1913), 270–98, 387–420.
Wikander, Stig, 'Sur le fonds commun indo-iranien des épopées de la Perse et de l'Inde', *La nouv. Clio*, I (1949–50) 310–29.
Yarshater, E. (Yār-shāṭir, I.), 'The Theme of Wine-Drinking and the Concept of the Beloved in Early Persian Poetry', *Studia Islamica*, 13 (1960), 43–53.
——, *Shiʿr-i fārsī dar ʿahd-i Shāhrukh (nīma-i avval-i qarn-i nuhum) yā āghāz-i inḥiṭāṭ dar shiʿr-i fārsī* (Tehran 1334) (Univ.).
Zajączkowski, A., *Orient jako źródło inspiracji w literaturze romantycznej doby mickiewiczowskiej* (Warsaw 1955).
Zand, M. I., 'Iskusstvo perevoda v tadzhikskoy poezii X v.', in *Rūdakī va zamoni ū* (B VIb, *s.v.* 'Rūdakī') (Stalinabad 1958), 152–67.
——, 'Jihathoyi falsafī dar nazmi asri X tojik', *ShS*, 1961/6, 120–9.

b. *Individual Authors: Studies and Texts*

Abdul Hai, Mohammad, 'Ibn-e-Tufayl's Story of Hayy', *Islamic Liter.*, 5/12, 357 *et seq.*
ʿAbdu'l-Vāsiʿ Jabalī, *Dīvān*, ed. by Dh. Ṣafā. I: *Qaṣīdas* (Tehran 1339); II: *Introd. and Indices* (Tehran 1341) (Univ.).
ʿAbdu'n-Naʿīm, *Niẓāmī al-Ganjavī* (Cairo 1954).
ʿĀbid, ʿAlī-khān, 'Ta'rīkh va sabab-i marg-i ʿUrfī-i Shīrāzī, I' [died of *ishāl* in 999/1590], *Vaḥīd*, 4/5 (1346), 455–8.
Abū-ʿAbdi'llāh az-Zanjānī, *Al-faylasūf al-fārisī al-kabīr: Ṣadru'd-dīn ash-Shīrāzī* (Damascus 1348/1930).
Abú Bakr ibn Tufajl, *Živý syn bdícího. Hajj ibn Jakzán*, Přel. Ivan Hrbek (Prague 1957).
Abū-Isḥāq "al-Aṭʿima", *Dīvān*, ed. by Mīrzā Ḥabīb Iṣfahānī (Istanbul 1303/1885). (Ḥikmat, 365. Cf. H. Ferté, *JA*, 1886); ≅.
Abu'l-Faraj Rūnī, *Dīvān*, ed. by [K.I.] Chāykīn (1304) (Arm.) (The first critical edition of a Persian poet ever published in Tehran).

Abû'l-Haitham Jorjânî, *Commentaire de la Qasîda ismaélienne d'– attribué à Moh. i. Sorkh de Nishapour (IVe/Xe–Ve/XIe siècles)*, ed. and comm. by H. Corbin and M. Mo'în (Bibl. Iran.) (Tehran–Paris 1955).
Abū-Sa'īd b. Abi'l-khayr, *Rubâ'îs* [92 poems]. Hrsg. und übers. von H. Ethé (München 1875–8) (Akad.); ≌.
——, *Sukhanān-i manẓūm*, ed. by S. Nafīsī (Tehran 1334).
——, *Abu Sajid Fadlullah ben Abulchajr i tegoż czterowiersze, przełożył z perskiego Damian Rolicz-Lieder* (Kraków 1895).
Ādamiyyat, Farīdūn, 'Andīshahā-i Ṭālibūf', *Sukhan*, 16 (1345), 454–64, 549–63, 691–701, 815–35.
Adīb Nīshāpūrī, *La'ālī-i maknūn yā dīvān-i* —, ed. by 'Alī Zarrīn-qalam (Tehran 1334–5).
Adīb Ṣābir Tirmidhī, *Dīvān*, ed. by 'Alī Qavīm (Tehran 1334). See *infra*, p. 800.
Adīb-Ṭūsī, Muḥ. Amīn, 'Tarānahā-i maḥallī', *NDAT*, 5/1 (1332), 49–101; 5/2, 138–68.
——, 'Fahlaviyyāt-i al-Mu'jam', *ibid.*, 6 (1333), 471–8.
——, 'Namūnaī chand az fahlaviyyāt', *ibid.*, 7 (1334), 251–73.
——, 'Fahlaviyyāt-i zabān-i ādharī dar qarn-i hashtum va nuhum', *ibid.*, 7 (1335), 460–82.
——, 'Muthallathāt-i Shaykh Sa'dī', [Arabic–Persian–Kāzirūnī], *ibid.*, 7 (1334), 157–89.
——, 'Fahlaviyyāt-i Maghribī-i Tabrīzī', *ibid.*, 8/2 (1335), 121–37.
——, 'Fahlaviyyāt-i Lurī' [Among these also Bābā Ṭāhir], *ibid.*, 10/1 (1337), 1–16.
——, 'Du qaṣīda ba-du lahja-i nīma-ādharī?', *ibid.*, 10/4 (1337), 367–417.
——, 'Du ghazal ba-lahja-i shīrāzī va chand tarāna-i nayrīzī' [Ḥāfiẓ, ed. Qazvīnī *ghazal* 438, *istiqbāl* to Quṭbu'd-dīn Shīrāzī], *ibid.*, 11/1 (1338), 1–18.
——, 'Si ghazal-i Iṣfahānī az Auḥadī-i Marāghī', *ibid.*, 15 (1342), 387–400.
—— 'Kāh-i malāḥat', *ibid.*, 17 (1344), 18 (1345), *passim* (in the dialect of Shiraz, 9th/15th cent.).
——, 'Si guftār-i ba-lahja-i Shīrāzī', *ibid.*, 17(1344), 149–82 (9th/15th cent.).
——, *Dah maqāla* (Collection of these and other articles of the same kind in book-form).
Adību'l-mamālik, *Dīvān-i kāmil*, ed. by Vaḥīd Dastgirdī (Tehran 1312) (Arm.).
Afḍalu'd-dīn Muḥ. Maraqī Kāshānī, *Muṣannafāt*, 2 vols., ed. by M. Mīnuvī and Yaḥyā Mahdavī (Tehran 1331–7) (Univ.).
——, *Les Quatrains de Baba Afzal-ed-Din Kashani, précédés d'une étude sur la vie et l'œuvre par S. Naficy* [in Persian] (Tehran 1933).
Affifi, A. E., *The Mystical Philosophy of Muḥyid Dīn Ibnul 'Arabī* (Cambridge 1939).
Afzal Iqbal, *The Life and Thought of Rûmî* (Lahore 1956).
Ahlī Shīrāzī, *Siḥr-i ḥalāl* (s.l. and n.d.; Lucknow 1926).
——, See Hilālī.
Aḥmad 'Alí, *The Haft Āsmán or History of the Masnawí of the Persians, being an Introduction to Nizámí's Iqbálnámeh i Sikandarí*, ed. by H. Blochmann (Calcutta 1873) (BI 80).
Ahmadov, Mirza, 'Az ghazaliyoti Darveshi Dehakī', *ShS*, 1961/6, 110–9.
Ahuja, Y. D., 'Early Years of Shaykh 'Irāqī's Life', *IC*, 30/2 (1956), 95–105.
——, 'Iraqi in India', *ibid.*, 32 (1958), 57–70.
——, 'Shaykh Iraqi's travels and his stay in Rum', *ibid.*, 33 (1959), 260–77.
Akhtar, Ahmedmian, *Studies: Islamic and Oriental* (Lahore 1945). From the contents: 'A Tract of Avicenna, transl. by 'Umar-i Khayyām'; 'Sa'dī's visit to Somnath'; 'The Arabic Poetry of Ḥāfiẓ' (= *IC*, 13 (1939), 222–37 = Pearson 24686).
Ākhund-zāda: see Fatḥ-'Alī Ā.
Alf layla-i fārsī, tr. by 'Abdu'l-Laṭīf Ṭassūjī, lith., 2 vols. (Bombay 1308/1891); (Tehran 1338); ≌.
'Alī-chelebī, *Hümāyūn-nāma* [In Ottoman-Turkish] (Būlāq 1254/1838–9; Istanbul 1293/1876).
Aliyev, G. Yu., '"Shirin va Khisrav"-i Amir Khisravi Dehlavī va "Khisrav va Shirin"-i Nizomii Ganjavī', *ShS*, 1957/10, 90–104. Cf. F.
——, *Legenda o Khosrove i Shirin v literaturakh narodov Vostoka* (Moscow 1960).

—— 'Ranniye khristianskiye istochniki legendï o Khosrau i Shirin', *SV*, 1957/6, 75–96.

——, 'Legenda o Khosrove i Shirin v "Shakhname" Firdousi', *UZIV*, 19 (1958), 190–210.

——, '"Anis al-kalb" Fuzuli i traditsii filosofskoy kasïdï' (With facsimile), *KS*, 44 (1961), 13–25.

Aliyev, Rustam M., 'Osnovnïye publikatsii "Golestana" Sa'di', *KS*, 1955/17, 83–91.

——, 'Novoye izdaniye "Gulistana" Sa'di', *SV*, 1956/6, 71–82.

——, '"Gulistan" Sa'di i kritika teksta', *UZIV*, 19 (1958), 89–152.

Aliyev, R. M. and Osmanov, M. N., *Omar Khayyam* (Moscow 1959).

Aliyev, S. M., 'K voprosu o vliyanii M. F. Akhundova na obshchestvennuyu mïsl' Irana XIX v.', *NAA*, 1963/4, 118–25.

Al-Kak (?), Viktūr, 'Badī'āt az-zamān. Baḥth ta'rīkhī taḥlīlī fī maqāmāt al-Hamadhānī', *Nuṣūṣ wa durūs*, 15 (Bayrūt 1961).

'Am'aq-i Bukhārā'ī, Shihābu'd-dīn, *Dīvān* (Tabriz 1347/1928).

——, *Dīvān*, ed. by S. Nafīsī (Tehran 1339).

Amīr-Niẓām, Ḥasan-'Alī-Khān, *Munsha'āt*, lith. (Tabriz 1325/1907).

Amonov, R., 'Qabri Rūdakī yoft shud...!', *ShS*, 1956/12, 62–9.

Āmūzgār, Sayyid Ḥus., *Muqaddima-i Tuḥfatu'l-khavāṭir va zubdatu'n-navādir-i Khāqānī* (Tehran 1333).

'Andalīb-i Kāshānī, *Dīvān*, ed. by Tīrdād Andīsha (Tehran 1343).

Andersen, Hugo, 'Sasanidisk Tradition i Firdausis Kongebog', *Øst og Vest* (Copenhagen 1945), 84–93.

Anṣārī, 'Abdu'llāh, *Munājāt (shāmil-i munājāt, pand, andarz)* (Tehran 1342). See also p. 459, note 110.

Anṣārī, Sharīfu'n-nisā Begum, *Ḥayāt va taṣnīfāt-i Mīrzā Abū-Ṭālib Kalīm-ī Hamadānī* (Haydarabad 1961).

Anvarī, *Dīvān*, ≌; ed. by S. Nafīsī ([Tehran] 1337).

——, *Dīvān*, ed. by Muḥ. T. Mudarris Raḍavī, 2 vols. (Tehran 1337–40).

——, Abu'l-Ḥas. Ḥusaynī Farāhānī, *Sharḥ-i mushkilāt*, ed. by Raḍavī (Tehran 1340) (Univ.).

——, 'Anvarī va S. 'Alā'u'd-dīn-i Ghūrī', *Yādgār*, I/5 (1323–4), 73–6.

——, Z. N. Vorozheykina, 'Neizdannïye stikhotvoreniya Anvari', in *V...konferentsiya po iranskoy filologii* (B VIa), 41–3.

Araslï, G. (=H.), 'Nizami i azerbaydzhanskiy fol'klor', *Niz. Gyandzh.*, Mat., 76–91 (in Russian) =*Niz. Gyanj.*, *Sbornik statey*, 9–28 (in Azerī) (*s.v.* 'Niẓāmī').

——, '"Leyli vë Mëcnun" hakkında', *Türk Dili Araştırmaları Yıllığı, Bell.*, 1958, 17–39.

——, *Böyük Azarbayjan shairi Füzuli* (Baku 1958) =(in Russian) *Velikiy azerbaydzhanskiy poet Fizuli* (Baku 1958).

Arberry, A. J., 'Junayd', *JRAS*, 1935, 499–507.

——, 'Orient Pearls at Random Strung' [Ḥāfiẓ], *BSOAS*, 11 (1943–6), 699–712.

——, 'Omar Again', *ibid.*, 14 (1952), 413–19.

——, 'Iraqi, Mystic Poet of Iran', *Proc. Iran. Soc.*, 2 (1938–45), 32–45.

——, 'Ḥāfiẓ and his English translations', *IC*, 20 (1946), 111–28, 229–49.

——, *Fitz-Gerald's "Salámán and Absál". The Versions of 1856 and 1879 with an introduction and a literal translation* (Cambridge 1956).

——, 'An Early Persian Epic', in *Mélanges Massé* (Tehran 1963), 11–6.

'Ārifī, *Gūy u chaugān yā Ḥālnāme. "The Ball and the Polo Stick" or "Book of Ecstasy"*, ed. by R. S. Greenshields (London 1931). – *The Ball and the Polo Stick*. Tr. by the same (London 1932).

Asadī, *Garshāsp-nāma*, ed. by Ḥabīb Yaghmā'ī (Tehran 1317). French tr.: *Le Livre de Gerchâsp, poème persan d'Asadî Junior de Toûs*, publié et traduit par Clément Huart, I (Paris 1926); II, trad. par H. Massé (Paris 1951).-See also p. 435, note 7,

Aṣafī Haravī, *Dīvān*, ed. by Hādī Arfa' (Tehran 1342).

'Āshiq Iṣfahānī (1107–81/1695–1768), *Dīvān*, ed. by Ḥusayn Makkī (Tehran 1318).

Ashurov, G. A., 'Resheniye osnovnogo voprosa filosofii Nasiri Khisravom (Na osnove analiza filosofskogo traktata "Zad-al-musafirin")', *IAN OON* (Dushanbe), 1963,2, 29–40.

——, *Filosofskiye vzglyadī Nosiri Khisrava (na osnove traktata "Zad-al-musafirin")* (Dushanbe 1965).
Asín Palacios, M., *Algazel: Dogmática, Moral, Ascética* (Zaragoza 1901).
'Asjadī, Abū-Naẓar 'Abdu'l-'Azīz b. Manṣūr, *Dīvān*, ed. by Ṭāhirī Shihāb, with introd. by S. Nafīsī (Tehran 1955).
Ateş, Ahm., 'Hâkânî', *İA*, 40. cüz (1948), 85–95.
——, 'Şâhnâme'nin yazılış tarihi ve Firdevsî'nin sultan Mahmud'a yazdığı hicviye meselesi hakkında', *Belleten*, 18/70 (1954), 159–78.
——, 'Yak mathnavī-i gum-shuda az daura-i Ghaznaviyān: Varqa va Gulshāh-i 'Ayyūqī', *MDAT*, 1/4 (1335), 1–13.
——, 'Farrukhī chi zamān ba-Chaghāniyān raft?', *MDAT*, 1339, 1–12 = (in Turkish) *ŞM*, 4(1961), 23–32.
——, 'Recueil de lettres de Xāqānī-i Şirwānī (munṣa'āt-i Xāqānī)', in *Trudī XXV. mezhdunar. kongressa vostokovedov*, II (Moscow 1963), 356–62. Cf. also Y. E. Bertel's, *Trudī* (Moscow 1962), 82–5.
Athīru'd-dīn Akhsīkatī, *Dīvān*, ed. by Ruknu'd-dīn Humāyūn-farrukh (Tehran 1337).
'Aṭṭār, *Kulliyyāt*, lith. (Lucknow 1872).
——, *Dīvān* (without the quatrains), ed. by S. Nafīsī (Tehran 1319; 3rd ed. 1339); ed. by T. Tafaḍḍulī (Tehran 1341; 1345).
——, *Mukhtār-nāma* (Quatrains, in the *Kulliyyāt*).
——, *Manṭiqu't-ṭayr*, ≅; ed. by Muḥ. Javād Mashkūr (Tehran 1337; 1341); ed. by S. Ṣādiq Gauharīn (Tehran 1342). – Tr. into Persian prose by Ni'matu'llāh Qāḍī (Shakīb) (Tehran 1343). – *Mantic Uttaïr; ou, Le langage des oiseaux, poème de philosophie religieuse, publié en persan par M. Garcin de Tassy* (Paris 1857). – Tr. by the same (Paris 1863). – *The Bird-Parliament*, tr. by E. Fitz-Gerald (Boston 1899). – *The Conference of the Birds: a Sufi Allegory*, being an Abridged Version by R. P. *Masani* (London 1924). – *Mantiq-ut-Tayīr*. Utg. (anast. reprint of the text-ed. by Garcin de Tassy) och öfversatt af E. Hermelin, 2 vols. (Stockholm 1929). – Turkish translations etc. mentioned by Agâh Sırrı Levend: *Gülşehrī, Manṭiqu't-ṭayr* (Ankara 1957), 15–26. – The most recent tr. by A. Gölpınarlı (Istanbul 1944).
——, *Ilahi-name. Die Gespräche des Königs mit seinen sechs Söhnen. Eine mystische Dichtung*, ed. by H. Ritter (Bibl. Isl., 12) (Istanbul 1940). – Ed. by F. Rūḥānī (Tehran 1340). – *Le livre divin*, trad. par F. Rouhani (Paris 1961).
——, *Ushtur-nāma*, ed. by Mahdī Muḥaqqiq (Tehran 1340).
——, *Khusrau-nāma*, ed. by Aḥm. Suhaylī Khvānsārī (Tehran 1340).
——, *Bulbul-nāma, Nuzhatu'l-aḥbāb, Miftāḥu'l-futūḥ*, lith. ([Tehran] 1312). – 'Kniga o solov'ye. Perevod: Y. E. Bertel's', *Vostok*, 1923/2, 5 *et seq*.
——, *Muṣībat-nāma*, ed. by Nūrānī Viṣāl (Tehran 1338). – Turkish tr. by Pīr Meḥemmed b. Yūsuf by order of Murād II.
——, *Asrār-nāma*, lith. (Tehran 1298/1880). – Ed. by Ṣādiq Gauharīn (Tehran 1338) (emendations *RK*, 2/5, 1338, 716–24).
——, *Bī-sar-nāma*, lith. (Tehran 1312).
——, *Pand-namèh, ou Le livre des conseils*..., traduit et publié par... Silvestre de Sacy (Paris 1819). – *Pand-nāma*, lithographs and translations: see Ethé (B V) 287, Arb. (B I). – *Pand-Nâmah*. Utg. (anast. reprint of the text-ed. by Silvestre de Sacy) och öfversatt och öfverförd till Romersk skrift af E. Hermelin, 2 vols. (Stockholm 1929).
——, *Maẓharu'l-'ajā'ib*, lith. (Tehran 1323/1905–6; 1345).
——, *Maẓharu'l-'ajā'ib* and *Maẓharu'l-asrār*. Ed. by Aḥm. Khvashnuvīs ('Imād) (Tehran 1344).
——, *Lisānu'l-ghayb* (together with *Miftāḥu'l-irāda*). Ed. by Aḥm. Khvashnuvīs ('Imād) (Tehran 1344).
——, *Tadhkiratu'l-Awliyá ("Memoirs of the Saints")*, ed. by R. A. Nicholson. With a critical intro-

duction by Muḥ. Qazwíní, 2 vols. (London–Leiden 1905–7). – Abridged and tr. into English by B. Behari (Lahore 1961). – Swedish tr. by E. Hermelin (1931–2). – Paul Klappstein, *Vier turkestanische Heilige, ein Beitrag zum Verständnis der islam. Mystik* (Türk. Bibl., 20) (Berlin 1919). – Jakob Hallauer, *Die Vita des Ibrahim b. Edhem, eine isl. Heiligenlegende* (Türk. Bibl., 24) (Leipzig 1925). Review by H. H. Schaeder, *Islamica*, 3 (1927), 282–94.

——, *Muslim Saints and Mystics. Episodes from the Tadhkirat al-Auliyā'* (*'Memorial of the Saints'*). Transl. by A. J. Arberry (London 1966).

Aubin, J., *Matériaux pour la biographie de Shâh Ni'matullâh Walî Kermânî.* Textes pers. avec une introd. (Bibl. iran., 7) (Theran-Paris 1956). See also *s.v.* 'Nūr-bakhsh'.

'Aufī, *Javāmi'u'l-ḥikāyāt va lavāmi'u'r-rivāyāt* [*Muntakhab* for high schools by Muḥ. T. Bahār], 1 (Tehran 1324). – Ed. by Muḥ. Mu'īn, 1 (Tehran 1335) (Univ.); (1340).

——, Niẓámu'ddín, Muḥ., *Introduction to the Jawámi'u'l-Ḥikáyát wa Lawámi'u'r-Riwáyát, a Critical Study of its Scope, Sources and Value* (London 1929).

——, *The Lubábu'l-albáb*, ed. by E. G. Browne and Muḥ. Qazvīnī, 2 vols. (London–Leiden 1903–6). – Ed. by S. Nafīsī. With *ta'līqāt* (Tehran 1334–5).

Auḥadī Iṣfahānī, *Jām-i Jam*, ed. by Vaḥīd Dastgirdī (Tehran 1307) (Arm.).

——, *Kulliyyāt*, ed. by S. Nafīsī (Tehran 1340).

——, *Dīvān*, ed. by Ḥamīd Sa'ādat (Tehran 1340). – Ed. by Sayyid Yūsha' (Univ. Madras 1951).

——, *Khulāṣa-i aḥvāl va muntakhab-i āthār ... va mathnavī-i Manṭiqu'l-'ushshāq yā Dah-nāma-i Auḥadī*, ed. by Maḥm. Farrukh (Mashhad 1335).

Avicenna, *Majmuayi she'rho*, with introd. by M. Zand (Stalinabad 1953) (Akad. Tadzh. SSR).

Āyatī Bīrjandī, Ḥājj Shaykh Muḥ. Ḥus., *Bahāristān dar ta'rīkh va tarjama-i rijāl-i Qā'ināt* (Tehran 1327).

Aynī, K. S., 'Rukopisnïye redaktsii proizvedeniy Badriddina Khilali', *Akhborot*, 1955/7, 29–49.

——, *Badriddin Khiloli* (Stalinabad 1957) (Bibliography, 191–8).

——, 'K izucheniyu klassicheskogo persidsko-tadzhikskogo eposa (ob unikal'noy rukopisi "Shakhriyarname")', *XXV mezhdunar. kongress vostokovedov. Dokladï delegatsii SSSR* (Moscow 1963) = (in Persian) *SSh*, 1964/8, 145–8.

Aynī, S., 'Ustod Rudakī', *ShS*, 1940/2-3. – 'Qabri Rudakī va dehayi Rūdak', *ibid.*, 1940/5.

——, *Dar borayi Firdavsī va Shohnomayi ū* (Stalinabad-Leningrad 1940).

——, *Shaykh Muslikhiddin Sa'diyi Sherazī* (Stalinabad 1941).

——, *Shaykhurrayis Abuali Sino*, 2nd ed. (Stalinabad-Leningrad 1941).

——, 'Maqolayi Sadriddin Aynī dar borayi Kamoli Khūjandī', *ShS*, 1957/5, 70–6.

'Ayyūqī, *Varqa u Gulshāh*, ed. by Dh. Ṣafā (Tehran 1343) (Univ.).

Āzād Kābulī, Muḥ. 'Alī, 'Ḥakīm Shifā'ī', *Arm.*, 7, 553–7.

Azizqulov, J., 'Munosibati "Sindbodnoma"-i Zahirī ba ab'yoti Rudakī', *SSh*, 1966/1, 133–8.

Azraqī, *Dīvān*, ed. by S. Nafīsī (Tehran 1336).

Bābā Kūhī Shīrāzī, *Dīvān*, lith. (*s.l.* 1347/1928; Shiraz 1333). – *Dīvān-i shaykh 'Alī mashhūr ba-Bābā Kūhī*, ed. by Muḥ. Taqī Ma'rifat, 3rd ed. (ba-taṣḥīḥ-i kāmil) (Shiraz 1331).

——, 'Dva gazeli Bābā Kūkhī Shīrāzī': Y. E. Bertel's, *DRAN-B*, 1924, 59–62.

Bābā Ṭāhir, *The Lament of Bābā Ṭāhir*, ed. and tr. by E. Heron-Allen, rendered into verse by Eliz. Curtis Brenton (London 1902).

——, *Dīvān-i kāmil-i bī-naẓīr*, with biography by Rashīd Yāsimī, ed. by Vaḥīd Dastgirdī (Tehran 1306; 1311; 1333). – *Les quatrains et ghazals*, traduits en arménien par R. Abrahamian (Tehran 1930). – *Poems of a Persian Sufi*, tr. by A. J. Arberry (Cambridge 1937; Tehran 1341). – *Pláč Bábá Táhirův čili Rubá'iját Bábá Táhira Hamadání ('Urján)*. Z pers. textu Edw. Heron-Allena přel. Dr. Josef Štýbr (Brno 1938). See also bibliogr. in *Enc. of Isl.* (B 1), *s.v.*

Bacher, W., 'Sa'dî-Studien', *ZDMG*, 30 (1876), 81–106.

——, *Sa'dîs Aphorismen und Sinngedichte* (Strassburg 1879).

Badī'u'z-zamān Furūzānfar, *Risāla dar taḥqīq-i aḥvāl va zindagānī-i maulānā Jalālu'd-dīn Muḥammad mashhūr ba-Maulavī* (Tehran 1315).
——, 'Qadīmtarīn iṭṭilā' az zindagī-i Khayyām', *NDAT*, 1/8-9 (1327), 1–29.
——, 'Sa'dī va Suhravardī', in *Sa'dī-nāma* (see *s.v.* 'Sa'dī'), 71–90.
——, *Ma'ākhidh-i qiṣaṣ u tamthīlāt-i Mathnavī* (Tehran 1333) (Univ.).
——, *Aḥādīth-i Mathnavī* (Tehran 1334) (Univ.).
——, 'Shi'r va shā'irī-i Rūdakī', *MDAT*, 6/3-4 (1338), 93–116.
——, *Sharḥ-i aḥvāl va naqd va taḥlīl-i āthār-i shaykh Farīdu'd-dīn Muḥ. 'Aṭṭār-i Nīshābūrī* (Tehran 1339–40). Abridged in *Ad-dirāsāt al-adabīyah*, 3 (1340), 265–93.
——, 'Muṣībat-nāma', *RK*, 4 (1340), 832–8.
——, 'Abū-'Alī Sīnā va taṣavvuf', *Yaghmā*, 7 (1333), 105–10, 155–9.
Bahār, Muḥ. Taqī, 'Shihāb-i Turshīzī', *Arm.*, 13, 36–44 and 2 contin.
——, *Firdausī-nāma* (Tehran 1345).
Bahār-mast, Aḥmad, *Farmān-dihī-i khudāvand-i jang sipahbad Firdausī*, I (Tehran 1313).
Bahā'u'd-dīn Muḥ. al-'Āmilī "Bahā'ī", *al-Kashkūl* (Qum 1379/1959).
——, *Pand-i ahl-i dānish u hūsh ba-zabān-i gurba u mūsh* (From the contents: 'Zākānī's Mūsh u gurba', 'Bahā'ī's Nān u ḥalvā', 'Shīr u shakar', 'Nān u panīr') (Miṣr 1346/1927).
——, *Kulliyyāt-i ash'ār-i fārsī va Mūsh u gurba*, ed. by M. Tauḥīdīpūr (Tehran 1337).
——, *Kulliyyāt*, ed. by Javāhirī (Tehran 1341).
Bahā'u'd-dīn Muḥ. Valad, *Ma'ārif*, ed. by Badī'u'z-zamān Furūzānfar, I (1333); II (1339).
——, *Mathnavī-i Valadī ... ma'rūf ba Valad-nāma*, ed. by Jalāl Humā'ī (Tehran 1315).
Bahā'u'llāh, *Haft vādī, Al-kalimātu'l-maknūna, Mathnavī* ([Cairo] 1332/1913).
——, *L'oeuvre de Bahaou'llāh. La très sainte tablette. Les paroles cachées. Les sept vallées du voyage vers Dieu. La lettre sur le Bayan*, trad. franç. p. H. Dreyfus (Paris 1923). – *Verborgene Worte. Worte der Weisheit. Gebete*, aus dem Englischen von Alice T. Schwarz u. Wilh. Herrigel, 3rd ed. (Stuttgart 1924). – *The Hidden Words of Baha'ullah*, transl. by Shoghi Effendi (London 1932).
——, Numerous editions and translations.
Bahmanyār, Aḥm., 'Zindagānī-i adabī-i Ṣāḥib b. 'Abbād', *MDAT*, 12 (1344), 237–83.
Bajraktarević, F., 'Ficdžerald i Omar Chajjam', *Strani Pregled*, I (1927), 101–14.
——, 'Firdusijev život i dela', *Srpska književna zadruga* (1928).
——, *Uticaj istoka na Getea. Književno-naučna studija* (Beograd 1938).
——, 'Chajjâm kod nas' ['Omar Khayyām with the Serbs and Croats], with German summary, *Anali filol. fakulteta*, 3 (1963), 7–22 (Beograd 1965).
Bakhtyār-nāma of Shamsu'd-dīn Muḥ. Daqā'iqī, ed. by Vaḥīd Dastgirdī. (Tehran 1310) (Arm.). – Bertel's Y. E., *Bakhtiar-name. Persidskiy tekst i slovar'* (Leningrad 1926).
——, The same: 'Novaya versiya Bakhtiār-nāme', *IAN OGN* (1929), 249–76.
——, Transl. by W. Ouseley (London 1801; Larshall 1883). – French tr. by M. Lescallier (Paris, an XIII [1805]). – *Bəkhtiyarnamə*, tr. into Azeri by the poet Fidā'ī, ed. by G. Mammeddi (Baku 1957).
Bal'amī: see *s.v.* 'Ṭabarī'.
Bāmdād, Muḥ. 'Alī, 'Khiṭāba' (On: Adīb-i Nīshāpūrī), *Arm.*, 7, 39–51.
——, *Ḥāfiẓ-shināsī yā ilhāmāt-i khvāja*, 2nd ed. (1338).
Baqoyev, M., 'Dostoni "Duvalronī va Khizrkhon"-i Khisravi Dehlavī', *ShS* 1957/5, 84–97; 1957/6, 98–112.
——, *Khusravi Dehlavī va dostoni ū "Duvalronī va Khizrkhon"* (Stalinabad 1958).
Bārādīn (Borodin), Ch. [!] G., 'Ḥakīm Nizārī-i Quhistānī', *FĪZ*, 6/2-3 (1337), 178–203.
Bartol'd, V. V. [W. Barthold], 'K istorii persidskogo eposa', *ZVORAO*, 22 (1913), 257–82 = 'Zur Geschichte des pers. Epos', deutsch von H. H. Schaeder, *ZDMG*, 98 (23) (1944), 121–57.
——, 'To the Question of early Persian Poetry', *BSOS*, 2 (1923), 836–8. (Cf. Yuriy N. Marr, 'Zabïtaya zametka akad. V. V. Bartol'da', *IAN OON*, 1933, 264–71.)

[Barzū-nāma]: *Il primo canto del Libro di Berzo...* Versione letterale di Vittorio Rugarli (Bologna 1899).

Basirov, R., 'Rūdakī dar osori shoyironi guzashtayi tojik', *ShS*, 1956/10, 70–6.

Bāstānī Rād, Ḥusayn, 'Ḥabsiyya-i Mujīru'd-dīn-i Baylaqānī', *Yādgār*, 2/6, 55–8.

Bausani, Alessandro, 'La rappresentazione della natura del poeta persiano Ḥāfiz', *OM*, 23 (1943), 28–39.

——, 'Two unpublished Qaṣīdehs by Furūġī Bisṭāmī and his son on the Pope', *ArOr.*, 30 (1962), 559–63.

Bayānī, Mahdī, 'Yak namūna-i nathr-i fārsī az daura-i Rūdakī yā qadīmtarīn nathr-i fārsī-i maujūd', *MDAT*, 6/3-4 (1338), 57–70.

Bayburdi, Ch. G., 'Rukopisi proizvedeniy Nizārī', *KS*, 65 (1964), 13–24.

——, *Zhizn' i tvorchestvo Nizari* (Moscow 1966).

Bayḍā'ī, Partau, 'Sharḥ-i ḥāl-i ustād Ṣabāḥī-i Bīdgulī-i Kāshānī' (d. 1208/1793–4?, 1218/1803–4?), *Arm.*, 18, 109–24.

——, 'Muḥtasham-i Kāshī', *ibid.*, 18, 465–75.

Beaurecueil, S. de Laugier de, *Khwadja Abdullah Ansari* (Beyrouth 1965).

Bergh, S. van den, 'De Tempels van het Licht door Soehrawerdi', *Tijdschrift v. Wijsbegeerte*, 10 (1916), 30–59.

Bertel's, A. Y., *Nasir-i Khosrov i ismailizm* (Moscow 1959).

——, 'Rudaki i Karmatī', in *Sb. "Rūdakī va zamoni ū"* (see *s.v.* 'Rūdakī'), 63–78.

Bertel's, Yevg. E. [E. Berthels], 'Ob odnom kommentarii na gazel' 'Aṭṭāra', *DRAN-B* (1924), 187–90.

——, 'Kommentariy na gazel' 'Attara', *DRAN-B* (1924), 126–9.

——, 'Sufiyskaya kosmogoniya u Ferideddina 'Attara', *Yafet.sb.*, 3, 81–98.

——, 'Eine wertvolle Handschrift von Farīdaddīn 'Aṭṭārs Dichtungen in der Öffentlichen Bibliothek zu Leningrad', *DAN-B* (1928), 33–8.

——, 'Farīdaddīn 'Aṭṭārs Khayyāṭ-nāma', *IAN OGN* (1929), 201–14.

——, 'Avitsenna i persidskaya literatura', *IAN OON*, 1–2 (1938), 74–94.

——, *Dzhami. Epokha, zhizn', tvorchestvo* (Stalinabad 1949).

——, 'Abdurrakhman Dzhami i yego druzhba s Navoyi', *IAN OLY* (1947), No. 6, 463–74.

——, 'Ferdovsi i yego tvorchestvo', in *"Ferdovsi". Sborn. stat. IVV* (Leningrad 1935), 97–118.

——, *Abu-l'-Kasim Firdovsi i yego tvorchestvo* (AN SSSR, Leningrad–Moscow, 1935).

——, 'Arabskiye stikhi Fuẓūlī', *ZKV*, 5 (1930), 39–71.

——, 'Kosmicheskiye mifï v gazeli Bābā Kūkhī', *DRAN-B* (1925), 43–5.

——, 'Poeziya mullï Mukhsin-i Fayẓ[=ḍ]-i Kāshānī', *Iran*, 1 (1926), 1–28.

——, 'Nevāi i 'Aṭṭār', in *Sb. Mir-Ali-Shir* (Leningrad 1928), 24–82.

——, 'Navoyi i Nizami', in *Sb. Alisher Navoyi* (Moscow–Leningrad 1946), 68–91.

——, *Izbrannïye trudï: Navoi i Dzhami* (Moscow 1965).

——, *Izbrannïye trudï: Nizami i Fuzuli* (Moscow 1962).

——, 'Istochniki "Leyli i Medzhnun" Nizami', in *"Nizami"*, Sbornik pervïy (see *s.v.* 'Niẓāmī'), 57–69.

——, 'Nizami i Firdousi', in *"Nizami"*, Sbornik vtoroy (see *s.v.* 'Niẓāmī'), 38–85 (=*Izbr. trudï*, 360–93).

——, 'Nizami i yego izucheniye (k 800-letnemu yubileyu)', *SV*, 1 (1940), 95–106.

——, *Velikiy azerbaydzhanskiy poet Nizami. Epokha, zhizn', tvorchestvo* (Baku 1940).

——, *Nizami* (Moscow 1947) (Molodaya gvardiya).

——, *Nizami. Tvorcheskiy put' poeta* (AN SSSR, Moscow 1956).

——, 'Rabota nad tekstom Nizami', *Niz. Gyandzh.*, Sbornik (see *s.v.* 'Niẓāmī'), 35–50.

——, 'Poetika Nizami', in *Niz. Gyandzh., Mat.* (see *s.v.* 'Niẓāmī'), 19–25.

——, 'Literatura epokhi Nizami', *IAN OLY* (1941), No. 2, 42–57.

——, 'Politicheskiye vzglyadï Nizami', *IAN OLY* (1941), No. 2, 22–41.

——, 'Kak zvali pervuyu zhenu Nizami?', in *Sbornik statey akad. Vl.Al. Gordlevskomu*, AN SSSR OLY (1953), 64–6.
——, 'Odna iz melkikh poem Senai v rukopisi Aziatskogo Muzeya' [Sayru'l-'ibād], *DRAN-B*, 25, 39–42.
——, 'Tarzi Afshar i yego tvorchestvo', *ZIV*, 3 (1935), 101–24.
——, 'Stil' epicheskikh poem 'Unṣurī', *DAN-B* (1929), 47–53.
——, 'Khakīm 'Unṣurī iz Balkhu'; cf. *SV*, 5 (1948), 201.
——, 'Obrazets tadzhikskoy khudozhestvennoy prozï XIII v.' [Sūzanī, Ẓahīrī's Sindbād-nāma], *KS*, 9 (1953), 37–47.
——, 'Pyatoye munazare Asadi Tusskogo', *UZIV*, 19 (1958), 55–88.
Bīdil: see D IIb.
Bīghamī, Maulānā Shaykh Ḥājjī Muḥ. b. Shaykh Aḥmad b. Maulānā 'Alī b. Ḥājjī Muḥ., *Dārāb-nāma*, ed. by Dh. Ṣafā, 2 vols. (Tehran 1339–42).
Bodrogligeti, A., 'Glosses on Sayf-i Sarāyī's Gülistān bi-t-türkī', *Acta Orient. Hung.*, 14 (1962), 207–18.
Boldïrev, A. N., 'Dva shirvanskikh poeta Nizami i Khakani', in *Pamyatniki epokhi Rustaveli*, red. Y. Orbeli (Leningrad 1938) (Ermit.), 111–38.
——, 'Dīvān Darvīsh'a Dikhakī', in *Trudï XXV mezhdunar. kongr. vostokoved.*, II (Moscow 1963), 342–8. (On the poet-workman of the years 1450–90.)
——, 'Persidskiye perevodï "Madzhalis-an-nafais" Navoi', *Ucheniye zapiski Len. Gos. Univ., orient. series*, fasc. 3 (1952).
Bolotnikov, A., 'Omar Khayyam. Filosof – poet – matematik', in *Lit. Irana* (B VIa), 179–211.
Bonelli, L., 'Di una recente pubblicazione persiana' [The Muntakhab of Shaybānī (*q.v.*)], *GSAI*, 5 (1891), 167–74.
Borecký, M.: see J. Rypka.
Boyce, Mary, 'A Novel Interpretation of Ḥāfiẓ', *BSOAS*, 15/2 (1953), 279–88.
Braginskiy, I. S., 'O tvorchestve Kamola Khodzhandi', in *OITL*, 239–61.
——, 'Zum Studium des Schaffens Kamol Hudschandis', in *Akten des XXIV. Int. Or.-Kongr. München* (Wiesbaden 1959), 499–505.
——, 'K izucheniyu tvorchestva Kamol Khudzhandi', *KS*, 27 (1958), 82–7.
——, 'Tarkibi gharbī-sharqī dar lirikai Gëte va Pushkin', *ShS*, 1963/7, 137–50.
Browne, E. G.: see A. T. Wilson (B I), and Pearson, *Index Isl.* (B I).
Burdach, K., *Zur Entstehungsgeschichte des West-östlichen Diwans. Drei Akademievorträge*, hrsg. von E. Grumach (Berlin 1955).
Burhān, Āzād 'Du nukta-i marbūṭ ba-sharḥ-i ḥāl-i shaykh Bahā'ī', *Yaghmā*, 13/3 (1339), 143–6.
Burzū: see Barzū.
Buzurg, Niyā 'Alī, 'Shihāb-i Turshīzī', *Arm.*, 6, 552–7.
Caferoğlu, A., 'XIXuncu asır büyük Azerî Reformatörü Mirza-Feth-Ali Ahundzade', *Annali* (Napoli) N.S., I (1940), 69–85.
Chaykin, K. I., 'Asadi starshiy i Asadi mladshiy', in *Sb. "Ferdovsi"* (1934), 119–60.
——, 'Nur-ed-Din Abd-or-Rakhman Dzhami', in *Lit. Irana* (B VIa), 421–6.
——, 'Ferdausi', *ibid.*, 75–88.
——, 'Khakani', *ibid.*, 245–7.
——, 'Sa'di', *ibid.*, 317–20, and introduction to the translation of the Būstān.
Cheyshvili, G., 'O gruzinskom perevode "Tarikhe Naderi" Mirza Mokhammed Mehdi-khana', *Trudï Univ. Tbil.*, 108 (1964), 397–404.
Christensen, A., *En persisk Satiriker fra Mongolertiden* ['Ubayd-i Zākānī] (Copenhagen 1924).
——, 'Les facéties de Ubaïd-i Zākānī', *Acta Or.*, 1924/3, 1–37.
——, *Recherches sur les Rubā'iyāt de 'Omar Ḫayyām* (Heidelberg 1905).

——, 'Critical Studies in the Rubá'iyát of 'Umar-i Khayyám. A revised Text with Engl. Transl.', *Hist.-fil. Medd.*, 14/1 (1927).
——, Further bibliogr.: see A. T. Wilson (B I).
Churchill, Sidney, 'A Modern Contribution to Persian Literature. Rizá Kulí Khán and his works', *JRAS*, 18 (1886), 196–206; 19 (1887), 163–4.
H. Corbin, *Avicenne et le récit visionnaire*, I: *Etudes sur le cycle des récits avicenniens*; II: *Le récit de Hayy ibn Yaqzan*. Texte arabe, version et commentaire en persan... (Tehran–Paris 1954).
Coyajee, Sir J. C., *Cults and Legends of Ancient Iran and China* (Bombay [1936]).
——, *Studies in Shahnameh* (Bombay [about 1940]).
Csillik, Barth., *Les manuscripts mineurs des rubâ'iyât de 'Omar Khayyâm dans la Bibl. Nationale* (Szeged 1933).
——, *The Principal Manuscripts of the rubá'iyát of 'Umar-i Khayyám in the Bibliothèque Nationale, Paris*, Vol. I (Szeged 1934).
——, 'The real 'Omar Khayyām', *Acta Or. Hung.*, 10 (1960), 59–77.
——, "Omar Khayyām miscellanea', *ibid.*, 11 (1960), 57–68.
Dabīr Siyāqī, Muḥ. (Manūchihr), 'Labībī va ash'ār-i ū', *Mihr*, 8 (1331), 310–2 and 2 contin.; in book-form 1332.
——, 'Sindbād-nāma-i Rūdakī', *Yaghmā*, 8 (1334), 218–23 and contin.
——, *Ganj-i bāz-yāfta*, I [on Labībī, Abū Shakūr, Daqīqī, Ghaḍā'irī, etc.] (Tehran 1334).
——, *Daqīqī va ash'ār-i ū* (Tehran 1342).
Dānish-puzhūh, Muḥ. Taqī, 'Navishtahā-i Bābā Afḍal', *Mihr*, 8 (1331), 433–6, 499–507.
——, 'Tarjama-i fārsī-i shashṣad-sāla-i Taurāt', *RK*, 5 (1341), 389–94.
Dashtī, 'Alī, *Naqshī az Ḥāfiẓ* (Tehran 1337; 4th ed. Tehran 1342).
——, *Qalam-rav-i Sa'dī* (Tehran 1339). – Arabic tr. Cairo 1964.
——, *Shā'irī dīr-āshnā* [Khāqānī] (Tehran 1341).
——, *Sayrī dar dīvān-i Shams*, 3rd ed. (Tehran 1343).
——, *Damī bā Khayyām* (Tehran 1344).
Dav(v)ānī: see Jalālu'd-dīn Muḥ. Dav(v)ānī.
Dāvarī farzand-i Viṣāl-i Shīrāzī, *Dīvān-i ash'ār*, ed. by Rūḥānī Viṣāl (Shiraz 1330).
Dāvarī, Naṣru'llāh, *Dar shinākht-i 'Ubayd-i Zākānī* (Mashhad 1344).
Demidchik, V., 'Tarjimayi osori Hofiz dar Pol'sha', *ShS*, 1959/9, 131–9.
Demirtaş, Faruk K., '"Ḫusrev ü Şīrīn" ve "Ferhād ü Şīrīn" yazan şairlerimiz', *Türk Dili* (1952).
Devek, S., 'Perviy yevropeyskiy perevod iz Nizami', *NAA*, 1961/3, 157–9.
Dhukā, Yaḥyā, 'Qaṭrān va nukhustīn mamdūḥ-i ū', *Sukhan*, 14 (1343), 763–8.
Dhu'l-Faqār Shirvānī, *A Facsimile of the Manuscript B. M. Or. 9777 of Dīwān i Ẕu'l-Faḵār. The Collected Poems*, ed. by E. Edwards (London 1934)
Dhu'l-qadr, Aḥm., *Vaḥshī shā'ir-i Kavīr* (Yazd 1342).
Djafarov, Dj., *Mirza Fatali Akhoundov* (Baku 1962) (and extensive commemorative literature).
Duda, Herbert W., *Ferhād und Shīrīn. Die literarische Geschichte eines persischen Sagenstoffes* [Text and tr. of an episode in Niẓāmī's Khusrau va Shīrīn] (Prague 1933).
Dunayevskiy, Y., 'Nezami', in *Lit. Irana* (B VIa), 259–72.
Durrī, J., 'Ba'ze ma'lumot dar borayi Nizorī' (With specimina), *ShS*, 1958/9, 140–54. See also: *Izv. AN Tadzh. SSR*, 1958/1.
D'yakonov, M. M., *Ferdousi. Zhizn' i tvorchestvo* (Moscow 1940).
Ethé, H., Khusravānī, Abū-Naṣr Gīlānī, Kisā'ī, Nāṣir-i Khusrau, Persian tenzones etc.: see Ethé (B V), 223, 282, 281 *et seq.*, 229.
Fakhru'd-dīn Gurgānī, *Vīs u Rāmīn*, ed. by Mujtabā Mīnuvī, I: *Text* (Tehran 1314; 1337). – Ed. by Muḥ. Ja'far Maḥjūb (Tehran 1337). – K. H. Graf, 'Wîs und Râmîn' [Analysis of the contents and

specimina in translation], *ZDMG*, 23 (1869), 375–433. – *Le Roman de Wîs et Râmîn*, trad. par H. Massé (Coll. UNESCO) (1959). – *Vis i Ramin*. Per. S. Lipkin (Moscow 1963).

——, Sargis T'mogveli, *Visramiani*. English by Sir Oliver Wardrop (London 1914) (rev. by N. Marr, *ZKV*, 1 (1925), 118–39). – *Visramiyani. Gruzinskiy roman 12 veka i persidskaya poema 11 veka Vis i Ramin*, tr. by B. T. Rudenko and M. M. D'yakonov (Moscow–Leningrad 1938). – *Visramiani. Tekst, issledovaniye i slovar'*, ed. by A. A. Gvakhariya and M. A. Todua (Tiflis 1962) (Georgian text with parallel passages in Persian); transl. from the Old-Georgian into Russian by Ts. Yordanishvili (Tiflis 1949; 1960).

——, *Vis va Romin* (Dushanbe 1966). (In Tajik script.)

Falakī Shirvānī, *Dīvān*. Ed. by Ṭāhirī Shahāb (Tehran 1345). – See also p. 783, *s.v.* 'Hādī Ḥasan'.

Farāmurz b. Khudā-dād b. 'Abdi'llāh: see below, *s.v.* 'Ṣadaqa'.

Farhād-Mīrzā, *Munsha'āt*, lith. (Bombay 1318/1900–1).

——, *Zanbīl* [A miscellany in Arabic and Persian of own work and that of others], lith. (Tehran 1318–29/1900–11).

——, See also below, *s.v.* 'W. Pinnock'.

Farhang-i Viṣāl, 'Dhukhru's-safah 'alā-ṭibbi'l-balah', *Arm.*, 14, 433–40 and 2 contin.

——, Cf. *ibid.*, 557 *et seq.* and 664 *et seq.*

Farrukhī Sīstānī, *Dīvān*, ed. by 'Alī 'Abdu'r-Rasūlī (Tehran 1311). – Ed. by Muḥ. Dabīr Siyāqī (Tehran 1335).

Farzad, Massud, *To translate Hafez* (Tehran 1935).

——, *Chand namūna az matn-i durust-i Ḥāfiẓ* (Cairo 1942).

Faṣīḥī, Ḥusayn Iḥsān, 'Shūrīda-i Shīrāzī', *Arm.*, 9, 77–92 and contin.

Fatḥ-'Alī Ākhund-zāda, *Tamthīlāt. Tarjama-i Mīrzā Ja'far Qarājadāghī* (Tehran 1291/1874). – *Komedii* [In Russian] (Tiflis 1953). – *Trois Comédies*, publ. avec un glossaire par C. Barbier de Meynard et S. Guyard (Paris 1886). – *Persian Plays (Vukalā-i murāfa'a, Khirs-i qūldūr-bāsān, M. Žūrdān) with Literal Engl. Transl. and Vocabulary*, by A. Rogers (London–Calcutta 1860).

——, *Vazir of Lankurán. A Persian Play. A Textbook of Modern Coll. Persian*, ed. with a gramm. introd., transl. and vocabulary by W. H. D. Haggard and G. Le Strange (London 1882, 1930). – Other editions and transl.: see Arberry (B I).

——, *Khirs-i qūldūr-bāsān*. Text and English tr. by K. M. Maitra (Lahore 1926).

——, *Sargudhasht-i mard-i khasīs. L'Avare, comédie persane*, texte publié et traduit avec un glossaire par A. Bricteux (Liège 1934). – English tr. by K. M. Maitra (Lahore 1923).

——, *Monsieur Jourdan, im pers. Texte mit Übers. und Wörterverzeichnis*, hrsg. von A. Wahrmund (Vienna 1889).

——, 'The Alchemist. A Persian Play', transl. by G. Le Strange, *JRAS*, 18 (1886), 103–26.

——, 'Histoire de Youssouf Chah, nouvelle historique. Texte azeri publié et traduit par Lucien Bouvat', *JA* 1903/1, 393–489. – English tr. by Edw. C. Ross, *JRAS*, 1895, 537–60.

Fatḥ-'Alī-Shāh, *Dīvān*, lith. ([Tehran] 1304/1887). – Ed. by Ghulām-Ḥusayn Javāhirī (Tehran 1337).

Fattāḥī Nīshāpūrī, *Ḥusn u dil (Schönheit und Herz.) Pers. Allegorie*, hrsg., übers., erklärt und mit Lâmi'îs türk. Bearbeitung verglichen von Rudolf Dvořák (Vienna 1889).

——, *Dastūr-i 'Ushshāq "The Book of Lovers". The Allegorical Romance of Princess Husn (Beauty) and Prince Dil (Heart)*, ed. by R. S. Greenshields (London 1926). – Muḥ. b. Yaḥyā Sībak Nīshābûrī, 'Risāla-i Ḥusn u dil' [Text], *Sukhan*, 13 (1341), 1047–60.

——, *Shabistān-i khiyāl* (Tashkent 1331/1912–3); = *Shabistān-i nikāt u gulistān-i lughāt*: see Arberry (B I). – "*Das Schlafgemach der Phantasie*", I: *Vom Glauben und Islam*. Übers. von H. Ethé (Leipzig 1865; 1868).

Fayḍī, *Nal Daman*, lith. ([Lucknow] 1877); ≅.

——, Specimens from his lyric poetry: *ShS*, 1961/5, 125–35.

Fighānī, Bābā, *Dīwān*, ed. with a preface in Urdu by Prof. Mana-Mōhana Lāl Māthar Dihlavī (Lahore [1932]). – Ed. by Suhaylī Khvānsārī (Tehran 1317; 1340).

——, *Ghazaliyyāt* (Tehran 1326).

——, *Les perles de la couronne. Choix de poésies, traduites pour la première fois avec une introduction* par Hocéyne-Azad (Paris 1903) (BOE).

Findariskī, "*Qaṣīda-i ḥikmiyya*". Comm. by (1) Ḥakīm 'Abbās Sharīf Dārābī Shīrāzī, *Tuḥfatu'l-murād*, ed. by Faḍlu'llāh Lā'iq (1338); (2) by Muḥ. Ṣāliḥ al-Khalkhālī, in *Majmū'a* ([Tehran] 1314) (see Harrassowitz, *Kat.* 430, 1931 [B I], 671).

Firdausī, *Shāh-nāma*, ed. M. Lumsden, I (Calcutta 1811); Turner Macan, I–IV (Calcutta 1829); J. Mohl, 7 vols. (Paris 1838–78); J. A. Vullers, I–II (Lugd. Bat. 1877–9); S. Landauer, III (*ibid.* 1884). – Ed. by Muḥ. Ramaḍānī, 6 vols. (Tehran 1311–2; reprint 1341). – A Revision of Vullers' Edition newly Collated with MSS., with the Persian Translation of the Latin Notes (A Continuation of Vullers' Edition, based on Turner Macan and Jules Mohl's Editions, and augmented by critical notes by Saïd Naficy), 10 vols. (Tehran 1313–5). – *Shāh-nāma*, ed. by Muḥ. Dabīr Siyāqī, 6 vols. (Tehran 1335); ed. "Amīr-i Kabīr", 7 vols. (Tehran 1341). – *Shākh-nāme. Kriticheskiy tekst*, I–V. Red. Ye. E. Bertel's *et al.* (Moscow 1960–7, to be continued). Cf. *KS*, 13 (1955), 3–71; *SV*, 1955/1, 88–95. See also *s.v.* 'Osmanov'. – *Khulāṣa-i Shāh-nāma-i Firdausī*, by Mīrzā Muḥ. 'Alī-Khān Furūghī (Dhukā'u'l-mulk), 2 vols. (Tehran 1313). – *Shohnoma. Dostoni Bahromi Chubin* [Based on a MS. from 1333 A.D.] (Stalinabad–Leningrad 1940). – *Shāh-nāma.* Ed. by J. Mohl. Repr. in pocket edition (Tehran 1345).

——, Translations (only recent and little known): *ash-Shāh-nāma*, Arab. tr. by Fatḥ b. 'Alī al-Bundārī, ed. by 'Abdu'l-Wahhāb 'Azzām, 2 vols. (Miṣr 1350/1932). – Swedish tr. by Ax. Er. Hermelin (1931). – *Das Buch der Könige*. Übers. U. von Witzleben [Selections] (Düsseldorf 1961). – *Kniha králů (Šáh-náme)*. Překládá a vysvětlivkami provází Jaromír Borecký, I (Prague 1910). – *Zál a Rúdábe*, tr. by Věra Kubíčková (Prague 1958). – Per. S. Sokolov, I (Moscow 1905). – *Shakh-name*, I: *Od nachala poemï do skazaniya o Sokhrabe*. Izd. podgotovili Ts. B. Banu [tr. into Russian verse], A. Lakhuti [red.], A. A. Starikov [epilogue, 593–644. Persian in *Payām-i navīn*, Tehran 1341] (Moscow 1957) (in the bibliography on p. 646 *et seq.* a list of Russian translations); II: *Ot skazaniya o Rosteme i Sokhrabe do skazaniya o Rosteme i khaqane China*. Per. Ts. B. Banu-Lakhuti, komm. A. A. Starikov (Moscow 1960); III: *Ot skazaniya o bitve Rostema s khakanom China do tsarstvovaniya Lokhraspa*. Per.: Ts. B. Banu-Lakhuti; komm.: idem and A. Azer (Moscow 1965). – *Shah-namê abo iran'ska knïha tsariv*, A. Krïms'kïy, I (L'viv 1896); again in the anthology *Pal'move Hïllya*; III (Kiev 1922), 26–118. – *Firdausis Kongebog*. Udvalgte sagn i metrisk gengivelse A. Christensen (Copenhagen 1931). – *Rustem i Suhrab*. Prev. F. Bajraktarević (Beograd 1928). – 'Opowieść o Bîżanie i Manîże, przetł. Alex. Frejman', *Wisła*, 15 (1901), 742–5, 746–8; 18 (1904), 153 *et seq.* – 'Zal i Rudabe, przeł. wierszem Fr. Machalski', *Stud. Ir.*, 3 (Tehran 1945); *Opowieść o miłości Zala i Rudabe*, przeł. Fr. Machalski [prose] (Wrocław–Kraków 1961). – *Bahrām-i Gūr u Āzāda*. Armenian tr. by Rub. Abrahamian (Tehran 1313). – A list of Uzbek translations: H. Homidyan, *SSh*, 1965/9, 128–40.

——, Zajączkowski, A., *Turecka wersja Šāh-nāme z Egiptu mameluckiego* [Facsimile] (Warsaw 1965); cf. 'Türk Dili Araştırmaları Yıllığı', *Belleten* 1966, 51–63 (French), 65–76 (Turkish).

——, *Yūsuf u Zalīkhā*, ≌; crit. ed. by H. Ethé, Fasc. I (Oxford 1908). – *Jussuf und Zuleicha. Romant. Heldengedicht*, übertr. von O. v. Schlechta-Wssehrd (Vienna 1889).

——, H. Ethé, 'Firdûsî als Lyriker', *SBAW*, phil.-hist. Kl. (München 1872), 273–304; 1873, 623–59.

——, 'Firdausī-nāma', *Mihr*, 2/5-6 (1313), 401–704. – *Kitāb-i hazāra-i Firdausī* (Tehran 1323). – *Ferdovsi, 934–1934* (Leningrad 1934) (IVV i Gos. Erm.).

——, L. T. Gyuzal'yan and M. M. D'yakonov, *Rukopisi Shakh-name v leningradskikh sobraniyakh* (AN SSSR, Leningrad 1934).

——, Bibliography: Arberry (B I); Ethé (B V), 231; *İA*; Krïmskiy (B V); Nöldeke (*q.v.*); *NY*. – Schubert, J.: '"Firdausī und seine Zeit". Eine Zusammenstellung von Firdausī-Literatur im Anschluß an die Ausstellung "..." i. d. Univ.-Bibl. zu Leipzig', *Buch und Schrift*, I (1938), 20–72.
"Firdausī-i thānī", Muḥ. 'Alī Ṭūsī, *Shāh-nāma-i Nādirī*, ed. by Aḥm. Suhaylī Khvānsārī (Tehran 1339).
Frye, R. N., 'The Andarz Nāme of Kāyūs b. Iskandar b. Kāpūs b. Vušmgīr', in *Serta Cantabrigiensia* (1954), 7–21.
Fuḍūlī, 'Fuzûlî'nin Farsça Divanı', ed. by A. N. Tarlan, *İslam Dergisi*, 1944, Nr. 25–26 *et seq*. – *Ash'ār. Muntakhab-i fārsī*, ed. by H. Ārāslī (Baku 1958). – *Gulchinī*, ed. by Rahim Hoshim (Stalinabad 1960). – *Äsärlär*, red. H. Araslï, I–III (Baku 1958) (in Vol. III the Persian divan transl. into Azeri verse); IV (Qaṣīdas) (1961). – *Farsça Divan*, edisyon kritik: Hasibe Mazioğlu (Ankara 1962). – 'Fuzûlî'nin bilinmeyen kasideleri': A. N. Tarlan, *IEFD*, 3 (1948/9), 193–209; 4 (1951), 251–64, and contin. – Further qaṣīdas: see *İA*, 37. cüz, 693.
——, *Leylī ve Mejnūn* [In Azeri], ≅. – Russian tr. by Anat. Starostin (Moscow 1958).
——, Selections from his lyrical poetry, tr. into Russian by the same.
——, *Sbornik Fuẓūlī* (Baku 1925).
——, Bibliography: *İA*, and A. Karahan (*q.v.*), IX *et seq.*, 287 *et seq.*
Furūghī Bisṭāmī, 'Abbās, [*Ghazaliyyāt*]. Printed after the *Dīvān* of Qā'ānī, lith. (Tehran 1274/1857; 1302/1884). – *Ghazaliyyāt*, ed. by Manṣūr Mushfiq, 2nd ed. (Tehran 1342).
——, *Dīvān*, ed. by 'Alī Ghaffārī (Tehran 1320); new ed. by Sayfi-Āzād (1337). – *Dīvān-i kāmil*, ed. by Ḥus. Nakha'ī (Tehran 1336; 1342).
Furūzānfar: see Badī'u'z-zamān.
Gaál László: *Az ezeréves Firdouszi. Tanulmány* [The millenary of Firdausi. A study] (Karcagi Gimnáziumi Értesítő 1935).
Gabrieli, Fr., 'Versioni da Niẓāmī', *Annali* (Napoli) 10 (1937/8), 31–72.
——, 'Note sul "Vīs u Rāmīn" di Faḫr ad-dīn Gurgānī', *RRAL*, VI/XV (1939), 168–88. – 'Sul poema persiano "Vis u Rāmīn"', *Annali* (Napoli), N.S., I (1940), 253–8.
——, 'Il valore letterario e storico del Farağ ba'da š-šidda di Tanūḫī', *RSO*, 19 (1940), 17–44.
——, 'Il settimo capitolo del Marzbān-Nāmeh', *RSO*, 19 (1940), 125–60.
——, 'Abū Nuwās, poeta 'Abbāside', *OM*, 33 (1953), 279–96.
Galimova, G., 'Stareyshaya rukopis' stikhov Khafiza [805–807/1403–1405!]', *PV*, 1959/4, 105–12.
Gardet, L., *La pensée religieuse d'Avicenne (Ibn Sīnā)* (Paris 1951) (Ét. de philos. médiévale, XVI).
——, *La connaissance mystique chez Ibn Sīnā et ses présupposés philosophiques* (Mémorial Avicenne II) (Cairo 1952).
Gauharīn, Sayyid Ṣādiq, *Farhang-i lughāt va ta'bīrāt-i Mathnavī*, I–IV (Tehran, in progress since 1337) (Univ.).
Genceli, Ali, 'Tebrizli Sâib', *Türk Amacı*, I, 33–7, 52–60.
Genko, A. N., 'Gruzinskaya versiya "Khosro i Shirin" Khosro Dekhlevi', *DAN-B*, 1924, 138–41.
Ghani, Q. [d. 1331], *Baḥth dar āthār u afkār u aḥvāl-i Ḥāfiẓ*, I: *Ta'rīkh-i 'aṣr-i Ḥāfiẓ*. W. introd. by Muḥ. Qazvīnī (Tehran 1321); II: *Ta'rīkh-i taṣavvuf* (Tehran 1330). – 2nd ed. (1340).
Ghazālī, Aḥmad, *Aphorismen über die Liebe*, hrsg. von Hellmut Ritter (Istanbul–Leipzig 1942) (Bibl. Isl., 15). – 'Risāla-i Savāniḥ', ed. by Īr. Afshār, *MDAT*, 14/3–4 (1345).
Ghufrānī al-Khurāsānī, *'Abdu'llāh b. al-Muqaffa'* (Cairo 1965). [In Arabic.]
Giunashvili, L. S., 'Zametki o zhenskikh obrazakh "Shakh-name"', *Trudï Univ. Tbil.*, 116 (1965), 181–97.
Goichon, A. M., *La philosophie d'Avicenne et son influence en Europe médiévale*, 2nd ed., rev. et corr. (Paris 1951).
——, *Le Récit de Ḥayy Ibn Yaqẓān* (Paris 1959).

Gölpınarlı, Abdülbâki, *Mevlânâ Celâleddîn. Hayatı, felsefesi, eserleri, eserlerinden seçmeler*, 3rd ed. (Istanbul 1959).

——, 'Mawlānā, Şams-i Tabrīzī ile altmış iki yaşında buluştu', *ŞM*, 3 (1959), 156–61.

Grunebaum, G. E. von, 'Firdausî's Concept of History', in *F. Köprülü Armağanı* (1953), 177–93 = *Islam. Essays* etc. (1955) (B II, *s.v.* 'von Grunebaum'), 168–84.

Gulchīn-i ma'ānī, Aḥm., 'Mīr Najāt-i Iṣfahānī', *Māh-nāma-i Vaḥīd*, 1/3 (1343), 33–9; 1/4, 27–8.

Gulizade, M. Y., *Nizami Gyandzhevi. Zhizn' i tvorchestvo* (Baku 1953).

——, *Lirika Fizuli. Avtoreferat* (Baku 1965) (Univ.).

Guseyni, Abul'fas, 'Yeshche raz ob avtore pervïkh persidskikh p'yes', *NAA*, 1965/6, 142–5.

Guseynov, Geydar, *O sotsial'nïkh vozzreniyakh Nizami* (AN AzSSR Baku 1946).

Gvakhariya, A. A., *Persidskiye istochniki gruzinskikh versiy "Yusufa i Zelikhi"* (AN Gruz. SSR., Tiflis, 1958) (in Georgian, with summary in Russian).

——, 'O poeticheskoy versii "Bakhtiar-name"', *Trudï Tbil. gos. univ.*, 91 (1960), 125–31.

——, '"Vis o Ramin" Fakhraddina Gorgani i "Khosrov i Shirin" Nizami Gyandzhevi', *Trudï Univ. Tbil.*, 116 (1965), 199–207.

Gvakhariya, A. A. and Todua, M. A., 'Znacheniye drevnegruzinskogo perevoda "Visramiani" dlya ustanovleniya kriticheskogo texta yego persidskogo originala "Vis u Ramin"', *Iranskaya filologiya* (B VIa) (Leningrad 1964), 104–110.

Habib, Mohammad, *Hazrat Amir Khusrau of Delhi* (Bombay 1927).

Hādī Ḥasan, I. *Falakī-i Shirwānī: His Time, Life and Works*; II. *Dīwān* (London 1929) (Furl. Fund 6, 9). Important additions in *IC*, 24 (1950), April, 77–107 and July, 145–86. See also *Majmū'a* and *Researches* (B VI, *s.v.* 'Hādī Ḥasan').

Hādī Sabzavārī, Ḥājjī Mullā, "Asrār" [d. 1295/1878], *Ghazaliyyāt*, lith. ([*s.l.*] 1299/1881).

——, *Dīvān*, ed. by Muḥ. Riḍā Dāyī Javād (Isfahan [1339]).

——, *Asrāru'l-ḥikma*, ed. by Abu'l-Ḥasan Sha'rānī (Tehran 1380/1960).

——, Autobiography: *Yādgār*, 3, 43–8.

Ḥāfiẓ, *Dīvān*, ed. by Sayyid 'Abdu'r-Raḥīm Khalkhālī [from a ms. of 827/1424] (Tehran 1306). – ed. by Muḥ. Qazvīnī and Qāsim Ghanī (Tehran 1320). – *Die Lieder des Hafis* (Vol. I = *Ghaz.*, 1–80, with the Turkish comm. by Sūdī), ed. by Herm. Brockhaus, 3 vols. (Leipzig 1854–60). – *Der Diwan ... im pers. Original*, hrsg., ins Deutsche metrisch übersetzt von Vinz. Ritter von Rosenzweig-Schwannau, 3 vols. (Vienna 1856–64). – *Ghazalhā-i Khvāja Ḥāfiẓ-i Shīrāzī* [152 ghazals from a MS. 813–4/1410–2], ed. by P. N. Khānlarī (Tehran 1337). – 'Chand ghazal-i aṣīl-i Ḥāfiẓ, ed. by P. N. Khānlarī', *Sukhan*, 1340, nr. 1–5. – *Ḥāfiẓ, tashrīḥ*, 3rd ed. (Tehran 1343). (The ghazals arranged according to subject-matter by 'Abdu'l-Ḥus. Hazhīr.)

——, *Fifty poems*. Texts and translations by A. J. Arberry (Cambridge 1947; 1953).

——, Turkish commentary by Sūdi, 3 vols. (Būlāq 1250/1834). Persian tr. by Mrs. 'Iṣmat Sattār-zāda, 2 vols. (Tehran 1341–42).

——, *The Dīwān...*, transl. with crit. and explanatory notes by H. Wilberforce Clarke, I–II (Calcutta 1891). The *'Awārifu-l-ma'ārif* by Shaikh Shahābu-d-dīn 'Umar b. Muḥammad-i-Sahrwardī, transl. (from the Arabic into Persian) by Maḥm. b. 'Alī-al-Kāshānī. Transl. by H. W. C. Vol. III (Calcutta 1891).

——, *Ghazelen des Hafis*, Übers. von Friedr. Rückert (München 1926) (42 unpublished ghazals, recovered by H. Kreyenborg). – *Gedichte aus dem Diwan*, übertr. von Rolf Dietrich Keil (Düsseldorf 1962). – Arthur Guy, *Les Poèmes érotiques ou ghazels en calque rhythmique et avec rime à la persane*, I (Paris 1927) (with comm. based on Sūdī). – *Z dîvânu Hâfize*, Přel. Jar. B. Košut a Jar. Vrchlický. Pozn. opatřil R. Dvořák (Prague 1881). – H. Massé, 'Vingt poèmes de Hafiz', *Cinquantenaire Fac. Lettres Alger*, 1932, 343–56. – *Les ghazels*, trad. p. Ch. Devillers (Paris 1959). – *Lirika*. Perevod i stat'ya Y. Dunayevskogo, *Acad.* (1935). – *Lirika*, tr. into Russian by M. Zand, S. Lipkin, and S. Shervinskiy (Moscow 1963). – Stallard, P. L., *Renderings from the Dewan of Khwaja Shamsu'ddin*

Muhammad Hafiz Shirazi (Oxford 1937). – Abdülbaki Gölpınarlı, *Hafiz Divanı* [Turkish introd., 1–39; tr. mainly based on the ed. by Khalkhālī and the MS. Aya Sofya 3945 of 813–4/1410–2] (Istanbul 1944) (Dünya edebiyatından tercemeler. Şark-İslâm klâsikleri, 4). – *Pyat'desyat gazeley. V novïkh perevodakh*, sostavleniye I. Braginskogo (Stalinabad 1949; 1955) (Klass. tadzh. lit.). – Arabic tr. by Ibr. Amīnu'sh-shavāribī (Cairo 1944; 1947). – Translations into Arabic, French and English in *Ad-dirāsāt al-adabīyah*, 4 (1962), 50–62, 301–16. – An. Zajączkowski, 'Liryka Hafiza. Gazelijāt', *Przegl. Orient.*, 2 [1949] (1950), 18–50; cz. II, 3 (1950), 26–44; 4 (8) (1953), 233–6. – Idem: *Gazeli wybrane Hafiza* (Warszawa 1957). – *Versek*. Tr. into Hungarian by Képes Géza, with introd. and notes by Bodrogligeti András, illustr. by Kondor Lajos (Budapest 1960).

——, Bibliography of the numerous editions, selections, commentaries, verse translations, etc.: Arberry (B I), Ethé (B V), *İA*, *NY*, in particular Krïmskiy, II (B V; up to 1924), and Krïms'kïy, *Khafïz* (see below).

Hakim, K. A., *The Metaphysics of Rumi. A Critical and Historical Sketch*, 2nd ed. (1951).

Ḥālī, Alṭāf Ḥusayn, *Ḥayāt-i Sa'dī*, tr. from the Urdu by Naṣru'llāh Surūsh (Tehran 1316).

Ḥallāj, Manṣūr, *Dīvān*, ed. by Valī'u'llāh Yūsufiyya (Tehran 1343). (Other Indian and Tehran editions also exist. The *Dīvān* is only attributed to Ḥallāj.)

Ḥamīdī (cf. *Yādgār*, 1/7, 25–8), *Maqāmāt* (Tehran 1290/1873–4); ≌. – Ed. by Sayyid 'Alī Akbar Abarqūyī (Isfahan, Fac. of Letters, 1339).

Hansen, Kurt Heinrich, 'Das iranische Königsbuch. Aufbau und Gestalt des Shahname von Firdosi', *Wiesbaden, Akad., Abh. d. Klasse d. Lit.* (1954), Nr. 3.

Ḥasan Ghaznavī (Ashraf), Sayyid, *Dīvān*, ed. by Taqī Mudarris Raḍavī (Tehran 1328) (Univ.).

Ḥasan Sanjarī Dihlavī, *Kulliyyāt*, Ind. lith. (see Khānlarī: *Taḥqīq* [B IV], 212). – See also Bibl. E VI.

Hashim, Rahim, *Imya proslavlennoye v vekakh* [Jāmī] (Dushanbe 1964). – In Tajik: *Haykali buzurgi nazm* (Dushanbe 1964).

Hāshimī, Muḥ. Yaḥyā, 'Ta'aththur ash-shā'ir al-Almānī Güte [= Goethe] bi-Ḥāfiẓ ash-Shīrāzī wa shu'arā' al-Furs', *Ad-dirāsāt al-adabīyah*, 4 (1962), 30–49.

Hātif-i Iṣfahānī, *Dīvān* (With biography by Rashīd Yāsimī) (Tehran 1307); (with biography by 'Abbās Iqbāl) (Tehran 1312) (Arm.).

——, Specimens: *ZDMG* (1851); *JA* (1856).

——, *Dirāsat wajīza*, ed. with introd. by Fīrūz Ḥarīrchū (Tehran 1343). (Three Arabic poems.)

Hātifī, *Lailí Majnún, a Persian Poem* [ed. by Sir W. Jones] (Calcutta 1788). – *Laylī va Majnun*, ed. by S. Asadulloyev (Dushanbe 1962). – ≌.

——, *Ẓafar-nāma*, lith. (Lucknow 1869). – See also p. 457, note 41.

Ḥazīn, Muḥ. 'Alī: see p. 458, note 104.

Henning, W. B., 'Die älteste persische Gedichthandschrift: eine neue Version von Barlaam und Joasaph', in *Akten des XXIV. Or.-Kongr. München* (Wiesbaden 1959), 305–07; Persian tr. by Iḥsān Yār-Shāṭir, *MDAT*, 5/4 (1337), 1–9.

Ḥikmat, 'A.-A., 'Shūrīda-i Shīrāzī', *Arm.*, 7, 355–65.

——, *Ruma'ū va Zhūliyat-i Shakispīr va muqāyasa bā Laylī u Majnūn-i Niẓāmī* (Tehran 1319).

——, *Jāmī* (Tehran 1320).

——, *Amīr 'Alī shīr-i Navā'ī* (Tehran 1326).

——, *Fitz-Gerald's Translation of Jami* [Salāmān u Absāl] (Tehran 1947).

——, 'Manābi'-i jadīd dar pīrāmūn-i ḥayāt-i Ḥāfiẓ', *MDA Shiraz*, 1341/7, 3–28.

Hikmet, Ism., Türk dilinde yazılan ilk Yusuf ve Züleyka', *Edibiyat Fakültesi Türk Dili ve Edebiyatı Dergisi*, 3/1–2 (1948), 211–30.

Hilālī, *Dīvān*, ed. by Kūhī Kirmānī (Tehran). ≌. – *Dīvān* (*bā du mathnavī: Pādshāh u darvīsh va Ṣifātu'l 'āshiqīn*), ed. by S. Nafīsī (Tehran 1337).

——, *Mathnavī-i Ṣifātu'l-'āshiqīn*, ed. by Kūhī Kirmānī (Tehran).

——, *Shāh u darvīsh*, lith. ([Tehran] 1321/1904); lith. ([*s.l.*] 1321) (together with *Gul u Jam* by Ahlī, etc.); ed. by Kūhī Kirmānī (Tehran). – German tr. by H. Ethé, in *Morgenländ. Studien* (Leipzig 1870), 197–282.

Horn, Paul, 'Der Dichter Sultan Selim I.', *ZDMG*, 60 (1906) 97–111.

Horst, Heribert, 'Arabische Briefe der Khorazmšāhs an den Kalifenhof aus der Feder des Rašīd ad-Dīn Waṭwāṭ', *ZDMG*, 116/1 (1966), 24–43.

Houtsma, M. Th., 'Some remarks on the Dīwān of Niẓāmī', in *'Ajab-nāma* (B VIa), 224–7.

Humā Shīrāzī, *Dīvān = Kitāb-i Shakaristān* [Lyric poetry], lith. ([Shiraz?] 1320/1902).

Humā'ī, Jalālu'd-dīn, 'Humā-i Shīrāzī', *Arm.*, 10, 217–33, 326–43 (the sons of Humā).

——, 'Muqaddima-i qadīm-i Akhlāq-i Nāṣirī', *MDAT*, 3/3 (1335), 17–25.

——, *Maqām-i Ḥāfiẓ* (Tehran 1343).

Humāmu'd-dīn Tabrīzī, *Dīvān*, ed. by Mu'ayyid Thābitī (1334).

Hūman, Maḥmūd, *Ḥāfiẓ chi mīgūyad?* (Tehran 1317).

——, *Ḥāfiẓ* ([Tehran] 1325) (review of the Qazvīnī-Ghanī ed., attempt at a chronology of 258 ghazals).

Humbert, Paul, *Observations sur le vocabulaire arabe du Châhnâmeh* (Neuchâtel 1953).

Ḥusayn b. Bāyqarā, *Divan-i Sultan Hüseyin Mirza Baykara "Hüseyinî"*, ed. by Ismail Hikmet Ertaylan (Istanbul 1946) (facsimile; in East-Turkish).

Ibn-i Sīnā: see Avicenna.

Ibn-i Yamīn, *Dīvān*, ed. by R. Yāsimī (Tehran 1317). – Ed. by S. Nafīsī (Tehran 1318).

——, *Muqaṭṭa'āt. 100 short Poems.* The Persian Text with Paraphrase by E. H. Rodwell (London 1933). – *Ibn Jemins Bruchstücke*, aus dem Pers. von Ott. M. von Schlechta-Wssehrd (Vienna 1852).

Ibrāhīm-Munshī, *Tadhkira-i Majdiyya* [Poets from the highest circles of the Court about 1850–85], lith. (Tehran 1303/1885). (Many lithographed portraits!)

Imronov, S., 'Ibni Yamin Far'yumadi i Ibni Yamin Shiburgani', in *IV Kongr. po iranskoy filologii* (Tashkent 1964), 71–3. – 'Ibni Yamini Faryumadī va Ibni Yamini Shiburgonī', *SSh*, 1964/12, 142-8 [in Tajik]. – 'Ibni Yamini Far'yumadī va ta'siri ū ba adabiyoti asri XV', in *V Konf. po iranskoy filologii* (Dushanbe 1966), 71–4. – 'Ibni Yamin – tarjuman' [As translator from Arabic], *SSh*, 1965/7, 108–11.

Iqbāl Āshtiyānī, 'Abbās, *Qābūs-i Vushmgīr-i Ziyārī* (Berlin 1924).

——, *Sharḥ-i ḥāl-i 'Abdu'llāh b. Muqaffa'* (Berlin 1926).

——, 'Sharḥ-i ḥāl-i Rashīd-i Vaṭvāṭ', *Arm.*, 11, 398–400 and contin.

——, 'Ta'rīkh-i vafāt-i Kamālu'd-dīn Ismā'īl', *Arm.*, 14, 8–13.

——, 'Zamān-i tavallud va avā'il-i zindagānī-i Sa'dī', in *Sa'dī-nāma* (see *s.v.* 'Sa'dī'), 11–32.

'Irāqī, *Kulliyyāt*, ed. by S. Nafīsī (Tehran 1335; 3rd ed. 1339).

——, *The Song of Lovers ('Ushshāq-Nāma)*, ed. and transl. into verse by A. J. Arberry (Isl. Res. Ass. Ser., 8) (London 1939).

Ishaque, M., series of articles (Shahīd, Rābi'a, Rūdakī, Kisā'ī, Mahsatī, Manūchihrī, Ni'matu'llāh, Qurratu'l-'Ayn etc.) in *Indo-Iranica* (since 1946).

Ishrāq-i Khāvarī, 'Abdu'l-Ḥamīd, 'Adīb-i Nīshābūrī', *Arm.*, 7, 234–45.

——, 'Ṣafā-i Iṣfahānī', *Arm.*, 7, 403–17.

Iskandar-nāma, ed. by Īraj Afshār (Tehran 1343): from VI/XIIth cent., Pseudo-Kallisthenes.

Ismā'īl, *Il Canzoniere di Šāh Ismā'īl Ḫaṭā'ī*, ed. by Tourkhan Gandjeï (Naples 1959).

Ismailzade, Dzh., 'K voprosu izucheniya zhizni i tvorchestva Yagma Dzhandagi', in *Voprosī iranskoy filologii* (B VIa), 279–90.

'Iṣmat: specimens *ShS*, 1961/9, 120–6.

Ivanow, W , 'Tabaqát of Ansárí in the Old Language of Herat', *JRAS*, 1923, 1–34, 337–82.

——, *Problems in Nasir-i Khusraw's Biography* (The Ism. Soc. Ser., B 10) (Bombay 1956).

Jabalī, see 'Abdu'l-Vāsi' Jabalī.

Jacob, G., 'Das Weinhaus nebst Zubehör nach den Gazelen des Ḥāfiẓ. Ein Beitrag zu einer Darstellung des altpersischen Lebens', in *Orient. Studien Th. Nöldeke* (Gieszen 1906), 1055–76.

Jalālu'd-dīn Muḥ. Dav(v)ānī, 'Sharḥ-i yak ghazal-i Khvāja Ḥāfiẓ', *Arm.*, 21, 365 *et seq.*

——, 'Du nāma-i bāstānī', *ibid.*, 22, 14–6.

Jalālu'd-dīn Muḥ. Rūmī "Maulavī", *The Mathnawí*, ed. from the oldest MSS. available with crit. notes, transl. and commentary by R. A. Nicholson, 8 vols. (London–Leiden 1925–40) (GMNS, 4). Review: H. Ritter, *OLZ*, 1928, 4–9; 1935, 243–6; 1941, 247–53. – *Kulliyyāt-i mathnavī-i ma'navī*, ed. by M. Darvīsh, 6 vols. (Tehran 1340). – *Daftar-i haftum az Mathnavī-i ma'navī-i Maulavī* [Spurious] (Bombay 1301/1883–4). – Khulāṣa-i Mathnavī, *Badī'u'z-zamān Furūzānfar* (Tehran 1321). – *Bāng-i nāy* (*Qiṣṣahā va dāstānhā*), 2 vols. ed. by M.-'A. Jamāl-zāda (Tehran 1337).

——, Translations. Turkish: Süleymān Naḥīfī (d. 1151/1738–9), I–VI and Ism. Ferrukhī (d. 1256/1840–1), VII (Būlāq 1268/1851) (together with the Persian text). Further old translations into Turkish: Dal Meḥmed (cf. Hammer-Purgstall, *Gesch. des Osm. Reiches*, III, 577); Shākir Meḥmed-ef. (cf. Ibr. Nejmī, *Tār. edeb. dersleri*, I (Istanbul 1338/1919–20), 262. – English and German: see Arberry (B I), Ethé (B V), *İA*, *NY*. – R. A. Nicholson, *Tales of mystic meaning, from the Mathnawi* (London 1931). – A. J. Arberry, *Tales from the Masnavi* (London 1961). – Dutch: R. van Brakell Buys, *Fragmenten uit de Masnawi* (Amsterdam 1952). – Swedish: by Ax. E. Hermelin, 4 vols. (Lund 1933–6). – Russian: *Pritchi*, tr. by Vl. Derzhavin, with intr. by N. Osmanov (Moscow 1957); idem, with preface by A. Bertel's (Moscow 1963). – Arabic (modern): 'Abdu'l-'Azīz Ṣāḥibu'l-javāhir, *Javāhiru'l-āthār*, 4 vols. (Tehran 1336–42) (Univ.).

——, Turkish commentaries: see H. Ritter, *İA*, *s.v.* 'Celâleddin R.'.

——, *Kulliyyāt-i Shams-i Tabrīz* (Lucknow 1302/1885) (1036 pp., only lyric poetry). – *Kulliyyāt-i Shams yā dīvān-i kabīr*, ed. by Badī'u'z-zamān Furūzānfar, 7 vols. (Tehran, 1336–45) (Univ.). – *Dīvān-i Shamsu'l-ḥaqā'iq* (Tabrīz 1281/1864). – *Ghazaliyyāt-i Shams-i Tabrīzī*, ed. by Manṣūr Mushfiq [incl. quatrains, a few studies and a commentary] (Tehran 1335). – *Maktab-i Shams* [Ghazals], ed. by S. A. Injū Shīrāzī (Tehran 1337). – *Selected Poems from the Dīvāni Shamsi Tabrīz*, ed. and transl. with an Introd., Notes and Appendices by R. A. Nicholson (Cambridge 1898). – *Sun of Tabriz. A lyrical introduction to higher metaphysics*, tr. by Sir Colin Garbett (on the basis of R. A. Nicholson's Selections) (Capetown 1956). – *Auswahl aus den Diwanen des grössten mystischen Dichters Persiens* (text, transl., notes) von Vinz. von Rosenzweig (Vienna 1838). – N. Martinovich, 'Noviy sbornik stikhov Dzhelal'-ed-dina Rumi', *ZVORAO*, 24 (1917), 1–28. – *Dîvân-i kebîr*, tr. into Turkish prose by Abdülbâki Gölpınarlı, 5 vols. (Istanbul 1957–60).

——, *Rubā'iyyāt*. Several Istanbul editions: see Karatay (B I). – L. Bogdanov, 'The Quatrains of Jalālu-d-dīn Rūmī' (Survey of the MSS.), *JASB*, 1935/1-2, 65–80. – 'Dselâl ed-Dīn Rûmî négysoros versei', *Székfoglaló Kégl Sándortól. Értekezések a nyelv- és széptudományok köréből* (Budapest), 19/10 (1907), 563–634.

——, *The Rubā'īyāt*. Select Translations into English Verse by A. J. Arberry (London 1949). – *Roubâ'yât*, traduit du persan par Assaf Hâlet Tchelebi (1950). – *Rubâîler*, tr. by A. Gölpınarlı (Istanbul 1964).

——, *Mevlânâ'nın Mektubları*, ed. by Ahmed Remzi Akyürek (Istanbul 1937). Extracts and review: M. Şerefeddin Yaltkaya, *TM*, 6 (1936–9), 323–45. – *Maktūbāt*, ed. by Yūs. Jamshīdī-pūr and Ghulām-Ḥusayn Amīn (1337).

——, *Majālis-i sab'a. Mevlânâ'nın yedi öğüdü*, ed. by Ahm. Remzi Akyürek (Istanbul 1937). – *Arm.*, 23, 109, etc.

——, *Fīhi mā fīhi*. R. A. Nicholson, 'The Table-tale of Jalálu'd-dín Rúmí', *JRAS*, Centen. Suppl. (1924), 225–32. – Ed. by Badī'u'z-zamān Furūzānfar (Tehran 1330) (Univ.); ed. Shirkat-i sihāmī (Tehran 1339). – Turkish tr. by A. Gölpınarlı (Istanbul 1959). – *Selections*, transl. ... with introd. and notes by R. A. Nicholson, ed. by A. J. Arberry (from the *Mathnavī*, the *Dīvān* and *Fīhi māfīhi* (London 1950). – *Discourses of Rumi*, tr. by A. J. Arberry (London 1961).

——, ʿA. A. Mushīr Salīmī, *Yād-nāma-i Maulavī*, Kumisyūn-i millī-i UNESCO (Tehran 1337).
——, Full bibliography: Krïmskiy (B v), III, 264 *et seq.*; Arberry (B I) and his *Class. Pers. Lit.* (B v), 454 *et seq.*
Jamālu'd-dīn Muḥ. b. ʿAbdu'r-Razzāq, *Dīvān*, ed. by Vaḥīd Dastgirdī (Tehran 1320) (Arm.).
Jāmī, *Kulliyyāt*, ≃.
——, *Dīvān*, ed. by H. Pizhmān (Tehran–Leiden 1317; 1335).
——, *Dīvān-i kāmil*, ed. by Hāshim Raḍī (Tehran 1341).
——, *Asarhoyi muntakhab*, 5 vols. (*Ghazaliyot* etc., I–II, *Haft avrang* III–V) (Dushanbe 1964).
——, Selections from the lyric poems, text and transl. by Friedr. Rückert, *ZDMG*, 1848–90; V. von Rosenzweig (Vienna 1848; 1858).
——, Y. E. Bertel's, 'Tolkovaniye Abd-ur Rakhmana Dzhami na pripisïvayemïye yemu chetverostishiya', *ZVORAO*, 26 (1925), 19–46.
——, *Bahāristān*, ≃. Ed. by M. Ṭabāṭabā'ī, lith. (Tehran 1311/1893). – Muḥ. ash-Shākir, *Hadiyyatu'l-ʿirfān dar sharḥ-i Bahāristān* [Turkish comm.] (Istanbul 1252/1836). – *Der Frühlingsgarten.* Selection and tr. by O. M. von Schlechta-Wssehrd (Vienna 1846; Tehran 1340). – Several English transl.: see Arberry (B I). – *Le Béharistan*, traduit par Henri Massé (Paris 1925). – *Bekharestan (Vesenniy sad)*. Perevod 14 otrïvkov, vstupit. stat' K. Chaykina [With the Persian text], *Acad.* (1935). – *Vesenniy sad (Bakharistan)*, tr. into Russian fr. Tajik (Fārsī) by M. Zand (Dushanbe 1964). – *Jarní zahrada* [Selections], přel. J. Marek, verše K. Bednář (Prague 1957).
——, *Haft aurang*, ed. by Murtaḍā Mudarris Gīlānī (Tehran 1338).
——, *Salāmān u Absāl*, ed. by Rashīd Yāsimī (Tehran 1306; 1319). – Ed. by F. Falconer (London 1850). – Ed. by Prof. Shaykh ʿAbdu'l-Ḳādir'e Sarfarāz (based on Falconer and Yāsimī) (Bombay 1936). – Translations: "– –", *poème allégorique persan*, traduit par Auguste Bricteux. Avec une introduction sur le mysticisme persan et la rhétorique persane (Paris 1911). – Older English translations: E. Fitzgerald (new ed. with introd. and literal transl. by A. J. Arberry (1956) and F. Falconer. – Summary of the contents: Īr. Afshār, *Sukhan*, 6/5 (1334), 439–43.
——, *Tuhfat ul Ahrār, The Gift of the Noble*, ed. by Forbes Falconer (London 1848). – ≃.
——, *Subḥatu'l-abrār*, lith. (Tehran 1315/1897). – ≃.
——, *Yūsuf u Zalīkhā*, ≃. – *Joseph und Suleïcha, hist.-romant. Gedicht* (hrsg. und) übers. von Vinz. Edl. von Rosenzweig (Vienna 1824). – *Youssouf et Zuleikha*, traduit en français par Auguste Bricteux (Paris 1927). – English: Ralph T. H. Griffith (London 1882); Alex. Rogers (London 1892).
——, *Laylī u Majnūn*. Translations: see Ethé (B v), 248.
——, *Khirad-nāma-i Sikandarī. Kniga mudrosti Iskandera*, per.: V. Derzhavin. Red. i vstup. stat'ya: L. Klimovich (Stalinabad 1949; 1955) (Klass. tadzh. lit.).
——, J. Bečka, 'Publications to celebrate the 550th Anniversary of the Birth of Abdurraḥmān Jāmī', *ArOr.*, 34 (1966), 606–11.
——, A set of studies on the occasion of the commemoration: *SSh*, 1964/12, 9–70; numerous other publications.
——, Bibliography: see Arberry (B I); *İA*; Krïmskiy (B v), III, 264 *et seq.*; *NY.*
Javādī, Ḥasan, *Muqāyasa-i Saʿdī va Ḥāfiẓ az naẓar-i ghazal-sarā'ī va sabk* (1333) (cf. *Sukhan*, 5, 651).
Javān-mard, ʿA., 'Yak munqid-i buzurg-i ijtimāʿī – ʿUbayd-i Zākānī', *Payk-i ṣulḥ*, 1, 37–46; *Satāra-i ṣulḥ*, 57–65.
Juvaynī, Alā'u'd-dīn Aṭā Malik, *Ta'rīkh-i Jahān-gushā*. See: Storey, II/2, 260–4. – *The History of the World-Conqueror*, tr. by J. A. Boyle, 2 vols. (Cambridge, Mass. 1958).
Kalīm, *Kulliyyāt*, ed. by H. Partau Bayḍā'ī (Tehran 1336).
Kalīla u Dimna: see *Index Isl.* (B I, *s.v.* 'Pearson'), 750, nrs. 23.847–60. – See also Bibl. F.
Kamāl Khujandī, *Dīvān*, ed. by ʿAzīz Daulatābādī (Tabriz 1337).
——, *Muntakhabot*, ed. by Sh. Husayn-zoda (Stalinabad 1955).

——, *Kamol' Khudzhandi*: *Izbrannaya lirika*. Per. A. Y. Adalis. Primechaniye i red. I. S. Braginskiy (Stalinabad 1949) (Klass. Tadzh. lit.).
Kamāliyān, Mahdī, 'Nuskha-badalhā-i dīvān-i Ḥāfiẓ' [ms. of 818/1415, Dillī], *FĪZ*, 6/2-3 (1337), 204–82.
Kamālu'd-dīn Ismā'īl Iṣfahānī, *Kulliyyāt* (Bombay 1307/1889). – ≅.
——, *Dīvān*, ed. by Vaḥīd Dastgirdī (Armaghān) (in preparation).
——, *The Hundred Love Songs*. Now first transl. by L. H. Gray and done into verse by Ethel W. Mumford (London 1903).
——, On his grave: *Arm.*, 11, 488–93, 640–50.
Kandī, Ghaffār, 'Dar bāra-i nāmahā-i Khāqānī', *FĪZ*, 12 (1343), 329–39.
Karahan, Abdülkadir, *Fuzulî. Muhiti, hayatı ve şahsiyeti* (Istanbul 1949) (Univ.).
Kāshifī, Ḥusayn Vā'iẓ, *Anwār-i Suhelī*; *or Lights of Canopus*, ed. by J. W. J. Ouseley (Hertford 1851). – *Kalīla u Dimna yā Anvār-i Suhaylī* (Berlin 1341/1923; repr. Tehran 1316; 1341). – *Fables tirées de l'Anouâri Souhaïlî d'el Ouâidh el Kâchifî*. Texte persan avec des notes en franç. par A. Raux (Paris 1915). – *Sagor ur "Anwār-i Suhailī"*, öfversättning från Persiskan of E. Hermelin (Stockholm 1929). – Numerous editions, educational adaptations, translations etc.: Arberry (B I), Ethé (B V), etc.
Kasravī Tabrīzī, 'Qaṭrān, shā'ir-i Ādharbāyjān', *Arm.*, 12, 45–51 and cont.
——, *Ḥāfiẓ chi mīgūyad?*, 4th ed. (Kit. 1335/6).
——, *Dar pīrāmūn-i "adabiyyāt"* (Tehran 1323; 1325; n.d.).
Kausar, In'amul Haq, 'Fughani's Life and Works', *Journ. of the Pakistan Hist. Society*, 10 (1962), 52–65, 213–46, 344–89; 11 (1963), 40–58, 127–38.
Kay-Kā'ūs b. Iskandar b. Qābūs, *The Nāṣīḥat-Nāma known as Qābūs-Nama*, ed. by R. Levy (London 1951). – Ed. by S. Nafīsī [from a MS. dated 750 h./1349–50] (Tehran 1342). – Ed. by 'Alī Ḥaṣūrī (Tehran 1343). – *A Mirror for Princes*, tr. by R. Levy (London 1951). – Russian tr. w. introd. and notes: Ye. E. Bertel's (Moscow 1963). – Cf. G. Lazard, *Anciens monuments* (B IV), 100–3 and *supra*, p. 428, note 12.
Kégl, Sándor (Alex. von Kegl), 'Šeibânî, ein moderner persischer Dichter des Pessimismus', *WZKM*, 6 (1892), 157–65.
——, 'Riẓâ Ḳulî Xân als Dichter', *WZKM*, 11 (1897), 63–74.
——, 'Viṣāl und seine Söhne, eine Dichterfamilie des modernen Persiens', *WZKM*, 12 (1898), 113–27.
——, 'Szenáji és a perzsa vallásos költészet' [Sanā'ī and Persian religious poetry], *MTA*, Értekezések 18/9 (1904).
——, 'Dselâleddîn Rûmî négysoros versei. Székfoglaló' [Jalālu'd-dīn Rūmī's rubā'īs. Inaugural address], *ibid.*, Értekezések 19/10 (1907), 563–634.
——, 'Emir Khoszrev', *ibid.* 21/10 (1911).
Khadizade, R., 'Neizvestnoye podrazheniye "Shakhname" Firdousi', *NAA*, 1961/4, 195–8.
Khālid, *Sharḥ-i 'Ishq-nāma-i ḥaḍrat-i Bahā'u'd-dīn Valad* [Turkish comm.] (Istanbul 1305/1887).
Khalīlu'llāh Khalīlī, *Aḥvāl va āthār-i Ḥakīm Sanā'ī* (Kābul 1936).
Khalkhālī, S. 'Abdu'r-Raḥīm, *Ḥāfiẓ-nāma* ([Tehran] 1320).
Khanikof, N., 'Mémoire sur Khâcâni, poète persan du XIIe s.', *JA*, 1864–5/4, 137–200; 5, 296–367.
Khānlarī, P. N., 'Du-baytīhā-i Bābā Ṭāhir', *Payām-i nau*, 1324/8, 9.
——, *Chand nukta dar taṣḥīḥ-i dīvān-i Ḥāfiẓ* ([Tehran] 1337) (Intishārāt-i "Sukhan"). Critical notes: Muḥ. Farzān, *RK*, 3/2 (1339), 229 *et seq.*
——, 'Hafiz de Chiraz', in *L'âme de l'Iran* (B VIa), 151–78.
Khāqānī, *Dīvān-i Ḥassānu'l-'Ajam*, ed. by 'Alī 'Abdu'r-Rasūlī (Tehran 1316). – Ed. by Muḥ. 'Abbāsī and Ḥusayn Nakha'ī (with biography, 26 pp.; indices, 874–923) (Tehran 1336) (Amīr-i kabīr). – *Dīvān-i Khāqānī-i Shīrvānī*, ed. by Ḍiyā'u'd-dīn Sajjādī (Tehran 1338).
——, *Tuḥfatu'l-'Irāqayn* (also with commentary), ≅. – Ed. by Y. Qarīb (Tehran 1333) (cf. *Sukhan*, 6, 1334, 368 *et seq.*). – Abjadi, Ismail Khan, *Kulliyat* IV. *Sharhi Tuhfati Iraqain* [1200/1785] (Madras

Univ. Islamic Series, No 16). – Ḥus. Amūzgār, *Muqaddima-i Tuḥfatu'l-khavāṭir va zubdatu'n-navāẓir yā Tuḥfatu'l-ʿIrāqayn-i Khāqānī* (Tehran 1333) (cf. *Sukhan, l.c.*, 464 *et seq.*).

——, *Aïwân-i-Madâin*, adapté et augmenté par quelques poètes contemporains (Berlin 1343/1924).

——, *Chetverostishiya Khakani*. Izdal i perevel K. G. Zaleman (Diss. St.-Petersburg 1875) (*ibid.*, bibliography).

——, *Khagani Shirvani. Sechilmish əsərləri* [tr. into Azeri] (Baku 1956).

——, *Izbrannïye proizvedeniya*, tr. by Vlad. Derzhavin (Baku 1959).

——, Specimens of scattered lyric poems: cf. Ethé (B v), 265.

Khaṭīb, Khalīl, *Rahbar-i ashʿār-i Farrukhī-i Sīstānī* (Tehran 1343).

Khayyām, ʿUmar, *Rubāʿiyyāt*, ed. by S. Nafīsī (with biography) (Tehran 1305–6). – Ed. by M.-ʿA. Furūghī and Q. Ghanī (Tehran 1321; 1340). – Ed. from a newly discovered MS. (dated 658/1259–60) by A. J. Arberry. With comparative English versions by E. Fitzgerald, E. H. Whinfield and the Editor (London 1949). – *Ruboyiyot*, ed. by M. Zand (from the MSS. of 604/1207 and 658/1259–60) (Stalinabad 1955). – *Rubāʿīyāt*, I (*Facsimile* [of the Cambridge MS. of 604/1207]); II: *Podgotovka teksta*, perevod i predisloviye: R. M. Aliyev i M.-N. Osmanov (Moscow 1959). – *Tarānahā-i Khayyām*, ed. by Ṣ. Hidāyat (Introd., 5–69) (Tehran 1313).

——, Some recent or little known translations: Albanian: cf. *RK*, 5 (1341), 987. – Arabic: Aḥmad Ṣarrāf, 3rd ed. (Baghdad 1961). – Armenian: Yūsuf-Khān Mirzoyants (Tehran, before 1929) (cf. *Iran*, 3, 240). – Azeri: cf. *Kit.*, 1335/6, 314. – Czech: *Rubáiját*, E. Fitzgeralda přel. J. Štýbr (Prague 1922). – *Čtyřverší Omara Chajjáma*, z perštiny přel. Josef Štýbr (Prague 1931; Brno 1938; Prague 1947). – *Čtyřverší Omara Chajjáma*, přel. Jaromír Borecký (Studií, poznámkami a vysvětlivkami doprovodil Miloš Borecký) (Prague 1945). – Danish: by Arth. Christensen (Copenhagen 1943). – Dutch: *Kwatrijnen*, vertaald door F. Pijl (1947). – *Rubaiyat*. Metrisch vertaald door J. A. Vooren. Met inleiding van E. F. Tijdens (Deventer 1966). – English: A new version, based upon recent discoveries, by A. J. Arberry (London 1952). – J. C. E. Bowen, *A New Selection* (London 1961). – French: R. Pascal, *Les Robâʿiyyât* (Rome 1958) (in French verse, with a facsimile of the Cambridge MS. of 604/1207). – *Les Quatrains*, trad. M. M. Fouladvand (Paris 1960). – *Les Rubaiyat d'Omar Khayyam d'Edward Fitzgerald* Trad. en vers français par Emil Désiron (Louvain 1964). – German: Walter von der Porten (Hamburg 1927). – Friedr. Rosen (Leipzig 1940). – "*Durchblättert ist des Lebens Buch*", B. Alavi – M. Remané. Nachworte von J. Rypka und B. Alavi (Berlin 1962). – Hungarian: Szabó Lőrinc, *Omar Khayyám Rubáiyát* [from E. Fitzgerald] (Budapest 1920). – Erődi Harrach Béla, *Keleti gyöngyök. Egy cynikus persa költő, Omer Chejjam költeményei* (Pest [?]). – Hegyi Endre, *Chajjám, Omer, Robáiyát. Forditotta, utószóval és jegyzetekkel ellátta* (Budapest 1958). – Italian: *Le Rubaiyyàt*, traduz. di Franc. Gabrieli (Firenze 1944). – *Quartine (Robâʿiyyât)*. A cura di Alessandro Bausani (*s.l.* 1956). – Kashmiri: cf. *RK*, 6 (1342), 209–11. – Polish: *Wybrane czterowiersze Omara Chajjama*, przełożył Andrzej Gawroński (Lwów 1933). – Russian: *Chetverostishiya*, per. O. Rumer (Moscow 1938). – *Izbrannoye*. Vvodnïy ocherk S. Morochnika (Stalinabad 1948; 1954). – Per. T. Zul'fikarov, *Gulistan*, 1962, No 1, 81–8 (Dushanbe 1962). – Serbo-Croatian: cf. F. Bajraktarević, *Prilozi za književnost*, 25/1-2 (1959), 146. – Slovak: *Múdrost' vína*, prel. E. B. Lukáč (bibliophile ed.). – Spanish: F. A. Propato, cf. *REI*, 5 (1931) = A 159.

——, Ambrose George Potter, *A Bibliography of the Rubáiyát of Omar Khayyám* (London 1929). (Since then many further editions and translations, see also Arberry.)

——, *Nowrūz Nāmah. The Persian New-Year Festival*, ed. by Mojtabâ Minowi (Tehran 1933).

——, *Kulliyyāt-i āthār-i pārsī*, ed. by Muḥ. ʿAbbāsī (Tehran 1338).

Khayyām-pūr, 'Yūsuf u Zalīkhā-i Firdausī', *NDAT*, 2 (1328), 191–229. – 'Yūsuf u Zalīkhā', *ibid.*, 10 (1337), 221–8, 418–33; 11 (1338), 39–68, 233–60; 12 (1339), 85–119. – 'Iḍāfātī bar silsila-i maqālāt-i "Yūsuf u Zalīkhā"', *ibid.*, 17/2 (1344), 186–7; cf. *ibid.*, 183–5 (Īraj Afshār) and 392–7 (continuation by Aḥmad Gulchīn-i maʿānī: Shāhīn's Y. u. Z., cf. Bibl. D IIb *s.v.* 'Shohin').

Khekmat, A. R., *Rasskaz o persidskom poete. Zhizn' i tvorchestvo Ibn Yamina* (Moscow 1965).

Khusrau, Amīr, *Kulliyyāt-i ʿanāṣir-i davāvīn-i Khusrau* [4 dīvāns in 1 vol.] (Cawnpore 1334/1916). – Dīvān-i kāmil, ed. by M. Darvīsh, preface by S. Nafīsī (Tehran [1343]). – (Odes 1–60). The Text with an Introduction, literal Translation and Notes. A. O. Koreishi (Bombay 1316/1901).
——, *Maṭlaʿuʾl-anvār* [Didact. mathnavī]. With comm. by Muḥ. Akram Multānī (Dihlī 1293/1876).
——, *Laylā Majnūn*: ≅, see Arberry (B I). – *Majnūn Laylī*, ed. by Muḥ. Ḥabību'r-Raḥmān-Khān (Aligarh 1335/1917). – *Majnūn u Lailī*, crit. ed. by T. A. Maḥramūf (Moscow 1964).
——, *Hasht bihisht*, ed. by Muḥ. Sul. Ashraf (Aligarh 1336/1918).
——, *Shīrīn i Khusrau*, krit. tekst, ed. by G. Yu. Aliyev (Moscow 1961).
——, *Qirānuʾs-saʿdayn*: see Arberry (B I), Harrassowitz (B I). – Ed. by S. Ḥasan Barnī (Aligarh 1918).
——, 'Miftāḥu'l-futūḥ', ed. by Yāsīn Niyāzī, *Orient. Coll. Mag.*, XII–XIII (1936–7).
——, *Duwal-Rānī va Khizr Khān* (= 'Ashīqa, 'Ishqiyya), ed. by Rashīd Aḥmad (Aligarh 1336/1917).
——, *The Nuh Sipihr. An Historical Mathnaví on the Reign of Mubárak Sháh*, ed. by Muh. Wahid Mirza (Islamic Res. Ass. Ser., 12) (Oxford–Calcutta 1949).
——, *Tughluq-náma*, ed. by S. Hashimi Faridabadi (Aurangabad 1933).
——, *Khazāʾinuʾl-futūḥ*, ed. by Syed Moinul Haq (Aligarh 1345/1925).
——, *Iʿjāz* [Epistolography I–II only] (Lucknow 1876). – See also p. 458, note 77.
Khusravānī Ṭurfa'ī, 'Alī Riḍā, 'Sharḥ-i ḥāl-i Amīr Mu'izzī', *Arm.*, 4, 529–48; 5, 15–30.
Khvājū Kirmānī, *Dīvān*, ed. by Aḥm. Suhaylī Khvānsārī (Tehran 1336).
——, *Muntakhab-i ghazaliyyāt*, ed. by Kūhī Kirmānī (Tehran 1306).
——, *Rauḍatuʾl-anvār*, ed. by Kūhī Kirmānī (Tehran 1306).
——, *Sām-nāma*, ed. by Khāḍi', with introd. by S. Nafīsī, 2 vols. (Bombay 1319–20).
Kirste, J., 'Über das Khodāi-nāme', *WZKM*, 10 (1896), 323–6.
Kishāvarz-i Ṣadr, *Kalīm-i Kāshānī*, cf. *Kitāb*, 1/7 (1335), 424.
Kiyā, S., 'Kuhnatarīn dast-navīs-i Lughat-i Furs', *MDAT*, 3/3 (1335), 1–9.
Klimovich, L., 'Nizami i yego poema "Iskender-name"', in *Iz istorii literatur sov. Vostoka* (Moscow 1959), 37–60.
Kobidze, D. I., *K voprosu o gruzinskoy versii Bahman-name* [Georgian, with Russian summary] (Tiflis, Inst. gruz lit., Liter. razïskaniya, IV, 1947), 317–36.
——, *Persidskiye istochniki gruzinskikh versiy "Shakh-name"* [Georgian, with Russian summary] (Tiflis 1959).
——, *Rudaki 857–1957* (Tiflis 1957).
——, *Jami, 1414–1492* (Tiflis 1964). (Both coll. publ. in Georgian, with Russian summary.)
Kodve-Khorb, R., 'Maulawis Mystik und seine Dialektik', in *Trudï XXV mezhdunar. kongressa vostokovedov*, II (Moscow 1963), 362–4.
Köprülü, M. Fuad' 'Fuzûlî', *İA* (1947), 37. cüz, 686–99.
——, 'Hâcû-i Kirmânî', *İA* (1948), 39. cüz, 36–40.
Košut Jaromír, *Hâfiz. Jeho život a jeho básně* (Prague 1881).
Kotetishvili, V. V., 'K voprosu o ponimanii sushchnosti poezii Khafeza', *Trudï Univ. Tbil.*, 99 (1964), 101–25. (With Russian summary.)
Kowalski, T., 'Les Turcs dans le Šāh-nāme', *ROr.*, 15 (1939–40), 84–99.
——, *Studia nad Šāh-nāme*, 2 vols. (Kraków 1952–3).
Krachkovskiy, I. Yul., 'Arabskiye perevodï Gulistāna', *DAN-B* (1924), 101 *et seq.*
——, 'Rannyaya istoriya povesti o Medjnune i Leyle v arabskoy literature', in *Alisher Navoyi* (1946), 31–67; German tr.: *Oriens*, 8/1 (1955), 1–50.
Krause, Max, 'Al-Biruni. Ein iran. Forscher des Mittelalters', *Isl.*, 26 (1942), 1–15.
Krïmskiy, A., 'Nizami i yego izucheniye', in *Niz. Gyandzh.*, *Sbornik* (see *s.v.* 'Niẓāmī'), 139–83.
Krïms'kïy, A., *Khafïz ta yoho pisni* (Kiev 1924) (With extensive bibliography.)
Kubíčková, V., *Qāānī, poète persan du XIXe siècle* (Prague 1954).
——, 'La qaṣīda à l'honneur de Wağīhuddīn Zangī', *ArOr.*, 20 (1952), 435–41.

Kūhī Kirmānī, Ḥ., *Tarānahā-i millī, "fahlaviyyāt"* (Tehran 1310).
——, *Haft-ṣad tarāna az tarānahā-i rūstā'ī-i Īrān* (Tehran 1327).
Kuliyev, Abbasali, *Abdurrakhman Dzhami* (Baku 1964). (In Azeri.)
Lazar Zhilber (= Gilbert Lazard), 'Du risolayi tibbiyi asri X dar forsiyi darī', *ShS*, 1958/10, 129–38 = 'Dva meditsinskikh traktata etc.', in *Rūdakī va zamoni ū* (see *s.v.* 'Rūdakī').
Lentz, Wolfg., *Goethes Noten und Abhandlungen zum West-östlichen Divan* (Hamburg 1958).
——, "Aṭṭār als Allegoriker. Bemerkungen zu Ritters "Meer der Seele"', *Isl.*, 35 (1960), 52–96.
Lescot, R., 'Quelques pages inédites de Djāmī', *BEO Damas*, 7–8 (1937/8), 177–94.
—— 'Chronologie de l'œuvre de Hafiz', *BEO Damas*, 10 (1944), 57–100.
Levend, A. S., 'Türk edebiyatında Leylâ ve Mecnûn yazan şairler', *Türk Dili Araştırmaları Yıllığı, Bell.* (1957), 105–13.
——, 'Attar ile Tutmacı'nın Gül ü Husrev mesnevileri', *ibid.*, 161–203.
——, 'Tutmacı'nın Gül ü Husrev mesnevisi', *VIII. Türk Dil Kurultayında okunan Bilimsel Bildiriler 1957* (Ankara 1960), 169–74.
——, *Arap, Fars ve Türk edebiyatlarında Leylâ ve Mecnun hikâyesi* (Ankara 1959).
——, *Ali Şir Navaî. I. Hayatı, sanatı ve kişiliği* (Ankara 1965).
Levy, R., 'A Prose Version of the Yūsuf and Zulaikhā Legend, ascribed to Pīr-i Anṣār of Harāt', *JRAS* (1929), 103–6.
Machalski, Fr., 'Uwagi o liczbie mnogiej rzeczowników w Safar-nama Nasir-i Xusraua', *ROr.*, 13 (1937), 123–8.
——, 'Tarjama-i rubā'iyyāt-i 'Umar-i Khayyām ba-zabān-i Lahistānī', *Majmū'a-i Anjuman-i Īrān-shināsī*, 1 (Tehran 1325).
Maftūn: see Shamsu'd-dīn Faqīr.
Maghribī, *Dīvān*, ≅, the more recent: *s.l.* 1344/1925.
——, *Kulliyyāt-i dīvān* (reprint of the ed. by Suhaylī) (1337).
Mahdī-khān Astarābādī: see p. 42g.
Maḥjūb, Muḥ. Ja'far, 'Kalīla u Dimna', *FĪZ*, 5/2 (1336).
——, 'Laylī u Majnūn-i Niẓāmī va Majnūn u Laylī-i Amīr Khusrau-i Dihlavī', *Sukhan*, 14 (1342), 620–37.
Maḥmūd-Khān Ṣabā, *Dīvān* (Tehran 1329) (Arm.).
Maḥmūd Shabistarī, *Gulshan-i Raz: The Mystic Rose Garden.* The Persian text, with an English translation and notes, chiefly from the comm. of Muh. b. Yahya Lahiji by E. W. Whinfield (London 1880). – *The Dialogue of the Gulshan-i Raz or Mystical Garden of Roses*, with the introduction to the Diwan of Be-Dil and selections from the Rubaiyat of Omar Khayyam, by Johnson-Pasha (Dublin 1908) (by E. A. Johnson, London 1887). – Further editions and translations: see Arberry (B 1). Moreover the Swedish tr. by Ax. Er. Hermelin (1926).
——, Comm. by Ḥājjī Mīrzā Ibrāhīm Sabzavārī, lith. (Tehran 1303/1885). – Comm. by Lāhijī, *Mafātīḥu'l-i'jāz*, with introd. by Kayvān Samī'ī (Tehran 1337).
——, 'Shāriḥān-i Gulshan-i rāz', *Arm.*, 32 (1342), 108–10.
——, *Mir'ātu'l-muḥaqqiqīn* (Shīrāz 1317).
Maḥmūdī Bakhtyārī, 'Alī-qulī, *Rāhī ba-maktab-i Ḥāfiẓ* (Tehran 1345).
Mahsatī Ganjavī, *Dīvān*, ed. by Ṭāhirī Shihāb (Tehran 1335; 1336).
——, *Ruba'ilər* (Baku 1940; 1957).
Majewska, Barbara, 'Gazele Hafiza v nieopublikowanym przekładzie Wiernikowskiego', *Przegl. Or.*, 1 (33) (1960), 39–68.
Majlisī: see Muḥ. Bāqir.
Makovel'skiy, A. O., 'Nizamiana', *Trudī Inst. filosofii AN AzSSR*, 1 (Baku 1945).
Maktabī Shīrāzī, *Laylī u Majnūn*, ≅. – Ed. by Ḥ. Kūhī Kirmānī (Tehran 1312). – Ed. by Ism. Ashraf (Shiraz [1343]).

——, *Kalimāt-i ʿaliyya-i gharrā* ["Author not certain"], ed. by Kūhī Kirmānī (Tehran 1313).
Mamed-zade, G. R., 'P'yesa "Kerim Shirei" i vopros o date vozniknoveniya pervogo dramaticheskogo proizvedeniya v Iranu', *V konf. po iranskoy filologii* (Dushanbe 1966), 77-8.
Manūchihrī, *Menoutchehri.* Texte, traduction par A. de Biberstein-Kazimirski (Paris 1886).
——, *Dīvān*, ed. [based on 21 MSS.] by Muḥ. Dabīr Siyāqī (Tehran 1326; 1338).
Marek, Jan, 'Amīr Muʿizzī. (Einige Verse im Vergleich zweier Traditionen)', *ArOr.*, 24 (1956), 252–71.
Marr, Y. N., 'Perevod gazeli Nizami iz rukopisi Instituta Vostokovedeniya AN SSSR', *Iranskiye yazïkï*, I, 144–5.
Marzbān b. Rustam, *The Marzubán-náme, a Book of Fables, originally compiled in the dialect of Ṭabaristán, and translated into Persian by Saʿdu'd-dín-i-Waráwíní*, ed. by Mírzá Muḥ. of Qazwín (London 1909) (GMS, 8).; reprints: Tehran 1332; 1337. – *The Tales of Marzuban*, transl. by Reub. Levy (London 1959).
Maskūb, Shāhrukh, *Muqaddama bar Rustam va Suhrāb* (Tehran 1344).
Masrūr, Ḥusayn, 'Sharḥ-i ḥāl-i Kamālu'd-dīn Ismāʿīl-i Iṣfahānī', *Arm.*, 7, 19–23 and contin.
——, 'Sharḥ-i ḥāl-i Auḥadī-i Marāgha'ī', *Arm.*, 9, 123–34.
Massé, H., *Essai sur le poète Saadi, suivi d'une bibliographie* (Paris 1919).
——, *Les Epopées Persanes. Ferdausi et l'épopée nationale* (Paris 1935).
——, 'Le voyage de Farhâd-Mîrzâ (Turquie, Égypte, Hedjaz)', in *Mélanges Gautier*, 348–56.
——, 'Quinze poésies de Qasim-ol-Anvar', in *Charisteria* (B VIa), 164–78.
——, 'Les versions persanes des contes d'animaux', in *L'Ame de l'Iran* (B VIa), 127–50.
Massignon, L., *La passion d'al Ḥosayn i. Manṣūr al-Ḥallādj, martyr mystique de l'islām*, 2 vols. (Paris 1922).
Masʿūd-i Saʿd-i Salmān, *Dīvān*, ≌. – Ed. by Rashīd Yāsimī (Tehran 1319, 1339).
——, *Ashʿār-i guzīda* [For high schools] ed. by R. Yāsimī ([Tehran] 1319).
McDonald, M. V., 'The Religious and Social Views [of] Nizami of Ganjeh', *Iran*, I (1963), 97–101.
Meier, F., 'Der Geistmensch bei dem persischen Dichter ʿAṭṭār', *Eranos-Jb.*, XIII (1945).
——, *Die schöne Mahsatī. Ein Beitrag zur Geschichte des persischen Vierzeilers*, I (Wiesbaden 1963).
——, 'A Difficult Quatrain of Mahsatî', in *Mélanges Massé* (Tehran 1963), 269–81.
Mijmar, *Dīvān*, lith. (Tehran [n.d.]; Tehran 1312/1895); w. introd. by M. Ṭabāṭabā'ī (Tehran 1345).
Miklukho-Maklay, N. D., 'O proiskhozhdenii "Dopolneniya" k "Tazkirat al-Avliyā" 'Aṭṭāra', *KS.* 22 (1956), 19–27.
Miller, B. V., 'O dialekte g. Shustera. Suficheskaya poema na shusterskom dialekte i opït grammaticheskoy kharakteristiki poslednego', *Iran*, 3 (1929), 71–93.
Minorsky, Vl., 'Bābā Ṭāhir-i 'Uryān', *EI*, 3, 661–4 = *Arm.*, 9, 569–88 = *İA*, 13. cüz, 166–70; id. *EI*, New Ed., *s.v.* 'Bābā Ṭ.',
——, 'The Poetry of Shāh Ismāʿīl', *BSOS*, 10 (1942), 1006a–53a.
——, 'L'épopée persane et la littérature populaire russe', in *Hazāra-i Fird.* (Tehran 1944), 48–57.
——, 'Khāqānī and Andronicus Comnenus', *BSOAS*, 11 (1945), 550–78 = *Iranica* (B VIa), 120–50; in Persian: *FĪZ*, I (1332).
——, 'Vīs u Rāmīn, a Parthian Romance', *ibid.*, 11 (1946), 741–63; 12 (1947), 20–35; 16 (1954), 91–2 = *Iranica*, 151–99; in Persian: *FĪZ*, 4/2 (1335), 113–72 = *Vīs u Rāmīn*, ed. by M. J. Maḥjūb, 391–440.
——, 'Pūr-i Bahā and his Poems', in *Charisteria* (B VIa), 186–201.
——, 'Pūr-i Bahā's Mongol Ode', *BSOAS*, 18/2 (1956), 261–78.
——, 'The Older Preface to the "Shāh-nāma"', in *Studi Orientalistici in onore di Giorgio Levi Della Vida*, II (Roma 1956), 159–79.
Mīnuvī, Mujtabā, 'Kitāb-i "Hazāra-i Firdausī" va buṭlān-i intisāb-i "Yusūf u Zalīkhā" ba-Firdausī', *Ruzgār-i nau*, 5/3 (1323), 16–36.

——, 'Vīs u Rāmīn', *Sukhan*, 6 (1333), 13–21; II. (Contents), *ibid.*, 6 (1334), 129–37.
——, 'Ijtimā'-i kavākib dar sāl-i 582', *MDAT*, 2/4 (1334), 16–53.
——, 'Yakī az fārsiyyāt-i Abū-Nuvās', in *Z.V. Togan'a Armağān* (Istanbul 1955), 437–50; *MDAT*, 1/3 (1333), 62–77.
——, 'Az khazā'in-i Turkiya', *MDAT*, 4/2 (1335), 42–75 (*i.a.* Bābā Ṭāhir, Niẓāmu'l-mulk, 'Umar-i Khayyām-i shā'ir).
——, 'Qiṣṣa-i Mūsh u gurba', *Yaghmā*, 7/8 (1336), separate print 20 pp.
——, 'Dar bāra-i mathnavī-i Taḥrīmatu'l-Qalam-i Ḥakīm Sanā'ī', *FĪZ*, 5/1 (1335), 5–15.
——, 'Kāpūs-nāma-i Frāi. Tamrīnī dar fann-i tazvīr-shināsī', *Yaghmā*, 9 (1335), 448–65, 481–93 (Turkish: *Şarkiyat Mecmuası*, 1958/2, 105–30).
——, 'Khāk-pāy-i sag-i ma'shūq (Jāmī)', *Yaghmā*, 12/11 (1338), 511–6.
——, 'Shaykh(i) San'ān', *MDAT*, 8/3 (1340), 11–13.
Mirzoyev, Abdulghanī, *Binoyī* (Stalinabad 1957).
——, *Abu Abdullo Rūdakī* (Stalinabad 1958) (in Russian characters) = *Abū-'Abdu'llāh Rūdakī* (Stalinabad 1958) (in Arabic characters).
——, *Abu-'Abdu'llāh Rūdakī va inkishāf-i ghazal dar 'aṣrhā-i X–XV* (Stalinabad 1957) = *Rudaki i rozvitiye gazeli v X–XV vv.* (Stalinabad 1958).
——, 'Novїy istochnik po literature Irana safevidskogo perioda', *Trudї XXV. mezhdun. kongr. vostokovedov*, II (Moscow 1963), 269–75.
——, ' "Shahroshūb" va asosi ijtimoii paydoishi on', *V konf. po iranskoy filologii* (Dushanbe 1966), 82–6.
Mishkātu'd-dīn, Abu'l-Ḥusayn, *Naẓarī ba-falsafa-i Ṣadru'd-dīn-i Shīrāzī (Mullā Ṣadrā)* (Tehran 1345).
Modjtehedy, Karim, *Afzaladdīn Kāshānī, philosophe iranien (XIIe–XIIIe siècles)* (Paris 1964).
Molé, M., 'Rustam a Kṛsāspa. Przyczynek do badań nad formacją eposu irańskiego', *Spraw. Pols. Ak. Umiej.*, 49 (1948), 269–72.
——, 'Garšāsp et les Sagsār' [The symbolism of the motifs in the *Garshāsp-nāma* is not yet Islamic, but no longer Orthodox-Zoroastrian], *La Nouvelle Clio*, 3 (1951), 128–33.
——, 'Un poème "persan" du Comte de Gobineau' ["Ferydun"→Kūsh-nāma], *ibid.*, 4 (1952), 116–30.
——, 'L'épopée iranienne après Firdōsī', *ibid.*, 5 (1953), 377–93.
——, 'Vīs u Rāmīn et l'histoire seldjoukide', *Annali* (Napoli), N.S., 9 (1960), 1–30.
Molière, *Tarjama-i Mīzāntrūp az āthār-i Mūliyer: Gudhārish-i Mardum-gurīz* [In verse] (Istanbul 1286/1869).
——, *Ḥikāyat-i ṭabīb-i ijbārī*, lith. (Tehran 1306/1888).
Mommsen, Momme, 'Studien zum West-östlichen Divan', *SBAW*, Berlin (1962).
Monteil, Vincent, 'Neuf Gazals de Hâfez', *REI*, 22 (1954), 21–57.
Morier, J. (cf. *Yādgār*, 1/5, 28–50), *The Adventures of Haji Baba of Isfahan*, transl. into Persian by Ḥājī Shaikh Aḥmad-i Kirmānī, and ed., with notes, by D. C. Phillott (Calcutta 1905; 1924). – *Maẓharu'l-'Ajam, Savāniḥ-i 'umrī-i Ḥājjī Bābā Iṣfahānī*, tr. by Mīrzā Asadu'llāh-Khān Shaukatu'l-vizāra (Bombay 1323/1905; 1329/1911). – Tr. by Mīrzā Khalīj Bey (Pakistan 1964).
Morochnik, S. B. and Rozenfel'd, B. A., *Omar Khayyam – poet, mїslitel', ucheniy* (Stalinabad 1957).
Mudarrisī Chahārdihī, Murt., *Zindagī va falsafa-i Ḥājj Mullā Hādī Sabzavārī* (Tehran 1334).
——, 'Farhād-Mīrzā', *Arm.*, 29/6 (1339), 257–61 and 4 contin.; 30/1 (1340), 11–8 (his liter. work) and 1 contin.
Muḥ. 'Alī Dā'ī'l-islām, "Urfī-i Shīrāzī', *Arm.*, 9, 321–30 and contin.
Muḥ. b. Badr al-Jājarmī, *Mu'nisu'l-aḥrār fī daqā'iqi'l-ash'ār*, ed. by Mīr Ṣāliḥ Ṭabībī, 1 (1337).
Muḥ. Bāqir b. Muḥ. Taqī Majlisī: see Arberry (B 1) and *NY*.
Muḥ. Ibn-Ghazi de Malatya, *Le Jardin des Esprits (Rawzat-al-'oqoul)*, 1ère partie publiée et trad. par H. Massé (Paris 1938).
Muḥaqqiq, M., 'Yād-dāshthāī dar bāra-i Marzbān-nāma', *FĪZ*, 8/1-2 (1339), 37–71.

——, "Alavī būdan-i Nāṣir-i Khusrau', *Yaghmā*, 14 (1340), nr. 153, 35–41.
Muḥsin Fayḍ, *Dīvān-i ash'ār*, lith. (Tehran 1348/1929). – Ed. by Asadu'llāh Shahshahānī (1337).
——, *Kulliyyāt ba-ḍamīma-i risāla-i Gulzār-i quds* (Tehran 1339).
——, (1) *Al-ḥaqā'iq fī maḥāsini'l-akhlāq*; (2) *Qurratu'l-'uyūn fi'l-ma'ārif va'l-ḥikam*; (3) *Miṣbāḥu'l-anẓār* (Tehran 1378/1960).
Muḥtasham Kāshī, *Dīvān* (Bombay 1304/1886; Tehran 1337).
——, 'Rubā'iyyāt-i sitta' [From the Tadhkira of Naṣrābādī], *Arm.*, 11, 271–2. On this M.N., 'Intiqād', *ibid.*, 351–2. See also *s.v.* 'Vaqār'.
Mu'īn, Muḥ., *Ḥāfiẓ-i shīrīn-sukhan* (Tehran 1319).
——, (Cited *ibid.*, 1361:) *Ganjīna-i 'irfān. Tafsīr-i dīvān-i Ḥāfiẓ.*
——, 'Burhānī va qaṣīda-i ū', *NDAT*, 1/1 (1327), 7–18.
——, 'Amīr Khusrau-i Dihlavī', *Mihr*, 8, 25–32 and contin.
——, 'Lughāt-i fārsī-i Ibn-i Sīnā va ta'thīr-i ānhā dar adabiyyāt', *MDAT*, 2/2 (1333), 1–38 (on p. 2: list of the oldest prose-works).
——, 'Yak qaṣīda-i Rūdakī [*būy-i jūy-i Mūliyān.*]', *ibid.*, 6/3-4 (1338), 71–92.
——, *Taḥlīl-i Haft paykar-i Niẓāmī*, 1 (Tehran 1338) (Univ.).
——, Lists of his numerous studies: *REI* (1951), 151 *et seq.*; *Bar-guzīda-i shi'r-i fārsī* (B VIa), on the cover.
Mu'izzī, *Dīvān*, ed. by 'Abbās Iqbāl (Tehran 1318).
Mukhtārī Ghaznavī, Ḥakīm 'Uthmān, *Dīvān*, ed. by Ruknu'd-dīn Humāyūn Farrukh (Tehran 1337). – Ed. by Jalālu'd-dīn Humā'ī (Tehran 1341).
Mullojonovi Shahristonī, 'Shairi asri XIV Ibni Yamin', *ShS*, 1960/8, 127–39.
Murtaḍavī, Man., '"Pīr" az naẓar-i Khvāja-i Shīrāzī', *NDAT*, 6/2 (1333), 154–88.
——, "Ishq dar dīvān-i Ḥāfiẓ', *ibid.*, 6/4 (1333), 395–434.
——, "Ishq az naẓar-i Maulānā Jalālu'd-dīn', *ibid.*, 7/1 (1334), 67–80.
——, "Ishq az naẓar-i Khvāja-i Shīrāz', *ibid.*, 81–96.
——, 'Ta'aththur-i Ḥāfiẓ az Sa'dī', *ibid.*, 8 (1335), 2–34, 165–80; 9/1 (1336), 59–72.
——, 'Yād-dāshtī dar bāra-i ta'aththur-i Khvāja Ḥāfiẓ az dāstān-i shaykh-i Ṣan'ān', *ibid.*, 7/4 (1335), 362–93 (see *s.v.* 'Mīnuvī').
——, 'Taḥlīl-i yakī az tamthīlāt-i Mathnavī', *ibid.*, 10 (1337), 133–64.
——, 'Īhām yā khaṣīṣa-i aṣlī-i sabk-i Ḥāfiẓ', *ibid.*, 11/2 (1338), 191–224, 485–500; 12 (1339), 65–84.
——, 'Yād-dāshthā-i marḥūm-i Qazvīnī', *ibid.*, 12/4 (1339), 401–60 [on 'Aṭṭār, *Muṣībat-nāma*, ed. 1354/1935].
——, 'Muqallidīn-i Shāh-nāma dar daura-i Mughūl va Tīmūrī va ta'rīkh-i manẓūm-i Shamsu'd-dīn-i Kāshānī', *Ibid.*, 14 (1341), 141–75, 323–52.
——, *Maktab-i Ḥāfiẓ yā muqaddama bar Ḥāfiẓ-shināsī* (Tehran 1344).
——, 'Naqsh bar āb', *NDAT*, 17 (1344), 419–39.
Mushtāq Iṣfahānī, *Dīvān*, ed. by Ḥus. Makkī (Tehran 1320).
Muẓaffaru'd-dīn-Shāh: see Storey, II/2, 346 *et seq.* To be added: *Duvvumīn safar-nāma* [1320/1902] ([Tehran] 1320/1902).
——, 'Safar-nāma ... az Tabrīz ba Khūy dar hangām-i vilāyat-i 'ahdī, ed. by H. Farmān-farmāiyān', *Yaghmā*, 16 (1342), 1–16.
Nafīsī, Sa'īd, 'Adīb Ṣābir-i Tirmidhī', *Arm.*, 4, 230–45; 294–306.
——, 'Jamālu'd-dīn 'Abdu'r-Razzāq', *ibid.*, 6, 109–18 and contin.
——, *Aḥvāl va muntakhab-i ash'ār-i Khvājū-i Kirmānī* (Tehran 1307).
——, *Aḥvāl va ash'ār-i Rūdakī-i Samarqandī*, 3 vols. (Tehran 1309–19) (cf. *Arm.*, 12, 199–206 and contin.; 2nd improved ed. 1341).
——, 'Madrasa-i Niẓāmiyya-i Baghdād', *Mihr*, 2/2 (1313), 117–27.
——, 'Majdu'd-dīn Hamgar-i Shīrāzī', *Mihr*, 2/10-12 (1313–14), 1055–60, 1117–23, 1213–20.

——, *Aḥvāl va ash'ār-i fārsī-i shaykh Bahā'ī* (Tehran 1316).
——, *Dar pīrāmūn-i ash'ār va aḥvāl-i Ḥāfiẓ* (Tehran 1321).
——, *Just-u-jū dar aḥvāl va āthār-i Farīdu'd-dīn 'Aṭṭār-i Nīshābūrī* (Tehran 1320).
——, 'Vazn-i Shāh-nāma-i Firdausī', *Dānish-nāma*, 2 (Tehran 1326), 123–48.
——, 'Le "Yûsuf et Zalîkhâ" attribué à Firdowsy', *ArOr.*, 18/3 (1950), 351–3.
——, 'Ta'rīkh-i durust-i dar-gudhasht-i Sa'dī', *MDAT*, 6/1 (1337), 64–82.
——, 'Chand nukta-i tāza dar bāra-i Rūdakī', *ibid.*, 6/3-4 (1338), 21–39.
——, 'Qadīmtarīn nuskhahā-i rubā'iyyāt-i 'Umar-i Khayyām', in *Trudī XXV. mezhdunar. kongressa vostokovedov*, II (Moscow 1963), 367–73.
Nafthatu'l-maṣdūr: see Nūru'd-dīn.
Na'imuddin, Sayyid, 'Some Unknown Qasidas of 'Urfi of Shiraz', *IC*, 30/4 (1956), 385–409; 33 (1959), 232–9.
Najāt Qumī, *Gul-i kushtī*, ed. by Ḥ. Kūhī Kirmānī (Tehran 1327). – Specimens: *Arm.*, 15, 180–2 and contin.
Nakhjavānī, Ḥus., "Abdu'r-Razzāq b. Dunbulī-i mutakhalliṣ ba "Maftūn"', *NDAT*, 2/1 (1328), 1–13.
——, 'Zindagānī va shakhṣiyyat-i Maliku'sh-shu'arā Fatḥ-'Alī-Khān Ṣabā', *ibid.*, 3/3-4 (1329), 66–76.
——, 'Khvāja Humāmu'd-dīn-i Tabrīzī', *ibid.*, 3/1-2 (1329) 36–46.
Nakhshabī (resp. Qādirī), *The Tooti Namah, or Tales of a Parrot*, ed. and transl. [by F. Gladwin] (London 1801). – *Les contes du perroquet*. Texte persan: L. Bogdanov (Paris 1927); idem, transl. "pour la première fois en français" (Paris 1948). – *Touti-Nameh ou les Contes du Perroquet de Ziya-ed-Din Nakhchabi d'après la réd. de Moh. Qaderi*, traduits par Henri Muller (Paris 1934). – *Skazki popugaya* [Selection, with vocabulary], ed. by V. A. Zhukovskiy (St.-Petersburg 1887; 1901). – *Das persische Papageienbuch*, übers. von C. J. L. Iken. Neudruck mit einer Einleitung von R. Schmidt, 2nd ed. (Berlin 1905). – Further texts and translations: see Arberry (B I), 544 *et seq.*, Ethé (B v), 325 *et seq.*; cf. Chauvin (B I), VIII.
Nashāṭ, *Ghazaliyyāt*: see Arberry (B I).
——, *Ganjīna*, lith. (Tehran 1282/1866).
——, *Ganjīna-i dīvān*, ed. by Ḥus. Nakha'ī (Tehran 1337).
Nāṣiḥ, Muḥ. 'Alī, 'Sharḥ-i ḥāl-i ḥakīm Khāqānī', *Arm.*, 5, 375–88 and contin.; 6, 98–102 and contin.
——, 'Ṣāḥib b. 'Abbād', *ibid.*, 8, 212–20 and contin.
Nāṣir-i Khusrau, *Dīvān-i ash'ār* [Qaṣīdas, qiṭ'as, Raushanā'ī-nāma, Sa'ādat-nāma, Risāla], ed. by Naṣru'llāh Taqavī, with introd. by Ḥas. Taqī-zāda and notes by 'A. Akb. Dih-khudā (Tehran 1304-7) (emendations: *Arm.*, 12, 271 *et seq*); repr. Tehran 1337. – Ed. by M. Darvīsh (Tehran 1339).
——, *Pānzdah qaṣīda az rūy-i qadīmtarīn nuskhahā-i khaṭṭī* (Tehran 1340).
——, Older editions and transl.: Ethé (B v), 281 *et seq.*
——, A. V. Zhukovskiy, 'Pesn' Nasiri Khosrova', *ZVORAO*, 4 (1890), 386–93.
——, *Sefer-Nameh. Relation du voyage*, publié, traduit et annoté par Ch. Schefer (Paris 1881). – Reprints: cf. Storey, 1138–41. – *Safar-nāma, Raushanā'ī-nāma, Sa'ādat-nāma* (Berlin 1341/1922) (Kāviyānī). Review by A. Semenov, *Iran*, 1, 215–24. – *Puteshestviye*. Russian transl. by Ye. E. Bertel's (Moscow 1935). – See also p. 463, note 18.
Nāṣiru'd-dīn-Shāh: see Storey, II/2, 340–2 and Bertel's, *Ocherk* (B v).
——, *Safar-nāma* (Isfahan 1343) (Andīsha).
——, *Dīvān*, ed. by Muḥ. Bāqir I'tiḍādī (1334).
——, *Dīvān-i kāmil-i ash'ār*, ed. by 'Alī Rāhjīrī (Qā'im-maqām), 2nd ed. ([Tehran] 1339).
Naṣru'llāh b. Muḥ., Abu'l-Ma'ālī, *Kalīla u Dimna*, ed. by 'Abdu'l-'Aẓīm Qarīb, 4th ed. (Tehran 1359/1940). – Ed. by Sayyid Ja'far Sajjādī (Tehran 1339). – Ed. by Ḥasan-zāda Āmulī (Tehran 1341). – Ed. by M. Mīnuvī (Tehran 1343) (Univ.). – See Arberry (B I) and Ethé (B v). On the Arabic verses in *Kalīla u Dimna* cf. Mahdavī Dāmghānī, *Yaghmā*, 16 (1342).

——, An. Zajączkowski, *Études sur la langue vieille-osmanlie*, I: *Morceaux choisis de la traduction ... de Calila et Dimna* (Kraków 1934). – Tr. into Azeri: Rəhim Sultanov (Baku 1960).

Navābī, Māhyār, 'Khāndān-i Viṣāl-i Shīrāzī', *NDAT*, 7 (1334), 190–239, 288–356, 392–459.

Navā'ī, 'Abdu'l-Ḥusayn, "Abdu'l-Vāsi'-i Jabalī', *Yādgār*, 1/3, 44–6.

——, 'Anvarī va nuskha-i 'Uyūnu'l-ḥikma-i Ibn-i Sīnā', *ibid.*, 2/7, 45–9.

——, 'Ḥabsiyya-i Shāh Shaykh Abu'l-Isḥāq', *Mihr*, 8 (1331), 543–7.

Navā'ī, 'Alī-shīr ("Fānī"), *Dīvān*, ed. by Ruknu'd-dīn Humāyūn Farrukh. With introd. by 'A.-A. Ḥikmat (Tehran 1342).

Nāẓir, Aḥmad, *Ẓuhūrī Turshīzī* [English] (Bombay). Cf. Catalogue of the bookseller "Ṭahūrī" (Tehran 1335), 14.

Naẓīrī Nīshāpūrī, *Ghazaliyyāt*, ≅, see Arberry (B I).

——, *Dīvān*, ed. by Maẓ. Muṣaffā (Tehran 1340).

Nicholson, R. A., *Studies in Islamic Mysticism* ('Abū Sa'īd b. Abi'l-Khayr', 1–76) (Cambridge 1921; reprint 1967).

——, *Studies in Islamic Poetry* ('An Early Persian Anthology [*Lubābu'l-albāb*]', 'The Meditations of Ma'arrī') (Cambridge 1921).

——, *A Persian Forerunner of Dante* [Sanā'ī] (Towyn-on-Sea 1944) (Persian tr.: *Yādgār*, 1/4, 1323–4, 48–57).

Nikitina, V., 'Oyid ba mas'alayi mahorati badeyiyi Nosiri Khisrav', *ShS*, 1957/8, 111–22.

——, 'Peyzazh v kasīde Nasir-i Khosrova', *Dokladī Vīsshey shkolī* (1961), 172 *et seq.*

Ni'matu'llāh, Shāh, *Dīvān*, ed. by Abu'l-Qāsim Vāfī 'Alī-shāh Sīrjānī (Tehran 1316). – Ed. by M. 'Ilmī (Tehran 1329).

Niẓāmī, Complete epics and *Ganjīna-i Ganjavī* (cont. biography, lyric poetry, and vocabulary), ed. by Vaḥīd Dastgirdī (Tehran 1313–8 and reprints).

——, *Kulliyyāt-i Khamsa* (Tehran 1341). – *Choix de vers de la Khamsa de Niẓāmī.* Texte persan, publié par M. Th. Houtsma (Leiden 1921).

——, *Pyat' poem* [Transl. of the Khamsa], ed. by Yevg. E. Bertel's and V. V. Gol'tsev (Moscow 1946). – *Izbrannīye proizvedeniya*, ed. by V. V. Gol'tsev and P. G. Skosīrev. Vstup. stat'ya i kom.
Yevg. E. Bertel'sa (Sovetskiy pisatel' 1947). – Turkish transl. of the Khamsa: Rodosī-zāde Meḥmed-efendi (cf. Brusalī Meḥ. Ṭāhir, *'Osm. Mü'ellifleri*, I, 315).

——, *Makhzanu'l-asrār*, ed. by N. Bland (London 1844). – Crit. ed. by A. A. Alizade (Baku 1960). – Ed. by Pizhmān Bakhtyārī (Tehran 1343). – *The Treasury of Mysteries*, transl. with introd. essay on the Life and Times of Nezāmī by G. H. Dārāb (London 1945). – *Sokrovishcha tayn.* Interlinear tr. by A. A. Romaskevich, the MS. kept in the Inst. lit. AN AzSSR. – *Sokrovishchnitsa tayn*, tr. by Marietta Shaginyan (Baku 1947). – Tr. by K. A. Lipskerov and S. V. Shervinskiy (Moscow 1959). – Turkish: M. Nuri Gençosman (Ankara 1946).

——, *Khosrov i Shirin.* Crit. ed. by L. A. Khetagurov (Baku 1960). – *Khusrau u Shīrīn*, ed. by Ḥus. Pizhmān Bakhtyārī (Tehran 1343). – Tr. by Konst. Lipskerov (Baku 1947); the same transl.: (a) with epilogue by L. I. Klimovich (Moscow 1953); (b) with epilogue by Yevg. E. Bertel's (Moscow 1955). – Turkish: Sabri Sevsevil (Istanbul 1955).

——, *Farhād u Shīrīn*: see H. W. Duda.

——, *Laylī u Majnūn.* Crit. text ed. by A. A. Alesker-zade and F. Babayev (Moscow 1965). – Ed. in Tajik script by A. Dehotī (Stalinabad 1947). *Khulāṣa-i Layli u Majnūn*, ed. by Jalāl Matīnī (Mashhad 1341). – *Lejla und Medshnun. Der berühmteste Liebesroman desMorgenlandes.* Aus dem Persischen übertragen von R. Gelpke (Zürich 1963) (ill.). – *The Story of Layla and Majnun.* Transl. from the Persian and ed. by R. Gelpke (1966). – Turkish prose-tr.: *Leylâ ile Mecnun*, tr. by Ali Nihat Tarlan (Istanbul 1943). – Russian: *Leyli i Medzhnun*, tr. by Pavel Antokol'skiy, with introd. and notes by Rustam Aliyev (Moscow 1957). – Azeri: tr. by Səməd Vurgun (Baku 1959).

——, *Heft Pejker. Ein romantisches Epos*, hrsg. von H. Ritter und J. Rypka (Prague 1934). – *Haft Paykar*, ed. by Pizhmān Bakhtyārī (Tehran 1344). – *The Haft Paikar (The Seven Beauties)*, transl. with a comm. by C. E. Wilson, 2 vols. (London 1924). – *Příběh panice*, přel. Jan Rypka a Vítězslav Nezval (Prague 1939) (bibliophile ed.). – *Sedm princezen*, přel. a doslovem opatřil Jan Rypka. Zbásnili Svat. Kadlec, Vlad. Holan a Jar. Seifert (Prague 1940; 1952; 1959). – *Sem'-krasavits*, per. Vlad. Derzhavin (Moscow 1959). – Per. Ryurik Ivnev. With introd. by M. Arif (Baku 1959). – *Rasskaz indiyskoy tsarevnï*, per. A. E. Gruzinskiy (Moscow 1952). – 'Sem' portretov. Novella ("Māhān")', per. Yevg. E. Bertel's, *Vostok*, 1923/3, 14–25. – *Die sieben Geschichten der sieben Prinzessinnen*, tr. by R. Gelpke (Zürich 1959). – *Terjeme-i ḥikāye-i Heft Peyker*, free tr. in prose by Yümnī (Istanbul 1289/1872; 1341/1922).

——, *Sharaf-nāma*, crit. ed. by A. A. Ali-zade (AN AzSSR, Baku 1947). – *The Sikandar Náma, E Bará* (sic!), *or Book of Alexander the Great*, transl. into prose by H. Wilberforce Clarke (London 1881). – *Iskanders Warägerfeldzug. Ein iranischer Heldensang des Mittelalters aus Niẓâmîs Iskender-nâme*, im Auszug metr. nachgebildet von Georg Jacob (Glückstadt [1934]). – *Sikandar-Nāmah I–XV*, öfversatt af Ax. Er. Hermelin (Lund [1933]).

——, *Iqbāl-nāma*, crit. ed. by F. Babayev (AN AzSSR, Baku 1947).

——, *Iskender-name*, per. Konst. Lipskerov. With epilogue by L. Klimovich (Moscow 1953) = I–II, with introd. by M. Y. Gulizade (AN AzSSR, Baku 1953). – *Iskender-name*. Chast' 1: *Sharaf-name*, Per. i red. Yevg. E. Bertel's (Baku 1940); Chast' 2: *Iqbal-name*, podstrochnïy per. A. K. Arends, red. Yevg. E. Bertel's (in MS.). – *Iskender-name*, prozaicheskiy pereskaz poemï: S. Mstislavskiy (Moscow–Leningrad 1942).

——, *Dīvān-i qaṣā'id va ghazaliyyāt*, ed. by S. Nafīsī (with full biography) (Tehran 1338). – 'Chand ghazal-i tāza az Niẓāmī-i Ganja'ī', ed. by J. Rypka, *Arm.*, 16 (1314), 1–24. – *Dīvān*, ed. by M. Ṭabāṭabā'ī (Tehran 1334). – Translations: *Lirika*, red. Y. E. Bertel's i K. A. Lipskerov (Moscow (1947). – *Chvály*, přel. Jan Rypka a Pavel Eisner (Prague 1953).

——, Gyuzal'dzhan, L. T., 'Dva otrïvka iz Nizami na izraztsakh XIII i XIV v.', *Epigr. Vost.*, 1953/7, 17–25.

——, *Nizami Gyandzhevi. Materialï nauchnoy konferentsii* (AN AzSSR, Baku 1947).

——, *Nizami Gyandzhevi. Sbornik Statey* (AN AzSSR, Baku 1947). – *Nizami (Sbornik)*, 4 vols. (Baku 1940–7) (in Azeri).

——, Bibliography: see Arberry (B I), the monographs by Bertel's (*q.v.*), Ethé (B V), Karatay (B I), and Krïmskiy (*q.v.*).

Niẓāmī 'Arūḍī, *Chahār maqāla*, ed. by Muḥ. Qazvīnī (Leiden–London 1910) (GMS, 11/1). – Rev. by M. Mu'īn (Tehran 1334) (Univ.); enlarged Tehran 1955–7 (cf. bibliography of other reprints: Introd., 80–3). – Ed. Iqbāl and Co. (Tehran 1339). – Rev. by 'Alī Ḥaṣūrī (Tehran 1343). – Rev. transl. by E. G. Browne, with abridged transl. of Qazvīnī's notes to the Persian text (London 1921) (GMS, 11/2). – Urdu transl. by Aḥm. Ḥasan Savātī (Delhi n.d.). – *Tib ilmi ve meşhur hekimlerin mahareti*, Turkish transl. of Book IV by Abdülbaki Gölpınarlı (Istanbul 1936). – *al-Maqālāt al-arba'*, Arabic transl. by 'Abdu'l-Wahhāb 'Azzām and Yaḥyā al-Khashshāb (Cairo 1368/1949). – *Sobraniye redkostey ili chetïre besedï*, Russian transl. by S. T. Bayevskiy and Z. N. Vorozheykina (Moscow 1963).

Niẓāmu'l-mulk, *Siyaru'l-mulūk (Siyāsat-nāma)*. Ed. by Hubert Darke (Tehran 1340). – *The Book of Government*. Transl. by Hubert Darke (New Haven 1960). – *Siyāsatnāma*. Übertragen von K. E. Schabinger, Freiherr von Schowingen (Freiburg-München 1960). – See also p. 428, note 13.

Nizārī, *Dastūr-nāma*: Yevg. E. Bertel's, in *Vostochnïy Sbornik* (Leningrad), 1, 37–104.

Nöldeke, Th., 'Über die Texte des Buches von den zehn Veziren [*Bakhtyārnāma*], besonders über eine alte persische Rezension desselben', *ZDMG*, 45 (1891), 97–143.

——, 'Das Iranische Nationalepos', in *GIPh*, II, 130–211; 2nd, separate ed. (Berlin 1920).

Nūr-bakhsh Kirmānī, Javād, *Zindagī va āthār-i janāb-i Shāh Ni'matu'llāh Valī-i Kirmānī* (1337).

Nūru'd-dīn Muḥ. Khvarandīzī Khurāsānī, *Nafthatu'l-maṣdūr*. With introd. and notes by Riḍā-qulī-Khān Hidāyat, lith. (1308/1890); ed. by Amīr Yazdgardī (Tehran 1343).

Odilov, N., *Jahonbinii Jalaliddin Rumi* (Dushanbe 1964).

Ol'denburg, Sergey, 'O persidskoy prozaicheskoy versii "Knigi Sindbada"', in *Sbornik V. R. Rozen* (St.-Petersburg 1897), 253–78.

Osmanov, M. N., 'Svodï iranskogo geroicheskogo eposa ("Khuday-name" i "Shakhname") kak istochniki "Shakhname" Firdousi', *UZIV*, 19 (1958), 153–89.

——, *Firdousi. Zhizn' i tvorchestvo* (Moscow 1959).

——, 'O narodnïkh tendentsiyakh v poeme Firdousi "Shakh-name"', *KS*, 2 (1952), 38–47.

——, 'Iz opïta textologicheskoy rabotï nad Shakh-name Firdousi', *PV*, 1960/3, 123–9.

Pâzewârî-i Mâzenderânî, Emîr, *Dîwân*, hrsg. von B. Dorn und Mirzâ Moh. Schafî (St.-Petersburg 1866). – *Kanzu'l-asrār yā dīvān-i Amīr Pāzvārī*, repr. in offset from the 1866 ed., with introd. by Man. Sutūda (Tehran 1337).

Perry, B. E., 'The Origin of the Book of Sindbad', *Fabula. Journal of Folktale Studies* (Berlin), III, Fasc. 1/12 (1960).

Pertsch, W., 'Über Nachšabî's Papageienbuch', *ZDMG*, 21 (1867), 505–51.

Pinnock, William, *Jām-i Jam* [Work on geogr. and hist.], tr. by Farhād-Mīrzā, lith. (Tehran 1272/1856).

Pizhmān Bakhtyārī, 'Masīḥ-i Kāshānī', *Arm.*, 13, 228–32 and contin.; 17, 601–8.

P.N., 'Nasab-nāma-i yak ghazal-i Ḥāfiẓ', *Sukhan*, 5 (1333), 736–41 (cf. *ibid.*, 6, 1334, 144–5).

Ptitsïn, G. V., 'K voprosu o geografii Shakh-Name', *TOV*, 4 (1947), 293–311.

Qā'ānī, *Dīvān* + *Ghazaliyyāt* of Furūghī, lith. (Tehran 1274/1857; 1302/1884). – *Dīvān* + *Kitāb-i parīshān*, lith. (Bombay 1277/1860; enlarged 1293/1876). – ≃.

——, *Dīvān* + poems by his son Muḥ. Ḥasan Sāmānī, ed. by Muḥ. Ja'far Maḥjūb (Tehran 1336). (Crit. notes by Ḥasan Qāḍī Ṭabāṭabā'ī, *NDAT*, 12/4, 1339, 503–12.)

——, *Parīshān*, ed. by Ism. Ashraf (Shiraz 1338).

——, Bibliography: see *s.v.* 'Kubíčková'.

——, *Arm.*, 17, 713–5 (on the date of his death).

Qābūs-nāma: see *s.v.* 'Kay-kā'ūs'.

Qā'im-maqām, *Munsha'āt* + *Dīvān*, lith. (Tabriz 1282/1866; 1294/1877). – Ed. by Jihāngīr al-Qā'im-maqāmī (1337). – Ed. by Mu'tamadu'd-daula Ḥājj Farhād-mīrzā (Tehran 1337).

——, Further letters: *Yaghmā*, 7 (1333), 438 *et seq.*; *ibid.*, 485 *et seq.*; *RK*, 5 (1341), 213 *et seq.*

——, *Dīvān-i shi'r* (With introd. by 'Abdu'l-Vahhāb al-Qā'im-maqāmī, 1–80) (Tehran, Arm., n.d. [about 1344/1926]).

——, 'Sharḥ-i ḥāl-i Nashāṭ-i Iṣfahānī Mu'tamadu'd-daula', *Arm.*, 9, 179–83.

Qārī, *Dīvān-i albisa*, ed. by Ḥabīb Iṣfahānī (Galaṭa 1303/1886).

Qāsim Mādiḥ, *Jihāngīr-nāma* (Bombay 1309/1892).

Qāsim-i Anvār, *Kulliyyāt*, ed. by S. Nafīsī (Tehran 1337).

Qaṭrān, *Dīvān*, ed. by Muḥ. Nakhjavānī (Tabriz 1333).

Qazvīnī, Muḥ., 'Mas'ūd-i-Sa'di Salman', transl. by E. G. Browne, *JRAS* (1905), 693–740; (1906), 11–51.

——, 'An Account of the Mu'nisu'l-Ahrar; a rare Persian MS.', *BSOS*, 5 (1928–30), 97–108.

——, 'Mamdūḥīn-i Shaykh Sa'd-ī- in *Sa'dī-nāma* (see *s.v.* 'Sa'dī') (Tehran 1317), 98–175 (partly superseded by 'Abb. Iqbāls study on Sa'dī (*q.v.*)).

——, 'Ḥāfiẓ va Sulṭān Aḥm. Jalā'ir', *Yādgār*, 1/1 (1323–4), 9–12.

——, 'Manūchihrī', *ibid.*, 1/2, 52–75.

——, 'Ba'ḍī taḍmīnhā-i Ḥāfiẓ' [On verses borrowed by Ḥ. from other poets], *ibid.*, 5, 67–72; 6, 62–71; 8, 60–72; 9, 65–78.

——, Many biographical notes in *Yādgār*.

Qiṣṣa-i chahār darvīsh (Bombay 1295/1878). – *Bāgh u bahār* (Bombay 1318/1900) (in both Amīr

Khusrau as author). – In Tajik: Stalinabad 1961. – In Urdu: Mir Amman Dihlawi, *Bagh-o-bahar*, ed. by Duncan Forbes (London 1846; 1860 etc.) (about 70 editions).
Rādūyānī: see B IV.
Radzhabov, M., *Mirovozzreniye Ubayda Zokoni* (AN Tadzh. SSR, Stalinabad 1958).
"Rājī", Bamūn 'Alī, *Ḥamla-i Ḥaydarī*, lith. (Bombay 1264/1848; 1266/1850).
Rashīdī Tabrīzī, Yār Aḥmad (9th/15th cent.), *Ṭarab-khāna. Rubā'iyyāt-i Ḥakīm Khayyām-i Nīshāpūrī*, ed. by Jalālu'd-dīn Humā'ī (Tehran 1342).
Rashīdu'd-dīn Vaṭvāṭ, *Ḥadā'iqu's-siḥr fī daqā'iqu'sh-shi'r* [Poetics], ed. by 'Abb. Iqbāl (Tehran 1308).
——, *Ali's hundert Sprüche arabisch und persisch paraphrasiert*, hrsg. und übers. von H. L. Fleischer (Leipzig 1837). – 'Ṣad kalima', *Arm.*, 21, 41–50 and contin.
——, 'Si sanad', *ibid.*, 19, 73–81.
——, *Nāmahā*, ed. by Qāsim Tūysarkānī (Tehran 1339) (Univ.).
——, *Dīvān* (+*Ḥadā'iqu'-s-siḥr*), ed. by S. Nafīsī (Tehran 1339).
Rasmussen, H., *Studier over Hafiz med Sideblik til andre persiske Lyrikere* (Copenhagen 1892).
Rāynart, Dr. [Reinert], 'Mas'ala-i tajdīd-i maṭla' dar Khāqānī', *MDAT*, 12/2 (1964), 126–49.
Rempis, Chr. H., 'Avicenna als Vorläufer 'Omar Chajjāms', in *Orient. Studien. Enno Littmann* (Leiden 1935), 149–56.
——, *'Omar Chajjām und seine Vierzeiler nach den ältesten Hss. aus dem Pers. verdeutscht* (Tübingen 1935).
——, *Beiträge zur Ḫayyām-Forschung* (Abh. für die Kunde des Morgenl., 22/1) (Leipzig 1937).
——, *Neue Beiträge zur Chajjām-Forschung* (Sammlung orient. Arbeiten, 17) (Leipzig 1943).
Resulzade Mehmed Emin, *Azerbaycan şairi Nizami* (Ankara 1951).
Reychman, Jan, 'Nowe przyczynki do dziejów zainteresowań Hafizem v Polsce na początku XIX wieku', *Przegl. Or.*, 2/42 (1962), 153–7.
——, 'Ludwik Spitznagel jako tłumacz Nizamiego', *Przegl. human.*, 4 (1964), 67–79.
Richter, G., *Persiens Mystiker Dschelāl-Eddīn Rūmī: eine Stildeutung in drei Vorträgen* (Breslau 1933).
Riḍā-qulī-Khān, *Farhang-i anjuman-ārāy-i Nāṣirī*, lith. (Tehran 1288/1871; 1338).
——, *Relation de l'ambassade au Kharezm (Khiwa)*, publ., trad. par Ch. Schefer, 2 vols. (Paris 1876–9).
——, *Majma'u'l-fuṣaḥā* [A comprehensive Tadhkira], 2 vols, lith. (Tehran 1295/1878); (Tehran n.d.); ed. by Maẓ. Muṣaffā (Tehran, from 1339 onwards).
——, *Rauḍatu'ṣ-ṣafā Nāṣirī*. IXth–Xth vols. (Tehran 1339–40).
——, *Riyāḍu'l-'ārifīn* [Biographies of Ṣūfī poets], lith. (Tehran 1305/1887; 1316/1898).
Rijā'ī, Aḥm. 'Alī, *Farhang-i ash'ār-i Ḥāfiẓ*, I: *Sharḥ-i muṣṭalaḥāt-i ṣūfiyya* (Tehran 1340).
Ritter, H., *Über die Bildersprache Niẓāmīs* (Berlin–Leipzig 1927).
——, 'Zur Frage der Echtheit der Vierzeiler 'Omar Chajjāms', *OLZ* (1929), 156–63.
——, 'Das Proömium des Maṭnawī-i Maulawī', *ZDMG*, 93 (1939), 169–96.
——, 'Die Aussprüche des Bāyezīd Bisṭāmī. Eine vorläufige Skizze', in *Festschr. Tschudi* (Wiesbaden 1954), 231–43.
——, *Das Meer der Seele. Mensch, Welt und Gott in den Geschichten des Farīduddīn 'Aṭṭār* (Leiden 1955).
——, 'Philologika: VIII: Anṣārī Herewī. – Senā'ī Ġaznewī', *Isl.*, 22 (1935), 89–105; 'IX: Die vier Suhrawardī. Ihre Werke in Stambuler Hss.', *ibid.*, 24 (1937), 270–86; 25 (1939), 38–86; 'X: Farīdaddīn 'Aṭṭār. (a) Zur Vita', *ibid.*, 25 (1939), 134–73; 'XI: Maulānā Ǧalāladdīn Rūmī u. sein Kreis', *ibid.*, 26 (1942), 116–58, 221–49 = *TM*, 7–8 (1940–2), 268–81. – 'Neue Lit. über Cal. Rûmî', *Oriens*, 13–4 (1960), 342 *et seq.*; 'XIV: Farīddudīn 'Aṭṭār, II', *Oriens*, 11/1–2 (1958), 1–76; 'XV: 'Aṭṭār, III.7. Der Dīwān (Mit Vergleich einiger Verse von Sanā'ī u. Ḥāfiẓ.)', *ibid.*, 12/1–2 (1959), 1–88; 'XVI: 'Aṭṭār. IV.8. Muxtārnāme. Pandnāme', *ibid.*, 13–14 (1961), 195–239.

——, Art. on 'Aṭṭār and Djalāl al-Dīn Rūmī, in *EI*, New Ed., *s.v.*; biographies in *İA*: Attâr, Câmî, Celâleddîn Rûmî, Dakîkî, Ferruhî, Firdevsî, Hâfiz.
Roemer, H. R., 'Probleme der Hafizforschung und der Stand ihrer Lösung', *Ak. d. Wiss. u. d. Lit. in Mainz, Abh. d. Kl. d. Lit.* (1951), 97–115.
Romaskevich, A., 'Persidskiy "tafsīr" Ṭabarī', *ZKV*, 5 (1930), 801–6.
——, 'Ocherk istorii izucheniya "Shakh-Name"', in *Ferdovsi* (see *s.v.* 'Firdausī') (1934), 13–50.
Root, Martha L., *Ṭáhirih the Pure, Irán's greatest Woman* [Qurratu'l-'Ayn] (Karachi? 1938) (bibliography of Bahā'ī literature, 102–13).
Ross, E. Denison, 'Rudaki and Pseudo-Rudaki [Qaṭrān]', *JRAS* (1924), 609–44.
——, 'A Qasida by Rudaki', *ibid.* (1926), 213–38.
——, 'An Arabic and a Persian metrical version of Burzoe's autobiography from "Kalila and Dimna"', *BSOS*, 4 (1926–8), 441–72.
Rozen, V.: see A III.
Rozenberg, F. A., 'O vine i pirakh v persidskoy natsional'noy epopeye', *Sbornik Muz. Antrop. i Etn.*, 5 (1918), 375–96.
Rozenfel'd, B. A. and A. F. Yushkevich, *Omar Khayyam* (Moscow 1965).
Rūdakī, *Dīvān*, lith. (*s.l.* 1315/1897).
——, (1) *Āthār-i Rūdakī* [in Arabic characters] = *Osori Rūdakī*; (2) *Ash'ori hamasroni Rūdakī*; (3) *Rūdakī va zamoni ū. (Majmu'ayi maqolaho) = Rudaki i yego epokha (Sbornik statey).* All three books ed. by A. Mirzoyev (Stalinabad 1958).
——, *Rudaki*, per. V. V. Derzhavin i V. V. Levik. Introd. etc. by I. S. Braginskiy (Stalinabad 1949; 1955) (Klass. tadzh. lit.)
——, *Izbrannoye*, per. V. Levik i S. Lipkin. With introd. by I. S. Braginskiy (Moscow 1957; 1958).
——, Numerous studies on the occasion of the Rūdakī commemoration publ. in *ShS*, 1958, espec. Fasc. 10 and apart from that also in the USSR and in Iran.
—— *Rudaki. Stikhi*, red. i komm.: I. S. Braginskiy. Sostavitel': D. S. Komissarov; per. V. V. Levik, S. I. Lipkin (S. V. Shervinskiy) (Moscow 1964).
—— *Rūdakī, 1100* (Univ. Tbilisi [Tiflis] 1957) (mostly only in Georgian).
—— R. O. Tal'man and A. Yunusov, *Rudaki (Ukazatel' literaturī)*; *Rūdakī (Fehristi adabiyot)*, ed. by A. M. Mirzoyev (Dushanbe 1965).
Rugarli, Vitt., 'Il Libro di Gershasp, poema di Asadi', *GSAI*, 9 (1895–6), 33–80.
——, 'Susen la cantatrice, episodio del Libro di Berzu', *ibid.*, 11 (1897–8), 15–33.
Rūḥānī Viṣāl, *Gulshan-i Viṣāl* [Selections from the poems of Viṣāl and his descendants] (Tehran 1319).
[Ruknā], 'Sharḥ-i ḥāl-i ḥakīm Ruknā', *Arm.*, 5, 437–9.
Rūnī: see Abu'l-faraj.
Rypka, J., 'Les sept princesses de Nizhami', in *L'Âme de l'Iran* (B VIa), 99–126.
——, 'Ḫāqānīs Madā'in-Qaṣīde rhetorisch beleuchtet', *ArOr.*, 27 (1959), 199–205.
——, 'Ritoricheskiye priyemī Firdausi', in *Sbornik I. A. Orbeli* (Moscow–Leningrad 1960), 427–32.
——, 'Textkritisches zu Niẓāmīs Haft Paykar, 3–4. Gesang', *ROr.*, 26 (1962), 85–96. – 'Der vierte Gesang von Niẓāmīs Haft Paikar neu übersetzt', *Oriens*, 15 (1962), 234–41.
——, 'Sukhan-rānī ... dar bāra-i Ḥāfiẓ', *MDAT*, 10 (1342), 385–96 (= *Furūgh-i tarbiyat*, Shiraz 1342/2 31–9).
——, 'Sukhan-rānī dar bāra-i Khāqānī', *MDAT*, *ibid.*, 397–405 (= *NDAT*, 15, 1342, 101–11).
——, 'Opīt tekstologicheskogo razbora pervoy glavī poemī "Haft paykar"', *KS*, 65 (1964), 147–55.
Rypka, J. and Borecký, M., 'Labíbí', *ArOr.*, 14 (1943), 261–307.
——, 'Farruḫī', *ibid.*, 16 (1947), 17–75.
Rzakulizade, S. D., *Obshchestvenno-politicheskiye i filosofskiye vzglyadī Khakani Shirvani* (Baku 1962).
Ṣabā Kāshānī, *Shāhanshāh-nāma*, lith. (Bombay [1890]).
——, *Gulshan-i Ṣabā*, ed. by Ḥ. Kūhī Kirmānī. With introd. by Muḥ. Bahār, 2nd ed. (Tehran 1313).

——, *Dīvān*, ed. by Muḥ. ʿAlī Najātī (Tehran 1341).

Ṣabāḥī Bīdgulī, *Dīvān*, ed. by Ḥus. Partau Bayḍā'ī (Tehran 1338).

Ṣābir Tirmidhī, Adīb, *Dīvān*, ed. by Muḥ. ʿAlī Nāṣiḥ (Tehran [1343]). – *Ashʿori muntakhab* (Dushanbe 1965). Introd. by Akhm. Abdulloyev. – See *supra*, p. 772.

Ṣabūrī, Ḥājj Mīrzā Muḥ. Kāẓim, *Dīvān*, ed. by Muḥ. Malik-zāda (Tehran 1342).

Ṣadaqa b. Abu'l-Qāsim Shīrāzī, *Kitāb-i Samak-i ʿAyyār* [adapted by Farāmurz-i Khudā-dād b. ʿAbdu'llāh al-Kātib al-Arrajānī 585/1189]. On the contents: *Sukhan*, 8/11-2 (1336), 1108–25.

——, 'Yād-dāshtī dar bāra-i nuskha-i kitāb-i Samak-i ʿAyyār', *ibid.*, 9/4 (1337), 333–6.

——, Crit. ed. by P. N. Khānlarī (Tehran 1339); 2nd ed., 4 vols. (Tehran 1345) (Univ.).

Saʿdī, *Kulliyyāt*, ed. by M.-ʿA. Furūghī (Tehran 1337, 1338, 1340, 1342).

——, *Ghazaliyyāt*, ed. by M.-ʿA. Furūghī (1318, 1343).

——, *Qaṣā'id*, ed. by M.-ʿA. Furūghī (repr. Tehran 1343).

——, *Matn-i kāmil-i dīvān u Gulistān u Būstān u Majālis*, ed. by Maẓ. Muṣaffā (based on the editions by Furūghī, Garakānī and Aliyev) (Tehran 1342).

——, *Le Boustân*. Texte persan avec un commentaire persan publ. par Ch. H. Graf (Vienna 1858). – Turk. comm. by Sūdī (Istanbul 1288/1871). – *Būstān*, transl. by G. S. Davie (London 1882). – *Bustan*, per. K. Chaykin (Moscow 1935). – *Lustgården*, öfversatt af E. H(ermelin) (Stockholm 1918). – *Stories from the Bustán together with Selections from Francis Gladwin's translation of Gulistán*, by R. Levy (London 1928). – Georgian, tr. by D. I. Kobidze (Tiflis 1964).

——, *Gulistān*, ed. by ʿAbdu'l-ʿAẓīm Garakānī ([Tehran] 1310). – *Gulistān*. Ed. by S. Nafīsī. 3rd ed. (Tehran 1345). – Scheich Saʿdi, *Hundertundeine Geschichte aus dem Rosengarten. Ein Brevier orientalischer Lebenskunst*. Auswahl und Übersetzung aus dem Persischen von Rudolf Gelpke (Zürich 1967) (ill.). – "From the oldest MSS. in the world", ed. by M.-ʿA. Furūghī (1316 and reprints). – Crit. text and tr. into Russian by R. M. Aliyev (Moscow 1959). – Ed. "Iqbāl", based on Furūghī and ʿAbdu'l-ʿAẓīm Qarīb [Garakānī]. (Tehran 1341). – Turk. comm. by Sūdī (Istanbul 1249/1833); + comm. by Shemʿi (in the margin) (Istanbul 1293/1876). – *Kings and Beggars*. The first two chapters of Saʿdī's Gulistān, transl. by A. J. Arberry (London 1945). – *The Gulistan or Rose Garden*, transl. by E. Rehatsek, ed. with a pref. by W. G. Archer. Intr. by G. M. Wickens (1964). – *Gulistan. Rozovïy sad*, tr. by Rustam Aliyev (prose) and Anatoliy Starostin (poems) (Moscow 1957). – *Gulistan. Izbrannïye rasskazï*, per. Y. E. Bertel's (Berlin 1923). – De Vincentiis, G., *Il roseto di Saʿdi, prima versione italiana dall'-originale persiano* (Napoli 1873) (not ment. by Ethé). – *Gulistan, to jest Ogród różany*, przeł. W. z. Bibersteina Kazimirski (Paris 1876) (not ment. by Ethé). – *Růžový sad*, přeložil J. Entlicher [Poems tr. by Fr. J. Rypáček] (Prague 1906) (torso). – *Peršana Saʿdího myšlenky o vychováni*, podávají J. Entlicher a F. J. Rypáček (Brno 1902). – *Myšlenky o lásce a mládi* [*Gul.*, 5th Chapter], přelozil J. Entlicher (Prague 1926). – *Růžová zahrada. Výběr z Bústánu a Gulistánu*, přel. Věra Kubíčková (Prague 1954). – Turkish tr.: *Seyfi Serâyî, Gülistan tercümesi*, ed. (in facsimile) by Feridun Nafiz Uzluk (Ankara 1954). – *Rauḍatu'l-ward*. Arabic tr. by M. al-Furātī (Damascus 1961).

——, *Ṭayyibāt*, ed. by L. W. King (Calcutta 1919–21); transl. by L. W. King (London 1926).

——, *Badā'iʿ*, ed. and transl. by L. W. King (Berlin 1304/1925).

——, *Pand-nāma*: *Saʿdīs Scroll of Wisdom*. Persian and English text, with introd. by A. N. Wollaston (London 1906). – ≅.

——, *Muslichiddin Saadi*, ed. by I. S. Braginskiy, transl. by K. A. Lipskerov (Stalinabad 1945; 1954).

——, 'Saʿdī-nāma', ed. by Ḥabīb Yaghmā'ī, *Taʿlīm va tarbiyat* (Tehran 1316), Fasc. 11–12.

——, Full bibliography: Krïmskiy (B v), III, 429–69 (till 1915), Massé (*q.v.*; 1919), Arberry (B I) and his *Class. Persian Lit.* (B v), Karatay (B I), *NY*, Ethé (B v).

Ṣādiq-Beg Afshār, *Qanūnu'ṣ-ṣuvar* [Didactical poem on miniature-painting and illumination], ed., with preface and Russian tr. by ʿĀdil Qāḍīyev (Baku 1963).

Ṣafā, Dh., "Amʿaq-i Bukhārā'ī', *Mihr*, 3 (1314), 177–81, 289–95, 405–11.

Ṣafā'ī Iṣfahānī, Ḥakīm, *Dīvān*, ed. by Aḥm. Suhaylī Khvānsārī (Tehran 1338).
Ṣafā'ī Malāyirī, Ibrāhīm, 'Shāṭir 'Abbās-i Ṣabūḥī', *Arm.*, 21, 155–7; cf. also *ibid.*, 201–5 (Muḥ. Amīn Riyāḥī).
——, 'Yak shāh dar qiyāfa-i yak shā'ir' [Fatḥ-'Alī-Shāh], *Arm.*, 29/3 (1339), 97–103.
Ṣafī, Fakhru'd-dīn 'Alī, *Laṭā'ifu't-ṭavā'if*, ed. by Aḥm. Gulchīn-i ma'ānī (Tehran 1336).
——, *Zanimatel'nīye rasskazī o raznīkh lyudyakh*. Russian transl. by M. Zand (Moscow 1966).
Saḥābī, *Rubā'iyyāt*. Many specimens: *Arm.*, 13 and 14.
Ṣā'ib Tabrīzī, *Kulliyyāt*. With introd. by Amīrī Fīrūzkūhī (Tehran 1333).
——, *Dīvān*. Ed. by Amīrī Fīrūzkūhī (Tehran 1345).
——, *Ash'ār-i bar-guzīda*, ed. with extensive introd. by Zaynu'd-dīn Mu'taman ([Tehran] 1320). – By the same: *Gulchīn*, lith. (Tehran 1333).
——, *Kitāb-i ash'ār-i bar-guzīda*. Selected by J. Āzmūn. Introd. by Nuṣratu'llāh Kāsimī, 3rd ed. (Tehran 1334).
——, On Ṣā'ibs grave: *Arm.*, 19, 259–60, 260–1, 338–40, 631–2.
Sajjādī, Ḍiyā'u'd-dīn, 'Nāmahā-i Khāqānī', *FĪZ* (1342), 5–33.
——, 'Sukhanī chand dar bāra-i Yaghmā-i Jandagī', *Sukhan*, 16 (1345), 469–77.
Salač, Antonín, 'Firdousī et la religion babylonienne', *ArOr.*, 18 (1950), 479–84.
Salīm I, *Dīvān-i Sulṭān Salīm*, ed. by P. Horn (Berlin 1904). See also Karatay (B I).
Salmān Sāvajī, *Juzv-i qaṣā'id* (for the B. A. Examination of 1910), ed. by Mīrzā Mahdī-khān (Bombay 1909/1327).
——, *Kulliyyāt* (Bombay n.d.), 236 pp.
——, *Kulliyyāt-i ash'ār*, ed. by Rashīd Yāsimī (Tehran 1337). – Ed. Avistā (Tehran n.d.).
——, *Dīvān*, ed. by Manṣūr Mushfiq (Tehran 1337).
Samoylovich, A. N., 'Persidskiy turkolog XVIII veka Mirza Mehdi-Khan', *Izv. Obshch. obsledovaniya i izucheniya Azerb.*, 5 (Baku 1927).
Sanā'ī, *Ḥadīqatu'l-ḥaqīqa*, ed. by Mudarris Raḍavī (Tehran 1329 and reprints). Review by H. Ritter: *Oriens*, 5 (1952), 190–2. – Lith. Bby. 1275 h. – Lith. Lūhārū 1290 h. (only the first book), with comm. by 'Alā'u'd-dīn Bahādur. – Lith. Lucknow 1304 h., with comm. by 'Abdu'l-Laṭīf al-'Abbāsī: *Laṭā'ifu'l-ḥadā'iq*. – *The First Book of the* "——"; *or, The Enclosed Garden of the Truth*, ed. and transl. by J. Stephenson (Calcutta 1911) (BI, N.S., 1272). – *Sanningens Inhägnade Örtargård*, öfversatt af Ax. Hermelin (1928) (Swedish). –
Muḥ. Taqī Mudarris Raḍavī, *Ta'līqāt-i Ḥadīqatu'l-ḥaqīqa* (Tehran 1345) (with an extensive commentary).
——, 'Kār-nāma', ed. with introd. by Mud. Raḍavī, *FĪZ*, 4/3 (1334), 297–354. ('*Kār-nāma*', Shiraz 1318, bears this title wrongly, the work it contains being in fact Shifā'ī's *Namakdān-i ḥaqīqat*).
——, *Sayru'l-'ibād ila'l-ma'ād*, ed. by S. Nafīsī (Tehran 1316).
——, *Ṭarīqu't-taḥqīq* (cf. Ethé (B v), 283), lith. ([Tehran] 1309/1891; Bombay. 1318 h.).
——, *Dīvān*, lith. (Tehran 1274/1858). – Ed. by Mud. Raḍavī (Tehran 1320; 2nd, revised ed. Tehran 1341). – Ed. by Maẓāhir Muṣaffā (Tehran 1336).
——, *Kulliyyāt* [Lyric Poetry] (Bombay 1328/1910).
——, Further bibliography: S. Nafīsī in the *ta'liqāt* to his ed. of 'Aufī, *Lubābu'l-albāb* (Tehran 1334–5), 719–22.
Ṣanī'u'd-daula: see Storey, II/1, 154 *et seq.*; II/2, 344 *et seq.*
as-Ṣarrāf, Aḥmad Ḥamīd, "*Umar al-Khayyām. Ḥayātuh, 'ilmuh, rubā'īyātuh*, 2nd ed. (Baghdad 1949).
Schabinger Freiherr von Schowingen, K. E. 'Tughrai (1061–1121/22), Wehklage über Zeit und Welt', *Hist. Jahrb.*, 83 (1964), 278–99.
Schaeder, H. H., *Goethes Erlebnis des Ostens* (Leipzig 1938).
——, 'Läßt sich die "seelische Entwicklung des Dichters Hafis" ermitteln?', *OLZ* (1942), 201–10 (against K. Stolz, *q.v.*).

Schimmel, Annemarie, *Die Bildersprache Dschelâladdîn Rûmîs* (Walldorf-Hessen 1950).

——, 'The Maulānā and the West', *Isl. Rev.*, 44 (1956/2), 1–3 (the transl. into West. Eur. languages).

——, *Mevlâna Celâlettin Rumî'nin şark ve garpta tesirleri* (Konferans) (Ankara 1963).

——, 'The Symbolical Language of Rūmī', in *Studies in Islam* (New Delhi 1964), 26–40.

——, 'Ta'thīr-i Maulānā Jalālu'd-dīn-i Balkhī dar adabiyyāt-i sharq va gharb', *Adab*, 14/3–4 (1345), 1–16.

Shafaq, Riḍā-zāda, *Farhang-i Shāh-nāma bā sharḥ-i ḥāl-i Firdausī* (Tehran 1320).

Shaginyan, Marietta, *Etyudï o Nizami* (AN Armyanskoy SSR, Yerevan 1935) (cont.: Gyote o Nizami, "Utopiya" Nizami, etc.).

Shāh Shujā', 'Āthār', *Arm.*, 15, 217–25.

Shāhī, Amīr: *Dīvān-i Amīr Shāhī-i Sabzvārī*, ed. (in facsimile) by Amir Mahdi Badi' (Lausanne 1962).

——, See Krïmskiy (B v), III, 118, and Karatay (B I).

Shamsu'd-dīn Faqīr "Maftūn", *The Story of Valeh and Hadijeh*, transl. by Mirza Mahomed and C. Spring Rice (London 1903).

Sharīf, *Rāḥatu'l-insān*, ed. by Ch. Schefer, *Chrest. Pers.*, I, 206–32. – 'Pand-nāma-i Anūshirvān', ed. by S. Nafīsī, *Mihr*, 2 (1313), 181–8, 254–64.

Sharif, A. A., 'Mirza-Fatali Akhundov (k 75-letiyu dnya smerti)', *KS*, 9 (1953), 3–18.

Shaukat, *Dīvān*. With biography by Maulavī Muḥ. Ṣāliḥ, lith. (Lucknow 1290/1873).

——, *Sharḥ-i qaṣā'id*, Muḥ. Murād b. Khalīl (Istanbul n.d.).

Shaybānī (his grave: *Arm.*, 11, 40): *Durj-i durar* [Stories and poems], lith. (*s.l.* 1300/1882).

——, *Muntakhab az majmū'a-i bayānāt-i Sh.* With introd. by Ism. Naṣīrī Qarājaṭāghī (Istanbul 1308–9/1890–1).

Shihābī, 'Alī Akbar, *Niẓāmī shā'ir-i dāstān-sarā* (Tehran 1334).

Shomuhamedov, Shoislom, *Hofiz Sheroziy* (Tashkent [1965?]).

Shoytov, A. M., 'Rol' M.-F. Akhundova v razvitii persidskoy progressivnoy literaturï', *KS*, 9 (1953), 58–65.

Shu'ā'u'l-mulk, 'Majd-i Hamgar', *Arm.*, 14, 97–102 and 3 contin.

——, 'Abu'l-'Alā-i Ganjavī', *ibid.*, 14, 705–13.

Shūrīda-i Shīrāzī, *Ghazaliyyāt*, 2nd ed. (Tehran 1337).

Sindbād-nāma: see *s.v.* '*Ẓahīrī*'; Chauvin (B I), VIII, and Ethé (B v), 216, 315.

——, Ed. with introd. by 'Alī Qavīm (Tehran 1333). – Per. M.-N. Osmanov, red. A. A. Starikov (Moscow 1960).

——, See also *s.v.* 'Bertel's'.

Sipihr, Muḥ. Taqī, *Nāsikhu't-tavārīkh*, see Storey II/2, 152–4; 343 and addenda; new ed. in many vols. (Tehran, since 1337).

Sirishk, M. (Shafī'ī Kadkanī), *Ḥazīn-i Lāhījī. Zindagānī va zībātarīn ghazalhā-i ū* (Mashhad 1342).

Siyāsī, 'Alī Akbar, 'Nafs u badan va rābiṭa-i ānhā bā yakdīgar dar naẓar-i Ibn-i Sīnā va dīgarān', *MDAT*, 1/2 (1332), 12–38.

——, 'Naẓar-i 'irfānī-i Ibn-i Sīnā dar ḥuṣūl-i ma'rifat va vuṣūl ba-ḥaqq', *ibid.*, 1/3 (1333), 1–17.

Smith, Margaret, *Rābi'a the Mystic* (Cambridge 1928).

——, *An Early Mystic of Baghdad* [al-Muḥāsibī] (London 1935).

——, *Al-Ghazālī, the Mystic* (London 1944).

Sourdel, D., 'La biographie d'Ibn al-Muqaffa' d'après les sources anciennes', *Arabica*, 1/3 (1954), 307–23.

Srivastava, A. L., 'Historicity of Deval Rani – Khizr Khan', *IC*, 30/1 (1956), 24–30.

Stackelberg, R. von, 'Neskol'ko slov o persidskom epose Visa i Ramin', *Drevnosti vostochnïye*, 2 (Moscow 1896).

Stolz, Karl, 'Die seelische Entwicklung des Dichters Hafiz', *WZKM*, 48 (1941), 97–120.

——, 'Die seelische Entwicklung des Dichters Hafiz läßt sich ermitteln', *OLZ*, 46 (1943), 97–103.

——, 'Der Diwan des ʿImāduddīn Faqīh', *WZKM*, 49 (1942), 31–71.

Suhaylī Khvānsārī, 'Bābā Fighānī', *Arm.*, 17, 474–5 and 4 contin.

——, 'Maliku'sh-shuʿarā Ḥakīm Shifā'ī-i Iṣfahānī', *ibid.*, 423–36.

——, 'Ḥiṣār-i Nāy: sharḥ-i ḥāl-i Masʿūd-i Saʿd-i Salmān', *ibid.*, 19, 113–23 and 6 contin.; 20, 123–8, 137.

Sulṭān Valad, *Valad-nāma* (= *Daftar* 1), ed. by Jalāl Humā'ī (Tehran 1315).

——, *Dîvân-i Sulṭân Veled* [Persian], ed. by Kilisli R. Bilge (Istanbul 1941).

——, *Divan-i türki-i Sultan Veled*, ed. by Veled Çelebi (İzbudak). (Review in *TM*, 2, 475–81.)

——, *Dīvān*, ed. by Aṣghar Rabbānī. Introd. by S. Nafīsī (Tehran 1338).

Sultanov, Rəhim, *Səʿdi yaradïjïlïğïnda "Gülüstan"* (Baku 1961).

Surūsh, *Dīvān ("Shamsu'l-manāqib")*. Introd. by Ḥusayn-qulī Kirmānshāhī (with a list of the works of Surūsh), lith. (Tehran 1300/1883). – *Dīvān*, ed. by M. J. Maḥjūb. Introd. by J. Humā'ī (1–90) and by the editor (91–208), 2 vols. (Tehran 1339–40).

Sūzanī Samarqandī, *Dīvān*, ed. by Nāṣiru'd-dīn-shāh Ḥusaynī (Tehran 1338; 1344).

Ṭabarī, *Chronique d'Abou-Djafar-Mo'hammed-ben-Djarîr-ben-Yazîd Tabarî* ... traduite sur la version persane d'Abou-Alî-Mo'hammed Bel'amî par H. Zotenberg, 4 vols. (Paris 1867–74). – Extensive bibliogr.: Storey, II/1, 61–5; Lazard, *Anciens Monuments* (B IV), 38–41.

Ṭabāṭabā'ī, Muḥ. Muḥīṭ, 'Mijmar', *Arm.*, 12, 474 *et seq.* and contin.; 13, 162–6.

——, 'Shihāb-i Turshīzī', *ibid.*, 13, 239–44 and contin. (against Bahār, *q.v.*).

——, 'Saḥābī-i Astarābādī', *ibid.*, 13, 617–20.

——, 'Ta'rīkh-i vafāt-i Qā'ānī va Viṣāl', *ibid.*, 18, 57–61.

——, "ʿAqīda-i dīnī-i Firdausī. Intiqād-i dānishmandān-i Urūpā'ī', in *Firdausī-nāma* (see *s.v.* 'Firdausī'), 635–72.

Ṭabāṭabā'ī Muṣṭafā, 'Dīvān-i Niẓāmī-i Ganjavī', *Yaghmā*, 1333 (Dai-māh).

Taeschner, Fr., 'Das Futuvvetnāme des persischen Dichters Hātifī', in *Festschr. G. Jacob* (Leipzig 1932), 304–16.

Tagirdzhanov, A. T., 'K voprosu o poeme Ferdousi "Yusuf i Zuleykha"', *SV*, 5 (1948), 334–8.

——, '"Divan" Baba Kukhi v issledovaniyakh V. A. Zhukovskogo', in *Ocherki po istorii russkogo vostokovedeniya. Sb. V. A. Zhukovskogo* (Moscow 1960), 59–62.

Tāju'l-Ḥalāvī, ʿAlī b. Muḥ., *Daqā'iquʿsh-shiʿr* [8th/14th cent.], ed. by S. Muḥ. Kāẓim Imām (Tehran 1341) (Univ.).

"Talibov", ʿAbdu'r-Raḥīm b. Shaykh Abū-Ṭālib, *Masā'ilu'l-ḥayāt* (Tiflis 1906).

Tanūkhī, *Faraj baʿda'sh-shidda*, tr. by Ḥus. b. Asʿad ad-Dihistānī, ≅; the most recent ed. by M. Mudīr (Tehran 1333). – Anon., 'Yak kitāb-i farāmūsh-shuda. Tarjama-i fārsī-i kitāb-i al-faraj baʿda'sh-shidda, ta'līf-i Ḥus. b. Asʿad-i Mu'ayyidī-i Dihistānī', *Yādgār*, 5/1-2, 49–61.

Ṭarab Iṣfahānī [son of Humā, died 1330/1911–12], *Dīvān*, ed. by Jalālu'd-dīn Humā'ī (Tehran 1342).

Tarbiyat, Muḥ. ʿAlī [d. 1358/1939–40: *Arm.*, 20, 433–8], 'Vāmiq u ʿAdhrā', *Arm.*, 12, 519–31.

——, 'Shaykh Maḥmūd-i Shabistarī', *Arm.*, 12, 601–11.

Tardov, V., 'Ferdausi i Mazdak', in *Lit. Irana* (B VIa), 126–48.

Ṭarsūsī, Abū-Ṭāhir Muḥ., *Dārāb-nāma*. Ed. by Dh. Ṣafā, I (Tehran 1344).

Ṭarzī Afshār, *Dīvān*, ed. with extens. introd. by [M.] Tamaddun (Riḍā'iyya 1309; 1338).

Taymas, A. Battal, 'Seyf Sarayi'nin Gülistan tercümesini gözden geçiriş', *Türk Dili Araştırmaları Yıllığı* (1955), 73–90 (Kipchak transl. from the 14th–15th cent.).

Timurtaş, Faruk K., 'Iran edebiyatında Husrev ü Şirin ve Ferhad ü Şirin yazan şairler', *ŞM*, 4 (1961), 73–86.

Todua, M. A., 'Podrazhaniya "Golestanu" v tadzhikskoy i persidskoy literature. Autoreferat', Gos. Univ. Tbilisi (Tiflis), *Kafedra pers. filol.* (1954).

Trever, K. V., 'Sasanidskiy Iran v Shakh-name', in *Sbornik "Firdovsi"* (see *s.v.* 'Firdausī') (Leningrad 1934), 177–96.

Turjānī-zāda, Aḥm., 'Ta'aththurāt-i Khāqānī az shu'arā-i tāzī va pārsī', *NDAT*, 10/2 (1337), 105–20.

Ṭūṭī-nāma: see Nakhshabī.

Tushishvili, L. N., 'Arabskiye leksicheskiye elementï v "Shakh-name" Firdousi', *Trudï Inst. yaz.-ved., seriya vost. yazïkov*, 1 (1954), 131–52 (Georgian, with Russian summary).

'Ubayd-i Zākānī, *Kulliyyāt*, ed. with biogr. by 'Abbās Iqbāl (Tehran 1321; 1332); + prose (Tehran 1331); the latter ed. with biogr. by M. Ferté (Tehran 1331). – *Kulliyyāt*, ed. by Parvīz Atābakī (Tehran 1337, 1343). – *Kulliyoti muntakhab*, ed. by Kh. M. Mirzozoda (Dushanbe 1963).

——, *'Ushshāq-nāma*, ed. by S. Nafīsī (Tehran 1334).

——, *Muntakhab-i laṭā'if* (Berlin 1343/1925).

——, *Mūsh u gurba*. In numerous lith. editions (E. Littmann, 'Der Katzenmäusekrieg, ein neu-arabisches Gedicht', *Die Welt des Buches* (1951), 231–59 [*Oriens*, 5, 125]). – *Katze und Maus*, aus dem Persischen übertr. von H. W. Duda (1947). – *Rats against cats*, transl. by Mas'ūd Farzād (London 1946).

——, F. Bajraktarević, 'Zakanijeve definicije', *Stvaranje* (Cetinje), 11 (1956), 500–4.

——, *Veselaya kniga*. Preface, notes and Russian tr. of the prose by N. Kondïreva, of the poems by G. Alekseyev, ed. by Yu. Borshchevskiy, ills. by I. Offengenden (Moscow 1965).

'Unṣurī, *Dīvān*, ed. by Yaḥyā Qarīb (Tehran 1323; 1341). – Ed. by Muḥ. Dabīr Siyāqī (Tehran 1342).

'Urfī, *Qaṣā'id* (With comm.) (Lahore 1924). – ≃.

——, *Nafaḥāt-i Shīrāz*, ed. by Ṣābir 'Alī, lith. (Lucknow 1930).

——, *Kulliyyāt*, ed. by Ghulām-Ḥus. Javāhirī (Tehran 1339) (cf. M. J. Maḥjūb, *RK*, 3/6 (1340), 343–54).

Vachha, P. B.: *Firdousi and the Shahname* (Bombay 1950).

Vaḥshī Bāfiqī, *Kulliyyāt-i ash'ār* [together with three epics], with intr. by Ism. Ḥamīdu'l-mulk, lith. (Tehran 1347/1928–9). – Ed. by M. H. 'Ilmī (Tehran 1333). – ≃.

——, *Farhād u Shīrīn va Khuld-i barīn*, ed. by Kūhī Kirmānī (Tehran 1334).

——, *Dīvān*, ed. by Ḥus. Nakha'ī (Tehran 1339; 1343).

Vaqār b. Viṣāl Shīrāzī, 'Sharḥ-i shash rubā'ī-i Muḥtasham', *Arm.*, 14, 713–22; 15, 73 *et seq.*, and contin.

Varasteh, Khosrow, *Le vrai visage d'Omar Khayyam* (Tehran [1337?]).

Vaṣṣāf: see p. 456, note 26.

——, 'Qaṣīda-i mausūm ba "Nuzhatu'l-abṣār fī 'ilmi'l-'arūḍ va'l-ash'ār"', ed. by Ḥus. Nakhjavānī, *NDAT*, 1/10, 43–68.

Veit, Friedr., 'Des Grafen von Platen Nachbildungen aus dem Diwan des Hafis', *Studien z. vergl. Lit.-Gesch.*, 7 (1908), 257–307, 390–438; 8, 145–224.

Vil'chevskiy, O. L. [† May 21st, 1964], 'Khakani. Nekotorïye chertï tvorchestva i mirovozzreniya poeta', *SV*, 1957/4, 62–76.

——, 'Khronogrammï Khakani', *Epigrafika Vostoka*, 13 (1960), 59–68.

——, 'Oda Khakani gruzinskomu tsaryu Dimitriyu I', in *Sb. Orbeli* (Moscow–Leningrad 1960), 56–60.

——, 'Iranskiye publikatsii proizvedeniy Khakani', *NAA*, 1964/3, 162–70.

——, 'Tyurkskaya tematika v tvorchestve Khakani', in *Iranskaya filologiya* (Leningrad 1964), 121–9.

Viṣāl, *Kulliyyāt*, lith. (*s.l.* and n.d.); + *Dīvān-i Khusrau-i Shīrāzī* (Tehran 1858 [?]).

——, *Dīvān*, Fol. (*s.l.* and n.d.), 760 pp.; + *Dīvān-i Taqī-i 'Alīābādī* (*s.l.* and n.d.) (without paging).

——, *Risāla fī rithā'i ahli bayti'l-'iṣma* [In verse], lith. (Bombay 1299/1882), 192 pp.; (Bombay, date illegible), 88 pp.

——, Vaḥshī's (*q.v.*) *Farhād u Shīrīn* finished by Viṣāl (cf., above, p. 298).

——, On the five sons of Viṣāl and their works: cf. the detailed study by Navābī (*q.v.*).

Vorozheykina, Z. N., 'Liricheskiye "fragmentï" Kamal al-Dina Ismaila Isfahani', *KS*, 67 (1963), 148–59.
——, 'O literaturnom nasledii Baba Kukhi i Baba Takhira', in *Iranskaya filologiya* (1964), 149–55.
Wahid, Muhammad, *The Life and Works of Amir Khusrau* (Calcutta 1935).
Wesselski, A., 'Quellen und Nachwirkungen der Haft paikar', *Isl.*, 22 (1934), 106–19 (more positive results: Yevg. E. Bertel's (*q.v.*), *Navoyi*, 81).
Wickens, G. M., 'The Persian Conception of Artistic Unity in Poetry and its Implications in other Fields', *BSOAS*, 14 (1952), 239–43.
——, 'An Analysis of Primary and Secondary Significations in the Third Ghazal of Ḥāfiẓ', *ibid.*, 627–38.
——, *Intiqāḍ al-i'tirāḍ* [Polemics against Mary Boyce, *q.v.*], rotogr., 15 pp.
——, 'The Sa'ādatnāmeh attributed to Nāṣir-i Khusrau', *The Isl. Quarterly*, 2 (1955), 177–232; 206–21 (transl. and critical explanation).
——, Article on Ḥāfiẓ in *EI*, New Ed. (1966).
Wolff, Fritz, *Glossar zu Firdosis Schahname*; Suppl.-Bd.: *Verskonkordanz* (Berlin 1935).
Yaghmā, *Kulliyyāt*, ed. by Ḥājjī Muḥ. Ismā'īl ([Tehran] 1283/1866; Tehran 1277/1860); reprint ed. by I'timādu's-salṭana (Tehran 1339). – *Tikkahā-i bar-guzīda*, ed. by 'Alī Muqaddam (Tehran 1313) (bibliophile ed.).
——, *Munsha'āt va ghazaliyyāt*, lith. (*s.l.* 1301–2/1884–5).
——, *Ghazaliyyāt va Sardāriyya*, ed. by Muḥ. Ḥus. Ṭabarī (Tehran 1337).
Yaghmā'ī, Ḥabīb, 'Sharḥ-i ḥāl-i Yaghmā', *Arm.*, 5, 404–18 and cont.; in book-form (Tehran n.d.).
Yakānī, Ism., *Nādira-i ayyām Ḥakīm 'Umar-i Khayyām va rubā'iyyāt-i ū* (Tehran 1342).
Yaltkaya, M. Şerefeddin, 'Kalimāt va ash'ār-i turkī-i Maulānā', *NDAT*, 3/5-6 (1329), 54–65; 3/8, 31–4; 4/1-2 (1330), 49–55. Tr. fr. Turkish (*TM*, 4, 1934, 111–67) by Khayyām-pūr.
Yāsimī, Rashīd, *Aḥvāl-i Ibn-i Yamīn* (Tehran 1303).
——, 'Bābā Ṭāhir-i 'Uryān', *Arm.*, 10, 66–70.
——, *Salmān-i Sāvajī* (Tehran n.d.).
Yūsufī, Gh.-Ḥus., *Farrukhī-i Sīstānī. Baḥthī dar sharḥ-i aḥvāl va rūzgār va shi'r-i ū* (Mashhad 1341).
Ẓahīr-i Fāryābī, *Kulliyyāt*, lith. (Lucknow 1331/1913).
——, *Dīvān*, lith. (Tehran 1324/1906). – Ed. by Taqī Bīnish (Mashhad 1337). – Ed. by Hāshim Raḍī (Tehran 1338).
az-Ẓahīrī as-Samarqandī, Muḥ. b. 'Alī, *Sindbādh-nāme*, ed. by Ahmed Ateş (Istanbul 1948) (Univ.). – Per. M.-N. Osmanov (Moscow 1960).
Ẓahīru'd-dīn Nīshāpūrī [d. about 582/1186], *Saljūq-nāma*, ed. by Ismā'īl-Khān Afshār Ḥamīdu'llāh (with appendix by Abū-Ḥamīd Muḥ. b. Ibrāhīm dated 599/1202–3) (Tehran 1332).
Zajączkowski, A., 'Najstarsza wersja turecka perskiego zbioru opowieści p. t. Marzubān-nāme', *Spraw. Polskiej Akad. Umiej.*, 41 (1936), 321–6.
——, 'Czterowiersze Awicenny. Z dziejów literatury irańskiej w Azji Środkowej', *Przegl. Or.*, 1952/4, 34–55.
——, 'Stareyshaya tyurkskaya versiya poemï Khosrev-u-Shirin Kutba', in *Charisteria* (B VIa), 387–96.
——, *Najstarsza wersja turecka Ḫusräv u Šīrīn Quṭba*, 3 vols. (Warsaw 1958–61).
——, 'Sur quelques proverbes turcs du "Ḫusrev-u-Šīrīn" de Nizami (dans l'original persan et la version turque de Qutb)', in *Jean Deny Armağanı* (Ankara 1958), 349–55.
——, 'A propos d'un épisode du Khusrau u Shirin de Nizami (Shīr-kushtan-i Khusrau dar bazmgāh)' in *Mélanges Massé* (Tehran 1963), 405–55.
——, *Turecka wersja Šāh-nāme z Egiptu Mameluckiego* (Warsaw 1965).
——, Numerous other studies.
Zakhoder, B. N., 'Yubileynaya literatura o Nizami', *Sov. Kniga*, 1948/12, 97–102.

Zand, M. I., 'Jihathoyi ziddikhilofatī va ijtimoī dar nazmi Rūdakī va hamasroni ū', *ShS*, 1956/12, 78–86, abridged from: 'Antikhalifatskiye i sotsial'no-oblichitel'nïye motivï v tadzhikskoy poezii X v.', *Trudï AN Tadzh. SSR*, 27 (1954), 185–223.

——, *Sohibqironi shoyirī – ustod Rūdakī* (Stalinabad 1957).

Zenker, R., 'Die Tristansage und das persische Epos von Wîs und Râmîn', *Roman. Forschungen*, 29 (1910), 321–99.

Zhukovskiy, V. A., *Ali Aukhadeddin Enveri. Materialï dlya yego biografii i kharakteristiki* (St.-Petersburg 1883).

——, 'Pesni kheratskogo startsa [Anṣārī]', *Vostochnïye Zametki* (1895), 79 *et seq.*

——, 'Mukhammad-Khasan-Khan (I'timad-al-Saltane)' [=Ṣanī'u'd-daula, *q.v.*], *ZVORAO*, 10 (1897), 187 *et seq.*

——, 'Omar Khayyam i "stranstvuyushchiye" chetverostishiya', in *Sbornik V. R. Rozen* (St.-Petersburg 1897), 325–63.

Ẓuhūrī Turshīzī, *Dīvān*, essays etc., see Arberry (B1).

——, *Se nathr*, text and English tr. by 'Abdu'l-Ghanī (F), 3, 305–467.

Zulālī, *Maḥmūd u Āyāz*, ed. by Muḥ. Ṣādiq 'Alī "Ghālib", lith. (Lucknow 1290/1874).

VII. PRINTING AND THE PERIODICAL PRESS

Bahār, *Sabk-shināsī* (B VIa), 3, 344 *et seq.*

Browne, E. G., *The Press and Poetry of Modern Persia, partly based on the MS. Work of Mirzá Muḥ. 'Alí Khán "Tarbiyat" of Tabriz* (Cambridge 1914).

Massé, H., art. 'Djarīda, II: Īrān', in *EI*, New Ed., II (1963).

Nakhjavānī, Ḥājj Ḥus., 'Ta'rīkhcha-i intishār-i rūz-nāmahā va majallāt dar Ādharbāyjān va Tabrīz', *NDAT*, 15 (1342), 1–14.

Rabino, H. L.: see B I.

Ṣadr-i Hāshimī, Muḥ., *Ta'rīkh-i jarā'id u majallāt-i Īrān*, 2 vols. (Isfahan 1327).

Tarbiyat, Muḥ. 'Alī [great-grandson of Mahdī-Khān, cf. *Arm.*, 20, 433–9], *Arm.*, 12, 369–81, 448–57; *Ta'līm u tarbiyat*, 4 (1313), 657–64, 721–5.

Yādgār, 1 (1323-4), no. 3, 49–54; no. 7, 6–17; 2 (1324–5), no. 1, 31–7.

VIII. AFGHANISTAN

'Adab va shi'r dar Afghānistān' [A set of articles and essays by several authors], *RK*, 7/2 (1343), 215–61.

Afghānistān, Anjuman-i Aryānā, Dā'iratu'l-ma'ārif (Kābul 1337/1958), 162–369.

de Dianous, H. J., 'La littérature afghane de langue persane', *Orient. Revue trimestrielle*, 8 (1964), no. 31, 137–71.

Gerasimova, A. and G. Girs, *Literatura Afganistana. Kratkiy ocherk* (Moscow 1963).

Kukhtina, T. I., *Bibliografiya Afghanistana. Literatura na russkom yazïke* (Moscow 1965).

Massé, H., 'L'Académie afghane et ses publications', *REI* (1939).

Namunayi ash'ori muosiri Afgon. Put together by H. Ne'matulloyev and R. Hoshim (Stalinabad 1958).

Obshchestvennïye motivï v sovremennoy literature Afganistana, red. G. F. Girs (AN SSSR, Moscow 1961).

C

VĚRA KUBÍČKOVÁ: PERSIAN LITERATURE OF THE 20TH CENTURY

Modern works in Persian prose and poetry that have already been referred to in the article are not included in the bibliography.

Afshār, Īraj, *Nathr-i fārsī-i muʿāṣir* (Tehran 1330).

——, See also B I.

Alavi, Bozorg, *Das Land der Rosen und Nachtigallen* (Berlin 1957).

——, 'Sar o tah-e yek karbās ya Eṣfahān-nāme', *OLZ*, 54 (1959), 52–6.

——, *Geschichte und Entwicklung der modernen persischen Literatur* (Berlin 1964).

ʿAqā'id u afkār dar bāra-i Ṣādiq Hidāyat. Intishārāt-i anjuman-i Gītī (Tehran 1313; 2nd ed. Tehran 1335).

Arberry, A. J., 'Modern Persian Poetry', *Life and Letters*, Dec. 1949.

Areshyan, S. G., 'Gor'kiy i literaturī Vostoka', *SV*, 3 (1945), 177–82.

Artz, P., *Wirtschaft und Verkehr Persiens* (Vienna 1934).

Atyeo, H. C., 'Political Developments in Iran 1951–54', *MEA*, 5 (1954), 249–59.

Aubin, E., *La Perse d'aujourd'hui* (Paris 1934).

Avery, P. W., 'Developments in Modern Persian Prose', *MW*, 45 (1955), 313–23.

——, *Modern Iran* (London 1965).

Badi, M., *Agrarnīye otnosheniya v sovremennom Irane* (Moscow 1959).

Bahār, M. T., *Sabk-shināsī yā ta'rīkh-i taṭavvur-i nathr-i fārsī*, III (Tehran 1331).

Balfour, J. M., *Recent Happenings in Persia* (London 1922).

Bausani, A.: see B II and B IV.

Bertel's, Y. E., *Ocherk istorii persidskoy literaturī* (Leningrad 1928).

——, 'Persidskiy istoricheskiy roman XX veka', *TMIV*, I (1932), III *et seq.*

Bombaci, A., 'Il poeta nazionalista 'Āref di Qazvīn', *OM*, 25 (1945), 42–53.

Borecký, M., 'Persian Prose since 1946', *MEJ*, 7 (1953), 235–44.

Braginskiy, I. S., 'K voprosu o razvitii metoda sotsialisticheskogo realisma v literaturakh zarubezhnogo Vostoka', *KS*, 17 (1955), 3–9.

——, See also: Komissarov.

Browne, E. G., *A Year amongst the Persians* (London 1893).

——, *The Persian Revolution 1905–1909* (Cambridge 1910).

——, *The Persian Crisis of December 1911* (Cambridge 1912).

——, *The Reign of Terror in Tabriz* (London 1912).
——, *The Press and Poetry of Modern Persia* (Cambridge 1914).
Chaykin, K. I., *Kratkiy ocherk noveyshey persidskoy literaturī* (Moscow 1928).
Christensen, A., *To iranske komedier fra Kadjarernes tid* (Copenhagen 1938) [Malkum-Khān].
Curzon, G. N., *Persia and the Persian Question* (London 1892).
Danish, H., *Sarāmadān-i sukhan* (Istanbul 1327/1909).
Daulatābādī, ʻA., 'Taḥavvul-i nathr-i fārsī dar nīm-qarn-i akhīr', *NDAT* (1332), 235 *et seq.*; (1333), 241 *et seq.*
Doroshenko, E. A., 'Ideologicheskiye osnovī iranskikh uchebnikov perioda pravleniya Reza-shakha Pekhlevi', *KS*, 14 (1955), 58 *et seq.*
Elwell-Sutton, L. P., 'Ta'rīkhcha-i tiātr dar Īrān', *Sukhan* (1335), 288 *et seq.*, 383 *et seq.*
——, *Modern Iran*, 2nd ed. (1942).
——, *Persian Oil* (London 1955).
E'tesam-zadeh, A. G., ''Ali Dachti, le nouveliste', *Journal de Téhéran* (Sept. 18th, 1945).
Essad Bey, *Reza Schah, Feldherr, Kaiser, Reformator* (Vienna 1936).
Farmanfarmaian, Ch., 'The Oil-industry and National Enterprise in Iran', *MEA* (1957), 333–342.
Filishtinskaya, Z. G., 'Maksim Gor'kiy v sovremennoy progressivnoy persidskoy literature', *KS*, 4 (1952), 45–51.
Fraser, D., *Persia and Turkey in Revolt* (London 1910).
Frye, R. N., 'Report on the Trip to Iran in Summer 1948', *Oriens*, 2 (1949), 204–15.
——, *Iran* (London 1954).
——, 'Islam in Iran', *MW*, 46 (1956), 5–12.
Gabriel, A., *Die Erforschung Persiens* (Vienna 1952).
Gadzhizade (Hacizade), Alibaba Gudrat-oglī, *Farruhi Yazdinin poeziyasī* (Baku 1965) (in Azeri); cf. *Voprosī iran. filol.* (B VIa), 299–307 (Azeri with Russian summary).
Gelpke, R., *Die iranische Prosaliteratur im 20. Jahrhundert*, I: *Grundlagen und Voraussetzungen* (Wiesbaden 1962).
Gibb, H. A. R. and H. Bowen, *Islamic Society and the West*, I: *Islamic Society in the Eighteenth Century*, 2 vols. (London–New York 1950–7).
Gordon, T. E., *The Reform Movement in Persia* (London 1907).
Grunebaum, G. E. von, 'The Problem of Cultural Influence', in *Charisteria Orientalia* (Prague 1956), 56–99.
Hamadānī, ʻA. R., *Ta'rīkh-i Īrān* (Tehran 1317).
Ḥamīdī, M., *Daryā-i gauhar* (Tehran 1330).
Hashtrūdī, M. Z., *Muntakhabāt-i āthār az navīsandagān va shuʻarā-i muʻāṣirīn* (Tehran 1342).
Hesse, Fr., *Persien. Entwicklung und Gegenwart* (Weltpolitische Bücherei) (Berlin 1932).
Ḥikmat, ʻA. A., 'Shiʻr-i fārsī dar ʻaṣr-i muʻāṣir', *NKNI* (Tehran 1325).
——, 'Some aspects of Modern Iran', *IC.*, 30 (1956), 365–84.
Hurewitz J. C., *Diplomacy in the Near and Middle East* (New York 1956).
Ibragimov A. A. and G. Mamedzade, *O podlinnom autore p'yes pripisīvayemīkh Mal'kom-khanu* (Baku 1956).
Il'yinskiy, G. N., 'Agrarnīye otnosheniya v Irane v kontse XIX – nachale XX veka', *UZIV*, 8 (1953), 113–45.
Iqbāl, ʻA., *Ta'rīkh-i nau* (Tehran 1327).
Īrānī, D. J., *Sukhanvarān-i daurān-i Pahlavī* (Bombay 1933).
——, 'The Renaissance of Persian poetry', in *Dr. Modi Memorial Volume* (Bombay 1930), 358–74.
Ishaque, M., *Sukhanvarān-i Īrān dar ʻaṣr-i ḥāḍir*, 2 vols. (Calcutta 1933–7).
——, *Modern Persian Poetry* (Calcutta 1943).
——, 'Bahar of Meshhed', *Indo-Iranica*, I/3 (1946–7), 41–51.

——, *Four Eminent Poetesses of Iran* (Calcutta 1950).
Ivanov, M. S., *Ocherk istorii Irana* (AN SSSR, Moscow 1952).
——, *Iranskaya revolyutsiya 1905–1911 godov* (Moscow 1957).
Ivanova, M. N., 'Germanskaya agressiya v Irane v godï pervoy mirovoy voynï', *KS*, 19 (1956), 14–27.
Jamālu'd dīn Afghānī, *Maqālāt-i Jamāliyya* (Tehran n.d.).
——, *Réfutation des matérialistes* (Paris 1956).
——, 'Philosophie de l'union nationale', *Orient* (1958/9), 123 *et seq.*
Jamāl-zāda, M. 'A., 'Mujaddid-i rastākhīz-i adabī: du rūmān-i tāza-i fārsī – Zībā (M. Ḥijāzī) va Tafrīḥāt-i shab (M. Mas'ūd)', *Kūshish*, 15 isfand. 1313.
——, *Ganj-i shāygān yā auḍā'-i iqtiṣādī-i Īrān* (Tehran 1335).
Kamshad, H., *Modern Persian Prose Literature* (Cambridge 1966) (with special reference to Ṣādiq Hidāyat).
Kasravī, A., *Ta'rīkh-i mashrūṭa-i Īrān*, 3 vols. (Tehran 1319–23).
Kazemzadeh, F., 'Recent Iranian Historiography', *MEA*, 7 (1956), 334–40.
Khalkhālī, 'A., *Tadhkira-i shu'arā'-i mu'āṣir-i Īrān* (Tehran 1334).
Khānlarī, P. N., 'Shā'irī', *Sukhan* (1332), 1–5.
——, 'Shi'r-i nau', *ibid.*, 9–10.
——, 'Nathr-i fārsī dar daura-i akhīr', *NKNI* (Tehran 1325).
Kishāvarz, S., *Zanānī ki ba fārsī shi'r gufta-and az Rābi'a tā Parvīn* (Tehran 1956).
Klyashtorina, V. B., 'Fol'klornïye zhanrï v demokraticheskoy poezii Irana perioda revolyutsii 1905–1911 gg.', *KS*, 22 (1956), 56–65.
——, 'Zhurnal Molla Nasredin i persidskaya politicheskaya satira', *KS*, 27 (1958), 31–41.
——, 'Saye – sovremennïy persidskiy poet', *KS*, 36 (1959), 33–44.
——, 'Imagery in 20th-Century Persian Poetry' [Bahār, Yūshīj], *CAR*, 13/3 (1965), 205–15. Transl. from *NAA*, 1965/1.
Komissarov, D. S., 'Obraz polozhitel'nogo geroya v sovremennoy persidskoy proze', *KS*, 17 (1955), 53–65.
——, *Sadek Khedayat. Izbrannoye* (Moscow 1957) (see also: Rozenfel'd).
——, 'O realisticheskoy tendentsii v sovremennoy persidskoy literature', *SV* (1958/3), 57–65.
——, 'Mokhammed Khedzhazi i yego "Sereshk"', *KS*, 27 (1958), 73–81.
——, *Ocherkï sovremennoy persidskoy prozï* (Moscow 1960).
——, I. Braginskiy and D. Komissarov, *Persidskaya literatura* (Moscow 1963).
Kubíčková, V., 'Un éclair de sourire sur un visage tragique' [Hidayat], in *Charisteria Orientalia* (Prague 1956), 142–8.
Kūhī, *Sūsiyālism va Īrān* (Tehran 1325).
Kuznetsov, A. A., 'Oktyabr' i ukrepleniye nezavisimosti Irana', *SV* (1957/5), 100–4.
Lāhūtī, A. Q., 'About myself', *Soviet Literature*, 9 (1954), 139 *et seq.*
——, 'Tvorcheskoye osvoyenie traditsiy klassikov', *Lit. gazeta* (August 31st, 1954).
Lambton, A. K. S., *Landlord and Peasant in Persia* (Oxford 1953).
Laurent, F., 'La politique actuelle de l'U.R.S.S. en Iran', *Orient*, 5 (1958), 47–57.
Law, D. G., 'A Persian Symposium', *AR*, 7 (1948).
——, 'Modern Persian Prose', *Life and Letters* (Dec. 1949).
Lazard, G., 'Ṣādiq Hidāyat, pīsh-rau-i reālism-i Īrān', *Sukhan* (1334/3), 194–8.
Lenczowski, G., *Russia and the West in Iran 1918–1948* (New York 1949).
——, *The Middle East in World Affairs* (New York 1953).
Lentz, W., 'Beobachtungen über den gedanklichen Aufbau einiger zeitgenössischer Prosastücke', *Isl.*, 30 (1952), 166–208.
Lescot, R., 'Notes sur la presse iranienne', *REI* (1938), 261–77.
——, *La réforme du vocabulaire en Iran* (Paris 1938).

——, 'Le roman et la nouvelle dans la littérature iranienne contemporaine', *BEO*, 9 (1943), 83–101.
Lewis, W. Th. and R. N. Frye, *The United States and Turkey and Iran* (Cambridge, Mass., 1952).
Litten, W., *Persien. Von der "pénétration pacifique" zum "Protektorat". Urkunden und Tatsachen der europäischen "pénétration pacifique" in Persien 1860–1919* (Berlin–Leipzig 1920).
Machalski, Fr., *Historyczna povieść perska* (Krakow 1952).
——, 'Šams et Ṭoġrā, roman historique de Moḥammad Bāqir Ḫosrovī', in *Charisteria Orientalia* (Prague 1956), 149–63.
——, 'Le modernisme dans l'oeuvre poétique de Mohammad Redā Ešqī', *FO*, 1 (1959), 62–86.
——, 'Nīmā Yūšīğ. Essai d'une caractéristique', *FO*, 2 (1961), 53 *et seq.*
——, 'New Poetry in Iran', *New Orient* (1965/2), 33 *et seq.*
——, 'Principaux genres et espèces de la prose persane contemporaine', in *Trudī XXV mezhdunarodn. Kongr. vostokovedov* (Moscow 1963), II, 278–80.
Malekpur, A., *Die Wirtschaftsverfassung Irans* (Berlin 1935).
Malkum-Khān, *Les comédies de Malkom Khan* ... trad. par A. Bricteux (Bibl. de la fac. de philos. et lettres de l'Univ. de Liège, Fasc. 53) (Paris 1933).
Marr, Y. H., 'Sovremennïye sredstva peredvizheniya izobrazhenii persidskikh poetov', *ZKV*, 5 (1930), 221–34.
Massé, H., 'Bibliographie des oeuvres persans', *REI* (1947–51).
——, 'La littérature persane d'aujourd'hui', *Cahiers du Sud* (Août-Sept. 1933).
Massignon, L., *Annuaire du monde musulman statistique, historique, social et économique*, 4th ed. (Paris 1955).
Mel'nikov, L. Y., 'Ispol'zovaniye Irana kak platsdarma protiv Sovetskiy Rossii', *SV* (1957/1), 145–55.
Millspaugh, A. C., *The American Task in Persia* (New York–London 1925).
——, *The Financial and Economic Situation of Persia* (London 1926).
Monteil, V., *Sâdeq Hedâyat* (Inst. franco-iranien, Tehran 1952).
——, *Le persan contemporain* (Paris 1955).
Mostafavi, R., 'Fiction in Contemporary Persian Literature', *MEA*, 2 (1951), 273–9.
Munibar, R., *Post-revolution Persian Verse* (Aligarh 1955).
——, 'Nīmā Yūshīj', *ArOr.*, 29 (1961), 53–63.
Musil, Al., *Země Arijcú – Nový Iran a nový Afganistan* (Prague 1936).
Nafīsī, Sa'īd, *Shāhkārhā-i nathr-i fārsī-i mu'āṣir* (Tehran 1330).
——, 'Le roman dans les littératures iraniennes', *Journal de Téhéran* (Oct.-Nov. 1939).
Nāẓimu'l-Islām Kirmānī, *Ta'rīkh-i bīdārī-i Īrāniyān* (Tehran 1954).
Nicolas, A. L. M., 'Balivernes persanes', *RMM*, 4 (1908), 261–70.
Nikitine, B., 'Le roman historique dans la littérature persane actuelle', *JA*, 223 (1933), 297–338.
——, *La nation iranienne* (Krakow 1949).
——, 'Les thèmes sociaux dans la littérature persane moderne', *OM*, 34 (1954), 225–37.
——, 'Farangshināsī ou l'Europe vue de Téhéran', in *Charisteria Orientalia* (Prague 1956), 210–26.
Nūrā'ī, H. Sh., 'Nāmahā-i Ṣādiq Hidāyat', *Sukhan* (1334), 191 *et seq.*
Osmanova, Z. G., 'Abulkasim Lakhuti', *SV* (1957/6), 74–86.
——, 'Farrokhi Yezdi. Zametki o zhizni i tvorchestve', *KS*, 27 (1958), 67–72.
Petrov, G. M., 'Materialï k sotsialno-ekonomicheskoy kharakteristike ostanov Irana', *KS*, 19 (1956), 78–89.
Peysikov, L. S., 'M. Bakhar kak uchennïy-filolog', *KS*, 36 (1959), 9–22.
Romaskevich, A., 'Literaturnoye dvizheniye v sovremennoy Persii', *Vostok*, 2 (1923), 92–100.
Rossi, Et., 'Il poeta persiano Irağ', *OM*, 23 (1943), 208–20.
Rossow, R. J., 'The Battle of Azerbaijan 1946', *MEJ* (1956), Winter, 17–32.
Rozenfel'd, A. Z., 'O khudozhestvennoy proze v persidskoy literature XX veka', *Vestnik Leningr. univ.*, 5 (1949).

——, 'Pushkin v persidskikh perevodakh', *ibid.*, 6 (1949).
——, 'Gor'kiy v sovremennoy persidskoy literature', *ibid.*, 8 (1951).
——, 'Sadek Khedayat. Opït kharakteristikï tvorchestva', *KS*, 17 (1955), 66–72.
——, 'A. P. Chekhov i sovremennaya persidskaya literatura', in *Pamyati akad. I. Yu. Krachkovskogo* (Leningrad 1958), 73–9.
Rypka, J., 'Aus der modernsten Belletristik Irans', *ArOr.*, 7 (1935), 302–13 [B. 'Alavī].
——, 'Parvín, novodobá básnířká perská', *Ceský časopis filologický*, 1 (1943), 187–95.
Sadiq Issa Khan, *Modern Persia and her Educational System* (New York 1931).
Ṣadr-i Hāshimī: see B VII.
Scarcia, G., '«Ḥağī Āqā» e «Būf-e kūr» i cosidetti due aspetti dell'opera dello scrittore contemporaneo persiano Ṣādeq Hedāyat', *Annali* (Napoli), N.S. (1958/9), 103–23.
Schaeder, H. H., *Die weltliche Stellung Persiens* (Königsberg 1929).
Shafaq, S. R., 'Patriotic Poetry in Modern Iran', *MEJ*, 6 (1952), 417–28.
Sharīf, A., '50 let so dnya osnovaniya zhurnala "Molla Nasreddin"', *KS*, 27 (1958), 23–30.
Shoytov, A. M., 'Rol' M. F. Akhundova v razvitii persidskoy progressivnoy literaturï', *KS*, 9 (1953), 58–65.
——, 'Nekotorïye osobennosti tvorcheskogo metoda Bozorga Alavi', *KS*, 36 (1959), 23–32.
Shuster, M., *The Strangling of Persia* (New York 1912).
Siasi, A., *La Perse au contact de l'Occident* (Paris 1931).
Smith, W. C., *Modern Islam in India* (London 1946).
Sovremennïy Iran, red. B. N. Zakhoder (AN SSSR, Moscow 1957).
Tabāṭabā'ī, M., *Majma'-i āthār-i Malkum-Khān* (Tehran 1327).
——, 'Modern Persian literature', *Indo-Iranica*, 5/1 (1951/2), 21–4.
Tagiryanov, A. T., 'Istoricheskiye korni persidskoy politicheskoy satirï', *Vestnik Leningr. univ.*, 8 (1952), 83 *et seq.*
Tahmāsp, A. A., *Ta'rīkh-i Riḍā-Shāh-i Pahlavī* (Tehran 1304–5).
Toynbee, A. G., *Survey of International Affairs 1920–23* (London 1924).
——, *The Islamic World since the Peace Settlement* (London 1924).
Vassighi, H., *M. A. Djamalzadeh, sa vie et son œuvre* (Tabriz 1955).
Vorozheykina, Z. N., 'O tvorchestve Iraj-Mirzï', *KS*, 17 (1955), 73–82.
——, *Iraj-mirza* (Moscow 1961).
Yāsimī, R., *Adabiyyāt-i mu'āṣir* (Tehran 1316).
——, *Shā'irī va maṭbū'āt-i jadīd* (Tehran n.d.).
——, 'La poésie contemporaine', in *L'âme de l'Iran* (Paris 1951).
Yaukacheva, M., 'Problema osvobozhdeniya iranskoy zehnshchinï v sovremennoy persidskoy proze', *KS*, 27 (1958), 42–9.
Zakhoder, B. N., 'Pervïy bibliograficheskiy zhurnal v Irane', *SV* (1957/1), 163–5.
——, 'Bakhar', *KS*, 36 (1959), 3 *et seq.*
Zaynu'l-'Ābidīn Mu'taman, *Shi'r va adab-i fārsī* (Tehran 1332).

D

JIŘÍ BEČKA: TAJIK LITERATURE FROM THE 16TH CENTURY TO THE PRESENT

This selected Bibliography primarily lists books and articles dealing with Tajik literature and history as they are analysed in this book. Tajik literary works have not been included, as they are listed in the text of the article. An exception has been made for anthologies, particularly of works of deceased writers or poets, which usually contain studies on these authors. The Bibliography has four parts: (I) History; (II) Literature (each of which has been subdivided into (a) General; (b) Pre-Revolutionary; (c) Post-Revolutionary); (III) Periodicals and Bibliographies ((a) Scholarly; (b) Literary; (c) Bibliographical Manuals); (IV) Books published in the Arabic script.

I. HISTORY OF CENTRAL ASIA

a. *General*

Aminov, A. M., 'K kharakteristike Sredneaziatskogo ekonomicheskogo rayona', *Uzbekistonda izhtimoiy fanlar* (1963/2), 5–12.

Bendrikov, K. J., *Ocherki po istorii narodnogo obrazovaniya v Turkestane (1864–1924 godī)* (Moscow 1960).

Bennigsen, A. and Chantal Quelquejay, *The Evolution of the Muslim Nationalities of the USSR and their Linguistic Problems* (Oxford 1961).

——, *La Presse et le mouvement national chez les Musulmans de Russie avant 1920* (Paris–The Hague 1964).

Bogomolova, K. A., *Bukhoro dar davrai Revolyutsiai burzhuazii demokratii fevralii soli 1917. Materialho oid ba ta'rikhi tojik* (Stalinabad 1957).

Bogoutdinov, A. M., *Ocherki po istorii tadzhikskoy filosofii* (Stalinabad 1961).

Chotonov, A., *O natsional'nīkh traditsiyakh narodov Sredney Azii* (Frunze 1964).

Gafurov, B. G., *Istoriya tadzhikskogo naroda v kratkom izlozhenii* (Moscow 1955). (Concise bibliography, 498–538.)

——, 'Adabiyoti khalqi tojik', *ShS* (1949/9).

——, *Nekotorīye voprosī natsional'noy politiki KPSS* (Moscow 1959).

Hayit, Baymirza, *Turkestan im XX. Jahrhundert* (Darmstadt 1956).

Istoriya tadzhikskogo naroda. Red. B. G. Gafurov and B. A. Litvinskiy (Moscow 1963–65).

Istoriya Uzbekskoy SSR., 2 vols. (Tashkent 1955–7).

Kolarz, Walter, *Russia and her Colonies*, 3rd ed. (London 1953).
Krader, Lawrence, *Peoples of Central Asia* (The Hague 1963).
Lenin, V. I., *O Sredney Azii i Uzbekistane* (Tashkent 1957).
Monteuil, Vincent, *Les Musulmanes soviétiques* (Paris 1957).
Nehru, Javaharlal, *The Discovery of India* (London 1951).
Novaya istoriya stran zarubezhnogo Vostoka, I and II (Moscow 1952).
Olzscha, Reiner and Georg Cleinow, *Turkestan* (Leipzig 1942).
Perepelitsïna, L. A., *Rol' russkoy kul'turï v razvitii kul'tur narodov Sredney Azii* (Moscow 1966).
Ross, Colin, *Der Weg nach Osten. Reise durch Russland, Ukraine, Transkaukasien, Persien, Buchara und Turkestan*, 2nd ed. (Leipzig 1924).
Schramm, Stuart and Hélène Carrère d'Encausse, *Le Marxisme et l'Asie* (Paris 1964).
Umarov, S., *Inkishofi ilm dar Tojikiston* (Stalinabad 1959).
Vakhabov, M. G., *Formirovaniye Uzbekskoy sotsialisticheskoy natsii* (Tashkent 1961). (For Engl. translation see *CAR*.)
Wheeler, Geoffrey, *The Modern History of Soviet Central Asia* (New York – Washington 1964).
Zentralasien (Frankfurt am Main 1966) (Fischer Weltgeschichte, 16).

b. *Pre-Revolutionary*

Abdoul-Kerim Boukhary, *Histoire de l'Asie Centrale*. Publié, traduit et annoté par Ch. Schefer, 2 vols. (Paris 1876). (Cf. *GIPh*, I, 407.)
Abdurrakhman-i Tali, *Istoriya Abulfeyz-khana*, transl. with preface and notes by A. A. Semenov (Tashkent 1959).
Amin-i Bukhari, Mir Mukhammad, *Ubaydulla-name*, Russian transl. by A. A. Semenov (Tashkent 1957).
Aminov, A. M., *Ekonomicheskoye razvitiye Sredney Azii (Kolonialnïy period)* (Tashkent 1959).
Bartol'd, V. V., *Turkestan down to the Mongol invasion*, transl. by H. A. R. Gibb, 2nd ed. (London 1928).
——, 'Narodnoye dvizheniye v Samarkande v 1365 g.', *ZVORAO*, 17 (1906), 1–19.
——, *Ulugbek i yego vremya* (Petrograd 1918) (Zapiski Ross. AN, ist.-fil.-otd., vol. 13/5).
——, 'Vostochno-iranskiy vopros', *Izv. Gos. Akad. Ist. mat. kul't.* (1922/2), 361–84.
——, 'Tadzhiki. Istoricheskiy ocherk', in *Tadzhikistan. Sbornik statey*, pod red. N. L. Korzhenevskogo (Tashkent 1925), 93–111.
——, *Istoriya kul'turnoy zhizni Turkestana* (Leningrad 1927).
——, 'Mir Ali Shir i politicheskaya zhizn'', in *Mir Ali Shir* (Leningrad 1928), 110–64.
——, *Herat unter Husein Baiqara, dem Timuriden*, Deutsche Bearbeitung von W. Hinz (Leipzig 1937) (Abh. für die Kunde des Morgenl., XXII/8).
——, *12 Vorlesungen über die Geschichte der Türken Mittelasiens*, Deutsche Bearbeitung von Th. Menzel (Berlin 1935).
Boldïrev, A. N., 'Memuarï Zayn-ad-dina Vosifi, kak istochnik dlya izucheniya kul'turnoy zhizni Sredney Azii i Khorasana na rubezhe XV–XVI vekov', *TOV* (1940/2), 204–74.
——, 'Ocherki iz zhizni geratskogo obshchestva', *TOV* (1947/4), 313–422.
Burnes, Alexandre M., *Voyages de l'Embouchure de l'Indus à Lahor, Caboul, Balkh et à Boukhara pendant les annees 1831, 1832, 1833*, transl. from the English (Paris 1835), in particular vols. II and III.
Carrère d'Encausse, Hélène, 'La politique culturelle du pouvoir tsariste au Turkestan (1867–1917)', *Cahiers du monde russe et soviétique*, 3 (1962). English summary: *CAR*, XI/4, 374–94.
Davidovich, Ye. A., 'Some Social and Economic Aspects of 16th Century Central Asia', *CAR*, XII/4 (1964), 265–70.

Erkayev, M., 'Ta'siri revolyutsiai yakūmi rus ba harakati ozodkhohii millii khalqhoi Osiyoi Miyona', *ShS* (1956/1), 30–8.
Fait, M., *Ruská Střední Asie* (Prague 1901).
——, *Středoasijští národové, zvláště na území ruském* (Prague 1910).
Fomchenko, A. P., *Russkie poseleniya v Bukharskom emirate* (Tashkent 1958).
Frye, Richard N., *Bukhara. The Medieval Achievement* (Norman, Okla., 1965).
Holdworth, Mary, *Turkestan in the Nineteenth Century. A Brief History of the Khanates of Bukhara, Kokand and Khiva* (Oxford 1959).
Iskandarov, B. I., *Iz istorii Bukharskogo emirata (Vostochnaya Bukhara i zapadnïy Pamir v kontse XIX veka)* (Moscow 1958).
——, 'O nekotorïkh izmeneniyakh v ekonomike vostochnoy Bukharï na rubezhe XIX–XX vv.', *Trudï Tadzh.*, 133 (1958), 3–140.
Ivanov, P. P., *Khozyaystvo dzhuybarskikh sheykhov* (Moscow–Leningrad 1954).
——, *Ocherki po istorii Sredney Azii (XVI – seredina XIX v.)* (Moscow 1958).
Khalfin, N. A., *Russia's Policy in Central Asia 1857–1868* (London 1964). Condensed English version by Hubert Evans of a work published Moscow 1960.
Kislyakov, N. A., 'Patrialkhal'no-feodal'nïye otnosheniya u osedlogo naseleniya Bukharskogo khanstva', *Trudï XXV mezhdunar. Kongr. vostokovedov*, III (Moscow 1963), 77–83.
——, 'Ishan – feodal vostochnoy Bukharï', *Trudï Tadzh. bazï AN SSSR* (1940/9), 3–27.
Madzhlisov, A., *Karategin nakanune ustanovleniya sovetskoy vlasti* (Stalinabad 1959).
Mir Mukhammad Amin-i Bukhari: see Amin-i Bukhari.
Mukhammad Yusuf Munshi, *Mukim-khanskaya istoriya*, annotated transl. by A. A. Semenov (AN UzSSR, Tashkent 1956).
Mukhsinova, K. Z., 'K istorii vïstuplenii Bukharskikh krest'yan protiv nalogovogo gneta v kontse XIX veka', *PV* (1959/1), 94–9.
Olliver, E. B., 'The Decline of the Sāmānīs and the Rise of the Ghaznawīs in Māvarā-un-Nahr and Part of Khurāsān', *JASB*, 55, 89 *et seq.*
Pahlen, K. K., *Mission to Turkestan: Being the Memoirs of Count ... 1908–1909* (New York 1964).
Petrov, P. I., 'Bukharskiy mukhtasib v nachale XX veka', *PV* (1959/1), 139–42.
Pierce, Richard A., *Russian Central Asia 1867–1917* (Berkeley–Los Angeles 1960).
Remez, I. A., *Vneshnaya torgovlya Bukharï do mirovoy voynï* (Tashkent 1922).
Rojkoff, M. V., 'La commerce de la Russie avec l'Asie Centrale dans les années 60 du XIXe siècle', *Cahiers d'histoire mondiale*, 9/4 (1966), 957–90.
Romodin, V. A., 'Nekotorïye istochniki po istorii Ferganï i Kokandskogo khanstva (XVI–XIX vv.) v rukopis'nïkh sobraniyakh Leningrada', *Trudï XXV mezhdunar. Kongr. vostokovedov*, III (Moscow 1963), 58–66.
Schuyler, E. S., *Turkistan* (New York 1876, reprint 1966).
Semenov, A. A., 'Rol' Russkogo naroda v razvitii khozyaystva i kul'turï narodov Sredney Azii do Velikoy Sotsialisticheskoy Revolyutsii', *Izv. Tadzh.* (1958/17), 3–9.
——, *Ocherk pozemel'no-podatnogo i nalogovogo ustroystva Bukharskogo khanstva* (Tashkent 1929).
Shams Bukhari Mirza, *O nekotorïkh sobïtiyakh v Bukhare, Chokande i Kashgare* (Zapiski Mirzï-Shemsa Bukhari), ed. by V. V. Grigor'yev (Kazan 1861). (Cf. *GIPh*, I, 407.)
Sokol, E. D., *The Revolt of 1916 in Russian Central Asia* (Baltimore 1954).
Sukhareva, O. A., *Bukhara. XIX – nachale XX v.* (Moscow 1966).
Ta'rīkh-i Badakhshān. 'Istoriya Badakhshana'. Photographic reprod. of the MS., with introd. and index by A. N. Boldïrev (Leningrad 1959).
Teufel, F., 'Quellenstudien zur neueren Geschichte der Chanate', *ZDMG*, 38 (1884), 235–381.
'The Peoples of Southern Turkmenistan and Khorasan in the 17th and 18th Centuries', *CAR*, VIII/3 (1960), 364–72.

Vambery, Arminius, *Reise in Mittelasien* (Leipzig 1865).
——, *Skizzen aus Mittelasien* (Leipzig 1868).
——, *His Life and Adventures written by Himself* (London 1884).
Vzaimootnosheniya narodov Sredney Azii i sopredel'nïkh stran Vostoka v nachale XX v., ed. by M. A. Babakhodzhayev (Tashkent 1963).
Yakubovskiy, A. Y., *Samarkand pri Timure i Timuridakh* (Leningrad 1933) (Ermit.).
——, 'Chertï obshchestvennoy i kul't. urnoy zhizni epokhi Alishera Navoi', in *Alisher Navoi* (Leningrad 1946), 5–30.
——, 'Voprosï periodizatsii istorii Sredney Azii v sredniye veka', *Kratkiye soobshcheniye Inst. istorii mat. kul't* (Moscow 1949).
——, 'Glavnïye voprosï izucheniya istorii razvitiya gorodov Sredney Azii', *AN SSSR, Tadzh. fil., Trudï*, 29 (1951), 3–18.
Yakunin, A. F., *Narodï Sredney Azii i Kazakhstana vo vtoroy polovine 19 veka* (Moscow 1954).
Yorck von Wartenburg, Maximilian Graf von, *Das Vordringen der russischen Macht in Asien* (Berlin 1900).
Zhdanko, T. A., 'Semi-nomadism in the History of Central Asia and Kazakhstan', *Trudï XXV mezhdunar. Kongr. vostokovedov*, III (Moscow 1963), 176–84.

c. *Post-Revolutionary*

Alim Khan, Said, *La voix de la Boukharie opprimée* (Paris 1919) (In French and Persian).
Aliyev, G. A., 'Razvitiye sotsialisticheskoy kul'turï v Tadzhikistane', *SV* (1955/3), 96–107.
Babakhodzhayev, A. Kh., *Proval angliiskoy antisovetskoy politiki v Sredney Azii i na Srednom Vostoke v period priznaniya sovetskogo gosudarstva de-fakto i de-yure (1921–4 gg.)* (Tashkent 1957).
Bailey, F. M., *Mission to Tashkent* (London 1946).
Castagné, J., *Les Basmachis* (Paris 1925).
——, 'La réforme agraire au Turkestan', *REI*, II (1928), 361–99.
——, 'Le mouvement de latinisation dans les républiques soviétiques musulmanes et les voisins', *REI*, II (1928), 559–95.
Conolly, Violet, *Soviet Asia* (Oxford 1942).
Forbes, Rosita, *Forbidden Road – Kabul to Samarkand* (London 1937).
Fučík, Julius, *V zemi milované. Reportáže ze Sovětského svazu* (Prague 1954).
Gafurov, B., *Nekotorïye voprosï natsional'noy politiki KPSS* (Moscow 1959).
Gafurov, B. G. and N. N. Prokhorov, *Tadzhikskiy narod v bor'be za svobodu i nezavisimost' svoey rodinï* (Stalinabad 1943).
——, *Padeniye Bukharskogo emirata* (Stalinabad 1940).
Gordiyenko, A. A., *Sozdaniye sovetskoy natsional'noy gosudarstvennosti v Sredney Azii* (Moscow 1959).
'Gumanitarnïe nauki v Tadzhikistane za 40 let sovetskoy vlasti', *Izv. Tadzh.* (1957/15), 3–25.
Ishanov, A. I., *Pobeda narodnoy sovetskoy revolyutsii v Bukhare* (Frunze 1957).
Kisch, E. E., *Asien gründlich verändert* (Berlin 1932).
Lenczkowski, George, *Russia and the West in Iran 1918–1948. A Study in Big-Power Rivalry* (Ithaca, N.Y., 1949).
Materialho oid ba ta'rikhi khalqi tojik (Davrai sovetī) (Stalinabad 1957).
Makashov, A., *Utverzhdenie sovetskoy vlasti v central'nom i yuzhnom Tadzhikistane* (Stalinabad 1957).
——, *Pervïy s'yezd KP(b) Tadzhikistana* (Stalinabad 1960).
Ocherk istorii sovetskogo Tadzhikistana (1917–1957 gg.) (Stalinabad 1957).
Pyaskovskiy, A. V., 'K voprosu o progressivnom znachenii prisoyedineniya Sredney Azii k Rossii', *VoIst.* (1959/8).

Shek, L. K., 'Iz istorii Sovetsko-Bukharskikh otnosheniy (1917–20 gg.)', *Trudï Sredneaziatskogo gosudarstvennogo Universiteta imeni Lenina*, 78, Ist. nauki, vol. 11.

Todzhikistoni sovetī respublikai shukufon dar Sharq (Stalinabad 1960).

Togan, A. Z. V., *Bugünkü Türkistan ve Yakin Mazisi* (Türk. Bil., 2) (1940).

Urazayev, Sh. Z., *Turkestanskaya ASSR – pervoye sotsialisticheskoye gosudarstvo v Sredney Azii* (Moscow 1961).

Zabulunov, R., *Taraqiyoti madaniyat dar Tojikiston dar davrai ba'di jang* (Stalinabad 1956).

Zenkovsky, Serge A., *Pan-turkism and Islam in Russia* (Harvard University Press, Cambridge, Mass., 1960).

II. LITERATURE

a. *General*

Adabiyoti tojik. Kitobi darsī (Stalinabad 1956).

Antologia tadzhikskoy poezii s drevnikh vremen do nashikh dney, ed. by I. Braginskiy, M. Rakhimi, M. Tursun-zade and S. Ulug-zade (Moscow 1951; 2nd ed. 1957).

Aragon, Louis, *Littérature soviétique* (Paris 1953).

Aynī, Sadriddin, *Namūna-i adabiyyāt-i tājīk 300–1200 h.* (1925; Moscow 1926).

Bennigsen, Alexandre and Ch. Lemercier-Quelquejay, *La presse et le mouvement national chez les Musulmans de Russie avant 1920* (Paris–The Hague 1964).

Bertel's, Ye. E., 'Literatura na persidskom yazïke v Sredney Azii', *SV* (1948), 199–228. German transl. by I. Engelke, *Mitteilungen des Inst. für Orientforschung*, 3/2 (1955), 180–221.

Braginskiy, I., 'Doir ba mas'alai ba davraho taqsim kardani ta'rikhi adabiyoti tojik', *ShS* (1947/2-3).

——, 'Nazare ba taraqqiyoti adabiyoti tojik', *ShS* (1947/4-5-7).

——, *Iz istorii tadzhikskoy narodnoy poezii* (Moscow 1956).

——, *Ocherki iz istorii tadzhikskoy literaturï* (Stalinabad 1956).

——, 'Literatura narodov Sovetskogo Vostoka v 20 veke', *Vestnik istorii mirovoy kul'turï* (1960/5), 3–16.

——, 'K izucheniyu uzbeksko-tadzhikskikh literaturnïkh svyazey', in *Vzaimosvyazī literatur Vostoka i Zapada* (Moscow 1961), 7–56.

Charoqhoi irfon, compiled by N. Ma'sumī (Stalinabad 1960).

Chotonov, A., *O natsional'nïkh traditsiakh narodov Sredney Azii* (Frunze 1964).

Fol'klori tojik, ed. by M. Tursunzoda and A. N. Boldïrev (Stalinabad 1957).

Hayit, B., 'Die jüngste özbekische Literatur', *CAJ*, 7 (1962/2), 119–52.

Hodizoda, R., 'S'yezdi XXII KPSS va ba'ze mas'alahoi omūkhtani merosia dabī', *ShS* (1962/9), 139–47.

Hodizoda, R., M. Shukurov and T. Abdujabborov, *Farhangi istilohoti adabiyotshinosī*, 2nd ed. (Dushanbe 1966).

Huseynzoda, Sh., *Bahs va andesha* (Dushanbe 1964).

——, 'Dar borai ba'ze lahzahoi asosii ta'rikhi adabiyoti tojik', *ShS* (1946/3).

Istoriya literatur narodov Sredney Azii i Kazakhstana, red. M. I. Bogdanova (Moscow 1960). The chapter on Tajik literature by I. S. Braginskiy.

Katalog vostochnïkh rukopisey AN Tadzh. SSR, 1, ed. by A. M. Mirzoyev and A. M. Boldïrev (Stalinabad 1960).

Klimovich, L. I., *Khrestomatiya po literature narodov SSSR*. [Tajik, Uzbek, Azeri, Turkmen, Kirghiz and Kazakh] (Moscow 1947).

——, *Iz istorii literatur Sovetskogo Vostoka* (Moscow 1959).

Madzhidi, R., *Literatura Uzbekistana. Doklad na pervom vsesoyuznom s'yezde sovetskikh pisateley* (Moscow 1934).

Ma'sumī, N., *Usuli ta'limi adabiyot dar sinfhoi V–VIII* (Stalinabad 1960).

——, *Jahonbinī va mahorat* (Dushanbe 1966).
Materialho doir ba adabiyoti tojik (Asarhoi Universiteti Davlatii ba nomi Alisher Navoī, S.N. 90, Kafedrai zabon va adabiyoti tojik) (Samarkand 1959).
Miklukho-Maklay, N. D. *et al*, 'Some rare Persian and Tajik MSS in the collection of the Leningrad branch of the Institute of Oriental Studies, the USSR Academy of Sciences', in *XXVth Intern. Congress of Orientalists* (Moscow 1960).
Miklukho-Maklay, N. D. (red.), *Persidskiye i tadzhikskiye rukopisī Instituta narodov Azii AN SSSR (Kratkiy alfavitnīy katalog)*, 2 vols. (Moscow 1964).
Mirzoyev, A., 'Oid ba ba'ze mas'alahoi merosi adabi va omukhta shudani on' [Lecture at the 4th Session of the Union of Tajik Writers], *ShS* (1959/4), 40–50.
Mirzozoda, Kh. M., *Mulohizaho dar borai adabiyot. Majmūai maqolaho* (Dushanbe 1963).
——, *Materialho az ta'rikhi adabiyoti tojik* (Dushanbe 1962).
Musul'mankov, R., *Sadhz i yego istoricheskoye razvitiye v tadzhikskoy proze.* Avtoreferat (Dushanbe 1966).
Namunahoi adabiyoti tojik [Latin script], ed. by S. Aynī, Kh. Mirzozoda, Javharizoda Suhaylī *et al.* (Stalinabad 1940).
Narodnīye khafizī Tadzhikistana (Stalinabad 1957).
Ocherki po istorii filosofskoy i obshchestvenno-politicheskoy mīsli narodov SSSR (Moscow 1955).
Orifī, M., *Az ta'rikhi afkori pedagogii khalqi tojik* (Dushanbe 1962).
Pagliaro, Antonino and Alessandro Bausani, *Storia della letteratura persiana* (Milano 1960).
Ponomareva, Z. V. and Z. A. Chernīkh, *Tadzhikskaya literatura. Rekomandatel'nīy ukazatel'* (Moscow 1961).
Pūlotov, T., *Guzashta va oyandai maorifi khalq dar Tojikiston* (Stalinabad 1960).
Scarcia, Gianroberto, 'Sguarda alla lirica tagica', *OM*, 45/3 (1965), 244–72.
Shukurov, M., *An'ana, khalqiyat va mahorat. Majmūai maqolaho* (Dushanbe 1964).
Sirus, S. I., *Rifma v tadzhikskoy poezii* (Stalinabad 1953).
——, *Arūzi tojikī. Tahqiqi intiqodī* (Dushanbe 1963).
Sobraniye vostochnīkh rukopisey Akademii Nauk Uzbekskoy SSR, I–7 (Tashkent 1952–64).
Stranitsī tadzhikskoy poezii. Izbrannīye perevodī, ed. by S. Lipkin (Stalinabad 1961).
Z dějin literatur Asie a Afriky, III: *Asijské literatury SSSR* (Prague 1963).
Zehnī, T. N., *San'athoi badeī dar she'ri tojikī* (Stalinabad 1960).

b. *Pre-Revolutionary*

Abdullayev, V. A., *Uzbekskaya literatura XVII–XVIII vekov v Khorezme* (Samarkand-Baku 1958). (Dissertation report.)
Abdullayev, V. and Sh. Shukurov, 'Mirzo Bedil – Sharqning mashhur shoiri va mutafakkiri', *Uzbekistonda izhtimoiy fanlar* (1964/8-9), 108–14.
Ahrorī, Zohir, 'Abdurahmon Mushfiqii Bukhoroī va Mushfiqihoi digar', *SSh* (1965/6), 121–8.
Akhtar, Khvāja 'Ibādu'llāh, *Bīdil* [In Urdu] (Inst. of Islam. Cult., Lahore, 1952).
Amirqulov, S., 'Jarayoni zindagii Hoziq. Majmūai korhoi ilmii aspiranton', *Pedagogicheskiy Inst. Dushanbe*, 36 (Dushanbe 1961), 3–22.
Aripov, M. (Orifī), *Iz istorii pedagogicheskoy mīsli tadzhikskogo naroda* (Dushanbe 1965).
Asirī, Toshkhoja, *Muntakhaboti ash'or*, ed. by J. Khojayev, with introd. by Z. Rajabov (Stalinabad 1960).
Aslanov, R., 'Aqidahoi ma'rifatparvarī – progressivii Saidahmad Siddiqī [Ajzī]', in *Ba'ze mas'alahoi zabon va adabiyoti tojik*, S.N., 114 (Samarkand 1961), 65–74.
Avezbaeva, R., 'Vozzreniya Akhmada Donisha na gosudarstvo', *Izv. Tadzh.*, 30 (1962), 76–93.
Aynī, Kamol, 'Rukopisnīye redaktsii proizvedeniy Badriddina Khiloli', *Izv. Tadzh.* (1955/7).

——, *Badriddin Khiloli* (Stalinabad 1957).
——, *Badriddin Hilolī. Osori muntakhab* (Stalinabad 1958).
Aynī, Khalida, *Bedil' i yego poema "Irfon"* (Stalinabad 1956).
Aynī, Sadriddin, 'Mirzo Abdulqodiri Bedil', *ShS* (1946/7 and 1947/1, 2, 3).
——, *Vosifī va khulosai "Badoe'-ul vaqoe'* (Stalinabad 1956).
——, *Mirzo Abdulqodir Bedil* (Stalinabad 1954).
Azizqulov, Jum'aboy, *Abdulqodirkhojai Savdo* (Stalinabad 1960).
Bausani, A., 'Note su Mirza Bedil', *Annali* (Napoli), N.S., 6 (1957), 163–91.
——, 'Note sulla natura in Bēdil', *Annali* (Napoli), N. S., 15 (1965), 215–28.
——, 'Bēdil as a narrator', *Yádnáme-ye Jan Rypka* (Prague 1967), 227–35.
Bečka, J., 'Soviet Studies on Ahmad Donish', *ArOr.*, 31 (1963), 483–7.
Bertel's, Ye. E., 'Chetverostishiya sheykha Nadzhmeddina Kubra', *DRAN-B* (1924), 36–9.
—— 'Rukopisï proizvedeniy Akhmada Kalle', *Trudï Tadzh. bazï AN SSSR*, III: *Lingvistika* (Moscow-Leningrad 1936), 9–28.
——, 'Literatura narodov Sredney Azii ot drevneyshikh vremën do XV veka n.e.', *Novïy Mir* (Moscow 1939), No. 6, 7, 9.
——, *Navoi. Opït tvorcheskoy biografii* (Moscow–Leningrad 1948).
——, *Ali Shir Nevai, Leyli ve Mecnun* [Introd. to the Russian transl. by S. Lipkin] (Tashkent 1943).
——, 'K voprosu ob "indiyskom stile" v persidskoy poezii', in *Charisteria* (B VIa), 56–9.
Bīdil, *Kulliyyāt* (Bombay 1299/1882).
——, *Majmū'a-i kalām musammā ba Dīvān-i Bīdil* (Bombay 1292/1875).
——, *Nikāt* (Lucknow 1287/1871).
——, "*Komde i Modan*", Russian transl. by L. M. Pen'kovskiy, preface by S. Aynī (Stalinabad 1949).
——, *Ruboiyot*, preface by M. Rahimī (Stalinabad 1961).
Binoī, Kamoliddin, *Hikoyot va tamsilot*, ed. by A. Mirzoyev (Dushanbe 1963).
Boldïrev, A. N., 'Masnavi tadzhikskogo poeta Fayyoza', *Trudï Tadzh. bazï AN SSSR* (1940/9), 55–64.
——, 'Tezkire Khasana Nisori, kak novïy istochnik dlya izucheniya kul'turnoy zhizni Sredney Azii XVI v.', *TOV* (1940/3), 291–300.
——, *Zaynaddin Vasifi. Tadzhikskiy pisatel' XVI v.* (Stalinabad 1957).
——, *Persidskiye perevodï "Madzhalis-an-nafais" Navoi* (Uchenïye zapiski LGU, 1952, No. 128) (Seria vost.-v. nauk, vïp. 3).
——, 'The 16th Century Tajik Writer Zainiddin Vasifi and His "Remarkable Tales" (Badai' al vaqai')', *New Orient Bimonthly* (Prague 1962), 75–8.
Boldïrev, A. N. and I. S. Braginskiy, 'Soobrazhenie o periodizatsii klassicheskoy persidsko-tadzhikskoy literaturï', *NAA* (1965/2), 100–10.
Braginskiy, I. S., 'Unsurhoi ejodiyoti badeii khalq dar osori khattii qadim va asrmiyonagii tojik', *ShS* (1954/10).
——, *Ocherki iz istorii tadzhikskoy literaturï* (Stalinabad 1956).
——, 'Unsurhoi badeī-khalqī dar adabiyoti tojikii asrhoi XVI–XVIII', *ShS* (1955/3).
——, 'Muborizai tendentsiahoi reaktsionī va taraqqiparvaronai adabiyoti tojik dar okhirhoi asri XIX va ibtidoi asri XX', *ShS* (1955/3).
——, 'Zur Frage der Periodisierung der Geschichte der persischen und tadshikischen Literatur', *XXVth Int. Congress of Orientalists* (Moscow 1960).
Dehotī, A., 'Dostoni ishqi bemarg' [On the poem Komde va Mudan], *ShS* (1946/1).
——, 'Chand sukhan dar borai omūzish va nashri osori guzashtagoni mo', *ShS* (1959/5), 134–8.
——, *Asarhoi muntakhab* (Stalinabad 1957).
Donish, Ahmad, *Asarhoi muntakhab*, ed. with introd. by R. Hodizoda (Stalinabad 1959).
——, *Porchaho az "Navodir-ul-vaqoe'"* (Stalinabad 1957).
——, *Puteshestviye iz Bukharï v Peterburg. Izbrannoye* (Stalinabad 1960).

——, *Risola yo mukhtasare az ta'rikhi saltanati khonadoni Manghitia*, ed. by A. Mirzoyev (Stalinabad 1960).
Fakhrii, Rūmonī, *Majmūai she'rho* (Dushanbe 1964).
Fattoyev, M., 'Shakuri – maorifparvar', in *Ba'ze mas'alahoi zabon va adabiyoti tojik*, S.N., 114 (Samarkand 1961), 75–84.
Fitrat Zardūz, *Ṭālib u Maṭlūb* (Tashkent 1917).
——, 'Kozurpisar', *SSh* (1966/10), 113–35.
Galimova, G., 'Dastnavisi noma'lum she'rhoi shoironi Kūhiston', *ShS* (1957/9), 116–24.
——, 'Literaturnoye naslediye Savdo', *Izv. Tadzh.* (1958/1).
——, 'Chernovaya tetrad Savdo', *Izv. Tadzh.* (1957/12).
Gandjeï, Tourkhan, 'Il canzoniere persiano di 'Alī Šīr Navā'ī', *Annali* (Napoli), N.S., 4 (1952), 142–54.
Ghafforov, Abdullojon, 'Zebunniso va muallifoni "Devoni Mahfī"', *SSh* (1966/4), 135–49.
Gulchin, ed. by A. Sharifī (Stalinabad 1959).
Ḥabībī, 'Abd al-Ḥayy, 'Muzakar-i asbāb-i Nisārī', *Āryānā* (1340/11), 1–12.
Hayrat, *Ash'ori muntakhab*, introd. by R. Hodizoda (Dushanbe 1964).
Hilolī, Badriddin, *Osori muntakhab*, ed. by K. Aynī (Stalinabad 1958).
Hodizoda, Rasul, *Istochniki k izucheniyu tadzhikskoy literaturï vtoroy polovinï XIX veka* (Stalinabad 1956).
——, 'Tazkira Vozekha "Tukhfat-ul-akhbob"', *Izv. Tadzh.* (1956/9).
——, 'Nuskhahoi khattii tazkirai Vozeh', *Izv. Tadzh.* (1957/12).
——, 'Raviai peshqadam dar adabiyoti nimai duyūmi asri XIX', *ShS* (1957/2).
——, 'Mutafakkiri buzurgi tojik' [A. Donish], *ShS* (1960/5), 142–53.
——, 'O pervoy chernovoy redaktsii "Navādir al-vaqāii" Ahmada Dānisha', *KS* Inst. Narodov Azii, 65 (1964), 176–83.
——, See also *s.v.* 'Donish'.
Hojī, Muhammadhusayni, *Asarhoi muntakhab*, ed. by S. Sulton (Dushanbe 1962).
Huseynzoda, Sh., 'Osnovnïye momentï razvitiya tadzhikskoy klassicheskoy literaturï', *Trudï Tadzh.*, 21 (1945).
——, *Sukhansaroi Panjrūd (Ba yodi ustod Rūdakī)* (Stalinabad 1958).
Karimov, Usmon, 'Mirzo Sodiq va masnavii "Dakhmai Shohon"', *SSh* (1965/5), 145–51.
Kayumov, Aziz, *Hoziq* [In Uzbek] (Tashkent 1957).
Khalīlī-i Afghān (Khalīlu'llāh Khalīlī), *Āthār-i Harāt*, 3 vols. (Herat 1309–10 A.H.).
Khodzhayev, Dzhamol, *Zhizn' i tvorchestvo poeta Tashkhodzhi Asiri* (Stalinabad 1957).
——, 'Toshkhoja Asirī va ejodiyoti ū', *ShS* (1957/1), 96–111.
Klimovich, L. I., 'Bedil' i yego poema "Komde i Modan"', in *Iz istorii literatur Sovetskogo Vostoka* (Moscow 1959), 159–78.
Koshif, Muhammadaminkhoja, *Ash'ori muntakhab*, introd. by Murtazo Nazirov (Dushanbe 1962).
Ma'sumī, N., *Adabiyoti tojik dar asri XVIII va nimai avvali asri XIX* (Dushanbe 1962).
Mirzayev, K. M., 'K voprosu ob ekonomicheskikh vozzreniyakh Mirzï Bedilya', *Izv. Uzb.* (1958/2).
Mirzoyev, A., *Sayido va maqomi ū dar ta'rikhi adabiyoti tojik* (Stalinabad 1947).
——, 'Tazkirai Maleho va ba'ze mas'alahoi ta'rikh', *ShS* (1946/1).
——, 'Shahroshub va "Shahroshub"-i Sayido', *ShS* (1948/2).
——, 'Dastkhati tozai yak masnavii Hilolī', *ShS* (1948/12).
——, 'Maleho – hamchun she'rfahm va sukhansanji asri XVII', *ShS* (1948/2).
——, *Adabiyot (XVI–XX vv.)* (Stalinabad 1948).
——, 'Yak asari tozai Ahmadi Donish', *Izv. Tadzh.* (1950/XXII).
——, 'Yak fakti muhimmi ta'siri madaniati rus dar nimai duyūmi asri XIX va sharti asosii omukhtani merosi adabī-ilmii Ahmadi Donish', *Trudï Tadzh.* (1951/XXIX).
——, 'Ibni Sino va "Badoe'-ul-vaqoe'"-i Muhammad Vosifī', *ShS* (1952/8-9-10-11).

——, *Pervaya redaktsiya "Navodir-ul-vakoe" i vremya yego sostavleniya. Sbornik statey* (Stalinabad 1953).
——, *Sayido Nasafi i yego mesto v istorii tadzhikskoy literaturï* (Stalinabad 1955).
——, 'Binoī va mas'alai tashakkulyobii shaksiyati fardī', *Izv. Tadzh.* (1955/7).
——, 'Binoī va munosibati ū ba mas'alahoi ilmu donish', *ShS* (1956/3), 73–87.
——, 'Binoī va mas'alai tanqidi zamoni feodalī', *Izv. Tadzh.* (1956/9).
——, *Binoī* (Stalinabad 1957).
——, 'Sayfii Bukhorī va roli ū dar adabiyoti doirahoi hunarmandī', *Izv. Tadzh.* (1957/7), 3–18.
——, 'Ob avtore "Shakhinshakh-name"', *Izv. Tadzh.* (1957/12).
——, 'Yak hujjati oid ba takhallusi Bedil', *Izv. Tadzh.* (1958/1).
——, 'Akhmad Donish o probleme vodï dlya Bukharï', *KS* Inst. narodov Azii, 65 (1964), 112–6.
Mirzozoda, Kh., 'Ahmad Makhdumi Donish mulaqqab ba Ahmadi Kalla', *BAS* (1936/3).
——, 'Shohini Kulobī', *ShS* (1948/7).
——, *Shamsiddin Shohin* (Stalinabad 1956).
Mujaddidī, 'Naqd-i Bēdil', *Adab* (Kabul, 1343/5–6), 117–29.
Muminov, I., 'Filosofskiye vzglyadï Mirzï Abdulkadïra Bedilya', *Trudï Uzb. gos. Univ.* (1946), N.S., 31 (ist.-fil.), Vol. 1, 3–13.
——, 'Izucheniye tvorchestva Mirzï Bedilya v Uzbekskoy i Tadzhikskoy SSR', *Izv. Uzb.* (1958/1).
Muqimov, R., 'Muhammadsharif Gulkhani va uning "Zarbulmasal" asari', *Ŭzbek adab. masalari* (1959), 292–325.
Mushfiqī, *Muntakhabot*, ed. with preface by Z. Ahrorov (Stalinabad 1958).
——, *Zahrkhandai Mushfiqī* (Stalinabad 1960).
Nazarov, H., 'She'rhoi Karim Devona', *ShS* (1957/4), 102–8.
——, *Dar justujūi Karim Devona* (Stalinabad 1958).
Ne'matzoda, T., *Dar borai Vozeh va asari ū "Savoneh-ul-masolik va farosikh-ul-mamolik"* (Stalinabad 1957).
——, '"Koni lazzat va khoni ne'mat"-i Vozeh', *Majmūai ilmī Univ. Davlat. Tojikiston ba nomi Lenin*, XXVI, Ser. fanhoi filol., nashri 2 (Stalinabad 1959), 53–8.
Ptitsïn, G. V., 'Poeticheskiye proizvedeniya Sayido kak istoricheskiy istochnik', *TOV*, 2 (1940), 275–83.
Qosimzoda, A., 'Ba'ze ma'lumothoi nav dar borai Ahmad Makhdumi Donish', *ShS* (1956/3).
Rajabov, Zarif, 'Ahmadi Donish ifodakunandai ghoyahoi islohot dar amorati Bukhoro', *ShS* (1948/6).
——, 'Odamoni peshqadami Osiyoi Miyona dar borai Rossia va madaniyati rus', *ShS* (1950/2).
——, *Poet-prosvetitel' tadzhikskogo naroda Asiri* (Stalinabad 1951).
——, *Iz istorii obshchestvenno-politicheskoy mïsli tadzhikskogo naroda vo vtoroy polovine XIX i nachale XX vv.* (Stalinabad 1957).
——, *Az ta'rikhi afkori jam'iyatī-siyosii khalqi tojik dar nimai duyūmi asri XIX va avvali asri XX* (Stalinabad 1959).
——, *Vïdayushchiysya prosvetitel' tadzhikskogo naroda Akhmad Donish* (Stalinabad 1961).
——, *Maorifparvar Ahmadi Donish* (Dushanbe 1964).
Rūmonī, Fakhrii, *Majmūai she'rho*, ed. by R. Jalil and R. Toshmatov (Dushanbe 1964).
Salimov, Yu., *Stanovlenie zhanra skazochnoy prozï v persidsko-tadzhikskoy literature* (Moscow 1964). (Dissertation report.)
Saljouqui, Fekri, 'Ostad Benay Heravi', *Afghanistan*, 9/3 (1954), 18–21.
Samoylovich, A., 'Sheybani-name. Persidskiy Unikum biblioteki Khivinskogo khana', *ZVORAO*, 19 (1910).
——, 'Iranskiy geroicheskiy epos v literaturakh tyurkskikh narodov Sredney Azii', in *Sbornik "Ferdovsi"*, 161–75.
——, 'Dramaticheskaya literatura Sartov', *Vost. imp. obshch. vostokovedeniya*, 5 (1916).
Sattorov, N., *Badriddin Hilolī* (Dushanbe 1962).

Savdo, *Muntakhabot*, ed. with introd. by Gul'sum Galimova (Stalinabad 1958).
Sayfiev, N., '"Abdullonoma" – hamchun sarchashmai adabī', *Izv. Tadzh.* (1963/4), 33–44.
——, 'Nakhlī va fikrhoi ijtimoī-siyosī dar ejodiyoti ū', *ShS* (1963/8), 118–32.
——, *Nakhli i yego tvorchestvo* (Samarkand 1963). (Dissertation report.)
Sayidoi Nasafī, *Devoni muntakhab*, ed. and introd. by A. Mirzoyev (Stalinabad 1944).
——, *Rasskaz o zhivotnïkh* (Stalinabad–Samarkand 1940).
Semenov, A. A., 'Zabïtïy sredne-aziatskiy filosof XVII v. i yego "Traktat o sokrïtom"' [Mushfiqī], *Izvestiya Obshchestva dlya izucheniya Tadzhikistana*, 1 (1926), 137–85.
——, *Persidskaya novella o Mir-Ali-Shire Nevai* (Tashkent 1926) (Tajik text, with Russian transl.).
——, 'K voprosu, kto bïl avtorom Tarikh i Sayid Raqim', in *Sbornik "V. V. Bartol'd". Obshchestvo dlya izucheniya Tadzhikistana* (Tashkent 1927).
——, 'Kurzer Abriss der neueren mittel-asiatisch-persischen (tadshikischen) Literatur (1500–1900)', *Litt. Orient.* (Harrassowitz), 46 (1931), 1–10.
Shohin, *Ash'ori muntakhab*, ed. with introd. by M. Rahimī (Stalinabad 1960).
Siddiqov, S., 'Tazkirai Sadri Ziyo', *SSh* (1966/1), 139–53.
Sodiq Munshī Mirzo, 'Ash'ori muntakhab', *SSh* (1966/9), 110–24.
Solov'yev, M., 'Nekotorïye voprosï istorii sredneaziatskikh literatur', *Novïy Mir*, 6 (1950).
Sulaymonova, Lola, *Fitrati Zardūzi Samarqandī* (Stalinabad 1960).
Tarlan, A. N., *Ali Šir Nevayi* (Istanbul 1942).
Usmon, Tojī, *Bistu se adiba* (Stalinabad 1957).
——, 'Dar borai shoirahoi gumnom', *TS*, 43 (1960), 3.
Valikhojaev, B., 'Qaidho judogona oid ba she'rhoi tojikii Makhmur', in *Materialho doir ba adabiyoti tojik* (Samarkand 1959), 39–53.
——, *Iz istorii razvitiya literaturno-kriticheskoy mïsli v Uzbekistane (XV–XIX vv.)* (Samarkand 1960).
Vāsifī, Zayn ad-dīn, *Badāī' al-vaqāī'*, crit. text ed. with introd. and index by A. N. Boldïrev, I and II (Moscow 1961).
Yuldashev, K., 'O sotsial'no-ekonomicheskikh vozzreniyakh Akhmada Donisha', *Uzbekistonda izhtimoiy fanlar* (1963/10), 55–8.
Zebunnisso, *She'rho* (Stalinabad 1940).
——, *Majmūai she'rho*, ed. with introd. by A. Sidqī (Stalinabad 1958).
Zuhuriddinov, A., 'Nozim va aqidahoi insonparvarii ū', *ShS* (1963/10), 144–51.
——, *Nozim i yego tvorchestvo*. Avtoreferat (Samarkand 1966).

c. *Soviet period*

Abdullo, Ghanī, 'Dar borai vazifahoi drammatorgia dar Tojikiston', *BAS* (1933/4), 8–13.
——, 'Dar borai ba'ze mas'alahoi drammaturgia', *BAS* (1935/4), 17–9. [Latin script.]
Abdullozoda, R., *Zarbulmasal va maqolho dar asarhoi Sadriddin Aynī* (Stalinabad 1958).
Adiboni Tojikiston (Dushanbe 1966).
Allworth, Edward, 'Reform and Revolution in Early Uzbek Drama', *CAR*, 12/2 (1964), 86–96.
Aminova, S., *Zhenskiye obrazī v tvorchestve S. Aynī* (Moscow 1957).
Amonov, Rajab, 'Ba'ze fikrho oid ba mas'alahoi fol'klorshinosii tojik', *ShS* (1952/9), 101–12.
——, 'Oid ba mavqei fol'klor dar "Yoddoshtho"-i S. Aynī', *Izv. Tadzh.* (1958/1), 43–51.
——, 'Qaidho dar borai munosibati adabiyoti sovetii tojik bo ejodiyoti dahanakii khalq', in *Hayot va adabiyot* [*q.v.*], 223–34.
——, 'Vazifai ta'khirnopaziri mo dar shohai omūkhtani va nashr kardani fol'klori tojik', *ShS* (1958/8) 145–51.
Amonov, R. and A. Sayfulloyev, *Suhaylī Javharizoda* (Stalinabad 1960).
Asrorī, V., 'Hayot va ejodiyoti Yusuf Vafo', *ShS* (1955/9), 86–113.

——, 'Hajv va mazhaka dar adabiyoti tojik', *ShS* (1957/6), 84–97, 116–28.
——, 'Namunai ruboiyoti khalqii zamoni sovetii havzai Zarafshon', in *Majmūai ilmī* (D 111a), 63–76.
——, 'Hajv dar adabiyoti tojik', in *Hayot va adabiyot* [*q.v.*].
Atokhon, S., 'Sohibi tab'i ravon' [Tillo Pūlodī], *ShS* (1962/5), 105–10.
Aul, Josef, 'Atádžán [*sic*] Sulajmán-i-Pajrau', *Nový život* (1954), 593–603. Tajik transl. ed. by S. Tabarov: *ShS* (1964/3), 143–6.
Ayyomi mo. Majmūai ocherkho (Stalinabad 1958).
Aynī, Sadriddin, *Ash'ori muntakhab* (Stalinabad 1958).
——, *Kulliyot*, Vols. 1–7, 10–11 (Dushanbe 1958–66).
Azizqulov, J. and Z. Mullojonova, *Fehrasti asarhoi S. Aynī va adabiyoti oid ba ū to okhiri soli 1961* (Dushanbe 1961).
Bečka, Jiři, 'Sadriddin Ajni', *Nový Orient*, 9 (1957), 140–1.
——, 'Die tadshikische Literatur nach der Grossen Sozialistischen Oktoberrevolution', *ILG*, 413–60.
——, 'Yoddoshti yak adib va olimi chekh dar borai Payrav Sulaymonī', *ShS* (1958/12), 120–3.
——, 'From the Reminiscences of Sadriddin Ayni', *New Orient Bimonthly* (Prague), 1 (1960/4), 18–20.
——, 'The Historical Veracity and Topicality of the *Novel Margi* sudkhūr by Sadriddin Aynī', *Yádnáme-ye Jan Rypka* (Prague 1967), 197–207.
——, 'Tradition in Margi sudkhūr, the Novel by Sadriddin Aynī', *ArOr.*, 35 (1967).
——, 'Islamic Schools in Central Asia', *New Orient* (Prague), 5 (1966), 186–90; 6 (1967), 49–56.
Boboyev, Yu., 'Ba'ze mulohizaho oid ba mahorati badeii navisanda', *ShS* (1952/6).
——, 'Oid ba mas'alai an'ana va navovarī dar ejodiyoti Mirzo Tursunzoda', *ShS* (1957/5), 98–112; 6, 113–22.
——, 'Doir ba mas'alai an'ana va navovarī (Dar misoli ejodiyoti Mirzo Tursunzoda)', in *Hayot va adabiyot* [*q.v.*], 53–83.
——, 'Jalol Ikromī – navisandai ma'ruf', *TS* (1959/225), 3.
——, *Mirzo Tursunzoda. Hayot va ejodiyoti ū* (Stalinabad 1961).
——, *Mirzo Tursun-zade. Kratkiy ocherk zhizni i tvorchestva* (Stalinabad 1961).
——, *Partiya, zamon va adabiyot* (Dushanbe 1964).
——, 'Nazare ba adabiyoti soli 1964', *TS* (1965/85), 3.
——, 'Quvvai hayotbahshi adabiyot', *ShS* (1964/4), 117–48.
Bobokalonova, Jonon, 'Ba'ze mulohizaho dar borai adabiyoti bachagoni sovetii tojik', in *Majmūai ilmī* (D 111a), 103–8.
——, *Tvorchestvo M. Mirshakara dlya detey* (Leningrad 1958).
Braginskiy, I., *Sadriddin Ayni, ocherk zhizni i tvorchestva* (AN Tadzh. SSR, Stalinabad 1954).
——, *Zhizn' i tvorchestvo Sadriddina Ayni* (Moscow 1959).
Davronov, S., *Metrika poezii Abulkasim Lakhuti*. Avtoreferat (Dushanbe 1966).
Demidchik, L. N., 'Sovremennaya tadzhikskaya dramaturgiya', *Izv. Tadzh.* (1957/15), 53–60.
——, 'Zarozhdeniye i stanovleniye tadzhikskoy dramaturgii (1929–1941 gg.)', in *Voprosī istorii tadzhikskoy*... [*q.v.*].
Den' poezii Tadzhikistana 1962, introd. by M. Tursunzoda (Dushanbe 1962).
Den' tadzhikskoy poezii (Stalinabad 1957).
Dungan (see also Rajabov, Z.), 'Dramaturgiyai jadidon', *BAS* (1936/6-7).
Germanetto, Giovanni, '*Ū* zinda ast' [A. Lohutī], *ShS* (1957/12), 88.
Hayot va adabiyot. Majmūai maqolahoi tanqidī-adabiyotshinosī, ed. by N. Ma'sumī and Yu. Boboyev (Stalinabad 1958).
Halimov, S., *S. Aynī – leksikograf* (Dushanbe 1964).
Hamdī, Ahmadjon, *Majmūai asarho*, ed. by J. Azizqulov (Dushanbe 1963).
Hasanov, I., 'Ba'ze khususiyathoi lughavii zaboni "Dukhtari otash"' [J. Ikromī], *SSh* (1964/9), 121–32.

Hodizoda, R., 'Dar yodi ustod' [S. Aynī], *ShS* (1963/3), 119–33.
Hoji, Bobo, 'Dar borai ejodiyoti Lutfī', *TS* (1959/141), 3.
Hoshim, R., 'Dar borai ejodiyoti Payrav Sulaymonī', *BAS* (1934/5-7), 37–40.
——, 'Yodoat ba khayr, Payrav', *ShS* (1959/4), 133–46.
——, *Nekotorïye voprosï stanovleniya tadzhikskoy sovetskoy literaturï* (Dushanbe 1963). (Dissertation report.)
——, 'Osori Aynī baroi bachagon', *ShS* (1963/4), 58–65.
——, 'Dar kūrai muborizaho (Bahrom Sirus)', *SSh* (1965/3), 119–23.
Huseynzoda, Sh., 'Lohūtī va metodi ejodiyoti ū', *BAS* (1932/2), 38–44.
——, 'Doir ba mas'alai taraqqiyoti nasri badeii tojik', *ShS* (1951/6).
——, 'Doir ba mas'alahoi adabiyotshinosii sovetii tojik dar solhoi ba'di jang', *Izv. Tadzh.* (1954/6).
——, 'Doir ba ba'ze mas'alahoi ejodii nazmi sovetii tojik dar solhoi bistūm', *Izv. Tadzh.* (1957/15), 27–39.
——, *Jalol Ikromī. Mukhtasar dar borai hayot va faoliyati adabii navisanda* (Stalinabad 1959).
——, 'Dar borai yak p'esai hajvii ustod Aynī', in *Majmūai ilmī. Univ. davl. Tojikiston*, 26,2 (1959), 3–18.
Ikromī, Jalol, 'Chand sukhan dar borai dramaturgiyai mo', *ShS* (1958/6), 105–9.
——, 'Dar borai ba'ze khususiyathoi nasri tojik', *ShS* (1958/11), 113–9.
——, 'Javonii nasri tojik', *ShS* (1964/1), 55–62.
Imomov, A., *Madaniyati shukufoni khalqi tojik* (Stalinabad 1959).
Isoyev, Ya., 'Lohutī – saroyandai revolyutsiyai Oktyabrī', *ShS* (1957/12), 92–105.
——, 'Lakhuti – poet revolyutsionnogo dvizheniya v Irane', *Uchenïye zap. Pedagog. Inst. Dushanbe*, 17,7 (Stalinabad 1957), 115–96.
——, 'Tabrizskiy divan Lakhuti', *Voprosï tadzh. yazïka i literaturï* (Pedagog. Inst. Dushanbe, Stalinabad 1959), 3–72.
Jashnomai Aynī [A volume in honour of S. Aynī] (*Izv. Tadzh.*, 1960/3); vol. II (1963); vol. III (1966).
Kalontarov, Y. I., 'Razvitiye tadzhikskoy pis'mennosti za godï sovetskoy vlasti', *Izv. Tadzh.* (1957/15).
Kamoliddinov, B., *Hakim Karim. Mukhtasare oid ba hayot, ejodiyot va uslubi adabī* (Dushanbe 1965).
Karim, Hakim, *Hikoyaho* (Stalinabad 1957).
Karimov, M., 'Taraqqiyoti matbuot dar Tojikiston', *TS* (1958/104).
Karimov, T., 'In'ikosi hodisoti ta'rikhī dar romani "Shūrob"', *ShS* (1964/7), 145–53.
Kedrina, Z. S., *Mirsaid Mirshakar. Kritiko-biograficheskiy ocherk* (Moscow 1954).
Khadi-Zade: see Hodizoda.
Khashimov, R. M.: see Hoshim, R.
Khromov, A., 'Lutfullo Buzurgzoda va faoliyati ilmī adabii ū', *ShS* (1958/2), 107–9.
Khudoydodov, B. and M. Najmiddinov, 'Shoiri boiste'dodi sovetii tojik' [Payrav Sulaymonī], *TS* (1954/87), 2.
Kirilov, V., 'Sukhan dar borai shoir' [M. Rahimī], *ShS* (1952/5), 111–4.
Lemenovskiy, A. G., 'Iz vospominaniy o Sadriddine Ayni', *Trudï Uzb. gos. Univ.*, N.S. 69, 61–75.
Lohūtī, A., *Tadzhikskaya literatura (Doklad na pervom vsesoyuznom s'yezde sovetskikh pisateley)* (Moscow 1934).
——, *Kulliyot*, Vols. 1–6 (Dushanbe 1960–3).
Levshina, Inna, 'Tadzhikskiy sovetskiy rasskaz', *Literaturnïy Tadzhikistan, Almanakh No 9* (Stalinabad 1956), 233–59.
——, 'Qaydho oid ba ta'rikhi taraqqiyoti hikoyai sovetii tojik', *ShS* (1955/12), 86–109.
——, *Nasrnavisoni sovetii tojik. Ocherkhoi tanqidī-biografī* (Stalinabad 1957).
——, 'Hikoya dar adabiyoti sovetii tojik', in *Hayot va adabiyot* [*q.v.*], 190–219.
Lutfī, Obidkhūjaev, *Asarhoi muntakhab*, introd. by R. Abdullozoda (Stalinabad 1959).
Maniyozov, A., *Publitsistika va nazmi ustod S. Aynī (1918–1921)* (Stalinabad 1958).

——, 'She'rhoi inqilobii S. Aynī', *Izv. Tadzh.* (1957/15), 41–52.
Maqolaho oid ba adabiyoti bachagona (Dushanbe 1967).
Ma'sumī, N., *Ocherkho oid ba inkishofi zaboni adabii tojik* (Stalinabad 1959).
——, 'Saidalī Valizoda va ejodiyoti ū', *ShS* (1949/2), 27–31.
——, *Muhammadjon Rahimī* (Stalinabad 1961).
——, 'Poem on the Transformation of Life', *Yádnáme-ye Jan Rypka* (Prague 1967), 209–17.
Ma'sumī, N. and Yu. Boboev, 'Nazmi sovetii tojik dar solhoi 1949–1957', *ShS* (1957/4), 118–31.
Mirshakar, Mirsaid, 'Baroi inkishofi minba'dai adabiyoti sovetii tojik', *ShS* (1950/9).
——, 'Dar borai ba'ze mas'alahoi adabiyoti bachagonai tojik', *ShS* (1952/12), 80–8.
——, 'Vazifai muhimmi adabiyoti mo', *ShS* (1949/2), 1–11.
——, 'Zametki k moey biografii', *Guliston* (1959/1), 182–95.
——, *Nishondihandai bibliografī* (Stalinabad 1960).
Mirsaidova, S., 'San'atkori boiste'dod (S. Saidmurodov)', *SSh* (1965/5), 103–8.
Mirzoyev, A., 'Nazmi sovetii tojik', *ShS* (1948/1).
Mirzozoda, Kh., *Habib Yusufī* (Stalinabad 1960).
——, *Mirsaid Mirshakar* (Dushanbe 1962).
——, 'Ba'ze mulohizaho dar borai nazmi soli 1949', *Majmūai ilmī*, 4/4 (Stalinabad 1954), 5–30.
——, 'Mulohizaho dar borai adabiyoti sovetii tojik', *Majmūai ilmī*, 2 (Stalinabad 1955), 3–40.
——, 'Qaydho oid ba nazmi javonon', *ShS* (1962/4), 145–52.
——, 'Mas'alahoi asosii inkishofi nazmi sovetii tojik dar solhoi 1917–1929', *Nazare ba ta'rikhi tojik. Majmuai maqolaho*, 45 (Dushanbe 1966). 3–64.
Morris, G. B., 'Writing in Central Asia', *Survey* (London), 1961, April-June, No. 36, 65–70.
Mulloqandov, M., 'Mulohizae chand dar borai sifathoi adibī va insonii Aynī', *SSh* (1965/4), 141–52.
Muqimov, R., 'Qaydho doir ba mahorati tiphoi satirikī ofaridani ustod Aynī', in *Ba'ze mas'alahoi zabon va adabiyoti tojik*, S.N. 133 (Samarkand 1963), 3–12.
——, 'Lohūtī va adabiyoti dahanaqii khalq', *ibid.*, 13–25.
Nafisī, S., 'Musohabat bo mardi buzurg', *ShS* (1963/4), 56–7.
Nasriddinov, B., 'Payrav Sulaymonī – saroyandai hayoti navi sotsialistī', *Majmūai korhoi ilmii aspiranton* (Stalinabad 1961), 35–45.
Nasrnavisoni sovetii tojik. Ocherkhoi tanqidī-biografī (Stalinabad 1957).
Nevskaya, B., 'Matbuoti Frantsiya dar borai ejodiyoti Sadriddin Aynī', *ShS* (1959/7), 141–6.
Nikitine, B., 'La littérature des musulmanes en URSS', *REI* (1934), 307–81.
Niyazov, Kh. N., *Put' Sadriddin Ayni – poeta* (Moscow 1965).
Niyozī, Sh., *Nazmi epikii tojik dar solhoi Jangi Buzurgi Vatanī* (Dushanbe 1965).
Niyozmuhammadov, B., 'Khususiyathoi zabonii ash'ori Mirzo Tursunzoda', *ShS* (1964/9), 106–20.
Nudel', Y., 'Hofizi khalq Bobo Yunus Khudoydodzoda', *ShS* (1958/6), 115–9.
Nurjonov, N., 'Az ta'rikhi teatri khalqii tojik', *ShS* (1958/5), 104–16.
——, 'Tadzhikskiy teatr v godī Velikoy otechestvennoy voynī', in *Iskusstvo tadzh. naroda*, 2 (Stalinabad 1960), 5–34.
——, 'Quvvahoi navi dramaturgiyai tojik', *ShS* (1963/1), 107–10.
——, 'Ba'ze mulohizaho oid ba vaz'iyati teatri tojik', *ShS* (1963/12), 128–39.
Ocherk istorii tadzhikskoy sovetskoy literaturī (AN Tadzh. SSR, Stalinabad, 1955).
Ocherk istorii tadzhikskoy sovetskoy literaturī [A large work containing *i.a.* monographs on S. Aynī, A. Lohūtī, M. Tursunzoda, S. Ulughzoda and M. Mirshakar] (Moscow 1961).
Ocherki ta'rikhi adabiyoti sovetii tojik, 2 vols. (Stalinabad 1956–7).
Osmanova, Z., *Mirzo Tursun-zade. Ocherk tvorchestva* (Moscow 1961).
——, 'Problemī traditsii i novatorstva v sovetskoy tadzhikskoy poezii', in *Sotsialisticheskiy realizm v literaturakh narodov SSSR* (Moscow 1962), 145–85.
Otakhonova, Kh., *Rahim Jalil va ejodiyoti ū (Hikoyaho va Odamoni jovid)* (Dushanbe 1962).

Pankina, V. P., 'Povest' "Smert' rostovshchika" – odno iz vïsshikh dostizheniy tvorchestva S. Aynī', *Izv. Tadzh.* (1957/15), 61–90.
Payrav, Sulaymonī, 'Maktubi kushoda ba idorai rūznomai "Tojikistoni Surkh"', *BAS* (1937/6), 22–3.
——, *Majmūai osor*, ed. by Lola Sulaymonī, with introd. by Rahim Hoshim (Stalinabad 1959).
Pechat' Tadzhikskoy SSR 1928–1958 (Stalinabad 1959).
P'yesï tadzhikskikh dramaturgov [Russian transl. of six Tajik dramas] (Stalinabad 1959).
Poetï sovetskogo Tadzhikistana, ed. by I. Braginskiy (Moscow 1950).
Qahhorī, A., 'Nazare ba ta'rikhi nashriyoti tojik', *SSh* (1964/10), 153–7.
Qalamhoi purumed [Chrestomathy of poems and tales by young Tajik authors] (Stalinabad 1957).
Qosimov, V., 'Iborahoi khalqī dar dostoni Mirzo Tursunzoda – "Hasani arobakash"', *Materialho D* (IIa), 127–33.
——, 'Ba'ze khususiyathoi zaboni she'rhoi hajvii Muhiddin Aminzoda', in *Ba'ze mas'alahoi zabon va adabiyoti tojik*, S.N., 114 (Samarkand 1961), 95–102.
Radzhabov: see Rajabov.
Rahimov, N., *Ideyno-khudozhestvennïye osobennosti romana Sadriddina Ayni "Dokhunda"* (Tashkent 1954).
Rahimzoda, B. and M. Farhat, 'Shoir vatanparvar' [Habib Yusufī], *ShS* (1955/3), 112–8.
Rahmat ba partiya (Stalinabad 1960).
Rajabov, Qayum, 'Ocherk – zhanri jangovar', *SSh* (1965/11), 145–56.
Rajabov (Radzhabov), Z., *K kharakteristike pervogo sovetskogo zhurnala na tadzhikskom yazïke "Plamya revolyutsii"* (Stalinabad 1959).
——, *Sadriddin Ayni – istorik tadzhikskogo naroda* (Stalinabad 1951).
——, *Nekotorïye stranitsï kul'turnoy zhizni sovetskogo Tadzhikistana (Materialï)* (Dushanbe 1964).
Rasskazï tadzhikskikh pisateley (Stalinabad 1957).
Sadriddin Aynī. Nishondodi bibliografī (Stalinabad 1956).
Said, Homid, *Ruboiyot*, ed. by S. Normatov (Stalinabad 1961).
Saloh, S., 'Ba'ze materialho doir ba hajvi solhoi bistūm va siiūm', *ShS* (1957/10), 106–19.
——, *Satira i yumor v tadzhikskoy periodike 30–20kh godov* (Dushanbe 1964). (Dissertation report.)
——, 'Dar borai zabon va uslubi romani "Shūrob"', *Izv. Tadzh.* (1961/4), 76–91.
Sarvar, M., *Ash'ori muntakhab*, ed. by M. Rahimī and M. Mirhaydarov (Dushanbe 1961).
Sayfulloyev, A., *Obrazi qahramononi musbati dar romanhoi ustod Sadriddin Aynī* (Stalinabad 1960).
——, *Mirzo Tursunzoda* (Stalinabad 1961).
——, 'Asirī – shoiri maorifparvar', *SSh* (1964/9), 29–37.
——, 'Dar zeri bayraqi realizmi sotsialistī', *SSh* (1964/10), 3–22.
——, *Romani ustod Sadriddin Aynī "Dokhunda"* (Dushanbe 1966).
Sbornik statey posvyashchennïkh 40-letiyu Velikogo Oktyabrya (Stalinabad 1957).
Sharifov, J., 'Adibe ki bo hayot barobar qadam mezanad' [Foteh Niyozī], *SSh* (1964/9), 38–47.
Shavkat, K., 'Nazmi tojik ba khizmati Jangi Buzurgi Vatanī', *SSh* (1965/5), 132–44.
Shavkat, N., 'Ba'ze khususiyathoi nazmi epikii tojik dar zamoni Jangi Buzurgi Vatanī', *ShS* (1956/9), 111–23; (1956/10), 94–101.
Shklovskiy, V., 'Qosim Lohutī', *BAS* (1937/9-10), 17–8.
Shukūhī, A., 'Saroyandai ishq va ozodī' [A. Lohūtī], *ShS* (1963/2), 122–9.
——, 'Nazm boyad chun dar'yoi sof boshad', *ShS* (1963/9), 56–62.
——, 'Hayoti mo va nasri mo', *ShS* (1964/1), 44–54.
Shukurov, M., 'Ba'ze mas'alahoi mahorati shoironi javon', *ShS* (1955/8), 67–77.
——, 'Doir ba mas'alai an'anahoi M. Gorkiy dar "Yoddoshtho"-i Sadriddin Aynī', *ShS* (1955/7), 70–85.

——, 'Dar borai povesti "Vafo" muvaffaqiyat va kambudihoi on', *Akhborot* (1956/9), 55–71.
——, 'Konflikt boyad to okhir inkishof doda shavad', *ShS* (1953/11), 99–103.
——, *Ob ideynïkh i khudozhestvennïkh osobennostyakh "Vospominaniy" S. Aynī* (Moscow 1954). (Dissertation report.)
——, 'Baroi lirikai balandi purehsos', *ShS* (1957/11), 107–21.
——, *Revolyutsiyai madanī dar Tojikiston (Ocherkho)* (Stalinabad 1957).
——, *Sotim Ulughzoda* (Stalinabad 1961).
——, 'Khalqiyati nazmi Mirzo Tursunzoda', *ShS* (1961/4-5).
——, 'Sukhan az lirika va mazmuni hayotii on', *SSh* (1965/2), 78–105.
——, 'Elements of Rhyming Prose in the Ëddostho of S. Aynī', *Yádnáme-ye Jan Rypka* (Prague 1967), 219–24.
Shukurov, M. and A. Edel'man, 'Taraqqiyoti navi nasri tojik', *ShS* (1957/4), 109–17.
Slovník spisovatelů národů SSSR (Prague 1966).
Sokolov, S. and V. Demidchik, 'Asarhoi Aynī dar Frantsiya', *ShS* (1961/11), 144–8.
Sovetskiye pisateli Tadzhikistana. Biograficheskiye spravki (Dekada tadzhikskoy literaturï v Moskve 1949), ed. by L. Klimovich (Stalinabad 1949).
Stranitsï tadzhikskoy poezii. Izbrannïye perevodï (Stalinabad 1961).
Tabarov, S., 'Roli Aynī dar taraqqii zaboni adabī va nasri sovetii tojik', *ShS* (1948/11), 7–11.
——, 'Oid ba mas'alai in'ikosi revolyutsiyai soli 1905 dar adabiyoti sovetii tojik', *ShS* (1955/6), 120–31.
——, 'Ba'ze qaidho dar borai uslubi dostonnavisii M. Tursunzoda va dostoni "Hasani arobakash"-i ū', *ShS* (1955/9), 114–29.
——, *Sadriddin Aynī – saroyandai Revolyutsiai Kabiri Sotsialistii Okt'yabr'* (Stalinabad 1958).
——, 'Yulius Fuchik – dūsti jonii khalqi sovetī', *TS* (1958/212), 4.
——, 'Adabiyoti sovetii tojik haqiqatan khalqī va realistist', *TS* (1958/209).
——, 'Ustodi mohiri hajv' [Rahim Jalil], *TS* (1959/139), 2.
——, *Payrav Sulaymonī (Ocherki hayot va ejodiyot)* (Dushanbe 1962). Reviewed in *ArOr.*, 31 (1963), 707.
——, *Mirsaid Mirshakar* (Dushanbe 1962).
——, *Hayot, adabiyot, realizm* (Dushanbe 1966).
Tadzhikskaya sovetskaya dramaturgiya [Russian transl. of seven successful Tajik plays and a treatise on Tajik drama by N. Klado] (Moscow 1957).
Tadzhikskaya sovetskaya literatura. Sbornik statey (Stalinabad 1954).
Tadzhikskiye ocherki, ed. by A. Odintsov (Stalinabad 1957).
Taronahoi navrūzī [preface, biographies and examples of the work of ten folk-poets], ed. by P. Amonov and S. Normatov (Stalinabad 1960).
Toshmuhammadov, F., 'Taqozoi zamon va mahorati dramaturg', *SSh* (1965/1), 128–39.
Tursunzoda, Mirzo, 'Baroi ghoyai balandi adabiyot', *ShS* (1947/5).
——, 'Baroi vatandūstii sovetī bar ziddi paneronizm', *ShS* (1949/3), 1–4.
——, 'Poeziyu na liniyu ognya', *Druzhba narodov* (1954/6), 255–65.
——, 'Hayot va adabiyot', *ShS* (1959/3), 98–133.
Ulughzoda, Sotim, 'Adabiyoti buzurgi khurdtarakonro ejod mekunem', *BAS* (1936/5), 24–7.
——, 'Baroi asarhoi sahnavii olisifat', *ShS* (1947/12), 21–6.
——, 'Dar borai mahorati dramaturg', *ShS* (1951/6), 113–9.
Usmon, Tojī, 'Yak moh bo Sadriddin Aynī (Khotirot)' *ShS* (1962/8), 94–118.
Usmonov, J., *Taraqqiyoti matbuoti soveti dar Tojikiston* (Stalinabad 1958).
Voprosï istorii tadzhikskoy sovetskoy dramaturgii i teatra (by N. Nurdzhanov and L. A. Demidchik) (Stalinabad 1957).
Wurmser, A., 'Orientale. Boukhara par Sadriddine Aini', *Les lettres françaises* (1956), No. 651, 2.

——, 'Splendeurs et misères de l'Orient' [On Aynī's *Margi sudkhūr*], *Les lettres françaises* (1958), No. 704, 2.
Yavich, M., 'Ocherk v 1958 godu', *Guliston* (1959/1), 219–22.
——, 'Sharqi khorijī dar nazmi tojik', *ShS* (1958/12), 124–34.
Yusupov, K., *Sotīm Ulug-zade i yego avtobiograficheskaya povest' "Utro nashey zhizni"* (Dushanbe 1964). (Dissertation report.)
——, 'Abdushukur Pirmuhammadzoda', *ShS* (1964/2), 82–7.
Zabulunov, R., *Taraqqiyoti madaniyat dar Tojikiston dar davrai ba'di jang* (Stalinabad 1956).
Zand, M. I., *Abulkosim Lakhuti (1887–1957)* (Stalinabad 1957).
——, *Pisateli Tadzhikistana* (Stalinabad 1957).

III. THE MOST IMPORTANT TAJIK PERIODICALS AND BIBLIOGRAPHIES

a. *Scholarly periodicals*

Akhboroti Akademiai fanhoi RSS Tojikiston. Shū'bai fanhoi jam'iyatī. Izvestiya Akademii nauk Tadzhikskoy SSR. Otdeleniye obshchestvennīkh nauk (Stalinabad, since 1961 Dushanbe).
Akhboroti Filiali tojikii Akademiai fanhoi SSSR. Izvestiya Tazhikskogo filiala Akademii nauk SSSR (Stalinabad, published from 1941 to 1952).
Majmūai ilmī. Instituti Davlatii pedagogii ba nomi T. G. Shevchenko. Fakul'teti zabon va adabiyot (shū'bai tojikī) (Dushanbe, publ. since 1940).
Nauchnīye trudī. V. I. Lenin nomidagi Toshkent davlat universiteti. Filologicheskiye nauki (Tashkent).
Trudī tadzhikskoy (tadzhikistanskoy) bazī Akademii nauk SSSR (Stalinabad, 1935–1940).
Trudī tadzhikskogo filiala Akademii nauk SSSR (Stalinabad, 1941–1951).
Trudī Akademii nauk Tadzhikskoy SSR. (Dushanbe, publ. since 1951).
Trudī uzbekskogo gosudarstvennogo Universiteta imeni Alishera Navoi (Samarkand).
Ūzbekistonda izhtimoiy fanlar. Obshchestvennīye nauki v Uzbekistane [A monthly containing articles on literature and history in Uzbek and Russian] (Tashkent, publ. since 1961).
UzSSR fanlar Akademiyasining akhboroti. Seriya obshchestvennīkh nauk (Tashkent, 1957–1960).

b. *Literary periodicals*

Baroi adabiyoti sotsialistī [Abbr. *BAS*]. See *Sharqi surkh.*
Guliston. A quarterly published by the Union of Tajik Writers. It contained Russian translations of Tajik literary works, examples of the works of Russian writers living in Tajikistan, as well as literary articles and reviews. Until 1958 it was called *Literaturnīy Tadzhikistan.* It ceased publication in 1961.
Khorpushtak. Monthly satirical magazine. Publ. in Dushanbe since 1953.
Komsomoli Tojikiston. Publ. three times a week in Dushanbe since 1929. Before 1956 it was called *Javononi Tojikiston.*
Madaniyati Tojikiston. Publ. monthly by the Ministry of Education and Culture of the Tajik SSR. It ceased publication in 1959.
Maorif va Madaniyat. Press organ of the Ministry of Education and Culture, publ. three times a week since 1957. It often contains literary articles and reviews [Abbr.: *M. va M.*].
Sadoi Sharq: see *Sharqi surkh.*
Sharqi surkh. Publ. monthly by the Union of Tajik Writers. 1932–1937 called *Baroi adabiyoti sotsialistī*, 1941–1945 not published. Since 1964 beginning with issue No. 5 called: *Sadoi Sharq* [Abbr.: *ShS*, *SSh* resp.].

Tojikiston. A monthly also containing literary articles, especially reviews. Publ. from 1956 to 1962. Since 1957 also publ. in a Russian version.

Tojikistoni Sovetī. A daily also containing occasional literary reviews and articles on literature. Publ. since 1925. Prior to 1955 it was called *Tojikistoni surkh* [Abbr.: *TS*].

Zanoni Tojikiston. Monthly magazine. 1932–1941 called *Bo rohi Leninī*, not publ. from 1942 to 1950. Contains also poetry and short stories.

c. *Bibliographical Manuals*

Bibliografiya izdaniy Tadzhikskoy Bazï i Tadzhikskogo filiala Akademii nauk SSSR. Knigi i stat'i 1933–1951 (Stalinabad 1952).

Bibliografiya izdaniy Akademii nauk Tadzhikskoy SSR. Knigi i stat'i 1951–1954 (Stalinabad 1955).

Leyvi, L. S. and N. S. Nazarova, *Nauka v sovetskom Tadzhikistane. Bibliograficheskiy ukazatel' 1951–1960* (Dushanbe 1963).

Shevchenko, Z. M. and M. V. Nikolayeva, *Katalog kandidatskikh i doktorskikh dissertatsiy zashchishchennïkh na materialakh Tadzhikskoy SSR (1934–1959)* (Stalinabad 1960).

Solnomai matbuoti RSS Tojikiston. A complete classified list of books and articles published in Tajikistan, in Tajik, Uzbek and Russian. Publ. quarterly since 1939.

IV. BOOKS PRINTED IN ARABIC SCRIPT

ʿAynī, Ṣadru'd-dīn, *Tahdhību'ṣ-ṣibyān* (Samarkand 1917).

——, *Ta'rīkh-i amīrān-i Manghītiyya-i Bukhārā* (Tashkent 1923).

——, *Namūna-i adabiyyāt-i Tājīk, 300–1200 h.* (Moscow 1926).

——, *Sargudhashta-i yak Tājīk-i kam-baghal yā ki Ādīna* (Samarkand 1927).

——, *Dākhūnda* (Kazan 1930).

——, *Marg-i sūd-khur* (Stalinabad 1936).

——, *Yād-dāshthā (qism I–IV)* (Stalinabad 1958–9).

——, *Maktab-i kuhna* (Dushanbe 1966).

Bihrūz, Muḥammad Ḥusayn, 'Adabiyyāt az Abu'l-faraj Sigzī ba baʿd', in *Afghānistān* (Kabul 1334/1955), 190–369.

Dānish, Aḥmad Makhdūm, *Risāla yā mukhtaṣarī az ta'rīkh-i silsilat-i khāndān-i Manghītiyya*, ed. by ʿAbdu'l-Ghanī Mīrzāyef (Stalinabad 1960).

Dihātī, ʿAbdu's-Salām, *Payāmhā-i dūstī. Shiʿrhā, shiʿrhā barāyi bachchagān, ḥikāyahā-i hajvī va khāṭirāt-i safarhā-i khārija* (Stalinabad 1959).

Fiṭrat, *Shūrish-i wāsiʿ* (Samarkand 1927).

——, *Daura-i ḥukm-rānī-i Amīr ʿĀlam-khān* (Tashkent–Stalinabad 1930).

Jalīl, Raḥīm, *Ādamān-i jāvīd* (Stalinabad 1959).

——, *Shūrāb* (Stalinabad 1960).

Jauharī-zāda, Suhaylī, *Barg-i sabz* (Stalinabad 1956).

Karīm, Ḥakīm, *Ḥikāyahā* (Stalinabad 1940).

Khalīlī Afghān (Khalīlu'llāh), *Āthār-i Harāt*, 3 vols. (1309–10).

Lāhūtī, Abu'l-Qāsim, *Adabiyyāt-i surkh* (Samarkand–Dushanbe 1927).

——, *Kreml va rubāʿiyyāt* (Samarkand–Dushanbe 1927).

——, *Mā ẓafar khāhīm kard* (Moscow 1931).

——, *Du nishān* (Moscow 1934).

——, *Hazār miṣraʿ* (Moscow 1935).

——, *Dīvān* (Moscow 1939; 1946; 1957).

——, *Jang-i ādamī-zād bā dīv* (Moscow 1944).

——, *Surūdhā-i āzādī va-ṣulḥ* (Moscow 1954).
Laṭīfahā-i Tājīkī. Tartīb-dihanda ʿAbduʾs-Salām Dihātī (Stalinabad 1958).
Mīr-shakar, Mīr-sayyid, *Bahār-i Tājīkistān* (Stalinabad 1958).
——, *ʿIshq-i dukhtar-i kūhsār* (Dushanbe 1966). Review: *Kāva*, 12–13, 154–5.
Mīrzāyef, ʿAbduʾl-Ghanī, *Rūdakī va inkishāf-i ghazal dar aṣrhā-i X–XV* (Stalinabad 1957).
——, *Abū ʿAbduʾllāh Rūdakī* (Stalinabad 1958).
Mushfiqī, ʿAbduʾr-Raḥīm, *Muntakhabāt. Tartīb-dihanda Z. Aḥrārofī* (Stalinabad 1959).
Namūna az tarānahā-i millī-i Tājīkī (Stalinabad 1957).
Namūnahā-i ashʿār-i shāʿirān-i Sovyetī-i Tājīk. Tartīb-dihanda Bahrām Sīrūs (Stalinabad 1958).
Payrau, Sulaymānī, *Ashʿār-i muntakhab* (Stalinabad 1959).
Qahhārī, A., *Āhanghā-i dūstī. Shiʿrhā* (Dushanbe 1965).
Qahhārūf, ʿAbduʾl-Aḥad, *Dar partau-i āzādī* (Dushanbe 1966).
Raḥīm-zāda, Bāqī, *Chashm-sār. Ashʿār-i muntakhab* (Stalinabad 1959).
Rubāʿiyyāt va du-baythā-i khalqī-i Tājīk (Stalinabad 1958).
Saudā, *Muntakhabāt. Jamʿ-kunanda va tartīb-dihanda Kulthūm ʿĀlimova* (Stalinabad 1959).
Taʾrīkh-i Badakhshān. Istoriya Badakhshana, ed. by A. N. Boldïrev (Leningrad 1959).
Tursūn-zāda, Mīrzā, *Ṣadā-i Āsiyā* (Stalinabad 1956).
——, *Chirāgh-i abadī* (Stalinabad 1958).
Ulūgh-zāda, Ṣātim, *Ṣubḥ-i javānī-i mā* (Stalinabad 1957).
——, *Qismat-i shāʿir* (Dushanbe 1963).
Vāṣifī, Zaynuʾd-dīn Maḥmūd, *Badāyiʿuʾl-vaqāyiʿ*, 2 vols., ed. with introd. and indices by A. Boldïrev (Moscow 1961).
Yūsufbekov, *Muʿārif-i khalqī-i Tājīkistān* (Dushanbe 1967).
Zhāla, *Zinda rūd* (Moscow 1960).

E

JAN MAREK: PERSIAN LITERATURE IN INDIA

(As a rule, titles mentioned in the sections B, C and D are not repeated here)

I. BIBLIOGRAPHY

Ghani, A. R., *Bibliography of Iqbal* (Lahore 1955).

Hasan, Khan Bahadur Maulvi Zafar, *Bibliography of Indo-Moslem History excluding Provincial Monarchies* (Calcutta 1932).

Sharma, Sri Ram, *A Bibliography of Mughal India (1526–1707)* (Bombay n.d.).

II. POLITICAL, ECONOMIC AND CULTURAL HISTORY

Abu'l-Faḍl, *Ā'īn-i Akbarī*, 2 vols. (Calcutta 1867–77). – *Ain-i Akbari* (Vol. I tr. by H. Blochmann; vols. II–III tr. by H. S. Jarrett) (Calcutta 1868–94).

——, *Akbar-nāma*, 3 vols., tr. by H. Beveridge (Calcutta 1897–1935).

'Afīf, *Ta'rīkh-i Fīrūz-shāhī* (Calcutta 1891).

Aziz Ahmad, *Studies in Islamic Culture in the Indian Environment* (Oxford 1964).

Badā'ūnī, 'Abdu'l-Qādir, *Muntakhabu't-tavārīkh*, 3 vols. (Calcutta 1864–9). – *Muntakhab al-tawarikh* (Vol. I tr. by G. Ranking; vol. II tr. by W. H. Lowe) (Calcutta 1884–98).

Banerji, S. K., *Humayun Badshah.* Vol. I: Oxford University Press; vol. II: Maxwell Comp. Lucknow (1941).

Baranī, Ḍiyā'u'd-dīn, *Ta'rīkh-i Fīrūz-shāhī* (Calcutta 1862).

Elliot, H. M., *The History of India as told by its own Historians*, ed. by J. Dowson, 8 vols. (London 1867–77).

Firishta, Abu'l-Qāsim, *Gulshan-i Ibrāhīmī* (Bombay 1831).

——, *Mahomedan Power in India*, Tr. by J. Briggs, 4 vols. (London 1829).

Gankovskiy, Yu. V., *Narodī Pakistana* (Moscow 1964).

Gankovskiy, Yu. V. and L. R. Gordon-Polonskaya, *A History of Pakistan* (Moscow 1964).

Goetz, H., 'Persia and India after the Conquest of Maḥmūd', in *The Legacy of Persia* (B VIa), 89–115.

Gordon-Polonskaya, L. R., *Musul'manskiye techeniya v obshchestvennoy mīsli Indii i Pakistana* (Moscow 1963).

Gulbadan Begam, *History of Humayun (Humāyūn-nāma)* (London 1902).

Husain, Mahdi, *The Rise and Fall of Muhammad bin Tughlaq* (London 1938).

——, *Tughluq Dynasty* (Calcutta 1963).

Ikram, S. M., *Muslim Civilization in India*, ed. by Ainslie T. Embree (New York–London 1964).
Jahn, K., *Rashīd al-Dīn's 'History of India'. Collected Essays with Facsimiles and Indices* (Central Asiatic Studies, x) (The Hague 1965).
Lal, K. S., *History of the Khaljīs (1290–1320)* (Allahabad 1950).
Lane-Poole, Stanley, *Mediaeval India under Mohammedan Rule (A.D. 712–1764)* (London 1906).
Malik, Hafeez, *Moslem Nationalism in India and Pakistan* (Washington 1963).
Niẓāmu'd-dīn Aḥmad, *Ṭabaqāt-i Akbarī*, tr. by De (Calcutta 1932–6).
Tūzuk-i Jahān-gīrī, tr. by Rogers and Beveridge, 2 vols. (London 1909–14).

III. RELIGION, MYSTICISM, SECTS

Horten, M., *Indische Strömungen in der islamischen Mystik* (Heidelberg 1927).
Husain, Yusuf, *L'Inde mystique au Moyen Age: hindous et musulmans* (1929).

IV. HISTORY OF LITERATURE

'Abdu'llāh, Sayyid, *Adabiyyāt-i fārsī mẽ Hinduõ ka ḥiṣṣa* (Delhi 1942).
Bausani, Alessandro, *Storia delle letterature del Pakistan* (Milano 1958).
Ethé, Hermann, *Die höfische und romantische Poesie der Perser* (Hamburg 1887).
Ghani, Muhammad Abdul, *A History of Persian Language and Literature at the Mughal Court*, vols. I–III [Bābur-Akbar] (Allahabad 1929–30).
——, *Premughal Persian Literature in Hindostan* (Allahabad n.d.).
Hadi Hasan, *Mughal Poetry: its cultural and historical value* (Madras 1951).
Husain, Iqbal, *Early Persian Poets of India* (Patna n.d.).
Husaini, Abdul Karim, *Persian Language in the Deccan* (Hyderabad 1934).
Ḥusayn, I'jāz, *Mukhtaṣar ta'rīkh-i adab-i Urdū*, 5th ed. (Delhi 1956).
Ikrāmu'l-Ḥaqq, *Shi'ru'l-'Ajam fi'l-Hind* (Multan n.d.).
Sadarangani, H. I., *Persian Poets of Sind* (Karachi 1956).

V. MONOGRAPHS

Abdul Ghani, *Life and Works of 'Abdulqādir Bēdil* (Lahore 1960).
Akhtar, Khvāja 'Abdu'llāh, *Bēdil ki shā'irī* (Lahore 1952).
Anikeyev, N. P., *Vīdayushchiysya mīslitel' i poet Mukhammad Iqbal* (Moscow 1959).
Enver, Ishrat Hasan, *The Metaphysics of Iqbal* (Lahore 1957).
Ghafforov, Abdullojon, *Hayot va ejodiyoti Mirza Asadullo Gholib* (Dushanbe 1965).
Habib, Mohammad, *Hazrat Amir Khusrau of Delhi* (Bombay 1927).
Hasrat, Bikramajit, *Dara Shikuh, Life and Works* (Calcutta 1955).
Iqbal as a Thinker [A Collection of Essays on Iqbal by eight scholars] (Lahore 1944).
Iqbal Singh, *The Ardent Pilgrim* (London 1951).
Ishaque, M., *Four Eminent Poetesses of Iran, with a brief survey of Iranian and Indian Poetesses of Neo-Persian* (Calcutta 1950).
Maitre, Luce Claude, *Introduction à la pensée d'Iqbal* (Paris 1955).
Naqī Muḥammad Khān Khurjavī, *Ḥayāt-i Khusrau* (Karachi 1956).
Qanungo, K. R., *Dārā Shukoh* (Calcutta 1934).
Sachchindananda Sinha, *Iqbal, The Poet and His Message* (Lahore 1958).

Saiyidain, K. G., *Iqbal's Educational Philosophy* (Lahore 1954).
Schimmel, A., *Gabriel's Wing* [With an exhaustive bibliography of Iqbal] (Leiden 1963).
Shiblī Nuʿmānī, *Savāniḥ-i Zību'n-nisā bēgam* (Lucknow n.d.).
Vahid, Syed Abdul, *Introduction to Iqbal* (Karachi 1954). – *Iqbal, His Art and Thought* (London 1952).

VI. TEXTS AND TRANSLATIONS

(The bibliography of Indian poets is to be supplemented from the sections B, C and D)

Abū Ṭālib Kalīm Kāshānī, *Dīvān-i Kalīm Kāshānī*, ed. by Bīzhan Taraqqī (Tehran 1958).
Amīr Khusrau Dihlavī, *Khazā'inu'l-futūḥ*, ed. by S. Muʿīnu'l-Ḥaqq (Aligarh 1927).
——, *Medzhnun i Leyli*, ed. by G. A. Magerramov (Moscow 1963).
——, *Nuh Sipihr*, ed. by M. Vaḥīd Mīrzā (Lucknow 1950).
——, *Tughluq-nāma*, ed. by S. Hāshimī Farīdābādī (Aurangabad 1933).
Bābur, *Sobraniye stikhotvoreniy imperatora Babura*, ed. by A. Samoylovich (Petrograd 1917).
Bābur-nāma, Memoirs of Zehir-ed-Din Muhammed Baber, tr. by J. Leyden and W. Erskine, 2 vols. (London 1826).
Badr-i Chāch, *Qaṣā'id*, ed. by Hādī ʿAlī (Cawnpore 1845; Lucknow 1907).
Bayrām Khān, *The Persian and Turkī Dīvāns of Bayrām Khān*, ed. by E. Denison Ross (Calcutta 1910).
Bowen, J. Ch. E., *The Golden Pomegranate* [Selections of Persian poetry] (Bombay 1957).
Dārā Shikūh, Muḥammad, *Majma-ul-Bahrain or the Mingling of the two Oceans*, ed. in the original Persian with English Transl., Notes and Vocabulary by M. Mahfuz-ul-Haq. (Bibl. Indica, Vol. 246) (Calcutta 1929).
——, *Risāla-i Ḥaqq-numā*, lith. (Lucknow, Nawal Kishore 1883; 1910).
——, *Safīnatu'l-auliyā*, lith. (Lucknow 1872; Lahore 1884; Cawnpore 1900).
——, *Ṭarīqatu'l-ḥaqīqat*, lith. (Gujrānvāla 1857).
——, *Shaṭḥiyyāt or Ḥasanātu'l-ʿārifīn*, lith. (Delhi, Mujtabai Press 1309 A.H.). – Engl. tr. by Pandit Sheo Narain, *Journal Panjab Hist. Soc.*, 2 (1913–14), 28 *et seq.*
Ḍiyā'u'd-dīn Nakhshabī Badā'ūnī, *Ṭūṭī-nāma*, tr. into English by M. Gerrans (London 1792).
Fayḍī, *Nal Daman*, lith. (Lucknow 1877; 1930).
Ghanī, Muḥammad Ṭāhir, *Dīvān*, lith. (Lucknow 1845).
Ghanīmat, Muḥammad Ikram, *Dīvān-i Ghanīmat*, ed. by Ghulām Rabbānī ʿAzīz (Lahore 1958).
——, *Nayrang-i ʿishq*, ed. by Ghulām Rabbānī ʿAzīz (Lahore 1962).
Hadi Hasan, *Qasim-i Kahi (868–988 A.H.), his life, time and works* (Hyderabad [Deccan.] 1953).
Ḥākim, ʿAbdu'l-Ḥakīm, *Tadhkira-i mardum-dīda*, ed. by Sayyid ʿAbdu'llāh (Lahore 1961).
Ḥasan Dihlavī, Amīr, *Dīvān* (Hyderabad 1933).
——, *Kulliyyāt*, ed. by Masʿūd ʿAlī Mahvī.
Husain, A. Mahdi, *ʿIṣāmī's Futūḥus-salāṭīn, the Shahname of Medieval India* (Agra 1938).
Ikram, Shaykh Muḥammad, *Armaghān-i Pāk* [Selections of Persian poetry from India] (Tehran 1333; Karachi 1955).
Indarjīt Munshī, *Nāma-i ʿishq*, ed. by Vaḥīd Qurayshī (Lahore 1959).
Iqbāl, Sir Muḥammad, *Asrār va Rumūz* (Lahore 1948). – *The Secrets of the Self*, tr. by Reynold A. Nicholson (London 1920; Lahore 1950, etc.). – *The Mysteries of Selflessness*, tr. by Arthur J. Arberry (London 1953).
——, *Payām-i Mashriq* (Hyderabad n.d.). – *Message de l'Orient*, traduit par Eva Meyerovitch et Mohammad Achena (Paris 1956). – *Botschaft des Ostens*, übersetzt von Annemarie Schimmel (Wiesbaden 1963). – *Poselství z Východu*, Czech tr. by Jan Marek and Kamil Bednář (Prague 1960). – *Risālatu'l-mashriq*, Arabic tr. by Abdul Wahab Azam Bey (Lahore 1951). – *Şarktan haber*, çeviren Ali Nihat Tarlan (Ankara 1956).

——, *Zabūr-i ʿAjam* (Lahore 1948). – *Persian Psalms*, tr. into English verse by A. J. Arberry (Lahore 1957).

——, *Jāvīd-nāma* (Lahore, Hyderabad). – *Das Buch der Ewigkeit*, übersetzt von A. Schimmel (Munich 1957). – *Il Poema Celeste*, traduzione dal testo Persiano e note del Alessandro Bausani (Rome 1952; Bari 1965). – *Le Livre de l'Éternité*, trad. par Eva Meyerovitch (Paris 1962).

——, *Musāfir. Pas chi bāyad kard ay aqvām-i sharq* (Lahore n.d.; Armaghān-i Ḥijāz, Lahore, 1946).

——, Selections: *Poems from Iqbal*, tr. by Victor G. Kiernan (London 1955). – *Poesie*, traduzione dal Persiano e dall' Urdu di Alessandro Bausani (Parma 1956). – *The Tulip of Sinai*, tr. by A. J. Arberry [A part of *Payām-i mashriq*] (London 1947).

ʿIṣāmī, *Futūḥuʾs-salāṭīn*, ed. by A. S. Usha (Madras 1948).

Jauhar Āftābchī, *Tadhkiratuʾl-vāqiʿāt* [Humayun's Memoirs], Urdu tr. by S. Moinul Haq (Karachi 1955).

Qāniʿ, Mīr ʿAlī Shīr, *Tadhkira-i maqālātuʾsh-shuʿarā*, ed. by S. Ḥusāmuʾd-dīn Rāshidī (Karachi 1957).

Sarkhush, *Kalimātuʾsh-shuʿarāʾ or Tadhkira-i Sarkhush* (Lahore 1942).

Sarmad, *Rubāʿiyyāt-i Sarmad*, ed. by Faḍl Maḥmūd Asīrī (Shantiniketan 1950).

Shaykh Muḥammad, *Muʾayyiduʾl-fuḍalā* (Lucknow n.d.).

ʿUrfī, Jamāluʾd-dīn Muḥammad, *Qaṣāʾid* (Lucknow 1845).

Vāqif, *Dīvān-i Vāqif*, ed. by Ghulām Rabbānī ʿAzīz (Lahore 1962).

Zībuʾn-nisā, *Dīvān-i makhfī*, lith. (Cawnpore 1345 h.) – *Majmūai sheʿrho*, ed. with introd. by A. Sidqī (Stalinabad 1958). – *The Diwan of Zeb-un-Nissa*, tr. by Magan Lal and Jessie Duncan Westbrook (London 1913).

Ẓuhūrī, *Si nathr-i Ẓuhūrī*, lith. (Lucknow 1259 h.).

VII. ARTICLES

Abbasov, A. M., 'Nekotorïye zamechaniya o zhizni i tvorchestve Hasana Dekhlevi', *Voprosï istorii i filosofii* (Baku 1966), 188–205.

Abdul Hakim, Kh., 'Concept of Love in Rumi and Iqbal', *IC*, 14 (1940), 266–73.

Abdu'l-Wali, Maulavi, 'Sarmad, His Life and Execution', *Indian Antiquary*, 39 (1910), 119–26.

Abdur Rahim, 'Mughal Relations with Persia', I–III, *IC*, 8 (1934); 9 (1935).

Abdur Rahman, S. Sabahuddin, 'Glimpses of Indo-Persian Literature', *Indo-Iranica*, 10/2 (1957).

——, 'Study of Hindu Learning and Religion in Indo-Persian Literature', *Indo-Iranica*, 14 (1961).

Abdus Sattar Khan, 'Tāj Rēzah', *IC*, 14 (1940), 359–66.

ʿĀbidī, S. Amīr Ḥasan, 'Mathnavī-i Mihr-o-māh by Maulana Pir Muhammad Awadhi', *Majalla-i ʿulūm-i islāmīyya*, 2/1 (1961).

——, 'The Influence of Hindi on Indo-Persian Literature in the Reign of Shah-Jahan', *Indo-Iranica*, 13/2 (1960).

——, 'Abū Ṭālib Kalīm Kāshānī', *Indo-Iranica*, 10 (1957), 25–40.

Ahuja, Y. D., 'Iraqi in India', *IC*, 32 (1958), 57–70.

——, 'Some Aspects of the Persian Prose Translation of Gita ascribed to Abul-Fazl', *Indo-Iranica*, 13/3 (1960).

Anikeyev, N. P., 'Obshchestvenno-politicheskiye vzglyadï Mukhammada Ikbala', *SV* (1958/3), 91–100.

Antonova, K., 'Dva issledovaniya o mogol'skoy poezii', in *Sbornik Literaturï Indii* (Moscow 1958), 249–58.

Asīrī, Faḍl Maḥmūd, 'Sarmad shahīd', *Vishvabhāratī Patrikā*, 6 (1947), 50–60.

Askari, Syed Hasan, 'Fresh Light on Shaikh Ali Hazin and his Tours in Eastern Hindustan', in *Proc.*

2nd Ind. Hist. Cong. (1938), 382–8. – 'The Political Significance of Hazin's Career in Eastern India', *Bengal Past and Present*, 63 (1949), 1–10.

Baqir, Muhammad, 'Munshī, the Author of Sussī Punnūn', *IC*, 17 (1943), 206–9.

Basu, K. K., 'The Court-Poets of Bijapur and their Philosophy', *IHRC Procs.*, 16 (1939), 158–63.

——, 'Quli Qutb Shah, a Poet-King of Golconda (1543 A.D. – 1550 A.D.)', *B. C. Law*, 1 (1945), 232–6.

Bausani, Alessandro, 'Mohammad Iqbāl's Message', *East and West*, 1 (1950), 137–40. – 'Dante and Iqbāl', *East and West*, 2 (1951), 77–81. – 'Satana nell'opera filosofico-poetica di Muhammad Iqbal', *RSO*, 30 (1955), 55–102.

——, 'Note su Mirzā Bēdil', *Annali* (Napoli), N.S., 6 (1954–56), 163–99.

Bilgrami, Sayid Wasi Ahmad, 'A Persian Poet of the Shāhābād District', *Journal of the Bihar and Orissa Research Society*, 2 (1916), 469–74.

Borah, M. I., 'An Account of the Immigration of Persian Poets into Bengal', *Dacca Univ. Studies*, 1 (1935), 141–50.

——, 'A Short Account of an Unpublished Romantic Masnavī of Amīr Ḥasan Dihlavī', *New Ind. Antiquary*, 2 (1939–40), 258–62. – 'The Life and Work of Amīr Ḥasan Dihlavī', *JASB*, 3/7 (1941), 1–59.

Bukhari, Syed Abdul Wahab, 'Persian in India, with Special Reference to the Contribution of Hindu Writers and Poets', *Annals of Oriental Research University of Madras*, 13 (1957), 27–38.

Courtois, V., 'Sir Muhammad Iqbal, poète, philosophe et apologiste indien', in *En Terre d'Islam* (1938), 327–50.

Desai, Z. A., 'The Story of Nala-Damayantī as told by Faiḍī and its Comparison with the Original Sanskrit Version', *Journal of the Oriental Institute* (Baroda), 8/1 (1958), 81–96. – 'Life and Works of Faiḍī', *Indo-Iranica*, 16/3 (1963), 1–35.

——, 'Salari – a thirteenth Century Persian Poet of India', *IC*, 36/4 (1962), 275–80.

Fakhru'z-zamān Bēgam, 'Mīr 'Alā'u'd-daula Kāmī Qazvīnī', *Majalla-i 'ulūm-i islāmiyya*, 1/1 (1960), 111–22.

Fück, J. W., 'Muhammad Iqbāl und der indomuslimische Modernismus', in *West-östliche Abh. R. Tschudi zum 70. Geburtstag* (Wiesbaden 1954), 356–65.

Gai, B. M., 'Development and Character of Persian Language and Literature in the State of Bombay', *IC*, 30 (1956), 211–38.

Ghauri, Iftikhar Ahmad, 'Responsibility of the 'Ulama for the Execution of Dara Shikoh', *JPHS*, 7/3 (1959), 221–2.

Ghose, Sudhin N., 'Faizi and Urfi, two of Akbar's Court Poets', *The Aryan Path*, 31/4 (1960), 153–6.

Gilani, Arifshah C. Syed, 'Persian Poetry of Ghalib', *Islamic Literature*, 7/9 (1955). – *Ghalib – His Life and Persian Poetry* (Karachi 1956).

Gorekar, N. S., 'Persian Poets of India', *Indo-Iranica*, 16/2 (1963), 66–85.

Hadi Hasan, 'The Unique Diwan of Humayun Badshah', *IC*, 25 (1951), 212–76.

——, 'Qasim-i Kahi, His Life, Time and Works', *IC*, 27 (1953), 99–131, 161–94, 199–224. – 'An Introduction to the Diwan of Qāsim-i Kāhī', *Indo-Iranica*, 8 (1955), 34–42.

Halim, A., 'History of Persian Literature during the Sayyid-Lodi Period (1414–1526)', *JPHS*, 3 (1955), 12–34.

——, 'Growth of Urdu Language and Literature during the Sayyid-Lodi Period', *JASP*, 3 (1958), 43–66.

Hasan, Mas'ud, 'Fard – a little known Persian Poet from Bihar', *Indo-Iranica*, 8 (1955), 25–42.

Hasan, Zafar, 'Manuscript Copy of the Divan of Dārā Shikūh', *JASB*, 3/5 (1939), 155–73.

Hashmi, B. A., 'Sarmad, His Life and Quatrains', *IC*, 7 (1933), 663–72; 8 (1934), 92–104.

Hasrat, Bikrama Jit, 'The Diwan and the Quatrains of Dara Shikoh', *IC*, 18 (1944), 145–66. – 'Dara Shukuh and Saints', *Vishvabharati Quarterly*, 4. – 'Mukalama Baba Lal va Dara Shukuh', *Vish-*

vabharati Quarterly, 9 (1949), 326–39. – 'Three little known Works of Dara Shikoh', *IC*, 25 (1951), 52–72.

Hidayat Hosain, M., 'Contemporary Historians during the Reign of the Emperor Shāh Jahān', *IC*, 15 (1941), 64–78.

Huda, M. Z., 'History of Persian Literature', *JPHS*, 9 (1961), 87–93, 170–5, 261–88.

Husain, Iqbal, 'Chandar Bhan Brahman, a Hindu Writer of Persian Prose and Verse', *IC*, 19 (1945), 115–22.

Husain, Mahdi, 'The Firdausī of India', *Indo-Iranica*, 1 (1947), 23–8.

Ikram, Sheykh Muhammad, 'Persian Literature in Bengal', *Pakistan*, 3/3 (1953), 27–31.

——, 'Persian Literary Heritage', in *The Cultural Heritage of Pakistan* (Karachi 1955), 92–118.

Jahn, K., 'On the Mythology and Religion of the Indians in the medieval Moslem Tradition', in *Mélanges Massé* (Tehran 1963), 1–13.

Kausar, Inamul Haq, 'Rabia Khuzdari, a prominent literary figure of medieval Baluchistan', *JPHS*, 9/1 (1961), 36–41.

——, 'Nāṭiq Makrānī', *JPHS*, 9/4 (1961), 296–301.

Kāẓmī, Tamkīn, 'Hindustān mẽ fārsī zabān aur adab kī taraqqī', *Ham qalam*, 1/3 (1960), 17–28.

Khaṭībī, Ḥusayn, 'Mukhtaṣarī rājiʿ ba-āthār va sabk-i ashʿār-i duktur Muḥammad Iqbāl Lāhaurī, shāʿir-i pārsī-gū-i Pākistān', *MDAT*, 1 (1332/1953), 57–68.

Lakhanpal, P. L., *Ghalib – the Man and His Verse* (New Delhi 1961).

Marek, Jan, 'The Date of Muḥammad Iqbāl's Birth', *ArOr.*, 26 (1958), 617–20.

Masani, R. P., 'Persian Poets in Indian Durbars', *Journal Univ. Bombay*, 1 (1932), 82–92.

Massignon, Louis and A. M. Kassim, 'Un essai de bloc islamo-hindou au XVIIe siècle: l'humanisme mystique du prince Dārā', *RMM*, 63 (1926), 1–14.

Mīnuvī, Mujtabā, 'Iqbāl-i Lāhaurī, shāʿir-i fārsī-gū-i Pākistān', *Yaghmā* (1327).

Mirza, Mohammad Wahid, 'Muṭahhar-i Karā kī shāʿirī', *Oriental College Magazine* (May 1935).

——, 'India and Her Muslim Poets', in *Woolner Commemorative Volume* (1940), 173–6.

Modi, Jivanji Jamshedji, 'King Akbar and the Persian Translations of Sanskrit Books', *Annals of the Bhandarkar Oriental Research Institute*, 6 (1925), 83–122.

Nadvi, Syed Suleyman, 'The Literary Progress of the Hindus under the Muslim Rule', *IC*, 12 (1938), 424–33; 13 (1939), 401–26.

Nafīsī, Saʿīd, 'Adabiyyāt dar Hindūstān', *Armaghān*, 10, 566–77, 609–35.

Naʿimuddin, Sayyid, 'Some Unpublished Verses of Babur', *IC*, 30 (1956), 44–50.

——, 'Some Unknown Qasidas of ʿUrfi of Shiraz', *IC*, 30 (1956), 385–409.

Narain, Pandit Sheo, 'Dārā Shikūh as an author', *JPHS*, 2/1, 26.

Nazir, Ahmad, 'Kitab-i Nauras', *IC*, 28 (1954), 333–71.

——, 'Taqi Awhadi', *IC*, 32 (1958), 276–94.

——, 'Mīr Jamālu'd-dīn Ḥusayn Injū Shīrāzī', *Majalla-i ʿulūm-i islāmiyya*, 1/1 (1960), 17–48.

——, 'Malik Qummī aur us kē nasharī risāle', *Oriental College Magazine*, 5/1 (1961).

Nāzukī, Mīr Ghulām Rasūl, 'Ghanī Kashmīrī', *Ājkal Urdū*, 14/1 (1955), 70–3.

Nicholson, R. A., 'Iqbal's Message of the East', *Islamica*, 1 (1924), 112–24.

Pal, Dharm, 'Poetry and Architecture in the Time of ʿAlā'ud-Dīn Khiljī', *IC*, 19 (1945), 245–60.

Pūlodova, Sharaf, 'Shoiri mashhuri Gholib', *ShS* (1961/9), 131–49.

Reyazul Hasan, 'Il poeta musulmano indiano Mohammed Iqbal (1873–1938)', *OM*, 20 (1940), 605–23.

Riazul Islam, 'A Survey in Outline of the Mystic Literature of the Sultanate', *JPHS*, 3 (1955), 201–8.

Ross, Denison E., 'Diwan-i Babur Padishah', *JRASB*, 6 (1910).

Roy Choudhury, M. L., 'The Hindu Contribution to Persian Literature', *Journal of the Bihar and Orissa Research Soc.*, 29 (1943), 120–6.

Roy, N. B., 'The Background of Iqbal's Poetry', *Vishvabharati Quarterly*, 20 (1955), 321–31.

Ṣafā'ī, Ibrāhīm, 'Farhang-i Īrān dar Hind', *Armaghān*, 29/4-5, 145–57.

Schimmel, Annemarie, 'Muhammad Iqbal. The Ascension of the Poet', *Welt des Islams*, N.S., 3 (1954), 145–57.

——, 'Babur Padishah, the Poet with an Account of the Poetical Talent in His Family', *IC*, 34 (1960), 125–38.

Shaikh, C. H., 'Literary Personages of Ahmadnagar', *Bulletin Deccan College Research Inst.*, 2 (1940–41), 383–96; 3 (1941–42), 212–8.

Sharma, Ram, 'A Little-known Persian Version of the Ramayan', *IC*, 7 (1933), 673–8.

Shaukat, Sameena, 'Mahārāja Chāndūlāl Shādān and His Persian Poetry', *IC*, 36/1 (1962), 54–64.

Shērvānī, Ḥabību'r-Raḥmān Khān, 'Qaṣā'id-i Muṭahhar-i Karā', *Ma'ārif* (August 1935).

Siddiqi, M. Aslam, 'Persian Press in India', *Indo-Iranica*, 2/2 (1947), 15–26.

Srivastava, A. L., 'Historicity of Deval Rani Khizr Khan', *IC*, 30 (1956), 24–30.

Storey, C. A., 'Abd al-Qadir Badā'ūnī and the Kathā-Saritsāgara', in *Woolner Commemoration Volume* (1940), 249–50.

Whittemore, R., 'Iqbal's Pantheism', *Rev. Metaphys. USA*, 9/4 (1956), 681–99.

Winter, H. J. J. and Arshad, Mirza, 'Concerning the Persian Version of Līlāvatī', *JASB Science*, 3/18 (1952), 1–10.

Zia-i-Ahmad, 'Development of Persian Literature during the Time of Akbar', *Allahabad Univ. Studies*, 3 (1927), 265–88.

F

JIŘÍ CEJPEK: IRANIAN FOLK-LITERATURE

Aarne, Antti, *Leitfaden der vgl. Märchenforschung* (Folklore Fellows Communications No 13) (Hamina 1913).

——, *Übersicht der Märchenliteratur* (FF Communications No 14) (Hamina 1914).

Abdullozoda, R., *Zarbulmasal va maqolho dar asarhoi Sadriddin Aynī* (Stalinabad 1958).

Abrahamian, Roubène, *Dialectes des Israélites de Hamadan et d'Ispahan et le dialecte de Baba Tahir* (Paris 1936).

Afganskiye narodnïye poslovitsï i pogovorki (Moscow 1961).

Afganskiye skazki, sostavitel' K. Lebedev (Moscow 1955).

Afsonahoi khalqii tojikī. Tartibdihandagon R. Amonov va K. Ulughzoda (Stalinabad 1957).

Ahmadov, Mahmud, 'Hofizi nomdori khalq Domullo Halim Ibodov', *ShS* (1958/5), 98–103.

Aliyev, G. Y., 'Ranniye khristianskiye istochniki legendï o Khosrove i Shirin', *SV* (1957/6), 87–96.

——, 'Iz istorii vozniknoveniya obraza Farkhada v literaturakh narodov Vostoka', *KS*, 27 (1958), 50–7.

——, 'Legenda o Khosrove i Shirin v "Shakhname" Firdousi', *UZIV*, 19 (1958), 190–210.

——, *Legenda o Khosrove i Shirin v literaturakh narodov Vostoka* (Moscow 1960).

Aliyev, Ghazanfar, 'Dar borai "Kalilavu Dimna"-i Rūdakī', *ShS* (1958/10), 117–26.

Alpamïsh, sostavitel' R. Amonov, perevod tekstov L. N. Demidchik (*Trudï Tadzh.*, CXVII) (Stalinabad 1959).

Amonov, R., 'Dar borai ejodiyoti shoiri khalqo Saidalī Valizoda', *Izv. Tadzh.* (1954/6), 109–25.

——, 'Oid ba mavqei fol'klor dar "Yoddoshtho"-i S. Aynī', *Izv. Tadzh.* (1958/1), 43–52.

——, 'Asrori ruboiyoti khalq', *SSh*, 37 (1964), 139–58.

——, 'Vazifahoi ta'khirnopaziri mo dar sohai omukhtan va nashr kardan fol'klori tojik', *ShS* (1958/8), 145–51.

——, 'Dostonhoi khalqī dar borai bahoduroni Chambuli Maston', *ShS* (1961/12), 141–51.

Anderson, Walter, *Zu Albert Wesselski's Angriffen auf die finnische folkloristische Forschungsmethode* (Commentationes Archivi traditionum populariorum Estoniae, 4) (Tartu 1935).

Andreyev, S. M., 'Sredneaziatskaya versiya Zolushki-Sandriljonï', in *Sbornik po Tadzhikistanu, otchet ekspeditsii 1925* (Tashkent 1927), I, 60–1.

Andreyev, M. S., *Tadzhiki dolinï Khuf (verkhovya Amu-Daryi)*, 1–2 (*Trudï Tadzh.*, VII, XLI) (Stalinabad 1953, 1958).

Andreyev, M. S. and Y. M. Peshchereva, *Yagnobskiye tekstī* (Moscow–Leningrad 1957).

Anekdotï mollï Nasreddina (Baku 1958).

Anekdotï o khodzhe Nasreddine, transl. from Turkish into Russian by V. A. Gordlevskiy, 2nd ed. (Moscow 1957).

Anikin, V. P., *Russkaya narodnaya skazka* (Moscow 1959).

——, *Russkiy bogatïrskiy epos* (Moscow 1964).

Anmerkungen zu den KHM der Brüder Grimm, neu bearbeitet von Johannes Bolte und Georg Polívka, unter Mitwirkung von Elisabeth Kutzer und Bernhard Heller, Bd. IV: *Zur Geschichte der Märchen I–VIII* (Leipzig 1930).

Antologiya azerbeydzhanskoy poezii, I (Moscow 1960).

Antologiya osetinskoy poezii (Moscow 1960).

Antologiya tadzhikskoy poezii, red. A. Bertel's and S. Shervinskiy (Moscow 1957). Cf. Aliyev, R., I. Braginskiy, and N. Osmanov, *Vstupitel'naya stat'ya*, 5–27 (1st ed.: Moscow 1951). Also other Anthologies of poetry: *Abkhazian anth.* (Moscow 1958); *Kabardinian anth.* (Moscow 1957); *Kirghiz anth.* (Moscow 1957); *Turkmenian anth.* (Moscow 1949); *Uzbek anth.* (Moscow 1950).

Asrori, V., 'Oid ba hayot va ejodiyoti shoiri khalq Yusuf Vafo', *Izv. Tadzh.*, 6 (1954), 85–107.

——, 'Mavqei afsonahoi khalqī dar ejodiyoti Sadriddin Aynī', *ShS* (1959/11), 138–48.

'Az afsonahoi khalqii tojik: Zani hunarmand. Boi zolim va Kali zirak. Savobjūy', Jamʿ kunanda R. Amonov, *ShS* (1956/3), 40–7.

'Az ruboyoti khalqii Afghoniston. Ba chop tayyorkunanda M. Kholov', *ShS* (1961/6), 84–92.

'Az ruboyoti khalqii tojik. Jamʿkunandagon M. Jorūbov, F. Murodov, J. Karimov', *ShS* (1963/9), 136–40.

'Az ruboyoti Kulōb. Jamʿkunanda M. Kholov', *ShS* (1962/2), 145–7.

'Az ruboyoti Qarotegin. Jamʿkunandagon Q. Hisomov, S. Fathulloyev', *ShS* (1963/11), 131–4.

Azerbeydzhanskiye skazki, sostavitel' Akhliman Akhundov, red. Oleg Erberg (Baku 1957).

Azerbeydzhanskiye skazki, sostavitel' Z. Akhmedov, red. Dzh. Il'drïmzade (Baku 1959).

Azerbeydzhanskiye tyurkskiye skazki (Moscow 1935).

'Badehai "Bobo-pirak". In badeharo marhum M. Kholov az hofizoni khalqī Ghaffurov Shakur, Bobokhalil vu Mirzolatif navishta giriftaast', *ShS* (1963/10), 84–8.

Baesecke, Georg, 'Die indogermanische Verwandtschaft des Hildebrandsliedes', *Nachr. Akad. der W. zu Göttingen*, phil.-hist. Kl., N.F., Fachgr. IV/3 (1940–41); Nr. 5 (1940), 139–53.

Bakayev, Ch. Kh., *Govor kurdov Turkmenii* (Moscow 1962).

——, *Yazïk azerbaydzhanskikh kurdov* (Moscow 1965).

Basile, Giambattista, *Das Pentameron*, übersetzt von Felix Liebrecht, hrsg. und mit einem Nachwort von Bruno Heinrich (Rudolstadt 1956).

Basset, René, *Mille et un contes, récits et légendes arabes*, 3 vols. (Paris 1924–6).

Baumgartner, Alexander, *Geschichte der Weltliteratur*, vol. I–II (Freiburg 1897).

Bédier, Joseph, *Les légendes épiques. Recherches sur la formation des chansons de geste*, 4 vols. (Paris 1908–13).

——, *Les Fabliaux. Études de littérature populaire et d'histoire littéraire du moyen-âge*, 5th ed. (Paris 1925).

Beidar, Paul, *Grammaire kurde* (Paris 1926).

Beludzhskiye skazki, sobrannïye I. I. Zarubinïm, 2 vols. (Moscow 1932–49).

Belyayev, V. M., *Afganskaya narodnaya muzïka* (Moscow 1960).

Bertel's, Ye. E., 'Persidskaya "lubochnaya" literatura', in *S. F. Ol'denburgu k pyatidesyatiletiyu ... deyatel'nosti 1882–1932* (Leningrad 1934), 83–94.

——, *Roman ob Aleksandre i yego glavnïye versii na vostoke* (Moscow–Leningrad 1948).

Bgazhba, Kh. S., 'Ob abkhazskom geroicheskom epose', in *Voprosï izucheniya eposa narodov SSSR. Sbornik statey* (Moscow 1958), 188–99.

Bibliografiya po kurdovedeniyu, sostavitel' Zh. S. Musaelyan (Moscow 1963).

Bichurin, N. Y. [Yakinf], *Sobraniye svedeniy o narodakh obitavshikh v Sredney Azii v drevniye vremena*, 3 vols. (Moscow–Leningrad 1950–3).
Bitlisi, Kharis, *Leyli i Madzhnun*. Perevod s kurdskogo, predisloviye i primechaniya M. B. Rudenko (Moscow 1965).
Bogatïrev, P. G., 'Nekotorïye zadachi sravnitel'nogo izucheniya eposa slavyanskikh narodov', in *Issledov. po slavyan. literaturoved. i fol'kloristike* (Moscow 1960), 211–51.
Bogdanova, M. I., *Ob epose narodov sovetskogo Vostoka* (Moscow 1960).
Boldïrev, A. N., 'Tadzhikskiy fol'klor v literature sov. Tadzhikistana', *Zhurnal Literaturnïy kritik* (1935/9), 115–23.
——, *Fol'klor i literatura Badakhshana. Tezisï dissertatsii* (Moscow 1941).
——, 'Badakhshanskiy fol'klor', *SV*, 5 (1948), 275–94.
——, 'Ustnïy epos Tadzhikistana', *Al'manakh Druzhba narodov*, I (Moscow).
——, 'Voprosï izucheniya tadzhikskogo narodnogo tvorchestva', *Trudï tadzh. filiala*, 29 (1951), 99–108.
——, 'Novopersidskiye obrabotki epicheskikh predaniy v Zapadnom Irane', *KS*, 67 (1963), 127–37.
Borovkov, A. K., 'Voprosï izucheniya turkoyazïchnogo eposa narodov Sredney Azii i Kazakhstana', in *Voprosï izucheniya eposa narodov SSSR. Sbornik statey* (Moscow 1958), 66–100.
Bouisson, M., *Le secret de Shéhérazade; les sources folkloriques des contes arabo-persans* (Paris 1961).
Bowra, Maurice, *Heldendichtung. Eine vergleichende Phänomenologie der heroischen Poesie aller Völker und Zeiten* (Stuttgart 1964).
Braginskiy, I. S., 'Zametki o tadzhikskom epose "Gurguli"', *KSIV*, 9 (1953), 48–57.
——, 'Ob izuchenii epicheskogo tvorchestva narodov Sov. Vostoka ("Gurguli" i "Geser")', *SV* (1955/3), 19–35.
——, *Iz istorii tadzhikskoy narodnoy poezii. Elementï narodno-poeticheskogo tvorchestva v pamyatnikakh drevney i srednevekovoy pis'mennosti* (Moscow 1956).
——, 'O tadzhikskom epose "Gurguli" i yego khudozhestvennïkh osobenostyakh', in *Vopr. izuch. eposa nar. SSSR* (Moscow 1958), 126–48.
——, *Ocherki iz istorii tadzhikskoy literaturï* (Stalinabad 1956).
——, 'Tadzhikskaya literatura', in *Istoriya literatur narodov Sredney Azii i Kazakhstana* (Moscow 1960), 21–107 (ustnoye nar. poet. tvorchestvo, 26–40).
Britayev, S., *Osetinskiye skazki* (Moscow–Leningrad 1951).
Busse, Bruno, 'Geschichtliches zum Hildebrandsliede', *Beiträge zur Gesch. der deutschen Sprache*, 26 (Halle 1901), 1–92.
Buzurg ibn Shakhriyar, *Chudesa Indii* (Moscow 1959).
Buzurgzoda, L. and R. Jalilov, *In'ikosi shūrishi Vose' dar fol'klor* (Stalinobod-Leningrad 1941).
Carnoy, A. J., *Iranian Mythology. The Mythology of all races*, ed. by L. H. Gray and G. F. Moore, VI (Boston 1917), 251–351.
Cejpek, Jiří, 'Ta'zije, pašijové hry stoupenců ší'y', *Nový Orient* (1951/9-10), 206–7.
——, 'Die verbale Periphrase als ein wichtiges Unterscheidungsmerkmal zwischen Neupersisch und Tāǧikisch', *ArOr.*, 24 (1956/2) 171–82.
——, 'Příspěvky ke studiu tadžické lidové slovesnosti', *Čs. etnografie*, 7 (1959), 29–58.
——, 'Lidová epika a současný Sovětský východ', *Nový Orient* (1960/9), 208–9.
——, 'Father–son combat as seen by an Iranist', in *Yádnámeye Jan Rypka* (Prague 1967), 247–54.
Chetverostishiya (Iz tadzhikskoy narodnoy liriki) (Stalinabad 1957).
Chicherov, V. I., 'Voprosï izucheniya eposa narodov SSSR', in *Vopr. izuch. eposa nar. SSSR* (Moscow 1958), 5–23.
——, *Voprosï teorii i istorii narodnogo tvorchestva* (Moscow 1959).
——, *Russkoye narodnoye tvorchestvo* (Moscow 1959).
——, 'Traditsiya i avtorskoye nachalo v fol'klore', *Sovetskaya etnografiya* (1946/2), 29–40.

——, 'Nekotorïye voprosï teorii eposa i sovremennïye issledovaniya nartskikh skazaniy osetin', *Izv. AN SSSR, otd. lit. i yaz.*, XI/5 (1952), 393–410.
Chikovani, Mikhail, *Amiraniani, gruzinskiy epos* (Tbilisi 1960).
Chistonho. Jamʿkunanda va tartibdihandagon Amonov va Kalontarov (Stalinabad 1956).
Chodzko, Alexander, *Specimens of the Popular Poetry of Persia* (London 1842).
Christensen, Arthur, *Recherches sur l'histoire légendaire des Iraniens* (Stockholm 1915).
——, *Le dialecte de Sämnān...* (Det Kgl. Danske Videnskabernes Selskab – Skrifter 7. raekke, histor. og filologisk Afd. II/4) (Copenhagen 1915).
——, *Les types du premier homme et du premier roi dans l'histoire légendaire des Iraniens* (Archives d'études orientales J. A. Lundell, XIV) (Stockholm 1917).
——, *Contes persans en langage populaire...* (Hist.-filol. Medd., I/3) (Copenhagen 1918).
——, *Textes ossètes* (Idem, VI/1) (Copenhagen 1921).
——, *Les dialectes d'Awromān et de Pāwä.* Textes recueillis par Åge Meyer Benedictsen... (Idem, VI/2) (Copenhagen 1921).
——, 'Júhí in the Persian literature', in *ʿAjabname* (B VIa).
——, *Contributions à la dialectologie iranienne,* I–II (Hist.-filol. Medd., XVII/2, XXI/3) (Copenhagen 1930–5).
——, *Les gestes des rois dans les traditions de l'Iran antique* (Paris 1936).
——, *Märchen aus Iran* (Jena 1939).
——, *Essai sur la démonologie iranienne* (Hist.-filol. Medd., XXVII/1) (Copenhagen 1941).
——, *Le premier chapitre du Vendidad et l'Histoire primitive des tribus iraniennes* (Idem, XXIX/4) (Copenhagen 1943).
——, *Persische Märchen* (Düsseldorf–Köln 1958).
——, 'La légende du sage Buzurğmihr', *Acta orientalia,* 8 (1930), 81–128.
Chukasvyan, B. L., 'Otzvuki iranskikh epicheskikh skazaniy v "Pismakh" Grigora Magistratosa', *PV* (1960/3), 150–5.
Cosquin, Emmanuel, 'Le prologue-cadre des Mille et une nuit. – Les légendes perses et le Livre d'Esther', *Revue biblique internat.* (Paris), N.S., 6 (1909), 7–49, 161–97.
Dalgat, N. B., 'K voprosu o narodnosti epicheskikh skazaniy i istoricheskikh pesen u narodov Sever. Kavkaza', in *Vopr. izuch. eposa nar. SSSR* (Moscow 1958), 200–8.
Dames, M. Longworth, *A Sketch of the Northern Balochi Language...* (Extra number *JASB*, 1880, I) (Calcutta 1881).
——, *Popular poetry of the Baloches*, 2 vols. (London 1907).
Dansker, O. L., 'Narodnaya pesnya tadzhikov Darvaza', *Izv. Tadzh.* 10-11 (1956), 137–52.
Darmesteter, James, *Afghan Life in Afghan Songs* (1887).
——, *Chants populaires des Afghans* (Paris 1888–90).
Dasturamal oid jamʿkardani ejodiyoti dahanakii khalq. Dar zeri tahriri ... Rajab Amonov (Stalinabad 1960).
David Sasunskiy. Armyanskiy narodnïy epos (Moscow 1957). (Cf. Orbeli, Iosif, *Armyanskiy narodnïy geroicheskiy epos,* 5–10.)
Davletov, K. S., *Fol'klor kak vid iskusstva* (Moscow 1966).
Dekhoti, A., *Tadzhikskiy narodnïy yumor* (Stalinabad 1958).
Demidchik, L. N., 'Zarozhdeniye i stanovleniye tadzhikskoy dramaturgii (1929–41 gg.)', *Vopr. ist. tadzh. sov. dramaturgii i teatra* (Stalinabad 1957), 63–284.
Dirr, Adolf, *Kaukasische Märchen* (Jena 1920).
Dovatur, A., *Povestvovatel'nïy i nauchnïy stil' Gerodota* (Leningrad 1957).
Drevniye avtorï o sredney Azii (VI v. do n.e. – III v. n.e.). Khrestomatiya pod red. L. V. Bazhenova (Tashkent 1940).
'Dubaythoi mardumi Afghoniston. Jamʿkunanda Bozor Sobirov', *ShS* (1963/12), 120–7.

Duda, Herbert W., 'Das persische Passionsspiel', *Zeitschrift für Missionskunde und Religionswissenschaft*, 49/4 (1934).
Dumézil, Georges, *Légendes sur les Nartes, suivies de cinq notes mythologiques* (Bibliothèque de l'Institut français de Léningrad, XI) (Paris 1930).
——, *Le Festin d'Immortalité. Étude de mythologie comparée indo-européenne* (Paris 1924).
Dvadtsat'pyat' rasskazov Vetalï, perevod s sanskr. I. Serebryakova (Moscow 1958).
Dvoryankov, N. A., 'Malang Dzhan – narodnïy poet Afganistana', *KS*, 37, *Afgan. sbornik* (Moscow 1960), 60–75.
Dzhalil, Dzhalile, 'Geroicheskiye pesni kurdov-yezidov o sobïtiyakh, svyazannïkh s pereseleniyem ikh predkov v Rossiyu v 30-kh godakh XIX veka', *Iranskaya filologiya* (Leningrad 1964), 130–43.
Dzhalil, Dzhamila, *Kurdskiye narodnïye pesni* (Moscow 1965).
Dzhalilov, O. Dzh., 'Kurdskiy geroicheskiy epos "Zlatorukiy khan"', *KS*, 67 (Moscow 1963), 171–7.
Dzhangoyev, A. A. and I. I. Tsukerman, 'Kurdskiye tekstï', in *Iranskiy sbornik k 70-letiyu I. I. Zarubina* (Moscow 1963), 219–48.
Eberhard, Wolfram and Pertev Naili Boratav, *Typen türkischer Volksmärchen* (Veröffentlichungen der orientalischen Kommission, V) (Wiesbaden 1953).
Edel'man, D. I., 'Yazgulyamskaya legenda ob Aleksandre', *KS*, 67 (Moscow 1963), 46–54.
——, *Yazgulyamskiy yazïk* (Moscow 1966).
Ejodiyoti dahanakii aholii Kūlob, jildi yakūm (Stalinabad 1956).
Elisséeff, N., *Thèmes et motifs des 1001 Nuits, essai de classification* (Beyrouth 1949).
Entsiklopedicheskiy muzïkal'nïy slovar'. Sostaviteli B. S. Shteynpress i I. M. Yampol'skiy (Moscow 1959).
Fatkhulloyev, Salohiddin, 'Gūrughlii tajikoni Afghoniston', *SSh* (1965/6), 96–103.
Ethé, Hermann, *Morgenländische Studien* (Leipzig 1870).
——, *Essays und Studien* (Berlin 1872).
——, Np. Lit.: see B v.
Filshtinskiy, I. M., *Arabskaya klassicheskaya literatura* (Moscow 1965).
Fol'klor kak iskusstvo slova. Otv. red. N. I. Kravtsov (Moscow 1966).
Fol'klori sokinoni sargahi Zarafshon, tartibdihanda R. Amonov (Stalinabad 1960).
Fol'klori tojik, tartibdihandagon: M. Tursunzoda va A. N. Boldïrev (Stalinabad 1957).
Gaffarov, Mirza Abdulla and Vl. Gordlevskiy, *Persidskiya poslovitsï* (Vostochnïye drevnosti, IV/1) (Moscow 1913).
Gafferberg, E. G., *Formï braka i svadebnïye obryadï u dzhemshidov i khazare* (Sov. etnografiya 1936, No. 1).
Galunov, R. A., 'Zūrkhāna – atleticheskaya arena Persii', *Iran*, I (Leningrad 1927), 87–110.
——, 'Pakhlavan Kachal' – persidskiy teatr petrushki', *Iran*, II (Leningrad 1928), 25–74.
——, 'Kheyme shab bāzī – persidskiy teatr marionetok', *Iran*, III (Leningrad 1929), 1–50.
——, 'Ma'rike Girī', *Iran*, III (Leningrad 1929), 94–106.
——, 'Narodnïy teatr Irana', *Sov. etnografiya* (1936), No. 4-5, 55–83.
Geiger, Wilhelm, 'Das Yātkār-i Zarīrān und sein Verhältnis zum Šāh-nāme', *Sitz.-Ber. d. philos., philol. u. hist. Classe d. bayr. A. d. W. zu München* (1890/2), 43–84.
Geissler, Friedmar, *Brautwerbung in der Weltliteratur* (Halle 1955).
Gennep, A. van, *La Formation des Légendes* (Paris 1910).
Gerasimova, A. S. and G. F. Girs, *Literatura Afganistana* (Moscow 1963).
Gerhardt, Mia J., *The art of Story-Telling. A literary study of the Thousand and One Nights* (Leiden 1963).
Gibbon, S. M., 'Some Persian folk-lore stories, concerning the ruins of Persepolis', *JASB* (1909/5), 279–97.
Gietmann, Gerhard, *Poetik und Mimik* (Kunstlehre, 2) (Freiburg i.B. 1900).

Goosens, R., 'Eléments iraniens et folkloriques dans le conte d'Omar al-No'mân', *Byzantion*, 9 (1934), 420–8.

Gor'kiy, Maksim, *Literaturno-kriticheskiye stat'yi*, red. M. Breytburg (Moscow 1937).

Görres, Joseph, *Mythengeschichte der asiatischen Welt*, hrsg. von Willibald Kirfel (Gesammelte Schriften, 5) (Köln 1935), 1–303.

Gozenpud, A. A., *Operniy slovar'* (Moscow – Leningrad 1965).

Gozzi, Carlo, *Skazki dlya teatra* (Moscow 1956). (Cf. Mokul'skiy, S., *Karlo Gotstsi i yego skazki dlya teatra*, 3–38).

Grabar'-Passek, M. Ye., *Antichnïye syuzhetï i formï v zapadnoyevropeyskoy literature* (Moscow 1966).

Grégoire, H. and R. Goosens, 'Byzantinisches Epos und arabischer Ritterroman', *ZDMG*, 88 (1934), 213–32.

Griechische Märchen, Fabeln, Schwänke und Novellen aus dem klassischen Altertum, ausgewählt und übertragen von Aug. Hausrath und Aug. Marx (Jena 1913).

Grierson, G. A., *Ishkashmi, Zebaki and Yazghulami* (London 1920).

Grigoryan, Roubik, *Recueil de chansons rustiques iraniennes* (Tehran 1948).

——, *Cinq chansons rustiques iraniennes* (Tehran 1949).

Grimm, Brüder, *Kinder- und Hausmärchen* (Berlin 1955).

Grintser, P. A., 'Literaturnïye i fol'klornïye svyazi sanskritskoy obramlennoy povesti', *Vzaimosvyazi literatur Vostoka i Zapada* (Moscow 1961), 182–234.

——, *Drevneindiyskaya proza (obramlennaya povest')* (Moscow 1963).

Gryunberg, A. L., *Jazïk severoazerbeydzhanskikh tatov* (Leningrad 1963).

Gumilev, L. N., 'Bakhram Chubin (Opït kritiki istochnikov)', *PV* (1960/3), 228–41.

Gurgani, Fakhriddin, *Vis i Ramin*, perevod s persidskogo S. Lipkina (Moscow 1963). (Cf. Braginskiy, I. S., *O "samoy beznravstvennoy" poeme i yeye smïsle*, 3–20.)

Gūrūghlī, *Dostani bahoduroni Chambuli Maston*, jildi 1. Navishtagirandagon M. Kholov va Q. Hisomov, ba chop tayyorkunanda Q. Hisomov, muharrir R. Amonov (Dushanbe 1962).

Gusev, V. Ye , 'Fol'klor kak istochnik izucheniya sotsial'noy psikhologii', *Problemï obshchestvennoy psikhologii* (Moscow 1965), 374–401.

——, *Estetika fol'klora* (Leningrad 1967).

Gusyev, V. Y., *Marksizm i russkaya fol'kloristika kontsa XIX – nachala XX veka* (Moscow–Leningrad 1961).

——, *Problemï fol'klora v istorii estetiki* (Moscow–Leningrad 1963).

Gvakhariya, A. A., 'O persidskikh i gruzinskikh versiyakh "Bakhram o Golandam",' *NAA* (1967/2), 113–6.

Habibov, A., 'Nosiri Khisrav va fol'klori Badakhshon', *ShS* (1960/9), 129–35.

Hackin, R. and A. A. Kohzad, *Légendes et coutumes afghanes* (Paris 1953).

Hadank, Karl, *Die Mundarten von Khunsâr, Mahallât, Natänz, Nâyîn, Sämnân, Sîvänd und Sô-Kohrûd* (Kurdisch-persische Forschungen [KPF], III/1, ("Nachlass Mann")) (Berlin–Leipzig 1926).

——, *Mundarten der Gûrân* … (KPF, III/2) (Berlin 1930).

——, *Mundarten der Zâzâ* … (KPF, III/4) (Berlin 1932).

Hamidzhanova, M., 'Devichnik (choygashtak) v Stalinabade', *Izv. Tadzh.*, 10-11 (1956), 103–9.

Hartman, S. S., *Gayōmart* (Uppsala 1953).

Hedayat, Sadek, 'Neirangistan', perevod s persidskogo, predisloviye i kommentariy N. A. Kislyakova, *TIE*, N.S., XXXIX (Peredneaziatskiy etnograf. sbornik 1) (Moscow 1958), 259–336.

Henning, W., 'Sogdian Tales', *BSOAS*, 11 (1943-6), 465–87.

Henninger, J., 'Über die völkerkundliche Bedeutung von 1001 Nacht', *Schweizer Archiv für Volkskunde*, 44 (1947), 35–65.

Hikayat, *Persische Schnurren* (Berlin 1918).

Hiltbrunner, Otto, *Kleines Lexikon der Antike* (Smlg. Dalp, Bd. 14) (Bern 1946).

Hole, Christina, *English Folk Heroes* (London 1948).
Horovitz, Josef, *Spuren griechischer Mimen im Orient* (Berlin 1905).
Horten, Max, *Die Philosophie des Islam in ihren Beziehungen zu den philosophischen Weltanschauungen des westlichen Orients* (Geschichte der Philosophie..., Bd. 4) (Munich 1924).
Huet, Gédéon, *Les contes populaires* (Paris 1923).
Huseynzoda, 'Rūdakī va fol'klori tojik', *ShS* (1958/10), 79–100.
Hüsing, Georg, *Iranische Mythologie.* Sonderabdruck aus *Gölls Illustrierter Mythologie*, 8th ed. (Leipzig 1905).
Indiyskiye narodnïye skazki v obrabotke S. F. Ol'denburga (Moscow 1956).
Indiyskiye skazki, perevod s yaz. urdu M. I. Klyaginoy-Kondrat'yevoy i V. L. Krasheninnikova (Moscow 1958).
Inostrantsev, K. A., *Persidskaya literaturnaya traditsiya v pervïye veka islama* (Zap. AN, VIII, A (VIII) 13) (St.-Petersburg 1909).
Isayev, M. I., *Digorskiy dialekt osetingskogo yazïka* (Moscow 1966).
Istoriya grecheskoy literaturï, 3 vols. (Moscow-Leningrad 1946, 1955, 1960).
Istoriya literatur narodov Sredney Azii i Kazakhstana (Moscow 1960).
Istoriya Severoosetinskoy ASSR, I (Moscow 1959).
Italyanskiye skazki, obrabotannïye Italo Kal'vino (Moscow 1959) (Jokes on Giuffà, 180–9).
Ivanov, M. S., *Plemena Farsa, kashkayskiye, khamse, kukhgaluye, mamasani* (TIE, N.S., LXIII) (Moscow 1961).
Ivanov, V., 'Neskol'ko obraztsov persidskoy narodnoy poezii', *ZVORAO*, 23 (1915), 1–28.
——, 'Some Persian Derwish Songs', *JSAB*, 23 (1927).
——, 'The Gabri dialect spoken by the Zoroastrians of Persia', *RSO*, 16, 31–97; 17, 1–39, 68–164.
Ivanova, S. Yu., 'Materialï po pendzhikentskomu govoru tadzhikskogo yazïka', *TIYa*, 6 (1956), 281–342.
Jacob, Georg, *Türkische Volksliteratur* (Berlin 1901).
——, *Geschichte des Schattentheaters im Morgen- und Abendland*, 2nd ed. (Hannover 1925).
Jolles, André, *Einfache Formen: Legende – Sage – Mythe – Rätsel – Spruch – Kasus – Memorabile – Märchen – Witz*, 2nd ed., durchgesehen von A. Schossig (Halle 1956).
Jomi, Abdurrahmon, 'Salomon va Absol. Doston', *SSh* (1964), 5, 63–78; 6, 72–88.
——, 'Yusuf va Zulaykho. Doston', *SSh* (1964), 9, 52–82; 11, 125–43; 12, 71–80.
Kahlo, Gerhard, *Die Wahrheit des Märchens. Grundsätzliche Betrachtung* (Halle 1954).
Kalila i Dimna, perevod s arab. I. Yu. Krachkovskogo i I. P. Kuz'mina. Stat'ya i primechaniya I. Yu. Krachkovskogo (Moscow–Leningrad 1934). – 2nd ed., with Preface by Ye. E. Bertel's (Moscow 1957).
Kaloyev, B. A., 'Motiv Amazonok v osetinskom nartovskom epose', *KSIE*, 32 (1959), 45–51.
Kanbu, Inayatullakh, *Kniga o vernïkh i nevernïkh zhenakh ili Bekhar-i danesh*, perevod s persidskogo i primechaniya M.-N. Osmanova (Moscow 1964).
Karrïyev, B. A., 'O proiskhozhdenii i rasprostranenii eposa "Keroglï"', in *Problemï sravn. filologii, sbornik statey ... V. M. Zhirmunskogo* (Moscow–Leningrad 1964), 444–50.
Kazakhskiy epos (Alma Ata 1958).
Kégl, Alex. von (Sándor), 'Muḥammed Hibelrûdî's Ǵâmi'-ul-tamṯîl. Die erste neupersische Sprichwörtersammlung', *ZDMG*, 48 (1894), 692–8.
——, 'A perzsa népdal', *Bp. MTA, Értekezések*, XVIII/3 (1899).
Khakhanov, A. S., *Ocherki po istorii gruzinskoy slovesnostï. I: Narodniy epos i apokrifï* (Moscow 1895).
Khani, Akhmed, *Mam i Zin*, kriticheskiy tekst, perevod, predisloviye i ukazateli M. B. Rudenko (Pamyatniki literaturï narodov Vostoka, tekstï, malaya seriya, XIII) (Moscow 1962).
Khudozhestvennaya literatura zarubezhnogo Vostoka. Bibliografiya perevodov na yazïki narodov SSSR (1918–1960) (Moscow 1963).

Kireyev, A. N., 'O bashkirskom epose "Alpamïsha"', in *Voprosï bashkirskoy filologii* (Moscow 1959), 52–9.
Kirgizskiy geroicheskiy epos Manas. Voprosï izucheniya eposa narodov SSSR. Sbornik statey (Moscow 1961).
Kirmānī, Kūhī, *Chahārdah afsāna az afsānahā-i rūstāī-i Īrān* (Tehran 1314).
——, *Haftṣad tarāna az tarānahā-i rūstāī-i Īrān* (Tehran 1327).
Kislyakov, N. A., 'Sadek Khedayat...', *Sov. etnogr.* (1949/2), 230–4.
——, 'Perezhitki matriarkhata v brachnïkh obryadakh narodov Sredney Azii', *KSIE*, 28 (1957), 21–7.
——, *Sem'ya i brak u tadzhikov* (TIE, 44) (Moscow–Leningrad 1959).
Klimchitskiy, S. I., 'Darvazskiye fakhlaviyot', *Trudï Tadzh. bazï AN SSSR*, IX (Moscow–Leningrad 1940), 65–93.
Klimovich, L. I., *Khrestomatiya po literature narodov SSSR* (Moscow 1947).
——, *Sovetskiye pisateli Tadzhikistana* (Stalinabad 1949).
——, 'Nizami i yego poema Iskender-name', in *Nizami, Iskender-name* (Moscow 1953), 733–58.
——, 'Zametki ob epicheskom tvorchestve narodov Sov. Vostoka', in *Vopr. izuch. eposa narodov SSSR. Sbornik statey* (Moscow 1958), 239–90.
——, *Iz istorii literatur sovetskogo Vostoka* (Moscow 1959) (On folk-poetry, 181–290).
——, *Islam*, 2nd ed. (Moscow 1963).
Klyashtorina, V. B., 'Fol'klornïye zhanrï v demokratïcheskoy poezii Irana perioda revolyutsii 1905–1911 gg.', *KS*, 22 (1956), 56–65.
Kniga moyego deda Korkuta. Oguzskiy geroicheskiy epos (Moscow–Leningrad 1962).
Kobidze, D., '"Shohnoma" dar zaboni gurjī', *ShS* (1958/2), 135–47.
Kokkyara, Dzhuzeppe, *Istoriya fol'kloristiki v Evrope*, perevod s italyanskogo A. Venediktova i M. Kirillovoy, redaktsiya i vstupitel'naya stat'ya E. Meletinskogo (Moscow 1960).
Koroglï, Kh. G., 'Ob iranskikh elementakh v narodnom tvorchestve turkmen', *Narodï Azii i Afriki* (1962/3), 135–8.
——, 'Dastan "Bakhrom va Gulandom" Saykali i yego istochnik', *NAA* (1967/2), 107–12.
Koryev, S., *Uzeir Gadzhibekov i yego operï* (Moscow 1952).
Kosven, M. O., 'Amazonki (istoriya legendï)', *Sovetskaya etnografiya* (1947), 2, 33–59; 3, 3–32.
Krachkovskiy, I. Y., 'Rannyaya istoriya povesti o Medzhnune i Leyle v arabskoy literature', in *Alisher Navoi, sbornik statey* (Moscow–Leningrad 1946), 31–67. German transl. by H. Ritter in *Oriens*, 8 (1955).
Krïms'kïy, Agatangel, *Pers'kïy teatr, zvidkï vin uzyavs' i yak rozvivavs'* (Zbirnïk istor. filol. viddilu Ukr. AN, No. 6) (Kiev 1925).
Krumbacher, Karl, *Geschichte der byzantinischen Litteratur von Justinian bis zum Ende des Oströmischen Reiches (527–1453)* (Hdbch. d. klass. Altertumswissenschaft, 9/1), 2nd ed. (Munich 1897).
Kurdoyev, K. and I. Tsukerman, 'Kurdskiye tekstï', in *Iranskiye yazïki*, II (Moscow–Leningrad 1950), 39–60.
——, 'Iz kurdskogo eposa', in *Iranskiy sbornik k 70-letiyu I. I. Zarubina* (Moscow 1963), 249–55.
Kurdskiye narodnïye skazki, zapis i obrabotka A. Dzhindi (Erevan 1959). (In Kurdish.)
Kurdskiye narodnïye skazki (Moscow 1967).
Kurdskiye narodnïye skazki, I, zapis, predisloviye i kommentariy A. Dzhindi (Erevan 1961). (In Kurdish.)
Kurdskiye skazki (Moscow 1959).
Kuznetsova, N. A., 'Remeslennïye risale', *KS*, 19 (1956), 90–3.
Kvyatkovskiy, A., *Poeticheskiy slovar'* (Moscow 1966).
Lahy-Hollebecque, M., *Le Féminisme de Schéhérazade* (Paris 1927).
Lakhuti, A., *Tadzhikskaya literatura* (Moscow 1934).

——, *Kuznets Kova* (Moscow–Leningrad 1941).
Lambertz, Maximilian, *Die Volksepik der Albaner* (Halle 1958).
Lammer, Hanns, *Wörterbuch der Antike* ... (Kröners Taschenausgabe, Bd. 96) (Leipzig 1933).
Larousse, Encyclopedia of Mythology (London 1959).
'Latifaho, Samad Ghanī jamʿ va tahrir kardaast', *ShS* (1955/10), 87–102.
'Latifaho. Jamʿ kunanda M. Boqiyev', *ShS* (1956/7), 72–3.
Latifahoi tojikī, jamʿ kunanda A. P. Dehotī (Stalinabad 1954).
Le Livre des Héros. Les légéndes sur les Nartes, traduit de l'ossète avec une introduction et des notes par Georges Dumézil (Paris 1965).
Lebedev, K. A., 'Afganskaya narodnaya poeziya', in *Voprosï yaz. i lit. stran Vostoka*, pod red. Y. V. Rozhdestvenskogo (Moscow 1958), 258–73.
Lenskiy, A., *Tadzhikskaya SSR. Muzïkal'naya kul'tura* (Moscow 1954; 2nd ed. 1957).
Lentz, Wolfgang, *Pamir-Dialekte*, I (Erg. Hft. zur *Zft. für vgl. Sprachf.*, Nr. 12) (Göttingen 1953).
——, *Auf dem Dach der Welt. Mit Phonograph und Kamera bei vergessenen Völkern des Pamir* (Berlin 1933).
Lesïn, V. M. and O. S. Pulïnets', *Slovnïk literaturoznavchïkh terminiv*, 2nd ed. (Kiev 1965).
v. d. Leyen, Frdr., *Das Märchen. Ein Versuch* (Leipzig 1911).
——, *Die Welt der Märchen*, 2 vols. (Düsseldorf 1953–4).
Libedinskiy, Yu., *Soslan Bogatïr, yego druz'ya i vragi. Skazochnaya povest' po motivam osetinskogo nartskogo eposa* (Moscow 1959).
Litten, Wilhelm, *Das Drama in Persien* (Berlin–Leipzig 1929).
Littmann, Enno, *Arabische Märchen. Aus mündlicher Überlieferung gesammelt und übertragen* (Leipzig 1957).
Ljungman, Waldemar, *Die schwedischen Volksmärchen. Herkunft und Geschichte* (Berlin 1961).
Lorimer, D. L. R. and E. O., *Persian tales. Written down for the first time in the original Kermani and Bakhtiari and translation* (London 1919).
Losev, A. F., *Antichnaya mifologiya v yeye istoricheskom razvitii* (Moscow 1957).
Lozovskaya, T. S., 'Mat' i dit'ya u sredne-aziatskikh yevreyev g. Samarkanda', *Sov. Aziya* (1930), kniga 3-4, 197–212; kn. 5-6, 245–60.
Lübker, Friedrich, *Reallexikon des klassischen Altertums*, 8th ed. (Berlin–Leipzig 1914).
Mackenzie, D. N., *Kurdish Dialect Studies*, II (London Oriental Studies, vol. 10) (London–New York Toronto 1962).
Makas, Hugo, *Kurdische Texte im Kurmânjî-Dialecte aus der Gegend von Märdîn* (St.-Petersburg–Leningrad 1897–1918–1924).
——, *Kurdische Studien. Materialien zu einer Gesch. der Spr. und Liter. des vorderen Orients*, I (Heidelberg 1900).
Malitskiy I., *Iz oblasti tadzhikskogo fol'klora* (Sbornik Turkest. vostoch. i-ta v chest A. E. Shmidta) (Tashkent 1923).
Mann, Oskar, *Die Tâjîk-Mundarten der Provinz Fars* (Kurdisch-persische Forschungen, I) (Berlin 1909).
——, *Die Mundart der Mukrî-Kurden* (Idem, IV/I) (Berlin 1909).
——, *Die Mundarten der Lur-Stämme* ... (Idem, II) (Berlin 1910).
Marquart, J., 'Beiträge zur Geschichte und Sage von Eran', *ZDMG*, 49 (1895), 628–73.
Marr, Yu. N., 'Koye-chto o Pekhlevan kechele i drugikh vidakh narodnogo teatra v Persii', *Iran*, II, 75–88.
Massé, Henri, *Contes en persan populaire, recueillis et traduits* (Paris 1925).
——, *Croyances et coutumes persanes suivies de contes et chansons populaires*, 2 vols. (Paris 1938).
——, 'Les versions persanes des contes d'animaux', in *L'âme de l'Iran* (Paris 1951), 129–49.
——, *Firdousi et l'épopée nationale* (Paris 1935).

Massignon, Louis, 'Le folklore chez les mystiques musulmans', in *Mélanges René Basset*, I (Paris 1923), 259–70.
Masson-Oursel, P. and Louise Morin, 'Mythology of ancient Persia', in *Larousse, Encyclopedia of Mythology* (London 1959), 321–38.
——, 'Mythology of India', *ibid.*, 339–92.
Matviychuk, N. F., *Tvorchestvo M. Gor'kogo i fol'klor* (Kiev 1959).
Meier, F., 'Turandot in Persien', *ZDMG*, 95 (1941), 1–27; 'Nachtrag', *ibid.*, 415–21.
Meletinskiy, Ye. M., *Geroy vol'shebnoy skazki. Proiskhozhdeniye obraza* (Moscow 1958).
——, *Proiskhozhdeniye geroicheskogo eposa. Ranniye formï i arkhaicheskiye pamyatniki* (Moscow 1963).
——, 'O drevneyshem tipe geroya v epose tyurko-mongol'skikh narodov Sibiri', in *Problemï sravn. filol. Sbornik statey k 70-letiyu V. M. Zhirmunskogo* (Moscow–Leningrad 1964), 426–43.
——, 'Narodnïy epos', *Teoriya literaturï, osnovnïye problemï v istoricheskom osveshchenii, rodï i zhanrï* (Moscow 1964), 50–96.
Melodii Pamira, sostaviteli N. M. Zubkov i A. S. Lenskiy (Tashkent–Stalinabad 1941).
Menzel, Theodor, *Meddâḥ, Schattentheater und Orta Ojunu. Eine kritische Übersicht über die Ergebnisse der jüngeren Forschung nebst neuen Beiträgen* (Prague 1941).
Mikhaylov, G. I., 'K voprosu ob evolyutsii mongol'skogo geroicheskogo eposa', in *Tyurko-mongol'skoye yazïkoznaniye i fol'kloristika* (Moscow 1960), 210–7.
Les Mille et un jours, contes persans, traduits en français par Pétis de la Croix ... Nouvelle édition, accompagnée de notes et de notices historiques par A. Loiseleur Deslongchamps, publié sous la direction de M. Aimé Martin (Paris 1838).
Miller, B. V., *Talïshskiye tekstï* (Moscow 1930).
——, 'Tatskiye tekstï', in *Iranskiye yazïki*, I (Moscow–Leningrad 1945), 107–26.
Miller, Vsevolod, *Ekskursï v oblast' russkago narodnago eposa* (Moscow 1892).
——, *Digorskiya skazaniya po zapisam digortsev...* (Trudï po vostokovedeniyu Lazarev. inst. vostoch. yaz., v. XI) (Moscow 1902).
——, 'Ocherki ariyskoy mifologii v svyazi s drevneyshey kul'turoy', *Izbr. trudï russkikh indologov-filologov* (Moscow 1962), 87–143.
Minorsky, V. F., 'L'épopée persane et la littérature populaire russe', *Iranica* (Publications of the University of Tehran, vol. 775) (Tehran 1964), 110–9.
——, 'Vīs-u-Rāmīn, a Parthian Romance', *ibid.*, 151–99. ("Drastically revised in very many places.")
Mironov, N., *Muzïka tadzhikov. Muzïkal'no-etnograf. materialï* (Stalinabad 1932).
Mirsaidov, S., 'Bayt hamchun zhanri fol'klori', *SSh* (1964/11), 149–57.
Mirshakar, Mirsaid, *Stikhotvoreniya i poemï* (Moscow 1951).
Mirzo-zade, Kh. M., *Rudaki – osnovopolozhnik tadzhikskoy klassicheskoy literaturï* (Moscow 1958).
Monogarova, L. F., 'Materialï po etnografii yazgulemtsov', in *Sredne-aziatskiy etnograf. sbornik*, II (*TIE*, 47) (Moscow 1959), 3–94.
Montet, E., *Le conte dans l'Orient musulman; étude littéraire et critique des 1001 nuits* (Paris–Genève 1930).
Morgenstierne, Georg, *Indo-iranian Frontier Languages*, vol. I–II (Oslo 1929–38).
Motif-Index of Folk-Literature. A Classification of Narrative Elements in Folktales, Ballads, Myths, Fables, Medieval Romances, Exempla, Fabliaux, Jest-Books and Local Legends, rev. and enlarged ed. by Stith Thompson, 6 vols. (Copenhagen 1955–8).
Munkácsi, Bernhard, 'Blüten der ossetischen Volksdichtung...', *Keleti Szemle*, 20, 1–88; 21, 1–160.
Nal'skiy, Y., 'Qaydho doir ba zhanri epikii nazmi khalqi tojik', *ShS* (1956/2), 95–114.
'Namunahoi az fol'klori Kangurt. Ba chop tayyorkunandagon Kh. Muhibov va Kh. Sharifov,' *SSh* (1964/6), 136–40.
Namunahoi fol'klori Darvoz (Dushanbe 1962).

'Namunahoi fol'klori diyori Rūdakī. Tartib dihandagon Muhammadjon Shukurov va Rajab Amonov', *ShS* (1958/8), 122–36.
Narodï Peredney Azii. Etnograf. ocherki (Moscow 1957).
Narodnaya poeziya Tadzhikistana, red. i predisloviye M. Yavich (Stalinabad 1949).
Nartï, kabardinskiy epos. Vstupitel'naya stat'ya, obshch. red. i podgotovka teksta S. A. Andreyeva-Krivicha (Moscow 1957).
Nartï. Epos osetinskogo naroda, izd. podgotovili V. I. Abayev i drugiye (Moscow 1957).
Nartskiye skazaniya. Osetinskiy narodnïy epos (Moscow 1949).
Navoi, Alisher, *Sem' planet, poema*, perevod s uzbek. Semena Lipkina, pod red., s predisloviyem i primechaniyami L. Klimovicha (Moscow 1954).
Neobïchaynïye priklyucheniya Nasretdina Afandi (Tashkent 1959).
Nicholson, O., 'Some Notes on the Arabian and Persian Folklore', *Fol'klore* (1930), 345–58.
Nikitine, Basile, *Les Kurdes. Étude sociologique et historique* (Paris 1956).
Nöldeke, Theodor, 'Das iranische Nationalepos', in *GIPh*, II/II,4, 130–211; 2nd, separate ed. (Berlin-Leipzig 1920).
——, *Burzōēs Einleitung zu dem Buche Kalīla wa Dimna*, übersetzt und erläutert (Strassbourg 1922).
Normatov, S., 'Afsonaho dar Afghoniston', *Izv. Tadzh.*, No. 4 (46), (Dushanbe 1966), 55–68.
Nurdzhanov, Nizam Kh., 'Istoki narodnogo teatra u tadzhikov. Po materialam Kulyabskoy oblasti', *KSIE*, 18 (1953), 103–9.
——, 'Zametki po khodzhentskomu kukol'nomu teatru', *Trudï Tadzh.*, 17 (1953), 167–76.
——, *Tadzhikskiy narodnïy teatr. Po materialam Kulyabskoy oblasti* (Moscow 1956).
——, 'Otchet o rabote vo vremya Garmskoy etnograf. ekspeditsii 1954 g.', *Izv. Tadzh.* (1956/10-11), 45–59.
——, 'Nekotorïye arkhaicheskiye chertï v tantsakh i pantomimakh gornïkh tadzhikov', *Izv. Tadzh.* (1956/10-11), 179–90.
——, 'Teatri khalqi tojik', *ShS* (1956/1), 87–95.
——, 'O bukharskom kukol'nom teatre', *Izv. Tadzh.* (1956/10-11), 191–219.
——, 'Materialï k istorii zarozhdeniya tadzhikskogo teatra i dramaturgii', in *Voprosï istorii tadzh. sov. dramaturgii i teatra* (Stalinabad 1957), 4–62.
——, 'Az ta'rikhi teatri khalqii tojik', *ShS* (1958/5), 104–16.
——, 'Tantsï tadzhikoy Kulyabskoy oblasti', *Izv. Tadzh.* (1953/3), 131–55.
Oberholzer, Otto, *Kleines Lexikon der Weltliteratur* (Smlg. Dalp, Bd. 15) (Bern 1946).
Ocherki po istorii SSSR: 1: *Pervobïtno-obshchinnïy stroy i drevneyshiye gosudarstva na territorii SSSR* (Moscow 1956). – 2: *III–IX vv.* (Moscow 1958). – 3: *IX–XIII vv.* (Moscow 1953). – 4: *XIV–XV vv.* (Moscow 1953). – 5: *Konets XV v. – nachalo XVII v.* (Moscow 1955). – 6: *XVII v.* (Moscow 1955). (Very important!)
Oestrup, J., *Studien über 1001 Nacht*, aus dem Dänischen übersetzt von O. Rescher (Stuttgart 1925).
Orlov, A. S., *Kazakhskiy geroicheskiy epos* (Moscow–Leningrad 1945).
Osetinskaya literatura, red. S. Britayev i S. Shenzinskiy (Moscow 1952).
Osetinskiye narodnïye skazki, perevod S. Britayeva i K. Kazbekova (Moscow 1951).
Osetinskïye narodnïye skazki, sostaviteli S. Britayev i G. Kaloev (Moscow 1959).
Osetinskiye narodnïye skazki, I–II (Stalinir 1959–60). (In Ossetian.)
Osetinskiye nartskiye skazaniya, per. v liter. obrabotke J. Libedinskogo (Moscow 1949).
Osmanov, M.-N., 'O narodnïkh tendentsiyakh v poeme Firdousi "Shakhname"', *KS*, 2 (1952), 38–48.
——, 'Svodï': see B VIb.
——, *Firdousi, zhizn' i tvorchestvo* (Moscow 1959).
Osmanova, Z., 'Geroiko-romanticheskaya traditsiya i sovremennost' (O natsional'nom nachale v persidsko-tadzhikskoy literature)', in *Problemï razvitiya literatur narodov SSSR* (Moscow 1964), 279–310.

Pakhalina, T. N., *Ishkashmiyskiy yazïk* (Moscow 1959).
——, 'Obraztsï sarïkol'skoy narodnoy poezii...', *KS*, 67 (Moscow 1963), 46–54.
——, 'K kharakteristike sarïkol'skogo dialekta', in *Iranskiy sbornik k 70-letiyu I. I. Zarubina* (Moscow 1963), 81–94.
——, *Sarïkol'skiy yazïk* (Moscow 1966).
Pamyatniki yugoosetinskogo narodnogo tvorchestva, 3 vols. (Stalinir 1929–30).
Pamyatniki narodnogo tvorchestva osetin. I (1925); II (1927); III (1928); IV (1930); V (1941).
Panchatantra, perevod s sanskrita... (Moscow 1958).
Paret, Rudi, *Die legendäre Maghāzi-Literatur. Arabische Dichtungen über die muslimischen Kriegszüge zu Mohammeds Zeit* (Tübingen 1930).
——, *Der Ritterroman von Umar an-Numan und seine Stellung zur Sammlung von 1001 Nacht* (Tübingen 1927).
Peredneaziatskiy etnograficheskiy sbornik, 1 (TIE, N.S., 39) (Moscow 1958).
Perry, B. E., 'The origin of the Book of Sindbad', *Fabula*, 3 (1960), 1–94.
Persidskiye anekdotï, perevod s persidskogo ... pod red. A. Kushina (Moscow 1963).
Persidskiye poslovitsï i pogovorki. Sostavleniye, perevod i kommentariy Kh. G. Koroglï (Moscow 1961).
Persidskiye skazki, sostavitel' N. Osmanov (Moscow 1958).
Persidskiye tesnifï, *zapisi Khatem Khana*, vstupitel'nïye stat'yi B. V. Millera i V. M. Belyayeva. Perevodï tekstov i primechaniya B. V. Millera, red. sbornika V. M. Belyayeva (Moscow 1964).
Persidskiy yumor, perevod s persidskogo ... pod red. i s predisloviyem Leonida Lencha (Moscow 1962).
Pfister, Friedrich, *Alexander der Grosse in den Offenbarungen der Griechen, Juden, Mohammedaner und Christen* (Dtsche Ak. der W. zu Berlin, Schriften der Sektion für Altertumswissenschaft, 3) (Berlin 1956).
Phillott, D. C., 'Persian Saws and Proverbs', *Memoirs ASB*, 1/15 (Calcutta 1906), 301–37.
Pizzi, Italo, *L'epopea persiana e la vita e i costumi dei tempi eroici di Persia. Studie e ricerche* (Firenze 1888).
Plutovka iz Bagdada, perevod s persidskogo ... predisloviye i primechaniya Yu. Borshchevskogo. Sostavitel' N. N. Tumanovich (Moscow 1963).
Poslovitsï i pogovorki narodov Vostoka (Moscow 1961).
Potanin, G. N., *Vostochïye motivï v srednevekovom yevropeyskom epose* (Moscow 1899).
Prášek, Justin V., *Geschichte der Meder und Perser bis zur Makedonischer Eroberung*, 2 vols. (Gotha 1906–10).
Printsipï tekstologicheskogo izucheniya fol'klora. Otv.red. B. N. Putilov (Moscow–Leningrad 1966).
Propp, V. Y., *Istoricheskiye korni vol'shebnoy skazki* (Leningrad 1946).
——, 'Osnovnïye etapï razvitiya rus. geroicheskogo eposa', in *Issledovaniya po slavyan. literaturoved. i fol'kloristike* (Moscow 1960), 284–311.
——, *Russkiy geroicheskoy epos* (Moscow 1955).
Pukhov, I. V., '"Olonkho" – narodnïy geroicheskiy epos yakutov', in *Voprosï izuch. eposa nar. SSSR* (Moscow 1958), 209–25.
——, *Yakutskiy geroicheskiy epos Olonkho. Osnovnïye obrazï* (Moscow 1962).
Pushkin i Gor'kiy o narodnom tvorchestve (Moscow 1938).
Rademacher, Ludwig, *Mythos und Sage bei den Griechen* (Brünn–Munich–Vienna 1938).
Rakhimov, M. R., 'Obïchai i obryadï, svyazannïye so smertyu i pokhoronami, u tadzhikov Kulyabskoy oblasti', *Izv. Tadzh.* (1953/3), 107–30.
——, 'Nekotorïye rezul'tatï rabotï vo vremya Garmskoy etnograf. ekspeditsii 1954 g.', *Izv. Tadzh.* (1956/10-11), 61–72.

——, 'Sledï drevnikh verovaniy v zemledel'cheskikh obïchayakh tadzhikov Karategina i Darvaza do revolyutsii', *Izv. Tadzh.* (1956/10-11), 73–83.
Raverty, H. G., *The Pushto Manual* (London 1880).
Rescher, Oskar, *Studien über den Inhalt von 1001 Nacht* (Berlin 1919).
Rohde, Erwin, *Der griechische Roman und seine Vorläufer* (Berlin 1960).
Romaskevich, A. A., 'Persidskiye narodnïye chetverostishiya', *ZVORAO*, 23, 313–47; 25, 145–228.
——, 'V. A. Zhukovskiy i persidskaya narodnaya poeziya', *ZVORAO*, 25.
——, 'Skazochniki v Persii', *Vostochnïye zapiski*, I (Leningrad 1927), 251–70.
——, 'Persidskiye narodnïye chetverostishiya', 3rd part: *ZKV*, III (1928), 305–66.
——, 'Persidskiye versii fablo "Constant du Hamel"', in *Sbornik ... Oldenburgu* (Leningrad 1934), 443–50.
——, *Persidskiye narodnïye skazki* (Moscow–Leningrad 1934).
——, 'Lar i yego dialekt', in *Iranskiye yazïki*, I (Moscow–Leningrad 1945), 31–86.
——, see also B VIb.
Rooth, Anna Birgitta, *The Cinderella Cycle* (Lund 1951).
Rossi, Ettore and Alessio Bombaci, *Elenco di drami religiosi persiani* (Fondo Mss. Vaticani Cerulli, Biblioteca apostolica Vaticana, Studi e testi, 209) (Città del Vaticano 1961).
Rozenfel'd, A. Z., *Persidskiye skazki* (Moscow 1956).
——, 'Darvazskiye govorï tadzhikskogo yazïka', *TIYa*, 6 (1956), 196–272.
——, *Persidskiye narodnïye skazki* (Tashkent 1958).
'Ruboī, zarbulmasal va maqolho. Jam'kunandagon: Razzoqberdī Burhonov, Gulmuhammad Barotov, Sa'dī Abdulazīzov, Bozor Sobirov, Ghulom Isoyev', *ShS* (1962/12), 127–38.
'Ruboyoti khalqii Eron. Ba chop tayyorkunandagon T. Isroilova, E. Shvarts', *ShS* (1962/6), 127–40.
'Ruboyyoti mardumi Hirot. Jam' va ba chop tayyorkunanda Sh. Kamolov', *ShS* (1963/9), 132–5.
Rudenko, M. B., *Opisaniye kurdskikh rukopisey leningradskikh sobraniy* (Moscow 1961) (On folk-poetry, 9–25).
Rumi, Dzhelaluddin, *Pritchi.* Perevod s persidskogo Vl. Derzhavina (Moscow 1963).
Russkoye narodnoye poeticheskoye tvorchestvo, pod. red P. G. Bogatïreva, 2nd ed. (Moscow 1956).
Russkoye narodnoye poeticheskoye tvorchestvo. Ocherki po istorii, I (Moscow 1953); II/1 (Moscow 1955); II/2 (Moscow 1956).
Safi, Ali, *Zanimatel'nïye rasskazï o raznïkh lyudyakh.* Perevod s persidskogo M. Zanda (Moscow 1966).
Samarin, Y., 'Pesni sov. Tadzhikistana, obzor', *Zhurnal Literaturnïy kritik* (1935/5), 176–207.
Sanakoyev, P. A., *Sovetskiy fol'klor Yugo-Osetii* (Tbilisi 1954).
Saussey, Edouard, *Littérature populaire turque* (Etudes orientales, publ. par l'Institut français d'archéologie de Stamboul, IV) (Paris 1936).
Schack, A. F. von, *Heldensagen von Firdousi*, 2nd ed. (Berlin 1865).
Schiller, Friedrich, 'Turandot, Prinzessin von China. Ein tragikomisches Märchen nach Gozzi', in *Fr. Sch. – Gedichte – Übersetzungen* (Reclam, Leipzig, n.d.), 208–94.
Schirmunski, Viktor, *Vergleichende Epenforschung*, I (Dt. Ak. der W. – Veröffentlichungen des Institutes für Dt. Volkskunde, Bd. 24) (Berlin 1961).
Schröder, F. R., *Die Parzivalfrage* (Munich 1928).
Schulthess, Friedrich, *Kalila und Dimna* (Berlin 1911).
Schulze, Fritz Willy, *Folklore. Zur Ableitung der Vorgeschichte einer Wissenschaftsbezeichnung* (Hallische Monographien, Nr. 10) (Halle 1949).
Semenov, A. A., *Etnografischekiye ocherki zarafshanskikh gor', Karategina i Darvaza* (Moscow 1903).
——, 'Detskiye pozdravitel'nïye stishki v bukharskikh maktabakh', *Izv. Tadzh.*, 10–11 (Stalinabad 1956), 95–102.
Sharifzoda, B., 'Shūrishi khalqī (Ba munosibati 70-solagii sar shudani Vose')', *ShS* (1956/3), 88–97.

Shohini Sherozī, 'Dostoni Ardasher va Ester', *ShS* (1958/3), 86–106; 4, 105–28.
——, 'Qissai "Yusuf va Zulaykho". Ba chop tayyorkunandagon Kh. Rahimī va N. Mulloqand', *ShS* (1964/2), 101–13.
Shukasaptati. Sem'desyat' rasskazov popugaya, perev. s sanskrita... (Moscow 1960).
Siabəndov, Semend, *Siabənd u Kheje. Kurdskaya nar. poema* (Erevan 1959). (In Kurdish.)
Sieg, Emil, *Die Sagenstoffe des Rgveda und die indische Itihâsa-Tradition*, I (Stuttgart 1902).
Sindbād-nāma: see *s.v.* 'Ẓahīrī' (B VIb).
Sirdar Ikbal Ali Shah, *Afghanistan of the Afghans* (London 1928).
Sirus, B. I., 'Ba'ze qaydhoi muqoisavī oid ba qofiyai fol'klor va adabiyoti klassikii tojik', *Izv. Tadzh.*, 7 (Stalinabad 1955), 19–27.
Skazki Indii, redaktor-sostavitel' V. A. Gakina (Moscow 1957).
Skazki i stikhi Afganistana, perevod s afg. (Moscow 1958).
Skazki narodov Vostoka (Moscow 1962).
Skjöld, Hannes, *Materialien zu den iranischen Pamirsprachen* (Lund 1936).
Sokolov, V. S., *Russkiy fol'klor* (Moscow 1941).
Sokolova, V. S., *Ocherki po fonetike iranskikh yazïkov*, 2 vols. (Moscow–Leningrad 1953).
——, *Rushanskiye i khufskiye tekstï i slovar'* (Moscow–Leningrad 1959).
——, *Bartangskiye i khufskiye tekstï i slovar'* (Moscow–Leningrad 1960).
Sorok devushek. Karakalpakskaya narodnaya poema... (Moscow 1951).
Sovetskiye kompozitorï. Kratkiy biografischekiy spravochnik. Sostaviteli G. Bernardt i A. Dolzhanskiy (Moscow 1957).
Spanner, Werner, *Das Märchen als Gattung* (Giessener Beiträge zur dt. Philologie, 68) (Giessen 1939).
Starikov, A. A., 'Firdousi i yego poema "Shakhname"', in *Firdousi, Shakhname*, I (Moscow 1957), 459–592.
Ṣubḥī, M , *Afsānahā*, 2 vols. (Tehran 1965).
——, *Afsānahā kuhan*, 2 vols. (Tehran 1965).
——, *Afsānahā-i Bū-'Alī-i Sīnā* (Tehran 1965).
——, *Dāstānhā-i milal* (Tehran 1948).
——, *Dizh-i khushrubā* (Tehran 1951).
——, *Dīvān-i Balkh* (Tehran 1952).
Sumane az har chamane. Tartibdihandagon A. Nazarova-Shirinova, R. Muharriron, N. Sharakmuhammadov, F. Murodova (Dushanbe 1966).
Surits, Ye. Ye., *Vse o balete. Slovar'-spravochnik* (Moscow–Leningrad 1966).
Swahn, Jan-Öjvind, *The Tale of Cupid and Psyche (ATh 425 and 428)* (Lund 1955).
Sykes, Ella C., 'Persian Folklore', *Folklore* (1901), 261–80.
Tadzhikskaya poeziya, per. Y. Sel'vinskogo, pod red. I. Braginskogo (Stalinabad 1949).
Tadzhikskiye narodnïye skazki. Sostavleniye i obrabotka R. Amonov i K. Ulugzade (Stalinabad 1957).
Tadzhikskiye narodnïye skazki. Perevod Klavdii Ulug-zade (Moscow 1964).
Tadzhikskiye skazki, sostavitel' R. Amonov (Moscow 1961).
Tadzhikskiy fol'klor. Sbornik, sost. M. Tursunzade i A. N. Boldïrev (Stalinabad 1954).
Tadzhikskiy narodnïy yumor, sobral A. Dekhoti (Stalinabad 1958).
Takhmasib, M., 'Problema narodnosti azerbeydzhanskikh dastanov i sovremennoye sostoyaniye issledovaniya ikh', in *Voprosï izucheniya eposa nar. SSSR* (Moscow 1958), 176–87.
'Taronahoi mardumi Asht. Jam' va ba chop tayyorkunanda N. Azimov', *SSh* (1965/5), 124–31.
'Taronahoi Samarqand. Ba chop tayyorkunanda Bahrom Shermuhammadov', *SSh* (1966/2), 103–9.
Tegethoff, Ernst, *Märchen, Schwänke und Fabeln* (Munich 1925).
Théatre persan. Choix de téaziés ou drames. Traduits pour la première fois du persan par A. Chodzko (Paris 1878).
Tkachenko, T. S., *Narodnïy tanets* (Moscow 1954).

Tokarev, S. A., *Etnografiya narodov SSSR.* (Moscow 1958).
Tolstov, S. P., *Po sledam drevnekhorezmiyskoy tsivilizatsii* (Moscow–Leningrad 1948).
Tolstoy, I. I., 'Chernomorskaya legenda o Gerakle i zmeyenogoy deve', *Stat'yi o fol'klore* (Moscow–Leningrad 1966), 232–48.
Trencsényi-Waldapfel, Imre, *Mifologiya*, perevod s vengerskogo (Moscow 1959).
Tsukerman. I, I., 'Tri kurdskiye skazki. Issledov. po istorii kul'turï narodov Vostoka', *Sbornik ... Orbeli* (Moscow–Leningrad 1960), 492–503.
Turetskiye narodnïye skazki, perevod ... N. Tsvetinovich (Moscow 1959).
Turetskiye narodnïye skazki, pod red. ... N. K. Dmitriyeva (Moscow 1967).
Tursun-zoda, M. and A. Dekhoti, *Vosstaniye Vose* (Moscow–Leningrad 1941).
The Types of the Folktale. A Classification and Bibliography. Antti Aarne's *Verzeichnis der Märchentypen* (FFC No 3) translated and enlarged by Stith Thompson (FF Communications, LXXV, No. 184) (Helsinki 1961).
Ukraiyins'ka narodna poetïchna tvorchist', I (Kiev 1958).
Uspenskaya, L. V., 'Karatagskiy govor tadzhikskogo yazïka', *Trudï Tadzh.*, 46 (Stalinabad 1956).
Ustnoye tvorchestvo narodov SSSR. Bibliograficheskiy ukazatel', sostavila E. R. Binkevich (Moscow 1940).
Ustnoye poeticheskoye tvorchestvo russkogo naroda. Khrestomatiya, sost. S. I. Vasilenok i V. M. Sidel'nikov (Moscow 1954).
Uygurskiye skazki, sostavitel' M. N. Kabirov (Alma Ata 1963).
Uzbekskiye narodnïye poemï (Tashkent 1958).
Uzbekskiye narodnïye skazki, v obrabotke i pod red. M. I. Sheverdina (Tashkent 1955).
Uzbekskiye narodnïye skazki, 2 vols. (Tashkent 1960–1).
Valitova, A. A., 'K voprosu o fol'klornïkh motivakh v poeme "Kudatgu Bilig"', *SV* (1958/5), 88–102.
——, 'Tatarskaya versiya eposa "Alpamïsh"', in *Tyurko-mongol'. yazïkozn. i fol'kloristika* (Moscow 1960), 173–209.
Vil'chevskiy, O. L., 'Mukrinskiye kurdï. Etnograficheskiy ocherk', in *Peredneaziatskiy etnogr. sbornik*, I (*TIE*, N.S., 39) (Moscow 1958), 180–222.
——, *Kurdï* (*TIE*, N.S., 67) (Moscow–Leningrad 1961).
Viroleaud, C., *Le théâtre persan ou le drama de Kerbéla* (Paris 1950).
Voprosï narodno-poeticheskogo tvorchestva. Problemï sootnosheniya fol'klora i deystvitel'nosti. Otv. redaktorï V. I. Chicherov i V. M. Sidel'nikov (Moscow 1960).
Vries, Jan de, *Heldenlied und Heldensage* (Smlg. Dalp, 78) (Bern–Munich 1961).
——, 'Das Motiv des Vater–Sohn-Kampfes im Hildebrandslied', *German.-roman. Monatsschrift*, 34 (1953), 257–74.
Wesendonk, O. G. von, *Das Weltbild der Iranier* (Geschichte der Philosophie, I/Ia) (Munich 1933).
Wesselski, Albert, *Versuch einer Theorie des Märchens* (Reichenberg 1931).
——, *Probleme der Sagenbildung* (Schweizer Archiv für Volkskunde, XXXV) (1936), Hft. 2-3.
——, *Märchen des Mittelalters* (Berlin 1925).
Winternitz, M., 'Das Märchen innerhalb der Erzählungsliteratur der Völker', *ArOr.*, 4 (1932), 225–49.
Wundt, Wilhelm, *'Das Märchen'. Zur Psychologie und Ethik, zehn ausgewählte Abschnitte.* Hrsg. und eingeleitet von Julius A. Wentzel (Leipzig 1911), 64–114.
Yershov, N. N., '"Tūi guldor" u kïstakozskikh tadzhikov', *Trudï Tadzh.*, 17 (Stalinabad 1963), 87–97.
Yershov, N. N., N. A. Kislyakov, Y. M. Peshchereva, and S. P. Rusyaykina, *Kul'tura i bït tadzhikskogo kolkhoznogo krest'yanstva* (*TIE*, N.S., 24) (Moscow 1954).
Yevseyev, V. Y., *Istoricheskiye osnovï karelo-finskogo eposa*, 2 vols. (Moscow–Leningrad 1957–60).
Zakani, Obeyd, *Veselaya kniga.* Perevod s persidskogo, predisloviye i primechaniya N. Kondïrevoy ... (Moscow 1965).
Zakaryan, K., *Kurdskiye narodnïye pesni* (Erevan 1938).

Zand, M. I., 'Oid ba masalhoi tendentsiyai khalqii dar adabiyoti tojik dar asrhoi VIII–IX', *ShS* (1953/6).

——, *Shest' vekov slavï. Ocherki persidsko-tadzhikskoy literaturï* (Moscow 1964).

Zarifov, Kh. T., 'K izucheniyu uzbekskogo narodnogo eposa', in *Vopr. izuch. eposa nar. SSSR* (Moscow 1958), 101–25.

Zarubin, I. I., *Oroshorskiye tekstï i slovar'* (Trudï Pamirskoy eksped. 1928 g., VI) (Leningrad 1930).

——, *Shugnanskiye tekstï i slovar'* (Moscow–Leningrad 1960).

——, 'K kharakteristike mundzhanskogo jazïka', Iran, I (Leningrad 1927), 111–200.

Zaydenshnur, E. Y., 'Fol'klor narodov Vostoka v tvorchestve L. N. Tolstogo', *SV* (1958/6), 57–65.

Zelenin, D. K., *Bibliograficheskiy ukazatel' russkoy etnograficheskoy literaturï ... 1700–1910 gg.* (Zap. R. geogr. obshch. po otd. etnogr., XI/1) (St.-Petersburg 1913).

——, 'Religiozno-magicheskaya funktsiya fol'klornïkh skazok', in *Sbornik ... Ol'denburgu* (Leningrad 1934), 216–40.

Zhdanko, T. A., 'Karakalpakskaya epicheskaya poema "Kïrk-kïz" kak istorikoetnograficheskiy istochnik', *KSIE*, 30 (1958), 110–20.

Zhirmunskiy, V. M., 'Problema fol'klora', in *Sbornik ... Ol'denburgu* (Leningrad 1934), 195–213.

——, 'Nekotorïye itogi izucheniya geroicheskogo eposa narodov Sredney Azii', in *Voprosï izuch. eposa nar. SSSR* (Moscow 1958), 24–65.

——, 'Kitabi Korkut i oguzskaya epicheskaya traditsiya', *SV* (1958/4), 90–101.

——, 'Epicheskoye tvorchestvo slavyan. narodov i problema stravnitel'nogo izucheniya eposa', in *Issledovaniya po slavyan. literaturovedeniyu i fol'kloristike* (Moscow 1960), 252–83.

——, *Skazaniye ob Alpamïshe i bogatïrskaya skazka* (Moscow 1960).

——, *Narodnïy geroicheskiy epos. Sravnitel'no-istoricheskiye ocherki* (Moscow–Leningrad 1962).

Zhirmunskiy, V. M. and Kh. T. Zarifov, *Uzbekskiy narodnïy geroicheskiy epos* (Moscow 1947).

Zhizn' Vikramï ili 32 istorii tsarskogo trona, perevod s sanskrita (Moscow 1960).

Zhukovskiy, V. A., *Materialï dlya izucheniya persidskikh narechiy*, 3 vols. (St.-Petersburg 1888–1922).

——, 'Kolïbel'nïye pesni i prichitaniya osedlago i kochevago naseleniya Persii', *Zhurnal Min. nar. prosveshcheniya 1889 janvar* (St.-Petersburg), 93–126.

——, 'Musul'manstvo Rustama Dastanovicha', *Zhivaya starina* (1891), 109–17.

——, *Obraztsï persidskago narodnago tvorchestva* (St.-Petersburg 1902).

Zweiundneunzig Anekdoten und Schwänke aus dem modernen Indien. Aus dem Persischen übersetzt von Johannes Hertel (Leipzig 1922).

Cf. also: Araslï – B VIb; Avesta – A I; Bartol'd (epos) – B VIb; Bertel's (Navoi) – B VIb; Coyajee – B VIb; Duda – B VIb; Eberman – B VIa; Gafurov – D Ia; Hansen – B VIb; Horn – B V; Christensen – B II; B VIa; Krïmskiy – B V; Marzbān – B VIb; Minorsky – B VIb; Molé – B VIb; Ibn an-Nadīm – A IV; Nikitine – D IIV; Niẓāmī – B VIb; Rempis – B VIa; Richter – B VIa; Rozen – A III; Spuler – B III; Suhtscheck – A III; Wikander – B VIa; Zenker – B VIb.

KEY TO THE SUBJECTS OF MONOGRAPHS AND ARTICLES IN THE PRECEDING BIBLIOGRAPHIES

(Names of authors etc. refer to B VIb, *unless otherwise indicated)*

'Abbās Marvazī: Barthold ("To the Question").
"*Abdullonoma*": Sayfiyev (D IIb).
'Abdu'l-Vasī' Jabalī: Navā'ī, 'Abdu'l-Ḥ.
Abū-Isḥāq, Shāh Shaykh-: Navā'ī, 'Abdu'l-Ḥ.
Abu'l-'Alā Ganjavī: Shu'ā'u'l-mulk.
Abu'l-Faḍl: Ahuja (E VII).
Abū-Muslim: Muḥ. 'Abdu'l-Ghanī (B II).
Abū-Naṣr: Ethé.
Abū-Nuvās: Gabrieli – Mīnuvī.
Abū-Sa'īd b. abi'l-Khayr: Nicholson.
Abū-Shakūr: Dabīr Siyāqī.
Adīb Nīshāpūrī: Bāmdād – Ishrāq.
Adīb Ṣābir: Nafīsī.
Afḍal, Bābā-: Dānish-puzhūh.
Aïnī*: *s. 'Aynī.
Afḍalu'd-dīn Kāshānī: Modjtehedy.
'Ajzī, Saidaḥmad Ṣiddīqī: Aslanov (D IIb).
Ākhund-zāda (Akhundov): *s. Fatḥ-'Alī Ā.*
'Alavī: Rypka (C) – Shoytov (C).
'Am'aq: Ṣafā.
Aminzoda: Qosimov (D IIc).
Amīr Khusrau Dihlavī: Aliyev, G. Yu. – Baqoyev – Genko – Habib (B VIb, E V) – Kégl – Maḥjūb – Mu'īn – Naqi (E V) – Srivastava (B VIb, E VII) – Wahid.
Anṣārī Haravī: de Beaurecueil – Ivanow – Levy – Ritter – Zhukovskiy.
Anvarī: Mīnuvī ("Ijt.") – Navā'ī, 'Abdu'l-Ḥ. – Vorozheykina – Zhukovskiy.
"*Arabian Nights*" *s.* "*Thousand and One Nights*".
'Ārif: Bombaci (C).
Asadī: Bertel's – Chaykin – Ethé ("Tenzonen") – Kiyā – Molé ("Garshāsp") – Rugarli – Rypka (B IV: "Mutaqārib").
Asīrī: Khodzhayev (D IIb) – Sayfulloyev (D IIc).
'Aṭṭār: Badī'u'z-zamān – Bertel's – Garcin de Tassy (B III) – Lentz – Levend – Meier – Miklukho-Maklay – Murtaḍavī – Nafīsī – Ritter.
'Aufī: Nicholson.
Auḥadī Marāghī: Adīb Ṭūsī – Masrūr.
Avadhī: 'Ābidī (E VII).
Avicenna: *s. Ibn Sīnā.*
Aynī, Sadriddin: Abdullozoda (D IIc, F) – Azizqulov/Mullojonova (D IIc) – Aminova (D IIc) – Amonov (D IIc) – Asrorī (F) – Bečka (D IIc) – Braginskiy (D IIc) – Halimov (D IIc) – Hodizoda (D IIc) – Hoshim (D IIc) – Huseynzoda (D IIc) – "Jashnomai Aynī" (D IIc) – Lemenovskiy (D IIc) – Maniyozov (D IIc) – Mulloqandov (D IIc) – Muqimov (D IIc) – Nevskaya (D IIc) – Niyazov (D IIc) – "Ocherk ist. tadzh. sov. lit." (D IIc) – Pankina (D IIc) – Rahimov (D IIc) – Rajabov (D IIc) – "Sadriddin Aynī" (D IIc) – Sayfulloyev (D IIc) – Sokolov/Demidchik (D IIc) – Shukurov (D Wurmser (D IIc).
Ayyūqī: Ateş.

Bābā-Ṭāhir: Abrahamian (F) – Adīb Ṭūsī – Khānlarī – Minorsky – Mīnuvī – Vorozheykina – Yāsimī.
Bābur: Na'imuddin (E VII) – Ross (E VII) – Schimmel (E VII).
Badā'ūnī: Storey (E VII).

Badī'u'z-zamān Hamadhānī: Al-Kak.
Bahār: Ishaque (C) – Klyashtorina – Peysikov (C) – Zakhoder (C).
Bahā'u'd-dīn "Bahā'ī": Burhān Āzād – Nafīsī.
Bahā'u'd-dīn Valad: Khālid.
Bahā'u'llāh: Esslemont (B iii).
"Bahman-nāma": Kobidze.
"Bahrām Chōbīn": Gumilev (F).
"Bahrām u Gulandām": Gvakhariya (F) – Koroghlï (F).
"Bakhtyār-nāma": Gvakhariya – Nöldeke.
Bal'amī: *s. Ṭabarī.*
Bannā'ī s. Binā'ī (Binoī).
Bāqillānī: von Grunebaum (B iv).
"Barlaam and Joasaph": Henning.
"Barzū-nāma": Rugarli.
Bāyazīd Bisṭāmī: Ritter.
Bīdil (Bēdil): Abdul Ghani (E v) – Abdullayev/Shukurov (D iib) – Akhtar (D iib, E v) – Ayni, Kh. (D iib) – Ayni, S. (D iib) – Bausani (D iib, E vii) – Dehotī (D iib) – Klimovich (D iib) – "Maḥmūd Shabistarī" – Mirzoyev (D iib) – Mujaddidī (D iib) – Muminov (D iib).
Bīnā'ī (Binoī): Mirzoyev (B vib, D iib) – Saljouqui (D iib).
Bīrūnī: Krause.
Bobo Yunus: *s. Khudoydodzoda.*
Burhānī: Mu'īn.
Buzurgmihr: Christensen (F).
Buzurgzoda: Khromov (D iic).

Chandar Bhān Brahman: Husain, I, (E vii).
Chāndūlāl Shādān: Shaukat (E vii).
Chekhov: Rozenfel'd (C).

Dānish (Donish), Aḥm. Kalla: Avezbayeva (D iib) – Bečka (D iib) – Bertel's (D iib) – Hodizoda (D iib) – Mirzoyev (D iib) – Mirzozoda (D iib) – Qosimzoda (D iib) – Rajabov (D iib) – Yuldashev (D iib).
Dante: Bertel's (Sanā'ī) – Nicholson.
Daqīqī: Dabīr Siyāqī – Ritter.
Dārā Shukōh: Ghauri (E vii) – Hasan, Z. (E vii) – Hasrat (E v, E vii) – Narain (E vii) – Qanungo (E v).
Darvīsh-i Dihakī: Ahmadov – Boldïrev.
Dashtī: E'tesam-zadeh (C).
Donish: *s. Dānish.*
Fahlaviyyāt: Adīb Ṭūsī – Kūhī Kirmānī.
Fakhru'd-dīn Gurgānī: Gabrieli – Gvakhariya – Gvakhariya/Todua – Minorsky – Mīnuvī – Molé – von Stackelberg – Zenker.
Falakī: Hādī.
Fard: Hasan, M. (E vii).
Farhād-Mīrzā: Kégl (B via: "Tanulmányok") – Massé – Mudarrisī – Pinnock.
Farhād u Shīrīn: Aliyev, G. Y. (F) – Duda – Timurtaş.
Farrukhī Sīstānī: Ateş – Khaṭīb – Ritter – Rypka/Borecký – Yūsufī.
Farrukhī Yazdī: Gadzhizade (C) – Osmanova (C).
Fatḥ-'Alī Ākhund-zāda (Akhundov): Aliyev, S. M. – Çaferoğlu – Djafarov – Sharif – Shoytov.
Fatḥ-'Alī Shāh: Safā'ī Malāyirī.
Fayḍī: Desai (E vii) – Ghose (E vii).
Fayyāḍ (Fayyoz): Boldïrev (D iib).
Fighānī, Bābā: Kausar – Suhaylī.
Firdausī: Aliyev, G. Y. (B vib, F) – Andersen – Ateş – Aynī, S. – Bahār, M. T. – Bahārmast – Bajraktarević – Bartol'd – Bertel's – Cejpek (F) – Chaykin – Christensen – Coyajee – D'yakonov – Gaál – Geissler (F) – Giunashvili – von Grunebaum – Hansen – Humbert – Khadizade – Khayyāmpūr ("Yūs. u Zal.") – Kobidze (B vib, F) – Kowalski – Massé – Minorsky – Mīnuvī ("Yūs. u Zal.") – Molé – Nafīsī ("Yūs. u Zal."; "Vazn") – Nöldeke – Osmanov (B vib, F) – Ptitsïn – Ringgren (B via) – Ritter – Romaskevich – Rozenberg – Rypka (B iv: "Mutaqārib"; B vib) – Ṣafā (B via) – Salač – Samoylovich (D iib) – Schack (F) – Shafaq – Starikov (F) – Ṭabāṭabā'ī Muḥīṭ – Tagirdzhanov ("Yūs. u Zal.") – Tardov – Trever – Tushishvili – Vachha – Wikander (B via) – Wolff – Zhukovskiy (F); *s. also Shāh-nāma.*
Fitrat-i Zardūz: Sulaymonova (D iib).
Fitzgerald: Arberry – Ḥikmat.
Fuchik: Tabarov (D iic).
Fuḍūlī: Aliyev, G. Yu. – Araslï – Bertel's – Gulizade – Karahan – Köprülü.
Furūghī Bisṭāmī: Bausani.

Gayōmart: Hartman (F).
Ghaḍā'irī: Dabīr Siyāqī.
Ghālib: Ghafforov (E v) – Gilani (E vii) – Lakhanpal (E vii) – Pūlodova (E vii).
Ghanī: Nāzukī (E vii).

Jāmī: Arberry – Bertel's – Blochmann (B IV) – Chaykin – Hashim – Ḥikmat – Kobidze – Kuliyev – Lescot – Mīnuvī – Ojha (B VIa) – Ritter.
Javharizoda: *s. Suhaylī.*
Junayd: Arberry.

"*Kalīla va Dimna*": Aliyev, Gh. (F) – "*L'Âme de l'Iran*" (B VIa: Massé) – Cejpek (F) – Chauvin (B I) – Maḥjūb – Nöldeke (F) – Schulthess (F).
Kalīm Hamadhānī (*Kāshānī*): Anṣārī, Sh. Bēgum – Kishāvarz.
Kalla: *s. Dānish.*
Kamāl Khujandī: Aynī, S. – Braginskiy.
Kamālu'd-dīn Ismā'īl: Iqbāl – Masrūr – Vorozheykina.
Kāmi Qazvīnī: Fakhru'z-zamān Bēgam (E VII).
Karim Devona: Nazarov (D IIb).
Karīm-Khān-Zand: Navā'ī (B II).
Kay-Kā'ūs: Frye – Iqbāl – Mīnuvī.
Khāqānī: Āmūzgār – Ateş – Boldïrev – Chaykin – Dashtī – Hādī Ḥasan (B VIa) – Kandī – Khanikof – Minorsky – Nāṣiḥ – Rāynart (Reinert) – Rypka – Rzakulizade – Turjānī-zāda – Vil'chevskiy.
Khayyām: Akhtar – Aliyev, R. M./Osmanov – Arberry – Badī'u'z-zamān – Bajraktarević – Bolotnikov – Christensen – Csillik – Dashtī – Machalski – "Maḥmūd Shabistarī" – Mīnuvī – Moročnik/Rozenfel'd – Nafīsī – Rashīdī Tabrīzī – Rempis – Ritter – aṣ-Ṣarrāf – Varasteh – Yakānī – Zhukovskiy.
"*Khudāy-nāma*": Kirste – Osmanov.
Khudoydodzoda, Bobo Yunus: Nudel' (D IIc).
Khusrau Dihlavī: *s. Amīr Kh. D.*
"*Khusrau u Shīrīn*": Aliyev, G. Y. (F) – Demirtaş – Timurtaş – Zajączkowski.
Khusravānī: Ethé.
Khusravī: Machalski (C).
Khvājū: Köprülü – Nafīsī.
Kisā'ī: Ethé – Ishaque.
Kūhī, Bābā-: Bertel's – Tagirdzhanov – Vorozheykina.
"*Kūsh-nāma*": Molé.

Labībī: Dabīr Siyāqī – Rypka/Borecký.
Lāhutī (*Lohūtī*): Davronov (D IIc) – Germanetto (D IIc) – Huseynzoda (D IIc) – Isoyev (D IIc) – Muqimov (D IIc) – "Ocherk ist. tadzh. sov. lit." (D IIc) – Osmanova (C) – Shklovskiy (D IIc) – Shukūhī (D IIc) – Zand (D IIc).
"*Laylī u Majnūn*": Bitlisi (F) – Fück (B IV) – Krachkovskiy – Levend – Maḥjūb.
Lutfī: Hoji (D IIc).

al-Ma'arrī: Nicholson.
Maftūn: Nakhjavānī.
Maghribī: Adīb Ṭūsī.
Mahdī-Khān: Cheyshvili – Samoylovich.
Maḥmūd Shabistarī: Tarbiyat.
Mahsatī: Ishaque (B VIb), C: "Poetesses") – Kishāvarz – Meier – Mushīr-i Sālimī.
Makhmūr: Valikhojayev (D IIb).
Maleho: Mirzoyev (D IIb).
Malang Jān: Dvoryankov (F).
Malik Qummī: Nazir (E VII).
Malkum-Khān: Christensen (C) – Ibragimov (C) – Ṭabāṭabā'ī (C).
Manūchihrī: Ishaque – Qazvīnī.
Marzbān: Gabrieli – Muḥaqqiq – Zajączkowski.
Masīḥ Kāshānī: Pizhmān.
Mas'ūd: Jamāl-zāda (C).
Mas'ūd-i Sa'd: Qazvīnī – Suhaylī.
Mijmar: Ṭabāṭabā'ī Muḥīṭ.
Mirshakar: Bobokalonova (D IIc) – Kedrina (D IIc) – Mirzozoda (D IIc) – "Ocherk ist. tadzh. sov. lit." (D IIc) – Tabarov (D IIc).
Muhammad Ḥasan Khān: Zhukovskiy.
Muḥāsibī: Smith.
Muḥsin-i Fayḍ: Bertel's.
Muḥtasham: Bayḍā'ī Vaqār.
Mu'izzī: Khusravānī – Marek.
Mujīr: Bāstānī-Rād.
Munshī: Baqir (E VII).
Mushfiqī: Ahrorī (D IIb) – Semenov (D IIb).
Muṭahhar-i Karā: Mirza (E VII) – Shervānī (E VII).

Najāt Iṣfahānī: Gulchīn-i ma'ānī.
Najmu'd-dīn Kubrā: Bertel's (D IIb).
Nakhlī: Sayfiyev (D IIb).
Nakhshabī: Chauvin (B I) – Pertsch.
Nartes, legends of the: "Antol. abkhazskoy, kabardinskoy poezii" (F) – Chicherov (F) – Dalgat (F) – Dumézil (F).
Nasafī: Palmer (B III).
Nashāṭ: Qā'im-maqām.
Nāṣir-i Khusrau: Ashurov – Bertel's, A. Y. – Ethé – Habibov (F) – Ivanow – Machalski –

Muḥaqqiq – Nikitina – Schaeder (B VIa) – Wickens.
Naṣīru'd-dīn Ṭūsī: Humā'ī.
Naṣru'llāh: Chauvin (B I: "Kalîlah").
Nāṭiq Makrānī: Kausar (E VII).
Navā'ī (*Navoī*): Bartol'd (D Ib) – Bertel's (D IIb) – Boldïrev (B VIb, D IIb) – Gandjeï (D IIb) – Ḥikmat – Levend – Semenov (D IIb) – Tarlan (D IIb) – Yakubovskiy (D Ib).
Nāẓim (*Nozim*): Zuhuriddinov (D IIb).
Ni'matu'llāh: Aubin – Ishaque – Nūr-bakhsh Kirmānī.
Nithārī (*Nisorī*): Boldïrev (D IIb) – Ḥabībī (D IIb).
Niyozī: Sharifov (D IIc).
Niẓāmī: 'Abdu'n-Na'īm – Aḥmad 'Alī – Aliyev (B VIb, F) – Araslï – Bertel's (B VIb, F) – Boldïrev – Devek – Duda – Dunayevskiy – Gabrieli – Geissler (F) – Gulizade – Guseynov – Gvakhariya – Ḥikmat – Houtsma – Iqbāl (B II) – Klimovich (B VIb, F) – Krachkovskiy (B VIb, F) – Krïmskiy – Maḥjūb – Makovel'skiy – Marr – McDonald – Mu'īn – Pfister (F) – Resulzade – Reychman – Ritter – Rypka (B IV, B VIa, B VIb) – Shaginyan – Shihābī – Ṭabāṭabā'ī Muṣṭ. – Wesselski – Zachoder – Zajączkowski; *s. also*: *"Farhād"* – *"Khusrau"* – *"Laylā"* – *"Turandot"*.
Niẓāmu'l-mulk: Falsafī (B VIa) – Mīnuvī – Nafīsī (Niẓāmiyya) – Rippe (B II) – Schabinger (B II) – Tauer (B II).
Nizārī: Bārādīn (Borodin) – Bayburdi – Durrī.
Nozim: *s. Nāẓim.*

Parvīn: Ishaque (C: "Poetesses") – Kishāvarz (B VIa) – Rypka (C).
Payrav Sulaymonī: Aul (D IIc) – Bečka (D IIc) – Hoshim (D IIc) – Khodoydodov/Najmiddinov (D IIc) – Nasriddinov (D IIc) – Tabarov (D IIc).
Pirmuhammadzoda: Yusupov (D IIc).
Platen, Graf von: Veit.
Proverbs: Kégl (F) – Phillot (F).
Pūlodī: Atokhon (D IIc).
Pūr-i Bahā: Kubíčková – Minorsky.
Pushkin: Braginskiy – Rozenfel'd (C).

Qā'ānī: "Furūghī" – Kégl (B VIa: "Tanulmányok") – Kubíčková – Ṭabāṭabā'ī Muḥīṭ.
Qābūs: Iqbāl.
"*Qābūs-nāma*": *s. Kay-Kā'ūs.*
Qāsim Kāhī: Hadi Hasan (E VI, E VII).
Qāsimu'l-anvār: Massé.
Qaṭrān: Dhukā – Kasravī (B VIa, B VIb) – Ross.
Quli Quṭb Shāh: Basu (E VII).
Qurratu'l-'ayn Ṭāhira: Ishaque (B VIb, C: "Poetesses") – Root.
Quṭb: Zajączkowski.

Rābi'a: Smith.
Rābi'a Quzdārī (*Khuzdārī*): Ishaque (B VIb, C: "Poetesses") – Kausar (E VII) – Kishāvarz (B VIa) – Meier ("Die schöne Mahsatī") – Mushīr-i Sālimī (B VIa).
Rahimī: Kirilov (D IIc) – Ma'sumī (D IIc).
Rāqim, Sayyid: Semënov (D IIb).
Rashīd-i Vaṭvāṭ: Horst – Iqbāl.
Rashīdu'd-dīn: Jahn (E II).
Riḍā-qulī Hidāyat: Churchill – Kégl.
Riyāḥī: Ṣafā'ī Malāyirī.
Rūdakī: Aliyev, Gh. (F) – Amonov – Aynī, S. – Azizqulov – Badī'u'z-zamān – Basirov – Bertel's, A. Y. – Dabīr Siyāqī – Huseynzoda (F) – Ishaque – Kobidze – Mirzoyev – Mirzozade (F) – Mu'īn – Nafīsī – "Namunahoi fol'klor" (F) – Ross – Tal'man/Yunusov (B I) – Zand.
Ruknā: *s. Masīḥ Kāshānī.*
Rustam: Maskūb.

Ṣabā: Nakhjavānī.
Ṣabāḥī: Bayḍā'ī.
Ṣabūḥī: Safā'ī Malāyirī.
Sa'dī: Adīb Ṭūsī – Akhtar – Aliyev, R. M. – Aynī, S. – Bacher – Badī'u'z-zamān – Chaykin – Dashtī – Ḥālī – Iqbāl – Javādī – Krachkovskiy – Massé – Murtaḍavī – Nafīsī – Qazvīnī – Sultanov – Taymas – Todua.
Ṣadrā (*Ṣadru'd-dīn*): Abū-'Abdi'llāh – Mishkātu'ddīn.
Sadri Ziyo: Siddiqov (D IIb).
Ṣafā Isfahānī: Ishrāq.
Saḥābī: Ṭabāṭabā'ī Muḥīṭ.
Ṣāḥib b. 'Abbād: Bahmanyār – Nāṣiḥ.
Ṣā'ib: Genceli.
Saidalī Valizoda: Amonov (F).
Saidmurodov: Mirsaidova (D IIc).

Salari: Desai (E VII).
Salmān-i Sāvajī: Yāsimī.
"*Sām-nāma*": Hādī Ḥasan (B VIa).
Sanā'ī: Bertel's – Khalīlu'llāh – Kégl – Mīnuvī – Nicholson – Ritter.
Ṣanī'u'd-daula: Zhukovskiy.
Sarmad: Abdu'l-Wali (E VII) – Asīrī (E VII) – Hashmi (E VII).
Saudā (*Savdo*): Azizqulov (D IIb) – Galimova (D IIb).
Sāya: Klyashtorina (C).
Sayf-i Sarāyī: Bodrogligeti – Taymas.
Sayf-ī Bukhārī: Blochmann (B IV) – Mirzoyev (D IIb).
Sayyidā Nasafī (*Sayyido*): Mirzoyev (D IIb) – Ptitsïn (D IIb).
Selim I: Horn.
Shahīd: Ishaque.
Shāhīn (*Shohin*): Khayyāmpūr – Mirzozoda (D IIb).
"*Shāh-nāma*": Maskūb – Osmanov; *s. also Firdausī* – "*Khudāy-nāma*".
"*Shahriyār-nāma*": Aynī, K. S.
Shakespeare: Ḥikmat.
Shams-i Qays: Adīb Ṭūsī ("Fahlaviyyāt").
Shamsu'd-dīn Kāshānī: Murtaḍavī.
Shaybānī: Bonelli – Kégl.
Shifā'ī: Āzād – Suhaylī.
Shihāb: Bahār – Buzurg Niyā – Ṭabāṭabā'ī Muḥīṭ.
Shohin: *s. Shāhīn.*
Shūrīda: Faṣīḥī – Ḥikmat.
"*Shūrob*": Karimov (D IIc) – Saloh (D IIc).
Ṣiddīqī: *s. 'Ajzī.*
"*Sindbād-nāma*": Bertel's – Dabīr Siyāqī – Ol'denburg – Perry; cf. B VIb *s.v.*
Sirus: Hoshim (D IIc).
Sodiq: Karimov (D IIb).
Suhaylī Javharizoda: Amonov/Sayfulloyev (D IIc).
Suhravardī: Badī'u'z-zamān – van den Bergh – "Ḥāfiẓ" (Wilberforce-Clarke) – Ritter.
Surūsh: Kégl (B VIa: "Tanulmányok").
Sūzanī: Bertel's.

Ṭabarī: Romaskevich.
Ṭāhir: *s. Bābā-Ṭ.*
Ṭāhira: *s. Qurratu'l-'ayn.*
Tāj Rēza: Abdus Sattar Khan (E VII).
Ṭālibūf: Ādamiyyat.
Tanūkhī: Gabrieli.
Ṭaqī Auḥadī: Nazir Ahmed (E VII).
Tarbiyat: Browne (B VII).
Ṭarzī Afshār: Bertel's – Kasravī (B VIa).
"*Taurāt*": Dānish-puzhūh.
ta'ziya: Baumgartner (F) – Cejpek (F) – Duda (F) – Krïms'kïy (F) – Litten (F) – *Théâtre persan* (F) – Virolleaud (F).
"*Thousand and One Nights*": Bouisson (F) – Cejpek (F) – Cosquin (F) – Eliséeff (F) – Gerhardt (F) – Henninger (F) – Lahy-Hollebecque (F) – Montet (F) – Oestrup (F) – Paret (F) – Rescher (F).
"*Tristan*": Zenker.
Ṭughrā'ī: Schabinger.
"*Turandot*": Gozzi (F) – Meier (F) – "Mille et un jour" (F) – Niẓāmī ("Haft Paykar") – Schiller (F).
Tursunzoda: Boboyev (D IIc) – Niyozmuhammadov (D IIc) – "Ocherk ist. tadzh. sov. lit." (D IIc) – Osmanova (D IIc) – Qosimov (D IIc) Sayfulloyev (D IIc) – Shukurov (D IIc) – Tabarov (D IIc).
"*Ṭūṭī-nāma*": Chauvin (B I) – Pertsch.
Tutmacı: Levend.

'Ubayd Zākānī: Bahā'u'd-dīn 'Āmilī – Christensen – Dāvarī – Javān-mard – Mīnuvī – Radzhabov.
Ulugh-Beg: Bartol'd (D Ib).
Ulughzoda: "Ocherk ist. tadzh. sov. lit." (D IIc) – Shukurov (D IIc) – Yusupov (D IIc).
'Unṣurī: Bertel's – Tarbiyat.
'Urfī: 'Ābid – Ghose (E VII) – Muḥammad 'Alī – Na'imuddin (B VIb, E VII) – Ojha (B VIa).
Uzeir Gadzhibekov: Korev (F).

Vāḍiḥ (*Vozeh*): Hodizoda (D IIb) – Ne'matzodah (D IIb).
Vafo: Asrorī (D IIc).
Valizoda: Ma'sumī (D IIc).
Vāṣifī (*Vosifī*): Aynī, S. (D IIb) – Boldïrev (D IIb) – Mirzoyev (D IIb).
"*Vīs u Rāmīn*": *s. Fakhru'd-dīn Gurgānī.*
Viṣāl: Kégl – Navābī – Rūḥānī Viṣāl – Ṭabāṭabā'ī Muḥīṭ.
Vozeh: *s. Vāḍiḥ.*

ADDENDA

RYPKA

Page 104, line 20:

On the importance of national tendencies see A. Nasreddinov, *Narodnaya tendentsiya v persidsko-tadzhikskoy klassicheskoy poezii XI–XII vv.* Author's report (Dushanbe 1966).

Page 112, line 29:

3rd/9th to beginning of 5th/11th century.

Page 117, lines 25–27:

"Una certa decadenza per la prosa persiana" (Bausani, *Storia*, 805, and *Sabk*, 2, 359).

Page 119, line 5:

Here I should like to draw attention with great emphasis to the treatise: Boldïrev, A. N. – Braginskiy, I. S., 'Soobrazheniya o periodizatsii klassicheskoy persidsko-tadzhikskoy literaturï', *NAA*, 1965,2, 100–110, to my knowledge the most complete essay on this theme. Unfortunately it was no longer practicable to make alterations in my classification.

Page 120, note 3:

R. S. Sultanov, *Slova tyurkskogo proiskhozhdeniya vstrechayushchiyesya v "Mesnevi" Dzhalaladdina Rumi* (Voprosï ir. filologii) (Baku 1966), 75–87. (Azerb. with Russian résumé.)

Page 121, note 32:

Shiblī (4,134) points out that nowhere do we come across the conception of freedom of thought etc.

Page 125, note 126:

M. I. Zand, *Shest' vyekov slavï*, 44 *et seq.*, has ingenious grounds for taking up a stand against the generally intransigent attitude towards the system of patronage.

Page 131, line 25:

With M. I. Zand (*Shest' vyekov*, 42) one must not ignore the fact that the Persian poets were bilingual, a somewhat later stage in the Shuʿūbite trends that succeeds the period of purely Arabic poetry and leads on to an exclusive use of Persian. The first of these bilingual poets is the already mentioned author Abu'l-Yanbaghī (beginning of the 9th century).

Page 137, line 17:

According to A. N. Boldïrev (B VI), Bashshār b. Burd wrote numerous verses in Persian in his youth.

Page 137, note 12:

In order to give publicity to their verse, the poets used to keep reciters (*rāvī*), a custom which the Iranians had adopted from the Arabs and of which there is already evidence in the 12th century. Bertel's, *Nizami* (1956), 125; idem, *Niz. i Fuz.*, 137; see below p. 109, note 12.

Page 138, note 31:

Philologically important because the verses contain words that belong to the earliest New Persian records.

Page 150, line 15:

See Bibl. D II and the new edition based on a MS of *Majlis-i Shūrā-i Millī* (Tehran 1345).

Page 167, note 9:

Now dealt with comprehensively by G. Lazard, *Les premiers poètes persans* (B VI).

Page 167, note 14:

Latterly: ʿAlī Akbar Mushīr Salīmī, *Shāʿirān-i kūr* (Tehran 1344).

Page 167, note 15:

A. Tohirdzhonov, 'Baʿze mas' alahoyi terjimayi holi Rūdakī,' *SSh*, 1966,1, 126–130 contradicts the assertion that either the rulers or the poets belonged to the Carmathians. Cf. A. T. Tagirdzhanov, 'K voprosu o karmatstve Nasra II ibn Akhmada Samani', *Ir. Fil.*, 1966, 167–182.

Page 168, note 37:

Siddīqī, Ghul.-Ḥus., 'Baʿḍī az kuhnatarīn āthār-i nathr-i fārsī tā pāyān-i qarn-i chahārum-i hijrī', *MDAT*, 13/4 (1345), 56–126. – G. Lazard, *La langue* (Bibl. B IV), 32–134: 'Les débuts de la prose persane.'

Page 168, note 38:

In facsimile publ. Tehran 1345 after a MS dating from 586/1190 (Library Mashhad, Āstān).

Page 168, note 39:
The torso of an anonymous *tafsīr* from the end of the 4th/10th century (Univ. Library Lahore) in facsimile publ. Tehran 1343.

Page 168, note 44:
P. G. Bulgakov, 'K biografii Bīrūnī', *NAA*, 1966,4, 195–200.

Page 169, note 50:
A. N. Boldïrev, *Novopersidskiye obrabotki epicheskikh predaniy v zapadnom Irane* (KS Inst. nar Azii, 67) (1964), 127–35.

Page 169, note 56:
See above, ad note 50.

Page 170, note 99:
Niẓāmī's critique: Bertel's Izbr. trudï, *Nizami i Fuzuli*, 352, 369.

Page 171, note 107:
Dīvān-i Mukhtārī, 799–844: 925 vv. from the *Shahryār-nāma*. – M. J. Maḥjūb, *Mathnavī-sarā'ī* (B VIa), 267: after his death, Chaykin's complete MS (sole extant copy) is said to have been temporarily lost sight of.

Page 190, line 25:
Better "il Maestro che sta sulle Montagne" (Bausani, *Storia*, 171).

Page 206, line 26:
It is the motif 'ubi sunt qui ante nos fuere', cf. R. Rakhimov, 'Motiv ubi sunt v persidsko-tadzhikskoy poezii', *V. konf. po iran. filologii*, 106–8.

Page 209, line 28:
According to B. Kh. Kuliyev, 'Zakhir Faryabi (k voprosu o gode rozhdeniya)', *NAA*, 1965,6, 145–6: 1160.

Page 210, line 39:
On *Makhzanu'l-asrār* in Persian and Turkish literature: Ye. E. Bertel's 'Izbr. trudï, *Nizami i Fuz.*, 204–14.

Page 211, line 21:
On *Laylī u Majnūn* in Arabic, Persian and Turkish literature: *s.v.* H. Araslï and Ye. E. Bertel's Izbr. trudï, *Niz. i Fuz.*, 275–313.

Page 217, note 45:
Khalīlī.

Page 219, note 116:
The following dates are derived from S. Nafīsī's detailed Preface to his edition of the *Dīvān*: Niẓāmī born 540/1145–6, died 598/1201–2 (p. 5, 65). Ra'īsa is not a proper

name but literally 'lady principal' or something of the sort (p. 3); similarly Āfāq (died before 578/1182–3) (p. 11 *et seq.*). *Makhzanu'l-asrār* (p. 74 *et seq.*) composed 552/1157–8 (perhaps 572/1176–7?). *Khusrau u Shīrīn* (p. 92, 119) started in 576/1180–1, completed after 587/1191 (!). *Laylī u Majnūn* (p. 99) 584/1188–9: *Sharaf-nāma* (p. 115), 597/1200–1; *Iqbāl-nāma* (p. 121 soon afterwards). The *Khamsa* contains 31,600 verses, the *Dīvān* 1989.

Page 222, line 13:

Special mention may be made here of Shaykh Ḥājjī Muḥ. b. Shaykh Aḥm. b. ʿAlī b. Ḥājjī Muḥ. Bīghamī's *Dārāh-nāma*, a revision of the story orally transmitted by Abū-Ṭāhir Muḥ. Ṭarsūsī (or Ṭarṭūsī) dating from the 8th–9th/14th–15th century (?); and further a novel on the poetess Mahsatī (see p. 199).

Page 222, line 20:

Ḥusayn b. Asʿad Dihistānī, between 651 and 669: *Yaghmā*, 7 (1333), 250 *et seq.*, 296 *et seq.* (M. Qazvini): S. Nafīsī, *Ta'rīkh-i naẓm va nathr*, 1, 186 adds al-Vīrī.

Page 224, note 10:

According to S. Nafīsī, *Ta'rīkh-i naẓm va nathr*, 1, 186: Ḥusayn b. Asʿad Dihistānī Alvīrī (?).

Page 225, note 15:

Shamsu'd-dīn Muḥ. Daqā'iqī Marvazī, *Rāḥatu'l-arvāḥ fī surūri'l-mifrāḥ "Bakhtiyār-nāma"*, ed. by Dh. Ṣafā (Publ. Univ.) (Tehran 1345).

Page 232, lines 16–17:

An enquiry into this: RK from 9/2 *et seq.*, 1345 onwards.

Page 234, line 32:

Dealing mainly with Bābā Ṭāhir is Kh. Guliyev's note, 'Iz vzaimosvyazi persidskoy poezii s ustnim narodnïm tvorchestvom', *V. konfer. po ir. fil.*, 1966, 50–1, in which we are shown the connection between Bābā Ṭāhir's quatrains and folk poetry.

Page 237, line 22:

ʿAṭṭār – already in the third generation, thus *laqab* and at the same time surname: S. Nafīsī, *Justujū*, 169.

Page 241, line 3:

In his critical edition of the *Kulliyyāt* Prof. Furūzānfar counts 33,135 verses.

Page 243, note 43:

Z. N. Vorozheykina, 'K voprosu o literaturnom nasledii Abdallakha Ansari', *IV. konfer. po ir. fil.* (Tashkent 1964), 68–70, does in fact establish the influence on Jāmī's *Yūsuf u Zalīkhā*. – *Ibid.* anti-despotic tone in Anṣārī's works.

Page 243, note 47:

Ye. E. Bertel's, Izbr. trudï, *Niz. i Fuz.*, 37, note 27, also considers the year 535/1140–1 as the most probable. Ṣafā, *Ta'rīkh*, 2, 559, arrives at the same date. Khāqānī's verse (*ibid.*, 356), according to which the year of his birth coincided with that of the death of Sanā'ī, would nevertheless indicate 525/1130–1 (thus S. Nafīsī, *Ta'rīkh-i naẓm u nathr.* 1, 103).

Page 244, note 69:

On the sources or models: *Mantiqu'ṭ-ṭayr*, ed. by Muh. Javād Mashkūr, 2nd ed. (Tehran 1962), p. 25 *et seq.* of the Preface.

Page 245, note 86:

Apart from occasional Turkish words or verses in Jalālu'd-dīn Rūmī, the section composed in Turkish in Sulṭān Valad's *Rabāb-nāma* is one of the earliest Turkish records in Anatolia (cf. above p. 120–3).

Page 259, line 23:

For more on *shahrāshūb*, see A. Mirzoyev, *Sayyido Nasafi* (Russian) 143 *et seq.*, 161.

Page 261, line 39:

According to B. Kuliyev, 'Zakhir Far'yabi i Salman Saveji', *IV. konfer. po ir. fil.*, 1964, 51 *et seq.*, and *Ir. filologiya* (Tashkent 1966), 314–328, Ẓahīr Fāryābī formed the main source of Sāvajī's inspiration.

Page 275, note 49:

M. Baqoyev, 'Khizmati shoistani taqdir', *SSh*, 1965,4, 153–8, confirms this and is unable to indicate any close connection between the *ghazals* of the two poets. The above-mentioned copy does not derive from Ḥāfiẓ' hand (Muḥ. Mu'in 1953, cited by M. Baqoyev).

Page 276, note 64:

Detailed, N. Sayfiyev, 'Gul va Navruz-i Jalal Tabib', *V. konfer. po ir. fil.* (1966), 110–3.

Page 285, line 35:

A. M. Abbasov, 'Nekotoriye svedeniya v poeme Abdullakh Hatifi "Temurname"', *V. konfer. po ir. fil.* (1966), 3–5.

Page 299, line 4:

More complete: Sayyid Jamālu'd-dīn Muḥ. 'Urfī.

Page 299, line 27:

Nal u Daman: better: 'recasting'. M. Qanoatov, '"Nal va Daman" va mavqei o dar ejodiyote Fayzī', *V. konfer. po ir. fil.* (1966), 127–8.

Page 300, line 35:

Nāẓim occupies an important place in the literary development and progressive social and political attitude of the orient in the 17th century. Humanism, philanthropy, criticism of society, antipathy towards force and despotism, a pantheism that regards life optimistically and affirmatively – these are the outstanding traits of his personality. Cf. Z. G. Rizayev, 'Nazim i Mashrab', *IV. konfer. po ir. fil.* (Tashkent 1964), 56–8; *Ir. fil.* (1966), 240–253.

Page 303, note 10:

A. Guliyev, 'Nekotorïye zamechaniya po povodu indiyskogo stil'a', *V. konfer. po ir. fil.* (1966), 47–50.

Page 304, note 31:

More recent literature: Bertel's, Izbr. trudï, *Niz. i Fuz.* 303, 493 *et seq.*

Page 304, note 34:

'Urfī's *mathnavīs* do not reach the level of his *qaṣīdas*, and are altogether of less value; the first of them (*Majma 'u'l-Akbar*), running in the track of *Makhzanu'l-asrār*, is extremely abstruse: bad verses but with a perfect technique (cf. Bertel's, Izbr. trudï, *Niz. i Fuz.*, 209, 15).

Page 304, note 44:

On Shaukat's biography (d. 1107/1695 or 1111/1699) and travels (Herat, Mashhad, Isfahan, Shiraz, Hindustan), see M. Akhmadov, in *V. konfer. po ir. fil.* (1966), 23–5.

Page 319, note 10:

Cf. Ethé, *GIPh*, 2, 338 *et seq.*

Page 319, note 13:

Since 1327 Prof. Dr. 'A. Khayyāmpūr has been publishing a series of *tadhkiras* in Tabriz. Up to date six numbers have appeared, most of them dealing with the 13th/19th century.

Page 330, line 2:

Other traditional dates of his death: 1272, 1273 (*Yaghma*, 7, 1333, 161).

Page 351, note 49:

Cf. also Farīdūn Ādamiyyat, 'Andīshahā-i Ṭālibūf', *Sukhan*, 16 (1345), Vols. 5–8. – Īraj Afshār, *Savād va bayāḍ* (*Majma'-i maqālāt*), I (Tehran 1344), where, among others, Ṭālibūf is discussed.

TAUER

Page 433, line 16:

The theory of poetry is also treated in the small book *Daqā'iqu'sh-shi'r*, 'Subtleties of the Poetry', by Muḥammad Tāju'l-Ḥalāvī, who probably lived in the 8th/14th century. Ed. by M. Kāẓim Imām (Tehran 1341).

Page 446, line 1:

The most detailed history on Nādir Shāh is the *Nāma-i ʿālamārā-i Nādirī*, 'The World-adorning Book of Nādir', by his contemporary, the vizier of Marv, Muḥammad Kāẓim. Ed. by N. D. Miklukho-Maklay, 3 vols. (Moscow 1960–66). His exploits are depicted in the *Shāh(anshāh)-nāma-i Nādirī*, 'The Book of King (of Kings) Nādir', by Muḥammad ʿAlī Ṭūsī, known as Firdausī-i thānī, who took part in all his campaigns. Ed. by Aḥmad Suhaylī Khvānsārī (Tehran 1339).

Page 453, line 13:

The *Sakīnatu'l-auliyā'*, 'The Spiritual Calm of the Saints', by Dārā Shikūh (*PL*, I, Nr. 1321/2), dealing with the lives of the famous saint of Lahore, Miyān Mīr, and his disciples, has been re-edited by Dr. Tarāchand and Sayyid Muḥammad Riḍā Jalālī Nā'īnī (Tehran 1344).

BEČKA

Page 491, line 18:

The most conspicuous characteristic in comparison with post-revolution literature is the long span of time during which the older literature developed and also the fact that the notion of national literature did not come to the fore in the sense we know it today.

Page 493, line 26:

The great progress of culture in the 16th century also forms an important chapter in the cultural history of present-day Afghanistan.

Page 502, line 20:

The work entitled *Badoeʿ-ul-vaqoeʿ* aroused a wide response. In Soviet libraries alone there are 28 manuscripts and three copies of the Uzbek translation. The importance of the work lies particularly in the author's having overcome the narrow, professional attitude through his wide outlook on and profound consideration of problems of social and cultural life in relation to Central Asia.

Page 546, line 3:

The present text was completed before 1963. During the proof-reading, contemporary literature in particular has been complemented by the addition of the most important new data up to 1966.

Page 550, line 26:

The mutual relationship between the literatures of the Soviet Union of Nations is influenced simultaneously by the forces of integration and disintegration – the latter to a certain degree from the second half of the 'fifties as a reaction to the apathy towards national individuality at the time of the personality cult. Disintegration is fostered also by the close link with tradition and folklore. On the other hand, writers of different nations are linked by a similar historical destiny, similar problems and very similar school education.

Page 553, line 4:

Up to the time of the Revolution the majority of writers were known under a pseudonym, a *takhallus*, as was the custom in Iran, Afghanistan and other countries. As examples we may quote Binoī, Bedil and Donish. Older authors too entered the literary arena after the Revolution under a pseudonym, including for instance Aĭnī, Munzim and Paĭrov. At present, however, young Tajik writers and poets, apart from a few exceptions such as Bahorī and Farhat, use no pseudonym. Some writers and scholars are known by their surname, which most often ends in -ov or -ev, for instance, Mirzoyev, Akobirov; the generation of writers that began their literary activities in the 'twenties and 'thirties most frequently write under their surnames, ending in the patronymic -zoda, for example, Tursunzoda, Rahimzoda, etc. Another type of name features the traditional *nisba*, an indication of origin, which is, however, attached to the name of the writer's father. As examples may be mentioned Rahimī, Qahhorī, etc. Some authors have taken as surname the unaltered name of their father, e.g. Ghaffor Mirzo, Qutbī Kirom, and others. In the case of poets the use of their personal name has become popular, for example Gulchehra Sulaĭmonova – who writes under the name of Gulchehra – and Khursheda Otakhonova, whose works appear under the name of Khursheda. (See A. Gafurov, *Lichnosobstvennye imena v tadzhikskom jazĭke*, Dushanbe 1964. Manuscript.)

Page 569, line 41:

A large selection from Aminzoda's poetry was published in 1964 under the title *Bahori dil*, 'The Heart's Spring', in honour of the poet's sixtieth birthday. In the foreword V. Asrorī draws attention to the importance of Aminzoda's translations of opera librettos, such as Tchaikovsky's *Eugene Onegin*, and a number of plays. The poet Aminzoda died suddenly in 1966.

Page 570, line 21:

Rahimī's love of traditional and small poetic forms is borne witness to by the collection *Roboiët va dubaĭtho*, 'Four Verses' (1965).

Page 573, line 38:

In 1966 extracts from a great new novel dealing with stories of the popular uprising at the end of last century were presented to Tajik readers. The book was named after its hero – *Vose'* (see *M. va M.*, 1966, 153,3, in serial form).

Page 575, line 24:

Ikromī was awarded the Rūdakī Prize for his novel *Dukhtari otash*. A Russian translation was published in 1965.

Page 579, line 30:
His large output included collections of poetry such as *Bo chashmoni tu*, 'Through your Eyes' (1963), and *She'rhoi nav*, 'New Poems' (1966), which, conforming to tradition, comprise a very wide range of genres, from the tender lyricism of *Modaram*, 'Mother', to battle poems serving the noblest human ideas.

Page 581, line 29:
The poet regularly publishes his poems in magazines, and in 1966 his new collection *Ishqi dukhtari kūhsor*, 'The Love of a Girl from the Mountains', appeared in book form in the Tajik and Arab scripts. The magazine *Kāveh* (Munich, 1345, 13-14, 154) published an interesting article on this collection, drawing attention to the differences between the contemporary Persian and Tajik languages.

Page 583, line 40:
In other poems Rahimzoda celebrates the beauty of his country and friendship among all nations. Since 1963 he has been publishing a series of short stories in serial form in *Sharqi Surkh*, the majority of which bear the common title *Az sarguzashthoi Soqī*, 'Soqī's Adventures', and describe life in the Tajik countryside.

Page 584, line 19:
From time to time poems by Pulodī devoted to special occasions appear in the press (the tradition of writing poems in honour of important events is still very much alive). In 1964 he published an interesting work entitled *Shoironi khalqii Badakhshon*, 'Folk Poets of Badakhshan'.

Page 586, line 8:
Farhat's poems written during a period covering almost two decades are contained in the collection *Taronahoi muhabbat*, 'The Melodies of Love' (1962). Another collection was published in 1964 under the title *Rūdi kūhī*, 'The Mountain Stream'.

Page 586, line 16:
Apart from poems for children and works devoted to the Azerbayjan countryside and his friendship for the people of that country, Bahorī has latterly written a number of short stories, including his first attempt at science fiction (*qissai fantastikī*), entitled *Jur'ati doktor Mansur*, 'Dr. Mansur's Decision' (1966), and finally also a drama from kolchoz life with the title *Rohi safed*, 'Happy Journey' (1966).

Page 586, line 27:
In the following years Shukūhī showed great creative activity. *Nafasi garm*, 'Hot Breath' (1964) clearly shows the poet's knowledge of classical poetry and folk works. In the same year he published, in cooperation with H. Askar, a novel entitled *Shahlo*, which describes the tragic fate of a Tajik girl of the same name who became the victim of enemies of the new life. Many of Shukūhī's poems have been published in magazines, and in recent years short stories of his have also appeared, such as *Imzoi*

shakhsī, 'Personal Signature' (1967), and other prose, including a large portion of the writer's last collection *Niyati naghz*, 'Good Intention' (1966). He was awarded the Rūdakī Prize for his lyrics.

Page 586, line 34:

In recent years Qahhorī has achieved great success, first with his *doston, Shabi pesh az marg*, 'The Night Preceding Death' (1965), which returns to the immortal theme of heroism in the Second World War, and secondly with his collection *Changhoi dūstī*, 'Songs of Friendship' (1065), which has also been published in Arabic script and has aroused the interest of Iranian readers. (See the review by Īraj Dehqān, *Kāveh*, Munich, 1345, 13-14, 152.)

Page 587, line 5:

In recent years too, Ansorī has written lyrical poetry and *dostons*. A selection of these was published under the title *Tori ilhom*, 'The Greatest Inspiration' (1963). A good work dating from 1966 is his one-act play *Shahr dar oghūshi tu*, 'The Town in Your Arms'.

Page 587, line 19:

Another work by the talented poetess was published in the collection entitled *Zinda rud*, 'The Live River' (1964–65) in Arabic script. She frequently makes use of free verse.

Page 587, line 27:

In recent years Nazarov has turned exclusively to prose; evidence is to be found in the novels *Yūldosh-Komandir*, 'Commander Yuldosh' (1964), *Targhal va Alo* (1965), and extracts from a great novel concerned with the transition to collective farming at the beginning of the 'thirties, bearing the title *Mirzo Rizo* (1964).

Page 587, line 32:

Untraditional poems can be found in Qanoat's *Dostoni otash*, 'A Doston on Fire' (1966).

Page 587, line 34:

Another of Kirom's collections, *Būi non*, 'The Scent of Bread' (1966), contains poems in the traditional spirit describing a journey through Kazakhstan.

Page 587, line 35:

Gulchehra published her delicate poems on the subjects of her mother, son, Nature, Bukhara, poems for children, and translations from Uzbek, as well as other poetry, in her first collection entitled *Nargis*, 'Narcissus' (1966).

Page 587, line 40:

The names of the poets encountered most frequently in the press include that of A'zam Sidqī (b. 1927) whose collection *Niholi orzu*, 'The Spring of Wishes' (1957), contains works from the years 1949–57, in particular poems on various concrete themes. He has also written a number of remarkable sketches and less successful short stories. In 1961 he extended his creative scope by writing a play on contemporary life – *Irodai zan*, 'A Woman's Will' – dealing with life in the fields. Another of his plays – *Suporishi Chk*, 'Order of Cheka' (1966) – is concerned with the struggles of the Soviet government against Basmachis in the 'twenties. [A. Sidqī was not cited in the text owing to an error in the translation – he is mentioned in the Czech edition (published in 1963).]

Page 588, line 34:

In recent years Muhammadiev has published a number of short stories in Tajik magazines as well as the novel *Dar on dun'ë*, 'In That World' (1966), which he wrote after making a pilgrimage to Mecca and Medina and which has an atheistic trend. It ranks among the documentary literary works (in Tajik *povesti hujjati*) that have aroused great response in Soviet and also Tajik literature.

Page 589, line 3:

Usmon Tojī has published a number of short stories in magazines as well as a novel entitled *Dukhtari niqobdor*, 'The Veiled Girl' (1965), which deals with the life and work of Robiai Balkhī, a 10th-century poet.

Page 589, line 9:

In the following years Akobirov wrote a number of short stories and novels; a collection of his short stories and reports has been published under the title *Qandak gul kard*, 'The Apricot Bloomed' (1965), as well as a long story entitled *Munira* (1966).

Page 589, line 12:

A certain success has been enjoyed by Ortiqov's novel *Guli sadbarg*, 'The Centifolious Rose' (1966). In the relatively weak sphere of Tajik literature of the short story type, the war tale entitled *Soldati noshinos*, 'The Unknown Soldier' (1966), by Hojī Sodiq can be considered a success.

Page 595, line 20:

Of late many plays have been written, one of the reasons for which undoubtedly lies in there being at present seven professional theatrical companies and more than six hundred amateur groups in Tajikistan, comprising altogether more than thirty thousand people. (See M. Nazarov, 'Qaĭdho oid ba hunarhoi zebo', *Sharqi Surkh* 1966,7, 106.) The majority of the plays have themes dealing with contemporary life, the minority are historical dramas, some of which are based on events of the Second World War. The new plays by Ghanī Abdullo, *Hurriyat*, 'Freedom' (1965), dealing with glorious battles that took place at the time of the Bukhara revolution in 1919–20, deserve mention. In them Lenin also appears for the first time. The historical plays by this author include *Rustam va Sūhrob* (1966), on a theme from Firdavsī's *Shāhnāma*. Another of his plays, entitled *Mo az bomi jahon*, 'We from the Roof of the World'

(1965), deals with the period of the last war. The experienced Saidmurodov wrote a documentary play on the stubborn struggles against the Basmachis entitled *Qissai Zaĭnabbibī*, 'The Story of Zaĭnabbibī' (1965), a work somewhat lacking in simplicity of structure. Among his successes we may count *Suporishi ChK*, 'Order of Cheka' (1966). A. Sidqī pays tribute to Soviet chekkists and Tajik patriotism in the first years of Soviet government. In recent years a number of plays has been written on the subjects of morality, love and the human character, examples being the successful play by A. Shukuhī, *Kuchaboghi oshiqon*, 'Lovers' Lane', and the already mentioned plays by F. Ansorī such as *Imtihon*, 'The Test' (1961). M. Rabiyev's play *Gulhoi atrofi shahr*, 'Flowers of the Suburbs' (1963), dealing with the contemporary life of young people, has not met with great success. Of works by the youngest playwrights, a large number of one-act plays and the drama *Sharori Khujand*, 'The Khujand Spark' (1964), by Sulton Safarov, about the Central Asian rebellion in 1916, have attracted considerable attention.

Page 600, line 3:

At the faculty of Tajik and eastern linguistics and literature at Dushanbe, B. Kamoliddinov is writing a literary-linguistic dissertation on contemporary Tajik literature. T. Ne'matzoda was the first to concern himself with the person and work of the 19th century poet Vozeh (p. 526) and S. Asadulloev with classical literature. The work of S. Aĭnī and modern Tajik literature are being dealt with by A. Manië̈zov, a scholar at the Institute of Tajik Language and Literature, while S. Niëzī has written several dissertations on Tajik literature dating from the Second World War period.

Page 605, note 104:

The 5th Assembly of the Union of Tajik Writers (*Ittifoqi navisandagoni Tojikiston*), held in April 1966, was attended by 33 poets, 13 prose-writers, 10 playwrights, 5 authors of books for children, 21 critics and scholars of literature, and 4 translators. Many of them, however, devote their attention to several of these fields (*M. va M.*, 1966,51, 4).

INDEX